# The Encyclopedia of

# Biblical Ethics

*General Editor*

## R.K. Harrison

# TESTAMENT BOOKS
NEW YORK

# LIST OF CONTRIBUTORS

| NAME | INITIALS |
|------|----------|
| | |

ANDERSON, J. K., M.A.  JKA
Vice-President, Probe Ministries International, Dallas, Texas

ANDERSON, S. D., Ph.D.  SDA
Bethel College, St. Paul, Minnesota

ATKINSON, D. J., Ph.D.  DA
Corpus Christi College, Oxford, United Kingdom

BILANIUK, P. B. T., D. Phil.  PB
St. Michael's College, Toronto, Canada

CAMERON, N. M.de S., Ph.D.  NMdeSC
Rutherford House, Edinburgh, United Kingdom

CAREY, G. L., Ph.D.  GC
Principal, Trinity College, Bristol, United Kingdom

CHALLICE, C. E., Ph.D.  CEC
University of Calgary, Canada

CONNERY, J. R., S.D.T.  JRC
Loyola University, Chicago, Illinois

ELWELL, W. A., Ph.D.  WAE
Wheaton College, Wheaton, Illinois

ESSENBURG, M., Ph.D.  ME
President, Covenant College, Chattanooga, Tennessee

FIELD, D. H., M.A.  DHF
Oak Hill College, Southgate, London, United Kingdom

FLETCHER, D. B., Ph.D.  DBF
Wheaton College, Wheaton, Illinois

GALLAGHER, J., S.T.D.  JG
St. Michael's College, Toronto, Canada

GALLAGHER, Sharon M., M.T.S.  SG
*Radix* Magazine, Berkeley, California

GAMBLE, A. J., LL.M.  AJG
Faculty of Law, University of Glasgow, United Kingdom

GELDARD, M. D., M.A.  MDG
St. John the Divine, Fairfield, Liverpool, United Kingdom

GILCHRIST, P. R., Ph.D.  PRG
Covenant College, Chattanooga, Tennessee

GUNDRY, S. N., S.T.D.  SNG
Zondervan Publishing House, Grand Rapids, Michigan

HAGNER, D. A., Ph.D.  DAH
Fuller Theological Seminary, Pasadena, California

HARRISON, R. K., Ph.D.  RKH
Wycliffe College, Toronto, Canada

HAYES, A. L., Ph.D.                                                          ALH
Wycliffe College, Toronto, Canada

HAYES, Morar M. Murray-, M.A.                                               MMM-H
Queen's Theological College, Kinston, Canada

HELM, P., M.A.                                                              PH
University of Liverpool, United Kingdom

HEXHAM, I., Ph.D.                                                           IH
University of Manitoba, Canada

HORNE, J. R., Ph.D.                                                         JRH
University of Waterloo, Canada

JONES, M. H., LL.B.                                                        MHJ
Faculty of Law, University of Glasgow, United Kingdom

LEGGE, Laura, Q.C.                                                         LL
Bencher *ex officio,* Law Society of Upper Canada

LIEFELD, W. L., Ph.D.                                                      WLL
Trinity Evangelical Divinity School, Deerfield, Illinois

LUND, N. J., Ph.D.                                                         NJL
Lutheran Bible Institute, Ahaheim, California

LUTTRELL, G. S., M.A.                                                      GSL
Thomas Nelson Publishers, Nashville, Tennessee

LUTZER, E. W., Ph.D.                                                       EWL
Moody Church, Chicago, Illinois

MACKAY, D. M., Ph.D.                                                       DMM
University of Keele, United Kingdom

MCQUILKIN, J. R., Ph.D.                                                    JRMcQ
President, Columbia Bible College, South Carolina

MCRAE, W. J., D.Min.                                                       WJM
President, Ontario Theological Seminary, Canada

MCCREADY, W. O., Ph.D.                                                     WOM
University of Calgary, Canada

MARTIN, N. D., Ph.D.                                                       NDM
Commonwealth Laboratory, Gore's Landing, Canada

MICHAELS, J. R., Ph.D.                                                     JRM
Southwest Missouri State University, Springfield, Missouri

MIKOLASKI, S. J., D. Phil.                                                 SJM
Carey Hall, University of British Columbia, Canada

MILLARD, C. J., LL.M.                                                      CJM
Solicitor of the Supreme Court of England and Wales, London, United Kingdom

MOO, D. J., Ph.D.                                                          DJM
Trinity Evangelical Divinity School, Deerfield, Illinois

MORRIS, L., Ph.D.                                                          LM
Ridley College, Melbourne, Australia

OSMOND, D. H., Ph.D.                                                    DHO
Department of Medicine, University of Toronto, Canada

PEEL, Alice, B.A.                                                       AP
Wycliffe College, Toronto, Canada

PEEL, D. N., Ph.D.                                                      DNP
Wycliffe College, Toronto, Canada

RAMSAY, W. M., Ph.D.                                                    WMR
Bethel College, McKenzie, Tennessee

ROBERTS, J. W., D.Min.                                                  JWR
Ministry of Correctional Services, Brampton, Canada

ROBERTS, Shelley E., LL.M.                                             SER
King's College, London, United Kingdom

RUNIONS, J. E., M.D.                                                    JER
Dept. of Psychiatry, University of British Columbia, Canada

SLATER, C. P., Ph.D.                                                    CPS
Trinity College, Toronto, Canada

STACKHOUSE, R. F., Ph.D.                                               RFS
Member of Parliament, Ottawa, Canada

THOMS, D. Elizabeth, LL.M.                                            DET
Barrister and Solicitor, Toronto, Canada

TOON, P., D. Phil.                                                      PT
Director of Post-Ordination Training, St. Edmundsbury and Ipswich Diocese,
United Kingdom

WENNBERG, R., Ph.D.                                                     RW
Westmont College, Santa Barbara, California

WHITLAM, T. W., Th.D.                                                  TWW
Wycliffe College, Toronto, Canada

# Preface

This book is a textbook of ethics for students and teachers as well as a practical manual for the average Christian. The various entries have been contributed by experts in their fields who have demonstrated an interest in writing ethics for the nonprofessional. Traditional Christian faith is held to be the norm for this volume. Thus, Christian values are not brought under question by the contributors, all of whom accept one or another of the church's historic creeds.

All the contributors, as Christians, are concerned professionally with the application as well as the teaching of ethics. Thus, this book is not merely descriptive, as some textbooks of ethics are; it is also prescriptive, in the sense of furnishing guidelines for behavior. Where different points of view exist on a given topic, authors were requested to explain them as objectively as possible, making allowance for the diversity of views that exist among Christians on some matters of ethical discussion.

Two different indexes at the back of the book add immeasurably to its value as a reference tool. A Personalities Index helps the reader locate quickly all the articles that mention specific persons or great ethical thinkers, such as Augustine or Immanuel Kant. A Scripture Index to the volume should help Bible teachers and ministers in their preparation of studies and sermons on ethical issues.

I wish to express my heartfelt thanks to the contributors, who responded so warmly to the invitation to write entries for this volume in spite of their busy schedules. A few even set aside other work in order to meet the rather restricted deadlines. For this gesture of confidence and cooperation I am deeply grateful. The incidence of personal tragedy and illness among the contributors made it necessary for the General Editor to undertake more of the entries than originally planned. Authors can be identified by their initials at the end of the various entries.

Mr. Gary Luttrell, editor at Thomas Nelson Publishers, supervised the production of this book at every stage. To him I owe an immense debt of gratitude. Finally, it is my privilege to express my deepest thanks to Mrs. Irene Crews, Principal's Secretary, Wycliffe College, for her painstaking work in connection with the manuscript; and to Mrs. Adrienne Taylor, Librarian of Wycliffe College, and to Miss Gayle Ford, her assistant, both of whom helped me so much in the production of this book. They responded cheerfully and promptly to my calls for help. Whatever success this book may enjoy will be due in no small measure to their own endeavors.

R. K. Harrison
General Editor
Wycliffe College
University of Toronto

# Publisher's Preface
# to the Revised Edition

The publication of the *Encyclopedia of Biblical and Christian Ethics* in 1987 offered scriptural guidance on ethical matters for some 540 topics. As time for another printing approached, it was felt that a modest revision would help the volume serve its readers better. This revision includes new entries, revision of others meriting it, corrections, and an increase in the number of cross-references throughout the book.

Entries added are "Acquired Immune Deficiency Syndrome (AIDS)" and "Homelessness." Those revised are "Abortion," "Addiction," "Civil Rights," "Contraception," "Euthanasia," "Fetal Rights," "Kinsey Report," "Nuclear Warfare," and "Population Control."

This revised edition is offered with the hope that it may help the people of God witness to the Gospel as effectively in ethical deeds as in words.

Following are the Contributors to this revision and the initials by which their work is identified:

BECKWITH, Francis J., Ph.D.  FJB
University of Nevada, Las Vegas

DIXON, Patrick, M.D.  PD
AIDS Care Education and Training, London, UK

HEMFELT, Robert, Ed.D.  RH
Minirth-Meier Clinic, Texas

PAYNE, Franklin (Ed), Jr., M.D.  FEP
The Medical College of Georgia, Augusta

PAYNE, Karl, M.Div.  KIP
Scott Memorial Baptist Church, El Cajon, California

SMITH, Janet, Ph.D.  JS
University of Dallas, Texas

SNIDER, Noah  NS
Author

WESTFALL, Bruce, B.A.  BW
Journalist

# The Encyclopedia of

# Biblical Ethics

# -A-

**ABORTION.** Abortion is a procedure which involves the premature expulsion of the fetus with the intent of bringing about its death. The most important United States Supreme Court decision concerning abortion is *Roe v. Wade* (1973). Recently, however, *Webster v. Reproductive Health Services* (1989) chipped away at Roe's foundation.

In *Roe,* the Court divided pregnancy into three trimesters. It ruled that aside from normal procedural guidelines (e.g., an abortion must be safely performed by a licensed physician) a state has no right to restrict abortion in the first six months of pregnancy. Thus a woman could have an abortion during the first six months of pregnancy for any reason. In the last trimester the state has a right, although not an obligation, to restrict abortions to only those cases in which the mother's health is jeopardized, since the state *may* have a legitimate interest in prenatal life. In sum, *Roe v. Wade* does not prevent a state from having unrestricted abortion for the entire nine months of pregnancy if it so chooses.

But the Court's "health restriction" is a restriction in name only. For it so broadly defined health in *Roe*'s companion decision, *Doe v. Bolton* (1973), that for all intents and purposes the current law in every state except Missouri allows for abortion on demand. In *Bolton* the court ruled that health must be taken in its broadest possible medical context, and must be defined "in light of all factors—physical, emotional, psychological, familial, and the woman's age—relevant to the well being of the patient. All these factors relate to health." Since all pregnancies have consequences for a woman's emotional and family situation, the court's health provision has the practical effect of legalizing abortion up until the time of birth if a woman can convince her physician that she needs the abortion to preserve her "emotional health."

On July 3, 1989, in *Webster,* the Court reversed (in a 5 to 4 vote) a lower court decision and upheld a Missouri statute which contained language that contradicted certain aspects of *Roe* and *Bolton,* such as *Roe*'s trimester breakdown and their permissive "health" provision which allows for third-trimester abortions. Although *Webster* neither overturned *Roe* nor affected the *Roe*-modeled statutes in states other than Missouri, it did invite other states to pass restrictive abortion laws which may be legally challenged and eventually serve as the impetus to finally overturn *Roe.* As of the publication of this article, several states have passed post-*Webster* laws restricting abortion, which are currently being challenged in the courts.

Ethicists who argue either for or against abortion focus on either one of two issues: (1) the moral status of the fetus; and (2) the bodily autonomy of the pregnant woman.

*The Moral Status of the Fetus.* Scientifically there is no doubt that the beginning of an individual human life begins at conception and does not end until natural death. At the moment of conception, when sperm and ovum cease to exist as individual entities, all human genetic characteristics are present in this tiny individual. No new genetic information is added to the individual from this moment until natural death. All that is needed, as with the rest of us, is food, water, air, and an environment which is conducive to survival.

The unborn human gradually develops from the moment of conception, as is true of humans at later stages, such as the development from infancy to childhood to adolescence. So it does not follow from the fact of human development that the unborn human is any less human than the infant, the child, or the adolescent, who are nonetheless fully human although they are gradually developing.

However, abortion-"rights" ethicists do not deny the *humanity* of the unborn. What they argue is that the fetus is not a *person* until some decisive moment after conception. Some argue that personhood does not arrive until brain waves are detected (40 to 43 days) or at sentience (10 weeks). Others define a person as a being who can do certain things, such as have consciousness, solve complex problems, and communicate, which would put the arrival of personhood quite possibly *after birth.* Although all these views agree that killing innocent persons is wrong, they disagree as to when a person comes into existence.

These human being/person distinctions are flawed for at least two reasons. First, they are completely arbitrary. There are no essential, only functional, grounds for declaring some humans non-persons. The unborn cannot walk, talk, think "abstractly," and early on they have no consciousness. But then again some adults and children temporarily lose these functions. Consequently, to make a distinction on functional grounds would justify killing such children and adults, although they are undoubtedly still persons.

Second, determining personhood by function confuses function with essence. Function is the result of essence, not the reverse. For example, imagine two newborn twins, Larry and Stacey. Larry attains self-consciousness and then lapses into a coma for eight years, after which he will come out. Stacey is born in a coma, never attaining self-consciousness, and will come out of it at the same moment as Larry. The only difference between Larry and Stacey is one of function—the former attained self-consciousness whereas the latter did not. Suppose one argues that it is permissible to kill Stacey but not Larry the day before they are set to come out of the coma. But this seems absurd. The difference between Larry and Stacey is functional only, not a difference in essence, and thus not morally relevant, precisely the same kind of difference between the unborn and the born. Consequently, the unborn are not humans who are potential persons, but human persons with great potential.

*The Bodily Autonomy of the Pregnant Woman.* Judith Jarvis Thomson argues that even if the fetus is a person with a right to life, this does not mean that a woman must be forced to use her bodily organs to sustain its life. Just as one does not have a right to use another's kidney if one's kidney has failed, the fetus, although having a basic right to life, does not have a right to life so strong that it outweighs the pregnant woman's right to personal bodily autonomy.

Thomson mistakenly assumes that one does not have a moral obligation to one's children unless one has volunteered for such a role. But consider the following. Suppose a couple has sex and uses many forms of contraception, but the woman conceives. She chooses not to abort, but the father is unaware of this decision (and legally, the father has no right to take part in the decision; see *Planned Parenthood of Missouri v. Danforth,* [1976]). Since after the child's birth he declines to provide child support, she seeks legal action. Although not *volunteering* for fatherhood, all child support laws in the United States would demand that he accept responsibility for his child's livelihood *precisely because* of his relationship to this child. Child-support laws assume that the child has a right to expect his parents' bodies to be an indirect resource for maintaining his existence. If the father repairs cars, the state will intervene if some of the effort he expends fixing cars is not used to provide food for his child.

Thus if the born child has a natural claim upon her father's body, why does not the fetus, who Thomson assumes is a person, also have a natural claim upon her mother's body? A court will not force a parent to donate a kidney to his dying child or force a pregnant woman to carry her child to term where there is a good chance that continuing the pregnancy will kill her or seriously impair her health. But these types of "dependence" on the parent's body are highly unusual and differ radically from ordinary pregnancy, since donating one's own kidney and giving up one's life are not part of the ordinary obligations associated with the *natural* and *ordinary* process of human development and parental nurturing. Hence, most who oppose abortion nevertheless believe that abortions to save the mother's life are morally justified, since it is a greater good that one live (the mother) rather than two die (both mother and child).

*Popular Arguments.* On a popular level, people justify abortion by arguing that many children are unwanted because of many reasons: economics, a pregnancy resulting from rape or incest, the deformation of the fetus, a pregnancy that is psychologically damaging to mother, etc. But all these reasons beg the question of the moral status of the fetus since the killing of born children is not morally justified for any of these reasons. The real question, then, is whether or not the unborn are persons. And if they are, then killing them can be justified only on the same grounds we justify the killing of born people

From a distinctively Christian point of view, the "rights" talk in the abortion controversy wrongly construes the relationship between unborn child and mother in adversarial terms, fetal rights vs. mother's rights, when the relationship is instead one of love. Neither the child nor the mother are seen as individuals competing to achieve autonomously independent existence, but as members of the Christian community, which is itself called to express love by protecting both child, a gift from God, and mother.

The Christian ethic from earliest times (cf. the *Didache* 2.2) opposed abortion as a part of its special concern for widows, orphans, the poor, and the unborn. Scripture proclaims God to be the author of life and witnesses to its high value even before birth (Ps. 139; Luke 1:42). Together Scripture and Christian tradition value children and the ethic of love and self-sacrifice highly, and thus conflict fundamentally with the choice to abort.

**Bibliography:** Beckwith, F., and Geisler, N., *Matters of Life and Death* (1992); Feinberg, J., (ed.), *The Problem of Abortion,* 2nd ed. (1984); Hauerwas, S., *Character and the Christian Life* (1989); Horan, D. *et al,* (eds.), *Abortion and the Constitution* (1987); Schwarz, S., *The Moral Question of Abortion* (1990).

See CONTRACEPTION; FETAL RIGHTS; INFANTICIDE; LIFE, SACREDNESS OF; MEDICAL ETHICS; MURDER.

F.J.B.

**ABSOLUTES, MORAL.** The phrase *moral absolute* is ambiguous. As conventionally used it is taken to mean a moral rule which applies, or is true, irrespective of culture or society. More precisely it means a moral rule enjoining or forbidding some type of action or specifying some value to which there are no exceptions, one which is obligatory in all circumstances (e.g., one ought never to steal). Someone who claimed that one ought never to steal, no matter what the consequences, would be a moral absolutist with respect to stealing, just as someone who held that all actions ought without exception to exemplify divine love or foster human happiness would hold these values absolutely.

In modern times there have been two sources of moral absolutes. One is some version of law theory, according to which certain actions are unnatural (e.g., saturation bombing) and ought never to be permitted, while other actions are natural (e.g., fidelity in marriage) and ought always to be observed. The other source is the moral philosophy of Immanuel Kant (1724-1804) according to which a good will, action in accordance with the moral law, is the only good in all circumstances. Because, according to Kant, a rational agent can never, for example, will that a maxim which permitted lying should become a universal law; therefore, one ought never to tell lies.

Besides general criticisms of natural law (on account of its vagueness) and of Kant's moral philosophy (that it is purely formal, abstract, and unhistorical), absolutism has been attacked on both factual and logical grounds. It has been argued that cultural diversity supports the view that human nature is both variable and datable. But if this criticism is intended to show that no moral rules are followed universally, then it may be misplaced because what is claimed by the absolutist is not that all people *do in fact* follow the same moral rules, but that all *ought* to. In any case the conclusions drawn from anthropological evidence can be overstated, for cultural differences may conceivably be different exemplifications of the same absolute value.

Objections have also been raised about how moral absolutes are to be recognized (by intuition? by reason? through conscience? education?). But perhaps the most damaging objection arises over the prospect of two or more absolute moral rules. If it is not possible to avoid conflicts between them, then how are such conflicts to be adjudicated?

The view that there are absolute moral rules is typically opposed by some version of consequentialism, according to which the rightness or wrongness of an action depends not on its character as an action but upon its consequences, for example, happiness or human welfare. Consequentialism can be thought of as the idea that there is only one absolute value in terms of which the morality of all actions is to be assessed. Rule-utilitarianism, the doctrine that those moral *rules* ought to be kept which have the best consequences even when particular actions may not have the best consequences, is an attempt to provide an intermediate position between consequentialism and absolutism.

Because of the multiplicity of divine commands in, for example, the Decalogue or in the moral teaching of Christ, it is hard to see how any one type of action can be regarded by the Christian as absolutely right or wrong. For what if the obligation to tell the truth conflicts with the obligation to preserve life? In fact to many divine commands, if not to all, mainstream Christian ethics has readily allowed exceptions. The command "Thou shalt not kill" has not been generally regarded as being disobeyed by the killing of an enemy in the furtherance of a just war or by capital punishment for certain criminal offenses. Christ's words citing the greatest of the commandments (Matt. 22:36-40) lend plausibility to the idea that such conflicts ought to be resolved by personal judgments about how best to exemplify love to God and love to mankind.

It might be held that if certain types of action or moral values are morally absolute in the sense indicated, then it follows that such moral absolutes ought to override every other sort of concern. Of course, this does not follow, and to maintain such a moralistic stance would require separate argument.

**Bibliography:** Geach, P. T., *The Virtues* (1977); Kant, I., *Groundwork of the Metaphysics of Morals*, trans. H. J. Paton (1948).

See ANTINOMIANISM; NORMS; PRINCIPLES, BIBLICAL; SITUATION ETHICS.

P.H.

**ABSOLUTION.** This term, derived from the Latin *absolvo*, "release from," has occurred in Christian history in two senses:

Because human sins are remitted through Christ's atoning work on Calvary (1 John 1:7), sinners who confess their offenses and claim the merits of Christ's redemption are liberated or absolved from their iniquities. It is God who absolves, since only He can forgive sins (cf. Mark 2:7). Yet Scripture also provides for mutual confession (James 5:16) and spiritual support for sinners through prayer. In the Reformed tradition, absolution, where practiced, comprised the declaration to the penitent sinner of God's absolving grace in Christ.

Early Roman Catholicism interpreted Christ's statement about forgiving and retaining sins (John 20:23) as a warrant for the priest to preside in judgment over an individual's transgressions (cf. Matt. 16:19; 18:18). Subsequently a tribunal of penance provided the framework for priestly absolution, and penance was accorded sacramental status.

In Patristic times, absolution involved the spiritual reinstatement of one laid under church censure and disbarred from communion because of heinous crimes.

See FORGIVENESS.

**ABSTINENCE.** Voluntary restraint from a particular thing or action, commonly involving foods, alcohol, drugs, and carnal relations.

The first scriptural instance of abstinence forbade the use of blood given to Noah (Gen. 9:4). The Israelites began abstaining later from eating the "sinew of the hip" (Gen. 32:32). Leviticus 11 required Israelites to abstain from certain foods to avoid uncleanness or possible fatal illnesses; the Law prohibited the ingestion of fat, blood, or entrails (Lev. 3:14-17; 7:3-5), as well as from anything consecrated to idols (Exod. 34:15). Priests officiating at the sanctuary were to abstain from alcohol (Lev. 10:9), and the Rechabites (Jer. 35) abstained from alcoholic beverages voluntarily.

Earliest Christians observed prohibitions of the Mosaic Law, although with Christ's coming all meats were deemed clean (Mark 7:19; Acts 10:15). The Council of Jerusalem acted to promote unity, restricting compulsory abstinence to "things polluted by idols . . . sexual immorality . . . things strangled, and . . . blood" (Acts 15:20).

Christian abstinence should result from personal spiritual guidance based on the Gospel (1 Cor. 10:23-24), not from religious prohibitions that actually undermine it (cf. Col. 2:20-23; 1 Tim. 4:1-3).

See ALCOHOLISM; CELIBACY; SEX; SMOKING; VICE.

**ACQUIRED IMMUNE DEFICIENCY SYNDROME** (AIDS). AIDS is the greatest threat to public health this century. First reported in five homosexual men in July 1981, it quickly became known as the "gay plague." The term AIDS was used in 1982, the virus HIV identified in 1983 and the first heterosexual case identified in Africa in 1985. At the same time scientists first realized that HIV could be transmitted in the blood and screening was started, too late for thousands given infected blood products or transfusions.

Most health campaigns started only from 1986 onwards, by which time it is estimated that at least six million were infected, one million in the U.S. By the end of 1991, one in 250 of the entire adult population of the world was already infected, three out of four through heterosexual activity. By the year 2000, out of 40 million expected infections, over 36 million will be among heterosexuals in developing countries, mainly Asia. Already countries in Africa are reporting that up to a third of all sexually active adults in some towns and cities are infected or dying.

The gay label is totally inappropriate and dangerously inaccurate; yet it continues to dominate the thinking of many Christians. Some have declared AIDS to be the wrath of God on the gay community—an illogical position to take in view of the fact that lesbians are the one group almost entirely protected from sexually transmitted HIV. If AIDS is the wrath of God, then syphilis was, too; or did syphilis cease to be an expression of God's wrath when penicillin was discovered? Another view is that AIDS is a sexually transmitted disease like any other, a part of our cause-and-effect world.

The Christian response to AIDS is demonstrated in the attitude of Jesus to the woman caught in adultery: "Neither do I condemn you. Go and sin no more." In the church we find it hard to love unconditionally, yet still maintain Jesus' teaching on behavior. We emphasize either God's love or God's standards; Jesus held to both.

To many Christians in other nations, the slowness of the church in the U.S. to respond compassionately to the AIDS problem is hard to understand. Because of a delay of up to 20 years between infection and death, almost any growing church can expect people in the congregation with AIDS as a result of previous life-styles. The nearest equivalent of a leper today is someone with AIDS: often thrown out of the home and deprived of a job by reactions of colleagues, rejected by family and friends, living in constant fear of assault or insult, coping with isolation, loneliness, and a slow uncertain death. No wonder suicide rates are so high among those with HIV.

Yet in many countries the church is starting to make a significant contribution to the care of those with AIDS and to effective prevention. Practical care to those dying at home is an opportunity to offer love to people who may have a very different world view. The church can play a key role in education by providing clear factual information, enabling people to make choices about protecting their health. Overseas missions are often well placed to make a major contribution to the AIDS fight in countries like Uganda and Malawi.

Many churches have been worried about the safety of the communion cup. Although saliva can contain HIV if the person is infected, the risk from kissing is considered to be immeasurably small and that from a shared cup even less. The church needs to show by example that HIV is an infection we need not fear unless we have sex or share a needle with an infected partner.

**Bibliography:** Dixon, Patrick, *The Whole Truth About AIDS* (1989); *Ibid., AIDS and You* (1991).

See HOMOSEXUALITY; SUFFERING; VENEREAL DISEASE.

P.D.

**ADDICTION.** An addiction is an exaggerated and pathological dependency of one human being upon another person, institution, substance, activity, or even series or pattern of interior mood states or thought patterns. These objects of the addiction are commonly referred to as the addiction agents. Much contemporary knowledge about addiction resulted from studies of one particular addiction agent (mood-altering chemical substances) and of their concomitant dependency patterns, such as alcoholism or classic drug addiction.

While for many decades the term *addiction* was understood to mean "drug addiction," recently behavioral scientists have acknowledged a far broader range of potential addiction agents. Not only a substance such as ethyl alcohol, but also an activity such as work can be such an agent. The workaholic forms an almost symbiotic dependency on certain activities or achievements that may closely parallel classic drug addiction.

Potential addiction agents include food (compulsive overeating and other eating disorders); activity, achievement (workaholism), rigid performance standards (perfectionism), the emphasis on form rather than substance in spiritual matters (religiosity, religious legalism, or spiritual addiction); erotic fantasy and arousal (sexual addiction); money (compulsive spending, hoarding, or shopping); and interpersonal relationships (codependent relationships, often involving the interchangeable relationship roles of victim, victimizer, and/or rescuer). None of these agents is necessarily addictive in and of itself. Reliance on these agents crosses an invisible line into the realm of addiction when the reliance is perceived as necessary for survival, identity, or the eradication of mental or emotional pain.

The addiction process is frequently understood as a cyclical phenomenon beginning with emotional pain and unresolved emotional neediness. Many theorists point to a painful or traumatic family-of-origin relationships as the deepest source of this pain, with the source identified as the "shame base." Addicts are drawn to the addiction agent as both a source of physical or emotional anesthesia for the shame-caused pain and as a surrogate means of providing identity and fulfillment. Although addicts may reach compulsively for the addiction agent in order to address both the old shame base as well as other contemporary sources of distress, the agent fails to truly resolve these problems. Addicts fail to treat the authentic source of discomfort, and the practice of the addiction generates new sources of pain in the form of fallout or consequences. This new pain adds to the old, and the addict relies more heavily on the addiction agent in a doomed effort to eliminate the ever-escalating pain. As this vicious cycle tightens its grip, addicts attempt to defend, rationalize, and deny the addictive properties of their behavior, further complicating addiction.

Besides denial, two other dynamics appear universally in addiction. Addicts may rapidly form a *tolerance* for the anesthetic effect of the agent; each time they recycle through the pain/anesthesia/fallout cycle, progressively larger doses of the agent are required. When addicts attempt to abstain from the agent, they experience the intensely unpleasant sensations accompanying *withdrawal*.

Withdrawal discomfort consists of the original shame, the added pain of the addiction cycle fallout, and a new sense of panic over the inability to function without the addiction. Withdrawal pain is usually so acute that addicts return to the shame or even elevated levels of dependency on the agent; and this return is usually accompanied by vigorous rationalizations justifying or denying the presence of the addiction.

Addictions are multidimensional, including physical (for example, the biochemical dependence on a drug), emotional (the emotional neediness which originates and propels the addiction), mental (the obsession with the addiction agent), behavioral (the compulsion to act out the addiction cycle), and spiritual dimensions. Modern Christian psychology recognizes that effective addiction treatment must arise from a spiritual foundation. This same recognition is explicit in the writings, teachings, and group dynamics of addiction self-help recovery groups such as Alcoholics Anonymous. These "Twelve Step" recovery organizations view the addiction as a false god and stress profound spiritual conversion and renewal as absolute prerequisites to lasting addiction recovery.

Churches can minister effectively if they learn about addiction, integrate this knowledge with their Gospel ministry, and minister to those caught in addiction without condemning them.

**Bibliography:** *Alcoholics Anonymous* (1976); Minirth, Frank *et al, Love Hunger: Recovery from Food Addiction* (1990); Hemfelt, Robert *et al, Love is a Choice: Recovery for Codependent Relationships* (1989); Arterburn, Steve, and Felton, Jack, *Toxic Faith: Understanding and Overcoming Religious Addiction* (1991); Hemfelt, Robert *et al, We Are Driven* (1991).

See ALCOHOLISM; DRUGS; HALLUCINATORY DRUGS; NARCOTICS.

R.E.H.

**ADULTERY.** Adultery is illicit sex outside marriage and, as well, in the Old Testament by the betrothed with a third party prior to the consummation of marriage. In the Bible sex belongs to marriage. Adultery is consistently prohibited and condemned in both Old and New Testaments.

In the Old Testament, the cornerstone of sexual morality is the seventh commandment, "Thou shalt not commit adultery" (Exod. 20:14; Deut. 5:18). Adultery was prohibited by law and was punishable by death (Lev. 18:20; 20:10; Deut. 22:22-24). This proscription endured late in Old Testament history (Ezek. 18:11-13; 22:11; Mal. 3:5). Fidelity is foremost a moral issue based on the foundations of family life following creation (Gen. 2:24). The Old Testament teaches that God intended a single male and a single female to contract a permanent spiritual union, that is to say, monogamous marriage. Adultery is a violation of this union. This prime moral issue takes precedence over social considerations such as the husband's or wife's individual sexual rights, the assurance that children are a husband's own, or the practice on grounds of the mores of polygamy or polyandry.

The seriousness with which adultery is viewed in the Old Testament is clear from the adultery of David with Bathsheba (2 Sam. 11—12; note David's confession in Ps. 51). By analogy, adultery is used as a symbol of spiritual unfaithfulness and religious backsliding (Jer. 3; 7:9-10; Ezek. 16:26; Hos. 4:11-19).

In the New Testament, Jesus reinforces prohibition of adultery (Matt. 19:18). By not only the actual deed, but by the thought in the heart one is equally culpable (Matt. 5:28); and whoever marries a divorced woman commits adultery with her (Matt. 5:32; Mark 10:11; Luke 16:18). The latter proscription condemns the easy dissolution of marriages and easy remarriage as being in fact adultery. Jesus forgave the woman taken in adultery (John 7:53—8:11) and thus brought even this serious moral lapse under divine grace and forgiveness. Jesus adds, however, "go and sin no more." Similarly, the conversion of the woman at the well of Samaria entailed her commitment to a new, moral lifestyle (John 4:16-26, 39). Paul states that remarriage after the death of a spouse is not adultery (Rom. 7:3; 1 Cor. 7:39).

Adultery is, however, a ground for divorce (Matt. 5:32; 19:9). It is likely that divorce in this case simply ratifies what has in fact already taken place, namely, sinful violation and dissolution of the marriage which is in the first instance a deeply spiritual covenant between contracting persons, rather than a church or civil formation. Forgiveness, reconciliation, and reaffirmation of fidelity may restore the marriage, without divorce occurring.

It is important to set the specific prohibition of adultery in its wider biblical context of prohibition of fornication, including the related vices of lust, indecency, and filthy talk. Exodus 20:10 is understood to include all fornication, which is also true of Paul's many references to sexual sinning. Of Paul's seven major lists of vices, five list fornication as the first vice, and this would include adultery (1 Cor. 5:11; 6:9; Gal. 5:19; Eph. 5:3; Col. 3:5; the other two lists are Rom. 1:19-31 and 2 Cor. 12:10). Someone who fornicates is not really, but is only "called," a brother (1 Cor. 5:11). The seriousness of this sin is clear from 1 Cor. 6:9-20: no fornicator or adulterer can inherit the kingdom of God. Paul goes on to say that because the Christian belongs to Christ and is indwelt by the Holy Spirit, his or her very body cannot be joined to a harlot as well.

It should be noted that the terms for fornication, adultery, and harlotry in the New Testament coincide (Luke 15:30; Acts 15:20, 29; 21:25; 1 Cor. 5:1; 6:13, 18; 7:2; 2 Cor. 12:21; 1 Tim. 1:10; 1 Thess. 4:3). Such prohibitions completely undercut modern attempts to relativize sexual morality as accommodation to varying situations or to glamorize deviant sexual behavior through euphemisms such as "making love" or to excuse it on pseudo-Freudian grounds that sex relieves tension and prevents neurotic guilt. Guilt is due not to abstaining from illicit acts, but from their practice. Forgiveness comes when sin is acknowledged and confessed; spiritual well-being ensues when a new, moral lifestyle is pursued.

Christians are urged to recognize and shun internal and external enticements to sexual sinning. Graphic examples are cited, as in the case of David and Bathsheba, and Samson and Delilah (Judg. 16). The tactics of adultery and fornication include womanly sinful wiles (Prov. 2:16-17; 7:6-23) and male lust (Job 24:15; 31:9; Matt. 5:28). The main vehicles of concupiscence are the eye and the heart, which must be set to see other persons differently from being lustful objects or persons craved sexually. The Scriptures warn against beautifying and justifying sinful desires or behavior.

Throughout the Scriptures such acts as murder and adultery are uniformly and equally condemned as morally wrong. Because sexual abuse was widespread in the Roman world, Christians' emphasis on sexual purity, among other virtues, won them deep respect. Such Christian virtue is as relevant today, and as practical, as it has always been.

When Athenagoras wrote his famous *Plea* to the Emperor Marcus Aurelius about A.D. 175, he declared what had been the Christian ideal and practical morality from New Testament days. Athenagoras pointed out that Christians seek to do more than restrain themselves from evil. They seek to have right relations among themselves and with their neighbors. Thus Christians regard each other as sons and daughters, as brothers and sisters, as fathers and mothers: "We feel it a matter of great importance that those, whom we thus think of as brothers and sisters and so on, should keep their bodies undefiled and uncorrupted." This is the expression of true love.

**Bibliography:** Athenagoras, *Plea* (c.175); Dewar, L., *New Testament Ethics* (1949); Henry, C., *Christian Personal Ethics (1957); Yankelovich, D., New Rules* (1981).

See MARRIAGE; SEXUAL MORALITY.

S.J.M.

**ADVERTISING.** At one time advertising was considered a positive force in society which informed people about goods and services. It was said to help create larger markets so that prices could be lowered as manufacturers took advantage of lower costs produced by greater demand. Recently, however, advertising has come to be viewed as undesirable propaganda and harmful to the public good. Vance Packard's 1957 book, *The Hidden Persuaders*, stands as a monumental attack on advertising and probably marks the beginning of popular criticism of the advertising industry.

Although many people see advertising as propaganda, it is important to notice the differences between the two. Propaganda exists to influence people in a systematic way by reducing the amount of discussion available and encouraging people to act on impulse. Thus, in Nazi Germany the government's propaganda machine was used to eliminate alternative interpretations and provide the German people with endless examples of the value of national socialism. As a result the national socialist view became the only possible interpretation of reality and led people to act accordingly.

By contrast, advertising exists within a framework of choice and alternative views. Although advertisers may want us to buy brand X, they must not only compete with brands Y and Z but also convince us that buying brand X is better than a different purchase. Thus, in selling video equipment the advertiser must not only convince me that their brand of video is better than all other competitors but also that I need a video and not a new car or a ten-year subscription to a magazine. Advertising is therefore very different in purpose and practice from propaganda.

Today advertising cannot be separated from marketing as a total approach. Fundamental to the concept of marketing is the belief that to gain and maintain customers, a product must meet a real need and provide the purchaser with lasting satisfaction. Unless a product is able to meet some needs and leave the purchaser with a satisfied feeling, that product will not survive. Successful marketing is based on the ethically justifiable position of providing satisfaction and meeting real needs.

Critics of advertising counter the claims of marketers by saying that "real needs" may well be "created needs" and that what is luxury today may well become a necessity tomorrow through advertising. In such cases the claim is made that advertising creates unnecessary needs and promotes mindless consumerism. If the world had unlimited resources such created needs might be justifiable; but given limited resources and the fact that millions of people are on the verge of starvation, can advertising still be justified?

Such a question is a good one but goes beyond the ethics of advertising to the problem of economic growth and the relationships among nations. Defenders of advertising would say that it is unrealistic to expect Western peoples to lower their standard of living and that even if they did there is little guarantee that this would help the Third World. Further, it can be argued that, by maintaining healthy economies in the West, advertising ultimately helps Third World peoples by creating demands for their goods and services.

More direct questions about the ethics of advertising concern the immense power advertisers are believed to wield over consumers. Here marketers and their critics sharply disagree. Most marketers and advertising executives argue that advertising is still very much a hit-or-miss affair. We know that in a general sense advertising works, but how it works and which advertisements will be successful is difficult to say. Critics, however, believe that advertisements manipulate people in undesirable ways.

Books like Judith Williamson's *Decoding Advertising* (1974) present a strong case against advertising by showing how advertisements use images to suggest sexual and violent activities which play upon primitive instincts and, in Christian terms, sinful desires. The explicit sexuality of many advertisements and the subtle suggestions that advertisements often convey about power, friendship, wealth, and a host of other human desires may indeed provide cause for concern.

From a Christian perspective, it appears that, while many advertisements may indeed violate Christian moral codes in their use of sex and appeals to greed, advertising as such is not unacceptable. What is needed is a concerted attempt by Christians to monitor advertisements and to judge their social impact in terms of truthfulness and the promotion of ethical values. If advertisements simply inform and enable people to make better choices in a complex technological society, then indeed they may serve a social role. If, however, they promote values which are bound to lead to the breakdown of society, then they need to be controlled. This however leads us to questions of censorship and goes beyond the scope of this article.

In conclusion, advertising can play a positive role in society; but it needs to be carefully monitored and judged by standards of truth, honesty, and moral integrity.

**Bibliography:** DeGoot, G., *The Persuaders Exposed* (1980); Engel, J., *Advertising* (1980); Hyman, A. and Johnson, M. B., *Advertising and Free Speech* (1977).

I.H.

**AFFLUENCE.** This word originated in a Latin verb *affluo*, meaning "to flow, run, flock toward," and was used in the Latin orators in the sense of "to have in abundance, to overflow," with an elevated rather than a pejorative connotation. In modern speech the term is used of wealth and implies respect, admiration, or downright resentment, depending upon the economic perspective of the user.

Through the ages the prospect of amassing great wealth has attracted persons of all races. Unscrupulous means have often been devised to satisfy human cupidity. Thus in ninth century B.C. Palestine, the greedy king Ahab (874-853 B.C.) participated in a contrived process initiated by his wife, Queen Jezebel, to illegally acquire a vineyard belonging to a certain Jezreelite named Naboth (1 Kings 21:1-16). By contrast, other Old Testament figures became affluent because of divine blessing, as with Abraham (Gen. 13:2). His wealth was based not merely upon his herds but also upon gold and silver, of which he had a substantial amount to be able to pay four hundred shekels of silver for the cave of Machpelah as a burial place for the deceased Sarah (Gen. 23:15-16).

Clearly it was not necessary for a person to own land in order to become rich in the ancient world, as the nomadic peoples of the Middle Bronze age (2000-1500 B.C.) and the caravan traders attest. But to become affluent frequently involved a great deal of hard work, uncertainty, and risk-taking, as is the case at the present day. Those who acquired wealth easily could lose it just as effortlessly, as the overthrow of the young king Rehoboam by Shishak of Egypt (1 Kings 14:25-26) illustrated.

While the means by which great riches could be amassed might come under moral condemnation in Old Testament times if they violated the general social ethic of the Sianai covenant, riches as such were regarded either as morally neutral, or as evidence of divine blessing. Only the motivating factors which underlay a person's affluence were subject to moral scrutiny. While the Old Testament prophets generally regarded riches as one of the factors that could occasion moral decadence in the individual, instructed no doubt by the example of Solomon, their preference for the values of the simpler and stricter nomadic life did not in itself preclude the amassing of wealth.

Nowhere in His teaching did Jesus condemn riches in themselves, and in His ministry He mingled with affluent and poor alike. What He did condemn, however, was the person who trusted in his wealth for security and salvation rather than acknowledging God as the source of his affluence (Deut. 8:17-18; Hos. 2:8) and basing his faith on God alone.

Affluence brings with it a certain degree of power that often results in the oppression of others in various ways. This did not escape the notice of the psalmist who commented pointedly on the way in which God deals with the misuse of affluence (Ps. 52:7). The counsel that people should not set their hearts upon riches should they increase (Ps. 62:10) applies to individuals in all ages, if only because of the fact that the love of money is the root of all evil (1 Tim. 6:9-10).

Since, however, money is one of God's precious gifts to humanity, it is at least worthy of consideration that there should and must be a godly use of affluence, just as there can be abuses of it. Here the devout Christian character of the individual is mandatory if wealth is to receive the most satisfying kind of stewardship, as is the firm resolve that one's affluence shall be sanctified by the process of tithing. This act not only invites divine blessing upon the resources of the donor; it also brings rich spiritual benefits and blessings in other ways (Mal. 3:10).

Those who interpret Christ's challenge to a single individual to sell all his possessions (Matt. 19:16-22) as a general command to them to dispose of all their possessions make a mistake that is as erroneous spiritually as it is devastating economically. The plain teaching of the Old Testament is that God does not demand all our financial resources. He is well satisfied with one-tenth given in love for Him and His creatures. He knows that if we were to donate everything to Him, we would then be forced to join the already swollen ranks of the impoverished, thereby making an already critical problem so much worse. But by remaining affluent, an individual is able to continue, hopefully for many years, to support those who are in economic need.

Affluent people, especially Christians, are frequently harrassed by other persons, some of them also professed Christians, who are constantly giving the impression that affluence is an evil that needs to be eradicated in the interests of high spirituality, social justice, or other considerations. This is not the teaching of Jesus about wealth. He recognized that economically deprived people would continue to exist and be the objects of charity periodically from others who had the will and the resources to support them (Mark 14:7). He also made it clear that He alone must be the one for whom the good work must really be done. Or, as Paul expressed it more plainly, if we give all our goods to feed the poor and are not activated by the altruistic love of Christ, it is of no profit whatever to us.

For an affluent person to monopolize his or her wealth to the neglect of others is morally wrong. Such an individual is not helping to bear the burdens of the poorer brother or sister for whom Christ also died. But even with the most dedicated and altruistic of motives there can be certain pitfalls associated with the distribution of monetary resources. Some reforming enthusiasts believe money should be applied in such a way as to enable people to assist themselves through some form of employment that will provide a sense of responsibility and some feeling of purpose in life. Unfortunately, the disbursing of charity money or of relief supplies so often does nothing more than address the needs of the moment and seldom satisfies the productive urges that normally healthy people possess. What is even more regrettable is the fact that, under some circumstances, the distribution of affluence actually demeans the recipients in the process.

Before any moral judgments are formulated, it is important for a distinction to be made between the appearance of affluence and its actuality. In the inflation-ravaged countries of South America, for example, a casual glance at average citizens on the street shows them to be neatly and attractively dressed. A closer examination, however, frequently reveals that the individuals concerned are commonly wearing what is probably the only dress or suit that they possess and that their footwear is of poor quality or in a serious state of disrepair. The United States as a country is the envy of people in the Third World because of the affluence which appears to be depicted by so many facets of American life. But for several years the country's deficit has been increasing annually, which casts quite a different light upon the supposed affluence of the United States.

It would seem prudent for the wealthy to avoid causing offense to their less fortunate fellows by maintaining a low profile in society, a procedure which some extremely wealthy individuals practice assiduously for their own security. There are others, however, who are so foolish as to flaunt their wealth, and worse still, to misuse it so that they exploit and corrupt those around them. As for the ones who criticize the affluent because of their wealth, a great deal of uninformed opinion and consequent bad judgment regarding the source, nature, and disposition of the wealth often underlies their pronouncements. It is not always easy to avoid the conclusion that the tirades of some of the more vocal opponents of affluence are motivated more by envy than by actual concern for the poor. Affluence thus presents moral problems for all concerned and would seem to need special wisdom and grace if it is to be handled in a manner that will glorify God and work toward the benefit of humanity.

See PROSPERITY; WEALTH.

**AGAPE.** The two most widely used words for love in the New Testament along with their cognates are *agape* and *philos*. The term *eros*, which was historically the common word for love in Greek along with *philos*, does not occur in the New Testament. The question about the lexical origin and meaning of *agape* and the significance of the absence of *eros* from the New Testament have produced vigorous discussion and conflicting scholarly opinion. Some have argued that *agape* is a providentially initiated and preserved term uniquely suitable to express divine love. Others have argued that *eros* was excluded from the New Testament because of its traditional sexual overtones. Still others maintain that the uses or nonuses of these terms are simply either historical accidents or the natural consequences of the evolution of language and that no term lexically is more spiritual or theological than any other.

The translators of the Septuagint, which is the pre-Christian era translation of the Old Testament into Greek, did not make such fine distinctions. They commonly used *agape* and its cognates for sexual love (Song of Sol. 2:4-5, 7; 5:8; 8:6), *eros*, and *philos* synonymously (Prov. 7:18). In Psalm 109:5 and Hosea 11:4 *agape* identifies human affection and loyalty and in Habakkuk 3:4 admiration for might. Plato used a form of *agape* to describe the love of a wolf for a lamb (*Phaedrus* 241d), which does not fit the exclusively spiritual connotations attached by some to *agape*.

Whether or not the absence of *eros* from the New Testament is a conscious omission is a matter of dispute. Its sexual overtones are clearly not the meaning for love which most New Testament references require. Some believe as well that its classical use for aspiration to the divine is not consistent with Christian spiritual aspiration or the meaning of grace. *Philos* is employed commonly for human affection, including the kiss of greeting. While earlier uses of *agape* embrace the normal range of human affection in the Septuagint, the total absence of *agape* from nonbiblical texts is puzzling. Only one occurrence has been cited and the broken state of the text has drawn vigorous denial that the occurrence is in fact *agape*. It would appear that *agape* was picked up in Christian vocabulary, perhaps from the Septuagint, as the ordinary word for love and that it and its older synonymn *philos* were used interchangeably (John 21:15, 17). *Agape*, meaning

love with the added dimension of being other-regarding, dominated use for redemptive love and Christian interpersonal love.

In the New Testament, *agape* is used for the highest form of love, including God's love to mankind (John 3:16; Rom. 5:8), God's love to Christ (John 15:9; 17:23, 26), Christ's love to mankind (John 15:9; Gal. 2:20; Eph. 2:4), man's love to God and Christ (John 14:23-24; 1 John 2:5), and men's love to one another (John 13:35; 1 John 3:14; 4:20). Notably, John and Paul use this word extensively in a natural and unforced way to express the truth about God's relationship to mankind, man's to God, and the best interpersonal relationships among men.

The single and most important characteristic of the love which *agape* identifies has to do with persons and personal relationships and the ethics of those relationships. This is crucial with respect to the biblical teaching about God, the world, and redemption.

Firstly, in the Bible, love is not God's way to the world ontologically. Regarding the nature of God, various forms of ancient and modern demythologizing reconstruct the interpersonal nature of love. To say that God is love or that God loves is thought to jeopardize the impassibility or simplicity of God's nature, which seemed unappealing to Plato. Ancient Gnostics theorized that the world is the product of the overflow of the divine essence or that the world derives from descending emanations from the primordial impassible divine principle. According to the Gnostics and contrary to traditional Christian teaching, desire enters only well down the scale in relation to the material, evil-infected world.

Secondly, neither is love the world's way to God. This was the role of *eros* in various Greek philosophical traditions. Man aspires to the beatific vision, to mystical union with the divine, hence the traditions which advocate the pursuit of absolute beauty or absolute truth through ecstatic flight of the soul. Paul Tillich, for example, denies that God personally loves. Tillich says that love is aspiration or drive to unity. Love is that attracting and impelling power which moves us toward reunion with God, which he defines as full actualization of individual life in a social context. While the concept of aspiration lends credence to the attracting power of transcendental ideals, it misses the active, gracious, other-regarding character of God's love.

Thirdly, love is not man's way to himself, though healing and reintegrating sin-broken persons is certainly a function of love. Love is not to be redefined to signify purely human personality dynamics and relationships. The final stage of contemporary demythologizing does precisely this. Some argue that to say that God is love is too anthropomorphic; rather, that God is love means that I believe in pure personal relationships or that I feel good about myself. In other words, the being of God and the love of God become functions of human nature and human relationships, not attributes of the God who creates, cares, loves, and redeems.

Love is the essence of God's nature, and this truth controls our understanding of all love. When John says "God is love" (1 John 4:8), this means more than that God loves men or that they love one another. It means that, as the living God, His inmost nature is love. In the Bible, far from protecting God from attribution of love to His nature in order to shield His impassibility, both testaments of Scripture freely declare that God is love and that He loves. There is no higher metaphysical reality than personhood. God is personal and He loves personally. On this text C. H. Dodd helpfully comments, "If the characteristic divine activity is that of loving, then God must be personal, for we cannot be loved by an abstraction, or by anything else less than a person."

This truth fits the full range of Christian teaching. God is triune, Father, Son, and Holy Spirit, and love is the essence of the divine interpersonal relations (John 17:23). God deals with mankind redemptively through his love (1 John 4:10). Consequently this love becomes the sphere of the Christian life (John 15:9), and this mode of God's dealing with us becomes the pattern of our own relationships with one another (1 John 4:16-21).

Love is essentially other-regarding. Anders Nygren and many others overdraw the distinction between *eros* as self-acquisitive and *agape* as value-conferring. J. M. Rist has shown that *eros* means more than sensual, self-seeking desire. Nevertheless, the other-regarding character of love as *agape* in biblical teaching is clear. Love is not so much value-creating as value affirming. Because men are sinners does not mean that they are of no value. Rather, the immense value which God placed upon mankind through creation is reaffirmed through redemptive love.

Redemptive love operates morally. While redemption originates in love, it is not achieved by display or attraction but by action, which is the cross. Hence the biblical epitome of love: if love, then persons; and if persons, then morality. Love in the Bible is holy love.

Paul has much to say about the ethics of the sphere of love into which Christians are redeemed (Eph. 6:23). Christians are the beloved of God (Rom. 1:7; 8:37-39), which means they are lovingly chosen through grace. God loves sinners (Rom. 5:8), and believing sinners themselves become repositories of God's love (Rom. 5:5; 15:30). Christian life operates within a range of new categories, including faith, hope, and love. These are not merely beliefs. They identify a new lifestyle, a new set of moral relationships among Christians and new ways of dealing with others (Gal. 5:22-23; 1 Thess. 1:3; 3:6).

The way of life which is infused by the love of God is Paul's great theme in 1 Corinthians 13. It should be borne in mind that Paul in this letter wrote to a factious church where some members were boasting super-spirituality. The most excellent way of life, he declared (1 Cor. 12:31), is not self-seeking. It is the way of love. This chapter not only defines love, it sets forth ethics that operate within the sphere of love. Here is true love for one's brother or sister or neighbor. Here is a true prescription for inner healing. Having concluded, Paul repeats, "Make love your aim" (1 Cor. 14:1).

What is the ethical prescription of 1 Corinthians 13? It begins with the infinite value of persons: if a man has no love (love regards persons as ends, not means), he is hollow despite all pretensions to abilities and gifts (vv. 1-3). Love is therefore the necessary inner essence of valid human existence. Paul identifies love in God and love in man; he draws no distinction between them. We may take it that 1 Corinthians 13 defines what Paul found in Christ.

Fourteen paired statements follow (vv. 4-7), which are ethical prescriptions as well as descriptions of love and how it works. Love is long-tempered and gentle; it seethes neither with jealousy nor envy; it makes no bragging display; it is not arrogantly puffed up nor is it unmannerly and tactless; love does not look out only for its own interests; it does not get angry easily or remain bitter long after a wrong; love does not store up resentment; love takes no pleasure in the wrongdoing of others; rather, it takes pleasure in the truth and in what is right; love forbears; it absorbs much; love believes the best rather than the worst when there is no proof. Love believes that good will finally prevail, which is the heart of hope. Love endures, despite the odds. Paul concludes (v. 8) that love never ends. Beyond all the things that men might prize, true personhood and full maturity embrace and are defined by the life of love. Love is the greatest virtue among the trilogy of faith, hope, and love (v. 13).

**Bibliography:** Morris, L., *Testaments of Love* (1981); Newlands, G. M., *Theology of the Love of God* (1980); Nygren, A., *Agape and Eros* (1953); Rist, J. M., *Eros and Psyche* (1964).

See EROS; LOVE.

S.J.M.

**AGED, CARE OF THE.** The practice of population control in Western countries in an attempt to approximate "zero growth" has combined with better geriatric care to focus attention on a steady increase in the numbers of elderly people in society. Currently, more than one in ten persons can be regarded as aged—a proportion that is unlikely to diminish in the future.

In the biblical world the elderly were respected because of their experience, and it was rare for this tradition to be questioned (Job 32:9). By contrast, the youth-orientation of modern society has diminished seriously the influence of the aged, frequently making them feel insecure, burdensome, and unwanted. Whereas the family formerly cared for its elderly members, the disintegration of home life, coupled with the lack of domestic help and the general need for most family members to work, has now reduced drastically the viability of this source of care. But an accepting family situation where Christian love is paramount is still the ideal environment for the elderly, whether sick or well.

Many people romanticize old age, forgetful of the ravages of body and mind that it can bring. Even when comparatively free from infirmity, the aged are often tormented by despair, bitter regrets, a sense of failure, and fear of death. Care of the aged, therefore, must not be thought of primarily in institutional terms, but as a ministry to personalities of a kind that will minimize the loss of status that old age brings and enable individuals to fulfill their days in security and dignity. Many old people feel insecure for spiritual rather than economic reasons. They need to experience, perhaps afresh, the renewing and invigorating presence of Christ in their lives.

Where family facilities do not exist, social services and government institutions of various kinds make valuable provision for the aged at varying degrees of cost. Some homes for senior citizens admit only paying residents who do not require health care, providing facilities that are adequate without being lavish. The majority of staff workers are dedicated and unselfish persons who strive to care for people in various stages of senility.

When the aged are ill, they are normally taken to chronic care wards of public hospitals or to other accommodations that cater to special needs. The dying of Calcutta, for example, have been provided for in an exemplary manner by the activities of Mother Teresa, as have the terminally ill in the renowned St. Christopher's Hospice in London, directed by Dame Cicely Saunders. In between these varieties of care for the ailing elderly are different kinds of nursing homes, clinics, and municipal facilities.

The Christian church, which fostered the hospital movement, has cared consistently for the aged. Modern church facilities in this area are impressive, not merely for their physical attributes, but also for the spiritual ministry extended to the aged residents. So valuable are the contributions of the churches in this important field of human welfare that they have received the ready support of government in various jurisdictions.

Care for the aged constitutes a fundamentally important area of witness and service for the Christian. Caring for the aged shows the love of Christ for the disadvantaged as well as the whole, reassuring them that they are continuing objects of God's redemptive love and care. A society bent on ignoring or avoiding death needs a theology that identifies death as part of the mystery of existence. The church should speak confidently to this situation from a personal experience of the resurrection power of Christ, which guarantees the believer victory over death (1 Cor. 15:57).

**Bibliography:** Clements, W. M., (ed.), *Ministry With the Aging* (1981); Freeman, C. B., *The*

*Senior Adult Years* (1979); Kubler-Ross, E., *On Death and Dying* (1970); du Boulay, S., *Cicely Saunders—The Founder of the Modern Hospice Movement* (1983); Stoddard, S., *The Hospice Movement* (1978).

**AGGRESSION.** Great ambiguity may attend the use of the term *aggression*, from describing a military action to the use of the term by a pacifist to advocate aggressive pacifism.

The negative connotations of the term go back to its root (*aggress*) as "attach" or "assault," in the sense that the aggressor initiates the attack. He makes it first, unprovoked, whether it is a military action, a fight, a quarrel, or the style of a relationship in which one of the parties is the aggressor and abuser.

Distinctions need to be made between the meaning of *aggression* and terms such as *opposition, conflict, tension, rivalry, resolution, initiative*, and *competition*, Harmony without tension is not mandated by the Christian ethos. At the same time, Christians reject the ancient dictum of Empedocles that conflict is metaphysically the father of all things, which concept is a key feature of Marxist ideology: thesis, antithesis, synthesis. Instead, Christians advocate reconciliation as the key to resolving a conflict—using tension creatively and morally to achieve progress. For Christians, the term *aggression* is used in a benign way, more as *initiative*, employed to cut through bureaucratic stalling or blundering; to encourage efficient, profitable enterprise in business; to provide assistance to the needy quickly, efficiently, and at the lowest cost; to reinforce the commitment of faith and pledge of loyalty to Christ (Matt. 10:14, 34-39; 11:12; Acts 5:29; Rom. 8:13; 1 Cor. 9:24-27; Eph. 6:12).

The roots and causes of human aggression are a matter of uncertainty and great disagreement among theologians, psychologists, psychiatrists, sociologists, and other students of human behavior. Christians believe that aggression, especially when rooted in anger, is a characteristic of sinful humanity not merely in the sense of having been produced or learned behaviorally but as rooted in a fallen nature. Man sins because he is alienated from God the Creator and Norm-giver. The result is aggression in the form· of war, interpersonal quarreling and violence, crime, and various forms of psychological violence. Christians believe the problem is best and most effectively dealt with at its root, in the heart of man (Matt. 15:19; Rom. 1:28-32; 3:9-20; Gal. 5:19-21) through redemption (Rom. 3:21-26; Gal. 5:22-26) and a life subsequently patterned after the teachings of Christ.

The image of the aggressive, swashbuckling North American capitalist, though true in a limited number of cases, does a disservice to the vast numbers of businessmen and businesswomen who create opportunity for others through efficient, competitive enterprise. There are theories of enterprise which advocate aggression as the most effective way to achieve efficiency and success. These are now largely discredited in favor of administration theory, which rejects multilayered levels of communication in which detached executives simply give orders aggressively for leadership. The new approach strives to create a corporate culture in which everyone feels a sense of ownership and responsibility to innovate, produce efficiently, and achieve excellence.

The cure for wrongful aggression is respect for persons and love. This is particularly important in family relations where children are first nurtured in the subtleties of human relationships. Modern pressures on the family raise new questions as to their effects upon the emotional tone of growing children. Do modern problems in family life inhibit the capacity to love and instead generate increased anger, depression, and, consequently, aggressive behavior? Some recent studies claim that day-care for small children, especially during the first three years of life, tends to produce a more aggressive personality. Others challenge this finding. Claims have been made that impersonal rearing, as was said to have occurred in early kibbutz experiments, produces flat emotions. In North American society, increased incidence of divorce, single-parent families, working mothers, and impermanent spousal relations are creating new conditions. Special attention will have to be given to propagating and nurturing love in children through precept and example while preserving creative tension, competition, and creativity.

**Bibliography:** Drucker, P. F., *Innovation and Entrepreneurship* (1985); Forbes, C., *The Religion of Power* (1983); Ouchi, W. G., *Theory Z* (1981); Pfeffer, J., *Power in Organizations* (1981).

S.J.M.

**ALCOHOLISM.** Alcoholism is a condition caused by a dependence upon alcohol which results in physical, emotional, and spiritual disturbance. It is also responsible for related interpersonal, economic, and social problems (e.g., family disintegration, accidents, violence, murder and suicide, unemployment, and poverty).

Alcoholism is a moral problem as well as a physiological disease. The moral choice comes in the actual choice to drink; the disease is the effect of the alcohol on a person's physical, emotional, moral, and spiritual health.

While the biblical writers reflect a variety of views of the use of alcohol, there are many injunctions against drinking wine or strong drink on particular occasions: at meetings (Lev. 10:9); in the inner court of the temple (Ezek. 44:21); for the time of a special consecration (Num. 6:3-20); during particular pregnancies (Judg. 13:4, Luke 1:15). Alcohol is recognized as potentially evil in Isaiah 5:22, 28:7 and in Proverbs 20:1: "Wine is a mocker, strong drink a brawler; and whoever is led astray by it is not wise." Proverbs 23:29-35 contains a description of an alcoholic.

Drunkenness is sometimes confused with the presence of the Spirit (1 Sam. 1:13-18; Acts 2:13).

Jesus uses wine as a teaching tool and as a sign for the people (Luke 5:37-39; John 2:1-11), but sees drunkenness as evil (Luke 12:45). Yet, in Matthew 15:11 we read, "It is not what goes into the mouth that defiles, but what comes out of the mouth." The effects of alcohol on behavior is the major problem which Christians should keep in mind as they work to overcome the forces of alcoholism in their communities.

Attitudes towards alcohol have varied through the history of the church. Some Christians, such as the early American Puritans, have seen alcohol as a "good creature of God" to be enjoyed along with the other fruits of the earth. On the other hand, the evangelical tradition in American Protestantism, with its desire for a new moral order and a new emphasis upon care for others, produced in the nineteenth century the Women's Christian Temperance Movement. A social analysis by this group revealed the evils of alcohol abuse: economic waste, diversion of grain to liquor production from food production, physical danger which faced the pioneer who was not alert, and psychoses and deaths which left families destitute.

Religious perfectionism underlay the temperance movement and provided roots for the founding of Alcoholics Anonymous (AA), a self-help organization begun in the belief that an alcoholic is trying to satisfy deep religious needs in the wrong way. AA uses an approach based upon the resources of alcoholics themselves who had met despair in the bottle but discovered hope in a spiritual force.

AA has been the single most effective agency in the control and treatment of alcoholism. It encourages victims to take one step at a time. First, they stop playing God by admitting their powerlessness and surrender control over their lives to God. Then they confess to God and to one another the sins they have committed under the influence of alcohol; they repent and make amends. They develop humility and begin to grow in their ability to trust, especially in a group committed to spiritual values—first trusting God, then other people. Because alcoholics must continue to exercise vigilance to avoid losing humility, AA members continue with the program after sobriety is established. Finally, alcoholics must pray for knowledge of God's will and the power to carry it out, and they take up the task of working with other alcoholics.

There has been a growth of treatment and research facilities which provide care for the alcoholic and family. Recently there has been special emphasis upon the care of the child of the alcoholic, since the child usually experiences trauma in the home, has difficulties in relating to others, loses self-esteem, and finally runs a high risk of becoming or marrying an alcoholic.

The spiritual factor in the use and abuse of alcohol is widely acknowledged. For example, a strong religious commitment on the part of young people acts as an effective control upon their drinking behavior. Most contemporary forms of treatment recognize the spiritual component as a factor in treatment.

There is no consensus among the churches on the issue of abstinence, but all agree on the need for sobriety (Titus 2:2-3). To be effective, the church's response must be comprehensive, interdisciplinary, and ecumenical. As Christians, we must be aware of our own drinking habits and how they might influence others either as an example, an encouragement, or a problem; Paul encourages the Romans to refrain from drinking wine if it causes another to stumble (Rom. 14:21).

The church has the necessary resources for a ministry to alcoholics and their families based upon characteristics that are specific to Christian communities. These include a caring fellowship based upon trust and commitment to spiritual values; a privileged relationship between the pastor and parishioner; the recognition of sin and the hope of forgiveness; a sound theology including an interpretation for suffering; the regular renewal of self-acceptance based upon our creation in the image of God, which gives each person value; the knowledge that there is a caring God; prayer; mission; closeness to God; regular liturgical experiences of transcendence; celebrations of the goodness of life; social and activity groups; and pastoral authority.

In the past Christian churches initiated concerned actions in response to the problem of alcoholism. Now secular agencies are initiating actions and are challenging the church to respond. It is our Christian responsibility to be actively involved in the prevention and eradication of this problem which has such severe moral and spiritual consequences.

**Bibliography:** Clinebell, H. J., Jr., *Quarterly Journal of Studies in Alcoholism* (1963), XXIV, pp. 473ff.; Drummond, T., *International Journal of Offender Therapy and Comparative Criminology* (1982), XXVI, No. 3, pp. 275–80; Graham, K., Jaggs, K., and Brook, R., *Canada's Mental Health* (1984), XXXII, No. 1., pp. 19–20; Rice, O.R., *Quarterly Journal of Studies in Alcoholism* (1944), V, pp. 250–56; Robinson, D. (ed.), *Alcohol Problems: Reviews, Research and Recommendations (1979).*

See ADDICTION; DRINKING, SOCIAL; DRUGS.

M.M. M-H.

**ALIENATION.** This is a general term which describes an act or state of estrangement, which has several usages. In law it designates the conveyance of property. This is matched in ethical theory by the dictum that, while some rights can be alienated, others, such as the right to freedom, may not or can not.

The philosopher Hegel maintained, with Plato, that nature was a self-alienated form of Absolute Mind. But he held that man, too, is alienated by not becoming the agency for communicating to the Absolute the knowledge necessary for dealienation. In that event every human product expresses alienation, since mankind's essence remains unfulfilled.

Marx went further in stating that man alienates himself not merely in religion, as Feuerbach maintained, but in social matters as well. These include economics, capital, law, and politics. He saw humanity's greatest alienation in the area of human labor—the processes and effects of which enslaved individuals and alienated them from their products and from each other in what Marx called "concrete alienation."

Biblical tradition described mankind's alienation from God as the result of man's disobedience (Gen. 3:11-24). Even in this calamity, however, the hope of reconciliation was promised (Gen. 3:15). It is possible that Hegel derived his concepts of alienation and disalienation from the Christian doctrine of original sin.

In the Old Testament alienation also described the conveyance of property (Ezek. 48:14), and the emotional trauma of marital infidelity (Jer. 6:8). The New Testament recognized the alienation *(allotrius)* of the person from God (Eph. 2:12; 4:18) because of sin, but emphasized equally that in the cross Jesus has reconciled the sinner to God (Col. 1:21). Paul's ministry of reconciliation (2 Cor. 5:19-20) was intended specifically to end human alienation and restore fellowship between man and God.

Alienation was formerly a psychiatric synonym for insanity. The term is now used for any form of personal or social deficit.

**Bibliography:** Feuerbach, L., *The Essence of Christianity* (1957 ed.); Marx, K., *Economic and Philosophical Manuscripts* (1844; first published in 1932).

See WAGES; WORK.

**ALLEGIANCE.** This term is derived from the Latin *ligare*, "to bind." In medieval Europe the term was used of the feudal obligations of a vassal to his overlord. Allegiance now describes a citizen's duty to a ruler or government. In a wider sense it denotes general loyalty to various organizations, including the Christian church, and even Christ himself. A specific form known as "express allegiance" is an obligation based upon an oath or an understanding given in direct, explicit terms.

The biblical teaching about fidelity to a ruler or government occurs in Romans 13:1-7. Just as the family is God's ideal basis of society, so a state headed by a strong leader (who need not be a Christian) can be used by God to promote divine ordinances. For the believer, the ultimate

Lord is Jesus Christ, who must be obeyed (Acts 5:29), although the legitimate claims of Caesar (Matt. 22:21) have to be recognized also.

See LOYALTY.

**ALMSGIVING.** The practice of subsidizing the poor is rooted in the Old Testament (Deut. 15:11; Job 29:13-16) as a meaning of the Hebrew *sedaqa*, "righteousness" (Deut. 24:13; Ps. 24:5; Prov. 10:2). Though the Law took every precaution to prevent alienation of property, there were still instances of poverty in Israel. These were covered by sabbatical year legislation (Exod. 23:11), tithings (Deut. 14:28-29), interest-free loans (Lev. 25:35-36), gleanings from fields and orchards (Lev. 23:22; Deut. 24:19-22), and other provisions reflecting the inalienable right of the poor to some of the earth's produce. By the eighth century B.C. almsgiving was considered virtuous (Isa. 58:4-7) and subsequently as a means of securing divine favor (Ezek. 18:7-9; Dan. 4:27).

In the New Testament, Christ enjoined almsgiving (*eleemosune*; Anglo-Saxon *aelmaesse*, hence "alms") upon his disciples, but prohibited Pharisaic ostentation (Matt. 6:1-4). Many would have died without this charity, especially widows (cf. Acts 6:1), the blind, and the infirm. Thus, Christian tradition rightly insists on the stewardship of almsgiving to the poor (Luke 6:30; 12:33; Acts 9:37), without subsidizing laziness (2 Thess. 3:10) or patronizing the recipients. The motivation of the donor matters more than the amount of the alms (Mark 12:44).

**ALTRUISM.** Altruism is to act with regard for others as a prime and consistent principle of action, in contrast to egoism which is to act systematically with regard to one's own interests.

The term originated in the period of the French Enlightenment in relation to social theory. Altruism, defined as selfless love and devotion to society, was advanced by Comte as a major cohesive social force. That man is by nature altruistic became a fundamental premise of nineteenth-century optimism. Altruism became part of the quest to perfect man socially by eradicating self-centered desire. Most socialist theory assumes the right of society to discipline self-centered desire, though some have advocated the right not only to discipline but to eradicate self-centered desire by chemical means, conditioning, or close regulation. For Marxist (communist) theorists it remains a dilemma as to how to combine a moral ought of devotion to society with historical, economic, and psychological inevitability (note the work of Ernst Bloch).

Some (e.g., A. L. Hilliard) reject altruism as intellectually and emotionally suicidal. They applaud the ancient hedonism of the Epicureans, though in a modern form. They argue that behaviorally all organisms, including man, in fact, seek their own satisfaction or gratification. Others concede that while psychological hedonism is the root of action, intelligence should lead men to conclude that self-gratification ought to be the motive for action. It remains a puzzle in the naturalistic ethics of R. B. Perry and John Dewey as to why anyone should care about anyone else.

Attempts to frame a behavioral explanation of altruism have led some to claim that concern, even self-sacrificing concern, for another (such as animal care for offspring) suggests that altruism may be biologically programmed into creatures, including man. It is therefore not a spiritual quality in the sense of answering to a divinely given ethical norm.

Still others, notably within the Catholic and other Christian monastic traditions, have advocated the view that altruistic concern for humanity can come only when one achieves total self-abnegation. On this view, love for God and for others is inconsistent with love for self.

In principle, Christian love is directed in a threefold manner: to God, to neighbor, to self (Matt. 22:37-39). Man is not seen in purely behavioral terms, though there is no denigration in the Bible of the creation nor of the human body and emotions. Fundamentally, God is love and God created man for love. This is reflected in God's care of man and His redemptive love for man. It is also to be reflected in human relationships. God loves us and through that love enables us to love others (1 John 4:16-21).

In practice, altruism should be the principle of action for the Christian. To act altruistically is to be systematically other-regarding. In its best sense this is not the product of neurotic self-flagellation, but is based on reflection, deep devotion to God, and love to others. Self-sacrifice, sharing what one has with others, and regarding others as better than oneself are not psychological aberrations. They are person-conserving and person-affirming attitudes that the Christian learns from God's prior love (Phil. 2:3-5).

**Bibliography:** a Kempis, T., *The Imitation of Christ*; Lewis, C. S., *The Four Loves* (1960); Merton, T., *Seeds of Contemplation* (1949); Neil, S., *The Christian Character* (1956).

See HEDONISM; LOVE; NATURALISM, ETHICS OF.

S.J.M.

**AMBITION.** This term arose from the Latin *ambire*, "to go about," used in ancient Rome in a political context of canvassing for votes. In contemporary language it describes the desire to attain some special objective or goal. Psychologically, ambition is a concentrated form of the purposiveness that normally occurs in healthy personalities. For ambition to be achieved, planning, dedication, effort, and dogged persistence are all necessary ingredients of the process, as for example in the pursuit of a career.

Ambition is sometimes fostered against a background of high idealism. Realized ambitions can frequently bring great benefit to humanity. But where ambition is governed by greed, self-interest, or pride, it becomes sinful and can frequently prove injurious to persons other than the individual thus motivated.

The athletic metaphors of the Pauline writings express the concepts of competition, training with a view to achieving a goal, persistence during the contest, and the hope of ultimate success (1 Cor. 9:24-27). When applied to the spiritual life, they affirm the legitimacy of human ambition for the spread of the Gospel and the acquisition of the imperishable crown of eternal life. For the Christian, therefore, the main thrust of ambition should be centered upon the zealous proclamation of Christ's redeeming and saving work, by which the Christian church is extended and God's eternal kingdom is realized.

It is comparatively easy for ambition to become distorted and depraved by that type of self-satisfaction which results in pride. Such "swelling excellence" (Heb. *ga on*) is generally a prelude to disaster (Prov. 16:18) and is the opposite of that humility (*tapeinophrosune*) which is enjoined upon the practicing Christian (cf. Eph. 4:2; 1 Pet. 5:5), whatever that individual's personal ambitions might be.

See PRIDE.

**AMUSEMENTS.** Amusements are generally understood as activities which provide temporary mental diversion of a pleasurable character. Except for the avowed hedonist, amusements are not normally part of the individual's daily routine. It is probably in such a circumstance that their chief value resides. Some would distinguish between the kind of frivolity that is frequently a concomitant of amusement and the more serious forms of recreation that also provide a diversion from routine living. A factor common to both may be that of different forms of play, these being especially important for children as a means of developing coordination and learning skills. Some adults use amusements and recreation in order to demonstrate their superiority or as a form of escapism. These approaches raise psychological as well as ethical queries.

The range of amusements is naturally wide and thus amenable to considerable choice. Certain pastimes which are diverting to some people have little or no significance for others. Yet all must be amenable to ethical evaluation, since human beings are moral creatures. If the sport, amusement, or hobby is potentially dangerous, cruel, dehumanizing, or debasing, it necessitates responsible and appropriate assessment. If the amusement leads to vice, corruption, or sin, it clearly violates the Christian ethic that demands a holy life on the part of the believer (1 Pet. 1:16).

The individual's judgment as to the value of society's amusements ought to be balanced. It should avoid the Puritan extreme of aversion from pleasure in general but at the same time

bring strict moral and esthetic standards to bear upon the situation under examination. For many Christians the overriding consideration involves stewardship of time. Time is not lost when doing God's will, but it is wasted when spent otherwise.

See LEISURE, RECREATION.

**ANGER.** The emotional arousal provoked by some form of threat or injury to an individual or others is commonly described as anger. The provoking factor may even have altruistic overtones, as when one becomes angry through considering the plight of the helpless, the poor, and the oppressed.

Young children frequently express anger when frustrated in their desires. This response also occurs in some adults when frustrated in goal-oriented behavior. Physiologically, anger produces responses in the sympathetic area of the autonomous nervous system. Anger brings a release of adrenalin from the renal body into the bloodstream. Blood sugar is also liberated, blood pressure rises, respiratory capacity and blood-clotting time are increased, waste is eliminated rapidly through perspiration, and the muscles become tense. Unresolved anger can have serious bodily consequences, especially when feelings of anger are repressed.

In antiquity anger was characteristic of the gods as well as human beings. The Hebrews used *anap* (Isa. 12:1; Ps. 2:12) and *haron ap* (Exod. 32:12) of God's anger, while *ap* ("nostril," which when dilated was regarded as the seat of anger) was employed of both human and divine wrath. These and other Hebrew terms were rendered indiscriminately in the New Testament by *thymos* and *orge*. Divine wrath was a basic ingredient of covenantal religion. This was Israel's punishment for violating the Sinai covenantal provisions (Deut. 7:4; 31:16-17) or the penalty for rejecting Christ's sovereign mercies under the New Covenant (John 3:36; Eph. 5:6).

Although God may be angry with His people, He is always ready to forgive the truly penitent and turn away his anger (Jer. 31:34; 1 John 1:9). While being "slow to anger" was considered virtuous (Prov. 14:29; 16:32), becoming angry was deemed preferable to taking vengeance (Rom. 12:19), perhaps in a blood-feud. Anger must always be short-lived (Ps. 4:4; Eph. 4:26), otherwise resentment and bitterness will replace Christian love, with possible somatic effects upon the individual. Even "righteous anger" should be vented sparingly, lest it convey the impression of self-righteousness.

**ANIMAL RIGHTS AND RESEARCH.** In recent years the work of experimental biologists, medical researchers, and others has been hampered by activists who object to the use of animals in research. They even threaten to curtail animal experimentation and with it the basic "rights" and expectations of health and lifesaving advances that could ultimately benefit millions of people and animals. Extremists also violate human rights by committing illegal acts of intimidation and violence against scientists and their families, vandalizing homes, research laboratories, and educational facilities.

Genuine animal lovers, including scientists, react to this strange situation with mixed feelings. They dislike the misrepresentations and extremism, but appreciate the outspoken concern for animals and the added incentives it provides to improve care, recognizing that human frailty always leaves room for improvement.

The place that animals occupy in research is a mysterious, misunderstood entity, partly because such scientists communicate poorly about their research. Through improper understanding, misguided opinions arise that animals should be replaced by computers or cell cultures, that we already know enough and do not need to know more, that animals are being sacrificed to satisfy scientific curiosity, or that such work is irrelevant to humans. These and other matters relating to animal rights in research can probably be approached best by a series of questions and answers.

*What is research?* Research involves reasoning and experimentation in such a way as to discover answers to the many questions confronting alert observers of nature. When it comes to the issues of life, suffering, and death, researchers need to understand reasons in order to improve life and postpone death. Only intellectual atrophy of the kind seen in retarded persons and societies can block out the basic human desire and need to do research.

*Is there any other way to knowledge?* The simple answer is no. There is no other way to knowledge—at least scientific knowledge. Everything we know today in any scientific field is the product of research, and everything that we shall know in the future will come to us from research. This reality is usually clouded by the fact that once a discovery is made, it quickly becomes commonplace and taken for granted. Soon forgotten are the flashes of creative genius that sparked the splendid discoveries, the lifetimes of painstaking labor, the experimental animals, and the millions of enabling dollars that brought health, life, and hope to millions.

*Can there be too much research?* In a word, no, because there cannot be too much curiosity. Such curiosity is mostly productive, occasionally frivolous, too little in relation to the need for it, or too much in proportion to the money available for it.

*Can research be controlled according to the country's financial ability to sustain it?* Research is a growth process which cannot be turned off and on, any more than that of a child. For one thing, it takes about ten years of university training to produce a high-level researcher. Uncertain funding discourages and diverts such trainees into other avenues, drying up the supply. Research pursued under such conditions is easily undermined both psychologically and logistically.

*Why are animals used in research?* Animals as well as humans reap the benefits of animal research. The rights of animals must surely include the right to better nutrition and health through modern research. There are millions of healthy household pets which, because of good nutrition, immunization, and medication, all pretested on other animals, will never suffer or die from rabies, distemper, hepatitis, viral and bacterial infections, or parasites. Animal research also contributes to the production of healthy farm animals from which come butter, milk, meat, cheese, and eggs to nourish our dependent urban populations. These animals survive because other animals were previously sacrificed in research.

*What rights have we to use animals?* Although man by divine decree exercises dominion over the animal world, nature is organized into food chains recognized by hunter and hunted alike. Before "civilization," in our hunter-gatherer days, we also took prey and were taken like the others. We remain an imperceptible part of a food chain. When humans took to agriculture we did so for greater convenience. It was easier to breed and herd animals than to hunt them down; but they were, and still are, with us for food.

If animals were not bred, they would not be there, and if they were not eaten or otherwise used by people, they would sooner or later be eaten by other animals in the wild. If domesticated, they are slaves. Animal rights activists cannot escape this reality, nor the harsh fact that their humanity also defines them as part of a food chain. The shrillest champion of them all has lived off animals and will continue to do so. Even vegetarians will doubtless drink milk, use leather goods, or benefit from the animal manure used to fertilize the grains or vegetables that keep them alive. In a thousand other ways, recognized or otherwise, they will exploit animals directly or indirectly.

If we did not exert mastery over animals, they would do so over us by eating up our food supplies, or even us! Animal pests contribute to disease and food shortages in countries that fail to control them. Even more attractive creatures such as birds in raspberry patches, raccoons in cornfields, or groundhogs in gardens, can swiftly deprive us of the fruits of our labor. Such grim realities also underscore the utter lack of realism and practicality of animal rights extremists whose urban blinkers allow them to "love animals and eat them too," with the added joy of imposing guilt on others.

A second basis for using animals is ownership, which confers rights as well as responsibilities. Employing animals in research is a mere extension of such rights of ownership, and arguments against one apply equally to the other. The Judeo-Christian perspective of humans as stewards of nature makes them keepers of God's world, entrusted with responsibility but also with the privilege of using animals for sacrifices and food. Animals are viewed, not as equal to human beings in any hierarchical sense, but as creatures for whom we are responsible. It is especially significant that the humane tradition, including animal rights concerns, have been nurtured substantially within the Judeo-Christian developed countries. In many other jurisdictions animal rights get even scantier attention than human rights.

*Do some animals have more rights than others?* Probably not. Dogs and cats have obvious appeal, but the fact that animal activists have focused on such animals suggests both an opportunism and an inconsistency, since, if they remain untouched, all other animals should be also.

*Are animals replaceable in research?* Absolutely not. Historically, much of what we know in any biological field is based on animal research. Isolated cells cannot substitute for living animals. Such cells are not served by a cardiovascular or nervous system, nor by the body's own hormones, which intricately regulate their metabolism. Since it is not the number of animals used that determines rightness or wrongness, and since cell culture work merely reduces the number of animals used, it obviously does not solve our animal problem.

*Is animal research applicable to humans?* A great deal of it is undeniably applicable. For example, the basic salt composition of our body fluids was investigated initially in small animals, paving the way for subsequent administration of compatible intravenous fluids. The depancreatectomized dogs of Banting and Best became diabetic, as would humans, and responded to insulin in a similar way. On this basis diabetics began to be treated successfully. Similarly, most of our nutritional knowledge involving the major nutrients and trace elements, minerals, vitamins, and fatty acids is based on animal work. Apart from this we would still be rampantly afflicted with rickets and all manner of mineral, nutritional, and vitamin deficiencies.

*What about the horror stories of cruelty to experimental animals?* In fact, most experiments are carried out and terminated under anesthesia, so that the animal feels no pain at all. Most other experiments involve no more pain than is endured by human beings who undergo similar procedures. Emotional, ethical, and scientific reasons encourage researchers to work with well-treated animals; and the sheer complexity of animal life generates in us a deep sense of reverence for it. Animal rights advocates are not the only ones who care, as indicated by the existence in universities and research centers of animal care committees, resident veterinarians, and the like, to say nothing of statutory monitoring bodies at various levels of government.

*Conclusion.* Animals are the basis of most biomedical research and cannot be replaced by cell cultures or computer models except in limited specialized cases. The justification for using animals is based on the basic laws of nature, rights of ownership, and the Judeo-Christian principles of responsible, compassionate stewardship—principles upon which our civilization is based. Such a privilege carries weighty responsibilities in terms of sound judgment in animal use and the prevention of unnecessary pain. For their part, animal activists should be consistent and coherent in their approach, mindful of the immense health and economic benefits they themselves enjoy because of animal experimentation.

D.H.O.

**ANNULMENT.** This term describes the invalidating of a marriage by lawful authority, which effectively declares it null and void from the date of the ceremony.

Court action is necessary for a secular annulment. In the process the marriage contract must be shown to have been impaired by some serious impediment such as bigamy, insanity, or nonconsummation of the marriage. Under some circumstances the continued absence of the spouse—when, for example, a man is serving a life sentence in prison—can furnish grounds for annulment proceedings.

Annulment is also provided for under church Canon Law. Genuine doubt as to the basic validity of the marriage due to concealed or open impediment must be demonstrated in the matrimonial court before an annulment decree can be considered. In the days when church marriages normally followed the publishing of banns, public opportunity was offered for the alleging of impediment, and to that extent the banns reduced conditions for possible annulment.

Church courts scrutinize cases in the light of the moral and canonical laws of Christian marriage. But as in civil actions a proper balance must be maintained between *de jure* and *de facto* considerations.

See DIVORCE; IMPEDIMENTS OF MARRIAGE; MARRIAGE.

**ANTINOMIANISM.** Antinomianism is the denial of obligation to the moral law. In practical terms, it is the easy excusing of lawless or immoral behavior. Antinomianism is implicit in some modern behavioral views of human nature and conduct which deny objective moral standards by means of rationalizations such as that good is any object of any interest.

Antinomianism is peculiarly a religious phenomenon in which what morally would be called wrong acts are justified religiously or theologically. Professing Christians have done this on a number of grounds.

*Firstly, by denying creation.* The created order, including the body, is held to be indifferent to the spirit and therefore bodily acts including licentiousness are matters of no consequence. In modern times super-Christians or Christians claiming superior spirituality are not infrequently guilty of such aberration because their illusion of spirituality tempts them to become a law to themselves.

*Secondly, by abasement and corruption of moral values (Isa. 5:20).* In this, attempts are made to justify evil acts such as fornication or adultery in the name of love and beauty; to venerate fertility and sexual intercourse; or to justify repression, cruelty, and genocide in the name of national or religious ideals.

*Thirdly, by biological or psychological special pleading.* This includes pleas such as that release of tension, human frailty, biological makeup, or overwhelming impulse in even normal people explains and presumably therefore justifies wrong acts.

*Fourthly, by dispensational rationalism.* Because some kingdom ideals are scarcely realizable until Christ's return, the inference is drawn that all ideals of the kingdom are neither presently realizable nor are they a present moral obligation.

*Fifthly, the traditional form of antinomianism, which is to misinterpret Paul's emphasis on grace in contrast to law.* This is the antinomianism which presumes on grace. Paul reacted swiftly and vigorously to the distortion of his teaching which said, "Why not do evil that good may come?" (Rom. 3:8). Such teaching is anathema (Rom. 6:1, 14). Paul, like James, makes clear that true faith without works is impossible (Rom. 6—8). We are justified by faith alone, but the faith which justifies is not alone.

Identification and rejection of antinomianism by Christians requires a clear sense of the gospel as to what are grace, faith, justification, and morality. Paul insists that salvation is received by faith alone and that good works must spring from faith. James insists that the faith which justifies must be authenticated by good works. In other words, *believe and behave.*

The moral law is not nullified by faith. The moral validity of the commandments is clear from Christ's words in Mark 7:21. Jesus lists at least five of the evils which are condemned by the Ten Commandments in this passage. As well, he joins obedience to the moral law with love for God and love for neighbor (Matt. 5:43; 19:19; 22:37). Paul deals extensively with the moral principles which are renewed and reinforced in each Christian's life and which are conveyed to each Christian by the Holy Spirit (Gal. 5:22-23). His lists of vices are as frequent, detailed, and prominent as his references to virtues.

Thus everywhere in Scripture the principle of freedom is balanced by the principle of obedient love based on the broad, undergirding premise that creation and morality derive from the same Creator and that it is therefore always better to do right than to do wrong.

Most Christians have succumbed to antinomianism to varying degrees at various times, and most churches have been tested by such views. Modern Christians are particularly vulnerable in view of the prevalent behavioral view of man that morals are merely functions of mores—that human beings are no more than behaviorally responding organisms whose bodily functions are no more and no less moral than the more of the community.

Christians believe that morality is grounded in the righteousness of God, not in Situational Ethics in which every person does what appears to be right in his own eyes. Christian morality is more than an expression of feeling. Thus Christians teach each other to avoid evil and to do good as an expression of the life of grace.

**Bibliography:** Fairlie, H., *The Seven Deadly Sins Today* (1978); Lewis, C. S., *Christian Morality* (1943); Mikolaski, S., *The Grace of God* (1966); Robinson, N. H. G., *Faith and Duty* (1950).

See SITUATION ETHICS.

S.J.M.

**ANTI-SEMITISM.** The term *anti-Semitism* was probably first coined by the German Wilhelm Marr in 1879 to describe campaigns against Jews in Europe. Today it is understood more broadly to embrace all kinds of hostility toward the Jewish people, including inward prejudice as well as outward discrimination.

To avoid confusion anti-Semitism should be carefully distinguished from anti-Judaism and anti-Zionism. Anti-Judaism is a religious concept; anti-Zionism is political; anti-Semitism is racial.

The pro-Arab backlash after the Six Day War in 1967, for example, was an anti-Zionist protest against the perceived elitism and colonialism of the State of Israel. Strictly speaking, it was not a symptom of anti-Semitic hate, because the Arabs, too, are Semites. True anti-Semitism was exemplified most obviously in the Nazis' eugenic aim to destroy the Jewish people in order to promote their "superior Aryan" stock.

Understood in its broadest context, anti-Semitism is far older than Christianity. The Old Testament book of Esther (see especially 3:8) reflects the hostility Jews have always attracted through their distinctive lifestyle. Supposed Jewish antipathy toward people of other nations also lay behind another serious and sustained period of persecution in the days of Antiochus IV Epiphanes (175-164 B.C.).

When Jesus was born, Jews made up more than 10 percent of the Roman Empire's population. Though they were exempt from various civic duties (especially on the Sabbath), their exclusiveness became an object of widespread suspicion, and their refusal to take part in emperor worship was interpreted as lack of patriotism.

The New Testament describes the tensions caused by the Christian gospel within Judaism. The gap between Christians and Jews widened considerably in the Patristic period, notably through the writings of Tertullian (died c. 220) and John Chrysostom (c. 347-407). In his tract

*Adversus Iudaeos* Tertullian claimed that God had rejected the Jews in favor of the church, while Chrysostom delivered eight violently anti-Semitic sermons which warned Christians against any contact with Jewish people.

Persecution of Jews in the Middle Ages was patchy. At first there was even some popular fraternizing between church and synagogue. In the ninth century Agobard disparagingly referred to Christians who not only celebrated the Sabbath with their Jewish neighbors but also claimed that they heard better sermons from the rabbis than they did from their priests.

The Crusades, however, marked a severe deterioration in relationships. Jewish quarters in Western Europe were attacked as homes of the "enemies of Jesus." The rise to power of the Dominican and Franciscan orders had a similar effect. Some Jews committed suicide as the only alternative to forcible conversion.

In the Reformation period Jews continued to suffer, though the prominence Calvin gave to the Old Testament in his political system added a little to their prestige. Luther, however, was more antagonistic. His theological quarrel with rabbinic Judaism spilled over into anti-Semitic pamphleteering. Among other things, he advocated the burning of synagogues "for the honor of God and of Christianity" and the confiscation of Jewish prayer books along with copies of the Talmud.

With the dawning of the Enlightenment, the lot of Jews in Western Europe improved. They were seen as oppressed victims of Christian intolerance. Accordingly, their status became a focal point of liberal attention, especially in France where, after the Revolution, legislation was passed to ensure that Jewish citizens would in the future enjoy equal rights. England, too, was relatively free from anti-Semitism in the nineteenth century.

Russia, however, remained openly anti-Semitic. A wave of persecution led to a great exodus of Jews westward, notably to America, where the Jewish population increased by fifteenfold between 1880 and 1900.

At this time, too, the seeds of Aryan racism were being sown in Germany. The ugly fruit appeared some decades later under Hitler. Systematic deportation of poorer Jews caused friction in the countries to which they emigrated. In 1941 the liquidation of all Jews became official Nazi party policy. In the resulting Holocaust, an estimated six million Jewish people perished.

The Holocaust has left a lasting mark on Jewish-Christian relations. As a result, the World Council of Churches (in 1948 and 1961) and the Second Vatican Council (in 1966) both issued strong statements condemning anti-Semitism. Individual theologians (particularly Moltmann, Schillebeeckx and Kung) have been quick to express contrition for the church's checked history of anti-Semitic hostility and for its failure to protest more strongly against Nazi atrocities. They see the restored State of Israel as an affirmation of life and hope for oppressed Jewry and press hard for inter-faith understanding.

The most common causes of anti-Semitic feeling among Christians have traditionally been the following:

*Anti-social behavior*. "Hatred of the human race" was a charge leveled against both Christians and Jews in the early Patristic period. It was based on the refusal of both groups to accept any object of worship other than the one true God. In the case of the Jews, however, this religious exclusiveness was also expressed socially in their dietary laws and ceremonial restrictions on mixing with Gentiles. Inevitably, exaggerated rumors of anti-social behavior followed closely upon the determination of strict Jews to maintain their distinctive lifestyle. Apart from the wilder accusations ("Jews poison wells" was a favorite in the fourteenth century), the close association of Jewish financiers with usury was frequent target of moral abuse in the church. In the Middle Ages, the verb "to Judaize" meant two things: to be a heretic and to lend money on interest.

*The blood libel*. In the earliest days of the church, it was strongly rumored (and not just by Christians) that the main reason for excluding Gentiles from the Temple at Jerusalem was because human sacrifices were offered there. In the twentieth century this allegation was embellished. Christian children, it was said, disappeared mysteriously at Passover time. A rash of capital trials resulted, where Jews stood accused of murdering Christians in order to obtain blood for their Passover and other rites. Despite the flimsy nature of the evidence, many defendants were executed and the charge of "blood libel" against Jews persisted spasmodically in Europe, until it became part of the Nazi party's official propaganda in the 1930's.

*Enemies of Jesus*. The New Testament provides plenty of fuel to fire those who represent Jews as Jesus Christ's enemies. The Gospel of John, in particular, often brands "the Jews" as Jesus' main antagonists. "You belong to your father, the Devil," He once told them (John 8:44). Taking their cue from verses like these, many early commentators identified hatred of Jews with hatred of evil—a Christian duty. This style of exegesis has led Rosemary Ruether to conclude that modern Christians will only free themselves from the shackles of anti-Semitism when they reject the New Testament's Christologies. "Anti-Judaism is the left hand of Christology," she writes.

*Deicide*. It is Matthew's Gospel, however, not John's, which preserves the most traditionally damaging indictment of the Jewish people. Faced with the shouts of "Crucify him!" at Jesus' trial, Pilate washed his hands of all moral responsibility. "Let his blood be on us," responded the Jews, *"and on our children!"* (Matt. 27:24-25). Paul, too, lays the responsibility for Jesus' death at the Jews' door (1 Thess. 2:14-16). That, he writes, has made them recipients of God's anger.

Again, from the earliest times Christian commentators have interpreted these New Testament texts in a strongly anti-Semitic way. Justin is typical of many. Jerusalem's fall, he tells his Jewish correspondent Trypho, was "in fairness and justice, for you have slain the Just One." Because of their implication in Jesus' death, the Jews are condemned to be homeless and to suffer for the rest of time.

Taken together, these four considerations have fed Christian hostility towards Jews for centuries. "If it is incumbent upon a good Christian to detest the Jews," commented Erasmus caustically, "then we are all good Christians."

As a case for anti-Semitism, however, they do not even begin to make theological and ethical sense. For one thing, Christians are clearly called to be on the side of truth and justice. More than that, a biblical ethic demands that all victims of injustice must be rescued and vindicated (Exod. 22:21-27; James 5:1-6). The history of anti-Semitism is a horrifying story of lies and scapegoating, culminating in the horrors of the Holocaust. The proper Christian response is repentance for the church's part in such displays of xenophobia and a greater vigilance and determination to champion oppressed minority groups (whether Jewish or not).

In addition to this, Christian integrity demands accuracy in interpreting and applying the teaching of the Bible. It is a caricature of the New Testament to portray it as an anti-Jewish manifesto. The Gospel writers only condemned those who opposed Jesus, not all members of the Jewish race (John 12:9-11). After all, Jesus was Himself a Jew, as were His first disciples. His attacks on the religious leaders of Judaism, as recorded in the Gospels, were well within the tradition of the Old Testament prophets. They, too, had exposed the hypocrisy of an unauthentic religion; but no one used that as evidence to accuse them of anti-Semitism.

Paul was especially proud to be a Jew (Rom. 9:1-5). Despite his doctrinal attacks on Judaizers, he presented the gospel as the fulfillment of Jewish Scripture. He continued to believe passionately that the Jewish people had a special place in God's future (Rom. 11).

Furthermore, the Bible requires Christians to judge anti-Semitism in the light of love and forgiveness. Jesus taught His disciples that their love should mirror His (John 15:12) and that their mercy should reflect His Father's (Luke 6:36). The Jewish leaders may have declared themselves His enemies and accepted responsibility for His death, but that did not stop Jesus loving them (Matt. 5:43-45) and praying that God would forgive His executioners (Luke 23:34). Anti-Semitism is a negation of the biblical love ethic which Jesus both taught and exemplified.

Finally, the Christian ethic demands an end to racism. Anti-Semitism is overtly racist, as Nazi propaganda so clearly displayed. The same radical division between Jew and Gentile was a feature of life in New Testament times as well (though in the Jewish world the roles of oppressor and oppressed were reversed). Jesus deliberately bridged that divide by His teaching (Luke 10:25-37), by His example (Matt. 8:5-13), and by His death (Eph. 2:11-22).

Christian ethics and anti-Semitism are therefore incompatible. There will always be tension between Jesus' claim to be the only way to salvation (John 14:6) and anyone who denies that claim. But radical religious disagreement must never lead to racial contempt. The kind of interfaith dialogue that leads to syncretism is no substitute for evangelism (Acts 1:8), but the Christian missionary task can never excuse prejudice.

**Bibliography:** Heinemann, J. *et al.*, *Encyclopedia Judaica*, vol. 3, pp. 87–161 (1972); Jocz, J., *Christians and Jews* (1966); *Ibid.*, *The Jewish People and Jesus Christ after Auschwitz* (1981); Pawlikowski, J.T., *What Are They Saying About Christian-Jewish Relations?* (1980).

D.H.F.

**ANXIETY.** Anxiety is a complex emotional state with apprehension or dread as its most prominent feature. Three different expressions of anxiety may be distinguished.

1) *Normal Anxiety.* Anxiety is a common manifestation in everyday life. Child analysts such as Melanie Klein argue that anxiety feelings are among the earliest an infant can experience. A child's anxieties normally arise from any threat to its dependence upon its mother. Anger, aggression, or separation may result in the fear of losing mother, and anxiety will set in.

In later years anxiety will erupt from a variety of circumstances including pressure, breakdown of relationships, unemployment, inability to cope, examination fears, and so on. If anxiety is not properly faced and handled, the ensuing and accumulating stress may result in overstrain, irritability, and poor quality of life, or even worse, in a breakdown or heart attack. Stress is now regarded as a major threat to health in the Western world. Indeed, in highly developed countries such as in Western Europe, the United States, and Canada it contributes significantly to premature death.

2) *Depressive Illnesses.* A more chronic manifestation of anxiety is found in various nervous and mental disorders. In fact, anxiety is the prime symptom of neurosis. This form of anxiety differs from the preceding description in two important ways.

First, acute anxiety is not always clearly associated with a motivating factor or an easily recognizable cause. The depressed person may give lucid reasons for the state of depression but the counselor will find the apparent causes ever-changing and shifting. Second, in a chronic anxiety state, the physical equivalents will be more observable. In normal experience anxiety will express itself in sweating, breathlessness, mild migraines, and so on. According to Freud, anxiety equivalents in chronic suffering may include heart disorders, excessive sweating, trembling and shaking, giddiness, and bladder and bowel irregularities. Stekel adds to this catalog excessive tiredness, deadness of fingers, muscular tics, extreme migraine attacks, and digestive problems.

The common factor in these anxiety states is the disruption of normal bodily functions with a corresponding feeling of helplessnes. Such types of anxiety will usually require expert counseling and, frequently, medical treatment. The wise pastor will know when the problem is beyond his capacity to assist.

3) *Metaphysical Anxiety.* In recent times philosophers and theologians have noted a form of dread caused by the world. The existentialist thinker Soren Kierkegaard popularized the notion of *angst* (a German word meaning fear, dread, or anxiety) to denote the fear which grips modern people transfixed by an apparently meaningless universe. It can be that feeling of numbness of horror in feeling, "If there is no God, then I am helpless and life has no meaning." Without question, this form of anxiety is very prevalent among our contemporaries and is possibly at the heart of what the poet W. H. Auden called "our anxiety ridden age."

*Biblical Teaching.* In the Bible no single word conveys the wide range of human worries and cares. However, anxiety is clearly in the story of the Fall. This may well be considered the starting point of anxiety in that mankind is separated from a secure and loving relationship and thrust forth to stand alone and insecure. It is also very probably there in Jacob's flight from the wrath of his brother, resulting in the mysterious night-long struggle with his divine adversary. This curious and immensely meaningful event is doubtless a state of anxiety which ends in Jacob's finding God's will and peace (Gen. 32:24). On the other hand, Saul's growing alienation from God and his awareness that David was a threat to his throne led to the kind of deep anxiety and strange behavior which we would describe as paranoid (1 Sam. 19:9).

In the New Testament the word which comes closest to our word "anxiety" is *merimna* (care, worry) which comes from the verb "to divide." This describes quite accurately the character of anxiety. The purposive drive of a healthy mind is diverted to a certain extent, due to the incidence of anxiety, by a concern for some distressing circumstances or perhaps a potentially hazardous situation which might threaten personal existence. Under such conditions the pursuit of normal goals has to be set aside somewhat while remedies are devised that will allay the individual's basic fears.

Christ's disciples were apparently worried about how they would survive economically without being able to work while they were fol-

lowing him. The Savior's response was to urge them to view discipleship in proper perspective, in the realization that a provident heavenly Father is well aware of fundamental human needs. "Seek first the kingdom of God and his righteousness," he advised, "and all these things shall be added to you" (Matt. 6:33). Paul repeats the same teaching in Phil. 4:6: "Have no anxiety about anything, but by prayer, supplication and thanksgiving let your requests be made known to God."

Anxiety, therefore, is seen by the Bible as an unnatural state because the Christian should know that the world is God's and that a heavenly purpose directs everything. At the theological level anxiety is without substance if God has all things under his control. Just as a small child is secure in the blackest circumstance if his parents are there, so the Christian may know "God's peace which passes all understanding" (Phil. 4:8).

Does this mean that we should never be anxious and that, if we are, we are sub-Christian? Not necessarily. Jesus knew anxiety in the Garden of Gethsemane. He gave us there an example of how we may cope with it—to face the problem in all its bleakness, place it before God in prayer, seek the support of others, and follow God's will even if it takes you to a cross.

**Bibliography:** Darling, H. W., *Man in His Right Mind* (1969); May, R. *The Meaning of Anxiety* (1950); McKeating, H., *Living with Guilt* (1970); Stekel, W., *Conditions of Anxiety* (1954).

G.C.

**APARTHEID.** This term, pronounced "uh-part-hate" and meaning "separateness," describes the political policy of the Republic of South Africa, whereby whites and nonwhites are segregated forcibly and accommodated in different residential areas. Only one-fifth of South Africa's population is white. The remaining persons have been classified by the government as either Bantus, Coloured, or Asians. Approximately one-sixth of the whites and one-half of the other classes live under rural conditions, while the remainder inhabit towns and cities.

The whites, sometimes called Europeans, are descendants of settlers from the Netherlands, Germany, Britain, and France. Migrations began in 1652 when Dutch settlers came to South Africa as farmers (*Boers*), sponsored by the Dutch East India Company. In 1806 Great Britain occupied the Cape of Good Hope in order to protect the trade route to the Orient.

Although Holland officially ceded the Cape Territory to Britain in 1814, the disgruntled Boers repudiated British rule and "trekked" inland to the Orange and Vaal rivers, where they established the Orange Free State and the South African Republic. The discovery of diamonds near Hopetown and gold in the Transvaal in 1866 demonstrated the richness of the natural resources.

The Boers fought two wars against the British. Although they won the first (1880-1881), they lost the second (1899-1902). Independence was within reach, however; and in 1906 the Orange Free State and the Transvaal became self-governing. In 1910 they joined with the British colonies of Natal and the Cape to become the Union of South Africa. In two World Wars the Union allied with the British and in the interval had begun a program of industrialization.

Political developments took a significant turn when Daniel Malan led his Nationalist party to victory in the 1948 elections and moved quickly to establish apartheid. In 1950 an Act of Parliament delineated separate areas where whites and nonwhites were allowed to live and established severe penalties for violation of this law, known as the Group Areas Act. The police received increasingly wide powers of search, arrest, and imprisonment, especially where nonwhites were suspected of misdemeanors. This caused mounting concern both inside and outside the Republic.

Johannes Strijdom, who succeeded Malan in 1954, used his Nationalist majority to restrict the rights of Coloured people to vote. A move towards even greater segregation came with the appointment of Prime Minister Hendrik Verwoerd in 1958, which led to eighteen months of tension and bloody riots, including an unsuccessful attempt on Verwoerd's life in 1960 by a white farmer. That same year South Africans voted to become a republic and in 1961 withdrew from the British Commonwealth following persistent criticism of the country's racial segregation policies. Such protests proved to have no effect upon the apartheid proposals of the South African minority white government, that has continued to exercise rigid control over the nonwhite majority.

The effect of the apartheid legislation has been to stigmatize four-fifths of the population by designating them "nonwhites" and dividing them into three principal groups. The largest section, comprising 11 million Bantus, some of whose ancestors had resisted white encroachment onto their territory as early as the eighteenth century, were either settled on government reserves in towns or cities specially allotted to them or as workers for white farmers. In 1953 the government passed an act that provided for their education.

The second largest class, the 1.5 million Coloureds, are descendants of a mixed group of indigenous Hottentots, Malay slaves, and others who intermarried with the early settlers. The final group, the Asians, are less than half a million strong and are descended from Indian laborers brought into Natal Province in the mid-nineteenth century to cultivate the sugar plantations. The religious ethic of the Dutch Reformed Church, the largest white religious denomination, has played a significant part in the formulation of South Africa's policies.

The effect of this situation has been that the white population has claimed the preponderance of the Republic, and the nonwhites live under severe restrictions. The Reserves set aside for them are meant in theory to afford the traditional freedoms enjoyed previously by the native peoples but in actuality are often places of crime, squalor, and human degradation. The government pledged to develop the Reserves socially, culturally, and economically to the point where they would become independent politically but this objective is unlikely to be realized in the near term if only because pitifully inadequate amounts of money have been expended on them. The burgeoning black population, estimated at 23 million, has outstripped available Reserve land, compelling individuals to seek living accommodation and employment on farms or in industries owned by whites, where they are frequently exploited ruthlessly.

A further attempt at constitutional reform occurred in 1984, when President Pieter Botha implemented legislation to allow South Africa's Coloureds and Indians a limited degree of power-sharing with the minority whites. This legislation disenfranchized the blacks completely, leaving them with no representation in Parliament and no civil rights. The blacks expressed their disapproval by an upsurge of racial violence, which had predictable consequences in arrests and imprisonments. Critics of apartheid such as Alan Boesak, Desmond Tutu, and Trevor Huddleston continued their spirited denunciations, especially outside South Africa. Bishop Tutu interpreted the award of the 1984 Nobel Peace Prize, not so much in terms of personal recognition, but as an indication that the world was winning its fight against what he described as the "totally evil, unchristian and immoral" policies of apartheid in South Africa.

The Christian churches generally have castigated apartheid as contrary to the Word of God, demonstrating in the process an unusual degree of unity. They have maintained that it is repulsive to the Christian ethic because its racial segregation policies inhibit human freedom, deny individual rights and social justice, disrupt family unity, neglect and abuse the poor, and obstruct the totality of fellowship in Christian worship. The South African Council of Churches in particular has assumed the role of the "voice of the voiceless," the true champions of the poor and oppressed blacks, and has spoken out vigorously against the resettlements, removals of power, and the social injustices that have resulted from apartheid. Tutu's attempt to confer respectability upon the banned African National Congress has encountered a challenge from the government to the effect that the South African Council of Churches is actually a political instrument being wielded to challenge the government's policies and is aided by international radicals and activists.

The vociferous condemnation of apartheid has almost completely drowned out any policy statements from the South African government, which itself claims to be Christian. In the light of this situation, some comments on the objectives of the Pretoria government made in 1984 by B. G. Fourie, South Africa's ambassador to the United States, are perhaps worth recording. In acknowledging the complexity of the social and political status of his homeland, he affirmed that South Africa was in a process of transformation and was looking for a political framework in which all its people, including blacks, could participate. He pointed out that President Botha was well aware of the deficiencies of the current constitution and recognized the need for political participation to be afforded to the black population so as to meet their demands for social justice. While the requests for political rights would not be ignored, government policy required that changes be made as peacefully as possible so as to bring economic and social progress to all the races in South Africa.

Fourie pointed out that already four black nations had acquired political independence from South African administration through referendums and elections and that the government had entered into consultation with a wide range of black leadership in an attempt to secure means for political participation by urban blacks. He also reported that, in the decade since 1970, blacks' share of total personal income rose from 25 per cent to 40 per cent, by contrast with the white population's share, which declined from 75 per cent to 60 per cent. During the same period the black high school population increased fivefold, and in 1983-1984 the government's education budget actually exceeded that set aside for defense. Job reservation for particular racial groups had now been abandoned; blacks are now legally entitled to form or join their own trade unions, and the principle of equal pay for equal work applies. Fourie indicated further that, while many parts of continental Africa are moribund economically and harrassed by famine and starvation, South Africa has provided employment for more than a million workers from other parts of Africa, many of whom are actually illegal immigrants.

It has been very easy for people in the Western world to crusade against apartheid. It has been described as "the kind of war that every American can fight and not get hurt." The occasional demonstrations and arrests in front of the South African Consulate in Washington seem to illustrate this remark. South Africa can be denounced quite safely as the last outpost of all the worst iniquities that the twentieth century reformers had supposedly corrected. Such a cause readily unites people of quite opposing faiths and political persuasions and gives new impetus to civil rights movements while diverting attention from pressing matters much closer to home.

Apartheid activists have tried to bring political and religious pressure on South Africa by such devices as boycotts of various kinds, public demonstrations, and outright political denunciation. Even the United States government was reported in 1984 to be moving away somewhat from the conciliatory position of constructive engagement and quiet diplomacy with regard to apartheid. But this may be nothing more than a discreet political gesture designed to appease local American activists.

The problem of how to deal with apartheid morally and objectively so that the best interests of all concerned parties are served is an extremely difficult one. The Pretoria government has made it abundantly clear that it will not bend to external political pressure, while for their part Western nations have too large an investment in South Africa to sever relations with the country completely. South Africa, for instance, is one of Great Britain's most important trading partners; and the British have been purchasing uranium secretly from the country despite government statements that no such trade existed. If the West were to break off all trade with South Africa, an economic and military opportunity of unprecedented proportions would be presented to the Soviet Union, which has not been at the forefront of attacks against apartheid, and which in any event has its own form of totalitarianism.

Many of those protesting apartheid, including black church leaders in the United States, have found it easy to bring pressure on the South African government in various ways. Very few, however, have a realistic master plan that could become operative immediately were apartheid to be abandoned. Particularly pressing problems for blacks in South Africa are the low academic performance of black students despite the money spent on education, the very high rate of crime and illegitimate births, and the general disintegration of social organization among the poor. These are urgent problem which demand attention of a kind that black leadership, whether inside or outside of South Africa, has been unable to provide, but which may yet emerge with the cooperation of the South African government.

In view of the fact that many opponents of apartheid present an incorrect historical view of the black South African population as an oppressed, indigenous people, it is worthy of record that there is no native South African people as such. All races are immigrants to the territory, the blacks being refugees from the nineteenth-century Zulu wars.

Apartheid is clearly a politico-social phenomenon with immense demographic, moral, and spiritual dimensions. No facile solution to the problems seems possible, and violent means to achieve supposedly democratic ends would in all probability bring further disasters upon those who need them the least. The voting system established by the Pretoria government is controlled so tightly that there is little chance of the white minority government being overthrown by democratic means, even though the parliament has now become tricameral with the inclusion of Coloured and Indian houses. Apartheid adherents protest that a preponderant black vote would swamp the country with inexperienced leaders, would destroy the present fragile political balance, and would plunge the country into anarchy. This argument could be used, of course, *pari passu*, by other totalitarian governments as justification for perpetuating their own political systems.

The moderates in the Pretoria government have proclaimed that they are following a path of tolerance, cooperation, and understanding. All Christians, therefore, should pray that these ideals may be realized quickly, so that the blacks may be afforded an opportunity to rehabilitate themselves with government help and with the other peoples of South Africa to move forward to a new era of peace and prosperity.

**Bibliography:** De Gruchy, J. W., *The Church Struggle in South Africa* (1978); De Gruchy, J. W., and Villa-Vicencio, C., (eds.), *Apartheid Is a Heresy* (1983); Marguard, L., *The Peoples and Policies of South Africa* (1969 ed.); Reeves, A., *South Africa—Yesterday and Tomorrow* (1962).

See CIVIL RIGHTS; RACE RELATIONS; SEGREGATION.

**APPETITE.** The desire, craving, or longing of the body or mind for satisfaction in specific areas of activity is known as appetite. The term is commonly used of physical or emotional appetite for food—a bodily response that is common to all except the anorexic. Appetite is also used euphemistically of desire for sexual fulfillment and less frequently for other purposive activities such as adventure. Physiologically, appetite involves a complex interaction of blood components and cerebral neurochemical activity.

For the Christian, appetite must be regulated carefully in accordance with the principle that the body is the temple of the Holy Spirit (1 Cor. 6:19). The believer should glorify God in every aspect of life. This means that rigorous control of appetite is mandatory if the physical and metaphysical aspects of personality are to function harmoniously to God's glory.

**ARMAMENT.** The notion of armament covers both defensive and offensive equipment to enable an individual, an army, or a nation to be effective in conflict, generally, warfare. In ancient times the soldier was equipped both defensively (with body armor and shield) and offensively (with spear and sword). The modern soldier has his equivalents for defense and attack, while the growing scale of conflict and advances in technology have brought to the center of the military and ethical stage the concept of nuclear deterrence.

The nation of Israel in Old Testament times used the weaponry and armor common to the peoples of the ancient Near East. Though Israel did not maintain a standing army until the time of Saul, her earlier leaders were able in time of national need to call together a volunteer army for conquest or to resist aggression.

One of the themes of the Old Testament prophets was that the nation should learn to depend upon God and not upon its military strength in alliance with foreign powers. During the period of the divided monarchy, a succession of such alliances was condemned. But this should not be read as a condemnation of the principle of armed defense, or indeed of collective defense, but rather of alliances with Gentile nations which were contracted out of a lack of trust in God and whose fruit was the intrusion of foreign gods into the national religious life of Israel.

The series of military defeats which are chronicled in the story of the divided monarchy and which continued until the destruction of Jerusalem in A.D. 70 were given to teach the nation that its religious identity and the fulfillment of its messianic hopes did not depend upon its military prowess. Conversely, national disaster resulted from religious infidelity.

The quickening pace of technological advance since biblical times has sharpened the ethical questions posed by the possession and use of weaponry. The medieval church, whose judgments on the ethics of warfare have been so influential, was concerned with weapons scarcely distinguishable from those of ancient Israel. The protection of noncombatants and the humane treatment of prisoners could be made a matter of policy for the warring party. These policies did not seriously prejudice the conduct of hostilities. This is no longer the case. The introduction of gas onto the battlefields of the First World War and the use of obliteration bombing during the Second have set the scene for the development of chemical, biological, and nuclear weaponry of awesome power.

The dilemma which now confronts decision-makers is that one of only two factors would seem to be sufficient to ensure that a potential adversary does not unleash a particular type of weapon in a future conflict: the mutually agreed destruction of such weaponry by the power that considers itself to be threatened, however little it may wish to have to use it.

To prevent the use of chemical weapons in time of conflict by $a$ against $b$, $b$ must itself possess them and threaten their use against $a$ in retaliation. $A$ might perhaps be persuaded to destroy its stocks in advance of hostilities or to refrain from use once they had broken out, but only in response to their possession also by $b$ and $b$'s declared intention to use such weapons in response to $a$'s use. If $b$ does not act in this way, in time of conflict $a$ will be the more likely to use these weapons to gain an advantage against a party which does not possess or has declared that it will not use them. In practical terms the near impossibility of verification of the destruction of, in particular, biological weapon stocks, makes their use in warfare both hazardous and unlikely.

This is a special case of the general deterrent argument, showing the need to match weapons and weapons systems (however unpleasant) against those of a potential adversary. The alternative lies between an acceptance of this strategy and the pacifist option.

The theological foundations of the possession and threatened use of armaments of every kind lie in the fact and universality of sin. An irreducible element in man's rebellion against God lies in man's desire for power, autonomy for himself, and authority over his fellows.

A chief function of the institution of the state is to place limits upon man's ambition to play the part of God by ruling His creatures. Within the nation this role is exercised by government and its administration of justice. Between the nations there is no such arbitrary authority, despite the establishment of international agencies and of international law. But the multiplicity of states and collections of states ensures that man's sinful desire is contained and his ambition thwarted, since a balance of power is established between nations, groups of nations, and empires in which it becomes self-defeating for one to seek power over another.

The possession of armaments, therefore, deters aggression on an international as on an individual level and has as its goal the maintenance of peace and order. This is one of the great ironies of sin.

See DISARMAMENT; MILITARISM; WAR.

N.M. de S.C.

**ARMINIAN ETHICS.** As a system of theology, Arminianism refers not only to the teaching of the Dutch pastor Jacob Arminius (1560-1609) but also to both the doctrines of the Remonstrants of Holland and to the Methodist and related denominations.

What is held in common and which is referred to as "Arminian" are the following emphases: (1) Christ died to make an atonement for the sin not of the elect only but for every human being; (2) every person has the freedom of will either to accept or reject the gospel of Jesus when he or she hears it; (3) every Christian must ensure that he or she remains within the body of Christ as a believer, for it is possible to cease to be a genuine Christian by negligence of one's duties towards God. The usual contrast with "Arminian" is "Calvinist."

In harmony with these theological principles, the major emphases within Arminian ethics are (1) The value, worth, and dignity of each human being whatever his or her background, race, or color. This bestowal of worth flows from the basic claim that Christ died for every person and in so doing demonstrated how much God loves each person. If God loves in such a way, so should we. (2) The importance of the right exercise of the person towards God, given free will. The strength of sin in human beings is such that there is a bias toward doing what does not please God; but given free will by God, it is the solemn duty of all men and women to accept the gospel and

then, assisted by grace, to accept the standards of the gospel. (3) The importance of obedience to God's will for personal salvation. Since there is always the possibility of losing the gift of eternal life and ceasing to be born of the Spirit, it is necessary for the believer to exercise his will to follow Christ and to walk in his way. Thus individual responsibility before God is fundamental.

Outside these basic emphases there is a wide spectrum of approaches to ethics within those of the Arminian tradition, just as there is among those of the Calvinist tradition.

**Bibliography:** Mott, S. C., *Biblical Ethics and Social Change* (1982); Harrison, A. W., *Arminianism* (1937).

P.T.

**ARTIFICIAL INSEMINATION.** This term describes the introduction into the female body of the semen of her husband, or conjointly with the sperm of some other man, by a means other than normal copulation procedures. The need for such a contingency may arise from the inability of the husband to fertilize his wife's ova, despite the fact that he can produce motile sperm. Such a condition could furnish the warrant for attempts to produce conception by nonnatural means. Where both partners are known to be fertile, the husband's sperm can be introduced by syringe into the uterus when the wife is ovulating; and this procedure, described professionally as AIH (artificial insemination, husband), has claimed a moderate rate of success.

Where the husband is infertile and his spouse desires to become pregnant, the husband's sperm are generally mixed with those of a donor, and then inserted into the wife's uterus. This procedure is known as AID (artificial insemination, donor) and may be available either as the result of fresh sperm or from a specimen that has been stored in a frozen state in a sperm bank.

Artificial insemination has been in vogue for a considerable number of years in animal husbandry, but it is far from being widely used among human beings for a variety of reasons. While a woman might be content to become pregnant by the AIH method, both she and her husband could well have emotional and moral misgivings about an AID pregnancy. In some jurisdictions the latter is illegal, while in others it is hedged about by qualifications that make the procedure of dubious legality.

The vast majority of married women wish to have children by their own husbands. When the AID procedure is suggested in the light of the husband's demonstrated infertility, the prospect of producing a child from the sperm of an unknown donor may be very disconcerting. This will be the case particularly where the woman regards the introduction of donor sperm as tantamount to adultery, a point of view held by many Christians.

While donor sperm is supposed to come from

individuals who have been screened carefully for possible genetic defects, there is, of course, no guarantee that the screening has excluded such liabilities. Were a child to be born with a genetic condition such as Down's syndrome, the mother could conceivably bring lawsuits against the operators of the sperm bank (if such facilities had been used) or the individual donor if his identity happened to be revealed, as well as the medical practitioner who performed the insemination. Considerable room is in fact left for litigation because of the general uncertainty of the law in these matters.

Although Roman Catholicism and Orthodox Judaism have generally opposed artificial insemination, especially AID, most Protestant bodies have been reluctant to make formal pronouncements on the matter, preferring instead to allow such arrangements as are made to be kept private between the individuals concerned and their doctor. This attitude, however, tends to place moral decision in the area of personal inclination or convenience, perhaps to the detriment of all concerned.

Many secular persons as well as convinced Christians maintain that AID procedures constitute adultery. Scripture has nothing to say about artificial insemination as such, although the deliberate prevention of conception on one occasion by means of *coitus interruptus* was dealt with severely because it defied God's will for that particular situation (Gen. 38:8-10). Some writers have maintained that Jesus only condemned the lustful desire that precipitates adultery and that therefore AID cannot be regarded as coming within that category.

But the uniform teaching in Scripture about sexuality is that a man's sperm belongs properly and exclusively in the body of the woman who is his lawful spouse, and carnal relations with any other woman are described in terms that depict a violation of the fundamental monogamous ideal. The reason why men make their sperm available for AID procedures, quite apart from any monetary gain that may be involved, is to produce children in women to whom they are not married and who will never be their spouses. While normal coition may be replaced by a syringe, the end result is still the same, and the donor is the *de facto* father of whatever offspring the female recipient produces. For the present writer at least, therefore, AID constitutes an adulterous procedure, and persons contemplating it should be counseled to consider adoption as an alternative.

**ASSASSINATION.** The term refers to political murders, usually of prominent persons, either to advance a cause or to express deep hostility. The term's origin is the Arabic, *hashshashin,* meaning "hashish-eaters," and refers to Muslim fanatics, intoxicated by hashish, sent to murder Christian leaders of the Crusades.

The practice of assassination, however, is as old as history. The Old Testament contains such episodes as Ehud's slaying of Eglon when Ehud received a divine commission to dispatch this ruler, who had tyrannized the Benjaminites for eighteen years. The book of Judges also describes Jael driving a pin through the temple of Sisera the Canaanite whom Deborah the prophetess and Barak had defeated in battle (Judg. 3:15-30; 4:17-22; 5:2-31).

Assassination was also part of the Roman Empire. Rulers such as Julius Caesar fell before the attack of those who could find no better way of removing a political opponent. In the Middle Ages, it was as familiar among Christians as among the Muslims. Thomas a Becket, for example, was slain to free the king of England from an archbishop and primate who dared to resist him in the name of the church.

Although Martin Luther insisted that no one had the right to take up arms against a tyrannical ruler, later Reformers justified assassination of kings who threatened their Protestant subjects. In a tract called "How Superior Powers Ought To Be Obeyed" (1558), Christopher Goodman justified rebellion against such authorities, even if it meant taking a king's life. To defend God's laws and precepts, he claimed, it was the duty of the people to "cut off every rotten member."

Two years earlier, a Church of England bishop, John Ponet, despairing of a future for Protestants under the relentless judgment of Queen Mary, had also argued that when all else failed, taking the monarch's life could be justified. It was, he argued, an act that could be considered a natural and conscientious act, one that was "grafted in the hearts of men."

Conversely, Roman Catholic champions of the Counter Reformation could make the same claim to defend rising against a heretical ruler, even if that should mean taking his life. Henry IV, albeit a Roman Catholic convert, was seen as too willing an ally to Protestant opponents of the Hapsburgs and consequently fell victim to an assassin's dagger.

This method of eliminating undesired rulers was, however, secularized along with the rest of Western culture following the Enlightenment. It became an exclusively political action in the West. In the past two centuries, most countries have lost prominent persons by assassination.

The killing of American presidents—Lincoln, Garfield, McKinley, and Kennedy—has encouraged the view that the United States is especially prone to this kind of violence, but the record does not support that claim. The British have lost at least one prime minister, Spencer Perceval. Even politically stable Canada has known such acts as the political murders of Thomas D'arcy McGee and Pierre Laporte.

World War I had many major causes, but it was initiated by the shooting of the Archduke Ferdinand at Sarajevo in what is now Yugoslavia. Assassinations have also blotted the histories of twentieth-century France, Italy, Egypt, Jordan, Iraq, Zaire, Uganda, India, and Japan.

This century has also seen a return to religiously motivated assassinations. Dietrich Bonhoeffer, a German theologian, was among those executed for complicity in the abortive attempt on Hitler's life. Only recently, the Mufti of Jerusalem, Sheikh Sa ad e-Din'el 'Alami, issued an order of divine deliverance to any Muslim who tried to take the life of President Hafez Assad of Syria, the assassin being assured of "a place in Paradise for eternity."

History thus indicates that assassination is part of the human scene. Facing it is, to quote an Italian king, "one of the risks of the job." It has not been peculiar to any period or country, nor is it a monopoly of a single religion, nor is it confined to secularists who deny all religion.

Assassination results from the frustration and despair of those who can see no other way of achieving their political objectives. Ironically, history does not offer assassins· much reason to think that murdering a ruler is ever the way to achieve the justice they seek.

**Bibliography:** Bell, J. B., *Assassin!* (1979); Havens, M. C., *et. al.*, *The Politics of Assassination* (1970); Heaps, W. A., *A Special Kind of Murder* (1969).

R.F.S.

**ASTROLOGY.** This ancient procedure for studying heavenly bodies with a view toward determining individual destiny originated in ancient Mesopotamia. From the time of Sargon of Agade (c. 2350 B.C.) lists of stars appeared in Old Babylonian astronomical texts. Less than a thousand years later the *Anu-Enlil* tablet series catalogued omens and predictions based on astronomical data. These sources were used outside Mesopotamia among the Syrians, Hittites, and Canaanites.

Horoscopes, or "celestial maps," were first devised in Babylonia about the fifth century B.C. These became popular throughout the Near East at a time when the zodiac, or circle of twelve constellations with their characteristic signs, had been devised. The movements of the planets in the zodiac, which were supposed to coincide with certain terrestrial happenings, provided for the ancients a basis for assessing individual personality and predicting the future. Some modern advocates still argue for the influence of the moon over the earth to a wider control of terrestrial phenomena by the planets; others deny such a possibility.

Astrology exerted some influence over the Hebrews (cf. Judg. 5:20), and Isaiah furnished an excellent description of an astrologer (Isa. 47:13). But the practices were forbidden by Mosaic law, along with other kinds of divination (Lev. 19:26; Deut. 18:10-14). Although the sun, moon, and stars were to be God's witnesses to the New Covenant (Jer. 31:35-36), they were not to be venerated. Despite such prohibitions against astrology, the Israelites still practiced it periodically (2 Kings 17:16; 23:4-5; Amos 5:26), especially at the turn of the Christian era. "Predictive astronomy" brought the eastern Magi to Christ's birthplace (Matt. 2:1-12); but for the Christian the Holy Spirit, not the stars, is the true guide to eternal life.

Modern astronomy, by revealing the vastness of space, has made astrology less credible. In Japan, astrologers have been forsaking the planets in favor of horoscopes based on blood types. The final word must come from a devotee, who, disillusioned, described astrology as "all Taurus."

**Bibliography:** Gleadow, R., *The Origin of the Zodiac* (1969).

See FORTUNE TELLING; MAGIC; OCCULTISM.

**ASYLUM.** Originally an asylum was a secure place to which one could go to escape danger. Ancient peoples generally provided locations where criminals could find freedom from retribution. The Hebrews established six such refuge cities to accommodate those guilty of accidental homicide (Num. 35:6-34; Deut. 4:41-44). This was a remarkably humane provision, since it avoided vengeance in terms of a blood-feud (Exod. 21:12; Lev. 24:17) by relatives of the deceased. When the High Priest died, the fugitive's guilt was wiped away automatically, thus enabling him to leave his refuge without penalty.

In medical terminology, asylum formerly described an institution in which the feeble and mentally infirm were confined for their own safety and that of others. The condition of many of these asylums was deplorable. In the Bedlam (Bethlehem) institution (1402, officially designated a lunatic asylum in 1547), inmates lived in an atmosphere of uproar and degradation, the violent patients being shackled and starved. The term is now obsolete, with medical emphasis being placed on treatment rather than refuge.

**ATHLETICS, CHRISTIAN PROBLEMS OF.** There is a new kind of religion in our culture that is both fascinating and flourishing. It is amateur and professional sports. The fans are the worshipers, the athletes are the priests, the arenas are the cathedrals, and the events are the order of service. Not only are tithes and offerings presented liberally and willingly, but dedication and sacrifice are demanded and offered as well. For the Christian, however, participation is increasingly problematic on two levels.

Philosophically, the worldly view of success and excellence involves winning, which often means at any price. A Christian perspective is far different. Biblical excellence (*arete*, Greek) features moral virtue (2 Pet. 1:5), and it involves doing whatever we do heartily as unto the Lord (Col. 3:23) and to the glory of God (1 Cor. 10:31). The story of Eric Liddell in *Chariots of Fire* illustrates dramatically the conflict between these two views of excellence and success. His Christian commitment to honor the Lord cost him a gold medal in a particular event. The intensity of the competition and the pressure to win often create intimidating standards within which a Christian athlete finds it difficult to practice without compromise.

Technically, there are several issues relating to sacrifice which give rise to thorny and controversial questions. What about Sunday sports? Is Sunday to be revered as a holy day, with much the same respect as the Old Testament Sabbath? Many Christians believe so and have strong convictions against athletics on the Lord's day. Others believe all days are alike, and that each day of the week is the Lord's day (Rom. 14:5). While these may feel at liberty to engage in sports on Sunday, ought they to exercise that liberty if it will be to the spiritual detriment of others? Does not the law of love dictate that they should relinquish their rights (1 Cor. 8—9)? If the manner of celebrating Sunday is a matter of Christian liberty as seems so from Romans 14:5 and Colossians 2:16, individuals must develop personal convictions before the Lord based on their knowledge, faith, and motivation to please the Lord. We must also manifest Christian attitudes toward others with contrary convictions, attitudes devoid of pride and condemnation (Rom. 14:3-4).

Every Christian ought to be outraged by extreme physical violence in specific sports. Christian football players, who are often asked how they can play such a violent sport, generally respond that it is not a violent sport—only a contact sport. As long as contact is within the rules of the game, and as long as the intention of the player is no to inflict bodily harm, there is no violence. While this is true as far as it goes, it may not go far enough. What was a contact sport has become a collision sport and can be a very dangerous one at that.

The 1983 Pan-American games held in Caracas, Venezuela, will be remembered as "the Great Steroid Bust." Nineteen athletes from ten countries were disqualified for drug use; fourteen were caught with traces of steroids in their systems. Anabolic (muscle building) steroids, such as testosterone, speed up the intake of proteins for muscle building and, when combined with heavy training, will increase body weight and muscle size. The International Olympic Committee laws state the use of steroids is illegal. The National Football League takes a peculiar stand when it states that players found to be using steroids "improperly" may be fined. Steroids are often prescribed in rehabilitation from chronic muscle disease and protection of blood cells during chemotherapy. To use them otherwise, however, is equivalent to cheating. It destroys the fine balance between athletes competing under a system of rules that creates an equality. More than this, there are several potential side effects which are too great a risk. The steroid craze is a further symptom of our need to win at any cost.

It, however, is only a small part of the much larger drug problem, involving cocaine and alcohol. Disobedience to the laws of the land and drunkenness are clearly condemned in the Bible (Rom. 13:2; 1 Pet. 2:13; Gal. 5:21). The Christian athlete is to remember that his body is the temple of the Holy Spirit. It is to be kept holy and used for the glory of God (1 Cor. 6:19-20).

Perhaps one of the most difficult and dangerous problems confronting Christian athletes today is exploitation. As they advance toward stardom the Christian world demands more and more of their athletes and other celebrities, using them for selfish purposes and offering them little in return. Our superstar mentality swallows them up into our cult of personality. Traveling from church to church, banquet to banquet, they give the same "success story" year after year. They may attract a crowd and boost the offering; but the returns are shallow and short-lived, while the athletes suffer from perpetual immaturity, spiritual pride, and radical inconsistencies in their lives. Their great need is to resist the pressure to perform and to pursue instead a pathway that will bring them to maturity in Christ.

Moderation is a Christian virtue expected of both participants and spectators (Phil. 4:5). While exercise and competition are important we must maintain a proper perspective as spiritual beings and emphasize exercising toward godliness (1 Tim. 4:8). It is wrong for Christians to give themselves over to a sport, even though it may be done in the name of excellence.

There is no other platform which provides greater opportunity to impact our society for Christ. The courage, consistency, and convictions of many Christian athletes is to be commended. They are not only in desperate need of our prayers; they are worthy of them as well.

**Bibliography**: Diehl, W., *Thank God, It's Monday* (1982).

W.J.M.

**ATOMIC ENERGY.** Energy can be defined as the capacity for doing work. Progressively through recorded history, but particularly since the industrial revolution, mankind has sought means whereby he does not supply that energy himself but derives it from some other source in nature.

The simplest source of energy to understand is probably gravitational potential energy. This is the type of energy used in an old-fashioned grandfather clock in which a heavy weight is pulled up on a chain. In the process of descending, the heavy weight rotates the wheels and swings the pendulum against the forces of friction. The amount of work done by the weight in descending is equal to the amount of work dissipated as heat by friction in the bearings of the clock.

This same form of potential energy is available when water in a lake or river at a high level is dammed and allowed to fall to a lower level in a controlled way. At least some of that energy is converted to electrical energy in the process of descending. This energy is made available for mankind to use for the many purposes for which we require energy to maintain our present-day quality of life.

Energy exists in many forms; for example, potential, kinetic (the energy of motion), electrical, and heat. Another form is chemical energy which exists by virtue of the energy present in atoms and molecules. Each atom consists of a nucleus that has a positive electrical charge. This charge is surrounded by a cloud of orbiting electrons in sufficient numbers to counterbalance the charge on the nucleus. But these atoms can become associated with each other and share their electron clouds.

This associated arrangement of nuclei and electrons (which we call a molecule) can have the electrons arranged in such a manner that they have a lower potential energy than when they are orbiting around the single atomic nucleus. When this happens, the difference in the potential energy between the two arrangements is given off as heat. This is what happens when a chemical element burns—its atoms combine with oxygen atoms forming molecules. The loss in potential energy of the electron cloud is given off as heat. The same sort of thing happens in any chemical reaction that produces heat. The final arrangement of the electrons has a lower potential energy than the initial potential energy, and the difference is given off as heat.

A similar sort of situation exists in the atomic nucleus itself. The nucleus consists of two types of elementary particles—protons (positively charged) and neutrons (which carry no charge). These are very tightly bound in a minutely small volume. In the case of very heavy atoms, such as radium, the energy of these particles in the nucleus is such that periodically one or more of these elementary particles breaks loose, emitting a burst of energy, in a process known as radioactivity.

Also, the energy of binding of the nucleus of these heavy atoms is such that if they could be split by some means, they would form two daughter atoms (of lighter elements) where the total potential energy would be lower. The loss in nuclear energy would be given off as kinetic energy of the particles plus electromagnetic energy (gamma rays), some of which could be converted into heat.

With the growth of knowledge of atomic structure, it was realized that it should be possible to obtain at least some of this energy by using the energy of the naturally occurring radioactivity (i.e. the high energy particles which are emitted from these elements) to collide with and break up other nuclei. This in turn would produce more high energy particles which in their turn would be used to break up yet more nuclei. This was first done in a cumulative fashion (i.e., the atom-splitting process quickly escalated to become out

of control) in 1945 in the first nuclear (or "Atomic") bombs.

Following the Second World War, the nuclear nations had the vision of "beating swords into ploughshares" and using this method of energy production (known as nuclear fission) in a controlled manner to generate electrical power. The industrialized nations, while contemplating their declining reserves of fossil fuels (oil, coal, natural gas) saw this process (nuclear energy) as providing the answer to their growing problems. At the same time the process offered virtually limitless power very inexpensively for the development of the nonindustrialized nations. Nuclear research was, at that time, at least partly redirected to that end. This resulted in the establishment of nuclear power stations in a number of countries. However, over the years since that period, significant negative aspects of this development have emerged:

1) The waste products from the nuclear fission process contain radioactive materials that are dangerous to life and which cannot be eliminated completely from the environment.

2) There is always a significant risk of an accident that can lead to a nuclear explosion or to the release of large quantities of radioactive materials into the environment (e.g., "Three Mile Island," March 28, 1979).

3) When the ability to produce industrially useful power from nuclear energy is in place, it is a comparatively simple matter to produce nuclear weapons by dividing a proportion of the materials and the effort to that end.

The advantage of the availability of the energy is obvious. But the ethical question now arises as to whether the disadvantages and dangers inherent in the process of making it available outweigh the advantages. Debate on this issue is prolific and often emotional. This debate is complicated by the existence of diverse special interest groups which include, on one side, those with financial interests in "conventional" power sources. On the other side are those who may obtain cheap power, as well as those individuals and nations who have invested resources in the development of nuclear energy and who stand to acquire substantial profit (or loss) themselves. In a democratically ordered society, we are called upon to evaluate these factors and to exercise our influence for or against the development of nuclear energy.

With regard to objection number one above, standards have been set up whereby a certain level of radiation is considered "safe," or at least acceptable. However, it has been pointed out that no level may in truth be considered safe because the effects are additive, meaning that a very low level of exposure over an extended period is just as bad as a higher level for a short period. Furthermore, this affects not only the present generation but also subsequent generations who could develop in a world with ever-increasing levels of harmful radiation with consequent increase in biological mutation. Virtually all of this biological mutation would represent a deterioration in higher biological life, particularly human.

While these criticisms can sometimes appear more emotional than valid, they are documentable. We have to answer the question, "Is it worth the risk?" Some put this more strongly, bearing in mind the future generations, and ask, "Are we *entitled* to take this risk?" A counter argument would be that in earlier generations mankind was not as conscious of the effects of industrialization as we are today. Many risks were taken which remain part of our lives but gave us the quality of life we now enjoy.

For example, the mining of coal and other minerals subjected the miners to very significant risks. Although these risks have been reduced considerably in present-day industry, they remain. The development of the automobile introduced risks, and although safety consciousness increases, this vehicle provides one of the greatest causes of accidental death in the developed world. One could cite many other examples.

Also it is noteworthy that many discoveries that we now regard as beneficial created significant fears in the people of their time. The Reverend Joseph Priestley (1733-1804) is regarded by modern chemists as a pioneer who contributed significantly in that field. But his work was viewed with fear and horror—even violence—by the general population of his time.

Thus the answer to objections numbers one and two above has to be the same as for any industrial development. Ethical considerations have to lead to an insistence on the acceptance of standards of safety. These safety standards, although they can never be absolute, must be governed by consideration for the health and safety of our own and future generations. Such standards will impinge on the economic viability of this energy source, making its attractiveness less overwhelming and indeed perhaps not profitable. But we must fight against the profit motive overriding the safety standards. While it has to be admitted that such altruism has not governed industrial development in the past, modern society now rightly demands this. Such concerns are now serious considerations in many aspects of industrial development (e.g., acid rain, water pollution, conservation of wildlife) and are particularly valid with regard to nuclear energy where unscrupulous development would have such devastating results.

The Christian ethical approach thus becomes a complex and difficult one. Loving our neighbor (Mark 12:30-31; Luke 10:27) might be said to involve making cheap nuclear power available to him at some risk to ourselves—also to him and indeed to the future of all humanity. In choosing to deprive him, we may say we have a duty to be our brother's keeper (Gen. 4:9); but we will then be accused of selfish paternalism. But some level of compromise between the world's socio-economic development through nuclear power, and

the dangers involved, has to be made. Any Christian ethical influence has to be to ensure that this is based on love and concern for the dignity, well-being, and health of mankind rather than on personal, corporate, or nationalistic gain.

With regard to objection number three above, there are many conflicting and opposing viewpoints. It has to be viewed in the broader context of the relationship between technological development and the demands of the military.

It is perhaps ironic that the exigencies of war, over the years, has provided the stimulus for significant scientific and technological advances and the provision of facilities which have been beneficial to society. In Roman times, the network of roads throughout Europe, including Britain, was built for military purposes. But these roads established communication for social and economical development after the military needs of the Romans had ceased to exist. Benjamin Thompson (later Count Rumford) realized the relationship between mechanical work and heat through the process of boring cannon.

The Crimean War led to the initiation of the nursing profession as we know it today. The First World War probably stimulated the development of the aircraft, and certainly the Second prompted great strides in aircraft design, particularly the jet engine. Medical problems of the trenches in World War I led to advances in treatment of all kinds of diseases. Although Fleming discovered penicillin in 1927, it was not until there was wartime concern to find the best antiseptics that interest was stimulated which led to its development for clinical use.

Some might call it cynical to ask if the United States government would have invested billions in the space research program had it not been for the possible military implications of the launching by the Soviet Union of Sputnik I. But it cannot be denied that whatever may be the reason for its inception, the space program has provided benefits to the world. These benefits include the stimulation of the search for peace, since communication (facilitated by satellites) helps understanding, which is one of the keys to peace. When considering the association between weapons and developing science and technology, even medical research cannot be eliminated because it is closely associated with chemical and germ warfare.

It was undoubtedly stimulation by perceived military needs that led ultimately to the development of nuclear energy for peaceful purposes. A continuing relationship between the two is likely to exist. We must now agree that despite the gifts that war has given to our social developments, we may not see this as a justification for military development being the first concern and social development arising as "fallout." This applies to all fields of technology. The perversion of our capabilities to military use will not be prevented totally until we have come to terms with the control of aggression. Thus in all these fields, but specifically in nuclear energy, we have to support and develop controls and safeguards by recognizing that what exists can never be returned to its former state. We must seek all the time to come to terms with the basic search for peace and render the perceived need for military uses less acceptable to all God's people.

Our attitude to the development of nuclear power must take into account the fact that it already exists and has become an integral part of the economy of a number of countries. If the magnitude of this program is to increase, the safeguards also must increase. In time the cost of these may ultimately outweigh the benefits. If and when this arises, an honest ethical code must insist on the development of alternative sources of power. This is essential, lest we compromise the health and safety of the world.

Some other factors must be mentioned. It cannot be denied that nuclear technology has been used constructively in biological and medical research, in the diagnosis of a growing number of human pathological conditions, and also in therapy, particularly cancer therapy. There can be no doubt about the benefit to human life arising from this application.

There is a further technical point. In addition to nuclear fission, nuclear fusion is also possible. When two hydrogen nuclei (single protons) are made to combine with two neutrons, a helium nucleus is formed, and a significant amount of energy is released. This can take place only under extreme conditions of temperature and pressure, but the energy yield is much greater than with nuclear fission. However, to date no method of controlling this reaction to provide useful energy has been developed. Its only manmade application is the so-called "Hydrogen" bomb that creates the megaton bombs of the nuclear arsenal. But this natural reaction does take place in outer space in the galaxies and stars. Such fusion represents the source of the earth's light and warmth which it receives from the sun.

**Bibliography**: Caldicott, H., *Nuclear Madness* (1982); Garrison, J., *From Hiroshima to Harrisburg* (1980); *The Darkness of God* (1982); *The Effects of Populations of Exposure to Low Levels of Ionizing Radiation*, BIER Committee, National Academy of Science (1972).

See NUCLEAR WARFARE.

C.E.C.

**AUTHENTICITY.** This word describes a situation or condition characterized by genuine authority or warrant, as opposed to that which is counterfeit or spurious. An authentic document is thus one that embodies true content, according to its title or description.

In ethics, Kierkegaard reflected the concept in terms of the responsible activity of one whose personal life is integrated and directed by conscience. Heidegger examined authenticity against a somewhat similar background, stressing the fi-

nite individual's responsibility for governing his own activities in a stable manner, independently of external forces. At a more specific level, Whitehead's "authentic feelings" described a direct, subjective, affective experience which for him conformed to a genuine emotional value-response.

See CONSCIENCE.

**AUTONOMY.** This term, the Greek word for "independence," is used in several disciplines. In biology it describes an independent organism such as the autonomic nervous system of the human body, which through its two antagonistic parts maintains a stable physical environment. In political theory, autonomy is used of a group or nation enjoying independence or the right of self-government.

In ethics, Kant's (1724-1804) support for freedom in political, religious, and intellectual affairs conflicted with duty, which for him was the essence of morality. To make the law of reason valid, he held that personal autonomy meant subordinating the will to that which maintained authority over it, i.e., the categorical imperative of conscience, instead of to ordinances external to the individual's will. The rational will possessed autonomy because it was free to legislate its own behavior, so that for Kant, autonomy was equal to freedom. This conclusion furnished the basis for his understanding of the autonomy of the moral law.

Adherents of ethical intuitionism describe an autonomy of ethics in terms of actions being either right or wrong ethically because these qualities are apparent intuitively and therefore not in need of ratiocination as to consequential value. For British moral philosophers such as H. Sidgwick (1838-1900) and G.E. Moore (1873-1958), intuitionism included any view that accepted ethical judgments based upon institutions as to the moral value of the things or activities.

For the Christian, autonomy must always be subordinated to the revealed will of God in Christ and not to a supposed "law of conscience," which can be misinformed, prejudiced, and culturally conditioned. The guidance of the Holy Spirit and God's Word must take precedence over reason as the arbiter of truth in life (John 16:13), because in Augustine's words, "I believe so as to understand," *(credo ut intellegam)*.

See ALTRUISM; CONSCIENCE.

**AVARICE.** The overwhelming desire to possess excessive amounts of material commodities, especially money, is known as avarice (Latin *avaritia*). The term is closely related to greed, which describes acquisitive and compulsive desires of body or mind. Avarice is a fundamentally selfish disposition that has much in common with covetousness, an attitude forbidden expressly in the Decalogue (Exod. 20:17; Deut. 5:21).

Avarice endows material things with a disproportionate value, thereby setting Mammon against God (Matt. 6:24). By contrast the Christian is exhorted to seek God's kingdom (Matt. 6:33), believing that a providential Father will satisfy needs rather than desires. Should riches increase, they must never become the principal object of individual affection (Ps. 62:10).

Paul castigated greed as idolatry (Col. 3:5), since it displaced God in the believer's life. Elsewhere he regarded it as a vice (Rom. 1:29; 1 Cor. 6:10; Gal. 5:3). The believer is to live a Christ-centered life, allowing everything else to become subordinate. Avarice was one of the classic "seven deadly sins."

See COVETOUSNESS; GREED; SELFISHNESS.

# -B-

**BEATITUDES**. The Beatitudes, the opening words of the Sermon on the Mount (Matt. 5:3-12; Luke 6:20-23), are affirmations of the true and deep happiness of those who receive the kingdom of God. The Beatitudes stand as a kind of preface to the most impressive compendium of the ethical teachings of Jesus ever assembled. They are above all statements of grace because they point to the present reality of the kingdom as a gift. The ethical imperatives of the Sermon therefore cannot be regarded as a new law that must be obeyed in order to bring in the kingdom or in order to experience the kingdom. As always in the Bible, grace precedes the call to righteousness.

If the Beatitudes are a prediction of grace, a kind of title-deed of possession of the kingdom, then it is wrong and potentially dangerous to think of them as involving ethical directives. The specific conditions described in the Beatitudes are not requirements to be met for entrance into the Kingdom. What those conditions describe is at bottom a *receptivity*. The kingdom comes to those who have nothing but open and empty hands; it comes to those who know their own unworthiness, who are nearly overwhelmed with their own, and who therefore have no hope but in the provision of God.

The Beatitudes thus describe a receptive state of mind, a condition that is presupposed in those who receive the kingdom. They tell us that reception of the kingdom can occur only when we are conscious of our ultimate and total dependence upon God. The virtues described in the Beatitudes are particularly instructive for Christians and may be said to provide a background to all New Testament ethics because they point to our absolute reliance upon God and thus provide the ground for, and the possibility of, an absolute and an unqualified discipleship.

There are nine Beatitudes in Matthew 5:3-12, although only eight separate characteristics; since the last two speak of those who are persecuted. The first four of these, which are more attitudinal in nature, may be distinguished from the last four, which can be considered more active; but the distinction is artificial and not as consistent as it could be. Nor is there any readily perceivable significance to the sequence of the Beatitudes as we find them in Matthew.

The first four speak of the needy, the powerless, the oppressed—in short, those who have no recourse but to throw themselves upon the mercy of God. Some scholars have accused Matthew of "spiritualizing" the first and fourth Beatitudes (Matt. 5:3, 6) by turning Luke's "poor" to "the poor in spirit" and Luke's "hunger" to "hunger and thirst for righteousness." But what Matthew has actually done is to focus more on the results of poverty and hunger without denying the literal causes.

It is the literally poor who are most likely to exhibit poverty of spirit and dependence upon God; thus "the poor in spirit" (a phrase found in the Qumran scrolls, 1QM 14:7) becomes another way of referring to "the righteous." Similarly, it is the literally hungry who are the most eager for God's righteousness (or better, "justice") to be manifested in the world.

It is possible, but hardly common, for the rich to exhibit such poverty of spirit and such a desire for God's messianic age. They seldom know this kind of absolute dependence upon God. Those who have plenty in this world are less likely to realize their true poverty and lack of resources. Unqualified discipleship will be correspondingly more difficult for them. This is the explanation of the complementary woes found in Luke 6:24-26.

The second Beatitude (Matt. 5:4) refers to those who mourn. This points most naturally not to mourning of every kind, but to mourning for the evil of the present world which is so desperately in need of messianic fulfillment. This condition of mourning reflects a helplessness and thus an ultimate dependency upon God for any alteration of present circumstances. This is not an ethical demand for mourning (nor is the exhortation to mourn and weep in James 4:9, which has particular references to the proud, double-minded sinner).

The third Beatitude (Matt. 5:5, virtually a quotation of Ps. 37:11) concerns "the meek," a designation nearly synonymous with "the poor in spirit" of the first Beatitude. Again in view is powerlessness and consequent dependence upon God. Meekness here means not softness or weakness, but an inner strength that seeks and trusts in the will of God. Jesus used the same word for "meek" to describe himself in Matthew 11:29 (the same word in the quotation of Zech. 9:9 is in Matt. 21:5).

In the fifth Beatitude (Matt. 5:7) we encounter for the first time a more active characteristic: "the merciful." To show deeds of mercy presupposes a position of power in relationship to others, is something hardly in accord with the remaining Beatitudes. The emphasis of this Beatitude must be on mercy in judging others. The point is that as God has been merciful in judging us, so are we to be merciful in judging others. This is clearly an important motif in the Sermon (Matt. 6:12, 14-15; see also 18:33) and is made explicit in Luke 6:36: "Be merciful, even as your Father is merciful" (see James 2:13).

The sixth Beatitude (Matt. 5:8) affirms the blessedness of "the pure in heart." This refers neither to moral nor to ritual purity, but to single-mindedness. The pure in heart are those who are totally committed to obeying God's will. Their discipleship is absolute. Of them it is true that they "seek first His kingdom and His righteousness" (Matt. 6:33).

We again encounter one of the more active characteristics of the recipients of the kingdom in the seventh Beatitude (Matt. 5:9), referring to "the peacemakers." Peace—that deep, comprehensive peace and ultimate well-being contained in the Hebrew notion of *shalom*—is one of the benefits of the dawning kingdom of God. To be a peacemaker is to exhibit in this age the eschatological peace that will exist in the future age. This realization of peace is possible only because of the present reality of the kingdom of grace.

James 3:18 sees peace in a similar way: "And the harvest of righteousness is sown in peace by those who make peace." Quite probably in the words of Jesus there is a deliberate contradiction of the Zealot argument that the kingdom would arrive only through a forceful confrontation with the Romans.

The eighth and ninth Beatitudes (Matt. 5:10-12) refer to the persecution of those who receive the kingdom and make it the center of their existence. To be persecuted for "righteousness' sake" (v. 10), says Jesus, is to be persecuted "on my account" (v. 11). It is to be persecuted for doing the will of God, defined now in the Gospel as following Jesus.

Clearly the Beatitudes, like the ethical teaching of Jesus, are inseparable from the eschatological fulfillment brought in the present experience of the kingdom. The tone of the Beatitudes is that of messianic fulfillment (see Isa. 61:1-2). The recipients of the kingdom are declared blessed *now* in advance of the future coming of the kingdom. The blessings of the kingdom, like the kingdom itself, are thus both present and future.

The Beatitudes, properly understood, articulate the foundation for ethics, but they are not themselves ethical stipulations. There is, of course, an ethical content implicit in the Beatitudes; and they anticipate some of the ethical teachings of Jesus in the sermon that follows as well as elsewhere in the Gospel. But the Beatitudes themselves are primarily indicatives rather than imperatives. They emphasize the conditions of a total dependence that moves most readily to total commitment—the kind of commitment alone worthy of the kingdom. Jesus best exemplifies this frame of mind and thus always remains the supreme paradigm of discipleship.

**Bibliography:** Guelich, R. A., *The Sermon on the Mount* (1982), pp. 62–118; Hunter, A. M., *A Pattern for Life* (1965), pp. 33–44; Schweizer, E., *The Good News According to Matthew* (E.T., 1975), pp. 79–98.

See JESUS, ETHICAL TEACHINGS AND EXAMPLE OF; NEW TESTAMENT ETHICS; POVERTY; RIGHTEOUSNESS; SERMON ON THE MOUNT.

D.A.H.

**BENEFICENCE.** This term is derived from the Latin *beneficentia*, describing the qualities of kindness and the honorable treatment of others, which include generosity, favor, and liberality. Beneficence is basically the practice of benevolence or "doing good." By derivation it also describes the result of that activity in terms of a kindly action or gift.

The New Testament exhorts the believer to perform good works (Matt. 5:16; Col. 1:10; 1 Tim. 5:10). Jesus went beyond the Law (Lev. 19:18) in extending acts of beneficence to one's enemies (Matt. 5:44) as well as to neighbors. By this means we reflect, although inadequately, God's generous grace in giving his only Son for our eternal salvation (John 3:16). Beneficence is thus a form of altruism, and all ethical schools advocate it in one manner or other.

See ALTRUISM; BENEVOLENCE.

**BENEVOLENCE.** The Latin term *benevolentia* ("well-willing") describes goodwill, kind conduct, and favor as a characteristic or disposition of a benefactor or donor. Benevolence thus constitutes an innate aspect of individual personality that finds objective expression in terms of beneficence. The emphasis of the term is upon the motivating element of character that produces the charitable response rather than the nature or quality of the response itself. The New Testament emphasizes the need for the Christian faith to be expressed in human society in terms of good works (1 Tim. 6:18; Titus 2:14) motivated by the love of Christ as an integral part of the believer's witness to the world (James 2:17).

See BENEFICENCE.

**BESTIALITY.** This term, otherwise known as zoophilia, describes any type of sexual contact between animals and human beings. It is a form of sexual perversion that occurred in antiquity among the Mesopotamians, Egyptians, Hittites, and Canaanites. The Mosaic Law specifically forbade bestiality (Lev. 18:23) and prescribed the death penalty for both animal and human offenders (Exod. 22:19; Lev. 20:15-16). Some scholars conjecture that the "lusts" of Romans 1:24 also included this particular sexual perversion.

Western culture has long condemned bestiality, regarding it in most jurisdictions as a statutory offense punishable by imprisonment. The incidence of bestiality appears more pronounced in rural areas, with men being greater offenders than women. Christian morality restricts acts of coition to human males and females within marriage in accordance with biblical precepts; it regards all other varieties of sexual congress as perversions. Bestiality must therefore be condemned on the grounds that it is prohibited in Scripture as well as being a criminal and antisocial activity that debases and perverts the human participants.

**Bibliography:** Kinsey, A. C. *et al.*, *Sexual Behavior in the Human Male* (1948); *ibid.*, *Sexual Behavior in the Human Female* (1953).

See SEXUAL MORALITY AND PERVERSIONS.

**BETTING.** Betting is the risking or wagering of money or some other article of value on a forecast that a specific future event will turn out as predicted. Betting is an essential component of gambling, a social system that often includes elaborate structures for the taking and paying off of bets. Gambling in some form is legal in the United States in forty-six states but is conducted illegally on a larger scale in all states, providing billions of dollars annually for organized crime.

Although some religious organizations conduct betting games such as bingo to raise money, many Protestants oppose betting and gambling, not because they are directly prohibited by the Bible, but because they are contrary to biblical principles. Since betting assumes chance, it denies a world of providential order (Isa. 65:11-12; Rom. 8:28-29; Col. 1:15-17). The unwarranted risk taken in most acts of betting is contrary to the principle of stewardship that humans are accountable to God for the use of their abilities and resources (Matt. 25:14-30). The gambler presumes that gain can be gotten for nothing, but the Bible ordains works as the proper means to material gain (Gen. 3:17; Eph. 4:28; 2 Thess. 3:10-12). Gambling is fostered by a love of money and covetousness that is condemned by the Ten Commandments (Exod. 20:17; Deut. 5:21), Jesus (Matt. 6:24; Luke 12:15; 16:13), Paul (Col. 3:5; 1 Tim. 6:10), and the writer of Hebrews (Heb. 13:5). Since betting is based on a reciprocal relationship, happiness for the winner implies unhappiness for the loser. Those who bet do not show love for their neighbor, especially the poor or unwary who are enticed to gamble when they cannot win. (Matt. 7:12; 19:19; 22:39; Luke 10:27; Rom. 13:9-10; Gal. 5:14; James 2:8.)

Gambling is addictive; it is estimated that as many as 10 million compulsive gamblers live in the United States. This compulsive behavior often not only leads to loss of income, but also to large debts, stealing, and ruined personal relations.

**Bibliography:** Bergler, E., *The Psychology of Gambling* (1958); Commission on the Review of the National Policy Toward Gambling, *Gambling in America: Final Report* (1976); Lundquist, C., *Silent Issues of the Church* (1985).

See also GAMBLING

S.D.A.

**BIGAMY.** When a person deliberately and consciously contracts a marriage with a second spouse while the first one is neither deceased nor legally divorced, the resultant situation is known as bigamy. Occasionally a spouse thought to be dead proves to be alive. If a marriage has occurred in the meantime, it is necessary to prove the seriousness of presumption of death in order to avoid a charge of bigamy.

The biblical ideal of marriage is monogamy (Gen. 2:24; Matt. 19:5-6). Christians and others have added to that understanding the concept of a lifelong union. For overseers of the church these conditions are mandatory (1 Tim. 3:2), since such leaders must set an example to believers.

Western Christendom prohibited bigamy. Prior to the time of George I (1714-1727), it was a capital offense in England. Subsequently, it became punishable by a term of imprisonment. The American colonists followed the earlier British tradition, but gradually they too replaced capital punishment for this crime with a prison sentence.

Polygamous marriages, common in some parts of the world, are essentially bigamous, whatever the presumed social justification. Bigamy cannot be condoned by any who submit to the authority of Scripture.

See MARRIAGE; MONOGAMY; POLYGAMY.

**BILLS OF RIGHTS.** A bill of rights is a constitutional document that legally establishes and defines the fundamental freedoms of the country to which it applies. One of the earliest bills was that set out in the first ten amendments to the U.S. Constitution; one of the most recent is the Canadian Charter of Rights and Freedoms. Both of these bills have been entrenched in their constitutions so that they have a superior status to all other legislation; no subsequent law can contradict or alter the provisions of the bill unless a special amendment process is invoked, requiring a vote of near unanimity.

When a bill of rights has been thus established, all existing and future laws may be challenged in court as potentially "unconstitutional." The subjects contained in bills of rights deal with democratic freedoms such as liberty, speech, religion, and association. They also can outline rights of equality among minority groups within a society and discuss the situations, such as arrest and detention, in which a country may infringe upon the rights of its citizens, provided certain procedural safeguards are followed. Covenants on human rights have also been adopted by groups of countries, such as the Common Market and United Nations.

Although the bill of rights is a modern concept, some of its underlying ideals can be traced to the Scriptures. In the Old Testament, legal codes tend to impose commandments rather than delineate rights; still, there are examples in the Bible of attempts to outline a system of fair criminal procedure (e.g., Num. 35). The New Testament also avoids the "selfish" orientation of individual rights. But in its teachings of responsibility toward one's fellow man and in Christ's example of fairness and compassion toward even the least desirable of society's minority groups, a duty is clearly imposed upon us to respect the dignity of each human being. We are taught that, in Christ, there is neither Jew nor Greek, slave nor free, male nor female (Gal. 3:28). Modern legislators have attempted to adapt these ideals to their societies through bills of rights.

Some may question the value of bills of rights when countries can draft model charters, then reduce them to empty rhetoric through restrictive interpretation, which effectively sanctions glaring human rights violations. Conversely, some countries such as Britain have an excellent human rights record without any written bill or constitution. A bill of rights can only be as effective as the sentiments of leaders and citizens dictate; if those sentiments are already fair and just, there scarcely seems a need to impose a codification of the status quo.

There can be certain disadvantages to having a bill of rights. If drafted in too much detail, it will quickly become a dated and inflexible voice from the past, attempting to guide a society in which its provisions are anachronistic. If a bill is too broad and sweeping, it may be dismissed as vague idealism, or else be subject to extensive judicial interpretation that removes legislative power from elected representatives and transfers it to judges.

However, the existence of even a poorly drafted or hopelessly idealistic bill can command a certain moral authority. An earnestly adopted bill of rights represents a commitment to human liberties. It fulfils the practical function of bringing various existing statutes into conformity with modern thought. A bill of rights may serve to guide and educate members of society toward greater tolerance and respect for human dignity. These ideals are unquestionably a heritage of the Christian tradition.

**Bibliography:** Zander, M., *A Bill of Rights?* (1985).

See CIVIL RIGHTS; HUMAN RIGHTS.

S.E.R.

**BIOETHICS.** The explosive growth of the life sciences in the past has brought with it ethical questions that man has never faced realistically before. Christians may be tempted to dramatize the situation in terms of "man attempting to play God," with emphasis on the element of human pride that easily creeps into the most well-meaning of utopian efforts; but this would disastrously oversimplify the problem. A biblical understanding of human stewardship indicates that any accession to our knowledge (not gained immorally) must be seen first and foremost as a gift or "talent" from our Master, to whom we are answerable for its proper exploitation. This does not

mean that "anything that can be done ought to be done," but it does mean that Christians need to have good reasons before excusing themselves from the *prima facie* duty to look for new ways of doing good with our new knowledge (Matt. 25:14-30). True, "godliness with contentment" is a Christian virtue (1 Tim. 6:6); but we must distinguish between contentment with the *unalterable* in the human condition, which is enjoined in Scripture, and complacency with the *alterable*, which is repeatedly condemned as slothful and lacking in compassion (James 4:17).

Among the possibilities that Christians have to consider in this spirit are the following pressing issues:

*Genetic engineering.* Hundreds of human diseases have a genetic origin, and perhaps 5 percent of all children are born with an identifiable genetic defect. In principle "genetic screening" of parents can forewarn them if they carry defective genes. Recombinant DNA technology is a long way from offering "gene repair" at the human level but may eventually make possible the design of genetic make-up "to order," eliminating such diseases as hemophilia or sickle cell anemia. There are marvelous scientific and medical advances which all Christians should welcome.

The Christian must of course resist any tendency to demean the dignity of human beings born with genetic defects or to reduce human procreation to the level of animal stockbreeding; but the dangers of such abuse cannot excuse us from considering what good it may be our Christian duty to do for "generations yet unborn" with the help of this new knowledge. Such compassionate efforts to ameliorate the human condition need have nothing to do with unbiblical notions of "the perfectibility of man."

Less obviously justifiable, and still very much in the realm of science fiction, is "cloning," whereby genetically identical human beings could in principle be multiplied indefinitely. The main ethical objection is not that cloning would "destroy individuality" (after all, identical human twins are still individuals), but that the cloned individuals would be denied many of the normal ingredients of family life and relationships, with quite unforeseeable consequences. Cloning is being introduced gradually for stockbreeding purposes.

*Artificial aids to conception.* Artificial insemination (AI) is now a well-established technique that allows a woman to become pregnant by semen either from her husband (AIH) or from a known or unknown donor (AID). As a remedy for childlessness it has an obvious compassionate purpose, but it raises many ethical questions. The long-term psychological effects of separating procreation from coitus, even in AIH, are as yet unknown. AID undertaken by agreement between husband and wife is clearly not adultery in the sense of unfaithfulness, though some Christians, both Roman Catholics and others, would still consider it a breach of the seventh commandment. Its psychological ramifications, however, are still less predictable. Again, if donor sperm is to be used at all, it would seem right to ensure that it is genetically "sound"; but how are criteria of "soundness" to be determined? A "sperm bank" stocked by Nobel prize winners, as currently proposed, cannot be guaranteed to offer fewer genetic risks than a random sample; and whether it would guarantee a happier or better breed of human beings is another matter.

In vitro fertilization (IVF) allows a woman's eggs (usually several at a time) to be fertilized outside her body and one or more then implanted in either her own or another uterus. Since eggs, sperm, and embryos can all be deep frozen, it is even possible in this way to raise progeny to parents long dead.

The technique raises complex ethical issues in several categories, and Christians as well as non-Christians differ as to the legitimacy of IVF. First come all the legal and moral implications of implantation in a surrogate mother who may not even be married. Whose is the child? Does growing and bearing it confer no right to it? Then there is the status of the "spare" embryos that are not implanted. Are there ethical objections or limits to their use in embryological research? Do they have "human rights"? Can they legitimately be deep frozen in a "bank" for possible future implantation? Does anyone have an obligation to ensure that a deep-frozen embryo is eventually implanted in some uterus, even if its progenitors are dead? It would be idle to pretend that Scripture gives explicit answers to such questions; but the Christian is bound to ask in every case what constraints are set, both positively and negatively by biblical principles (compassion, stewardship, "counting the cost," etc.). Their implications are often far from obvious, and in an imperfect universe we must be prepared for some degree of tension between principles that point in conflicting directions. In an overpopulated world, for example, it may well be questioned how much of scarce medical resources should be devoted to costly efforts to relieve infertility.

*Contraception and abortion.* The catastrophic prospect of unlimited world population growth has spurred new developments in contraceptive technology. Many of these involve the prevention of implantation or early removal of the embryo, which some would consider equivalent to abortion.

*Psychosurgery and Euthanasia.* The ethics of interference with the bodies of mature persons is of course a quite different issue from that of abortion. Modern techniques for the relief of suffering have removed much of the pressure to legalize "mercy killing," though they can raise ethical problems of their own. Psychosurgery (the division of selected fiber pathways in the brain), which can stop a patient from being worried by incurable pain, may also render him incapable of caring ever again about anything else, resulting in

effect in the premature death of his spiritual faculties. For these reasons psychosurgery has largely given place to methods that use drugs to achieve similar but less irreversible effects.

*"Spare part surgery."* To meet the need of living patients by giving them corneas, kidneys, or other tissues from a dead body does not for most people raise ethical problems. What is increasingly problematic is the choice of criteria by which to recognize the donor as "dead." Where freshness of transplanted tissue is all-important, there are humane reasons for pushing as early as possible the point at which the donor's body may be dismantled. Is it ethically obligatory to wait for death, or even for irreversible coma, if the donor is certainly moribund and willing to give tissue now? Christians with John 15:13 in mind might not find it easy to raise convincing objections. On the other hand there is an obvious need to retain protection for the patient who might otherwise fear that his prospects of recovery would be jeopardized by his value as a source of spare parts.

**Bibliography:** Anderson, J. K., *Genetic Engineering* (1982); Anderson, N., *Issues of Life and Death* (1976); Ellison, C. W., (ed), *Modifying Man; Implications and Ethics* (1978); Mackay, D. M., *Human Science and Human Dignity* (1979).

See ABORTION; ARTIFICIAL INSEMINATION; BRAIN RESEARCH; CLONING; CONTRACEPTION; EUTHANASIA; GENETIC ENGINEERING; MEDICAL ETHICS; SURROGATE MOTHERHOOD; TRANSPLANTING OF ORGANS.

D.M.M.

**BIOLOGICAL WARFARE.** Strictly speaking, this term describes the use of living organisms, such as germs and viruses, to attack and destroy people, plants, and animals. The concept is surprisingly old, an early example occurring when the Mongols contaminated the Genoese with bubonic plague at the siege of Caffa (1347), thereby causing the Black Death to spread into Europe. Louis XIV was reputed to have been offered an early bacteriological agent for military purposes by an Italian scientist, but he declined to use it. In World War I the Germans infected Allied cavalry with an eruptive equine disease (glanders), but with little lasting success. In the Korean war (1950-1953) the Chinese alleged the use of biological agents by American forces, but could not adduce proof.

Biological warfare nowadays also includes chemical agents such as defoliants, poison gases, and nerve gases. Phosgene and chlorine gases were used in World War I; but the most notorious substance was mustard gas, a compound of sulphur, carbon, hydrogen, and chlorine, which the Germans directed against Allied soldiers with deadly effect. In World War II, gases were manufactured both by the Germans and the Allies but were not utilized. Other gases that have come into production include the "blood gases," which produce a dangerous oxygen imbalance in the blood, and less toxic substances such as the lacrimators ("tear gas") that can be used for crowd control and specific emergencies of a local nature. Phosphorus preparations were used effectively as defoliants by the Allies in World War II.

Chemical agents are more effective weapons than biological ones because they do not require an incubation period, as would be the case for bubonic plague, anthrax, typhoid, equine encephalitis, and other pathogens. Chemical weapons are infinitely more lethal than their biological counterparts, and because of their practicality and predictability can be employed for strategic or tactical purposes.

The implications of biological warfare are so devastating for humanity as to make the very thought of their deployment utterly abhorrent to all rational people. The United Nations has studied the problem carefully and has urged an end to the proliferation of such weaponry. This appeal will be supported by all Christians who include ecological and humanitarian concerns in their proclamation of the gospel of Christ.

**Bibliography:** *Chemical and Bacteriological (Biological) Weapons and the Effects of their Possible Use,* Report of the Secretary General, United Nations (1969); Rose, S., (ed.), *CBW: Chemical and Biological Warfare* (1968).

See WAR.

**BIRTH CONTROL.** (See **CONTRACEPTION**).

**BLASPHEMY.** This constitutes a deliberate slandering, reviling or cursing of the name, being, or work of God, who is Father, Son, and Holy Spirit. As such it is condemned in the Old Testament and New Testament and traditionally has been punishable by law in Western countries, though such prosecutions have been uncommon in recent times. Blasphemy is immoral because it is a flagrant rejection of the One who is Creator, Redeemer, and Judge.

The term *blasphemy* is derived from the Greek noun *blasphemo,* "to harm one's reputation." The ancient Greeks used the term to denote the "mockery" or "insult" of a person; they also used it to refer to any depreciation of the gods' nature and their powers. In this sense, *blaspheme* became a technical term in both Jewish and Christian circles.

Blasphemy against the God of Abraham is condemned in the Law of Moses (Lev. 24:10-13; 1 Kings 21:9-10) and punishable by stoning to death (the fate of Stephen the martyr, Acts 6:11; 7:58). The name of God, which reflects his nature and character, is to be blessed ("Blessed art thou, O Lord...") and hallowed ("Hallowed be thy name..."), not cursed and reviled. In the New Testament it is considered blasphemy against God to revile Jesus the Christ (Mark 15:29-30), to oppose the content and progress of the gospel (1

Tim 1:13; Acts 26:11), and to bring discredit upon Christianity (Rom 2:24; James 2:7; 2 Pet. 2:2; Titus 2:5).

Further, there is the special sin of blasphemy against the Holy Spirit which, unlike other forms of blasphemy, is unforgivable. This sin involves calling demonic that which is obviously and clearly the work and presence of the living God (Matt. 12:32; Mark 3:28). It is to stare into the light and call it darkness. Because of their warped sense of values, the Jewish leaders accused Jesus of blasphemy because he presumed to forgive sins (Matt 9:3; Mark 2:7) and because He claimed to be the Messiah (Matt. 26:63-65; John 10:33, 36).

Obviously, given the existence of the living and holy Lord, blasphemy is always a serious sin. It is a difficult question as to whether in a highly secularized Western society, where many people have little or no sense of the existence of God and of themselves as contingent beings, blasphemy should be an offense in penal law. In Islamic countries blasphemy is punished. But there is little will within Western countries, even where there are laws against blasphemy on the statute book, to punish those who publicly blaspheme. Until there is a greater consciousness of God within Western society, Christians would be unwise to press for the revival, implementation, or introduction of penal laws against blasphemy. As an alternative, they do have the spiritual weapons of the Spirit to fight against such sin (Eph. 6:10-11).

P. T.

**BLESSEDNESS.** This idea or concept refers to the state of a person who tries to please God by the way he thinks, feels, or behaves. In His Sermon on the Mount, Jesus gave a series of descriptions of blessedness. These brief descriptions are known as the Beatitudes. He implied through these teachings that blessedness, or happiness, comes to a person as a by-product of a life of righteousness that is committed to the will of God.

Another great truth that emerges from the Beatitudes is that blessedness is not a state to be reached only after death. It can be fully experienced in this life. "Blessed are the poor in spirit," Jesus declared, "for theirs is the kingdom of heaven" (Matt. 5:3, RSV). Those who live in humble submission to God, fully conscious of their weaknesses and human limitations, will participate in God's royal rule in the world today—not at some distant point in the future. The poor in spirit are those with whom God walks in rich fellowship throughout all the days of their lives.

The apostle Paul also added an interesting note about the blessed life that all Christians should experience. In his speech to the elders at Ephesus, he quoted these words of Jesus, "It is more blessed to give than to receive" (Acts 20:35, RSV). While these words do not appear in the Gospels, they must be the authentic words of Jesus because they express so clearly His philosophy of service. His entire life was an unbroken symphony of service to others. To become a disciple of Jesus even today is to commit oneself to a life of love and dedicated service on behalf of others.

Those who seek the state of blessedness described by Jesus as if it is something to be earned and possessed will never find it. It comes only to those who humble themselves in total devotion to God and His will for their lives. "Blessed are those who hunger and thirst for righteousness," Jesus said, "for they shall be satisfied" (Matt. 5:6, RSV).

**BODY.** This term ordinarily denotes the physical expression of a person. A human being does not have a body, but rather exists as a body. However the relationship and distinction between flesh and spirit (or body and mind, or body and soul) are stated, Christian teaching is that a person always exists bodily, be it in this age in a body subject to sin and death or in the age to come in an immortal, resurrected body (1 Cor. 15).

The fact that God has ordained that human beings exist as bodies and express themselves through bodies produces moral implications. God's commands are addressed to person as persons in and with bodies, not as pure spirits. Thus there ought to be positive concern for the health of the body and the removal of sickness and disease, expressed historically in the Christian involvement in hospitals and medical care. At the same time there should be a recognition of the need for discipline, since the appetites and desires expressed through the body can easily get out of control (1 Cor. 9:27). This involves controlling the desire for food, drink, sex, exercise, work, and pleasure as well as setting aside all gluttony, drunkenness, perversion, laziness, and laxity.

For the Christian there is a further incentive for holiness expressed through the body. The Holy Spirit comes to dwell in the body of the believer and so he can be called "the temple of the Holy Spirit" (1 Cor. 6:15, 19). As such he ought to be set apart wholly for the Lord and to offer himself as a living sacrifice (Rom. 12:1). Two extremes must be avoided. One is the semi-glorification of the body, expressed in the modern cult of beauty clinics and health clubs. The other is the treatment of the body as if it were evil, as witnessed in extreme forms of asceticism. From the Bible the general principles concerning the nature and purpose of the human body may be learned. How these are applied will vary in different cultures, for example, the amount of the body that may be uncovered publicly.

P. T.

**BOYCOTT, SOCIAL AND RELIGIOUS IMPLICATIONS OF.** The term owes its origin to Charles Stewart Parnell, who coined it in 1880 to describe the ostracizing by his neighbors of a certain Captain Boycott (1832-1897). Boycott was employed as an Irish landlord's agent and was prominent in the disturbances of the Land League in Ireland at that period.

From an activity centered upon an individual to demonstrate communal displeasure, the term has now come to describe specific protest movements directed against organizations and industrial concerns. Where a boycott is organized on an international scale, it is usually spoken of in terms of sanctions or an embargo.

As an instrument of protest the boycott has been used by Christians as well as others. Thus attempts are made to force the South African government to change its policies on apartheid through a well-publicized boycott of goods coming from that country. Multinational corporations have yielded to public pressure and have discontinued the sale of certain products to Third World nations.

Boycotts can have positive social and religious value if they are directed at redressing demonstrable abuses in society. But in a fallen world it is not always easy to identify the real moral issues in given situations, with the result that boycotts occasionally support causes other than those originally in view. Indiscriminate use of the boycott can undoubtedly be harmful, since the innocent are often affected alone with the guilty.

While engaging in boycott, the Christian must consider each case carefully on its own merits, avoid self-righteousness, and resist manipulation by political rather than social and religious forces. The aim should be to bring alleged injustices to the notice of the appropriate authorities in a responsible manner without generating class or civil strife. A boycott may not always be the best way to address a moral or ethical issue.

**BRAIN RESEARCH.** The human brain, the "control center" of the body, comprises a tightly interlocked cooperative community of 10,000 million or more nerve cells. Each of these cells is a minute transmitter/receiver of electrical and chemical signals with links to hundreds or even thousands of neighbors. Faced with such complexity, brain research has had to develop many subdisciplines. Neurochemists, for example, study mechanisms whereby signals between cells are transmitted or blocked by different drugs. Neurophysiologists record the electrical activity of cells and try to crack some of the codes in which information is represented. Computer scientists and psychologists develop theoretical models of the ways in which intelligent behavior, including the recognition of sights and sounds, could be organized by computational networks of nerve cells.

Because human nerve cells are similar to those of other species, our knowledge of brain mechanisms has gained enormously from studies in humanely anesthetized animals. Research into the organization of the brains of animals as a working whole has thrown a flood of light on the mechanisms underlying our emotions and drives, as well as our diverse capacities for action and reaction to the changing world around us. Much has been learned also from the effects of accidental damage to the human brain itself, particularly with regard to the localization of brain functions. This helps the neurosurgeons to minimize the loss of function when brain surgery is required for the removal of tumors and the like.

Although still in its infancy, brain research is today one of the fastest-growing fields of science. The human brain is a self-programming computational or information-processing system, quite different in many respects from our digital computers and vastly more complex. But it is not less mechanistic in its functions than other biological structures such as the heart or the kidneys. Even the new science of robotics is contributing some useful thought models for our understanding of brain organization. Although most cerebral computing operations are distributed over a large population of cells, certain major functions are segregated geographically. Most automatic bodily processes, like the control of breathing or digestion, are regulated by structures in the base of the brain. The spinal cord and cerebellum have hundreds of millions of nerve cells involved in the control of movements. But these cells are not essential for the maintenance of consciousness, which depends on the interplay between the cerebral hemispheres and deeper structures. Each hemisphere of the brain controls the limbs on the opposite side of the body; speech is normally controlled by the left hemisphere. There is some evidence that appreciation of spatial and musical patterns depends more on the right hemisphere. The extent of hemispheric specialization, however, is often exaggerated.

Even in its present early phase, brain science holds much promise for the relief of human suffering and treatment of mental illness. Both its presuppositions and its successes, however, have raised a number of ethical questions. First, it might be thought that this mechanistic approach leaves no part for mental activity to play in the determination of human behavior; but this would be a mistake. Just as a mechanistic explanation of a computer's working does not deny that its behavior is determined by the equation it is solving, so brain science does not deny, but presupposes that our thinking and choosing determines at least some of our behavior.

In the brain (as in a computer) we have a complex system that demands analysis in quite different categories at several different levels. The claims that human behavior is determined (in part) by mental activity and that the behavior of individual brain cells is determined by physical laws provide complementary explanations, each applicable at its own level and in its own categories. There is thus no need to suppose that the brain has some special organ through which it acts upon, and is acted upon by, "the mind," considered as an entity inhabiting another "world." Biblical data also emphasize the unity of our human nature, while distinguishing between its bodily, mental, and spiritual aspects of significance.

Secondly, however, physical intervention, either by applying electric currents, administering drugs, or by cutting out parts of the brain, can radically affect a patient's personality. In principle this is nothing new, but it breeds new kinds of ethical questions. Cutting connections to the frontal lobes of the brain, for example, may destroy a patient's capacity for reflective action. He "doesn't care" any more. How much of the brain must remain undamaged, then, if a patient is to be held responsible for his actions? How can benefits and costs be balanced when radical surgery is contemplated? What kinds of intervention would be always unethical? Conversely, could it sometimes be unethical to *refuse* to intervene?

A particularly dramatic effect is produced by cutting the *corpus callosum*—the thick bundle of fibers linking left and right brain hemispheres—as a way of preventing epileptic seizures from spreading from one side to the other. The patient's "speech center" remains linked only with the left-hemisphere system, receiving signals from his right side and controlling his right limbs. Therefore, he may verbally deny seeing signals flashed briefly to his left, even though his left hand responds correctly to them. This "split brain syndrome" is sometimes taken to mean that the patient has become "two persons." In fact, there are many vital lower brain structures, including some involved in emotional assessment, which are left undivided and maintain considerable integration of the personality. The popular notion that the two half-patients could be held morally responsible as separate agents has scant basis in the facts.

Thirdly, although the physical correlates of mental illness are still obscure and controversial, there is growing evidence that not only brain tumors and the like but also genetic factors can be responsible for abnormalities of brain function, including some forms of schizophrenia. Whether these clues may lead to effective (as distinct from less critical) chemical remedies for any mental disorders remains to be seen. From a Christian standpoint there is every reason to hope that they will. Their success would in no way imply, as has sometimes been suggested, that science is taking over the domain of religion. The gospel has just as relevant a message for the psychiatrically normal as for the sick.

Fourthly, what of the "normal" person? Could mechanistic brain science one day make our future decisions predictable? For most practical purposes the answer is no. Prediction of brain states in detail, even if we understood everything about brain mechanisms, would require far more information than could ever be extracted from an intact brain. At the level of the nerve cells, for example, at least 100 million million ($10^{14}$) data would be required. In especially simple cases, however, where we are interested only in knowing which way a single decision will go and are content with probabilities rather than certainties, behavioral science may be expected to show increasing predictive success. Advertising technology already exploits this with obvious ethical implications, not least for mass evangelists.

But how much does the predictability of our actions matter for human responsibility? It is true that since 1927 Heisenberg's well-known Uncertainty Principle has virtually ruled out strict determinism in physics. To invoke this as a solution to the problem of free will, however, would be philosophically dubious. Free action is not necessarily or typically random nor even unpredictable. The question is whether in the light of brain science all our actions are not just predictable by others but *inevitable for us*. The mistake often made is to equate *predictability* with *inevitability*. Even if a brain scientist could (secretly) predict the immediate future of your brain in full detail, he cannot claim that his prediction is something you would be correct to accept as inevitable and mistaken to disbelieve if only you knew it. The reason is that (on the working assumption of brain science itself) the state of your brain (unlike the rest of the physical world) must change according to what you think and believe or disbelieve. Hence, no unchanging description of the immediate future of your brain could be equally accurate, whether or not believed by you. In that sense the brain scientist's secret prediction, even if valid for him, is not at all inevitable for you. For you, the immediate future of your brain, and all that follows from it, is indeterminate until determined by your thinking, valuing, and deciding. What he would be correct to believe is not what you are correct to believe. The situation here is relativistic. It is logically as fallacious to deny human responsibility on grounds of the (alleged) physical determinacy of brain function as to do so on grounds of the sovereignty of God.

Finally, it is sometimes thought that because brain research seeks to correlate conscious experience with specific states of the physical brain, it must deny, at least implicitly, that man is a being with an eternal destiny. This however would be as illogical as to suppose that the destruction of a computer must make it impossible for the program it embodied to be "resurrected." The death of the body doubtless brings to an end—in this world—the sequence of experience that has been embodied in it. But nothing in brain science denies the possibility that the same individual could find himself re-embodied in the resurrection to eternal life if the Creator so wills it.

**Bibliography:** Buser, P. A., and Rougeul-Buser, A., (eds.), *Cerebral Correlates of Conscious Experience* (1978); Jones, D. G., *Our Fragile Brains* (1981); Mackay, D. M., *Human Science and Human Dignity* (1979); *Brains, Machines and Persons* (1980).

D. M. M.

**BRAINWASHING.** This term is a slang designation of the process which replaces previously held opinions and convictions with those deemed more acceptable by the person or persons in charge of the process of thought control. While some individuals may be indoctrinated in this way more easily than others, a certain degree of coercion is always necessary. The length of time needed to establish a satisfactory change of opinion or lifestyle could conceivably extend over a period of months or years.

Brainwashing is generally, though not uniformly, associated with totalitarian regimes, where political or social dissidents are known to have been subjected to various forms of duress in order to bring about fundamental change of outlook. The indoctrination may vary in duration and in degrees of intensity; but the basic aim is the reconstruction of an individual's or a group's mental, moral, and spiritual outlook. In some circumstances the indoctrinators resort to physical or mental torture, confinement, the use of mind-disorienting chemicals, electric shock, and an intensive regimen of personality restructuring by means of psychological techniques.

The expected result of this process is that individuals or groups will abandon their basic opinions and attitudes concerning political, social, or other issues and embrace *ex animo* the new form of indoctrination. It is a marked feature of such brainwashing that the new ideas that have been accepted, perhaps with less conviction than might appear at first sight, are of a doctrinaire, regimented form. Although these ideas are presented with an uncompromising demand for implicit observance, they may actually be inferior ideologically, intellectually, and pragmatically to those concepts which they have replaced.

Procedures which many have identified with political brainwashing are not unknown among certain contemporary religious groups. If reports of victims of these processes who subsequently have recanted are to be believed, the indoctrination techniques employed by such groups can match in intensity and duration what allegedly transpires in totalitarian regimes.

This is hardly surprising, since religious conviction and motivation constitute very powerful forces within the human personality when they are aroused. Consequently, an authoritarian religious leader with charismatic gifts can sway individuals who have less dominant personalities by a demand for implicit obedience to the commands, real or imaginary, of whatever deity he or she purports to be promoting. Recalcitrant followers, or some would-be converts, sometimes need a more personal, concentrated indoctrination, which commonly involves various forms of physical and psychological punishment. Cult leaders generally have no compunction whatever about addressing themselves to this task.

Communications media such as radio, television, and the press can and do conspire from time to time, particularly in totalitarian regimes, to present to the public certain socially or politically "approved views" as a means of influencing or controlling opinion or espousing a particular type of philosophy. By misrepresenting, concealing, or ignoring opposing ideas or beliefs, it is hoped that the general public can be manipulated into the acceptance of propositions that serve the interests of government, political parties, or certain groups in society. There is also an important sense in which such media manipulation can be construed legitimately as an overt form of censorship.

There are in addition other, less vicious forms of mental indoctrination with which everyone is beset as the result of modern advertising. The purpose, while less radical than the kind of political or religious thought control described above, is nevertheless of the same general order; namely, to persuade an individual or a group to accept the sponsor's view of the superiority of his product over all other competitors. Mental acceptance of the proposition, it is hoped, will lead to an emotional commitment to the product. The motivation, of course, is one of economic power. Although in a "free" society there is no necessarily significant social or perhaps even moral danger, the usual caution of *caveat emptor* ("let the buyer beware") still needs to be entertained. There does tend, however, to be an important element of deception where, unknown to the consumer, a company markets two allegedly competing brands that are actually manufactured in the same plant from the same basic ingredients.

The principal moral and ethical objection to brainwashing is that the coercion and thought control involved interfere so radically with individual freedom as to bring about its destruction. Those who practice brainwashing are frequently bullies and dictators who have serious personality deficits. It is the duty of Christians to deal with such persons in a manner that will safeguard the dignity, individuality, and freedom of the weaker members of society.

See DEPROGRAMMING; MIND CONTROL.

**BRIBERY.** Bribery is the bestowing of money or favor upon a person who is in a position of trust (for example a judge or government official), in order to pervert his judgment or corrupt his conduct. It is an act intended to make a person act illegally, unjustly, or immorally. As such it is condemned in the Law of Moses: "You shall take no bribe, for a bribe blinds officials and subverts the cause of those who are in the right" (Exod. 23:8; Deut. 16:19). The practice of giving gifts to judges in order to sway their judgment in one's favor is denounced by the prophets of Israel (the prince and the judge ask for a bribe but must not be given one Mic. 3:11; 7:3). Likewise, in most countries in the modern world this form of bribery, especially of those who administer justice, is theoretically a serious offense in law.

Bribery, however, may also mean the giving of a gift with the hope of inducing or influencing another, as for example, to make a business deal, to buy certain products, or to vote for a specific person. In certain business transactions between Western companies and certain Third World and Arab/Muslim countries, no progress can be made in business negotiations without the giving of appropriate gifts. In such business deals there would appear to be nothing immoral in giving gifts. But the practice, since it is wasteful of resources and open to abuse, should be discouraged. In personal relations the giving of gifts to gain favor need not be immoral but could be unwise. For the Christian, who is committed to seeing God's righteousness (Matt. 6:33), the giving of gifts to gain favor is not appropriate behavior.

See HONESTY; JUSTICE.

**BROTHERHOOD.** Because there is a link between the children of one father, it is right that the children have a special affection among themselves. The Bible teaches that God is Father. Since there is but one God, He is accordingly the Father of all (Eph. 4:6). All mankind is united in a brotherhood that rests on the fact that one God created them in His own image. Color, creed, culture, or nationality, whether rich or poor, slave or free is irrelevant.

The Fall has, however, impaired and fractured this relationship. Humans sin against one another instead of living in brotherhood. But Christ's atoning work restores the broken relationship and establishes a new brotherhood marked by love (1 Pet. 2:17). Indeed the term "brotherly love" takes on a new meaning in the New Testament. Whereas the ancient world referred to affection within the physical family, in the New Testament love binds together those who are in Christ. Because they have received the great love seen on the cross, they respond with love to God and to their fellows. They show in their fellowship what real brotherhood means.

The brotherhood of man, real though it is, has been grievously impaired by sin. It is imperative, then, that Christians, who have been brought into real brotherhood in Christ, should so live as to bring that brotherhood to others.

L. M.

**BUSINESS ETHICS.** Are business ethics different from personal ethics? Many writers argue that they are not. What is different is the range of problems to which the businessman must apply ethical judgments. Over the past thirty years the business world has shown an increasing awareness of the need to develop ethical sensitivity among businessmen. In 1959 the Ford Foundation and Carnegie Corporation jointly sponsored a study in "The Education of American Businessmen," which urged that business training take into account the need for managers to develop "a personal philosophy or ethical foundation." At that time only a few courses existed which taught managers ethics. By 1982, however, over 317 American business schools were offering courses in business ethics. Various corporations, like the Lockheed-California Company, had hired ethicists to establish training and development programs.

The need for ethical instruction of managers has been highlighted by various studies in recent years. Typical of these is David J. Fritzsche and Helmut Becker's empirical study, "Linking Management Behaviour to Ethical Philosophy" (*American Academy of Management Journal*, 1984, vol. 27, no. 1). In this work the authors show that most managers make ethical decisions on the basis of act utilitarianism.

Act utilitarianism makes ethical judgments solely on the outcome or consequences of a particular act. Fritzsche and Becker show that managers following an act utilitarian philosophy tended to accept the "necessity" of paying bribes, were willing to pollute the environment when a competitive advantage could be gained, and were generally unwilling "to blow the whistle" even when human life was involved in the possible outcome of certain acts which they knew but in which they were not directly involved. As a consequence of this study, the authors argue that the "almost total reliance of managers on utilitarian ethics is not in the best interest of society." They suggest that an attempt be made to educate managers to think in terms of rule utilitarianism rather than act utilitarianism. Rule utilitarianism makes ethical judgments based on a theory of justice and rights rather than consequences. It is at this point in the debate about business ethics that a Christian can contribute to the discussion.

Although Christian ethics originate with biblical teachings, their application to the type of situation which arises in business is a relatively new phenomenon. Therefore, when Christians look to the Bible for guidance on business issues, they find few examples which can be directly applied to contemporary concerns beyond a general emphasis on honesty and truth. However, as Harold L. Johnston has shown in "Can the Businessman Apply Christianity?" (*Harvard Business Review*, September–October, 1957), Christian theology can provide a general framework within which ethical reflection and the discussion of business issues takes place. Johnston stresses the practical importance of beliefs like the doctrine of creation and the nature of man in understanding the human situation and formulating an ethical philosophy.

Christian history also provides some guidelines that may be suggestive in discussing recent issues. Thus in the Middle Ages an ethic was developed which regulated commerce and discussed such issues as a just wage and the fair price of goods. Therefore, in the works of St. Thomas Aquinas and other medieval writers, we can find useful guidelines for developing our ethics.

Following the Reformation there was a tendency to continue medieval practices and accept existing Roman Catholic teachings on society and business. But gradually, as society became more complex, new issues arose and a theological emphasis on such things as a person's calling and the duty of industry, linked to a growing individualism, led to theological justifications of competition and the "hidden hand" of Adam Smith.

In the early part of the nineteenth century there was a massive breakdown in Christian traditional teaching on social and economic issues, with the result that utilitarian and other secular views gained dominance in Western society. Resisting this trend, the work of F. D. Maurice, whose *The Kingdom of Christ* (1838) inspired British Christian Socialism, stands out. Later in the century, the Roman Catholic Church issued *Rerum Novarum* (1891), which dealt with the relationship between labor and capital, and attempted to apply medieval insights to modern society. The Dutch Calvinist tradition also produced significant works that attempted to develop a Christian ethic for the modern world. Among these Abraham Kuyper's *Christianity and the Class Struggle* (1891) and his *Lectures on Calvinism* (1898) are examples of an attempt to develop a theory of society that goes beyond the purely organic view of society that inspired both Christian socialism and *Rerum Novarum*. Kuyper retains aspects of an organic social theory but fuses them with mechanistic imagery and a more positive evaluation of the modern world. In North America, Walter Rauschenbusch's *Christianity and the Social Crisis* (1907) presented yet another attempt to give a Christian interpretation of the modern world. Rauschenbusch typifies the social gospel movement in America.

In this century, the Christian socialist tradition in Britain received considerable support from William Temple, the Archbishop of Canterbury. His book *Christianity and the Social Order* (1942) was highly influential in shaping modern Anglican thought. Reinhold Niebuhr played a similar role in shaping modern North American thinking about business and society, especially with his book *Children of Light and Children of Darkness* (1944). More recently works like D. L. Mundy's *Christianity and Economic Problems* (1956), Phillip Wogaman's *The Great Economic Debate* (1977), Ron Sider's *Rich Christians in an Age of Hunger* (1977), Michael Novak's *The Spirit of Democratic Capitalism* (1982), and Brian Griffith's *Morality and the Marketplace* (1982) have kept alive the debate about business ethics and modern society at the macro level of generalized philosophical positions.

But theorizing about macro-social-economic problems is of little help to people facing day-to-day problems. Therefore, several Christian writers have attempted to tackle the complex issue of daily ethical decision making.

Donald Jones, of Drew University, has produced two invaluable volumes entitled, *A Bibli-*

*ography of Business Ethics* (1977; 1982) which cover the periods 1971-1975 and 1976-1980. He has also written and edited several books such as *Doing Ethics in Business* (1981). A more popular practical work is Oliver F. Williams and John W. Houck's, *Full Value: Cases in Christian Business Ethics* (1978). Equally practical is the emphasis of the Mennonite Economic Development Associates, which, unlike most other Christian businessmen's organizations, is concerned with applying Christian principles to concrete situations rather than simply enjoying fellowship. They publish several useful booklets on Christianity and business such as *The Business Person, the Christian, and the Church* (1982), as well as a valuable quarterly magazine, *The Marketplace* (Box M, Akron, PA. 17501, U.S.A.), which frequently comments on ethical issues in business.

In conclusion, the area of business ethics is not radically different from personal ethics. But it does require considerable and sustained efforts by Christians to apply Christian ethical teachings to specific situations in business. Christian managers and workers need help and advice in living in the business world. Such help and encouragement will include a recognition of the value of Christian fellowship but must go beyond sharing experiences to ethical reflection and the practical application of Christian principles to daily life. Just as secular managers are developing ethical training programs, so too Christian organizations must develop similar programs for Christians and anyone else who cares to take them. It is in the development of such programs that the greatest challenge in the area of business ethics faces the church today.

**Bibliography:** Baumhart, R. S., S. J., *An Honest Profit* (1968); Beauchamp T. L., and N. E. Bowie, *Ethical Theory and Business* (1979); Beene, R., *The Ethic of Democratic Capitalism* (1981); Reeck, D., *Ethics for Professionals: A Christian Perspective* (1980).

See COMPUTER ETHICS; ECOLOGY; TECHNOLOGY, ETHICS OF.

P.H.

# -C-

**CALUMNY.** This term originated in the Latin *calumnia* which had a basic meaning of trickery or deception and which was used in Roman law to mean a subterfuge, a misrepresentation, or a false statement. Where verbal utterances were involved, the Romans understood a calumny to describe a false accusation, a malicious charge not grounded in fact, or some form of legal action that was not *bona fide* in character and perhaps even designed to subvert or impede the judicial process.

In modern times a calumny is·an utterance involving false charges or misrepresentations of fact which are designed to injure, impair, or damage the character or reputation of a person. Thus a calumny is synonymous with the concept of defamation, without actually falling into the category of meretricious falsehood. A calumny also accords with the legal use of the term "detraction" to describe the utilizing of false or slanderous material in such a way as to result in possible harm to an individual's reputation. By "slander" is meant the kind of malicious spoken report that uses false charges, misrepresentations of fact, and allegations that cannot be substantiated in order to defame or damage a person.

Calumny is clearly a dishonest activity that seeks to injure or destroy an individual who is innocent of the charges or misrepresentations involved. Not merely is it dishonest because it perpetrates unjust or untrue concepts, but it is a violation of God's express prohibition in the ninth commandment of the Decalogue against false witness in connection with one's neighbors (Exod. 20:16). The New Testament gives the positive aspect of that teaching by showing that Christ's love in the believer does not work ill towards his neighbor (Rom. 13:10).

**CANON LAW.** This title describes a formulation of rules, a decree, or a constitution that has been drawn up by the highest ecclesiastical authority. The "law" is fundamentally what the Bible teaches about man's behavior as a moral creature, and from this body of instruction came further rules and regulations which were held to be valuable for the life of the believer. Informal behavioral codes of this sort were evidently known in the apostolic period (see Gal. 6:15-16; Phil. 3:16) and set the pattern for a more developed corpus of rules later on.

The word "canon" claims a venerable history, going all the way back to the Sumerian *GI.NA*, which originally meant a reed (see Job 40:21) and which appeared in a similar form in other ancient Near Eastern languages. When used figuratively it described something straight or upright that could even have been employed in measuring. The Greek *kanon* had a particularly wide range of meanings, including a list, a rule, boundary, standard, tax assessment, and chronological table. The church Fathers used the word to describe biblical law, articles of faith, church doctrines, exemplary individuals, catalogs, tables of contents, and lists of saints. Only about A.D. 352 was the term "canon" used of the divinely inspired Scriptures by Athanasius in the Decrees of Nicea, section 18.

Canon law is thus seen to comprise a body of legislation dealing with the divine view of human behavior that has been formulated by ecclesiastical authority and made binding upon the particular group from which it has emerged. From the Nicene concept of canon law as the corpus of current regulations that governed Christian discipline came the association of canon law with divine law (*ius divinum*), and with sacred law (*ius sacrum*). After the tenth century these formulations of laws were also known as the sacred canons (*sacri canones*), while from the end of the twelfth century the term canon law (*ius canonicum*) became current in the Roman Catholic Church to describe the integration of ecclesiastical rules and regulations with the discipline of legal procedure.

Traditionally this formulation was traced to the Decretum of Gratian (1140) and continued the principle of papal centralization which was established in the eleventh century. The sole authority for formulating canon law in the Roman Catholic Church is still vested in the Pope and the bishops acting in concert. Modern canon law deals with such areas of ecclesiastical concern as liturgy, the personal lives of clergy and followers, penalties for infractions of canon law, and judicial matters such as marriage, divorce, and annulment.

The highly systematized form of Roman Catholic canon law is reflected to a lesser extent in some other denominations, where many of the same basic issues are covered in a collection of enactments. Whether elaborate or not, the primary purpose of such legislation is simply to ensure that church affairs are conducted in an appropriate and orderly manner. Where serious issues are at stake, it is then possible to use such a mechanism as a basis for a hearing in a regularly constituted church court instead of having important matters decided unsystematically and possibly on an *ad hoc* basis. Many of the church lawyers who function when church courts are called into service are also trained in various areas of common law. Whether this be the case or not, however, formal legal representation is normally always available for litigants.

It is axiomatic that no denomination should be regarded as essentially identical with its legal formulations, since they are obviously not creedal statements; but having arrived at them by proper processes of reasoning and debate, any denomination should certainly be prepared to be governed by them for the sake of decency and order. As social circumstances change, various aspects of canon law can be modified while leaving unimpaired the permanent elements of divine law.

**CAPITAL PUNISHMENT.** The most radical and far-reaching form of human punishment is that which deprives an individual of his or her existence. Capital punishment is so named because it reflects a method of execution by which the head (Latin *caput*) was crushed, severed, or otherwise fatally mutilated. In Roman law the *res capitalis* was a crime punishable to the least extent by the loss of civil rights and to the greatest by the execution of the offender. In either event the penalty was regarded as severe, since even the loss of civil rights generally entailed banishment.

In the ancient Near East the deity associated with a particular community sanctioned the laws governing the people who lived in the area. Thus the stele containing the legislation instituted by Hammurabi depicted Shamash, the Babylonian sun deity, investing the ruler with the authority to formulate and execute justice in the land. Much of Near Eastern jurisprudence was in the form of case law, beginning with a phrase such as, "If a man . . ." and in general did not differentiate sharply between what would now be called civil and criminal law. To a large extent the emphasis of ancient Near Eastern law was upon the necessity for the injured party to be compensated.

Among the Hebrews, this principle formed an important aspect of the usage of the verb *shalam* when it occurred in a legal sense. A more common word, *yasar*, applied to any kind of chastisement or punishment and on rare occasions might even refer to instruction, perhaps accompanied by blows from a rod. The concept of punishment or revenge, usually with God as the subject, was expressed by the vigorous verb *naqam*; and such retribution was generally of a capital nature.

Ancient Near Eastern nations varied in the degree of severity which they attached to social crimes. Negligence, resulting in damage to property or loss of life, could comprise a capital crime in some circumstances (Exod. 21:29) and was thus regarded normally as a serious offense. Among the Hittites, capital punishment was prescribed for a homosexual who violated his son or for a man who committed incest with his mother or his children. Certain forms of bestiality were condoned in Hittite society, such as coition with a horse or a mule; but by contrast similar behavior with a pig was deemed a capital offense for the offender, although not for the animal. But whatever variations of opinion there may have been about particular social practices, opinion in the ancient Near East was united in regarding murder as a capital crime; and there appear to have been very few instances in which the offender did not receive the death penalty.

Although under Hebrew law a person could also be put to death for adultery (Lev. 20:10; Deut. 22:24), female harlotry if the offender was a priest's daughter (Lev. 21:9), homosexuality (Lev. 20:13), the rape of an unmarried woman away from the protection of her home (Deut. 22:25-27), and in certain cases of incest (Lev. 20:14), the crime for which capital punishment was consistently prescribed was murder. The warrant for this procedure was set out early in human history (Gen. 9:6), and it is of great significance because of its antiquity for any consideration of capital punishment.

In the first instance, it specifies that murder is essentially a serious crime against the Creator, in whose image humanity was made. Secondly, it establishes not so much the innate sanctity of life as the value of the individual's existence. One life is worth no more and no less than another's, so that while the murderer may be executed, his or her family members will be protected from the terror of a blood feud that could possibly continue for generations. Finally, the proscription insures that only the prime offender will be punished on the basis of retribution rather than possible rehabilitation.

The legal sanctions by which a murderer could be executed for his or her crime were continued in the Decalogue, where the sixth commandment (Exod. 20:13) specifically prohibited murder, using phraseology characteristic of what scholars call apodictic or prohibitive law. Some modern versions render the edict "You shall not kill," but this is an incorrect and inadequate translation of the Hebrew verb *ratsah*, which is generally used in the Old Testament specifically of murder. So specialized is this verb that it is not even employed to describe such acts as the killing of enemy soldiers in battle or the inflicting of death upon a criminal. The commandment is therefore a clear and absolute prohibition of murder and is followed in Exodus 21:12 by the injunction that the individual guilty of such a crime must suffer capital punishment.

"Degrees" of murder of the kind which sometimes occur in Western legislation did not appear clearly among the Hebrews. One possible provision for what might perhaps be described as "second degree" murder appears in Exodus 21:22-25, where a pregnant woman could conceivably be injured fatally in a fight between two men, one of whom would presumably be her husband. In such cases the principle of *lex talionis* was applicable, so that if the woman did in fact sustain fatal injuries, the offending male paid the penalty with his own life. Again the prescription "eye for eye, tooth for tooth" specified the maximum penalty to be exacted retributively on a strictly individual basis, at which point the affair would be deemed to be settled.

The Hebrews distinguished carefully between murder, which in current Western usage is modified by some such term as "premeditated," and an act of manslaughter, in which the death of the victim was accidental rather than deliberate. Provision was made during the Mosaic period for an individual guilty of manslaughter to obtain refuge in one of six refugee cities (Exod. 21:13; Num. 35:11-15). There he was safe as long as the current high priest was in office (Num. 35:22-25), after which he was free to return to his home. This is quite clearly a different situation from that legislated for in the case of the murderer, for whom there was no alternative to capital punishment (Num. 35:31).

On some occasions the line separating murder from manslaughter could become somewhat indefinite. In the case of a thief breaking into a house at night, the owner was within his rights if he killed the intruder in process of defending his property, and no penalty would be attached to such a contingency. If, however, the burglar was caught intruding during daylight and was killed, a penalty would be imposed on the householder because the changed conditions could possibly leave room for premeditation (Exod. 22:3). But even in the legislation, the tenuous nature of the situation was such that no particular penalty for the daylight killing of a burglar was specified. This would imply that, at worst, such a contingency was treated as manslaughter rather than murder.

New Testament Greek words expressing the concept of punishment as such are *kolasis* and *timoria*, while *dike*, which is commonly used of judgment, most probably had an associated meaning of punishment. In secular Greek usage the root from which *kolasis* came meant "to check, punish, chastise, or discipline"; and in the New Testament it is the common term for punishment (Matt. 25:46; Acts 22:5; 1 John 4:18). *Timoria*, which occurs only in Hebrews, seems to imply punishment in the sense of vengeance. The New Testament authors were at one with their Old Testament precursors in regarding criminal behavior as synonymous with rebellion against God's laws, thereby envisaging wrongdoing in terms of theological categories. On this interpretation, crimes against humanity were not restricted to a particular social dimension, but were offenses that had been committed against God himself.

Of those deeds that were prohibited in the Mosaic legislation, murder continued to be a capital crime. Nowhere in his teachings does Jesus repudiate or modify the sixth commandment, and this attitude is consonant with his avowed mission of fulfilling rather than destroying the Law (Matt. 5:17). Nor did he encourage his followers at any time to disobey the injunctions of the Decalogue, since much of his moral and spiritual teaching was based upon it, as his summary of the Law indicates (Matt. 22:37-40). But quite aside from his support for the prohibition of murder and the punishment of the offender according to Hebrew law, Jesus made the Christian life more arduous by demanding that motivation, as well as implicit obedience of the Law, be regarded as a dominant part of the believer's behavior. This meant that, if the motivation was wrong, the individual was already in a state of sin, regardless of whether the act had been committed (Matt. 5:28).

An appeal is made periodically to the Lord's "new commandment" (John 13:34), sometimes styled the "law of love," as though that principle overrode all other considerations such as natural or divine justice. Even a brief perusal of the passage in question will show that Christ is speaking about Christians loving their brothers and sisters in the faith, rather than behaving toward them in an unchristian manner. It does not contain prescriptions of magnanimity toward felons, murderers, and other criminals; and any attempt to invoke such a "law of love" in order to cover behavior that is condemned ethically or morally in Scripture is a theological perversion.

All of this is not to say that Christ was unconcerned with such offenders as felons (whose dubious company he kept on the cross), adulterers, and others who were objects of social ostracism. Indeed, his broadening of Christian responsibility toward society included loving one's enemies (Matt. 5:44), appeasing the immediate needs of persistent beggars (Matt. 5:40, 42), accommodating the urges of the obsessive-compulsive (Matt. 5:41), taking the line of passive resistance to insure survival in a time of weakness (Matt. 5:39), and in general showing forbearance towards perverse humanity.

Had Christ wished to repudiate the sixth commandment, he could have done so in his pronouncements as recorded in Matthew 5:21. Instead, he includes in the judgment that will overtake the murderer those who are angry with their fellows without cause and those who hurl abuse at others indiscriminately. To emphasize his complete commitment to the precepts of the Law, Jesus warned his followers about the grave dangers associated with even the slightest attempts at relaxing these commandments (Matt. 5:19).

In his teachings, the apostle Paul emphasized the role that the secular state played in crime and punishment and, against a background of usage in the Old Testament, pronounced firmly about the nature of the authority which upheld the sanctions. In secular society just as much as in the ancient religious community of Israel, the rulers received their authority from God; and from this it followed for Paul that they would never be a threat to people of good conduct. If, however, the citizen was not a lawabiding individual and persisted in wrongdoing, that person should be afraid, since the ruler does not wield his authority to no serious purpose (Rom. 13:1-4).

To summarize the foregoing observations, it

can be said that capital punishment has a solid theological and social basis in Scripture (Gen. 9:5-6; Num. 35:33) and carries with it the purpose of emphasizing the importance and the intrinsic value of human life as fashioned in the divine image. Such enactments as require or support the death penalty in Scripture enhance the character of individual life by endeavoring to protect it; and in no sense can they be represented as unethical, immoral, or inhumane in character. Nothing that the ancient Hebrew Law said about murder or the penalties attaching thereto was modified in any way in the teachings of Jesus. It is therefore legitimate and proper to presume that capital punishment is one element that is basic to the Christian ethic.

In contradistinction to the biblical view, a non-Christian "doctrine" of humanity has furnished the theoretical basis for attempts to abolish capital punishment on the general grounds that it comprises immoral, unusual, and cruel punishment. This standpoint regards the life of the murderer as of greater value than that of his or her victim, interprets capital punishment as an instrument of racism and class prejudice. In some jurisdictions, prosecuting attorneys are seen as "politicians" whose electoral career stands or falls by the "number of heads that roll." Impassioned pleas by jurists attempt to commend rehabilitation as a replacement for the supposed violence of execution, in apparent unawareness that it is at present impossible to rehabilitate chromosome aberration or mental retardation. Retributive justice is interpreted by this liberal humanistic, nonbiblical view in terms of vengeance often, as noted above, with racial overtones.

Some opponents of capital punishment seem to imply that the execution of a murderer is much too great a price to pay for the crime committed and that the need for punishment, if any, is amply satisfied merely by apprehending the criminal. Others who oppose the death sentence for murder look vaguely and simplistically to the prison system for some kind of reform or rehabilitation of the murderer. In those jurisdictions where murderers are returned to public life after a period of incarceration, the rate of recidivism lends little support to such expectations.

A particularly superficial view of capital punishment is the one that proclaims that it does not serve as a deterrent. Quite clearly the word *deterrent* needs to be defined very carefully under such circumstances. The present writer can only say that he has still to hear of any executed murderer who committed yet another capital offense, which would indicate that capital punishment has some degree of success as a deterrent. As far as statistics are concerned, it is impossible to measure with any accuracy the deterrent or nondeterrent effect of capital punishment on anyone other than the murderer and hence any claims about the nondeterrent effect of capital punishment simply cannot be supported by evidence of a convincing nature.

Some secular humanists profess to be overwrought by the notion that an innocent person might be executed by mistake, and hence the safest way to avoid this contingency is to abolish capital punishment altogether. By the same logic any form of incarceration should also be abolished, to save society the embarrassment of imprisoning someone wrongly. The dilemma posed by such a situation can be avoided very easily by following the Old Testament tradition, which distinguished carefully between murder and manslaughter and made proper provision for both categories of offenders. Since such a procedure has long been a part of modern criminal legislation, there would seem to be nothing exceptional about applying it to doubtful cases.

A good deal of current debate about capital punishment, especially in the United States, seems to be dealing not so much with the morality of executing murderers as with the manner in which the legal community has become embroiled in the mechanics of prosecuting murderers. This situation is made even more complex by the variety of legal traditions that exist across the country. Complaints are also made that the system is frequently manipulated by attorneys to produce what allegedly results in discriminating behavior toward minorities. While all of this may be true, the real issue is with the theory of capital punishment, not the mechanics of American courts; and it is incumbent on the legal community to put its own house in order so that the law may be applied appropriately. At such a point, American lawyers could also look profitably and critically at the time and money-consuming system of appeals, which sometimes only terminate with the natural death of the criminal under prosecution.

The liberal humanist cause relating to the abolition of capital punishment has also been espoused widely by some clergy, theologians, and others as part of a great crusade to reform society. Periodically some greater or lesser churchman will address any listening audience and proclaim the abhorrent nature of capital punishment. This liberal philosophy has even been adopted uncritically by various groups of Christian bishops, who have issued periodic denunciations of capital punishment with all the authority that their office is deemed to possess. Although historically the function of a bishop in the Christian church was that of the supreme teacher of the faith, it is merely a matter of record that most modern bishops are not conspicuous for their theological acumen. Those members of the episcopate who support the abolition of capital punishment for whatever reason are quite clearly thinking and acting in direct contravention of the teachings of Scripture.

One argument that is commonly advocated against capital punishment is the statement that "violence begets violence." The reasoning behind this approach appears to be that if capital punishment is abolished, there will be considerably less cause for violence in society, including murder. This simplistic assumption constitutes a gross misreading of human nature, which has always been, and will continue to be, homicidal in character. While violence may or may not provoke reciprocal action, it can also put an end to violence. The brutality and inhumanity of the Hitler regime in World War II was ultimately terminated by even stronger forces than the Nazis were able to mount. The lesson has been learned, and that kind of tyranny has not been repeated since. In the case of capital punishment, it is no longer necessary to think of the terminating of a murderer's existence as an act of violence, since modern methods of execution are so sophisticated as to enable a murderer to die painlessly within a few seconds.

As in so many other areas of life, the issue is an ideological one; and the choice rests between the values represented by a secular theory of criminality and those enshrined in biblical law. From the evidence presented above, there can surely be no doubt for the Christian that capital punishment is both moral and legal. Thus the view that would promote the abolition of the death penalty is in fact advocating that the relevant biblical teaching is in fact fallacious. Given such a premise, it is a very simple matter to deny truth or validity to any or all parts of Scripture at will.

See CHRISTIAN ETHICS; CIVIL RIGHTS; OLD TESTAMENT ETHICS; SERMON ON THE MOUNT; TEN COMMANDMENTS.

**CAPITAL SINS.** For some time the capital sins have been listed in Catholic tradition as pride, covetousness or greed, lust, anger, gluttony, envy, and sloth.

Both the Old Testament and the New Testament speak of the sins later called "capital" but neither made any attempt at classifying them systematically or listing them under this heading. There were indeed in the Old Testament sins to which a "capital" (death) sentence was attached, but this was not the understanding of the capital sins listed by the Fathers of the church. Nor were they considered capital because they were deadly or serious. Capital sins might be mortal, but they might also not be. They were called capital because they were the heads (*capita*) or sources of sin. In this sense they come closer to habits or inclinations to sin than actual sin. Evagrius Ponticus (A.D. 345-399) wrote of eight such sins in his *De octo vitiosis cogitationibus*. The theme of capital sins was quite common in the Egyptian desert of the time.

The tradition of eight capital sins was brought to the West by John Cassian (A.D. 360-435), although John Climacus later reduced the number to seven. To Gregory the Great (A.D. 604) who in his *Moralia* also followed this number, pride was not just a capital sin but the source of all sin. Vainglory, therefore, was the first capital sin. There have also been other variations as well.

For instance, there have been different interpretations of the capital sin called *tristitia*, literally, sadness, or perhaps even some kind of depression. Some associated it with what is now called *sloth*; others identified it with *envy*. It does not appear as such in lists today.

While the capital sins were given considerable emphasis among the Fathers, especially in preaching, they never received the same emphasis in academic treatises on moral theology. This may well have been due to the negative emphasis on sin involved in approaching the moral life. It may also have been due to the difficulty of identifying, for example, a sin of anger, apart from some other norm. Anger is sinful only when it is "inordinate," which can only be judged from its result. Also, the same actual sin may be the result of envy or sloth. So, while a list of capital sins may be helpful pastorally, they may not actually specify a sin as such.

Since the time of the Fathers of the church, academic moral theology has moved away from the capital sins as a structure. Thomas built his moral theology around the virtues, moral as well as cardinal. Later moral theologies were built around the commandments of the Old Testament. More recently, however, the emphasis has been on the commandment of love of the New Testament. The moral life in this context is seen as a response to the Christian vocation to love.

The moral theology used in Catholic education had traditionally devoted space to the capital sins but usually only to relate them to some other structure which they had adopted. One would have to search a long time today to find a modern treatise built around the capital sins. But it would be a mistake to overlook the real contribution this classification can make to the study of the moral person.

See ACTUAL SIN; AVARICE; ANGER; COVETOUSNESS; ENVY; GLUTTONY; GREED; LUST; PRIDE; SLOTH; SIN.

J.R.C.

**CARDINAL VIRTUES.** In Christian tradition the cardinal virtues are wisdom (or prudence), justice, temperance, and fortitude. The adjective *cardinal* is derived from the Latin *cardo*, the pivot and socket which enabled a door to turn, and hence, in late Latin, the central point upon which everything else depends or turns. In this sense of a "hinge," whatever is cardinal is pivotal to all other relevant considerations.

The word *virtue* also has a lengthy history, being the English form of the Latin *virtus* (literally, "manhood"), a term that summarized all that was excellent in human beings. This concept looked back to the Greek word *arete*, which encompassed nobility or rank, people or things that were excellent or famous, meritorious individuals, and to a lesser extent, the concept of exemplary moral behavior.

The fourfold system defined above is attributable to Greek ethical speculation, occurring first in the reported teachings of Socrates. In the *Republic*, Plato enunciated the four virtues that were set out in *The Laws* as follows: "Wisdom is the chief and leader; next follows temperance, and from the union of these two with courage springs justice. These four virtues take precedence in the class of divine goods." Although Aristotle adopted the Platonic virtues with some minor modifications, he accorded them only a rather general treatment in his *Ethics* and did not systematize them.

The Latin authors followed the trend of Greek ethical thought, and in this respect Cicero was representative. His definition of virtue stated that "each man should so conduct himself that fortitude appears in labors and dangers, temperance in forgoing pleasures, prudence in the choice between good and evil, justice in giving to every man his own." Among Christian authors, Ambrose (397) was probably the first to use the phrase "cardinal virtues" in connection with the Lukan Beatitudes (*quattuor virtutes cardinales*), and in this he was followed by Augustine (430). In the medieval period Thomas Aquinas defined "cardinal" generally as constituting the qualities basic to all the moral virtues; but he also related the term more specifically to the perceived kind of rational good that the particular virtue seeks out.

In the biblical literature, in the Old Testament, wisdom is commended as a divine attribute that the believer is exhorted to possess. But it was not necessarily a spiritual quality, since the word *hokhmah* meant manual dexterity as well as intellectual capacities and could even be used of nonreligious persons (Exod. 26:3; 31:3), the aged (Job 12:12), and also of the cunning of animals (Prov. 30:24). Although a wise person need not necessarily be religious, the wisdom most admired among the Hebrews was a gift divinely revealed to mankind. Paul recognized a form of natural wisdom (*sophia*) in contemporary pagan philosophy (1 Cor. 1:20; 2:5), but contrasted the place of the Holy Spirit in the believer's life in opening the mind to receive the riches of divine wisdom (1 Cor. 12:8; Eph. 1:17).

Justice was a corollary of covenant law in the Old Testament and appears under such terms as *mishpat* (Job 36:17), *tsedeq* (Job 8:3; Ps. 89:14), and *tsedaqah* (Gen. 18:19; 2 Sam. 8:15). It was regarded as one of the fundamental attributes of a supremely moral God and, along with humility and the exercise of mercy, constituted the Lord's basic requirement of the believer (Mic. 6:8). The just person was commended consistently throughout Scripture, and the principle of the just living by faith (Hab. 2:4) was emphasized in Paul's writings (Rom. 1:17; Gal. 3:11).

Of the remaining Greek virtues as reflected in Scripture, temperance in the sense of self-restraint (*enkrateia*) was regarded by Paul as an eminently important aspect of Christian character (Gal. 5:23; 1 Cor. 9:25; Titus 1:8). Paul also urged the older men to be prudent in judgment (*sophron*, Titus 2:2). Fortitude has long been required of God's servants, hence the exhortations to strength when the Israelites were about to possess the Promised Land (Deut. 11:8; 31:6, 7; Josh. 1:6, 9) and on repeated occasions when the Lord's servants were being commissioned for a particular task (Hag. 2:4; Zech. 8:9, 13). Quite frequently human beings would urge each other to be strong in the face of adversity (1 Sam. 4:9; 2 Chron. 32:7; Isa. 35:4). The good soldier of Jesus Christ is commanded to manifest fortitude (2 Tim. 2:3), and in continuing in this manner will ultimately attain to salvation (Mark 13:13).

While scriptural parallels can thus be found for the classic Greek virtues, it is important to note that the abstract concept of virtue, so prominent in pagan ethical discussion, is virtually absent from Scripture. The Septuagint Greek version used *arete* to translate *hodh* in Habakkuk 3:3 and Zechariah 6:13, where "glory" and "kingly honor" respectively are actually being described. Similarly, *arete* appeared as the Greek rendering of *tehillah* ("praise") in Isaiah 42:8, 12; 43:21; and 63:7, where the Hebrew is actually a plural form. The Septuagint translation clearly took some liberties with the sense of the Hebrew text on such occasions.

In the New Testament, *arete* describes divine "excellence" (RSV, 2 Pet. 1:3; NKJV has "virtue") and renown (1 Pet. 2:9), which the Christian is required to proclaim. As an abstract concept it is translated "excellence" by the RSV of Philippians 4:8 and "virtue" in 2 Pet. 1:5 (RSV; NKJV). These are the only New Testament occurrences of *arete* and they reflect the nature of Christ's work in the believer rather than representing "virtue" as an independent ethical quantum. In short, the New Testament emphasis is upon virtues as the fruit of the Holy Spirit's work in the believer's life, and not on the attainment of some abstract ideal of personality and behavior which might be called "virtue." The medieval Schoolmen quite properly remedied the deficit of pagan philosophy by adding faith, hope, and love to the list of the four classical virtues that came to be known as "cardinal."

**CASUISTRY.** This term designates the method of solving problems both of right and wrong. Specifically, it refers to removing feelings of guilt or uncertainty by the systematic application of moral or theological principles to specific cases. In developed casuistry, general laws or principles are posited; and then possible exceptions, modifications, or extenuating circumstances are recognized as possibly justifying departure from the strict obedience to the basic moral laws or principles. Considering the moral law, "You shall not bear false witness" as an example, possible exceptions could include telling a lie to save the lives of people who are hidden away in a time of war or telling a lie to divert a marauding army from finding a village in the forest. Considering uncertainty, a common case of conscience faced by Protestant pastors in the seventeenth century was, "How do I know that I am one of the elect?" This was solved by applying a series of tests from the New Testament which revealed whether a person is a child of God, for example, that he loves the brethren (1 John 3:14).

Casuistry has been an important part of Roman Catholic moral theology. Many manuals have been provided for the use of priests and confessors to help them to apply general moral principles as well as to recognize possible exceptions to them. However, the provision of details of exceptions has, at times, been so bountiful that the whole system of casuistry has been brought into disrepute. For example, in the seventeenth century, Blaise Pascal (1623-62) launched a powerful attack upon Jesuit casuistry in his *Provincial Letters*. One legacy of this has been that casuistry has not always had a good reputation, even within Roman Catholicism.

It is possible to find a simple kind of casuistry in the New Testament. In his dealings with the Pharisees, Jesus showed the right kind of concern for cases of conscience (Matt. 12:9-14; Mark 10:2-10) and also condemned the abuse of exceptions (Mark 7:1-13). St. Paul also used a basic casuistry (Rom. 13—14; 1 Cor. 12; Philem.). It is such teaching that has been the basis of casuistry with Protestantism, especially in Puritanism and Anglicanism but also in Lutheranism and other traditions. However, since casuistry can give the impression of being based more on law than gospel, it is usually unwelcome in modern Protestantism. It is also unwelcome both to the supporters of situation ethics and to those who want simplistic solutions to complex moral issues.

**Bibliography:** Waddams, H., *A New Introduction to Moral Theology* (1972); Kirk, K. E., *Conscience and Its Problems: An Introduction to Casuistry* (1936).

P.T.

**CATEGORICAL IMPERATIVE.** This is a phrase used by Immanuel Kant (1724-1803), the great German philosopher, in his teaching on morals. It is found in his *Groundwork of the Metaphysic of Morals* (1785) and *Metaphysic of Morals* (1797). Kant rejected the view that an action has to be judged by its results and consequences. Instead, he insisted that the action itself has to proceed from a good will, that is, where the human will is intent on obeying the moral law because it is the moral law. This has been described as "duty for duty's sake." It may produce happiness or unhappiness; but the results are secondary, for the good will is primary.

The meaning of the categorical imperative is clearer when it is contrasted with the "hypothetical imperative." The latter is of the form: "Take Concorde if you wish to fly across the Atlantic very quickly." One is invited to act in a certain way in order to achieve a desired result. In comparison, the categorical imperative commands unconditionally and says, "Do not kill," or "Do not steal," or "Tell the truth." Here the motive for action is primarily that of respect for the moral law and submission to its demands.

It would be a mistake to think that Kant based his teaching on duty for duty's sake on revelation from God. While there was room in his teaching for a moral argument for the existence of God, he did not deduce his concept of the categorical imperative from belief in God. Rather, it was deduced from his metaphysical teaching on *a priori* knowledge. For example, he argued that it is wrong to tell lies because if all of us lied when it suited us, the result would be chaotic, without any distinction between truth and falsehood. His principle was: "Act as if the maxim of your action were to become, by your will, universal law." This supplies a necessary condition for a moral principle—that we should only adopt and act on principles which everyone should adopt. However, it does not tell us which of such principles we ought to adopt at any one time in a specific situation. Thus it may be said that the operation of the categorical imperative is best understood not as a source of moral principles but rather as a test of those principles we have or may adopt.

*Bibliography:* Paton, H. J., *The Categorical Imperative* (1947).

P.T.

**CELIBACY.** Celibacy is the renunciation of marriage undertaken with the intention of practicing perfect chastity. In the Roman Catholic Church the vocation to celibacy is chosen for the good of the kingdom. Although celibacy was not recognized as a way of life in the Old Testament, the teaching and life of Christ undoubtedly were the driving influence in the church in recognizing celibacy as a vocation. Important also were the exhortations and example of St. Paul.

Celibacy is a way of life which is open to all who can live it. In the history of the church it has never been considered obligatory, nor has it in any way involved an implicit condemnation of sex or marriage. On the other hand, along with poverty and obedience, it has traditionally been a requirement for the vocation to what the church calls the religious life or state. In this life, however, the emphasis is more on chastity; and Roman Catholic religious orders take a vow of chastity, not simply a promise or vow not to marry.

Although it was not demanded in the first few centuries, celibacy has been a requirement since that time for the priesthood in the Latin church. In the Eastern church it has been a requirement only for bishops. The requirement for bishops is found in the codes of the emperors Theodotius II and Justinian and in the Synod of Trulla (A.D. 692). Although in the Eastern church they cannot be bishops, married men are allowed to be ordained to the priesthood. But celibacy is expected of anyone unmarried when ordained.

**Bibliography:** Egentur, R., *Furrow* (1965) XVI, pp. 731–49; Weber, L., *Sacramentum Mundi* (1968) I, pp. 275–80.

J.R.C.

**CENSORSHIP.** In its most developed form, censorship is the active result of a value judgment which seeks to prohibit the general usage of certain statements, ideas, or opinions, whether they occur orally or in written form. The need for such action allegedly arises because the censoring authority regards the objects of its attention as a potential or actual threat to official policy or public morality, or possibly to both. It constitutes a form of choice made by one group for another. What makes censorship so significant is the fact that it could be imposed rigorously upon a much larger social configuration were the proper authority available for such a purpose. In some political jurisdictions censorship plays a significant part in controlling what people see, read, and believe, while in others it has been used, especially in time of war, to prevent the dissemination of information which might assist the enemy or impair national defense.

As an attempt to impose the will of an individual or a group upon others, censorship has had a lengthy history. In ancient Egypt, only those accounts of battles which depicted the pharaoh in a favorable light were allowed to appear as inscriptions on temple walls, thus constituting the "official" record of the events. In the Old Testament, King Jehoiakim of Judah censored those portions of the first edition of Jeremiah's prophecy that offended him by cutting them out of the scroll with a knife and burning them in the presence of his courtiers (Jer. 36:20-25). In the New Testament period, converts to Christianity in Ephesus engaged in a communal form of censorship by destroying scrolls and books having to do with magic (Acts 19:19) after Paul had preached the gospel to them.

The ancient Greeks held to a form of censorship, as illustrated in Plato's *Republic*, Book II, where the very first step to be taken in formulating the ideal educational system was to establish a censorship of written fiction. Under this procedure good stories would be acceptable for teaching the young, and bad ones would be rejected. For Plato, the tales that were in current use were mostly unfit for serious consideration by the state censors. Among the Romans, the Latin verb *censeo*, from which "censor" is derived, probably originated from a word describing the numbering of people by hundreds, as in a census. *Censeo* was also used widely of land and monetary assessments, tax rates, and the like. When it came to be employed in connection with Senate deliberations and decisions, it frequently described opinions that were expressed and the right that the individual had to impart his opinions. Among the Latin orators and poets, the noun *censor* described not merely the two Roman magistrates who bore that title, but alluded figuratively to anyone considered to be a rigid judge of morality.

As the arbiter of faith and morals for European Christendom, the medieval Roman Catholic Church developed a system of censorship that had its roots in such situations as the Council of Nicea (A.D. 325). The purpose was to perpetuate doctrinal orthodoxy as legislated by papal authority; and in practice it acted either to examine a work before publication (*censura praevia*), or to suppress it after publication (*censura repressiva*) if it contained offensive passages. Discipline in this area was strict, and even the reading of the Bible in the vernacular was prohibited to the Roman Catholic faithful. The reorganization of censorship and the banning of certain books resulted in the publication in 1564 of the *Tridentine Index*, which contained the regulations governing censorship. These, along with associated penalties for infractions of the *Index*, were made binding upon authors, printers, and booksellers.

In his *Areopagitica*, John Milton argued in 1664 that the licensing of printers was itself a form of censorship that inhibited the development of truth and that just persons of good faith ought not to fear the consequences should licensing be removed. A more perceptive view of human nature, however, was expressed in 1733 by James Bramston, who coined the following aphorism: "Can statutes keep the British press in awe, when that sells best that's most against the law?" More than a century later, in a ponderous statement on the subject in his essay *On Liberty*, John Stuart Mill implied that the suppression of certain opinions indicated that the censoring agent was by his very actions claiming infallibility. A contemporary author, the English historian Macaulay, noted that the British press had, during the preceding century and a half, enjoyed increasing liberty, while its readership had become much more strict in matters of propriety during that same period.

There are very few individuals who would quarrel with the notion that censorship should be retained where questions of national security are involved and that offenders should be punished. But in the area of what may be considered public or private morality, there is a great division of opinion in modern pluralistic societies. Censorship in such instances is directed mainly at what is considered pornographic, but it also deals with the acts that are depicted by the various mediums.

There is a considerable amount of hypocrisy where censorship is concerned. Pornographers make enormous sums of money from sensational representations of human vice and accordingly are condemned from time to time by the same governments that reap large tax revenues from the sale and distribution of pornographic items. At other times, stern advocates of private enterprise clamor for government to legislate public morality, while those of a socialist outlook who demand "cradle to grave" government regulation of society suddenly appear as advocates for free enterprise where morality is concerned. Quite frequently the same individuals who support freedom in terms of explicit descriptions of sexual activity in literature or graphic representations on film are among the first to deny liberty to those who wish to be equally explicit in racist publications. Surely if censorship is to be credible, there ought to be some degree of consistency in the proceedings.

Because all of us are censors in the sheer exercise of personal choice, it follows that there has never been a time in civilized society when some form of censorship, private or public, did not exist. Although public opinion shifts periodically, it seems inevitable that censorship will continue to be a part of human life. The import of James Bramston's aphorism seems to be not whether we shall employ censorship, but rather what will be the most functional form that censorship can adopt.

The question is easier for the Christian to answer than anyone else because the Scriptures instruct the believer in appropriate behavior. The Christian is to live a life of holiness (1 Pet. 1:16; Lev. 11:44), avoid gratification of fleshly lusts (Rom. 13:14), be pure in word (Eph. 4:29) as well as in deed, and generally be transformed from a carnal to a spiritual person by God's renewing grace (Rom. 12:2).

Laws are only as effective as the support which public opinion bestows upon them. A certain segment of the public will always insist upon carnal gratification, whatever restraints may be imposed. For these people censorship merely impedes the process of self-satisfaction somewhat. Where there is a perceived need for the prurient, there will always be persons more than willing to meet that need for an appropriate amount of money.

The person who is serious about censorship will have to realize first of all that it is far easier to change laws than to modify human attitudes. Having faced that fact, the would-be reformer will then be confronted with a challenge to evangelization in the best sense of that term that only the most dedicated Christian will be able to fulfil.

See BOYCOTT; MIND CONTROL; PORNOGRAPHY.

**CHANCE.** Chance is generally regarded as some fortuitous happening that occurs outside human control. Its unusual character arises from the fact that it is not part of any pattern or relationship that typifies normal life. It is not so much the event, circumstance, or situation that is necessarily as bizarre as its relationship in time or space to other aspects of life. Indeed, the circumstantial nature of the occasion implies often a lack of human control.

In contrast to the modern humanist view that chance is accidental and without purpose, the ancient Greeks included in their Pantheon a god to whom chance events were attributed. This god was named *Tyche* ("chance," "fortune"), and among the Romans was known as *Fortuna*. The chance in question could be good or bad, as the context of events determined.

Until comparatively recent times physicists and others spoke of chance as though it were a random, unregulated quantity entirely fortuitous in nature. More careful probability studies, however, have revealed that chance is by no means as indeterminate as was once supposed, and scientists now speak cautiously about the "laws of chance." One result of this type of study is that so-called "accidents" are now deemed to have specific causal factors.

The philosophical monism of the ancient Hebrews in relating everything to God's activity absolutely precluded the notion of uncontrolled chance. For the Christian who believes that God notices the plight of the insignificant sparrow (Luke 12:6), a chance event is either no more than an occurrence which is part of the experience of many other people, or it is a concurrence of phenomena which often appears fortuitous merely because it is unexpected.

Some Christians are convinced that chance events are actually part of a rigid predestination ordained by God. Many others prefer to regard chance occurrences as a salutary reminder that many aspects of existence are totally outside the bounds of human control. In such a case the believer, therefore, needs to walk by faith and in the power of God, so that no event, whether good or ill, can separate him or her from God's provident love and care.

See FREEDOM.

**CHARACTER.** Character is used to describe the various facets of human personality as they are apperceived socially. Character has been defined as the sum of the attributes that make individuals distinctive and can comprise a genetically based amalgam of such personality factors as high moral and ethical standards, loyalty, altruism, fidelity, and the like on the positive side, and egocentric behavior, lust, criminal intent, greed, and similar negative factors on the other. An individual's character may be recognized not merely by the preponderance of negative over positive features, or vice-versa, but also by the motivation which governs individual activity, with its recurring possibility of "hidden agenda." Thus an egocentric base to individual character can be expected from the start, since one result of Adam's rebellion against God was the instituting of a genetic pattern within human nature whereby we love darkness rather than light (John 3:19). While perhaps appearing desirous of doing good, we actually find ourselves performing evil deeds (Rom. 7:19). It is from this self-destroying condition that Christ would have us be saved by His grace (Eph. 2:8) and renewed in our minds (Rom. 12:2).

The ancient covenant established by God with Israel on Mount Sinai was intended to form the character of individual and community living by insistence upon a holy life (Lev. 11:44) and obedience to the known will of God (Exod. 23:21). The Old Testament enshrined the ideal person's character in terms of the attributes of the young David. The New King James Version renders these as "skillful in playing (that is, a musical instrument), a mighty man of valor, a man of war, prudent in speech, and a handsome person; and the LORD is with him" (1 Sam. 16:18). These represented the six qualities of the ideal Hebrew aristocrat and in effect comprised the standard by which character was to be judged.

The New Testament has much to say about the difference between Christian and pagan character (Rom. 13:12-14; Gal. 5:16-24), with especial emphasis upon the motivating factors in personality, as brought out in the Sermon on the Mount (Matt. 5—6). In the Pauline writings emphasis is laid upon the transforming effects that Christ's saving grace has in human life, and the believer is urged to live in a manner that exemplifies conspicuous spiritual gifts (Gal. 5:22-23; Eph. 5:15-21; Col. 3:12-17). Such qualities constitute the basis of a truly Christian character.

**CHARITY, WORKS OF.** The Latin word *caritas* originally meant "high price, costliness," and only later come to describe "esteem, love, or affection." In classical Greek *charis* portrayed graciousness, good will, or favor, whether given or received. In the New Testament it was a characteristic designation of divine grace, having both a subjective (Luke 2:52; Acts 7:10) and an objective (Rom. 5:2; 1 Pet. 5:12) perspective.

In the best New Testament tradition, works of charity are practical expressions of concern and altruism based on an appreciation of our common humanity, our love for God (1 John 4:19), and our love for our neighbor (Lev. 19:18; Deut. 15:4, 11; 1 John 3:14). Charitable works were among the earliest practical applications of the Christian faith, directed at needy believers (Acts 2:44-45; 4:32-36) and, ultimately, at Hellenist widows (Acts 6:1). As a demonstration of pure and undefiled religion, charitable acts toward widows and orphans, two highly vulnerable segments of the population, were commended in James 1:27.

Works of charity are commonly extended by Christians to such needy persons as the poor and those unable to help themselves, such as the retarded, the disabled, and the disadvantaged. Social programs in modern Western societies are based broadly upon the Judeo-Christian ethic, and it is worthy of note that those societies which follow a different ideology are far less conspicuous for their deeds of charity. As a proper noun, the term *charity* can mean either that which is given as part of a charitable exercise, or, in a legal sense, any kind of institution that is devoted to charitable works.

For the Christian, works of charity should comprise an expression of a person's love for God and his or her neighbors (Matt. 22:37-39). As such, it ought to be marked by generosity, understanding, tolerance, and genuine altruism. These are performed most effectively when handled with tact, discretion, and a sense of privacy (Matt. 6:1-4), losing their value when the intentions of the donor are well publicized in advance.

See PHILANTHROPY.

**CHASTENING.** This term is derived ultimately from the Latin *castigare*, "to punish," the word itself being a combination of *castus*, "pure," and *agere*, "to lead, drive." Chastening is therefore some sort of punitive activity intended to direct the recipient toward a purer state of heart and mind. In Scripture the concept involves a person being subjected by God to calamity, deprivation, psychic or emotional pain, and the like, so that the outcome may be a stronger faith, a more resolute character, or a firmer appreciation of moral and spiritual principles. It is thus distinguished from the self-induced activity envisaged by Socrates and Plato, in which the body was mortified so that the soul might live. The King James Version of Hebrews 12:6 rendered the Greek *paideuo* by "chasteneth," in the general tradition of the Septuagint. The implication is that God allows suffering, pain, and calamity to occur in believers' lives so that, by profiting from chastening as a spiritual discipline, they may indeed become true disciples in the faith and learn obedience from the things which they suffer.

**CHASTITY.** This term relates predominantly to purity in sexual matters, though it also carries some other derived meanings such as artistic or ethical purity. Originating in the Latin *castus*, "pure," it is used in the narrowest sense of individuals who abstain from sexual relations and also from thoughts or activities that are likely to provoke lubricious behavior. In a less comprehensive way it describes the preservation of virginity in an unmarried woman and abstention from carnal intercourse with single men. Within the marriage relationship the term denotes sexuality as practiced exclusively by the husband and wife, while for the widow or widower the virtue of chastity finds expression in continence.

In the Old Testament, violations of chastity were treated with great severity (Deut. 22:20-29) in order to forestall in Israel the kind of idolatry that had corrupted Canaanite life and religion. But the incursions of foreign women into Israel from the time of Solomon depraved the Hebrew people and, along with the accompanying idolatry, brought the nation into severe decline. Postexilic Judaism under Ezra (Ezra 10) sought to purify Israelite stock. This struggle continued into New Testament times, where the traditional

Hebrew ideals of chastity and sexual purity stood in stark contrast to the profligacy of the pagan world.

It is important to remember that chastity is not merely a matter of abstaining from, or circumscribing, certain physical acts, but as with all behavior it carries for the Christian a correlative degree of emotional and motivational involvement. Thus a man is not chaste if he is thinking libidinous thoughts about a woman, although not actually engaged physically in sexual activity with her (Matt. 5:27-28). According to Paul, matrimony was provided by God so as to enable the potentially incontinent to live lives of chastity and purity (1 Cor. 7:1-10), and in Hebrews it is spoken of as honorable among all and pure in its sexual aspects (Heb. 13:4). By using the marriage symbol of the Christian church as the bride of Christ, which he had purchased with his own blood, Paul showed that the relationship of fidelity that existed between them was based on God's love as manifested on Calvary. Where the church, through wantonness and disobedience, does not behave in a chaste manner toward its Lord and Master, it has violated divine love, as ancient Israel did frequently through its apostasy and idolatry, and consequently the church can expect to be punished unless the chaste relationship is restored.

In the medieval church the various monastic rules usually included chastity in the list of prescribed virtues; but it was commonly interpreted sexually, and seldom in terms of gluttony or drunkenness, which themselves constitute carnal indulgence.

**CHEATING.** Cheating involves any kind of deceptive maneuver or trick in which fraud plays a part and which enables an individual or a group to gain temporary or permanent advantage over others. Such behavior is characterized as dishonest because it seeks to gain its objective by means that violate established rules of procedure and norms of rectitude and fairness. It thus constitutes a subversive attack upon morality which, under certain circumstances, can have wide social and political implications.

Cheating appeared early in human history as one manifestation of mankind's depravity. In the early biblical period, Jacob helped his mother Rebekah to perpetrate an act of deception upon his aged father. As a consequence of this deed, Jacob cheated his brother Esau out of his family blessing (Gen. 27:1-40) and fulfilled his birthname as "Supplanter." At a somewhat later time, group fraud was perpetrated upon Joshua and his supporters by the citizens of Gibeon, an important Horite settlement in Canaan. Fearing extermination by the Israelites, they pretended to have come from a distant land in order to make a covenant with Joshua and actually achieved their objective until the dishonesty was exposed (Josh. 9:1-27). Rather than repay cheating with perfidy, Joshua placed the new allies in a servile position in Hebrew society as a punishment.

Cheating is widespread in human society and is often associated with lying. In those cultures where Christian canons of honesty are disregarded, it is very easy for individuals to establish norms in terms of ends and means and to give ethical justification to the process by some such dictum as, "if it works for me, it is right." Cheating and fraud are thus justifiable as long as the perpetrator is not caught in the act and thereby has his or her purposes frustrated. In many societies cheating is regarded as a way of life that indicates how "smart" the successful cheat is; and many aspects of fraud, such as those associated with the criminal manipulation of computers in order to obtain private or classified information, are perpetrated in the most deliberate and calculated fashion.

In educational circles, cheating is an especially serious problem because it erodes academic standards and places a premium on dishonesty. While those in authority endeavor to institute preventative measures, the techniques for deception are usually far in advance of those for prevention. Sometimes the act of cheating is the most blatant and obvious kind. The writer heard of an undergraduate at an Indian university who stationed a huge white dog beside him as he wrote his examinations. Although he was seen to be cheating, the presence of the dog made it impossible for the monitor to interfere with the process. During the author's undergraduate years, a tutor at a British university was bribed to impersonate a student and write his final examinations. The deception was only discovered when the tutor was unfortunate enough to sit near a window fan which blew off his false beard and exposed his identity. While these two examples are rather unsophisticated illustrations of cheating, they serve to show the lengths to which some individuals will go in disregarding the rights of others as they seek to achieve their own goals.

A particularly despicable form of cheating is that which seeks to elicit a positive emotional response from others while perpetrating calculated and deliberate fraud. At a prominent North American exhibition some years ago, a young woman was being taken through the grounds in a wheelchair which was pushed by two women friends. As a gesture of kindness the three were escorted to the head of waiting lines, ushered through the cafeterias, and given other concessions that civilized people normally accord the incapacitated. As the trio neared the exit gates at the end of a long and tiring day, the wheelchair suddenly went out of control on a slope and pitched its occupant out. To the astonishment of bystanders who were rushing to help, the supposedly incapacitated young woman picked herself up hurriedly and ran with her two companions to the nearby exits, to the anger and indignation of those who had witnessed the occurrence.

Of the many other forms of cheating, brief notice should be taken of that which is actually a euphemism for sexual immorality. It is by no means an inadequate description of the activity involved, however; and where it refers to adultery it reflects the deception, selfishness, and dishonesty of the offenders in the light of the solemn marital commitments undertaken at an earlier time.

For the Christian, any form of cheating, however minor it may appear, demonstrates a selfish, and often cynical, intent to break laws or established principles in order to gain personal advantage. This attitude is certainly not that of the individual who worships God in obedience and holiness, nor is it a characteristic of one who loves his neighbor as himself. Cheating in any area of life can be, and often is, a costly, self-demeaning procedure that can have serious repercussions in the lives of others than the offender and therefore has no place in the life of the Christian believer.

See COMPUTER ETHICS; EDUCATION AND MORALITY.

**CHILDLIKENESS.** Traditionally childlikeness has been described in terms of the innocence, trust, and openness associated with the young of the species *homo sapiens*. Unfortunately these characteristics are by no means typical of young children, but can be seen to be a part of a complex which includes fear, anger, greed, cruelty, and a predominant selfishness. Far from being *innocent*, young children are commonly scheming, devious, vicious, and disobedient, making evident to any discerning observer the evil nature that they have inherited as a consequence of the Fall.

Childlikeness as a virtue has been proclaimed by reference to Christ's actions in blessing children and threatening all those who would harm them. The children who followed Jesus must have done so out of considerable curiosity, and no doubt in some cases they loved and obeyed him. This attitude stood in marked contrast to that of the juvenile delinquents of ancient Bethel (2 Kings 2:23-24) who reviled Elisha and rejected his message. When Christ spoke of the kingdom in terms of children (Mark 10:14-16), he was clearly thinking of dependent, helpless children who in the best Hebrew tradition would love and honor their parents and cherish the ancient ideals of family life. By contrast with powerful and imposing adults, who manipulate people and situations alike and try to take the kingdom of heaven by force, the true children of Christ are those loving and obedient ones in whose very weakness Christ's strength is made perfect. This kind of childlikeness, stripped of all romantic pretensions, must characterize the lives of believers as they grow into Christ in trust, innocence of evil, obedience, and holiness of life.

**CHILDREN, ABUSE OF.** Scripture calls on parents to nurture their children for God, not to abuse them (Eph. 6:4; Matt. 18:3-10). Humans, like some animals, are trained for this by creation—a quality which the Apostle denotes as "natural affection" (Rom. 1:31).

The child beater is usually a parent suffering from some form of self-hatred brought about in many instances by abuse in his or her own childhood. In disciplining children, parents tend to imitate the way their parents treated them, especially in times of extreme frustration and stress. The cycle can be broken by the grace of God who changes lives (2 Cor. 5:17), coupled with help from an agency like Parents Anonymous or from a Christian psychiatrist.

Sex abusers of children are nearly always known and trusted adults, including parents, and usually male. Unfortunately, some mothers say and do nothing about their husband's sexual abuse of their daughters, perhaps out of fear, as a form of denial, or because they are relieved from their husband's sexual demands. A friend or spouse who suspects any kind of child abuse should report it to the Children's Aid Society or to public health authorities in order to set in motion rehabilitative treatment for the adult and therapy for the child. James Dobson urges "tough love" in such reporting, undeterred by fear of spouse's or friend's wrath or dislike. The reporter may indeed save a child.

Nurses, doctors, social workers, teachers, and others who suspect physical child abuse but do not report it are negligent and quite justifiably liable in most Western countries to penalties of the law. Symptoms of violent abuse such as bruises, welts, burns, inadequate clothing, and hunger should arouse suspicion. Children who report sexual abuse should be believed. A child's psychological withdrawal or strange remarks and comments should be probed gently by professional child workers for possible sexual abuse.

Lay persons cannot be expected to recognize the rare Ehlers-Danlos syndrome, a genetic weakness in connective tissue by which children bruise easily, causing their condition at times to be attributed to parent brutality. Parents of children with this syndrome may expect to be suspected of abuse unless they take steps to make the facts known.

A type of child abuse that may easily escape detection is emotional manipulation and rejection. Churches should continually educate their membership about this problem (Luke 1:17).

**Bibliography:** Dobson, J., *Love Must Be Tough* (1983); Morris, R., (ed.), *Encyclopedia of Social Work,* 16th ed. (1971), articles on "Mental Health and Illness in Children," "Protective Services for Children," and "Sexual Deviance"; Fortune, M. M., *Sexual Abuse Prevention* (1984); Hyde, M. O., *Sexual Abuse, Let's Talk About It* (1984); Sutherland, R., "Our Abused Children: How To Recognize Them" in *Focus on the Family* (February, 1984).

D.N.P.

**CHILDREN, REARING OF.** Children are a gift from God (Gen. 4:1; Ps. 127:3) to be brought up in the fear and nurture of the Lord. They are not their parents' property, as Western legal systems, following ancient Roman law, presuppose. On the contrary, they belong to God and are especially beloved by Him (Mark 10:14-16). Rearing them is a sacred stewardship designated by God (Deut. 6:3-7; 1 Sam. 1:11; Mark 10:13; Eph. 6:1-3). Scripture affirms that children are neither entirely bad nor inherently good. Understanding this will save parents from confused thinking with respect to their parental duties.

Christians ought to be vitally concerned on behalf not only of their own, but of all children, to affirm through legislation and other avenues the right of children to receive love, care, education, and other essentials of healthy life and development. Adults tend to segregate and ignore children in subtle ways. Schools, the prime loci of child segregation, can become juvenile ghettos which at times breed as many problems as they overcome.

Germaine Greer rightly suggests that adults in Western society appear to have a profound aversion to children as intruders detrimental to their lifestyles. Wherever this attitude exists it undoubtedly is due to an overvaluation of consumerism and ostentation, and an undervaluing of relationships. Moreover, since adults tend to reproduce their own consumer appetites in children, they actually thus exacerbate the latter's capacity to be burdensome. Christian parents, therefore, are faced with a formidable cultural challenge in their efforts to affirm children as God's welcome gifts, a holy trust from Him, and to value them far more than anything else in all creation. Parents need to be fully alert to the social and educational problems that exist and to trust God for promised strength to exercise their stewardship well.

*The Holy Spirit and Training.* Success in godly parenting does not depend entirely on parental expertise, although parents do have the responsibility of striving for excellence in understanding and nurturing their young (Phil. 1:10). Christian parents can accept the sound advice that they place less than complete confidence in books about child rearing and trust more their own commonsense knowledge and instincts. With minds immersed in the principles and values of Scripture, Christian parents can offer to God their best child-rearing efforts and trust His grace to use them for the children's benefit.

Parents must encourage children in moral effort and obedience (Rom. 1:5; Heb. 5:9) but realize that external adult pressure alone will not encourage their children's commitment and attitudes toward God. Only the grace of the Holy Spirit can effect that inner transformation. The parents' main obligation is to provide carefully

the kind of formation that, in the hands of God, can produce the desired inner transformation. Christian parents should monitor and take appropriate action toward the information and values being taught in their children's schools. Nonchristian values, particularly concerning sex and material wealth, have found their way into many textbooks and courses, even into some Sunday school curricula. Vigilance is essential, even within the household of faith.

Modern psychologists affirm scriptural principles in asserting that a child needs to know that he or she is fully accepted, loved, wanted, worthwhile, and forgiven, and that there is meaning to his or her life. The child who does not receive such treatment is likely to grow up lacking in confidence. Christianity that is lived out in the home supplies these common human needs. Continuous negative criticism and punishment, on the other hand, can "provoke a child unto wrath" (Eph. 6:4). If God accepts us in Christ, parents must do the same for their children, not merely telling them of their love, but demonstrating it by their behavior (Rom. 5:8; 15:7; 1 John 3:18). This behavior calls for hugs, family fun, and the inclusion of children in most social and religious activities.

Christian parents must guard against being so intent on "doing a good job" as parents that their children begin to feel like objects being "worked on," rather than persons with whom to relate in love and enjoyment. Echoing this caution, Spock admonishes parents to love children as they are. That, after all, is how God loves us. This will not spoil them because an integral part of our loving will be, as James Dobson insists, appropriate and firm discipline. Spoiling happens when the parent is afraid to use commonsense discipline or has a pathological need to be manipulated by the child. Parents who use Dr. Spock or other child psychologists as an excuse for complete permissiveness disregard their clear teachings about parental firmness.

*Discipline and Punishment.* "Spare the rod and spoil the child," is a well-known saying, mistakenly believed by many to be a quotation from Scripture. Actually the Bible declares that only "betimes," that is, promptly, is corporal punishment appropriate (Prov. 13:24; 29:15) which approximates to what Dr. Spock also advises. Spock rightly indicates no rule of thumb about punishment—either that it always works (as the strict disciplinary school might hold) or that it never works (as the permissive school would assert). The benefit of its presence or absence depends greatly on the general attitude of the parents to their children. Punishment never should be the constant and only method of formation. Its beneficial use is mainly as an occasional strong additional reminder that standards must be maintained and that the parents are definitely "in charge." Sparing the rod completely may tend to spoil the child; but counting on the rod alone can ruin him or her, engendering the very opposite of faith and trust in God. Punishment that originates entirely from parental resentment of children or from timidity in the God-given parental role will inevitably prove detrimental. Adults whose faith is in the rod, not God, whether that rod is a literal one or in the form of emotionally manipulative behavior, should seek professional Christian counseling to deal with their own inner emotional and spiritual problems. However, when discipline is administered in love with realistic understanding based on wide experience of children, the results can only be good. An important caution is not to expect understanding and behavior of children which, at a given stage of development, they are developmentally incapable.

Parents have to be ready to loosen the reins of external control gradually and appropriately until the child can stand in freedom and commitment as a Christian and a responsible citizen. Moral development will come only partially by guiding the child's increasing capacity to sort out conflicting rights of individuals and groups and by internalizing the ethics of the faith community. It will come mainly, as Craig Dykstra suggests, by sharing with the child a vision of who he or she is in Christ and the destiny to which he or she is called as a believer guided by Scripture and empowered by the Spirit.

*Parental Goals in Child Rearing.* The chief goal of Christian child rearing is that each child will believe in Christ as Savior who brings pardon and acceptance with God; as Lord to be followed in personal commitment; and as supplier of resources to live justly, to maintain truth, and to witness and exercise whatever gifts He gives.

Parents should take fullest advantage of the known tendency of children, as Spock reminds us, to "do grown-up things." Children are more likely to do as their parents do than merely as they say. Parents should therefore give major attention to changing themselves by the grace of God, acknowledging their faults, and requesting the support and prayers of the whole family. For this reason, Scripture, while referring occasionally to the important task of forming children for God, places greatest emphasis on the need of adults themselves to repent, believe, and behave as God's chosen. With a little further effort, the children's transformation will follow in due course (2 Tim. 1:5). It follows that intensive and continuous adult education is essential for Christian parents, not only to learn how to nurture their children in the faith, but also to use every means available to fulfill their own destiny and purpose in God.

Christian children need to realize themselves as members of the body of Christ and as responsible members of society. This goal will be hampered if their nurture takes place exclusively in the nuclear family. Here we can learn from other cultures. Children in Oriental and African extended families learn from their earliest days to deal confidently in relationships not only with members of their immediate nuclear family but with the larger kinship and community groups of which their nuclear family is a part. Western Christian families could benefit much by adopting aspects of this healthy nurturing pattern, examples of which can be found in the Scriptures themselves, and experience more deeply their common life in the body of Christ.

*The Family: God's Agent of Child Formation.* The primary context of a child's formation is the family where essential personality and character qualities such as trust, self-worth, and sharing have their beginnings and are nourished. Faith itself begins as God's gift to children through their parents (2 Tim. 1:5). In Bible days the first and primary educational agency clearly was the family. Later, synagogue schools were created to supplement and extend the home education. Education was thus understood as nurture in a believing community. The classical Greek pattern, by contrast, was to educate an elite minority. Congregations and national churches, as well as schools, should affirm the efforts and values of Christian parents, not compete with them.

In modern terminology the family is a "system." Over a century ago Horace Bushnell described it graphically as an organism in which the beliefs and attitudes of parents have tremendous and far-reaching effect. An affirming and disciplined family environment can, under the leadership of believing parents, produce children who are secure enough to exercise their God-given abilities throughout life and self-confident enough to risk vulnerability and sensitivity to others. The parents' accessibility to their children, both physically and emotionally, is supremely important. A child's repeated experiences of his or her parents' obvious pleasure at his or her presence encourage that child and go far toward developing a positive self-image. This probably is the greatest gift a parent can give.

Children are not helped by parents who let their charges' demands exhaust their energies. Parents must exercise stewardship before God with respect to their own needs as well as their children's. Father and mother must expect responsible behavior from their children according to the latter's changing capacity. Not to expect this is truly to spoil both them and the family's life together. Again, firm and reasonable control is the best evidence of parental love.

*The Crisis of Parenthood.* The arrival of the first baby in most Western homes could be categorized as a crisis. Many Western couples today seem unready for serious marriage commitments and particularly ill-prepared for parenthood. Married persons really need years of previous participation in caring for children, whether siblings or the offspring of community families, to help them cope with the sudden transition from being lovers to nurturers. More primitive societies provide this perforce. The churches have a responsibility to advocate the changes needed to make possible such lifelong education in nurturing.

*Adolescence.* Adolescents present parents with probably the greatest of all challenges in child rearing. At this stage, childhood dependence begins to give way to independent thinking and commitments. Enforcing obedience, though sometimes regrettably necessary, is a less-than-ideal living arrangement. Parents should learn in advance to be two-way communicators and to hear their children. Such attitudes and skills do not develop overnight but must be learned early. Continuing education in them, both formal and informal, is a never-ending Christian obligation.

The thinking adolescent's chief question is often, "Is there anything in this world worth committing myself to?" Christian parents know that there is, but just telling their children about the kingdom will not bring commitment to it. The secret is to be fellow disciples, fellow learners, and fellow believers with them; to be coordinators of the family band of disciples, not authoritarian pontificators (Matt. 23:8-12). This collaborative attitude is all-the-more imperative because, as Mead points out, in today's world there are precious few elders alive who truthfully know more about what adolescents are experiencing than do the adolescents and young people themselves. With the inner resources of the Spirit and adequate support within the extended family of God, members of each nuclear family will be able to deal initially with the worldliness with which media and peer groups inexorably bombard them.

The most effective way of dealing with these pervasive secular influences is by frank and open comparison of the "ways of the Gentiles" (1 Thess. 4:5) with the family's espoused Christian way. Parents can also support and aid their children in the choice of peer groups and band together to provide much-needed supervised facilities for youth to meet for their own programs. A know-it-all authoritarian imposition of leadership is out of the question.

*Sex Education.* Because sex is such a foundational aspect of God's creation (Gen. 1:28), sex education for their children is a moral obligation of all Christian parents. The educational goal will be to inculcate in children the awareness that sexual activity within God's design for marriage and the family is good, healthy, moral, and enjoyable. Outside of that it is ultimately harmful.

Sex education should not be left until adolescence. It is a lifelong enterprise, about which adults never cease learning and which even toddlers are capable of insight. The biological mechanics of reproduction are an important but minor part of sex education. The crucial lesson is the lesson of love, agape, the relationships of total positive regard taught by Christ. Children can learn from infancy that husband-wife relationships exist in the context of caring commitment that has its source in God. The biological "facts of life" will then be perceived in the proper context of marital fidelity and family devotion to Christ.

**Bibliography:** Bushnell, H., *Christian Nurture* (1979); Dobson, J., *Dare to Discipline* (1982); Dykstra, C., *Vision and Character, A Christian Educator's Alternative to Kohlberg* (1981); Galinsky, E., *Between Generations: Six Stages of Parenthood* (1980); Ginot, H. G., *Between Parent and Child* (1965); Peel, D. N., *The Ministry of Listening* (1980); Richard, D., *Has Sex Education Failed Our Teenagers?* (1989); Whitehead, M., and McGraw, O., *Foundations for Family Life Education* (1991).

See FAMILY; MARRIAGE; ORPHANS; PARENTHOOD.

D.N.P.

**CHIVALRY.** Originating in the late Latin word *caballarius,* "horseman," it described the armored cavalry of the medieval period. The meaning was transferred subsequently from a unit of mounted warriors to an elaboration of the illustrious and distinguished characteristics of a knight at arms and came to its highest degree of development in the system of knighthood.

At the time of the Crusades the Roman Catholic Church made the bearing of arms compatible with religious faith and in the rituals for the consecration of a knight invested chivalry with a religious character. The knight of that period had as his goal the recovery of Palestinian sites from Moslem occupation, and the oath of service that he swore in this connection was seldom more than three years in duration.

In the Romantic period, chivalry lost some of its specifically religious character, and this was replaced by an emphasis upon love. Court troubadours hastened the degeneration of earlier ideals of chivalry by associating it with the devoted, though often distant, service of an honorable lady, who could well be the wife of a king or a noble lord. With the decline of the use of cavalry in warfare from the fourteenth century, the practice of chivalry and courtly love degenerated further. In modern times chivalry describes the ancient knightly ideals of honor, fidelity, magnanimity, kindness to one's enemies, consideration for the lowly and weak, and a sense of compassion for vulnerable members of society, especially women and children. All these characteristics are in harmony with Christ's teachings in the Sermon on the Mount (Matt. 5—7) and are important elements of all sincere Christian behavior.

**CHOICE.** Choice is a conscious or unconscious act of the individual will whereby a decision is made to prefer one object or course of action above another one. For choice to be real within the course of normal human experience there must be more than one possible object from which to choose, and the selecting individual must be free to make a decision without being hampered by external pressures of other forms of harassment. In the light of these remarks there can be neither genuine choice nor an opportunity for exercising individual freedom in the kind of "democratic" elections conducted in Russia, where the ordinary voter is confronted with a preselected list of candidates which he or she is required to endorse without the option of any modification at all.

Freedom is thus an essential ingredient of decisions involving choice, and this in turn rests upon the nature of the human will. It is common for theologians, ethicists, and others to speak in terms of "free will." But this description is rather gratuitous at best, since human beings never experience the will in any other sense than "free." Professional ethicists have therefore identified two characteristics of human will and have designated them by the Latin names *liberum arbitrium* and *voluntas*. The former indicates the kind of freedom which enables an individual to respond spontaneously to any stimulus, object, or occasion without prior ratiocination or cogitation. Because of its spontaneous nature it is, of course, necessarily unreflective in character. But where cogitation and conscious action formed by intent are involved, the will then manifests its character as *voluntas* in an act of choice.

Many ethicists have asserted that good and evil can only be predicated on choices motivated by *voluntas*, and while that may be true in a narrow sense, it is also possible to assign moral value to the involuntary acts of choice by the human will. Insofar as these impulses arise from genuine altruism, they may be said to possess potentially good moral value. But the egocentric nature of the bulk of human motivation is such that individual reaction is normally governed by purely selfish considerations. Even ratiocinative choice need not necessarily be either correct or good, of course, and is normally influenced by social background, religious beliefs, education, prejudice, and other factors.

God exercised conscious choice in selecting the ancient Israelites as his people (Deut. 10:15; Ezek. 20:5) and revealing to them his nature and will. They in turn were urged to choose life by being obedient to him and manifesting a condition of holiness in their dealings. But as a consequence of rebellion and apostasy, the Hebrews were set aside, to be replaced by the Christian church as the vehicle of divine revelation. Again, the disciples were informed that Christ had chosen them for the task of witness (John 15:16; 1 Pet. 2:4), and hence the church became regarded as a chosen generation (1 Pet. 2:9). Whenever people are challenged by the preaching of the cross to make a decision for Christ as the Savior and Lord of their lives, whatever is ultimately chosen partakes of the nature of *voluntas*, making the acceptance or rejection of Christ a deliberate, conscious act.

See ABORTION; FREEDOM; FREE WILL.

**CHRISTIAN ETHICS, HISTORY OF.** In the world of early Christianity, religion was mostly a matter of temple cults that promoted gods and goddesses for all occasions. Some worshipers discerned a single divine force behind these powers but polytheism was commonly accepted. Questions of behavior and ethics were more a matter of the pursuit of ultimate happiness than obeying commands from a transcendent source. In this milieu, Jews and Christians appeared to be atheists, because their beliefs and behavior differed so radically from the dominant polytheistic culture. Nonetheless, the apostle Paul wrote in Greek and reflected many Hellenistic traits. Debate among scholars has shifted from interpreting Paul wholly in Hellenistic terms, or wholly in Judaic terms, to the present consensus that both worlds influenced him. The relevance of this issue for ethics is clear, especially when Paul writes on questions of conscience. Some hear in Paul echoes of Stoic doctrine concerning a rational principle pervading the universe, of which every human being has some awareness.

The Prologue of the Fourth Gospel suggests that John was directly or indirectly familiar with the kind of thinking found in Philo of Alexandria. This Jewish scholar linked Bible study with the concept of the *Logos* or divine mediator between God and creation. This method underlay the allegorical method of interpreting the Bible until the time of the Reformation. The allegorical method virtually equated the ethical teachings of the Mosaic commandments in the Torah (Law) with the wisdom of the Greek philosophers, especially Plato and Aristotle (c. 400 B.C.). In matters of ethics, Aristotle's prudential analyses of virtues and vices, coupled with Stoic conceptions of reason ruling emotion, formed the basis of Christian thought. In cosmology and discussions of the relation of God to the world and the nature of the soul, Plato and the later Neoplatonists became the dominant influence. These Greek sources gave a conceptual framework for the growing monastic movement following the era of the early martyrs. Neoplatonism posited a heavenly reality behind the distracting world of appearances and drew a sharp distinction between affairs of the flesh and concerns of the spirit in a way that seemed already certified by Paul.

Because of its minority status, the early church was more preoccupied with personal conduct than with social ethics. The second-century composition *The Shepherd of Hermas* is preoccupied with the effect of postbaptismal sin on an individual's chances for salvation. Out of this concern grew the penitential system and concepts of purgatory, which later came under attack from Martin Luther. Also in this period the *Didache* illustrates the overriding concern in the Western church on the practicality of normative ethics. Prescriptive rules for local order and personal growth were considered more crucial than "meta-ethical" questions concerning a hierarchy of ethical values.

The early Latin theologians in the Western church reflected a practical Roman outlook on everyday matters, while at the same time drawing on Greek philosophy and Hellenistic mystery religions for their cosmology and eschatology. Tertullian's famous cry "What has Athens to do with Jerusalem?" did not reflect the general consensus, which followed instead the lead of Clement of Alexandria, Origen, and the Cappadocian Fathers. The most permanently influential Latin theologian was Augustine of Hippo. Writing at the end of the fourth century, he responded to the challenges of the declining power of the Roman Empire and the concerns of a now-established Catholic Church. It is often said that the Reformation was Augustine against himself, the bishop concerned with church order against the theologian concerned with the priority of grace.

Augustine followed his predecessors in drawing on Old Testament patterns for guidance on topics relatively untouched in the New Testament. The title of his famous apologetic work on the theology of history, *The City of God*, originated in his studies of the Psalms. Augustine's emphasis on the doctrine of creation reflected the desire of the Christian church to take the middle ground between the worldly materialism of the political arena and the otherworldliness of the Hellenistic mysteries. The latter identified evil with matter and set asceticism as the model for the truly religious individual. In his *Confessions*, Augustine used the image of life as an earthly pilgrimage and as a time of preparation for heavenly bliss. For him pride, a spiritual factor, is the cause of evil in both Adam and the devil. To this Christ's incarnation is the antitype and our model for humility and grace. The ethical norm in personal life thus becomes the ideal of imitating Jesus, while the political norm becomes that of the theocratic ideal identified with the Israelite monarchy of David.

In his theology, Augustine made extensive use of Neoplatonic thought, which contained important consequences for subsequent theology. It clearly gave priority to spiritual realities and established a concept of eternity as timelessness, making God's lordship over history highly problematic. Augustine carried this line of thinking to the point of asserting a doctrine of double predestination. This doctrine, assigning some to heaven and the rest to hell, was challenged by the British monk Pelagius, because it seemed to undercut all moral effort and personal responsibility. On systematic grounds, Augustine won the argument for the unqualified priority of grace in Christ and the universality of original sin through Adam, thus justifying the practice of infant baptism. However, the church prudently adopted a more moderate approach in ethics, which led to a semi-Pelagian position, that is, one in which grace combined with human effort leads to right living. The theoretical underpinning was finally provided in the thirteenth century by the other great Latin theologian, Thomas Aquinas, whose influence has continued into the present.

Thomas Aquinas absorbed the new knowledge of Aristotle that was coming into Europe from the Muslim world. Through Thomas Aquinas, a system developed that combined theology and philosophy. This "scholastic synthesis" produced a view that moved toward God through natural as well as supernatural means. Grace supplements nature to the point that the Fall does not obliterate the good of creation completely.

The Aristotelian heritage, mediated through the Latin Christianity of Thomas, emphasized an ethic of virtues, rather than an ethic of duties. By this is meant the building up of strengths of character or habits through active human effort in response to divine grace. All of these activities are aimed at that blessedness which enjoys the beatific vision of God's goodness for eternity.

The system that Thomas developed judged actions as means to natural or supernatural ends. For example, the end of sexual union must be procreation. Hence, contraception is inherently immoral. The purpose of celibacy must be a sacramental realization of Christ's priestly role, such that a married priesthood becomes a contradiction or confusion of the natural with the supernatural order. On specific questions, such as usury, the system casuistically classifies sins into mortal and venial. The theological virtues faith, hope, and love need the added impetus of divine grace. The cardinal virtues wisdom, justice, fortitude, and temperance can be acquired by any right thinking person and are only augmented by grace. The effect of such classifications was to direct attention, through the self-examination of the confessional, to specific sins and penitential remedies, rather than to sin as a state of alienation between creature and Creator pervading all specific actions. Purgatory was posited as the place for spiritual perfection for those not fully sanctified at the time of death.

In the medieval synthesis that became normative for centuries in Catholicism, law was understood as the custom or the inner *telos* (end) of our being. The theory of natural law was developed to account for the various categories acknowledged: laws of nature proper to our organic existence, positive laws enacted by governments, revealed law given in Scripture, and custom (*ius gentium*). Nature is sufficiently unaffected by the Fall so that the "Book of Nature" is open to rational investigation and is wholly consistent with the Word of God as revealed in the Bible. In the political sphere, the equal standing of a natural institution (the state) and a supernatural one (the church) made for ambiguities that took centuries of confrontation between pope and emperor to resolve.

Even though ethical actions are in conformity with God's will, in Thomistic thought they do not neccessarily assure the beatific vision. Jesus Christ is the sole mediator between God and humankind. Through ethical action, people may share in the merits of Jesus' sacrifice and draw nearer to salvation.

During the late medieval period, witchcraft ceased to be a civil matter between individuals and was seen as a challenge to church order. As such, it came under the institution of the Inquisition which resulted in widespread persecution, especially of women, as in the case of Joan of Arc (1412-1431) in France.

The medieval synthesis came under attack from church philosophers who subordinated intellect to will. In the fourteenth century, John Duns Scotus and William of Occam [Ockham] turned reason against itself. Nominalism, mysticism, and the increasing emphasis on individual salvation set the stage for Luther's revolt against the penitential system and a return to voluntarism in matters of faith. Luther's liberation from the burden of sin and his emphasis on justification by grace alone, received in faith, originated in his fresh reading of the Bible in Hebrew and Greek. The biblical usage of righteousness (*dikaiosune*), in contrast to the Latin understanding of justice (*iustitia*), no longer had a juridical sense for him. Instead righteousness identified our relationship to God through Christ, as opposed to our moral and pious behavior in the fallen world.

Martin Luther (1483-1546) departed from previous critics of corruption in the Catholic hierarchy with his conclusion that the papacy as an institution, and not just individual popes as sinners, is a work of the devil. For all Reformers, the church erred when it ascribed to its earthly presence a glory that properly pertains only to its heavenly promise. Nature, therefore, remains unredeemed for the duration of history, which must see the last of Satan's rule. Grace does not supplement nature, as for the Thomists, but comes in a moment-by-moment reception of the biblical revelation of Christ as sole Head and legitimating Authority in the church. The result was Luther's paradoxical declaration that we are simultaneously sinners and justified persons (*simul iustus et peccator*). There are no grades of sanctity setting the "religious" above the "secular" in the visible world. Consequently, Luther articulated a distinctive doctrine of vocation consistent with the priesthood of all believers. We are all called to be Christ to our neighbors, not just those who are ordained, and every occupation is a godly service in the eyes of the Lord, whether it be that of hangman or housewife.

Although Luther was the instigator and chief polemicist of the Reformation, its definitive systematic theology came later in the *Institutes of the Christian Religion* written by John Calvin (1509-1564). Trained in law, Calvin was the dominant voice in Geneva, which he sought to make the center of a theocratic state, basing its laws solely on Scripture. The resulting patriarchal and presbyterian form of polity saw the state not just as a restrainer of wickedness, enabling the gospel to be preached, but as a positive proponent of the virtuous lifestyle expected of a community of saints. Whereas Lutheran theology maintains an unresolvable dualism between the perfection of heavenly life and the universality of sin in this world, Calvin placed more emphasis on sanctification, as the working out of grace in the lives of the elect. Luther's radical contrast between gospel and law led to mistrust of all "works righteousness." The only righteous work is Christ's death upon the cross, which we appropriate by grace through faith and obedience to God's Word. The two clear uses of the law for Luther become (1) to convict us of sin and (2) to restrain the wicked while the gospel is preached. Scholars debate whether Luther himself allowed a third use. Certainly for Calvin the third use, that of the law as guide to right conduct, was vital to the community of saints in this world. The resulting Puritanism in social thought had an important impact in Britain and later North America.

Calvin followed Augustine's logic concerning predestination and the universal corruption of nature through the Fall. The latter emphasis in politics led to a system of checks and balances influential in the formulation of the United States Constitution. No organization, according to Calvin, is exempt from the threat of corruption. Hence each must be kept in check by the others. Calvin consistently emphasized that the purpose of creation is to glorify God and that predestination to heaven or hell is not contingent on good works, since we are saved by sheer grace. However, the fruits of saving grace necessarily show in sober, industrious, charitable, and godly behavior, summed up in what Max Weber (1864-1920) dubbed "the Protestant ethic." Weber's argument was that the Reformation insistence that all vocations are religious meant the release of much energy, previously channeled into monasticism, into the business world. Calvin himself maintained traditional religious injunctions against usury. But the parable of the talents seemed to many to endorse the kind of capitalistic enterprise which became characteristic of the Protestant districts of Europe and their transplants in North America.

Calvinistic theology so stresses the glory of God that what is right must be determined by reference to God's expressed revelation. It is right because God wills it, not that God wills it because it is right. Consequently, once given political power, Calvinistic arbiters of Scripture dealt quite arbitrarily with dissidents. As Luther sided with the princes in Germany during the Peasants Revolt (1524-1525), so Calvin had Michael Servetus burned at the stake in 1553 for advocating an early version of Unitarianism. However, the religious wars between Catholics and Protestants throughout Europe in the next century discredited both sides in the eyes of many, especially those on the so-called "left wing" of the Reformation. Menno Simons (1496-1561) was the Anabaptist for whom the communalistic and pacifist Mennonites were named. In the same mold, George Fox (1624-1691) emphasized the inner light of Christ and power of the Holy Spirit as contrasted with all externals, such as written words in either Scripture or papal encylicals. Among his followers, known as the Quakers, or Society of Friends, women became equal leaders in the community. The American Quaker John Woolman (1720-1772) later applied the same insights to a call for the abolition of slavery and a more humane treatment of prisoners and mental patients. To escape persecution as conscientious objectors in this time of war, many Protestant groups emigrated to North America, especially into the Midwest. The Hutterites, for instance, insulated themselves as far as possible from the rest of the world on communal farms, seeking to live strictly by the literal commands of Scripture.

Among intellectuals, the narrowing on both sides following the religious wars led to a mistrust of religious "enthusiasm" and a rationalistic turn toward deism. David Hume (1711-1776) still declared that "reason is and ought to be the slave of the passions," but listed fear, rather than love, as the mainspring of religion. Immanuel Kant (1724-1804) attempted to give a rational basis to ethics by translating the Golden Rule into what he termed "the categorical imperative," placing the emphasis on duty for duty's sake. His key was moral consistency: always act on a rule that could be endorsed without contradiction as a universal law of nature. By this maxim, lying, for instance, could be shown to be self-defeating. This "deontological" position was contrasted with a prudential, "teleological" ethics, in which the ends justify the means. Kant in practice identified religion with ethics, attempting to defend the freedom of moral agency against the determinism of those like Hume, who considered all of nature, including human nature, to be subject to a mechanistic law of cause and effect. Since virtue in this life is not rewarded, Kant postulated immortality instituted by God as the state in which duty and happiness coincide.

Following the Scottish moralists' emphasis on common sense, the Englishman, Jeremy Bentham (1748-1832) attempted to formulate a "hedonic calculus" which would give a more scientific basis for ethics. In his introduction to the *Principles of Morals and Legislation* he stressed the natural pressures of pleasure and pain, as well as the moral distinction between right and wrong, which he based on the utilitarian principle. This declares the common end to be the greatest happiness of the greatest number, encouraging each individual to pursue maximum pleasure within the constraints of not causing suffering to others. As against the moralism of the Puritans, such hedonism was grounded in a secularized doctrine of creation, according to which individual self-interest naturally harmonizes with the interests of all. In political economy this emphasis on freedom for private enterprise found its classical expression in Adam Smith's *An Inquiry into the Nature and Causes of the Wealth of Nations* (1776).

The same stress on individualism, but with more emphasis on piety and devotion, is found in the many works written during the early modern period. Among Puritans, John Bunyan (1628-1688) was influential through his work *Pilgrim's Progress*, in which the women have such names as Prudence, Hope, Mercy, Innocent, and Charity. In North America, Jonathan Edwards (1703-1758) tied the Calvinistic concern for grace to the experience of individual conversion. His works *The Freedom of the Will* and *The Nature of True Virtue* continue to be studied as the first American moral theology of consequence. In both Britain and North America, by far the most influential preachers and hymn writers were the Wesley brothers, John (1703-1791) and Charles (1707-1788). Their movement, called Methodism because of the stress on self-examination concerning the assurance of salvation and the experience of grace, was well adapted to the patterns of settlement in North America, which generally outran the European and New England structure of parishes and theocratic colonies.

In European theology for the next generation, the dominant voice was that of Friedrich Schleiermacher (1768-1834). Against Kant, Schleiermacher stressed Jesus' God-consciousness and the creaturely feeling of absolute dependence. These themes were continued at mid-century in the work of the Danish philosopher of religion, Soren Kierkegaard (1813-1855), who classified Kant's moral phase of humanity as a stage above animal passion, but a stage below individual faith. In *Fear and Trembling*, Kierkegaard described Abraham's faith as a "teleological suspension of the ethical," since God's command to sacrifice Isaac went beyond conventional norms for fathers and sons, focusing on the uniqueness of Abraham's decision in faith. Against Hegel's portrayal of religion as the culmination of human culture, Kierkegaard stressed the nonrational nature of the faith-response to divine transcendence. Because of this, Kierkegaard ranks as a forerunner of twentieth-century existentialism, in which "doing your own thing" takes precedence over "doing the done thing." Both Schleiermacher and Kierkegaard reflect the romantic movement in modern thought, stressing passion over reason in reaction to the enlightenment rationalism of Kant and his followers.

Also on the rationalist side in the nineteenth century was John Stuart Mill (1806-1873). His *Utilitarianism* reformulated Bentham's teleological ethic, arguing for a qualitative superiority of human experience with the maxim, "better to be Socrates dissatisfied than a pig satisfied." In Mill and in William James (1842-1910), the American pragmatist, we see a growing interest in psychology as a science of human behavior. In pragmatism, truth is a value; and value is determined by reference to what works. The focus in ethics comes to be a matter of judgment on the basis of the best information available, rather than deduction from biblical maxims or intuitive norms.

Throughout the nineteenth century, the most influential figure for theology and religious philosophy was G. W. F. Hegel (1770-1831). Where Mill and others looked to individual fulfillment, Hegel read world history as the key to the self-realization of the divine Spirit in the organization of the modern state. Civilization is the triumph of mind over matter in art, morality, law, and religion. In Britain, this "idealist" metaphysics was most powerfully formulated by F. H. Bradley (1846-1924). In his *Ethical Studies* he shows how the individual gains significance through participation in the community, which emerges through the experience of conflict and failure. In America the same stress on community was articulated by Josiah Royce (1855-1916), a contemporary of William James at Harvard, whose *Philosophy of Loyalty* stressed the unity of personal and community interests. All of these writers looked for laws of behavior in the social structures of personal development which indicate the immanence of the divine in human experience. History is the march toward freedom in which all the demands of humanity are reconciled, namely the demands of nature and the demands of society, by transformation into "higher" cultural forms of expression, especially religion and art.

Against such philosophical speculation, the most powerful challenge came from the sciences. The evolutionary conception of history seemed to many confirmed by Darwin's *Origin of the Species* (1859). The pressure of the industrial revolution and the attempt to use biology as a key to economics led Karl Marx (1818-1883) and Friedrich Engels (1820-1895) to repudiate the theistic presuppositions of Hegelian thought. The state came to be viewed as an oppressive weapon of the few against the many. Freedom now meant the dissolution of the state and ultimate anarchy. In a secularized version of biblical apocalyptic, the culmination of history would take place in a final, violent conflict between the forces of good and evil. Marx and Hegel read the laws of history as a pattern of alienation and reconciliation of the individual with the group. But Marx identified the key as the conception of labor, not religion, which was treated only as a symptom of the underlying conflict.

Secularization in personal ethics to many European thinkers meant a return to Greek and Latin classics. Friedrich Nietzsche (1844-1900) found the contrast between Apollos and Dionysios in Greek myth as exemplifying the rational and the passional. In such works as *The Birth of Tragedy* and The Genealogy of Morals, Nietzsche portrayed morality as the attempt of the common herd to suppress the emerging *Übermenschen* of culture, for whom might is right. Where Nietzsche was an atheistic existentialist, for whom "God is dead" because we have killed him (so stated in *Thus Spake Zarathustra*), some twentieth-century followers, notably the Nazis or National Socialists, gave a racial and political twist to such thought, glorifying the genius of the Aryan peoples in a way that Nietzsche never intended. On the political side, Nietzsche's views were anticipated by Thomas Hobbes (1588-1679), whose *Leviathan* portrays human beings as brutish and materialistic, only kept under control by dictators or absolute sovereigns. In the absence of any natural moral order, Hobbes allowed for revolt against rulers, setting, with Jean Jacques Rousseau (1712-1778), the stage for modern revolutionary movements. Rousseau mistrusted law and romanticized the state of nature, regarding a "social contract" as the basis for social order.

During the nineteenth century, Christian thinkers reflected the secular trend in their study of Scripture. Among educated Protestants, Scripture became a warrant for a this-worldly identification of the kingdom of God with evolutionary, cultural progress. Repudiating Hegelian metaphysics and reviving Kant's moralism, Albrecht Ritschl (1822-1889) focused thought on the kingdom of God in this world and on the church as the community of reconciliation, striving for freedom guided by love. Adolf von Harnack (1851-1930), in *The Essence of Christianity*, epitomized this liberal theological trend by reducing all to the fatherhood of God and the brotherhood of man. In North America, Walter Rauschenbusch (1861-1918) taught the perfectibility of humanity through the social gospel, in such books as *Christianizing the Social Order*. Christian concern over the abuses of the industrial revolution led many, such as the Anglican F. D. Maurice (1805-1872), to advocate a loose form of Christian socialism, out of which grew Christian support for trade unions, the co-operative movement, working class educational ventures, and the Young Men's and Young Women's Christian Associations. Among Protestants, perhaps the most powerful movement was the Women's Christian Temperance Union, founded in 1874, which led to the legal prohibition of the sale of drugs and alcohol in the United States (1919-1933).

Liberal theology foundered on the evidence of historical criticism, as shown by Albert Schweitzer (1875-1965), that ethics cannot be separated from eschatology. Schweitzer advocated a reverence for life which he found in the mystical strand of Pauline thought. Mysticism, loosely defined, was the third category, along with church and sect, used by Ernst Troeltsch (1865-1923) in his influential *The Social Teaching of the Christian Churches*. Whereas churches are organized as schools for sinners, sects are societies of saints, each one intolerant of the backsliding of its spiritual cousins. Troeltsch's historical relativism concerning the absoluteness of Christianity was carried on by his North American exponent, H. Richard Niebuhr (1894-1962), who used the term "denomination" to depict the inclusive types of church organization found in countries that recognize no established church. His *Christ and Culture* surveys Christian ethics under the rubric of a fivefold typology, favoring "Christ the

Transformer of Culture" over both "Christ Against Culture' and "the Christ of Culture."

World War I and the challenge of Marxism turned theologians to renewed emphasis on the transcendence of God and the sinfulness of individual and communal history. The best-known "crisis" or dialectical theologians were Karl Barth (1886-1968), Reinhold Niebuhr (1892-1971, Richard's brother), and Paul Tillich (1886-1965). Barth's *Epistle to the Romans* showed the influence of Kierkegaard, while his massive *Church Dogmatics* attempted a thorough integration of theology and ethics through the God-manhood of Jesus Christ. Barth was a principal author of the Barmen Declaration of 1934, affirming the sole lordship of Jesus against prevailing German Christian enthusiasm for the Fuehrer, Adolf Hitler. Barth's younger contemporary on that occasion, Dietrich Bonhoeffer (1906-1945) became famous for his posthumous *Letters and Papers from Prison*, in which he carried further his interest in *communitas* or *koinonia* as the key to ethics and emphasized the need for costly grace, to offset Christian accommodations to worldly triumphalism.

Reinhold Niebuhr's *Nature and Destiny of Man* returned to the Augustinian analysis of pride and original sin as a corrective to the Marxist emphasis on material causes of alienation. Niebuhr broke with what he termed utopianism to urge United States entry into World War II on the grounds that Christian realism requires the restraint of tyranny in history. After he was expelled from Germany for his involvement in Religious Socialist opposition to the Nazis, Tillich became Niebuhr's colleague at Union Theological Seminary in New York. Tillich articulated the Protestant Principle as the biblical theme of prophetic faith and paraphrased the doctrine of justification by grace through faith as affirming "the courage to be," in spite of the anxiety of fate, guilt, and meaninglessness. Of the next generation, the French lay theologian, Jacques Ellul (1912- ) has maintained a Calvinist stance on questions concerning technology and the philosophy of law. In Germany, since World War II the most prolific Lutheran author on theological questions, including biomedical ethics, has been Helmut Thielicke (1908- ).

Between World Wars, the French philosopher Henri Bergson (1859-1941) and Russian Orthodox expatriate Nicholas Berdyaev (1874-1948) were read widely. Bergson contrasted "open" and "closed" societies in his analyses of ethics. The latter fall into mechanical routines and absolutistic authoritarianism, while the former follow intuitively the "elan vital" that leads us to maximize diversity. Berdyaev repudiated his early espousal of Marxism on the basis of an existentialistic sense of freedom grounded in Neoplatonic mysticism. Among Roman Catholics, Jacques Maritain (1882-1973) popularized a Neo-Thomist brand of humanism and, while in the United States during World War II, became an influential supporter of the radical neighborhood organizer, Saul Alinsky (1909-1972). Two non-Christians of the period were most influential on the history of ethics. Mahatma Gandhi (1869-1948) promoted a program of nonviolent conflict resolution which was later adopted by Martin Luther King, Jr. (1929-1968) in the struggle for civil rights on the part of American black people. Martin Buber (1878-1965), the Jewish existentialist, contrasted I-You and I-It relationships as the key to understanding the life of dialogue between God and his people found in all truly religious communities.

Undermining traditional assumptions of freedom and responsibility in the modern period has been the psychoanalytic movement, founded by Sigmund Freud (1856-1939) in Vienna. What previously were thought to be moral flaws came to be considered sicknesses arising from "the unconscious." However, existential psychology, advocated for instance by Viktor Frankl, has reaffirmed the need to accept responsibility as part of a cure. Contemporary authors, such as Thomas Szasz, are drawing attention to the ethical implications of leaving too much power in the hands of psychiatrists. (John C. Hoffman, *Ethical Confrontation in Counseling*, 1979, points out that Freud's fight was with moralism, not morality.) Freud's main rival, C. G. Jung (1875-1961) concentrated on the mythic power of dreams in a way that seems more open to religion, as an integrative force for the individual, but is at odds with orthodox Christian faith and any genuinely altruistic ethic.

Contemporary ethicists since World War II have had to wrestle as never before with the moral implications of modern technology. Most obvious among these are the problems raised for the traditional just war theory by nuclear weapons. Roland Bainton's *Christian Attitudes To War* (1960) surveys the history of thought on its subject. On medical ethics, Paul Ramsey (1913- ) and Joseph Fletcher (1905- ) have led the debates, Ramsey representing a somewhat conservative position against Fletcher's advocacy of "situational" ethics. The ramifications of medical research on human embryos and transplants of nonhumanoid tissue are only now coming under serious consideration. How to define the right to life in relation to both conception and expiration is a question that divides ethicists across denominational lines. Related topics are population control, developmental ethics for the Third World, and abortion.

Among evangelicals in North America, E. J. Carnell (1919- ) and Carl F. Henry (1913- ) have spoken for the previous generation, insisting that the Bible provides us with an objective basis for moral judgment based on divine revelation. Henry found the love ethic of the Sermon on the Mount entirely consistent with the lasting intent of the Mosaic Code. The pedagogic, political, and didactic uses of the Law find their fulfillment through the guidance of the Holy Spirit, even though Christian expositors may disagree at times over the choice of biblical text used to warrant a decision. As a result of the war in Vietnam and the challenge of urban ghettos, contemporary evangelicals are increasingly concerned with social ethics. They are still seeking faithfulness to biblical norms while admitting the difficulty of deriving specific prescriptions for contemporary problems directly from God's revealed Word, the Bible.

In ethical theory, Christian theologians are beginning to reject both teleological and deontological philosophical orientations, in favor of a biblical reading of salvation history. This concept was articulated by Oscar Cullman (1902- ), among others, and now appears under the rubric of "narrative theology," as in the work of Stanley Hauerwas (1940- ). An instructive essay on this theme is Thomas W. Ogletree's *The Use of the Bible in Christian Ethics*. Ogletree discusses covenantal fidelity and Pauline ethics in the context of the eschatological horizon of Christian faith. The present trends reflect a renewed interest in the formation of character, contributing to right decisions under unpredictable conditions, rather than perpetuating attempts to enunciate timeless rules of conduct. Principles of love and justice are indeed universal, ethical theorists now argue against relativistic anthropologies. But in biblical thinking, their application hinges on the prophetic wisdom of judges in the tradition of Solomon. In short, patterns of lives in faithful communities through the ages, not abstract arguments and rules, are how the Spirit shapes Christian ethics in ways consistent with both the eternal covenant and the incarnate truth.

The most notable directions in ethical research in the latter half of the twentieth century have come in response to various liberation theologies, among women and blacks in the United States, and from African, Asian, and Latin American theologians. In Latin America, the principal concern of such Catholic leaders as Gustavo Gutierrez, Juan Luis Segundo, and Jon Sobrino is to ally the church with what is termed "the option for the poor." Among Protestants, Jüngen Moltmann in Germany and Jose Miguez Bonino in Argentina are best known, the latter drawing on themes from the Fourth Gospel for a critical response to Marxism. Among women in America, the Catholic Margaret Farley at Yale and Protestant Beverley Wildung Harrison at Union Theological Seminary have concentrated on ethical questions. James H. Cone at Union Theological Seminary is representative of the black theologians and Kosuke Koyama of Asian thinkers. The best-known conservative critics of liberation ethics are probably the Catholic Michael Novak and the Lutheran Richard John Neuhaus. The latter, with the sociologist Peter Berger, wrote *Against the World and for the World* as a challenge to facile assumptions in modern theology. Few, if any, of these names will be remembered a generation hence, but collectively they have forced social

ethicists to pay closer attention than before to the hard data of economics and politics.

Finally, the impact of other traditions on Christian thought is reshaping the context of ethical thinking in various ways. David Little and Sumner B. Twiss have tried to focus discussion in one topic area with *Comparative Religious Ethics*. On the theology of culture in relation to missions, Charles H. Kraft's *Christianity in Culture* reflects his experience in Africa and expertise in linguistics. Again, as African and Asian theologians find their own voices, their critique of Western choices of topics (such as, nuclear pacifism over developmental ethics) is likely to become sharper on questions of content and more concrete in matters of theory.

**Bibliography:** Curran, C. E., and McCormick, R., (eds.), *The Use of Scripture in Moral Theology* (1984); Gustafson, J. M., *Theology and Christian Ethics* (1974); Long, E. L., Jr., *A Survey of Christian Ethics* (rev. ed., 1984); Ramsey, P., *Basic Christian Ethics* (1950).

C.P.S.; T.W.W.

**CHURCH AND STATE.** Tensions between church and state are by no means a modern phenomenon but in fact can be traced at least as far back as the third millennium B.C. in Mesopotamia. A reform document from ancient Lagash, produced about 2350 *B.C.* during the reign of Urukagina, described the redressing of a whole range of abuses perpetrated by the previous regime. One aspect of this had been an attempt by the king to usurp the powers of the temple priests, and it is interesting that in this very early conflict between church and state the citizens of Lagash supported the former against the latter. Many centuries subsequent to this event, the Palestinian Jews of the Maccabean period found themselves in violent conflict with their Seleucid rulers over what were predominantly religious issues, and only after the Maccabeans (Hasmoneans) had expelled the Syrians from Judea in 153 B.C. was a measure of peace restored.

Jesus Christ addressed himself to the problem of church-state relations, teaching that the believer has in fact a duty to both bodies (Matt. 22:21). It is ironic that His own life became a pawn in the relations between temple and Roman governor. In the period of the primitive church, the Christians endured sporadic persecutions from imperial Rome, and it was only in the fourth century under Constantine that such opposition ended when Christianity became the official religion of the Empire.

Questions involving the relationship between church and state were still matters of lively concern, however. Augustine endeavored to provide a theoretical basis for the relationship in his *De Civitate Dei* ("City of God"), in which he enunciated the responsibility of the state for civil matters and that of the church for spiritual concerns. This type of dualism was to have important implications for other areas of theology at a later period.

In 494 Pope Gelasius used the imagery of two swords, the temporal and the spiritual, to claim that rulers needed priestly power for the sake of their own eternal destiny, while priests needed the power of the state in the cause of temporal affairs. But Gelasius clearly gave precedence to priestly power, since it enabled rulers to be justified at the final evaluation of individual affairs. This attitude has been deemed important because it constituted the doctrinaire foundation for the subsequent Holy Roman Empire. Matters came to a head during the 1075 dispute between Henry IV and Pope Gregory VII, in which Henry insisted upon his right to exercise lay investiture, while Gregory asserted the complete supremacy of his office.

The sixteenth-century Reformers were largely successful in challenging the right of Roman ecclesiastics to dominate the political scene of any country. Luther was somewhat deficient in evaluating biblical teaching on church and state, but Calvin not only expounded it in his *Institutes*, he also endeavored to exemplify it in his model community of Geneva. Concurrently with this, the European Anabaptists demanded a total separation of church and state, a position that they continue to maintain.

The British philosopher John Locke (1632-1704) also argued for separation, partly because he felt the hopelessness of the notion that church and state could be united in a country whose inhabitants claimed to be Christian but in fact were divided into denominations. Locke's solution was to apply the concept of toleration to the problem. In his celebrated *Letter Concerning Toleration* he argued that the state should have no part in church polity because such matters were beyond its proper jurisdiction and that legal coercion would be wrong in any event. In the same way the church had no real right to interfere with the government, even where moral persuasion was involved. The main emphasis of Locke's argument was that there had long been a distinction between the roles of church and state, and the fact of that distinction ought to make for the separation of the two bodies and the exclusion of religion from the province of the civil power.

It has been suggested that the turmoil of his day, both in England and on the continent of Europe, led Locke to urge that the state's powers should be restricted to matters of civil importance, such interests being defined in his *Letter* as "life, liberty, health, and indolence of body; and the possession of outward things such as money, lands, houses, furniture, and the like." Conversely, he stated, the concerns of the church have always been with the internal, spiritual life and the care of souls, a responsibility which, he argued, had been given by God to the church, and not to the state. The inner convictions of persons are the essence of true religion, and these must be the product of moral persuasion and conviction,

not of civil compulsion, which he regarded as alien to the ideals and example of Christ.

Toleration, by contrast, was in harmony with the gospel; and he presented his plea in a disarmingly simple manner. In civil affairs, he stated, errors of judgment or policy seldom result in uproar or insurrection. By contrast, people held such a serious view of what they deemed to be religious error that they frequently went to violent lengths to quell it. By applying principles of toleration, Locke wondered whether in fact it would not be possible for people to accept each other's alleged doctrinal errors but continue to live together in peace.

Locke's concept of the church, however, differed from that which had dominated the Holy Roman Empire, where in a Christian country church and state were to all intents and purposes one. Locke defined the church as "a free and voluntary society of men joining themselves together of their own accord in order to the public worshipping of God in such a manner as they judge themselves acceptable to Him, and effectual to the salvation of their souls." For Locke, therefore, the church was just like any other voluntary society, with the important difference from earlier days that it was now split up into what amounted to different religious denominations. Each of these would be free to establish its own polity and share the same civil rights and freedoms without any discrimination. The various church denominations would be free to criticize each other and proselytize but would be prohibited from using physical coercion. Interestingly enough, Locke's main concern was with people of Christian persuasion, and he refused to allow toleration to atheists on the ground that a belief in God was the common bond that ensured the keeping of oaths and covenants.

The first settlers of the American colonies arrived with a vision of establishing a holy commonwealth, reflecting the theocratic ideal of the Sinai covenant in the Mosaic period. They wanted to be free to live under divine rule as exemplified in the Puritan tenets, but they were unwilling to extend religious toleration to others. This principle was only established in 1636 by Roger Williams, who founded Rhode Island. Locke's advocacy of the separation of church and state had a far-reaching effect upon the colonists, and it ultimately became enshrined in the United States Constitution. The First Amendment, enacted by Congress in 1787, was not adopted without some resistance; and it was only in 1832 that Massachusetts discontinued its state church. The separation of church and state has been rationalized as being in the best interests of peace and harmony in a pluralistic society, while at the same time allowing religion to flourish unopposed.

Separation of church and state has been in effect generally in British Commonwealth countries outside the United Kingdom, largely because the Anglican denomination was in a minority. This was particularly the case in Canada, despite abortive attempts by the early settlers to gain state support for the Anglican religion. In Australia, the earliest clergy were Church of England chaplains to the guards and prisoners of the penal colony and as such were under the command of the governor. By 1823 the religious pluralism of the country made formal separation of church and state advisable.

Not all processes resulting in the separation of church from state have been so reasonable and peaceful as the foregoing. There are times when the state is the sworn ideological enemy of the church, and either harasses it or endeavors to exterminate it. Until the early fourth century the Roman emperors regarded membership of the Christian church as a crime against the state, and known Christians were persecuted accordingly. The most familiar and dramatic modern rupture between church and state occurred in Russia after the 1917 revolution. For some centuries prior to that time the Russian Orthodox Church had been under czarist control to the point where, by 1800, all clergy were in effect civil servants.

This was swept away in 1918, when the new Communist government enacted a separation of the church from the state and took steps to restrict the influence that the clergy had exercised previously. Atheism became the approved religious position of the state, and attempts were made to repress the Christian faith with varying degrees of severity. By 1935 the zeal for persecution was lessening; and in World War II, in a desperate attempt to gain the friendship of the Christian West, a more conciliatory stand was adopted towards the Russian Orthodox Church and other religious bodies. Religious groups in Russia are still the object of periodic persecution; but despite the official stance of political hostility toward them, the state recognizes clearly, if not openly, the need to bridge the gap between church and state to some extent if only for propaganda purposes in the Western world. Such cleavage as there is, therefore, is neither absolute nor final.

By contrast with the foregoing, a notable example of the union of church and state is to be seen in England, where the church is under state control, participates to varying degrees in the political process, has its bishops and archbishops formally appointed by the state, and receives a certain amount of financial support from the British government. This union goes back to the very roots of the Church of England as an indigenous religious body and was fundamentally important in the days of Elizabeth I for preserving the unity of Britain against outside political and military threats. Puritan objections to such an "established" church rested largely on their reluctance to accept the authority of the queen and Parliament over the church.

In a classic defense of the establishment, Richard Hooker's *Laws of Ecclesiastical Polity* demonstrated that, in a Christian country, there was nothing intrinsically antagonistic between the concepts of church and state. Indeed, for him they were complementary; and under such conditions he saw nothing improper in the head of state also being the head of the church. To allay Puritan fears of an all-powerful temporal monarch, Hooker pointed out that even rulers of state are themselves under law.

His principal concern was so to envisage church and state that neither was inferior to the other and that both should work together for the order and welfare of the British nation. In this latter regard he had in mind the political and social turmoil of contemporary Europe, which was to become worse rather than better. It was his advocacy of the establishment, followed by such champions of the cause as Edmund Burke and Thomas Arnold, that preserved Britain from the kind of civil strife that wracked other, larger countries.

The Church of England establishment has survived largely because of its adaptability. It has been granted wide powers of self-government by the state, but its senior appointees continue to be nominated from Downing Street. Needless to say, these recommendations normally come in the first instance from church sources, although prime ministers have been known to make independent appointments on political grounds. Popular opinion in Britain and elsewhere notwithstanding, the clergy are not remunerated from tax sources or hidden state funds. Indeed, in earlier times the church possessed vast holdings of property, much of which was confiscated by the state when the monasteries were dissolved. In the eighteenth century Queen Anne contributed a large amount of money for church use, and this became known as "Queen Anne's Bounty." It provided the fiscal base for the modern Church of England, and the capital has been expanded greatly by judicious investment on the part of the church commissioners, who manage these funds. As in countries where church and state are separated, the only British clergy who receive state salaries are employees of the armed forces and public institutions of various kinds. In Norway and Sweden, by contrast, which still retain their national churches, the clergy are remunerated from the government coffers but are still able to exercise autonomy in certain ecclesiastical matters.

Periodically in Britain voices are heard demanding that the church be "disestablished." Accordingly, it is important to realize that the only legally "established" feature of the Church of England is its liturgy and doctrinal confession; and these can only be modified by an act of Parliament. Freedom from state control, it is urged, would allow the church to pursue its own affairs without any external hindrance. It would also, however, open the way for cultic hotheads, political activists, and religious cranks to wreak havoc on the ecclesiastical fabric without having to be concerned about the impediment of civil legal restrictions. The result would be to bring a situation that is already dangerously pluralistic into open chaos. The fact is that the well-known antinomianism of Church of England clerics needs to be controlled by the more sober and balanced judgments of experienced state officials.

From the foregoing discussion it will appear that, for many centuries, relations between church and state have been matters of great concern for those involved. While sometimes appearing as allies and at other times opponents, neither has been indifferent to the existence and importance of the other. The reason for this involves ethical considerations in the sense that neither can act on behalf of society as though the other did not exist. While the Christian church recognizes that the legitimate powers of the state are legislated by God (Rom. 13:1-7), it is also sensitive to the corrupting potential of power and accordingly must be vigilant lest the state should exceed its proper functions. In addition, the church can act as the conscience of the state, urging it to use its secular powers for the greater benefit of its citizens and perhaps even for persons beyond its own immediate borders. Conversely, when the church is corrupt and decadent, it is in the distinct interests of the state to reform it and redirect it to its true functions.

However ardently it may be proclaimed that church and state have their own separate functions from which they should not depart, it is evident that such a view is naive and impracticable. It would be simply immoral for the church to withdraw into a cocoon of cultic self-interest and ignore the pressing social, personal, and racial problems of the age. While the church may sometimes be at odds with state policies, the privileges of life in Western democratic societies allow the church to make proper representation to the state on specific matters and to expect a hearing from responsible officials who themselves are not infrequently Christians.

What is often overlooked in modern society is the way in which church and state cooperate for the welfare of all concerned. Thus the state makes special provision for the church to minister to members of the armed forces as well as to inmates of penal institutions and to the staff and patients of hospitals. The American Constitution notwithstanding, oaths are administered in courts of the United States on the Bible, a practice which is also followed at the inauguration of a president. Even more surprising is the fact that a chaplain opens the daily sessions of the American Congress with the recitation of prayer.

Even in situations where the ideology of the state may be so different from that of the church that it makes any form of cooperation very difficult, it still remains true that neither can behave as though it were in total isolation from the other. If the separation of church and state is to be entertained under any other circumstances, it should be based on the clear understanding that both parties are independent in their activities without being mutually exclusive and that both have a vitally important function to fulfill, sometimes jointly and sometimes alone, in working toward the improvement of human society.

**Bibliography:** Ehler, S. Z. and Morrall, J., *Church and State through the Ages* (1951); Morrison, K. F., *The Two Kingdoms* (1964); Stackhouse, R. F., *Christianity and Politics* (1966); Stokes, A. P. and Pfeffer, L., *Church and State in the United States* (1964).

**CHURCH DISCIPLINE (PROTESTANT).** Procedural guidelines for use where Christians commit misdemeanors or fall into sin have been in existence since the time of Jesus (Matt. 18:15-17) and were reinforced in the teachings of Paul as a result of specific problems that occurred in some of the churches he had visited (1 Cor. 5:1-5; 2 Thess. 3:6; 1 Tim. 5:19; 2 Tim. 2:25).

The corruption of human nature is such as to beset the saints continually and demands the sustained submission of the personality to Jesus Christ at all points. One danger to which some Christians are particularly susceptible is antinomianism, which in general assumes that, because of the new birth in Christ, the believer is under no obligation to obey the moral law. Divine grace is supposed in some fashion to override such considerations, which only apparently apply to lesser mortals, thus making the believer free to indulge in whatever behavior suits the needs of the moment without regard for any other than purely personal considerations.

This misunderstanding of the relationship between law and grace troubled the Corinthian church (1 Cor. 5:1-5) and has been in evidence among Christians in various ways ever since. When disruptive behavior of any kind occurs in the body of Christ, it is important for it to be dealt with as expeditiously as possible, so that the offender may be reproved and rehabilitated, or at the worst, expelled from the company of believers.

The definition of an offense will vary considerably, depending upon the openness of the fellowship, but quite clearly doctrinal heresy would be offensive in a group that laid stress upon doctrinal purity. In such an eventuality the offender could well be disciplined by being asked to give a reasoned account of his or her position against the background of Scripture, and possibly denominational tradition, and to abide by the verdict of the remaining members of the group. Ecclesiastical courts have sometimes been convened formally to deal with such matters, and the alleged offender has been judged according to canon law. Less formal assemblies have been content with a summary "reading out" of the delinquent member on the basis of an adverse decision.

In some of the older religious denominations, church discipline is normally in the hands of a bishop or legal officer appointed as his surrogate.

Such discipline applies to both clergy and laity and the punishment imposed after due hearing is deemed to be binding morally upon the offender, regardless of any possible additional involvements under civil law. The most serious penalty that can be prescribed is excommunication, which among other things prevents the convicted person from "approaching the sacraments." In some denominations this is considered a very heavy price to pay for an alleged misdemeanor, however proper the verdict may appear to be.

In an earlier day church discipline was often exercised in a forbidding, even spectacular manner, with the delinquent being punished in a variety of ways, some of them of a severe nature. A more tolerant attitude has appeared at the end of the twentieth century, due perhaps to the blurring of distinctions between right and wrong in so many areas of contemporary life and behavior. As a result, a person accused of what is regarded as a crime against morality is generally called to account for such activities by his or her denomination or church authority before any further action is taken. When guilt has been established, appropriate penalties are then imposed.

In cases of grave moral offenses committed by the clergy, the person who exercises authority generally removes the man or woman involved from active duty immediately when the facts become known and, after due consideration, recommends some course of action which the offender is expected to undertake voluntarily. Where aberrant behavior seems to call for psychiatric treatment, steps are taken to insure that the person concerned receives proper medical care.

In those instances where the moral problem is the result of addiction to alcohol or to mind-disorienting chemicals, some form of rehabilitation is prescribed at special centers. If the offense is sex related, such as fornication or adultery, the delinquent person is usually required to resign from his or her position immediately and could also be expelled subsequently from the larger group when guilt has been established. The intention behind a request for resignation in such cases is not so much to presume guilt as to insure that the alleged offender and any family members are protected as much as possible from the publicity that normally attends such occurrences. Embezzlement is often dealt with by means of dismissal; and the culprit is not infrequently prosecuted under civil statutes, especially if a large amount of money has been stolen.

Such disciplinary steps are often traumatic for the church authority as well as for the alleged offender and consequently are normally surrounded by a great deal of circumspection so as not to cause unnecessary offense to the body of Christ. Such action as is taken is, of course, independent of any civil suits which may be launched by an aggrieved party. While the offense should be handled discreetly and according to properly established procedures rather than *ad hoc* action, an attitude of Christian charity and genuine help in the direction of treatment or rehabilitation must be extended to one who is demonstrably a weaker brother or sister.

See ANTINOMIANISM; CANON LAW.

## CHURCH DISCIPLINE (ROMAN CATHOLIC).

Church discipline focuses on the conduct expected of the Christian. It flows from doctrine and belief, but it is not entirely identified with it. The basis for discipline is in the authority granted by Christ to the Apostles to regulate the Christian communities.

Present church discipline in the Latin Church (the Eastern Church has its own code) is contained in the Code of Canon Law published in 1983. Prior to that the regulation came from a code promulgated in 1918. The present code contains 1,752 canons (compared with 2,414 in the code of 1918) regulating the life of the Christian. It is divided into seven books which are further divided into parts, sections, titles, chapters, and articles. The word *canon* comes from the Greek word meaning "rule, norm, or measure."

Only the pope in unison with the bishops can legislate for the whole church, which is guided, Roman Catholics believe, by the Holy Spirit. The code is meant to be a means through which this guidance comes to the individual member or group. The sources from which the canons are drawn are the divine or biblical law, natural law, and laws of other societies and custom.

As is true of laws in general, Roman Catholics consider themselves bound in conscience by these laws. The obligation varies according to the seriousness of the matter involved. Thus, for instance, Catholics feel that they are bound by the laws of fast and abstinence and judge that in violating them without a justifying reason, they are committing sin. The same is true of the other canons of the code.

An individual bishop may pass laws for his own diocese, but in themselves these do not bind Catholics in other dioceses. In passing laws, also, the local bishop may not go contrary to the universal law of the church. If he does, the law has no force, since the first obligation of the Catholic is to the universal law of the church.

The purpose of the new code of 1983 was to bring church law in line with the spirit of Vatican II. It would be impossible to go into any detail to show the difference between the new code and the old code. Suffice it to say here that the new code is built more around the dignity of the human person. Because it is easy for law to turn into legalism, many felt that church law prior to Vatican II was becoming an end unto itself, thus unduly subordinating the person. While Vatican II still recognized the need for law, it was also concerned about the value and dignity of the human person. The thinking underlying the new code was law is for the good of the person, not vice versa.

**Bibliography:** Buckley, J., *et al., Catholic En-*

*cyclopedia* (1967) III, pp. 29–53; Schaeffer, F., *Catholic Encyclopedia* (1910) IX, pp. 56–68.

J.R.C.

**CIVIL DISOBEDIENCE.** By this term is meant a conscious demonstration of disloyalty toward some enactment, statute, or ordinance promulgated by a body that has power to make legally binding regulations. Civil disobedience is specific in character because it describes defiance of promulgations enacted by the *civitas*, namely the state or body politic. Through disobedience of particular ordinances it poses a direct challenge to the authority of the promulgating body.

Civil disobedience can sometimes be minor in nature, involving the protest of one individual in connection with some enactment which is considered unjust or oppressive. An act of this nature could involve, for example, the withholding of civic taxes as a protest against waste, mismanagement, or political corruption, whether real or imaginary. Multiple involvement in civil disobedience normally takes such forms as protest marches when they have been declared illegal, disruptive "sit-in" demonstrations which involve trespass upon property, and similar antisocial activities. In a more serious political activist form, civil disobedience results in riots, rebellion, and general insurrection.

A marked feature of those who engage in civil disobedience is the superior moral attitude that is generally manifested toward certain aspects of existence. For one reason or other their experience of life has led them to think that the most effective way of changing the current political or social order to suit their own ideas and preferences is by violating statutes that were instituted for the general protection of persons and property. Confident in the supreme rightness of their cause, they have no qualms about harassing or victimizing those who disagree with them. Where they are involved in riots or insurrection of any significant degree, they commit murder and atrocities without any compunction and in general show a complete disregard for private property. Because civil disobedience represents a fundamental challenge to established processes of law and order, clashes with the police and military personnel are not infrequently the consequences of demonstrations that have been inspired by political activists, among whom communist agitators are usually prominent as rear-end leaders.

The kind of moral superiority that is often typical of those who become involved in civil disobedience is generally fostered by "causes" of various kinds. The so-called peace movement has made a virtue out of promoting disarmament in the Western world but has ignored studiously the progress made by some communist nations in rearming and in proliferating atomic weaponry. Thus some such object as the cruise missile, for example, can generate an incredible outpouring of hysteria among peace activists, who go to great lengths by picketing, trespassing, and using other forms of harassment to promote their own "cause," but on a totally selfish basis.

If civil disobedience is conducted in an orderly, nonviolent manner, it can draw attention to the fact that at least one segment of the population has a grievance about an issue that may well commend itself to the attention of others. But even though the protest may be peaceful, if it is illegal on various grounds there is no guarantee that the cause being espoused will commend itself immediately if at all to law-abiding citizens, and there is always the possibility that it may produce a countermovement of serious proportions. Civil disobedience activities such as the passive resistance tactics employed in India by Gandhi against the British, or the illegal marches of Martin Luther King in the United States, undoubtedly achieved their goal in large measure; but the overall cost was high, and the problems at which the acts of civil disobedience were directed have by no means been solved by these attempts. It goes without saying that Western democracies are the most tolerant of any jurisdictions in the matter of civil disobedience, and the totalitarian regimes the most repressive.

Although many who purport to be Christians participate in acts of civil disobedience, the New Testament makes it clear that temporal power operates in its legitimate capacity of maintaining justice and order in society as an agent of God (Rom. 13:1-12) and that therefore absolute justice must remain an ideal to be pursued. But if the state operates under divine authority, rebellion against its enactments can, for the Christian, be construed readily as apostasy. Yet in democratic institutions it is permissible for Christians to make proper representations to government, and in many cases submissions are welcomed. Individuals can also call attention to perceived injustices by means of test cases in the courts without having to resort to acts of violence, and if inequities have been demonstrated it is then the responsibility of government to redress the situation. It is difficult to believe that Christians honor their Lord by burning buildings, pillaging, and even killing in the process of demonstrating their displeasure with law and statutes. Instead, the Christian will use whatever processes of lawful procedure are available in society and effect change in an orderly manner so as to avoid that type of anarchy that is destructive of all law.

**CIVIL RIGHTS.** Civil rights are those rights which all citizens of a society must *legally* possess in order for that society to be a just society. Citizens of all governments are naturally entitled to these rights. In the American tradition, they are said to be grounded in natural rights, rights with which human beings are endowed either by their Creator or by Nature, rights that are legitimate whether or not any government acknowledges them. Martin Luther King, Jr. (1929-1968) understood civil rights in this way: "A just law is a manmade code that squares with the moral law or the law of God. . . . To put it in the terms of Saint Thomas Aquinas, an unjust law is a human law that is not rooted in eternal and natural law." Hence, for King, a civil right is simply the government's legal acknowledgment of an existing natural right. In the philosopher's language, a civil right is a positive law manifestation of natural law.

This view is articulated in the Declaration of Independence (1776), which underlies the Constitution and which makes several claims about natural rights and their relationship to government: 1) Because all men are created equal by their Creator, they possess certain unalienable rights; 2) Among these rights are life, liberty, and the pursuit of happiness; 3) Since these rights are unalienable, the state cannot create them, but must secure them; 4) The state derives its power to secure these rights from the consent of the governed; and 5) The governed have a right to alter the government or form a new one if it violates natural rights.

Notice that these natural rights are not justified by their *utility*. One does not, for example, establish the freedom of religion as a natural right because it has social benefit. But rather, freedom of religion has a social benefit because it is a natural right.

The Constitution (1789) outlines how these three basic rights—life, liberty, and the pursuit of happiness—are best secured in the securing of more specific rights, such as those found in the First Amendment: freedom of religion, speech, press, assembly, and petition. When a citizen is denied these and other fundamental rights for arbitrary and/or irrelevant reasons (such as race, creed, color, gender, national origin, etc.), that citizen has been denied her civil rights.

Although the language of rights, which originated in the Enlightenment, is not found in the Bible, the concept of rights is taught there. For example, though the Bible does not say that one has a "right to own private property," it does forbid stealing, an act which is possible only if the thief's victim in fact owns the stolen property. This is because in many cases duties imply rights. If I have a duty not to steal from you, this implies that you have a right to own something. Therefore, most of the commands of Scripture, such as those found in the Ten Commandments, imply correlative rights. Consequently, the Bible implies that human beings possess rights to property, truth, life, etc. It follows then that any government which tramples on these rights violates both its citizens and the laws of God.

Certain legal philosophers and jurists, such as the late Chief Justice Oliver Wendell Holmes, argue that civil rights are not grounded in natural rights but are merely artifacts created by societies and governments in the constitutions, social contracts, and statutes they choose to accept. This view is called *legal positivism*. But if this view is correct, then the Declaration of Independence is a sham, and the Nazi defense at the Nuremberg war crimes trials after WWII was philosophically legitimate. The Nazis defended themselves by arguing that they were "only following the law." They appealed to legal positivism.

The civil rights movement of late twentieth-century America focused first on the predicament of African-Americans, who were denied full legal personhood under Southern slavery and the Supreme Court's *Dred Scott* decision (*Scott v. Sandford*, 60 U.S. [19 How.] 393 [1857]). Although the Fourteenth Amendment was passed in 1868, and African-Americans were granted full Constitutional rights, for decades after, blacks were still denied their civil rights. They were forced to live in segregated areas, attend segregated schools, dine at segregated lunch counters, and sit at the back of the bus. On the basis of skin color only they were denied jobs and school entrance.

To remedy the denial of the civil rights of not only blacks, but women as well as other minorities, arguably the two most important events are the following: (1) the U.S. Supreme Court's *Brown v. the Board of Education* (347 U.S. 483 [1954]) in which the Court ruled racial segregation unconstitutional; and (2) the passage of the Civil Rights Act of 1964. Part of Title VII of this act reads:

It shall be an unlawful employment practice for an employer—

(1) to fail to refuse to hire or to discharge any individual, or otherwise to discriminate against any individual with respect to his compensation, terms, conditions, or privileges of employment, because of such individual's race, color, religion, sex, or national origin; or

(2) to limit, segregate, or classify his employees or applicants for employment in any way which would deprive or tend to deprive any individual of employment opportunities or otherwise adversely affect his status as an employee, because of such individual's race, color, religion, or national origin.

Although a vast majority of Americans support the 1964 Act, since its passage a giant rift has occurred in the civil rights community over the question of *affirmative action,* a policy requiring employers to hire a certain number of blacks and women in order to redress past discrimination. Even though the Supreme Court in *United Steelworkers v. Weber* (443 U.S. 193 [1979]) declared affirmative action constitutional, critics insist that affirmative action is illegal according to the 1964 law, which says in subsection 703(j) of Title VII that no employer is required to "grant preferential treatment to any individual or group on account of any imbalance which may exist" between the number of employees in such groups and "the total number or percentage of persons of such race, color, religion, sex, or national origin in any community, State, section or other area."

Therefore, the fundamental question concerning affirmative action is *not,* "Does it work?," but rather, "which basis for civil rights is more consistent with both our constitutional tradition and the 1964 Civil Rights Act: civil rights based on a principle of equality (all persons, created equal by their Creator, possess certain unalienable rights) or on a principle of preferential treatment?''

Where should the Christian stand on civil rights? Concerning policies such as affirmative action well-meaning Christians can disagree. However, when it comes to standing with those individuals who have been denied their civil rights for reasons that are arbitrary, bigoted, and/or irrational, Christians should be in the forefront demanding justice.

What about "gay rights" or "abortion rights"? The Christian should examine each claim critically, taking into consideration how the principle of equality can be applied. In the case of gay rights, the question is not whether people who practice homosexuality have equal rights under the law. This is indisputable. But rather, does the state have an obligation to treat their homosexual behavior as fundamental to their nature, as salient a feature as race? If not, does the state have a right to favor certain forms of behavior, such as heterosexual monogamy, for the good of the community? It is possible, therefore, to say that people who practice homosexuality have civil rights by virtue of being persons but that there is no such thing as gay rights because there is no such thing as "gay persons."

Whether abortion rights are fundamental to civil rights is contingent upon the nature of the unborn. If they are persons, then there is no such thing as abortion rights, since such a "right" would result in the unjust killing of another person.

**Bibliography:** Dworkin, R., *Taking Rights Seriously* (1978); Glendon, M. A., *Rights Talk: The Impoverishment of American Political Discourse* (1991); King, M. L. Jr., "Letter from the Birmingham Jail," in *The Right Thing to Do*, J. Rachels, ed. (1989), pp. 236-253; Sowell, T., ed. *Civil Rights: Rhetoric or Reality?* (1984); Strauss, L., *Natural Right and History* (1953); Thomas, C., "The Higher Law Background of the Privileges and Immunities Clause of the Fourteenth Amendment," *Harvard Journal of Law and Public Policy* 12 (Winter 1989): 63-70.

See BILL OF RIGHTS; HUMAN RIGHTS.

F.J.B.

**CLONING.** The term *clone* describes a group of identical cells that have come from a common ancestor. Cloning is thus a process by which this identity is fostered and proliferated within a scientifically regulated environment. There are two types of cloning, the first being a natural process which is demonstrated in multiple births whenever the babies are "identical" genetically, that is to say, monozygotic, rather than being "fraternal" or dizygotic.

The second type of cloning is of an artificial, mechanical nature, involving nuclear transplantation and cellular bodies. As practiced in the laboratory, the nucleus of a living body cell is placed inside an unfertilized egg cell from which the nucleus has been extracted. If the procedure is a success, the host (egg) cell then adapts the genetic characteristics of the body cell nucleus, whereupon the fertilized egg cell is cultivated to full term growth.

Because cloning involves special techniques and great skills, there is a high rate of failure. As part of a larger program of genetic manipulation, cloning has been applied to livestock breeding, but the results are unconvincing at the present. More favorable prospects have emerged from salmon-cloning experiments conducted in Japan in 1983, using a modified technique that Britain scientists had abandoned. Salmon are regarded as ideal subjects for such experiments, since they produce thousands of large, accessible eggs that can be fertilized quite readily away from the fish's body. The eggs are radiated according to special techniques in order to modify the genetic structure. The results of these procedures have shown that it is apparently easier for the scientists to produce female rather than male fry. Theoretically this type of experimentation can be applied to any animal's eggs that can be fertilized externally, though to what extent it will become widespread is far from certain.

Cloning has already found medical applications. Through experiments with certain kinds of rodents, American scientists have been able to clone the gene for myelin basic protein, the fatty tissue that insulates the nerve cells. When myelin is deficient or absent, it permits a short-circuiting in the nervous system that results in a variety of neurological disorders, including multiple sclerosis. If this disease is indeed genetic, as seems indicated by its familial incidence in some cases, it should be possible in theory to employ the myelin basic protein as a means of testing the genetic view of origins of the disease. But as researchers have already pointed out, even if a defective myelin basic protein gene is discovered in people suffering from multiple sclerosis, the substitution of a normal gene cannot be guaranteed to rectify all, or perhaps even any, of the difficulties brought on by multiple sclerosis.

Beginning in 1984, the cloning of human skin has been particularly successful. In that year scientists cloned large sheets of smooth pink skin from small pieces that had been scraped from the bodies of two badly burned children. Cloning was the skin-replacement procedure of choice, since there was an inadequate amount of skin available from the childrens' bodies for grafting; and skin taken from other donors would have been rejected by the victims' immune systems. The process allowed doctors to produce sufficient skin within a three-week period to cover the patients' entire bodies.

Cloning in the foregoing areas would seem to be unexceptionable and even highly beneficial. But when the concept of cloning involves multiple embryonic engineering in human beings, ethical questions begin to arise. Anything that would weaken the strength or diminish the integrity of the biological family is contrary to the purposes of the Creator, who established the family concept as the building block of human society. It would therefore be improper for fundamental decisions about human reproduction and parenting to be removed from the family and made the responsibility of the laboratory.

Many Christians would argue that under no circumstances should medical or scientific techniques attempt to produce genetically identical human beings, since this would distort the natural processes of reproduction and could lead, in unscrupulous hands, to a program of mass selective breeding. In terms of heredity and character, such a process would deny a child's right to familial individuality, whether that right be for better or worse. In order to guard against the possibility of multiple selective breeding, the process of cloning as a permitted or delegated function leading to human procreation ought to be restricted to a single clone, and any multiples should be disposed of in consultation with the parents. In any event, cloning ought to be regarded as ethical if it is being undertaken as a means of circumventing the transmission of hereditary disease. No laboratory, clinic, or hospital should have anything approaching complete autonomy in decisions relating to cloning, if only to avoid the charge of medical experimentation for its own sake and the infringing of individual rights.

**COERCION.** This term describes any type of force or pressure to which an individual may be subjected in order to produce a form of activity or an end result which is in conflict with the exercise of free choice. Coercion should be distinguished from compulsion, which while it may have external physical characteristics is often used to describe internal impulses which are translated into activity that is often irrational and morbid.

Coercion may comprise physical force, or the threat of it, but can be recognized equally as a psychological phenomenon, whether proceeding from one's equals in the form of peer pressure, from criminal sources such as attempts at blackmail, or from the abuse of state power, as in a dictatorship. From whatever source coercion is being applied, the freedom of choice traditionally associated with individual acts of will is being thwarted or denied. Jesus resisted coercion at his trial before Pilate and urged his followers to fear only the one who can destroy body and soul in hell, instead of being able to coerce the body alone (Matt. 10:28). In the Sermon on the Mount, Jesus showed how the believer should deal with coercion by going the celebrated "second mile" (Matt. 5:41). This is probably best interpreted as a concession to the obsessive-compulsive behavior of an individual and not to brutal physical coercion by a captor.

See CHOICE; SERMON ON THE MOUNT.

**COHABITATION.** This term traditionally describes the dwelling together under one roof and the sharing of a common life together of a husband and wife. In recent times the word has been enlarged in scope to cover any couple (heterosexual or homosexual) who choose to live together in one place. Thus cohabitation now has the common meaning of the act of living with, and in particular sleeping with, another person of the same or opposite sex in a permanent or semi-permanent relationship.

Thus a young heterosexual couple will cohabit to see whether they can "make it together" in a lifelong arrangement; or a heterosexual couple, who cannot legally marry, will cohabit in order to share a common life together. Homosexual couples will cohabit because this is what they find themselves needing and wanting. The variety of forms of cohabiting is large today in the Western world, and most people accept it as normal or permissable.

Legal problems which are not easily solved are connected with many such relationships, such as the custody and care of any children born to, or adopted by, those not legally married and the question of the ownership of property. There are social and psychological difficulties also, especially in the long term, for those who indulge themselves in one form or another of this new sexual freedom.

God's plan and purpose for the happiness of man and woman as well as for the increase of the human race requires that only those who are bound together in marriage should cohabit. Then, from a Christian perspective, other forms of cohabitation, whether heterosexual or homosexual, are immoral and sinful (Heb. 13:4; Gal. 5:19). Furthermore, Christians are obliged, as a minimum, not to encourage these relationships (for example, by renting a house for such immoral cohabitation). In addition, by the example of genuinely Christian married cohabitation, believers are to commend God's will and purpose. Of course, it is permissible and often good that members of the same sex share a house or apartment together. What is condemned by God is not sharing, but immoral cohabitation.

P.T.

**COLLECTIVISM.** Collectivism is a social and economic theory and is sometimes called socialism. Sometimes advocated on religious grounds, collectivism theorizes that the people as a whole own and control the means of production and distribution. This contrasts sharply with capitalism, which advocates private ownership for profit of most means of production and distribution and resists central planning and state control.

Historically, collectivist theories and ideals abound, from Plato's *Republic* to various versions of modern socialism and Marxism and to Christian communes in their various forms.

The most common modern political form of collectivism is Marxism, usually in its Leninist form. Marxist collectivism (communism) is based solidly upon a materialist metaphysic, including historical and economic determinism, except for its expectation of a utopian social end. The traditional concept of absolute ethics and rights is regarded as a reflection of ruling class interests. Religion is viewed as an opiate that consoles the oppressed in their misery. Power alone is regarded as the key to social reform and is usually grasped by a small minority allegedly held in the name of the people. All citizens theoretically share in decision making in collectives, though in reality they become employees of the state. Modern collectivist states produce their own entrenched ruling class, as observed by Milovan Djilas, the former vice-president of Marxist Yugoslavia, in his biting 1957 expose, *The New Class* (for which he was imprisoned).

In modern times, collectivism advocated on grounds of Christian teaching ranges from democratic socialism in Western Europe, Britain, and Canada, to political liberalism and Christian communes. Many other versions have been added to the traditional Mennonite and Hutterite communes. Arguments against ownership and free enterprise by means of appeals to the monastic movement and to early church fathers have tended to be one-sided. For example, the money raising tactics of Jerome when he built his monastery at Bethlehem rivaled modern religious television fund raising methods. The religious sanction of greed in the name of a utopian collective model is particularly odious.

Contemporary liberation theology is usually allied with a collectivist social and political model. Liberation theologians favor Marxist economics in relation to their thesis that truth from God can be discovered only within solutions to present-day political and social problems. The claim that personal freedom and freedom from economic repression flourish under collectivist regimes flies in the face of the facts. It is striking that liberation theory runs hand in hand with decrease in personal liberty and vast increase in enslavement and torture.

Peter Bauer, a British economist, argues that modern socialist and liberation theories that are advocated in religious guise amount to the legitimation of envy. He has demonstrated that psychological and cultural factors in many cases precondition whole societies against economic growth. The studies of the American sociologist Thomas Sowell arrive at similar conclusions.

There is a superficial resemblance between secular and Christian collectivist theories in that both are utopian. Each in its own way depends upon the unwarranted assumption that human beings are universally altruistic and the assumption of the prior validity of the will of the whole group as against the individual will. On one side this ig-nores original sin, and on the other side it ignores human propensity to selfishness and abuse of power (note the novels of the Mennonite, Rudy Wiebe). Collectivist societies boast about their elections, which are usually a formality; but few have safeguards to eject leaders, as happens in democracies. Collectivist societies discourage pluralism, and the right to say no is rare.

The inevitable formation of massive, entrenched, and self-serving bureaucracies that blunt initiative is a serious problem in modern collectivist societies. An unsolved problem of socialist countries is how to incorporate incentive into a system which plans from the top. The smothering effects of a closed system tend to starve the system itself. In eastern European bloc countries, moonlighting in addition to working at state jobs is a modern expression of how incentives draw people to productive work which jeopardizes central planning. It is instructive that such utopian societies require walls and strict regulations to prevent people from emigrating.

Christians, like others, adapt to many different political and social models. Christians are morally committed to freedom, justice, equitable treatment in an economy, and to the principle of love of neighbor to help those less fortunate than themselves. At the same time, Christians recognize that humans are imperfect, sinful, and at times exploitative and repressive. Thus from long experience, Christians realize that utopian schemes are not only inadequate but are not mandated by biblical teaching.

The dark side of human nature must be kept in check. Thus human society, short of Christ's promised kingdom, must always insure that a system of checks and balances is jealously guarded as well as maintain the hope that principles of freedom, justice, enterprise, and love of neighbor prevail. In human society altruism and self-interest will always be present together and will be in frequent tension. A great value of democratic capitalism is the advantage of the impersonal nature of the market economy that the economist Paul Heyne describes as "a social system in which people do not care about most of those for whom they care." When motivated by self-interest to do their best work and to produce the best product competitively in a free economy, people tend to serve the needs of others best.

**Bibliography:** Popper, K. R., *The Open Society and Its Enemies*, 2 vols. (1945); Novack, M., *Capitalism and Socialism* (1979); Gutierrez, G., *A Theology of Liberation* (1981); Bauer, P., *Reality and Rhetoric* (1984).

S.J.M.

**COLONIALISM, COLONIZATION.** A colony is an expatriate group of persons who are attempting to recreate a way of life, perhaps comparable to the one familiar from earlier days, in a new environment that is at some distance from the homeland. In the ancient Near East the Assyrians maintained control of their conquered lands by transporting groups of native peoples to exile in Assyria and replacing them with persons loyal to the empire. This process occurred in connection with the Samaritans (2 Kings 17:24-33), an Assyrian group transplanted in conquered Israelite territory by Sargon of Assyria (722-705 B.C.). Colonies established at subsequent periods in different parts of the world arose from such diverse circumstances as the expansion of trade, military conquest, and religious persecution.

As distinct from colonization, the term *colonialism* describes the intent or motivation, whether of a political, military, or social nature, which leads the colonizing power to acquire and maintain territorial holdings. Colonization sometimes results in oppression and exploitation, especially where the colonies are established among people of different races from that of the imperial power. Where discrimination and exploitation are practiced, the urge for independence and self-determination soon becomes apparent and, if pursued to a conclusion, can result in bloodshed and severely oppressive measures by the colonizing power. Not all colonization is sinister in character, however, and can in fact bring a great degree of social organization and stability to the colony. An ideal situation occurs where the colony is allowed to develop to the point where self-government can be achieved in a responsible and peaceful manner.

**COLOR BAR.** In this expression the word *bar* is used of something that interposes, prevents, or excludes. Hence a color bar is an enactment that prohibits persons of a particular color from taking part freely in the entire range of activities that are practiced by those who are not of that color. Such a bar can be applied equally to majorities as well as minorities, provided that the enacting authority possesses the power to implement the regulations that seek to establish the color bar. While not all areas of social or political life in the dominant group may be closed to those of a different color, the effect is to institute racial segregation and convey to the barred segment of the population the idea that it is inferior, because of the color differential, to others in that society. The color bar has not infrequently been practiced by white persons living in a majority population of a different color as a means of monopolizing or controlling influential political, economic, or social positions in that society.

For the Christian the concept of a color bar violates the basic New Testament teaching that all believers are one in Christ Jesus, regardless of race or color (Gal. 3:28). This is not to say, of course, that all persons, whatever their race, possess qualities that are common and uniform, but this teaching expressly prohibits racism in any form and the exploitation that so commonly accompanies such an attitude.

See APARTHEID; EQUALITY; RACE RELATIONS; RACISM.

**COMMANDMENTS.** For Christians, the nature of God defines what is good (Mark 10:18) and the will of God defines what is right. He alone has supreme moral authority.

This explains why so much of the Bible's ethical teaching is phrased as command, rather than statement. The moral philosopher sets out theories in his own name. The Bible, in contrast, makes demands on God's name. The philosopher must support a thesis about fidelity in marriage, for example, with solid reasoning if he expects to be taken seriously. The Old Testament simply demands, "You shall not commit adultery" (Exod. 20:14), without any supporting argument. The assumption that the command expresses God's will is enough to establish its ethical validity and authority.

In Scripture, all ethical commands are doctrinally based. The revelation of God's own nature provides the foundation on which His moral demands are built. This is supremely so in the case of the key biblical injunctions to the holy (Lev. 11:44-45; 19:2; Matt. 5:48) and to love (Eph. 5:1-2; Luke 6:36). In each case, the basic instruction is to imitate God. So while some moralists say "Do what I tell you," and a few dare to add "Do as I do," God goes a step further: "Be as I am."

The doctrine of man also features strongly in the Bible as a basis for ethical directives. Because man and woman are created in God's image (Gen. 1:26-27), His laws for living are inscribed indelibly upon human nature (Rom. 2:14-15). This provides the basis for a Christian approach to natural law theory.

The theocentric nature of the Bible's ethical commands also determines man's chief motive for obeying them. In Scripture, God's demands are set firmly in a context of love. The Ten Commandments, for example, begin not with an imperative but with a reminder of God's loving rescue of Israel from Egypt. The appeal is therefore for men and women to obey God's commands willingly, not grudgingly, in response to and in gratitude for His amazing acts of saving love.

More specifically, different parts of the Bible highlight different aspects of God's demands. The Old Testament law vividly expresses the comprehensiveness of His will. Alongside commands that we recognize as purely ethical come regulations governing worship and instructions for life in society (including directions for government, for management of the economy, and for the care of the land).

The four Gospels, on the other hand, reveal a different emphasis. In reaction to Pharisaic legalism, Jesus stressed the inwardness of God's demands. He commanded an end to sexual fantasizing and vicious thoughts, as well as acts of adultery and murder (Matt. 5:21-22, 27-28). When asked to choose the greatest of the Old Testament's 613 rabbinically recognized commands, He selected two that challenged all outward law-keeping, that lacked inward compassion (Mark 12:28-31)

The Epistles, as well, have a slightly different emphasis in the demands they make on Christian behavior. Paul, especially, spells out the detailed application of God's will, often in imperative form. Unlike Jesus, he goes into enormous detail when he bans different kinds of wrong behavior (for example, sins of speech—see Rom. 1:29-30; Eph. 4:29; 5:4; Col. 3:8).

Great care must be taken in applying the command of Scripture to contemporary ethical issues. In particular, it is important to avoid both legalistic and antinomian approaches.

The legalist insists on applying the full force of every biblical command, irrespective of its original context. Apart from the practical difficulty of coping with situations where no relevant rule is to be found in Scripture, this method leads its exponents to conclusions that most Christians would find unacceptable (for example, advocating the death penalty for young delinquents—Deut. 21:18-21).

At the other extreme, the antinomian finds no binding force at all in any of the Bible's commands. He may base this conclusion on an existentialist premise, seeking God's direct guidance in the situation over and above any fixed, written rule or regulation (1 Cor. 14:37-38). Again, most Christians would find this position untenable. It hardly does justice to Jesus' estimate of the Old Testament law's continuing validity (Matt. 5:17-20)

Seeking to avoid the traps of legalism and antinomianism, some have adopted a selective approach. This assumes that distinctions can be made within the corpus of the Bible's commands. Some of them demand strict obedience, while others do not. The Old Testament law, for example, was divided by the European reformers into three categories: the ceremonial, the civil, (both of which are no longer binding on Christians), and the moral (which is still binding, particularly the Decalogue). Similarly, Jesus' commands were subdivided into *mandata* (binding), *exempla* (merely illustrative), and *consilia* (applying to individuals only).

The selective method has much to commend it. But problems arise because the Bible does not categorize its commands quite so neatly. As a result, there is room for disagreement about which commands belong to the categories that demand absolute obedience.

In recent years, the paradigmatic approach has rightly gained most favor. This assumes that every command in the Bible is based on some principle that has universal validity because it reflects God's nature and expresses His will. The interpreter's task, therefore, is first to identify the underlying principle and then to recast it into a relevant imperative for modern times. Sometimes the result is simply repetition and reinforcement (for example, the ban on adultery). In other cases the application may be quite different (in relating the command to build parapets around roofs, Deuteronomy 22:8, to safety precautions for modern tower blocks).

**Bibliography:** Field, D. H., *Free to Do Right* (1973); Smedes, L., *Mere Morality* (1983); Wright, C. J. H., *Living as the People of God* (1983); White, R. E. O., *Biblical Ethics* (1979).

D.H.F.

**COMMON GOOD.** The term *common* in this expression relates primarily to the constituted community and to the general degree of participation that characterizes its activities. The common good, therefore, describes the well-being that is common to each member of the group. In ethical and political theory each member should be able to aspire to the ideal of the common good and also be in a position to contribute to its realization.

The ideal has found expression at various times in human history, in the communal organization of the primitive Christian church (Acts 4:32-35), in more developed religious communities of later periods, and also in the beginnings of doctrinaire socialism. The philosophical movement known as Utilitarianism adopted a hedonistic position under Jeremy Bentham (1748-1842) in identifying the greatest good for the greatest number of people as constituting the "good life." A more mature development of Utilitarianism placed greater stress on esthetics and interpersonal relationships, from which the common good would be nurtured, rather than from psychological hedonism.

**COMMON-LAW MARRIAGE.** This designation describes a marital union which has been entered into by a man and woman without the benefit of an ecclesiastical or civil ceremony and which generally has no attestation as to validity in the form of written undertakings or the certification of witnesses. In many jurisdictions a marriage would be regarded as legally valid technically if the bride and groom had pledged themselves to each other in the presence of at least two witnesses. But by dispensing with even simple legalizing ceremonies, the participants in common-law marriages find that their union is not recognized as legal in many countries or states. The civil ceremonies are important for preserving the order and stability of society in establishing approved relationships, while the religious ceremonies add a dimension of spiritual strength to the union inasmuch as the contractual obligations are made in the presence of God.

A common-law marriage deprives both participants of these extremely important elements and in effect makes each party highly vulnerable to the whims and passing fancies of the other. Because the relationship is seldom protected by legal statutes, neither party has any recourse when the relationship is dissolved. Women who bear children under such conditions are highly vulnerable, and it is the exception rather than the rule for common-law marriages to be much more than a temporary arrangement. It is possible for there to be conditions where such a marriage would be contracted in good faith, but in that event it ought to be legalized at the earliest opportunity for the protection of those concerned.

Most Christians would find common-law marriages reprehensible from a moral standpoint, since sexual gratification unfettered by the obligations of law seems to be the predominant concern. Such unions would also be regarded as undersirable where they were prohibited by law. Furthermore, no responsible Christian couple could countenance the insecurity that characterizes a marital relationship that has not been contracted in God's presence and is unprotected by social statutes.

**COMMUNITY.** A broad definition of *community* is that of a group which cherishes certain common ideals and practices and lives in an associative relationship which may vary in closeness depending upon the size of the community. From very early times people lived together as a family, a clan, or a tribe, and established community relationships that were based largely upon what would now be styled a "theory of social contract." People lived together in groups for their own preservation, but also as a means of enriching and developing their overall resources, especially in sedentary communities. The ancient Near Eastern city-states, consisting of a city and its environs, not infrequently developed into places of high culture as at Ur, Mari, Nuzi, Ebla, Babylon, and elsewhere. The ancient Greek community was exemplified by the *polis*, in which every citizen was expected to make some sort of contribution to community well-being. Most communities in the ancient world had small populations, and it is doubtful if Plato and Socrates could have conceived of a true *polis* as large as twelve thousand inhabitants. Such a community by its very size would have defeated the ideals of closeness and civic interaction.

Communities have arisen from time to time for religious as well as purely social reasons, but with comparable objectives of service and mutual support in view. The primitive Christian church was one such community which practiced a form of commensalism and social service to underprivileged Christians in Jerusalem (Acts 2:44-46). In the medieval period monastic communities arose which perpetuated the religious ideals of the individuals or groups who founded them.

While many look upon community living as an ideal form of existence, it manifests certain deficiencies. By its very nature it tends to isolate its members from the exigencies of daily life as experienced by noncommunity members and hinders those who belong to it from a legitimate expression of individuality by its insistence upon conformity to rules, some of which can be quite stringent. As a result the members tend to lean upon the institution for support, and if they are suddenly separated from the group they not infrequently experience emotional difficulties. For insecure persons community living is probably the best means of survival, but the very weakness of such individuals leaves them open to exploitation by more powerful, and even unscrupulous, members of the community, as is the case with certain modern quasi-religious sects.

While the concept of community may have certain aspects that are beneficial socially and that, having regard to the nature of modern society, demand the participation of people as a whole, it should not be expected to have universal appeal. Although it is obviously important for persons to be in association with others in order to be healthy mentally and emotionally, there are some for whom even a modest degree of community regimentation results in profound frustration. The parameters necessary for beneficial participation in community living will therefore vary between individuals and will need to be observed carefully if the best interests of both the participants and the community itself are to be served in the fullest sense.

**COMPASSION.** This is the virtue expressed in a sympathetic consciousness of the need or distress of another person with a desire to remove or alleviate it. The Lord is compassionate as well as merciful (James 5:11; Ps. 103:8). This is well illustrated in the parable of the lost son (Luke 15:11-31) in which the father "was filled with compassion" for the prodigal young man (v. 20) and wanted both to remove his distress and welcome him back into the family home.

The Lord Jesus is compassionate both toward individuals in need (for example, the widow of Nain, Luke 7:13) and toward groups of people who reflect a common need (for example, the harassed and helpless crowd, Matt. 9:36). Thus, in imitation of God the Father and of Jesus, the incarnate Son, Christians are urged to "clothe yourselves with compassion" (Col. 3:12; 1 Pet. 3:8; 1 John 3:17). Thus compassion may be described as a particular expression of genuine love which both feels the agony of another and enters into that agony in order to help.

To say this does not imply that compassion is an impossible virtue for non-Christians to reflect. Since all are made in God's image, all are capable of expressing to some degree this God-like virtue. However, the true character of compassion is only possible when a human being is assisted by the indwelling Holy Spirit in imitation of the Lord Jesus. Within any Christian community compassion ought to be present in terms of the depth of mutual care and concern which believers have one for another. The fact that Paul commanded "Clothe yourselves with compassion," suggests that Christians have consciously to pray and work to express this virtue.

Compassion for those who are both without God's salvation and also in one or another form of real human need ought to flow from the Christian community and from each individual believer as part of that general love for the neighbor which Christian faith and commitment require. Thus compassion ought to produce both caring evangelism and relief of human need (for example, in famines, disasters, and catastrophes as well as in specific individual cases).

P.T.

**COMPETITION.** The normally healthy individual's personality is marked by purposiveness, one aspect of which is a goal-identifying activity that has positive fulfillment as a concomitant. Because of genetic, social, and environmental factors, no two individuals are exactly alike in personality drives, even where identical siblings are concerned. When normally healthy people are thus brought together in community, whether it be kindergarten or the business and professional world, the scene is set for competitive activity.

As observed in young children, competition is a necessary and desirable element in personality growth because it stimulates imagination and energy as goals are being pursued. Because competition involves more than one participant, it emerges as an activity in which several members of a group are striving against one another in order to gain superiority. In the process certain character factors such as aggression, drive, persistence, greed, honesty or the lack of it, and selfishness come into play; and unless they are under proper control they can prejudice the outcome.

While the mechanical success of a participant might illustrate one aspect of competition, it does not describe the whole process by any means. Failure to achieve a competitive goal can be an extremely important factor in an individual's learning experience, for when it is taken seriously as part of the developmental process it enables the person concerned to undertake a critical evaluation of his or her performance in the light of others' achievements. On the negative side there are certain cultures where failure to succeed in competition besmirches personal, family, or company honor; and this sometimes results in suicide.

A great deal of competition in life is entered into by people who are not fully in touch with reality, either because of personality deficits or as a consequence of inadequate training and experience. Under such conditions competitive failure will force some re-examination of motivation and of native ability for the task. If competition demonstrates to individuals the nature and extent of their limitations and suggests that for the sake of mental health they should learn to live well within those limitations, an extremely important function will have been served by the experience. The result could well be identified in the words of an old American proverb: "If at first you don't succeed, try something easier."

Competition is the essence of the capitalistic world of economics; and where competition is stifled or prohibited, as in the classical Marxist economies, social life begins to stagnate because individual initiative has been thwarted by the political system. To maintain proper economic balance there must always be independent groups of vendors and purchasers. Where one group gains a monopoly, whether it involves the pricing or supplying of commodities, a state of economic competition no longer exists. Western democracies have enacted antitrust legislation in order to control business monopolies in the interests of a balanced economy.

Because competition is so deeply rooted in human character, the Christian will need to be aware of the weakness of mankind's inherited nature in terms of dishonesty, selfishness, greed, and the like. The Old Testament prescribed fair business practices (Deut. 25:15; Prov. 11:1), and these have long since been adopted by Western societies. At its highest level, competition needs to be leavened by consideration for one's neighbor in the light of God's law of love (cf. Rom. 13:10), and then it is a beneficial instrument of human society.

**COMPUTER ETHICS.** The computer revolution has been spectacular and swift. The first electronic digital computer weighed 30 tons, contained 18,000 vacuum tubes, gobbled 140,000 watts of electricity, and cost $847,000. Less than forty years later, many hand-held calculators have comparable computing power for a few dollars.

But the rapid development and proliferation of computing power has also raised some significant ethical questions. As a society we need to think clearly about these issues, but we often ignore them or become confused. Somehow people's ethical discernment becomes blurred when computers are involved.

It is often helpful to realize that computer fraud is merely a new field with old problems. Computer crimes are often nothing more than fraud, larceny, and embezzlement carried out by more sophisticated means. They usually involve changing addresses, records, or files. In short, they are old-fashioned crimes using high technology.

One set of ethical concerns arises from the centralization of information. Governmental agencies, banks, and businesses use their computers to collect information on its citizens and customers. There is nothing inherently wrong with that, if it can be kept confidential and is not used for immoral actions. Unfortunately, this is sometimes difficult to guarantee.

In an information-based society, the centralization of information can be as dangerous as the centralization of power. Given sinful man (Rom. 3:23) in a fallen world (Gen. 3), we should be concerned about the collection and manipulation of information. When Hitler's Gestapo began rounding up millions of Jews, information about their religious affiliation was stored in shoe boxes. U. S. Census Bureau punch cards were used at the beginning of World War II to round up Japanese-Americans living on the West Coast. Modern technology would make this task much easier. Governmental agencies routinely collect information about ethnic origin, race, religion, gross income, and even political preference.

Moreover, the problem is not limited to just governmental agencies. Many banking systems, for example, utilize electronic funds transfer systems. The current plans to link these systems together into a national system could also provide a means of tracking the actions of citizens. A centralized banking network could fulfill nearly every information-need a malevolent dictator might have.

A related problem arises from the confidentiality of computer records. Computer records can be abused like any other system. Reputations built up over a lifetime can be ruined by computer errors, and often there is little recourse for the victim. In 1974, the U. S. Congress passed the Privacy Act which allows citizens to find out what records federal bureaucracies have on them and correct errors. But much more is needed than this particular act.

In the recent past, most of that information was centralized and required the expertise of the "high priests of FORTRAN" to utilize it. Now more people have access to information due to increasing numbers of personal computers. This will have many interesting sociological ramifications, but it is also creating a set of troubling ethical questions. The proliferation of computers which can tie into other computers provides more opportunities for computerized crime.

The news media have reported numerous instances in which computer "hackers" have been able to gain access to confidential (and supposedly secure) computer systems and obtain or interfere with the data banks. Fortunately, most cases involved only curious teenagers, but it is likely that this may be a developing area of crime. Criminals use computer access to forge documents, change records, and draft checks. They could use computers for blackmail by holding files for ransom and threaten to destroy them if their demands are not met. Unless better methods of security are found, professional criminals will begin to crack computer security codes and gain quick access into sensitive files.

As with most technological breakthroughs, engineers have outrun lawmakers. Computer deployment has created a number of legal questions. First, there is the problem of establishing penalties for computer crime. Typically, intellectual property has a different status in our criminal justice system. Perhaps we need to evaluate the notion that ideas and information need not be protected in the same way as property. Legislators need to enact computer information protection laws which will deter criminals, or even curious computer "hackers," from breaking into confidential records.

A second legal problem arises from the question of jurisdiction. Telecommunication allows information to be shared across state and even international borders. There are few federal statutes governing this area, and less than half of the states have laws dealing with information abuse. Enforcement will also be a problem because of the previously stated problem of jurisdiction, because police departments rarely train their personnel in the area of computer abuse and fraud, and because of lack of personnel. Computers are almost as ubiquitous as telephones or photocopiers.

Computer fraud raises questions about the role of insurance companies as well. How does one insure an electronic asset? What value does computer information have? These are questions that will have to be addressed in the future.

At present there are no definitive essays or books which set forth a biblical perspective on computer ethics. But a few principles could provide a beginning foundation. The first principle is that one should never do with computers that which one would consider immoral without them. An act is not justified because a computer had made it easier to achieve. If it is immoral for someone to rummage though another person's desk, then it is equally unethical for them to search another's computer files. If it is illegal to violate copyright law and photocopy a book, then it is equally wrong to copy a disk of computer software.

A second principle is that information should be treated as something that has value. People who use computers to obtain unauthorized information often do not realize that what they are doing is wrong. Since information is not a tangible object and can be shared, it does not seem to be stealing, since it does not deprive anyone of anything. Yet in an information-based society, we must not forget that information is a valuable asset. Stealing information should carry legal penalties similar to those for stealing tangible objects.

A third principle is that computers are merely a tool to be used, not a technology to be worshiped. God's mandate to us is to use technology wisely within His creation (Gen. 1:28). Many commentators express concern that within an information society, we may be tempted to replace ethics with statistics.

Massive banks of computer data already exert a powerful influence on public policy. Christians must resist society's tendency to undermine the moral basis of right and wrong with facts and figures. Unfortunately, there is growing evidence that the computer revolution has been a contributing factor in the change from a moral foundation to a statistical one. The adoption of consensus ethics (51 percent) makes it right and the overuse of cost-benefit analysis (modernized form of utilitarianism) give evidence of this shift.

Christians, therefore, must work to prevent our world from being conformed to the computer but instead must transform our society with Christian values (Rom. 12:1-2).

J.K.A.

**CONCUBINAGE.** In the ancient world concubinage was a social system whereby a man could take another woman for purposes of procreating a family if his wife proved to be infertile over a period of time. This procedure was not infrequently provided for in Babylonian marriage contracts and illustrates the behavior of Abram when Sarai, his legal wife, was unable to bear him children (Gen. 16:1-3). The concubine was regarded as a member of the family, and under Mesopotamian law her expulsion was forbidden. This accounts for Abram's anxiety as he yielded to pressure from Sarai to expel Hagar and her son (Gen. 21:10-11). The concubine was therefore not a harlot, but a member of the family who was at the disposal of the patriarch for purposes of procreation. She had no status as a legal wife, however, and when her children were born they were delivered symbolically on the legal wife's knees to afford them proper legitimacy.

In modern usage concubinage describes a sexual relationship between a male and a female which has not been characterized by either a civil or ecclesiastical marriage. Common-law relationships are considered by ethicists to fall into this general category of concubinage. They have no legal standing in most Western countries; and the relationship, which is based predominantly upon carnal desire, does not afford either party proper security. Monogamy is the biblical ideal for sexual activity and the procreation of children (Gen. 2:24), and any deviation from that norm defies God's plan for order and general stability in human society.

See COMMON-LAW MARRIAGE; POLYGAMY.

**CONCUPISCENCE.** This archaic term, occurring in Elizabethan English to translate the New Testament Greek word *epithumia* (Rom. 7:7; Col. 3:5), came into the language through the Latin verb *cupio*, "desire." While in New Testament usage the word carries the sinister connotation of sexual passions, desire (Rom. 1:24; 1 Thess. 4:5), or uncontrolled lust (1 Pet. 2:11), it is also amenable to a more neutral interpretation in terms of normal desires, whether for food, companionship (Luke 22:15), or the things of this world in general. Because desire is almost always selfish, the Christian has to submit this part of his or her personality to the will of Christ. Where concupiscence is of a specifically sexual character, it is possible to commit fornication or adultery in the mind alone (Matt. 5:28), and thus sin against God. If concupiscence takes the form of greed for the things of this world, it displaces the sole lordship of Christ over the believer's life and thoughts. Unless the desire being entertained is in strict accord with the will of God for the individual Christian, it is sin and must be avoided accordingly.

**CONFESSION.** The meaning of confession is rooted in the spiritual life of God's people in both testaments. There are three foci: worshiping, praising, and blessing God (Ps. 89:1-3); declaring faith in God and Christ (Matt. 16:16; John 1:34; Rom. 10:9; Phil. 2:11; 1 John 4:15); and acknowledging sin and guilt as the mark of repentance toward God and man (Lev. 26:40-42; Neh. 9:1-3; Pss. 32; 51; Acts 2:37-38). It is in this latter sense that John the Baptist called people to repentance (Matt. 3:1-6), that men and women everywhere are invited to turn to God in Christ, and that Christians confess their sins to God and to one another.

Auricular confession, which means "to the ear" (of the priest), as practiced in the Roman Catholic Church since the late Middle Ages, evolved from various forms of priestly and lay confessional traditions. Its danger lies in the communicant's forming the perception that he is confessing to the priest rather than directly to God, which perception may be reinforced by the priest's words "I absolve thee." (The earlier form of absolution was "May the Lord absolve thee.")

Some Reformation churches did not totally abandon the practice of auricular confession to a priest; but their emphasis changed dramatically to general congregational confession and absolution, along with encouragement to be reconciled to one another and to make restitution wherever possible. The danger in this is that confession may be practiced in a general, formal manner, without becoming deeply personal.

Smaller or larger group confession runs the risk of inciting recurrent hysteria, of encouraging the ceaseless raking over of feelings of guilt and inadequacy, and of catering to the prurient interests of hearers.

Each of the many forms of confessions may be helpful if practiced in an uncorrupted way and with careful attention to the biblical truths relating to Christ's atonement and the nature of forgiveness and reconciliation.

The validity of confession rests on the premise that men and women are morally answerable to God and to one another, that they are responsible to one another as neighbors, and that reconciliation between man and God and man and man is God's redemptive purpose. At bottom, confession rests on the truth that forgiveness is possible and that confession and forgiveness permanently remove the stain of sin.

Confession and forgiveness are essential to the moral integrity of the soul, to the emotional health of the whole person, and to the well-being of the church as the household of faith. This is especially true for those who believe that they have committed the unpardonable sin (though often this is not understood in its biblical sense). Recognition of one's guilt is the first step to healing;

confession and reconciliation to God and to others is the second.

Sin isolates and creates mistrust. Repentance, confession, and forgiveness create the environment of love where persons can be whole (1 John 1:9-10).

**Bibliography:** Baillie, J., *A Diary of Private Prayer*; Mowrer, O. H., *The Crisis in Psychology and Religion* (1961); Stott, J., *Confess Your Sins* (1964).

S.J.M.

**CONFLICT OF INTEREST AND DUTIES.** This predicament arises when a person is confronted with the prospect of performing two ethically irreconcilable activities. Such a conflict would arise, for example, if a dedicated peace activist who also had a great respect for private property. were required, as part of a "peace" demonstration, to burn down or blow up a building as evidence of his or her commitment to the "cause." Similarly, a lawyer who attempted to represent both sides in a lawsuit would experience a conflict of interests. A fairly common occurrence for the Christian is one in which a believer is asked to "tell a white lie," or to conceal or misrepresent data so as to save a friend from serious consequences. There is obviously a conflict between the obligation not to bear false witness (Exod. 20:16) and the desire to rescue the friend from his or her predicament.

Scripture does not legislate for such situations in detail, but instead offers ethical standards such as love, justice, and mercy (Mic. 6:8; Matt. 23:23) by which the believer is to be guided. Christ's words "no man can serve two masters" have an important bearing upon conflict of interests and duties. Where conflict appears to arise, the Christian will choose, as the Lord leads, to do whatever serves the highest interests of revealed spiritual truth and justice. Business persons and politicians, who are particularly vulnerable to such conflicts, must make strenuous efforts to prevent personal gain from conflicting with the responsibilities of office. This can be accomplished most readily by avoiding those situations which give promise of conflict. Many jurisdictions have regulations designed to provide guidance in cases where there might be some conflict of interest or duty.

**CONFORMITY.** A state of conformity exists when the ideals or actions cherished by an individual or group are made to harmonize or correspond with those of another body, whether larger or smaller. There need not be complete and detailed identification of ideals for conformity to exist, and a general acceptance of the principles or modes of action *ex animo* normally preserves the integrity of conformity while allowing for legitimate minor variations.

Ethicists generally view conformity from two aspects. External conformity merely involves correspondence or coincidence in outward behavior only, whereas internal conformity focuses more upon the ideals, customs, beliefs, and general values which are normally the principal concern of *ex animo* acceptance. Too rigid an application of the concept of conformity can stifle individuality and incentive and perhaps even bring ultimate disvalue into the larger community which is being governed by the idea of conformity.

In British Christianity the sixteenth century saw persistent efforts on the part of Church of England authorities to enforce conformity to Anglican liturgy and precepts upon Roman Catholics, Anabaptists, Presbyterians, and others. Those who refused to enter into such a relationship were described as "nonconformists" and were persecuted in various ways. Even in the nineteenth century, persons who refused to conform to Anglican liturgical and doctrinal tenets were denied admission to the universities of Oxford and Cambridge.

In an insecure modern society, where any deviation from the generally accepted norm poses an enormous threat to many people, conformity to the mores of one's peer group is a matter of great importance. Only the strong-willed, the unconventional, and the individualist are able to examine conformity critically and reject those aspects of it that they find erroneous or reprehensible. The Christian is urged not to be conformed to the ideals and ethos of this world, but to be transformed by spiritual renewal (Rom. 2:3; 12:2), so as to conform to the image of Christ (Rom. 8:20). Conformity to social, religious, or political ideals or practices need not be a particular problem for the Christian, provided that he or she is required only to conform in those matters that are lawful and honest.

**CONSCIENCE.** The voice of conscience is something that all persons experience, but explanations of the conscience vary enormously. For some it is a sixth sense; for others it is the voice of reason or of desire. In his famous treatment of the matter Bishop Joseph Butler (1692-1752) claimed that conscience provided a distinctive motive for action, different from both passion and self-love. The universality of conscience has led some to argue that it is part of the natural law, even that it is the voice of God. Although there is some biblical support for such a view (Rom. 2), this must be carefully qualified by the Bible's recognition of the diversity of the moral verdicts given by the conscience. Although the conscience may, along with other factors, provide an individual with some inkling of the divine law, this is both perverted and suppressed by him, though not to such an extent that he is freed from all responsibility to keep it. So conscience, to be the voice of God, needs informing both from Scripture and from experience. Conscience does not therefore merely record and express emotional or other responses to moral situations; it may be changed through reasoning about facts and principles.

The term *suneidesis*, "conscience" in the writings of Paul (Rom. 2:15; 1 Cor: 8:7, 10, 12), has origins in paganism, where it meant the experience of remorse for bad actions. But Paul recast this to include the ability to direct or justify moral conduct (Rom. 2:15; 2 Cor. 1:12). Though the word is unique to him in the New Testament, essentially the same concept can be found in references to the heart both in the New and Old Testaments (for example, Ps. 19:2; Prov. 12:18; Mark 16:14; Heb. 4:12). The heart or conscience is part of the *imago dei*, part of man's natural make-up. Thus it is foreign to Scripture to suppose that the conscience is the product of certain circumstances such as a strict upbringing as a child, or of some psychological deficiency.

Although the conscience as such is not the product of such factors, and Scripture insists that it is wrong to make a person act against his or her conscience (1 Cor. 8:7), it also recognizes the possibility of a "weak conscience" (1 Cor. 8:10). A weak conscience is not properly informed and regards as being morally right what God's laws condemns, or morally wrong what God's law allows or commands. Superstitious or licentious consciences each are weak. Further, while an informed conscience plays a critical role in the conviction of sin (and is, thus, an experience of the wrath of God, as the dialectical theology of Karl Barth stresses), the New Testament also refers to a clear conscience, "void of offence" (Acts 24:10).

In both Roman Catholic and orthodox Protestant moral theology, conscience has been held to function through the discernment of general rules and their application to particular circumstances, the "practical syllogism." For example, smugglers ought to be punished (principle); Hornblower is a smuggler (particular fact), therefore Hornblower ought to be punished (moral judgment). The practice of casuistry that grew up in the medieval church classified sins with various penances but resulted in dulling the conscience. Luther's agony was that of a conscience suddenly sharpened by the Word of God. The casuistry that developed in Protestantism associated with such names as William Ames (1576-1633) and Richard Baxter (1615-1691) attempted to work this Reformation principle out in great detail using much of the formal framework of pre-Reformation moral theology. In the Roman Catholic Church of the Counter-Reformation, casuistry again became luxuriant and notorious, prominence being given to the principle that the end justifies the means. These practices were mercilessly exposed by Blaise Pascal (1623-1662) in his *Provincial Letters* (1657) to such effect that "casuistry" and "Jesuitry" have since that time become synonymous with moral trickery.

The assertion of the freedom of the individual conscience at the time of the Reformation inevitably led to claims for freedom to act in accordance with one's conscience, initially in worship and later in a greater range of matters. This resulted in the religious and cultural "pluralism" that is characteristic of modern Western democracies. There clearly must be political limits to allowing the freedom of conscience to express itself, though such a definition is a matter of continuing debate.

**Bibliography:** Baxter, R., *The Christian Dictionary*, (1673); Butler, J., *Fifteen Sermons*, (1726); Pierce, C. A., *Conscience in the New Testament* (1955); Raphael, D. D., *The Moral Sense, (1947)*.

P.H.

**CONSCIENTIOUS OBJECTION.** A conscientious objector is a person, Christian or non-Christian, who refuses to go to war because he or she believes that killing is wrong. Christians who object to military service as a matter of conscience usually do so on grounds of a no-exception interpretation of the sixth commandment ("Thou shalt not kill") and an interpretation of the teachings of Jesus which applies principles of peace and nonresistance to every human situation without exception (Matt. 5:9).

It is important to note that where conscientious objection is legally accepted it is done solely on moral or religious grounds or both, but not on political grounds. The conscientious objector refuses military service because he or she believes war and killing to be wrong on moral and religious grounds, not because he or she objects to the political policies of the government. Governments have been reluctant to grant conscientious-objector status on political grounds. Conscientious objection is a public policy issue primarily when universal conscription for military service is in force.

Historically, conscientious objectors have been severely punished and abused. This included beatings, torture, imprisonment, confiscation of property and even execution in Western countries up to the twentieth century. Such treatment was most severe under totalitarian regimes. Sometimes conscientious objection (or refusing to swear an oath in a court of law) was used as an excuse to practice religious persecution. The widespread persecution of minority evangelical groups such as Nazarenes in some European countries earlier in this century is a case in point.

Western democratic societies have gradually relaxed laws and provided legal exemption from combat duty for conscientious objectors. In many cases alternative or noncombat service is required in lieu of combat duty. In most cases concession against military service is granted on religious grounds. Recently, especially during the Vietnam War, conscientious objection on purely moral grounds has increased. Granting conscientious-objector status and exemption on other than grounds of conscience has proved to be a thorny issue. In England, very often a corroborating statement made to a clergyman has been required. Until suspension of the draft in the United States, a legal declaration by the individual usually made before a tribunal was accepted.

Interpretation of conscientious objection varies. Some pacifists regard conscientious objection as a narrow category of a broader and more desirable conviction, namely, nonresistance as a lifestyle. Some are selective conscientious objectors: they will fight in some wars but not in others. Some will engage in noncombat military service; others will not. Some countries, such as Britain, have allowed for substitute nonmilitary social service at home or abroad during the prescribed period of conscripted service. The cyclical nature of attitudes is instructive. During peacetime conscription the percentage of conscientious objectors tends to rise; during wartime the percentage falls. For example, in the United States during World War II, less than half of conscripted Mennonites chose alternative service, while in the 1950s this figure rose to over 80 percent.

While the majority of the population, including Christians, reject conscientious objection in a democratic society which is committed to justice, allowance for it is still made in democratic societies. Vigorous criticism has been leveled against conscientious-objection practices in the past. These practices include payment of commutation fees by conscientious objectors, which were sometimes bribes to escape military service. On occasions the money was used by the state to finance war. Another practice found by critics to be objectionable was the recruiting and paying of a substitute to serve in place of the conscientious objector. This practice is regarded by critics as solicitation or hiring of a mercenary.

Other criticisms are directed at the theological, moral, and social arguments of conscientious objectors. The state is divinely sanctioned, as Christian conscientious objectors usually agree, in Scriptures such as Romans 13:1-7 and 1 Peter 2:13-17, and it has the right and obligation to punish evildoers. It is argued therefore that Christians have the moral obligation to honor justice by participating in the punishment of wrongdoers. Others insist that a distinction must be drawn between the ideals of personal ethics among Christians and the realities of life in an evil-infected world. It is wrong to interpret John 17:16 in such a way as to excuse Christians from citizenship and societal duties, which are seen to be moral obligations just as the quality of Christian interpersonal relations is a moral responsibility. While just punishment is an evil to the evildoer who is being punished, because it is just it is not an absolute evil. The forcible restraint of evil is necessary, and is morally incumbent upon Christians as well as upon the state. Hence the Christian cannot be excused from any and all acts of justice. Morally, the Christian cannot enjoy the benefits of a just society and at the same time disown responsibility for maintaining justice. Advocates of pacifism are accused of one-sidedly emphasizing social and economic justice and of failing to uphold retributive justice. They are also charged with overplaying the importance of physical violence while missing the psychological violence which characterizes human relations generally, even in utopian groups.

In the United States and Canada the current establishment of the military as volunteer forces has greatly lessened the tensions created by conscription and conscientious objection.

**Bibliography:** Eidsmoe, J., *God and Caesar* (1984); Hormus, J.M., *It Is Not Lawful for Me to Fight* (1980); Kaufman, D. D., *The Tax Dilemma: Praying for Peace, Paying for War* (1978); Niebanck, R. J., *Conscience, War and the Selective Objector* (1968).

S.J.M.

**CONSENT.** In general usage the term *consent* implies concurrence in or support for some course of action or a proposal that will lead to such a situation. Ethicists normally consider consent to have been based upon a careful assessment of all the factors involved, and therefore it is a more complex act of volition than the giving of permission, which need not involve a great deal of reflection. Consent need not be fully *ex animo* in nature, for there are many occasions where consent is given only partially or with some reservations. Where psychological or other duress is applied to secure assent to some scheme, such approbation cannot be considered consent legally, since it did not partake of the nature of voluntary acquiescence. What is known in law as the age of consent describes a stage of human existence at which approval, especially for sexual seduction, is able to be given implicitly or explicitly as a voluntary act. But in this, as in so many other instances, it is not always easy to differentiate between permission as an expedient for extricating oneself from a difficult situation and the kind of overall agreement that characterizes consent.

All of this is obviously very important for the contractual issues that arise from human relationships. In areas of government it is often very difficult for an individual to consent to policies or proposed courses of action to which conscientious objection can be made to some degree. Consent in marriage, which ought emphatically to be wholehearted, is sometimes marked by the kind of devious reservations that become obvious in subsequent divorce proceedings. Doctors, lawyers, and clergy also find themselves consenting on occasions to policies or programs to which they cannot give full emotional assent. This situation raises its own ethical problems.

In a fallen world, few sets of circumstances can be such as to receive unquestioning and unanimous support from participants. In cases of doubt, the Christian will pray for guidance from the Holy Spirit and will seek to apply the moral principles of honesty, integrity, and truth before making an informed decision. As a result, it may well be that consent will prove impossible, in which eventuality an agreement to differ would probably constitute a legitimate conclusion to the matter in question.

**CONTENTMENT.** This word is commonly defined in terms of general satisfaction with one's estate or condition in life which produces a pleasing, or at the least an easy, tranquil state of existence. In the Old Testament the ideal of contentment was expressed by the concept of "every man under his vine and under his fig tree" (1 Kings 4:25), secure and free from external threats of destruction. But it was a false sense of security that brought defeat upon the relaxed citizens of Laish by the tribe of Dan (Judg. 18:27), which suggests that successful contentment should always be marked by a certain dynamic quality.

While Paul had professedly learned contentment (Phil. 4:11), namely self-sufficieny in Christ, this did not prevent him from witnessing vigorously to the gospel of Christ. Godliness with contentment is described as "great gain" (1 Tim. 6:6, KJV) in that it indicates a life rooted in Christ that is untainted by greed for financial gain. Contentment comes from complete trust in the ability of our heavenly Father to provide for our necessities (Matt. 6:25-34), as distinct from our desires or wants. This is one of the graces of a truly Christian character. But because the latter must be in a constant state of development, there can never come a time when the believer will be content with contentment. In its highest form it will constitute one by-product of a life lived in the faith and power of Christ, rather than being the object or goal of human striving.

**CONTINENCE.** The basic meaning of *continence* is control in relation to the body or the emotions. In the most obvious physical sense, continence is used in a medical sense to describe the control exercised by the autonomic (parasympathetic) nervous system over the bladder and bowels. A much older use, however, had to do with sexual functions, in which continence came to be equated with chastity. In the Old Testament, continence was enjoined upon the Israelites periodically, as with the giving of the Law upon Mount Sinai (Exod. 19:15), or when their armies were involved in fighting a war (2 Sam. 11:11).

Continence may have been a way of life for those who were eunuchs for the sake of the kingdom (Matt. 19:12), but a more tolerable regime of abstention was recommended by Paul as part of spiritual growth within marriage (1 Cor. 7:5). Continence was even recommended by Paul as a worthy substitute for marriage for those intending to serve the Lord without being unduly distracted by the by the implications of matrimony. Continence was not elevated above sexuality by this suggestion, however, but was merely advanced as

an alternative way of life that was open to the believer.

A departure from biblical teaching occurred in the medieval period, when under monastic influences continence was elevated to improper heights, being regarded as more virtuous than sexual relations. The imposition by the Roman Catholic Church of celibacy upon its clergy and religious orders has perpetuated this distorted view of continence.

Scripture teaches that outside the marriage relationship continent behavior is mandatory for the Christian, and that within marriage chastity must be practiced. This latter may include continence of one degree or another by mutual consent.

See CHASTITY; MARRIAGE; SEX.

**CONTRACEPTION.** Modern concepts of "birth control" have gained considerable social acceptance because of the movement started by Margaret Sanger early in the 20th century. Its goals advocated that "procreation of the diseased, the feeble-minded, and the poor be stopped." Today that movement exits as "family planning," formally represented by the international organization of Planned Parenthood, whose agenda is anti-Christian, anti-family, and pro-abortion.

By contrast, God's direction for His people in Scripture is clear. He is intimately involved with the formation of unborn children (Ps. 139:13-16). "Children are a gift of the Lord" and a "reward"; "a full quiver" of them is a "blessing" (Ps. 127:3-5). God plans the lives of people even before they are born (Jer. 1:5). Even salvation is "for you and your children" (Acts 2:39).

Thus God expects and will bless families with children. *The modern couple who is physically able to have children has no biblical justification to choose to be childless.* To "be fruitful and multiply" (Gen. 1:28) is directed not only at Christians but also to non-Christians, since it was given before the Fall (Gen. 3) and after the Flood (Gen. 9:1).

With this background, *stewardship of procreation* (birth control) *is neither endorsed nor prohibited by Scripture.* Man's responsibility is not just to let "nature take its course," but consciously to order his life toward the fulfillment of the divine plan. Thus, the number of children that a couple has and the timing of their birth is permissible, *as long as other biblical principles are not violated.* Given the fact that 2.2 children per couple are necessary to maintain the current world population (ZPG or Zero Population Growth), more than two children per family seems a reasonable goal, especially since twenty percent of married couples are physically unable to have children.

Some circumstances seem to allow for timing of birth. A child too early in one's marriage may not be wise (Deut. 24:5). Successive pregnancies may be too hard on some women with physical problems. Family income may be believed insufficient to provide for many children. (However, most estimates of resources needed for raising children are greatly exaggerated). Completion of higher education requirements seems a sufficient reason for a *short* postponement of children. Inherited genetic diseases *may be* a reason not to have children, but medical and spiritual counseling is necessary because this area is complicated.

However, this control cannot be argued to extend to unmarried women and men. Fornication and adultery are condemned by God (Exod. 20:14; 1 Cor. 6:15-20). The use of birth control to prevent one consequence of these sins is not ethically acceptable (Rom. 3:8).

*Birth control methods.* Birth control methods generally fall into two types: those that prevent fertilization of the egg (conception) and those that prevent implantation of the fertilized egg into the uterus (abortifacient). Since individual human life begins at conception (Gen. 4:1; Ps. 51:5; Matt. 1:20), abortifacients are not an ethical choice. These methods include surgical abortion by various means and at various stages of fetal development, the intrauterine contraceptive device (IUD), the "mini pill" (containing a progestin only), subcutaneous injection of estrogens and progestins, the "morning after" pill (a high dose of estrogen or progestin), and the new French abortifacient, RU-486.

*Coitus interruptus* is the oldest form of contraception. Onan's punishment for this act was for his failure to fulfill his levirate obligation, not the act itself (Gen. 38:8-9). Thus, *coitus interruptus* is morally acceptable but practically not reliable as it requires considerable discipline for the man.

The rhythm method is the only form of birth control acceptable to Roman Catholic teaching but also common to Protestants. With some modern adaptations such as temperature monitoring and testing of vaginal mucous, its effectiveness increases. The periodic abstinence required by the method is itself endorsed by the apostle Paul when practiced *by mutual consent* (1 Cor. 7:5).

Other morally acceptable forms of birth control include the use of condoms, diaphragms, cervical caps, and spermicides (foams and jellies). Only minor problems (proper fitting and irritation) are associated with these methods, but their ability to prevent conception is limited by the efficacy of the methods themselves and their practical implementation before and during sexual passion. Breast feeding has a feedback mechanism that can prevent ovulation, but as a single form of birth control, it may be the least reliable.

The most effective and most controversial form of birth control among Christians today is the birth control pill (oral contraceptives). Generally, they contain both an estrogen and a progestin. Their primary method of action is to prevent ovulation. Secondary actions include the prevention of sperm moving to an egg (if ovulation does occur) and alteration of the lining of the uterus to prevent implantation (if ovulation and fertilization occurs). While much has been made of potential side effects of "the pill," women who do not smoke and are under 35 years of age appear at little risk of serious side effects. The pill even has positive effects to prevent ovarian cancer, benign breast disease, and ectopic pregnancy.

The controversy rages over the question, "Are oral contraceptives abortifacients?" If ovulation does occur in women using oral contraceptives, it is rare (in the range of 1 in 250 cycles). The likelihood that sperm can survive the hostile uterine and tubal environment created by the hormonal effects to reach the egg is remote.

However, millions of women on the pill make for a large number of potential abortions (non-implantation), despite the rarity. If only 1 in 1000 cycles results in conception, but 10 million women have 130 million cycles (28 days) each year, 130 abortions will result. A consistent pro-life position (individual human life begins at conception) would appear to reject this position.

In the final analysis, the almost 100-percent efficacy of the birth control pill must be weighed against the *potential* (not proven) for abortion of a fertilized egg. If pregnancy must be absolutely prevented and sterilization is not an option, then birth control pills are morally acceptable. If, however, pregnancy needs only to be *statistically* delayed (the vast majority of cases), then methods other than oral contraceptives ought to be chosen.

The last two forms of birth control involve surgery: tubal ligation and vasectomy. While many of these procedures can be reversed with the microsurgical techniques available today, a decision for one or the other should only be made with the serious intention to renounce future pregnancies. Whether tubal ligation or vasectomy is chosen involves many factors that can be made only within the context of individual marriages.

**Bibliography:** Davis, J. J., *Evangelical Ethics* (1985); Payne, F., *Making Biblical Decisions* (1989); Provan, C., *The Bible and Birth Control* (1989).

See ABORTION; HUMANE VITAE; POPULATION CONTROL; PROCREATION; STERILIZATION.

F.E.P.

**CONTRACTS.** A contract is an agreement between two or more parties which is legally binding and creates legal relationships between those parties. Common examples are sale, employment, and construction contracts. Different legal systems have rules which differ in some considerable detail as to the requirements for validity of contracts in general or of certain kinds of contracts. These rules cover such issues as the proper parties to a contract, the formalities (if any) which are required, the terms usually applied to particular contracts and how intention to create legal relations is established. Some legal systems recognize the legal effect of promises, that is, unilateral voluntary obligations as well as contracts. Others restrict legal obligation to bilateral or multilateral arrangements, thus making agreement of the essence of legal obligation. Particularly in the Anglo-American or common-law legal systems this feature of agreement is established by an analysis of offers and acceptances of contractual terms. A key feature of the Anglo-American approach is also the need for consideration to effect legal validity, that is, there must be some payment or equivalent (however formal) involved in the arrangement. Civilian legal systems, that is, those deriving from the law of ancient Rome, do not usually make consideration an essential feature of contracts.

In the nineteenth century the development of industry and commerce in the Western world brought about an increase in the legal importance of contract. Furthermore, such developments were also connected to a free market approach to the economy, de-emphasizing legal regulation by the state, commonly called *laissez-faire*. An important aspect of this general approach was to give great importance to two legal ideas called sanctity of contract and freedom of contract. These emphasized that parties should be free to make whatever agreement they wished, and once made it should be legally enforced. Certain qualifications were recognized, but these were seen as being as limited as possible. In most modern legal systems there has been an increasing tendency to limit the freedom of contract by increasing legal controls over contracts. This whole process has considerable ethical implications.

The traditional qualifications which existed even in the heyday of freedom of contract related to such matters as the parties to the contract and its terms. There were protections for contracting parties under full age or lacking in full mental ability. Similarly contracts could be vitiated by such factors as duress, drunkenness, or fraud. Likewise contracts whose whole purpose was immoral or illegal or contrary to the basic policies of the legal system were denied legal effect. These exceptions tended to be strictly interpreted, and an agreement between parties of full age and capacity was generally enforced in the terms in which it was made, however unfair to one party it may have seemed.

The new approach to contract has been to recognize that freedom of contract can be a formal and one-sided freedom and to accept that contracts are often made in a situation of unequal bargaining power between the parties. This applies particularly in contracts of employment as between employer and employee and in many consumer contracts, for example, sale, hire, and hire-purchase, as between the supplier and the consumer. Different legal techniques have been applied in different legal systems to prevent the abuse of bargaining power where the stronger party imposes a one-sided contract on the other. Most modern economies have legislation restrict-ing the growth and operations of monopolies, for example, the antitrust legislation of the United States of America such as the Sherman Act and Clayton Act. Some legal systems have developed the concept of duress to include not only the pressure of physical force and fear or actual fraud but also overwhelming economic pressure or a disparity in economic power of a threatening character and have refused legal validity to contracts made in these circumstances. Another approach has been to allow the courts power to reopen certain contracts and regulate the rights of parties rather than merely enforcing agreed terms. Yet another technique is to impose a standard set of contractual terms by law and allow at most minimal deviation from them. Certain contractual clauses can be forbidden, especially those excluding rights otherwise conferred by the general law, or the courts can be given a general power to prevent reliance or such exclusion clauses if they are seen as unconscionable or not fair and reasonable. Sometimes a so-called cooling off period is allowed whereby, for example, a consumer can withdraw from a contract he has entered into without any penalty. These various approaches have been followed particularly with regard to the so-called standard form or adhesion contract, where the contractual terms are imposed on one party and not truly agreed by both. Such clauses are essential in modern business.

It is submitted that the principle of sanctity of contract is ethically acceptable, but that certain restrictions upon it to prevent its abuse are also ethically demanded, and the general modern approach of recognizing the reality of a lack of true freedom of contract is to be commended. Abridging formal contractual freedom creates conditions for true contractual freedom to operate. The law has a necessary function in establishing fair contractual terms in common, everyday transactions.

A.J.G.

**CONVENTIONAL MORALITY.** Conventional morality is that set of patterns of behavior and of attitudes that are presumed by society as being what ought to be done, that are largely done, and that become the basis of legitimate expectations. Within society there may be groups of subcultures having their own (stricter or laxer) conventional moralities, for example, the armed forces or legislative assemblies. Often what is regarded as conventional morality embraces only a part of what is truly of moral importance and regards as included in morality what in fact is not. Thus, conventional morality may neglect covetousness and overemphasize standards of sexual morality. It may also exaggerate the idea of personal honor and regard as a moral issue what is a mere social convention or a rule of etiquette. The standards of conventional morality may be set or influenced in various ways at different times, for example, by the media, by the churches, or by some influential individual or family.

How conventional morality varies in time, between cultures, or between subgroups within a culture, is a matter for careful empirical research. For even where such apparent differences exist, they may not indicate differences in moral standards so much as different applications of the same moral principle called forth by different sets of circumstances. Although differences over marriage, divorce, and birth control may be said to show the existence of conflicting moral principles, these principles may in fact be attempts to exemplify the same or very similar moral values.

Conventional morality has a more definite sense when it refers to voluntary obligations, as in marriage or in the monastic life. The standards of conduct to which a person commits himself are very different from those which prevail in society at large. Included in this narrower sense of "conventional" are standards of professional care and conduct, for example, in the judiciary and in nursing.

If conventional morality is identical with custom and law, then moral reform of behavior or legislation of that society becomes difficult, if not impossible. For such reform is possible only where law and custom are capable of being assessed critically by moral standards.

To the extent that there is one conventional morality prevailing in some area of society, terms such as "good" and "bad" will have a definite meaning. In such a situation, to describe someone as a good man is to convey something fairly precise about his moral character. The existence of such a moral consensus is frequently said to be threatened by the growth of pluralistic societies in which different subcultures, espousing different sets of moral value, exist uneasily side by side. While such differences are characteristic of many modern Western societies, both their uniqueness and their strength can easily be exaggerated. It could be argued, for example, that the pluralism of the United Kingdom in the twentieth century is no greater than that of seventeenth-century Holland. Although the line between matters of personal and group morality as against those of the society in general may be hard to draw, this "pluralism" reflects difference of personal morality and lifestyle adopted within a *common* legal and political framework.

For some thinkers all morality is a mere matter of convention in that moral rules are constituted solely by tacit or explicit social agreement and do not have any objective status either from reason, nature, or the will of God.

The stance of the Christian church toward conventional morality has been somewhat ambivalent, perhaps echoing the ambivalence of the New Testament itself. On the one hand, the existence of such morality in a fallen and sinful world has been regarded as the gift of God's restraining grace, something to be received with thanksgiving. Such morality, and the respect for law and decency that goes with it, makes life tolerable. It provides a framework within which human culture can exist and somewhat flourish, the family can retain its identity, and the church continue her mission. It is infinitely preferable to the hellish anarchy which would and does result when all divine restraint is lifted.

On the other hand, the Christian church has from time to time stood over against the prevailing morality of the day and has assessed it as critically as Christ did the conventional morality of the Pharisees. The stance of Luther against indulgences and of the Confessing Church against Hitler's Germany are noteworthy instances. The church has asked and must continue to ask whether the standards of conventional morality, her own conventional morality included, are biblical standards; and whether the motives and intentions which give rise to such morality are proper, or whether there are, as there were with the Pharisees of Christ's day, warped moral standards, hypocrisy, and legalism.

**Bibliography:** Kaye, B. N., and Wenham, G. J., (eds.), *Law, Morality and the Bible* (1978).

P.H.

**COPYRIGHT INFRINGEMENT.** Copyright is a legal right to prevent copying. The right is given, either automatically or subject to certain formalities, to the creator of an original "work." The scope of copyright protection varies from country to country; but protected works generally include not only material of aesthetic significance such as poetry, musical compositions, and paintings, but also more mundane creations such as railway timetables, computer programs, and even the design of purely functional objects such as chairs and boxes. Copyright frequently is assigned to a third party such as a publisher in return for a lump sum payment or continuing royalty.

Infringement, or "breach," of copyright occurs when anyone, without prior authorization, uses anything to which the copyright owner has the exclusive right. This usually covers not merely direct reproduction but also the making of an adaptation or translation of a work. Copyright does not, however, create absolute monopolies because protection is only available for the form of expression of ideas and not for ideas themselves.

The reason why copyright infringement has become a contemporary ethical issue is that, for very many people, noncompliance with copyright statutes is considered to be far less serious than disregard for other rights or duties. Indeed, the unathorized photocopying of printed works, the reproduction of copyright recordings, and the manufacture of many protected works probably occurs most often without any thought of the moral significance of these acts. Many Christian individuals, organizations, and churches routinely flout both the spirit and the letter of copyright laws.

As for the ethics of such behavior, a starting

point might be the general undesirability of Christians ignoring legislation enacted by legitimate civil authorities. In his letter to the church in Rome, the apostle Paul placed considerable emphasis on obedience to the state (Rom. 13:1-3). Compliance with the requirements of the law should be motivated not only by fear of punishment but also by conscience (Rom. 13:5). This general obligation to abide by human laws is, of course, qualified by the corresponding duty to render to God what is God's (Matt. 22:21; Mark 12:17; Luke 20:25). Should the two systems of law conflict, God's must prevail, and thus there may be situations in which "civil disobedience" is excusable or perhaps even necessary for the Christian.

Can copyright infringement ever be justified in such terms? If they were to consider seriously the implications of their conduct, Christians would have to choose between three alternative conclusions. As a justification for ignoring copyright laws completely, a person might seek to demonstrate that such laws are in basic ethical conflict with some biblical principle. The second conclusion, which might provide a reason for copyright infringement on a more selective basis, would be that the consequences of a particular application of a copyright law are manifestly unjust. The third option, however, is to conclude that to infringe copyright is to violate another person's rights in an inexcusable manner and that acts of infringement cannot be justified.

Apart from the general presumption that the laws of the state should be obeyed, what biblical principles can be brought to bear on this issue? Copyright is understood in terms of property and is usually classified in law as a form of "intellectual property." Analyzed in such terms, infringement of copyright may be viewed, morally at least, as tantamount to theft.

It need hardly be stated that stealing is condemned in the Bible from the Ten Commandments onward (Exod. 20:15; Matt. 19:18; Rom. 2:21; Eph. 4:28). Yet, mainly because of the intangibility of much of the subject matter it covers, infringement of copyright is in many ways quite unlike theft. In most jurisdictions, for something to be stolen it must be taken without authority from its owner with the intention of permanently depriving that person of it. Copyright can be infringed, however, without anything being physically "taken" and without the owner being deprived of anything tangible at all.

In other respects, payment of copyright royalties is more closely analogous to payment of a worker's wages. Certainly in both cases a person is being compensated for work done and may seek to make a living accordingly. Failure to pay wages was strongly condemned by the Old Testament prophets (Jer. 22:13; Mal. 3:5); and in the New Testament the general principle that a laborer is worthy of his hire is echoed in both the Gospels and Epistles (Luke 10:2; 1 Tim. 5:18). Thus it might be said that a composer or author

has as much right to receive royalties as any other worker has to receive wages or a salary. This analogy also is imperfect, however, as remuneration is normally only paid once in respect of a given task or period of employment. In marked contrast, the right to receive copyright royalties usually continues for many years after the creation of a copyright work; and in most countries it will subsist long after the creator of the work has died.

Yet, whichever theoretical analysis is used, it is unlikely that a convincing argument could be sustained for disregarding the requirements of copyright laws completely. What about the specific ground for noncompliance? It is sometimes claimed, for example, that songs and other musical compositions written by Christians for use in church services should be considered a "gift" from God to be shared by all free of charge. This proposition can be countered in at least two ways.

Firstly, the argument confuses the general creative skill of the writer or composer, which is indeed a gift from God, with the work which is produced by the application of that skill. If the latter can be taken without compensation, then logically a Christian should not expect to be paid for any goods or services provided to another Christian.

Secondly, where Christian songwriters or composers nevertheless feel strongly that certain works are direct gifts from God (and they should perhaps be the judge of that), they can always disclaim copyright and make the work freely available. Alternatively, copyright might be assigned for a token consideration to a church or Christian charitable trust which can then apply any royalty earnings directly for Christian purposes. Both these options are to be preferred to a casual or deliberate disregard for rights clearly established in law.

**Bibliography:** Breyer, 84 *Harvard Law Review* (1970), pp. 281–351; Ladd, D., *Copyright* (1983), pp. 289–300; Law, S. and Lives, E., *Keep Music Legal* (1982); Patterson, P., *Copyright in Historical Perspective* (1968).

See PLAGIARISM.

C.J.M.

**CORPORAL PUNISHMENT.** This expression describes a penalty whereby the offending individual's body (Latin *corpus*) is punished in some manner, normally by beating or flogging. This type of punishment contrasts with the imposition of a fine or a sentence of probation. In its mildest form corporal punishment is very ancient, being a part of ancient Sumerian education. In third millennium B.C. Sumerian schools, a disciplinarian known as the "big brother" kept order and rapped rowdy students with a rod, a form of discipline which found its way into the educational systems of the Levant and Egypt. In the latter country in antiquity, almost any activity in life was accompanied by blows from a whip or a stick and was regarded as a normal part of work. Thus the Hebrews who were made to work on construction projects after the Joseph era ended (Exod. 1:11) were not being discriminated against and subjected to brutal physical treatment, as has often been suggested, but were in fact being treated as ordinary Egyptian workpeople. Corporal punishment is still dispensed in Turkish schools along traditional lines, and interestingly enough is said to promote a bond of respect between teacher and pupil. The biblical statements about punishment (Prov. 13:24; Heb. 12:5-9), therefore, need to be assessed against such a cultural background and hence to be distinguished from the more serious prescriptions in which flogging occurred as a punishment for wrongdoing (Deut. 21:18; 22:18). Even under these conditions a statutory limit was imposed in order to maintain the dignity of the offender (Deut. 25:1-3).

Whipping or flogging has been used widely in society for punishing, perhaps all too readily, those thought guilty of antisocial or criminal activity. Undoubtedly such penalties would have a deterrent effect in many cases, as with the use of the British "cat o' nine tails," a form of lash to which those who underwent it never reputedly returned for further punishment of that type. But while such treatment may draw the attention of the deliquent to the fact that his or her behavior is undesirable, it may not always be the best way of correcting the emotionally or mentally unstable, if indeed that is a possibility.

Corporal punishment can degenerate very easily into a terrifying brutalizing act of the strong over the weak and helpless; and if it is performed under the influence of mind-disorienting chemicals, such as when a drunken parent beats his or her children, the effect of the activity has gone far beyond the biblical intent, which was to build up rather than destroy relationships. Except in households governed by secular permissive concepts, most Christian parents punish their children physically from time to time in their early years, but normally in the kind of love with which God deals with his errant children. Physical punishment in schools still exists in some areas, although it is seldom applied with the abandon that marked nineteenth-century British education. As a threat to the unruly the strap or cane may well have some value, but it is clearly inappropriate for disciplining a child who cannot read because of some such problem as undiagnosed dyslexia, as has sometimes happened.

Corporal punishment, whether for young or old, can have an immediacy about it that concentrates the attention of the person being punished upon the offense that has been committed. But unless it has a consequent remedial effect, its rehabilitative value for the recipient must be suspect, and therefore it should not be prescribed routinely.

**CORPORATE RESPONSIBILITY.** In the past it was generally believed that corporations were acting responsibly if they performed their stated task efficiently and, where appropriate, made a profit for shareholders. Following World War II the idea grew that corporations were also responsible for providing employment and protecting their workers. In the 1960s a new view of corporate responsibility understood corporations as major agents of social change and called upon them to solve the problems of society in general.

Traditionally, Christians have been very conservative in their view of corporate responsibility. Through the influence of magazines like *Sojourners* and *The Other Side* and books like Ron Sider's *Rich Christians in an Age of Hunger* (1977), however, a more radical approach to corporate responsibility has emerged. This new outlook can be seen in Miriam Aidney's *God's Foreign Policy* (1984), where Christians are encouraged to pressure corporations to take action toward solving social problems and encouraging certain forms of economic development in the Third World. In reaction to the views of Sider and similar writers, Franky Schaeffer in *Bad News for Modern Man* (1984) and R. J. Rushdoony in *The Politics of Guilt and Pity* (1970) have sought to return to the older view of the noninvolvement of corporations in social issues.

Between these two opposing camps are people like Michael Novak, whose books *The Spirit of Democratic Capitalism* and *Toward a Theology of the Corporation* (1982) seek to offer a Christian defense of the corporation, while at the same time recognizing some corporate responsibility for particular social problems created by corporations themselves.

Any discussion of the social responsibility of corporations needs to consider and distinguish three different situations where corporate responsibility is involved. These are: situations where corporations can exercise a positive role to solve a problem which they helped create; marginal situations where the solution to a particular problem may produce new problems, and situations where corporations are held responsible for social problems that they have not created and that are beyond their competence to solve.

In the first case, corporations may be held responsible for direct impacts which they have on society. Thus, many cases of environmental pollution, industrial safety, and other problems are in their long-term interest to solve. Here it is important to identify accurately the social impact and to show realistically how the problem may be solved. This is the duty of corporate management, and where the problems are beyond the capacity of a particular firm, due to such things as increased costs which would reduce their ability to compete, then legislation may be necessary to insure justice.

Marginal situations are those where the costs of solving a problem are unjustifiable in terms of either the problem itself or other problems created in attempting to solve the original one. Here we are faced with either the abandonment of an enterprise or the acceptance of unavoidable social costs. For example, mining involves great social costs to any society in terms of death and disease. But unless we decide that we can continue to live without minerals, mining will persist. In this situation corporate responsibility will be to minimize the costs, but it would be unrealistic to ask for them to abolish them altogether.

The final type of situation is where demands are made for corporations to exercise responsibility for problems which they neither created nor have the means to solve. Here we need to recognize that a healthy corporation cannot exist in a sick society. Consequently, attempts by corporations to solve social problems under such conditions are inevitably self-defeating. Corporations have neither the expertise nor the political authority to deal with certain issues. By attempting to do so they simply create discontent, and when they fail, disillusionment. Many issues of Third World development and "justice" in society probably fall into this category and should not be tackled through corporate action.

In conclusion, the issue of corporate responsibility is a complex matter where Christians often feel a need to take a prophetic stance. However, in doing so they may simply increase corporate involvement in the political process and fail to achieve the desired end. On the other hand, to hold that corporations have no responsibility for their social impact is equally wrong. What is needed in this debate is a definition of the problems for which corporations may be held responsible and how these problems may be solved.

**Bibliography:** Drucker, P. F., *The Concept of the Corporation* (1982); *The End of Economic Man* (1939); *Management: Tasks, Responsibilities, Practices* (1974); Heilbroner, R. L., *et.al.*, *In the Name of Profit* (1972).

I.H.

**COURAGE.** Courage is a positive emotional response to specific situations involving fear or apprehension that is based upon intrinsic strength of personality or conviction of purpose and can find expression in a physical or intellectual manner. Because courage is frequently associated with strength, it is a prerequisite for a successful confrontation of situations fraught with potential or actual danger. By its character courage demonstrates a repudiation of the paralyzing effects of fear, and when brought to bear upon particular circumstances involves a commitment to action that gives promise of success in dealing with the problems at issue.

As a prerequisite for the accomplishing of deeds of high resolve, courage based on strength was enjoined of the Hebrew leader Joshua (Josh. 1:6, where the Hebrew term *ematz*, "be confirmed," involved bravery in the face of danger as well as moral conviction in pursuit of a goal. With the addition of the word for "heart" (*lebh*),

Amos could speak of the courageous people who nevertheless would flee from divine punishment (Amos 2:16, KJV). Elsewhere courage was associated with strength and was thus synonymous with the Hebrew verb *hazaq*, "be strong" (Josh. 26:6). Taking courage in the sense of showing himself strong was ascribed to King Asa in suppressing idolatrous practices in Judah (2 Chron. 15:8). While courage was often referred to in connection with military exploits, it clearly had application to many other circumstances in life also.

For the ancient Greeks, courage (*andreia*) was included with wisdom, temperance, and justice as one of the four pagan cardinal virtues. The Greek philosophers tried to give courage a moral content by requiring it to be the result of ratiocination rather than a mere automatic biological response. Rational choice, therefore, was the deciding factor in any ethical evaluation of courage. The pagan term *andreia* does not occur in the New Testament, and consequently the word occurred infrequently in the King James Version (Acts 28:15). But the ancient Hebrew concept of strength through trust in the Lord is commended continually (1 Cor. 16:13; Eph. 6:10), and the Christian is urged to follow God's leading boldly, in the belief that no weapon formed against him or her can prosper (Isa. 54:17). Such faith gives strength of purpose and the power, that is, courage, to carry it through.

See CARDINAL VIRTUES.

**COURTESY.** In common parlance *courtesy* is understood to signify the exercise of polite or considerate behavior toward others. It is based upon concepts of etiquette, which were themselves rules for acceptable behavior in medieval European courts. Courtesy was thus courtly conduct, particularly with reference to behavior among and toward ladies, with due consideration for others being an important feature. This contrasted strikingly with the blustering, arrogant, self-important conduct generally exhibited by those who either ignored or violated the canons of courtesy.

To some extent its origins reflected the nature of medieval church liturgies with their established rituals, proprieties, and sense of order. When courtesy was formulated in terms of everyday life, it exemplified a secular "grace" as distinct from the ecclesiastical variety. But it was only when what was practiced in terms of etiquette or chivalry was thought of as morally desirable behavior that courtesy could claim any ethical, as distinct from purely social, value.

The altruism of Christianity makes consideration for the needs of others a matter of paramount concern. By accepting Christ as Savior and Lord, the believer has died to self and henceforth should be striving to win others for the kingdom of Christ. The credibility of that witness turns in no small measure upon the extent to which we are kind, considerate of the less privileged, understanding, unselfish, and loving in our relationships (1 Cor. 13:4; Eph. 4:32; Col. 3:12-13). Where these factors are present, common courtesies will appear readily, and the believer's behavior will be truly Christian.

See CHIVALRY.

**COVETOUSNESS.** This word may be defined in terms of the greed or avarice which results from the jealous desire to possess something that others have already, or that constitutes the object of passionate longing. The aspirations of the covetous individual may be directed at animate and inanimate objects alike, as indicated by the tenth commandment (Exod. 20:17; Deut. 5:21), in which covetousness was expressly forbidden to the Israelites. While this commandment relates specifically to the possessions of others, the teachings of Jesus make it clear that lusting after any kind of possessions carries with it grave spiritual dangers (Matt. 6:19-24; Luke 12:15,). As with other aspects of Christ's teaching, what is condemned is not the object of desire so much as the motivating forces of greed, jealousy, and the like, that have provoked the desire. In the moral instruction of Paul, covetousness was castigated as one of the most serious of human vices (Rom. 1:29-32; 1 Cor. 6:9; 2 Cor. 12:10; Eph. 4:31).

Covetousness is completely wrong for the Christian because it inculcates behavior which is the exact opposite of that demanded by Christ. Instead of giving liberally to others and sharing material and spiritual blessings as part of the message of the kingdom, the covetous person spends an inordinate amount of time and energy in heaping up treasures on earth, contrary to the express instructions of Christ (Matt. 6:19-21). As the pursuit of possessions becomes increasingly oppressive, the individual concerned becomes a worshiper of created things rather than the Creator, which, of course, constitutes idolatry (Rom. 1:25). Covetousness, unfortunately, can usually be measured in more than purely personal dimensions, as the illegal acquisition of Naboth's vineyard by the greedy king Ahab of Israel (1 Kings 21:1-16). For him, as for many others since, his covetousness had serious social implications and ultimately led to his undoing. The obvious antidote to incipient covetousness is for the individual to establish a disciplined practice of unselfish, liberal giving in a demonstration of the desire to serve God rather than mammon.

**CRIME.** The committing of a crime involves some form of violation of statutory law and as such is directed at the public, whether on an individual or a collective basis. While the nature of the crime may vary greatly, the fact that it has been committed shows that public welfare has been violated or even endangered in some manner and the order and harmony threatened to that extent. It has been traditional among ethicists to make a distinction between sin, vice, and crime in a manner which regards sin as rebellion against God, vice as an offense against oneself, and crime as a violation of social legislation of some variety.

The fact of crime is a stark illustration of the depravity of human nature and, not surprisingly, is almost as old as humanity itself. The first crime recorded in Scripture is murder, which even without the benefit of formal legislation at that stage was so heinous as to demand vengeance (Gen. 4:11-16). Subsequently murder was established as a capital crime, the appropriate penalty for which was the death of the murderer (Gen. 9:6). This principle enunciates the worth of a person by stating that the life of the murderer is of no greater or lesser value than that of the victim and that justice has been satisfied under circumstances where the offender, and he or she alone, has been executed for the crime committed. From that time forward murder has been regarded as the most serious crime to be committed against society and therefore the one that demanded the most stringent punishment.

Even a casual perusal of such ancient Near Eastern legislation as has survived shows that many types of crime were in existence in the third millennium B.C. The ancient Sumerians waged a constant battle for law and order, but the fragmentary codes of Lipit-Ishtar and Eshnunna show that the theory of social contract upon which they were based was violated repeatedly by such characteristically human features as greed, lust, oppression of the weak, corruption, and general moral depravity.

The most detailed list of crimes in second-millennium-B.C. Mesopotamia and their corresponding punishments was contained in the celebrated law code of Hammurabi (c. 1790-1750 B.C.), the last vigorous king of the First Babylonian dynasty. Among the Israelites, Hebrew law was established definitively in the Mosaic period and contained a detailed account of various types of offenses against society, of which murder continued to be the chief. Yet while petty theft might be considered inconsequential by comparison, it was still a crime and therefore punishable under the law (Exod. 22:4, 7). In point of fact it is wrong to think of petty theft as a minor social irritation at any time in ancient history because of its widespread occurrence. Even as late as the sixth century B.C. the prophet Zechariah was pronouncing curses upon thieves (Zech. 5:3), and it was only with the ascendancy of Moslem culture that the definitive solution to theft was reached. In general it can be said that certain types of crime, such as murder and treason, were illegal in all ancient societies, while in other areas such as sexual morality, the attitudes of different cultures varied considerably. Thus homosexuality was abhorrent to Hebrew tradition as defined in the law of Moses (Lev. 20:13), but was a prominent feature of Canaanite, Greek, and Roman life, being firmly enshrined in their religious rites.

The advance of cultural and technological knowledge in the ancient Near East did nothing to inhibit the growth of crime, whether of the terrorist variety or the less spectacular violations of public order. It is not without significance that Christ's companions in death at Calvary were two thieves (Matt. 27:38; Mark 15:27), whose offenses must have been somewhat significant to have merited so dramatic a punishment. Yet despite the callousness with which punishments were meted out to criminals, it is worth noting that teachings of Jesus expressed compassion for the prisoner and the condemned (Matt. 25:36), as indeed the petitions of the ancient psalmist had done (Ps. 79:11).

By some well-intentioned modern social reformers, crime has been interpreted as the product of a deprived environment in the criminal. Remove that deprivation, it has been argued, and crime will largely disappear. A more careful assessment of the situation, however, has demonstrated the falsity of such a supposition. Crime is not necessarily the product of poverty or an underprivileged childhood lifestyle, for it is seen equally under conditions that exhibit affluence and opportunity. But there can be no mistaking the fact that crime is the concomitant of fallen human nature and is therefore in the end a moral as well as a social issue. The sophistication of modern society is now such that it is possible for persons to pursue a genteel lifestyle while violating, consciously and deliberately, known legislative enactments. Sometimes these offenders are caught by sheer accident and, when on trail, are revealed to have occupied positions of public trust. Such criminality, needless to say, generally encounters a stern reception from the judiciary.

Of those criminals who are apprehended, males are unquestionably in the majority. Male crime includes all types of offenses from murder to petty trespass, and the perpetrators come from all walks of life. Due to various attempts at legal reform during this century, the prison population in many Western countries has declined in terms of percentage of the population. This, however, has been offset by the large increase in the birth rate since World War II, and the result is that the existing prison facilities are far from adequate for purposes of incarceration. The consequent overcrowding presents serious safety and discipline problems for inmates and guards alike, and these are particularly noticeable during summer heat. Attempts to offset the hazards associated with the overcrowding of prisons have included such measures as shorter sentences followed by mandatory parole, or the imposition of fines instead of incarceration. But whatever steps are taken, they tend to call into question the entire system of justice and the place that imprisonment has in it.

From very early times the concept of a prison was a secure place (Hebrew *masger*; Ps. 142:7; Isa. 24:22) where offenders were put under restraint (Hebrew *asur*, Judg. 16:21; Jer. 37:25) so that they were no longer in contact with society.

In the ancient world prisons were usually located in the basement of some large building such as a palace, but in Palestine offenders were not infrequently confined in disused wells or cisterns (Jer. 38:6). Such containers were forbidding, unsanitary places that were deemed fit only for a criminal who might never again see daylight. Their purposes was to prevent the possibility of further crime on the part of the imprisoned person, and as such they served as detention centers. The ancient Near Eastern system of justice was concerned primarily with punishment or restitution, and the concept of rehabilitation of the criminal formed no part of the cultural situation.

Although great advances have been made in the intervening years in the accommodating of criminals, prisons are still regarded basically as places of detention for criminals, although some institutions do provide some work programs for inmates. While penal theory has undergone significant changes in recent decades, the punishment of the offender seems to take precedence in the traditional manner in many jurisdictions over significant attempts to rehabilitate the prisoner. It is true, of course, that criminals are normally aware that being apprehended is only a preliminary to punishment, unless their cases are dismissed in court. Much penal theory appears to rest on the proposition that crime must be seen to be unprofitable, and the only way for the criminal element of society to appreciate the reality of this dictum is for emphasis to be laid upon punishment.

It is all the more unfortunate for advocates of rehabilitation that the rate of recidivism is so discouragingly high. According to some estimates as many as 60 per cent of all convicted criminals return to prison for crimes committed subsequent to their original discharge. While many modern prisons have commendable recreational and rehabilitation facilities, the choice of programs designed to enable a prisoner to survive on "the outside" when released is sometimes most unfortunate. Thus some prisoners are able to receive instruction in the operation of computers, which would seem to be an open invitation to the criminal mind to investigate a whole new field of antisocial endeavor.

Sociologists and psychologists have shown considerable interest in studies relating to crime and not least in the motivating forces that govern the criminal mind. In the process they have contrived to dispel some time-honored beliefs, such as the notion that certain criminals can be identified as such because they exhibit a peculiar shape of forehead or ears. Having laid these ideas to rest, scientists have become much more concerned with genetic experiments which seem to indicate that habitual criminals exhibit a certain abnormal pattern in their chromosome structure. If on this basis the tendency to criminal behavior is "in the blood," so to speak, it would seem overly optimistic, if not actually downright naive, to expect a change of genetic structure to result either from the imposition of punishment or the optimistic application of a rehabilitation program. Some doubt, however, has been cast on the validity of the genetic findings, and some attention has been given to the possibility of dietary factors in early life as having a bearing upon the development of the criminal personality. Whatever the cause may be, the necessity for dealing with an apprehended offender seems to point to segregation from the general public as the most effective immediate means of forestalling future crime on the part of the person involved.

Another tradition that has been shown to be fallacious is that crime proceeds predominantly from situations of poverty and that to reduce or even eliminate crime all that is needed is a program of social assistance that will remedy poverty quickly. While it is true that some criminals have emerged from a background of social deprivation, the nature of much modern crime is such that it attracts the "white-collar" workers—businessmen, doctors, lawyers, and others. Such crime, therefore, does not stem from a "deprived childhood" so much as the conscious choice by a mind that is basically depraved of a way of life that is criminal in character. So frequently, it would appear, that basic motivation for crime is not need but greed.

Profiles of male prisoners have been drawn up, and while they can only be expected to present a general picture, their implications are significant. In North American prisons the average age of the inmate appears to be between nineteen and twenty-seven years. He would probably be unmarried or separated, and if married he would be likely to have a common-law partner rather than a legally wedded wife. In eight cases out of ten his offense would be primarily against property, and any violence done to people would be coincidental. Conviction could thus result from arrest after robbery (with or without violence), breaking and entering premises, arson, motor vehicle theft, or willful damage. Of the crimes against property only about 25 per cent are solved and the culprits charged, as compared with 75 per cent in instances of violent crime. Many murders are not the work of total strangers, but of someone known to the victim, possibly a relative. Contrary to popular opinion, most men are not incarcerated for violent crime, but for offenses against property. Even more interesting is the fact that an estimated 30 per cent of the men in prison are there because of nonpayment of fines.

Most researchers agree that at least 70 per cent of all crime is committed by people acting under the influence of mind-disorienting chemicals or alcohol. From the foregoing it would appear that a very small number of men need to be incarcerated for the protection of society. Conversely, a large number of people are imprisoned because of a reluctance on the part of the authorities to develop more creative sanctions. This face comes into prominence when North American rates of incarceration are compared with those of other democratic countries. For every 100,000 of the population, Canada imprisons 150 while the United States incarcerates 270. On the same basis of reckoning France has 64 prison inmates, Italy 65, Great Britain 87, Japan 46, and the Netherlands 28. This startling statistic does not necessarily mean that North America is a more crime-ridden society; it could show that imprisonment is relied on too heavily in these countries as a means of dealing with crime.

Female crime has always been much smaller quantitatively than that of males, partly for sociological reasons as well as temperamental ones. The main distinction between male and female crime at present, however, turns on accessibility. In an earlier period females were sometimes guilty of devious behavior, prostitution, theft, and the occasional act of murder. But females have now become much more aggressive in society and are just as likely to be numbered among the terrorist groups as to be caught perpetrating serious computer fraud. Indeed, as women penetrate the work force increasingly and have access to all the opportunities for criminal behavior that men have experienced, they can be expected to commit crimes that hitherto were regarded specifically as "male." In addition to being open to crimes involving morality, women have been participating increasingly in the lucrative drug trade.

The ideal way of treating crime, of course, is to prevent it. One approach toward the realization of this goal was indicated by the discovery that about 80 per cent of convicted felons had also been found guilty previously of some minor offense, and this had generally occurred when they were young children. The first step toward preventing crime must be taken by the Christian church and must comprise a concerted program of evangelism and biblical instruction directed specifically at the youth of the nation. The Ten Commandments and the teachings of Jesus will be at the forefront of this educational program, supplemented by other biblical precepts about moral and spiritual integrity, honesty, and the duty that the Christian has toward others in society. In the process the church will recognize as allies the numerous organizations which, from a more secular point of view, are also aiming toward the same general goal. Only when the problem of crime is attacked at its very roots, namely at the level of potential criminals, can there be any hope of significant improvement and success in the enterprise.

See CAPITAL PUNISHMENT; CRIMINAL PERSONALITY; CRIMINALITY, FEMALE; JUSTICE; PRISONERS, RIGHTS OF; RAPE; THEFT.

J.W.R.

**CRIMINAL PERSONALITY.** The causes of criminal behavior have been a source of speculation as long as civilizations have existed. The pendulum of public opinion swings back and forth between rehabilitation and tougher laws with harsher penalties. With each swing there develop new theories to rationalize the action.

If the research is read as identifying the contributing factors that influence the choice to engage in criminal behavior, it is easier to reconcile these factors with Christian values. The alternative is to say that the criminal is totally predetermined by biological or social factors that rob him or her of free will.

Over the last century, there was a belief among some experts that people were born criminals. They attempted to identify physical characteristics common to criminals, but this research proved inconclusive. In more recent times it was suggested that criminals have special chromosome patterns. Again evidence for an XYY syndrome or other chromosome anomaly remains inconclusive. There is growing evidence that nutrition has an influence on behavior. The majority of people in prison would be victims of our fastfood culture or of malnutrition because of excessive use of drugs or alcohol that suppress appetite. Likewise, high traces of metal in the bloodstream are thought to influence behavior. However, these links of nutrition to criminal behavior are still inconclusive.

From a sociological perspective it is pointed out that many criminals come from what are identified as bad neighborhoods. It is thought that strong peer pressure reinforces antisocial behavior and converts deterrents such as imprisonment into norms or rites of passage. Ramsey Clark, while Attorney General of the U.S.A., noted that in most cities 80 per cent of those arrested came from 2 per cent of the population. This may suggest an uneven application of the law but also underlines the fact that many criminals come from what would be identified as economically underprivileged areas. Because schools in these areas are often beset by disciplinary problems, it is difficult to create good learning environments. Those with learning disabilities become lost in what is experienced by the teacher as a lack of motivation and a resistance to learning by the school population. With poor education and poor work habits these people become the first victims of any economic recession and learn to adjust to unemployment. Crime becomes an alternative form of employment. Finally, inadequate parenting and broken homes are cited as causes of criminality. The same has been alleged about the influence of television, which raises expectations of the good life and desentitizes people to violence, which may then become the means of achieving the good things.

While there is truth to all of these theories, they are proved inadequate by the exceptions to the rule, for there are those who grow up in these same situations and do not become criminals. Clearly no biological, sociological, or psychological theory is in itself sufficient to explain why a person becomes a criminal. It can be said that the factors noted earlier drastically reduce the options a person has or believes he or she has in making a choice. In that context, the options of crime often appear more attractive than they would if other factors were more positive.

**Bibliography:** Samenow, S.E., *Inside the Criminal Mind* (1984); Yochelson, S., and Samenow, S. E., *The Criminal Personality* (1977).

J.W.R.

**CRIMINALITY, FEMALE.** In the past the difference in patterns of criminality between men and women was more clear-cut. There was some evidence that women were socially conditioned to take fewer risks and were more vulnerable to social disapproval. However, during the Second World War more women were forced to assume positions formerly held by men, and social roles began to change.

Traditionally women were most often charged with morals offenses, petty pilfering, and some fraud. Today the opportunity for women to commit crime is equal to that of men, and the statistics show a narrowing of the gap. Even for women who stay at home to rear families, the temptations have increased. Large, impersonal stores in their effort to make people buy also make it easier to steal, and for public relations reasons are reluctant to prosecute other than persistent offenders.

There has also been a change in attitude of the courts toward women offenders. In the past a man was eight times more likely to be convicted than a woman. However, with mandatory sentences and a challenge to this misplaced chivalry from the women's liberation movement, this ration has been reduced greatly. It must also be noted that women appearing in court are more likely than men to rank as first offenders and thus receive more lenient responses from the court.

Finally, the percentage of women convicted of crime has increased three times over that of men since World War II. However, this increase is based on a much smaller number to start with and is, in fact, not as dramatic as the numbers suggest.

**Bibliography:** Radzinowicz, L., and King, J., *The Growth of Crime* (1977).

J.W.R.

**CRUELTY.** This term describes the inflicting of unnecessary pain or punishment upon a human being or animal. Thus it is often the opposite of clemency (moderation in punishing the guilty). Physical cruelty has existed throughout the history of the human race; but it surfaces particularly in the actions of corrupt and godless regimes where prisoners are subjected to torture, citizens severely maltreated, and so on. It is also expressed in personal relations when, for example, a parent, guardian, or stranger will treat a child violently, doing great harm.

Whatever may be the motive or state of mind

of the one who is cruel, cruelty is offensive to God and to genuine civilization. But cruelty is not only physical. There is a growing recognition in Western society and law of the existence of mental cruelty, even among apparently well-mannered and behaved people. This can take a variety of forms but often consists in the continual humiliation of a person so that his or her personal dignity and esteem are severely and deeply impaired. The scars from such cruelty can last longer and be deeper than those arising from physical cruelty. Again, the infliction of mental cruelty is offensive to God and to genuine civilization. A human being is not merely an assembly of flesh and bones but a creature made in the image of God, who is called by his Creator to do unto others as he would have others do to him.

While there is much sentimental talk about cruelty to animals it must be added that it is wrong in God's sight to maltreat animals by causing them needless suffering. Here the sinfulness does not consist in the violation of the rights and dignity of the animal but in the conduct of the one who is cruel. Under God, human beings have a duty to act humanely toward animals.

P.T.

**CURSING.** In the ancient world cursing involved the use of an oath, an imprecation, or an execration in order to bring about punishment, retribution, or penalty for disobedience upon an individual or a group of offenders. Such curses were based upon implied or actual divine sanction, and so superstitious were the ancient Near Eastern peoples generally that the curses often had a dramatic psychological effect. Only the Hebrews, because of their distinctive belief in the sovereignty of the God of Sinai, were able to resist such negative suggestions, as in the case of the young David, who remained undisturbed when the Philistine warrior Goliath cursed him by his gods (1 Sam. 17:43).

An interesting example of the multiple cursing of a nation's enemies is seen in the Execration Texts of the ancient Egyptians. Dated between 1990 and 1790 B.C. and recovered in fragmentary form, these curses had been inscribed on jars which were then smashed ceremonially, perhaps as the curses themselves were being recited in public. International treaties of the Hittite variety contained a section of curses which the vassal participating in the treaty could expect to encounter should he violate the provisions of the agreement. The Mosaic covenant in Deuteronomy 28 followed the same pattern, with a large section of curses outweighing in typical Hittite fashion the shorter list of blessings (verses 2-14) that would accrue if the treaty provisions were honored. The Hebrew word *alah* implies that such a curse was in fact an execration, and in some instances it was used in the sense of an oath as well (Num. 5:21; Neh. 10:29; Ezek. 17:13), particularly where the provisions of the Sinai covenant were involved.

The concept of cursing also occurred in a less

dramatic sense to describe a general denigration or reviling of a person or group, with the implication that those affected by such a curse could be regarded as people of little or no esteem. Curses of this kind were generally of human origin apart from some divine utterances (Gen. 8:21; 12:3; Exod. 21:27), but if delivered by a prophet (Deut. 23:4) or a judge (Judg. 9:19-21) they were felt to carry some form of divine sanction and could only be disregarded at great risk.

Such vilification seems to have inspired many of the curses in antiquity and was no doubt only effective because of the high degree of psychological suggestibility that the ancient peoples exhibited. This feature was still prominent in New Testament times, as in Acts 23:12, where a group of Jewish fanatics placed themselves under a curse (*anathema*) of abstinence from food until they had killed Paul. Such an action declared them publicly accursed if their goal was not achieved and was in fact a very serious undertaking. An equally solemn and misguided outburst marked the response of Peter to his identification as a Galilean by a palace maid at the trial of Jesus (Matt. 26:74; Mark 14:71). The Greek term preserved by Mark (*anathematizo*) means "to regard as thoroughly accursed," as distinct from the swearing (*omnumi*) which in this instance most probably amounted to a general vilification of the people and circumstances connected with Christ's arrest.

As a means whereby the speaker could give emphasis and authority to his or her pronouncements, cursing was apparently quite widespread in the days of Christ, and consequently he addressed himself to the ethical problems of such activity. In forbidding the cursing of parents (Matt. 15:4; Mark 7:10) he condemned those who spoke evil of their fathers or mothers, in defiance of the fifth commandment (Exod. 20:12). Not content with this kind of prohibition, he supplied the definitive antidote to any form of human execration, imprecation, or vilification, which is to pronounce divine blessing upon the one uttering the curse (Matt. 5:44). Paul went one step further in urging the believer not to indulge in any form of cursing, following the instruction of Christ that prohibited the swearing of oaths in any form (Matt. 5:34). Instead of calling upon heaven to witness this or that situation, the Christian should be a person of such recognizable integrity that a simple yes or no should guarantee the reliability of the occasion without further embellishment. On such a basis the Christian is in a preeminent position to make an affirmation of loyalty or a pledge of veracity where the situation warrants it.

**CUSTOM.** A custom is a form of tradition, whether of thought or behavior, that has become a habit in ordinary life processes or in religious functions. While some ethicists maintain that customs survive because they enshrine certain values, the passing of time and the changes that occur in social attitudes render many customs obsolete, thereby modifying whatever intrinsic values they may have possessed. Where customs are based upon traditional superstitious beliefs, they frequently represent disvalue rather than value. It is important, therefore, to avoid the assumption that a custom is necessarily something of good moral value. While changes may occur to customs as a result of new trends in social life, such changes may actually be harmful to morals, a situation that confronted the Jews when Hellenism swept across the Near East in the fourth century B.C.

Customs which are generally conducive to law and order are important for the stability of individual and community life. For those who follow the example of Jesus, attendance at places of worship is mandatory (Luke 4:16), for it is under such circumstances that the believer is able to honor God, receive instruction in the faith, and enjoy concourse with fellow Christians in an atmosphere of devotion and worship. But even though the customs produced by such associations may be biblically based, they can and do appear in various forms and can even degenerate and become corrupt with the passing of time. Such customs are then unlawful (Acts 16:21) and in need of reform according to scriptural standards. Such reformation should take into account the possibility that the desired spiritual values may not necessarily be preserved, even though the exact cultural form of the biblical period had been followed, insofar as that form was known.

At the risk of encountering the disapproval of one's peers, it seems important for the Christian to examine critically the customary features of his or her life in order to determine the extent to which they glorify God. Only those customs which fulfill this high ideal should be allowed to influence the believer's life, and the rest should be discarded resolutely.

**CYBERNETICS.** This Greek term, meaning "one who steers," describes the branch of study which examines the character and direction of controls in human society, especially where the transmission of information is concerned. In the latter area, in which computers are exerting an extremely important influence, the "steersman" under scrutiny is the one who feeds information into the computer. The ethics of cybernetics in such cases would be concerned with motivation, and also with the possibility of social manipulation by unscrupulous politicians, financiers, and others. Cybernetics recognizes that the computer is a nonmoral instrument that can only execute those programs prepared for it.

The attempt to link computers across the world in such a manner as to give them access to enormous data bases must be a matter of concern to those involved in cybernetics. The apparent ease with which the most complicated computer access codes can be broken raises urgent problems about illegal accessibility of information and the use to which it can be put by unscrupulous persons. Perhaps the most fundamental question of all is: "Who shall steer the steersman?" Clearly cybernetics is an area of activity in which Christians ought to be involved at the very highest level.

See COMPUTER ETHICS.

**CYNICISM.** This may be understood in two ways. Historical cynicism was the system of ethics of the Cynics (*kynikoi*), the disciples of Diogenes of Sinope (c. 400-325 B.C.) who was known as *kyon* (a dog) because of his shamelessness. For the Cynics, happiness consisted of living according to nature and satisfying basic and most fundamental natural wants in the simplest possible manner. They held that the reduction of individual wants to a natural minimum required self-discipline but brought as a result self-sufficiency and freedom. They rejected civilization, were critical of the ways of life it encouraged and required, and were prepared to do in public what they did in private. Diogenes masturbated in public to make the point. They were the first thinkers to reject human slavery, regarding it as against nature.

As a modern phenomenon however, cyncism is an attitude of contempt and distrust of human nature and motivation. It can exist minimally in a person about particular matters, or it can exist as a highly pessimistic attitude and approach to life in general.

Whether in a lesser or greater degree, cynicism is contrary to Christian ethics. To be pessimistic about human nature in certain situations and times may be justified, but to be wholly pessimistic all the time is wrong, for it denies the fundamental belief that, being made in the image of God, human beings are capable of some good, even though they are sinners at heart. Cynicism in its modern forms is often the exaggerated or excessive development of what in essence is fundamentally true; namely, that individuals are not perfect and are often motivated by self-interest.

The connection between the historical system and the modern phenomenon is to be seen in the disposition to be critical and find fault in people, as well as a general attitude of contempt and surliness.

P.T.

# –D–

**DANCING.** This form of bodily activity entails rhythmic movement which can be undertaken independently or in conjunction with others. It can be performed in silence or to the accompaniment of drums and musical instruments. Its style may vary from the elegant and graceful arabesque of classical ballet to the wild gyrations of certain modern styles of dancing.

In the ancient world dancing was an acceptable activity for both males and females. In Canaan, male priests sought communion with their god Baal by whirling around in a frenzied dance until they collapsed (1 Kings 18:26-28). In Babylonia and Egypt women danced in processions, while among the Greeks priestesses sometimes danced licentiously prior to acting as prostitutes. Hebrew men and women participated in dancing, both in processions and as part of temple worship (Ps. 150:4), and even David is reputed to have danced in the presence of the ark (2 Sam. 6:14) in such a manner as to offend his wife Michal. The term *dance* seems to be an inadequate rendering of what was evidently exuberant cavorting. It is important to note that nowhere in the ancient world did men dance with women in the manner that is fashionable today.

Dancing as a religious activity was not prominent in early Christianity, probably because of its pagan licentious associations. Some modern sects such as the now-extinct American Shakers engage in various dance contortions as part of their worship, but attempts to incorporate religious dance as an integral part of worship have met with what is generally an unenthusiastic response.

**DEATH.** Although death is universal for human beings and other creatures, it is seen in Scripture not as a natural part of human existence, but as an enemy. Death is the penalty for sin, both for the original human parents and for their descendants. Presumably had mankind not fallen, death would not be our lot. St. Paul sees Christ's resurrection as the conquest of death (1 Cor. 15:51-58; 2 Tim. 1:10). St. John's Revelation depicts Christ at the last day as conquering death, the last great enemy (Rev. 21:1-4).

During periods of widespread death from plagues, war, and disease, cultures have been preoccupied with death. Although the macabre and morbid have been popular images in such times, our period tends to sequester death. The dying are segregated in institutions until they die, when elaborate ceremonials at considerable expense mark their passing.

When does death occur? The determination of death is not primarily a medical question but more a philosophical one. The moment of death traditionally has been defined as the cessation of heartbeat. Modern biomedical technology and its life-prolonging devices have called for a newer definition of death, since biological systems can be prolonged artificially. Individuals can thus be kept biologically "alive" when it is questionable whether they are viable persons. For example, respiration and heartbeat can be sustained mechanically for a person with dramatically diminished brain functioning. This creates significant personal, ethical, and legal problems. Can we begin grieving for Grandmother as if she were dead? Is it appropriate to discontinue life-support treatment for this patient?

In an attempt to provide a definition of death, an ad hoc committee of the Harvard Medical School has developed the concept of "brain death," fixing death as the final and irreversible loss of brain function. While constituting a reasonable suggestion for determining when death occurs, this move is clearly a new development in the criteria of death, with philosophical implications. It assumes that rationality and consciousness are related to the brain and that they are definitive of what makes a truly human life. This criterion has been challenged by Robert M. Veatch, who sees it as only one of four possible definitions of death. Veatch defines death as irreversible cessation of such functions as the flow of vital fluids, the loss of the capacity for bodily activity and social interaction, and the cessation of consciousness. Others, such as Hans Jonas, are suspicious of the Harvard criteria because they fear it will lead to the use of patients as living "cadaver donors" of organs for transplantation, whom Willard Gaylin of the Hastings Center has referred to as "neomorts."

Most Americans die in institutions, often as the result of protracted and progressively debilitating illnesses. This entails a fearful deterioration, a loss of control over one's environment and decisions affecting one's welfare, and the loss of control over such basic physiological processes as feeding and waste elimination. Many such individuals would not have lived to face these indignities before the advent of sophisticated biomedical technologies. Such factors have led to a variety of innovations in the theory of death, of the ethics of treating dying patients, and of practical care for the dying. One such innovation has been the movement toward "death with dignity," a term that generally refers to reserving to the patient the right to make decisions about the treatment he is to receive at the end of life.

Controversy about treatment toward the end of an individual's life has been intense. One major practical and theoretical problem in this area has to do with the patient's capacity for true consent at a moment when he may be highly medicated, despondent, incoherent, or unconscious. This has led to the so-called "Living Will," a document prepared in advance of such illness which expresses the patient's wishes not to receive "extraordinary treatment" that, in his view, will not promise extended life but which will only prolong death. In its popular versions, the document expresses a naturalistic view that death is just the final phase of life. Questions abound concerning the binding status of such a document. Should the physician follow the Living Will when the patient evidences a desire to go on living, or should he follow the expressed desires of the moment?

Thanatology, the study of death and the dying process, has been popularlized by Elisabeth Kubler-Ross. Kubler-Ross believes that people facing terminal illness pass through five stages in their coping with approaching death: denial and isolation, anger, bargaining, depression, and acceptance. Such findings have been valuable for those engaged in pastoral care with the dying and have helped to provide support for the hospice movement. The hospice, pioneered by Cicely Saunders, is an attempt to provide a nonhospital environment where death can be faced with human care, supportive counseling, and minimal medication.

A few philosophers have contemplated the significance of death, some by viewing it as a passage to a better existence, others by characterizing it as a hopeless annihilation. Socrates welcomed death as the soul's liberation from mortal existence, while more recently Martin Heidegger understood death as annihilation and the awareness of one's own death as the beginning of true freedom. Human existence, according to Heidegger, is a "being towards death," a conscious awareness of impending nonbeing which when faced can give meaning to present life.

The Christian hope by which we face death is sharply at odds with the secularistic attitude that characterizes such writing as the Living Will, with its ready acceptance of death as a natural part of life. The Christian sees death as an evil, an enemy, and looks forward eagerly to Christ's victory over it. In the meantime, Christians have much to do to confront the alienation and isolation of the dying and their families with the comforting hope of Christ and the love of his people.

**Bibliography:** Beauchamp, T. L., and Walters, L., eds., *Contemporary Issues in Bioethics* (2nd ed., 1982); Choron, J., *Death and Western Thought* (1963); Hamilton, M. P., and Reid, H. F., *A Hospice Handbook* (1980); Kubler-Ross, E., *On Death and Dying* (1970); Olson,

R. G., *"Death,"* in Edwards, P., ed., *The Encyclopedia of Philosophy* (1967).

See AGED, CARE OF THE; EUTHANASIA.

D.B.F.

**DECEPTION.** Coming from a Latin root *capio*, "to take, capture," the term *deception* describes a situation in which one is persuaded of the veracity of something that is actually false. Deception is thus a calculated and deliberate misrepresentation of people and circumstances alike. Hence it partakes of the nature of fraud and selfishness on the part of the perpetrator. It seeks to gain an advantage by direct lying or by distorting the truth so that someone is wrongfully deprived or cheated because of having been persuaded by incomplete or inaccurate information. Even when a person is far from convinced about the *bona fide* of the deceiving party, he or she can still be misled by accepting a portion of the suggested proposition.

Where unscrupulous individuals are concerned, there is virtually no limit to the potential for deception in interpersonal relationships. All that is required for situations to be manipulated to a deceiver's advantage is a degree of ignorance or a lack of proper information on the part of the other person or persons involved.

Espionage is an obvious area of activity where successful deception of a potential or actual enemy is a major objective. Consequently powerful nations go to extreme lengths to misinform or pervert and misrepresent situations and purposes in an attempt to pursue their own selfish goals successfully. The business world offers an open invitation to fiscal deception, which is sometimes brought to a fine art in company balance sheets when words are manipulated in order to place corporate finances and prospects in a better light than is actually the case.

Advertising is yet another field where deception prevails; and this situation has actually led to the establishing of ethical standards for advertisers which, if violated, can result in charges of fraud. The field of science, which is supposed to deal with data in a disinterested and objective manner, is unfortunately riddled with the kind of deception that ignores or suppresses data hostile to the hypothesis being promoted or that actually falsifies results of experiments. In the area of social relationships, deception is at its most serious level morally when it involves clandestine marital infidelity.

In Scripture, deception basically constitutes a false witness, and this is condemned in the ninth commandment (Exod. 20:16) and is therefore dishonest. Deceit constitutes treachery and falsehood (Prov. 11:18; 14:15) and is the work of evil persons who through envy pervert the truth (Mark 7:22; Rom. 1:29). The practicing Christian will be careful to maintain a tongue free from deception in dealing with society (Ps. 15:2-3), and will avoid all those evil works that proceed from selfish, perverted hearts and lying lips. To avoid deception, the believer will strive to live a life of altruistic love that does no ill to his or her neighbor (Rom. 13:10) and will behave honestly and truthfully in all things.

See BUSINESS ETHICS; COMPUTER ETHICS.

**DECISION MAKING, ETHICAL.** A decision is an ethical one when it concerns conduct that has major consequences for human well-being. The term *ethics* is often used synonymously with *morals,* but, strictly speaking, *morals* refers to the conduct itself while *ethics* refers to the study of that moral conduct. Etiquette is similar to morality in that it deals with behavior that is approved or disapproved by society; it differs in that it lacks a strong sense of obligation. Civil law is similar to morality in that it deals with social standards that are obligatory for human beings, although it is obligatory in a different way. Civil law may or may not be constructed in accord with moral standards. In fact, civil laws may be patently immoral, such as the laws of apartheid in South Africa. It is normally the case that obedience to the civil law is morally obligatory.

Ethics can be divided into three categories: descriptive, critical, and normative. Descriptive or scientific ethics refers to a factual study of moral behavior, a characteristic of the social sciences. Critical ethics refers to the analysis and critique of how moral decisions are made and justified, and how moral language is used. Normative ethics attempts to set forth those characteristics that constitute proper moral norms, decisions, actions, and character. Critical ethics should precede normative ethics; the analysis of how people *do* make moral decisions should precede how people *ought to* make moral decisions. Normative ethics, however, should not be based on descriptive ethics. The way people do behave does not determine how they should behave. This is especially true within a Christian perspective because of the effects of the Fall on all human action.

An important aspect of ethical decision making is the requirement that the decision maker be able to justify his or her decision. This usually takes the form of bringing a specific case under a more general rule or principle. It is possible to distinguish four elements within this ethical decision making process. The first element is the moral situation or case under consideration; for example, whether Mrs. Johnson should have an abortion because she is likely to bear a seriously malformed child. The second element consists of the rules under which the cases fall; for example, abortions, except when performed to save the life of the mother, are immoral or it is always wrong to destroy the life of another human being. Morality is rule-bound in the sense that what is right for one individual in a specific situation is also right for a similar individual in similar circumstances. Moral rules will fall under other moral rules that have greater scope; for example, rules regarding abortion will fall under rules regarding life-taking.

The principles used to determine the moral rightness of the rules constitute the third element. Twentieth-century philosophers distinguish between utilitarian and deontological principles or approaches to moral decision making. In the utilitarian approach, actions or rules are determined to be morally right by their results or consequences, that is, the alternative which produces the greatest balance of good over evil is judged to be the morally correct choice. Capital punishment might be justified, for example, because of its benefits to society in reducing the incidence of murder. In the deontological approach, the determination is made on a factor other than results or consequences; for example, an action is morally right because it is in accord with conscience or the will of God. The fourth element of ethical decision making consists of the bases upon which one determines the rules and principles to follow. For the Christian, the basis rests in the moral character of God, and right action is defined by the will of God.

The question that confronts the Christian is how to determine the will of God for a specific moral situation. Three sources are possible: conscience, the Bible, and nature. Conscience, according to most psychologists, is the internalization of authority. It will reflect in large measure, then, the standards of the internalized authorities and will be only as trustworthy as they are. Conscience is a mechanism given by God that makes us feel guilty when we behave in ways contrary to our internal moral standards (John 8:9; Rom. 2:15). We should follow our conscience, then, when its standards coincide with the will of God. Paul sought "a conscience void of offense toward God, and toward men" (Acts 24:16; see also Acts 23:1; Rom. 9:1; 2 Cor. 1:12; 2 Tim. 1:3) and commended those with a pure conscience (1 Tim. 1:5, 19; 3:9; see also Heb. 10:22; 1 Pet. 3:16, 21).

The primary source for determining the will of God for moral situations is the Bible, but Christians differ on how the Bible is to be interpreted and used. The Bible was written in another language and time and to a culture different from ours. Many contemporary problems, such as nuclear war or genetic engineering, did not exist in biblical times. Even when the problems are parallel, it is unwise to apply the biblical texts directly. For example, if one were to resolve the problems of capital punishment by directly applying texts from the Bible, then we would execute children who curse their parents (Exod. 21:17), adulterers (Lev. 20:10), and those who work on the Sabbath day (Exod. 35:2).

The approach to the Bible which should be taken is to analyze the cultural situation and the meaning of the text to determine the underlying moral principles. Passages should be interpreted in light of the larger context, including the context of the whole Bible. Scripture must be used to interpret Scripture. The teachings of Matthew 5 on nonretaliation must be interpreted in light of the government's legitimate use of the sword in Romans 13 and vice versa. Attention must be paid to the progression of revelation, but this does not rule out the moral principles underlying the laws in the Pentateuch. The standard for marriage is monogamy even though Abraham was a polygamist, as the sacred character of marriage is illustrated in the Old Testament laws pertaining to adultery. Most of the Bible, and not just the distinctly moral passages, is relevant to moral questions because morality is integral to all of life. For example, the parables and life of Jesus tell us much about the ethics of human relationships.

Nature or general revelation is a source for determining the will of God because the created order reflects the mind and character of God. Ethical decisions often pertain to human well-being within social structures, such as the family, business and trade, and the state, that are part of the created order. Appropriate human action within these structures can be discovered through a study of the ways that the structures operate effectively; for example, one's moral obligations to family members can be determined through a study of effective families. The use of general revelation is limited because of the effects of sin and must be guided by principles gained from the Bible.

Love and justice are the two underlying biblical principles that should be used to develop, interpret, and apply moral rules. They are both central to the character of God and have God as their source (Deut. 32:4; Ps. 103:6; Isa. 9:6-7; 45:21; Zeph. 3:5; John 3:16; 1 John 4:7-10). They also presume that human beings have individual and corporate worth because God loves them and because they bear the image of God (Gen. 1:26-27; Pss. 8:4-8; 139:14-18).

The biblical idea of love (*agape*), not to be confused with romantic (*eros*) or even brotherly love (*philia*), is an act of will that seeks sacrificially the growth and well-being of others quite apart from who they are or what they can do for us (Deut. 10:19; Matt. 5:44; John 15:12-17; 1 Thess. 3:12). Love rules out a moral life directed toward self-interest, but not a concern for one's own growth and well-being, because the command is to "love thy neighbor as thyself" (Lev. 19:18, 34; Matt. 19:19; Mark 12:31; Luke 10:27). The principle of love embodies the Ten Commandments but extends them beyond literalistic rule-keeping (Matt. 5:17-48; 22:36-40; 23:23; Rom. 13:8-10; Gal. 5:14).

Justice is a deontological principle that requires equity of treatment to all human beings. In most of the Old Testament this takes the form of a concern for those who are most easily maltreated within society, particularly the alien, the widow, and the orphan (Exod. 22:21-27; 23:6, 9; Lev. 19:9-11, 13-15, 35-36; Deut. 10:17-19; 14:28-29; 24:17-22; 25:13-16; 26:12-13; 27:18-19; Ps.

146:7-9; Isa. 1:11-20; Jer. 22:3; Amos 5:11-20; Zech. 8:9-10; see also Luke 4:16-21; James 1:26-27). Rights are derived from the principle of justice. The Ten Commandments, along with related passages, give all human beings rights to such things as life, sanctity of marriage, and property (Exod. 20:13-15; Lev. 19:11; 20:10-12; 24:17; Num. 35:9-34; Deut. 5:17-19; 19:14; 22:22-27; 25:13-16; 27:17). Love and justice must undergird our moral character as well as our moral behavior, even as they do for God. Proper moral behavior includes proper motives that come from a heart directed toward God as well as following moral rules and principles (Luke 6:45; 1 Pet. 1:22; Matt. 5:27-30; 15:10-20).

Proper moral action is not limited to Christians, a fact that is possible because of the common grace of God. Nevertheless, Christians have the advantage of the inner working of the Holy Spirit and God's act of grace in Christ that enables them to respond in loving obedience to His will.

**Bibliography:** Barry, V., *Applying Ethics: A Text With Readings,* 2nd ed., (1985); Birch, B., and Rasmussen, L., *Bible and Ethics in the Christian Life* (1976); Frankena, W., *Ethics,* 2nd ed. (1973); Holmes, A., *Ethics: Approaching Moral Decisions* (1984).

S.D.A.

**DEFOLIATION.** Defoliation is the process whereby foliage is removed from trees, shrubs, and plants, usually through the use of chemicals. It was employed on a large scale as part of military campaigning in Europe in World War II (1939-1945), at which time chemical substances including phosphorus were dropped by Allied planes upon German crops and forested areas suspected of concealing troops and equipment. The United States forces employed herbicides extensively in Vietnam for the same purpose, but in the process managed to ruin huge mangrove and timber forests in South Vietnam as well as bringing a large segment of the population to the brink of starvation. What had appeared to be a satisfactory solution to the problem of monitoring enemy troop movements and depriving the invaders of food turned into disaster for the South Vietnamese by limiting their own supplies and causing serious ecological disturbance. As a result the defoliation program was discontinued in 1971.

A new and unforeseen defoliant has emerged on the ecological scene to bring grave concern to environmentalists and politicians alike. Known as acid rain, it is produced when millions of tons of sulphur dioxide and nitrogen oxide in the form of smoke emissions from smelters and coal-fired industrial plants combine with other pollutants in the atmosphere and fall back to earth in the form of a corrosive rain. This type of air pollution has allegedly brought considerable damage to trees and forests in the Western world, as well as polluting lakes and rivers and causing structural damage to buildings. Where trees are not actually killed by acid rain defoliation, they tend to exhibit a significant decline in tree diameter growth. As can be expected, not all scientists attribute this damage to acid rain, but do not suggest credible alternatives.

Acid rain is clearly an important threat to the ecological balance of the earth; and if its effects are to be halted, much more effort to prevent nitrogen emissions must be expended than has been the case previously. The Christian has a particular responsibility in this regard to exercise proper stewardship of the earth which has been committed to his care by God (Gen. 1:28), the creator and sustainer of all life. The damage already caused to the environment by centuries of abuse is of a very serious nature, and society is now paying for the callous exploitation of the earth's resources. God's people, therefore, should humble themselves, pray, and repent, in the expectation that God will hear from heaven and heal their land (2 Chron. 7:14).

See ECOLOGY.

**DEMONOLOGY.** Belief in personal or other intelligent forms of evil forces which are beyond our knowledge is common in most religions of the world.

The majority of Christians believe in the existence of angels, who are divine agents for good, and the devil and demons, who are agents of evil. Christians reject idealism, monism, and dualism in part because these philosophies deal inadequately with the origin and nature of evil. Given the Christian premise of the creation of the world by God, the Fall must have been an event in time. The idea of creaturely rebellion permitted by God, that is, the premundane fall of an angelic being (Satan) or the fall of Adam or both, therefore, is seen to be as reasonable an explanation of the origin of evil as any other. For Christians, the working of evil in the world takes place through the bad wills of fallen creatures and through the damaging impersonal forces of the evil-infected creation.

The healing ministry of Jesus included cure of disease, restoration of disability, and release from demonic power. There appear to be distinctions drawn in the Gospel accounts between demonic possession and insanity (Matt. 4:24; 17:15) and between possession and other forms of illness. Some scholars argue that this awareness is evident from the fact that Jesus customarily commands the demon whereas he customarily touches the sick (Matt. 8:14-17; Mark 1:40-41; 7:24-37; Luke 11:14-26). Debate continues as to how much of Jesus' healing dealt with physical causes, psychological factors, demonic powers, or combinations of these.

Medieval thought and practice continues to influence powerfully modern thought, language, and practice regarding the demonic. However, modern understanding of medieval thought tends to be distorted due to oversimplification and lack of knowledge.

The variety of abnormal phenomena compelled medieval people, and compels us, to distinguish differing abnormal conditions by asking whether the causes are hereditary, physical (including chemical, such as the body tumors of the Middle Ages), dietary, psychological, moral, or demonic. All these elements were factored into medieval theory to a greater or lesser degree. Unlike some modern faith healers, most medieval theologians and clergy were too sophisticated to attribute most or all illness and insanity to demonic power. They distinguished between permanent mental incapacity, rage which quickly abates, insanity (those out of touch with reality), compulsive behavior, and *menta capti*, that is, when one is under the power of the devil or some other power. It is from this latter language alongside the terminology of the New Testament that our language of possession and obsession derives.

T. K. Oesterreich says that traditionally there are three key signs of demon possession: changed facial form, usually made grotesque; change of voice (sometimes a mimicking of another person); and, crucially, displacement of the usual personal identity of the person by a new and alien self. This last point forces the observer to make the difficult judgment of distinguishing among epilepsy, ecstasy, furor, the fool, hysteria, insanity, and possession. As well, the possession may be spontaneous (invaded by the evil agent) or voluntary (yielded to or induced by the subject); it may be unconscious (not remembered later) or lucid; it may be possession by demons, other human spirits, or animal spirits (zoanthropy or lycanthropy), imagined or real (note Dan. 4:28-37).

When correlated with modern concepts these received ideas create great complexity and ambiguity. The secular inclination is to dismiss them, although a wide range of authorities, Christian and non-Christian alike, are reluctant to dismiss demon possession altogether as mythology or as hysteria.

The modern secular mood is to regard demons as the reification of evil powers or, as in Freudian theory, subterranean forces which defy or suspend the superego. However, modern humanists are dismayed, as are many Christians, at the rise of widespread interest in demonology, spiritism, astrology, and other paranormal and deterministic theories.

Some claim that this is due to the direction of thought taken by post-Freudian man about himself. The ancients believed that some disturbed people were possessed by the devil and could be delivered through penitence, prayer, and divine power. Modern man sees the devil to be part of his soul; to comprise the dark recesses from which emanate all the guilt, anxieties, fears, violence, and insecurity which plague mankind. The split between the ego and the superego is native to the soul; it is a fact of nature. This, critics of the modern mood say, is too great a burden, too intolerable for mankind to bear. Hence there has occurred a turning away from the mood of cultivated rational guilt to the irrational, a move which also took place in Greek and Roman times.

Most Christians believe that alien powers which may assault the soul exist. Indeed, some Christian theologians believe that if not all suicide is demonically instigated. It was the purpose of Christ to triumph over the kingdom of evil and this he has accomplished through his death and resurrection. The Christian is therefore part of an army whose moral victory is not only assured; it is already won through the cross. Christ has repulsed the demonic kingdom and broken its power (Col. 2:14-15). C. S. Lewis has expressed this theme in highly literate form in *The Screwtape Letters*. Many Christians believe that demon activity is regionalized and that where the kingdom of Christ is planted—in individual lives, homes, communities, society—the forces of evil are held in check.

Christian, non-Christian, psychiatric, and religious authorities uniformly caution against dalliance with forces of evil or amateur attempts at exorcism. M. Scott Peck emphasizes that as was the case traditionally in the Christian church where informed insight and spiritual credibility in rare cases called for exorcism, this may be done. But in all cases it must be attempted only by professionally competent psychotherapists and devout persons of great piety, spiritual strength, and moral courage.

**Bibliography:** Alexander, W. M., *Demonic Possession in the New Testament* (1980); Martin, M., *Hostage to the Devil* (1976); Neaman, J. S., *Suggestion of the Devil* (1975); Peck, M. S., *People of the Lie* (1983).

S.J.M.

**DEONTOLOGICAL ETHICS.** *Deontological* is derived from the Greek word *deontos*, a "duty," and thus characterizes an ethical outlook in which the notion of an obligation to keep a moral rule or principle is fundamental. Such an outlook is to be contrasted with teleological ethics according to which ethical rightness consists in the achieving of certain ends such as human happiness, or human welfare, and not in the performance of certain kinds of actions no matter what the consequences. According to deontological ethics, duty is both the reason and the motive for right action. As the "sense of duty," it provides one, and in some versions the only, acceptable motive for performing the action in question.

Deonotological ethics received its classical expression in the moral philosophy of Immanuel Kant, according to whom to act out of duty is to act in accordance with moral law: "I ought never to act except in such a way that I can also will that my maxim should become a universal law." Such a law is "legislated" (i.e., subscribed to) by all persons insofar as they are rational, and observance of the law is one of the chief expressions of human freedom or autonomy. The imperatives of morality are categorical, their obligatoriness being independent of the desire for any particular states of affairs. On some interpretations of Kant, duty never coincides with inclination. According to Kant, the feeling that duty is onerous arises out of the fact that human beings are imperfectly rational, experiencing the conflict between duty and personal inclination which reveals an "unholy will." All individual moral duties, such as the duty never to tell a lie, are to be derived from the moral law. The success of such derivations is a matter of controversy, and Kant's moral philosophy is often criticized for being purely formal and ahistorical.

There are certain structural similarities between Kant's ethics and Christianity. For example, the conflict between duty and inclination corresponds to that between the "old man" and the "new man" in Romans 7; and both Kant and Christian ethics understand freedom partly in moral terms. However, Christian ethics has no conception of duty for duty's sake. Although one's duty to God embraces a manifold of other duties, it is claimed in Christianity that these are deducible from the idea of duty to God. According to Christianity, duty is not to be performed for duty's sake; but for God's sake and for the sake of men and women who are made in the image of God. The motive for such actions is to be the fear and love of God, not the sense of duty in the abstract, Kantian manner. Not only is there a structural similarity between aspects of deonological ethics and Christian ethics, there is also a historical link. The moral maxims which according to Kant are derivable from the moral law are similar to the tenets of Christian morality.

**Bibliography:** Broad, C. D., *Five Types of Ethical Theory* (1930); Kant, I., *Lectures on Ethics*, trans. L. Infield (1930); Ross, W. D., *The Right and the Good* (1930).

P.H.

**DEPROGRAMMING.** This process is an attempt to reverse what is thought to be the emotional and habituative damage done to the mind of a person who has been subjected to some form of suggestive control, whether by political, religious, or other agencies. The aim of deprogramming is not merely to eradicate the traces of indoctrination as far as possible, but to substitute more orthodox or desirable value norms. In this respect deprogramming is distinct from debriefing, which merely involves the acquiring of information in the form of report, frequently of an oral nature, from the person who is being interrogated without prejudice to any values other than accuracy in factual matters.

While political and cultic indoctrination may be so severe as to make an interlude of deprogramming desirable or necessary, the fact is that because all human beings are creatures of habit, they may find it necessary on occasions to submit to a certain degree of mental reorientation in order to rectify habits of body or mind that are potentially or actually damaging to personal well-being. As a consequence, deprogramming now has important medical applications, especially for psychologists who are engaged in behavior modification programs and for psychotherapists. One such technique is based upon the innovative notion that the body can program the brain and thereby reverse undesirable acquired tendencies. The Feldenkrais Method, as it is called, employs a series of small, gentle exercises and movements to correct poor habits of posture, gait, and general mobility that individuals have acquired over the years. This form of deprogramming, which has been used by musicians, athletes, dancers, and people with such ailments as cerebral palsy, arthritis, multiple sclerosis, and back pain, is amazingly therapeutic if somewhat controversial in nature.

The Christian must be constantly aware of the lordship of Christ in his or her life and should only submit to that kind of programming or indoctrination which builds up the believer in the body of Christ. All thoughts must be brought into bondage to Christ, and anything that is disruptive of Christian values will be rejected in a process of personal critical deprogramming, in order that the individual's mind might be obedient to God's will and sanctified by the presence of the Holy Spirit.

See BRAINWASHING, MIND CONTROL.

**DESIRE.** This term describes an emotional response that includes elements of admiration, longing, envy, appreciation, lust, and covetousness, depending upon the circumstances under which desire finds expression. Ever since the time of Aristotle (384-322 B.C.) the relative priority of value and desire has been a matter of debate in value theory. Put simply as a question, do we desire a thing because we value it, or do we value something because we desire it?

As with other similar questions, a straightforward polarizing of value and desire represents a simplistic attempt to fathom the nature of human emotional and moral response. It assumes that value and desire are single, independent, and unrelated entities until they are brought together by a specific stimulus. In point of fact, values and desires co-relate psychologically from a person's earliest years; and it is therefore improper both emotionally and behaviorally to purport to isolate them. Instead of prioritizing the one in terms of the other, both should be regarded as different facets of a complex individual response mechanism which may even exhibit internal conflict in the decision process. At different stages in life one may be expected to take precedence over the other, but on a relative rather than an absolute basis.

The Scriptures make it clear that the desire of the believer must be for the highest levels of morality and spirituality as revealed in the Decalogue (Exod. 20:1-17) and the teachings of Jesus, especially in the Sermon on the Mount (Matt. 5—7). These enactments indicate the true nature of value as it resides in God and also show those things that are the legitimate objects of desire. A life spent in holiness and obedience to God in the service of one's neighbors represented the Old Testament ideals of value and desire. The Christian will be guided by the desires of the indwelling Holy Spirit for his or her own life (Rom. 8:9) and thus will avoid the intellectual and carnal desires that attract the unbeliever (Rom. 13:14). Because the believer's sinful desires have been crucified with Christ (Gal. 5:24), the highest value to be achieved is the consummation of eternal life with Christ, and the most commendable desire that the Christian can entertain is that of fulfilling the evangelistic and social responsibilities of membership in the Christian church.

**DESPAIR.** From a psychological standpoint despair is the antithesis of hope. Whereas the latter produces positive expectations for the present and future and provokes upsurges of energy and creativity, despair negates the possibility of any productive activity. It is nihilistic in character because of its conviction that life contains nothing of positive value and at the best will have a negative result. Those who are caught in moods of despair may have been forced into that condition by the pressure of external circumstances with which they are unable to cope, such as the sudden collapse of a marriage, a serious failure in business, or the unexpected loss of a loved one through death.

The sense of helplessness which is represented by despair may also have clinical overtones if the person in the throes of such an experience is the victim of autogenous depressive interludes. These are phases of depression which tend to occur without warning, with little or no apparent provocation, and which the sufferer seems powerless to prevent. In the darkest moments of such experiences the victim often feels and expresses the absolute hopelessness of his or her position and is certain that existence has absolutely nothing to offer.

There are times, however, when the sense of despair about the future is not specifically pathological, but is actually the product of the individual's experience, for which he or she is largely responsible. This often occurs when one has been unable to achieve an expected or proclaimed goal, and the despair follows from the realization that the ambition was not matched by the ability to bring about a successful conclusion. For those who have exaggerated expectations about the extent to which society in general will support them in their aspirations, a confrontation with the reality of the situation, where it becomes evident that society seems to be totally indifferent to any sense of responsibility in the matter, can bring about a state of grave despair. This is particularly agonizing for people living under conditions of abject poverty who receive very little remuneration for the work that they are able to do, see no hope of escape from their circumstances and have no expectation of financial deliverance from external sources. Only rarely does a sense of despair seem to arise because persons are so convicted of sin in their lives that they feel convinced that they have lost eternal salvation. Far more common is the carping questioning of divine justice by those who have lived dissolute and wanton lives or who have followed divine injunctions in an eclectic fashion, neglecting those which were not to their taste and giving lip service to others. The question, commonly and often ignorantly posed, "Can God be a God of love if he allows this or that to happen?" often represents the reaction of despair that results from a shallow understanding of divine action in human society. Finally, the kind of nihilism that is represented by despair is sometimes adopted as a pose by existentialist philosophers and has more of an intellectual than an emotional quality.

The Christian antidote to despair is the hope of new life in Jesus Christ, who enables the ones that walk in his love to achieve staggering goals (Phil. 4:13). When the power of the Holy Spirit strengthens and enriches human frailty, guiding it according to God's will for the individual, the sense of support from Jesus Christ, who has overcome the worst adversity that the world could heap upon him, provides the practicing Christian with all that is needed for confidence and hope in the future.

**DETERMINISM.** This philosophical approach to the problems of existence states that human actions are basically the consequence of antecedent causation. Determinism has appeared in numerous forms over the centuries, but the basic premise is still the assertion that people do not make free choices in life.

Of the three forms that will be noted briefly here, naturalistic determinism had its roots in Greek philosophy with the atomic speculations of Democritus in the fifth century B.C. and came into prominence with the nineteenth-century scientific developments in Europe. Such a view adopts a mathematical configuration of behavior, in which human beings are held to be part of the mechanism governing the universe, and like it can therefore be quantified in terms of mathematical equations.

The sequence of cause and effect typifies known physical behavior, and since humanity is one element of this sequence, all human conduct must be determined necessarily by prior causes. These may be of an environmental kind, as with upbringing and general cultural influences, or of a hereditary, that is, genetic variety.

Many advocates of behavioristic psychology maintain this view, and while they are usually careful to concede that human beings make choices in their lifetimes, they deny that these choices are independent, free, or otherwise unconditioned, being for them the products of heredity and environment. For these naturalistic determinists the concept of "ought" has no normal or ethical significance, since it allows for a latitude in choice which determinism fundamentally denies. More serious for the adherents to this view is the objection that thought, according to their presuppositions, has emerged from non-ratiocinative origins such as the environment. As a consequence, thought has to be regarded as basically nonrational, and this makes it impossible to know whether naturalistic determinism, and all other branches of thought for that matter, can ever be regarded as true or false. Such a self-defeating philosophy is not likely to inspire confidence in its would-be advocates.

A teleological form of determinism was first advanced by the Stoics, who held to the view that the universe was under the control of a Supreme Reason or Cosmic Logos. This Reason, they argued, has so constituted all things by intelligent planning that there can be no free will in the strictest sense of that term. On this supposition, whatever occurs in life has been planned by the Cosmic Logos to happen, and whatever does not happen was not part of the cosmic master plan. Human beings were regarded as totally depraved by nature, but because mankind contained a tiny spark of the divine fire, a life lived according to what was apperceived of the Supreme Reason was morally good and ethically proper. It is through knowledge of natural processes that human beings come at length to be virtuous and able to live in harmony with their natural surroundings. This form of materialistic determinism even had its own eschatology, because the Stoics believed in the fiery termination of the cosmos, after which a fresh beginning of a similar nature would occur.

In the nineteenth century Hegel (1770-1831) expounded a rational determinism that had some points of contact with the Stoic outlook. His idealistic philosophy regarded phenomena as the expression of absolute reality, which for him was God. History was an example of divine providence which managed to control antithetic elements by resolving them into a higher level of cultural and spiritual expression through a process of synthesis. For Hegel, choice was real only as the expression of mind and was subject to the workings of God's providential order.

Theistic determinism, which also had elements in common with Stoicism, maintained that all events are not merely overruled by God, but are in fact caused by him, since he foreordains what will happen. Advocates of this position have sometimes observed that human free will contradicts divine sovereignty unless human freedom constitutes the power to fulfill one's desires, which in this view are caused by God in any event.

Theistic determinism has several shortcomings, one of which is the defining of human freedom in terms of desire-fulfillment. The circumstances of life are often such that a person is obliged to perform tasks that are contrary to his or her desires, as for example in a time of war. But even unpleasant duties under such conditions seldom lack for volunteers who place duty and service to others above personal desire. Paul pointed to the difficulties in his own life (Rom. 7:19) as an example of how desire can be overruled by temptation in matters of choice, despite all attempts to act in accordance with God's will. While freedom of choice is God's gift to humanity (Matt. 23:37; Rom. 7:18; 1 Pet. 5:2), it can be abused because of the power of evil, as an early example in human history demonstrated (Gen. 3).

Rightly or wrongly, the *imago dei* or image of God in man includes the facility for choosing and for acting upon such choices for weal or woe. Furthermore, God does not control each facet of human activity by a minute, rigid form of predestination, but sustains the believer in his or her freedom of choice and provides grace whereby the individual can be guided in making right choices which will glorify God.

See FREE WILL.

**DETERRENTS, MORALITY OF.** A deterrent is some fact or principle which causes an individual or a group to abstain from, or be impeded by, action that otherwise would be indulged in without any hesitation. The word is derived from the Latin *terreo,* "to frighten," "put in fear of," "to deter by terror," and was common in Roman speech and writings. This general sense is reflected in English usage, and the fact that there is an element of fear attached to a deterrent implies that it is commonly used to halt evil plans. Good, constructive activity may be impeded for various reasons, but the word *deterrent* is not normally used in such situations.

Because, therefore, a deterrent is generally associated with the prevention of something bad or harmful, it is an obvious and legitimate subject for moral debate. Human beings are confronted with deterring situations from childhood. They are protected from injury and death by a wide variety of devices and persons and sheltered from unwise action by rules and regulations which are intended to be obeyed. In rough-and-tumble school play, for example, there is usually some adult available to monitor the situation and deter the activities of the sadist or the bully. In adult life laws have been formulated to have the same effect, and those who are caught violating them are punished accordingly. The world abounds in such mechanical deterrents as locks, bolts, bars, electrified fences, and a great assembly of alarm systems. All these things operate for the protection of the person who installs them and as a general deterrent to theft, vandalism, and the like. They are justified morally on the ground that they can be expected to prevent some form of misbehavior, and in everyday life they have become unexceptional.

But the principal area in which the morality of deterrents is discussed has to do with the present state of nuclear weaponry and the apparent willingness of the two superpowers, the United States and Russia, to employ such weapons should the need arise. These two nations are the prime consideration of this article, although it is realized that other countries possess atomic weapons and could well employ them on an independent basis to settle their own military conflicts. Since World War II (1939-1945), Russia and the United States have built up an awesome stock of nuclear weapons in the interests of what may be regarded as deterrence. Because each nation is well aware of the devastating nature of a nuclear counterattack, neither is willing to indulge in the risk of war through direct confrontation. Unfortunately the nations involved do not feel defended by this situation to any great extent and consequently have been in constant competition to build better and more numerous atomic weapons, as well as devising effective warning systems and means of intercepting missiles.

So terrified have many people become at the thought of global annihilation that since World War II there has been much dissatisfaction expressed regarding the policies of deterrence espoused by Western nations, both from an economic and an ethical standpoint. Interestingly enough, the policies of the Soviet Union seldom come in for scrutiny and protest in these areas. Concomitant with this is an increase in pacifism, not all of it from Christian sources by any means, which has been directed at the young and others untried in battle, to convey the impression that nuclear weaponry is downright immoral and should be abandoned completely.

Those who were conscientious objectors in World War II are still mostly prepared to allow others to lay down their lives for them, but the young secular or Christian pacifist has to be assessed on different grounds. Due to the socialist tendencies that swept Europe after World War II, millions of people have absorbed uncritically the Russian propaganda that the Soviets are a peace-loving people whose only desire is to protect themselves against the crass, expansionist imperialism of the United States. The fact is, of course, that Russian propaganda has been belied thoroughly by such events as the military occupation of the east European countries of Hungary, Czechoslovakia, and Poland, as well as the blatant and ruthless invasion of Afghanistan, all of which was undertaken daringly in the face of atomic deterrents. Nonpacifist political commentators have pointed out repeatedly that the Russians are hard negotiators, who in sports and politics alike employ every dubious device possible in order to gain their ends. In the political arena, the Russians quite clearly have as their overall objective the domination of the world, and all their activities are directed strictly at attaining this goal.

Despite the fact that the Marxist ideology of the Russians has proved to be a political and economic disaster in those parts of the world where it has been applied, the Soviets never avert their gaze from the prospect of world domination and will not therefore undertake any kind of negotiation that will not turn out advantageously for them. These sober considerations must never be forgotten either by pacifists or nonpacifists. The fact that the United States possesses such atomic weaponry as to give the Soviet leaders pause for reflection is an indication of the power of deterrents and holds out hope for some degree of success in negotiations about disarmament.

Against the alleged evils of nuclear deterrence it has been argued by some authorities in the ethical field and elsewhere that the real threat to peace comes from what has been styled the "moral gesturists." These individuals suggest that it would be morally advantageous to abandon nuclear deterrents as a gesture of good will (for the secular humanists) or Christian love (for the Christian pacifists). This in turn, it is argued, would bring moral pressure to bear upon the Soviet Union, which would be so Christian and gentlemanly as to follow this lead and indulge in unilaterial nuclear disarmament. To date, the present writer has not encountered any "moral gesturist" who has reflected upon the international significance of the unbelievable hilarity with which such action would be received by members of the Warsaw Pact, who would have their objective of world domination handed to them on the nicest and most courteous of moral grounds without even a request for such a windfall.

Critics of "moral gesturism," aside from calling attention to the naiveté of the position, have pointed out the potentially disastrous effects of a sudden alteration in the balance of atomic power between the United States and Russia, which in their view would constitute an open invitation to the Warsaw Pact powers to occupy the whole of Europe without opposition, and institute a dark age of even greater horror for the unwilling participants than the Nazi regime which precipitated World War II. Overall it would appear that the ethics of such a procedure as "moral gesturism" need to be given much more serious and penetrating consideration than has been the case among pacifists generally. Advocates ought, among other things, to answer the question of whether it is more preferable ethically to hold out deterrence as a threat in order to maintain some sort of peace, or in abandoning it to invite the horrors of what the pacifists fear most, namely a devastating war which would wipe them out. At the same time they might also reflect upon the conditions of life were the United States, along with the rest of humanity, to become enslaved to Russian communism.

The Christian church, which is so frequently either undecided or at odds about moral and ethical issues, has been compelled by the force of events to consider the morality of nuclear deterrence. The three-million-member Lutheran Church in America, for example, gave solid support in 1985 to a policy statement accepting the possession of atomic weapons as a necessary evil in order to prevent a nuclear war. In 1982 the Roman Catholic Church issued a statement in which deterrents were regarded as acceptable if accompanied by disarmament measures. The following year the Roman Catholic bishops endorsed a "strictly conditional moral acceptance of nuclear deterrence." By contrast, the World Council of Churches assembled in Vancouver in 1983 resolved that the concept of deterrence, the credibility of which depended upon the possible use of nuclear weapons, was to be regarded as morally unacceptable and incapable of safeguarding peace in the long term.

There is clearly much room for debate upon the matter of deterrence, but in the end it will be settled by politicians and militarists, who will or will not wield the weapons, and not by the weapons themselves. Experience of ordinary life indicates that in the arena of fallen humanity, the stronger a person is, the less likely he or she is to be preyed upon by bullies, opportunists, sadists, and others. Advocates of unilateral atomic disarmament by the United States might also reflect upon the fact that it was only the possession of superior weaponry in the form of the atomic bomb by the Americans that prevented the Russian Communists from making even larger territorial acquisitions after World War II than they actually did, which could quite possibly have spread to the North American continent.

**DIALECTICAL ETHICS.** The term *dialectic* comes from the Greek word for conversation. In the hands of Plato, the dialectic or Socractic method became famous. Plato's writings consisted of Socrates, the protagonist, seeking the unchanging essence of a quality such as justice, piety, or courage through a question-and-answer procedure. A dialectic method was also used in the medieval period by Abelard and others who set propositions in opposition to each other in the search for truth. In more recent times, dialectic is associated with the thought of Fichte, Schelling, Hegel, and Marx, who presented their doctrines using the triadic relationship of a thesis, antithesis, and synthesis. Marx used the concept of the dialectic to describe the movement of history, substituting matter for Hegel's "spirit."

The term *dialectical ethics* refers specifically to the ethical positions of the Neo-orthodox or dialectical theologians. Neo-orthodoxy arose after World War I, first in Europe, then in the United States, as a reaction against a liberal Protestantism that attempted to develop a coherent, rational, and optimistic understanding of the Christian faith that was in accord with Western science and culture.

A key source for Neo-orthodox ideas was the writings of Soren Kierkegaard (1813-1855), the Danish theologian who rejected the view that theological propositions, religious formulations, or creeds constitute the true essence of Christianity. Instead, the theological statements of the faith are paradoxical—the idea, for example, that God would come in human form is a paradox that reason cannot comprehend. Basic to his view is the concept of the single person from whom God demands a decision in a highly dialectical situation. This is illustrated by Abraham's confrontation with God that resulted in Abraham's willingness to sacrifice his son Isaac, even though this contravened ethical standards.

The leading figure associated with Neo-orthodoxy is Karl Barth (1886-1968). According to his dialectical method, truth is posed as a series of paradoxes, for example, the infinite became finite, God became human, and eternity entered time. Because of the tension of the dialectic, the individual discovers the ultimate truth of the transcendent God through a crisis experience and recognizes God's rejection of all human endeavor in science, morals, and religion. Barth rejected all autonomous human ethics as a hypocritical and self-justifying failure. In contrast, he suggested true morality begins with a response of faith to the Word of God, to which the words of the Bible bear witness. Ethics is necessarily theological; it can only stem from the knowledge of Jesus Christ as creator and redeemer. Human beings are called to shape their actions in response to the obedience of Jesus Christ, who fulfilled the law in their place. They are to choose what God has chosen them to be.

A second significant dialectical theologian is Emil Brunner (1889-1966), who embraced Barthianism in the twenties, but sharply disagreed with Barth in the thirties over Barth's rejection of natural theology. For Brunner, all human efforts to establish a "natural ethic" must be rejected because they are the attempts of "man in revolt" to be independent from God. Christian morality, in contrast, consists of a response by a person of faith to a command from God in a concrete situation. Each situation is unique; the content of God's command cannot be known beforehand. It is received each time afresh from the voice of the Spirit within a situation of faith. The commands of God are not found in moral principles, statements of law, or even in the dictates of Scripture. We may gain insight from the law and the ways that God made known His will in the past, but these insights cannot define the content of God's will for a new situation.

Other theologians, Rudolf Bultmann, Paul Tillich, Reinhold Niebuhr, and Dietrich Bonhoeffer, have also been identified either directly or indirectly with Neo-orthodoxy and thus with dialectical ethics.

**Bibliography:** Brunner, E., *The Divine Imperative* (1937); Kierkegaard, S., *Fear and Trembling* (1983); Long, E., *A Survey of Christian Ethics* (1967); Oden, T., *The Promise of Barth: The Ethics of Freedom* (1969).

                                                    S.D.A.

**DISARMAMENT.** The horror of warfare has led men to pray for the day when swords will be beaten into ploughshares and spears into pruning hooks. In the Bible, where war is a major theme, this hope is eschatological and related to the dawn of the messianic age. Disarmament will follow the establishment of the kingdom (Isa. 2:3-5). The modern idea that a degree of disarming will itself maintain peace and discourage war contains an element of truth—and also an element of fallacy.

It is true that the development of modern weaponry has raised the stakes of warfare to infinity. Even the conflicts of the two great World Wars, hitherto the models of "total war," pale in comparison with the prospect of nuclear, chemical, and biological conflagration. It is claimed that the very possession of such weapons makes war more likely, yet it is hard to see how a high level of armament on both sides raises the likelihood of the outbreak of war above that which would exist were the level lower but in similar balance. It is not weapons, but conflicts of interest, that cause wars.

The general effect of the vast increases in sophistication and destructive power of post-war weaponry has made the outbreak of war correspondingly less likely. The nuclear deterrent strategy has for forty years prevented war, both between the two great powers and on the European continent. There have, indeed, been many smaller wars, some involving client states of the super powers; but the enormous risks involved with nuclear armaments has always succeeded in preventing them and their major allies from engaging one another.

The scene has been set for attempts at disarmament between the major powers by earlier treaties, such as the 1925 Geneva Protocol on gas warfare (agreed in the aftermath of the horrors of gas warfare in the trenches of the First World War) and more recent bans on nuclear tests in the atmosphere, in outer space, and underwater. Treaties also inhibit the spread of nuclear technology and the deployment of antiballistic missile defenses in the United States and the Soviet Union. In the wake of these and other agreements, negotiated balanced reductions in both nuclear and conventional forces are sought. Both super powers have a major concern in the limitation of their spending on armaments, since the so-called arms race is a very costly exercise. It is naive to believe, however that were it not spent on arms the sums released would go to aid the needy.

Agreed and mutual reductions in arms levels have more than financial advantages. While competition and conflict of interest cause wars, a climate of mutual trust and dialogue can prevent them. It is in this context that disarmament negotiations are important. Disarmament agreements need to be the fruit of a lessening of international tension before they can become also its cause. It is, however, possible for agreements to have the opposite effect of that for which they are intended. While it is a catalyst and not a cause of war, an imbalance of armament can be a dangerous outcome of disarmament initiatives. The strategic nuclear balance is the present example of the traditional notion of a balance of power, which is an essential for peace between powerful competitors. Anything which upsets that balance, or leads one side to believe it has been upset, is destabilizing and can bring about the very thing it is intent upon avoiding. This is the gravest objection to notions of "unilateral" disarmament which are current in some Christian and other circles. Even the unilateral abandonment of nuclear defense by one of the major European powers, particularly France or Britain which maintain their own strategic nuclear defenses, could result in serious destabilization.

The morality of deterrence is complex and is interwoven with strategic considerations. In this discussion we must simplify both. The Christian rightly feels abhorrence when confronted with the possibility of the mass destruction of civilian targets as portrayed in some nuclear scenarios. At the same time, he is aware that if a certain strategic assessment of the bombing of Hiroshima and Nagasaki is accepted (and that is a strategic and military, not a moral, judgment), the nonpacifist Christian could accept the necessity of that dreadful act, mainly that it prevented the much greater casualties that would have been involved in an invasion of Japan. Such a strategic judgment may be questioned, but the acceptance of civilian casualties for overriding military reasons is possible in principle. It is at points like this that the Just War theory appears inapplicable, since its assumption that lines can be drawn between combatants and noncombatants in wars is no longer applicable when most of the combatants are conscripts and most of the civilian populace is heavily engaged in the war effort.

Yet the morality of deterrence does not hinge upon the acceptability of the mass destruction of civilian targets. Nuclear weapons, especially strategic weapons, are designed not to be used in warfare, but to maintain the peace by keeping the balance of power. The primary intention of nuclear power is therefore not the use of the weapons, but the discouragement of aggression. Deterrence need not even imply an intention to use the weapons *if* there is aggression. As a matter of fact we do not know whether the political decision would be taken to launch a strategic response in any given circumstance, whatever the declared intentions of the leaders of the nuclear power may be. Even if the intention were declared merely as a bluff, the deterrent affect would still be maintained.

What has helped many Christians in their assessment of this awesome matter has been a consideration of the alternative to some kind of nuclear deterrent strategy. It is illusory to believe that unilateral limitation or abandonment of the deterrent would produce any corresponding response from the other side, since nations act in their own interests. What is likely, rather, is that any lowering of the West's guard would lead to aggression on the part of those who threaten her security and bring about war—that one thing which those who desire disarmament least intend.

Against this background many have concluded that for all the moral and military perplexity inherent in the strategic *status quo*, any response that would imbalance it is as morally reprehensible as it is strategically foolish.

See ARMAMENT; FORCE, ETHICAL USE OF; JUST WAR CRITERIA; MILITARY SERVICE; WAR.

N.M. de S.C.

**DISCRIMINATION.** By the vicissitudes of our language, *discrimination* has acquired a pejorative meaning. Most often, in modern speech, discrimination means an irrational differentiation based on prejudices related to race, creed, or sex. They are not based on any empirically tested performance.

Ignorance and insecurity often lead to fear of the implications of a given problem. Thought is a necessary prerequisite to informed choice and proper discrimination. The result of unconsidered decisions is discrimination in its negative sense, based on our existent prejudices.

Christians are called upon to discriminate between good and evil. But such discrimination must take into account Christian values. Of course, this discrimination must be taken in its positive sense of making a distinction between unlike things (Lev. 1).

In the history of every nation there are instances of irrational prejudices against identifiable groups of people. The victims of such discrimination have often been subjected to economic and physical suffering. Slavery is one of the most degrading forms and blatant examples of discrimination between races. Until the late nineteenth century, slavery existed in nations in which the majority of the population professed to be Christian. The elimination of slavery in Christian society was effected only after great struggles in lawmaking bodies and on the battlefield.

The Jewish people, as an identifiable religious group, have long suffered from irrational prejudice, becoming the object of resentment and envy by the insecure in the societies in which they live. The most recent culmination of this suffering was the Holocaust during the Nazi era which occurred in a supposedly civilized and Christianized Europe.

Women have been victims of irrational discrimination. The need to protect and care for women bound to a childbearing role was interpreted to mean that they were inferior to men. Laws discriminatory against women excluded them from the normal legal rights afforded to men. Women came to be regarded not only as physically different but intellectually inferior. Now, enlightened governments in the Western world have been legislating against all forms of discrimination based on sex. Efforts are also being made in such jurisdictions to enforce these laws.

It is a sad reflection on the Christian church that among Christians we have not given effect to the teaching of Christianity relevant to discrimination (Rom. 3:22; 10:12). The ideal state would be one in which Christians by their voluntary behavior followed Christian teachings and eliminated all cruel or irrational prejudices. This ideal state is far from being achieved and, accordingly, legislation prohibiting cruelty to others is essential.

Where governments legislate against discrimination, often a new form of discrimination is created, and the majority become the victims of minorities. Affirmative action has been developed with the laudable ideal of insuring acceptance in employment for women and minority groups. However, the possibility arises that persons may be placed in positions of employment not because of aptitude but because of race or sex. Such placements may eventually work to the detriment of the given group of which the person is a member, especially if that person is not qualified for the job. In their demand for equal opportunity in job placements, women and minority groups may bring about improper discrimination, in turn, against the long-time employee deserving of promotion. Caution must be exercised to ensure that all persons of ability have equal opportunity in employment, regardless of race, creed, or sex.

Laws against discrimination will only succeed when the majority of the members of a society are educated in giving due thought to any choice or evaluation they make. In fact, the ability to discriminate, in its positive sense of distinguishing between things, is a useful tool in fighting irrational judgments. Christians must be able to distinguish between good and evil in thinking about what is acceptable and unacceptable. In Ezekiel 22:26, we read the basic exhortation to separate things into categories and distinguish between good and evil. Both the existence of slavery and the murder of Jews in Nazi Germany occurred in Christian countries because Christians had abandoned their obligation to think in order to distinguish good from evil.

Christians must accept all persons, regardless of race, creed, or sex, as belonging to God. Such tolerance of differences is necessary; but we must also never compromise our conviction in the teaching of Christ, with its proper obligations and values. Ultimately, the problems of discrimination (in its negative sense) find a certain resolution for Christians in the attempt to fulfill God's law as given in the new commandment: "If ye fulfill the royal law according to the scripture, thou shall love thy neighbour as thyself, ye do well" (James 2:8).

**Bibliography:** Boulding, E., *The Underside of History: A View of Women Through Time* (1976); Brown, H. C., *Christians Only: A Study in Prejudice* (1931); Peterson, O., *Ethnic Chauvinism: The Reactionary Impulse* (1977); Sartre, J. P., *Anti-Semite and Jew* (1948 tr.); Whittaker, B. (ed.), *The Fourth World: Victims of Group Oppression* (1972).

L.L.

**DISINTERESTEDNESS.** To speak of a person as being disinterested is to describe someone who is professedly without any bias regarding a particular issue or a given situation. Such an individual is an impartial participant or observer and is able to function in this way because he or she has no personal interest in the outcome of the situation. The fact that a person may claim disinterestedness in some area of activity should not be taken as a declaration of noninterest, of course. In actual fact the individual may be keenly interested in the outcome of events, but not to the point where personal concerns might clash with the best interests of the situation.

The Christian is required to serve his or her Savior in the finest traditions of disinterestedness, seeking only God's glory and the salvation of fellow members of society. The story of the Good Samaritan (Luke 10:25-37) illustrates disinterestedness characterized by altruism. The actions of the Samaritan brought him no special benefit or personal recognition, but were a response to the plight of one in deep need without any thought of recompense. Whereas the worldly person might ask: "What is in it for me?" the Christian, by contrast, witnesses selflessly and without hope of personal gain in ministering the gospel of Christ to others.

See ALTRUISM.

**DISPENSATIONAL ETHICS.** Dispensational ethics is not a distinct body of ethical teaching for two reasons. First, the distinguishing feature of dispensationalism is its approach to biblical interpretation, not its ethical principles. It is possible for dispensationalists to take different approaches to ethics but still agree on how they interpret the Bible. Second, dispensationalism is a broad movement consisting of differing interpretative opinions which have been modified over the decades. It is therefore difficult to identify a specific body of doctrine that is held by all dispensationalists.

Dispensationalism derives its name from the view that God works out His purpose in history through a succession of economies or dispensations. Although dispensationalists disagree on the number of dispensations, all would distinguish between the dispensation of Mosaic law; the dispensation of grace (the age of the church); and the dispensation of the millenial kingdom. This kingdom is realized through the reign of Christ on earth. It is preceded by the tribulation, prior to which, according to most dispensationalists, the church will be raptured. In their approach to biblical interpretation, dispensationalists distinguish sharply between Israel and the church, and between the Scriptures that apply to each.

An implication of these doctines is that traditional ethical theory does not have a primary role in most dispensational teaching. The task of Christians during the age of the church is primarily the saving of souls rather than working for the moral betterment of mankind. In addition, because the world is becoming increasingly evil and Christ is expected soon, dispensationalists traditionally have not been active in attempts to reform society through social action. This was particularly true of dispensationalists in the early decades of the twentieth century who reacted against the teachings of the social gospel which identified social reform with the Christian message.

The dispensational approach to biblical interpretation has some implications for the basis of ethics. The distinction between Mosaic law for Israel and the age of grace for the church implies that even though a dispensationalist would likely recognize some universal features in the Mosaic law, it is unlikely that he would use the Decalogue as the primary basis for an ethical theory. Neither will the Sermon on the Mount serve this function because Jesus uttered it in the dispensation of law before His death and Resurrection so that its principles, especially in any political sense, are intended primarily for the coming messianic kingdom. It is not completely irrelevant for the church, according to Charles Ryrie; but this application is secondary. The dispensationalist would most probably derive principles for Christian living from a literal interpretation of all Scripture, but primarily from the letters of the apostles to the church in the New Testament.

**Bibliography:** Clouse, R., *Christian Scholar's Review* (1983), 12:1, pp. 3–16; Ryrie, C., *Dispensationalism* (1965); Saucy, R., *TSF Bulletin* (1984), 7:4, pp. 10–11; 7:5, pp. 6–7.

S.D.A.

**DIVORCE.** Divorce is legal dissolution of the marriage bond with right of remarriage. No Old Testament law institutes divorce. The clearest biblical statement about divorce is Malachi 2:16, "I hate divorce, says the LORD the God of Israel."

Two broad perspectives determine the understanding of marriage and divorce, namely, utilitarian and creationist points of view.

The utilitarian perspective accepts the common-sense notion that monogamous marriage fits best our notions of love, provides emotional stability, and suits family rearing. Nevertheless where, as an empirical fact, marriage no longer exists, divorce is simply a recognition of that fact.

The creationist perspective holds that marriage is a gift of God in creation to the human race and that monogamous marriage, as a bond between two covenanting persons, is intended to be permanent (Gen. 2:24). However, biblical teaching focuses not upon the married state as an abstraction but as a unique kind of personal relationship involving deep, loving commitment to each other. Divorce is a concession to human failure where love has been annihilated. Divorce is thus a necessary evil.

Deuteronomy 24:1-4 does not institute divorce but only controls it, apparently to protect the woman. The bill of divorcement may have been intended as a procedure to discourage hasty acts as well as to regulate actions. "Defilement" which precludes remarriage to the same man (Deut. 24:4) may mean that the first marriage was not really annulled and that her second marriage was really a defaulting on the first. This statute on divorce is one of a series of statutes assembled in the latter part of the book, but without interpretation. It may well reflect compromise to regulate common marriage failure. Subsequent Jewish argument divided among those of strict interpretation that divorce is granted only for cause of adultery (School of Shammai) and those of broader interpretation that divorce may be granted for every cause (School of Hillel).

These are issues which stand behind the challenge to Christ on the question of divorce by the Pharisees (Matt. 19:3-12; Mark 10:1-12) and our Lord's other pronouncements (Matt. 5:31-32; Luke 16:18). The Pharisees posed a dilemma in which He could be criticized for being too strict or too loose. Crucial implications and statements of His words are as follows: the divine aim of marriage as expressed in Genesis 2:24 is reaffirmed by Jesus to be a lifelong union between one man and one woman. "The Creator made them male and female from the beginning." The first man and the first woman were intended solely for each other. Equality between man and woman as to obligation and responsibility is implied. Divorce is allowed on grounds of adultery. Other divorce is merely a concession to hardness of hearts. Remarriage following divorce except for cause of fornication is itself adultery.

Thus, while Jesus concedes the empirical facts of the casuistry embodied in the deuteronomic code, he does not concede that easy divorce was Moses' wish nor that it is the divine purpose. Divorce had to be conceded because of human frailty and was therefore regulated in the Mosaic code. In dealing with the dilemma posed, Jesus says that there is a cause which justifies divorce, but not just any whim ("for every cause").

There follows in Matthew a difficult passage (19:10-12). The disciples expostulate that marriage difficulties combined with such a strict rule concerning divorce might tempt men not to marry. (Instead, they would presumably live common-law in order to avoid such a strict code.) Jesus' reply has been construed to refer to celibacy, though Paul says he had no command respecting celibacy (1 Cor. 7:25). The passage probably belongs to the context of a pronouncement on self-denial for the sake of the kingdom. In it, however, is an important observation on human frailty. Jesus states that not all can take this (Matt. 19:5), but let him do so who can. Not everyone can have a fulfilled marriage. There may be burdens of marriage for some that are too great to bear.

In 1 Corinthians 7, an enigmatic chapter, Paul refers to celibacy, marriage, separation, and divorce. We do not know the specific questions the Corinthians posed. Remaining single is an honorable lifestyle but marriage is normal, he says. Marriage entails obligations, and each partner has his or her rights. Paul's charge to those who are married (vv. 10-11) is direct: no separation or divorce (perhaps this is to some who thought celibacy a higher spiritual state). Every attempt should be made to preserve a mixed marriage if the unbelieving spouse wishes to preserve the marriage (vv. 12-16). If not, it may be fairly inferred that Paul accepts separation or divorce as a necessary evil. In that case the forsaken partner is no longer bound by the marriage. These appear to be matters of what is humanly possible and of what is common sense (v. 25).

What is to be said about the indissolubility of marriage and Christian faith and practice? The facts of human frailty rule out unconditional self-committal for life. Nevertheless, utilitarian marriage falls below the Christian ideal because it falls below the Christian understanding of true love. To make of the married state a metaphysical abstraction, or a binding contract, or a necessary convention for society's good, does not address the issue that primarily marriage is a gift of the Creator, and that He blesses it as we choose it and experience the mysterious unity He intended (Gen. 2:24).

Every marriage is the same. To call marriage "sacramental" does not add anything to it. "One flesh" applies to marriage in general. This, it appears, is the force of Christ's teaching in Matthew 19:3-12 and Mark 10:1-12. Our Lord cast a bright light on the fact of creation. God intended that one man and one woman should enjoy a unique, deeply personal, unified life in their mutual self-giving. When that fails, men and women must seek reconciliation. If reconciliation is not possible, human frailty may dictate dissolution of the marriage with whatever safeguards right-thinking society can devise.

The Christian position involves more than a single paradox. The "one flesh" teaching is a matter of biblical revelation; yet Christians believe in only one kind of marriage for all mankind. The indissoluble nature of the "one flesh" union is the professed Christian ideal; yet sadly

not a few modern Christians themselves have been unable to honor it.

The struggles of the various Christian traditions with these issues is legendary. Some, such as the Eastern Orthodox and most Protestants, allow divorce for the cause of adultery. Others, such as the Roman Catholic Church, deny divorce altogether but have devised a complicated and often generous system of annulment. In no case has any Christian tradition satisfactorily resolved the issue of the status of the vows taken in marriage. The result is that most Christians yield the matter to the courts, thus assigning to the courts a higher spiritual authority than claimed by any church.

Christians ought to understand "except it be for fornication" not as a policy legitimizing divorce but as a concession to human frailty. Likewise, Christians must not too quickly take cognizance of the remnants of sin in human life to speed movement to divorce. Marriage makes demands, often calls for heroic qualities, stands for more than the achievement of happiness, and teaches that love and fidelity are the most precious realities of life. Without them human beings are spiritually and emotionally maimed.

Rules that facilitate severing the bond of marriage, though sometimes necessary, must not become the norm of the church or of society. Rather, the pressure of family, church, and society must be exerted, and easy emotional escape routes cut off, to keep married couples together for their own good as well as for the good of the family and the community.

While Christians are bound to seek help for themselves and for threatened marriages, some problems may be humanly intractable. These include annihilating evils such as philandering, alcoholism, violence, cruelty, psychotic or serious neurotic conditions, homosexuality, impotence, sociopathic behavior, abandonment, extended imprisonment, incest, and abortion without consent of the husband. There is no warrant in Scripture to submit to such evils. In some cases spiritual heroism on the part of a suffering spouse may be redemptive. Where redemptive steps prove fruitless, most Christians understand the Scriptures to allow merciful escape from such evils.

Where divorce occurs, the burden for just dealing is very great. Maintaining communication by divorcing and divorced parents is a moral obligation so that the well-being of the children can be put first, including decisions about property, maintenance, and access. Parents can never divorce their children. No matter how amicable the parting between parents, the children suffer severely. Communication is also important to fair division of money and property especially where a homemaker, after midlife, is expected to enter the work force, having devoted herself for years to her husband's career or business and to a family.

**Bibliography:** Church of England report, *Marriage, Divorce and the Church* (1971); Green, W., *The Christian and Divorce* (1981); Rambo, L. R., *The Divorcing Christian* (1983); Swihart, J. J. and Brigham, S. L., *Helping Children of Divorce* (1982).

See ADULTERY; ANNULMENT; MARRIAGE.

S.J.M.

**DOUBLEMINDEDNESS.** This condition can be explained most appropriately by reference to its opposite, singlemindedness, which in Christian life means that everything one does must be performed consciously to God's glory and to that alone (1 Cor. 10:31). The quality required for such dedication is known in the New Testament as *haplotes,* meaning "singleness of heart" or "freedom from duplicity" in life and service (Eph. 6:5; Col. 3:22). For the true Christian there can be no room for anything other than committed, uncompromising service to Jesus and to him alone, in the belief that he is the only master to be served. By contrast with this, the person stigmatized as "doubleminded" (*dipsuchos,* James 1:8; 4:8) is literally a "two-souled" individual. Because such persons are serving mammon as well as God, they are unstable and unreliable in their ways. Their untrustworthy nature makes them unsatisfactory emissaries of the gospel of eternal salvation, and the Christian is warned to avoid such behavior personally and to beware of those who exhibit it.

**DOUBT.** Doubt is sometimes internal, a state of heart and mind whereby we remain uncertain when we ought to be certain; it is sometimes external, because there is not enough evidence for us to make a definitive judgment.

This second form of doubt is Aristotle's "judicious doubt," the mean between skepticism and dogmatism. This form of doubt constantly confronts the researcher. The scientist, for example, who is pressing forward into new territory must constantly be on guard against the temptation to jump to premature conclusions; and he must equally be on guard against refusing to accept the evidence of the facts when a point has been demonstrated.

Judicious doubt is an essential part of the Christian position. Christians have been divided, for example, over the important question of baptism. Some believe that immersion is the only acceptable form, others see affusion as meant by some texts. Some hold that only believers should be baptized, while others think that the children of believers are legitimate candidates for this rite. While it is proper for every Christian to come to a conclusion based on the evidence, it is not appropriate to affirm that there is no room for others to doubt that conclusion. The main lines of Christian teaching are very plain, but there are some subjects on which it is possible to have different opinions. It would seem that it is this sort of controversy that Paul has in mind when he speaks of "doubtful disputations" (Rom. 14:1, KJV).

The New Testament often sets doubt over against faith; and in such contexts, doubt is blameworthy. Thus Matthew records that when Peter took his eyes off Jesus and, looking at the storm, began to sink, Jesus addressed him in these terms: "O man of little faith, why did you doubt?" (Matt. 14:31). Firm faith would have prevented doubt. In similar fashion, when it comes to removing mountains, for him who "does not doubt in his heart, but believes that what he says will come to pass, it will be done for him" (Mark 11:23; Matt. 21:21). The point here is that the disciple be a committed person. He has come to see that God acts decisively in Christ; salvation is a good gift that is received by faith. It is not some peripheral teaching which may be accepted or rejected at will. Without faith, it is impossible to be a Christian (Heb. 11:6). In this sense, a doubter denies what is at the heart of the Christian way; it places oneself outside the number of believers.

Christian faith has consequences for the daily decisions the believer makes. For example, in the first century, many Christians regarded an idol as nothing and therefore considered nothing wrong in eating meat that had been offered to a nonexistent deity. Other Christians, however, believed the idol represented an evil reality. This believer felt that he did wrong eating meat offered to idols. "He who has doubt is condemned, if he eats, because he does not act from faith; for whatever does not proceed from faith is sin" (Rom. 14:23). If the believer lives by faith, any personal scruple not contradicting faith is to be respected.

There are some areas of life where doubt is quite wrong. William James could say, "Skepticism in moral matters is an ally of immorality. Who is not for us is against." Again, Sir William Hamilton lays it down that "Doubt, as a permanent state of mind, would be, in fact, little better than an intellectual death. The mind lives as it believes."

Even more than the mind is involved. The Christian cannot deny the central place of faith in all of life and the consequent impossibility of doubt in some areas. This does not mean that the Christian always lives in a serenity beyond the reach of doubt. But such doubt is fleeting; it is faith that is constant and characteristic.

**Bibliography:** Baillie, D. M., *Faith in God* (1964), pp. 165–96; Wilde, N. and Starbuck, E. D., *Encyclopedia of Religion and Ethics*, vol. 4, pp. 862–65.

L.M.

**DRAFT.** In fiscal circles this term means the drawing or transfer of money by a written order which is transacted through a financial institution. In military parlance it describes a unit of men drawn from barracks or other reserves in order to supply reinforcement or for other purposes. The United States government uses the term as synonymous with conscription, which is the compulsory enlistment of personnel for military service. This practice of "drafting" has been in use for many centuries throughout civilized nations when the need for troops was urgent, and among some modern peoples it is still in force. Those drafted undertake basic military training and serve in various capacities for a short period of time. The procedure ensures that there will always be a reserve of trained personnel upon which the nation can draw immediately during an emergency. Some Western nations endeavor to avoid conscription in peacetime, relying instead upon voluntary enlistment in the armed forces.

See MILITARY SERVICE.

**DRINKING, SOCIAL.** This phrase describes the imbibing of alcoholic beverages in the context of recreational activities of various kinds, involving more than one person.

The form and meaning of drinking alcoholic beverages are culturally defined: the kind, amount and rate of intake, the time and place of drinking, the accompanying ritual, the sex and age of the drinker, and the role behavior.

Across cultures, social drinking seems to be more acceptable for men than for women. In many societies, men are far more likely to be heavy drinkers than women, although the postwar period has seen increases among women, adolescents, and residents of rural areas. It tends to be more common among peer groups than in family groups. Social drinking generally symbolizes durable social solidarity. In North America roughly four out of five adults drink socially at least once a month. Solitary drinking is less common and usually considered less healthy than social drinking.

Social drinking can divide one group or class from others in a society. Society will also judge the appropriateness of particular groups differently. While a middle class couple sharing a bottle of wine may be described as social drinkers, two "skid row" inhabitants engaged in the same action would not.

Social drinking has a variety of purposes. Drinking can be used to differentiate social contexts, as when a drink marks the ending of work and the beginning of relaxation. For Japanese men, even a small amount of social drinking may release demonstrations of affection. For some it seems to help to create a pleasant atmosphere and does not produce guilt or ambivalence in the drinker. For example, among the Kofyar of northern Nigeria, beer is seen to be an essential ingredient of their lives, and necessary to reach God. On the other hand, some of the Pueblo tribes of the American southwest regard alcohol as destructive and unnecessary and banned it from their communities for several years.

The benefits of social drinking seem to be short term in nature, while the long term effects are often negative. There are "social drinkers" who have hurt others by inappropriate behavior, offered models of drunkenness to their children, wasted time, had accidents, and generally isolated themselves from their families and friends. In Western countries, studies have shown a consistent increase in the amount of alcohol consumed and a correspondingly high rate of abuse.

There has been a general assumption that as long as alcohol is consumed in the company of others, the drinker is not an alcoholic. Recently, however, there has been a shift to use the phrase "problem drinker" to describe a social drinker who imbibes too much. Researchers are beginning to raise questions about the assumed safety of drinking in a group.

The disease concept supporting the belief that problem drinkers or alcoholics are distinct from normal social drinkers is appealing to the alcohol industry, because it shifts the focus of the problem from the bottle to the drinker. This leads to the conclusion that increased consumption by "normal" drinkers would not affect alcohol problems. Treatment is provided to encourage the problem drinker to abstain but not to prevent others from drinking socially. The expansion of the treatment system thus may be seen as a kind of cultural alibi for the relaxing of controls. The tension in control between health concerns and economic concerns means that the government benefits economically through tax revenues while at the same time trying to protect the health and welfare of its citizens.

In North America, there has been a move to accept more drinking as "social drinking" in the 1960s and 1970s, which has been followed in the 1980s by a rising concern about the amount of drinking and its effects. This can be documented in the patterns of various governments' legislative changes: first to lower the legal drinking age and then to raise it. The response to heavy social drinking and its effects has been followed historically by movements to eradicate the use of alcohol altogether. Lately, various organizations have sprung up to press for more stringent controls of drinking drivers.

Alcoholic beverages are used in the Bible in a variety of ways that seem to be acceptable to God; however, God also gives strict orders against their abuse. The churches have been ambivalent about the use of alcohol socially. Some do not use it at all. Some do not use it in church but use it socially in other settings. Others use it in worship and serve it socially in church and elsewhere.

Because alcohol problems will become more of a social and moral issue in the future, Christians must respond to the raised awareness of the effects of alcohol abuse in society. Prevention is better than attempts to control problem drinkers. Treatment facilities will not continue to increase at the same rate as the number of problem drinkers. It will be important for Christians to apply pressure on government policy to reinforce the more restrictive popular sentiments about drinking that are increasingly prevalent today. Christians must also press for change in the environment of social drinking (particularly that created through the use of advertising) to lower the risk of adverse consequences. In addition, Christians need to press for sanctions against alcohol-induced violence.

The churches must continue to offer opportunities for spiritual wholeness and an understanding of the fullness of life of which Jesus speaks (John 10:10) as the true way of relating in the world. Abundant life is denied by the abuse of alcohol and limited severely by frequent drinking. Our bodies are our earthly temples; we are called to care for them as such.

Paul urges us to live our lives so as not to be a stumbling block to others (Rom. 14:13). The Christian is called to ask, "Is my drinking interfering with my love of God or of others?" If the answer to this question is yes, then the Christian is called to make a responsible change in drinking behavior.

**Bibliography:** The Australian Foundation on Alcoholism and Drug Dependence, *Man, Drugs and Society* (1981); Makela, K. *et al.*, *Alcohol, Society and the State* (1981); "The Spiritual Dimensions of Alcoholic Recovery", *Virginia Theological Seminary's Symposium* (March 1982).

See ALCOHOLISM.

M.M.M.-H

**DRUGS.** The concern of this article is with mind-disorienting chemicals rather than with therapeutic substances prescribed by a doctor. It attempts to list the more common psychoactive substances in current use and to take some note of their effect upon individuals and society.

Of the illegal drugs on the market, marijuana is still probably the most widely used, although it appears to be decreasing somewhat in popularity. This substance is derived from the leaves and flowery tops of the *Cannabis sativa* or Indian hemp plant. In street parlance it is known as "pot," "weed," "hemp," and "grass," and is ingested by smoking. The resins and oils of cannabis are known as hashish, which was used in the Orient for many centuries before it became popular in the West. Researchers report that marijuana contains up to 47 per cent more carcinogens than ordinary tobacco and thus can be reckoned as one of the causes of pulmonary carcinoma. The effects of the plant begin to be felt about fifteen minutes after smoking and may be maintained for between two and five hours, after which further ingestion is required.

The majority of drug addicts begin with marijuana and progress to such addictive substances as heroin. A member of the opium family, heroin was used originally as a painkiller until it was found to possess far greater addictive properties than morphine, another opium derived substance which has only one-tenth the pharmacological potency of heroin. Heroin is often known as "horse," "H," "junk," and "white stuff," and involves great expense, and sometimes criminal activity, to satisfy the physical and emotional craving it causes. When ingested it produces violent bodily reactions which culminate in delusions and frightening hallucinations. Many Third World countries find it highly profitable to grow opium poppies and export them in raw form to Europe and the United States.

Cocaine is now appearing in more potent forms on the illicit drug market. Known popularly as "coke," "snow," or "gold dust," it is obtained from a South American bush, *Erythroxylon coca,* and was reputedly used medically by Sigmund Freud in the treatment of depression and anxiety. It is rather expensive to produce and consequently is often adulterated with amphetamines and other "fillers." Cocaine can be sniffed or injected into the bloodstream ("mainlined"), sometimes with lethal results. Although many beginners see cocaine as a "benign drug," it is in fact very addictive; and its popularity has made it the largest single source of illegal income among United States dealers. The substance has been judged quite properly as a grave threat to the fabric of American society, especially since people in responsible positions are often caught in its grip. Because the period of euphoria experienced when the substance is ingested is of brief duration, lasting in fact for only a few minutes, the addict is compelled to use cocaine frequently in order to maintain the sensation of pleasure. Sometimes cocaine is combined with a drug such as heroin to prolong the experience of euphoria, and the resulting substance is then frequently known as a "speedball." Addicts often suffer from drug-induced convulsions and respiratory viruses and experience painful physical withdrawal symptoms should they attempt to abandon the drug.

Drugs that stimulate the central nervous system are readily available and include amphetamines, caffeine, methamphetamine, and ritalin. In street jargon they are known as "uppers," "meth," "speed," "bennies," and the like. These stimulants are generally swallowed, injected, or inhaled. Persons addicted to such substances find it very hard to discontinue their use and discover that withdrawal symptoms include acute depression and general malaise.

A group of sedative drugs that acts as depressants of the central nervous system include the barbiturates. The psychological effect of such substances is to produce muscular relaxation, a lessening of inhibitions, and a general sense of well-being. Depressants of this kind can be obtained easily, and, as far as the barbiturates are concerned, prove to be every bit as addictive as heroin. Mixing barbiturates with alcohol can have grave consequences, as some addicts have discovered to their cost. Of the sedative drugs available, tranquilizers such as Librium and Valium are in common usage for relief of tension in various ways. Some medical authorities believe that they are over-prescribed, especially in the case of Valium, which is twice as strong as Librium. In large doses both drugs can produce addiction without the user realizing it.

An important and widely used class of mind-altering chemicals is known as the psychedelics or hallucinogens. They act on the brain to distort perception to varying degrees and cause illusions, hallucinations, and so-called "mystical experiences." Probably the best known member of the class is LSD (lysergic acid diethymanine), derived from a fungus that spoils rye grain. This fungus, *claviceps purpurea,* contains a significant number of useful medicinal substances, including the nonhallucinogenic lysergic acid. But the LSD derivative is a powerful mind-altering chemical that is reportedly two hundred times stronger than cocaine. It can cause serious personality disorientation, paranoia, and can even cause a person to attempt suicide. The supposed experience of mystical transcendence is not infrequently followed by terrifying fears of temporary or permanent insanity. When this illegal, psychedelic substance is in the hands of street dealers, its relative strength and purity are completely unknown quantities, since they have not been calibrated scientifically; and therefore the result is a drug of potentially great danger. Other illusion-producing substances include mescaline, peyote, and psilocybin, which have vegetable origins, as well as an extremely strong veterinary anesthetic with the clinical name of phencyclidine, but known widely as PCP or "angel dust." It is apparently easy and cheap to manufacture illegally, and it is so powerful that it must be diluted by means of additives such as LSD. Needless to say, PCP has devastating effects upon the central nervous system and produces changes of personality, depression, hallucinations, that can cause a person to commit homicide or suicide.

The most widely used psychoactive substance in the world is, interestingly enough, ethyl alcohol in its various forms. The fact that alcohol ingestion seems to be so acceptable socially everywhere except in Moslem countries still does not detract from its seriousness as an addictive substance. Chemically it functions as a central nervous system depressant which affects judgment, modifies inhibitions, delays reflexes, and induces lethargy, depression, or hostility, depending upon individual reaction to the drug. Alcoholism is the major cause of injury and absenteeism in industry and has been responsible for a vast array of social and family problems. Many crimes are committed under the influence of alcohol, which is regarded by some experts as the third most potentially dangerous drug, following the inhalants and "mainline" speed (methamphetamine). Psychiatric patients frequently have a history of serious drinking, and alcoholics are generally in much worse bodily and emotional health than nondrinkers. Alcohol is included in this article as a drug because most teenage drug addicts are reported to have begun their mind-altering experiences with alcohol.

Symptoms of drug abuse are readily recognizable, ranging from unusual psychological factors such as abrupt changes of mood or a withdrawal from reality to physical phenomena such as tremors, hyperventilation, stupor, convulsions, and hallucinations. Because of the potency of the substances involved, professional help should be sought immediately for the addicted.

Christian opinion is apt to be ambivalent about the "drug scene." While it is recognized as a serious social problem, some observers think that the addicts should simply be left to end the way of life that they have chosen. Others, feeling that the victims of drug abuse may have been lured into addiction unknowingly, are willing to make strenuous efforts to rehabilitate them. These persons have already made important contributions to the crusade against drug use, but they often feel that much more concern for the problem needs to be expressed by society as a whole.

For the Christian, the first onslaught against drug use must begin in the family, where parents must set an example of sobriety and high morality for their children to follow. When the latter feel loved, secure, and accepted at home, peer pressure to indulge in various forms of drugs, applied by weak-willed persons who have already succumbed to the habit, will be easier to resist, even though the temptation to "explore" may be present. Christians need to realize that the substances described briefly in this article are all highly toxic, many of them to a degree that the ordinary medical practitioner seldom really understands. If Christians are to speak credibly to the drug situation, they first need to be well informed, which unfortunately all too few are.

In a fallen world, drug abuse is only one symptom of humanity's sinful nature and alienation from God. In an age where people are striving for personal identity, freedom, and self-determination, it is ironic that they are content to bring both their bodies and minds into a kind of slavery that frequently destroys both. The Christian is exhorted to stand in the liberty which results from personal acceptance of Christ's atoning work on the cross and is warned against entanglement in anything that might bind, inhibit, or enslave (Gal. 5:1). Believers need to take seriously the Christian doctrine of the body as the temple of the Holy Spirit of God (1 Cor. 6:19) and ponder the penalties that accompany its defilement. We are commanded to glorify God in our bodies as we submit to His will in our lives, and we must not merely proclaim this lofty ideal but must practice it. The experience of Jesus Christ as Savior and Lord and the personal guidance of the Holy Spirit in the believer's life must be presented convincingly as spiritual realities which alone will satisfy those who are looking for "mystical transcendence" and which will build up the believer in the body of Christ instead of abandoning him or her to addiction, bodily degeneration, and possible premature death. At another level of ministry to society, Christians should press for a much more radical control over the supply of illicit drugs on the world market; and instead of blaming young people for the growing problem of drugs in contemporary life should instead be prosecuting rigorously those corrupt, selfish, mercenary adults who are enslaving these weak and helpless victims of their greed.

See ADDICTION; DRINKING, SOCIAL; HALLUCINATORY DRUGS; NARCOTICS.

**DUTY.** Most systems of ethics find a place for duty, but there is controversy over whether duty is a central ethical concept. If it is, is the duty in question an absolute or overriding duty, or only a *prima facie* duty? Duty is often contrasted with pleasure or inclination and sometimes with merit (Luke 17:10). Duty is central to Kant's ethics, according to which a morally right action is one that is done in accordance with the moral law, irrespective of the personal inclinations of the agent or of the likely consequences. Certain more modern moral philosophers (e.g., W. D. Ross) give a central place to *prima facie* duty, which may be overridden by one or more of a variety of considerations. There is further controversy over whether, granted the centrality of duty in ethics, the recognition that some action is a duty provides or ought to provide a sufficient motive for performing the action in question.

In a less precisely philosophical sense, a duty is an action or type of action that ought to be performed even though it might be inconvenient or unpleasant to do, or which one may for some other reason be disinclined to do. Hence, a person may regard it as his or her duty to look after aged parents, to start work punctually, or to vote.

But the recognition of the centrality or importance of *duty* is of little help if it is impossible, for whatever reason, to specify *duties*. Kant thought, probably mistakenly, that certain specific duties (e.g. the duty not to tell a lie) were derivable from his moral law. Others have sought to derive duties from nature. Whether such attempts succeed or not, a broad contrast may be drawn between those duties which are held to be inseparable from being a person (e.g., duties to one's parents or to one's country) and those which arise as a consequence of a person's free decision, as part of a promise or contract (e.g., duties to a specific woman as one's wife or to

one's children). The recognition of a range of such duties does not by itself argue that moral rightness consists in performing them. The place in morality of love, sympathy, and friendship also *ought* to be considered.

One of the central conceptual questions about duty and duties is: does having a duty imply the ability to perform that duty? Does "ought" imply "can"? For many cases, it is plausible to suppose that this implication holds. If a person is physically incapable of looking after his aged parents, it is implausible to suppose that he has an obligation to do so. He might plausibly be supposed to have had an obligation not to allow himself to be incapacitated where this was avoidable, or to insure the care of the parents in other ways. Despite the plausibility of the implication, however, Augustinians and Calvinists (in their controversies with the Pelagians and the Arminians respectively) have taken what they believe to be the biblical view that inability does not limit obligation. Though a person, because of his sin, cannot love God with all his heart, mind, soul, and strength, nevertheless he is obliged to do so, and is culpable for not doing so.

The other main conceptual question about duty has to do with the relation between duty and rights. Does every obligation create a right in someone else? Does a person's duty to care for his aged parents mean that the parents have a right to be cared for? And does a person's duty not to be cruel to animals confer on them a right to be treated humanely? Perhaps it is more plausible to support the view not that obligations confer rights but that moral rights, if there are such, delimit obligations. If a person's rights are flouted, this ought not to be done.

In Christian morality there is controversy over whether duty or love is paramount. Perhaps this confusion is caused by a failure to distinguish the *rule* of morality, which is the law of God in nature and through Scripture, from the *motive* in morality, which is to be love to God and gratitude to Him.

**Bibliography:** Helm, P. (ed.), *Divine Commands and Morality* (1981); Moore, G. E., *Ethics* (1949); Prichard, N. A., *Moral Obligation* (1949); Ross, W. D., *Foundations of Ethics* (1939).

See AGAPE; RESPONSIBILITY.

P.H.

# –E–

**EARLY CHRISTIAN ETHICS.** Christianity came into a world of ideas and sophisticated ethical systems. Ancient schools that were based on Democritus, Plato, and Aristotle, such as the Stoics and Epicureans, produced distinct and popular ethical theories that continue to influence modern thinkers.

How did it come about that as a result of the life and teachings of Jesus and the activities of his undistinguished followers, the ancient cults and schools were displaced? The republican nature of the Roman Empire and its legendary rule of law helped to transcend regional religious-ethnic sentiments. Early Christian writers such as Justin Martyr and Athenagoras make a strong point of the principle of universal justice in their plea for toleration. Ease of travel, the social withdrawal of the aristocratic class, and the emergence of a new entrepreneurial social group stimulated the cross-fertilization of ideas including the spread of Christianity.

More importantly, key features of philosophical traditions fostered the denigration of human personality and elementary morality. The philosophical schools tended to reinforce the impression that the universe is indifferent to individuals. Idealism advocated the view that existence is a form of nonbeing, while materialism through its determinism encouraged a fatalistic view of life and a belief in such practices as astrology.

The religious cults of the empire (Diana, Mithra, Adonis, Isis, Eleusis, and many others) were impersonal and ritualistic. Transcendental absorption, ritual ecstasy, and ritual asceticism tended to diminish the worth of the individual and to be a cover for orgiastic practices. The Christian conventicles became a powerful magnet to non-Christians because of their fellowship and personal purity. The Christian doctrine of creation with its corollaries that God is personal, that He personally cares for and judges man, that He loves mankind redemptively in Christ, and that as a forgiven sinner man can live in harmony with God and his fellows, furnished ancient people with a distinct intellectual, emotional, and moral alternative.

Criticism has been directed against early Christian writers by alleging that they diminish salvation by grace alone and instead articulate Christianity in legalistic and moralistic terms. For the most part, this view is mistaken. For example, the teaching about the Two Ways, the way of love to God and neighbor and the way of death, of the *Didache* runs parallel to the teaching of the book of James in the New Testament. If there is a frequent appeal for perfection in early writers, this should be judged in relation to the then-widespread immoral practices and the pastoral need to urge vigilance, morality, and integrity of Christian commitment. They expressed their faith in relation to issues that shaped perception and thinking. Thus at the end of the second century A.D., Clement of Alexandria presented Christ as The Instructor. Clement did not intend to exclude the cross but, in the fertile intellectual climate of a great educational center, he interpreted Christ to the non-Christian mind.

Three examples of ethical exhortation and discussion may be cited:

Firstly, concerning Christian actions and interpersonal relations. The so-called First Epistle of Clement is the earliest extant item of Christian literature outside the New Testament. It is not an episcopal document; rather, it is a congregational letter from the Christians of the church at Rome to the Christians in the church at Corinth. The situation at Corinth reflects Paul's earlier concerns in his two letters to Corinth, though now certain elders had been ejected from office and a younger group had assumed leadership in the church.

The letter is filled with Old Testament and secular allusions and appeals based on obedience to Christ. Pride, envy, and sedition are wrong. The Lord commands repentance, following the example of obedient biblical heroes of faith such as Abraham. The Holy Spirit honors the gentle and longsuffering. Consider the example of Christ's own humility and submission. There is order and harmony in nature and subordination and gradations of rank in the army as well as in other human relationships. The evicted elders should be restored to their places. These ethical injunctions are not episcopal pronouncements but appeals to faith, loyalty to Christ, a Christ-like pattern of humility, and common sense.

In the letter, the Corinthians are repeatedly addressed as "brethren," the exhortation "let us" occurs over sixty times, and the term *beloved* recurs many times as well. The theme of the letter is renewal of brotherly love, not direction from Rome. Allied with the fraternal appeal are pleas to re-establish mission as their priority, and to reshape attitudes and relationships. Ethical behavior is seen to be an ingredient essential to effectively "preaching the good news that the kingdom of God is coming."

Hallmarks of early influential Christian congregations were kerygmatic integrity, egalitarian loving concern, and high moral standards that reached out with welcoming and renewing hands of love.

Secondly, concerning interpretation of the Christian faith to non-Christians. An unknown Christian of the early second century addressed a letter to Diognetus. Christians, he says, despise gods fashioned in the image of their makers' passions. Propitiatory sacrifices to such gods insult the intelligence. It is immoral to try to buy off the gods or to gaze at the stars in order to cater astrologically to one's own whims. Devotees employ superstition simply to gratify human passions and justify moral weaknesses.

There follows a remarkable statement in *Diognetus* 5—6 about the place of Christians in the world. Christians are not eccentrics, but are like their fellow-citizens in any society. To be sure, their mores differ from those of the world, but more important are the spiritual qualities which their faith produces in them. Christians believe that God personally creates, cares for, redeems, and will finally judge all men for their deeds. God saves men by neither coercion nor deception, but by love and persuasion. Such love evokes answering devotion to truth and goodness, so that Christians would rather die in the arena than renounce their faith.

Life is viewed from the standpoint of a divine purpose, not of fatalism; as under divine providence, not as victims of capricious nature or gods. God is nurse, father, teacher, counselor, physician, mind, light, honor, glory, strength, and life. To those who yearn for faith, their response is moved by love: love for Him who wrought the sweet exchange in sending the Son to die for them, which makes men debtors to limitless grace. The true Christian understands that while his lot is cast on earth, God rules in heaven. Therefore, he admires the heavenly virtues and is unafraid to rebuke evil and wrong, whether in himself or around him.

Thirdly, concerning the defense of Christian faith and values, about 175-177 A.D. a *Plea* on behalf of Christianity was submitted to the emperor Marcus Aurelius at Athens by Athenagoras, who was trained in philosophy and had become a Christian. It should be borne in mind that Marcus Aurelius was the last of the great Stoic ethicists.

At the outset, Athenagoras pleads for justice on the grounds of traditional Stoic and empirical commitment to equity. By law even ridiculous beliefs were tolerated. It is not beliefs but wrongdoing that merits penalty and punishment, says Athenagoras. Christians, on the other hand, "suffer unjustly and contrary to all law and reason." Despite such mistreatment, Christians are taught not to return blow for blow but to be kind to those who oppress them and who pour out unfounded accusations upon them. Christians espouse principles of justice, rather than arbitrary acts of malice.

Athenagoras argues that the atheism charged against Christians is false. Christians distinguish God from matter, and he cites well-known pagan sources that satirize the irrationalities and immoralities attributed to the gods. Such behavior is merely an attempt to explain away or to justify human immorality, which Christians do not practice. They regard adultery, homosexuality, and pederasty as outrageous. The strong chase the weaker, he says, and "outrage those with the more graceful and handsome bodies." These practices Roman laws also condemned but were unable to control.

Christians strive not to violate personhood, and they set a value upon human life. Athenagoras states a beautiful and vital Christian principle: through genuine love, Christians regard one another as sons and daughters, brothers and sisters, fathers and mothers. Therefore, "it is a matter of great importance that those, whom we thus think of as brothers and sisters and so on, should keep their bodies undefiled and uncorrupted." Christians will neither exploit nor kill. They "regard the fetus in the womb as a living thing and therefore the object of God's care." How then can they slay it? Children are God's gift. How then can unwanted infants be left on hillsides exposed to die or be eaten by animals, as was commonly done by the Greeks and Romans?

Athenagoras goes on to argue that the Christian virtues of love and goodness are neither merely abstract principles, nor ascetic ideals, nor hair-splitting verbal distinctions. Christians value the creation and the beauty of the human body as God's work. The "order, harmony, greatness, color, form, and arrangement of the world" give ample reason to adore God. He adds, "beautiful, indeed, is the world, in all its embracing grandeur." Yet, it is not the world but its Maker who should be worshipped. Men by avarice and immorality destroy beauty by unreasoning passion.

Some remarkable parallels between the modern and early Christian worlds are closer than at any intervening time. Ease of conversion from cult to cult was a feature of life in the second and third centuries A.D. Especially noteworthy was the quest for personal identity. The cultic religions and ethical systems were lonely and impersonal. Aspiring to displace the individual's ordinary social identity through ecstacy or transcendental participation in the divine was a common theme among devotees. This quest for a new identity tended to diminish the ultimate worth of the individual and his daily ethical responsibility.

Christian attitudes and practices contrasted sharply with the mood of the times. Christians were radically egalitarian; they displayed a powerful sense of community and affirmation of one another; their devotion to God was complete; and their ethical principles were life-transforming.

**Bibliography:** Chadwick, H., *The Early Church* (1967); Judge, E. A., *The Social Pattern of the Christian Groups in the First Century* (1960); Oates, W. J., (ed.), *The Stoic and Epicurean Philosophers* (1940); Richardson, C. C., (ed.), *Early Christian Fathers* (1950).

S.J.M.

**EASTERN ORTHODOX ETHICS.** There is no real distinction in Eastern Orthodoxy between moral, pastoral, ascetical, and mystical theology, or between Christian obligations and the evangelical counsels. Therefore, there is a tendency to imitate the ontological perfection and holiness of the Triadic God, which are the foundation of the morality and holiness of all rational creatures. Consequently moral theology is a corollary to dogmatic theology, for orthopraxis follows orthodoxy. "Ethics" is usually understood as a philosophical term.

Orthodox moral theology perceives a wide field of Christian morality ranging from the minimum, or the Decalogue (Deut. 5:6-21), to the maximum, or the Beatitudes (Matt. 5:3-12). Within these Orthodox confines, one is free to choose the most convenient, acceptable, or subjectively possible moral teaching and practice.

Since the monastic rules and letters of St. Basil the Great (A.D. 379), Orthodox Christians formed their consciences under the guidance of spiritual fathers, directors, or elders, that is to say, monks who had the right to administer the Sacrament of Penance. Soon they became masters of Orthodox moral teaching and created an extensive penitential literature, such as *Penitential of John the Faster* (A.D. 595). This led to "monasticization" of moral theology as applied to laity. This trend was strengthened by the teaching and practice of St. Theodore of Studion and the promoters of cenobitism (life in a religious community), social virtues, and personal sacrifice.

There also emerged *hesychasm* (hesychia-quietude, tranquillity), an ascetic and mystical teaching and psychosomatic practice resembling Yoga. Here the quiet, contrite, and inner prayer or meditation was bringing the mystic into the presence of God, his uncreated energies, and contemplation of the uncreated divine light by prescribed physical exercises, flexing of muscles, control of breathing and heartbeat, the lotus sitting position, and a constant repetition of the Jesus Prayer: "Lord, Jesus Christ, the Son of God, have mercy on me," or an equivalent formula.

The sources of Orthodox moral theology are: Sacred Scriptures, liturgical books, writings of the Church Fathers (especially of St. Basil the Great, St. John Chrysostom, St. John Climacus, Pseudo-Dionysius the Areopagite, Pseudo-Macarius, St. Maximus the Confessor, St. Theodore of Studion, St. Symeon the New Theologian, and St. Gregory Palamas); the symbolic books, that is, "Orthodox Confession of Faith" of Peter Mohyla (Mogila), the Metropolitan of Kiev (1646), and the Acts of the Synod of Jerusalem of 1672; canonical collection *Pedalion* (Slavic *Kormchaia kniga*); *Philokalia* of Nikodemus Hagiorites (1809); and the *Dukhovnyi reglament* of Peter the Great (1721), etc.

From the seventeenth century onward, Greek, Ukrainian, and Russian Orthodox theologians started to compose moral theological treatises and manuals, which in many instances were imitations or adaptations of Catholic and Protestant catechisms and moral theological works. At the same time there grew a polemical literature against the Catholic and the Protestant moral teaching, especially against casuistry, Jesuit theology, probabilism, the scholastic method, and the sufficiency of attrition for confession.

Orthodox morality is communal and mystical in character and establishes a distinct Orthodox ethos. Hence the dominant position of liturgies, which to Orthodox Christians are the schools of morality, asceticism, and mysticism. The liturgies do this by the texts, rubrics, gestures, utensils, icons, and architecture, and especially by Scriptural lectures and preaching. Here the faithful can learn the threefold path of salvation, which consists of purification (Greek *katharsis*), illumination (*ellampsis*), and vision (*theoria*), as the first step, of unification (*henosis*), as the second step, and of divinization (*theosis*), as the third step. Purification implies a conversion and cleansing of body and soul of sin and evil desires. Illumination is a process of permeation by the divine light of the heart, mind, and soul. Vision implies contemplation of the Triadic God as the absolute truth, supreme goodness, and infinite beauty. This constitutes a participation in the Divine Wisdom. Unification is a process of coming ever closer to the Triadic God as to the merciful Father, redeeming Brother, and sanctifying Spirit. Finally, theosis or divinization (not deification), leads Christians through moral life to the holiness and glory of God. It is the sanctifying activity of the Trinity which transfigures by grace the moral conduct and introduces a process of assimilation to God the Father of the whole human person and of mankind, through the mediation of Jesus Christ and in the Holy Spirit. Thus the human being becomes an image and likeness of God and Christ.

The focal point and foundation of Orthodox morality and moral theology is the mystery of, and life in, Jesus Christ, the Second Person of the Most Holy Trinity, the inhominized Logos, the God-man, the crucified, resurrected, and exalted Lord, Messiah, and Savior. He is the creating, renewing, sanctifying, and fulfilling source and power, who is the ideal example of moral activity and life for His mystical members on their way to eschatological fulfillment in His kingdom and the family of God. The mystical union with Christ and imitation of Him help to comprehend and existentially realize in the Holy Spirit His moral teaching and His law of love to God, mankind, and all creation.

The Holy Spirit is the dynamic and moving power of the cosmos, the church, and each person. He is the Lord and Giver of both the natural life and the life of grace. He is the Heavenly King, Consoler, the Spirit of truth, goodness, and beauty, and the treasury of blessings, including the moral and holy life. His fruits are "love, joy, peace, patience, kindness, goodness, faithfulness, gentleness, and self-control" (Gal. 5:22-23). His gifts are wisdom, knowledge, faith, healing, working of miracles, prophecy, distinguishing of spirits, various tongues, and their interpretation (1 Cor. 12:4-11). Thus life in the Holy Spirit is the source and foundation of a moral, virtuous, and holy life for all Orthodox Christians. His gracious activity comes to them as a call, warning, strengthening, consolation, or illumination. He opens their minds and hearts to the Word of God and causes them to repent with prayerful contrition (Acts 2:40; Rom. 8:28-30; 1 Cor. 14:3). He also gives them internal witness of their adoptive divine filiation (Rom. 8:16; 1 John 3:19-24).

Prayer is the pinnacle of religious and moral activity for all Orthodox Christians. It is a mysterious and loving gift of God the Father through the Son and in the Holy Spirit, which comes to us as a supernatural call in faith, hope, and love. It develops into an intimate and personal polylogue with the Tri-Personal God, which includes His praises, petitions, and thanksgiving. Prayer is also the expression of participation in His inner life, light, and love, and ascends from us to God the Father, as to the Head of the Divine Family, through the Son and in the Holy Spirit.

Today Eastern Orthodoxy condemns astrology, occult rites, homosexuality, premarital sexual relations, pornography, marital unfaithfulness, abortions, child abuse, mercy killing, and cremation. It permits divorce for grave reasons, but prohibits tetragamy. Contraception is a controversial issue left to the discretion of the confessor and the penitent. Capital punishment has been tolerated in the past but a strong movement is in existence today opposing it on moral, legal, and psychological grounds.

**Bibliography:** Bilaniuk, P. B. T., *Studies in Eastern Christianity*, I, (1977); II (1982); III (1983); Harakas, S. S., *Contemporary Moral Issues Facing the Orthodox Christian* (1982); *Ibid., Towards Transfigured Life* (1983); Spidlik, T., *New Catholic Encyclopedia* (1967), IX, pp. 1126–28; Zuzek, I., *Ibid.*, IX, pp. 1125–26.

P.B.T.B.

**ECOLOGY.** The study of relationships among organisms, and between organisms and their environment is ecology. Man takes his place among these relationships.

The *divine origin* of biological relationships is established in Genesis 1:9-25, and the role of Christ is set forth in Colossians 1:16-20 and Hebrews 1:3. God's Son was not only instrumental in the establishment of the natural order but continues to express Himself through it as He gives it existence.

The recorded history of man's systematic learning about these relationships spans the time from Theophrastus in the fourth century B.C. to the present. The German biologist Haeckel in 1866 coined the word *okologie* from the Greek *oikos* (home) to refer to the habitats of plants and animals. The development of ecology as a scientific discipline has been relatively recent. Elton in Britain and Clements and Shelford in America are the most famous pioneers, and all belong to the first part of the twentieth century.

While man's dominance over other species has been built into the system by God (Gen. 1:28), this has not had much more than local impact on the environment until recently. Now, in the latter part of the twentieth century, man's technological development coupled with his high rate of population increase have placed him in the position where his stewardship of the environment is as crucial to the survival of life on earth as is his management of nuclear energy.

The environment in which organisms live consists of physical factors and biotic factors. Physical factors include temperature, light, and moisture. Most living things have a fairly narrow range of tolerance for these factors. As man removes the earth's forests, resulting changes in physical factors affect the biota, usually adversely. The use of three shifts of ten thousand men each to clear forests in Lebanon during the reign of Solomon (1 Kings 5) undoubtedly had something to do with the transition of much of the region to desert.

Other physical factors include properties of the media—water, soil, air—in which organisms live. Chemical solutes in bodies of water affect their suitability for aquatic life; exposure to wind erosion, as in the Sahara, destroys the fertility of the soil; and the cutting of trees reduces oxygen in the air. Most of the oxygen in the atmosphere comes from photosynthesis by trees, with tropical forests providing for the current shortfall in the industrialized northern hemisphere.

Biotic factors in the environment include the interrelationships of plants, insects, birds, mammals, and other animals in both natural and cultivated areas. Man's efforts to control certain pest species have commonly resulted in ever more resistant genetic strains of these species. It is probable that man's attempt to make himself independent of the natural environment has in fact made him increasingly insensitive to it and ever more at risk to ecological catastrophies such as oxygen deficit, water contamination, and destruction of soil.

A particular set of environmental conditions occurring in an area is called a habitat. There are marine habitats, freshwater habitats, and land habitats. Marine habitats are the most stable in terms of chemical composition, temperature, and light. Since there is more light near the surface, plants are found there, and so the oxygen photosynthesized by the plants is concentrated near the surface. In the depths there is little oxygen and few animals.

In freshwater habitats plants and animals must have adaptations to keep excess water out of their tissues. Temperature and dissolved chemicals are more variable than in marine habitats due to smaller size of freshwater bodies. Turbidity varies with condition, thus affecting light. Organisms living in freshwater habitats must be adaptable to variable conditions.

Land habitats are the most variable of all. Temperatures fluctuate daily and seasonally, water conservation is especially important, and plants and animals sort themselves out into a variety of niches according to their adaptations to these conditions.

The ecological distribution of living things on the earth is thus highly organized, and those species that have similar requirements and adaptations tend to group themselves together in *communities*. The community is the whole group of plants and animals living in a particular location or habitat. There are desert communities, grassland communities, deciduous forest communities, and so forth. Within each community there is a multitude of niches such as the forest floor, herbs, shrubs, tree trunks, and canopy. Each niche is appropriate to certain species for various activities such as feeding and nesting. Furthermore, communities themselves are not scattered at random but result from combinations of factors in each place, one of the most important being the history of the area.

Communities are dynamic. There is constant competition among member organisms for light, moisture, nutrients, and various niche requirements such as nesting sites. With certain exceptions, such as areas of soil erosion, there is a built-in tendency for bare areas to become clothed with vegetation. This produces further changes as photosynthesis traps more solar energy, light penetrating the foliage is reduced, and debris accumulates on the ground. These changes militate against the continuing presence of those plants and animals which found the conditions attractive in the first place and encourage other species to succeed them. Thus a succession of communities occurs until a dominant one is established, able to reproduce itself indefinitely in the conditions of its own making.

In this way God has given to the planet a kind of self-healing capability. When an area has been damaged by natural or manmade causes such as fire or disease, there is at hand provision for reinvasion of that area by organisms, surrounding it in an orderly succession of communities leading up to re-establishment of the climax, or a dominant community. Unfortunately from an ecological viewpoint, present-day forestry practice usually tries to hold forest succession to early stages because tree species most valuable for commercial wood products occur in these stages. Climax forests are thus disappearing, along with the various plants and animals that depend upon them, and the gene pool for all these biota is growing smaller. Ethics here must concern itself with short-term profits and long-term disaster.

One of the worst offenders in environmental destruction is the agricultural industry. Its usual practice is to try to bring every possible meter into cultivation. This means eliminating fence rows, reducing wood lots, draining wetlands, and using chemical sprays both on cultivated ground and uncultivated areas nearby. The ecological result of this is to destroy the natural biota, lower the water table in the ground, expose the cultivated land to wind erosion, and generally produce an ecological desert. So far the agricultural industry has been almost completely closed to discussion of these issues. The answer usually given is that current policies are dictated by economics. So long as agriculture is unwilling to consider the long-term benefits of alternative policies, this stands as one of the world's most glaring examples of contempt of ethics related to ecology.

The source of energy for all life processes on earth is the sun. Green plants capture this energy that comes as light and convert it by photosynthesis to chemical energy. From the leaves of plants it then passes through the earth's system of energy flow. Green plants are thus "producers." Animals are "consumers," gaining their energy by eating plants. Primary consumers feed directly upon plants; secondary consumers feed on primary; and there may be tertiary consumers as well. As plants and animals die, some energy is committed to the soil to be returned to the system via the roots of other plants. But the various life processes of organisms also produce heat, which is energy lost to the atmosphere and eventually to outer space. Survival of life on the planet is directly related to the flow of energy from the sun through the various components of the energy system on earth.

While it is true that the sun is gradually burning out, God has made provision for the energy requirements of the world for a very long time to come, if a long future should be in His purposes. On the other hand the energy available at each level in the system at any time is limited by the vegetation. Energy requirements in excess of this can often be met by stored supplies, including fossil sources, as long as they last; but these too are limited. Man's practice of taking what he wants now as if there were no tomorrow could in fact jeopardize tomorrow. Use of energy at all levels must be monitored carefully, and a new respect for green vegetation as the ultimate means of supply is urgently needed.

The dominance of man in relation to other living things has been built into the system by God (Gen. 1:26-28). The ark (Gen. 6:19—7:16) reflects the fact that man is not only dominant over other life, but also dependent upon it. It is reasonable to assume that God values other species for themselves (Luke 12:6), but it is also clear that other living things are essential to man's survival.

The role of man is that of steward of the environment. The greatest wisdom is needed in the management of water, soil, and air, plants and animals so that the productivity of the environment is maintained at the highest possible level. This challenges man's capabilities to the utmost since he is confronted with a gigantic complex of interacting processes. It also challenges man's ethical integrity, since pressure groups are constantly seeking to increase short-term profits by sacrificing long-term goals.

**Bibliography:** Clements, F. E. and Shelford, V. E., *Bio-Ecology* (1939); Elton, C., *Animal Ecology* (1927); Kendeigh, S. C., *Ecology, With Special Reference to Animals and Man* (1974); Smith, R. L., *Ecology and Field Biology* (1980).
See DEFOLIATION; TECHNOLOGY, ETHICS OF.
N.D.M.

**EDUCATION AND MORALITY.** "Train up a child in the way he should go, and when he is old he will not depart from it" (Prov. 22:6).
*Man's nature and moral character.* "What is man that you are mindful of him, and the son of man that you should visit him" (Ps. 8:4)? To train a child in the way he should go, we must understand the nature of children and the nature of man so that training can be directed to the desired result. Man may be classified more properly as *homo religiosus* than as *homo sapiens*. He is rational, social, esthetic, and free and therefore a responsible and moral being, dependent upon God. He reflects the moral image of God and has been given dominion over the creation. Cornelius Jaarsma concurs with this, stating that man has the capacity for moral knowledge, is capable of making moral decisions, and possesses moral affections.

What is the function of man? As the paragon of creation and the image bearer of God, man should glorify his Creator by fulfilling the cultural mandate, by being fruitful, and by exercising dominion over the creation (Gen. 1:28). Man functions as God's representative on earth and must rule in a way that reflects God's being; His wisdom, power, justice, holiness, goodness, and truth. Jaarsma adds a second function as well, stating that man is also to serve as creation's representative to God. As creation's representative, man must acknowledge all that God is, must receive God's blessings with a thankful heart, and must have intimate communion with the Almighty.

As a result of man's fall into sin, he is estranged from God, from himself, from humanity, and from the rest of creation. Depraved man does not act properly as God's faithful representative to the creation, but now rules in a flawed manner and is inclined to seek his own glory. No longer does man function well as the creation's representative to God either, for he is now inclined by nature to refuse acknowledgment of God's sovereignty. In his state of estrangement and ignorance, man is in need of redemption to bring about reconciliation to God and is in need of education to help him fulfill his dual representative role. This education is inextricably linked to morality.
*The purpose of education and its relationship*

*to morality.* It is noteworthy that traditional definitions of "educate" sometimes include the following: (1) to provide schooling, and (2) to develop mentally and morally, especially by formal training. Contemporary educational theory often attempts to ignore morality, but such is futile because of the inherent relationship between the two. The question is never, "Shall we teach morality?" but rather, "What type of morality shall we teach?" It is significant that educational theory today emphasizes knowledge as a means to "changed behavior" rather than an end in itself. Such jargon has heavy moral overtones.

We accept these definitions of "morality" also: (1) principles of conduct, and (2) conformity to the rules of right and wrong conduct. It is impossible for any program of formal and comprehensive education to avoid dealing with issues of morality, even though some absurd efforts are made to do so. One example of this occurred in the state of Georgia during 1984, when a county school system decided to restrict or prohibit discussion of nine controversial topics, including religion, abortion, and homosexuality.

In contrast to such thinking, Jay Adams says that "education has as its function the task of introducing people to Christ's liberating, refreshing teaching about life in all of its perspectives, which will enable them to enter into the occupying and controlling activities that were the substance of the creation commandment. This redemptive work of Christ in believers enables them to give God His full weight in all these endeavors." He also says that "the purposes of Christian education are to help students to understand and relate to God, to man, and to the rest of creation in terms of the biblical parameters of creation and redemption."

Norman de Jong's definition is similar. He views education as "the recreation and development of the true understandings and relationships between God and man, man and fellowman, and man and the physical universe." He concludes that "any education which is not Christian is not education."

It is readily apparent that non-Christian educators will disagree with the above definitions, but it should also be noted that some Christian educators appear to find these definitions too narrow. Indeed, an evangelical Christian man who is the administrator of a large American high school said in a 1984 interview, "To be perfectly honest, if I were flying from Washington to Miami, I wouldn't be overly concerned about whether my pilot was a Christian or not. My concern would be can he fly the plane. I feel the same way about education. You do kids a disservice by not giving them the best education they can get to go with the Christian training they receive at home" (*Christianity Today*, September 7, 1984, p. 23). It is difficult to reconcile such reasoning with the assertion that education and morality are inextricably linked together.

The relationship of education and morality is

best understood when we reflect upon the biblical concept of wisdom. "Wisdom is the principal thing; therefore, get wisdom, and with all your getting get understanding" (Prov. 4:7). What is this wisdom that the Lord says is "the principal thing"? The dictionary defines wisdom as "knowledge of what is true or right, coupled with good judgment." The antonyms of wisdom are foolishness, stupidity, and ignorance. The biblical concept of wisdom involves understanding, discretion, judgment, and more. In the first chapter of Proverbs we are told that "the fear of the Lord is the beginning of knowledge, but fools despise wisdom and instruction." Psalm 111 contains the same thought but adds a new dimension: "The fear of the LORD is the beginning of wisdom; a good understanding have all they who do His commandments." Wisdom is to be rooted in the fear of God; and it obviously involves more than the mere accrual of knowledge, for it said that those who obey the commandments of God have good understanding.

The biblical concept of wisdom also involves a relation. To know God means much more than simply to know about Him, for even the demons have that type of knowledge, says James, and they tremble. "Who is wise and understanding among you?" asks James. "Let him show it by his good life, by deeds done in the humility that comes from wisdom.... The wisdom that comes from heaven is first of all pure, then peace loving, considerate, submissive, full of mercy and good fruit, impartial and sincere" (James 3:13, 15).

*Current theory and practice in moral education.* The public schools of America today in general are not striving to help students get the wisdom described above. They are not teaching a biblically based morality. In order to understand American schools today, one must acknowledge the enormous and powerful influence that writers such as Piaget, Dewey, and Kohlberg have had upon educators. As a graduate student at the University of Chicago in the 1950s, Lawrence Kohlberg became fascinated by Piaget's studies of moral development. He decided to expand upon Piaget's original research by devising moral dilemmas that would be appropriate for older children. After analyzing the responses of ten- to sixteen-year-olds to the stories he had written, Kohlberg eventually, in 1963, developed a description of six stages of moral reasoning:

1. *Punishment-Obedience Orientation.* The physical consequences of an action determine its goodness or badness. Those in authority have superior power and should be obeyed.
2. *Instrumental Relativist Orientation.* An action is judged to be right if it is instrumental in satisfying one's own needs or involves an even exchange. Obeying rules should bring some sort of benefit in return.
3. *Good Boy—Nice Girl Orientation.* The right action is one that would be carried out by someone whose behavior is likely to please or impress others.
4. *Law and Order Orientation.* To maintain the social order, fixed rules must be established and obeyed. It is necessary to respect authority.
5. *Social Contract Orientation.* Rules needed to maintain the social order should be based not upon blind obedience to authority but upon mutual agreements.
6. *Universal Ethical Principle Orientation.* Moral decisions should be made in terms of self-chosen ethical principles. Once principles are chosen, they should be applied in consistent ways.

Kohlberg's "moral dilemmas" can be quite complex or as simple as "Why shouldn't you steal from a store?" Answers to that question will range from "You might get caught" (stage 1) to "You need to weigh all the factors and then try to make the most appropriate decision in a given situation. Sometimes it would be morally wrong *not* to steal" (stage 6).

He formed three rules emerging from his research: (1) the sequence of stages is invariant for everyone; (2) nobody ever reverts to an earlier stage after having been in a later one; and (3) nobody ever skips a stage.

Why are the writings of this Harvard School of Education professor so popular and so widely accepted? Nicholas Wolterstorff believes that the answer lies partly in the fact that Kohlberg's theory goes counter to our preconceptions at many points, making it a striking theory. And, says Wolterstorff, "...it also addresses itself seriously to moral *reasoning*...and since most research on moral education has been conducted within the orientation of either behaviorism or psychoanalysis, both of which regard the role of reason in human life with profound skepticism, the Piaget/Kohlberg theory has seemed to many like a powerful gust of fresh air blowing away a stale fog. Then, too, Kohlberg presents the strategy of moral education he recommends as itself making no disputable moral commitments; and that has seemed a godsend to public school administrators and teachers in a morally and religiously diverse society."

Perhaps Kohlberg's basic point is that it is never right *as such* or wrong *as such* to do something. Instead, actions are only right or wrong relative to a certain principle for action....Morality for him is nothing more than a human creation. There is no objective law behind it....Kohlberg nowhere recognizes any dark side to the human self—no pride, no impulse to self-aggrandizement, no wish to serve oneself at the cost of the other....Kohlberg never tires of insisting that teachers should concern themselves exclusively with the *form* of a child's moral reasoning, not with the *content*....it is the moral *reasoning* of the student, not *behavior*, which should be of concern in a program of moral education.

*Characteristics of a biblically based moral education.* Has it always been so in America? No. Our earliest schools had a strong religious orientation. Absolute standards, biblical standards were recognized and taught. The reading material found in the old "Horn Book" and in the "McGuffey Readers" was designed to promote the moral standards of God's Word. And there was no debate over the nature of man. Young children learned that "in Adam's fall, we sinned all." Indeed, the earliest schools were established so that children would be able to read the Bible. The plan for schooling in the Massachusetts Bay Colony in 1647 was commonly referred to as "The Old Deluder Satan Act," for it was designed to teach all children to read and thus enable them to read the Word of God and be fortified to fight off the devil.

Harvard University, where Kohlberg now teaches, was established in 1636; and a student of that era was "to be plainly instructed, and earnestly pressed to consider well, that the maine end of his life and studies is to know God and Jesus Christ which is eternal life...and therefore to lay Christ in the bottome, as the only foundation of all sound knowledge and learning." Other early American colleges had similar purposes and objectives. In the early 1700s Yale stated as its primary goal "that every student shall consider the main end of his study, to wit to know God in Jesus Christ and answerably to lead a Godly, sober life." A 1754 statement by the president of Columbia dealt with the goals of "sobriety, godliness, and righteousness of life."

American society today faces moral problems of enormous proportions, problems ranging from abortion and homosexuality to the failure to pay financial debts. Most of the babies born during 1983 in Washington, D. C., were born out of wedlock. Thousands more were aborted. What America is reaping today is certainly in large measure due to the failure of parents, churches, and schools to give proper moral training and direction to children and young people in recent decades.

**Bibliography:** Adams, J. E., *Back to the Blackboard* (1982); de Jong, N., *Education in the Truth* (1969); Jaarsma, C., *Fundamentals in Christian Education* (1953); Kohlberg, L., *The Philosophy of Moral Development* (1981); Wolterstorff, N., *Educating for Responsible Action* (1980).

See CHILDREN, REARING OF.

M.E.

**EGALITARIANISM.** Egalitarianism is the view that all human beings are like each other in essential respects and should be accorded similar treatment. Equality of human beings may be viewed as an empirical claim; that is, human beings are like each other in some ways, whether physically, intellectually or psychologically. In most ways, of course, humans are not equal to each other. They differ in physical size, intellectual ability, wealth, and education. The claim of the egalitarian is not that human beings are equal to each other in all things, but only in certain essential respects. The Stoics, for example, considered all humans to be equal because they possess a spark of the divine, or reason, and thus are equally capable of virtue.

Equality of human beings may also be viewed as an ideal. In spite of their many differences and inequalities, each and every human being has the same intrinsic value. It is in this sense that Thomas Jefferson's "all men are created equal" takes on its political meaning. The egalitarian ideal must be a driving principle for any Christian ethic because it follows from the essential Christian belief in the creation of all men and women in God's image (Gen. 1:27), in the fall of all humans into sin (Rom. 3:23), and in God's love for all the world that resulted in Christ's death on the cross (John 3:16). This ideal is also central to Paul's conception of the church where "there is neither Jew nor Greek, there is neither bond nor free, there is neither male nor female: for ye are all one in Christ Jesus" (Gal. 3:28; Col. 3:11). In taking this view, Paul opposed the ethnic Jews who saw themselves as being a superior race because they were God's chosen people.

The ideal of equality is a major principle within modern western political thought. According to Locke's social contract theory, a view that influenced the founders of the American government, political authority is derived from the consent of individuals who are equal within a state of nature, but agree to be governed by those whom they choose from their own number. This principle of the sovereignty of the people that is essential to democracy assumes that no specific individual has been given the right to rule, either by nature or by God. The doctrine of inalienable rights also rests on the assumption that all individuals have equal intrinsic value and thus an equal claim to life, freedom, property, and unbiased treatment by law and the courts. It is because of this equal claim of all people to a fair distribution of the benefits and burdens of a society and to impartial treatment within that society that justice becomes the fundamental social virtue in a democratic society.

It is inevitable that within fallen societies, the biblical ideal for human equality will not be achieved. Groups of individuals who are of a different race, sex or tribe will be accorded less than equal treatment. The principle of equality is typically asserted where a specific inequality is evident, such as when blacks are unable to vote or women receive less pay than men for the same work. The children of Israel were commanded to give special consideration to the needs of the alien, the widow, and the orphan, that is, those who did not have equal political and economic status with the adult males (Exod. 22:21-27; Deut. 10:17-19; 14:28-29; 24:19-22; 26:12-13; 27:18-19). They were condemned when they failed to do so (Isa. 1:15-23; Jer. 7:3-8; 22:3;

Amos 2:6-16; 4:1-3; 5:11-15; Zech. 7:8-14; Mal. 3:5). The model of concern for the oppressed is God himself who freed the children of Israel from their slavery in Egypt (Exod. 3:7-9; Deut. 26:5-9) and who takes special interest in all types of people who have unequal standing in society (Ps. 9:9; 10:17-18; 103:6; 146:7-9; Luke 4:16-21; James 1:27; 2:1-9).

**Bibliography:** Abernathy, G., (ed.), *The Idea of Equality: An Anthology* (1959); Brandt, R., *Social Justice* (1962); Scanzoni, L. and Hardesty, N., *All We're Meant To Be: A Biblical Approach to Women's Liberation* (1974); Tawney, R., *Equality* (1931).

S.D.A.

**EMANCIPATION OF WOMEN.** Emancipation of women sometimes means specifically the movement for women's suffrage (right to vote) in the late nineteenth and early twentieth centuries. More generally it means the movement toward valuing women equally with men and removing institutional and cultural restrictions on women's social roles. The present article embraces this more inclusive meaning. In this sense the emancipation of women includes their achievement of equal treatment legally, educationally, economically, and vocationally. Historically, at least until this century, Christian women have been among the leaders in the emancipation of women, often as a by-product of their efforts to impress other Christian values upon society, such as peace, justice, temperance, and care for the weak. Because of their distinctive social situation in history, women have also often had special insights into the living of the Christian life, which are now finding increasing expression in biblical studies and theology.

*Scripture and Interpretation.* The proper role that women should play in society has been a controversial one for many Christians. Four historic views may be discerned.

The first is that the scriptural norm is the subordination of women. This view can be argued on two grounds. The "supralapsarian" idea is that woman was inferior to or dependent on man in the Garden of Eden, having been created later in time, out of his body, and as a helpmate to him (1 Cor. 11:8). The "infralapsarian" idea is that woman may have been equal with man in Paradise but is subordinate after the Fall because of her greater transgression (1 Tim. 2:14).

The second view is that, whatever their situation either in nature or after the Fall, in the order of redemption women are equal with men. "There is neither male nor female; for you are all one in Christ Jesus" (Gal. 3:28).

The third is that Scripture does not lay down permanent precepts for the role of women in church and society. This appears to be the view of the Protestant reformer John Calvin and is related to the gospel message of freedom from the law.

The fourth is that the attitudes of the biblical writers to the issue changed over a period of time according to their historical circumstances. Since Scripture is consistent as to essentials, this view implies that the role of women is inessential and is theologically equivalent to the third view. These four views are not necessarily mutually exclusive.

Recently the first view has come under increasing criticism, on the grounds that it rests on an inaccurate understanding of the Hebrew text of Genesis. For instance, the biblical scholar, Phyllis Trible, challenges the interpretation that man was created first, woman second. She argues that the word "Adam" (related to the Hebrew *adamah*, "earth") is accurately translated, "earth creature," a human being with neither maleness nor femaleness. Genesis 2:7 would properly be translated, "The Lord God formed the earth creature (*adam*) from the dust of the ground (*adamah*)..."

In the second stage of creation, this earth creature was separated into male and female. Thus in Genesis 2:22 male and female are distinguished (*ishshah*, woman, and *ish*, man). She also challenges the interpretation that woman was more responsible than man for the Fall. A closer reading sees both the woman and the man disobedient, with the woman willing to shoulder responsibility while the man attempted to shift blame onto the woman and onto God ("the woman whom You gave to be with me...," Gen. 3:12). In consequence, God placed a curse upon the serpent and the man. For the woman, the curse formula is missing; instead God prophesied that she would have pain in childbirth and would remember the unity and mutuality of the relationship she had had with the man before the Fall. Thus God's original intention for men and women was a relationship of mutuality and obedience to God.

Although many Christian traditions have used biblical passages to legitimize a subordinate role for women, many recent interpretations have become more sensitized to the numerous passages in the Bible that teach us something of the importance of women. For example, Deborah is portrayed as a strong judge in war and a just leader of her people over many years of peace and prosperity (Judg. 4:5). The prophetess Miriam, the sister of Moses, led her people into the wilderness singing and dancing and playing the timbrel (Exod. 15:20-21). Sarah gave birth to a son in her old age and thereby mothered a nation (Gen. 17:18). The daughters of Zelophedad were given by God the right to inherit their father's property (Num. 26:33—27:11). Many other women in the Hebrew Scriptures are active participants in the history of the people of God.

There are some difficult Pauline texts which sometimes appear inconsistent. On one hand, Ephesians 5:22-27 seems to subordinate women to men, although its statement of husbands' duty to their wives is, for the time, quite radical. On the other hand, Paul speaks of many women leaders of the churches (1 Cor. 1:11; Col. 4:15; Rom. 16:1-5). Paul names one woman, Junia, an apostle (Rom. 16:7, although some translators have changed her name to the masculine version, Junius. On the one hand, Paul places restrictions on women concerning speaking in church (1 Cor. 14:34). On the other hand, he tells women that when they do speak in church they should wear a veil, the symbol of respectability and authority (1 Cor. 11:5).

There are no questionable teachings of Jesus, however. Jesus talked with women, taught them (Luke 10:38-42; John 4:8-24), consoled them (John 11:19), accepted their hospitality (Luke 10:38), valued their intellectual ability and reasoned faith (John 4, Jesus' most challenging discussion), raised their status (John 8:3-7), welcomed their devotion (Mark 14:3-9), and gave them authority and mission (John 4 and other instances). After the Resurrection, He appeared first to a woman (John 20:10-18). The only person in the Gospels to convince Jesus to change His mind is the Syrophoenecian woman (Mark 7:24-30). Women figure in many Gospel stories as followers of Jesus, although not numbered among the Twelve, probably since they were not counted in census or in synagogue congregations.

There are many instances in Scripture of feminine language and imagery for God: "God created humankind in God's own image, male and female" (Gen. 1:27); female pronouns for God as Wisdom in Proverbs and elsewhere; a feminine word for the Spirit of God (*ruach*); and statements that God will give comfort like a mother (Isa. 49:15; 66:11-13).

*Women and Christian History.* Early church frescoes, mosaics, and inscriptions show women as bishops and celebrating the Eucharist—although later hands often painted long beards and male clothing over the women. As time removed the early church from the life and teachings of Jesus, women were often pushed into the background. At any given time, however, there were forces working to include women as well as forces working to exclude them. For example, the second-century writer Tertullian called woman the "gateway to the devil"; but some early Christian groups recognized the gifts of women and accepted them as participants in the church's ministry. The influx of certain Greek ideas into the church in the fourth century led some theologians to devalue women; but the rise of monasticism around the same time gave women alternatives to their secular social roles, including prayer, meditation, visions, and charitable works. During the Reformation, Protestants dissolved women's religious orders, but allowed the marriage of clergy, so that ministers' wives often shared in their husbands' work.

Evangelical and lay movements in the church often brought women into roles of leadership, since the inspiration of the Spirit was in those cases more important than institutional legitimation. Mysticism in the Middle Ages, the English

Lollards in the fourteenth century, the Swiss Anabaptists in the sixteenth century, the Quakers and the Port-Royal group in the seventeenth century, the Methodists in the eighteenth century, and the Holiness Movement in the nineteenth century are such examples. Susannah Wesley, "the mother of Methodism," led Bible studies and devotions and wrote theological reflections. Phoebe Palmer founded the Holiness Movement, from which have sprung such groups as the Church of the Nazarene, the Salvation Army, and the Pentecostal Assemblies.

Economic and other social circumstances have influenced the roles of women correspondingly. In agricultural societies women were valued as part of the productive unit, namely, the family, and enjoyed security and partnership. Industrialization, however, separated men, women, and children, emphasized inequalities, and removed some household tasks from the home and thus from the purview of women. Industrialization gave women the option of working outside the home, but often for lower pay and in less attractive jobs than men. Increased competition led to deteriorating labor conditions and increased immigration forced women out of the factories altogether. With the rise of professionalism, women lost control of even more tasks that had traditionally been theirs. For example, as the care of the sick became professionalized, women were excluded from the ranks of the medical profession. Changes in law also affected the status of women. The rise of equity jurisprudence in the late eighteenth century gave women a status independent of their husbands, as well as more rights to hold property in some jurisdictions. In 1929, Canadian women won the right to be generally considered "persons" under the law.

The emancipation of women began making its greatest headway in the nineteenth century. Christian women influenced by Quakerism, Methodism, and other movements began to analyze society from a Christian perspective to identify reasons for social problems. The widespread abuse of alcohol and slavery appeared to them to be significant causes. "For God, Home and Country," was the motto of the Women's Christian Temperance Movement, as women moved into every aspect of public life including education, labor reform, and the social work movement. They intended to make changes that would protect their homes and improve people's lives, particularly those of women and children, and especially among the lower classes. Once women began to lobby within the political sphere, they soon realized that they would not be successful unless they could vote; therefore in Britain and North America the suffrage movement began. Suffrage was finally granted to women in 1918 in Canada, 1920 in the United States, 1928 in Britain, and still later in many developing countries. In the United States distilleries were energetic in their opposition to women's suffrage, and indeed women's suffrage was followed by prohibition.

The emancipation of women has included their assumption of greater responsibilities in the church. Their involvement in the mission of the church in the world is especially significant. In the nineteenth and twentieth centuries they formed study and support groups in all the major denominations. They were active in raising funds, although it was sometimes men who decided how to disburse them. Many women's missionary societies took bold and creative initiatives. In Canada, for example, they pioneered ecumenical missionary training, and during the Second World War they provided spiritual guidance, medical care, and education for interned Japanese-Canadians when many churches were not supportive. The women's missionary societies have left a legacy among church women's groups of Bible study and an educated concern for people in other countries. There is a strong network of concerned Christian women all over the world, sustained by organizations such as the Fellowship of the Lost Coin and the World Council of Churches.

There have been other options for women within the church. Religious orders have offered an alternative to family life from a very early period. Some denominations are structured so that laity, including women, can exercise authority. Many denominations have moved to ordain women (the Congregational Church in the United States in 1845, the United Church of Canada in 1936, the Episcopal Church in the United States in 1977, the Pentecostal Assemblies of Canada in 1984).

Although there has been a women's movement distinctly within the secular arena in the twentieth century, its strongest roots are in the Christian feminist movement of the nineteenth century. Christian women today are rediscovering these nonsecular roots. They are finding ways to carry values from their faith into public life, instead of abdicating to a secular environment hostile to those values.

In the Third World, women experience a double oppression: they are powerless in the face of the First World and of the men in their own societies. This common experience appears to cut across barriers of race, culture, age, and class. *The Christian Response.* The church has on the whole reinforced women in family life and offered varying degrees of support to women who tried to take their Christian values and their Christian commitment from the home to the public sphere. It has been slower to affirm women in ecclesiastical structures; but that movement, too, now seems well under way.

Many ostensibly women's issues of the present day are also Christian issues: violence against women and children (rape, prostitution, pornography, and domestic violence), peace, political repression and torture, equality of economic treatment, the exploitation of Third World women through prostitution and through unfair labor practices, and the promotion of chemical milk substitutes for the nursing of infants. In some issues, such as abortion and so-called sexual rights, many Christian feminists will take a different perspective from many secular feminists. Where the values are congruent and the perceived needs of the world are of joint concern, Christian women and men are called to work together with all those who labor toward good.

As Christians we are all bidden to labor with one another for the reign of God. Christian women have a particular role to play in promoting life-giving values in the public as well as the private sphere.

**Bibliography**: Melder, K. E., *Beginnings of Sisterhood* (1977); Nunnally-Cox, J., *Foremothers: Women of the Bible* (1981); Ruether, R. R., *New Woman/New Earth* (1975); Tavard, G. and Trible, P., *God and the Rhetoric of Sexuality* (1978).

M.M.M.-H.

**EMPLOYMENT.** In formal terms, work is to be defined in terms of man's dominion over nature and the service of his fellow man. Thus it seems right to make a distinction between work and employment. Human activities that involve man in subduing his environment, in caring for his neighbor, and in the development of community life are to be considered as work. Whether or not they are done for direct financial reward is strictly a secondary factor.

This proper conceptual distinction, however, should not lead us to denigrate the importance of providing opportunities for work that are linked with the maintenance of one's economic livelihood, whether this takes the form of self-sufficiency, barter in kind, self-employment, or wage-earning employment. Throughout, Scripture assumes the importance of this connection between work and economic sustenance. In primitive Israelite society, it was the responsibility of families to develop their land (the land which was, in ultimate terms, God's and which had been allocated by him to different tribes, Lev. 25:23) as their most fundamental means of economic support. But few societies are maintained without some forms of wage-earning employment, which in modern industrial society have become the norm. The Bible affirms the importance of work for wages and insists that the wage earner be treated justly.

Because work for economic sustenance is such an important human endeavor, it is a primary source of many of the important social benefits associated with work in general. It often offers to the individual not only economic viability but also an experience of community and a sense of social belonging, a source of structure and continuity in life, and a means of developing his or her talents and potentialities in contributing to the well-being of society as a whole.

The notion of full employment is not at all easy to define. What school-leaving age and what age of retirement are presupposed? Does it entail provision of employment for more than one individual per nuclear household? How many labor hours per week are implied? In considering this issue, Christian social ethics point us toward the importance of maintaining the fundamental connection between work and the distribution of wealth. The payment of social benefit where society has failed to provide appropriate opportunities for labor is supported by some social thinkers. But the important link between work and the maintenance of livelihood does suggest that in future planning we should treat the notion of the social wage, or what some commentators call the "social dividend," with extreme moral caution. This would necessitate, in effect, a financially and culturally upgraded social benefit paid to a proportion of the population as a "normal" state of affairs.

**Bibliography:** Bleakley, D., *In Place of Work* (1981); Church of England, General Synod, *Work or What: A Christian Examination of the Employment Crisis* (1977); Large, P., *The Micro Revolution* (1980); Moltmann, J., "The First Liberated Men in Creation," in *Theology and Joy* (1973).

See UNEMPLOYMENT; WAGES; WORK.

M.D.G.

**ENCYCLICALS.** The word is taken from the Latin adjective *encyclicus,* meaning "circular"; the Latin term, *litterae encyclicae,* means "circular letters." The name is given to a letter addressed by the pope to Roman Catholic Church authorities all over the world, although it may also be limited to the hierarchy of a single country or a federation of nations. Some encyclicals (e.g., *Pacem in terris*) have even been addressed to all men of good will. The purpose of an encyclical is to condemn some doctrinal error, to inform the faithful through the hierarchy of some unfavorable government legislation, or to explain the meaning of certain conduct for Roman Catholics. Papal letters have been written to the whole Church from early Christianity, but the modern usage of the encyclical goes back to Benedict XIV (1740), who used the form frequently. After Benedict it was not used with any frequency until the time of Pius IX. Most of the encyclicals have been written in Latin but some (e.g., *Non abbiamo bisogno* and *Mit brennender Sorge* on fascism) have been written in modern languages, which is becoming more common. Encyclicals are usually named after the first two words which appear, for example, *Quadragesimo anno, Humanae vitae.* The introductory words, however, may give no clue to the topic discussed. As a result English translations will have their own title, such as, *On The Social Order,* or *On the Regulation of Birth.* In the preparation of encyclicals the pope may depend on individuals, groups of scholars, or his own ingenuity.

Ordinarily, encyclicals are not used to define doctrine and hence are not considered infallible. They are, however, generally intended for all the faithful who are expected to give them assent, obedience, and respect because of the importance of the truth they present. A respectful silence is not enough. In the encyclical *Humani generis,* Pius XII warned that what is contained in encyclical letters, even though part of his ordinary teaching, calls for assent. On the other hand, since encyclicals are not infallible statements, dissent is theoretically possible; but the burden of proof would be on the dissenter. Encyclicals may, of course, contain infallible teaching for other reasons.

Interpretation of encyclicals may be difficult. Statements made in an encyclical are to be understood in the light of the context of the encyclical itself, other writings of the pontiff, and contemporary theological interpretation.

**Bibliography:** Carlen, C., *The Papal Encyclicals* (1981); Freemantle, A., *Papal Encyclicals in their Historical Context* (1956); Malone, G. K., *Catholic Encyclopedia* (1967), V, pp. 332–33.

J.R.C.

**ENEMY.** An enemy is one who is opposed ideologically to another person or group and manifests this antagonism by showing hostility in a variety of ways. In general use the term *enemy* carries serious connotations with it, whether at a personal level or in terms of the community or nation. Enemies can be passive in the sense that, while they are in radical opposition to a concept or a group of people, they restrict their activities to verbal attacks and do not engage in violent counteractivities. The aggressive enemy, however, makes his or her presence felt by means of rebellion, terrorism, antisocial activities, and sometimes actual war. For order to be restored the enemy must be checked and the enemy's depredations halted, often at considerable cost. If a national enemy is allowed to invade and destroy at will, the result is the enslavement of the victim population and on occasions acts of genocide.

In the ancient world to have an enemy was always a serious matter, since because of the general view of the cheapness of human existence it was not infrequently a matter of life or death. This accounts for the apprehension which David (Pss. 25:2, 19; 38:19) and others felt about the presence and activities of their enemies. Because of the distinctive, nonidolatrous nature of Hebrew covenantal life, pagan nations were inimical by their presence and way of living to the kind of obedience and holiness which God demanded of his people (Lev. 11:44). Within the nation itself there arose apostate leaders who rejected the call of the prophets for repentance and a return to covenantal faith, and these enemies of righteousness were the reason for the ultimate collapse of the monarchy and the tragedy of exile.

In the New Testament an enemy (*echthros*) could be of a military character (Luke 19:43), a personal nature (Rom. 12:19-21; Gal. 4:16), or those who were opposed to the rule of God (Acts 13:10; Phil. 3:18). At the supernatural level both Satan (Matt. 13:39; Luke 10:19) and physical death (1 Cor. 15:25-28) are described as enemies of the Christian. Jesus taught believers to love their enemies (Matt. 5:43-44) rather than hate them, as was traditional, and this principle was also emphasized by Paul (Rom. 12:19-21). When it is practiced seriously by the Christian, it often produces startling results and great blessing.

**ENJOYMENT.** This term describes an emotional response to pleasure, satisfaction, and general positive affectivity to certain aspects of living. It occurs under a wide variety of circumstances, and consequently appears under many forms. Different types of physical recreational activity produce great enjoyment for some persons, while for others intellectual and esthetic pursuits fulfill the same purpose. A normally healthy person can expect to find enjoyment in some aspect of life and work, but this is not true of individuals suffering from depressive psychoses, for whom life is often a tremendous burden.

The Christian, above everyone else, ought to be able to rejoice in the works of the Creator and in the opportunities that are afforded for service and witness in society. Enjoyment is therefore a perfectly legitimate experience for the Christian, but it should be a consequence of life activity and not a goal. The Christian is admonished not to be a lover of pleasure rather than a lover of God (2 Tim. 3:4; Titus 3:3). Hedonism as a tacit or actual objective of life diverts energy from the primary task of proclaiming the gospel, and exalts self-interest instead of Christ's message of love and forgiveness. Enjoyment is therefore only most satisfying when it emerges as a consequence of mature Christian living.

See LEISURE; RECREATION.

**ENTREPRENEURSHIP.** The role of the entrepreneur is integral to the free enterprise economy. While all modern economies are mixed, that is, they are neither wholly socialist nor wholly capitalist, entrepreneurs are in principle excluded from socialist economies. Free enterprise allows free choice to entrepreneurs, consumers, and workers to buy and sell goods and services for their own advantage. In practice, greed and exploitation are muted by societal forces that tend to reward those who furnish that which is socially beneficial, though democratic societies try to ensure the maintenance of a free market and to censure abuse through laws.

The entrepreneur is a risk taker. He is prepared to undertake, to venture, and to try something untried. The entrepreneur is the vital link and catalyst between capital and labor. Incentive creates opportunity; that is, the entrepreneur's pursuit of his own self-interest tends to benefit others as well.

The role of the entrepreneur is criticized by some because the primary incentive is seen to be venture for profit that is then further defined as greed. However, profit serves a function beyond income. Profit is also a signal of efficiency and of having met public need or demand satisfactorily. To interpret the risk taking of the entrepreneur as being solely for profit is unfair. Some entrepreneurs are greedy; but most venture for reasons beyond profit including a sense of achievement, to create opportunity for others, to create or invent something new, and to contribute to the economy and to the well-being of their own country.

For the Christian, important ethical considerations follow from the role of the entrepreneur. The first is diligence and self-reliance that are part of the biblical work ethic. No Christian should be an idler (2 Thess. 3:6). This means that he should produce more than he consumes so as to be able to help others who are not so fortunate (1 Cor. 16:2; Eph. 4:28). Self-reliance does not exclude accepting help when one is in need; but it does reject exploiting the system when productive work of some kind is available. Paul does not say that those who are unable to work should not eat; only that those who refuse to work do not deserve to eat (2 Thess. 3:10).

Productivity is more than a profit-oriented concept; it is a term reinforced by powerful ethics. The Christian is expected to be productive in the important sense of creating opportunity for others. This means more than merely avoiding repressive tactics (Mic. 2:2; Amos 2:7; 5:12). It means targeting prosperity as a goal for others as well as for oneself as the natural by-product of personal initiative. "The plans of the diligent lead surely to abundance" (Prov. 21:5). The evangelical revival of the late eighteenth and the nineteenth centuries evoked from Christians new diligence, productivity, stewardship of capital, and social concern. Paul's denunciation of avarice (1 Tim. 6:6-10) is balanced by his insistence that Christians be diligent.

Competition sharpens one's wits and stimulates efficient use of resources. Because it forces effective planning, competition and incentive-oriented planning by individuals and local enterprise are vastly more efficient than the planning of centralized bureaucracies. Enterprise thus accommodates a better use of human resources that fosters human development, creativity, and fulfillment. The greatest waste is the waste of human resources and potential.

For the Christian entrepreneur as for others, life is filled with moral choices. These include commitment to justice, fairness, honesty, and kindness. A crucial issue is that of priorities. Does the drive to succeed solely concern acquisition of property, making a great deal of money, or controlling a business empire? Or does the Christian entrepreneur see business as his or her contribution to the well-being of society alongside his or her loving commitment to marriage, family, friends, and the ongoing work of the kingdom of God?

**Bibliography:** Kirzner, I. M., *Competition and Entrepreneurship* (1973); Novak, M., (ed.), *The Spirit of Democratic Capitalism* (1982); Ouchi, W., *Theory Z* (1981); Peters, T. J. and Waterman, R. H., *In Search of Excellence* (1982).

S.J.M.

**ENVY.** Envy is generally thought of as the embittered dislike or deeply jealous admiration of something that another person possesses, whether of a material or nonmaterial order. It is a particular concomitant of selfish, insecure, and undisciplined personalities, and if unchecked can result in badly ruptured relationships and even violence. It is closely related to covetousness, which is emphatically forbidden by the tenth commandment (Exod. 20:17).

The Gospel records indicate that Christ was arrested and crucified because of bitter envy and hostility on the part of the religious authorities (Matt. 27:18), a fact which was not lost on the governor of Judea (Mark 15:10). In the New Testament Epistles, envy comes in for particular criticism by Paul, who classes it as unholy behavior, along with deceit, murder, fornication, and "all unrighteousness" (Rom. 1:29). So serious an offense was envying for Paul that he included it in his catalog of "fleshly works" (Gal. 4:19-21), which disbarred a person from inheriting the kingdom of God and which contrasted forcibly with the "fruit of the Spirit" (Gal. 4:22-23). James was equally pointed in regarding "every evil work" as the result of envying and the inevitable strife that followed (James 3:16). He further indicated that the propensity for envying was part of fallen human nature (James 4:5), but showed equally that divine grace is sufficient to conquer this evil. It seems clear from Scripture, therefore, that there can be absolutely no place for envy in the believer's life.

**EQUALITY.** Equality is a condition in which there is recognized to be an identity of value, status, quantity, or function between objects that are being compared or contrasted. Equality can be applied to inanimate or abstract things, as when Job stated that gold and crystal could not equal wisdom (Job 28:17), or concretely to human beings, such as a friend (Ps. 55:13). The affirmation of equality is thus based upon a ratiocinative act which recognizes, *inter alia*, specific correspondence of value.

From a purely biological standpoint, the unqualified affirmation that all people are born equal is simply untrue. It would be more correct to affirm that most people come into the world in the same manner, but such a statement obviously lacks the sweep of a grand rhetorical utterance. The fact is that human beings exhibit vast variations in their genetic inheritance factors, with the result that millions of people are at a disadvantage in terms of upbringing, intellectual ability, physical health, and so on, to say nothing about

such matters as religious development and social standing. Clearly any ideological concept of the equality of all human beings needs either radical revision or an interpretation which corresponds to the realities of life.

Lawyers and ethicists have generally adopted the position that equality, as defined for example in the Constitution of the United States, means that all persons have equal rights under the law. By implication as citizens, they can also be understood to have equal responsibilities in society. For the ethicists there is an added dimension that all people have in common, and that is an inherited nature that has been tainted by sin to produce rebellion, egotism, and apostasy. All people are therefore equal as sinners in the sight of God (Rom. 3:23), and to attempt to deny this fact is to tell a falsehood (1 John 1:10). But because of God's love to humanity as revealed in the scriptural covenants, people are also equal as objects of his redeeming and saving grace. When men and women confess their sins and claim Jesus as their personal Savior and Lord, they enter into another relationship of equality as fellow members of the Christian church.

In this community inheritance factors and social opportunities are transcended completely by God's grace in Christ, which makes new creatures of those whose lives are committed to him. The old way of existence, with all its failures, is blotted out; and the future in Christ is gloriously new (2 Cor. 5:17). As though this were insufficient, the organic unity and equality of this group is a matter of emphasis in the New Testament, where Paul points out that national and civic boundaries are obliterated as the church, in spiritual fellowship, submits itself to the lordship of Christ. But again, equality in the grace of Christ makes each believer equally responsible under the law of saving love. There can thus be no apostasy or antinomianism, but instead a realization of the awesome task that is imposed upon the individual Christian to penetrate society with the good news of forgiveness of sin and eternal life in Christ.

Despite the affirmation that in Christ male and female differences are subsumed under the larger concern for Christian witness in the world, the church has generally been slow to realize the implications of this matter as far as women are concerned. Despite the witness of the Reformation to this effect, European women had few rights and those living in Moslem cultures scarcely any at all. Emancipation of women, aiming at some sort of social and political equality with men, progressed very slowly over several centuries; and it was only with the enfranchisement of women that a significant advance occurred. An increased participation by women in formal programs of higher education was followed by the promotion of women to various public offices. But in religious circles, some of the older denominations consistently refused to admit women to ordination, a position that is still maintained by the Roman Catholic Church and some Protestant groups.

Those female activists who insist upon making equality a goal rather than a means for service might profit from observing the example of Jesus Christ, who thought that equality with God was not some sort of prize that one should grasp avidly. Instead he assumed human form and nature, albeit sinlessly, and fulfilled that great service of eternal salvation which was beyond the abilities of human beings to perform (Phil. 2:6-10). This is the attitude of mind that Paul earnestly desired to see among Christians and is still an ideal for those aspiring to equality.

**EROS.** This is a pre-Christian, classical Greek term for "love," which appeared in the writings of Plato and others, but is not found in the New Testament. It is the basis of the word *erotic,* and as such reflects the selfish passion and undisguised lust of ancient Greek sexuality, with its persistent emphasis upon carnal gratification. In their sensuous activities the Greeks frequently indulged in such perversions as homosexuality and lesbianism, both of which were forbidden to the ancient Israelites (Lev. 20:13) because they were not merely violations of covenant morality but also were potential causes of idolatry because of their association with pagan religious practices.

Such a term as *eros* clearly does not belong in the vocabulary of the New Testament, although occasional allusions to immoral erotic behavior do occur in the Epistles (Rom. 1:26-29). The sexual practices which a Christian is encouraged to follow preclude perversions of all kinds and give sanction to carnal relations only within the scope of married life. Pagan eroticism is therefore inimical to dedicated Christian living and must be avoided in all its forms.

See AGAPE; MARRIAGE; SEX.

**ESCHATOLOGY AND ETHICS.** There are three points of the kingdom and related ethics in the Bible: Old Testament theocracy and kingdom expectation, fulfillment in the life and ministry of Jesus, and the eschatological event of Christ's second coming to inaugurate the final kingdom. The several meanings of the biblical term "kingdom" and related kingdom ethics have been reduced in modern times to platitudes and sometimes to theological confusion, even contradiction.

In the Old Testament God is king, which signifies both the prerogative of His divine right to rule and the sphere of His rule which is all creation, including men and nations. Notable passages such as Psalms 2 and 24 state this unambiguously. Extensive biblical documentation is possible (1 Sam. 12:12; Pss. 10:16; 44:4; 103:19; 149:2; Isa. 43:15; Jer. 10:7; Mal. 1:14).

Major themes of the Old Testament kingdom vision are righteousness and truth, judgment and redemption, and hope and renewal. The travail of nature in an evil-infected world; national social injustice; religious perversions such as idolatry and superficial ritual; international upheaval and war; and personal sins such as avarice, heartlessness, and impurity receive and are promised ultimate divine judgment. Judgment, however, is tempered by grace and promise of healing. God calls men to repentance, faith, and obedience. Often the appeal combines the themes of renewal and justice with hope for a new day when God will truly be king and men will willingly obey His laws (Isa. 2; 43). The principles of the final kingdom ought to affect present attitudes and behavior.

While in the Old Testament the coming kingdom is God's in the broadest sense and some Old Testament writers do not include messianic references, most interpreters of the Old Testament agree that the concepts of kingdom and Messiah belong together (Isa. 9:6-7; 32:1; Jer. 23:5; 30:9; Dan. 7:13-14; Zech. 14:9). The kingdom vision includes restoration of balance in the forces of nature. The greatest emphasis is placed upon reconciliation of man to God and renewal of human personality to do good. Great stress is placed upon righteousness, social justice, personal morality, and spiritual fidelity. Kingdom ethics in the Old Testament are never merely legal; they are always renewal ethics. God wants the hearts of his people; their obedience will follow.

This strand of Old Testament teaching is at the heart of kingdom expectation and realization in the life and teaching of Jesus (Zech. 9:9; Matt. 21:5). Jesus radically transformed conceptions of the kingdom from a political and economic ideal to personal renewal, a sustained spiritual relationship with God, and obedience to him. While Jesus confirms certain signs of the kingdom (Matt. 10:5-15; 11:2-6; Luke 4:16-30), He declares that the first priority of the kingdom is spiritual and moral renewal (Matt. 6:33; Mark 1:15; Luke 17:21). Nevertheless a powerful eschatological motif pervades Christ's teaching. There is indeed to be a coming kingdom and He is its true king, now revealed, who finally will be enthroned. This truth also serves as a sanctifying expectation, a presently morally purifying hope (1 John 3:1-3).

An important link between the Old Testament and the New Testament regarding the kingdom ideal is the place of the Holy Spirit. The new age is the age of the Spirit, which most Christians understand was inaugurated at Pentecost (Ezek. 36:27; 37:14; Joel 2:28-29; Acts 2:17-21). The Spirit energizes redeemed and restored mankind. The advent of Christ indeed marks inauguration of the kingdom, and Pentecost indeed marks the birth of the church. However, Pentecost is not the primary sign but the consequent sign of the Spirit. The primary sign of the Spirit is Christ Himself. His advent not only marks inauguration of the kingdom, but it also discloses historically the new man for the new age: the spirit-bearing humanity of Christ, the file-leader of the new humanity. Kingdom ethics are the ethics of the new spirit-endowed humanity.

Thus in Scripture there is a conscious analogy drawn between the life of Christ and the life of each Christian. Christ was begotten of the Spirit, baptized in the Spirit, taught and did mighty works by the Spirit, and quickened from the dead by the Spirit. The same is true of each Christian. The analogy of Romans 6:1-4, which speaks of entering upon new life, has its climactic interpretation in Romans 8:11. The Spirit in each Christian is the Spirit of Christ. The Spirit is author of the law of Christ. The aim of the Spirit is to duplicate in each life the spirit-bearing humanity of the incarnate Lord. Thus the greatest sign of the Spirit's presence is not unusual phenomena but the permanent moral transformation of life.

The kingdom ethic combines expectation and fulfillment. It gathers rather than scatters, conserves rather than discards. Christ came not to destroy but to fulfill the law. Similarly, Paul does not jettison but honors the moral values of the law. The principle of justification by faith does not sidestep morality. It embraces it and makes possible the morally transformed life by the power of the Spirit. It is therefore inadequate when dealing with the Sermon on the Mount to evade its moral principles as at present altogether impossible to realize and to project them wholly to a future kingdom age. The kingdom ethics that Jesus espouses parallel the ethics of the life in the Spirit which the epistles envisage.

While it is possible to draw instructive parallels between lists of proscribed vices in the teaching of Jesus and in the Epistles, especially Paul's, the power of kingdom ethics resides in their positive quality. First and foremost is their inward base: "the good man out of his good treasure brings forth evil" (Matt. 12:35). The primary virtue of this treasure of the heart is love, not as pure emotion, but as a personal relationship based on the integrity of moral commitment. It is love to God and love to neighbor (Matt. 22:37; Mark 12:30-31; Luke 10:27-28).

Corollaries of this inward spiritual and moral dedication include deep hunger to know and fulfill the righteousness of God, transcultural kindness and mercy, a peaceable and unrancorous disposition, integrity of moral purpose rather than moral duplicity, humility, and a forgiving spirit. These virtues, spoken by Christ in the Sermon on the Mount and the Beatitudes, coincide with the graces listed by Paul (Gal. 5:21-26), Peter (2 Pet. 1:5-11), and other writers in the New Testament. Early church literature, such as Clement of Rome's First Epistle and the Epistle to Diognetus, convey powerfully the same sentiments. To be a part of God's kingdom entails earnest aspiration to reflect its principles in life through God's help.

The ancient world was furnished richly with ideals, including attractive ethical ideals, in Judaism and the various schools of Greco-Roman culture. Christianity did not offer merely abstract ideals, but the power by means of which its ideals could actually be realized. This is the meaning of the life in Christ as the life in the Spirit. The fact that the world is still an evil-infected world and that Christians are still sin-prone reinforces to the Christian the importance of his dedication and re-dedication to kingdom ideals. Diognetus the enquirer is told in the epistle addressed to him that "Christians dwell in the world, but do not belong to the world." This is the eschatological nature and impact of kingdom ethics. Christians and their values really belong to another world. Nevertheless, they are solidly a part of this world and strive to realize Christ's ideals, which are epitomized in the phrase "the law of Christ" (Gal. 6:2), in their own lives, in their relationship with one another, and in their dealings with other people.

**Bibliography:** Hunter, A. M., *A Pattern for Life* (1953); Ladd, G. E., *A Theology of the New Testament* (1974); Schnackenburg, R., *Present and Future Aspects of New Testament Theology* (1966); Wilder, A. N., *Eschatology and Ethics in the Teaching of Jesus* (1950).

See LOVE; SERMON ON THE MOUNT.

S.J.M.

**ETHICAL LANGUAGE.** The philosopher's concern with the language with which we conduct our business has generated significant findings in the areas of ethics. Philosophers have always shown a strong interest in the meaning and justification of the concepts which we use in ethics; such as Socrates' painstaking inquiries into the meanings of "justice," "piety," and the like. The attention of philosophers today is more concentrated in the language-conscious analytical tradition of the Anglo-Saxon world.

A signal event in the history of ethical reflection was the attempt by the logical positivist school of philosophy to ban ethics entirely from the realm of cognitive discourse, of truth and falsity. Logical positivists such as A. G. N. Flew and A. J. Ayer advocated a thesis about language which advanced the verifiability principle by which any proposition which purported to be "true" could be assessed. Only propositions that allowed empirical testing could even aspire to truth; those untestable by sense experience were not false, but meaningless. These include, notably, the propositions of metaphysics, religion, and ethics. This position with regard to ethics was known broadly as noncognitivism, since it held that ethical claims are not in the realm of knowledge at all.

What then was to be said about the judgments and claims that we make about right and wrong, good and bad? According to the noncognitivists, they are mere expressions of our attitudes and feelings toward the actions in question and therefore no different in kind from smiles or disapproving grunts. From this theory we have inherited the popular saying, "It's only a value judgment," which expresses the view that value judgments are not significant, since they more closely resemble judgments of taste than weighty claims.

Emotivism was drastically amended as additional attention to the use of language in ethics contradicted the simple emotivist claim. It also suffered, as did noncognitivism in general, from the rather complete rejection of logical positivism by philosophers. Careful study of language cast strong doubt on the simple emotivist claim. When we call apartheid wrong, for example, are we merely giving vent to our personal and subjective feelings about the institution? We also at least seem to be implying that our attitudes are commendable to others. We do attempt to present our moral beliefs as reasonable and in some way objective. This is done by pointing to facts that we take to support our moral claims. ("Apartheid leads to unnecessary and undeserved suffering of persons solely on the basis of their color.") Others who recognize those facts can be expected to accept our judgment as well.

Prescriptivism, as found in R. M. Hare, accepted some of the noncognitivist's claims but pointed to other aspects of language that seemed to give ethics more objectivity. When a person makes a claim about the wrongness of apartheid, he does more than express his feelings or even recommend them to others. Hare notes that when we condemn apartheid, in addition to expressing our feelings, we appeal to a universal principle as a guide to action and make an assertion supportable by certain sorts of reasons or criteria. Noncognitivism fails to account for the fact that to call apartheid wrong is also implicitly to denounce other actions which fall under the same general principle. It also fails to recognize the extent to which moral claims presuppose the support of rational grounds.

Descriptivism attempted to advance beyond prescriptivism by closing the logical gap between the facts about a thing and the evaluation of the thing. Thus, how we judge something depends on our description of it. As descriptivist Phillippa Foot argues, if we describe a social institution as harmful, this indicates an inclination to be against the institution. Value judgments, then, are logically connected to descriptive statements.

The analysis of ethical language has had at least this major effect on ethical theory: in addition to elucidating the structure of moral discourse in interesting ways, it has shown that built in to the logic of ethical evaluation itself is evidence of objectivity.

**Bibliography:** Ayer, A. J., *Language, Truth, and Logic* (1936); Frankena, W. K., *Ethics* (2nd. ed., 1973); Hare, R. M., *The Language of Morals* (1952); MacIntyre, A., *After Virtue* (1983); Stevenson, C. L., *Ethics and Language* (1944); Taylor, P. W., *Principles of Ethics* (1975).

                                                              D.B.F.

**ETHOS.** This is the normal Greek word for "custom" and therefore describes the various traditions in which people grow up and by which they live. Religion is usually a part of any national ethos, although it is usually suppressed in totalitarian states. The characteristic activities of a country include traditions and practices that frequently differ in nature from those of other peoples and lend color and dimension to civic life. While most of the culture in Western nations rests upon some sort of Christian foundation, many elements have become secularized to the point where they may present difficulties for forthright Christian participation. Totalitarian states often impose an ideological ethos on their citizens that conflicts with other traditional secular values, and this also can produce tensions for Christians and non-Christians alike.

An ethos familiar to most people in Western society is the so-called Protestant work ethic, which is identified with capitalistic ideals. Of Puritan origin, this ethos emphasizes that thrift and hard work are of positive ethical value and are in harmony with biblical teachings (2 Thess. 3:10; 2 Tim. 2:15, 21).

**EUGENICS.** This term comes from two Greek words meaning "well born." Eugenics is the scientific attempt to produce superior offspring by processes of selective breeding and is related particularly to members of the species *homo sapiens*. Eugenics arose from nineteenth-century experimentation with animals in attempts to weed out detrimental inherited factors and concentrate as many good qualities as possible in the breed of animal involved.

As applied to human beings, eugenics concentrates upon encouraging marriage and reproduction between individuals with strong hereditary, that is, genetic, tendencies. Conversely, people who suffer from genetically transmitted disease would be discouraged from marrying and procreating. This natural desire for a reasonably healthy population has been reflected in statutes enacted in many jurisdictions prohibiting the marriage of the certifiably insane or the severely retarded.

It is probably true to say that nobody would choose to enter deliberately into marriage with a mentally deficient individual, or one who was handicapped by a crippling neurological disease. To that extent, therefore, eugenics is being practiced in a rudimentary manner on the basis of simple choice after inspection. Most people are unaware that nature has its own eugenics, which works by the various species discouraging the continued existence of their sick and weak members. In the same way, many badly deformed or diseased babies do not survive the birth experience for long unless their existence is protracted by artificial means of life support.

As a scientific program for upgrading the physical and mental qualities of the population, eugenics came into prominence under the Nazi regime in Germany prior to World War II (1939-

1945). In the process of developing a "master race," the German planners liquidated the persons they considered least desirable by means of genocide, euthanasia, and sterilization. In the expectation of victory over Britain, the Germans also planned to exterminate most of the British women, leaving only an elite female group which would be mated with their German male counterparts. But with an Allied victory these plans miscarried.

Advocates of eugenics often exhibit simplistic notions about their subject. One of these is that the matching of so-called "superior" individuals will necessarily result in "superior" offspring. But so complex is the human genetic structure that in mating, genes that have been long recessive can become dominant by mechanisms that are entirely unknown, and vice versa. Because the nature and direction of these genetic tendencies is not merely unknown, but also unpredictable and uncontrollable in consequence, it is very easy for the desired results to be thwarted completely. Even more serious for ethicists is the question as to who decides whether a person is superior or not. In the hands of an unscrupulous leader of a totalitarian state the criteria could be varied to suit the immediate situation, and ultimately nobody would be immune from the danger of extermination.

It appears to be the safest course to restrict genetic manipulation to animal and plant breeding, where better livestock and crops can hopefully be obtained by the kind of selective reproduction that has been practiced for some time. It is in God's mercy that human beings are poor candidates for purposes of genetic engineering. Whereas for mammals modern techniques introduce the new donor gene into the egg at the time of fertilization, for human beings this would be an entirely unsatisfactory approach to the problems of manipulation. Because human genetic defects are only observable long after conception has occurred, they would be detected much too late in fetal development to be prevented, and in such cases abortion would then have to be considered.

Even if a manipulative experiment were to be successful, scientists simply do not know the extent to which certain desirable traits of character are under genetic control, or what in fact the nature of the determining influence actually is. Should it be proved ultimately that behavior is influenced genetically, the scientists would then be involved in maneuvering a multiplicity of different genes without being able to predict or control the nature of the outcome. Under such conditions it would be virtually impossible for anyone to attempt direct genetic manipulation on a proper scientific basis.

Clearly the practical and moral problems associated with eugenics as it might be practiced on a scientific level are very serious. The image of God in humankind is defaced when human beings are equated with animals and plants as suitable subjects for genetic experimentation, and the Christian will resist such attempts vigorously. By virtue of being the product of divine creation (Gen. 1:23; 2:7), human beings are in a category *sui generis*. Although the human genetic pool is very seriously polluted, the transforming power of Christ's redeeming love makes all things new (2 Cor. 5:17; Rev. 21:5), and for the Christian this promise applies to the entire personality. While it obviously does not remove established genetic defects, it can and does have important mitigating influences by providing us with the grace and love to deal with them and to heal some of their more obtuse manifestations.

See BIOETHICS; GENETIC ENGINEERING.

**EUTHANASIA.** In 1990 physician Jack Kevorkian made headlines nationwide with the use of his "suicide machine" on a middle-aged Michigan woman who had been recently diagnosed for Alzheimer's disease. Calling his practice "medicide," Kevorkian engaged in a form of euthanasia which is rarely, if ever, approved of by medical ethicists. Nevertheless, his actions have brought to the forefront the moral question of whether euthanasia of any sort is ever justified.

The word *euthanasia* comes from two Greek words, *eu* and *thanatos*, which translated literally means "good death" or "happy death." Today euthanasia is defined as an act which brings about the death of a terminally ill person either suffering tremendously or near death. Death is brought about either by actively causing the patient's death, such as giving a lethal injection or removing oxygen from a room, or by passively causing the patient's death, such as withdrawing or withholding treatment which is perceived as useless. The former is known as *active euthanasia* while the latter is known as *passive euthanasia*. In passive euthanasia the *intent* is not to kill but simply to relieve the patient of an unnecessary burden and to permit nature to take its course.

In decisions concerning the withdrawing or withholding of treatment, intentions are an integral part in judging the morality of the act. For example, if a man receiving chemotherapy which will extend his life only a few months chooses to withdraw treatment for the sake of not undergoing the physical pain which almost always accompanies the treatment, then he has chosen passive euthanasia, for his intention is not to die but to relieve pain, although the decision to withdraw treatment will most certainly hasten death. On the other hand, suppose another man in a similar situation requests a lethal injection in addition to withdrawing treatment. In this case, he has chosen death, and hence has chosen active euthanasia, for he intends to end his life prematurely rather than merely to relieve pain.

The difference between the first man and the second man is a difference between choosing life without pain (although the cancer will eventually kill the first man) and choosing death (i.e., it is the lethal injection and *not* the cancer which kills the second man). Although not all so-called cases of passive and active euthanasia are as clear-cut, the above clearly shows that there is a fundamental moral difference between passive and active euthanasia.

Ethicists see both these types of euthanasia as being either voluntary, involuntary, or nonvoluntary. *Voluntary* euthanasia occurs when a fully informed competent patient freely *consents* either to withdraw/withhold treatment (passive euthanasia) or to actively hasten death by any number of means, such as a lethal injection (active euthanasia). Euthanasia is *involuntary* when it is forced upon a patient (whether it is passive or active) *against* his or her free will. *Nonvoluntary* euthanasia is performed on a patient (whether it is passive or active) *without* but not against his or her consent (for example, where a patient is in a persistent vegetative state and has not given any prior indication of what his or her wishes might be, such as through a living will).

Hence, there are six types of euthanasia: (1) voluntary active euthanasia; (2) voluntary passive euthanasia; (3) involuntary passive euthanasia; (4) involuntary active euthanasia; (5) nonvoluntary passive euthanasia; and (6) nonvoluntary active euthanasia. The last four types, associated by most people with the Nazi euthanasia programs, are rarely, if ever defended by any major medical ethicist in the United States today.

The Bible does not mention the words "suicide" or "euthanasia," but it seems apparent that its teachings do condemn both suicide and most forms of euthanasia.

First, since the Bible specifically condemns murder (Exod. 20:13), and suicide is a form of homicide, it seems reasonable to conclude that the Bible also prohibits suicide.

Second, even the most desperate believer in the Bible who desired death never considered suicide a morally valid option. Take for example Jonah's prayer: "O LORD, please take my life from me, for death is better to me than life" (Jonah 4:3 NASB; see also Job 3).

Third, the Bible records five cases of suicide: Abimelech (Judg. 9:50-56), Saul and his armor-bearer (1 Sam. 31:1-6; 2 Sam. 1:1-15; 1 Chron. 10:1-13); Zimri (1 Kings 16:18-19); Ahithophel (2 Sam. 17:23); and Judas (Matt. 27:3-10; Acts 1:18-19). But as R. N. Wennberg has pointed out, "in each case of suicide recorded in Scripture, death represents a tragic end to a life that did not (at least in its latter stages) meet with God's approval."

The Bible, however, does not teach that people have an absolute moral obligation always to accept treatment that would sustain life artificially. For example, it does not seem inconsistent with the Bible for somebody to refuse to take a pill (were it available) which would double her life span. Likewise, there does not seem to be a moral obligation to undergo chemotherapy or to receive kidney dialysis treatment, although it may be wise or desirable to accept such treatment.

Since the Bible does teach that God has appointed that all will eventually suffer the natural consequences of disease and mortality (Gen. 3; Rom. 5), it seems consistent with biblical teaching to accept them. After all, we must all do so eventually. It seems then, from a Christian perspective, that only passive euthanasia is justified.

**Bibliography:** Beckwith, F. J., and Geisler, N. L., *Matters of Life and Death* (1992); Moreland, J. P., and Geisler, N. L., *The Life and Death Debate* (1990); President's Commission for the Study of Ethical Problems in Medicine and Biomedical and Behavioral Research, *Deciding to Forgo Life-Sustaining Treatment* (1983); Wennberg, R. N., *Terminal Choices* (1989).

See AGED, CARE OF; RIGHT TO DIE; SUICIDE.

F.J.B.

**EVANGELISM, ETHICAL ASPECTS OF.** Evangelism has been defined as "spreading the good news that Jesus Christ died for our sins and was raised from the dead according to the Scriptures and now offers the forgiveness of sins and the liberating gift of the Spirit to all who repent and believe." As such, it is the activity of the disciples of Jesus who belong to His church. The aim of this activity is to enroll more members in that church. Because evangelism is both the activity of Christ Himself through His ambassadors (Mark 16:20) and the commendation of Christ and life in His name by His disciples (Matt. 28:19-20), the method, content, and context of it must be deemed to be important and to have moral content. The following statements help to identify that moral content.

1. Those who preach the gospel concerning Jesus ought to be people who are both committed to Him and are examples of the life produced by the power of the gospel. This would appear to be self-evident, but within the history of Protestantism there are many examples of evangelists whose way of life hardly commended the One whom they claimed to preach. The apostle Paul urged Timothy to be an evangelist and also told him to pursue righteousness, faith, love, and peace (2 Tim. 2:22; 4:5).

2. The community of believers (to which the preacher or evangelist belongs and to which converts to Christ will be introduced) ought to exem-

plify all aspects of the gospel. This again would appear to be self-evident, but it has always been easier to give lip service to it than to make sure it exists in practice. Jesus expected His disciples to be the light of the world (Matt. 6:14). Paul spoke of the local church as a letter from Christ to be read by all men in order for them to know the truth and way of salvation (2 Cor. 3:3).

3. Public evangelistic activity ought only to be supported by institutions, businesses, and individuals of integrity. Mass evangelism certainly needs much money and support from important parts of society in order to succeed. However, this support ought not to be sought at the cost of compromising the claims of Jesus Christ as proclaimed in the gospel.

4. Advertising of evangelistic meetings and personalities ought always to be honest and never to dishonor Christ. The normal manner of advertising goods in a competitive, consumer society is hardly appropriate for the commending of meetings where Christ will be uplifted. This is because it is based on a value system contrary to Christian values.

5. Technological aids ought not to dominate evangelistic activity so that the value of the individual person is effectively denied, or that its societal dimensions are effectively forgotten. There must be a central place given to the encounter of the evangelized with the evangelist.

6. Reporting of meetings and of the number of enquirers or converts ought to be governed by the most scrupulous guidelines of honesty. Bearing in mind the parable of the sower and the four types of ground on to which the seed fell, there is need for caution and care in the claims made for the results of evangelistic activity.

7. The recipients of the message ought to be treated with profound respect since, while being sinners, they are also made in God's image and are those for whom Christ died. When there is genuine love for sinners in the hearts of those who bring the good news, then there will be wholesome respect for the hearers. Such respect does not diminish enthusiasm for evangelism; rather, it controls the methods used and the style of the way Christ is offered. For example, aggression, compulsion, and racial discrimination will not be present.

8. The gospel ought to be preached to people as having both soul and body, living in this world in preparation for the next world. The gospel is good news of the kingdom of God. Although the kingdom will come in fullness only after the second coming of Christ, the rule of God in this age covers more than the human soul. People have bodies and live in particular circumstances and localities. They may be poor or rich, sick or in good health, maltreated or well-treated. These circumstances matter, and the gospel cannot be offered to people without some concern and care being extended to their own particular circumstances. This is particularly true where there is obvious injustice, deprivation, and disease. If the gospel is preached within the love of the neighbor, which God requires of the church, then evangelism will not be isolated from care for the people in their total circumstances.

9. Evangelists ought to make a thorough study of the culture, social background, religious views, and economic position of the people they will be, or are, evangelizing. For example, preaching the gospel in a Muslim country requires a different approach than in a Hindu or Buddhist country. Though the success of evangelism depends ultimately on the presence of the Holy Spirit, there is a moral obligation upon those evangelizing to do all they can to make the work of the Spirit more direct and effective, as well as to show their respect for the hearers by knowing their culture and context.

10. All engaged in evangelism ought to be conscious that their righteous and loving Lord is involved with them and that everything done should be done in His name and according to His mind and standards.

**Bibliography:** *The Grand Rapids Report: Evangelism and Social Responsibility* (Lausanne Committee for World Evangelization and World Evangelical Fellowship, 1982); Mott, S. C., *Biblical Ethics and Social Change* (1982).

P.T.

**EVIL.** As a metaphysical entity, evil is diametrically opposed to good in nature and function. It has important ramifications for the natural order of creation (Rom. 8:22) as well as for human beings. Evil is an immensely powerful and pervasive force, which appears to be the message proclaimed by one of the prophet Haggai's oracles (Hag. 2:12-14). No satisfactory explanation of the origin of evil has ever been devised, and even Scripture merely hints at the matter in relationship to the evil experienced by moral beings.

It first appeared in human society as the result of a successful attempt to persuade the mother of all living (Gen. 3:20) to disobey a divine injunction. The tempter assumed a guise which was apparently familiar to the woman and was trusted in consequence. Only when the deception was exposed was the true nature of the tempter and the act of temptation made apparent. In the Genesis account, God possessed the power to impose a curse upon all the participants in the act of disobedience and extended this to the earth itself. It is important for Christian theology to realize that the earth is permanently under a divine curse and is only secondarily in the power of the evil one. Elsewhere the tempter is known as the "adversary" (*hassatan*), or in English versions by the more familiar name of Satan. Elsewhere Satan tempted the second Adam as he had beguiled the first, but without success (Matt. 4:1-11; Mark 1:13; Luke 4:1-13), and was described by the Synoptic writers as "the devil." In New Testament times the Jews used the name Beelzebul to describe the "chief of the devils" (Luke 11:15).

Some Christian expositors have seen in the oracle of Ezekiel against the king of Tyre (Ezek. 28:13-19) an allusion to the origin of moral evil, but the passage in question is part of an extended prophetic condemnation (Ezek. 26:2—28:19) of the sins of ancient Canaan and thus deals with conditions occurring within a specific period of human history. Jesus Christ was equally enigmatic about the origin of evil, contenting himself with the assertion that he beheld Satan as lightning falling from heaven (Luke 10:18).

The moral evil that humankind experiences includes stupidity, ignorance, disease, suffering, obduracy, selfishness, and sin in the form of rebellion against the known and revealed will of God. Evil only becomes a "problem" if one believes the scriptural account of the self-revelation of God as holy, just, omnipotent, omniscient, and loving, whose mercy is over all his works. For those who reject such a God, evil has to be dismissed, generally in reductionist terms, as an "error of mortal mind," an illusion, or some such state as "nonbeing." These explanations may appear persuasive in a purely philosophical setting, but they have an uncomfortably hollow ring to them when some aspect of moral evil becomes a grim reality in individual experience.

Even for many Christians the fact of moral evil presents difficulties for faith, due partly to grossly inadequate biblical teaching, and also to unrealistic social perceptions that evil is something that always happens to others, not to oneself. Paul has stated the underlying concept of the second law of thermodynamics (entropy) quite clearly (Rom. 8:22), and has included humanity within its scope. By disobeying God's covenantal laws of hygiene, people have polluted the human genetic pool to an alarming extent and have corrupted themselves with mind-disorienting chemicals. So stupid and self-willed are human beings generally that they are even threatening to bring certain social diseases into being in epidemic proportions, in defiance of God's commands to the contrary. Before raising questions about God's love in the face of the enormous presence of evil in the world, people in general, including Christians, need to assess their own responsibilities as causative agents and determine whether in fact they are serving the God of love or the evil one.

Jesus formulated no teaching as such about the "problem of evil," but instead He dealt with it in the most practical and definitive manner. He became human in order to redress the damage done by our ancestors, and the records of His life show Him rejecting and defeating evil at every turn. His death was an atonement for humanity's sin (Mark 10:45), and His resurrection was the final victory over both sin and death. The believer cannot expect to receive better treatment in this life than the Master (John 15:20), although by God's provident mercy most of us do. Although we may be living in the faith and power of Jesus Christ, we shall still continue to be open to temptation, as He was, but we now have the means whereby sin

can be halted and conquered in our lives. Since in normal Christian experience moral evil is the consequence of sin, continuous spiritual cleansing through the atoning blood of Christ furnishes the means by which evil can be blotted out of our existence.

**Bibliography:** Petit, F., *The Problem of Evil* (1959); Pike, N., (ed.), *God and Evil* (1964).

**EXISTENTIAL ETHICS.** Basically a twentieth-century movement, existentialism has its roots in the nineteenth century with such figures as Soren Kierkegaard (1813-1855) and Friedrich Nietzsche (1844-1900). But it is in the present century that existentialism made its impact on the intellectual world.

The rise of existentialism corresponds with an altered consciousness that was precipitated by the tragedy of the First World War. This new outlook involved a disenchantment with the hitherto prevailing optimism, a deepening appreciation of the tragedy of the human condition, and a growing conviction that reason was inadequate to serve as a guide to life. In this congenial environment, existentialism made its inroads, finding able exponents among both humanists and religious philosophers, including such major figures as Jean-Paul Sartre (1905-1980), Jacques Maritain (1882-1973), Gabriel Marcel (1889-1973), Karl Jaspers (1883-1969), and Martin Heidegger (1889-1976).

All these writers endorsed a radical sense of freedom. What am I to be? What am I to live for? What am I to do with my existence? What values shall I affirm? There was seen to be no rationally correct answer to these questions. Rather, the individual is free to select any answer without fear of contradiction by reason. Thus there is a freedom from rational determinism. The individual can select an answer to these questions and live it out in his or her life, free from the dictates of heredity and environment. For individuals are not, the existentialist contends, the product of physical and social forces that shape them and mold them. Rather, we shape and mold ourselves. Thus, there is affirmed a freedom from causal determinism. This twofold freedom is enunciated in the famous existentialist catch phrase "existence precedes essence." That is to say, one first exists in the world and then one determines one's essence as a moral, spiritual, and social being. My essence precedes me neither as a rational concept dictating what I ought to be, nor as a social/physical force controlling what I will be.

As for moral norms, we do not demonstrate them rationally, but choose them in a radical act of freedom. The existentialist would argue that ultimate norms cannot be demonstrated. If they are ultimate, there is nothing to which an appeal can be made in order to substantiate them. At some point reasoning must come to an end, for we cannot go on proving all our beliefs *ad infinitum*. Thus, the only option left for us is to select randomly those norms that we shall use to guide our lives. This selection is arbitrary, and no selection is better than any other. So, affirming a certain set of moral standards and committing oneself to them are groundless acts that cannot be guided by either argument or authorities.

A closely connected existentialist theme is that of responsibility. For if I am free to create my own value system, I must as a consequence assume responsibility for the system that I create. Since my choices are utterly free from causally and rationally determining factors, it follows that I alone am the creator of my moral universe and that I alone am to assume responsibility for what I have created. Sartre introduced the term "bad faith" to characterize those who fail to assume this responsibility. These are people who seek to evade responsibility by fleeing to determinism. They protest that they could not help themselves because of environmental and hereditary factors and, therefore, that they are not to be blamed for what they do and are. Others argue that there is no choice in a given moral matter since reason dictates that this norm be accepted, this value be endorsed, or this decision be made. But all this is only bad faith, prompted by the anguish and forlornness that comes when one is forced to create one's own moral universe without reason or authorities to guide one. For authorities and reasons provide us with a comfort and a security in contrast to the agony that is ours when acknowledging the terrifying scope of our freedom. But to recognize one's freedom, to reject the blandishments of determinism, and to accept total responsibility for the value system one has created, is to live authentically and is the moral antithesis of bad faith.

Christian response to such teachings is mixed. While recognizing the need to accept responsibility for the life one has chosen to live, Christians nevertheless will wish to qualify existentialist claims that present actions are wholly disconnected from past happenings and conditions. Human freedom is not absolute in that sense. Such a view borders on Pelagianism, a view which has historically been rejected by the Christian community because of its failure to take adequately into account the impact of sin on the human condition. Similarly, the existentialist doctrine of absolute freedom fails to take seriously the human condition with its strong propensity to sin. It is the reality of the sinful human condition that creates the necessity for divine grace. For it is not within unaided human power simply to realize any and all moral ideals. In this regard the human condition is even more desperate than the existentialist realizes.

Further, the Christian community dissents from the existentialist claim that moral standards are no more than a human creation. For if there is a loving, holy, and just God, then moral standards have an objective basis, namely, the character of God. The Christian does not need to capitulate to the existentialist position even should it be the case that ultimate moral norms cannot be demonstrated. The critical assumption made by the existentialist here is that if a proposition cannot be demonstrated, then it cannot be known and is therefore arbitrarily affirmed. There is good reason, however, to reject this assumption. It must be the case that we know some propositions independently of formal argument and proof-giving, or else we know nothing at all. For argument must terminate at some point because an endless chain of reason-giving is not a possible route to knowledge. That is, there must be noninferential knowledge that is immediately apprehended as true without any inference being drawn from other knowledge that we possess. If there is no such noninferential knowledge, then, because traversing an infinite chain of argumentation is not a possibility, we are left with no knowledge at all. In that case the claims made by existentialists are not knowledge and can be ignored. On the other hand, if we conclude that there is knowledge and therefore that there is also noninferential knowledge, we must be open to the possibility that basic moral norms are a species of this very kind of knowledge.

Another theme frequently found in existentialist literature is that of individualism. Finding classical expression in the writings of Nietzsche, it is a theme widely used in existentialist fiction as well. Individualism is to be viewed in contrast to the thought of most moralists for whom virtue is conformity to an ideal or a set of norms that is the same for everyone. To the extent then that we are good, virtuous, or moral, we become like one another because we are all converging upon a common moral goal. This standard view of morality is repudiated by exponents of existentialist individualism. In its place is substituted one that rejects models and standards, stressing those qualities that are not shared by others but are the individual's alone. The great threat to individualism is living a life dictated by the expectations of others, where one succumbs to the social pressure to conform to commonly shared ideals. Though the task is not viewed as easy, one is to search for those features about oneself that are unique. A clue to those features is found in the tendency to suppress certain dimensions of ourselves in response to social pressure. Here one is likely to find a characteristic that needs to be liberated and given unchecked expression. To do so marks the beginning of self-discovery and the start of a journey that leads one-knows-not-where. Fear of the unknown may prompt many, the existentialist warns, to seek the security and the comfort of the well-worn path of moral consensus.

Existentialist individualism is at odds with the Christian emphasis on a common moral pattern. In the case of Christianity, there is uplifted for all humanity a divinely ordained Exemplar, the person of Christ, who loves God with all His being and loves His neighbor as He loves Himself. But to uplift the model of Christ and to offer a set of universal moral norms, as Christianity does, is not to advocate a stifling or boring uniformity. We need to distinguish between personality and character. At the level of character, there is to be fundamental agreement as to type, for the love modeled in Christ is to be embodied in us all. At the level of personality there is much room for divergence. Whereas good characters are to be alike, acceptable personalities need not be. Therefore, the same type of loving character can find individual expression through varying personalities, and thus the expression of that love is open to limitless variations. Further, it needs to be observed that one can be uniquely perverse as well as uniquely good. Uniqueness is not itself a moral quality worthy of praise. Finally, one will detect a note of *hubris* in the existentialist call to be unique. For only God is unique; and no matter how odd, different, or iconoclastic we may think we are, still if we are honest, we shall discover that we are only one among many of exactly the same type.

**Bibliography:** Barrett, W., *What is Existentialism* (1964); Hunnex, M. D., *Existentialism and Christian Belief* (1969); Olson, R. G., *An Introduction to Existentialism* (1962); Roubiczek, P., *Existentialism For and Against* (1964); Williams, J. R., *Existentialism and Christian Faith* (1965).

R.W.

**EXPEDIENCE.** This term describes suitability or advisability in a general sense, and in common usage indicates an attitude of mind that is prepared to modify a strictly legal interpretation of behavior in favor of one that seems more desirable or effective politically. It must not be construed as an attempt to break or ignore the law, but rather to enable law to serve more effectively the larger social goals in view. It is a simple fact that, in an increasingly complex society, situations arise continually in human relationships that are not covered adequately by laws or regulations and which therefore require special consideration for the well-being of those concerned. This latter is particularly important where political considerations are at stake, as was illustrated in the case of Jesus Christ. Because he constituted a serious threat to the religious status quo in Jerusalem, the high priest Caiaphas decided that it was expedient for one person, Jesus, to die rather than expose the entire nation to the very real threat of destruction (John 11:50).

In dealing with the social problems that the Corinthian Christians faced in a pagan society, Paul drew an important distinction between the lawful and the expedient. The larger area of what in theory was lawful needed to be modified by a consideration of what was actually advisable. In this instance the latter involved the edifying of the entire Christian community by Paul's own example, lest the "weaker brother" be diminished rather than built up in the faith (1 Cor. 10:23). In another instance Paul used expediency to avoid a narrow legalism (1 Cor. 6:12) and to dispel the impression that he might actually be boasting (2 Cor. 12:1).

**EXTORTION.** This word is based upon the Latin verb *torquere,* "to twist," and describes a process by which something is extracted by force. The historical concomitant of extortion has in fact been violence, whether of a brutal physical kind or the more subtle but equally effective psychological variety. In the Old Testament the extortioner (*mutz*) was dreaded as the individual who would wring out every possible bit of gain, but Isaiah predicted the end of such practices in an oracle against Moab (Isa. 16:4). In a similar vein Ezekiel (22:12) foretold punishment upon Israel's princes because of their extortion (*osheq,* "oppression"). Conversely he also prophesied that a son who had refused to follow his father in idolatry, oppression, violence, and extortion would live and not die (Ezek. 18:16-17).

In his denunciation of the scribes and Pharisees, Jesus not only described them as hypocrites, but accused them of being filled with extortion (Matt. 23:25). The Greek term employed (*harpage*) means "snatching away," which again reflects the violence implicit in extortion. In other New Testament occurrences the extortioner was classed with the covetous, idolaters, and drunkards (1 Cor. 5:10-11), and denied the inheritance of God's kingdom along with them (1 Cor. 6:10).

Extortion, however practiced, is an unjust exploitation of people who are usually unable to defend themselves for one reason or other. It is an evil, aggressive activity which is largely motivated by selfishness and greed and should neither be encouraged nor condoned by the practicing Christian.

See CRIME; DECEPTION; GREED.

# –F–

**FAITHFULNESS.** In secular society faithfulness implies a commitment to certain ideals, relationships, or courses of action, and the ability to continue supporting them even in the face of adverse circumstances. If fidelity to causes is to be anything more than a transient matter, it demands determination and a tenacity of purpose to see the issues through to a satisfactory conclusion.

In the spiritual life faithfulness typifies a person in whose life the fact of faith in the saving and sustaining power of God is dominant and persistent. Faithfulness is one of the supreme values that characterize God's revealed nature and remains independent of human attitudes toward him, since whatever people may or may not believe, God cannot deny his own fidelity (2 Tim. 2:13). This characteristic was in abundant evidence throughout Israel's history (Deut. 7:9; Ps. 119:86, 138) and contrasted sharply with the unfaithfulness of the chosen people to the Sinai covenant, a measure of apostasy which ultimately brought about their rejection and replacement with the Christian church.

But there were outstanding examples of stability and fidelity among God's ancient people, including Moses (Num. 12:7; Heb. 3:5), Hananiah (Neh. 7:2), David (1 Sam. 2:35; 22:14), Daniel (Dan. 6:4), and many others. The pious Israelite recognized that as part of his witness he must proclaim God's faithfulness (*emunah*) to those around, whether under normal circumstances (Pss. 40:10; 89:1; 92:2) or in the midst of calamity (Lam. 3:23).

Faithfulness occupied an important place in Christ's teachings, which is understandable in the light of the Israelites' long apostasy. It is never to be considered an isolated act, but characteristic of a life of faith in Christ (Hab. 2:4). It was often related to stewardship (Matt. 24:25; Luke 16:10), and the blessings of faithfulness were depicted parabolically as being of far greater magnitude than the act of fidelity itself (Luke 19:17-19). This emphasis was continued in Paul's writings, where faithfulness was made a prime requisite for stewardship (1 Cor. 4:2). A truly Christian life is one in which a faithful servant lives in communion with his faithful Lord, and it is important for believers to understand that the prime commitment in all witness and ministry is not success, but faithfulness. The truth and fidelity of God's nature is not unnaturally expressed in his scriptural utterances (Titus 1:9; 3:8; Rev. 22:6) through the Holy Spirit, who is described as the faithful and true witness (Rev. 3:14).

**FALL OF MAN.** In the Bible the Fall is a historical event in which Adam rebelled against God (Gen. 3). Through this act Adam and all of mankind consequently lost their original divinely given innocence and have experienced the doleful conditions which follow from sin: guilt, condemnation, painful conditions of life and environment, and finally death.

The original temptation is attributed in the Bible to the devil, disguised as a serpent. That God created the first couple and that the Fall was historical is assumed (Luke 3:38; Rom. 5:14; 1 Cor. 15:22, 45; 1 Tim. 2:13). In principle, the logic of the Fall of man and the logic of a premundane angelic fall (John 8:44; 2 Pet. 2:4; Jude 6; Rev. 20:1-2) are the same. To take it out of history is to end up with either dualism (that good and evil co-exist eternally) or monism (that good and evil are jointly encompassed in one undifferentiated whole). Given the Christian premises of the creation of the world by God, personhood, freedom and moral responsibility, the Fall, whether premundane or the Fall of man, must have been an event in time.

In modern times even those who have taken the Fall account to be mythological have expressed growing admiration for its theological implications, psychological insights, moral perceptions, and its cosmological and philosophical uniqueness.

This uniqueness centers upon the moral nature of man and his moral relation to God. The central issue is perversion of man's nature, which was created originally in the image of God. Whatever else this may mean, personhood is essential to the biblical model. Man is created to be an intelligent, moral, and purposing self. Corruption of this image by sin does not mean that something has happened to man; rather, that something has happened in man (Mark 7:21). The evil comes willfully from within. Evil is not merely a metaphysical state, but is a moral condition due to disobedience. This condition has been universal since the Fall. Hence the present contradiction in human nature. Man is capable of great good; nevertheless, man is dogged by his proneness to evil.

The possibility of sin is in itself a tribute to the greatness that man was given by God, who made man akin to Himself (Ps. 8:5). God made a free spirit in contrast to the rest of the animal creation. Man's uniqueness is apparent in his intelligence (including science and the practical applications of his knowledge), his creativity (including art and culture), and his ability to discriminate between right and wrong.

The dark side since the Fall is that man has become loveless, frustrated, and perverse. There have ensued repeated acts that reflect the Fall (1 Cor. 10:12; 1 Tim. 3:6; Heb. 4:11).

Why man fell remains a mystery. Answers include pride, independence from God, unbelief, concupiscence, and disobedience. Despite man's continuing perversity, God graciously purposes human redemption and renewal through Christ's sacrificial death. Renewal comes not by educational and social reform, nor by psychological or psychiatric reprogramming, as helpful as these may be, nor by adjusting any universal chemical imbalance in the brain as some have thought to do. Rather, the new man for the new age comes by redemption. Paul dramatically contrasts all that has come to the race through Adam's disobedience and the Fall with what has come to the race through Christ and His obedience (Rom. 5:12-21). Paul does not envision a behaviorally induced change, but a permanent moral transformation of human life through the power of Jesus Christ.

**Bibliography:** Babbage S. B., *Man in Nature and Grace* (1957); Cave, S., *The Christian Estimate of Man* (1944); MacKay, D. M., *Human Science and Human Dignity* (1979); Mikolaski, S. J., *The Grace of God* (1965).

S.J.M.

**FALSE WITNESS.** Duplicity, deception, and lying are in total contradiction to the morality of the divine nature, and accordingly such activity is condemned in the Decalogue (Exod. 20:16). The kind of falsity envisaged seems to be that of misrepresentation or duplicity, while in the parallel passage in Deuteronomy 5:17 the term implies something devoid of value. False testimony was obviously so damaging that the presence of witnesses in order to establish the factual veracity of a situation was highly desirable (Deut. 17:6; 19:15). The prevalence of false witnesses in Israel can be judged by the number of references to it in Scripture (Pss. 27:12; 35:11; Prov. 19:5, 9; 21:28), hence the importance of punishment for such an offense. The law of Deuteronomy 19:15-19 prescribed that when the guilt of a false witness had been established, the penalty that would have been imposed on the accused had the testimony been true was to be inflicted upon the lying witness.

False witnesses abounded when Jesus Christ was on trial for his life, but their testimony was so patently untrue and contradictory that even the Jewish authorities felt compelled to reject it (Mark 14:56-59). Elsewhere New Testament references to false witnesses are invariably to the ninth commandment (Matt. 19:18; Mark 10:19; Rom. 13:9). In modern society it is recognized as so serious an offense as to be punishable by law when a witness is under oath. The Christian is required to be a true witness to divine grace, to avoid falsehood, and to speak truth with his or her neighbor (Eph. 4:25).

**FAMILY.** Biblical writers found it unnecessary to promote the institution of the family, but rather took it very much for granted. Their assumptions were based on the order of creation in which man and wife in faithfulness to God and each other would enjoy and raise children as part of God's purpose in creation and in the superintendence of His world (Gen. 1:28; 2:24; Pss. 112:9; 103:13, 17). Direct teachings about family ethics are to be found throughout Scripture (see especially Exod. 20:12; Deut. 6:4-7; Eph. 5:21—6:8; 1 Tim. 5:8).

The deepest and most intimate communion of humans with their Creator is depicted often in family imagery: father and son (Matt. 11:27); bridegroom (Matt. 9:15); bride (Isa. 62:5); children of God (Matt. 5:9); brethren (Rom. 8:29); parent interacting with child and the motherly nature of God (Isa. 66:12-13; Hos. 11:1-2). Unfaithfulness to God is described in family terms as well, for example, "playing the harlot" (Isa. 1:21-23) and disloyalty as sons (Isa. 1:4). Some of Jesus' best-known parables incorporate family metaphors (Luke 15:11-32). All this suggests very strongly that God has created the family as the most suitable situation in which one can learn the true meaning of divine and human love and the values of the kingdom and family of God Himself (Deut 6:2, 6-7). The family has all the potential of being a small colony of heaven, a mini communion of saints, a training ground for the Christian's life in the present and in eternity, provided that Christ's teaching, power, and love are known and experienced there.

In considering family relationships and ethical responsibilities, the focus of attention is usually on husband, wife, and children of the nuclear family. It is essential, however, that others, particularly the elderly, be included in all our thinking and planning about family life. The apostle Paul writes harshly about Christians who neglect their own blood relations, particularly the elderly (1 Tim. 5:8). The local congregation, as well as the national church, therefore, has an obligation to support and enable families to be sensitive to their care responsibilities to the elderly. It is not possible to generalize on practical action to be taken in this area, but only to assert that the obligation to do something is a Christian family duty. In many instances there is a crying need in the church and in society for the skills and experience that senior citizens have, which go to waste because no one mobilizes them. Maggie Kuhn and her "Grey Panthers" are a rebuke to a very neglectful and unresourceful society.

Parents are responsible for nurturing their children in the faith and fear of God, in personal growth, in responsible citizenship, and in church membership. This parental responsibility cannot be transferred to the local congregation, though of course the local parish can and must provide some Christian education and give strong support and guidance to parents in this most basic Christian family duty. The most effective locus of

Christian education remains in the home (Deut. 6:6-7; Eph. 6:4; 2 Tim. 1:5).

*The Nuclear Family and the Family of God.* In the Scriptures the nuclear and/or extended family of blood relationships finds its meaning and purpose within the eternal family of God. That divine family, which on earth might ideally be identified with the church, in turn has the moral responsibility of supporting the nuclear family so as to enhance its participation in the larger family. We see this in the New Testament Epistles where immediate family concerns are colored by the intensity of the overarching need to be ready when Christ comes again. Indeed, every Christian activity in every aspect of life, family, and other matters, found its meaning in the light of that reality.

Life in the nuclear family, therefore, is not an end in itself. This principle is by no means demeaning to the nuclear family. On the contrary, it enhances the family's value and motivates its members with a power that transcends human effort (Eph. 3:20). These biblical truths and values provide a powerful basis and vision for the ethic of the Christian family today.

*The Modern Family.* There is widespread concern for the family in Western society today, both in Christian and non-Christian circles. When compared with the efforts put into building the nuclear family in ancient and medieval times, the enormous anxious energy poured into this enterprise today is unique in history. For instance, the widespread modern expectation that all families should be primary communities of deep intimacy is something new. It may be that ever-increasing available leisure time, longevity, and years spent in education make this intimacy a more attainable goal. These heavier emotional demands on the nuclear family call more insistently than ever for the high qualities of Christian relationship: love, caring, confession, forgiveness, patience—as well as for means of grace such as family prayer, Bible reading, worship, and active fellowship in the life of the church.

Modern nuclear Christian families need assurance of how their life together fits into the larger plan of God. The churches need to be intensely aware of deleterious cultural inroads into Christian values and interpersonal family relationships and to create new ways of supporting families of the congregation and the community. In earlier ages, especially before the so-called "Enlightment," the security of being part of something "bigger and beyond" was much more prevalent in families than it is now. The sense of cosmic participation was felt to be one of the "givens" of life. Christians today need to recapture and nurture this sense of eternal meaning as a basis for Christian family ethics, though not necessarily in precisely the same terms. They need a coherent and cohesive world view, God-centered and purposeful. God has revealed a basis for such a world view through the Scriptures, including a vision and hope for the future that surpasses anything of purely human manufacture.

Today's family members do not, generally speaking, have the "advantage" that earlier generations had of being desperately needed for the comfort and financial security of the family unit. The main contribution of contemporary family members to each other is more relational and spiritual: giving and receiving love and affection, a sense of belonging and acceptance, self-disciplined and responsible participation in the family community, and mutual accountability under God. Today, we have time and energy for these relational activities that family members of previous generations lacked because of the shortness of life, poverty, and inferior technology. What we so desperately need are the personal graces to use them.

Today about half the marriages in America end in divorce. The situation in other Western lands is no more encouraging. Many families are now "single-parent" and fatherless, which very often causes poverty and always involves the loss of an important element in a child's development: having a male parent. Similar problems no doubt occur when children are deprived of a mother figure. Psychologically and spiritually, both are needed; and efforts should always be made to see that children have the nurture of both male and female adults, if not their own parents then adoptive mothers and fathers or step-parents.

When divorce, desertion, death, or some other calamity occurs, the wider Christian family, the church, must rally around to minister healing, forgiveness, and whatever emergency or surrogate relationships and services might in compassion be needed. But always by the grace of God and by faith, some effort can and must be made to begin a new start and to provide members of the fractured family with the supports they need in Christ.

*Extending the Family Network.* Some of the disastrous consequences of the family break-up can be relieved by people who "look out for each other" and give affirmation, affection, and fellowship. The church often functions as a coordinating agency to bring people together for such support and should see this as one of its most valuable ministries. Even healthy nuclear Christian families need the support and backing of other persons in networks extending beyond immediate blood relationships and cohabitation.

*Christian Family and Secular State.* Since the nuclear family is the foundation of the state and of civilized society, the health of families is an obligation upon Christians not only from the point of view of their faith, but also as concerned citizens of their country. Christians will therefore feel obligated to contend for the propagation of Christian family values in government though the democratic process. Some state governments affirm and encourage stable family life through public education and the proclamation of special days or seasons dedicated to the study and renewal of family life. One such state is the Province of Ontario, Canada, where the lieutenant governor annually proclaims the month of May as "Family Unity Month." Through the appropriate governmental agency, Ontario provides information and guidelines for schools and churches to build up family values. Christians' cooperation in such projects is an essential obligation, though admittedly only part of their happy duty as the people of God. The laws promulgated by legislatures and pronouncements made by them send powerful messages to the people, particularly to the children of the land. This is only one reason why it is incumbent upon Christian citizens to ensure that values thus taught by the laws of the land and by government propaganda be such that they encourage the populace to respect two essential bulwarks of the state and of God's kingdom, namely marriage and the family.

*Personal and Social Formation*. The Christian citizen will also be concerned that the influences of society contribute to the kind of personal formation that is desirable from the Christian point of view. These influences include such matters as formal education; laws governing marriages, divorces, the rights of women and of the unborn; and compulsory schooling. The formation which our children receive in home, school, and society is part of the raw material which we offer to God to use in the transformation of their lives by the Holy Spirit. Parents must assume responsibility in those political and social activities which so greatly affect the formation of persons in the family and in society.

*Obligations of Family Members*. In general terms, Christian family members have an obligation, in love to Christ and to each other, to build one another up in the Lord and enable rather than hinder each other's growth as Christian persons. The pithy admonitions to household members in Ephesians 5:21—6:9 have perennial application to family ethics. The husband still needs to give major attention to how he expresses love to his wife, fulfilling a deep need of the wife and mother to be treated as a wanted and highly regarded person—a need, incidentally, shared to various degrees by every living human being! The wife in her turn must give attention to respecting the husband; children need to obey parents, because they're still learning the basics of life; fathers ought to participate in the discipline, nurturing, and education of children and not to provoke them by demeaning "putdowns" and neglect.

Current spiritual and psychological understanding affirms the ancient truth, newly rediscovered in our day, that all family members need in their hearts before God to forgive each other, and particularly their parents (dead or alive) for hidden hurts, real or imaginary. To forgive and be forgiven, to love and be loved are probably the most compelling needs of individuals in families today and absolutely basic to Christian family ethics (Matt. 6:14-15; Luke 15:28; Eph. 4:32).

Though the learning of skills and techniques of interrelationships are not the final answer in the improvement of family relationships, when used with loving motivation they can enhance the quality of family life and strengthen relationships. Workshops and courses in human relations, group development, group discussion and participation training, and above all in the ministry of attentive, affirming, and active listening, can help family members understand each other and change their habits in ways that will enhance genuine Christian love.

*Clergy Families*. Clergy in particular should pay attention to their family life. If through preoccupation with the many needs of parish members a pastor neglects the emotional and spiritual needs of his or her own family, then the efforts he or she is making to build up parishioners in fellowship and faith can be undermined. The congregation for its part as the larger family of God has the duty to minister to its pastor by accepting the obligation to share the burdens as well as the joys of ministry as a true priesthood of all believers (1 Pet. 2:9) and to support the pastor in his or her family obligations as well as the duties to the congregation.

*Formal Family Education*. Those who have the aptitude and inclination, which may possibly be discerned as components of a divine vocation, may take the initiative in organizing and leading family life symposia and involve Christians through various adult education methods in intentional enhancement of their family life in Christ. The methods used might be study groups, either topical or Bible-based, university or community college extension courses, private or collective viewing of relevant television and other programs, and frequent discussions between spouses and among family members. An essential basis for all such educational enterprises will always be personal consecration to God's way in Christ, regular study of the Scriptures (2 Tim. 2:15; 3:15-17), and openness to being continually transformed by His Word (Rom. 12:2; James 1:18). Growth in ethical family living does not happen automatically with acceptance of Christ as Savior and the indwelling of the Holy Spirit. This growth has to be intentionally pursued, as is abundantly evident from the many exhortations in Scripture to purposeful, decisive effort to learn and live the way of Christ (Matt. 9:13; 11:29; 1 Cor. 4:6; 2 Cor. 6:1; Eph. 4:20-24).

**Bibliography:** Christenson, L. (ed.), *The Christian Family* (1970); Curran, D., *Traits of a Healthy Family* (1983); Dobson, J., (ed.), *Focus on the Family* (a monthly periodical) Address: Colorado Springs, CO 80995; Gray, M., and Moberg, D. O., *The Church and the Older Person* (1962); Hessel, D., (ed.), *Maggie Kuhn on Aging* (1977); Martin, T. M., *Christian Family Values* (1984); Nicholi, A. N., "Moral and Mental Health Values" in *Christian Medical Society Journal* (1981) 12, p. 2; Peel, N., *The Ministry of Lis-*

*tening* (1980); Rossman, P., *Family Survival: Coping with Stress* (1984).

See CHILDREN, REARING OF; MARRIAGE; ORPHANS.
D.N.P.

## FAMILY PLANNING. (see CONTRACEPTION).

**FANATICISM.** *Fanaticism* is a religious word derived from *fanum*, the Latin for "shrine," and *fanaticus*, which means "inspired by a deity." It soon lost its specifically religious sense, however, and has now come to mean "wild enthusiasm" about anything.

It is difficult to define fanaticism more closely because the idea behind the word introduces a spectrum of meaning, ranging from committed devotion at one end of the scale to dangerous eccentricity at the other. One person's hero is another person's misguided lunatic.

The word "enthusiasm" provides an interesting parallel. Methodism today is a respected Christian denomination. But when the eighteenth-century Methodists were called "enthusiasts" by their contemporaries, the term was used with anything but respect. The drive, zeal, and initiative we admire so much in John Wesley today was regarded in his own time as a particularly destructive brand of fanaticism.

It is not surprising, then, to discover that the Bible's words for "zeal" can have good and bad meanings. Both the Hebrew *quin'a* and the Greek *zelos* can mean either "wholehearted devotion" or "blazing jealousy," depending on the context (see 2 Sam. 21:2 and 1 Cor. 12:31 for the good sense and Gen. 26:14 and Acts 5:17 for the bad).

What, then, is the criterion for distinguishing the right from the wrong? Certainly not the degree of fervor and commitment which is involved. In retrospect, we can see that the criticisms of the early Methodists' fanaticism revealed far more about their critics' spiritual poverty than about the enthusiasts' own excesses. Jesus, too, was noted for His totally committed intensity, so much so that He incurred the charges of madness and demon possession (Mark 3:21; John 10:20). It would be wrong to condemn commitment simply because of the lengths to which it goes.

Jesus' example does, in fact, provide important guidelines in defining the right kind of zeal for which Christians should strive. In the first place, His enthusiasm was divinely inspired and God-directed. He was "filled with the Holy Spirit" (Luke 4:1), eaten up with zeal for learning about God (Luke 2:49), and totally absorbed with His vocation, even though it led to death (Luke 9:51; 12:50). Secondly, he was fanatically preoccupied with the needs of others. In putting their needs first, He went hungry (John 4:31-35), worked tirelessly (Mark 1:38), and disregarded His own personal safety (Mark 1:41; John 13:1).

If this is fanaticism, Jesus plainly showed that He expected His disciples to share it. Their love

for God had to be total (Mark 12:30; Luke 9:60-62). Their commitment to Him needed to eclipse the closest human relationship (Luke 14:26). And their love for others had to be as intense as His love for them (John 15:12-17).

The later books of the New Testament expand this theme helpfully on the Godward side, Christians must be filled to the point of intoxication with the Holy Spirit (Acts 2:4, 13; Eph. 5:18). They should be obsessed with God's calling (2 Pet. 1:10), eagerly desire His gifts (1 Cor. 12:31) and strive to display godly qualities in their lifestyle (2 Pet. 1:5-7). On the manward side, their zeal ought to show itself both in peace keeping within the church (Eph. 4:3) and devoted care for the poor (Gal. 2:10). This kind of religious enthusiasm is not only defensible, according to the New Testament, it is mandatory. In Paul's words, "Never be lacking in zeal, but keep your spiritual fervor, serving the Lord" (Rom. 12:11).

Against this biblical background, we can see more clearly what can make fanaticism wrong. Above all, enthusiasm is suspect on Christian grounds whenever it is not directed by love for God and love for others.

Most obviously, there are those who are obsessed with God-substitutes. They give to things (like money) or to people (like political leaders) the abandoned dedication that belongs to God alone.

Less obviously, enthusiasm can be misdirected even when it is motivated by good intentions. It may be that an individual ignores his own fallibility in discerning God's will and moves away in a dedicated but hopelessly wrong direction. Mistakes have been made in that respect by those who believe that they have received a direct revelation from God. This becomes especially serious when their special disclosures contradict the clear directives of Scripture.

In addition, well-motivated fanaticism is wrong when it is unbalanced. More heat than light is generated in discussions on many ethical issues when one principle looms so large that others become blurred. Some dedicated pacifists, for example, have never thought about the claims of justice in their zeal to stop all killing. Others in the pro-life camp see the issue of the fetus's sanctity so clearly that they totally ignore the needs of a woman, threatened, perhaps, by terminal illness, with an unwanted pregnancy. This is not to say that stands for pacifism and against abortion are wrong, but simply to question all fanatical pressure groups whose enthusiasms are myopic. Paul himself came to recognize that his zeal for Judaism was wrong because it was rooted in only half of the truth (Acts 22:3-5; Gal. 1:13-14; Phil. 3:3-7).

Any kind of zeal that treats others unlovingly must likewise come under the condemnation of a Christian ethic. That must include those whose fierce stand on matters of personal principle wounds friends (Rom. 14:13-23), as well as those whose religious devotion leads them to hate and persecute others who do not share their beliefs. Paul sums up well: "It is fine to be zealous—provided the purpose is good" (Gal. 4:18).

**Bibliography:** Bauder, W., *DNTT* vol. 3, pp. 1166ff., (1978); Knox, R. A., *Enthusiasm* (1951).

D.H.F.

**FANTASY.** A fantasy is an exercise of the imagination that often exhibits extravagant overtones. It may take the form of a highly romantic escape from reality into a situation of dreamlike character, where the person who is fantasizing is experiencing pleasurable emotions. He or she is generally the central character in the episode, and the effects are imagined to be positive rather than negative. In some persons it can serve as a form of creativity and fulfill a useful therapeutic purpose if the individual leads an otherwise dull existence. There are even some occasions when fantasies can function as the basis for poetry or other forms of artistic expression.

Some psychologists have maintained that a certain degree of fantasizing is valuable in preserving the emotional balance of persons who live and work under great pressure. Its apparent benefit is that it provides a secret retreat for the mind, to which it can retire when stresses are becoming intolerable and regroup its psychic forces. The daydreams that the majority of people seem to have can be regarded as fantasies, particularly if they exhibit an extravagant component that does not correspond with the individual's real life. Fantasies should be distinguished from hallucinations, which are psychotic phenomena because they treat as real the sensory perception of objects or stimuli which have no existence outside the psyche of the sufferer.

The danger of fantasy is that it can become increasingly a vehicle for escaping from the responsibilities of daily life by those who engage in it, unless the fantasizing is kept under strict control. If the values of the fantasy world intrude perceptibly into a person's relationships with others, a good deal of damage can result from a failure to recognize the fantasy for what it actually is. While the Christian is no more exempt from romantic dreaming than anyone else and may indeed find great relief in imagining processes and scenes in the afterlife, it is important for the believer to remember that he or she is an emissary of God in a fallen world. Consequently the reality of the situation that sinners are dying without ever having heard of the saving gospel of Christ must be kept uppermost in the mind always. Responsible stewardship of time in a witnessing ministry to society allows precious little opportunity for indulging in selfish, romantic daydreams as we are confronted with the sin, degradation, and desperate need of those around us. Christ is the eternal reality, and as we grow into him in grace and love, the need to indulge in escapism diminishes, to be replaced by a sense of real and close communion with the Lord.

**FATE.** Those who believe in fate regard it as some inscrutable power, metaphysical influence, or life force that governs individual destiny and from which there is no ultimate escape. In classical mythology the concept of fate (Greek *moira*) was enshrined in the activities of three goddesses, one of which spun the thread of life, another determined its proper length, and a third severed it. However much people might attempt to propitiate these goddesses in order to extend their lifespan, it was all to no avail because fate decided the date of a person's death. Any representation of the Fates in statuary understandably represented them as unsmiling and dour.

The concept of fatalism, that is, the notion that all events and consequences in human life are predetermined, found philosophical expression among the Stoics. Being pantheists as well as fatalists, they attributed the determining of circumstances to the divine activity that possessed all of life and did not restrict fatalism to the actual time of one's death. For the Stoics, the belief in fate was not just a passive acceptance of all occurrences as inevitable. Indeed, if fate was to have its proper place in an individual's life, the cooperation of that person was considered a necessary ingredient.

The Christian believes that all events are under God's control and that not even the smallest detail escapes his observation (Matt. 10:30; Luke 12:6, 7). While to some the death of Christ might appear to have been a cruel act of fate, the Scriptures make it clear that it was the outcome of a preconceived plan (1 Cor. 15:3) for human salvation. Although evil persons appeared to have thwarted God's design by killing the promised Messiah, they were actually principals in the course of action that brought the plan to fruition (Acts 4:28). Christians cannot accept fatalism or pessimism as valid explanations of life's occurrences, because they have the promise of Scripture that everything works together for good to those who love God, to those who are the called according to his purpose (Rom. 8:28). The Christian's destiny is not in an inevitable death, but in a glorious eternity in the nearer presence of God where death is swallowed up in victory (1 Cor. 15:54).

Christians also reject fatalistic tenets on moral grounds in the sense that if everything is regarded as inevitable, it also includes the area of moral decision. If one thinks it right to bow to the inevitable, whatever that may be, one is thereby relieved of all ethical responsibility and freed from any culpability that might attach itself to a wrong decision. The result is a pitiably inert individual, helpless in the face of any prevailing circumstance, and unable to exercise or implement moral judgments. Part of the problem arises in determining precisely what is inevitable and what is not. If, according to the celebrated maxim, there are actually only two inevitable circumstances in life, there is still an enormous amount of scope left for moral and ethical decision.

There are times, of course, when submission to the trend of events is the only prudent way of dealing with the situation. Thus Amos (5:13) recognized that in the coming day of judgment the wise person would remain silent, because it would be an evil time and not propitious for protest or counteraction. Similarly Jesus Christ did not judge in any compelling rhetoric when he was on trial for his life in front of the Jewish and Roman authorities (Matt. 27:12; Mark 15:3). Both the prophet and the Savior knew that a time of silence is followed by a time of speaking (Eccles. 3:7) and that under God's providence the goals that had been planned would be accomplished, even at the expense of suffering and death. Complete trust in the power of God to save and keep is the antidote to moral inertia and the passivity and pessimism that characterize fatalism.

See NECESSITY.

**FEAR.** Fear is generally described as an emotional reaction of the autonomic nervous system that is produced by a sense of danger, impending calamity, or some dire emergency. It is often accompanied by certain changes which may include fainting, hysterical outbursts, vomiting, intestinal disturbance, and even cardiac arrest. Some psychologists describe fear as a negative emotion because it produces reactions that are disturbing or damaging. Many experts regard fear as a learned emotional reaction, on the theory that children are born without emotions and only acquire them through confronting certain situations in life. Other psychologists will concede that such reactions as the fear of doctors or dentists are learned or acquired emotional responses, but that they are qualitatively different from what is experienced when a person is suddenly confronted by grave danger. The age and environmental background of the person must always be considered when assessing the nature and degree of fear.

From a physiological standpoint the impact of fear causes the adrenal gland, located on top of the kidney, to secrete adrenalin from its medulla into the bloodstream. As a consequence the heart beats more quickly as the body automatically prepares to defend itself. Blood pressure rises dramatically, breathing becomes more rapid, sugar is released into the blood, and the skeletal muscles absorb blood from the abdominal area. Other accompanying physical changes may include pallor and active paralysis of the muscles.

Powerful emotions such as fear can damage both the physical tissues and the personality. Stomach ulcers, for example, are often ascribed to the tensions engendered by prolonged fear and the worry that frequently accompanies it. Fear can also be seriously damaging to creativity by causing a blockage of thought processes and inhibiting the kind of expression necessary for the successful prosecution of a project. To see someone literally paralyzed by fear is to witness a human being in an unbelievably piteous state of helplessness.

The Scripture has strong, reassuring statements for those persons in the grip of fear in the affirmation that perfect love casts out fear (1 John 4:18). The individual who abides in Christ's love, therefore, has the complete defense against the physical and psychological depredations of fear. If a person can say, with Paul, "I can do all things through Christ who strengthens me" (Phil. 4:13), the need for an emotional reaction of fear simply does not arise. But as with Paul, a prolonged period of growth in Christ is mandatory before such a state of emotional maturity is achieved.

**FEMINISM.** The dictionary defines feminism as the theory of the political, economic, and social equality of the sexes, and organized activity on behalf of women's rights and interests.

American feminism has its genesis in two distinct historic movements. One, the suffrage movement of the last century, was led in the main by Christian women who were fighting for the right to vote and to have a voice in society. The ideas they had about their basic equality were based on biblical principles. For instance, suffrage leader Sarah M. Grimke defined the argument thus:

> Here then I plant myself. God created us equal; he created us free agents; he is our Lawgiver, our King and our Judge, and to him alone is woman bound to be in subjection, and to him alone is she accountable for the use of those talents with which her Heavenly Father has entrusted her.

As Christians, these women were concerned with moral issues in society yet found themselves powerless and without a voice, because, as women, they were disenfranchised. After a long battle, they won the right to vote in 1920 and the women's movement died down.

The movement was reborn under different auspices in the late 1960s as one of many secular liberation movements. The feminist rhetoric of that era was often marked by a typical militancy and stridency.

Documents like the 1968 SCUM manifesto, for instance, described "the utter uselessness and banality of the male." Others called for the abolishment of marriage and the family. This kind of rhetoric, however, represented only a small fraction of women describing themselves as feminist, even in the sixties.

The National Organization for Women (NOW), founded in 1966, seems to represent the views of many feminists. NOW's primary goal has been to have the Equal Rights Amendment to the U.S. Constitution ratified.

The other demands raised by NOW's first national conference in 1967 included: (1) enforce the law banning sex discrimination in employment; (2) ensure maternity leave rights in employment and social security benefits; (3) legislate tax deduction for home and child care expenses for working parents; (4) provide child day care centers; (5) guarantee equal and unsegregated education; (6) insure equal job training opportunities and allowances for women in poverty; (7) provide for the right of women to control their reproductive lives.

It is interesting to note that most of the NOW demands are concerned with economic justice and help for mothers in the work force. Women work outside the home for a variety of reasons, including a sense of achievement and the need to develop skills and talents. Many women, however, work out of economic necessity. Changing sexual mores, the rising divorce rate, economic pressures, and other social problems have forced many women into the work force. Two out of three poor adults in the United States are women, many of them single heads of families. It is unjust to pay women less than men because of an idealized view of the kind of society that no longer exists for many people—that of an intact nuclear family with a male providing the income.

Some Christians have become anti-feminist in reaction to the extreme feminist lesbian separatists who form a small but vocal minority of the movement. Other Christians, while rejecting that extreme stance, identify themselves as feminist because they believe that women should have equal political, economic, and social rights.

A number of women with a biblically based sense of a woman's worth would call themselves Christian or evangelical feminists. These groups claim that their purpose is to present God's teaching on female-male equality to the whole body of Christ's church and to call both women and men to mutual submission and active discipleship.

As Christians, when we evaluate women's issues, we must start by looking at how Jesus Himself treated women. Many of His followers, supporters, and friends were women (Matt. 27:55; Luke 8:2-3; 10:38-42). His teaching and actions toward women often cut through the sexual discrimination of His day (John 8:1-11).

We also have New Testament examples of the active role that women played in the early church. Philip's four daughters prophesied (Acts 21:9-10), Phoebe was a deaconess or minister (Rom. 16:1-2), and churches mentioned in the New Testament were founded in the homes of women.

While broader areas of service in the church are possible for women today, we must not forget the contribution they have made to missions. Most church women's organizations grew out of their concern for missions. This is one of the greatest legacies which women have left the modern church.

In taking a stance on the issues raised by feminism, it is important not to conform unquestioningly to either secular feminist attitudes or the reactionary movement against them, but rather to evaluate each issue in light of Scripture. At the same time, we need to be aware of changes in our society which create new injustices that must be dealt with.

Many secular feminists reject Christianity as a "male" religion which encourages discrimination against women. It is the responsibility of the church as Christ's body on earth to show that we treat women with the same justice, love, and respect as He did, as witness to a watching world.

S.M.G.

See CIVIL RIGHTS; WOMEN, STATUS OF.

**FETAL RIGHTS.** Recent medical research indicates that tissue from the brains of fetuses could provide considerable assistance to individuals suffering from such diseases as Alzheimer's and Parkinson's. It is also possible to transplant organs, such as livers, from fetus to fetus. To date, the U.S. government has sustained a highly controversial ban against the use of fetal tissue for research purposes or for purposes of transplantation. This decision has met with great opposition from those who think that it is cruel and inhumane not to provide whatever relief possible to those suffering from various debilitating diseases. The availability of massive amounts of fetal tissue from aborted fetuses seems a great resource to many. Those who believe abortion to be a morally permissible act are not troubled by the charge that use of aborted fetal tissue amounts to complicity in abortion. Since they do not believe the fetus is a person, they maintain that it is permissible to use fetal tissue much in the same way one could use the hair gathered from the floor of a barber shop. They see use of fetal tissue as transforming what seems to be needless waste into a compassionate good.

Those opposed to the use of fetal tissue for purposes of research and transplantation have three major objections: 1) the fetus is not being respected as a human person of intrinsic worth but is being treated as an instrument; 2) use of fetal tissue amounts to complicity in abortion and demand for the use of such tissues will legitimate the abortion industry; 3) the ready access to tissue from aborted fetuses will lessen the effort to find alternative sources of treatment for sufferers of Alzheimer's, etc.

The question of the personhood of the fetus in respect to fetal rights is the same as that for abortion. Science has indisputably demonstrated that the fetus is a human being (and it can be argued that personhood is coextensive with humanity). Several times in Scripture fetal life is recognized as precious to God. For instance, the psalmist (138) praises God, "who created my inmost self, and put me together in my mother's womb"; Luke 1:42 reports that John the Baptist "leapt in the womb" upon hearing the voice of his Savior's mother. Is not the humanity of the fetus being denied in the very act of abortion, and then its humanity being exploited for the purposes of transplantation?

Yet, that the fetus is a person does not necessarily rule out therapeutic or experimental use of fetal tissue. Use of human tissue, organs, and bodily parts for transplantation and research is common and universally approved as ethical. One necessary provision for the morality of such actions is that the source of the tissue, etc., or a proxy acting in the agent's interest, give free consent. How can the mother of an aborted fetus, the appropriate proxy, be presumed to have the best interests of her child in mind?

For decades ethicists have rejected using data gathered by Nazi scientists. They argue that it further demeans those individuals killed by the Nazis to use what was learned from their murdered bodies. In the use of fetal tissue, are we not benefitting from crimes committed against the most defenseless and innocent among us?

Fetal tissue for purposes of research and transplantation can be obtained from spontaneous miscarriages and artificially generated cell-lines. The acquisition of such is difficult for many reasons (e.g., spontaneous miscarriages do not happen at convenient times and fetuses that are spontaneously aborted often have genetic defects), but not impossible. If the medical industry becomes dependent on fetal tissue for alleviating suffering, will it not become less likely that alternative treatments will be found and even more difficult to put an end to abortion?

A related issue is the practice of conceiving babies with the intent of using their tissue to assist persons already born. For instance, one highly publicized case featured the conception of a child with the hopes that the child's bone marrow would provide relief for a sibling suffering from bone cancer. This choice is ethically problematic for several reasons. Since the couple was not going to abort the unborn child if there was a marrow mismatch, many argue that the baby was not being used instrumentally but was truly loved.

Nonetheless, since the procedure for a marrow transplant involves considerable pain and risk, there is a question whether it is right to expose a baby to such pain and risk for a procedure that is not beneficial to himself. Yet, were the child loved unconditionally for himself, and if the parents were extending their own principles of Christian charity through their child, it seems that conceiving a child to help another child is within the realm of moral acceptability.

Currently the use of fetal tissue and organs is inextricably linked with abortion; until abortion becomes illegal, it will be difficult to extend to the unborn the respect due them as persons and difficult to assess any other acts where it seems that the child is being used as an instrument rather than a person with intrinsic worth.

**Bibliography:** Burtchaell, J., *The Giving and Taking of Life* (1989); Kearney, W. and Caplan, A., *Emerging Issues in Biomedical Policy* (1992), 262-85; O'Donovan, O., *Begotten or Made?* (1984); Ramsey, P., *The Ethics of Fetal Research* (1975); Smith, J., *Critical Issues in Contemporary Health Care* (1989), 253-68.

See ABORTION; FEMINISM; GENETIC ENGINEERING; HUMAN SUBJECT RESEARCH; SURROGATE MOTHERHOOD.

J.S.

**FIDELITY.** This term is derived directly from its Latin counterpart *fidelitas*, which means "loyalty," "faithfulness," or "trustworthiness." Fidelity is a quality of character that has been prized throughout human history. It has been celebrated in song and story, enshrined in proverbial sayings, and dignified by being included among spiritual qualities. It is based upon a resoluteness of mind that, having made a commitment to a person or an ideal, guards that pledge jealously and remains true to it no matter what circumstances may arise. Whether or not the cause or the person is worthy of such loyalty is not the point at issue, for many individuals have given their lives for tawdry and unworthy causes. What characterizes fidelity is the unwavering, persistent nature of the allegiance.

In the Old Testament, faithfulness (*emunah*) was one of the distinguishing characteristics of God's nature, being explicitly lauded in Israel's psalms (Pss. 36:5; 89:2; 119:90). Along with righteousness it was one of the ethical qualities that marked out the Messiah as a moral champion, wearing the belt that demonstrated his wrestling prowess (Isa. 11:5). In the New Testament, God's fidelity and justice are proved by his willingness to cleanse the penitent sinner from all iniquity (1 John 1:9), since his abiding commitment is to righteousness and holiness.

Fidelity is an essential ingredient of the social order. Without this virtue, civilization would be impossible. Loyalty and fidelity lift a person from preoccupation with self and focus his thoughts on others and the higher good.

Because fidelity must always have some object of allegiance, it is particularly important as a factor in contractual obligations. For this reason faithfulness in the marriage relationship has always been a matter of great significance, and this was never made clearer in Scripture than in the description of Hosea's marriage to a harlot who, after a time, seems to have reverted to her immoral ways. What is particularly poignant about Hosea's situation is that his marital distress became a parabolic illustration of the infidelity that God had experienced with his people Israel as they abandoned the ideals of the Sinai covenant for pagan Canaanite worship.

Marital fidelity, with which this entry is concerned predominantly, demands the kind of commitment and mutual trust that will survive the worst crises that can occur in the union. When solemnized before God, a marriage assumes a sacred relationship because in it is depicted the relationship between Christ and his church (Eph. 5:23-32). Its integrity must be preserved, despite all attractions to the contrary, if the participants are not to fall into the snare of covenant repudiation that brought about ancient Israel's destruction. Some marriage relationships require an enormous degree of commitment to the original ideal, and often those participants who do not possess the necessary moral fiber find what to them are easy and justifiable ways of pursuing infidelity. The fact that such conduct is reprehensible to God seems a matter of complete indifference, and this should be of great concern to North American Christians especially, who have by far the highest divorce and remarriage rate of any Christian group.

See ADULTERY; DIVORCE; MARRIAGE.

**FOOLISHNESS.** This is the kind of behavior that can be expected from a fool. While it may contain elements that are entertaining, foolishness always has a negative character or quality to it because it is not in contact with existential reality. There is a certain amount of unwarranted levity to foolishness and a basic lack of seriousness which, after a time, makes foolish behavior very irritating. Some individuals disport themselves continually in the manner of medieval court jesters, believing that they are making some sort of positive contribution to the situation by misguided attempts at humor. In the area of decision making, foolish judgments are commonly made on the basis of little or no evidence, being predominantly the result of emotional reactions, flippancy, stupidity, prejudice, ignorance, and the like, with predictable results.

If this is true of secular life, it is equally the case with spiritual matters. In the Old Testament, the fool (Hebrew *nabal*, "empty") denies God's existence (Ps. 14:1) and consequently pursues a selfish way of life that is devoid of or deficient in spiritual values (Prov. 12:15). The Hebrew poets and sages berated the fool consistently, using language which showed that, for them, the real characteristics of a fool were the obvious deficiencies in the fool's moral nature, hence the association of foolishness with emptiness or stupidity (1 Sam. 25:25; Prov. 15:2).

The New Testament continued the emphasis of the Hebrew sages that foolishness was ultimately a moral deficiency. Those who treated the preaching of Christ's saving gospel with contempt were castigated for regarding the good news as foolishness (Greek *moria*, 1 Cor. 1:18-23; 2:14). In point of fact, such persons were actually demonstrating their folly for all to see by casting away the opportunity of claiming eternal salvation.

**FORBEARANCE.** Forbearance results when one abstains from a certain course of action or thought, or when one exercises restraint or patience under a variety of circumstances. The term is less commonly used now than in the period of the King James Bible, in which it occurs in a number of instances to describe the actions of both God and humans. Thus God instructed Ezekiel to refrain from mourning on his wife's death (Ezek. 24:17), while the Israelite prophets advised the king of Israel to fight against Ramoth-gilead rather than to forbear (1 Kings 22:6). Job questioned the value of patience or restraint in his affliction, since to forbear availed him nothing (Job 16:6), while the poor of the flock in Zechariah's oracle were instructed to pay the prophet his price or discontinue the association (Zech. 11:11-12).

In the New Testament, God's forbearance with sinners was described as riches (Rom. 2:4), because his delay in executing the deserved judgment upon human iniquity affords the sinner ample opportunity to repent and be saved (Rom. 3:25). The believer is counseled to exercise similar restraint (Eph. 6:9) and great patience in dealing with other members of the Christian community (Eph. 4:2; Col. 3:13). By this means the love of God is manifested because we are willing to be patient and forgive others, just as God has done with us.

**FORCE, ETHICAL USE OF.** Force is the power to attack, conquer, compel, or punish. This may be done by means of sheer personal physical strength, force of arms, maneuver or entrapment, psychological coercion, or lawful authority. The legitimate use of force is based upon morally and legally valid authority backed by physical power or force of arms. Immoral and illegal use of force includes violation of persons, various criminal acts, unjust war, anarchy, terrorism, and psychological violence. This can occur between nations or within communities, churches, families, and in the work place.

Pacifists, Christian and non-Christian, claim that there can be no justification for the use of force. Christians of the peace groups differ significantly among themselves as to how much force, if any, an individual may use; whether self-defense is ever legitimate; whether one may physically discipline children; whether the state may punish criminals (including the question of capital punishment); and whether Christians ought to be involved in enforcing the binding power of law.

Critics of pacifist, nonresistance, and nonviolence perspectives allege that absorption with the question of physical force allows such groups to ignore the practice of psychological violence within their own ranks. A damaging criticism is the observation that the claim that force and punishment are inconsistent with the New Testament law of love creates a disjunction between Christians and the legitimate responsibilities and obligations of the state. Pacifism is alleged to be utopian and unrealistic. A nation made up of sinful men and women cannot be run solely on the basis of the law of love. As well, this view creates an unbridgeable gulf between Old Testament and New Testament teaching, furnishing no basis for faith in the continuity of ethical and moral principles from Old Testament to New Testament literature, nor any justification for the historical judgments of God upon evildoers through disaster and war.

For Christians, the crucial question is the meaning of the law of love (Gal. 5:6) as the crystallization of Jesus' ethical teaching in the Sermon on the Mount. All Christians believe that love and peace are God's will for men. No Christian defends naked violence. What stance must the Christian take when he has his feet planted in two worlds, the evil-infected world of fallen humanity and the kingdom of God?

Those who reject the pacifist claim do not thereby reject peace. They believe that it is a moral obligation to fashion laws which justly withstand and punish evil; and that Christians have the freedom, indeed the obligation, in a just state to participate in the proper coercive functions of the state as soldiers, judges, police officers, sheriffs, and guards.

On this view the importance of love and peace as obligations placed upon Christians is not diminished. They are put into the broader perspective of biblical teaching which embraces obligations wider than those which define ideal character and ideal relations. The Sermon on the Mount is thus understood to deal with personal, one-on-one relations, not with state relations or general non-Christian relationships. The Sermon on the Mount does enjoin peace. It is significant, however, that such matters as war, capital punishment, and punishment of evildoers are not specifically proscribed. It is clear that God judged Israel for idolatry, injustice, immorality, and other vices, but not for self-defense or just war. To separate God's commands to judge, punish, or go to war from fundamental morality creates a theological impasse in biblical interpretation.

The state is divinely sanctioned to maintain and promote justice and to punish evildoers (Rom. 13:1-7; 1 Pet. 2:13-17). How far does this extend? To which matters does this authority apply? What role may or ought Christians to have in the work of the state? Ought the Christian acting as an individual ever use force? Most Christians maintain that their faith and instinct to reject the use of force in personal relations runs parallel with their obligation to uphold justice and to participate in the restraint of evil even if force is necessary. Thus nonviolence as a norm in personal ethics,

submission to violence when persecuted, and refusal to participate in unjust acts or causes, cohere with the right to self-defense and obligation to restrain evil.

The power of the state to compel is not in itself evil. Each situation must be judged in light of the moral principles of justice and equity, and in relation to political and religious freedom.

Most Christians believe themselves justified to go to war in defense of their country and to prevent the conquest of others by totalitarian regimes. The march to political freedom has been long and bloody. Few who now enjoy democracy and freedom are prepared to yield them.

The right to self-defense and the defense of life is fundamental to existence in an evil-infected world. As contradictory as it may seem, the right to restrain, including the power to kill, is moral and killing may itself, paradoxically, be a just act. This does not justify personal vengeance or war crimes. The faith that life is God's gift does not of itself entail the obligation to yield life to any and every act of violence. Rather, it entails the obligation to shelter life, nourish it, and under law to avenge its abuse or violent extinction. To take life in some cases may be the only way to avoid betraying the moral trust of which humanity is heir. The idea that it is never right to use lethal force squares neither with biblical precept and practice nor with the considered moral conviction of humanity. Nevertheless, the burden of proof to justify the taking of life rests with him who takes life. Thus in a hostage-taking in democratic countries every effort is made to talk the hostage-taker skillfully into surrender, and lethal force is reserved as a desperate measure to protect the lives of hostages and others.

A difficulty alleged of no-defense and no-punishment theory is that it tends to institutionalize coercion and violence and to encourage anarchy. The compromise solution advocated by some Christians, that the state has the God-given right and duty to punish evildoers but that Christians ought to excuse themselves from these duties, is singularly unconvincing to most people and absurd to some.

Law and penalty express the right of society to protect itself and to punish evil deeds. Punishment must be seen for what it is, namely, punishment for wrongdoing. Punishment can indeed serve more than one function. It can aid reformation and deter evildoing. However, the ultimate moral justification of punishment must be, first, that it vindicates the law and, second, that it brings just (graded and appropriate) retribution upon the wrongdoer.

**Bibliography:** Bainton, R. H., *Christian Attitudes To War and Peace* (1960); Cleary, E. L., *Crisis and Change: The Church in Latin America Today* (1985); Clouse, R. G., (ed.), *War: Four Christian Views* (1981); Yoder, J. H., *The Politics of Jesus* (1972).

See ARMAMENT; JUST WAR CRITERIA; PACIFISM; SERMON ON THE MOUNT.

S.J.M.

**FORGIVENESS.** There is no verbal solution to sin in the Bible. Forgiveness is not merely spoken; something happens so that forgiveness becomes possible. The crucial factor is that sin is forgiven as it is borne (John 1:29). This is based upon a previous objective decision to forgive sin lovingly. This is as true of human forgiveness as it is of divine forgiveness, because true human forgiveness is a copy of God's forgiveness and is made possible by it.

In the Bible sacrifice and atonement are the ground of forgiveness and reconciliation. All of these have their possibility in the unbounded grace of God (Exod. 34:6-7; Num. 14:17-19; Neh. 9:17; Ps. 86:15). In the Old Testament, grace, atonement, and forgiveness belong together (Lev. 17:11; cf. Heb. 9:22). The unity of the Scriptures and fulfillment of their promises devolve upon Christ the Lamb of God whose death on the cross is the final sacrifice for the sins of the world (Matt. 26:28; Acts 2:36-38; Eph. 1-7; 1 John 4:10). That the Suffering Servant of Isaiah 53 is the Son of man who comes to give His life a ransom for many (Mark 10:45) is the vital link in the biblical message of redemption, forgiveness, and reconciliation.

God's forgiveness and human forgiveness interlock (Matt. 6:12, 14-15; Luke 17:3-4; Eph. 4:32). Man's being forgiven entails his having a forgiving spirit toward his fellows. The righteousness of God is more than legal rectitude, for it embraces mercy and grace. For this reason Jesus, in Matthew 5:38-48, urges His followers to practice love and forgiveness rather than stark justice (an eye for an eye) or vindictiveness. This meaning of forgiveness is integral to the ethical life of the Christian and is built upon the spiritual foundation of reconciliation with God. Forgiveness and reconciliation through Christ bridge the gap between God and man and between man and man to overcome the distance and alienation due to race, culture, and religion (Eph. 2:11-22).

Previously "sons of disobedience" (Eph. 2:2), Christians enter the blessings of loving obedience as the children of God (Rom. 1:5; 1 Pet. 1:2). This obedience is not acquiescence to arbitrary rules. Rather it is joyful participation in doing good as the expression of true freedom. Forgiveness releases from guilt, comdemnation, and fear of death. The forgiven sinner can be at peace with himself because he is at peace with God and is able to forgive himself as well (Pss. 32; 51). This is the theme of Paul's powerful argument in Romans 5:1-11. While there may be contrived, self-imposed kinds of guilt which can be exposed and dispelled verbally, the real guilt of which Paul speaks can be dealt with only by grace, atonement, and faith.

Deliverance and freedom are goals of forgiveness (Col. 1:13). The "washing" (forgiveness) of

1 Corinthians 6:11 relates to the "all things are lawful...but I will not be enslaved by anything" of verse 12 (RSV). Freedom from sin means freedom for righteousness (Rom. 6:18; 8:11-15).

Forgiveness liberates for hope (Rom. 5:3-5). Sin creates more than the conditions of individual guilt and death. The dispersed consequences of evil acts spread out in widening rings, having unforeseen and uncontrollable consequences. Forgiveness includes for the sinner the faith that God through His redeeming activity can assuage these effects and turn their power to good. Therefore each forgiven person can enter his Christian vocation as a co-worker with God, confident that what he puts his hand to will not fail (Rom. 8:28).

Forgiveness is in itself a triumph over evil. A new power is released into the world and the moral affairs of men through the cross, namely, the power of vicarious love and burden bearing. To act vicariously epitomizes the genius of forgiveness. The heart of forgiveness is that sin is forgiven as it is borne, hence its costliness. When one person is forgiven by another, the injured party absorbs the evil done to him and converts its energy for good. This is a major element of the ethical substructure of the New Testament. If someone strikes you on the cheek, turn the other; render to no man evil for evil, but good for evil (Rom. 12:17; Gal. 6:10; 1 Thess. 5:15; 1 Pet. 3:9-12). To absorb evil redemptively is to triumph over evil and convert the powers of human life from evil by grace for good.

**Bibliography:** Brunner, E., *Our Faith* (1936); Hodgson, L., *Christian Faith and Practice* (1950); Marshall, I. H., *The Work of Christ* (1969); Stott, J., *Men Made New* (1966).

S.J.M.

**FORNICATION.** This word comes from the Latin noun *fornix,* which was used predominantly in architecture to describe an arch or a vault. Sometimes it was employed of a series of arches such as would occur in an arcade and infrequently of an arched doorway or other similar aperture in a wall. A subsidiary use of *fornix* by Horace and other Latin poets was with reference to a brothel. Since such places of whoredom were normally situated in underground vaults (*fornix*), the mention of a vault could constitute an oblique reference to immorality. It would therefore appear that fornication was an activity that was associated with such a vaulted building.

Another suggestion which extends this general interpretation is that, since many of the public baths had arched enclosures for the *sudoria,* or places in the hot baths where patrons could perspire in order to lose weight, fornication was something that literally took place beneath the arches. Since the Roman poets had given a sinister connotation to *fornix,* it would be highly probable that the activity described as fornication included homosexual practices. It is difficult to recover an explicit statement about this particular matter from contemporary literary sources, however, although the inference would hardly be surprising in view of the gross sexual abuse that passed for entertainment at fashionable Roman banquets in the imperial period. When Latin reached the medieval ecclesiastical stage the term *fornicatio* was used either of a vaulted arch or of whoredom and fornication.

Attention must now be given to the New Testament term for fornication, which is *porneia*. To trace its ancestry back to classical times is difficult, since it seldom occurred in the literature. There is thus no proper means of comparing classical and Hellenistic usages of the term, other than to suggest, as lexicographers have done, that in classical Greek *porneia* apparently meant prostitution originally. Only at a later time, presumably in the Hellenistic period, it is alleged, was the term applied to unlawful carnal relations generally.

Some biblical commentators have confused the issue further by stating that in Matthew 5:32 *porneia* was used interchangeably with *moicheia*, "adultery." The text in question reads: "Whoever divorces his wife except for the cause of fornication (*porneia*) makes her commit adultery (*moicheia*)." On the supposition that the two words are actually being used interchangeably, what Christ was apparently saying is that anyone who divorces his spouse except for adultery causes her to become an adulteress when she remarries. This is ludicrous reasoning, because if the two words carry the same meaning the woman is already an adulteress because of *porneia* and does not need to remarry in order to qualify as an adulteress (*moicheia*).

Quite clearly the sense of the passage demands a recognition of the fact that the two words being used convey quite different meanings. This is made plain in Matthew 15:19 and Mark 7:21, where *porneia* is distinguished from *moicheia,* as also in 1 Corinthians 6:9. If they occur as separate and distinct entities in a list of vices, it is difficult to believe that they suddenly become identical in meaning in another part of Christ's teaching on the subject.

In Matthew 19:9 a divorced man who remarried committed adultery unless the cause of divorce was *porneia*. His divorced wife also became an adulteress (*moicheia*) if she remarried. In this passage, so far from the words being used interchangeably, *porneia* is the cause of a sequence which under certain conditions results in *moicheia*. The latter, adultery, only occurs as an effect if the divorced person remarries, and if not, the individual cannot be charged with that moral offense. But *porneia* has already been committed, is still the cause of the divorce, and remains such regardless of remarriage. Two words carrying quite different senses, therefore, would seem quite clearly to be involved.

There is also a textual matter that merits some consideration where Matthew 19:9 is concerned.

If the phrase "except for fornication" is removed from the verse, the resultant smooth rendering is identical in content with what is generally regarded as the earliest form of Christ's teaching in Mark 10:11-12. This leads to the question as to whether the exception relating to fornication was ever part of Christ's original doctrine of marriage, or whether it was inserted at an early stage of the composition of Matthew's Gospel to reflect the interests of a more theologically liberal group of Jewish Christians who followed the traditions of the Hillel school regarding divorce. But whether the phrase "except for fornication" was part of the earliest draft of Matthew's Gospel or not, it has become enshrined in the manuscript tradition and must therefore be retained until firm textual evidence furnishes indications to the contrary. In any event there can be no doubt as to the seriousness of *porneia* for the New Testament writers. While it occurred in connection with other vices (1 Cor. 6:9), it was the only sin from which the Christian was bidden to flee (1 Cor. 6:18). Its deeply engrained nature was emphasized by Jesus, who taught that *porneia* came from the heart and defiled the entire personality (Matt. 15:19-20; Mark 7:21-22).

From the foregoing discussion there seems to be substantial reason for thinking that the Greek terms rendered "fornication" (*porneia*) and "adultery" (*moicheia*) in some English versions are actually describing two quite different kinds of sexual immorality, and therefore cannot be regarded as synonymous in meaning. There seems little doubt in the minds of lexicographers and commentators that *moicheia* is correctly translated by "adultery." A related verb form is used in Mark 10:11-12 of adultery, and is comprehensive enough to include either sex as subject. What is being described is a carnal relationship between a divorced man and another woman of unspecified marital status, or between a divorced woman and another man within a marriage relationship. It is evidently the fact of the prior marriage of one partner that makes a subsequent marriage an adulterous union if the previous spouse is still alive.

But with *porneia* the meaning is quite different, since marriage or nonmarriage does not seem to have any bearing upon its efficacy for evil. *Porneia* is treated as a separate vice in Christ's teaching (Matt. 15:19; Mark 7:21), and it proves to be one that not merely brings sin into a person's life but can also disrupt a marriage relationship as well. Perhaps some insight into the true meaning of *porneia* can be gained by noting the verb *porneuo* as used in Mark 10:9, 1 Corinthians 6:18, 10:8, and Revelation 2:14-20. The meaning suggested by the context seems to be that of hiring out the body for immoral purposes. If *porneia* was a female offense, the commonest form of sexual transgression would be prostitution, which would result in adultery if a married man was involved.

But having regard to the wide range of sexual

license in the Greco-Roman world, it would be wrong culturally to restrict *porneia* to females. Therefore if males were also to be covered by this designation, *porneia* would not merely describe prostitution on the part of men, but would include the various perversions characteristic of homosexuality. Again the difference between the terms for fornication and adultery is brought into focus. In the passages under immediate discussion, *porneia* seems to allude to a far wider range of sexual offenses, of which *moicheia* is only one. It is probably more correct to think of *porneia* in terms of trafficking in sexual vice for monetary gain, which in that event would include prostitution and homosexuality, but not adultery. Such a wide range of perversions could well have occurred "beneath the arches," either of the public baths in Roman times or the vaulted structures that accommodated the harlots.

In the nature of the situation it is hardly surprising that there was no single term in Greek to express the concept of homosexuality. Thus Paul used *arsenokoitos*, a variant form of the rare classical *arrenokoitos*, twice only (1 Cor. 6:9; 1 Tim. 1:10), and this is reasonably comprehensive in meaning ("sodomites," NKJV, RSV; "sexually immoral, perverts," NIV). In the same verse he also employed *malakos*, probably with the meaning of "degenerately obscene" (1 Cor. 6:9; "homosexuals," NKJV, RSV; "male prostitutes," NIV). While both Greek words may have conveyed different facets of perversion in Paul's day, the term *porneia* would have been sufficiently comprehensive to embrace both of them and even to have included male and female homosexuals as well.

If the above interpretation of a fundamental difference of meaning between *porneia* and *moicheia* is correct, it would go far toward explaining the severe condemnation under which *porneia* fell in the teachings of Christ and the apostles. Whereas adultery was condemned by the law (Exod. 20:14), the prohibition of whoredom and homosexuality occupied a rather less prominent position in the Mosaic legislation. Yet it was these moral offenses that were castigated so thoroughly by the prophets and which, through the influence of Canaanite religion, brought both the northern and southern kingdoms to ruin. Therefore it was fundamentally important for the New Testament writers to identify *porneia* correctly and to list it separately from adultery, since while the latter was a sin, the former was a deadly perversion.

In the last analysis it must be admitted that the meaning of *porneia* as understood in New Testament times is not clear to modern scholarship. It does seem incorrect, however, to assert that *porneia* and *moicheia* are used synonymously anywhere in the New Testament. Conversely, a better understanding of the passages in question is gained by regarding them as separate terms that have distinctively different meanings. In modern English usage adultery is generally employed of carnal relations between a married man and a woman other than his wife, whether married or not. Fornication normally describes voluntary sexual contact between an unmarried person and a member of the opposite sex.

**FORTITUDE.** This term is derived directly from the Latin *fortitudo*, which in turn came from an adjective *fortis*, meaning "strong," "sturdy." Latin authors understood the adjective to describe both physical and mental qualities. Thus someone who was strong physically exhibited muscular strength and powers of endurance. An individual who was strong mentally or morally was a person of high resolve who was resourceful and courageous enough to accomplish whatever objectives he or she had in view.

If fortitude is to have any abiding moral value, it cannot consist of physical attributes alone, desirable as these may be. It must be tested by confrontation with difficulty, hardship, temptation, and perhaps, as with Job, a degree of personal catastrophe. Under such conditions the moral fiber of the person is tried, and the degree of courage, endurance, resolution, and bravery is established. Not all those who begin experiences that demand fortitude are able to bring them to a successful conclusion. Even comparatively minor tests of endurance and resourcefulness can show that, while the spirit may be willing, the flesh is weak (Matt. 26:41; Mark 14:38).

Strength and courage were urged upon Joshua as he was commissioned for his conquest of Canaan (Josh. 1:6, 9, 18), and the same was true for the people of Jerusalem when Hezekiah called for resistance against Sennacherib (2 Chron. 32:7). Similarly the Christian is bidden to be strong in the Lord and in his mighty power (Eph. 6:10) and in the grace that is in Christ Jesus (2 Tim. 2:1) so as to be victorious in the struggle against evil and sin.

**FORTUNE TELLING.** The urge to know what the future holds is a very common feature of human existence. From a very early period attempts were made through the use of astrologer-priests to divine what the future might be for certain specific projects, and this was especially important in time of war. The Mesopotamians developed a number of techniques, including horoscopes, in an attempt to achieve this goal, and other contemporary nations shared in the general endeavor to probe into the future. Even biblical figures were not exempt from this kind of interest, as with Joseph (Gen. 44:5, 15), who used a divining cup, and King Saul (1 Sam. 28:7), who participated in a séance immediately before his death.

With the exception of the Israelites, all contemporary cultures were highly superstitious, and in such a climate the purveyors of astrological or other forecasts of the future prospered on the fears and gullibility of the populace. While many were doubtless charlatans, telling the listeners what they desired to hear, there were others who had psychic gifts of prediction and "second sight." A second-millennium-B.C. school for training divinatory priests existed at Mari in Syria, and it was from this establishment that Balaam was apparently secured to prophesy against the Israelites (Num. 22:5-6). Divination was forbidden under the law of Moses (Deut. 18:10), because the chosen people were ordered to be obedient to God's revealed will and live as a brotherly community characterized by the ethical quality of divine holiness. Despite this injunction, by the second century B.C. the Jews had adopted pagan astrological superstitions to the point where they were employing the signs of the zodiac. The only New Testament reference to divination (Acts 16:16) involved a young Philippian woman who told fortunes for money and who was dispossessed of her gift by Paul (Acts 16:18).

Modern fortune tellers use various time-honored techniques as tools of the trade, but the material objects employed such as cards, crystals, and the like, are usually diversions as the fortune teller attempts by nondirective interrogation to establish the pattern of the person's character or life. Contrary to expectations, fortune telling of this variety is extremely simple, even for the comparatively inexperienced operator, because of the gullibility of the clients. There are some psychics, however, who have a definite gift of "seeing" and employ their material adjuncts merely as a means of focusing more clearly their mental images of the client's future that they apperceive. Psychics of this kind are apt to be disturbingly perceptive about a person's past life and disastrously accurate about the future.

Christians should feel no need to indulge in any form of fortune telling, because the future is in God's hands; and we are required to obey his will and spend our lives serving him in faith and love. It is no part of our commitment to try to divine what the next step might be, but to trust the Holy Spirit to guide us into all truth (John 16:13). In God's mercy the future is normally hidden, and what is required of us is the faith and courage to be able to face what the coming days may hold as we witness in society for Christ.

See ASTROLOGY; MAGIC; OCCULTISM.

**FREE WILL.** In the West, three major philosophical traditions dominate discussion of freedom of the will: materialist, idealist, and creationist. Each brings to the discussion certain prior assumptions as to antecedent psychological and physiological conditions which determine the outcome of the argument.

Materialism, whether in its ancient atomistic or in its modern naturalistic form, sees the world as the product of a series of inexorable cause-effect events which do not allow for contingency related to the exercise of free will. Psychological components of existence are made out to be completely functions of physiological necessity whether mechanical, chemical, or neurological. Contingency may be allowed for in the sense of limited chance events, such as postulating that a primordial atom unaccountably swerved to produce atomic interaction and the present universe. Nevertheless, nature is ruled by laws of necessity and is a closed system.

Modern versions of materialism include Marxist theories of historical and economic necessity (E. H. Carr), psychological determinism (B. F. Skinner), instrumentalists (John Dewey), and various philosophical versions of biological determinism in which the mind is seen to be solely a function of physical processes in the brain (Russell Brain, Gilbert Ryle). These views leave little room for duty and "ought." Morality is defined in terms of mores and behavioral responses, usually hedonistically, rather than as answering to transcendental or divinely sanctioned ethical norms.

Traditional forms of idealism tend to denigrate the physical world and to elevate mind or cosmic reason as the divine element of the universe as well as being transpersonal. In the mind of God there scarcely can be any contingencies, and therefore freedom in the sense that events may occur at the choice of a finite being which are against the will of God is an illusion (Spinoza). As the expression of the mind of God, the best of all possible worlds is already here (Leibniz).

Modern forms of idealism have sought to incorporate a scientific view of the world in their attempts to embrace transcendental forms within the evolutionary process, as in recent finite god theories (A. N. Whitehead, Charles Hartshorne). In these views the possibility of free will is expressed as part of a series of antinomies relating to the emerging absolute will of God.

Systems of idealism tend to absorb finite acts into divine ones and thereby emptying free will of significance. Critics of modern attempts to express Christianity metaphysically in categories of philosophical idealism include Leonard Hodgson, Gustave Weigel, and Kenneth Hamilton.

Modern rejection of free will and reduction of mind to physical functions of the brain have evoked a strong reaction and a significant literature, including studies by Austin Farrer, Arthur Koestler, John Beloff, H. D. Lewis, J. R. Smythies, Ian Ramsey, Donald MacKay, John Eccleds, and Karl Popper.

Christian creationism rejects materialist and idealist attempts to cancel or to rephrase radically the meaning of free will. In the Christian revelation, persons and personal relations are the highest level of reality, hence the strategic role of grace. In this view grace is the primary mode of relationship between God and the world, in virtue of which He remains free and the world remains real. Grace is also the primary mode of human interpersonal relations, in virtue of which men allow freedom to one another. Thus grace, freedom, and responsibility are correlative concepts.

Augustine reiterates this theme in his *Confessions* (7.2). Only when based upon the categories of freedom, sin, responsibility, and redemption could his soul find peace and his mind rest, because these allowed him to make sense of his experience in contrast to the reductionist idealist philosophy of the Manicheans, which had attracted him earlier.

For Christians, freedom is a function or capacity of spiritual beings. Persons are spiritual beings. To be a person is to be a self-conscious spiritual reality with the power of rational thought and capable of purposeful activity which is morally qualified. Freedom involves the reality of contingency in the world order and the recognition that things may go this way or that depending upon the choice of a spiritual being. Persons as spiritual beings are free in contrast to matter. This is the fundamental distinction between spirit and matter: the difference between that which is active and that which is passive; between that which is self-moved and that which is moved upon (such as being programmed or conditioned).

Spiritual beings are more or less free, that is, they are more or less spiritual. Christians are called upon to spiritualize their bodily life, which means to act in terms of moral and other ideals. Thus there is a further meaning of freedom, namely, the difference between spiritual bondage and spiritual liberty. As spiritual beings, persons in the image of God are intended to utilize the elements of a dependable world to increase freedom.

A scientifically dependable world and the reality of persons and their freedom are the truth of the way things are to the Christian. Increase of control can lead to increase of freedom, whether it is control of one's own life or of the environment. Actions and goals are to be morally qualified by the will of God. God's purposes have at their center the creation of free good persons who share His life and work. The Christian sees it as a moral ideal to relate to and to treat others as persons altruistically, through love, for their full development in freedom.

For the Christian there are three practical issues which impinge upon understanding free will and the morality of choice. Firstly, modern psychological explanations of wrong behavior and purely sociological explanations of social ills have failed. Anna Russell aptly satirizes such explanations in her "Psychiatric Folksong":

> But now I'm happy; I have learned the lesson this has taught;
>
> that everything I do that's wrong is someone else's fault.

A proper sense of responsibility and guilt is now seen by many to be the first step to healing and to freedom. On this view the term "free" is virtually superfluous. The self knows itself in the immediacy of its own intuition. It reflects on its own immediate acts in relation to motive and ends. The self knows not only that the body is acting, but also that the action has been willed.

Two sustained themes in the Bible are moral responsibility for wayward behavior and clarity as to the question of moral choice. Many biblical examples focus on these two issues: David's dramatic confession of adultery and murder in Psalm 51 clearly pinpoints his freedom of choice and his guilt: "I know my transgressions, and my sin is ever before me" (v. 3 RSV). The prodigal son accepts that his alienation was his own choice (Luke 15:18). Judas acknowledges that his betrayal of Jesus was his own action (Matt. 27:4). Wrongdoing entails freely taken wrong moral choice. Augustine concludes that 'nothing can make the mind the consumption of lust but its own will and free choice" (*On Free Will* 1.11). He was a shrewd diagnostician to conclude that imperfect commitment to do good results in imperfect command to will good (*Confessions* 8.9).

Secondly, A. N. Whitehead has argued that the emergence of the modern scientific world view is tied closely to the medieval conception of a providentially governed and therefore dependable world order, based on the Christian doctrine of creation. Modern man accepts the Christian premise that the world order does not function capriciously and that what happens here under given conditions will happen there under the same conditions. Therefore, far from evading the truth of the conditioned response, Christians embrace it. However, Christians embrace the behavioral principle not to empty freedom of its meaning but with a view to heightening freedom. Conditioning can be used to increase freedom and maximize good. Habits of devotion, well-balanced meals, buckling a seat belt, and exercising the body, all work for good. Such behavioral responses help to maximize freedom. Bad habits limit freedom. Nevertheless, a major thesis of biblical teaching is that we are responsible for the evil conditioning to which we become slaves. We know that we are freely conditioning ourselves and that we may reach the point or series of points at which there is loss of freedom and control. For this, too, we are responsible. Paul's statement concerning morally wrong conditioning is "all things are lawful for me but I will not be enslaved by anything...all things are lawful, but not all things are helpful" (1 Cor. 6:12; 10:23-25).

Thirdly, freedom combined with the truth of providentially dependable world order provides opportunity to maximize good socially, scientifically, and politically. Christians can accept the contingencies of life as opportunities to be co-workers with God in shaping the future. Fatalism and historical and economic inevitability are not Christian points of view. The Christian ought to consider the whole of life as dedicated to God. So viewed, life becomes a providentially overshadowed pathway through thousands of options. By freely choosing among them in relation to moral and spiritual ends, the Christian as a co-worker with God can make a valuable contribution to the present and future well-being of others.

**Bibliography:** Farrer, A., *The Freedom of the Will* (1957); Hodgson, L., *For Faith and Freedom*, Vol. I (1956); Popper, K. R. and Eccles, J. C., *The Self and Its Brain* (1977); Schelling, T. C., *Choice and Consequence* (1984).

S.J.M.

**FREEDOM.** The free will versus determinism debate is of ancient vintage and continues to be a controversial topic among theologians, philosophers, social scientists, and others. The outcome of the debate has crucial implications for the existence of human moral responsibility and consequently for the coherence of Christian theology. For if we are not "free" in a certain significant sense of this term, then we are not responsible moral agents who can incur guilt, stand in need of forgiveness, deserve blame (or praise), become fitting objects of punishment (or reward), and so on. Such a conclusion would require a radical revision of the common view of ourselves as moral agents, and it would be at fundamental odds with the biblical emphasis on human accountability before God. But while it is agreed that human responsibility requires freedom in some sense, disagreement enters over: (1) the relevant sense in which we must be free in order to be responsible, and (2) whether we actually are free in the sense required.

A brief taxonomy of the positions available to one in this debate is in order. First, there is the hard determinism position. Here it is argued that all events, including human actions, are causally necessitated and that no one is free. If no one is free, then no one is ever morally responsible. A person choosing between two courses of action can only choose one of them, that is to say, the one that in fact is chosen. The choice is predetermined by social, genetic, or supernatural factors over which the individual ultimately has no control. Therefore, moral responsibility is a myth. Such a position, however, undercuts the possibility of human accountability before God. Indeed, none of the central notions of the Christian faith would make sense in such a view. Sin, guilt, forgiveness, and atonement all presuppose human responsibility. Therefore, hard determinism, with its denial of moral responsibility, is incompatible with basic Christian doctrine.

The second position is the libertarian position. The libertarian responds to the hard determinist by asking, "How can a person ever be responsible?" The libertarian rejects causal determinism and affirms that people are free, if not always, at least sometimes. Not all human actions are causally necessitated and people, because they are sometimes free, are also sometimes morally responsible. For the libertarian then, the relevant sense of "free" is "free from necessitating causes," or what is called categorical freedom.

We do have such freedom, it is claimed, when we are confronted by situations of moral temptation (for example, to continue on a health-required diet versus indulging in a desire for some diet-forbidden food). We may or may not be free on other occasions, but then those other occasions are claimed not to be relevant to the assessment of moral responsibility. The libertarian position is popular among Christians who view people as having a genuine ability to make or withhold a deliberate conscious response to God and who seek to place the blame for the failure of some to respond solely on the human agent. Since a free response to the gospel—a free response being the only kind of response that is morally and spiritually significant—cannot be causally necessitated, therefore we cannot blame God for not doing what is logically impossible to do, namely, guarantee a positive human response.

A third position, and a version of determinism that some Christians have found attractive, is called "soft-determinism." This view affirms the truth of determinism, but also the truth of personal moral responsibility. We need not choose between the two, it is argued. Rather, we can and ought to affirm both. As a philosophical doctrine this dual affirmation has been attributed to such well-known philosophers as Aristotle, Hobbes, Leibniz, Locke, and Hume. It also has many able advocates among contemporary philosophers. The most careful theological exponent of this position was Jonathan Edwards. Part of its appeal for Christians is that it enables the Christian community to affirm two propositions that it may be very interested in affirming: (1) God is in sovereign control of all events, predetermining all things, including the response that people make to the gospel; (2) human beings are morally accountable to God for their moral and spiritual decisions. Soft-determinism enables one to make this twofold claim. Libertarianism and hard-determinism, on the other hand, preclude it.

Theological versions of soft-determinism often appeal to mystery in articulating their position. It is claimed to be a mystery how such notions as freedom, responsibility, divine sovereignty, and predestination all fit together. Scripture however, teaches each of them; and we are to affirm them regardless of our inability to make a coherent whole out of the conceptual parts. Though attractive to some Christians, others find the theological implications of this view unacceptable. For according to this version of determinism, a decision to embrace the gospel can be causally necessitated by God but still remain fully free. This is a mystery, but it is a biblically required one. However, if God can causally necessitate a free positive response to the gospel, then it becomes difficult to declare that God loves each person and wants each person to repent and embrace the gospel. For wherever there is a person who finally rejects the gospel, there we also have a person that God could have determined to respond freely but chose not to. How, then, the critic demands, can we proceed to say that God wants that individual to repent and embrace His love? We no longer have, it would seem, an all-loving God who wants none to perish but all to repent. However, if one is of a more Calvinistic persuasion, then one may be of the conviction that God does not actually want each individual to repent. In defense of such a view, it would be argued that God cannot be faulted for not saving those He could have saved but chooses not to, for the basic reason that God Himself is the standard of right and wrong. If God decides not to bring a person to faith in Christ, then that decision is beyond critical reproach simply because it is God's decision.

The doctrine of original sin is another crucial doctrine that raises questions central to this debate. For is the biblical notion of original sin compatible with the free (in the categorical sense) exercise of human agency, or is it not? It may be properly granted that unaided human will, unassisted by common or special redemptive grace, can do no good thing. But is it also the case that the human will has been rendered so dead and unresponsive by the effects of sin that it can be moved to the good only by overwhelming forces, either divine or naturalistic? To risk an analogy, are the morally and spiritually lost more like unconscious drowning swimmers in need of the total saving activity of a lifeguard (the lifeguard does it all), or are they more like conscious drowning swimmers who cannot save themselves but can successfully impede any assistance by failing to cooperate (the lifeguard can save the swimmer only with the cooperation of the swimmer)? This brief theological discourse, though far from complete, enables us to see how the critical issues in choosing between libertarianism and soft-determinism are deeply rooted in some very basic theological doctrines. These are doctrines about which Christians do not always agree.

Soft-determinists often move beyond the invocation of mystery and attempt to give an interpretation of freedom that does not render freedom and determinism mutually exclusive notions. It has been argued, to provide but one example, that "freedom to do what one chooses to do" is a sense of freedom sufficient for moral responsibility. This definition has the advantage, from a soft-determinist's perspective, that one can be both determined and free: determined, because the choice made is causally necessitated, but still free because there are no impediments to the successful execution of one's choice, once made. But this attempt and all other attempts to define freedom in a manner compatible with determinism will remain unconvincing to libertarians (and probably to most people), because these attempts always leave in place just these problematic features: causal necessity, inevitability, predeterminism, and the centrality of antecedent causal factors over which the agent has no control.

**Bibliography:** Edwards, J., *Freedom of the Will* (1957); Farrer, A. M., *The Freedom of the Will* (1958); Van Inwagen, P., *An Essay on Free Will* (1983).

See BILLS OF RIGHTS; CHOICE; DETERMINISM.

R.W.

**FREEDOM, RELIGIOUS.** Religious freedom is the immunity from coercion (by government or others in society), in order that an individual may not be forced to act contrary to his beliefs and that, positively, he is allowed within due limits to act in accordance with his beliefs. Expressed in terms of rights, it is the right to accept or change beliefs and to live in accordance with those beliefs without external constraint or coercion. Such a positive, civil freedom is not to be confused with the inner freedom of the Christian, who, ruled by the Holy Spirit, is free from the guilt and power of sin in the service of Jesus Christ (Gal. 5:1). Religious freedom is related to other civil freedoms such as those of speech, assembly, and political affiliation and activity. The "Universal Declaration of Human Rights" of the United Nations speaks of "the right to freedom of thought, conscience and religion."

Today in most Western countries religious freedom exists and is guaranteed by a constitution or civil law. In most communist countries it also exists theoretically in law, but is rarely allowed to be more than the right to public worship within controlled guidelines. In many Muslim countries there is no religious freedom either in law or practice, except for foreigners with residence permits; only conversions to Islam are allowed.

In the history of the West, religious freedom is relatively new. At the time of the Reformation of the sixteenth century, Protestant rulers insisted on uniformity of religion, doctrine, and worship in order to preserve national unity. Separatists of a Protestant or Catholic kind were punished. However, by the seventeenth century, there came religious toleration in which those who did not accept the religion of the ruler or government were allowed to practice their religion within a legally defined framework. Thus in England, to be a Protestant Nonconformist or Roman Catholic was possible, but only with a very restricted freedom. Eventually full religious freedom came in the nineteenth century, when no legal penalties were attached to being one or another kind of Christian or being a Jew, Muslim, agnostic, or atheist. In the Bill of Rights, the First Amendment affirms religious liberty: "Congress shall make no law respecting an establishment of religion or restricting the free exercise thereof."

It is perhaps true to say that the development of modern religious freedom has occurred both because of the insights of those Protestants who were persecuted by their fellow Protestants (for example, the radical reformers, Anabaptists, Mennonites, Nonconformists) and of the results of the growing secularization of the West. It is, however, possible and right to offer a Christian argument for the practice of religious freedom in all countries and societies. This has been attempted by the World Council of Churches in "Declarations on Religious Liberty," made at the Amsterdam (1948) and New Delhi (1961) Assemblies. But the clearest statement has come from the Second Vatican Council in its justly famous document, *Declaration on Religious Freedom* (1965) often known by its opening Latin words, *Dignitatis Humanae Personae*. In this it is stated:

> It is in accordance with their dignity as persons—that is beings endowed with reason and free will and therefore privileged to bear personal responsibility—that all men should be at once impelled by nature and also bound by a moral obligation to seek the truth, especially religious truth. They are also bound to adhere to the truth, once it is known, and to order their whole lives in accord with the demands of truth. However, men cannot discharge these obligations in a manner in keeping with their own nature unless they enjoy immunity from external coercion as well as psychological freedom. Therefore, the right to religious freedom has its foundation, not in the subjective disposition of the person, but in his very nature. In consequence, the right to this immunity continues to exist in those who do not live up to their obligation of seeking the truth and adhering to it. Nor is the exercise of this right to be impeded, provided that the just requirements of public order are observed.

Thus there should be freedom for the Catholic, the Protestant, the Jew, the Muslim and even for the atheist.

**Bibliography:** Bainton, R. H., *The Travail of Religious Liberty* (1951); *Documents of Vatican II* (ed. W. M. Abbott, 1972), pp. 672–700, with the "Response" by F. H. Littell.

P.T.

**FRIENDSHIP.** A friend is an individual who is kindly disposed toward another person or persons and behaves toward that person or those persons in an amicable, kindly manner which is known as friendship. Some ethicists define friendship as a form of love, and while there is certainly biblical precedent for such a position, the love displayed in friendship must be distinguished from the kind of close affection manifested by members of a family or by people who are deeply attached to each other emotionally.

The Hebrew term *ahab* described friends on numerous occasions (2 Sam. 19:6; Esther 5:10, 14; Prov. 18:24), but an even commoner word was *rea,* "companion," matched in the New Testament by *hetairos.* The predominant Greek word for friend, however, was *philos,* which carried with it the sense of benevolence and warm affection without reaching the levels of family or sexual love. Inherent in friendship was a sense of loyalty, commitment, and forgiveness that could be expected to survive disagreements and disappointments; and these characteristics were exemplified by Christ in his dealings with his disciples. Unworthy as these followers were, Jesus dignified them by calling them his friends (John 15:14-15).

Jesus also used the concept of friendship to demonstrate the highest nature of love, which was not sexual in character but supremely altruistic: "Greater love has no one than this, than to lay down one's life for his friends" (John 15:13, NKJV). In enunciating this principle, which has inspired many persons since that time, Jesus was also foreshadowing the vicarious atonement for human sin that he accomplished at Calvary. This saving act extends to every believer the privilege that was accorded to Abraham, who by his faith in God was accounted righteous and was designated "the friend of God" (James 2:23). If we obey Christ implicitly we are his friends (John 15:14), and he will reveal God's will to us. Conversely, if the believer becomes friendly with those powers that oppose the divine purpose for humanity, he or she thereby becomes at enmity with God (James 4:4).

# –G–

**GAMBLING.** Scripture provides no specific prohibition against gambling. Christian abhorrence of it derives purely from the believer's consecration to Kingdom values of stewardship, character, and social responsibility.

By right of creation and redemption, humanity, and indeed the universe in totality, belong to God in Christ. Our obligation is to use all resources to make adequate caring provision for our environment, especially for people. Irresponsible use of God's provision at any level of social existence is a sin, falling short of divinely mandated obligations both to neighbor and to Creator (Luke 10:27).

Investments of any kind in enterprises the outcomes of which depend on artificially created chance constitute pure gambling. Roulette is an example. Though horserace betting and blackjack do involve certain skills, the element of chance in them also is still very high.

All forms of gambling involve gain to the few and loss to the many without the creation of any real product or benefit, save perhaps a questionable thrill. Its promoters and managers have to appeal to the sinful motivation of covetousness in order to make it repay their own very often considerable investment. Gambling violates the principle of fair return for labor and investment, and the ethics of stewardship and work (Eph. 4:28; 2 Thess. 3:9-12). Gambling also can lead to neglect of family responsibilities, a grievous sin in the eyes of God (1 Tim. 5:8; 2 Cor. 12:14).

The word *gamble* is often used loosely and inaccurately of other activities, such as unavoidable risks taken by farmers or business persons. There is, however, a difference between such a "risk" and a true "gamble." For, while in farming and in business one attempts to *remove* the element of chance as much as is humanly possible, the objective in true gambling is exactly the opposite.

The worst form of gambling is the government-sponsored kind. Governments should be in the business of encouraging productive labor and fair distribution of wealth, not in enticing people by means of seductive advertising to crave unearned income through the "luck of the draw." This enticement is one which crime syndicates contemplate with glee, for it provides them with free advertising to promote the gambling habit and serves to increase the rate of participation in illegal gambling.

Christians should not gamble as a matter of principle, even in apparently harmless church raffles, which in a sense have been the thin edge of the wedge in gaining public acceptance for more mammoth legalized gambling operations. It is a great temptation to use gambling as a painless way to raise money for a "good cause" such as a new church building or for crippled children or the elderly. It is a matter of faith, however, not to offer that to God which has cost us nothing (2 Sam. 24:24). Christians should not only avoid gambling; they should use moral suasion in the church and political power in the state to diminish rather than expand the socially deleterious gambling climate. As a service to society, they should work also to alleviate the social conditions and spiritual sicknesses that foster the temptation to gamble.

A final word about psychopathic gamblers. These are neurotic people with an unconscious wish to lose. A Christian who for whatever reason develops such a neurosis should seek the help of a competent Christian psychotherapist.

**Bibliography:** Bergler, E., *The Psychology of Gambling* (1957); *Christians and Gambling*, A Working Party Report, National Council for Social Aid (1983); Clark, P., "The End of the Rainbow" in the *United Church Observer* (Toronto, July 1976); McKenna, D., "Gambling: Parasite on Public Morals" in *Christianity Today* (August 20, 1973).

D.N.P.

**GENEROSITY.** The emotional forces that motivate generosity are somewhat complex, but are rooted in a personality that cherishes high ideals and is prepared to make significant personal sacrifices in order to see them attained. Generosity therefore not merely involves unselfishness, but employs an active, complementary component of liberality that helps to make generosity specific. The generous person shares habitually, sometimes to his or her disadvantage, and the resultant generosity can at times produce some embarrassment on the part of the recipient. While freedom in giving is a typical mark of the generous person, the motivation for generosity may not always be of the most altruistic order. Many people who appear generous are actually endeavoring to purchase friendship, repute, positions, and so on, and are often quite insecure personalities. Other individuals are rather irresponsible temperamentally and lavish money and affection in a profuse manner that lacks discrimination.

While generosity is not a biblical term, the spirit of giving freely is expressed clearly in Scripture and not least in the voluntary death of Christ, which justifies the penitent sinner freely

(Rom. 3:24). Generosity is commanded by Christ of all his true followers in the admonition; "Freely you have received, freely give" (Matt. 10:8), and this establishes a standard for all Christian behavior.

**GENETIC ENGINEERING.** Genetic engineering involves any manipulation of genetic material in an attempt to modify the structure of an organism or aid in the transmission of genetic information. This field, therefore, can be divided into two distinct areas. The first is genetic manipulation. This would include traditional practices of breeding various plants and animals as well as the newer techniques of gene splicing (recombinant DNA research) and cloning. The second field is artificial reproduction. This includes such practices as artificial insemination (AIH, AID), artificial sex selection, surrogate parenting, in vitro fertilization (the method used to create "test tube babies"), and embryo transfer.

*Gene splicing* is a very powerful tool in the hands of scientists. As with any form of technology, it offers great benefits but also raises grave concerns. On the positive side, gene splicing offers some tremendous benefits. Scientists, for example, using these techniques have redesigned bacteria so they can efficiently produce medically important substances like insulin, interferon, or human growth hormone. This reduces the cost and allows scientists to produce materials that had previously been extremely scarce. Botanists are using these techniques to develop new plant species. Other scientists are working on improving the efficiency of photosynthesis to increase crop yields as well as giving certain crops nitrogen fixation capacities, which will reduce the need for fertilizer. Gene splicing is being used to improve industrial processes. It is also used to design organisms that can provide alternative means of energy production or can neutralize pollutants. Also, it will be an extremely useful tool in basic scientific and medical research.

On the negative side, however, are concerns about the danger of such a powerful form of technology. Gene splicing not only allows mankind to make minor modifications of life forms, it allows scientists to create entirely new forms of life as well. The former can be justified as a logical extension of the cultural mandate (Gen. 1:27-28). The latter moves man dangerously close to usurping the role of the Creator (Gen. 3). This latter attitude often results from an evolutionary world view. Scientists assume that since life on this planet is the result of millions of years of chance, surely they, as intelligent scientists can do a much better job of designing life in their sophisticated laboratories. Such a view is illustrated by Julian Huxley's hope that someday scientists would fill the "position of business manager for the cosmic process of evolution."

At this point, Christians must raise grave questions. Although we have powerful technological capabilities, we often lack the wisdom and moral capacity to use them correctly. Given finite wisdom and sinful human behavior, we could easily slide toward dire consequences. We therefore need firm guidelines to control the implementation of gene splicing technology. Our dominion over the created order does not include taking over the office of Creator and playing genetic roulette with God's creation. While tremendous benefits will accompany gene splicing, we must question the wisdom of wholesale genetic engineering of the biosphere.

*Artificial reproduction* encompasses a host of various techniques and has concerned people ever since Aldous Huxley wrote *Brave New World* in 1932. A half-century later, many of his prophecies seem to be coming true. Techniques have been developed to deal with male and female infertility. Infertility is a chronic health care problem and vast amounts of money are invested by couples desiring to have children. Though they have the same goal, each technique varies from the other in some important details.

Artificial insemination is used for male infertility. In some cases, the sperm of the husband (AIH) is collected, treated, and injected back into the wife. But in most cases, artificial insemination involves a donor (AID). In some cases, the sperm can be frozen for future use in a sperm bank. Artificial sex selection, previously used for animals, is now available to humans. When sperm is collected, the X-sperm, which would produce a female, is separated from the Y-sperm, which would produce a male. Although the technique is not perfect, it can increase the probability that couples could have a child of a predetermined sex. Surrogate parenting utilizes artificial insemination to deal with female infertility. In this case, the husband's sperm is utilized to fertilize a surrogate mother who will carry the child and give it up at birth.

Embryo transfer is very similar to surrogate parenting. The major difference is that the surrogate mother merely carries the embryo for a few days and then the embryo is flushed out of the surrogate and transferred to the infertile wife. In vitro fertilization is a procedure in which eggs are surgically removed from the wife and fertilized by the husband's sperm in a Petri dish. After a period of time, one or more embryos are transferred to the woman's womb. In some cases, not all of the embryos are used and can be frozen for future use.

The goal of artificial reproduction is certainly laudable. Research to aid childless couples is a worthy goal. But Christians must insure that the means by which we achieve that goal are also moral. Too often reproductive specialists let the end justify the means. Each individual technique has its own difficulties, but two major ethical concerns surface with nearly each technique described. The first is the issue of the sanctity of life. Some of these techniques destroy large numbers of fertilized embryos. Moreover, the success rates of such things as embryo transfer and in vitro fertilization are very low. Some clinics also use a procedure known as hyperfertilization in which a number of eggs are fertilized. After one or two embryos are used, the rest are destroyed or sometimes frozen. Such procedures also raise troubling sanctity of life questions if we accept the biblical teaching that embryos and fetuses share humanity with us (Pss. 51:5; 139).

A second major ethical concern is over the moral integrity of the family. Many of these techniques involve third parties. Artificial insemination, and especially surrogate parenting and embryo transfer, involve other parties in the reproductive event. Many Christians feel that such arrangements violate the biblical prescriptions for marriage and family (Gen. 2). In normal procreation, the communication of love, the union of sexual intimacy, and the desire for children are all merged together in the bounds of matrimony. There is security and intimacy within those relationships. This foundation is more easily threatened by developing techniques of artificial reproduction. The technology, if utilized, should be done with a concern for the sanctity of human life and the moral integrity of the family. Simply because we can do the procedure provides little moral justification for carrying it out.

In many cases, other options should be pursued. For example, if the fallopian tubes are blocked, a woman can have corrective surgery (tuboplasty). Other women might avail themselves of various drug treatments and other newly developed surgical procedures. In cases where medicine can provide little help, couples might still consider adoption.

**Bibliography:** Anderson, J. K., *Genetic Engineering* (1982); Lester, L. P., with Hefley, J. C., *Cloning: Miracle or Menace?* (1980).

See CLONING; MEDICAL ETHICS; SURROGATE MOTHERHOOD.

J.K.A.

**GENOCIDE.** This is the destruction of a racial or ethnic group, a practice that has not been uncommon in human history. It is often committed in the context of war, but may also be conducted by a government against its own people. The term also refers to the practice of singling out individuals for destruction on the basis of their race, even if no attempt is made to annihilate the race as a whole; and to the attempt to exterminate the cultural identity of a people. In some cases, it is the result of unintended but willing complicity by a government in the destruction of groups whose survival is seen as inimical to "progress," as is often the case with primitive tribes and peasant peoples. Genocide clearly is a moral atrocity both for its violation of respect for human life, in disobedience to the sixth commandment, and for its invidious racism. In addition, it deprives humanity of much of its divinely ordained diversity and richness.

In the biblical record, cultural identity is seen as so extremely significant that the survival and prospering of one's people is more important than virtually any personal matter. Few concerns could compete in importance with that of being a member of a "people" with an identifiable set of ancestors and descendants. Few terrors could compare with being "cut off" from one's people, left without an identity as a member of one's group. God's most significant promise to Abraham was that he would make of him "a great nation," whose descendants would be as numerous as the stars (Gen. 12:1-3; 15:5). The psalmist calls upon the Lord to "save thy people, and bless thy heritage," (Ps. 28:9, RSV). Perhaps the worst curse he could call upon the depraved enemies of God and His people was that "their camp" be made "a desolation," with "no one" left to "dwell in their tents" (Ps. 69:25).

Many groups have been targets of genocide, perhaps none so persistently as the Jews. The Book of Esther tells of a plot by the wicked courtier Haman, in which he obtained the permission of the Persian king Ahasuerus to destroy the Jewish people. The victory of Queen Esther, herself a Jew, over this attempt is celebrated today in the Jewish feast of Purim. In more recent times, Jews dispersed throughout the world have been the victims of genocidal attacks, pogroms, and persecutions. These culminated in the staggeringly evil Holocaust of Adolph Hitler and his Nazi regime, in which more than six millions Jews, as well as people from such ethnic groups as the Gypsies, lost their lives. In view of the Holocaust, many Jews believe that evangelism targeted at their numbers smacks of cultural genocide.

A variety of ethnic groups in the past or present have been made to suffer under genocidal policies, including the North American Indian in the face of the westward expansion of European settlers, present-day Indian tribes in Central America such as the Meskito, and the Tasaday of the Phillipines. Interest in stopping the spread of genocidal activity has been generated by anthropological as well as moral concerns. Groups such as Survival, International and Cultural Survival work to identify groups victimized by genocide and to intervene on their behalf.

**Bibliography:** Bragg, W. in Sine, T., (ed.), *The Church, in Response to Human Need* (1983); Frankena, W. K. in Temkin, O., Frankena, W. K., and Kadish, S. H., *Respect for Life in Medicine, Philosophy, and the Law* (1976); Smedes, L., *Mere Morality* (1984).

D.B.F.

**GENTLENESS.** Gentleness is a quality of the caring individual in which a mild, quiet, and kind approach to people and situations is adopted instead of an aggressive, blustering, violent one. It is a quality that is peculiarly Christian, as contrasted, for example, with the traditions of pagan Greek culture, which thought of gentleness as an effeminate trait. Since the male image that the Greeks chose to foster was that of a virile, rough, belligerent, bawdy individual, there could obviously be little place in the male character for such a quality as gentleness.

In the Old Testament two references (2 Sam. 22:36; Ps. 18:35) used the word *anah* in the sense of humility, while in one other instance (2 Sam. 18:3) the term *lebh* conveys the impression of kindness and mildness. The New Testament word *epieikeia* implies a yielding that is influenced by tolerance and forbearance. *Gentleness* thus involves a quiet, nonaggressive attitude of mind that is based on Christ's nature (2 Cor. 10:1) and is therefore commended in Scripture for Christians to exemplify (Titus 3:2; James 3:17).

**GLUTTONY.** This term describes the attributes or conduct of a glutton, a word which comes from the Latin verb *glutio*, "to swallow." Gluttony is therefore used principally of the avid devouring of food, although by transference it can be applied to other things which encourage a voracious appetite, such as work.

In the medieval period gluttony was listed as one of the seven deadly sins. Gluttony is an obvious form of physical appetite, and since the medieval clergy were forbidden by church law to indulge in sexual relations, they tended to compensate for this loss by gratifying themselves with another aspect of appetite. But gluttony was castigated in secular circles also, among those who were married as well as the single, and not least in wealthy and aristocratic circles, since as ethicists and moralists frequently point out, gluttony is a rich person's sin.

In the Old Testament gluttony (*zalal*) and alcoholism went hand in hand (Deut. 21:20; Prov. 23:21), a tradition that was still evident in Christ's time (Matt. 11:19; Luke 7:34). Gluttony is sinful for the Christian because its excesses defile the body, which is the temple of the Holy Spirit (1 Cor. 3:16-17). It is peculiarly selfish, and therefore ignores the needs and concerns of others in society, all of which is sin. Finally, it violates the injunction that the Christian should be living a temperate and sober life in this present world (Titus 2:2).

**GNOSTIC ETHICS.** Gnosticism is a term used to describe a religious and philosophical system that flourished at the turn of the Christian era. It was particularly influential from the second to the fourth centuries A.D. when it gained popularity in some Christian communities. It should be noted that gnosticism reflected a great diversity of teachings and beliefs, and thus it is difficult to establish one clear example of it.

The name is derived from the Greek word *gnosis*, "to know." Gnosticism characteristically offers "special or deep knowledge" in order to gain salvation. By receiving *gnosis*, one learns of the true inner self that stands in sharp contrast to the material self. The most common feature of gnosticism is an overriding belief in dualism, on individual terms as well as cosmic. Not only is the individual in tension with the self, but that person is out of harmony with the rest of the world. Gnosticism rejects the Judeo-Christian belief that this world and humanity is the result of a creative act of God. Rather, the gnostic views the world as the result of chaos, and the true God (or divine principle, depending on the gnostic system being examined) is far removed from humanity. Alienation is the true state of the human condition. Hans Jonas has paralleled the gnostic sense of alienation with that of the modern existentialist. Whether that is correct or not, the ancient gnostic's ultimate goal was to escape from the evil world in which he existed.

Through a redeemer figure, *gnosis* is given which instructs the recipient as to the divine spark that is at the core of every human. Once this knowledge is gained, liberation has been achieved. Very frequently, secret rites and special initiations passed the "knowledge" from individual to individual. However, self-discovery was encouraged, as innovation was a high mark of spirituality with gnostic circles. Once *gnosis* had been gained, the goal in life was to wait for death, when the material self would finally free the divine inner self to return to its heavenly origins.

During the second to the fourth centuries when Christianity was particularly involved with gnosticism and a struggle for orthodoxy (Irenaeus, *Against Heresies;* Tertullian *Against Marcion, Against Valentinus, Prescription of Heresies;* Clement of Alexandria, *Miscellanies;* Eusebius, *Ecclesiastical History*), the heresies of the gnostics were often characterized in two ways. On the one hand, there were ascetic tendencies that attempted to control natural bodily instincts, believed to be evil and in opposition to the divine inner self. The aim of the moral life was to be detached from this contaminated world. On the other hand, some gnostics had libertine attitudes that let human nature go its own direction without control. The inner self was detached through "knowledge" from the material body. In both cases, the gnostics claimed knowledge and individual experience. Very frequently the air of superiority led to divisions within a religious community.

In the late eighteenth century and early nineteenth century, fragments of gnostic writings were discovered. The largest and most significant gnostic library, however, was found in 1945 at Nag Hammadi in Egypt. This library has given substantial insight into gnostic beliefs and practices.

It is possible that parts of 1 Corinthians, Colossians, and Jude were addressing gnostic problems within early Christianity.

**Bibliography:** Jonas, H., *The Gnostic Religion* (1963); Pagels, E., *The Gnostic Gospels* (1979); Robinson, J., *The Nag Hammadi Library* (1977); Wilson, R. M., *Gnosis and the New Testament* (1968).

W.O.M.

**GOLDEN RULE.** The precept that is described by this celebrated title occurs in Christ's teachings about human relationships. In Matthew 7:12, as part of the Sermon on the Mount, Jesus told his disciples that whatever they wanted others to do to them, they themselves should first have set the example. For Christ, doing unto others as one would have them do in return constituted the essence of the Old Testament legal and prophetic teaching. The reference to the Law is supposedly to Leviticus 19:18, where the Israelites were instructed to love their neighbors as themselves, but Christ's words added a new dimension to the ancient teaching.

Consequently self is no longer the standard by which motivation is to be measured, but instead a degree of reflection is required as to the kind of treatment that one would like to receive were he or she to be in the position of the donor. Since self-interest would naturally expect kindness and goodness from others, the best way to ensure a like response is to anticipate others in practicing such things. The Golden Rule is thus one of the most important ethical precepts by which the Christian ought to live.

It has been pointed out frequently by writers that the Rule was not unknown to the pagan world, occurring in Oriental and European authors alike. When it is quoted, however, it usually appears in a negative form such as "Do not do to others what you would not have them do to you." The traditional title, "Golden Rule," is of modern origin, occurring first during the sixteenth century.

**GOOD, GOODNESS.** These terms occur commonly in Scripture, and describe one of the high ethical values present in the revealed nature of God (Pss. 25:8; 100:5; 135:3). They represent a standard of positive moral and spiritual quality by which people and events can be judged. Thus God's unsullied creation when completed was described as "very good," and thereafter the adjective *tob* was used to describe high quality situations of a physical or moral order that approximated to perfection. Goodness is that attribute which characterizes the activity of a morally and ethically upright person, and expresses itself in kindness, generosity, consideration, acts of altruism, and love, all of which are characteristic of God's relationship to his people Israel.

Believers in the New Testament period were convinced similarly of the goodness of God (Rom. 11:22; 1 Tim. 4:4) as expressed in both material and spiritual blessings. By that time the adjective seems to have become part of a title or a respectful form of address to persons of perceived superior rank or quality. This was apparently the case with the anonymous individual who addressed Jesus as "Good Master" (Matt. 19:16; Mark 10:17; Luke 18:18), only to be reminded of the true source of such high ethical characteristics. For the Christian goodness is among the fruits of the Spirit (Gal. 5:22; Eph. 5:9) which marks a sanctified life.

**GOOD NEIGHBOR.** The spirit of this concept was at the center of all life in the covenant community of ancient Israel. People were required to live in obedience to God's will, and to exhibit the spiritual quality of holiness in all their dealings. They were to ensure that nobody suffered from economic deprivation (Deut. 15:7-11) and were ordered to deal justly and kindly with the stranger and the sojourner (Exod. 20:10; Lev. 19:34). The ethical code in these matters was summed up in the saying, "You shall love your neighbor as yourself" (Lev. 19:18, NKJV). The Hebrew *rea*, "neighbor," carried much the same meaning as in modern times, including someone in close physical, topographical, or spiritual proximity, a companion, fellow, or someone of equal standing.

The teachings of Jesus added a new dimension to the ancient Levitical precept by subsuming all the teachings of the law and prophecy under the concept of an individual's love to God and to his or her neighbor (Matt. 22:37-40). As a practical example of the character and behavior of a good neighbor, Jesus told the story of a generous-hearted Samaritan (Luke 10:30-36), which included a devastating criticism of the priests and Levites, who above all others ought to have been exemplifying the law of the good neighbor. The lawyer who had initiated the whole discussion was told in no uncertain terms to go and live in the spirit of the altruistic Samaritan. The New Testament urges the believer to apply the law of Christ's love to all areas of life consistently, and thereby to fulfill both the spirit and duties of a good neighbor.

**GOOD WORKS.** In the community of ancient Israel, the practical application of the regulations concerning holy living issued in works of charity, justice, and social concern as befitted a "kingdom of priests and a holy nation" (Exod. 19:6). Unfortunately these good works were impeded by continued lapses from the high moral standards of the Sinai covenant due to idolatry and apostasy, and it was only after both Israel and Judah had been punished by exile that a stricter application of the ancient law was possible once more. From the time of Ezra (fifth century B.C.) the law became central to Jewish faith, and by the time of Christ justification with God was thought to be possible if a person had kept scrupulously every provision of the written and oral traditions of the law. Salvation was thus possible as the result of mechanical human works in this view, quite independently of faith in God.

Jesus repudiated this position by showing that God looked for love, faith, and obedience in his followers, and that those who paraded good deeds with a view to a reward would lose rather than benefit (Matt. 6:1). Paul was explicit about the relationship of works and faith in the matter of eternal salvation in Ephesians 2:8-9, stating that it is the product of grace through faith as a divine gift, not as a consequence of human works, lest anyone should boast because of having superior opportunities for exercising charitable deeds.

Some interpreters have seen a contradiction between Paul's teaching about justification (Rom. 3:28; Gal. 2:16) and the statement in James 2:24 that a person is justified by works. But what James is discussing is works wrought upon the basis of a justified, righteous life, for which he used as an example no less significant a person than Abraham, who by believing God was accorded justification and righteousness. The Christian is urged to show by works of love and justice that he or she is indeed regenerate through the atoning work of Christ. Such a living testimony will produce fruit unto holiness and in the end everlasting life (Rom. 6:22).

**GOSPEL.** The Greek word *evangelion*, which is translated "gospel" in the New Testament and which strictly means "good news," was used originally for the reward given to the messenger who brought good tidings. But in the New Testament it means the good news itself, a usage we find also in the Old Testament: "The Spirit of the Lord God is upon me, because the Lord has anointed me to bring good tidings to the afflicted..." (Isa. 61:1, RSV), words which Jesus applied to his own ministry (Luke 4:18-21). Mark says that Jesus came "preaching the gospel of God" (Mark 1:14), a gospel which may also be called "the gospel of Jesus Christ" (Mark 1:1) or "the gospel of the kingdom" (Matt. 4:23). It is linked with a call to repentance (Mark 1:15); those who respond to the good news of God or of Christ turn away from sin and self-centeredness and set themselves to obey God. It is impossible to take the kingdom seriously and at the same time to pursue selfish aims (Mark 8:34-35). If God is really sovereign, then that has significant implications for the whole of life.

It is Paul who has most to say about the gospel (sixty of the seventy-six New Testament occurrences of *gospel* are found in the Pauline corpus). He is insistent that there is but one gospel (1 Cor. 15:11; Gal. 1:6-7). Luke reports him as calling it "the gospel of the grace of God" (Acts 20:24), and the whole of Paul's writings testifies to the centrality of grace. For him what mattered most of all was that Christ died for our sins and that He rose triumphant (1 Cor. 15:3-10). Paul said emphatically that this was the Christian message, no matter who preached it (1 Cor. 15:11).

The gospel does not open up the way to antinomianism. One cannot say, "I am saved by grace, and therefore it does not matter how I live." For Paul, the gospel is the power of God at work (Rom. 1:16; 1 Thess. 1:5). He exhorts the Philippians, "Let your manner of life be worthy of the gospel of Christ" (Phil. 1:27). Repeatedly, he links the gospel with truth (Gal. 2:5, 14; Col. 1:5). This means that the preachers were proclaiming no falsehood when they preached the gospel, but it also means that truth is to have its place in the lives of those who receive it. But it is scarcely necessary to belabor the point. Paul's letters are full of exhortations to upright living, the kind of living that necessarily follows on reception of the gospel of God's grace. The preachers did not work on promising material (1 Cor. 1:26-29; 6:9-11), but the gospel wrought such a transformation in the lives of believers that their characteristic designation came to be "the saints."

**Bibliography:** Freidrich, G., *TDNT*, 2, pp. 707-37; Green, M., *Evangelism in the Early Church* (1970).

L.M.

**GRACE.** Divine grace is God's free, unmerited favor (Eph. 2:8). According to the Christian gospel, mankind in sin is both guilty and polluted. His redemption is effected by His justification by the grace of God though faith in Jesus Christ. Through such faith, sin is pardoned and perfect righteousness is imputed. Being freed from the guilt of sin, God's grace, through the co-instrumentality of the word of God and the Holy Spirit, renews the individual morally and spiritually, a process that continues unfinished until death and that will be consummated in glory at the second coming of Christ. The Roman Catholic Church denies that justification is a forensic act, involving only a change in status before God, and claims that it involves subjective renewal as well (sanctifying grace). In the eyes of Protestants however, this is unbiblical in that it undercuts justification by faith alone; it undermines the finished work of Christ; it is legalistic in its practical effects; and it makes impossible a personal assurance of salvation. Roman Catholicism, for its part, charges the Protestant view with being antinomian. This fails to appreciate that although justification and sanctification are conceptually distinct, and vitally so, they are also inseparable in practice.

From this summary of the theology of grace it can be seen that the saving grace of God has important ethical implications. How deep these implications run is also a matter of continuing controversy in the Christian church between those who regard divine grace as needed to provide moral assistance for the Christian and those who regard it as needed thoroughly to renew and re-create the moral personality of the individual.

Of what does such renewal consist? Of reforming and educating the conscience through the law of God (Gal. 5:16-24), by removing superstitious and unbiblical standards, and of motivating and directing the individual to keep God's law. The law is kept not out of a fruitless desire to justify the individual, but out of a knowledge of what that law is and out of gratitude to God for redeeming him from the consequences of a failure to keep it. The Christian recognizes that the law touches not merely the outward conduct, but the inner motive, the "heart." Having been loved much, the Christian loves in return; a love expressed in a desire to keep God's law, but a desire that is often thwarted by the remaining evil of his heart (Rom. 7).

For though there is no conceptual impossibility in the Christian being totally and completely renewed in this life—for the power of God is not limited—it is not God's will to bring about such sinless perfection before death. But a position of this sort is denied by all "perfectionists." Modern perfectionism stems from the Wesleyan branch of the eighteenth-century evangelical revival, though earlier forms of it can be found in the teachings of the radical sects of the continental Reformation and of the Commonwealth period in England. Perfectionists claim that it is possible for the Christian to live a life of "entire sanctification," without sin, though this is sometimes modified to "without known sin" or even "without deliberate sin." Such a position, it is argued by Augustinians, fails to take account of the strength of indwelling sin in the regenerate.

At the other extreme, antinomians hold that, being under grace and freed from the law in Christ, the Christian is no longer under any obligation to keep the law of God. Antinomianism, like perfectionism, has taken a variety of forms. Occasionally it seems to have led to overtly licentious behavior. More often it has amounted to no more than the claim that the idea of duty, or law-keeping, has no place in the Christian life, or that the Decalogue has been replaced as the Christian's rule of life by the precepts of Christ and of the Apostles. Modern "situation ethics" can be regarded as one form of antinomianism, as can certain aspects of the theological ethics of Karl Barth.

Besides the grace of God, which operates in the moral renewing of the regenerate, the moral state of society and culture at large is said by some to be the result of the "common grace" of God, which restrains sinful tendencies and enables family, political, and church life to proceed and human culture to survive and at times to flourish. "Common grace" in this sense was developed in detail by the Dutch Calvinist Abraham Kuyper (1837-1920). Thinkers within this tradition distinguish sharply between common grace and natural law. Insofar as they wish to insist that common grace is grace and is not the product of unaided ("natural") human powers then they are right to do so; but the moral standard of common grace is presumably that of the law of God, of which natural law (in one sense of this term) might plausibly be regarded as one expression.

**Bibliography:** Kevan, E., *The Grace of Law* (1964); Kuyper, A., *Calvinism* (1899); Warfield, B. B., *Studies in Perfectionism* (2 vols) (1931); Williams, N. P., *The Grace of God* (1930).

P.H.

**GRATITUDE.** This word is based upon a Latin word *gratus*, one meaning of which is "thanks," or simply "thankful." Gratitude is therefore a conscious emotional response of thanksgiving in a situation where provision of some kind, perhaps even generous and unexpected, has been made. Under such conditions religiously inclined persons often express their thanks to God, as well as to other individuals.

Christians should be especially thankful to God for having been created and redeemed and chosen through Christ's saving grace to enjoy his precious gift of eternal life. In all of this believers ought to rejoice that their daily lives are under the special care of the Holy Spirit, undeserving as they might be. Accordingly Christians can be expected to express their gratitude in continual thanksgiving (1 Thess. 5:16). Whether offered in song or not (Eph. 5:19-20), such gratitude should not be made a spiritual end in itself, but ought to furnish a pleasant if brief interlude in the continuous service of Christ and his church in the world.

**GREED.** Greed can be described psychologically as a compulsive or insatiable desire to possess certain things that present an attractive appearance. This urge may take the form of covetousness, prohibited by the tenth commandment (Exod. 20:17), which is a jealous desire for the property or possessions of another person. If greed is described as avarice, it constitutes a desperate desire for money, while if it is stigmatized as gluttony it indicates a person's obsessive urge to consume food. All these are vices, and one or two were actually included in the catalog of deadly sins which Pope Gregory the Great compiled.

Greed is evil because it substitutes material things for the place of honor that the Creator ought to have in an individual's life and is therefore idolatry (Col. 3:5), an offense also prohibited in the Decalogue (Exod. 20:4-5). Because of his stress on temperance and moderation (1 Cor. 9:25; Phil. 4:5), Paul condemned greed as an unwarranted excess, and in his list of vices he rated it only second to fornication and adultery (cf. Rom. 1:29-31; Gal. 5:19-21; Col. 3:5). Greed should be held in abhorrence by all practicing Christians if only for the broad reason that it leads to apostasy by substituting self for God.

See AVARICE.

**GUILT.** Guilt is the consequence or the effect of a shameful act, either real or imaginary. The word itself comes from an Anglo-Saxon root *gylt*, meaning "to pay." That is, the individual feels a sense of blame and either wants to discharge it, or is forced to do so by society. As a technical word *guilt* is used in three principal ways: feelings, moral failings, and legal responsibilities.

*Guilt as Feelings.* We may feel guilty even though there has been no overt act of wickedness or crime. Sigmund Freud considered guilt to be the most important problem in the evolution of human life. Accustomed as he was to dealing with neurotic and seriously disturbed people, he dismissed the idea that it had any real or objective basis. Because the universe was a closed system, with no objective or eternal values, guilt was a wrong emotion and should be eradicated if a person was to find wholeness.

*Guilt as a Moral Response.* Needless to say, Freud's views have not been generally shared because it is clear that guilt is not always neurotic or baseless. The American psychiatrist Rollo May, for example, viewed guilt feelings in a healthy person as a positive constructive emotion. It is, he argued, an awareness between what *is* and what *ought to be*. O. H. Mowrer developed this further. Moral guilt, he asserted, is not the invention of the church or Bible, but is the universal condition of the human soul. Whereas to Freud guilt is illusory, for May and Mowrer it is real and must be faced. Guilt, of course, is inevitably connected with conscience. In the early development of the conscience, morality is, at first, borrowed. Our parents' approval and disapproval are our first guides in moral behavior. If the parents are too dominating or restricting, the guilt feelings built up over many years may poison adult life, creating further guilt, accusing and condemning our total way of life. However, the normal mature person usually progresses from borrowed moral codes to a personal morality, accepting standards of right or wrong on the basis of the love of the good and the consideration of others.

*Guilt in Law.* For the lawyer, studying behavior from the viewpoint of social laws, "guilt" as a feeling or as the transgression of a moral failure may be considered irrelevant. He is concerned with the breaking of law, and it is conceivable that a man may feel guilty but be blameless in the eyes of the state. Conversely, it is possible for a person to be guilty of a crime yet be morally innocent. Thus, in an oppressive society, a Christian may feel it is necessary to oppose the state and thus face its condemnation, yet be innocent before God.

*A Christian Perspective on Guilt.* Our standing before God is one of guilt. Before Him each one of us is culpable for deeds that have violated His moral law: "None is righteous, no, not one" (Rom. 3:10, RSV). Sin's legacy is estrangement from God and broken social relationships. The Christian thus views guilt as going much deeper than individual misdemeanors based upon inherited behavior patterns. Mankind belongs to God by a moral bond that we have broken time and time again, and we share in the accumulated sin of mankind against a loving and holy heavenly Father. But the contribution of Christianity is that the power and effect of sin has been dealt with by Christ. Through His life and service, culminating in His death on the cross, the way has been opened for man to enter into a vital and liberating relationship with God, because forgiveness is ours in Christ.

Does this mean that guilt is a wrong emotion for the Christian? Not at all. Christ "breaks the power of canceled sin and sets the prisoner free," but because the Christian life, like any other life, is a journey through a sinful and fallen world, no one will ever arrive at a position of total freedom from feelings of guilt. As Paul Tournier points out, guilt and grace are experienced simultaneously. Grace removes condemnation, but we will continue to experience feelings of unworthiness and failure. All of us, then, need God's grace and daily forgiveness through the cross to grow to maturity and acceptance of ourselves as children of God.

**Bibliography:** Darling, H. W., *Man in his Right Mind* (1969); France, M., *The Paradox of Guilt* (1967); May, R., *The Meaning of Anxiety* (1950); Mowrer, O. H., *Morality and Mental Health* (1967); Tournier, P., *Guilt and Grace* (1962).

See CONSCIENCE; SIN.

G.C.

# -H-

**HABIT.** A habit may be described as an established tendency or a particular practice that characterizes an individual's way of life. Habits are psychologically generated in that they comprise response mechanisms that at first may be of a primitive motor nature. As habits are developed by being repeated over a period of time, they may prove to have positive or negative effects. As learned rather than instinctive behavior they can be evaluated for moral and social worth, and because habit responses are relatively uncomplicated psychologically they can, be changed by behavior-modification techniques.

Because of their particular psychological origin, habits must be distinguished from traditions and customs, which are culturally conditioned phenomena. Some habits arise, of course, from a cultural background, as for example the smoking of cigarettes or the drinking of beer in those communities where such activities are regarded as normal. Other habits can be self-imposed, whether as an act of personal discipline or not, and these can include a regimen of exercise, diet, spiritual activities such as regular prayer and worship, and similar forms of continued, repetitive behavior. Many habits, good and bad alike, arise from one's family background, and if habits are to be good servants rather than bad masters they need to be evaluated critically from time to time. Depending upon a person's emotional and spiritual development, the models upon which the habits were based originally may well prove to have been inadequate.

Habits have an obviously important bearing upon character, and for the believer whose goal is to attain to the measure of Christ's fullness (Eph. 4:13) only those habits which promote positive spiritual growth can be countenanced. Vicious habits (Rom. 1:29-31) will be replaced by those which reflect Christ's character (Gal. 5:22-23) as regular rather than occasional or sporadic expressions of the believer's life. In this activity the Christian has the special advantage over the self-reforming unbeliever of the power of God's Holy Spirit to perform and sustain the inward renewal of personality (Rom. 13:12-14; Eph. 3:16-17).

**HALLUCINATORY DRUGS.** These chemical substances cause distortion of perception (illusions) and false perceptions (hallucinations).

In addition to naturally occurring hallucinogens (such as "magic mushrooms"), many hallucinatory drugs have been synthesized in the laboratory. During the 1960s and 1970s, the use of many of these drugs became epidemic. Lysergic acid (LSD), mescaline, and phencyclidine (PCP or "angel dust") were used widely by young people. These drugs induce a delirium in which hallucinations, usually visual, are prominent.

Other drugs, not so clearly hallucinogenic, have also been used widely—notably cannabis ("marijuana," "hash," "pot"), amphetamine drugs ("speed"), and cocaine ("coke"). These drugs alter consciousness, but hallucinations tend to be secondary and are associated with heavy use.

The quest for intense personal "peak experiences," mystical experiences of "new birth" and "cosmic oneness," and the desire to escape from the immense anxiety of a nuclear age appear to be prominent reasons for the use of these drugs among intellectuals. Among adolescents the use of hallucinogens is more experimental (and tragic). The role-modelling of prominent entertainers and group pressure have made drug use attractive for many adolescents. The loss of parental guidance and of effective moral standards in the community have further contributed to the epidemic.

There is no clear reference to hallucinogenic drugs in the Bible. Nevertheless, it is not hard to criticize the use of these drugs on the basis of intention, of effect, and of consequence.

The quest for intense individual experience is not the product of Christianity but of humanism. At bottom the quest for "peak experience" and "self-actualization'" is based on preoccupation with self. The quest to escape from a frightening situation is contrary to the Christian willingness to confront the worst possible human situation in the power of Christ. Christianity, under the impulse of the Incarnation, plunges into all reality and proclaims the redeeming lordship of Jesus Christ. Social pressure is conformity to "this present evil age" and contrary to Christ's call to discipleship, to be ruled by the will of God alone.

Hallucinogenic drugs bear horrifying consequences. Their potential to induce dependency, shared with alcohol and sedatives; the danger of acute psychosis with its melange of terrifying hallucinations, appalling emotions, and uncontrollable impulses; and the risk of chronic mental illness in vulnerable persons make their use unacceptable. Voluntary loss of control is abhorrent to the Christian who desires to put himself under the control of the Holy Spirit. The quest for spiritual experience apart from God is full of spiritual danger. The Evil One can exploit any state of consciousness to effect distraction from God.

Christians should avoid the use of these drugs on both practical and religious grounds. The authentically Christian experience is rooted in God, expands awareness of reality, brings one more effectively into contact with human need, enhances human relationships, preserves integrity of body and mind, and endures anxiety and suffering in the fellowship of Christ's cross.

**Bibliography:** Gilman, A. G., *et al.*, (eds.), *Goodman and Gilman's The Pharmacological Basis of Therapeutics* (6th ed., 1980), pp. 560–69; Heath, R. G., *Archives of General Psychiatry* (1972) 26:577–84; Petersen, R. C., *Marihuana Research Findings* (1976) pp. 128–78.

J.E.R.

**HAPPINESS.** This term is the usual rendering of the pagan Greek term *eudaimonia* and is related to *eudaimon*, which literally means a "goodly demon." In classical times *eudaimonia* was interpreted to mean "good fortune" as opposed to the depredations of evil influences. While the distinction between eudaimonism (in which happiness is the goal of life) and hedonism (in which pleasure is the end of all striving) was blurred in antiquity, as it is today, such was not the case with Aristotle. He more than any other Greek thinker exalted happiness as the highest object of human endeavor. Unfortunately his concept has been misunderstood and distorted over the centuries by improper sentimentality. Thus while Aristotle has been assumed to be recommending wisdom, virtue, pleasure, and the like as a means to happiness, and thereby investing human endeavor with some sort of ethical and metaphysical respectability, the facts of the case are actually quite different. In the brawling, inebriated, lustful society of his day, all that Aristotle meant by *happiness* was simply the pragmatic notion of "living better."

Happiness is actually quite difficult to define, in spite of several whimsical attempts, and in the process admits of numerous subjective elements. Most persons, mindful of the adversity that life provides in abundance, would perhaps think of happiness as a transitory phase of positive emotional stimulation, to be associated with a particular individual or circumstance. Others of a more pragmatic outlook would be content to describe it in terms such as "job-satisfaction," without any attempt to impose mystic qualities on happiness. But on analysis it is usually conceded to be the consequence rather than the cause of a process.

The Old Testament contains over a dozen instances where the word *asher* and its cognates have been rendered by *happy* or *happiness* in many English versions. While the general sense involves satisfaction, gratification, contentment, and the like, it also seems to include an element of euphoria, as with the visit of the queen of Sheba to Solomon's court (1 Kings 10:8; 2 Chron. 9:7). Gratitude also seems to have played a part in human happiness (Job 5:17; Ps. 127:5).

In the New Testament *happy* was used in the King James Version to translate the Greek word *makarios*, as in John 13:17, Romans 14:22, and elsewhere. This is an unfortunate rendering, to say the least, because *makarios* means "blessed" and indicates a divine reward of joy and peace as the outcome of a particular type of life as lived in the power of Christ. Closer examination reveals that there is no Greek word in the New Testament corresponding to the pagan *eudaimonia*, if only because all demons in the New Testament were regarded uniformly as evil. In the New King James Version the word *makarios* has accordingly been rendered predominantly by *blessed*. This action could well be interpreted as "taking happiness out of the Bible," but sound linguistic practices offer no alternative. The Christian is nowhere urged in Scripture to make happiness the goal of his or her life, but if positive feelings occur as a consequence of diligent Christian living (John 13:17), the believer can be gratified by the fact of divine blessing. Conversely the lack of any significant euphoria in one's Christian life should not be taken as a necessary indication of failure, since individual faith is not governed by subjective emotional fluctuations but by the power of God.

**HATE.** Hate is an emotional response that is characterized by a bitter dislike of some person or situation. It is usually a complex reaction that includes fear, a sense of insecurity, feelings of intense hostility where rejection has occurred, and deep anger directed at those individuals or events that have brought about failure or personal calamity. Where the anger becomes chronic and assumes the form of resentment, it can have severe effects upon the individual's personality and circulatory system, producing hypertension and hardening of the arteries because of the action of the autonomic nervous system.

Hatred need not always result in negative values, however, if only because its exercise under proper circumstances can be a very valuable aid to Christian living. This is seen in Scripture where hating covetousness was one aspect of integrity (Exod. 18:21), along with detesting evil (Ps. 45:7; Amos 5:15) and lying (Ps. 119:63). The Hebrew term *sane* seems to imply a hearty emotional abhorrence of the particular object or situation whereas the kind mentioned in Genesis 27:41; 50:19 relates more to opposition of a general nature.

Certainly in Old Testament times a strong hatred of evil was essential for the survival of the Israelites, who were constantly subjected to the blandishments of pagan Canaanite idolatry (Deut. 12:31). Hatred, therefore, was legitimate for the Hebrews as a means of protecting the spiritual and ethical ideals of the Sinai covenant, whether it involved the repudiation of false gods or the rejection of temptations offered by pagan neighboring nations.

In the New Testament Christ taught his disciples to meet hatred with goodness (Matt. 5:44; Luke 6:27), and this applied especially to one's enemies, who were traditionally legitimate objects of hatred. Because Christ claimed the overlordship of the believer's life, he demanded total renunciation of property, other relationships, and even the believer's life (Luke 14:26) as evidence of commitment. Only when all other factors were subservient to his supreme will could they be countenanced as part of the believer's experience. Christ promised his followers that they would encounter hatred because of their allegiance to him (Matt. 24:9; Luke 21:17) and urged them not to be surprised when this occurred (John 15:18). Christians must love as Christ has loved them, and the only hatred permissible is the utter detestation of whatever is contrary to the revealed nature and purpose of God. Hatred in other respects is tantamount to murder (1 John 3:15) and is forbidden to the Christian along with other moral evils (Gal. 5:20).

**HEART TRANSPLANTATION.** The transplanting of bodily organs from a donor to a compatible recipient has been open to certain objections ever since the procedures began. Many people think that it is reprehensible for someone to be walking around with an organ from another person's body working inside them, even if it is sustaining life. Others wonder whether or not the donor's life, however minimal it might have been in its final stages, has in some way been sacrificed in order to allow the transplanting procedures to commence. Still others question the essential "rightness" of trading such personal items as portions of the body under any circumstances.

But if there is any concern at all about organ transplantation it is probably greatest where the heart is involved. This organ is crucial to the survival of the body (unlike a spleen, for example) and a transplant demands great surgical expertise and careful postoperative treatment from an experienced medical team if the patient is to survive. The heart also tends to be regarded differently because it is traditionally, although not biblically, the locale of emotion and love. Because of these factors, heart transplantation has been accorded far greater publicity than that attending other organs.

If, however, no ethical objection is raised in connection with the transplanting of other parts of the body, it would seem inconsistent to place the heart in a special category and forbid any attempts at transplantation. But from other points the procedure might be open to ethical objection, especially if it was viewed as experimental in nature, as with the implantation of a purely mechanical or electronic heart. In addition, the fact that the survival rate of cardiac transplant patients is discouragingly low might be urged against the propriety of the procedure. Indeed, some transplant patients have been reported subsequent to the operation as questioning the value of the entire procedure, especially where strokes

and hypertension have been experienced as side effects.

Needless to say, Scripture gives no guidance as to the rightness of heart transplants, and therefore any ethical issues will have to be decided on other grounds. In the opinion of some persons, heart transplantation could only be justified if it prolonged the patient's life significantly and improved the quality of that life to a noticeable degree, and these factors are not entirely in evidence at the time of writing. But for those whose evaluation of physical existence is such that every possible minute by which death is deferred is of incalculable significance, heart transplantation will continue to be a consideration of high priority.

**HEBREW ETHICS** (see **JEWISH ETHICS**).

**HEDONISM.** This term is derived directly from the Greek word *hedone,* which actually occurs only three times in the Greek New Testament (Luke 8:14; Titus 3:3; 2 Pet. 2:13) in a plural form and once (2 Pet. 2:13) in the singular. In all these occurrences it has the basic meaning of "sweetness," "pleasure," "enjoyment." Hedonism therefore is the dogma that pleasure is the principal good in human life. What is generally meant by pleasure is the delight, gratification, or enjoyment that results from indulgence in any one of a wide range of activities that give opportunity for emotional satisfaction. Where the hedonistic reaction is one of pleasurable affectivity, humor, laughter, and general gaiety are a normal part of the experience. But hedonism can also exhibit a pronounced sensual aspect in which self-indulgence in food, drink, and lascivious behavior play an important part. If this type of outlook characterizes the lifestyle of a particular person it is known technically as egotistic hedonism.

From the nature of the term it is evident that the basic hedonistic concepts were shaped by Greek culture. The germ of hedonism appears among the Sophists of Plato's time, but the movement came to full flower among the Cyrenaics. Greek culture is depicted frequently in idealistic terms as sensitive and beautiful, adorned by brilliantly executed statuary and dominated by elegant columned buildings. In reality Greek life was hard, coarse, and brutal, marked by an astonishingly high degree of illiteracy and only relieved culturally by the presence of Near Eastern slaves, including women captured in wars who brought some breadth of education and refinement to the homes of the wealthy. The weakest and least developed aspect of Greek culture was religion, the concepts and ideals of which were greatly debased by comparison with Hebrew spiritual traditions.

Drunkenness, lechery, and homosexuality were prominent features of Greek life, and for the egotistical hedonists constituted the main content of pleasure. The Cyrenaics were explicit exponents of this gross, sensual way of life and were followed to a more moderate extent by the Epicureans. Neither group troubled to define pleasure explicitly, however, and this defect has haunted all forms of hedonism including Jeremy Bentham's psychological hedonism and John Stuart Mill's Utilitarianism.

With this background in view it is small wonder that the New Testament condemned the love of pleasure (2 Tim. 3:4; Titus 3:3; 2 Pet. 2:13) as a gross indulgence which would result in spiritual death (1 Tim. 5:6). Instead of partaking in worldly enjoyments even to a moderate degree, the Christian is commanded to follow the self-denying life of Jesus Christ (Mark 8:34), to forswear luxury and personal indulgence, and to live a life of sacrifice in the faith of Christ and in service to others.

**HEREDITY.** Long seen as belonging to the domain of fate or "God's will," heredity has been placed by modern science in the realm of human control, and decisions must now be made about the sorts of offspring we are to have. An increased understanding of the processes by which genetic traits are passed on, along with new therapeutic options, have enabled us to take action in the realm of human reproduction. How should such knowledge be used? The availability of techniques to detect genetic abnormalities in the womb, coupled with the legality of abortion on demand, has made it possible to detect and destroy fetuses that have genetic diseases.

What options are open to humanity, now that we understand much of the hereditary transmission of genetic traits and have linked certain traits to diseases disastrous to life? Twenty per cent of the approximately 250,000 genetically defective births each year in the United States come from known genetic causes; and the suffering of these children, along with the emotional and economic burden they place on others, calls for action. Methods of controlling genetic disease include genetic screening and counseling, prenatal diagnosis, genetic surgery, and the use of new reproductive techniques. Genetic screening seeks to identify individuals who carry genetic diseases. A carrier is one who suffers no ill effects, yet contains the genetic material for disease that he or she can pass along to any offspring. They may be carriers of hemophilia, sickle cell anemia, or Tay-Sachs disease, to name a few. Screening can also identify those who suffer from a genetic disease. At the present time every infant born in the United States is screened for phenylketonuria (PKU), a serious metabolic disorder that affects about .08 per cent of births and which, left untreated, will result in severe mental retardation. By means of screening, affected infants can be identified and treated.

Genetic counseling is conducted by counselors trained in genetics and counseling who determine the risks that people will incur for passing genetic diseases to their offspring. Since diseases such as PKU, sickle cell anemia, and Tay-Sachs disease are transmitted along the lines of Mendelian transmission genetics, the likelihood of conceiving affected children can be specified and communicated to potential parents. While the couple is allowed to make the decision, the counselor explains the risks and options, including the option of aborting the affected fetus should one be conceived. Because of this option, some persons who would otherwise not have dared to risk the chance of having a genetically defective child will attempt to bear children.

Prenatal diagnosis gives reliable information about the genetic characteristics of the fetus in the womb. Fetal cells suspended in amniotic fluid are withdrawn by means of a needle and are analyzed for their genetic makeup. Presently there is little that can be done for affected children, and the information is used primarily for abortion decisions. It is hoped that more positive and therapeutic uses for such information will be found.

Genetic surgery, or gene repair, is an anticipated technique for the direct manipulation of human genes. At the least, it may enable physicians to repair gene defects. It is also speculated with some alarm, however, that positive "improvements" could someday be engineered in the types of persons we will have. Less futuristic is AID (artificial insemination by donor), which would substitute the sperm of a noncarrier for that of a carrier to eliminate the risk that the couple's child will have genetic disease.

What are the moral dimensions of such issues? Christians certainly affirm the value of childbearing in the family context and support measures to reduce suffering and disease. Genetic screening and counseling would meet little resistance from Christians unless such practices become coercive, as if the state were to become involved in deciding whether couples at risk would be allowed to have children. Christians will differ on prenatal diagnosis, especially when used to identify defective fetuses for abortion, since this singles out the weaker individuals for destruction. Some will be moved by the consideration that it holds the promise of enabling couples who otherwise would be unwilling to take a chance of having a child to do so. AID is controversial, seen by some as an application of an Old Testament principle of helping others have children when the male is incapable of being a father and by others as a violation of the marriage bond.

Ethical questions about the revolution in genetic knowledge and technology are certain to loom even larger in the future, not least in regard to eugenic attempts to "improve" the race according to someone's idea of human perfection. Christians will continue to consider this a dangerous overstepping of creaturely limitations placed upon humanity by God.

**Bibliography:** Fletcher, J., *The Ethics of Genetic Control: Ending Reproductive Roulette* (1974); Ramsey, P., *Fabricated Man: The Ethics of Ge-

*netic Control* (1970); Reilly, P., *Genetics, Law and Social Policy* (1977).

D.B.F.

**HERMENEUTICS, ETHICS AND.** Definitions of ethical behavior for most people in most societies are based on the traditions of that society. Most fallen human beings tend to revise their behavioral standards in the direction of personal preference to the limits of formal civil or informal cultural restraints. Academicians, on the other hand, have built extensive systems of ethics, based on various philosophies. But for the Christian who accepts the final authority of Scripture, ethics must be derived from the teaching of the Bible. This means that hermeneutics, the science (and art) of interpreting the Bible, is basic to any kind of biblically authentic ethical standards.

Historically, the purpose of Bible interpretation was simply to understand the meaning intended by the author. In recent decades it has become increasingly apparent that an accurate understanding of each biblical author's intended meaning will not of itself produce an authoritative biblical norm. Other questions must be asked: "For what audience was this teaching intended?" and "What response does God desire from His people today?"

In other words, the traditional scope of hermeneutics must be broadened to include not only principles for interpreting scriptural meaning, but principles for applying scriptural teaching. Meaning is the foundation, but significance for Christians today must also be determined. This expanded concept of hermeneutics, becomes the indispensable foundation for the building of any authentic biblical ethic.

What teachings of Scripture were meant for all believers of all ages? If Scripture is to maintain its own independent authority and not be subject to re-interpretation on the basis of external criteria, every teaching of Scripture should be received as normative for contemporary ethical behavior, unless the Scripture itself limits the audience or the application. Scripture does limit many teachings through subsequent teaching. The Mosaic ceremonial, civic, and health laws were set aside by Jesus Christ and His apostles, for example. Again, the immediate context may limit the intended recipients. For example, Christ and Paul advocated the single life, but only for those who have a special gift. It is especially important to notice that historical events and teachings given in specific historical contexts are not, merely by their inclusion in Scripture, normative for all believers of all time. That the people of the early church shared all things in common is not of itself a mandate for all Christians of all time to do the same. The teaching of Scripture, then, is normative for contemporary ethical behavior, unless Scripture itself in some way sets aside a particular teaching or category of teaching.

Another task of hermeneutics is to determine the response God desires for today, namely in terms of specific ethical norms. The easiest way to derive ethical norms from Scripture is by the direct application of explicit teaching or commandments. "Thou shall not steal" is clear enough and needs only to be obeyed. But the principles of Scripture are just as important as the commands. Some principles are in the form of a command, such as, "Be kind to one another." The specific behavior is not spelled out in the command, but the general principle is an ethical norm for the Christian: he must behave in kind ways toward his fellows. Principles may be derived from direct commands or combinations of commands. "Pray for the king" may not be applied directly in a society in which there is no king, but may be legitimately recognized as a principle that would require prayer for the president or others in authority.

Ethical principles may also be derived from historic events. The record of some human behavior does not of itself create an ethical norm. Only as Scripture endorses or condemns that behavior, and usually only if Scripture explains the reason for that commendation or condemnation, may the event be taken as normative. For example, the fact that Joseph imposed one of the most oppressive regimes of all history of the Egyptians, using grain he had originally taken from the people to bring them to total servitude to the Pharaoh, may not be viewed as a model for other despots, nor as approval of such behavior. The action is simply recorded, without giving God's viewpoint on it. On the other hand, when David took Bathsheba, a legitimate action for an absolute monarch, God revealed his view of this as a terrible sin. The principle to be derived is not only that God opposes adultery, but that He opposes wrong doing on the part of the wealthy, powerful, and those who might otherwise do as they pleased. This is a historical event interpreted ethically by Scripture itself.

The record of God's own activity is a limited source of deriving ethical principles from historic events. For example, if Jesus Christ did something, that behavior cannot be said to be ethically wrong, at least not under all circumstances. Again, when God commanded Israel to go to war, He did not thereby give validation to any and all warfare. On the other hand, a principle may be derived that war is not inherently sinful under all circumstances at all times, since God Himself wages war.

In these ways, ethical principles may be derived from Scripture, in the form of direct commands, principles derived from biblical teaching, and principles derived from historical events that are interpreted by Scripture as being good or evil.

Authentic principles for understanding the meaning intended by biblical authors, the audience God intended, and the response He desires today, when faithfully used, will yield valid biblical ethical norms.

**Bibliography:** Kaiser, W. C., Jr., *Toward an Exegetical Theology, Biblical Exegesis for Preaching and Teaching* (1981); McQuilkin, R., *An Introduction to Hermeneutics; Understanding and Applying the Bible* (1983), pp. 239–72; Thiselton, A. C., *The Two Horizons: New Testament Hermeneutics and Philosophical Description* (1980).

J.R.Mc Q.

**HEROISM.** The concepts underlying this term are Greek and originate in the word *heros,* which described a man who possessed godlike or superhuman qualities. Such a person had demonstrated his valor in military campaigns and on many different battlefields, and his courage, ingenuity, and sheer powers of physical endurance caused legends about him to gain currency. Especially commemorated in this way were the valiant warriors of Greek battles who perished on the field and were either burned at the site or carried home on their shields for interment. Heroism was thus that composite of qualities which characterized their deeds of valor and self-sacrifice for their native land. It bespoke qualities of bravery, steadfastness of purpose, strength of personality, and an ability to confront grave anger without fear. These features (along with other, less desirable ones) epitomized Greek masculinity, and in hero-worship were held up for public adulation and emulation.

Every nation has its heroes, and the Hebrews were no exception. The Epistle to the Hebrews catalogs the more outstanding champions of the faith (Heb. 11:3-40) in an unabashed testimony to the power in which all of them wrought mighty deeds of heroism for God. The Christian is consistently enjoined to participate in such heroic actions for the kingdom of God, to the point where the only explicit role model of a Christian in Scripture is that of a soldier, armed offensively and defensively (Eph. 6:13-17). The testimony and witness of God's ancient heroes is held out to the believer as an incentive to join the fray against the powers of darkness, looking unto Jesus, the author and finisher of our faith (Heb. 12:3).

**HIPPOCRATIC OATH, THE.** Hippocrates, "Father of Medicine," was a Greek physician born on the Greek Aegean island of Cos about 460 B.C., and who died in Larissa, Thessaly, about 377 B.C. He contributed to medicine's ethical and scientific enrichment, freeing it from superstition, "philosophy," and religious rites.

The Oath perpetuating his name appears in writings attributed to him, although some antedated him, and some were possibly added after his death. Elements of the Oath may be late enough to be related to the Asclepiads, an order of Greek physician-priests in the hermitage of Asclepiades, a Greek physician who practiced in Rome about 250 years after Hippocrates' death. Interestingly, it was Asclepius, whose Roman name was Aesculapius, of Greek mythology, the son of Apollo and god of medicine, whose staff with a single serpent encircling it is the symbol of the medical profession.

Edelstein suggests the actual dates for the Oath could range from the sixteenth century B.C. to the first century A.D., though he favors a post-Pythagorean era, roughly fourth century B.C., or later. Pythagoras, born at Samos almost one hundred years before Hippocrates, had a special interest in medicine. Edelstein suggests, however, that the Oath reflects views not necessarily those of Pythagoras or the later Neo-Pythagoreans, but views attributed to him by fourth-century writers, such as Plato and Aristotle and their disciples.

Whether the Oath was originally intended for use in family guilds of physicians or, in Edelstein's view, as an "ideal program designed without regard for any particular time or place," over the centuries countless physicians have taken the Oath, although not all schools provide it nor do all graduates elect to take it. Edited versions are used, some omitting references to deities, others the prohibition of abortions.

The original Oath was two-fold: On the one hand specifying the duties of the pupil toward his teacher and kin and to continuing the transmission of medical knowledge; on the other hand, briefly summarizing medical ethics, setting forth rules for the treatment of the sick. While the Hippocratic Oath represents ancient ideals of a fairly small segment of a particular society, it today reflects more a sense of justice rather than contemporary ideas of duty or charity, Christian or otherwise.

*Duties of the pupil toward his teacher.* The pupil promises to regard his teacher as equal to his parents, to share his life with him, supporting him if he should need it. He also vows to hold his teacher's children as equal to his brothers, and to teach them the art of medicine without fee and covenant if they should wish. He promises to impart precepts, oral instruction, and all other learning to his own sons, and to those who have taken the Oath according to medical law, but to no one else.

To understand this passage, we must recall that medicine, like most other ancient arts, was passed from father to son in closed family guilds. When outsiders were admitted, they were expected to participate fully in the responsibilities of the "real" children, defined in the Oath. Aside from the incidental issue of whether guilds themselves were ethically sound, the current significance of this part of the Oath would appear to be limited for purposes of this present discussion.

*Rules concerning poison and abortion.* Most modern interpretations agree that the intent in this passage is to discourage physicians from assisting their patients in committing suicide, and from making criminal attempts on their patients' lives. Apparently, poisoning was frequent in antiquity; laws against it were relatively ineffective, as proof of poisoning required expertise that did not exist.

Abortion was practiced freely in Greek and Roman societies with many physicians prescribing and giving abortive remedies. Greek and Roman law and religion did not protect the unborn child. Ancient religion was as indifferent to feticide as to suicide. The Platonists, Cynics, Stoics, Aristotelians, and Epicureans also condoned or tolerated feticide and suicide. Only the Pythagoreans opposed both, demonstrating their heavy influence on the Oath during its evolution. The Pythagoreans considered it their duty to beget children to provide future worshippers of their gods. They held that embryos were animate beings from the moment of conception, and that sex in marriage was solely to produce children.

Similarly, suicide was a sin against gods who had allocated life and therefore expected it to be preserved. All these beliefs would obviously militate against abortion and suicide on grounds that are not necessarily defensible by those of Judeo-Christian persuasion today, who can respect the fruits of the Oath but cannot defend its roots.

*General rules of the ethical code.* In the first part, mention is made of diet, drugs, and cutting, otherwise designated as dietetics, pharmacology, and surgery. The second part deals with the physician's personal conduct in relation to his patients, with special reference to sexual behavior and confidentiality.

In this section Edelstein perceives the Pythagorean hierarchical medical priorities. Diet was of primary importance for health, drugs secondary, and cutting (surgery) last. They defined bodily appetites as propensities of the soul, cravings for "the presence or absence of certain things" which could grow out of control. The unbridled satisfaction of these would bring forth consequences, such as the illnesses.

Frowning on drugs may hark back to abortive agents, while the clause concerning lithotomy (surgical removal of a stone) may draw a line between different branches of medicine, particularly the practice of "internal medicine" versus surgery. Alternatively, it has been suggested that the surgical prohibition is directed obliquely against castration and the moral problems it raises, whether intentional or incidental while removing a stone from the genito-urinary system. In either case, the intent of the Oath was to ensure that proper expertise be applied with maximum chances of preserving the patient.

Finally, the pleas for justice, sexual continence, and confidentiality are seen as having both a utilitarian and a moral basis. Injustice and mischief-making are to be shunned, and the patient's dignity, reputation, and confidence are to be protected. The physician is to keep to himself all that he hears and sees during the treatment of his patients.

*Comment.* The Hippocratic Oath justly deserves its reputation as a standard of decency in medical practice, even though its origins are pa-

gan, probably rooted in an extinct Pythagorean philosophy. It has no claim to authority, other than its wisdom, at least in parts, as recognized in the light of historic Judeo-Christian teaching. Thus it is treated as current medical sentiment and changed to suit current social standards. Physicians who swear it can suit their practice to acceptable norms, or they may choose not to swear it at all, or having sworn, not to follow through when social pressure to do so is not compelling.

Such a compromise is most obvious in the abortion issue, but applies equally in other ways. For instance, individual interpretations of "what is the good of the sick" or what it means to hold oneself aloof from wrong and corruption is highly subjective. It could be argued that the ethical value of the Oath depends heavily on the prior ethic of the physician.

A physician might ask, "Why should I take the Oath seriously?" considering its ancient roots. The Oath leaves out much that pertains to the personal morality of the physician, as well as to issues in this practice. Clearly, a more comprehensive ethic based on timeless realities and applicable to the continuum of human experience would be more helpful. Christians believe the Judeo-Christian Scriptures provide that ethic.

## Hippocratic Oath

I swear by Apollo the physician, by Aesculapius, by Hygeia, by Panacea, by all the gods and goddesses, that, according to the best of my ability and judgment, I will adhere to this oath and guarantee: to hold the one who taught me this art equally precious to me as my parents; to share my assets with him and, if need be, to see to his needs; to treat his children in the same manner as my brothers and to teach them this art free of charge or stipulation, if they desire to learn it; that by maxim, lecture and every other method of teaching, I will bestow a knowledge of the art to my own sons, to the sons of my teacher and to disciples who are bound by a contract and oath, according to the law of medicine and to no one else; I will adhere to that method of treatment which, to the best of my ability and judgment, I consider beneficial for my patients and I will disavow whatever is harmful and illegal; I will administer no fatal medicine to anyone even if solicited, nor will I offer such advice; in addition, I will not provide a woman with an implement useful for abortion.

I will live my life and practice my art with purity and reverence. I will not operate on someone who is suffering from a stone but will leave this to be done by those who perform such work. Whatever house I enter, I will go therein for the benefit of the sick and I will stand free from any voluntary criminal action and corrupt deed and the seduction of females or males, be they slaves or free. I will not divulge anything that, in connection with my profession or otherwise, I may see or hear of the lives of men which should not be revealed, on the belief that all such things should be kept secret.

So long as I continue to be true to this oath, may I be granted the happiness of life, the practice of my art and the continuing respect of all men. But if I forswear and violate this oath, may my fate be the opposite.

## A Revised Oath

I do solemnly swear by whatever I hold most sacred, that I will be loyal to the profession of medicine and just and generous to its members.

That I will lead my life and practise my Art in uprightness and honour.

That into whatsoever home I shall be for the good of the sick and the well to the utmost of my powers and that I will hold myself aloof from wrong and from corruption and from the tempting of others to vice.

That I will exercise my Art, solely for the cure of my patients and the prevention of disease and will give no drugs and perform no operation for a criminal purpose and far less suggest such thing.

That whatsoever I shall see or hear of the lives of men is not fitting to be spoken, I will keep inviolably secret.

These things I do promise and in proportion as I am faithful to this oath, may happiness and good repute be ever mine, the opposite if I shall be forsworn.

**Bibliography:** Edelstein, L., "The Hippocratic Oath: Text, Translation and Interpretation," in Siegerist, H. E., (ed.), *Supplement to the Bulletin of the History of Medicine*, No. 1, (1943), pp. 1–64; Jones, W. H. S., *Proceedings of the British Academy*, XXXI, (1945), pp. 1–23; *Stedman's Medical Dictionary*, 21st. ed., (1966).

D.H.O.

**HOLINESS.** The common though derived meaning of holiness is purity, integrity, moral perfection, and sanctity. The terms *sanctification* and *holiness* are, for the most part, synonymous. Tension continues as to whether holiness is best defined in negative terms such as "freedom from defect" or in positive terms. While most Christians tend in principle to emphasize the latter, the ways in which the holy life is defined in the practice of specific virtues remains a matter of dispute.

Modern perceptions as to what constitutes the holy life encompass the range of historical misconceptions. Some make special signs or unusual phenomena necessary conditions of higher holiness, though Paul insists that gifts are apportioned by the Holy Spirit and are not obtainable by wheedling God (1 Cor. 12:11). Indeed, he insists not only that no Christian can have all spiritual gifts, but that no gift such as miracles, healings, or tongues is the prerogative of either

every or any Christian. It is clear that "no" is the only possible answer to Paul's rhetorical questions in 1 Corinthians 12:29-30. Thus unusual phenomena may be part of the holy life, but they are not routinely a condition of the holy life.

Another claim which recurs generation after generation is the conviction that holiness and some form of abstinence are inextricably tied together. Individuals and groups have been thought, or they have thought themselves, to be more holy if they practice fasting, infliction of pain or discomfort on themselves, a strict regimen, and abstinence, including celibacy or even abstinence from sex within marriage. Paul probably had such "super-Christians" in mind when he cautioned against unnatural and ego-satisfying practices in 1 Corinthians 7. Monastic and other devotional literature is replete with testimonials that no ascetic ideal of itself produces or sustains holiness. Nevertheless, many who aspire to holiness attest to the legitimate place that self-examination, self-denial, commitment, and sacrifice can have. It is cultic forms of ascetic practices without moral change that prove to be self-defeating (Isa. 1:10-20).

A final misconception is to envision holiness as static perfection, the mirror image of an abstract ideal. Holiness certainly concerns character formation; however, in the Bible holiness is not presented as static perfection. Holiness is not merely a flight into a trans-world state of being. Rather, it is solidly embedded in this world and includes a process of becoming, of development and growth. More than this, holiness is active in the sense of service or ministry. Holy men and women are servants of God, not mirror images of abstract sanctity. There is a distinct contrast between some medieval and modern conceptions of holiness. A pale, drawn, eyes-downcast, madonna-like visage conflicts with the robust character of holiness one finds in prophets such as Amos and apostles such as Paul.

The Old Testament and the New Testament parallel each other as to the meaning of the holy. The holiness of God is His separateness, transcendence, and unapproachableness. He is God, which means that He is not dependent upon the creation for His life. It means also that God is awesome. From this there follows the conception of holiness as moral perfection. These two ideas, otherness and moral perfection, combine in the meaning of the standard Old Testament declarations that God is holy or the Holy One of Israel (Lev. 10:1-3; Ps. 111:9; Isa. 6:3; 41:14; 43:14-15; Ezek. 36:20-23). The New Testament parallels include Jesus' prayers "Holy Father" (John 17:11) and "hallowed be thy name" (Matt. 6:9).

There follows the moral imperative that God who is holy requires holiness in His people: "You shall be holy, for I am holy" (Lev. 11:44, NKJV; cf. Deut. 14:2; Jer. 2:3; Hab. 1:12-13). Peter repeats the demand: "As he who called you is holy, be holy yourselves in all your conduct; since it is written, 'you shall be holy, for I am holy'" (1 Pet. 1:15-16, RSV; note Heb. 12:10, 18-24). In the presence of the holy God, men and women become aware of their absolute profaneness and their need for cleansing and renewal. Holiness is the meaning that is assigned to the term *saints* (Rom. 1:7; 1 Cor. 1:2; Eph. 5:3) whose sanctified lives in the church comprise a holy temple in the Lord (Eph. 2:21).

Christian holiness is uniquely mediator and redemption centered, in contrast to other purely contemplative or ascetic sanctification ideals. Christian holiness is Christ-centered in two crucial senses: Christ is the pattern of holiness and Christ by His cross makes holiness possible for sinners. In both of these senses the Holy Spirit plays the crucial role, in the life of Christ as well as in the lives of Christians.

Firstly, as the bearer of the Spirit or the man of the Spirit, Christ in His humanity marks the onset of the new age and the new humanity. This is the primary and essential meaning of sanctification. Whatever follows in the Christian will be a duplication by the Holy Spirit of the qualities of Christ's incarnate life (Luke 4:18-21; Rom. 8:9-11). Secondly, Christ not only died for all; the death He died amounts to our own judgment of death and death to sin. Paul declares that the all for whom Christ died themselves died in that death (2 Cor. 5:14). This is the root of sanctification: death to sin (Rom. 6:1-11; Titus 2:14), death to the world in its alienation from God (Gal. 1:4; 6:14), and death to the carnal self (Gal. 2:19-20). In the Bible, sanctification is impossible apart from redemption. In practical ethical terms this death means responsiveness to new values in a new realm, which is to say the values of the kingdom of God.

Christ, the bearer of the Spirit, is as well the giver of the Spirit (John 14:26; 15:26; 16:7-14). Holiness defines that quality of life that ensues from the graces of the Spirit. For the Christian, the graces are always Christ-centered, not induced merely by contemplation, ascetic practices, nor simply by response to the numinous. This new reality and new relationship with God are the meaning of the metaphors that describe the presence of the sanctifying Spirit in each Christian's life: each Christian is baptized in the Spirit (Acts 2:38; 1 Cor. 12:13), sealed by the Spirit (Eph. 1:13-14; 4:30; 2 Cor. 5:5) and indwelt by the Spirit (Rom. 5:5; 1 Cor. 3:16). Essentially these terms all mean the same thing: each Christian is now indwelt by Christ through the Spirit, which reality is the power of the new holy life.

Thus salvation and development, justification and sanctification, Christ's work for us and Christ's work in us, and the once-for-all and progression are linked in the New Testament. There is a striking example of these truths in Hebrews 10. The Christian is sanctified once-for-all through Christ's cross (verse 10). Being related to Christ in this way, the Christian is also in the process of being sanctified (verse 14). The sixteenth-century Anglican theologian Richard Hooker expressed this truth succintly: "the righteousness wherewith we shall be clothed in the world to come is both perfect and inherent; that whereby here we are justified is perfect but not inherent; that whereby we are sanctified, inherent, but not perfect."

Permanent moral change is the indispensible outward mark of holiness and answers to the inner renewal of the heart and will by God. Justification is free but can never be an excuse for license (Rom. 5:1; 6:1). Grace is costly, and the price of redemption ought to be reflected in commitment to a holy life (1 Cor. 6:19-20). In practical terms the fruit of the Spirit and the Christ-like moral virtues coincide as the true description of a holy life (Gal. 5:16-25; 2 Pet. 1:3-11). Entailed are moral purity (1 Cor. 6:9-20), the obedience of faith (2 Cor. 10:5; 1 Pet. 1:2), and the great trilogy of faith, hope, and love (1 Cor. 12:31; 13; Gal. 5:14).

**Bibliography:** Baillie, J., *A Diary of Private Devotion* (1949); Barclay, W., *Epilogues and Prayers* (1963); Hallesby, O., *Religious or Christian* (1954); Tozer, A. W., *The Knowledge of the Holy* (1961).

S.J.M.

**HOMELESSNESS.** In simplest terms, homelessness refers to persons' lack of the kind of shelter that a particular culture judges to be adequate for its members. Narrowly, this definition would apply in the U.S. only to "street people," those without the shelter of any building reasonably well sealed against the elements; while broadly, the definition could include all who do not have the kind of shelter that prompts them to say, "This is *home,* where I feel safe." In this view, the homeless would then include those staying in shelters for the homeless, inmates in prison, and those living unwillingly in grossly substandard housing.

Given this range of definitions and given the difficulty of accounting for all who fulfill any definition, the estimates of the number of the homeless in the U.S. vary widely. The federal government estimates that 700,000 people sleep on the street nightly, while advocacy groups estimate that number to be as high as six million. The U.S. General Accounting Office reports that 310,000 children were homeless in 1989, but to many this figure seems low. Indirect evidence supporting a figure higher than the government's comes from the U.S. Conference of Mayors, which reported an increase in demand for emergency food of 22 percent in 1990 and another 26 percent in 1991, while demand for shelter increased 24 percent in 1990 and 13 percent in 1991. Shelter providers report that the numbers of families with children account for the area of greatest growth in shelter use.

Traditionally homelessness has been thought to be a condition of only the perpetually poor; and some economists and political leaders accept it as natural and an even necessary product of social change and progress. Certainly present economic conditions and the technological changes related to them have brought persons from all socio-economic strata into the membership of the homeless. And financial counselors warn that many today who have run up moderate consumer debt and feel relatively secure are themselves only a few weeks away from being homeless, should they lose and not be able to replace their jobs.

Answers to the problem of homelessness from the perspectives of macroeconomics and government policy are complex and lie beyond the scope of this article, but Scripture can guide the Christian community as it attempts to respond to this evil from the perspective of biblical faith.

While the poor will always be with us, the Lord has commanded His people to be generous and kind. The Old Testament law stipulates that the corners of the fields were to be set apart for gleaning by the poor and that each Sabbath year called for the cancelling of debt and the return of land to the family to which it was given by God. Christ's model prayer emphasizes the forgiveness of debt, any debt, and leads us to ask for forgiveness for ourselves that is proportional to that we give to others.

Christians must not fall into the worldly trap of dismissing their need to be generous and kind by judging that the poor are poor because they deserve to be poor, or that the homeless are without roof because of their lack of planning. Lazy hands and lovers of pleasure will often become poor or hungry (Prov. 10:4; 21:7; 2 Thess. 3:10), but properly diagnosing the immediate cause of such problems does not substitute for a ministry of mercy. Besides those poor or homeless because of their lack of diligence are the many who experience economic reversals or sickness through no fault of their own. We are warned against rejecting or mocking any of these (Ps. 14:6; Prov. 17:5).

No Christian, rich or poor, is excused from the mandate to assist according to his or her individual ability (Ps. 82:3-4; Prov. 11:25). In 2 Corinthians 8:1-15, Paul encourages the church to lead in helping each other and applauds the grace of the Macedonian churches who gave in spite of their extreme poverty.

Jesus spent a great deal of time on the street. He lived and walked with the poor, and his response to the needy was shown in Matt. 25:31-46 when he promised eternal life to those who helped the least of his servants and rejection to those who would not. Jesus' call to love our neighbor as ourselves underlies the story of the Samaritan (Luke 10:25-37). In it we learn that our neighbor is anyone in need; none are to be excluded from "neighbor;" and that to follow Jesus is to follow the Samaritan's example.

**Bibliography:** Snider, N., *When There's No Place Like Home: An Autobiography of the Homeless* (1991).

See CIVIL RIGHTS; HUMAN RIGHTS; SUFFERING; UNEMPLOYMENT; WORK.

N.S.

**HOMOSEXUALITY.** This term describes the propensity for sexual relations with members of one's own sex. It can be found among both males and females, but in the instance of females is often described as lesbianism, a term that comes from *Lesbos*, the ancient Greek island inhabited solely by women.

Although there is much more open discussion about homosexuality in the twentieth century than in previous times, there is sufficient reference to it in ancient documents to indicate how long a history it has had. Plato's *Symposium* is an example of how widely known and accepted was the love of man for man among the ancient Greeks. Although its references are critical, the scriptural record provides further evidence that homosexuality is not a modern phenomenon.

The frequently used synonym, *sodomy*, comes from the apparent homosexual activity among the men of Sodom (Gen. 19), and the Holiness Code's strictures were severe enough to suggest that the need for this discipline may have been great, with nothing short of the death penalty being imposed (Lev. 18:22; 20:13). Although some scholars question these references as evidence of Old Testament judgment on homosexuality, the traditional interpretation fits Judaism's general teaching on sexuality. This teaching understood sexual intercourse as not only a way of expressing a loving relationship, but also as a divinely appointed way of creating new life (Gen. 1:28). The judgment on Onan for spilling his seed on the ground was because of the value that Hebrew tradition put on semen as the source of life (Gen. 38:10).

New Testament teaching is just as negative. In 1 Corinthians, for example, Paul condemns male prostitutes and homosexuals (1 Cor. 6:9-11). He also judges it as unnatural in the first chapter of his epistle to the Romans (1:24-32). Homosexuals are included elsewhere among the immoral persons who, Paul says, deserve judgment by God (1 Tim. 1:10). These references are important because they show how all New Testament teaching about homosexuality is critical. There is no example in it of approval, acceptance, or even tolerance.

Throughout Christian history this disapproval has continued to be the case, with church attitudes varying in the severity of their judgments on homosexuality but not in the negativity. In the patristic era, for example, freedom from homosexuality was seen as a mark of the Christian's ethical superiority to the wanton way of life that converts had left. In this period, sexuality was generally viewed as an example of fleshly inferiority to the spiritual ideal that Christians should seek, and it is not surprising that sexual deviation received no word of approval. Monks were thus taught not only to avoid the sexual enticements of women, but also of other men. Basil of Caesarea instructed them to answer other men with downcast eyes so that they might not be allured by gazing at the face of a potential male lover.

During this period, the Pauline understanding of homosexuality as unnatural gained increased authority. John Chrysostom condemned it as a vice by which a man lost his true masculine nature or else debased it in a way contrary to God's design. Patristic references, like scriptural ones, were directed, however, to the practice of homosexuality, not to the desire itself. There was no condemnation of the person who kept this propensity in check, Christian judgment instead being imposed strictly on those who yielded to its pressures. There was no discussion of this distinction, but the various references indicate the thinking of the writers that it is a certain kind of behavior that they are condemning.

In the medieval period, more attention was given to justifying this condemnation on theological grounds. Thomas Aquinas elaborated how an act, to be natural, must serve the end which is natural to it. A natural end for sexual relations must include having children, since the fertilizing of the ovum by semen is a necessary possibility of sexual intercourse. It may not occur, but it must nonetheless be intended by the man and woman, at least to the extent of not interfering with its possibility. Homosexual relations cannot be natural, therefore, since they are an indulgence of lust that does not permit the sex organs to be used for their natural end. Penalties for such homosexual acts as mutual masturbation was imposed in the laws regulating monastic communities, and penitential codes affecting secular clergy and laity also included penalties for homosexual acts.

In Protestant countries, homosexual behavior became a criminal matter as the government took on more responsibility for regulating private behavior. Buggery became a capital offense in England in 1533 and remained a crime in Britain, as it did in many Western countries, until well into the twentieth century. Perhaps as a result of such hazards, homosexual behavior was driven underground, and in the modern period there was little reference to it until the mid-twentieth century. It became known as "the vice that dare not be named." Oscar Wilde's imprisonment and disgrace as a homosexual in the late Victorian era seems to have resulted partly from his determination to publicize what his generation preferred to keep hidden.

As a result, it was commonly assumed that homosexuality was an infrequently found deviance, known but seldom discovered. At the beginning of World War II, United States army authorities could thus claim that only a minuscule number of personnel were involved. The Kinsey report on sexual behavior among males, however, rebutted that claim by quoting a significant number of interviews in which the man reported to having one or more homosexual experiences. A second Kinsey report on sexual behavior among females indicated how widespread lesbianism was among women.

The Kinsey reports were harbingers of a growing desire in the West, especially in North America, to discuss sexual matters openly, free from the inhibitions of previous times. This led to both political and church authorities reviewing the assumptions of legal codes and Christian teaching on homosexuality, one result of which was a widespread willingness to reform the laws affecting homosexuals.

In several countries, legal penalties against homosexual behavior were modified so that relations between consenting adults in private ceased to be subject to legal penalties. Britain, the United States, and Canada were among the Western countries that made major changes in their law codes affecting homosexuals. It became widely acknowledged that an act might be considered a sin by the church, but need not be thought of as a crime by the government. It was also felt that homosexuals should be freed from the threat of blackmail, exploitation, and unemployment through their sexual behavior being treated as criminal.

With such thinking, most churches either agreed or passively accepted. Most have not, however, significantly changed their teaching on homosexual behavior, except to accept more clearly the distinction between a person having a homosexual orientation and his indulging in homosexual acts. It is now more readily appreciated that a person should not be condemned for an inclination that may be part of him, even though he may be judged for yielding to what most Christian thought still regards as not only deviant but unacceptable.

Most churches have not moved in the direction of approving homosexual behavior as an alternative for Christians. These have not provided for a rite of homosexual marriage, nor acknowledged the right of clergy to have homosexual relations if they wish. In spite of some theologians arguing that mutual love can mean that a homosexual relationship is not sinful, most churches have not responded by making significant changes in their teaching or policies.

On the pastoral side, however, there is a greater desire to minister to homosexuals who wish to find release from this inclination. The behavioral and medical sciences have not yet found a definitive explanation for homosexuality, nor any certain treatment that can lead to a homosexual changing his behavior. But they have attempted to promote the concept of the homosexual as a person who is not necessarily sick nor evil, and who may behave acceptably in every other way. Because of this pressure from behavioral and medical science, the churches are thus generally less strident in their condemnation of homosexuality and much more positive in their pastoral concern for the homosexual, although they still generally condemn the behavior as unnatural and sinful.

To add to their general disrepute, homosexuals have more recently been accused of transmitting AIDS (Acquired Immune Deficiency Syndrome) by having allegedly contaminated the entire blood transfusion system in Australia. The United States National Institutes of Health have reported that in Central Africa, however, almost all cases of AIDS in the region have been transmitted by heterosexual activity. While homosexual men predominate among the seven thousand or so individuals who have fallen victim to AIDS in the United States, with fewer than 150 cases being reported at the time of writing among American heterosexuals, the pathological picture is somewhat different in Haiti, where both homosexual and heterosexual transmission have been documented medically. AIDS would thus appear in part to be yet another disease that can be transmitted sexually, with the homosexual element of the population being at greater risk.

**Bibliography:** Bailey, D., *Homosexuality and the Western Christian Tradition* (1975); Edwards, J., "Eros Deified," *Christianity Today,* May 27, 1991: 14-15; Pittenger, N., *Time for Consent* (1974); Stott, J., *Involvement, Vol. II: Social and Sexual Relationships in the Modern World* (1985); Thielicke, H., *Ethics of Sex* (1978).

See ACQUIRED IMMUNE DEFICIENCY SYNDROME (AIDS); KINSEY REPORT; LESBIANISM; SEXUAL MORALITY AND PERVERSIONS.

R.F.S.

**HONESTY.** This term, which describes moral uprightness, is derived from the Latin *honor,* meaning "a mark of respect" or "token of esteem," which would be bestowed upon persons or inanimate objects. In Roman religious usage the word referred to offerings made to deities or the performing of due rites and ceremonies. The noun *honestas* denoted respectability, esteem, and probity of character, as demonstrated in both public and private life.

Honesty can only be articulated properly against a recognized background of truth, which furnishes the requisite ethical and moral standards. Secular society establishes behavioral codes in certain areas, and these enable honesty to be evaluated pragmatically. The New Testament teachings demand that believers live honestly in word and deed, as people whose lives are under public scrutiny (Rom. 12:17; 13:13). All pretense, guile, and hypocrisy came in for severe condemnation by Jesus (Mark 2:27; 6:14), who himself set an example of honesty before God and requires the same of his followers.

**HONOR.** Derived from the same Latin root as "honesty," the word follows more closely the meaning of its linguistic progenitor in pointing to acclaim, glory, high esteem, respect, or exalted position. Honor is bestowed upon individuals or groups and sometimes on inanimate structures when they are dedicated for a particular purpose, especially that of commemoration.

Honors have been conferred upon worthy people for many centuries, and in ancient Hebrew law the people were commanded to honor their parents (Exod. 20:12) if they wished to prosper in the homeland. Kings and famous persons (Esth. 1:4; Dan. 4:36) were accorded the honor due their positions, while God's personage was marked by glory and honor (1 Chron. 16:27). Jesus claimed honor from God (John 8:54), but warned his disciples that a prophet has no honor in his homeland (John 4:44). Paul taught that God's gift of eternal life would come to those who in patient witness were seeking glory, honor, and immortality (Rom. 2:7). Rulers are to be given the loyalty appropriate to their office (1 Pet. 2:13, 17); servants are to respect their masters (1 Tim. 6:1), believers are to prefer one another in courtesy and honor (Rom. 12:10), and husbands and wives are required to behave similarly (1 Pet. 3:7).

**HOPE.** Hope can be defined as expectation that has its roots in confidence and desire. While hope may often be presented as an abstract category, in practice it is seldom thought of in an isolated context. Hope normally has an object in view, which may vary from sheer physical or emotional survival to the acquisition of some special object or the attainment of a particular goal. To be realistic, hope must be sustained and enriched by a degree of trust, whether in some metaphysical force or in one's ability to achieve the objective in view. Hope is one of the creative properties of a healthy, purposive personality, and in sick persons the emergence of a sense of hope for the future is an important sign of healing.

In the Old Testament, the hope of God's ancient people was grounded upon the conviction that the mighty Creator of the universe was also the Lord of human history. He was the hope of Israel's ancestors (Jer. 50:7) and would continue to be (Joel 3:16) as long as his people were faithful to the covenant. The righteous person could therefore look with confidence to God for protection and blessing (Ps. 71:5; Jer. 17:7). Yet not all human expectation was matched by prompt fulfillment, and the Hebrew sage noted in a celebrated proverb the frustrations experienced under such conditions (Prov. 13:12).

In the New Testament God continued to be the ground of the believer's hope (Rom. 15:13). The indwelling Christ was affirmed by Paul as the hope of future glory (Col. 1:27). The hopelessness experienced by unbelievers can be transformed by the atoning blood of the cross (Eph. 2:12-14), bringing spiritual peace and the reconciliation of the sinner with God. On this basis the

Christian can live in the full assurance of hope until death (Heb. 6:11). There is also a hope that belongs peculiarly to the worldwide community of Christians, namely that at Christ's second coming to judge humanity, the Christian church will be saved for eternity because of the hope laid up for the believer in heaven (Col. 1:5). The evangelistic witness of the Christian requires each one to be able to speak rationally and persuasively about his or her hope of salvation in Christ (1 Pet. 3:15).

**HOSPITALITY.** This term normally describes the cordial invitation to food and shelter that is extended by a host to a guest. Hospitality was an important feature of ancient Near Eastern life, where travel was attended by constant hazards. Scripture contains numerous allusions to the treatment of guests by hosts, such as footwashing and the preparation of a choice meal (Gen. 18:1-9), the kissing of a guest (Luke 7:45), and the anointing of the head with oil (Luke 7:46). Strangers and friends alike were accorded a welcome, but guests were expected to behave considerately, without abusing the privileges of hospitality.

The word itself occurs only in the New Testament, in the Greek form of *philoxenia,* "love of strangers," and in all instances expresses the typical generosity of ancient Near Eastern culture toward travelers. The Christian is instructed to manifest a hospitable disposition (Rom. 12:13) and to be ungrudging in dispensing such generosity (1 Pet. 4:9). Bishops or overseers in the primitive Christian church were required to be hospitable (1 Tim. 3:2; Titus 1:8). The English term is derived from the Latin root *hospes,* "a host," "one who entertains a stranger," and thereby extends *hospitalitas.* Closely related is the *hospitium,* a lodging or inn where guests were cared for, which became the basis of a peculiarly Christian institution, the hospital.

**HOUSEHOLD CODES.** Every community, including the household, needs rules by which to regulate its life (Judg. 21:25). The reasons are not only psychological and sociological, but also, and basically, theological. The Christian household will follow the divine moral law, which Scripture depicts as a schoolmaster who leads people to Christ (Gal. 3:23—4:7). Christian parents are responsible by God's authority for creating household rules that form their children's thinking and habits, making them harmonize with God's known will (Eph. 6:1-9; 1 Tim. 3:4). Some regulations are necessary because of the fallenness of human nature (Rom. 7:7-25; 1 Tim. 1:9-11,); others are simply agreed-on or designated ways of cooperating in the home, in the power of the new nature in Christ (Rom. 12:9-11; 15:2; 2 Cor. 4:17; Gal. 6:2, 10; Eph. 4:22-24; 5:2).

God uses the regime of law, beginning with household codes, to lead persons to understand and receive His grace. Law both teaches standards and reveals sin. It leads under God to repentance and atonement through the cross, by faith in Christ. No law, no grace. Both Old and New Testaments bear this out. The widespread experiences of permissiveness and gracelessness in society attest to the truth of this dictum. Household codes generally are not written down though in some instances it would be useful if they were.

A most important code is that by which the spouses in a family (and other elders, either related or not, if there are any) agree to make executive decisions. The procedures adopted affect the tone of the entire household. While it is the Christian father's divinely designated responsibility to be "head," the *style* of headship that he exhibits and is able to execute depends on many factors. These include the ambient culture, his own intelligence, and the intelligence and leadership ability of his spouse and older household members. Whether or not the executive head is present, it is the duty of all household members to support and encourage each other in observance of the family code: little children by obedience, mature members through willing collaboration and appropriate guidance to those less mature.

Examples of matters beyond the moral law that require regulation in the Christian household are: mealtime, manner of saying grace at meals, family prayers, bedtime, bathroom times, use of television, church attendance, dating, noise control, invitation of guests for meals and overnight visits, ways of managing conflict, and so on. There is a moral obligation to abide by these ways of living in love together in addition to supporting each other in the observance of the moral law.

**Bibliography:** Bushnell, H., *Christian Nurture* (1979); Curran, D., *Traits of a Healthy Family* (1983); Dobson, J., *Dare to Discipline* (1982); Ginot, H. G., *Between Parent and Child* (1965).

See FAMILY.

D.N.P.

**HUMAN NATURE.** In the history of ideas, a great deal of ink has been spilt over the question, what is a human person? Boethius, a sixth-century Christian philosopher, defined *person* as "an individual substance of a rational nature." This led to an understanding of human nature as something static, formed by and under the control of rational principles. This view is sometimes referred to as a "theory of being" (ontology). Drawing upon Aristotelian ideas in the thirteenth century, Thomas Aquinas followed Boethius's idea and argued for an analogy between the human person and God. All nature, including human nature, was an object of knowledge, therefore we could make certain assumptions about God's nature on the basis of what we know about human nature.

The Bible however, has no theory of being as such. Indeed, it is possible to argue that it talks more of "human becomings" than "human beings." It has a dynamic understanding of human nature, and this is seen in the diversity of terms given to describe anthropology. A number of terms reveal this emphasis upon phenomenology (that is, humanity viewed from the perspective of what we observe). First, humanity is described as standing within the natural order. The Bible speaks of mankind as "flesh" (*basar*); we are made of the "dust of the earth" (Gen. 2:7; cf. Ps. 104:29). The second description is that of man as "soul" (*nephesh*). This interesting word has a number of meanings, its basic meaning being life (1 Kings 19:14). This may be seen in Jesus' teaching about discipleship where the Greek equivalent *psyche* is used: "Take no thought for your life [psyche], what you shall eat or what you shall put on" (Matt. 6:25). Both *nephesh* and *psyche* point beyond man as a physical being and describe him as someone with spiritual needs and drives (Ps. 103:1).

The third term used of man's nature is that of *spirit* (Old Testament, *ruach*; New Testament, *pneuma*). The main thrust of this word is that we are beings who stand apart from the rest of creation because we share God's spiritual nature. Old Testament teaching about this is imprecise; the spirit is usually associated with powerful men like Gideon and Samson (Judg. 6:34; 14:6) or with the prophets (Jer. 1). Ezekiel, however looks ahead to the day when the people of God will have a new heart and spirit (11:19; 36:26). It is left to the New Testament to develop this important anthropology. Paul particularly stresses the spiritual side of man's nature. Indeed, H. W. Robinson declared that Paul's doctrine of the Spirit is "his most important and characteristic contribution to Christian anthropology" (see such passages as Rom. 8:1-7; Gal. 5:16f).

Within Christian thought, however, the term that has reinforced these terms as expressing the idea that mankind is a unique and eternal being is the concept of humanity as the image of God. This mysterious term, which makes its entrance in the opening chapter of the Bible (Gen. 1:26), most probably means that mankind was meant to share God's life, and, alone of all creation can appreciate righteousness, goodness, and love. But all these terms speak of an openness about man's nature; his reach extends beyond his nature. In his mortality he is aware of immortal strivings (Eccles. 3:11), because sin has disrupted the harmonious relationship between God and man. Thus, in Christian thought about man, pessimism and optimism jostle side by side. Mankind can only find the true fulfillment of his nature in God. This, of course, contrasts sharply with the idea of human nature in secularism. There, a great deal of optimism is found concerning man's capabilities, but gross pessimism concerning his fate: no God, no hope, and no eternal destiny.

**Bibliography:** Anderson, R. S., *On Being Human* (1983); Carey, G. L., *I Believe in Man* (1977); Fichter, J., *Man the Image of God* (1978).

G.C.

**HUMAN RIGHTS.** Human rights are morally authorized claims that apply equally to all people by virtue of their being human individuals. The language of rights has been a mainstay of ethical, legal, and political controversy since at least the eighteenth century. Attempts to give political force to human rights have included the French "Declaration of the Rights of Man," the United States Constitution with amendments, the "Four Freedoms," the United Nations "Declaration of Human Rights," and the contemporary movement for legal recognition of civil rights and the rights of such groups as patients and consumers.

Rights are called "human" when they are claims made in the name of morality. They are applicable equally to all, not merely granted by arrangement and agreement. A person can be said to have, for example, the moral right to freedom even if legally it is not respected. Human rights claim to be recognized by all persons, not just by some, and are generally to protect against interference with the individual pursuit of a good, rather than actually entitling one to its possession. Rights generally entail correlative duties; a right to freedom, for example, implies a duty on the part of others not to coerce.

The concept of universal moral rights, like that of the Trinity, appears only obliquely in Scripture. In support of the concept of rights, Scripture speaks of all persons as being equally in God's image (Gen. 1:27) and the prohibitions in the Decalogue against killing, adultery, theft, false witness, and covetousness protect all against such infringements without regard to rank or privilege (Exod. 20:3-17). Biblical references to rights often refer to special rights of individuals in particular contexts (Deut 21:17; Ps. 9:4; Ezek. 21:27; 2 Cor. 10:8; 12:11-13; Philem. 8-14), although the psalmist is assured that "the LORD will maintain the right of the poor" (Ps. 140:12).

Rights are sometimes treated as "trump cards" in sociopolitical debate. The assertion of a putative right that covers the situation in question is expected by the right-bearer to be recognized and to settle the issue. Perhaps in response to the combination of the power and the vagueness of the concept, a minority of moral philosophers from Jeremy Bentham to the contemporary Alistair MacIntyre has been skeptical of rights. Bentham, responding to the French Declaration of the Rights of Man, called the concept "nonsense on stilts," while MacIntyre has called rights "fictions." Yet, there is reason to be concerned that without a place for rights in moral thought and practice, there is scant protection for individuals when their interests conflict with those of the stronger or of the group. In contemporary moral philosophy, rights have won renewed respect, perhaps because of their usefulness in the struggles against oppression and grave need that have characterized the past several decades.

Human rights are the strongest types of moral claim that can be made, because they protect basic goods necessary to living a truly human life. Historically in the Western moral and legal tradition, all people were held to have rights to life, liberty and property, as well as rights derivative of these, such as that to privacy; and this fact was tied in a belief in human dignity. If a human being is to be treated as a person, he or she must be entitled to claim as rights those basic requirements needed to pursue a life of his or her own design and choice. To be at the will of another in these basic areas of human concern is to suffer a serious affront to one's dignity, since it insults and diminishes one's capacity to live as a being who is the equal of others.

The most vexing question in the use of the concept of rights, where the assertion of conflicting claims often becomes heated, concerns how conflicting rights are to be adjudicated. Does the right of a defendant at trial in need of information germane to his case outweigh the right of a newsman to keep confidential his sources? Does the right to life of the fetus outweigh the right of a woman to control her own body? Does the right of the physician to practice his profession as he chooses outweigh a needy patient's right to be treated? Is there any right to a minimal standard of food, clothing, and health care?

Many ways have been suggested to resolve these disputes. One approach would be to ascertain first that the claimed rights are indeed valid, and then to weigh them against one another in terms of seriousness as interpreted as relevance to the basic requirements for human life. A right to life, for example, would outweigh a right to freedom in most circumstances. Christian concerns are relevant here. It is false and misleading to claim that a Christian individual "has no rights," particularly in cases of conflict, although there may well be many circumstances in which one might well choose to waive observance of all that they entail. While Christians should be in the vanguard of concern for the rights of all, a Christian attitude toward one's own rights must be moderated by a love that is willing to consider the needs of others as well as one's own legitimate claims (Phil. 2).

**Bibliography:** Gewirth, A., *Human Rights* (1982); Holmes, A. F., *Ethics* (1984); Lyons, D., (ed.), *Rights* (1979); Marshall, P., *Human Rights Theories in Christian Perspective* (1983); Melden, A. I., (ed.), *Human Rights* (1970); Smedes, L. B., *Mere Morality* (1983); Wolterstorff, N., *Until Justice and Peace Embrace* (1984).

D.B.F.

**HUMAN SUBJECT RESEARCH.** Human subject research is the use of persons as experimental subjects in scientific investigation. Re-search using people in this way is conducted both in biomedical and behavioral science. Biomedical research on persons has been of incalculably great benefit to public welfare, having undergirded the advance of modern medicine and leading to dramatic developments in the diagnosis and treatment of disease, preceding the introduction of such therapeutic innovations as cold remedies, surgical techniques, and the artificial heart. In the social sciences, such research has furnished an increased understanding of individual and group behavior and has led to innovations in intervention and therapy for a variety of behavioral disorders.

Nonetheless, human subject research is presently conducted in an environment that is substantially circumscribed by the imposed restrictions of ethical codes and specific regulations. Research on human subjects is conducted under a manifold of ethical pronouncements as embodied in codes such as the Nuremberg Code and the Declaration of Helsinki. There is also a newly stirred concern for the general situation of patients in the United States as expressed in the Patients' Bill of Rights, which deals with clinical research, among other things. Federal agencies have imposed specific mandates for compliance with regulations protecting subjects.

Human subject research is thus both positively regarded and held in suspicion in modern society. Although before 1960 there was but slight public or legal attention to biomedical research, there now exists a significant body of legal regulation, as well as the attention of such major federal agencies as the United States Food and Drug Administration, the National Institutes of Health, and the Department of Health and Human Services, all of which serve to protect the rights and interests of subjects. How is the anomaly of this positive regard and suspicion to be understood?

Several events have occurred to raise concern about the ethical acceptability of research on persons. The civilized world was horrified to learn in the wake of the Second World War that Nazi political and academic establishments had conducted excruciatingly painful and lethal experiments on their Jewish captives without the slightest regard for their welfare and dignity, a discovery that led to the Nuremberg Code regulating future research. Nazi Germany was not alone in performing such research. Henry Beecher shook the medical world with a 1966 article in the *New England Journal of Medicine* that documented unethical research among prestigious and highly qualified medical scientists.

It has also come to light that the National Institutes of Health conducted a study on syphilis in Tuskeegee, Alabama, in which a group of rural black males were used without their knowledge in a long-term study of the degenerative effects of venereal disease. In the now-famous Willowbrook study in which institutionalized retarded children were infected with hepatitis, it transpires that all the procedures were done without the consent of subjects, nor, it seems, with adequate concern for their welfare. More generally, Bernard Barber found in a study conducted in the 1970s that while a majority of researchers were ethically careful, "inadequate ethical concern" could be documented among a significant minority who posed excessive risk to subjects in relation to expected benefits and who were careless in securing consent.

Such facts bode ill for any attempt to allow human subject research to proceed without some form of public scrutiny and review, although several researchers have objected to such outside attention. Human subject research seems to be ethically questionable in the following ways, thus being liable to lead to unethical treatment of subjects, even by well-intentioned researchers. First, it can compromise the liberty of subjects, either by coercing them overtly or subtly into participation, or by deceiving them to ensure their cooperation. Second, it can threaten a greater or lesser degree of risk or harm to the subject. Third, it can amount to a violation of the researcher's primary obligation to place the interest of the individual patient above other concerns, even scientific ones that promise humanitarian benefit. This is based on the traditional maxim, *primum non nocere* ("above all, do no harm"), which has been interpreted as a prohibition against doing something to the patient not for his benefit.

While it is widely agreed that ethical research on human subjects must proceed with their fully informed consent, some researchers question this requirement, partially because they believe the average subject to be unable to sufficiently understand the research to be able to give consent that is truly informed. Alternative justifications for the practice of human subject research have been advanced, including a utilitarian argument that would justify the use of people in research, even without their knowledge or consent, by appeal to the good to be produced by this experiment. A simply utilitarian appeal will not suffice, however, even on utilitarian grounds, because if done publicly it would bring about such unintended harms as the decrease in trust in physicians and other assaults on the integrity of health care delivery. These would ultimately threaten to outweigh the good produced, and privately would lead to abuse that similarly would threaten to produce more harm than good. More fundamentally, it would violate human rights to the liberty and security of persons.

Justifiable human subject research must meet the following standards: it must be designed to achieve an end that will promote human benefit, must have a favorable likelihood of success, and must seek benefits commensurate with the risks involved. It must be conducted by competent professionals who take care of the interests of subjects and enable them to make well-informed decisions to participate. Subjects must be enlisted with their free consent, based on genuine knowledge of risks and discomforts of the research, as

well as the purposes to be achieved; and these will not be coerced, manipulated, or exploited. Further, special care must be taken when research is conducted on captive populations such as those in prisons, or on the mentally ill or institutionally dependent, because of the great potential for abuse.

**Bibliography:** Beecher, H. K., "Ethics and Clinical Research," *New England Journal of Medicine*, 274 (1966): 1354–60; *Daedelus*, Spring 1969, vol. 98; Fletcher, D. B., "Ethical Aspects of Human Subject Research in Biomedicine," unpublished Ph.D. dissertation (1984); Katz, J., *et al*, (eds.), *Experimentation with Human Beings* (1972).

D.B.F.

**HUMANAE VITAE.** *Humanae vitae* is the Latin title of "The Encyclical Letter of His Holiness, Pope Paul VI, on the right order of the procreation of children," which was published on July 25, 1968, in the Vatican and sent to all parts of the Roman Catholic Church. Because it opposed all forms of artificial birth control, it caused intense discussion and disagreement within the church. There are three parts to the Letter.

In Part I the Pope acknowledges that married couples, who collaborate freely and responsibly with God the Creator in the duty of transmitting human life, face special difficulties in the modern world. In short, they face the question: Has the time not come when the size of families should be regulated by human will and intelligence, making use of artificial techniques, rather than through the specific rhythms of the parents' bodies? To this and like questions the Pope claims that there are answers within the teaching of the church—teaching that is based on the natural law as illuminated and enriched by the light of divine revelation.

Part II begins with a summary of the sanctity and purpose of marriage before teaching on responsible parenthood is presented. It declares: "God has wisely ordered the laws of nature and the incidence of fertility in such a way that successive births are already naturally spaced through the inherent operation of these laws." It proceeds to require that "in any use whatever of marriage there must be no impairment of its natural capacity to procreate human life." Thus all forms of artificial birth control, together with abortion and sterilization, are condemned as against God's (natural) law. However, it is affirmed that "the Church teaches that married couples may take advantage of the natural cycles immanent in the reproductive system and use their marriage at precisely those times that are infertile, and in this way control birth." The Pope recognizes that this is a teaching that is not easy to follow, but he claims that "by vindicating the integrity of the moral law of marriage, the

Church is convinced that she is contributing to the creation of a truly human civilization."

Part III is entitled "Pastoral Directives" but begins with an acknowledgment that to obey the divine law requires of married couples both the recognition of the true blessings of family life and a complete mastery over themselves and their emotions. Self-denial or self-discipline has many good effects, including the fostering in husband and wife of thoughtfulness and loving consideration for one another. Following this important emphasis, there are appeals to rulers of nations, scientists, educators, Christian husbands and wives, doctors and nurses, and bishops and priests to take this teaching seriously and seek to implement it.

Popes since Paul VI have endorsed this teaching. In the Western world however, theologians have opposed it and many laity apparently have ignored it. Thus it has caused great divisions between Roman Catholic academic theologians and the hierarchy, and some believe that it has caused a loss of membership for the Roman Catholic Church in North America.

**Bibliography:** Curran, C. E., "Moral Theology in the Light of Reactions to *Humanae Vitae*" in *Transition and Tradition in Moral Theology* (1979); Selling, J. A., "The Reaction to *Humanae Vitae*" (S.T.D. thesis, Catholic University of Louvain, 1977); Hildebrand, D. Von, *The Encyclical "Humanae Vitae": A Sign of Contradiction* (1969); Smith, Janet, *Humanae Vitae: A Generation Later* (1991).

P.T.

**HUMANISM.** Historically, humanism is associated with the Renaissance, a period of learning that originated during the second half of the fifteenth century in Europe and came to be centered chiefly in Rome, Venice, and Florence. This revival of humane learning embraced not only the fine arts and classical literature, but also the natural sciences and morals. It was humane in that the rebirth emphasized a concern for human values and emotions as exemplified in the arts and in society, building upon one aspect of the medieval nature-grace scheme. Mankind was seen as the source of virtue, and also as the discoverer, in both the scientific and geographical senses. It was a rebirth in that both the case and, partly, the effect of this movement lay in the revival of the classics. With this, naturally enough, there went a rekindling of interest in the classical languages and in Hebrew, in the successful search for Latin manuscripts, in the formation and growth of libraries, and in the beginning of textual criticism. Renaissance humanism was thus very largely an academic movement of educators concerned with the renewal of the curriculum, of textual scholars, and of both musical and visual artists. In education, the place of grammar and rhetoric was constrasted favorably with the logic and metaphysics of the scholastics.

The revival of interest in the classics and in classical languages gave birth almost incidentally to a renewed study of the Bible in its original languages and to an interest in translating it into the vernacular languages of Europe. This was coincidental with, and an undoubted spur to, the progress of the Protestant Reformation in Europe, with its emphasis upon *sola scriptura*, the supreme authority of Holy Scripture. Erasmus (1461-1536) exemplifies both the extent and the limits of the influence of such humanism. He was a man of letters, not a theologian, who remained throughout his life a loyal but not uncritical member of the Roman Catholic Church, and who saw the Christian church primarily as an agency for the promotion of moral goodness. He was appalled by its then-current grossness and superstition, and was an advocate of such reforms as would bring it back to what he saw as its true purpose. His work as a Bible translator was but one aspect of this. He stopped short, however, of the thorough-going Augustinianism of Martin Luther, with its biblical emphasis on the bondage of the will to sin, the necessity for the return to purity and power of the biblical gospel of justification by faith alone, and the program of church reform that commitment to the supreme authority of Scripture entailed.

Besides the influence of humanism on the Reformation in the ways indicated, it is noteworthy that several of the Reformers, such as John Calvin were educated as humanists or under the influence of humanism. Later humanists such as Ramus (1515-1572) exercised some influence in the development of the theological methods of Reformed theology.

In its more modern usage, humanism has its roots in the Enlightenment of the eighteenth century. According to this usage human beings are not simply a chief source of value, but the only source; and people must be set free from the thralldom of every authority except their own theoretical and practical reason. While in the first instance not explicitly secular and atheistic, this humanism was thoroughly this-worldly. God was thought of in deistic terms, as the creator of the regular-running physical cosmos, or as made in the image of mankind and who will act to rectify present moral evils. The extent to which this anthropocentrism can partly be laid at the door of Protestant pietism is debatable and debated, but the influence of pietism upon a key figure such as Immanuel Kant (1724-1804) is undoubted. In its further more self-consciously developed form, secular humanism, humanism takes more extreme positions. The universe is not created, but exists as a brute fact. Mankind is a part of nature. The species *homo sapiens* is not made in the image of God, and does not contain a divine spark. Science, including the social sciences, provides the only route to knowledge of the universe. Mankind's end lies not beyond the universe, in the knowledge and service of God, but solely in some form of self-realization. These tenets conceal various differences among humanists, chiefly of a moral and political kind. Such humanism could without exaggeration be called a religion in that it claims that its tenets express basic or ultimate truths about the nature of reality.

While the sources of secular humanism lie in the Enlightenment, various other historical movements may accurately be called humanistic; and these also, in a measure, have contributed to the modern view. Among these are the humanism of Ludwig Feuerbach (1804-1872) and Karl Marx (1818-1883), claiming that mankind is dehumanized by circumstances, either individual or social and economic. As a result of this, the people concerned seek relief and compensation in the rejection of a mythical fantasy world from their false-consciousness. It is the job of a truly scientific philosophy to rid him of this, which it can only do, according to Marx, by a revolutionary overthrow of these circumstances that lead to the creation of the myths. Jean Paul Sartre (1905-1980) claimed that his secular existentialism was a species of humanism, and many psychologists and psychoanalysts work within a humanist framework.

Apart from its general anti-supernaturalism, secular humanism does not entail one definite ethical position. Some humanists, despite their scientism, believe in free will while others are determinists. Some are individualistic and libertarian, while others are socialists. At its most secular and militant, humanism campaigns against religious influences in state agencies such as state education. Others support the freedom of church and state and public life in general. In these areas and others such as movements to secure the freedom of the press, freedom of information, and civil liberties humanists are often found joining forces with some Christians. Such campaigns are frequently conducted by humanists for several reasons, not all of which are compatible. Some stress a libertarian, laissez-faire approach while others favor a greater degree of influence for centralized, state institutions. Some claim that capitalism tends to the maximization of human liberties, while others argue that the dehumanizing effects of individualism and capitalism must be transformed by a socialist revolution in which people become what they are not at present, truly themselves. But what unites these diverse movements and emphases is the conviction that mankind itself is the source of those moral values in terms of which human society is to be ordered, and that there is no higher source of human value, either in God or in some transcendent realm. More radically, humanists in effect deny mankind's fallenness, asserting innate goodness and self-sufficiency of the specis instead, while conceding that barriers, either social, individual, or both, exist that prevent its full-flowering.

Despite important differences, it can be seen from this that there are important lines of continuity between the humanism of the Renaissance and that of the Enlightenment, notably in an almost exclusive preoccupation with this world and the possession of general optimism about human powers and virtues.

What are the points of contact between humanism, whether Renaissance or secular, and Christianity? Besides the obvious ways in which Christians and humanists may find themselves in alliance over concrete political and social issues, there are at least two ways in which it makes sense to speak of a Christian humanism. According to Christianity, mankind is made in the image of God, and therefore any movement of thought that does not do justice to mankind's embodiment in physical flesh, to human rationality and moral agency, and to individuality may be said by a Christian to be dehumanizing. Christianity stresses that mankind is not a part of nature in the sense that human life can be explained wholly in terms of the laws of physics and chemistry, but rather it is unique in being made in God's image, in righteousness and true holiness. But the values in question—righteousness and holiness—are not the creation of mankind, they are derived from God; and true humanity is to be found in a renewal of the divine image in the knowledge and service of God through Jesus Christ. For a human being true liberty, knowledge, and wisdom lie in the service of God.

A second point of contact between humanism and Christianity lies in the recognition that the confession that the eternal Son of God became flesh, taking a fully human yet sinless nature is, central to the Christian faith. God became man, identifying Himself with His creation for the purposes of its redemption. Furthermore, the Christian church confesses that Christ is now seated in power at the Father's right hand, having elevated human nature to glory. From these two truths, mankind made in the image of God and God incarnate in Jesus Christ, it is clear that there are no grounds from within the Christian faith to justify any dehumanizing practices, whether it be medieval asceticism or the exploitation of child labor in Victorian England, which have often had the explicit, and more often the tacit, approval of Christians. There are no grounds for supposing that the Christian faith devalues or debases human nature. But at the same time it judges that the failures of humanity are due ultimately not to environmental factors, genetically based malformations, or plain ignorance, but to sin, that is, rebellion against the Creator. The Christian faith sees the gaining, or rather re-gaining, of true humanity not as a process of amelioration, but as a crucial result of the work and the Spirit of Jesus Christ, the God-man. Nor is such Christian humanism to be construed in individualistic terms. God's purpose in Christ, the second Adam, is the creation of a new humanity, a new family with Christ as its head.

**Bibliography:** Ayer, A. J., (ed.), *The Humanist Outlook* (1968); Blackham, H. J., (ed.), *Humanism* (1968); Cassirer, E., Kristeller P. O., and Randall, J. H., (eds.), *The Renaissance Philosophy of Man* (1948); Jaeger, W., *Humanism and Theology* (1943).

P.H.

**HUMANITARIANISM.** This word, which is closely related to the Latin word *humanitas*, "human nature," "the condition of being mortal," describes the ideology that is devoted to human welfare and that strives accordingly to improve the conditions under which people live and work. Humanitarian concerns include the support of causes such as famine and disaster relief, the provision of medical assistance to underprivileged nations, work among refugees, and the establishing of overseas agrarian projects, to name a few activities.

While some of these are the work of secular organizations, the Christian church has long been prominent in humanitarian endeavors and was working among deprived people in foreign lands on a missionary basis long before the earliest secular humanitarian societies were organized. The evangelical outreach of Christianity demands that the believer must take the gospel message "into all the world," in a mission of preaching, teaching, and healing (Matt. 28:19-20), bringing God's justice and peace to humanity. Many missionary Christians have made the supreme sacrifice in order to carry the gospel of Christ to their fellow human beings and thereby have demonstrated the highest order of love toward them (John 15:13).

**HUMILITY.** This word, which means "meekness" or "lowliness of mind," has itself a rather humble derivation from the Latin. Its root is *humus*, meaning "the ground," and hence the noun *humilitas* meant "nearness to the ground." For the Romans *humility* understandably carried negative connotations with it, such as shallowness, meanness, insignificance, and abjectness. Among the Greeks, humility (*tapeinophrosune*) fared even worse, being regarded as a servile characteristic exhibited only by slaves and women. The coarse, brawling, sensuous Greeks dismissed humility as an effeminate attribute that was unworthy of a virile male.

In the Old Testament humility was often associated with affliction, which brought a person into a low condition of life (Deut. 8:2-3). Humbling oneself through fasting (Ps. 35:13) was sometimes adopted as a spiritual discipline in Israel. But in the main the humble were the destitute, poor, underprivileged of the land for whom humility possessed no virtue whatever.

The teachings of Christ encouraged the faithful humble to believe that God would exalt them in due time (Matt. 18:4; Luke 14:11), and our Lord's mother was a significant example of God's power to achieve this transformation of roles (Luke 1:52). By his death Jesus gave a completely new meaning to humility. Although he was God, he humbled himself to the level of a human slave and was obedient to his Father's will up to the very point of death on Calvary (Phil. 2:8). Christ's saving atonement converts not merely individuals, but even the very words of human speech. *Tapeinophrosune* is no longer an effeminate, nondescript quality of life, but one of the supreme elements of Christ's character. The concept of humility has been transformed completely from the submissive attitude of a slave by one who suffered a slave's death. He exalted lowliness of mind to high virtue because of his obedience to God's will and demands as a consequence that his followers be "clothed with humility" (1 Pet. 5:5).

As with so many other facets of life, humility needs to be assessed carefully because there is a false as well as a true variety. Thus for a reasonably gifted person to pretend that he or she is unable to perform certain tasks or to achieve a particular level of proficiency when it is well within his or her competence to do so is not merely false humility, but also constitutes hypocrisy and lying. True humility for the Christian demands a proper confrontation with reality so as to avoid prevarication or false pride in the matter of "lowliness of mind." Probably the best definition of humility was supplied by Paul when he urged believers not to think of themselves more highly than they ought to think, "but to think soberly, as God has dealt to each one a measure of faith." (Rom. 12:3, NKJV). In their struggle to grow in the grace and favor of Christ, this kind of humility is made incumbent upon all believes without any exception.

See MEEKNESS.

**HUNTING.** Hunting is most commonly associated with the pursuit and either capture or slaughter of various types of animals. The kinds of hunting that have provoked ethical comment, and even spirited opposition, are those sometimes known as "blood-sports." Those persons who are persuaded by notions of the innate sanctity of all life forms feel it a fundamental violation of ethics for such life to be taken, whether out of necessity or for other reasons. Curiously enough, such persons entertain a double standard of values, esteeming mammalian life superior to vegetable life, and therefore preferring the latter for human sustenance in apparent unawareness of the fact that in the process of ingestion, a different form of organic life is still being taken.

Those who are governed by biblical principles, however, point out that part of the human mandate over nature is the use of the animal and vegetable creation for food (Gen. 2:28-29). Where the hunting of animals is a necessity for human survival, it can surely be no more unethical than the plucking of a fruit from a tree or the uprooting of a legume from a garden. Ethical considerations do enter into the matter, however, when persons, in the name of "sport," engage in the wanton killing of animals or birds with no other thought than the achieving or surpassing of a "quota." Poachers who slaughter wild animals or birds, especially if they endanger the survival of the species in the process, are displaying wanton disregard for human responsibilities toward God's creation, as well as being frequently in serious violation of civil statutes. Killing wild animals for any purpose other than for food or for maintaining human livelihood is difficult to justify ethically, unless it constitutes an officially authorized and executed form of population control that is essential for maintaining a proper ecological balance. Even the latter type of activity meets with vigorous opposition from time to time by well-intentioned but otherwise poorly informed persons.

Within recent years there has been a spate of opposition to the use of animals for hunting and killing other animals, especially where horses and hounds, or harriers, are used to hunt rabbits, hares, and foxes. In Britain, anti-blood-sport pickets have taken to harassing the hunters and spreading false animal scents so as to confuse the hounds, thereby thwarting the success of the hunt. It is difficult to know if those who are picketing really have the welfare of animals at heart when they save some and disable others, or whether in fact the motivation is much deeper, consisting of a "class" protest by persons who feel deeply inferior socially to the ladies and gentlemen who are elegantly attired in hunting pinks and mounted upon horses.

Hunting to hounds has been a popular sport in wealthy circles in Britain for centuries and in the United States since colonial times, although in both countries it is carried out nowadays on a greatly reduced scale. Even centuries ago in Britain, hunting had its detractors, such as the well-known Dr. Samuel Johnson. this taciturn individual, who loved to pontificate on all sorts of subjects, is reported to have delivered himself of the following aphorism regarding fox hunting: "It is very strange, and very melancholy, that the paucity of human pleasures should persuade us ever to call hunting one of them." Since Johnson was too obese even to mount a horse, he could hardly have been said to be speaking from personal experience.

The unbelievably maudlin sentimentalizing of some animal life in modern times has resulted in an imbalanced, highly emotional view of the original purpose of hunting. Rabbits, hares, and foxes are basically vermin. All are a potential, and sometimes actual, menace to health, especially when their numbers begin to multiply and necessitate control. Rabbits are subject to an illness know as myxomatosis, which in epidemic form decimates the rabbit population. The hare in the United States carries a virus that in humans produces tularemia, an ailment marked by chills, swollen glands, fever, and general malaise. While it is not usually fatal, it can certainly be very debilitating. The fox is well known for spreading rabies, and just as notorious for his predilection for the farmers' chickens, and is therefore a double nuisance. The urbanizing of countries such as Britain has brought about its own form of animal control, so that modern hunts are largely social occasions.

Quite apart from the merits or otherwise of the actual hunt, it is in fact supported by an industry that furnishes substantial employment in its numerous branches. The breeding of hounds, harriers, and hunting horses is a skilled and lucrative business in its own right, to which an enormous amount of time, talent, and experience is devoted. In a day when some breeds of hounds are in danger of following the superb Quarme harriers into extinction, great attention is paid to the purely scientific aspects of breeding and rearing stock.

**HYPNOSIS: LEGAL AND ETHICAL ISSUES.** The term "neuro-hypnotism" was first coined in 1842 by Dr. James Braid, a medical practitioner in Manchester, England. The practice of hypnotic trance inducement was in use, however, at least a century earlier. An awareness of the phenomenon of spontaneous trance dates back to Old Testament times. The present century has been marked by an increase in both the use and respectability of hypnotism as a therapeutic tool in the fields of psychiatry, medicine, and dentistry. In the last three decades hypnotism has also been used to a limited but increasing extent in criminal investigations. Despite their long history and current popularity, however, remarkably little is known about either hypnosis itself (the hypnotic state) or of the means by which it is induced (hypnotism).

Over the years more than a dozen distinct theories have been advanced to explain the workings of hypnosis, and there is still little consensus in the academic literature on the subject. The phenomenon is often popularly understood as a kind of "waking sleep." Physiologically, however, the hypnotic state is in many ways quite unlike sleep. Perhaps all that can be said with certainty is that hypnosis is a process or state of heightened suggestibility that occurs somewhere along the line between full awareness and complete unconsciousness. Precisely where on this line a given individual is hypnotized may depend very much on that person's personality and general openness to suggestion. Where one person hypnotizes another, the relationship between the two will of course be highly significant; although it should not be forgotten that hypnosis can apparently be self-induced or even occur quite spontaneously.

Since the term *hypnosis* only dates back a century and a half, there is obviously no express reference to the phenomenon in the Bible. There are, however, references in both Old and New Testaments to visions and trances being experienced by people who were apparently fully awake at the time (Num. 24:4; Acts 10:3, 10; 22:17; Rev. 1). Modern accounts of waking visions and trances are, however, often treated with suspicion by Christians, at least by many in the conservative Protestant traditions. This is perhaps due to a general unease with the supernatural and a distrust of phenomena that cannot be fully and rationally explained, including hypnosis. Moreover, the Bible contains stern warnings against dabbling in the occult world, and for some Christians hypnotism seems to be one of many manifestation of spiritualism (Deut. 18:10-12).

Both these interpretations may, however, be based on little more than fear of the unknown and a reluctance to admit that the subconscious plays a highly significant role in normal behavior and mental health. Perhaps a better view is that hypnosis is in itself a spiritually neutral phenomenon that may be used for good or evil purposes. Where induced by a hypnotist, attention should perhaps be focused less on the characteristics of the hypnotic state and more on the integrity and motivation of the person conducting the hypnotic session. Provided it is practiced by a reputable medical practitioner for legitimate therapeutic purposes, hypnotism may be of significant benefit to a patient. In addition to its obvious use in hypnotherapy, hypnotism is increasingly being used, for example, in dentistry, as a useful alternative to anesthetic drugs, especially if the latter would cause medical complications.

A more controversial application of hypnotism is in the realm of criminal investigations. Some American police forces, for example, have for many years employed hypnosis as an investigative tool. It is principally used in attempts to obtain information from witnesses who might otherwise be unable to recall either traumatic events in their entirely, or specific details of incidents they have witnessed. There have been a few dramatic illustrations of the possible benefits of such methods. In one much-publicized case, for example, a party of kidnaped schoolchildren was quickly found after a witness recalled under hypnosis the license plate numbers of two vans used by the kidnapers.

A distinction should be drawn, however, between such situations where hypnosis is used simply as a means of obtaining leads for further investigations, and cases where previously hypnotized witnesses and even suspects themselves are then called to testify in a criminal trial. Given that under hypnosis a person may be highly susceptible to suggestions made by the hypnotist, there is a significant danger that memory recall will be altered and a person's subsequent reliability as a witness will be jeopardized. Under Old Testament law considerable emphasis was placed on ensuring the reliability of witnesses in criminal cases (Deut. 19:15-20), and there should be a similar concern for evidentiary safeguards today.

If, however, hypnotism of a suspect or other potential witness holds out the only hope for establishing the truth about an incident, steps should be taken to minimize the risk of recall becoming distorted under hypnosis. These might include keeping a separate record of information obtained prior to hypnosis, using an independant hypnotist (unlike present practices where police officers are sometimes trained to conduct their own hypnosis sessions), and videotaping the entire interaction between hypnotist and subject so that bias introduced in questioning can be subsequently identified.

**Bibliography:** Kroger, W. S., *Clinical and Experimental Hypnosis* (1977); Millard, C. J., *Canadian Criminology Forum* (1982), 4:2, pp. 103–14; Newbold, G., *In the Service of Medicine* (1983), 29:2, pp. 16–20; Orne, M. T., *International Journal of Clinical and Experimental Hypnosis* (1979), 27, p. 311.

C.J.M.

**HYPOCRISY.** Hypocrisy is an act that involves a good deal of pretense, particularly if a person is endeavoring to convey the impression of innocence or virtue in a situation where that is patently false.

The word *hypocrisy* is derived directly from the Greek term *hupocrites,* "an actor," and can be understood against the background of classical Greek theater. There was always an element of unreality in the staged performances, whether they were tragedies or comedies. The actors, of whom there were seldom more than three on the stage at any one time, always wore masks to illustrate the roles that they were portraying. Thus tragedy required serious masks and comedy more amusing ones, but in each case the emotions were exaggerated so that the audience could not mistake the situation. Men always played the parts that had been written for females; and judged by the extravagant characterization and the style of diction in the original, the acting must at the very least have been stiff and perfunctory, which was a far cry from normal Greek life. An actor, therefore, was portraying an artificial situation and ultimately gave his professional designation to other social activities involving pretense or dissimulation.

In the Old Testament, hypocrisy generally implied the practice of deceit or profanity (Prov. 11:9; Isa. 32:6), and this sense was found in the New Testament also. Jesus accused the Pharisees of hypocrisy (Matt. 23:14) and warned his followers against imitating such behavior (Matt 6:2, 5, 10). A more serious condemnation of the scribes and Pharisees was in connection with their role of hindering others from following his teaching (Matt. 23:13).

There is a great deal of hypocrisy in human society, often euphemized as role-playing, and of this the Christian should beware. Christ demands absolute honesty of his followers in word and deed and spurns anything that would turn the divine truth into a lie (Rom. 1:25). Accordingly the Christian must reject hypocrisy in favor of speaking the truth in love (Eph. 4:15) and should be able to demonstrate Christian empathy (Rom.

12:15) instead of presenting a mask to society. The Christian faith is characterized by supreme reality and demands genuine persons, not hypocrites, as its ministrants.

# –I–

**IDEALISTIC ETHICS.** Specifically, idealistic ethics is that ethical outlook derived from or associated with philosophical idealism. According to absolute (as opposed to subjective) idealism, the human mind is not passive in its perception of the world, but is active in the constructing of (or more weakly, in the inevitable interpreting of) the object of knowledge. So while there is a residual sense in which reality is independent of any human mind, such reality is unintelligible and intractable except as it is given sense by the human mind. Such idealism, characteristic of Friedrich Hegel (1770-1831) and his followers, inherits the "Copernican revolution" of Immanuel Kant (1724-1804), in which the human mind, and not the external world, is the epistemological axis, but denies the intelligibility or plausibility of Kant's doctrine of the "thing-in-itself." By contrast with Kant, Hegel gives prominence to the idea that ethics is not an individualistic affair, and that it cannot be divorced from society (because individuals themselves cannot be), nor indeed divorced from the state. Ethics is in its nature, as well as in its application, a collective affair. Hence there is in Hegel, as opposed to Kant, a fusion of individual, social, and political morality, as well as a sense of historical continuity and an awareness of actual moral diversity.

According to idealistic ethics, moral freedom is not to be understood in terms of an individual's ability to do what he pleases (the liberal, laissez-faire understanding of freedom), but as an individual's self-realization that can only be achieved in a definite social and political context. Nineteenth- and twentieth-century idealists such as T. H. Green (1836-1882) and F. H. Bradley (1846-1924), upholding a mild form of Hegelianism, opposed utilitarianism, the idea that moral rightness consists in the maximizing of an individual's pleasure or happiness. Such a view was regarded by them both as individualist and sentimentalist. Rather, since true individuality is constituted by a person's relationship with other persons in society, true ethical fulfillment is necessarily social. Idealists in Britain during this period were generally drawn to some version of welfare socialism, though it is hard to see how socialism is *required* by their moral philosophy. But whatever the variations between different forms of idealism, the stress was monistic—the unifying character of mind transcending mere individual preferences and utilities.

Such a moral outlook finds it difficult to make a place for personal morality and for the possibility of conflict between the claims of the individual conscience and the wider morality. It is also emphatically Pelagian, for moral change is to be achieved through self-effort. Hegel saw this moral change in historical and religious terms, the growth of moral love of the New Testament out of the immoral or amoral ethic of law of the Old Testament. This change corresponded, in Hegel's eyes, to the shift from the legalism of Kant to his own position, but paradoxically Kantian legalism is only avoided, in Hegel's eyes, by an ethic that is embodied in the nation-state.

In a more general sense the phrase "idealistic ethics" may refer to a set of moral standards that are desirable but not at present attained or attainable. Such an outlook would embrace various kinds of utopianism and moral and social optimism, involving, perhaps, the requirement of a radically changed human nature. An ethic that had as its aim universal world peace, or the elimination of meat-eating on moral grounds, for instance, might be regarded as idealistic in this sense. Christian ethics is only idealistic to the extent that the eschatological goals transcend present reality in ways that are at present unimaginable, but which will be attained not through human self-renovation but by divine grace.

**Bibliography:** Bradley, F. H., *Ethical Studies* (1876); Richter, M., *The Politics of Conscience* (1964); Walsh, W. H., *Hegelian Ethics* (1969).

P.H.

**IDOLATRY.** Idolatry literally means "to worship an idol" and is condemned in Scripture as an unwarranted challenge to the uniqueness of the only true God. In theology "idolatry" is viewed as commencing with the Fall. The Fall was an act of rebellion that was man's attempt to dethrone God and substitute himself. "You will be like God;" said the tempter, "knowing good and evil" (Gen. 3:5). The centrality of God was replaced, therefore, by egocentricity. Our world begins and ends with ourselves.

It was therefore inevitable that in the development of Israel's religion idolatry became a major source of conflict. The foundation of the covenant began with Yahweh's insistence that "I am the Lord your God, you shall have no other gods but me" (Exod. 20:1). It is clear from this and other passages of the same period that the worship of false gods was always a problem for the Israelites, although in Israel's eyes their God was supreme and greatest of all. So the elderly Joshua exhorted his people to put away other gods and serve the Lord: "choose this day whom you will serve...the gods of the Amorites in whose land you dwell; but as for me and my house, we will serve the LORD" (Josh. 24:15). Even at this stage of Israel's experience of God, a strong ethical element is discernible in its awareness that to follow Yahweh implied the intention to follow His laws and ordinances. Thus the Decalogue begins by commanding the Israelites to worship Yahweh alone, and then it goes on to outline civil and religious duties binding upon the people of God. It is noteworthy that the second commandment forbids the worship of God under any visible form (Exod. 20:4).

One of the favorite themes of the Old Testament prophets is that there is only one God, Yahweh, and He alone exists and is Lord of all. So Isaiah 44 ridicules the gods of the heathen. In a biting satire on other gods, Isaiah mocks the vain efforts of pagan craftsmen to fashion gods or images. Such practices are delusions and folly. Yet, although this might be the considered verdict of godly men and women of the time, idolatry was a very serious problem separating Yahweh from His people. Jeremiah speaks for the Lord in his condemnation of their rejection of him: "Be appalled...for my people have committed two evils. They have forsaken me, the fountain of living waters, and hewed out cisterns for themselves, broken cisterns which cannot hold water" (Jer. 2:12-13). The book of Hosea, likewise, invokes God's wrath on those who walk after other gods: "I am the Lord your God from the land of Egypt; you know no God but me, and besides me there is no savior" (13:4; see also Rom. 1:18 for another striking condemnation of idolatry).

But what is the meaning of idolatry in our world today? Rebellion against the true God remains at the heart of human sin. Man is, as Luther once said, "incurvatus in se," that is, selfishly inclined toward himself. Modern man may congratulate himself that he has no need for God, but it belongs to his nature to find another object for his worship. If he is not worshiping the true God, he is busy at the shrine of other gods, created after his likeness. Luther's apt phrase, "Der Mensch hat immer Gott oder Abgott" (man always has either God or idol), goes to the heart of our existence. In his Larger Catechism, Luther develops this theme: "That to which your heart clings and entrusts itself, is your God."

In Scripture, idolatry is considered to possess strong ethical consequences. In Galatians 5:20 it is described as one of the fruits of the flesh (see also 1 Thess. 1:9). We must acknowledge that ethical implications are inevitable. If God is Lord, His obligations are total and binding; conversely, if we worship another god or merely ourselves, we will accept the moral norms appropriate to our beliefs.

**Bibliography:** Carey, G. L., *I Believe in Man* (1977).

G.C.

**ILLEGITIMACY.** This term describes a state or condition of being illegitimate, that is to say, unlawful, improper, or irregular. While illegitimacy can be employed to describe acts that are illegal in various ways, its principal usage has to do with children that are born outside a legal marriage relationship. This situation is also known as bastardy, a term allegedly derived from a French word meaning "packsaddle child," which is presumably a reference to the unusual or irregular origin of the offspring.

In the Old Testament, illegitimacy among the Israelites was generally the result of harlotry (Gen. 38:24), although sometimes an act of adultery produced that result, as in the case of David and Bathsheba (2 Sam. 11:5). Peoples of incestuous origin such as Ammon and Moab (Gen. 19:31-38) were regarded as illegitimate, and occasionally the term was applied to foreign nations of dubious origin. Illegitimacy was a serious offense in Israel because it violated the holiness of the chosen people and debased them to the level of the surrounding idolatrous peoples. Accordingly the descendants of the illegitimate child down to the tenth generation were forbidden to enter into the congregation of the Lord (Deut. 23:2).

The only specific use of the concept of bastardy in the New Testament (Heb. 12:8) has to do with the believer's proper response to the chastening that comes from God. It is the sons who have to be disciplined, and those who do not receive such discipline are therefore illegitimate and not true members of the household. The genuineness, legality, and propriety of the Christian experience is thus demonstrated graphically. The Christian doctrine of marriage forbids the procreation of children out of wedlock.

See ABORTION; MARRIAGE; SURROGATE MOTHERHOOD.

**IMMODESTY.** This noun describes something that is indelicate or indecorous because it does not conform to standards of unassuming behavior, propriety, or restrained conduct. Thus boastful statements can be just as immodest as indecent gestures because of their inappropriate nature. Since modesty carries with it a sense of suitability and rightness, immodesty manifests itself at the least as bad taste and at the worst as shameful, imprudent behavior.

Immodesty sometimes exhibits itself as a rebellion against tradition or authority and thus can be seen in indecorous displays of the human body under the guise of entertainment. Where immodesty has obvious sexual overtones it can arouse erotic impulses in certain persons while appearing repulsive to others. It may constitute temptations for the weak, but people who are secure emotionally and resolute in character regard immodesty as a lapse of good taste or evidence of poor upbringing.

Having in mind the possibility of temptation, the New Testament instructs female Christians to dress in a modest, unassuming manner (1 Tim. 2:9), as befits persons whose minds are centered on Christ. Indeed, any form of immodesty is inappropriate for the practicing Christian, since it is antagonistic to the humility and pureness of outlook which characterized the life of the believer's supreme Exemplar.

**IMMORALITY.** This term designates general moral wrong or evil in terms of the violation of established principles or norms that define moral values and practices. In a more specific sense immorality refers to sexual transgressions of various kinds.

In the ancient world sexual promiscuity was common and was encouraged by the licentious cult worship of pagan religions such as Canaanite Baalism. Because of God's desire to keep his covenant people from such morally degrading activities and preserve a sense of holiness and ethical purity in the community, elaborate legislation was enacted (Lev. 18:3-23) which stated explicitly what was acceptable moral behavior and what was not. These rules were still in effect in the time of Christ, and hence his hearers needed no explanation of his strictures against adultery. Christ added a new dimension to immorality, however, by teaching that the motive or thought was the equivalent of the deed (Matt. 5:28).

The immoral behavior of pagans is mentioned many times in the New Testament, and its character can be judged from the list of vices that Paul drew up (Rom. 1:29-31; 1 Cor. 6:9-10; Gal. 5:19-21). Sexual sins are prominent in these listings, including fornication, adultery, lasciviousness, and homosexuality, all of which are attributed to a depraved human nature. By contrast the Christian is to exercise chaste sexual behavior within the context of monogamous marriage and is required to maintain the body as the temple of God's Holy Spirit (1 Cor. 6:18-19).

See ADULTERY; CHASTITY; FORNICATION; HOMOSEXUALITY; MARRIAGE; SEX.

**IMPEDIMENTS OF MARRIAGE.** An impediment is something that hinders or retards activity of various kinds, and a marriage impediment constitutes a condition, circumstance, or situation that prevents lawful matrimony from taking place. Impediments have been established by church law for many centuries and have been adopted, with some modifications, into the statutory law of many civil jurisdictions. The basis of these enactments can be found in such Old Testament passages as Leviticus 18:6-18, which sets out the ancient Mosaic regulations relating to kindred and affinity. The fundamental concern seems to have been the avoidance of genetic damage through inbreeding, and the principles set forth have stood the test of time. The legislation had a sociological intent also, it would appear, by preventing the accumulation of wealth and property by a very few families through intermarriage of close relatives.

Impediments of marriage normally constitute proposed relationships within the prohibited degrees of affinity and consanguinity, and in traditional ecclesiastical marriage ceremonies the bride and groom are required to declare publicly that no such impediment exists. A similar declaration is also usually required at the time that application is made for a marriage license. On this basis the clergyman can officiate in good conscience and cannot be charged with violating the civil law should some impediment be alleged and proved subsequently. Another impediment to a marriage obviously occurs when one party to the proposed union is already wedded to a living, undivorced spouse. Occasionally attempts are made to contract a marriage with some feeble-minded person for a variety of reasons, but many jurisdictions prohibit the insane from marrying.

The sanctity of Christian marriage is such that no impediment of any kind ought to be present. In any event, the marriage relationship is often difficult enough to sustain without the presence of such adverse factors as impediments, however mild or insignificant they may be thought to be. In an ethical and unimpeded marriage, men and women should devote themselves to each other and to God in purity and honesty of heart and mind, so that those whom God has joined may never be parted.

**IMPERIALISM.** This word originated with the Latin *imperator*, "commander in chief," "general," or "emperor," as the title of the supreme commander of the military and naval forces of imperial Rome. The concept of imperialism is older by many centuries, however, having first occurred in fourth-millennium-B.C. Mesopotamia. It originated in the conquest of one city-state by another, and within a few centuries clusters of city-states were living under the control of a central ruler. The ancient Akkadian, Babylonian, and Assyrian empires grew through conquests of neighboring territories, and this pattern was followed throughout the ancient Near East.

Assyria, Babylonia, Persia, and Greece succeeded each other as the mightiest empires of the world, and Rome became the most powerful and extensive of them all. Rome brought the concept of imperialism to its highest point of development, and imperialism was never exceeded by later empires. Colonies in various countries helped the spread of imperialism in ancient as well as in more modern times, and these communities often arose because of the need to expand trade. Some nations become obsessed with the thought of world domination, and thus acquire territory by force, as has been the case with Communist Russia and her satellite states. Other nations such as America build their empires on commercial and cultural foundations without taking formal possession of vast territorial expanses which would be difficult and costly to administer. Imperial tendencies lurk in the minds of many people and result in business, literary, financial, and other empires. They are the product of the same kind of aggressiveness and emotional drive that established the ancient Near Eastern empires and often share the same visions of grandeur. Many modern commercial empires have brought great benefit to society, but all such structures carry with them the seeds of their own decay and need constant internal renewal if they are to survive and prosper.

Christ spoke of heaven in imperialistic terms as a "kingdom" and accordingly urged his followers to seek God's kingdom and his righteousness (Matt. 6:33). In the apocalyptic visions of John, the Lamb of God was described as Lord of lords and King of kings (Rev. 17:14) and would bear that special designation as his title (Rev. 19:16). Entrepreneurial instincts and talents need present no ethical or moral problems for the Christian provided that the dedicated service of Christ is the first and absolute priority in life. This being the case, the Christian can confidently expect divine blessing upon his or her labors for the kingdom (Matt. 6:33).

See COLONIALISM; COLONIZATION.

**IMPULSE.** In its generally accepted sense, an impulse is a sudden, impetuous will to undertake some form of activity without having given the matter proper consideration. The action which results from impulse need not necessarily be wrong, but it is nevertheless deemed inadvisable because it was not preceded by adequate reflection on the matter. Impulses are considered to be generated from emotional surges or mental fluctuations that are poorly understood. For the Christian, impulses can just as readily comprise instant guidance by the Holy Spirit on some matter, although such would appear to one schooled in worldly and materialistic values to be something entirely different.

Impulses need not be as dramatic and spontaneous as they are commonly depicted. They are often the product of latent envy, greed, or longing that has either been suppressed for various reasons or has not been aroused adequately by the appropriate mental or emotional stimuli. Once the latter are present, the latent longing is satisfied by a quick decision which is actually the product of a period of unconscious deliberation. Much modern advertising is designed to "create a need" for a particular product or service, and in consequence much of the "impulse buying" is largely the product of earlier psychological suggestion.

Irrational impulses, quite apart from the possibility of indicating personality disorders, are wrong for Christians to exhibit. The believer is commanded to worship God with the heart (that is, with purpose, intelligence, and will), with the mind (that is, rationally), and is assured that divine peace will follow such activity. Impulsive behavior is generally regarded in Scripture as foolish (Prov. 13:3; 14:16-17), and the advice of an ancient Greek town official to his fellow Ephesians to avoid rash action is appropriate for all Christians (Acts 19:36). Irrational impulses must never be substituted for speedy action in the Lord's service; neither must the impetuous, unguarded word (Col. 4:6) hinder the Christian's witness for Christ.

**IMPURITY.** Impurity constitutes a state of defilement or adulteration, whether of inanimate substances such as materials or of human beings in terms of thought or behavior. However modest the amount of contaminant in a substance, it still conveys a condition of impurity that will impair, if not actually nullify, the use to which the substance may be put. Thus a contaminated lubricating fluid that is introduced into a highly sensitive mechanism can cause serious damage within a short period of time.

If this is true of mechanical contrivances it is even more so with human beings, who already bear the liability of having inherited a sinful nature. To entertain any impurity in thought, word, or deed is to live contrary to the nature of God, whose very word is pure (Ps. 119:140; Prov. 30:5). Jesus commended purity of heart (Matt. 5:8), with the implication that impurity banished the offender from the divine presence. If the believer is to do everything in word or deed to God's glory, as Paul exhorted (Col. 3:17), there can be no place for impurity of mind, since this, according to Christ's teachings, is where impurity originates (Matt. 15:18; Mark 7:21).

**INCEST.** This term denotes sexual relations between persons who, because of family membership, are forbidden such indulgences by law. Modern statutes prohibiting incest are based on Old Testament legislation (Lev. 18:6-18; 20:10-21), which was intended to protect the moral integrity of marriage and family relationships. Consequently incest was defined in terms of a recognized blood relationship of parent and child, brother and sister, half-brother and half-sister, grandparent and grandchild, aunts and uncles, daughters-in-law, and stepchildren. Church law subsequently extended the list to include first cousins, nephews, and nieces. Incest was part of Canaanite sexuality (Lev. 18:24) and was normal in the Egyptian royal household. The ancient Hebrews sometimes recorded incestuous alliances (Gen. 19:30-35; 35:22; 2 Sam. 13:7-14; Ezek. 22:10-11), as did the early Christian church (1 Cor. 5:1-5).

In modern society in the United States, where no uniformity exists among states regarding the kinship degrees of prohibited relationships, two-thirds of reported cases comprise father-daughter incest, and the increasing incidence of the offense reflects the sexual permissiveness of the times. Some social workers have estimated that one in four women and one in ten men have been subjected to incestuous abuse as children. According to statistics, at least 97 per cent of those who molest children sexually are men, three quarters of whom are well known to and trusted by the victim.

These males do not correspond to a stereotype, which makes recognition of them all the more difficult. Thus affectionate grandfathers have been known to take advantage of their relationship with a granddaughter and engage in incestual practices with her. Incest, however, is not confined to males, for mothers and grandmothers also seduce children in the family, although with far less frequency. Females from the age of six onwards are at particular risk of incest, and adolescent girls are frequent targets of sexual abuse by stepfathers or paramours of the mother.

The physical character and severity of the incestual attack will naturally vary with the age and sexual development of the victim and the physical or mental condition of the offender. The female child's position is particularly vulnerable, for not merely does she lose the right to exercise exclusive ownership of her body, but by submitting to the threats of a male who is more powerful physically and socially than she, she lays herself open to repeated abuse for an indefinite period. Because of the consequent sense of frustration and abhorrence, some victims of incest attempt suicide.

All too frequently, complaints by those who have been molested are ignored, hushed up, or greeted with frank incredulity that "such a nice old man as granddad" could possibly be guilty of incest. The same sense of powerlessness that precluded the child from forestalling the incestuous attack in the first place now prevents him or her from obtaining a fair hearing as the result of a complaint. In consequence social workers report a further emotional factor to add to the fear, abhorrence, and revulsion attached to incest, namely a sense of guilt on the part of the victim that arises from the feeling that he or she was the cause of the entire affair. Females especially are said to be prone to imagine that because of their powerless and dependent position in society, they are somehow to blame for the sexual abuse that they have experienced.

Incest is an evil, immoral act that flaunts human lust and defies God's commandments regarding appropriate sexual behavior. It degrades and degenerates the moral values of family life and callously and brutally exploits persons who are helpless to protect themselves. For most incest victims the experience is definitely harmful, although a few who have not been particularly frightened or brutalized in the process have professed to have experienced a certain degree of enjoyment. But for the vast majority, the emotional and spiritual effects are decidedly traumatic and can produce depressive-suicidal reactions, sexual promiscuity, somatic complaints of a gynecological nature, and considerable marital discord in the adult patient. Suggestions that incest may not be harmful come, amazingly enough, from psy-

chiatrists who are treating incest victims.

The feelings of shame and rage that fill the child victims are often projected into adult life, and in some jurisdictions they are finding an expression in legal action against the offender with a view to securing some form of compensation. Fortunately, the recognition of incest as a moral and social problem of the greatest urgency is making it possible for comparatively young victims to be accorded credibility in court. Evidence from such children is being elicited increasingly through the use of dolls with male and female sexual characteristics, which the child manipulates in order to demonstrate to the court the actual nature of the alleged offense. When confronted with this type of evidence the offender not infrequently confesses to the crime, and conviction is the normal consequence.

Not all of these attempts by the victims to gain redress through legal action are successful in their objectives if only because in numerous instances too great an interval of time has elapsed between the alleged offense(s) and the trial itself. On some occasions the outcome of the action is prejudiced because the defendant is in such tenuous mental or physical health that the most that could be expected would be for him to be placed on probation, instead of having to serve a term in prison.

The nature of the offense is so serious that those who are guilty of incest should be punished to the limits of the law. Financial compensation for damages that may have been contingent upon the offense(s) are being sought increasingly by complainants, and for good reasons. Quite apart from the mental, emotional, and spiritual traumata that are well-recognized features of the incest victim's personality, there is the very real possibility that he or she may have contracted herpes, gonorrhea, syphilis, or the acquired immune deficiency syndrome (AIDS) from the person committing the assault.

What has been seen by some as a rather less injurious form of incest is the variety that is indulged in by siblings. This activity can range from mutual fondling of erotic areas as children to full coition as adults; but even this is almost always attended by guilt, often as part of a larger characterological disturbance. While the element of violence may be mitigated, or even absent altogether, the nature of the sexual contact still violates the legal degrees of sexual relationship. The abhorrent crime of incest, which often arises from complex family situations, demands the full weight of legal, moral, medical, and religious sanctions in order to secure the proper punishment of the offender and the rehabilitation of the victim.

**Bibliography:** Bass, E. and Thornton, L., (eds.), *I Never Told Anyone* (1984); Butler, S., *Conspiracy of Silence* (1978); Henderson, J., *Canadian Journal of Psychiatry* (1983), 28:1, pp. 34–40; Renshaw, D. C., *Incest: Understanding* *and Treatment* (1982); Rush, F., *The Best Kept Secret* (1980); Watters, W. W., *Canadian Journal of Psychiatry* (1983), 28:6, pp. 501-4.

**INDEPENDENCE.** This term refers to the modern political philosophy that a nation should govern its own affairs to promote the highest development of its citizens. Following an era of colonial expansion in the 1700's and 1800's, many nations achieved their independence since the beginning of this century.

**INDIFFERENCE.** This term expresses a basic sense of impartiality with regard to particular matters at issue. The individual who manifests indifference demonstrates no observable regard for, or opposition to, whatever is being mooted, and is most probably not genuinely interested in the issue at all. Indifference implies a complete lack of emotional involvement, and this would help to explain the resultant lack of activity. Such neutrality can also be adopted as a means of concealing an individual's real feelings about an issue or as a method of avoiding censure for possibly having made a wrong choice. Indifference is characterized by its apathy or lack of concern and must therefore be distinguished from disinterestedness. This latter term is used to describe those who are not influenced in particular situations by considerations of self-interest or personal bias. In a word, disinterestedness implies impartiality.

In the parable of the Good Samaritan (Luke 10:30-37), Jesus criticized the studied indifference of the priest and Levite to the dire needs of the wounded Samaritan. This parable illustrated Jesus' teaching that where God's kingdom was concerned there could be no indifference. Involvement was mandatory, and those who were not for Christ were against Him (Matt. 12:30). All who hear the message of eternal salvation through Jesus' atoning work on the cross but reject it because of indifference are ultimately enemies of the gospel. The parable of the judgment (Matt. 25:42-46) indicates the seriousness with which God regards indifference to the claims of Christ and the severity of the punishment that will follow.

**INDIVIDUALISM.** This term describes the view that a person exists only or primarily for himself or herself. In moral terms this means that what is right and wrong is determined by such a view of life. Since this outlook on life is endemic, if not dominant, in Western society, it seeps into religious faith and practice. Here it usually manifests itself in a heavy emphasis upon the vertical relation with God ("born again," and so on), with little or no complementary emphasis upon the expression of new life and moral standards in the church and world.

The importance of the individual as an individual is much greater in modern society than it was in ancient times, when membership of the tribe, clan, or race was primary. The concern for the human person as an individual, together with his rights and freedoms, has grown both from the Judeo-Christian tradition and from the Western philosophical and rational tradition. Individualism is the excessive development or exaggeration of this concern and involves the lack of emphasis on the individual as a person-in-community.

In the Old Testament we can see the position of the individual Israelite as a member of the covenant community, gaining his or her position from that membership (Exod. 19:3-6). We can also see that there is a complementary emphasis upon the individual as a person who is alone before God and open to God and thus knows personal guilt and responsibility and can also know a personal calling from God (Deut. 24:17; Jer. 15:17; 31:31-34; Ezek. 18:1-4). Jesus emphasized the value of the individual before and to God (Matt. 6:25-33), taught the need for personal, private prayer and discipline (Matt. 6:5-13), and expected judgment of individual actions (Matt. 25:31-46). Yet He also gathered around Him His little flock of disciples, taught that membership of the kingdom of God is membership of God's society, and said that serving the least of His brethren was to serve Himself (Matt. 10:1-15; Matt. 25:45; Luke 10:1f). Likewise the apostles emphasized the need for personal, individual repentance, faith, and faithfulness (Acts 2:38; 17:30; Rom. 10:9), but complemented it with teaching on membership of the body of Christ, of the household of faith and of the kingdom of God (Rom. 12:4-8; 1 Tim. 3:15). Thus Christian life is personal and communal, not individualistic. Christ is served via the brother and the neighbor, and so self-interest comes last of all. Individualism should not be justified or defended by reference to the Christian tradition.

There is, however, justification of a kind to be found for individualism in parts of the Western intellectual tradition, especially that of the Enlightenment. In fact one of the legacies of the Enlightenment of the seventeenth and eighteenth centuries in Western society has been the great emphasis upon the autonomy of man and his rights and freedoms. This can slip, and has so easily slipped, into emphasis upon self-interest alone. At the other end of the pendulum from individualism is collectivism, which also is a false view of the relation of the person to society. Finally, it is important to recognize that an insuperable problem of a philosophy of individualism is death—the inescapable fate of the individual; the final assault on his freedom and dignity.

**Bibliography:** Carey, G., *I Believe in Man* (1977); Dewey, J., *Individualism, Old and New* (1930); Macquarrie, J., *In Search of Humanity* (1982).

P.T.

**INEQUALITY.** Inequality is an unjust variation with regard to both animate and inanimate phenomena. Objects can exhibit quantitative in-equality in terms of linear measurement, weight, volume, purity, and many other factors. Among human beings the degree of inequality is even greater because of nonquantitative factors that emerge from interpersonal relationships.

While the concept of the equality of all mem-bers of the species *homo sapiens* may be a pictur-esque objective for politicians, social theorists, and others, it is unfortunately unrealistic in prac-tice. Genetic and cultural factors interpose to make it clear that vast differences exist between people, and this makes necessary a careful defi-nition of equality if it is to be true to human expe-rience.

Inequality under the law is probably the most serious handicap under which many people labor, and in some regimes this involves the exploitation of women on a serious scale, particularly if they are accorded few if any natural rights. This latter situation began to be rectified by the teachings and example of Christ, who gave an unprece-dented degree of dignity to womanhood. Paul's teachings showed that sexual inequality is re-moved by Christ's atoning death (Gal. 3:28) and that the previous state of the wife's inequality of standing must be rectified by her husband's love and respect (Eph. 5:25; Col. 3:19).

**INFANTICIDE.** This term normally de-scribes the killing of newborn children or infants, although anti-abortionists have used it in a moral evaluation of the destruction of a fetus by abor-tion. But in this connection, as some ethicists have maintained, a less judgmental and more technically accurate term would be *feticide*. In-fanticide can also apply to the exposure of young, unwanted children by the parents, such as was practiced in ancient Greece and elsewhere, as well as to the sacrificial rites of the ancient Near East by which children were burned as a sacrifice to the gods. In the Old Testament the offering of children to Moloch was emphatically prohibited (Lev. 18:21; 20:2-5; Deut. 12:31; 18:10) because it was grossly idolatrous as well as inhuman and homicidal. Despite this, the detestable practice was still being continued until the period of the exile (Jer. 32:35; Ezek. 16:20-21).

A practical illustration of the value of young life was afforded in the case of Abram's prepara-tion to sacrifice his son Isaac, the long-awaited child of promise (Gen. 22:1-12), where the im-plicit obedience of the father to God's com-mands, rather than the death of the son, was the real point at issue. The high value which Hebrew parents attached to their children (Ps. 127:3; Isa. 49:15) contrasted strongly with the widely prac-ticed infanticide in other nations up to and beyond the early Christian period. Interestingly enough, however, infanticide as a moral problem was not discussed by the New Testament authors.

Infanticide is murder and would thus come un-der the prohibition of murder in the Decalogue (Exod. 20:13). But even in Old Testament times it was distinguished from the kind of condition in which a pregnant woman aborted her fetus as the result of an accident (Exod. 21:22), for which eventually a fine was imposed if the person who caused this accident could be traced. Similar mis-fortunes occur in modern pregnancies, where the fetus is destroyed inadvertently through the mis-use of drugs.

See ABORTION; FETAL RIGHTS; MURDER.

**INNOCENCE.** The Bible knows more than one kind of innocence. Absolute innocence is found in Christ: "He committed no sin; no guile was found on his lips. When he was reviled, he did not revile in return; when he suffered, he did not threaten; but he trusted to him who judges justly" (1 Pet. 2:22-23). This kind of innocence is an example for all believers (v. 21), but in this life it is found only in Christ.

A very different kind of innocence is that of the impotent. There are those who are weak in body or mind and who are unable to perform cer-tain acts of wrongdoing. As regards those acts they are innocent, but their innocence is scarcely praiseworthy. It arises from incapacity rather than from any victory over wrong. It is this kind of innocence we see in childhood. It is beautiful and we do well to be thankful for it. But it is not that kind of innocence to which people aspire who live in a real world where evil is strong.

Sometimes the Bible records claims to inno-cence, as when the psalmist says, "I wash my hands in innocence, and go about thy altar, O Lord, singing aloud a song of thanksgiving, and telling all thy wondrous deeds" (Ps. 26:6-7; also see 73:13). This kind of claim is to be understood in the light of the general Old Testament teaching on the sinfulness of all mankind (1 Kings 8:46; Ps. 53:3). A sense of the universality and the se-riousness of sin pervades the Old Testament, a feature that is noticeably lacking from other liter-atures of antiquity. But sin is not the last word. The psalmist could pray, "Create in me a clean heart, O God, and put a new and right spirit within me" (Ps. 51:10). Innocence must be un-derstood in the light of the goodness of God. He does not leave the sinner alone in his sinfulness, but when he cries out for help, God gives it to him.

In the New Testament the idea of innocence is conveyed by a number of terms. Thus the writers may use *dikaios,* which means "righteous" (Luke 23:47), or *katharos* "clean" (Acts 18:6); they may prefer *akeraios* "unmixed" and thus "pure" (Phil. 2:15), or *athos* "without penalty" (Matt. 27:4). They are if anything even more clear than the Old Testament writers on the un-iversality of sin, for it is central to their preaching that Christ went to the cross to save sinners (Rom. 3:23). Believers are innocent in the sense that they have been forgiven, restored, created anew: "If any one is in Christ, he is a new crea-tion" (2 Cor. 5:17). The powerful, saving, creative work of Christ has brought about a new situation in which sin has been put away, and there is a power at work that enables the believer to walk in new ways (Rom. 1:16; 6:14). Perhaps we could say that the innocence that was lost in the first Adam has been restored in Christ, the last Adam (1 Cor. 15:22, 45).

There is more. In the New Testament there is a strong eschatological emphasis, which means that we are to see innocence not only as a moral quality to some extent achieved here and now through Christ's saving work, but also as something that will be brought to its consummation only when Christ returns. Paul speaks of being "guiltless in the day of our Lord Jesus Christ" (1 Cor. 1:8; see also 1 Thess. 5:23), while Jude has a memorable ascription of glory to "him who is able to keep you from falling and to present you without blemish before the presence of his glory with rejoicing" (Jude 24).

**Bibliography:** Ottley, R. L., *Encyclopedia of Religion and Ethics*, 7 pp. 329–30; Trench, R. C., *Synonyms of the New Testament* (1880), pp. 204–9; Young, F. W., *Interpreter's Dictionary of the Bible*, 2, pp. 704–5.

L.M.

**INSTRUMENTAL GOOD.** An instrumental good is usually regarded as a means of securing some superior form of value and which itself partakes of the nature of goodness in a distinctive manner. In ethical discussion, the higher form of value is often described as intrinsic or essential good, since it constitutes an end in itself. Thus, if God were to be considered in himself as intrinsic good, those means by which such goodness could be sought (as, for example commitment to his will, forgiveness, worship, scriptural study, and the like) would constitute instrumental goods. They would not be ends in themselves, since the intrinsic good is God alone, but would assist as vehicles in the understanding and attainment of the intrinsic good.

Some ethicists have expressed doubt as to whether or not means and ends can be differentiated carefully enough to distinguish between levels of value, but this should present no significant problem for the Christian. Scripture reveals God as necessary being, who by definition is the absolute or intrinsic good. He is the ground of all being; and humanity, as the highest of all his created orders, partakes of the nature of contingent being. God has provided fallen humanity with a means by which eternal salvation can be obtained, namely the substitutionary death of Christ for sinners. This constitutes an instrumental good through which the high goal of attainment to intrinsic value (1 John 3:2) is made possible. The instrumental goods which Scripture commands the Christian to observe (Gal. 5:22-23; Col. 3:12-17) constitute the divinely appointed means by which the supreme value of life

in eternity with God becomes the property of the believer.

**INSURRECTION.** This term is sometimes employed as a description of rebellion in its early stages. As such it would comprise a developmental phase of revolt against established authority which could blossom into wholesale civil war, given the appropriate circumstances. Insurrection may therefore be understood in terms of isolated protest groups which may erupt into violence in an attempt to challenge civil law in some area. If this insurgent movement attracts popular support and becomes truly violent, it could be met by severe reprisals from the authority that is being challenged.

In the time of Christ there were numerous terrorist groups that were attempting to stir up trouble against the Roman occupying forces. The underlying idea seems to have been the overthrowal of the hated ruling nation and the establishment of an autonomous Jewish state. In any event this notion proved to be unrealistic, because the Romans brought an effective end to the state in A.D. 70.

At the time of Christ's trial a man named Barabbas had been one of a group of insurgents (*sustasiastes*) and had been paid for committing murder in the insurrection (*stasis*). To pacify the crowds that were demanding Jesus' death, Pilate released Barabbas and crucified Jesus (Mark 15:6-15). Another turbulent Jewish group made Paul the excuse for insurrection when Gallio was proconsul of Achaia (Acts 18:12). In this case also a limited uprising seems to have been involved.

The Scriptures teach that civil authorities govern by divine warrant (Rom. 13:3; 1 Pet. 2:13-14), and therefore the believer must observe the laws that are enacted. If corrupt governments gain power by default, only passive resistance can be countenanced until the time comes when effective changes can be made.

**INTENTION.** A determination or resolve to act in a certain way; thus both the mind (judging that something is desirable and attainable) and the will (resolving to attain that end) are involved. In traditional moral theology certain phrases have been used to delineate various aspects of intention.

*Actual Intention.* This is the free resolve or determination involving both mind and will, so that what is actually done is influenced by the original judgment of the mind. Thus one may judge that to pray to God in secret is right. One then determines to do so and actually finds a secret place in which to speak to God as person to person.

*Habitual Intention.* This is the continuing resolve of mind and will to act in a way that is desirable, but indicates a failure to put the resolution into definite activity and toward a completion. Thus one may determine to visit a sick person, but for one reason or other never actually reaches that person's house.

*Interpretative Intention.* This describes the intention that would have been made and effected had the full circumstances been known when a decision had to be made. Thus it may be said that one would have been more lenient and understanding with Jack had it been known that he came from a broken home.

*Virtual Intention.* This is a resolve or determination once made that continues to influence action long after consciousness of the original resolution has been lost. Thus one may have intended years ago to say prayers each morning, and how, having got into the habit of so doing, is no longer consciously aware of that original intention.

Today, in the aftermath of the influence of various schools of psychology upon Western culture, it is more difficult to be clear and precise as to the nature of human intention. However, its importance in ethics arises from the generally held conviction that attributing blame for an act ought to take intention into consideration. Thus is one guilty of murder if in seeking to shoot an alligator a man was actually shot instead? One may intend to say a word of comfort to a mourner who may take it as a word of discomfort. Examples could be multiplied. They serve to make us aware that to define intention comprehensively is notoriously difficult.

Bearing this in mind, the Christian begins from the premise that everything about him, including his thinking, willing, and acting is known to God. Further, he knows that all that he thinks and wills and acts is to be guided by God's will and empowered, as well as purified, by the presence of the Holy Spirit. Thus he knows that he is to pray for a pure heart, an obedient will, and wisdom to govern his intentions.

**Bibliography:** Toon, P., *Your Conscience as Your Guide* (1983).

P.T.

**INTERCOURSE.** In the broadest sense this term simply describes communication at any given level. It can be effected between two individuals or between participants in a group meeting. Intercourse can describe the kind of communication that takes place in business or commerce, where people meet in multiples for discussion and decision. At an even higher social level, the term can be used of the intercommunication between the representatives of nations, whether in small units or in an international forum. The essence of intercourse is that there should be more than one person present and that this should be characterized by resultant communication, whether it is ultimately meaningful or not.

Because intercourse is essentially a social act, it has become used increasingly as a term in current speech to describe acts of sexual congress.

This is a particular use of the term *intercourse,* however, and should not be regarded as its basic meaning.

See MARRIAGE; SEX.

**INTERIM ETHIC** (German, *Interimsethik*). The view that much of the moral teaching of Jesus, being influenced by His belief that the end of the world was near, has an emergency character and thus was only intended for the interim period from the time when He spoke until the end. On this basis, the teaching of Jesus is an eschatological interim ethic having no immediate relevance for modern people, who (it is claimed) cannot share the eschatological vision of Jesus. In his *Die Predigt Jesu vom Reich Gottes* (1892) Johannes Weiss put this forward as a doctrine that Jesus taught, namely, that in the expectation of the imminent end, disciples of the kingdom should live wholly by the principles enunciated in the Sermon on the Mount (Matt. 5—7) and therefore give up earthly possessions, positions, and advantages. Albert Schweitzer developed this viewpoint in his *Das Messianitas und Leidensgeheimnis* (1901) and *Von Reimarus zu Wrede* (1906). He argued that Jesus was not a "Weltbejaher" but a "Weltverneiner" (not a "world-affirmer" but a "world-denier"), and that He disassociated Himself from this world and its civilization in order to be concerned for one reality—the kingdom of God. Thus the special and peculiar character of the teaching of Jesus was a negative attitude to family, the state, and property, and a moral position only suitable for a short, interim period.

This extreme way of interpreting the teaching of Jesus has not stood the test of time or scrutiny. Certainly Jesus linked His call for repentance with the arrival of the kingdom, but this does not mean that his teaching concerning the moral life of disciples had only temporary validity. People lost in selfishness and material pursuits need a radical conversion in order to know God truly and discover his will. In fact this theory of the interim ethic makes Jesus into a kind of psychological monster, and his character becomes an insoluble enigma.

**Bibliography:** Filson, F. V., *Jesus Christ, the Risen Lord* (1956); Schweitzer, A., *The Mystery of the Kingdom of God* (1925); *Ibid., The Quest of the Historical Jesus* (1910); Weiss, J., *Jesus' Proclamation of the Kingdom of God* (1971).

P.T.

**INTERMARRIAGE, RACIAL.** Marriage may be described as the union between a man and a woman that is contracted legally and in public for a lifetime. Commonly marriage is solemnized by ecclesiastical ceremonies in a church, chapel, or other appropriate location. One purpose of marriage is to legitimize the birth of children, though of course there are other social aspects that are also in view. In Christian theology the estate of matrimony is the only legal sphere for the exercise of sexual relations.

While both Old and New Testaments stress the permanence and indissolubility of marriage and extol monogamy as the ideal (Gen. 2:24), nothing is said about the union of one person with another of a different race or color. The nature of skin coloration in the ancient Near East being what it was, it is doubtful if interracial marriage posed a serious problem. The ancient Sumerians, for example, were apparently a swarthy, dark-haired people, and using this kind of dark complexion as a standard it would only be in tropical areas of Africa that the significant presence of melanin pigment in human tissues would be noticed.

Even so, this did not prevent Abraham from entering into sexual congress with an Egyptian household servant in order to produce a male child for the family (Gen. 16:4). Similarly, the object of the king's amorous intentions in the Song of Solomon was described in the elegant language of the King James Version as "black but comely" (Song of Sol. 1:5). The so-called white race probably only originated in the Middle Bronze Age with Esau (Gen. 25:25), who was described as "ruddy" or "red." In modern terminology he would be described as a pinkish-white mutation and would be distinctive on that account, hence the mention in Genesis. Royal marriages in Bible times must have occasioned a good deal of miscegenation, to say nothing of the migratory movements in the third and second millennia B.C.

While the Old Testament says nothing that would formally affirm or deny racial intermarriage, the New Testament teaches explicitly that racial differences are meaningless in the fellowship of Christian believers (Gal. 3:28). There is therefore no *a priori* reason why Christians of different racial origins should not marry, if other considerations that are common to all unions have been resolved satisfactorily. But in a mixed marriage there are certain social concerns to be borne in mind that would not apply otherwise, such as the general familial acceptability of an interracial marriage and the reception that would be encountered where local prejudice prohibits racially mixed unions. While the man and the woman might be able to survive social hostility, it would be quite a different matter for any children that they might have. In such a case the best option would seem to involve moving to a community where racial intermarriage is tolerated. At the moment when one asks if such a marriage "ought" to take place, the matter has been removed from the area of emotion and made the subject of ethical decision. The expected future environment will have much to do with determining the nature of the choice, but it is nevertheless a sad fact that a great many interracial marriages encounter friction and hostility, even in supposedly Christian circles.

**INTUITION.** This word is used to describe the instantaneous apperception by the human mind of data, impressions, judgments, and the like, without the necessity of utilizing any intervening ratiocinative processes. While the term originated from the Latin verb *intueor*, used of mental activity to mean "contemplate" or "consider," the modern understanding of intuition emphasizes the strict spontaneity of the response to an appropriate mental stimulus. Since immediacy is the characteristic feature of intuition, it could be assumed that the information intuited has been arrived at without any prior mental conditioning, experience, or knowledge, a position adopted by Hegel. The intuitionism of Plato, by contrast, depended upon the preexistence of perfect forms (ideas) "in the heavens," which humans were able to apperceive by intuition, albeit imperfectly. For Kant, such intuition was limited to concepts of time and space.

More modern studies, whether in ethics or behavioral psychology, have done little to explain the nature and psychodynamics of intuition. The problem that besets the experimental psychologist subsists in the fact that it is virtually impossible to quantify intuition, and this disability renders it less amenable to study by scientific method than is desirable. Such investigation as has been undertaken, however, seems to conflict with the "blank tablet" view of the mind as maintained by the old sensationalists Hobbes and Locke and points instead to some accumulated basis of knowledge that is perhaps lurking in the "unconscious mind."

In the light of the information that the RNA molecule transmits memory, the product of intuition being the result of genetic prompting must now be considered seriously by the investigator. In that event the intuition would be a recall of experience acquired in an earlier generation and would not be totally new and independent of the individual's experience. Intuition is usually credited to persons of an artistic or sensitive nature, but this is not easy to demonstrate experimentally, and in any event such a theoretical base will have to be broadened in the light of genetic knowledge. Women are normally much more amenable to intuition than men, as many a husband can testify to his embarrassment.

Probably the best ancient description of intuitive response based upon divine knowledge is found in the prophet Isaiah: "Before they call, I will answer; and while they are still speaking, I will hear" (Isa. 65:24, NKJV). This verse indicates the working of the divine mind by showing that God apperceives phenomena intuitively as the Supreme Reason.

**ISOLATIONISM.** To be isolated is to be kept separate or placed apart from other persons or things. Isolationism as a political doctrine or policy urges that a particular nation be set apart from all other countries so that it can pursue an independent form of existence. Adopting this doctrine would involve a renunciation of existing commercial ties. Under such conditions, whatever crises might arise in the rest of the world would be of no concern to the isolationist nation, which having stated its position publicly would feel under no obligation to engage in any form of activity that would compromise its isolationist stand. Such a position is attractive to the parochially minded and to those who are intent upon the exclusive pursuit of selfish gain. Isolationism also appeals to those who view altruism as a waste of resources on unworthy people or who themselves are too mean and inconsiderate to help others to bear their burdens.

In practical terms, however, isolationism is an unworkable system, because no nation on earth is sufficiently wealthy or endued with natural resources to be able to stand in splendid isolation from the rest of humanity. The pride and sinfulness of humanity have produced wars (James 4:1), which by their nature and scope have demanded moral action by other nations, who have cooperated as allies in their attempts to bring peace to the situation. To have stood aside indifferently and witnessed one act of genocide after another being perpetrated by a ruthless aggressor would have been to provoke agonized outcries of moral indignation from other nations.

Isolationism is impractical for another reason. While all the major powers of the world are already aligned politically, they still need to trade their resources with each other and literally cannot afford to be totally independent of one another. Only the small nations of the world can afford the luxury of contemplating isolationism as a political policy, but this is largely a dream where it occurs, since because of their smallness such nations depend upon donor nations for much of their existence. Isolationism is therefore an impossibility as long as trading is a necessity. Were any country to adopt that policy wholeheartedly, it would soon find itself in a cultural, industrial, and technological backwater.

In the ancient world Egypt was probably the most isolationist of the high cultures, predominantly for topographical reasons. Yet the Egyptians realized the necessity for trading and for maintaining a political and military presence far away from their national borders. Though they were often prosperous when others were experiencing famine (Gen. 42:2), they still depended heavily upon imported slave labor for their massive construction projects (Exod. 1:9-11). For the Christian evangelist, who is commanded to take the message of salvation throughout the world (Matt. 28:19), isolationism is the enemy of the gospel of Christ in negating all the altruistic values which Christ's atoning work enshrines.

**I-THOU.** This term was made famous by the Jewish philosopher, Martin Buber, who, in his poem-book *I and Thou* (published in 1923), distinguished between two attitudes people can have to the outside world. The first, I-IT, described an attitude of detachment and disinterestedness. That is to say, I may look at the world, or the person that I am talking to, or the work I do, as things that only confront me as objects; they are outside me, and they do not affect my inner being or my real concerns. The I-THOU relationship, however, is an attitude of receptiveness, of commitment and trust, that sees the world, people, and things as being in a close and intimate bond.

On this structure Buber built his ethical theory. He was not opposed to the I-IT approach because, as he saw it, it was necessary for mankind to explore the world in a scientific and disinterested way. But on its own, this approach was not enough for authentic existence. Authentic existence, or the truly human life, may only be experienced in an I-THOU bond with the world around. This alone is the basis for ethics. From this flows human responsibility, love, care, and real communication. Furthermore, through this discovery of trust through commitment, the eternal THOU may be known. Indeed, Buber's complaint about modern life was that by destroying the bond between the individual and the world around, we had cut ourselves off from the living God. We must, he said, begin to penetrate existence by loving. Only then will we find the signs of God there. They are spoken into life and are not above it.

Buber's thought has had a profound influence upon existential thinkers, as well as upon some Protestant theologians, including Reinhold Niebuhr, Paul Tillich, and Karl Barth.

**Bibliography:** Brunner, E., *The Divine-Human Encounter* (1943); Erickson, M., *Christian Theology* Vol. 1 (1983).

G.C.

# -J-

**JEALOUSY.** This term describes an emotional reaction of passionate envy in connection with persons or things. It is mentioned frequently in the Old Testament, generally in a negative context (Prov. 6:34; Song of Sol. 8:6), although in reference to God it describes his determination to keep his people to himself, untainted by contact with heathenism (cf. Zech. 1:14; 8:2). In the Decalogue the divine claim to be a "jealous God" (Exod. 20:5; 34:14; Deut. 4:24) may not imply a zeal for the spiritual integrity of the Israelites so much as the affirmation that God is a deity who maintains his own rights within the framework of the covenant relationship. In that event the reciprocal nature of the Sinai agreement (Exod. 24:3-8) is incorporated into Israel's founding legislation.

Jealousy was feared in Old Testament times because of its destructive character (Num. 25:11; Ezek. 25:23). It was particularly dangerous when it manifested itself in a mentally deranged personality in the form of homicidal tendencies, as with King Saul (1 Sam. 18:11; 19:2; 20:33).

In New Testament times it was the jealousy of the religious leaders in Jerusalem that caused Jesus to be arrested (Matt. 27:18). A similar reaction was experienced by the Jewish leaders in Antioch during the visit of Barnabas and Paul (Acts 13:45-50). The "jealousy" (*zelos*) of 2 Corinthians 11:2, KJV, should be more properly rendered by "zealous," as the Greek word implies.

**JESUS, ETHICAL TEACHING AND EXAMPLE OF.** The necessary framework for understanding the ethical teaching of Jesus is the proclamation that dominated His ministry from beginning to end: "The kingdom of God [or heaven] is at hand." This was the message He began to proclaim when He came into Galilee after the imprisonment of John the Baptist (Matt. 4:17; Mark 1:15). Matthew's Gospel represents it also as the message He gave to His twelve disciples to proclaim on their first missionary circuit among "the lost sheep of the house of Israel" (Matt. 10:6-7). Luke mentions the same formula in connection with the activity of seventy other disciples whom Jesus sent ahead to prepare His way as He journeyed from Galilee to Jerusalem (Luke 10:9, 11). Later, as Jesus and His disciples approached Jerusalem, some naturally concluded that "the kingdom of God was going to appear immediately" (Luke 19:11). It is to this message that the Gospel writers are referring when they use such expressions as "the gospel [or good news] of the kingdom" (Matt. 4:23; 9:35; 24:14; Luke 4:43; 8:1; 16:16), "the gospel of God" (Mark 1:14), or simply "the gospel" (Mark 1:15; 8:35; 10:29; 13:10; 14:9).

The centrality of Jesus' proclamation of the nearness of the kingdom of God means that the rest of His teaching—including His ethical demand—was based on the assumption that very soon, God would inaugurate a new age in which He would rule the world directly and immediately. Everything evil would be destroyed, and God's will would come to perfect realization on earth. In a word, Jesus' vision—and therefore the foundation of His ethics—was eschatological (from the Greek word *eschatos,* "last"). He invited His hearers to live every day as if it were the last day of their lives.

The ethical imperative based on the nearness of the kingdom of God in Jesus' proclamation was, "Repent" (Mark 1:15; Matt. 4:17; see also Mark 6:12; Matt. 11:20-21/Luke 10:13; Matt. 12:41/Luke 11:32; Luke 13:3, 5). The call to repentance was already central in the proclamation of John the Baptist (Mark 1:4/Luke 3:3), and Matthew attributes to John the same formula Jesus used: "Repent, for the kingdom of heaven is at hand" (Matt. 3:2). The repentance that John demanded was to express itself in specific actions, those who heard him were required to "produce fruit worthy of repentance" (Matt. 3:8/Luke 3:8). He said that "every tree that does not produce good fruit is cut down and thrown into the fire" (Matt. 3:10/Luke 3:9). Luke's Gospel includes several examples of such "fruit": those who have extra food or clothing must share with those who have none; tax collectors must not collect more than is their due; Roman soldiers must be content with their wages and not extort money from civilians entrusted to their care and authority (Luke 3:10-14).

Jesus too is represented in the Gospels as requiring "fruit" from those who responded to His proclamation (Matt. 7:16-20; 12:33-35; Luke 6:43-45; John 15:1-17), and it is likely that the specific examples attributed to John the Baptist were His as well. But in several ways His ethical teaching went further and deeper than that of John—at least to the extent that John's teaching is preserved and known from the Gospel tradition. First, Jesus refers to "fruit" (presumably the fruit of repentance) not as something important for its own sake but as an index to the state of a person's heart (Matt. 12:34/Luke 6:45; see also Mark 7:15/Matt. 15:11). This may have been implicit in the teaching of John as well, but Jesus makes a special point of it. Second, Jesus placed love, and most remarkably the love of enemies, at the very center of His ethical teaching.

Both of these tendencies are present in the most extensive collection of Jesus' ethical teachings to be found anywhere in the New Testament, the "Sermon on the Mount" (Matt. 5—7) as well as the briefer "Sermon on the Plain" (Luke 6:17-49). These somewhat parallel discourses are noteworthy first of all for the way they begin. Before confronting His hearers with any kind of ethical demand, Jesus first addresses them with a series of blessings, or Beatitudes (Matt. 5:1-16), or with a two-part series of beatitudes and woes (Luke 6:17-26). In either case the principle is maintained that radical grace, the grace of the kingdom of God, precedes the radical demand for repentance and a life pleasing to God. The Beatitudes are not primarily a call to the hearers to be poor in spirit, mourners, meek, hungry for justice, merciful, pure in heart, peacemakers, and persecuted for the cause of justice; they are rather a word of consolation to all who, out of whatever circumstances or necessity, already are those things.

Matthew's Beatitudes can be divided into two groups of four, each group ending with a reference to "justice" or "righteousness." The focus is on those who "hunger and thirst for justice" (Matt. 5:6) and on those "persecuted for the cause of justice" (5:10). Both sets are in the third person, but in verse 11, there is an abrupt shift to the second person: "Blessed are you...." The effect is to link the hearers (understood as Jesus' disciples, vv. 1-2) closely to the persecuted prophets and righteous of Israel's past (vv. 10, 12). Jesus' disciples are here identified as those who have enemies, who suffer at their enemies' hands (v. 10), and who consequently cry out, like the sufferers in many of the Psalms, for justice and vindication (v. 6). As "salt of the earth" and "light of the world," they bear their testimony to all people (Greek, *anthropoi,* vv. 13b, 16), the natural enemies of the kingdom and the King they represent (vv. 13-16). Jesus connects this testimony with their "good deeds" (v. 16), but the good deeds are not defined or specified until the section that follows (vv. 17-48).

The heart of the ethical demand of Jesus in Matthew's Sermon on the Mount is found in the six so-called "antitheses" of 5:21-48. This section is as close as Jesus comes in the Gospels to an ethical system or a formal set of moral requirements. He takes as His starting point the Jewish Scriptures, or "the law and the prophets" (v. 17). On the one hand He affirms without qualification the absolute authority of the written text of Scripture (v. 18), but on the other He claims for Himself an absolute authority over this written text as its supreme interpreter ("It has been said.... but I say to you," vv. 21-22, 27-28, 31-32, 33-34, 38-39, 43-44). Obedience to the Scripture so interpreted ("one of the least of these commandments," v. 19) is the core of Jesus' ethic and the way of entrance into the king-

dom of God. This higher justice (justice surpassing that of the scribes and Pharisees, v. 20) is immediately set forth in the antitheses of verses 21-48. Though not every antithesis focuses on the love of enemies, the unifying theme from the reinterpretation of murder in verses 21-26, to the section on nonretaliation in verses 38-42, to the explicit final command in verses 43-48 to "love your enemies," is the proper response of a disciple of Jesus toward "those who denounce you and persecute you and say all kinds of evil falsely against you for my sake" (v. 11).

Jesus' reinterpretation of the sixth commandment of the Decalogue, "You shall not kill," is more than simply an internalization of the command. He does internalize the command in verse 22 by equating murder with an attitude of anger toward one's brother or sister in the believing community, but He goes farther. Not only the inward attitude of mind, but a careless or destructive word such as *fool* (Aramaic, *raka*) is tantamount to the taking of a person's life. It matters not only what is in one's heart but how the heart's attitude expresses itself in speech and action (Matt. 12:32, 34, 36).

Jesus extends the interpretation yet another step in verses 23-26: not only anger or a destructive word, but the failure to take positive steps toward reconciliation, is the same as murder. This is true both within and outside the community of faith. Jesus requires of those who would be His disciples that instead of treating their brothers and sisters as enemies (vv. 23-24), they treat even their enemies as they would their brothers or sisters (vv. 25-26). This imperative of reconciliation He expresses first in the form of a possible real-life situation in the Jewish community (vv. 23-24), and then in the form of a brief parable in which the command is depicted as an example of prudence, a swift accommodation to the practical realities of a situation (vv. 25-26; Luke 12:57-59).

The reality of which the parable speaks is the theme of Jesus' ministry, the imminent dawning of the kingdom of God. "The kingdom is at hand; there is no time to lose!" Jesus' hearers must make peace with their enemies before it is too late, or they will find that the kingdom of God means for them judgment instead of grace. This appears to represent Jesus' interpretation of what it means to "repent" in view of the kingdom's approach (see also the parable in Luke 14:31-32 about a king preparing for war). You must, He says, make your peace first with God, the invading "enemy" whom you have long displeased, and second with your human enemies. You must never ask where the responsibility for reconciliation lies, for it always lies with you. Failure to seek that reconciliation makes you no better than a murderer!

The antitheses continue with prohibitions of two kinds of aggression of a man against a woman: lust and divorce (5:27-32). The violent invasion of a woman's person implicit in the male lust that Jesus condemns can be seen in the parallel between the right eye (the instrument of lust) and the right hand (the instrument of violence) in verses 29-30. In a somewhat different vein, the prohibition of oaths in verses 33-37 alludes to possible courtroom situations in which oaths served as weapons against legal adversaries. But the centrality of the command to love one's enemies becomes explicit only in the last two of the antitheses, with the principle of nonretaliation in verses 38-42 and the explicit love command in verses 43-48.

The command to "love your enemies" is particularly striking in contrast to instructions in some forms of sectarian (not orthodox) Judaism to hate those who do not belong to one's own faith community (e.g., the command in the Qumran Manual of Discipline [1 QS 1.9-10] to "love all the children of light"—the members of the community—and to "hate all the children of darkness"—the outsiders). What is also striking is that the sweeping summary command to "be perfect, as your heavenly Father is perfect" (Matt. 5:48) is given precisely in connection with the command to love enemies. Luke bears this out with his corresponding command, "Be merciful, just as your Father is merciful" (Luke 6:36). The love of enemies is the heart of what Jesus understands to be the very imitation of God Himself. The love of God for His enemies is illustrated in Matthew's Gospel from the sphere of the natural creation: God shines the sun and pours the rain on good and evil people alike (5:45). But Paul, in the Epistle to the Romans, makes the point more emphatically and in the sphere of redemption: "For one would scarcely [have to] die for the sake of a righteous [innocent] person—though for a good person someone might conceivably dare to die; but God commends his love to us, in that while we were still sinners, Christ died for us. How much more, then, being now justified by his blood, we shall be saved by his life! For if, when we were enemies, we were reconciled to God by the death of his Son, how much more, being reconciled, shall we be saved by his life!" (Rom. 5:7-10). The heart of the Christian gospel, for Paul, is that God loved His enemies, and that the enemies whom He has loved are none other than those now reconciled to Him, the Gentile Christian communities to which Paul ministers. Though Paul does not immediately draw the implication that those so loved must in turn love their enemies, he comes to this implication quite clearly seven chapters later (Rom. 12:17-21).

The requirement that Jesus' disciples love their enemies is, if anything, even more conspicuous in Luke's Gospel than in Matthew. After the beatitudes and woes (Luke 6:20-26), instead of a measured interpretation of the Jewish law by means of six antitheses (as in Matt. 5:17-48), Luke represents Jesus as coming immediately and intensely to the single supreme command: "Love your enemies, do good to those who hate you, bless those who curse you, pray for those who denounce you. When someone strikes you on one cheek, turn the other also, and when someone takes away your coat, do not withhold your cloak" (6:27-29). The same theme continues as far as verse 36, the Lukan parallel to the command to be perfect in Matt. 5:48, and beyond that to verses 37-38, paralleled somewhat later in the Sermon on the Mount in Matthew 7:1-5. The material in Luke 6:27-36 corresponds not to the six antitheses of Matthew 5:21-48 as a whole, but to the last two in particular (5:39-48, focusing exclusively on nonretaliation and the love of enemies) and, briefly, in verse 31, to Matthew 7:12 and what has come to be called the "Golden Rule": "And treat people just the way you want them to treat you."

For Matthew, this principle (essentially the equivalent of the love of one's enemies) summed up "the law and the prophets," the Hebrew Scriptures in their entirety (5:17-20, 7:12). Though Luke does not link the ethical teaching of Jesus to the Scriptures in the same explicit way, he achieves much the same result in another passage in which Jesus shows an inquiring scribe the way to eternal life (Mark 12:28-34/Matt. 22:34-40/Luke 10:25-28). In response to the scribe's question, Jesus asks, "What is written in the Law? How do you read it?" (Luke 10:26). The scribe replies with words drawn from Deuteronomy 6:5 and Leviticus 19:18: "You shall love the Lord your God with all your heart, and all your soul, and all your strength, and your neighbor as yourself" (Luke 10:27). Mark 12:29-31 and Matthew 22:37-39 are similar except that (a) they distinguish between love of God and love of neighbor as the "first" and "second" commands, respectively; and (b) they attribute the statement of the two commands of the law to Jesus Himself rather than to the inquiring scribe. And in Matthew alone Jesus adds, characteristically, "On these two commands depend all the law and the prophets" (22:40). Luke, however, appends to the incident a further exchange between Jesus and the scribe, an exchange found in no other Gospel, in the form of a parable. The scribe, "seeking to justify himself," pursues the matter with the question, "Who is my neighbor?" (Luke 10:29), and Jesus uses the parable of the Good Samaritan (10:30-37) to define the neighbor precisely as one's enemy, exemplified in the case of a Jew and the hated Samaritans. By means of this parable, the scribe's reading of the law is reinterpreted and radicalized as if to say, "You shall love the Lord your God with all your heart, and all your soul, and all your strength, and all your mind, and your *enemy* as yourself." Though Luke perhaps does not emphasize quite as strongly as Matthew (or Mark) the continuity between Jesus' ethic and that of the Hebrew Scriptures, he stresses even more than they the centrality of Jesus' command to love enemies. The theme is least evident in Mark's Gospel, in all likelihood simply because Mark gives the least attention to Jesus' teaching, and has no equivalent to Matthew's "Sermon on the Mount" or Luke's "Sermon on the Plain."

If the love of enemies is central in the ethical teaching of Jesus, it is natural to ask what Jesus meant by this command and how He intended it to be realized. It is hard to imagine love for one's enemies in the sense of natural (or supernatural) affection, or deep emotional attachment. Such affection would tend to contradict the initial premise that they are enemies, or, if it did not, would appear to give evidence of something bordering on masochism. The enemies are specifically defined in the relevant contexts as "those who hate you," "those who curse you," "those who denounce you," and "those who persecute you" (Matt. 5:43; Luke 6:27). The focus of Jesus' pronouncement is not on good or loving *feelings* but on *actions*. (Curses or physical abuse do not make even a saint feel good or loving!) The imperative, "love," is immediately explained by the imperatives that follow: "pray for" in Matthew; "do good," "bless," and "pray for" in Luke.

The larger context (preceding in Matthew, following in Luke) provides specific illustrations of the behavior Jesus has in mind: turning the other cheek when struck by one's enemy, or giving up one's possessions or one's personal freedom to an aggressor (Matt. 5:38-42; Luke 6:29-30). The principle that comes to expression here is that of non-resistance or nonretaliation. Those who intend to live by the ethics of Jesus must not return evil for evil, or meet force with force (especially Matt. 5:39: "Do not resist the evil person"). The principle applies to real-life situations in the physical world; in a different setting, where spiritual warfare is in view, the Epistle of James (ascribed to Jesus' brother) contains the admonition, "Resist the devil, and he will flee from you," framed by commands to "Be subject, therefore, to God," and "Draw near to God, and he will draw near to you" (James 4:7-8). But in Jesus' perspective, the imminent coming of the kingdom of God means that the protection of those who belong to God, and the punishing of their adversaries, is in God's hands. For Jesus' followers to retaliate when they are wronged, or to contend for their "rights," or even defend themselves against unfair treatment, is in His eyes neither necessary nor appropriate.

This principle, so conspicuous in Jesus' teaching, is echoed in other parts of the New Testament. The apostle Paul, in his epistle to the Romans, when he finally comes to discuss the ethical implications of God's love and redemption of his enemies, writes, "Do not return evil for evil to anyone....do not take vengeance, beloved, but leave room for the wrath, for it is written, 'Vengeance is mine, I will repay, says the Lord.' No, if your enemy is hungry, feed him; if he is thirsty, give him a drink, for in doing so you will heap coals of fire on his head. Do not be overcome by evil, but overcome evil with good" (Rom. 12:17, 19-21). Paul highlights the link between the command to love enemies and Jesus'

proclamation of the nearness of the kingdom of God with his reference to the eschatological "wrath" of God that will punish the evil oppressor and vindicate the oppressed. He also makes the point that nonresistance is itself a way of resisting evil: to retaliate in kind is to adopt the oppressor's evil standards, and so to be overcome by evil; the only way to resist evil effectively and legitimately is to return good for evil. Even though Paul does not refer explicitly to a saying of Jesus, his argument in this passage represents the earliest known interpretation of Jesus' command to love one's enemies, earlier in fact than any of the Gospels. The sayings of Jesus found in the Gospels, moreover, suggest that the implications Paul has drawn from Jesus' words are valid ones.

The principle of nonretaliation is demonstrated not only in the teaching of Jesus, but in His behavior as well. The testimony of all the Gospels that when he was arrested, interrogated, and executed by His enemies, He made no attempt to resist, is all the more remarkable in view of the conviction of the early Christians that He was the all-powerful Lord and Son of God. When His disciples (in the face of His consistent teaching) tried to defend Him with the sword against the Roman soldiers who had come to arrest Him, in three of the Gospels He restrains them (Matt. 26:52-54/Luke 22:41/John 18:10-11; only Mark 14:47 records the incident without Jesus' reaction). In Matthew, He explains, "All who take the sword shall die by the sword," adding "Or do you think that I cannot ask my Father and he will provide me even now with twelve legions of angels?" In John's Gospel, Jesus tells Pontius Pilate that if the kingdom of which He testified were an earthly kingdom, His "officers" (i.e., His disciples) would fight to protect Him from the Jewish temple authorities (John 18:36); the fact that they do not is evidence that His kingdom comes from somewhere else (from above or from heaven, as with Jesus Himself). In each case the principle of nonretaliation is seen in connection with the divine power of Jesus and of the kingdom He proclaims.

The First Epistle of Peter similarly attributes to Jesus a pattern of behavior at the time of His passion that Christians are intended to follow: "That is what you are called to do, for Christ also suffered for you, leaving you an example, that you might follow in his footsteps. He committed no sin, nor was deceit ever found on his lips. He was insulted, but he hurled no insults in return; in his suffering he made no threats, but left himself in the hands of him who judges justly" (1 Peter 2:21-23). In the next chapter, the Christian readers of the epistle are told, "Do not repay a wrong with a wrong, or trade insult for insult, but respond instead with a blessing, for this is what you are called to do, so that you in turn may inherit blessing" (3:9). The imperative of nonretaliation is here grounded not only in the example of Jesus of Nazareth but in the firm hope of divine vindication. To live in this way is to risk putting oneself at a grave disadvantage in a selfish and competitive world, but the consistent expectation of the New Testament writers is that God will intervene to vindicate His people and reward their obedient lifestyle. Just as Jesus "left himself in the hands of him who judges justly" (2:23), so His followers, when they "suffer according to the will of God," are to "entrust their lives to the faithful Creator by doing good" (4:19). Though the terminology of loving one's enemies does not occur in First Peter, the notion of "doing good" functions virtually as its equivalent (2:15, 20; 3:6, 17).

The love command, and in particular the command to love enemies, is the heart of Jesus' ethical teaching, but not the whole of it. From one point of view, the love of enemies can be subsumed under the broader category of renunciation. To respond to one's enemies in the way that Jesus requires is to renounce vengeance. Where the Hebrew Scriptures had set careful limits to retaliation or the taking of vengeance ("an eye for an eye, a tooth for a tooth"), Jesus takes the more radical step of eliminating it altogether. Renunciation can be defined as giving up voluntarily something one believes he is entitled to, whether the redress of grievances, home and family, material possessions, or, in the most extreme cases, life itself. The first of these occupies the central place in the teaching of Jesus because it is so clearly the extension of the activity of God Himself, who extends radical grace and forgiveness to His enemies. But in certain Gospel passages, Jesus demands renunciation in the other, more obvious ways as well. If the love of enemies is rooted in the attitude of God and modeled in the behavior of Jesus, the other forms of renunciation—of possessions and home, of family and marriage, and of one's very life—are also rooted in Jesus' mission and experience.

The renunciation of family and material possessions is conspicuous in the call to discipleship from the very beginning of Jesus' Galilean ministry. "Follow me," He commands the brothers Simon and Andrew by the lake, "and I will make you fishers of men" (Mark 1:17/Matt. 4:19; see also Luke 5:10). In the very act of making a word play of their occupation as fishermen, He calls them away from that occupation and livelihood to travel with Him and become His disciples. Simon and Andrew left their nets, the tools of their trade and their means of livelihood, to follow Him, while James and John left their father Zebedee (Mark 1:18, 20/Matt. 4:20, 22; see also Luke 5:11, where Simon and the brothers James and John left "everything").

Jesus' parable of the banquet in Luke 14:15-24 mentions three types of excuses by which the invited guests refused the host's invitation. One man said, "I have bought a field, and I must go out and see it" (v. 18); another, "I have bought five yoke of oxen and I have to try them out" (v. 19); a third said, "I have married a wife, and so I cannot come" (v. 20). The effect is to focus attention on the things in life that often stand in the way of Jesus' call to discipleship. Jesus adds, "If anyone comes to me and does not hate his father and mother and wife and children and brothers and sisters, and even his own life, he cannot be my disciple" (14:26). The same principle is expressed somewhat less radically in Matthew 10:37-38: "The person who loves father or mother more than me is not worthy of me, and the person who loves son or daughter more than me is not worthy of me, and whoever does not take up his cross and follow me is not worthy of me." Jesus' ethic is not an ethic of hatred, as hatred is commonly understood. The one who commanded his disciples to love each other, their neighbors, and even their enemies, can hardly have urged on them hatred of their own closest relatives. But Jesus is represented as calling his disciples to renounce their commitment to family and loved ones in favor of a single-minded commitment to God and to the proclamation of His kingdom. All other loves are like hatred in comparison with the all-encompassing love that motivates them to follow Jesus and share in His mission.

Mark's Gospel looks back on Jesus' call to discipleship in much the same way: "There is no one who has left home or brothers or sisters or mother or father or children or fields for my sake and for the sake of the gospel, who will not receive back a hundred times over, now in this age, homes and brothers and sisters and mothers and children and fields, with hardships, and in the age to come eternal life" (Mark 10:30).

The mention of the wife in Luke 14:20 and 26 (and in them alone) is striking. Divorce for the sake of Christ is not unknown in later legends about Jesus and the apostles in which celibacy has become one of the principal Christian virtues (e.g., the apocryphal Acts of Paul and Thecla from the third century A.D.). But neither Luke's Gospel nor the Acts of the Apostles shows evidence of fostering such views. It is likely instead that just as "hating" one's relatives does not refer to a commitment to their destruction but simply to loving Jesus more, so "leaving" a wife is used in these passages for a decision not to marry rather than the break-up of an existing marriage. The radical, even offensive, way of putting things is thoroughly characteristic of Jesus, though in this instance it appears that only Luke has preserved His shocking terminology. Matthew and Mark may have left it out because of the danger of misunderstanding.

That the saying was misunderstood is suggested by a question that the Pharisees asked Jesus about divorce. Was it ever lawful, they wanted to know, for a man to divorce his wife (Mark 10:2/Matt. 19:3)? In reply, Jesus assumes a role that is otherwise unknown to Him in the Gospels, the role of a legislator. The question is whether divorce is lawful, and Jesus' simple and direct answer is that it is not. Here alone in the

Gospels, He makes a legal ruling on a question that is put to Him without shifting the terms of the discussion. His more typical response is to challenge the questioner's assumptions, or to make a pronouncement that in some way cuts across the usual alternatives. The Sabbath is made for human beings not human beings for the Sabbath! It is not what goes into a person that defiles a person, but what comes out! But here Jesus meets the question head on and in the same terms in which it is asked. Why is His answer so uncharacteristic? The most plausible explanation is that He wants to guard, as carefully and clearly as he possibly can, against a dangerous misunderstanding of His own teaching. Nothing that He has said in His proclamation or His call to discipleship should be interpreted to mean that it is legitimate to leave one's wife (or husband), even for the sake of the kingdom of God. The marriage relationship, grounded in a divine command as old as creation (Gen. 2:24), is a sacred bond: "What God has joined together, let no human being separate" (Mark 10:9).

A second stage of the discussion takes place later in private between Jesus and His disciples. When they ask Him about the answer He had given to the Pharisees, He explains Himself further in even more direct terms: "Whoever divorces his wife and marries another commits adultery against her; and if she marries another man after she has divorced her husband, she commits adultery" (Mark 10:11-12). What began as a debate with His opponents over the correct interpretation of the law ends as a personal warning to His disciples. They in particular must not violate the sacred principle that marriage makes a man and a woman one flesh. Specifically, they must not divorce their wives even for the sake of the kingdom of God! Above all, they must not fall victim to the tragic irony of leaving a wife for such lofty motives only to turn around and marry someone else. Those who do such things must be called by their right names—not disciples, but adulterers.

It is no accident that this passage is placed in the larger context not of ethical teaching in general or of debates over the law, but of Jesus' teaching near the end of His ministry on the subject of discipleship and its implications (Mark 9:33-50; 10:13-45). The uncompromising, even legalistic, character of Jesus' pronouncement on divorce is perhaps the result of contemplating the possible misinterpretation (by His opponents) or abuse (by His disciples) of Jesus' own principle of renunciation as applied to marriage.

The best known and most widely discussed difference between Mark and Matthew in this passage is Matthew's addition of the words, "except for immorality" (Matt. 19:9). This addition is compatible, however, with Mark's main point that dedication to the kingdom of God is not a valid reason for divorce. An equally distinctive feature of Matthew's account is that if Mark refers only implicitly to the possibility of the renunciation of marriage in the passage about divorce, Matthew does so explicitly and directly (Matt. 19:10-12). Matthew merges the two stages of the Markan discussion into one, so that the blunt characterization of divorce and remarriage as adultery, no less than the scholarly debate over the implications of Genesis 2:24, is addressed to the Pharisees, who first raised the question. But Matthew still brings the disciples in for a second stage to the discussion. He preserves Mark's two-stage presentation even though his are not the same two stages. The disciples comment that in view of what Jesus has just said, it is better not to marry. Their point is not that it is better from a purely selfish or pragmatic standpoint, but that it is better for the sake of the kingdom of heaven. Those who do not marry are more free to respond to the call of the kingdom and to do the work that full commitment to it requires. Where the second stage of the discussion in Mark had addressed the disciples' question negatively—absolutely no divorce, even for the lofty cause of God's kingdom—stage two in Matthew addresses it positively—though divorce is not an option, celibacy for the sake of the kingdom is, though only for some (vv. 11-12). Thus each of the synoptic Gospels bears its own distinctive witness to Jesus' affirmation of celibacy in connection with the call to discipleship. It was precisely this affirmation that made it necessary for Him to affirm also, and in the strongest possible terms, the indissolubility of marriage.

If Jesus called His hearers to the renunciation of family, and even to celibacy as a possible option, He also called them to the renunciation of wealth and property. To the man who asked Him, "Good teacher, what must I do to inherit eternal life?" He focused on the designation "good" and pointed him to God, the single source of all goodness, and to several of the Ten Commandments (Mark 10:18-19/Matt. 19:17-19/Luke 18:19-20). To acknowledge God alone as good is to trace all mercy and kindness to Him and to say with the psalmist, "O give thanks to the Lord, for he is good, for his mercy endures forever" (Ps. 107:1). Goodness here, like perfection in Matthew 5:48, is defined not abstractly, but in terms of giving—to the poor and to all who are in need, even to enemies. When a person has obeyed all the commandments, the one thing still necessary is to become God's imitator in this respect, with the recognition that God's goodness is primary and one's own goodness merely derivative. Jesus told the man who asked Him the way to eternal life to renounce material possessions, to sell all that he had and give the money to the poor, and to follow Jesus (Mark 10:21/Matt. 19:21/Luke 18:22). It was easier, He explained to His disciples, for a camel to go through the eye of a needle than for someone rich to enter the kingdom of God (Mark 10:25/Matt. 19:24/Luke 18:25). God's kingdom is a gift that only He can give, and it must be received in poverty, as a little child would receive it (Mark 10:15/Luke 18:17; see also Matt. 18:3).

At the heart of Jesus' ethic was the renunciation of all the external symbols of self-worth: home, family, material possessions, and the "natural" right of justice or retaliation. He renounced these things Himself, and required of His followers the willingness to follow in the same path. "Foxes have holes," He said to one inquirer, "and birds of the air have nests, but the Son of man has nowhere to lay his head....No one who puts his hand to the plow and looks back is fit for the kingdom of God" (Luke 9:58, 62). The ultimate renunciation is of course the renunciation of life itself, and here too Jesus Himself set the example.

Before He suffered and died, He signified the mode of His death by depicting His disciples as taking up their crosses and following in His train like condemned criminals (Mark 8:34-37/Matt. 16:24-46/Luke 9:23-25). It is striking that the cross as an instrument of execution is mentioned in connection with them *before* it is mentioned in connection with Jesus. At the heart of His demand is an irony: those who try to "play it safe" will die, while those who risk—or even lose— their lives for Jesus and His message of the kingdom of God will live (in addition to Mark 8:34-37 and parallels, see also Matt. 10:39; Luke 17:33). *Life* in these passages as characteristically in the Old Testament refers without distinction to physical life and eternal life, but the Gospel of John makes the same point while bringing the distinction out clearly: "Whoever loves his life loses it, and whoever hates his life in this world will keep it for eternal life" (John 12:25). "Hating" one's own life, the logical extension of "hating" one's parents or wife or children (Luke 14:26), means living solely for the sake of Jesus, putting the kingdom of God that He proclaims ahead of every other allegiance.

For such radical discipleship, Jesus Himself was the model—most clearly in His death on the cross, but in many less dramatic ways as well. He described Himself as without a home, and without a place even to sleep (Matt. 8:20/Luke 9:58). He left His family for a new circle of friends committed to do the will of God (Mark 3:33-35/ Matt. 12:48-50/Luke 8:21). Looking back on His life, Paul could say, "Though he was rich, for us he became poor, so that we, through his poverty, might become rich" (2 Cor. 8:9; see also Phil. 2:7-8). In a metaphor, He saw Himself as a seed of grain that fell to the ground, died, and then sprang up to bear fruit (John 12:24). But His metaphor was not exhausted in His individual experience. He claimed that He would draw everyone to Himself and His cross (12:32); consequently, the seed of grain portrayed His followers' experience as well as His own. They too, He indicated, would "die" in order to live and bear fruit (12:24-26). They would become His imitators, as He was God's imitator. They would practice renunciation and the love of enemies because God

did so first, namely, when He gave up His only Son so that sinners might live. The ethic that Jesus taught is the extension both of the life that He lived and the gospel of the kingdom of God that He proclaimed.

Because Jesus' ministry was dominated by the sense of the nearness of the kingdom of God, and of the end of the present world order, it is not a "practical" ethic by which human society can function and perpetuate itself. Its preservation in the New Testament, however, testifies to the fact that the early Christians, in the decades following His resurrection, considered it an ethic that should govern their own behavior both among themselves and in the larger society of which they were a part.

There is no possible basis, therefore, on which Christians of subsequent generations who profess to follow the authority of the New Testament, can dismiss the life and teaching of Jesus as either impossible, impractical, or irrelevant to the ethical and political decisions that are theirs to make in their own time. In an age of cold war, power politics, and nuclear stalemate on a worldwide scale, it is difficult to see how a society that loves its enemies can hope to survive. Retaliation, or at least the threat of it, is part of the social compact of the free world and the totalitarian world alike; but in this compact the follower of Jesus has no part. Here the moral person and immoral society part company. Nowhere more clearly than at this point, the teaching of Jesus says "No" to the world and to all its standards. The world regards His negation as foolish and those who obey Him by turning the other cheek to their enemies as fools. Only Christian faith, with its persistent vision of a day when "the kingdom of the world has become the kingdom of our Lord and of his Christ, and he shall reign forever and ever" (Rev. 11:15), vindicates the ethic of Jesus and gives it validity in a world of sin and death.

**Bibliography:** Furnish, V. P., *The Love Command in the New Testament* (1972); Hiers, R., *Jesus and Ethics: Four Interpretations* (1968); Houlden, J., *Ethics in the New Testament* (1977); Knox, J., *The Ethics of Jesus in the Teaching of the Church* (1961); Manson, T. W., *Ethics and the Gospel* (1960); Marshall, L. H., *The Challenge of New Testament Ethics* (1946); Perkins, P., *Love Commands in the New Testament* (1982); Piper, J., *"Love Your Enemies": Jesus' Love Command in the Synoptic Gospels and the Early Christian Paraenesis* (1979); Sanders, J. T., *Ethics in the New Testament* (1965); Schelkle, K. H., *Theology of the New Testament: III. Morality* (1970); Schnackenburg, R., *The Moral Teaching of the New Testament* (1965); Wilder, A. N., *Eschatology and Ethics in the Teaching of Jesus* (rev. ed., 1950); Yoder, J. H., *The Politics of Jesus* (1972).

See FORGIVENESS; SERMON ON THE MOUNT.

J.R.M.

**JEWISH ETHICS.** The etymology of the word *Jew* comes from the Old French *giu*, which probably has its origins in the Latin *judaeus*, which in turn is based on the Greek *Ioudaios*. The Greek is a reasonable transliteration of the Hebrew *Yehudi*.

This designation of the descendants of Abraham, Isaac, and Jacob became popular in postexilic periods, when the citizens of the Babylonian and the Persian province of Judah were referred to by this name. It can also be used to refer to Jewish people from approximately 500 B.C. to the present. In regard to ethics, the emphasis of this article will be on the centuries at the turn of the Christian era, when Jewish belief and practice was conditioned by Palestinian and Babylonian rabbis. The Judaism of this period was most influential in setting the tone for further generations.

Jewish ethics at the turn of the Christian era were conditioned by the received traditions of the Hebrew Bible. The prime influence was the belief in a monotheistic religious system that gave the ethics of Judaism a theocentric or "one God" emphasis. This stood in contrast to the majority of other ancient religious systems that had a polytheistic basis for ethics, and with many gods came a greater possibility of a fragmented ethic. The particular view of the Jewish God was that He was a moral God. This would have significant impact when the rabbis encouraged Jews to imitate God in their ethical behavior. Israel was a special nation and the Jew was a unique individual, for God had stipulated in the scriptures that they were to be holy, "You shall be holy, because I, the Lord your God, am holy" (Lev. 19:2; see also Exod. 19:6; Deut. 14:2).

A second ethical influence from the biblical period was the belief that the Jewish God revealed Himself to humanity. Revelation was understood to be specific, historical, and purposeful. The revelation is frequently referred to as Torah, and this Hebrew word is commonly translated as "law." However, for our discussion it might more appropriately be defined as "path" or "way," for Torah was understood to be "the way" that Jews were to behave in their response to God and in their dealings with their fellow humans. Torah had to do with both dimensions and it was detailed for both possibilities. Revelation included an ethical code. Basic to Jewish ethics is the belief that God defines right and wrong. The ethical system that was established was a response of a "holy people" to their "holy God."

Very early in the Hebrew Bible it was made clear that this universe operates under a moral order. The rabbinic emphasis on ethics included the belief that humanity, both physically and spiritually, was God's pre-eminent creation without any inherent imperfection. There is no concept of a fall and regeneration mentality. Sin is the erring from the "establishing path," from Torah. Erring is resolved through repentance, and this is followed by forgiveness from God. The rabbis discuss two tendencies in humanity. One is *yezer tov*, or "good desire" that stands in tension to *yezer hara*, or "evil desire."

There is a sense in which the debate has to do with whether the human is self-sufficient or somehow a dependent creature. The resolution to the tension is twofold. On the one hand, the individual must choose between the two possibilities by free will as to which desire will dominate. Evil, according to the rabbis, must be a real possibility, or otherwise righteous deeds cease to be a virtue in any real sense. On the other hand, God has provided for the righteous person through the giving of the commandments. A commandment (*mitzvat*) is the response to God within the context of the covenant. The sense of the word implies an action. The thrust of observance of the commandments was not perfection, but response to the initiative of God through His revelation at Sinai. By keeping the commandments, good desires will be the dominant force in ethical decisions. Again, it needs to be emphasized that the rabbis called on people to imitate God in holiness, righteousness, compassion, and lovingkindness. This was possible because humans had been created in God's likeness.

The application of ethical principles function on two levels. On one level, ethics have to do with the individual and individual concerns. The commandments had included very specific requirements that defined a "covenant person" in regard to such topics as marriage and family obligations. On another level, Jewish ethics reflect a strong consciousness of community responsibilities. The "covenant person" was responsible to others who were part of the "covenant community." The morality of the individual was set within the context of the society and the two dimensions were understood to be interdependent. One of the main concerns of rabbinic teachings on ethics is that the Jewish person was accountable to the socially and economically disadvantaged (the stranger, the poor, the widow, and the orphan; see also Exod. 22:21; Lev. 19:18, 34; *Moed Katan* 6a). One of the famous sayings of Rabbi Hillel (ca. 30 B.C.-A.D. 10) is "what is hateful to you, do not do to your fellow."

**Bibliography:** Kadushin, M., *The Rabbinic Mind* (1972); Moore, G. E., *Judaism in the First Centuries of the Christian Era* (2 vols., 1971); Neusner, J., *Understanding Jewish Theology* (1973); Schechter, S., *Aspects of Rabbinic Theology* (1961).

W.O.M.

**JOY.** This term is derived from the Latin term *gaudeo*, "be glad," "rejoice," and expresses pleasure or general satisfaction with persons or situations in life. The concept is rendered in the Old Testament by several different words which express rejoicing appropriate to festivities (1 Sam. 18:6; Ezra 3:13), whether associated with holy days (Ps. 42:4), predictions of divine blessing upon the holy city of Jerusalem (Isa. 65:18), deliverance from national enemies (Esth. 8:16), or even the private satisfaction experienced by the private Israelite as he contemplated God's presence (Ps. 16:11). Gratitude, laughter, rejoicing, shouting, and singing are all elements of joy at various times and not least when joy has ethical overtones such as occur when a righteous person performs acts of justice (Prov. 21:15).

Gladness is also an ingredient of the joy mentioned in the New Testament, as on the occasion when the fetus moved vigorously in Elizabeth's womb as she heard the voice of her relative Mary (Luke 1:41, 44), who was soon to become the mother of Jesus. But the word most commonly used to express joy (*chara*), is related to the Greek noun *charis*, which is commonly translated "grace." While there was normally an ethical quality to grace in the Old Testament, the association of joy with divine grace in the Gospels and Epistles adds a distinctive spiritual dimension to the term.

The heralding of human salvation in the form of the infant Jesus taught that his followers would experience joy through keeping his commandments (John 15:11), thereby sharing his own joy that resulted from obedience to his Father's will. So satisfying was this relationship characterized by *charis* that Christ willingly endured the shame of crucifixion (Heb. 12:2). Along with righteousness and peace, joy in the Holy Spirit is of the essence of Christ's kingdom (Rom. 13:17) and is manifested in the heavenly places when a sinner repents of iniquity (Luke 15:10). Whatever elements of gladness or jubilation joy may have, the New Testament seems to indicate that at its highest level it is a product of the spiritual relationship between Christ and the believer and is therefore not transient after the fashion of worldly satisfaction.

**JUST WAR CRITERIA.** The "Just War" tradition in Christian ethics attempts to set out the minimal conditions under which participation in a war could be compatible with a Christian's conscience. It does not seek to justify all wars, but rather to restrict severely engagement in wars by the requirements of justice.

*History.* The tradition has its roots in the writings of the pagan Cicero, who set out several criteria justifying the waging of war as a last resort in the defense of national security. These included the need for a formal declaration of war, the aim of securing a just peace, and the humane treatment of prisoners.

It was not until the time of Ambrose (340-397) and Augustine (354-430) that the Just War doctrine became established in Christian thinking. Until then—that is for the first three centuries of the Christian era—the weight of theological opinion was opposed to Christian participation in military service. Around A.D. 300, however, the situation of Christians in the Roman Empire required a radical rethinking of the previous paci-

fist stance. The decision of Constantine to make Christianity the official religion of the Empire made it imperative for Christians to clarify the church's relationship to the secular authority. Augustine lived during the barbarian invasions of the Empire and concluded that war for the vindication of justice must sometimes be a Christian duty. Augustine had a radical understanding of the nature of human sin and recognized that no war could ever be completely just. Nonetheless, and although he longed for peace, he believed that God's justice requires that evil be restrained, if necessary by force, and that it is not impossible to please God while engaging in military service.

The Just War doctrine was developed by Thomas Aquinas (1225-1274), whose teaching remains the basis for Catholic moral theology. He emphasized the permissibility of war for defense and believed that in order for such a war to be just, three things are necessary: the authority of the sovereign; a just cause; and a right intention (to wage war not in order to conquer, but to secure peace). On the basis of Aquinas's teaching, several Counter-Reformation theologians, among whom the Spaniards Vitoria (1483-1546) and Suarez (1548-1617) are particularly notable, identified certain conditions that have to be observed if a war is to be waged justly. Their thinking was used by the Dutch lawyer Grotius, whose *On the Law of War and Peace* (1625) laid down rules of justice in war that have found expression in subsequent international conventions.

Luther and Calvin shared the Just War tradition of Augustine, agreeing with him on the sinful nature of man and making much of the Pauline teaching that the state is an instrument of order and justice in the hands of God. Calvin explicitly extrapolates from Romans 13:4 (in which Paul argues that the state is the servant of God to restrain evil) to justify the state's coercive use of force to restrain the evildoer who threatens from without. For Luther and Calvin, warfare is understood as a sort of external policing. Since the time of the Reformation and Counter-Reformation, theological work on the Just War tradition has been sparse. It was revived in both Catholic and Protestant theology in the period between World Wars in this century.

*Criteria for a Just War.* We can summarize the main emphases of the tradition thus: (1) The tradition does not offer a justification of all wars. There is a distinction to be made between a "just war" and the crusading militarism of a "holy war." The professed aim of a just war is peace through the vindication of justice. (2) There are circumstances in which the proper authority of the state may use force in defense of its people. (3) War may only be waged by legitimate civil authority, and there must be a formal declaration of war. (4) The purpose for which the war is fought must be just. (5) The recourse to war must be the very last resort. (6) The motive of the war must be just. (7) There must be reasonable hope of success. (8) The good consequence to be expected from going to war must outweigh the evils incurred in waging it. (9) Violence must only be directed toward those in arms. The "immunity of noncombatants" must be preserved as far as possible. (10) The war must be waged in such a way that only the minimum force needed to achieve the aims of the war may be used.

*Christian principles underlying the doctrine.* (1) God is a just God who cares about justice. It is a Christian obligation to work toward justice, especially for the poor and the oppressed (Ps. 98:1-2; Isa. 10:1-21; Luke 1:52). (2) The sinful nature of man and the fallenness of our social order mean that men and societies do act unjustly. There is an acquisitive and aggressive side to our nature that needs to be restrained (James 4:1-6). (3) True peace is based upon a right and just ordering of society (Ps. 85:10; James 3:18; Isa. 11:4-11). (4) God has ordained the authorities of the state to a specific and limited role in upholding order and punishing evil (Rom. 13:1; 1 Pet. 2:13-17). (5) At all times the state is subject to the authority of God and to the priority of human values (Rev. 13). War can only be waged as a lesser evil, in such a way that the "Spirit of the peacemaker" (Augustine; Matt. 5:9) is preserved. This requires, for example, the humane treatment of prisoners and the immunity of noncombatants that respects the divine commandment against the shedding of innocent blood (Exod. 20:13; Isa. 59:7-8; Rom. 3:15; Matt. 27:4). (6) The cross of Christ displays the willingness of God to wage war on the powers of evil to the point of self-sacrifice (Col. 2:15; Eph. 6:10-20).

*Pacifist criticisms of the Just War tradition.* Luther and Calvin's view of the relationship between church and state was rejected by Anabaptists such as Menno Simons (1496-1561). Many of today's Christian pacifists are in the Mennonite tradition. Their rejection of the Just War thinking often includes the following: (1) Jesus made no distinction between private and public morality. His command "Do not resist one who is evil" applies socially as much as personally (Matt. 5:39, 44). (2) The Old Testament, to which recourse is often made to justify war, for example in Augustine and Calvin, in fact points more characteristically to the way God worked by miracle (for example, at the Exodus) through his peoples' vulnerability and their trust in Him rather than chariots (Exod. 14:13ff; Judg. 7:19f). (3) Jesus sets aside his power; His example of nonretaliation is the Christian response to evil (Matt. 27:11-14). (4) The role of the state is to maintain order within society. It is illegitimate to extrapolate from Romans 13 questions of international warfare. (5) The Christian way is the way of witness to the peacemaking gospel of love. The church is to "overcome evil with good" (Rom. 12:21). (6) The way of the cross is the way of self-giving love and nonviolent resistance to violence (John 15:13).

There are, of course, many different emphases among those who espouse both the Just War and the Christian pacifist traditions. In general, however, the former believe that pacifists have too optimistic a view of human nature and have a separatist understanding of the relation of church to state. The latter tend to believe that Christians of the Just War tradition do not take the radical nature of the gospel seriously enough and have failed adequately to distinguish the role of the church as witness from the role of the state as civil authority. While both traditions acknowledge the need for some coercive force in the maintenance of order, pacifists forbid the state to kill. It is obvious that many of the criteria of the Just War tradition were more relevant to the personalized wars of the Middle Ages than they could be to total technological warfare in the modern world. The thinking underlying the tradition, however, and in particular the principles of discrimination (noncombatant immunity) and proportion, form the basis for some current military procedures. It was to these principles that Bishop Bell appealed in the British House of Commons in 1944 in his denunciation of the Allied obliteration bombing of Hamburg and Berlin.

*Could a nuclear war ever be a Just War?* If modern weapons could be targeted accurately, if the force used is the minimum necessary to achieve the goal of immobilizing an aggressor, and if the distinction between combatants and noncombatants can be maintained (recognizing the inevitable accidental loss of some noncombatant life), then the Just War theory accepts that, as a last resort, defensive and limited action against unjust aggression can be justified.

How does this apply to nuclear weapons? It might be that an accurately targeted counterforce *tactical* nuclear weapon, directed against an aggressor army in the middle of an uninhabitable desert, would be no more immoral than the use of a conventional weapon. But with the uncertain risks of escalation once a nuclear weapon is used, with the indiscriminate radiation hazards inevitable, and with the probability that conventional weapons could achieve the same effect, the use of tactical weapons on any likely battlefield scenario (for example, in Europe) could not be justified within the terms of this tradition.

The question of the use of *strategic* weapons that are indiscriminate by design is much clearer. "No one could justify pushing the button, no matter who pushes it or for what reason" (L. Smedes). There are no circumstances in which it could be regarded as permissible to launch an indiscriminate nuclear attack. This view is based partly on the criteria of discrimination and proportion, congruent as they are with the biblical prohibitions against shedding innocent blood, and the requirements of justice. It is based also on the consideration that the concept of a Just War is meaningful only so long as defense is possible. If, as would be inevitable in a strategic nuclear exchange, defense became identical with self-destruction, then the whole concept of a defensive war becomes absurd. "There can be no such thing as just mutual obliteration" (Archbishop Runcie). Furthermore, if the Just War tradition is right in pointing to the means by which God desires this world order to be preserved, namely the means of justice, then for man to take to himself the prerogative not only of intrinsically unjust actions, but to act in such a way that any possibility for the preservation of a just and ordered society is abandoned, is for man to play God and so succumb to the demonic.

**Bibliography:** Bainton, R. H., *Christian Attitudes to War and Peace* (1961); Holmes, A., *War and Christian Ethics* (1978); Paskins, B. and Dockrill, M., *The Ethics of War* (1981); Ramsey, P., *War and the Christian Conscience* (1961); Walzer, M., *Just and Unjust Wars* (1980).

D.A.

**JUSTICE.** Two very closely allied ideas are present in this word, both in everyday speech and biblical usage. There are the formal and substantial aspects of justice. The first can be expanded to the phrase "administration of justice" and involves fairness in procedure and general due process of law. The second aspect demands that there be actual fairness and equity embedded in the rules of law and that these be properly enforced. Both concepts are closely related to the idea of "rights." Justice in both of its related senses involves the securing and vindicating of rights. Justice may therefore be described in terms of the maintenance of rights in a fair manner. In turn this involves such dimensions as distributive justice (the distribution of rewards and advantages), remedial justice (the setting right of wrongs), and punitive or retributive justice (the penalizing of wrong conduct and wrongdoers).

Even a fairly casual reader of the Old Testament will observe a deep concern with law and justice. For the Christian, such concern expressed in the biblical material, rather than philosophical speculation should form the basis of a concept of justice. Of great importance is the emphasis that God Himself is a God of justice. Justice is thus a pivotal feature of a Christian social ethic. Although there are certain qualifications in using the Old Testament material today, it is submitted that in principle it can be applied outside its immediate theocratic setting.

Great stress is laid firstly on formal justice or due process of law. The primary text is probably Exodus 18:13-27 where, on his father-in-law's advice, Moses delegated the task of deciding disputes to capable judges. All but the hardest disputes were committed to them, and their key qualifications were trustworthiness and incorruptibility. Emphasis is consistently laid on scrupulous impartiality, especially as between rich and poor, a note echoed in the New Testament (Lev. 19:15; Deut. 16:18-20; James 2:1-13). There is a constant stress in the Old Testament on the dangers of bribery and its effect in destroying

proper and impartial justice (Exod. 23:8). Samuel, for example, can protest his integrity by asserting his freedom from bribery (1 Sam. 12:1-5). Those who exercised judicial functions always had to be aware that it was in God's name that they thus acted, and this demanded absolute impartiality and strict fairness in accord with God's own character (2 Chron. 19:4-11). Paul is at pains to remind us that God's own final judgment will be marked by these features in perfection (Rom. 2:11). The prophets denounce the failure of the nation to live up to these ideals (for example, Isa. 1:23; 5:7). This is especially true of the witness of Amos to the northern kingdom, Israel; but the same note is struck by Micah to her southern counterpart, Judah. The concern for due process of law and proper procedural fairness is also reflected in the legislation regarding witnesses, as well as that about judges. The prohibition against false witness in the Decalogue (Exod. 20:16) doubtless has ramifications beyond perjury but it certainly includes it (Exod. 23:1-3; Deut. 19:17-21). Likewise the law of Israel required corroboration of all essential matters in dispute (Deut. 17:6; 19:15). Certain modern legal systems retain this requirement. It must always be borne in mind that decisions in ancient Israelite judicial procedure were ultimately seen as the decisions of God. This was because the decision reached was based on God's revealed will, either in a case of real difficulty specifically asked for and given in regard to that case (for example, Deut. 17:8-13), or more generally by application of His law or earlier special revelations used as precedents. Thus the administration of justice in the Old Testament was altogether theocentric in principle.

Closely linked with the failure to administer justice in a fair manner in the indictment of the prophets is the unequal results that arose in the lawsuits and especially the oppression of the poor (Amos 2:6-7). This demonstrates a concern for substantial justice, namely, that all will have their rights respected. This is related to the idea of impartiality. The poor are not placed in a privileged position, nor are they the objects of favoritism. Nonetheless, in practice they were those who were most likely to suffer deprivation of rights. They had no human source to redress the balance or assert their cause due to the breakdown of the proper administration of law. Thus they were cast on God, who takes up their cause (for example, Pss. 68:5; 82:3). This explains the special concern for the poor on the part of Amos and the other prophets of the eighth century B.C. It formed part of their call for the return of the nation to the standards and norms of God's righteousness (for example, Amos 5:24). This involved a return to the law where the same concern finds a large place, no doubt for the same reasons. It is reflected in many of the detailed prescriptions on economic and social life, as well as even in the ritual regulations (such as Exod. 22:25-27; Lev. 19:9-10; 19:13-19; 25:8-55). In general it can be stated that the standard of justice and source of rights was God's revealed law, ultimately resting on His character.

The application of all this to modern conditions requires some discussion. Clearly, unless one accepts on biblical grounds the appropriateness of an enforcement of the fully theocratic system in modern society, which the present writer does not, some qualification has to be made to a full application. The following points may be relevant. Human government of any form is a divine institution (Gen. 9:6; Rom. 13:1-7). Thus, its administration is within God's concern. Secondly, the great concern for justice and righteousness as discussed is ultimately based on the character of God Himself. Thirdly, Israel was intended ethically, as well as religiously, to be an example and enlightenment to the nations. Finally even in the Old Testament there is concern over the denial of rights by pagan nations (see especially Amos 1:1—2:3). It is submitted that these conditions support a guarded application of the general principles found in the Old Testament.

These conditions suggest that a proper and impartial system of administration of justice is ethically demanded. Implicitly, the state should provide suitable facilities for the settlement of disputes and should provide efficient and fair procedures giving all involved an equal opportunity to state their case. The independence of judicial officers should be ensured and their freedom from bias and corruption emphasized. There should be no discrimination in access to these facilities, and this probably demands, at the least, fair access to legal advice and representation, at state expense if necessary.

The highly professional judicial and legal structures of modern states are considerably different from the more localized judicial system of Old Testament times, but it is submitted that the principles discussed support these modern implications. Indeed it is in countries with a long Christian heritage that these concepts of due process and equal protection of the laws have become embedded in law and constitutional documents. In modern conditions these standards of judicial procedure and behavior are emphasized by international agreements on human rights. The detailed application of these ethical principles will differ according to different legal cultures and traditions. It is submitted that there is a special role for Christians professionally involved to seek to ensure that the standards are observed so far as possible, and that, in all discussions of the apparent detail of legal procedure, they are kept in mind as undergirding standards.

One more precise ethical dilemma in this area is the modern application of Paul's strictures against use of the law courts of pagan Corinth by members of the Corinthian church (1 Cor. 6:1-8). It is the view of the present writer that this passage precludes the raising of litigation between committed Christians in secular courts, and that a much more preferable course for settlement of such issues is conciliation or arbitration within a Christian framework. Should that not be possible, the wronged party appears to be obliged to accept the position and not seek redress secularly. It appears unduly literal to restrict the passage to members of the same local congregation.

On the other hand, it does not *per se* preclude use of the law courts by Christians if another believer is not involved, nor does it necessarily prevent the defending of an action in appropriate situations. The general ethical imperatives of the Sermon on the Mount obviously have a bearing on these issues as well (Matt. 5:38-42). The very existence of the problem demonstrates that in the New Testament age the theocratic social and legal order no longer applies. However, the practical challenge of the passage is that Christians should be competent to handle disputes among themselves properly and justly (Matt. 18:15-18).

There are also general principles of substantial justice revealed in the theocratic system that should be reflected in modern legal orders. These should include the recognition of the importance of the individual, the recognition of a role for private property, protection against exploitation of the weak or underprivileged, and the maintenance of proper standards or behavior in commerce and employment. The detailed embodiment of these standards, and possibly the mutual balancing of them, is not an easy task; and one may fairly expect diversity of opinion as to their application in a complex economic and social order, unlike the agrarian society of ancient Israel. Dogmatism is thus to be avoided, but a recognition that God is a God of justice demands an assertion of these, His standards, even in modern societies. A consequent beneficial effect is to be expected (Prov. 14:34). One must await a future era before they will be fully displayed in perfect justice (Isa. 9:7; 2 Peter 3:13).

**Bibliography:** Anderson, Sir N., *Liberty, Law and Justice* (1978); Henry, C. F. H., *God, Revelation and Authority*, Vol. 6, (1983); Rawls, J., *A Theory of Justice* (1971); Smedes, L., *Mere Morality* (1983); Snaith, N., *Distinctive Ideas of the Old Testament*, (1944); Wright, C. J. H., *Living as the People of God* (1983).

See SERMON ON THE MOUNT.

A.J.G.

**JUSTIFICATION AND ETHICS.** The relation of justification and ethics becomes a problem when God's grace seems to leave no room for moral responsibility. The apostle Paul was accused of destroying ethics by teaching justification by faith (Rom. 3:8); Luther faced similar accusations. Since the Christian's justification before God is entirely by grace, based upon Christ's work and not one's own (Rom. 1:16-17; Eph. 2:8), is moral effort thus excluded from the Christian life? Certainly not! Although one's engrafting into Christ is entirely a gift, Christ Himself asserts that abiding in Him and bearing fruit does require commitment and perseverance (Luke 9:23-24; 13:23-24: John 15:1-18). It is thus a mistake to separate faith from effort. How can anyone truly believe in Christ without striving to follow and obey Him (Matt. 7:21; Luke 6:46; John 14:15, 21, 23; James 2:17, 26)? The unique thing about the effort of faith, however, is that the Holy Spirit continually leads the believer to seek grace anew and to put all his trust in Christ alone (John 15:5).

In response to the antinomian idea that Christians need not put forth any moral effort, Paul stresses the Christian's mandatory break with sin (Rom. 6:1-11), and he calls upon believers to "yield" themselves to God for sanctification (Rom. 6:12-19; 12:1-21). Similarly, Luther stressed that faith itself—a holy trust in Jesus Christ—demands the most rigorous effort. "There is no such Christ," Luther said, "that died for sinners who do not, after the forgiveness of sins, desist from sins and lead a new life" (*LW*, Vol. 41, p. 114). Dietrich Bonhoeffer raised the same warning about the false security of "cheap grace" in *The Cost of Discipleship*.

**Bibliography:** Berkhof, H., *Christian Faith* (1979); Bonhoeffer, D., *The Cost of Discipleship* (1959); Luther, M., "On the Councils and the Church," *Luther's Works*, Vol. 41 (1966), pp. 143ff.; *Ibid.*, "Against the Antinomians," *Luther's Works*, Vol. 47 (1971), pp. 107–10.

N.J.L.

**JUVENILE DELINQUENCY.** To speak of delinquency in general is to describe aberrant behavior from both a negative and a positive perspective. Negatively speaking, a person is regarded as delinquent when he or she fails to discharge an assigned responsibility or perform a duty. The positive definition of delinquency entails the actual committing of an indictable offense as defined by the particular culture. Juvenile delinquency is usually of a "positive" character and indicates unlawful acts committed by young people. The age beyond which a person is no longer a juvenile (Latin *iuvenis*, "young," "youthful,") varies considerably in different jurisdictions and is subject to periodic review by legislators. In general, juveniles are under eighteen years of age in most Western countries, even where the age of majority is regarded as twenty-one. Juvenile crime includes various kinds of theft, computer fraud, vandalism, drug trafficking, prostitution, truancy, assault, and sometimes murder.

The young criminal has been the object of much study by sociologists, doctors, lawyers, psychologists, and others in an attempt to understand the psychodynamics of such delinquency. Some investigators have established two broad classes of offenders, comprising the "individual" and the "gang." The former may come from a middle-class background and becomes delin-

quent because of "unconscious drives" or through fiscal necessity, especially if that individual has become involved with addictive drugs. The latter comprises a group of antisocial individuals who operate with financial considerations primarily in view. Since they are generally involved in drug trafficking as well as other matters, their motivation is explicit and violent and lacks any of the refinement of "unconscious drives."

External factors affecting or provoking juvenile delinquency have been envisaged in terms of such social deficits as unemployment, broken homes, poverty, the use of alcohol and mind-disorienting chemicals, illiteracy, or a low level of education. The general effect of the background where some of the above factors are daily realities has also been urged as a strong argument for the incidence of juvenile delinquency. Internal causation has been considered with reference to genetics and character, and these factors are gaining increasing attention as a result of the discovery that a deprived social environment is not necessarily the cause of juvenile delinquency. Indeed, some types of crime such as computer fraud demand levels of education and social standing that are out of reach of the fiscally impoverished. Thus a lesser emphasis upon the human environment and a greater stress upon motivation is being encountered in studies of juvenile delinquency. Genetic experiments with adult criminals have endeavored to describe delinquent behavior in terms of aberrant chromosomes, but some of the findings have been disputed. A few studies have suggested that negative social or environmental factors prompt someone with criminal tendencies to undertake illegal acts, but this does not account adequately for the fact that so-called middle-class crime does not proceed from a background of social deprivation.

The Christian church has failed to permeate society with the gospel as effectively as it should and therefore needs to devote far more energy to the task of combating juvenile delinquency than has been the case heretofore. Of primary concern in such an enterprise will be consistent emphasis upon the sanctity of Christian marriage and the responsibilities that parents have toward each other and their children (Eph. 5:22-28; 6:1-4). The Christian family ought to be established as a model for all to observe and the principle of obedience to the revealed will of God for human behavior proclaimed uncompromisingly. Christian parents must spend far less time in selfish indulgence and devote greater effort to bringing up their children in the knowledge and fear of the Lord. Once young people have been won for the kingdom of Christ, they can turn endeavor to evangelize their peers and thus minimize the works of the devil in human society.

**Bibliography:** Cohen, A. K., *Delinquent Boys* (1961 ed.); *Juvenile Delinquency* (United

States Congress, Senate Committe on the Judiciary, 1980 ed.); Shaw, C. R. and McKay, H. D., *Juvenile Delinquency and Urban Areas* (1980).

See CHILDREN, REARING OF; CRIMINAL PERSONALITY; FAMILY.

# –K–

**KIDNAPPING.** This is a slang American term which was coined originally to describe the theft of a child or children. It has gained currency in the present century because of the frequency of the act, though the crime itself is of great antiquity. This type of offense is perpetrated for a number of reasons, and the term is now applied to the theft of adults as well as children.

The victims are abducted by force and are held captive, normally for monetary ransom. In such a case the abductor communicates by one means or other with the household or company from which the person has been kidnapped, and establishes ransom demands. Where a highly placed business executive has been kidnapped by terrorists and is being held for ransom, the demands may be made of the individual's employer or of a state or national government. Police forces are also at work to apprehend the kidnapper and restore the victim to his or her previous place in society. The use of sophisticated electronic equipment, backed by the skill, daring, and resources of the police, frequently resolves the crime satisfactorily.

On other occasions where young children are involved, the kidnapper may well be an estranged parent or some other relative, and under such conditions the abduction is nonviolent. So unobtrusive is the deed that not infrequently some years elapse before the location of the kidnapper is discovered.

Abhorrent as kidnapping is, its most disturbing feature occurs where the victim is murdered because ransom demands have not been met. Parents of young children that have been abducted forcibly experience agonizing terror and deep apprehension for the welfare of their offspring. In cases where the victims are never recovered, the parents frequently experience devastating emotional and sometimes spiritual reactions.

What the Old Testament called "manstealing" was regarded as a capital crime (Exod. 21:16), regardless of whether or not the victim was murdered. The abduction of children would have been looked upon with equal horror, particularly since the Hebrews set a high value upon the possession of offspring (Ps. 127:3-5). Similarly Christians, who have lofty ideals for family life, would condemn kidnapping as one of the most reprehensible of crimes, especially if it was accompanied by the murder of the victim. In most Western countries kidnapping is dealt with very severely by the courts.

**KINDNESS.** This word describes gentleness, benevolence, friendliness, consideration, and the like, as attributes of character or behavior. Kindness is typical of generous, unselfish individuals who seek to serve others and contrasts forcibly with the harsh selfishness of the aggressive egotist. While it may readily be admired as an abstract quality, kindness is best appreciated within interpersonal relationships.

Kindness is a quality of both God and humans that can be seen throughout Scripture. Human kindness is sometimes depicted as reciprocal (Gen. 21:33; Josh. 2:12), but on other occasions is apparently a spontaneous expression of gratitude (2 Sam. 9:3). As a divine attribute, kindness underlies all of God's dealings with sinful humanity (Neh. 9:17) and was especially the motivating force of the Sinai covenant by which the Israelite tribes became the chosen people (Exod. 19—20). Even though the nation was to become apostate subsequently, God's kindness (*hesed*) to sinners expressed itself in a promise of redemption (Isa. 54:7-8). The New Testament authors stressed God's kindness in terms of the atoning work of Christ on Calvary (Eph. 2:7; Titus 3:4-5). As the believer grows in the grace of the Savior, kindness (*chrestotes*) must be demonstrated as a mark of Christian character (Col. 3:12).

**KINSEY REPORT.** When Alfred Kinsey published his two voluminous reports on human sexuality in 1948 and 1952, they created quite a stir. The findings contrasted markedly with what most Americans believed about sex. Kinsey suggested that one in ten Americans were homosexual and that extramarital sex, adult-child sex, and bestiality (sex with animals) were much more common than earlier believed.

Kinsey's research is a common foundation for today's sex education programs in American schools. The figure for homosexuality is often quoted and Kinsey often cited as a means of legitimizing deviant sexual behavior. But critics suggest that the studies, which relied on extensive interviews with thousands of people, are seriously flawed. The sampling included an unusually high proportion of prison inmates, who are more likely than most Americans to have homosexual experiences. Many were even sex offenders. Those who volunteered to be questioned extensively about their sexual experience are also likely to be more sexually adventurous and out of the mainstream. Most disturbing, Kinsey's studies encouraged sexual experimentation with children as young as two months, to prove that children could experience adult sexual satisfaction. His ex-associate Gershon Legman criticized Kinsey as not a researcher but a propagandist who sought to justify promiscuous sexual attitudes and behaviors.

While no one would claim that sexuality in America conforms to the Christian ideal of monogamous marriage, neither do Kinsey's studies, it is argued, portray reality accurately.

**Bibliography:** Kinsey, A. C. *et al., Sexual Behavior in the Human Male* (1948); *Ibid., Sexual Behavior in the Human Female* (1953); Reisman, Judith, and Eichel, Edward, *Kinsey, Sex and Fraud: The Indoctrination of a People* (1990).

See ADULTERY; HOMOSEXUALITY; PROMISCUITY; SEXUAL MORALITY.

B.W.

**KISS, KISSING.** Kissing (Latin *osculatio*) is a friendly gesture by which the lips of one person are placed upon the cheek or lips of another. Because it is in the nature of an intimate activity, it is not normally practiced among strangers, being sometimes replaced by a handshake or a formal embrace.

Certain kisses are of a purely ceremonial nature, as when the hand of some important personage or a church authority is kissed as a ritual procedure. But other kisses, especially those placed firmly upon the mouth, have a much more personal meaning. The tissues of the lips can be stimulated erotically by means of kissing, which often forms a prelude to coitus. Hence the mouth serves as an erogenous zone under such conditions.

Because of the intimacy of the activity, germs as well as affection can be transmitted by kissing, and many physicians blame outbreaks of mononucleosis on this sort of activity. There is also some question as to whether in fact the herpes simplex II virus can be spread by kissing as well as by other means.

Kissing in Old Testament times probably involved touching another person's cheek with the lips, although the mouth would doubtless be kissed during coitus. The kiss was regarded commonly as a gesture of sincerity and friendship, hence the shocking nature of Judas's betrayal of Christ with a kiss (Luke 22:48). In early Christian worship the "holy kiss" represented a token of fellowship in Christ, and this meaning was also applied to greetings between believers outside the context of worship. Some Christians still practice the "kiss of peace" in liturgical ceremonies, while others exclude it rigorously. To be most meaningful, kissing should always signify a loving, conscious relationship, and therefore casual osculation ought to be avoided if it merely betokens shallowness and insincerity, neither of which glorifies Christ.

**KU KLUX KLAN.** This organization is specifically American in character, but the first two elements of the name are derived from the Greek word *kuklos*, "circle." Originating in Tennessee in 1866, it was intended in the first instance as a social club for veterans of the Civil War. It was organized in 1867 as the "Invisible Empire of the South" and had an impressive hierarchy under the control of a Grand Wizard.

When freed blacks and others from the North gained political control in the South, Klansmen terrorized them and their allies by draping themselves and their horses in white as they rode in the darkness, threatening violence. Blacks and others were tortured and lynched; but this activity soon subsided, and in 1869 the Klan was disbanded, by which time the southern whites had regained political control.

But the spirit of racism had by no means disappeared, and in 1915 the Ku Klux Klan was revitalized in Georgia. It became a vigorous political force which spread across the United States and was used as a vehicle for wielding power by numerous persons who were aspiring to office in government. Blacks, or Negroes as they were known officially in those days, were no longer the main targets of the Klansmen, who also directed their activities at political radicals, Roman Catholics, Jews, and other people who were thought undesirable. In addition to a renewal of flogging and lynching, the Klansmen burned crosses in front of the homes or businesses of their opponents; and this, along with their white robes, became symbolic of their activity. After a decade, enthusiasm for this kind of racism began to wane, and the organization changed its name in 1928 to "Knights of the Great Forest." In 1944 the organization was dissolved when it was unable to meet its taxation responsibilities to the United States government.

Despite such a rebuff, the ethos of the Klansmen managed to survive, and after World War II the Klan was reorganized in 1949 in Alabama. Klansmen resumed their activities against blacks and their supporters, persisting in their traditional behavior even after members of the Klan were arrested, prosecuted, and imprisoned. Klansmen were bitterly opposed to any attempts at racial desegregation, and impetus was given to their movement when the United States Supreme Court made racial segregation in public schools illegal in 1954. Klansmen were involved in civil rights activities in the southern States in the 1960s and came under further scrutiny by federal and state officials. Although they normally deny any affiliation with the traditional Ku Klux Klan, men and women are still being arrested and indicted in connection with racist-inspired incidents that include cross burnings, the firing of shots, threatening telephone calls, and the like.

All the objections that Christians can raise in connection with racism can be alleged against the Ku Klux Klan movement. No sincere believer could support such violence, terrorism, and murder for one moment. Christians must obey civil rights legislation, however unappealing or distasteful that legislation may be thought to be, and must apply Christ's law of love for one's neighbor to all situations (James 2:8), especially those involving racial conflict.

See RACISM; SECRET SOCIETIES.

# -L-

**LAW, BIBLICAL.** Before discussing the ethical consequences of the biblical law, it is necessary to state that the ancient Hebrew religion viewed that God was lord over this universe and not subject to the whims and fate of natural consequence. Rather, the Hebrew God was viewed as the creator of the universe who demonstrated reason and rationality both through His character and in His creation. In addition to this view of God, they also believed that their God involved Himself in the affairs of humans in direct and purposeful ways that could be verified through the heroes and patriarchs of the ancestors. Just as creation was reasonable and rational, so God's dealings with humanity was believed to be reasonable and for the good of humanity. The sacred scripture of the Hebrews has to do with recounting God's interaction with individuals and groups of individuals, and in all cases God was viewed as taking an initiative toward humanity that revealed His nature and character. The consequences of this revelation was that the "way" or "response" of humanity to God's initiative was established. By responding to God in the appropriate manner, humans would be declared "righteous," which had to do with "right" living, according to God's commands to his people, as well as in the human-to-human dimension.

The essence of the "divine law" in the early stages of Judaism can be summarized in the following list: (1) a prohibition of worshiping gods other than the Hebrew God, (2) blaspheming the name of God, (3) cursing judges, (4) murder, (5) incest and adultery, and (6) robbery. Eventually, a seventh law was added to the list that prohibited the eating of flesh with the blood of life in it. These laws are sometimes referred to as commandments or laws of Noah, since they were viewed as the basic requirement for human conduct after the flood episode. In the later stages of Judaism, the term "righteous Gentile" would be applied to non-Jews who kept these commandments. The point to recognize about the laws of Noah is that two dimensions of human conduct and morality are addressed. The first dimension emphasizes a profound loyalty and allegiance to the Hebrew God. The God of self-revelation required a commitment to Him that excluded any other "god" possibility. On another level, and in consequence of the dedication to the Hebrew God, human-to-human relationships were established and clarified. The ethical demands included a commitment to the sanctity of life and human rights, while value was also placed on family and property.

At Sinai, the early revelation to the patriarchs was expanded to encompass a community context. The "divine law" was the foundation and the constitution of a people and an emerging nation. Later rabbinic sources will suggest that the revelation of Sinai had been offered to all nations, but it was only the Hebrews who were willing to receive it. This particular tradition has two consequences. Firstly, it emphasizes that all humanity is somehow included in the revelation and ultimately must respond to what was expressed in the Mosaic law. Secondly, Israel, as the chosen people of revelation, had a responsibility to demonstrate and witness the outcome of the encounter with God at Sinai.

The revelation of Sinai is referred to as the receiving of Torah. Traditionally, *Torah* has been translated into English as "law" (following the Greek, *nomos*). Although law is a reasonable rendering of Torah, it expresses a legislative meaning that is not fully appropriate to an understanding of the essence of the Sinai narratives. Torah might be better translated as "way" or "directive," and in both cases it would emphasis the sense of responding to revelation in the appropriate manner. Torah is the directive for being fully human. It is the way and the source for knowing the nature of things, whether of day-to-day concern or in regard to matters of ultimate concern. Torah is a light unto one's path. Regrettably, the translation of Torah as "law" has frequently been viewed by non-Jews as a negative term that prohibits human expression, confining behavior, spiritual character to a list of negations. However, this estimation is far from the positive character of Torah. The revelation at Sinai stipulates what is expected of humans in the horizontal dimension (people to people) as well as the vertical dimension (God to people). It is essential to recognize that biblical Judaism emphasized the reasonableness of Torah as the directive for humanity.

In later biblical Judaism, Torah is equated and identified as wisdom (Deut. 4:6; Prov. 8:22; Eccles. 24:23, 32). The essence of Torah as the source for wisdom in the ways of God and in human relationships is well stated in the extra-canonical book of Fourth Maccabees: "Wisdom, next, is the knowledge of divine and human matters...This, is turn is education in the law [Torah], by which we learn divine matters reverently and human affairs to our advantage" (1:16-17).

What is interesting to note is that Torah as the "way" of life given by God is understood to regulate the ethical behavior of the collective people. In order to be part of the covenant community, it was necessary to acknowledge the primacy of Torah in defining and regulating the chosen people of revelation. When calamity and tragedy struck during the Assyrian and Babylonian exiles, the writing prophets of the Hebrew Bible assessed the political, military, and social dilemma as linked substantially to the morality of Israel. The Torah had demanded certain consequences contingent upon the receiving of revelation. The consequences included justice, mercy, lovingkindness toward each other, and a full commitment and loyalty to the Hebrew God. The failure to live up to the expectations of Torah led to the exiles of 722 B.C. (northern Israel) and 587 B.C. (southern Judah). The historical sketch of ancient Judaism was decided by the moral condition of the people. The revelation contained in Torah included ethical responsibility. Not only the knowledge but the practice of Torah was the mark of the profound relationship between Judaism and their God.

Within the synoptic Gospels the subject of Torah goes in two directions. On the one hand, Jesus recognizes the validity of the Mosaic law and encourages his audience to follow it. This is demonstrated most forcefully in Matthew 5:19 where he states, "Whoever then relaxes one of the least of these commandments [in reference to the first two sections of Torah, law and the prophets] and teaches men so, shall be called least in the kingdom of heaven; but he who does them and teaches them shall be called great in the kingdom of heaven" (RSV).

Jesus set His own teachings, however, over and above that of the Mosaic law. In the Sermon on the Mount (starting particularly at Matt. 5:21), Jesus re-interprets the Torah in light of His eschatological status of messiah. It is this messianic restatement of Torah that separates Jesus from His contemporary religious peers, and the messianic claim on Torah ultimately leads to His execution by the Jerusalem religious authorities (Matt. 8:18-22; 15:1-20; 19:9; Mark 3:1-6; 7:1-23; Luke 9:59). The radical eschatological demand by Jesus that humanity must respond to His teaching (perhaps it could be expressed as "His Torah") as the Son of man produces the split between ancient Judaism and early Christianity. However, the ethical demand of Jesus' teaching is a call to morality of a high order, as it includes the stipulation that whoever is angry with his brother shall be liable to judgment (Matt. 5:22), and if anyone strikes the right cheek, then the other cheek must be offered to the offender also (Matt. 5:39).

The "law" and its place in early Christianity is a crucial issue for the first-century church. The essential and important point is that salvation was not gained by adherence to the Mosaic law. While that had never been a presupposition in Judaism (the grace of God was not earned by keeping the law; the obedience to Torah was the response to God's goodness), it would appear that certain aspects of the law (circumcision and dietary laws) were being used by some Christians to determine membership and admittance into the early church. The context of the Pauline letters on this topic presupposes the primacy of belief in Jesus as Christ and it is that claim that Paul reaffirms in his discussion on "law." However, once the conditions for "entrance" into Christianity are settled, Paul appeals to the law as the "guide" and directive for moral living. In this sense, both the Torah of Moses and the Torah of Jesus (the Hebrew Bible radicalized by Jesus' messianic claims) become the basis of biblical Christian ethics.

**Bibliography:** Gundry, R.H., *The Use of the Old Testament in St. Matthew's Gospel* (1967); Meyer, B. F., *The Aims of Jesus* (1979); Moore, G. F., *Judaism in the First Centuries of the Christian Era*, vol. 1 (1971); Neusner, J., *The Way of Torah: An Introduction to Judaism* (1974); *Ibid., Understanding Jewish Theology* (1973); Sanders, E. P., *Paul, the Law, and the Jewish People* (1983).

W.O.M.

**LAW AND GOSPEL.** This phrase refers to the natural tension between God's demands for righteousness in man and His promise of justification or salvation for man through Jesus Christ. This tension is dealt with extensively by the apostle Paul. He taught that man cannot achieve righteousness on his own by keeping the law (Rom. 3:30; Gal. 3:10). Rather, we are justified by the gospel, the good news of God's work of redemption through Jesus Christ.

**LAW, CIVIL.** The term *civil law* is ambiguous. Historically it refers to Roman Law and the legal systems that have derived many of their rules and attitudes from Roman Law are known as civilian systems. More generally, it covers the internal laws of a country and not the framework of rules and treaties known as international law. It is in this second sense that the term is used in common law jurisdictions. Sometimes "civil law" may relate to all aspects of internal law, and at other times the meaning given to it may not include all areas, such as criminal law or administrative law.

The spread of Roman Law throughout much of Europe was not accomplished so much by conquests of the Roman armies in the early centuries A.D. as by the rise and spread of scholarship in the period from the eleventh to the seventeenth centuries. Roman Law had been codified and reformed by the emperor Justinian in the sixth century A.D. and was therefore available to scholars in a form that became known as the *Corpus Juris Civilis*. In addition to the *Corpus Juris Civilis* there were and are works of other Roman writers in existence, for example, the Institutes of Gaius that belonged to the second century A.D. Roman Law provided a ready source of legal principles for students, teachers, legal writers, and judges. These principles became part of the fabric of European legal systems in different ways. Academics or scholars imparted them to their students who accepted the principles as a basis on which to make legal decisions. In the eighteenth and nineteenth centuries some of the European countries developed codes that expressed ideas and principles taken from Roman Law.

It is important to recognize that, in a civilian system of law, the law has not been generally viewed as judge-made, nor regarded as merely that which judges do. Law is seen more as a matter to be resolved by debate about competing principles. The doctrines of precedent and "stare decisis" whereby a judge is treated as bound to follow on earlier decisions of the courts are, perhaps, less important in civilian systems than in common law jurisdictions.

Important issues arise from the value placed upon Roman Law and the approach to precedent partially favored by the civilian lawyers. Firstly, Roman Law was and is entitled to a high place of honor among students of the law. One jurist has stated,

> Roman law, next to Christianity, was the greatest factor in the creation of modern civilization, and it is the greatest intellectual legacy of Rome (Buckland, *Journal of the Society of Public Teachers of Law*, 25 [1931]).

There are, however, various legal problems tackled by modern legislation that are not answered by Roman Law and, indeed, some areas of modern law differ radically from Roman ideas. It has been found necessary to develop concepts to deal with monopolies, insurance and no-fault liability, one-sided contractual freedom, and the need for consumer protection. Although Roman Law may now be regarded as deficient in many aspects, it must still be considered worthy of study and respect. Even those who would not accord it the place given by Buckland must admit that, without a knowledge of Roman Law, the task of explaining "the creation of modern civilization" is impossible.

Secondly, the civilian approach to precedent requires further comment. A full discussion of this topic cannot be undertaken in this article. A basic justification of the doctrine of precedent is fairness; that is to say, that the courts having treated one person in a particular way in a given set of circumstances should treat another in similar or identical circumstances in the same way. The difficulty with this justification is that it does not give sufficient weight to the rightness of the principles or rules applied. To treat two people wrongly may be fair, but fairness hardly justifies wrong treatment. A civilian lawyer in contrast to an exponent of the common law (or judge-made law created by precedent) would place considerable emphasis on the rightness of a rule or principle rather than on the fairness of applying the same rule or principle a second time. In the United Kingdom, where the English common law approach to precedent has been spread to civilian

Scotland, the highest court, the House of Lords, has modified the doctrine of precedent to allow a departure from earlier decisions that are thought to have given rise to injustice. Any attempt, however, to argue too strongly against the doctrine of precedent will undermine fairness; and if the courts reject the doctrine, they may undermine confidence in the administration of justice.

Another aspect of the doctrine of precedent is that a lower court is bound by a previous decision of a higher court. Without such a practice, the whole purpose of having appellate courts would be thwarted.

The relationship of the doctrine of precedent to legislation and legal codes is important. If the decisions of the courts when applying the legislation and legal codes are given binding force for the future, it is possible that the decisions may supplant the legislation or codes and reduce the enactments of the legislature to secondary sources of law. Underlying any discussion of this relationship is the fundamental question of the source or authority within a society.

One of the central questions that must be faced by legal philosophers is simply "What is law?" Various schools of thought have tackled the question, proposed numerous views on the meaning of the questions, and discussed many answers. The range of responses extends over natural law, positivism, realism, and sociological theories, to name but a few. At stake in this debate is the understanding of man, language, and its meaning, and authority. The importance of the question is often seen in the context of a discussion of law, religion, and morality. Such a discussion raises issues of fundamental human rights and the recognition and treatment of minorities. Attention has been focused on these issues by two opposite sets of circumstances. On the one hand, there has been the advent of government led by religious fundamentalists (as in Iran) who do not separate state and religion, and on the other hand there have been the controversies on abortion, divorce, obscenity, capital punishment, and homosexuality in Western societies, particularly in the United States, where state and religion remain separate, at least in legal formulations.

Of the arguments for a separation of law and religion, four will be mentioned. Firstly, arguments against the validity of religious claims and the meaningfulness of religious statements often stem from a denial of the existence of God and the fact of revelation. Unless God exists, there is no sense in building laws on religious claims. Secondly, it may be argued that law and morality belong to different spheres. A rule may be accepted as law even though it does not reflect a person's religious beliefs. Thirdly, adoption of a religious basis for law may lead to the persecution of those who reject the religion. It may create intolerance. Fourthly, some contend that the enforcement of religious views is either impossible or likely to detract from the commitment of the individual, which religion requires. Such arguments do not require that the law must never express a standpoint also held by religion. They merely suggest that when deciding on the content of law, legislators and judges need not, and perhaps should not, consider religious views.

On the other side of the debate, it is arguable that unless the law reflects the religious or moral concepts of a society, it may fall into disrepute. Secondly, there may be a modern trend toward the recognition of fundamental rights. An appeal to such rights may express an understanding of man that is akin to the concepts of religion and is certainly an assertion of morality. In this context, the question becomes not whether it is permissible to refer to fundamental belief in legislation, but how far one may go in legislating for fundamental belief. The argument does not yield the conclusion that religion and law may be brought together, but it does enable one to assert one's own basic beliefs, religious or otherwise, in a discussion of law. Thirdly, it is sometimes suggested that there is a distinction between private and public morality, and that the law that regulates public conduct need not reflect private views and beliefs. The distinction is obscure, and it follows that the conduct of a person in public life will be consistent with his private life. Whatever protest may be used to justify a public stance, that stance will be consistent with a person's basic beliefs. The separation of law and religion and morality is artificial and may lead to people hiding or disguising their true motives and reasons. Fourthly, Christians, who believe that the lordship of Christ is not restricted to spiritual matters, will argue that Christian belief should be expressed in law and politics.

A common misunderstanding is that the law of a country will contain answers to every problem that may arise. Many matters remain for decision or legislation. Furthermore, no society has a perfect set of laws. Even were there perfect laws, corrupt persons would soon enforce them harshly and for their own ends. Unless people acknowledge their own weaknesses and self-interest in the process of law making, laws can become instruments of oppression.

M.H.J.

## LAW, THREEFOLD USE OF THE.

The term *threefold use of the law* (*triplex usus legis*) is thought to have been coined by Philip Melanchthon, Martin Luther's close friend and associate. Melanchthon (1497-1560), and also John Calvin (1509-1564), employed this term to distinguish among God's different uses of law (that is, God's will expressed as command). Both men identified three uses, although they numbered them differently and gave somewhat different emphases. These are commonly called the political (or civil), the spiritual (or theological), and the moral (or didactic) uses of the law.

The first use is the exercise of social and political discipline and punishment. Melanchthon, following Luther, thought of the political use of the law as logically falling in first place. Calvin, however, designated this as the second use, thus interchanging Melanchthon's first and second uses. In this use the law functions to restrain sin and maintain order in the world. God has ordained earthly government for this purpose (Matt. 22:17-21; Rom. 13:1-7; 1 Tim. 2:1-4; Titus 3:1-11; 1 Pet. 2:13-17).

The second use of the law is the proclamation of God's wrath against sin. In this use the accusing voice of the law works within the sinner to reveal sin and destroy self-righteous pride (Rom. 3:19, 20; 7:7; Gal. 2:19). Both Luther and Melanchthon call this the "chief use of the law," a designation that Calvin reserves for the third use. Whereas the first use of the law is concerned with external force, the second is concerned with internal conviction. But the ultimate purpose of both is to bring the sinner to see his need for Christ and to be saved (Gal. 3:23, 24; 1 Tim. 2:1-4). Like the first use, the second use is thus directed primarily at unbelievers (1 Tim. 1:8-11). Insofar as a Christian walks into the Spirit and lives by faith in Christ, he knows freedom from the curse, bondage, and condemnation of the law (Rom. 5:1; 8:1, 2; Gal. 3:10-14; 5:1, 18). Nevertheless, the reformers agree that this use, the proclamation of God's wrath against sin, must continue in the church. Although it should no longer terrify those who have already been driven to Christ, it will keep them from false security. It is through this use of the law, Calvin said, that "the grace of God...is rendered sweeter." Furthermore, there are always unbelievers among the flock for whom the terror of the law is a necessary prerequisite to faith in Christ.

The reformers' third use of the law applies only to Christians. It is the call to Christians to "put off" the old nature and flee from sin. This use is necessary because Christians are still sinners who are continually tempted to return to the flesh (namely, the rule of self). But this use of the law is only possible because they are reborn with a new nature that delights in the law and desires to be rid of the flesh (Rom. 7:22-25; Col. 3:5-10). The third use is the exhortation to continue in grace, to resist the flesh, and to yield to the Spirit (Rom. 6:12-14; 8:12-14). Inevitably, this exhortation includes moral guidance (Rom. 12:14—13:14; Gal. 5:16—6:2; Eph. 4:25—6:9; Col. 3:5—4:6; 1 Thess. 4:1-8). It also includes the warning that those who return to the flesh, whether in legalistic or lawless ways, "will not inherit the kingdom of God" (1 Cor. 6:9-10; Gal. 3:1-10; 5:19-21; Eph. 5:5). The moral law is thus valid for the Christian, not as a means of salvation, but as a guide in sanctification.

Calvin specifies this use of the law as a "daily instruction" in God's will and a continuing exhortation to obedience, both of which are necessary because of the flesh. Melanchthon emphasizes the Christian's need for help to distinguish God-given moral directives from human ones. He also speaks of the use of the law in the "exercise of faith," in daily repentance, and in the battle against the flesh.

Since about 1950 the third use of the law has come under attack as unevangelical and legalistic. This may be attributed in part to misunderstanding and also to the influence of moral relativism. An evangelical understanding of the third use recognizes that the Christian, justified by the grace of God through faith in Jesus Christ, is no longer *under* the law but now *in* it. To be "in Christ" is to be in Him who fulfilled perfectly the law (Matt. 5:17; see also Jer. 31:33). It is through faith in Christ that the commandments are fulfilled in the Spirit-led life (Rom. 8:4; Gal. 5:14, 16). The law is not the means of justification, or of sanctification. But it reveals the need for salvation (first and second uses) and provides a guide for sanctification (third use). To those who denied this in his own day, Luther said: "Since Christ has come, not to get rid of the law, but to fulfill it, he comes in vain if the law is not to be fulfilled in us."

The three uses of the law have different applications for Christian ethics. The political use confirms the need for corporal and capital punishment and also "just war" as necessary consequences of God's work to restrain sin and maintain order in the world. The life and destiny of man fall under God's rule alone, even when carried out by human agents (Gen. 9:6; Rom. 13:3-4). The spiritual use provides a safeguard against moral hypocrisy, legalism, and utopianism. A truly good (namely, God-pleasing) life is only possible through the death of Christ, who suffered God's wrath for the sinner. The third use affirms the need for moral guidance and discipline in the church because of the Christian's battle with the flesh. However, it is important to recognize that the "flesh" against which the law warns can take both legalistic and lawless forms. The third use is a guide in both areas. In matters of "opinion" (for example, food, drink, dress), we are not to pass judgment or make laws for one another (Rom. 14; 1 Cor. 8). Here the law guards against loveless legalism. However, when a fellow Christian strays into what Scripture clearly identifies as sin, loving correction is commanded (Matt. 18:15-20; 1 Cor. 5:1—6:11; Gal. 6:1). Here the law guards against lawlessness. This latter use is particularly relevant in times of great moral ambiguity and compromise with sin. Today, for example, the third use of the law is particularly relevant in addressing issues like abortion, homosexuality, adultery, and divorce.

**Bibliography:** Allen, J., (ed. and trans.), *Institutes of the Christian Religion by John Calvin*, 8th ed. (1949), Vol. 1, pp. 382–92; Bockmuehl, K., "Keeping His Commandments," *Crux*, XVII/3 (Sept., 1981), pp. 17–25; Manschreck, C. L., (ed. and trans.), *Melanchthon on Christian Doctrine: Loci Communes 1555* (1965), pp. 122–28; Tappert, T. G., (ed. and trans.), *The Book of Concord* (1959), pp. 479–81, 563–68.

N.J.L.

**LEGAL ETHICS, PROFESSIONAL.** Members of the legal professions in the conduct of their businesses are not only governed by the rules and principles of the legal systems in which they practice, but also by the ethical rules of their professional bodies. Sometimes, the rules of the legal systems may be treated as ethical rules, particularly when the professional bodies enforce such rules in addition to any sanctions given by the courts. The penalties imposed by the professions may be harsher than the judgments of society or the courts because the power of the legal professions to exclude a person from membership may prevent a lawyer from pursuing a livelihood for which he has trained.

Ethics must not be confined to rules and principles that may be enforced. The concept of "standards" may be vague and obscure, but nonetheless important. Although standards may not be identified easily and may vary throughout a group of lawyers, the activities, pressures, and declarations of a professional body may tend to produce a common denominator of standards.

To understand legal ethics one must have some understanding of the nature of the legal professions and their work. In many legal systems, there is no distinction between those who practice in the courts and those who conduct broadly based practices of giving advise, looking after the money and affairs of clients, and securing that transactions, including the purchase and sale of houses and land, are carried out in accordance with the law. The legal systems of the United Kingdom draw a distinction between the specialist court pleader, known in Scotland as advocate and in the remainder of the country as barrister, and the general practitioner, known as solicitor. There is clearly an overlap of the ethical rules, principles, and standards applying to both court pleader and general practitioner, but there may be special principles applicable only to one of the types of practice. Thus, barristers and advocates who do not handle the money of clients are not subject to the strict accounting rules affecting solicitors. Where there is no division of labor, the lawyers may be subject to the one code.

Sources of ethical rules can include international declarations. The Declaration of Perugia, which was created by the lawyers of the European Community, and the Code of Ethics of the International Bar Association are examples in point. They have wider application than the rules of any professional body. The Code of the International Bar Association does not override the rules or ethics of local bodies.

The topic of legal ethics is broad, covering legal rules, standards, professional rules and principles, and international statements, and no set of ethics will necessarily apply to all lawyers in the one country. It is, therefore, only possible to identify a few salient principles and problems. The Declaration of Perugia identifies four main sets of professional duties; namely, to the client, to the courts, to the fellow members of the profession, and to the public at large.

The duties to the clients are numerous. It is essential that the lawyer exercises proper skill and care in the formulation of the advice given to clients. Furthermore, in acting for clients, he must ensure that there is no conflict of interest. A conflict of interest arises acutely when a lawyer acts for more than one party to a transaction. Thus a lawyer should not negotiate on behalf of both parties to a purchase and sale agreement.

In court, a lawyer may not represent both sides of a case and, indeed, in some may not represent joint defenders or pursuers. The problem of conflict of interest may also be seen in circumstances where a lawyer has a personal interest in the outcome of the transaction conducted for the clients. Thus, it is generally improper to draft a will in which substantial property of the client is left to the lawyer on the client's death.

A jealously guarded duty of lawyers to their clients is the duty of confidentiality. It is not only a duty but also a privilege in the sense that, in many countries, courts cannot compel a lawyer to disclose the contents of communications between the lawyer and his client. The secrecy of legal business ensures that the accused person can speak freely with a lawyer without fear that the slightest ill-advised phrase will become the basis of a prosecution case and that the person involved in a civil transaction need not worry that, by speaking to a lawyer, others interested in competing with him will gain an advantage. Confidentiality may ensure that an aged client is not placed under pressure by those excluded from the will.

Frequently, people inquire how it is that an honest lawyer can defend a guilty client. Fewer ask how it is that an honest prosecutor can prosecute an innocent person. The answer to both questions is the same. A lawyer representing a case to the court is not asserting his personal belief in the truth of the case. It is for the court to decide wherein lies the truth. The role of the lawyer is to present fairly the case of his client, and he must never turn himself into a judge. Great evil would result were lawyers to decide on the truth of their clients' causes. Innocent clients would be forced to plead guilty or be unrepresented; and the forensic process, established in law to determine what is true, would be made redundant. A lawyer may, however, advise the client that the position is hopeless and need not defend someone who asserts privately his guilt.

The lawyer may decide to withdraw from a case because the client is uncooperative and refuses the lawyer's advice. In such situations, however, it is considered improper to withdraw in such a way as to hurt the interests of the client.

The duties to the courts are numerous. The first duty is truthfulness. It is improper to suggest or propose things as facts that are known to be false. That does not mean that one need detail facts that are unfavorable to the client. It is the task of the opponent to refer to such facts. A lawyer should not add personal conviction to the case of the client. Thus a lawyer should not argue that he knows his client's story to be true when all he knows is that there is evidence to support the story. He, however, may argue that the evidence favors his client.

When arguing points of law, a lawyer ought to refer the court to decided cases, statutes, and other authorities that appear to contradict his case as well as to those that support the case. The skill in debate lies not in ignoring difficult authorities, but in showing why it is that they should not be followed by the court.

In addition to truthfulness and honesty, a lawyer should be polite both to the judges, to the juries, and to his opponents. Such behavior will lend authority to the case rather than detract from it and will help the business of the court to run smoothly. It is reason for the case that must be displayed, not the temper and pique of the lawyer. The ethical code of the International Bar Association makes it clear that respect for the court must always be set alongside the fearless defense of a client.

A lawyer has two principal duties toward other professional colleagues. He must seek to maintain the honor of his profession and avoid bringing it into disrepute. Of the many duties, the other chosen one is the duty to refrain from attracting business unfairly. Sometimes it is said that a lawyer must not tout for business. Traditionally, lawyers have not been allowed to advertise, and the view has been expressed that they should win clients by establishing a good reputation. The modern practice is, however, to permit advertising. In the United Kingdom, there are strict rules governing advertising.

It is easier to speak of duties to the public than to identify them. The Declaration of Perugia explains that the legal profession should try to preserve its independence and freedom while accepting proper regulation. Such independence and freedom is regarded as essential if lawyers are to preserve the freedom and rights of others. The difficulty for many people is that, unless the state pays the lawyer, they cannot obtain legal representation; and once the state pays the bills, it may seek to exercise some control over lawyers.

Finally, there are many specific rules that have been omitted, and it is important to recognize that different countries have ethical codes containing rules that others may reject.

**Bibliography:** *Code of Professional Responsibility by State* (American Bar Association, National Center for Professional Responsibility, 1980); *The Judicial Response to Lawyer Misconduct* (American Bar Association, National Center for Professional Responsibility, 1984); Patterson, L. R., *The Law of Professional Responsibility* (1982); Pirsig, M. E. and Kirwin, K. F., *Cases and Materials on Professional Responsibility* (1984); *Professional Conduct Handbook* (The Law Society of Manitoba, 1982); *Profes-*

*sional Conduct Handbook* (The Law Society of Upper Canada, 1983); *Recent Ethics Opinions* (American Bar Association, National Center for Professional Responsibility, 1982).

M.H.J.

**LEGALISM.** In an ethical context *legalism* is a term of reproach. To be labeled a *legalist* is judged to be wanting in some way. Accordingly, one would not apply the term to oneself, unless confessing a fault. It does not, however, have a single and unambiguous meaning. It can, for instance, designate an overemphasis on abstaining from evil acts, to the neglect and underestimation of doing what is positively good. This is exemplified by the person who sees virtue as consisting primarily in what is not done. The term also can refer to the conviction that an action is morally acceptable as long as it is not prohibited by the nation's laws. A case in point is the individual who concludes that because abortion is legally permissible, it must for that very reason be morally permissible.

More commonly, however, the term is used to refer to those who adhere rigidly to moral rules and do not exercise sufficient flexibility in the application of those rules to the human situation. In this regard, the term *legalism* does not specify a moral doctrine with a determinate content, but is a relative notion. Thus someone is a *legalist* who consistently applies rules more strictly than you yourself, just as someone is a *laxist* who consistently applies moral rules more loosely than you do. In recent years the term has been largely expropriated by advocates of situation ethics to characterize all those who operate with a greater respect for moral rules than they themselves do. But this only raised the question, "How strict or how loose should one be in the application of moral rules?" Those who judge situationism to be too loose with its denial that there is anything intrinsically wrong with such acts as lying, stealing, or promise-breaking, but also find Kantian absolutism too strict with its claim that moral rules never permit exceptions, may be attracted to a middle ground. Thus it can be argued that moral rules permit exceptions when they conflict with other more stringent moral rules, so that in such circumstances one is free to choose the stronger of the competing obligations, setting aside the weaker. To this can be added the corollary that catastrophic circumstances may release one from obligations that are otherwise binding. For example, one can justifiably lie in order to save the life of an innocent person against a murderous intruder.

Often accompanying the use of the term *legalist* is the implicit suggestion that the offending party is not sufficiently motivated by compassion or human concern. The legalist, the charge goes, either lacks compassion or stifles it in order to adhere to moral rules in situations where human beings are better served by departing from them. The alleged fault is one of placing rules before people and their needs. It is undeniable that moral rules can be used to mask a cruel insensitivity to human need, and Christians should be alert to the possibility. However, at the same time, there are legitimate moral restrictions that rightly apply to our humanitarian efforts. To sell all one has and in the process fail to pay one's legitimate debts in order to give generously to a worthy cause would not be justified, even if overall human welfare was furthered thereby. For one ought to pay one's debts, in spite of the fact that by not doing so one can make a more significant reduction in human suffering than otherwise would be the case. This indicates that not all acts that further overall human welfare are permissible, but actually may be morally objectionable. To label those who see matters this way as *legalists* does not contribute to the debate, but only presupposes what is at issue.

**Bibliography:** Fletcher, J., *Situation Ethics* (1966); Grisez, G. and Shaw, R., *Beyond the New Morality* (1980); Ramsey, P., *Deeds and Rules in Christian Ethics* (1967).

R.W.

**LEISURE.** Christians in Western society are beginning to recognize the need for a theology of leisure and play, but only the general outlines of that theology seem to be available now.

First, there is a difficulty in defining leisure. It may be seen as that part of a person's life that is not devoted to earning money, performing necessary duties (in home, society, church, and so on), and sleeping. However, such available time is probably better called discretionary time, since leisure involves a state of mind. Leisure cannot be imposed but must arise from personal desire. Its content may vary from meditation to swimming, and from gardening to acting. Genuine leisure is only possible where people are above the poverty line. Since most Westerners have been lifted above this line in modern times, the reality of leisure (once the prerogative of the rich) has become a "problem" to face; and accordingly, leisure industries have grown tremendously in modern times. There is not merely the leisure of those who are in paid employment, but there is the leisure of the growing number of those who have retired from paid employment and expect to live long lives. It has been rightly observed that, from a mental and emotional standpoint, we have not fully accepted our new leisure for what it is, namely, an opportunity to do and enjoy, a chance to realize the full benefits to be derived from the leisure we have now and will have subsequently in even greater abundance.

Second, a positive attitude to, and use of, leisure in order to relax and to play will necessarily be integrated to a positive attitude to work (both paid employment and work in home, church, society, and so on). Certain attitudes are unsatisfactory, such as, "Work is no more than a necessary means for living. What makes life worth living is the enjoyment of leisure"; and "Work is work and pleasure is pleasure and should not be mixed." The better approach would seem to be that of, "Work makes leisure pleasurable, and leisure gives new energy to work. Thus one should work faithfully and enjoy leisure to the full."

Third, the biblical basis for a theology of leisure seems not yet to be fully articulated. In his important book, *The Christian at Play*, R. K. Johnston points to the rest of the Sabbath, the advise of Qoheleth (Ecclesiastes), the portrayal of human love in the Song of Songs, the festivals and celebrations of Israel, and the practice of friendship by Jesus.

**Bibliography:** Johnston, R. K., *The Christian at Play* (1983); Smedes, L., "Theology and the Playful Life," in Orlebeke, C. and Smedes, L., (eds.), *God and the Good* (1975).

P.T.

**LESBIANISM.** Lesbianism refers to the attraction of women into a primary love relationship with other women. Until this century, lesbianism referred to homosexual activity among women. It now includes homosexual orientation among women, whether or not expressed physically.

The term derives from the Greek island Lesbos, which in the ancient world was sometimes governed and inhabited largely by women. Its most famous citizen was the female lyric poet Sappho (sixth century B.C.), whose love poetry has been much admired by classicists and others.

The original of lesbianism in a clinical sense, as of male homosexuality, is controversial. During the nineteenth century there began to be two schools of thought: one that it was psycho-social, the other that it was genetic. The debate is ongoing.

Lesbianism through the ages, as distinct from male homosexuality, has remained virtually invisible to modern historical scholarship. It was rarely reported and rarely addressed as an issue. No doubt this is partly because the role of women in society has been poorly documented.

Generally, the law has simply ignored lesbian behavior and so have most Christian theologians. This may have been because lesbianism has not been seen as a threat to procreation in the same way as male homosexual behavior, which involves the loss of semen. It may also have been because male homosexuals have had a greater reputation for profligacy than lesbians.

Few Christians would want to promote lesbian behavior as a social norm. Nevertheless, whatever their position on the issue, Christians are called to offer love and spiritual sustenance to all.

The apostle Paul made it clear that God's wrath is directed against all types of ungodliness and unrighteousness, including homosexual behavior. "God gave them up to dishonorable passion," he declared. "Their women exchanged natural relations for unnatural, and the men likewise gave up natural relations with women and were consumed with passion for one another" (Rom. 1:26, 27). The stark picture that Paul paints is of lesbians and homosexuals being consumed by their own lust.

However, Paul also showed that homosexuals and lesbians are not beyond the reach of God's love and redemption. The good news is the gospel of Christ, which is God's power to save all who repent and turn from their wicked ways. In his first letter to the Corinthians, Paul mentioned such grave offenses as idolatry, adultery, and homosexuality. "And such were some of you," he declared. "But you were washed, you were sanctified, you were justified in the name of the Lord Jesus Christ and in the Spirit of our God" (1 Cor. 6:11, RSV).

Paul's contrast between the darkness of this sin and the light of God's love is a good model for all Christians to follow in their attitude. Homosexual activity is a heinous sin, but this doesn't relieve us of our responsibility to work and pray for the redemption of the sinner.

**Bibliography:** Boswell, J., *Christianity, Social Tolerance and Homosexuality* (1981); Parrinder, G., *Sex in the World's Religions* (1980); Thielicke, H., *The Ethics of Sex* (1964).

See HOMOSEXUALITY; PROMISCUITY; SEX; SEXUAL MORALITY AND PERVERSIONS.

**LIBEL.** The law recognizes a right to take legal action for damage to one's reputation in two situations: slander, where the defamatory remarks have only been spoken, and libel, where they have been printed or recorded in more permanent form. In order for a libel suit to succeed, the comments in question must have constituted an attack on the person's own character or reputation, such as would tend to lower him in the estimation of right-thinking members of society. The principal defenses to a defamation action are "truth"—the proven veracity of the remarks made—"fair comment"—nonmalicious statements about matters of public concern, published in the interests of listener, speaker, or society—"privilege"—an accurate report of court or government proceedings—and "consent"—including the implicit consent given by those who voluntarily assume positions in the public eye.

The ethical objections to defamatory comments about one's fellow man begin with the commandment "Thou shalt not bear false witness against thy neighbor" (Deut. 5:20). Slanderers are frequently condemned throughout the Bible because they bring unrest and dissension by making false accusations against their leaders (Num. 14:36; Ps. 101:5; Prov. 10:18; Jer. 6:28).

In the modern era of instantaneous and widespread news transmission, it is especially important to thwart libelous publications that are willing to unjustly damage a person in the eyes of millions, all for the sake of sensationalist rumor. However, the withholding of unfavorable information about a person or event can also constitute a sort of false witness. If we are to make responsible decisions about our society, we must be given material from which to judge those in the public eye. Journalists should not be restrained through the fear of libel suits from reporting the shortcomings of our leaders. This applies to factual comments as well as to some unsubstantiated rumors of questionable activities that we can only hear about through others, but that may require our attention and investigation. Thus, the traditional defenses to defamation remain important. If the media are encouraged to exercise their responsibilities in an ethical manner, then open commentary will safeguard the freedom of the press, of speech, and of society itself.

**Bibliography:** *Duncan and Neill on Defamation,* 2nd ed., (1983); Street, H., *Freedom, the Individual and the Law,* 5th ed., (1982).

S.E.R.

**LIBERALISM, ETHICAL.** The term "liberal," when used in an ethical context, is generally interpreted to refer to those persons who advocate a wide degree of freedom by the individual in making decisions about ethical matters. Extreme ethical liberalism denies the validity of such concepts as a strict ethical code and the ethical requirements of God's Law. They prefer instead to let circumstances and the rational power of man's mind dictate what is right and wrong in specific situations.

**LIBERTY.** While the terms *freedom* and *liberty* are often used interchangeably, *freedom* is philosophically the broader term, encompassing the meanings of *liberty*. Freedom is a function or capacity of spiritual beings. Persons are spiritual beings. To be a person is to be a rational, self-conscious spiritual reality capable of purposeful activity which is morally qualified. Freedom involves the reality of contingency in the world order—that things may go this way or that depending upon the choice of a spiritual being—in contrast to the freedom-denying determinism of idealism and materialism.

Liberty is freedom from fate, necessity, or arbitrary control. It is the right to choose, which choice makes a difference to the course of events. This broad definition embraces a wide range of issues. They may be vital issues such as religious liberty, freedom of the press, civil liberties, political freedom, liberty to move from one place to another, liberty to choose a vocation, or issues which may be important or trivial such as social drinking, use of tobacco, or addiction to soap operas.

A moral person, including the Christian, acknowledges that there are limits within which freedom may be exercised. Thus definitions of liberty such as "the right to do anything," "exemption from compulsion," "the power to do as one likes," and "subject only to the laws of nature" are inadequate. Human actions ought to be qualified morally. The Christian prizes his or her liberty as God's gift and aims to enhance freedom through the moral utilization of the elements of

the scientifically dependable world. Therefore increase of the control of one's actions in relation to moral and spiritual ideals and ends leads to increase of freedom. These ideals reflect the will of God for the maximizing of good in the world. In this respect Christians see themselves as co-workers with God, redeemed to be free, good persons who share God's life and work. God's providential oversight of a scientifically dependable world and the reality of persons who are responsible to utilize their freedom in moral ways are the truth of the way things are to the Christian.

In the New Testament, liberty in Christ is a crucial issue. Salvation is by grace alone and is salvation to liberty. This is a major Pauline theme (Rom. 3:21-26; Gal. 5:1), in contrast to the treadmill of legalistically imposed religious observances which cannot justify a person before God (Acts 15:10-11).

Nevertheless, freedom in Christ does not signify that Christians are free to do anything at all. The freedom of grace is not license to sin, but a call to spiritual liberty which is bounded by the grace of Christ. Paul says, "you were called to freedom, brethren; only do not use your freedom as an opportunity for the flesh, but through love be servants of one another" (Gal. 5:13; note 5:13-25 and Rom. 6).

Three major points follow from these New Testament truths:

First, true liberty excludes the practice of those things which are distinctly sinful. In chapters 5—6 of his first letter to the Corinthians, Paul rebukes the church for tolerating certain abuses of liberty. This highlights the apparently paradoxical truth that using freedom to sin is really bondage and that the life of freedom is the moral life. Paul's seven lists of vices make sobering reading: Romans 1:29-32; 1 Corinthians 5:11-13; 6:9-11; 2 Corinthians 12:20-21; Galatians 5:19-21; Ephesians 4:31 and 5:3; Colossians 3:5-9.

Second, true liberty avoids the practice of those things which tend to enslave. Here Christians give full credence to the modern principle of the conditioned response. However, Christians believe that they are responsible for the ways in which they condition themselves into irresponsible, immoral, or illegal behavior. For example, small amounts of mood modifiers, or a little social drinking, or the occasional cigarette may lead to addiction. The Christian principle is, "All things are lawful to me but I will not be enslaved by anything" (1 Cor. 6:12). This is a sober injunction to moderation or total abstinence.

Third, true liberty takes into account the effects of actions upon others. This is the significance of Paul's question of whether an act or habit is edifying or unedifying. He counters the aphorism "all things are lawful for me" with the rejoinder "but not all things are helpful" (1 Cor. 6:12; 10:23). The example he employs is instructive (1 Cor. 10:23—11:1): Pagan meat vendors first offered their goods to the gods before selling them at the public market. The question arises, Ought a Christian to eat meat previously dedicated to a pagan god? The answer is, Of course we know that an idol is a nonentity and that the offering of the meat makes it neither better nor worse. Nevertheless, the Christian who understands the best use of his or her liberty will refrain from eating such meat if eating it offends a Christian who has scruples about that sort of thing.

This appears to proscribe personal liberty by the mores and sometimes foibles of others. It may well do so, though no Christian is bound completely or permanently by the erratic or irrational behavior of others. Nevertheless, the issue is one of love and edification, not merely of personal rights. The Christian can say, "I am free," but can also choose to say, "I am ready to limit my freedom and to shape my habits and interests so as to be helpful to myself and to others."

For Christians, liberty is a primary value (2 Cor. 3:17). It may be said that a key purpose of the Creator is to create free, good persons who manifest life as temples of the Holy Spirit (1 Cor. 3:16-17).

**Bibliography:** Fromm, E., *The Fear of Freedom* (1963); Gibbs, M., *Christians With Secular Power* (1981); Mill, J. S., *On Liberty* (1859); Miller, A. O., (ed.), *The Christian Declaration on Human Rights* (1977).

S.J.M.

**LICENSE, LICENTIOUSNESS.** This term, derived from the Latin *licet*, "it is lawful," is used in several senses, one of which signifies the granting of legal permission for the performance of certain duties. The authorizing body which sanctions such a procedure often issues a written certificate to that effect, which is known as a license. The fact that the license has been issued merely indicates that the licensee is authorized to function within the terms set out in the license and gives no guarantee as to the quality or effectiveness of the permitted functions.

A common use of *license* has to do with the transgressing of bounds of decency or sexual morality, the indulgence in which is known as *licentiousness*. This is the translation of the New Testament Greek term *aselgeia* in some modern English versions of Mark 7:22, Romans 13:13, and Galatians 5:19, where indecency or flagrant immorality are being condemned.

License is characterized not merely by sexual immorality as such, but also by a clear and deliberate defiance of behavioral canons established both by God and by society. In condemning licentiousness the New Testament teaches that Christian liberty does not permit the believer to continue in sin (Rom. 6:1). A life of spiritual holiness demands purity in thought, word, and deed, thereby expressly prohibiting the believer from indulging in licentious behavior.

**LIFE, SACREDNESS OF.** Life may be defined as a dynamic biological property which characterizes the existence of plants, animals, and human beings as long as they continue to function actively. Once this vital principle of existence has departed from the organism concerned, it is not possible in the normal course of events to restore it, and in consequence deterioration and decay overtake the tissues. In common experience the life principle is constantly at risk, and as a result the various organisms exercise some innate defense mechanisms to counter the possibility of extinction. These are not always completely adequate, however, and even if they are on occasions they merely postpone the inevitable fact of death for the organism under consideration. The presence of life seems to be correlative with the urge for survival, and this would appear to indicate that life in general is possessed of some intrinsic worth, quite apart from subsidiary manifestations in terms of procreation, productivity, and the like.

If this can be predicated of plants and animals, it can be asserted confidently in the case of human beings. The biblical doctrine of creation regards life as a property of the divine Creator with which all organic forms were endowed. Humanity as a special creation was formed from constituent elements already present in the ground (Gen. 2:7), with the qualitative addition of the "living breath" of God which afforded the species its uniqueness in the created universe. This very special attribute was described in the Hebrew as *nephesh hayyah*, a term that is unfortunately not easy to translate properly. Many versions use the expression *living soul*, following the tradition of the King James Version, but this raises metaphysical problems that the Hebrew does not appear to contain. *Nephesh* can often be translated quite properly as "self," and if personhood or identity were to be understood it would be consistent with humanity's uniqueness. Occasionally the phrase was used of animals also, perhaps in the recognition that they partook somewhat of the faculties of humans by being mobile and able to communicate in a very elementary manner. In both cases the term *hayyah* ("living") does no more than recognize in them the presence of a vital principle which enables them to function actively and which is the gift of the Creator.

But because humanity is stated expressly to have been created in the image of God (Gen. 1:26), unlike any other aspect of creation, the *nephesh hayyah* is not merely a natural endowment but an active aspect of God's own being. To be a "living self" or a "living person" means that, as distinct from all other forms of organic life, human beings possess an element of deity in their nature that enables reciprocal communication to take place between creature and Creator. Among other attributes it ensures that the individual's personhood is not destroyed by death, but instead returns to the Creator (Eccles. 12:7) while the physical component reassumes its original form (Gen. 3:19).

To recognize that human personality has been endowed with an element of the divine nature is one consideration. But to say that, in consequence, human life is supremely sacred is quite another. In the first instance the concept of *sacredness* will need to be liberated from all its modern accretions of meaning and defined carefully in terms of what it signified to God's ancient people who first became acquainted with it. In the process it will be observed that *sanctity* and *sacredness* are not specifically biblical terms in the sense that *holiness* is, for example. Secondly, whatever may be thought of humanity's pristine moral and spiritual condition, the fact of human rebellion against God, resulting in what theologians have styled as "the Fall" (Gen. 3), produced a qualitative alteration in the nature of *homo sapiens* that required no less an achievement than the substitutionary atonement for sin through Christ's death in order that humans might become reconciled to God (2 Cor. 5:18-19). Whatever qualities of sacredness attached to our earliest progenitors at the beginning were certainly impaired to a serious degree at a very early period, and the subsequent phases of human history were marked by violence and corruption which depicted human life unmistakably as cheap and sinful.

In spite of these circumstances, God was able to speak to humans, and there were occasions when individuals or small groups responded to the communication with varying degrees of obedience. Interestingly enough, the first recorded crime in Scripture (Gen. 4:8) shows the complete disregard for the image of God in his brother that Cain manifested, an example that was to be followed by Lamech (Gen. 4:23). In subsequent generations the people became so perverse and corrupt that God came close to destroying all of them, whether they bore his *imago* or not, in a great deluge. If the human spirit partook of such sacredness as some expositors imagine, it would have been out of character for God to have brought about such extermination. In the event, the wicked were destroyed and eight righteous persons comprising Noah and his family were saved (Gen. 6:8-11; 2 Pet. 2:5). It would thus appear that sacredness and corruption cannot cohere realistically in an individual and that, for the image of God to be manifested, a person must be just and perfect, living in obedience to God's will. The unique character of the *imago dei*, with its ability to receive communications from God, provides for these very contingencies (Gen. 6:9).

Yet despite the prevalence of sin in human life, it is possible to make some qualitative assessment of an individual's existence, and it is interesting that the image of God in humans is appealed to in this connection. In a number of postdiluvian instructions to Noah, God deals with the punishment to be inflicted in cases of capital crime (Gen. 9:5-6), stipulating that whoever sheds man's blood, by man shall his blood be shed. Such a procedure has complete divine sanction because God's image in humans has been ruthlessly violated by the act of murder, and therefore it is God who legislates the restitution. It should be noted that only one life, that of the murderer, is to be forfeited as a penalty, and not those of his family, clan, or tribe.

Whatever may be thought about the inherent "sacredness" of the *imago dei*, it is apparently not so sacrosanct or inviolable as to prevent a murderer from suffering the penalty of death. What this prescription does, however, is to evaluate human existence in terms of individual worth. Each life has value, but the consistency of the race demands that no life shall be worth either more or less than any other individual life. Human existence may not be characterized by conspicuous sanctity, but it evidently does possess quantitative as well as qualitative value.

This intrinsic worth is recognized in the Mosaic legislation, as for example in the statute protecting the dignity of the prisoner by limiting the number of blows to be inflicted by way of punishment (Deut. 25:2, 3). But nowhere does the law teach that, because human life is so supremely sacred, nothing must be done that will terminate it; and every effort must be made to preserve it, no matter what the circumstances. Murder was prohibited (Exod. 20:13; Deut. 5:17), and the guilty person was to be punished by execution when apprehended (Exod. 21:12), but only on the strict condition of "life for life" (Exod. 21:23).

In his teachings Jesus supported the enactments of the law, and significantly enough did not repudiate capital punishment in the process. Indeed, he proclaimed that motive had now to be taken into consideration, so that an adulterous or homicidal intent was to be regarded as the equivalent of the crime itself (Matt. 5:28). At no time in his ministry did Jesus teach or assume that human life is so sacred as to be inviolable. In point of fact, instead of being sympathetic toward some Galileans whom Pilate had murdered, he demanded repentance of his hearers lest they should also perish similarly (Luke 13:1-3). What Christ did require of his followers was faith, obedience, and holiness of life; and he promised the gift of the Holy Spirit to guide them into all truth (John 14:16-26). In the Epistles, the innate sacredness of life is ignored in favor of exhortations to believers to live so as to manifest the fruit of the Spirit and reject the defiling works of the flesh (Gal. 5:16-26). In other words, the writers are not so much concerned with sacredness as with sanctification.

The concept of the "innate sacredness of human life" has therefore no place in Scripture (whereas the *imago dei* has) and can only be maintained by misinterpreting or misunderstanding certain biblical precepts. It is a prominent feature of certain Oriental religions, however, including Hinduism; and when extended in its crudest form to include "all" life it is beset by the illogical superstitions associated with reincarnation. If, therefore, life is not innately sacred, there can be no objection to the killing of animal or insect pests, to capital punishment carried out by duly constituted authority, or to participation in war at the summons of the state. It must be quite clear, however, that where human life is taken it must not be on an independent or unilateral basis, but must be grounded in lawful authority.

See ABORTION; CAPITAL PUNISHMENT; FETAL RIGHTS.

**LIFEBOAT ETHICS.** This rather curious ethical subject has arisen out of the larger consideration of population growth and its implications. Statistics which indicate that the world's population is increasing by significant proportions annually have led many thoughtful people to question the ability of the earth's food productivity to sustain such growth indefinitely. Pressing though this concern may be, it is by no means new. As an economic treatise the problem was given its classic expression by Thomas R. Malthus in his *Essay on the Principle of Population*, published in 1798.

Malthus was a clergyman of the Church of England who subsequently became a teacher of history and economics. His interest in the problems of population arose from his view that population tended to increase more quickly than the food supplies available to sustain it. Were the world's population to reach significant proportions, food shortages and actual famine conditions would result. Since it seemed impossible to Malthus for food production to outstrip population growth, the only way in which a reasonable balance could be obtained was to reduce the numbers of human beings through wars or as a consequence of natural disasters of various kinds. Interestingly enough, Malthus rejected the idea of limiting the size of families by what nowadays is called birth control.

In Malthus's day the enormous ability of even a small, selected area of the earth's surface to produce ample supplies of food was still unrecognized. Despite the exponential growth of the world's population, economists and agriculturalists maintain that improved farming techniques, combined with good administration and distribution facilities, can prevent the ravages of famine from ravaging the world's population. But there are others, including conservationists, who are anxious about the ability of available land to sustain the needs of the burgeoning human race indefinitely.

"Lifeboat ethics" reflects this latter concern and looks, perhaps with unnecessary pessimism, to the time when the shortages that Malthus envisaged will be a reality. If there are too many people for the available supplies, it is asked, who will be fed and who will not? Perhaps inspired by the reality of events in World War II, the situation is likened to a lifeboat drifting on the ocean after a ship has been torpedoed. There are men in the water, swimming toward the lifeboat and crying out pathetically to be picked up. But unfortunately there are too many of them for the capacity of the lifeboat, and if everyone is taken aboard the lifeboat will founder and all will be lost. The ethical dilemma is basically that encountered in medicine from time to time and can be crystallized in the question "Who shall live?" The instinct of self-preservation is unlikely to prompt the first people aboard the lifeboat to surrender their places so that latecomers may live, and therefore some must die if some are to be saved. Yet there are Christians and others who have been known to give their lifejackets at a time of shipwreck to others who do not have any, so that they might be saved as the donors drowned. An analogous ethical dilemma was solved concerning the death of Christ by the dictum of Caiaphas that it was better for one man to die rather than that the nation should perish (John 11:50). Christians should be in the forefront of projects that would forestall or alleviate world hunger, but equally they should be concerned with propagating the concept of realistic family planning. For only if population increases are limited severely will the disastrous pragmatism of "lifeboat ethics" ever be avoided.

See POPULATION CONCERNS.

**LOANS, MORAL OBLIGATIONS OF.** Lending and borrowing are major financial activities, not only of private individuals and institutions, but also of governments. Recent years have witnessed the expansion of the provision of credit. Strictly, a loan is only one method of obtaining credit. Hire purchase, the credit card, and arrangements to defer payments for purchases have largely replaced the moneylender and pawnbroker. Loans to purchase homes and land and to finance businesses can be sought from the banks and other institutions. The securities given for credit have developed from the simple deposit of movables or chattels to more complex schemes involving the assignation of life policies to security. Guarantors are probably less frequently sought than at one time. An exception to the declining use of guarantors arises in situations where a lender will seek a guarantee from the directors and shareholders of a limited company.

Behind the expansion of credit has been the desire to defeat the bad effects of inflation by settling a liability for major investments at as early a date as possible. The expectation has been that inflation will work in the borrower's favor by reducing the value of subsequent repayments. Another motivation that explains the increase in borrowing is the wish to gain the use of assets quickly. Things should be enjoyed now, even if that means paying later.

Societies have found it necessary to control the grant of credit and protect the borrower from exploitation. In the Old Testament, there are clear prohibitions against charging interest on a loan (Lev. 25:26; Deut. 20:19). This prohibition is limited to loans between brother Israelites. It is stated in Deuteronomy that interest may be charged on loans to foreigners. Proverbs 22 offers discouragement to anyone thinking of becoming a borrower or guarantor. In verse 7 it is explained that "the rich rule over the poor, and the borrower is the servant of the lender." Verses 26 and 27 contain severe warnings for the guarantor: "Do not be a man who strikes hands in pledge or puts up security for debts; if you lack the means to pay, your very bed will be snatched from you." Nehemiah illustrates some of the problems that have arisen through overindebtedness.

Modern societies have also developed consumer credit laws. The aim of the laws is to protect the borrower and possibly the guarantor. Borrowers are often in a weaker financial position than lenders and may only too easily be persuaded by enthusiastic and overoptimistic salesmen to enter apparently advantageous transactions. At the same time, there are ways of stating an interest rate that disguises its real effect on the borrower. The temptation to acquire is so strong that people can in a short time overextend their indebtedness. Thus the laws may protect the individual by allowing a borrower time to reflect on his decision and cancel an agreement. Excessive interest may be struck down by law. The law may demand that certain information be clearly presented to a borrower if the contract of loan is to be valid. Similar protections may be offered to a guarantor.

Many responsible institutions go beyond the strict requirements of the law and investigate the circumstances of a would-be borrower to make sure that the loan can be repaid. Additional protection may be available to a borrower or his family through insurance or life assurance.

Perhaps the major problem that borrowers might face would be a period of deflation when they would be trapped by loans of values greatly exceeding the values of their assets. Borrowers would then lose some freedom of mobility. Even selling up would not pay off their loans.

In summary, the moral obligations of the borrower are to examine his ability to pay before undertaking indedtedness and to ensure that he does not become the slave of the financial institutions. The lender must be careful not to induce the weak into becoming borrowers and must avoid excessive rates of interest.

M.H.J.

**LONGSUFFERING.** This archaic word, which has been dropped from most modern biblical translations, is a graphic rendering of the Greek *makrothumia*, meaning literally "long in temper." In this word *long* is the equivalent of *patient*, and the Greek term is analogous to the Hebrew *erek aph*, or "long of countenance," "long of anger." The expression is used of God consist-

ently and in Exodus 34:6 constitutes a self-revelation of his character, for which the Israelites should have been far more grateful than they were. Like other ancient nomadic and seminomadic peoples, the Hebrews lived by custom and personal inclination rather than by law. Even though at Sinai they had promised implicit obedience to the provisions of the covenant (Exod. 24:7), they had no clear concept of what was involved, as their many subsequent acts of apostasy showed. In his mercy God warned them repeatedly of the penalties attached to idolatry and the repudiation of the covenant. When all efforts proved fruitless and God's patience finally came to an end, he sent the curses attached to covenant violation (Deut. 28:15-68) upon them.

Jesus gave no specific teaching concerning longsuffering, but exemplified it unmistakably in his life. Paul, however, commended those who by patient well-doing seek the glory of the kingdom (Rom. 2:7) and included longsuffering in his list of spiritual fruits (Gal. 5:22). Indeed, his concept of the Christian's vocation included meekness and exemplary patience (Col. 1:11; 3:12) in imitation of Christ's life. Patience with fellow Christians is, as Paul discovered, often as demanding (Eph. 4:12) as it is with members of secular society.

**LORD'S PRAYER, THE.** The Lord's Prayer is the title given two similar (though not identical) prayers that our Lord taught his disciples. Contemporary studies of the Lord's Prayer usually center on such matters as the theological significance of its differing forms in Matthew and Luke, comparative studies between Jewish and Christian prayers, and detailed exegetical issues. We shall observe here only such matters as are directly beneficial in understanding and applying the prayer ethically today.

The tradition history of the Lord's Prayer (that is, the way in which the words of the prayer were transmitted first in oral and then perhaps in some intermediate written form) is important in critical scholarship. It is debated whether our Lord taught the Lord's Prayer once, in which case the differences in wording are due to changes caused by literary or theological intentions, or simply unintentionally in the course of transmission, or whether the Lord taught the prayer in slightly different forms on two or more occasions. The latter would fit the circumstances of an itinerant teacher, would explain the differences, but would not rule out appropriate modifications in the respective contexts of Matthew and Luke. In either case, it is the final form in the canonical Gospels that is important for our purposes here. In each setting our understanding of the Lord's Prayer is helped by giving attention to the context. Conversely, the prayer forwards the teaching of the respective passages.

The Lord's Prayer in Matthew 6:9-13 lies near the center of the Sermon on the Mount. Since the main function of this sermon is to establish the true nature of righteousness and the ethical standards that God expects of people in his kingdom, we may expect that the Lord's Prayer will contribute toward this purpose. But human ethical behavior is determined only with reference to the character of God himself. Therefore both the sermon and the Lord's Prayer contain teaching about the parental nature of God as Father and about our relationship to him.

This relationship bears not only on prayer but on other religious practices as well. The context of the Lord's Prayer is Jesus' teaching on this larger subject. Jewish piety was expressed, as we know also from the writings of postbiblical Judaism, not only in prayer but also in such practices as fasting and the giving of alms to needy persons. The heavenly Father does not reward those who practice their piety for public observation and approval (v. 1). Giving to the needy (vv. 2-4) and fasting (vv. 16-18) are to be done without ostentation. While alms were normally given to beggars publicly in the street, and while a person would probably be seen outside during a day of fasting, prayer can be done in seclusion (v. 6). The context of the prayer in Matthew, therefore, is, in diminishing concentric circles: Jesus' teaching about God's standards of righteousness, his teaching about the practice of religious piety, and his teaching about prayer.

Not only the Jewish people, who were Jesus' audience in the Gospel setting, but also pagans attempted to establish and maintain a relationship with a divine being. Several times in the sermon the Lord made a comparison between the ethical behavior of his hearers and that of the pagans. He described this behavior in terms of their relationship to people (Matt. 5:47), to things (6:32), and the God himself (5:7-8). It is this latter relationship that is in view as Jesus introduces the Lord's Prayer. The pagan babbles, that is, pours out a stream of words or sounds intended to get his god's attention (v. 7). One reason that Jesus teaches his prayer is to help us give expression to our true relationship with God as Father.

Given this context, it is appropriate that the prayer is introduced with the word, *houtos*, meaning, "in this manner" (Matt. 6:9). Jesus does not teach the prayer here so much to provide a precise *form* as to show *how* one may pray with true piety before our heavenly Father.

In Luke, the prayer is not offered as part of a larger unit of teaching, but is in direct response to the disciples' request for teaching on prayer, that is, to be taught a prayer. A teacher's theology can be given succinct expression in a prayer. Therefore Jesus' introduction is, "When you pray, say..." (Luke 11:2). The Lord's Prayer can therefore appropriately either be followed in substance, as Matthew implies, or be repeated exactly, as seem to be indicated in Luke.

The prayer opens with three so-called "Thou petitions," the prayers concerned with the glory of God. The position of these before the "We petitions," offered on behalf of the petitioner, is ob-

viously significant. The form of address, "Father" (Luke) or "Father in heaven" (Matthew) expresses Jesus' teaching and also his practice. The Jewish people did have a concept of God as a father (Deut. 32:6; Ps. 103:13; Isa. 63:3; Hos. 11:1; Mal. 2:10 in the Old Testament; *Ta'anit* 23b in the Babylonian Talmud). But Jesus taught an individual personal relationship with God as Father and certainly expressed a unique relationship with God himself (Matt. 11:27; Luke 2:49). The Sermon on the Mount contains further implications of the fatherhood of God as Jesus encourages his followers to trust God completely for daily needs and their future security (vv. 25-34).

The plural "*our* Father" in Matthew suggests the corporate nature of this prayer. Cyprian (third century) commented that Jesus did not intend prayer to be made *singillatim* or *privatim*. It has been proposed that this probably means not "individual" and "private" prayer, as often construed, but "individualistic" and "self-centered" (in accordance both with Scripture and with the other teachings of Cyprian). Jesus had just spoken of the need to avoid the ostentation of those who paraded their piety in public and in that connection advised modest prayer in one's room. But that was not intended as a substitute for corporate prayer, since elsewhere Scripture does describe examples (Acts 1:14; 12:12). It is appropriate that the family of the heavenly Father should talk with him together.

The first petition, "Hallowed be your name," is of immense significance. It epitomizes the repeated imperative in the Old Testament that the name of God should be known and honored throughout the entire world. To "hallow" means to acknowledge as (or, in some contexts, actually to make) holy (1 Pet. 3:15). God revealed his name in Exodus 3:13-15. It was his intention that Israel should proclaim his name and extend his reputation. God's reputation was indeed a concern to some, for example, Moses (Num. 14:15-19), Hezekiah (2 Kings 19:19), and David (Ps. 86:8-10). In this last passage, David anticipates the time when "all the nations" will worship God and "will bring glory to your name."

Israel should have devoted herself to the sublime task of hallowing the name of God among the nations. This sadly did not happen, and so God had (so to speak) to do it himself: "I will show the holiness of my great name, which has been profaned among the nations, the name you have profaned among them. Then the nations will know that I am the LORD... when I show myself holy through you before their eyes" (Ezek. 36:23). To hallow the name of God among the nations has been the great missionary task of the people of God from the time of the Old Testament through the present. Also in daily life Christians are to glorify God in all they do. The meaning of *glorify* is to "ascribe glory to God, to enhance God's reputation." To call God, who is holy, our Father has an ethical implication. Peter follows his injunction to holiness (quoting "Be holy because I am holy" from Lev. 11:44, 45; 19:2; 20:7) with "Since you call on a Father who judges each man's work impartially, live...in reverent fear" (1 Pet. 1:17). The Lord's Prayer thus opens with an expression of the high calling of the people of God. It is not only a petition, but an act of worship and a commitment to bring glory to God in daily life.

God's name will be hallowed throughout the world when his "kingdom come [s]" and when his "will [is] done on earth as it is in heaven." These two next petitions are thus closely linked with the first. This is seen already in Psalm 145, which connects the praising of God's "holy name" (v. 21) with God's kingship (v. 1) and kingdom (vv. 11-13). Jesus' conquest of the powers of darkness indicated the arrival of the kingdom (Matt. 12:28; Luke 11:20). Yet the time when God's "Anointed" will rule the nations with a rod of iron (Ps. 2:9) is still future. The believer can therefore pray for both (1) the effective power of God's kingdom today in the lives of those who have been "brought...into the kingdom of the Son he loves" (Col. 1:13) and (2) the coming of God's righteous kingdom at the return of Christ. It is only as God is obeyed as the rightful King, whether over the individual believer, over the church, or over the world, that God's will is done. Thus both individual and social ethics are involved in the petitions about the coming of the kingdom and the accomplishment of God's will.

Since God's rule implies universal justice, it is understandable why those who forward a theology of liberation draw on the Lord's Prayer as a resource. The need for justice, especially in various Third World countries, is without controversy. So is the need for daily bread, the petition that immediately follows. There can be little doubt of the desperate need for Christians to offer the Lord's Prayer. Any difference of opinion does not center on the need for God's holiness, kingdom, and will, but rather (1) *theologically* on differences concerning the nature and coming of the kingdom and (2) *politically* on the responsibility of the church in this age to be an instrument of social justice.

The petition concerning daily bread is expressed in slightly but significantly different words in Matthew and in Luke. The tense aspect of the verb *give* in Matthew is once and for all (aorist) but continuous or repeated (present) in Luke. There is a corresponding difference in the time reference. Matthew has the word *today* (*semeron*), while Luke has *each day* (*kath' hemeran*). The effect of this difference is to imply a simple, perhaps single, act and time of giving in Matthew and a repeated daily trust in God for continuing provision of need in Luke. Some see in Matthew a reference to the future event of the coming of the kingdom, which is not demanded, but certainly compatible with the eschatological (that is, future) aspect of preceding petitions.

There is some uncertainty over the meaning of the Greek word usually translated "daily," which does not significantly affect the ethical meaning of the prayer.

The petition concerning forgiveness also contains different wording in the two Gospels. These do not constitute a problem. The use of *debts* in Matthew where Luke has *sins* is due to the familiar concept of sin as debt in Jewish thought. There is, however, a problem inherent in the words "as we also have forgiven" (Matthew) and "for we also forgive" (Luke). It has been supposed that this places the Lord's Prayer on "legal" ground, which, in turn, would imply that it is not suitable for believers in the "age of grace," but must apply to the kingdom in a Jewish framework. Such a point of view overlooks the fact that the Lord's Prayer is a "family prayer," that is, those who pray it are already children of the heavenly Father. The forgiveness sought involves relationships between child and Father and between siblings in the heavenly family. A human analogy would be the disfavor children who squabble among themselves incur from their parents. It is clear from 1 John 1:8—2:21 that forgiveness is a continuing element in the Christian life. The importance of relationships between believers also finds emphasis in Matthew 18:15-20, where, significantly, prayer has an important part. Scripture teaches that while we can not earn the right to be heard in prayer, certain wrong attitudes or relationships can obstruct prayer and forgiveness.

The "temptation" against which we should pray is not enticement to sin. Certainly God would not so entice us anyway, even if we did not pray, for it is unthinkable that he would tempt anyone in that sense (James 1:13-15). The word group that includes the word, *temptation* (*peirasmos*) has to do basically with testing in the relevant pre-Christian literature. Yet one can yield to pressure and sin, so that element is not completely ruled out. The idea that this refers to the great testing at the time of eschatological tribulation is unlikely since the definite article (found in Rev. 3:20) is not used with the word here. The petition here probably is to be kept not *from* but *during* testing, that is, kept from succumbing to it (1 Cor. 10:13; 2 Pet. 2:9). The petition for deliverance from evil probably refers not to abstract evil but to the evil one, because the Greek preposition translated "from" implies a person and because *evil* has the definite article. The concluding ascription of praise in Matthew is probably a later addition, apparently derived from 1 Chronicles 29:10-13.

The Lord's Prayer is, not surprisingly, similar in some respects to Jewish prayers of that period. Both naturally contain allusions to the Old Testament. The Jewish prayer known as the Kaddish contains the petition, "May he let his kingdom rule in your lifetime and in your days and in the lifetime of the whole house of Israel, speedily and soon." The Eighteen Benedictions also contains some ideas found in the Lord's Prayer. Jewish and Christian scholars emphasize the differences. The fact that the very context for the Lord's Prayer, the Gospels, teaches that the Messiah has come gives the Lord's Prayer a significance other prayers could not have.

The use of the prayer in the early church is attested as early as the *Didache* or *Teaching of the Twelve Apostles* (first part of the second century according to current opinion). It appears there in connection with baptism. It still remains the model prayer for Christians. It is appropriately named the *"Lord's* Prayer"—even though it was not recorded as a prayer Jesus used himself—because it is the prayer, and the only one, he taught.

**Bibliography:** Boff, L., *The Lord's Prayer: The Prayer of Integral Liberation* (1983); Guelich, R. A., *The Sermon on the Mount* (1982); Jeremias, J., *The Prayers of Jesus* (1978); Petuchowski, J. and Brocke, M., *The Lord's Prayer and Jewish Liturgy* (1978).

W.L.L.

**LOTTERY.** A lottery is a form of gambling which has often been used as a means of collecting money for a "good cause," but which now, in some areas, has become an end in itself. Its name was derived from the "lot" that was cast to determine winners in a process of chance selection from tickets or tokens that had been purchased by the participants. A lottery in Britain in the time of King James I helped to fund some early settlers in the American colonies, and charitable objectives have formed the excuse for this sort of gambling ever since.

Where lotteries operate legally they are patronized heavily and are often able to lure participants by offering the prospect of winning large sums of money, which are free of tax in some parts of the world. Only a very small percentage of the population refuses to indulge in such activities where they are permitted by law.

All the criticisms leveled against gambling in general apply to lotteries also and perhaps even more pointedly since the appeal to the individual's greed for instant wealth is so crass. The true Christian prefers to acquire money by honest labor (Eph. 4:28) and strives to avoid avarice and covetousness in all its forms. He or she is sufficiently mature to disburse money in a manner that will glorify God, mindful of the fact that even during Christ's dying agonies on the cross, Roman soldiers were gambling for his seamless robe, with no other concern that that of trying to satisfy a momentary covetousness (John 19:23-24).

**LOVE.** Poets, essayists, and novelists of all ages celebrate love as the greatest human emotion. Paul says that love is the highest virtue (1 Cor. 13:13). Differing and sometimes conflicting value systems as to the nature, place, and practice of love make for ambiguity in modern times.

Commonly understood, love is a feeling that is aroused by perceived attractive qualities in someone or something. Nevertheless, love is often powerfully evoked by the unbeauteous and wounded, even the grotesque. Love is a liking or affection for, an emotional attachment to, or sexual passion for a person of the opposite sex. Love is a wife or sweetheart. Love is friendship and personal appreciation.

Theologically, love is God's benevolence to men and His gracious action to redeem mankind. Man's chief end is to love God. Love is the affection Christians have for each other in the brotherhood as well as others outside.

Fundamentally, love is a function of persons and personal relations. This is the generic difference between Christianity on one side and systems of idealism and materialism on the other: Christians declare that personhood is the highest reality in the universe. God is love, and love is the ultimate state and activity of man (1 John 4:7-21). For Christians, love and ethics are jointly necessary parts of the sphere of persons and personal relations. They require each other. In materialist and behaviorist systems, love technically is a purely behavioral, value-free response. In idealist systems love is a needless complication of impersonal transcendental ideals. In Christian faith love is allowed its full emotional quotient on a sound moral footing and is not placed on a lower metaphysical level.

In the Old Testament God's love (*aheb*) embraces a wide range of meanings: affection, provision, mercy, care, redemption. These aspects show that God's love is personal, benevolent, saving, and moral. He loves individuals such as Abraham and David (1 Sam. 13:14; Isa. 41:8), those who trust Him (Ps. 60:5), and His beloved Israel (Isa. 63:9; Jer. 31:3). God's love places upon men the burden of loving obedience as their proper response to God's love (Deut. 4:37, 40; 7:12-13). Hosea's message is particularly poignant: God loves Israel still, even though she has played the harlot spiritually, and His enduring love will finally bring her back to Himself. God loves not only Israel; His love is universal (Deut. 33:3; Isa. 42:4-7).

The Old Testament is replete with terms that are synonymous with love and convey the truth about God's benevolence: loving-kindness (Deut. 5:10); mercy (Ps. 25:6); faithfulness (Lam. 3:23); and graciousness (Ps. 9:13). Many metaphors and images reinforce the truth about God's love. He cares for His children as a vinedresser cares for a vineyard, a shepherd for his sheep, or a physician for the sick. Above all, God cares for men as a father cares lovingly for his own child (Ps. 103:13).

In the New Testament *philos* and *agape* are the main terms used for love. The term *philos* and its cognates mean friendship, a beautiful relationship, to cherish. For example, the love of Jesus for Lazarus (John 11:3, 36), the father's love for the son (John 5:20), God's love to men (John

16:27), and Christian love for Christ (1 Cor. 16:22).

*Agape* dominates New Testament theological and ethical use. Love originates within the Godhead (John 14:31; 17:26). Love is the nature of God (1 John 4:8). God loves men savingly in Christ (Rom. 8:37; Eph. 2:4; 1 John 3:1, 16). It is man's duty to love God (Matt. 22:37; 1 John 4:19). Love to Christ is the heart of Christian faith (Eph. 6:24; 1 Pet. 1:8). Love is fundamental to Christian personal relationships (John 13:34; 1 Pet. 1:22; 1 John 3:11, 21).

The biblical characteristics of God's love set its ethical parameters. Love is given freely (Rom. 5:8), universal (John 3:16), sacrificial (Gal. 2:20), saving (Eph. 2:4), unfailing (Rom. 8:39), and purifying (2 Thess. 2:13). In short, God's love is person-centered and person-conserving on the moral footing of spiritual restoration. Appropriate human response is love that includes devoted loyalty to God (Matt. 6:24), affectionate obedience to God (John 14:15), and genuine care, matching His, for one's fellowman (1 John 4:12, 21). Love is the identifying mark of Christian communities (Eph. 4:16).

The most complete listing of the characteristics of love is in 1 Corinthians 13. Other parallel characteristics are: importuning on behalf of another (Philem. 9), restricting one's own liberty for the sake of another's welfare (Rom. 14:15), obligation to forgive (2 Cor. 2:7-8), sincerity (Rom. 12:9), unity (Phil. 2:2), and help (Heb. 6:10).

Love in the Bible is not defined or described in abstract terms. Its nature and characteristics are stated concretely. These convey not only the nature of love but the ethics of love as well. We should consider the following:

*Love to God.* "You shall love the Lord your God with all your heart, and with all your soul, and with all your mind...you shall love your neighbor as yourself" (Matt. 22:37-39). Christian ethics rests upon these two major premises, the second following from and enabled by the first. To love God is to give oneself up wholly to Him through faith and obedience. Love becomes the air one breathes for life, hence the capacity to love others. Love for God constitutes not only the saving response of faith to His redeeming grace in Christ it comprises as well the new mood of personality. From within this new mood one can react appropriately to specific situations and recognize and react appropriately to specific need. The Old Testament term for this attitude is "loving-kindness," which matches the meaning Paul gives to love as preferring always to think the best rather than the worst (1 Cor. 13:4-7).

*Self-love.* Modern definitions of love often begin with self-love. This ego-centered, narcissistic trend has gone so far as to say that the key to effective living is a proper self-image. While only a distortion of biblical teaching denigrates human personality, including the emotions, contemporary narcissism misses the crucial place that self-

sacrifice must have in a proper ethical life (Matt. 10:39; Mark 8:34; John 15:13). True understanding of self through love leads to self-sacrifice, without which nothing effective in life can be built, whether it is marriage, family, relationships, or a career. In Scripture, prideful egocentricity is contrasted with the fully realized life. For example, Paul puts down classical male chauvinist pride by elevating the virtues of humility and self-giving (Phil. 2:3), which were thought to be appropriate only for women and slaves.

*Romantic love.* There has been a distinct ascetic strain in Western Christendom. Eastern and evangelical Christian thought have generally accepted the ethical legitimacy of romantic love more readily than have large segments of the Catholic and evangelical perfectionist traditions, though in recent years Catholic writers have sought to relate eros to human love. There are still those, including some evangelicals, who accept the Song of Solomon only as an allegory rather than as a literal celebration of romantic love, which it is.

Samuel Bulter, the nineteenth-century essayist, remarked that "God is Love, I dare say. But what a mischievous devil love is." The writer in Proverbs ponders the mystery of awakening romantic love (30:18-19). Scripture combines wholesome appreciation for budding romantic love with chastity and reservation of sex to marriage (1 Cor. 7:9). The seeking of a bride for Isaac (Gen. 24, note vv. 62-67) results in a tender, romantic meeting and marriage. Jacob fell in love with Rachel and persisted until he had won her (Gen. 29:9-12, 28). Ruth loved Boaz and won his heart (Ruth 3). At the same time, the dangers of wrongly directed romantic love are pointed out as in the case of Samson's infatuation with Delilah (Judg. 16) and David's adulterous liaison with Bathsheba (2 Sam. 11—12).

Young people need encouragement to develop the arts of romantic love chastely and need emotional support in seasons of despair when romantic love fails. There is no reason to discourage romantic love but every reason to guide it helpfully and to nurture it in marriage. Modern debasement of the term "making love," which now often means fornication, should encourage Christians to recapture the sweetness, innocence, and high moral virtues of romantic love.

*Married love.* Christian marriage entails love in which the connubial partners share their lives fully and in which conjugal relations are the ongoing expression of their true love. Christian understanding of the created order places high priority on love in marriage and the achievement of delicate mutual understanding and fulfillment of emotional needs. This is the main point of Paul's discussion about marriage in 1 Corinthians 7. Married love should be self-giving and self-sacrificing (Eph. 5:25). It includes mutual bearing of burdens and responsibilities as well as mutual sharing of joys. It can fairly be said that love in marriage creates a new psychic entity that husband and wife share mutually, so that when bereaved the remaining partner feels as though part of him or her has died (Mark 10:6-9). Paul has in mind such unique love, intimacy, and trust when he employs the analogy of love in marriage to illustrate the love of Christ for the church (Eph. 5:21-33).

*Family love.* Husbands and wives, parents and children are urged to love one another (Ps. 103:13; Eph. 5:28; 6:4). Christian family love was unique in the ancient world. Jesus taught that the claims of husband and wife transcend even the ties to mother and father. This is not well understood by some modern parents, though it is a clear statement by Christ with regard to the social and ethical order of the kingdom of God.

Children are God's gift (Isa. 8:18). One of the most beautiful statements in Scripture is that of Cornelius, who gathered his household to hear Peter, "Now therefore we are all here present in the sight of God, to hear all that you have been commanded by the Lord" (Acts 10:33). Modern self-seeking finds children to be a burden. Christian love gives self to the interests of others, notably through family love.

*Fraternal love.* Love for one another within the Christian community is the badge of Christian society. Love creates the condition in which fellowship is nurtured (Col. 1:4; 2 Thess. 1:3). It is the witness of the earliest Christians, as in the *Plea* addressed to the emperor Marcus Aurelius by Athenagoras, that to regard one another as father, mother, brother, or sister is a sure way to protect the moral integrity of each person. A Christian would not wish to do to his own that which is morally demeaning. The concept of brotherhood and sisterhood among Christians is a powerful incentive to moral behavior.

*Neighbor love.* As noted earlier, the second part of the great love commandment is to love your neighbor as yourself (Matt. 19:19; 22:39). Paul repeats the commandment (Rom. 13:9), as does James (2:8). To love your neighbor as yourself means to desire for him nothing less than you desire for yourself. This is as much a missionary exhortation as it is an exhortation to loving care. The Christian ought to desire for others the same spiritual blessings he himself enjoys, and he ought to regard other persons as objects of love in the additional sense of caring and equitable treatment.

*Love to enemies.* This is the most dramatic of Jesus' teachings (Matt. 5:43-48; Luke 6:27-36). To love an enemy is to exercise the same love whereby God has first loved us as rebellious and often hurtful sinners. Such love absorbs the evil, which is the moral center of sacrifice and atonement. Forgiveness occurs first in the heart of the injured party and only then is it offered to the offender. Such love aims at spiritual renewal and reconciliation. Enmity is rendered ultimately powerless, even if the enemy remains an enemy despite such love. A fundamental principle of Christian ethics is the power of love to absorb evil

and to convert its power for good through forgiveness (Matt. 5:38-42; Rom. 12:17; 1 Thess. 5:15).

*Love of truth.* For Christians perception of and commitment to truth is as much a moral issue as it is an intellectual one. P. T. Forsyth remarked that the truth we see depends upon the men we are. It is one thing to see that something is true, but it is another to act upon it. True love is committed to truth and to that which is right (1 Cor. 13:6; Eph. 4:15; 1 John 5:3). A Christian must love truth and hate falsehood. Paul joins together the concepts of showing love and having a good conscience (1 Tim. 1:5).

Love of truth embraces mercy, not merely rectitude or unfeeling justice. Jesus taught that the righteousness of His followers must exceed the righteousness of the scribes and Pharisees, which amounted to legal rectitude. Christian love of truth includes the plus factor of grace and love.

Finally, Christian love is person-centered and redemptive. Only within the bonds of affection combined with morality can persons grow to full spiritual and emotional maturity. Love forgives, heals, restores, reconciles, and builds. Love commits to the highest, best, and holiest: "whoever keeps his word, in him truly love for God is perfected" (1 John 2:5).

**Bibliography:** Lasch, C., *The Culture of Narcissism* (1978); Lewis, C. S., *The Four Loves* (1960); Morris, L., *Testaments of Love* (1981); Yankelovich, D., *New Rules* (1981).

S.J.M.

**LOYALTY.** Wholehearted fidelity in one's allegiance to a person, cause, institution, or ideal is the essence of loyalty. Loyalty is widely believed to be a virtue and a praiseworthy character trait, because it is also widely believed that there are those to whom loyalty is properly due, or there are causes for which loyalty is fitting. Loyalty is not, however, an unqualified good. This is so because loyalty always has an object—one is always loyal to someone or to something. Whether loyalty is a virtue depends in large measure upon there being a proper match between one's loyalty and the object of that loyalty. Where there is a mismatch between the two, there we have something less than a virtue, possibly even a vice. Thus the total corrupt nature of an object may altogether disqualify it as a legitimate object of one's loyalty. In this regard, a wholehearted fidelity to the Nazi cause or to the mafia would be a perverted loyalty.

In other instances the finite nature of the object will place limitations upon the form that loyalty should take. For example, loyalty to a social club should not prompt one to sacrifice one's life or jeopardize one's financial future. This would be an exaggerated loyalty. In yet other stances, loyalty ought to take the form of criticism and correction. To serve one's country faithfully in the pursuit of ignoble ends would be blind loyalty. Loyalty is not to be uncritical of its object, forgetting the difference between right and wrong. On the contrary, when loyal patriots judge their country to be in the service of a mistaken or unjust cause, they will, as an expression of their loyalty, be willing to assist their country sacrificially in recharting her course. But in such circumstances it is not merely that they want just and good ends to prevail, but they want their country to serve those ends.

For the Christian, loyalty to the God and Father of Jesus Christ, and to His purposes in the world, is the sole object of a supreme loyalty and is the basis for testing the adequacy of all lesser loyalties. Other possible objects of loyalty include family, friends, country, and community. Each of these can be expressions of God's purposes in the world; and to the extent that our loyalty is linked with those purposes and is expressive of the divine will for human relationships, it may be deemed morally appropriate.

**Bibliography:** Bryant, S., "Loyalty," in Hastings, J., *Encyclopedia of Religion and Ethics* (1916), VIII, pp. 183–88; Rashdall, H., *Theory of Good and Evil* (1924).

R.W.

**LUST.** This term describes the emotion of lascivious passion when used in a sexual context or feelings of vehement desire when applied to a longing for inanimate or esthetic things. In the King James Version the word was used as a translation of the Hebrew *nephesh*, "soul," "self," "desire," as in Exodus 15:9 and Psalm 78:18. In Psalm 78:30 a direct object of desire was implied, whereas in Psalm 81:12 the meaning seems to be that of lewd imagination or perhaps blatant apostasy.

In the New Testament the common Greek word *epithumia*, "desire," was employed frequently to describe sensuous passion, against which believers were warned consistently. This situation is hardly surprising in view of the enormous amount of vice and sexual perversion which typified Greek and Roman culture. Paul quite obviously alluded to these corruptions in Romans 1:24-27 and elsewhere and took every opportunity of denouncing them to his readers. Lust is an extremely destructive spiritual influence and must be avoided at all costs by the Christian (1 Pet. 2:11), who instead must follow righteousness (2 Tim. 2:22), having crucified the flesh with its affections and lusts (Gal. 5:24, KJV). In the medieval Roman Catholic Church lust was classified as one of the seven deadly sins.

**LUTHERAN ETHICS.** Luther's chief contribution to Christian ethics was his emphasis upon the Christian life as one of thanksgiving. He believed that the behavior of the Christian is a gift, the "fruit" of a living faith in Jesus, and the result of His presence in the heart. At the same time, Luther's realism about the continuing sinfulness of the forgiven sinner led him to view the Christian life as a battle, in which thanksgiving

alternates with repentance. In spite of differences in Lutheran emphases since Luther's death (for example, in orthodoxy, pietism, rationalism, and existentialism), there are several key motifs that have continued to characterize Lutheran ethics.

*A Faith Ethic.* At the hub of these ideas is the doctrine of justification by faith. Lutherans have always stressed this truth as the spring from which the rest of Christian life and doctrine flows. "Good works cannot make a man good," Luther said. "Only a good man can perform truly good works." Thus, there can be no distinctly "Christian" ethics until people are converted and reborn in Christ. Through faith in Christ as one's sin-bearer, a sinner is grafted into Christ and made a new creature. Christ Himself is the source of this new life (that is, the vine), which makes a new ethical life possible (that is, the fruit, Matt. 7:17-18; 12:33; John 15:1-17; Rom. 11:17-24). Sometimes this emphasis on the spontaneity of the new life may seem, incorrectly, to deny moral effort on the part of the believer.

*An Ethics of Thanksgiving.* Because they thus view the Christian life as a gift, Lutherans consider thanksgiving to be the chief motive for Christian behavior. Those who follow Christ have been and are being freed from the bondage of self-interest. They have surrendered themselves to God and claimed Christ's death and resurrection as their own (Rom. 6:1-11). Since they are reunited, through Christ, with a merciful God who provides for all their needs, they need no longer worry about themselves. Now Christ calls them to direct their efforts toward the neighbor.

*A Two-Kingdom Ethic.* While Lutherans have always rejected the medieval distinction between a higher and lower Christian morality, they have sometimes been accused of substituting a double standard of their own. Luther did teach a twofold morality that distinguishes between the public "office" and the private "person." Although Luther's early thought tended to be somewhat dualistic, he developed a positive understanding of the two kingdoms as two dimensions of life in which every Christian participates. Each of the areas has a particular ethical focus.

On the one hand, Luther associated the inner life of the Christian with sanctification, or repentance, the daily battle with sin, self, Satan, and the world. In his Large Catechism, Luther refers to this as the "daily baptism," based upon Romans 6:1-23 and Colossians 3:1-17. Founded upon personal experience, and Paul's testimony in Romans 7:15-25, Luther believed that the Christian remains a sinner, at the same time that he is justified before God by faith in Christ (that is *simul iustus et peccator*). However, this is not an excuse to continue to walk in sin. On the contrary, throughout his life the Christian is called to fight against and "put off" his old love of sin and self and to "put on" his new identity in Christ. Each day Christ calls the believer to offer up "self" to die (Luke 9:23-24). Although Luther did believe that there must be progress in sanctification, he regarded the progress to be chiefly a growing awareness of one's sin and a corresponding growth of dependence upon Christ.

On the other hand, Luther associated the outer, public life of the Christian with vocation. Corresponding to the ongoing repentance for sin is an ongoing thanksgiving for Jesus, the Savior from sin. One of Luther's most helpful ideas is that God redeems all honorable vocations as places for expressing this thanksgiving.

*An Ethic of Moral Absolutes.* Because Luther regarded the Ten Commandments as the constitutional basis of earthly government, written in the hearts and minds of all people, he did not think that Christian ethics are necessarily different—in external respects—from the best natural ethics. The most distinctive feature of Christian ethics is the new source and motivation for doing good. However, Luther believed that natural law (that is, the law written on the heart) has become distorted by sin. God therefore provided the clear and certain revelation of His moral will in the Ten Commandments and other absolutes. Christ further clarified God's will in the Sermon on the Mount, revealing that the commandments must be kept in the heart as well.

Based upon the words of Christ and Paul, Luther taught that love is the fulfillment of the law (Mark 12:31; Rom. 13:8-10). However, Luther did not endorse a situation ethics based upon love alone. On the contrary, he regarded the Ten Commandments as an infallible guide that reveals the essential nature of love. For example, the three chief parts of his catechism are: (1) The Ten Commandments; (2) The Apostles' Creed; (3) The Lord's Prayer. Luther explains that in the first part God reveals what is required of us, in the second what He has provided for us. In the third part God commands that we pray continually, for obedience to keep the first, and for faith to believe the second. This indicates that Luther did recognize a "third use of the law." That is, Luther believed that in Scripture God has revealed moral absolutes that Christians ought to use as a guide for living. Luther also emphasized this conviction in his opposition to antinomians and in his appeals for church discipline.

**Bibliography:** Althaus, P., *The Ethics of Martin Luther* (1972); Bonhoeffer, D., *Ethics* (1955); *Ibid., The Cost of Discipleship* (1959); Koeberle, A., *The Quest for Holiness* (1936/38); Luther, M., *The Freedom of a Christian* (1520); *Ibid., The Large Catechism* (1529); *Ibid., Against the Antinomians* (1539); Thielicke, H., *Theological Ethics*, Vol. 1 (1979).

See ANTINOMIANISM; JUSTIFICATION AND ETHICS; LAW, THREEFOLD USE OF THE; ORDERS OF GOD; TWOFOLD REIGN OF GOD.

N.J.L.

**LYING.** Lying is one of the most serious forms of deception to be practiced by the human species. It can assume verbal or nonverbal guises, but its intent is still to proclaim something known to be false. Verbal lying consists of uttering statements which in part or whole are known by the person making them to be contrary to fact. In a court of law this type of false witness when given under oath is known as perjury, and because it is fundamentally inimical to the interests of justice it comprises a very serious offense.

The nonverbal form is sometimes described as "acting a lie" and is a hypocritical procedure which by the nature of its histrionic actions is intended to convey misrepresentation and deception. Yet another variety of lying is the so-called white lie. This euphemism for untruth purports to excuse the deception involved in the telling of a lie by the supposition that the motive, if not the actual deed, is worthy. Whether such an evaluation is justifiable subjectively or not, the fact remains that if such a procedure is used frequently, the distinction between "white" and "black" lies becomes blurred easily. This has led to the aphorism that those who tell white lies soon become color blind.

Lying was always abhorrent to the ideals of God's ancient covenant people. False witness was prohibited in the Ten Commandments (Exod. 20:16), and its prevalence in society was condemned uniformly by prophets and sages alike (Hos. 12:1; Amos 2:4; Prov. 14:5; 19:9). It was abhorrent because it represented something diametrically opposed to the ethical nature of the God who is truth (Deut. 32:4; Isa. 65:16).

In New Testament times Paul urged upon his hearers the veracity of his witness (Rom. 9:1; 1 Tim. 2:7) and demanded that the Christian should put away lying (Col. 3:9) and speak the truth with his or her neighbor consistently (Eph. 4:25). If believers obey this injunction from the emissary of the God of truth, they will be outstanding in a world of liars, deceivers, and assorted prevaricators.

See DECEPTION; TRUTHFULNESS.

**LYNCHING.** This title originated in an American procedure known as "Lynch's law" and consists of the summary execution, without due process of law, of one or more persons for alleged contravention of local laws or traditions. Those accused of such violations were generally arrested under conditions of violence and either given a sham trial or no trial at all before being dragged out to be executed. In American tradition this was by hanging, which was in effect death by strangulation. Lynching was often the concomitant of racial antagonism, and for some time prior to the American Civil War black persons were lynched for no other reason than a demonstration of the supposed supremacy of the white race.

The biblical tradition, based upon written law promulgated by God, abhors acts of terrorism and lawlessness, especially when they result in murder. The execution of criminals is only sanctioned when a capital crime has been committed and the offender has been tried and convicted (Num. 35:30; Deut. 17:6). The punishment then becomes a function of the state, and not of any individuals or terrorist groups (Num. 15:36). Execution merely on the basis of race in the absence of any statutory offense is reprehensible to Christian morality as an act of murder, and therefore all believers, mindful of Christ's own death at the hands of a mob, will do all in their power to repudiate and obliterate lynching.

See CIVIL RIGHTS; KU KLUX KLAN; MURDER; SECRET SOCIETIES.

# –M–

**MAGIC.** Magic is the attempt to manipulate spirits or occult forces of nature in such a way as to accomplish the will of the person doing the manipulation. It is a form of compensation for human inadequacy in the face of hostile forces. In one form or other magic must be as old as humanity. Cave paintings from paleolithic times depict animals struck with darts and the like, evidently an attempt to obtain the same result in hunting. Magic is found among all the ancient peoples of whom we have knowledge, and it persists into modern times.

Magic is often confused with religion. Some followers of every religion appear to view their religion as a form of magic, that is, as a way of constraining a superior power or powers to do the will of the worshiper. All such attempts are indeed forms of magic. But religion proper is altogether different; the worshiper endeavors to do the will of the deity, whom he sees as supreme; he is not trying to constrain the object of worship to do his own will.

In the environment of the ancient Near East, magic was universally held to be a legitimate practice, and the gods themselves practiced magic. For example, in Sumero-Akkadian literature we read of a great contest between Marduk and Tiamat, in which Tiamat used a charm and recited a spell, while Marduk, holding a red talisman between his lips, proved the better magician and won a decisive victory. Among the Canaanites there was the story of how Mot, the god of sterility, killed Baal, the god of fertility. Anath, Baal's sister, slew Mot, ground him up in a hand mill, and scattered his ashes on the land. The crops grew and thus gave evidence that Baal was alive again. This sympathetic magic has obvious importance for a fertility cult.

Magic could take many forms; and it is interesting, in view of the general attitude of the nations round about, that they were all forbidden to the Israelites. "There shall not be found among you any one who burns his son or his daughter as an offering, any one who practices divination, a soothsayer, or an augur, or a sorcerer, or a charmer, or a medium, or a wizard, or a necromancer. For whoever does these things is an abomination to the Lord; and because of these abominable practices the Lord your God is driving them out before you" (Deut. 18:10-12). There is discussion as to the precise meanings of each of these terms, but none as to the thoroughgoing nature of the prohibition of magical practices. It is because of their practice of magic that Yahweh is driving the Canaanites out from before the Israelites. His abhorrence of all forms of magic is a corollary of the central truth of Old Testament religion. Yahweh is the one God; there can be no thought of rival gods fighting against one another and employing magical arts in order to prevail. It is the will of Yahweh that is done; the worshiper cannot manipulate such a great God. He can only submit to Him and try to do His will. The Old Testament never addresses itself to the question of whether the magical arts are a sham. It is enough that they are wrong and that the people of God will have nothing to do with them. Sometimes, however, the Israelites engaged in such practices, as when Saul consulted the medium at Endor (1 Sam. 28:7-25), but this was always condemned.

Magic, of course, persisted into New Testament times, and it was just as much part of the world in which the servants of God lived then as it was in Old Testament times. There are specific references to practitioners of the magic arts, such as Simon Magus (Acts 8:18-24) and Elymas (or Bar-Jesus, Acts 13:4-12). The attitude of New Testament writers to magic may be gathered from Paul's address to Elymas: "You son of the devil, you enemy of all righteousness, full of all deceit and villainy, will you not stop making crooked the straight paths of the Lord?" (Acts 13:10). Paul includes sorcery among the "works of the flesh" (Gal. 5:19-21), and thus classes it with a variety of immoral forms of conduct. Sorcerers are excluded from the heavenly city and have their place in the lake of fire (Rev. 21:8; 22:15).

It is clear that magic has no place in biblical religion. Magic cannot fit into a religion that tells of a God who loves sinners so much that He sent His Son to die on a cross to put away their sin. Calvary is evidence of the love of God and of His will to give us all that is good. There is no place alongside this for the use of practices meant to constrain Him into doing the will of the worshiper. Sometimes professing Christians attempt to use prayer to get their own way, which is to see it as a form of magic. The use of amulets (like rabbit's foot charms) and the cult of "luck" are other survivals of magic that are out of harmony with the Christian way.

**Bibliography:** Kitchen, K. A., *Interpreter's Dictionary of the Bible*, 2, pp. 931–35; Mendelsohn, I., *Interpreter's Dictionary of the Bible*, 3, pp. 223–25; Wright, J. S. and Brown, C., *New International Dictionary of New Testament Theology*, 2, pp. 552–62.

L.M.

**MAGNANIMITY.** This term is derived directly from the Latin *magnanimitas,* meaning "greatness of soul," as used by the Roman orators. In employing this expression they were merely adopting the Greek concept of condescension on the part of a benefactor or a person known for high-principled behavior. For the Romans, an individual who possessed this enlargement of the mind could be counted upon to disregard trivialities as being inferior to his or her principles or avowed way of life.

Magnanimity is usually associated with strong persons such as victors in battle or outstanding leaders in other areas of life who are largely independent of their surroundings. It was reflected, for example, in the actions of David toward Mephibosheth (2 Sam. 9:1-7), the generosity and kindness that Elisha demonstrated toward his Syrian captives (2 Kings 6:18-23), and the prayer of the crucified Jesus that God would forgive his executioners (Luke 23:34).

Magnanimity most properly belongs to the individual who has had his or her perspective broadened by submission to Christ as Savior and Lord. Not merely is such a person immeasurably enriched by divine grace, but is all the more able to contemplate eternal rather than temporal things, thereby establishing a different set of values and priorities from those of the unbeliever. For some Christian ethicists magnanimity involves longsuffering (1 Cor. 13:4), while for others it includes generosity, hospitality, and condescension in grace to inferiors (Rom. 12:13, 16).

**MALICE.** Originating in a common Latin word *malum* ("something evil," "bad"), the word *malice* is normally understood to imply an intent or an expression of ill will by which harm, suffering, or affliction may come upon some other person. Malice was a common form of hatred in antiquity, expressing itself under such guises as evil gossip (Ps. 41:5-8), rejoicing over someone's plight at a time of misfortune (Obad. 12-14), or reviling and blaspheming God (Ps. 139:20). An especially dangerous form of malice in Hebrew society was that involving the actions of a lying witness. Despite the prohibition of false testimony by the law (Exod. 20:16; 23:1), it was found necessary to enact a careful legal procedure containing a punishment designed to discourage such activity in the future (Deut. 19:16-21).

In the New Testament Epistles the Greek word *kakia,* "badness," "evil," was rendered by *malice* in the King James Version. Believers are warned to "put off" malice (Col. 3:8) or urged to lay it aside (1 Pet. 2:1) along with other forms of evil. In a metaphorical expression, Paul equates malice with leaven in order to show how little of it is needed to produce a widespread effect (1 Cor. 5:8). Later in the same letter Paul urged Christ's followers to be as innocent as children where malice is concerned, and instead to be mature in spiritual understanding (1 Cor. 14:20). Because

of its association with envy, hatred, and a general lack of charity, malice is an evil that will blight Christian witness and therefore should be shunned.

**MAMMON.** This Greek term, the *mammonas* of the New Testament, is actually a Semitic loan word, being borrowed directly from the Aramaic. The sense of the original is that of abundant wealth or great material prosperity, and it occurred frequently in the Targums, though not in Old Testament Aramaic. Certainly by the time of Christ the word had become synonymous with great riches (Matt. 6:24; Luke 16:9, 11, 13). In the Sermon on the Mount Christ warned about divided loyalties in his service. This is because his claims are unique and exclusive, demanding all of the believer's resources. The disciple has to follow and serve his Lord with undivided attention and energy, and cannot allow the pursuit of material gain to interfere with the task of proclaiming the gospel. If the pursuit of the kingdom is given priority (Matt. 6:33) and the other things that are to be added include riches, that is clearly God's will for the individual. In such an event the *mammonas* will be subject to stewardship in the normal manner and will serve the best interests of God's kingdom.

Christ did not condemn riches as such in his teachings because for him money was a morally neutral commodity. But those who made it the center of their lives by pursuing it deliberately incurred censure because of the motivation which governed their use of money. For such persons, mammon had usurped the place which God ought to occupy lawfully, and they had become its slaves *(douloi).* The warning uttered by Paul about the uncertainty of riches is a timely reminder of the Lord's words. Yet the believer should never feel embarrassed if he or she happens to possess great wealth, as long as it is submitted, along with everything else that the individual has, to the absolute overlordship of Christ. Mammon is only deceitful or destructive when it is elevated above its legitimate position in life and becomes an object of idolatrous veneration.

See WEALTH.

**MARRIAGE.** Holy Scripture depicts marriage as a lifelong human male-female covenant relationship established by God in creation. Most wedding ceremonies describe its purpose in their opening exhortations: that husband and wife should be joined in a sexual union as "one flesh" (Gen. 1:26-28; 2:24; Mark 10:6-8), with the normal consequence that children would be procreated and nurtured in the faith and love of God. The union would be a total one of body, mind, and spirit, a mutual caring and support in all the joys and tragedies of life. As such, it has ramifications for the physical, emotional, and spiritual health and welfare, not only of participating individuals and their families, but of society as a whole.

The basic requirement for a marriage in God's will is lifelong commitment to the marriage partner. This may be termed "covenant-love," which is the basis of stability in marriage and, hence, in society. Other considerations such as romance and temperamental compatibility are of course important. Romantic love adds enjoyment to covenant love. Without the latter, though, it soon sours. Romance gives added incentive to marriage partners to fulfill the gracious purposes of God enunciated above. Erotic love in a marriage (see the Song of Solomon) is an undeniable asset if enjoyed within the parameters of God's design of faithfulness and monogamy.

Of equal or greater importance are the divinely assigned duties that husband and wife have to each other. Modern marriage services still require from the bride and groom solemn vows that in the future they will show Christ-like, self-sacrificing, genuine love or caring to one another, according to the revealed will of God, rather than assurances that they are attracted to each other. Only in the recent romantic age of Western society has marital duty widely received second priority to love understood as sensuous attraction, thus setting sensation and emotion above moral will. Modern marriages would on the whole be more successful if couples entered them with their sentimentality and eroticism subordinated to, but not eliminated by, glad and holy commitment to God and each other. Churches, and governments to the extent that it is within their province, have the duty to encourage such thinking through every avenue open to them, such as the school system, and Christian education in church and home.

Some Christians regard the marriage bond as a legislation imposed by Christ. Others hold that Jesus legislated nothing, but rather called His followers to strive for the ideal intended by God in creation. In connection with the marriage ideal, Jesus exposed our sinful tendency to use rather than serve one another, citing this sad reality as the reason why God regretfully inspired Moses to legislate permission for divorce (Mark 10:4-5).

Yet we must remember that Christ always acted compassionately and urged compassion for the weak and fallen. He also provided the way, through repentance and faith, to forgiveness and reconciliation to God by his cross and to victory by His Spirit over the power of sin. How churches and governments put this all together, balancing necessary legislation based on moral values (Matt. 19:8; Rom. 13:1-7; 2 Tim. 1:8-11) with pastoral compassion, must be worked out variously in different ages and circumstances. But the balance between legal rigor and pastoral concern must always be made in the light of full commitment to the ideal set forth by Christ.

The state has a stake in the regulation of marriages, and the Christian is bound to comply with its laws insofar as they do not make impossible the living out of commitment to Christ's ideal (Rom. 13:1-7). It is both unreasonable and defiant for any couple to refuse legal marriage with the argument that the essence of a relationship is commitment, not a marriage certificate. Indeed, refusal to make a commitment in writing throws doubt on the genuineness of that commitment. The legal ceremony represented by that "scrap of paper" (as some derisively call it) is in reality an outward and visible sign of the couple's inward spiritual commitment, as well as being an acknowledgment of common membership in an ordered society in which, according to God's will, every couple has responsibilities and obligations.

A common-law marriage, that is, one not solemnized by church or state, nevertheless may be a true marriage in the way that Isaac's marriage to Rebekah was a true marriage, though apparently solemnized only by sexual intercourse (Gen. 24:67). Nevertheless, to insist today on "marrying" in that manner is to show contempt for the basic concept of order in human society, for one's community obligations and loyalties to the Christian congregation, to the nation under God, and to future generations of children who learn their values more from what they see adults do than from what they hear adults say. It should be realized that according to Scripture every act of mutually consenting sexual intercourse is a becoming "one flesh" (1 Cor. 6:16). In this sense, therefore, there is no such thing as premarital sex. To copulate is itself to "marry," however temporary or nonexistent the commitment. Much human agony ensues from ignorance and disregard of this divine principle. Spiritual and emotional pain results when the "one flesh" of a relationship is "ripped apart," the latter phrase being the very one many people use in describing the break-up of a so-called nonmarital sexual relationship. In the short or long haul, someone always gets hurt. Indeed many suffer, and society suffers with them. This hurt can be prevented by honoring completely the Christian marriage ideal, both in practice and in education.

Within the marriage bond, wife and husband enjoy spiritual equality before God (Gal. 3:28), having equal value and status in His sight and equally free access to Him though faith. This equality and its practical ramifications continuously challenge Christians in the nature and quality of their relationships to each other. Christians, above all other peoples, ought to be ready to accommodate currently received concepts of marriage and the family to a growing understanding of God's will, neither arrogantly presuming that present cultural understandings are perfect, nor casting aside perennial truths already apprehended. We should do this much in the same way as earlier Christians worked out the reality of spiritual equality with regard to slavery. We should continue resolutely to deal with the manifold gross and subtle enslavements that people, both within and without the marriage relationship, impose on one another, even, at times, in the name of religion.

The scriptural concept of family headship (1 Cor. 11:3; Eph. 5:23) has been variously understood in different cultures and ages. It seems clear from Galatians 3:28 and Ephesians 5:21 that the husband's headship has nothing to do with any supposed instrinsic or achieved superior worth or ability. On the contrary, it is a headship of designated status among equals, to be exercised accordingly with sensitivity, understanding, and full acknowledgment of the worth of the wife. The model is Christ, the Servant, who gave His life for His people (Mark 10:45; Eph. 5:25). Conversely, the wife's respect toward her husband as family head must be given not in servility, but as a full equal, in love and full, willing collaboration. Christ the Servant is her model too.

It would help modern husbands and wives to understand that the Christian concept of headship in the home is not necessarily to be identified absolutely with leadership, a function that can be practiced and shared in the marriage by both spouses, even by children, without in any way undermining the husband's status as head. To grasp this reality it is necessary to understand what Christian leadership really is.

True leadership, far from being a way of controlling, manipulating, or domineering others, is the firm, sensitive use of whatever status, ability, authority, power, and interpersonal skill one happens legitimately to possess in order, as servant-enabler, to build others up in the spirit of Christ, inspiring them to action, and enabling them to fulfill the individual and social destinies to which God has called them. It may actually happen, and often does, that the main leader, that is, the most influential servant-enabler in a marriage, is the wife and mother. Many women in Scripture fit this category almost to perfection, and under God many women today are true leaders in their families, their communities, their churches, and the nation. Of course the husband himself may combine leadership skill with his status as head. With such personal resources at his disposal he ought to encourage his wife in love to exercise her gifts completely, in full confidence that she for her part will always support him in his weighty responsibility as family head.

Christians are bound to do all that is humanly possible to cooperate with God's purpose for the holy estate of matrimony. Public, church, and home education are basic to this process. Individually, Christians can witness and support friends' marriages by their presence and prayers; they can influence their own children, godchildren, and other young persons in wholesome attitudes toward marriage. They can at all times by precept and example urge positive conflict resolution and reconciliation between marriage partners. They can uphold the discipline of the community of faith and work prayerfully to restore to fellowship any who have broken its rules and alienated themselves. They can encourage couples having problems to use professional counselors skilled in helping to preserve family life. Finally, they can be faithful themselves as spouses. Educational opportunities for adults might include the Marriage Preparation Courses run by various denominations to help prepare young people for future marriage responsibilities and Marriage Encounter Weekends designed to help make good marriages better. All such organized efforts contribute to a social ambience favoring lasting marriages.

Paul, in Ephesians 5:21-33, pinpoints certain specific and evidently widespread deficiencies in husband-wife behaviors that need to be overcome, namely that husbands generally need to learn better how to show love and consideration to their wives, and wives to learn genuine respect for their husbands. Of course, all humans need love and respect; but if it be asked what each sex perennially lacks most from the other, for the women it probably would be tender love, for the men respect. It is not widely realized that many of the identity difficulties experienced by men today could be due in part to their not being accorded the needed respect of which Paul writes. Since in modern society women have less economic need for men than previously, one of the latter's traditionally apparent reasons for self-respect seems to be taken away. This being so, a wife, by subtly or grossly withholding personal respect for her husband can at worst devastate his sense of worth, or at least evoke in the depths of his psyche a resentment that neither he nor she fully understands but of which both are vaguely aware. Of course, both need respect and a sense of worth. Both need the security and support of a dependable and stable marriage relationship in order to cope in the emotionally lacerating rough-and-tumble of society today. Christian spouses should make extra-special efforts to provide that support and understanding for one another.

Each marriage partner has sexual "rights" too. Paul insists that each partner must take care to give these to the other (1 Cor. 7:3-5; compare Prov. 5:15-20). They should do this not legalistically, of necessity, nor demandingly, but in a spirit of genuine caring for the other's needs. Sexual relationships are an aspect of interpersonal communication, an expression of the quality of the marriage as a whole. They form an absolutely basic and extremely important area of married life; one in which marriage partners can deeply "know" each other (Gen. 4:1), and, in true Christian love, minister to one another. It would seem that in this spirit even married prison inmates should be accorded their conjugal rights, which in many instances they are.

**Bibliography:** Brow, R., *Living Totally Without Guilt* (1983); Clinebell, H. J. and Clinebell, C. H., *The Intimate Marriage* (1970); Dobson, J., *What Wives Wish Their Husbands Knew About Women* (1975); Ibid., *Straight Talk to Men and*

*Their Wives* (1980); Gottlieb, A., "What Men Need From Women," *McCall's* (October, 1983); Mead, M., *Male and Female* (1949).

See FAMILY; PROCREATION.

D.N.P.

**MASS MEDIA, ETHICS OF.** By the mass media we understand traditional newspapers, magazines, best-selling books that are mass produced, radio, television, cassette recordings, video, and modern electronic communication systems. Because of the nature and newness of much of the technology involved in producing the messages these media convey, the ethical issues involved are extremely complex and have received little attention from Christians. Therefore, there is no tradition of reflection upon which we can draw to evaluate modern mass media from a Christian perspective.

The difficulties involved in modern media ethics are well illustrated by the story of a Norwegian evangelist who visited Britain in the mid-1960s. He shocked his audiences by asking why British Christians accepted the general assessment that president Nasser of Egypt was the devil incarnate. "Didn't they know" he asked "that Nasser protected Egyptian Christians from persecution by fanatical Muslims?"

The point of this story is that, in the mid-1960s, Nasser was seen as an opponent of British imperial interests and therefore bad. On this issue all political parties in Britain agreed. Therefore, in reporting the news, British writers and commentators reflected the common feeling in the country about the evil nature of Nasser's rule. Individually, many newsmen honestly reported the situation as they saw it. Without realizing it, they reflected the last vestiges of an outlook derived from a dying empire. The news focused on Nasser's dispute with Britain over the Suez Canal and ignored other things he was doing in Egypt. What the Norwegian saw in this situation was a different picture. Freed from local prejudice and emotional involvement, he looked as a Christian at Egypt and saw things that he regarded as good. Therefore he judged the situation in terms of the welfare of the Christian church.

It does not matter whether the Norwegian's assessment of the situation was correct or not. What the story illustrates in a vivid way is the complexity of making ethical decisions in a global village. The Christian church is universal; therefore any news or media reporting ought to reflect the interests of the church worldwide and not Christian opinions influenced by local nationalism. Yet we are all social beings, and our personal ethics exist within fixed social contexts. To transcend existing nationalisms and create a Christian media that presents the views of the church universal is a pressing need today.

Although Christians have paid little attention to the problems of objectivity in the media, various non-Christian groups have produced studies that illustrate the vastly complicated problem before us. In Scotland, the Glasgow Media Group has produced several studies, such as *Bad News* (1976), which show how a desire to attract readers and television viewers distorts news coverage by encouraging media networks to concentrate on the sensational and violent issues. Similarly in America, The Media Institute has produced works like *Energy Coverage-Media Panic* (1983), which show how the media misreported the energy situation in the 1970s. Studies like these could be read as a conspiracy theory in which the media is attempting to corrupt and confuse society. But the authors of these works are at pains to point out that often the very complexity of modern life and the social pressures upon both media and audiences alike produce results that, while generally harmful, are unintended.

The misreporting that can often be seen today is usually not the result of single decisions or the deliberate actions of individuals. Rather, situations exist where multiple decisions by a large number of individuals, each of which may be honest and truthful, produce untruthful and dishonest results. Developing a way of ethical decision making in a complex society is therefore a pressing need for which there is no easy answer. One can only pray that, as technology advances and individual educational levels rise, access to information may increase and checks and balances will be created to counter the inherent confusions of today's situation.

Another problem in assessing media ethics concerns the effects of visual images on human psychology. George Gallup states in *Religion in America 1984* that the National Institutes of Mental Health have concluded from over 2,500 separate studies that "violence on television does lead to aggressive behavior." This being the case, what ought to be done to curb television and video violence, pornography, and other vices? Clearly, questions of censorship and press freedom are involved. Christians must decide whether the good of the community should prevail over individual freedoms. This question, however, raises additional issues such as whether individual liberty, in the long run, promotes communal good.

Another question raised by advanced media techniques involves the right of nations to exclude "undesirable" influences. To what extent should governments be able to control the spread of satellite television, video tapes, and the like? What is the relationship between political independence, national sovereignty, and the new technologies of the mass media? Finally, the growth of electronic mail, libraries, and communication systems raises a host of new problems. Who owns a book when it is stored electronically in a data bank? Does the author, the user, or the company that owns the data bank have ultimate ownership? And what happens if a company simply decides to erase an electronically stored piece of literature?

There are no easy solutions to these and other difficult ethical issues surrounding the mass media. Although general Christian principles about truth, honesty, and so on hold true, their application in specific situations needs considerable thought and hard work. This task is surely one that must occupy the minds of leading Christian thinkers for at least the rest of this century.

**Bibliography:** Baker, R. T., *The Christian as a Journalist* (1960); Cohen, S. and Young, J., *The Manufacture of News* (1981); Ellul, J., *Propaganda* (1969); Swain, B. M., *Reporter's Ethics* (1978).

See CENSORSHIP; COPYRIGHT INFRINGEMENT.

I.H.

**MASTURBATION.** This word is derived directly from the Latin *masturbator,* meaning "one who defiles himself." It was a part of the homosexual activities of the Imperial period, although it is not singled out for mention in Paul's list of vices (Rom. 1:26-31). Masturbation involves sexual self-stimulation in either males or females and is a common means of reducing excessive sexual tension when the normal sexuality of married life is unavailable. In a clinical setting it is seen as one ingredient of certain forms of cerebral dysfunction when it assumes compulsive proportions.

Because of its unnatural character as an act of individual indulgence as contrasted with the act of coitus between a male and a female, as well as its associations with pagan religions, the Christian church regarded masturbation as sinful. Up to the later part of the nineteenth century its practice was considered to be harmful physically, but this idea has now been discarded in most quarters. Much more serious are the moral and psychological effects, however. Jesus taught that even to look upon a woman (or a man, *pari passu*) with lust in the heart is precisely the same as having committed adultery with her (Matt. 5:28). If therefore a person masturbates and has the mental image of a particular person in view, the effect is the same morally as though actual adultery or fornication had taken place. This situation applies to living people and presumably would have no ethical significance in the case of a widower or widow longing for carnal relations with his or her deceased spouse and using sexual self-stimulation as a substitute.

The believer who is endeavoring to hold the mystery of the faith in a pure conscience (1 Tim. 3:9, KJV) will naturally desire to avoid anything that could lead to impurity of thought, word, or deed. As indicated above, masturbation provides serious pitfalls in this respect, and the believer is therefore urged to ensure that his or her love is one of fervent purity in Christ's service (1 Pet. 1:22).

**MATERIALISM.** Most people throughout history have tended toward an extreme in relating to the physical world. The majority opinion has moved toward unrealistic expectations of benefits to be derived from material possessions, while a minority viewpoint has viewed the material as evil. The Bible holds middle ground between these two extremes.

God created the material world and pronounced it good (Gen. 1:10, 12, 18, 21, 25, 31). He has ever affirmed the human body and possessions, contrary to the distortions of Greek philosophers and the medieval church, which created a dualism affirming the realm of the spirit and setting it over and against the necessary evil of the material world.

The vast majority of humankind, however, has not accepted this view of the material, but rather has tended to idolize some aspects of the material world. Paul pronounces the judgment of God on those who substitute worship of created matter for worship of the Creator (Rom. 1:25). God created man with a desire to enjoy the material world of food, sex, and the whole vast treasure house of creation. When pursued in biblical ways, the material world is a good gift of God. But when some material thing such as money, land, a house, an automobile, an object of art, one's own body, or that of another usurps the position that belongs only to God, appreciation of the material has become materialism.

A materialist need not bow down to an idol, but merely hold some material thing as of higher value than one's allegiance to God. Most Christians probably do not do this at a conscious philosophical level; but when the choices of life are made so that the acquisition, use, or protection of something material takes precedence over choices to benefit God, His kingdom, and others, the person is a materialist.

The biblical term for this is *coveteousness*. To covet is to desire to get or keep that which is not in the will of God for the possessor. It should be terrifying to the typical materialist, preoccupied with the affluent, "good life," ignoring the poor of the world, to read what God says of the covetous person. In Scripture, covetousness is so terrible a sin that it separates a person from God (Rom. 1:29, 32), destroys community (James 4:1-4), breaks fellowship in the church (2 Pet. 2:14-22), is the just object of church discipline (1 Cor. 5:10-11), and brings the wrath of God on mankind in this age (Col. 3:5-6) and the wrath of God on the covetous person in eternity (1 Cor. 6:9-10). It is a special temptation for the Christian minister and rightly debars him from service (2 Cor. 7:21; 1 Thess. 2:5; 1 Tim. 3:3). It is a form of idolatry, substituting things for the living God (Eph. 5:5; Col. 3:5).

Why does God hold so strongly against materialism? There are several reasons. To give primary attention to possessions or wished-for possessions, must be the ultimate insult to God. It is not another being that has usurped His place, not even an ideology or cause, but a dumb object. Furthermore, covetousness is a root sin that inevitably leads on to all varieties of sin: cheating, stealing, immorality, murder. In the final analysis, materialism or covetousness is a cancer that destroys the person who permits it to take up residence in his mind.

The antidote is for a God-centered way of life to replace a material-centered way of life. Love, not as a warm feeling, but as a way of life, displaces materialism. Covetousness is out to get, love to give. The materialist uses people to acquire things, the Christian uses things to help people. Biblical love is choosing to act consistently in behalf of the long-term welfare of others, even at personal sacrifice. To be God-centered and people-oriented is the best cure for the cancer of materialism.

**Bibliography:** Mooneyham, W. S., *What Do You Say to a Hungry World?* (1975); White, J., *The Golden Cow* (1979).

J.R.McQ.

**MATURITY.** Originating in the Latin word *maturitas,* "ripeness," "maturity," this word describes the fruition of a process of growth and development. In a purely physical sense all organic life is subject to the cycles of formation, of which maturity is the climax, but in *homo sapiens* there is no necessary correlation between the physical and the emotional or spiritual. Thus a person of advanced age can exhibit only an elementary stage of spiritual growth and is sometimes poorly developed at the emotional level.

The Scriptures speak of maturity in various ways. The emphasis upon "manly" behavior (1 Sam. 4:9; 1 Cor. 16:3) or being adult in understanding (1 Cor. 14:20) is an indication of the goal of maturity that God desires his followers to attain. This process commences with spiritual rebirth (John 3:3), which admits a person into the Christian church and marks the beginning of a life of growth in the Holy Spirit. Strict obedience to God's will and a conscious attempt to live a life of holiness are mandatory for spiritual growth. Paul's statement concerning the gifts given for ministry (Eph. 4:11-13) shows that Christ desires the believer to strive for "perfection." This constitutes Christian maturity as demanded in the Sermon on the Mount (Matt. 5:48), where the word *teleios* means "fully developed in all aspects of the personality" and is thus the equivalent of the Hebrew *tam,* as descriptive of Jacob in Genesis 25:27. Clearly it is a goal that will challenge the best efforts of every believer.

**MEAN, DOCTRINE OF THE.** By the term *mean* a mathematician would understand what others would describe as an "average." It is thought of more precisely as a point equidistant from two extremes. The so-called doctrine of the mean has to do with a state of being or a course of action that lies between two extreme positions. It was pivotal to the ethical thought of Aristotle (384-322 B.C.) and was dealt with at some length in Book II of his *Nicomachean Ethics.* According

to his teachings, the functioning of moral concepts and behavior as dictated by the human reason can be expected to result in a balanced life of goodness. The "golden" or "happy" mean ensured this expectation by commending the kind of moderation that would avoid extremes of any kind. Aristotle stressed the general nature of the principle and cautioned against the idea that the mean could always be found midway between opposite positions.

While the doctrine was no doubt meant to moderate the rough, licentious, belligerent character of contemporary Greek life, its effect would only be felt by the very small, elite group of intellectuals, since most of the population was illiterate in Aristotle's time. Moderation would actually not be as difficult for the Greeks to achieve as for later cultures, since the high degree of professional expertise found in various walks of modern life was unknown and would have been discouraged in any case. Or, as Aristotle himself put it, a man should be able to play the flute, but not too well. Moderation was ultimately defined by an appeal to the actions of a "reasonable man," a concept which subsequently found its way into British common law.

As a principle of life, moderation is beset by the difficulty of ethical subjectivism. What is moderate for one is not for another. Some courses of action are absolutely right or wrong from the beginning, and for such the concept of moderation is meaningless. In the matter of holiness or sanctification, for instance, the mean is always the highest point of development in the believer's life, since nonholiness or nonsanctification as an extreme for comparative purposes would negate the entire spiritual concept. In the same way, a woman cannot choose to remain "a little bit pregnant," because, as with the spiritual life, she is in a condition that is mandated by and toward growth.

The Scriptures, so far from promoting moderation, encourage believers to live their lives in uncompromising participation (Eccles. 9:10), doing things heartily (literally, "from the soul," "from the person") as unto God and not humans (Col. 3:23). Christians are to aim at a high level of spiritual maturity (Matt. 5:48), because the exacting standards specified by God for human behavior do not admit of halfhearted participation. Indeed, in Revelation 3:16, the Christian community at Laodicea was to be rejected violently by God for following the precise ethic that Aristotle had advocated.

See MODERATION.

**MEDICAL ETHICS.** The first recorded formulation of medical ethics is probably that of Hippocrates (ca. 462-357 B.C.), in which guidance was given to his students about appropriate behavior in medical practice. This time-honored formulation is now sadly out of date in wording if not exactly in intent, and not all graduating medical students honor it. With the growth in importance of medicine's purely social aspects, as well as the proliferation of medical and surgical techniques that were unheard of until the third quarter of the twentieth century, new and perplexing ethical issues have come to the forefront. Unfortunately many of these are not restricted to purely medical considerations, but have political, social, legal, and economic implications as well.

The list of problems that present moral dilemmas is daunting. To the familiar ones of abortion, genetic engineering, contraception, drug abuse, euthanasia, organ transplantation, and resuscitation can be added the management of congenital deformities, surgical change of human sex, various kinds of addiction, the care of handicapped and mentally infirm people, experiments connected with the stages of fetal development, the treatment of sexual deviates, vivisection, and last but not least the urgent problem of confidentiality in the age of computer data bases.

Most physicians at graduation generally concede that they are ill-prepared to meet the public's expectation that they must give firm leadership in such ethical matters. Although some instruction in medical ethics is offered as part of the undergraduate training, it is seldom considered adequate. This situation is unfortunately a by-product of the sheer technicality and scientific nature of the very training that leads to the ethical dilemmas. So overcrowded are the curricula to which the medical undergraduates are subjected that there is very little time available for reflecting upon the ethical problems that have become an inseparable part of modern medicine.

It is obviously beyond the scope of an article such as this to survey the issues of medical ethics in any depth. Nevertheless some areas of importance will be examined in an attempt to bring clarity to a complex and difficult moral situation. Matters involving human fertilization and reproduction are understandably of great concern to most people, and not least for those who stand ethically in the Judeo-Christian tradition, with its high view of the value of children (Ps. 127:3; Matt. 19:14). Many Christians affirm that some form of contraceptive usage is mandatory, since for them carnal relations have a recreational as well as a procreational aspect.

Even the Roman Catholic Church concedes that contraception may be practiced under certain conditions, but in so doing has prescribed a method which places great restraints upon married couples at a time when the woman is ovulating and is therefore more disposed to coitus than at any other time in her monthly cycle. Consequently many Roman Catholics have repudiated papal instructions on this matter, and at the risk of incurring ecclesiastical censure have opted for more satisfactory forms of contraception. Medical counselors who are consulted in such matters face the possibility of having to encourage married couples to disregard the advice of church leaders, however well-meant, and thereby to arouse feelings of guilt because of the use of unauthorized contraceptive devices.

Closely related to the prevention of conception is the question of the fate of an unwanted fetus, regardless of the identity of the father. The Roman Catholic Church opposes abortion uncompromisingly, but other Christians do not always share this view. Even those who favor it under some conditions recognize its dangers and thus are generally opposed to its use as a form of contraception. Those individuals who uphold the sacredness of all life regard the fetus as a person, albeit potentially, from the moment when the sperm fertilizes the egg, and therefore for them fetal life is sacrosanct. Others, recognizing the potentiality of fetal existence, prefer to think that the embryo becomes a true person, as distinct from privileged human tissue, at the time of birth. A situation that has legal as well as moral implications arises from the ability of doctors to save twenty-week-old fetuses. This technological development may compel a revision of the legal definition of the viability of the fetus, and could bring about changes in the abortion laws in those jurisdictions where abortions are permitted up to the twenty-ninth week of pregnancy. By lowering the fetus's age of viability, the technology has produced an embarrassing interval between the earliest period at which a premature infant can be expected to survive and the latest date by which legal abortion can occur. The increasing ability of doctors to treat the unborn for conditions such as urinary tract blockage, hydrocephalus, metabolic disorders, and other defects suggests that the fetus as a person in its own right, which could also involve moral and legal factors. But even this may have little or no significance in the end, since fewer than 1 per cent of all abortions are performed after the twentieth week of pregnancy.

Serious moral problems have arisen in connection with such procedures as AID (artificial insemination by donor). Many medical personnel have no compunction about administering to a woman some donor sperm mixed with that of her husband. In cases of conception the legal question of legitimacy can be raised, as well as the moral issue of possible adultery. Associated with this matter is the problem of the rights and responsibilities of motherhood consequent upon the donating or transferring of sperms or eggs, which again can raise serious legal issues as well as feelings of guilt and general emotional conflict. Most Christians regard AID conception as a constituting adultery, but as in so many other areas the denominations have been unwilling to make pronouncements upon a matter which is clearly divisive. By contrast, AIH (artificial insemination by husband) carries no legal or moral objections to it where it is used to overcome ejaculation difficulties on the part of the husband.

Many legal, medical, and ecclesiastical authorities are opposed to the artificial cloning of human beings, except for the remote possibility of bypassing genetic disease. In such an event only one clone is recommended for use, with any remaining ones being destroyed. Those who stress the sanctity of all life could well object to this procedure on moral grounds.

Concern is expressed periodically about the use of human embryos for research purposes, and the moral issues resulting from such procedures. The degree of concern will depend upon whether the fetus is viewed as a potential or as an actual person. If the former, the parents are normally counseled that it is ethically permissible for the embryo to be utilized for experimentation if the results can be expected to promote the growth of a subsequent healthy fetus in the donor mother or in other comparable women. Once more, religious beliefs and personal feelings will produce a variety of responses.

One other matter that should be considered is the ethical dilemma that is raised by the determined attempts to prolong life at all costs. This aspiration was characteristic of medicine in the pretechnological era and can be realized even more fully with the array of sophisticated equipment currently available to the doctor. But the modern physician now has to assess the justification, ethically as well as medically, when in a given patient the line separating life from death has become blurred. Can a doctor be commended for resuscitating a clinically dead person, only to have that individual exist in a comatose condition for a prolonged period of time? Can a practitioner come under moral censure for recommending the discontinuance of life-support techniques for a person suffering irreparable brain damage because of an anoxic cerebral cortex? What right do doctors have to discourage someone suffering from a terminal illness who wishes to end his or her life expeditiously? Why in cases of terminal illness should it be thought proper to use only those drugs that will result in "death later" rather than "death now"?

Again, is it ethical to preserve and prolong life whatever the cost and possibly in continued defiance of the sufferer's wishes? Or should a revised system of medical ethics focus upon the quality of the patient's remaining life instead of merely lengthening it? Can doctors, who professedly under oath have committed themselves to the health of human beings, consider it ethical to be involved in research which will ensure that chemical and biological warfare will become even more deadly than at present?

It is very easy to raise these and many more questions in this general area, but difficult to discover any satisfying answers. Scripture gives little or no guidance about the specific problems raised in this discussion, simply because they were not germane to the lives or the faith of people in biblical times. What Scripture as a whole does is to concentrate upon an appeal for individuals to commit themselves and their activities to God and thereafter to live in obedience to what his revealed will is for them. The Christian's body is stated specifically to be the temple of God's Holy Spirit (1 Cor. 6:19) and therefore must be respected and treated as such. Any kind of physical or mental abuse is therefore wrong, and whatever treatment is accorded the body or mind must conform to this consideration. But even this principle is open to subjective modification by Christians, especially among antinomians.

Where decisions have to be made, whether by individuals or groups, perhaps the only general principle that can be advanced to assist ethical decision is the determination to do everything to help patients to glorify God in their bodies and spirits (1 Cor. 6:20). This will involve a sympathetic understanding of their immediate needs and a careful assessment of their entire situation as they themselves are experiencing it, and not as it might appear to be to an external observer or how it ought to be according to doctrinaire conceptions.

See ABORTION; BIOLOGICAL WARFARE; CONTRACEPTION; EUTHANASIA; GENETIC ENGINEERING; HEART TRANSPLANTATION; LIFE, SACREDNESS OF; POPULATION CONTROL.

**MEEKNESS.** This quality of character is generally associated with mildness of disposition or a generally submissive spirit. In the Judeo-Christian tradition meekness is often depicted as synonymous with humility, and those who manifested this attitude were promised food (Ps. 22:26), divine guidance (Ps. 25:9), the earth as their inheritance (Ps. 37:11, quoted by Jesus in Matt. 5:5), and God's gift of salvation (Ps. 149:4). Moses was described as being more meek than anyone else (Num. 12:3), but there is some question as to whether humility is involved here. Perhaps the meaning of *anaw* in this case is "more harassed," "more troubled," or even "more humiliated."

In the New Testament meekness is associated by the self-testimony of Christ with humility (Matt. 11:29) and exemplified further at the time of his triumphal entry into Jerusalem on the back of a donkey, an animal ridden by a warrior (Matt. 21:5). The Christian is urged to receive the "ingrafted word" ("implanted word," RSV) with meekness (James 1:21) and to manifest meekness and self-control (Gal. 5:23) as a fruit of the Spirit. The meek Christian will not be self-assertive or unduly aggressive any more than Christ was, nor will he or she be seeking continually for revenge. Meekness must not be mistaken for weakness, because the meek individual has God's backing where strength or vindication are concerned. For those ambitious and energetic Christians who have tried to emulate it, meekness is by no means an easy virtue to acquire.

See HUMILITY.

**MENTAL RESERVATION.** To have reservations about someone or something means that one is not fully certain or absolutely convinced of the integrity of that person or thing. One cannot therefore offer an unqualified endorsement if called upon to do so, and while the hesitation may be expressed in a tacit or implied form, it is real nonetheless. It is possible that circumstances attendant upon the particular situation may admit of some qualification or deviation from the norm, but despite this it is impossible to make whole-hearted commendation, participation, or acceptance.

The matter of reservation can have important moral consequences on occasions, especially when specific mental reservation is involved. This phrase describes an implied, nonverbal qualification in an individual's mind of the professed understanding of a statement or a policy and is applied especially to the swearing of oaths and the giving of assent to other analogous statements.

Mental reservation under such conditions is not the same as perjury, since this involves verbalizing untrue statements under oath, but it does indicate that the individual who employs it has not expressed *ex animo* agreement with the proceedings requiring his consent. Mental reservation is as important to the church as to the judiciary, where in assenting to the denominational requirements for ordination a candidate may reserve assent in his or her mind because of uncertainty about the integrity of some doctrinal statement or ecclesiastical practice. Mental reservation has also been perceived as a threat to the bona fide nature of membership in certain societies, and as a result the initiate is often required to swear that he or she accepts the commitments of membership without equivocation or mental reservation.

Since Christ demands total and uncompromising submission to the claims of his lordship, it is important for the would-be initiate to understand as far as possible the implications of his or her actions before making a firm decision for Christ as Savior and Lord. So many lapses from the faith occur because the individuals concerned were poorly instructed in the nature of discipleship. Single-minded, complete devotion to Christ is mandatory, if only because nobody can serve two masters ultimately (Matt. 6:24).

**MERCY.** In common parlance mercy is generally associated with the compassion that would restrain an individual from participating in some severe or brutal form of activity or which would urge him or her to assist one who had fallen victim to such hardship. But the meaning in Scripture is quite different, because it describes the character of the motivating force underlying God's self-revelation to humanity.

The typical Hebrew word for "mercy" is *hesed,* and it is notable for the general inability of translators to render effectively in a single word. While "love," "loving-kindness," "compassion," and "loyalty" have been used, they fail to define adequately the fundamental importance of this element of God's character. It is that quality of al-

truistic grace from which everything else proceeds in God's relationship with humanity. It was *hesed* which led the Israelites from Egypt (Exod. 15:13) to Mount Sinai and which underlay the covenant relationship by which the Israelites became the chosen people (Exod. 20:6; 34:7). This association of *hesed* and the covenant was brought to Israel's attention periodically (Deut. 7:9; 1 Kings 8:23; Neh. 1:5; Isa. 55:3; Dan. 9:4), and the tragedy of apostasy and idolatry in the nation's turbulent history was that it actually involved a rejection of God's covenant *hesed* with its associated qualities of grace, faithfulness, love, divine blessing, prosperity, and so on.

The complex of qualities characterizing *hesed* reappears in the New Testament term *eleos,* commonly translated "mercy," "pity," "kindness," or "beneficence." Again it is best understood against a background of covenantal obligations, especially in the new covenant instituted by Christ's death. God's love for fallen humanity was of such an altruistic, compassionate nature that no price was too high to pay for human redemption and salvation (John 3:16).

God's mercy proceeds from his own essential freedom (Exod. 33:19; Rom. 9:15) and benefits all who submit their lives to his revealed will. Under both covenants God desires his followers to exhibit *hesed* and *eleos* in all their dealings, proclaiming these qualities for the differing ages to which they referred as paramount and making it abundantly clear that no amount of ritual or cultic ceremony can form an acceptable substitute for the divine characteristic of mercy (Hos. 6:6; Matt. 9:13; 12:7). In Christ's followers mercy can be seen in terms of consideration for the plight of those in difficulties, in the alleviating of poverty, and in the correcting of injustice where possible. These represent only a small selection from the wide range of tasks that can be undertaken through Christ's love in the service of others.

**MERIT.** This term originated in the Latin verb *mereor,* which originally meant "to acquire," and was used in a military sense to describe the way in which a man accumulated pay by serving as a soldier. From the notion of earning money came the sense of merit or reward, and by the time of Cicero it was used commonly of "being entitled to" or "deserving of" something. These meanings are still in use, but to them has been added the concept of praiseworthy quality or commendable excellence. Outstanding service of various kinds can now be recognized by the award of some such decoration as an "Order of Merit."

In theological discussion merit is related to good works in terms of their value as a means of obtaining eternal salvation. This in itself is unexceptionable, since it is a feature of many pagan religions. In Hebrew culture good works were recognized as part of covenantal community living, but the true welfare of the nation depended upon its monotheism and its strict observance of God's laws. With the growth of the Pharisaic party in the pre-Christian period there emerged a soteriological interpretation of good works which maintained that if a person kept all the injunctions of the written and oral law, salvation was assured without further need of divine grace. It was this type of theology, rather than the sincerity and dedication of the Pharisees themselves, that led Jesus to criticize their religion as shallow.

The New Testament makes it abundantly clear that the dominant soteriological influence is God's redeeming grace, mediated through Christ's vicarious atonement for sin on Calvary. Paul stated flatly that persons are saved by grace through faith as a divine gift rather than through human works, lest anyone should be able to boast (Eph. 2:8-9). Arguing from the emphasis on works in the epistle of James (2:18-26), some interpreters have purported to see a conflict between the teachings of James and Paul on this matter. But closer examination shows that Paul was discussing faith as an antecedent to good works, whereas James was emphasizing good works as a corollary of a vigorous faith.

In the medieval period the Roman Catholic Church laid great emphasis upon meritorious works, and the Roman sacrament of penance involved the performance of certain prescribed duties as a means of atoning for the sins confessed. The Protestant reformers restated the biblical doctrine of God's saving grace through faith in Christ and pointed out that humanity's corrupt nature could not begin to claim merit in God's sight without Christ's atonement. The Roman Catholic teaching regarding "works of supererogation," which are voluntary works above and beyond God's formal requirements, came in for sharp criticism in Article XIV of the Church of England's Thirty-nine Articles of faith. It showed the impossibility of doing more for God's sake than duty required by quoting the Lord's words, "We are unprofitable servants" (Luke 17:10).

Good works are meritorious for the Christian only insofar as they are grounded in the faith of Christ and are truly altruistic in nature. They cannot "earn" salvation, since that is a gift that must be accepted by faith. Good works undertaken from a purely human or secular point of view without reference to divine grace have no merit whatever with God.

**MILITARISM.** From the earliest days of the church, Christians have been divided in their attitudes toward war and armed forces. Generally speaking, major Roman Catholic, Orthodox, and Protestant groups have supported the legitimacy of armed forces as an arm of the divinely sanctioned state, provided that the state is committed to the principles of truth and justice. Christians of the older Anabaptist and some European Pietist traditions and modern peace groups have held mixed attitudes. Most Christians now reject the legitimacy of any nation's building up armed might for purposes of conquest. Some pacifists reject the concept of armed forces altogether. Most Christians affirm the necessity in a evil-infected world of a nation's maintaining adequate armed forces to protect itself and its democratic allies.

Since 1974 the United States armed forces have operated effectively on a completely voluntary basis. It is assumed that the draft will be reactivated by the Congress only in the event of a national emergency. In Canada the armed forces also operate on the basis of voluntary enlistment. However, conscripts were not sent overseas from Canada during World War II, due to the peculiarities of the French-Canadian question in Canadian politics.

Christians usually disapprove of service as mercenaries and the private sale of arms to mercenaries. While they are divided on the question, most Christians accept that sometimes it may be necessary for a Christian to participate reluctantly in revolutionary activity against oppression.

Attractive features of military service are disciplined training, the inculcation of honor, and the values of nationhood. In the Western democratic countries, bloodthirsty training and propaganda are not matters of policy. The forces themselves are run by competent officers who appreciate full well the horrors of war. It is important to maintain a powerful ethical sense and a sense of honor within the military. This is a noteworthy feature of Western military traditions. It is equally important to make the military subservient to elected government. Thus a sense of national decency and honor, a national mindset committed to peace, and democratically elected political control of armed forces are the best protection against dominance by militarists.

Historically, attitudes to armed forces, including attitudes among Christians, run in cycles. Whenever enemies or potential enemies appear to threaten, most Christians encourage and participate in the expansion of armed forces. During peacetime, as in the period 1918-1939, powerful peace movements emerge which insist on disarmament. A similar cycle has been occurring since the end of World War II in 1945.

The development, use, and continuing threat of nuclear arms have added new dimensions to the militarist threat. Totalitarian regimes now pose the danger of global disaster as the possession of nuclear arms widens. The policy of the major world powers since World War II has been deterrence, that is, mutual assured destruction of the aggressor (MAD). Totalitarian nations are accused of unnecessarily building up huge armies, subverting the democratic process, and militarily dominating their neighbors. For this reason security since World War II has been found in force, rather than in trust, mutual aid, and unarmed competition.

Satellite TV makes more difficult the waging of war in the future by democratic societies because the offending horrors of war are brought home to people directly and almost instantly. Conversely, such communications capabilities when completely controlled by government increase the capability of totalitarian regimes to foster hatred and to incite to brutality and war.

Longing for peace, aversion to violence, and fear of holocaust are the shared sentiments of most people everywhere. Nevertheless, it is an error to think that despite the terrors of mutual assured destruction all nations will logically choose peace, and most Christians are not satisfied that the pacifist option is justified morally or biblically.

Since the Vietnam War, powerful forces in the West have advocated disarmament, even unilaterally. Others point out that totalitarian governments have armed themselves heavily. Thus the debate over the legitimacy of military preparedness will go on into the twenty-first century.

One of the most poignant of post-World War II statements is that of President Dwight D. Eisenhower on April 16, 1953, as he contemplated the opportunity for peaceful coexistence in the world after the death of Joseph Stalin. President Eisenhower had been the Supreme Allied Commander during World War II. More than thirty years later his comments are again widely quoted: "Every gun that is made, every warship launched, every rocket fired signifies, in the final sense, a theft from those who hunger and are not fed, those who are cold and are not clothed. This world in arms is not spending money alone. It is spending the sweat of its laborers, the genius of its scientists, and hopes of its children.... This is not a way of life at all, in any true sense. Under the cloud of threatening war, it is humanity hanging from a cross of iron."

Nevertheless, his comments are set in the context of an address reminding his hearers and potential totalitarian adversaries that self-defense is a moral constraint placed upon free people which they cannot avoid despite their preference for a new era of mutual trust and disarmament. This sentiment reflects the reality of world and human conditions which most Christians perceive to be the case.

**Bibliography:** Chomsky, N., *For Reasons of State* (1973); Curry, D. C., *Evangelicals and the Bishops' Pastoral Letter* (1984); Dyson, F., *Weapons and Hope* (1984); Novak, M., *Moral Clarity in the Nuclear Age* (1983).

S.J.M.

**MILITARY CHAPLAINCY.** A chaplain is a member of the clergy who has the responsibility for officiating in a chapel or church and ministering under the license or authority of a specific denomination or other accredited group. Depending upon the circumstances, the ministration may be restricted in scope, with the minister performing only a few of the functions which he or she is legally permitted to exercise.

A military chaplaincy enables an ordained person to minister to one group or other of the armed forces. His or her work would naturally involve the arranging and conducting of divine worship along denominational lines, in cooperation with the chaplains of other faiths. In addition to parade services and the occasional wedding or funeral, the chaplain is engaged in a surprising amount of social work for members of his or her unit, as well as specific pastoral counseling and the visiting of patients in the sick bay or hospital.

The chaplain is a very important person in the larger task of maintaining morale, and though most service personnel may have little or no interest in the chaplain's faith, they normally accord him or her considerable personal respect which transcends mere considerations of rank. For clergy with a liking for military life, a chaplaincy in the armed services offers unusual opportunities for ministering the gospel of Jesus Christ to all ranks under a surprising variety of conditions, especially in a theater of war. It is mandatory for the chaplain to possess a robust Christian faith, a good education, high moral standards, and an ability to meet people from a perspective of genuine Christian love.

**MILITARY SERVICE.** From earliest times men have banded together to defend themselves, or to attack others, according to their perceived common interests. In primitive communities this is generally seen as the main duty of adult males, and there is no distinction between voluntary and involuntary military duty. It is a result of the development of more sophisticated societies that military service becomes an involuntary duty. This development occurred in ancient Israel. At the time of the Exodus and conquest, the entire available manpower of the tribes bore arms and joined in battle; but by the time of the monarchy under Saul, a small standing army was constituted and, in time of emergency, supplemented by a general levy.

The ethic of pacifism comes to a head during forced conscription into military service, whether in war and national emergency or to maintain a standing army in peacetime. It is not for pacifists only, however, that obligatory military service raises difficult questions. Whether the criteria are those of traditional Just War theory or some other, the Christian will judge the morality of the purposes for which conscription operates. If the particular conflict or the general policy of the state is in his conscientious judgment immoral, the Christian's attitude to military service (voluntary or involuntary) will tend toward that of the pacifist. There are, however, further considerations that should play their part in this thinking, chiefly those that arise from the Christian understanding of the state and its authority.

According to the position enunciated in the New Testament (Rom. 13:1-7) the state is instituted by God and, whether or not its leaders acknowledge Him, it should command the respect of its people, believers included. Such respect must not be unconditional (Acts 4:19), but its conditionality is severely limited. So, one of the major themes of the New Testament, taken up by the early apologists, is that believers can be good citizens of the pagan empire. It is therefore essential that the Christian be circumspect in the ethical assessment of state policy. Even in a representative democracy, the determination of policy does not lie with the individual, but with the government. The individual is often in no position to come to a proper assessment of the justice or otherwise of particular policy decisions. He needs to be very sure of his ground before venturing to deny his service to the state on account of conscience. If he finds himself convinced that the state's military purposes are fundamentally unjust, he may be unable to offer the state the service that is normally his duty. But it must be recognized that this is exceptional behavior and does not imply that the individual must be in agreement with the policy of the state, or indeed must agree that that policy is morally acceptable, before he can associate himself with it. That would be a recipe for the very chaos that the state is constituted by God to avoid.

The pacifist position is more straightforward. It involves the repudiation of war for any cause, though the degree to which it involves pacifists in refusal to bear arms, or to engage in the use of force of any kind (for example, in police actions, whether civil or military) may vary. Where "military service" can be confined to roles that do not involve the bearing of arms, the pacifist may be prepared to enlist in catering, or, more likely, in medical work. Others will not accept such alternatives, but refuse to participate in any way, either in military activity or in civilian activity, that will free another civilian for military duties. In the context of the modern concept of total war, there are probably no pursuits that will prove acceptable, except the imprisonment that may ultimately result.

The pacifism that was widespread in the early church before the conversion of the Roman Empire has since been maintained largely in two traditions, one resulting from the "radical" Reformation, and represented today chiefly by the Mennonites, and the other by the Quakers, the group that arose in England at the time of the Civil War (mid-seventeenth century). Both groups are numerically very small but have exercised considerable influence in keeping the pacifist option on the church's agenda. The development of nuclear and other modern weaponry of appalling and often indiscriminate destructive power has recently thrust to the fore the pacifist critique of conventional Christian moral thinking.

The pacifist position has generally been repudiated by Christian moralists on a number of grounds. (a) It rests on a false polarization of Old and New Testaments and lies uneasily with the fact that war, while seen as an evil that will one day be no more, is a very major theme in Old Testament history, often at the explicit command of God. (b) Its use of the teaching of Jesus is naive, such that principles intended to govern personal relations are applied indiscriminately to states and to individuals acting in their service. This approach would logically involve, among other things, the repudiation of police and judicial power to restrain and punish wrongdoing, something that is specifically upheld in the New Testament (Rom. 13). It also involves inexact exegesis of such passages as the Sermon on the Mount. (c) It involves an abdication of responsibility for the protection of the weak and defenseless, which is a prime biblical duty and must not be confused with self-sacrifice. (d) It ignores the evidence in the New Testament that our Lord and the apostles were unconcerned with the question, such that men on military service, including centurions and other officers, were contacted and sometimes converted without receiving any injunction to leave the service of the Empire. Their occupation is regarded as irrelevant.

See ARMAMENT; DISARMAMENT; JUST WAR CRITERIA; WAR.

N.M.deS.C.

**MIND CONTROL.** Mind control has in a sense always been with us. In many ways and with varying success we have persistently attempted to control the behavior and influence the beliefs of others. Techniques have included everything from suggestion and persuasion to threats and rewards to such manipulative techniques as seduction, coercion, and, more recently, brainwashing.

Today, mind control, or as it is more commonly referred to, behavioral control, makes use of recent scientific understandings and technologies to effect changes of a sort undreamed of a few years ago. Behavior control can be divided into two sorts: information control, which attempts to influence people, working within their capacity for voluntary choice, and appealing to the person's capacity to think, judge, and decide; and coercive control, which works directly on the brain, on behavior, or on the subconscious to achieve the desired change. Coercive control causes most of the newer ethical problems.

Coercive behavioral control is achieved by using a variety of technologies and scientific understandings having to do with brain physiology, subconscious processes, and deep psychological states. Examples of direct intervention in the human brain include electroconvulsive treatment (ECT; also known as "shock therapy"), electrostimulation of the brain by implanting electrodes into the brain (ESB), and psychosurgery (surgery on the brain to change behavior or attitudes). In ECT, ESB, and psychosurgery, recent discoveries in the relationship between brain changes and behavioral and attitudinal alterations have been put to use to alter aggressive behavior patterns or extreme anxiety.

Other therapeutic interventions yielded by technology include the use of psychotropic drugs, such as tranquilizers and antidepressants, which are much more widely used than the exotic therapies mentioned above. Although milder in degree, the widespread use of alcohol and nicotine are examples of the application of psychotropic drugs, as is the use of the widely prescribed Valium and the impressive array of antipsychotic drugs that treat such chronic psychoses as schizophrenia, mania, and paranoia. They are surprisingly effective in helping relieve the symptoms of these disorders.

Other psychotropic drugs are the medications, such as tranquilizers, used to relieve acute anxieties in individuals who are usually considered normal.

In addition to these pharmacological therapies, recent years have seen the advance of behavior therapy stemming from behavioristic psychology, often used in treatment of persistent "bad habits" such as smoking, overeating, and homosexual attraction, in which positive or negative reinforcement of behaviors to develop or end them.

Another recent development has been the technology of subliminal suggestion, in which messages designed to change behavior are inserted into visual or auditory background. Research shows that these messages are entirely hidden to the conscious mind but are registered in the subconscious. This has been used in department store background music to discourage shoplifting and has been used illegally in commercials for snacks during the showing of films in theaters.

Ethical issues in the use of behavioral control lie in several areas. First and fundamental to the others, is the implication of such coercive technologies for the concept of autonomy. Is it appropriate to compromise people's freedom in this way? Christians believe that persons are moral agents who are to be held responsible for their actions, and thus are metaphysically free in their moral choices. These technologies threaten to deny metaphysical and political liberties more subtly than those of past ages. Related to this point is a political one, since technology for control must itself be governed. If we accept the reductionistic view of man often associated with such technologies, that people are but psychophysical organisms to be manipulated, as B. F. Skinner and others suggest, we are in the position that C. S. Lewis warned of in *The Abolition of Man,* facing the totalitarian implications of the technology and its underlying philosophy.

Another question that arises is: What sorts of problems will be dealt with by such techniques? Do we use them for all kinds of behavioral disorders, or only those that seem to stem from biological malfunction? Many argue that the use of such control to alter attitudes and emotions is a symptom of our tendency to "medicalize" social problems. A better way, it is argued, is to look to social and environmental factors so as to enable us to deal with adjustment problems. An example of this is the use of drugs for "hyperactive" children. It is suspected that the extremely high incidence of the use of the drug in many schools evidences a failure to look at the true environmental causes of disorderly classroom behavior.

**Bibliography:** Delgado, J., *Physical Control of the Mind* (1969); Lewis, C. S., *The Abolition of Man* (1947); London, P., *Behavior Control* (1969); Mark, V., *The Case for Psychosurgery, Boston University Law Review* 54:217–30; Skinner, B. F., *Beyond Freedom and Dignity* (1971).

See BRAINWASHING; DRUGS; HYPNOSIS.

D.B.F.

**MINORITY RIGHTS.** Recognition of minority rights has come from an increasing awareness of individual rights. Society is starting to recognize that making all individuals equal at law does not necessarily give them equality, because by virtue of their membership in a certain group some individuals are thereby disadvantaged. Thus, some recognition has to be made of the minority group's needs. Minority rights are group rather than individual rights.

Religious minorities were the first to acquire recognition. In England the state church is the Church of England. In the nineteenth century discriminatory legislation against Jews and Roman Catholics was abolished. While prayers are still compulsory in schools at the beginning of the day, parents who so choose may have their children withdrawn from them. In Canada and the United States there is separation of church and state, and religious toleration is the policy although some sects have suffered serious discrimination in the past.

Religious toleration was followed by recognition of minority racial and cultural groups. Such groups also do not wish to be assimilated with the majority. Policies of anti-discrimination have evolved, slowly and painfully. While they may not remove prejudice they do provide a means of obtaining equality. Thus, discrimination in housing, employment, education, and so on on the grounds of race is prohibited and sanctions are imposed where it is found to exist.

In Canada the rights of French-Canadians now receive a much greater level of protection than formerly. Indians in both Canada and the United States have always received special treatment. However, they remain very disadvantaged in terms of education, housing, and employment. With the recognition and protection of racial and cultural groups, there have also grown demands for recognition and support of social groups with common qualities that result in discrimination against them.

Women are gradually taking their proper place in society. England is more advanced than Canada and the United States in this regard, partly as a result of the influence of the European Economic Community. It has legislation prohibiting direct and indirect sexual discrimination. In Canada the Charter of Rights prohibits sexual discrimination and the federal government urges a policy of equal employment, while some provincial legislation reflects the changing status of women. In the U.S. the proposed Equal Rights Amendment has lost some momentum and the federal government is not a strong proponent of such rights.

Various interest groups are becoming more vocal in pursuing their aims, such as the handicapped, the elderly, and inmates in mental institutions; and there seems to be a trend toward recognizing the validity of their concerns. Thus, society in some ways is becoming more caring and accommodating of its minorities.

The rights of minorities and disadvantaged groups were provided for in Old Testament laws. Thus, widows, orphans, and foreigners were not to be oppressed (Exod. 22:23-24), understanding and help were to be given to the handicapped (Lev. 19:14), and the poor were not to be exploited (Deut. 24:12-14). Jesus extended this concept of caring by advocating that the disadvantaged outcasts of society be fully accepted by it.

**Bibliography:** Bayefsky, A. F., *The Impact of the European Convention on Human Rights in the U.K.*, Ottawa Law Review, XIII (1981), p. 507; Schmeiser, D. A., *Civil Liberties in Canada* (1964); Sigler, J. A., *Minority Rights. A Comprehensive Analysis* (1983); Stevens, I. N. and Yardley, D. C. M., *The Protection of Liberty* (1982).

D.E.T.

**MIXED MARRIAGES (RELIGIOUS).** Just as marriage between an Israelite and a Gentile was abhorred in Old Testament times, so marriages between Jews and anyone else are forbidden by Orthodox Judaism. Either the Jew must separate from the Jewish community, or the Gentile must become a Jew by conversion and baptism. Such proselyte baptism dates from pre-Christian times, the convert immersing himself under living water with not a hair or a cell not being covered by the water. This immersion signified the death of the old Gentile, followed then by new birth as a Jew.

Although Conservative and Reformed branches of Judaism provide ways for Gentile converts to join the Jewish community, there has been less pressure for them to make the transfer. It is reported that it is more frequent that the Jewish partner to such a mixed marriage will identify more with the Gentile culture, although not necessarily with the Christian faith.

"Mixed marriages" have not been welcomed by the Roman Catholic Church when they mean marriage between one of its members and anyone outside its ranks, even though he or she be a professing Christian. In the encyclical, *Casti con-*

*nubi,* Pope Pius XI affirmed the ban on such marriages by canon law and referred to the provision of dispensations from this ban as the only acceptable circumstance under which a Roman Catholic might contract such a marriage.

This dispensation involved usually four commitments by the couple to be married: a promise by the non-Roman Catholic party not to influence the other partner to leave the Roman church; a promise by the Roman Catholic party to attempt the conversion of the other partner to Roman Catholicism; an undertaking that any children of the marriage will be baptized and educated as Roman Catholics; and an agreement that no civil or non-Roman Catholic ceremony will be conducted.

In general most non-Roman Catholic churches have not made similar demands of their members and have cordially accepted the right of church members to marry members of other communions and to be married by their clergy. In the face of the Roman Catholic demands, however, many churches have called on their people not to accede to the promises required by the Roman church. Typical of them has been this statement by the bishops of the Anglican Communion assembled in the 1948 Lambeth Conference:

> ...the religious education and spiritual training of their children by word and example is a paramount duty of parents and should never be neglected nor left entirely to others. It sometimes happens that, as a condition of marriage, one of the partners is required to sign a declaration that children born of the marriage will be brought up in the practice of a religious system in which he or she does not believe. To give such an undertaking is sin...We strongly deprecate such mixed marriages, and we assert that in no circumstances should an Anglican give any undertaking, as a condition of marriage, that the children should be brought up in the practice of another Communion."

The Lambeth Conference committee, dealing with mixed marriages, also studied the matter of Christians marrying members of other religions and agreed that these mixed marriages should be forbidden, except in cases approved by the bishop of the diocese, who has the power of granting dispensation.

R.F.S.

**MODERATION.** This term is one of several that are derived from the Latin root *moderor,* meaning "to set bounds to," "check," "moderate." Moderation is thus a state, condition, or attitude which is marked by restraint, or a lack of obvious extremes. For such a condition to obtain there certainly have to be proper parameters established, whether these are tacit or explicit, and a conscious control over whatever features are bounded by these limitations.

As an ethical proposition, moderation is not infrequently a part of self-reformation programs instituted by individuals who lack the determination or ability to abstain completely from whatever has prompted the need for change. Such a procedure can only be successful if it is monitored strictly, and since extremes are abhorrent to moderation, the effort is likely to be self-defeating.

The notion of adopting a policy of moderation in everything was Greek in origin and was central to the ethical teaching of Aristotle (384-322 B.C.). This dogma, known as the Golden Mean, was an attempt to bring some refinement in the form of the "good life" to the illiterate, licentious, aggressive braggarts that formed the bulk of the ancient Greek population. For Aristotle moderation lay at some point between two extremes in life, and he illustrated his precept by regarding self-control as the mean between suppression of appetite on the one hand and overindulgence on the other. The principle of moderation, however, did not claim for Aristotle any universal validity and in some moral issues such as murder had no validity at all, since that act was a crime under any circumstances.

The very subjectivity of moderation makes it at best a very uncertain secular guide to morality. The Bible encourages the believer to adopt high rather than moderate standards in life (Eccles. 9:10; 2 Tim. 2:15) and live in uncompromised submission to God's leading. For the Christian, moderation is an example of how the good can become the enemy of the best. The word *moderation* occurs once only in the King James Version (Phil. 4:5), for the Greek word *epieikes,* meaning "flexibility," "adaptability," "complaisance."

See MEAN, DOCTRINE OF THE.

**MODERNISM, ETHICAL.** Modernism is a general theological outlook rather than a specific set of doctrines. The aim of modernism is the reworking of traditional Christian beliefs derived from the New Testament and embodied in the classical creeds and confessions of the church, in order to make these intelligible and acceptable to the modern scientific and moral sensibility. Modernism takes its rise, within Protestantism, from the "moral religion" of Immanuel Kant (1724-1804), though traces of the modernist "spirit" can be found in some earlier thinkers, notably in latitudinarians and Socinians, and in English deism. Kant denied that it was possible to have knowledge of God, either by means of natural theology, or by an appeal to divine revelation. Rather, religion was understood as logically ancillary to morality, a "postulate" of the practical reason. Morality, in turn, is understandable in terms of a principle of universalisability. "Act in such a way that you always treat humanity, whether in your own person or in the person of any other, never simply as a means, but always at the same time as an end." Kant may be said to have initiated the search for the essence of religion in morality. Such morality is not understood either in terms of natural law, revealed law, or even utilitarian calculation, but in terms of a law that is the creation of the autonomous, rational man.

The moral individualism of Kant was fleshed out into corporate terms by the first influential post-Kantian theologian, F. D. E. Schleiermacher (1768-1834). The cooperative character of ethics was stressed, as was the corporate character of sin, which came to be a substitute for the traditional doctrine of original sin. But the dominant post-Kantian theological influence was exercised by Albrecht Ritschl (1822-1889). Ritschl was influenced by neo-Kantian idealism and based his largely ethical view of Christianity on a reconstruction of the so-called "Jesus of History," a human teacher as distinct from the divinized "Christ of Faith." Jesus trusted supremely in God's love and manifested the paradigm God-man relation. To follow this Jesus is to be delivered from the mechanism and naturalism of modern thought so dominated by science. Unlike Schleiermacher, Ritschl's starting point is not the Christian consciousness, the feeling of absolute dependence, but Jesus' gospel of the kingdom, his preaching of "the moral unification of the human race, through action prompted by universal love to our neighbor."

Ritschl's procedure illustrates vividly another characteristic of modernism, namely a preparedness to handle the text of the New Testament "critically," often in the light of certain principles derived *a priori* from philosophical sources. Thus, not only did the "Jesus of History" come to be opposed to the "Christ of Faith," but different ethical strands of the Old Testament were discerned and often assigned to different sources, and the teaching of the "Jesus of History" was opposed to the theology of Paul.

Thus the metaphysical and ethical categories of the Bible and especially the New Testament—creation, fall, and redemption through the sacrificial work of the eternal Son of God made flesh—were reduced to or replaced by categories that were essentially ethical and ameliorative. Jesus is not the eternal Son of God made flesh for the redemption of sinners, but a moral teacher with a vision of divine love who was put to death for His idealism, who gave in His death an unparalleled example of self-giving love, but who had the misfortune to be deified by His early followers. The Christian life is not to be understood in terms of the need to be justified by grace and the need for new birth and sanctification, but in terms of the imitation of Christ and the bringing in of the kingdom of God, understood wholly in immanent terms, by cooperative social action. Thus, viewed as a religion, modernism is Pelagian, anthropocentric, and places an almost exclusive stress on the immanence of God.

In the United States ethical modernism is largely identified with the "social gospel" movement, prominent members of which were Walter Rauschenbusch (1861-1918), Washington Gladden

(1836-1918), and H. E. Fosdick (1816-1918). While these men were part of a worldwide emphasis on the social aspects of Christianity at this time, it is not clear that their thought was notably dependent upon that of Germans such as Schleiermacher and Ritschl. Rather, the impetus came from an attempt to recast the gospel in a way that was thought to be more relevant to the solving of the social problems of rapid industrial expansion in the United States during this period. Both the degree of confidence that such problems could be overcome by social action and the degree of social change that was thought to be necessary to achieve the desired goals varied considerably from thinker to thinker. Thus Rauschenbusch, for example, while an advocate of some version of Christian socialism, and therefore keen to strengthen the hand of various federal agencies, was not optimistic about actually achieving socialism.

One influence upon the social gospel in the United States was undoubtedly the modernistic tendencies at work in England at this time. These came through the impact of idealist philosophy, through figures such as S. T. Coleridge (1772-1834), John Caird (1820-1898), Edward Caird (1835-1908), and most notably F. D. Maurice (1805-1872). These influences tended to reinforce the native liberal and "broad church' tendencies both within the Church of England and in some areas of nonconformity.

Insofar as ethical modernism was part of a wider optimistic social climate, its impact was severely weakened by the two World Wars and by the rise of Barthian and Barth-inspired theology. Yet the need for a continued restatement of the Christian faith in terms that are acceptable to people who have "come of age" has continued to be stressed by popular radical theologians such as J. A. T. Robinson, using lines of thought derived from diverse religious thinkers such as Bultmann, Bonhoeffer (1906-1945), and Paul Tillich (1886-1965), but especially those with an existentialist orientation. This has led to situation ethics in which, again in typical modernist fashion, divine law is opposed to love, the immanence of God is stressed; and there is an emphasis (albeit somewhat muted) on the need for social reconstruction.

From an orthodox Christian point of view modernist ethics may be criticized for capitulating to the spirit of the age, indeed to the spirit of successive ages. God's law is not used to arrest and convict the sinner and to herald God's mercy to the soul, but it is distorted by alien philosophical influences, or abandoned altogether. More generally, ethical modernism turns its back upon the metaphysical and ontological underpinnings of Christian ethics. Critics of modernism from the Barthian side can often be accused fairly of irrationalism, particularly in their neglect of the ethical implications of the biblical teaching on creation, while those from the side of conservative Protestantism have often been obscurantist

and legalistic, imposing on the biblical ethic a number of moral and behavioral taboos, and have often been exclusively individualistic in their ethical teaching.

"Modernism" in the Roman Catholic Church refers to a movement that arose at the beginning of this century and that was sympathetic to higher criticism, reacting against the traditional Aristotelianism and Thomism of Roman Catholic theology, with its emphasis on natural law. For the modernists, Roman dogmas came to be symbols to inspire a moral response. Leading thinkers were A. F. Loisy (1857-1940), F. Von Hugel (1852-1925), and G. H. Tyrrell (1861-1909). The movement was officially condemned in the papal encyclical *Pascendi* of Pius X in 1907.

**Bibliography:** Kant, I., *Religion Within the Limits of Reason Alone* (1934); Reardon, B. M. G., (ed.), *Liberal Protestantism* (1968); Ritschl, A., *The Christian Doctrine of Justification and Reconciliation* (1900); Schleiermacher, F. D. E., *The Christian Faith* (1928).

P.H.

**MODESTY.** The idea of modesty is based upon a mode, which in ethics indicates a manner of proper procedure or a form in which something is manifested. The term *mode* is derived from the Latin *modus,* which has to do broadly with standards of measurement, regulations, or the manner in which things are done. Modesty is thus one way of behaving and in general is characterized by unassuming conduct, self-depreciation, and inconspicuousness.

As a moral quality modesty is based upon perceived values which for fallen humanity resist attainment while attracting endeavor. The individual's resultant behavior generally seems to call for some sort of apology which is seldom articulated, but manifests a certain embarrassment or shame when it is. Where modesty involves a shrinking from what is indecorous, it is the high value of purity that has fallen short of attainment, either in the individual involved or in others.

Modesty is not a quality that secular society covets because of the brash, aggressive, and largely vulgar character of modern life. By contrast the Christian vocation encourages a realistic self-evaluation (Rom. 12:3) which will prevent overpowering pride and encourage sober, considerate behavior in society, based on the high values of truth, honesty, and love. The only instance of the term in the King James Version is in 1 Timothy 2:9, where the Greek *kosmios* means "what is decent," "fitting," as applied to women's clothing.

**MONOGAMY.** This term is a compound of two Greek words, *monos* and *gamos,* meaning "single marriage." It comprises a technical description of the biblical ideal of marriage, which is the lifelong union of a man and a woman in an exclusive relationship (Gen. 2:24). This basic statement was modified legally and culturally by the understanding that the man must be either single or a widower and the woman unmarried or a widow. If a man were to have more than one wife at a time, the relationship would technically be a polygamous one; and if a woman were to be married to more than one man at one and the same time, the union would be regarded as polyandrous.

Exceptions to monogamy occurred periodically in the Old Testament period, principally among royalty. David had four wives (1 Sam. 25:43-44; 2 Sam. 11:27), and Solomon was notorious for the number of foreign women whom he married (1 Kings 11:1-3). Even in the New Testament period, when monogamy was the normal marital pattern, King Herod reportedly had nine wives during his troubled reign.

Monogamy has many values, not the least of which is the obligation of husband and wife to be loving and loyal to each other. Just as no man can serve two masters, so no man can love two women equally at the same time. In polygamous situations, household jealousies and factions are the norm, which so far from being conducive to pleasant relationships are the breeding ground for jealousy, violence, and the like. Jesus commended the monogamous ideal of the Old Testament (Matt. 19:5), as did Paul (Eph. 5:31), and stressed the exclusive nature of the relationship (Matt. 19:9; Mark 10:11-12). The biblical ideal restores the equality and personal dignity of the woman and serves as an illustration of the spiritual relationship that exists between Christ and his church (Eph. 5:22-33).

**MORTAL SIN.** This title designates a type of sin which in medieval Roman Catholic moral theology could not be pardoned and consequently resulted in spiritual death or deprivation of sanctifying grace. Such transgression stood in contrast to venial sin which could be forgiven (Latin *venia,* "pardon") by a priest after confession. Mortal (Latin *mors,* "death") or deadly offenses were considered to be fundamental in nature and to have been committed willingly and in complete knowledge of the guilt incurred. So heinous were mortal sins considered to be by the Roman casuists that eternal damnation resulted from them unless a timely repentance and forgiveness took place.

While the classification of sin into venial and mortal categories was no doubt meant for the guidance and edification of the Roman Catholic faithful, it tends to obscure the nature of sin as revealed in Scripture. First and foremost sin constitutes for humanity a state of alienation from God as well as an act or acts of wrongdoing (Ps. 51:1-9; Isa. 6:5; Luke 5:8). Sin occurs because the human heart has been corrupted (Jer. 17:9) and therefore in its egocentric unregenerate state expresses itself characteristically in rebellion against God. Sin is grounded in unbelief, which according to Paul determined its scope and character (Rom. 14:23). Chronic unbelief was described in Scripture as "hardness of heart" (Exod. 7:14; Mark 16:14), which is really obduracy of will, the heart being regarded by the Hebrews as the locale of intelligence and will. This attitude reflects a complete unwillingness to obey God or to respect the needs of other people, thereby giving sin a social as well as a personal dimension. Paul cataloged the more obvious forms of spiritual transgression for the benefit of his readers (Gal. 5:19-21; Eph. 5:3-5), warning them that divine wrath would be the consequence of such activity (Rom. 11:18).

It seems evident from Scripture that all sin leads to death (John 8:24; Rom. 6:23), and therefore even the slightest sin is deadly if it remains unforgiven. But Scripture also assures the sinner that Christ's shed blood also avails for cleansing (1 John 1:7) and that the only sin for which there is no forgiveness is the one committed against the Holy Spirit, which presumably is a conscious and complete rejection of God's covenanted mercies in Christ.

**MORTIFICATION.** In ascetic theology a rigorous form of self-discipline known as mortification aims at nullifying as far as possible the sinful acts of the flesh. Based on two Latin words, *mors,* "death," and *facere,* "to make," it aims to "make dead" all those tendencies that lead the believer into sin. The word *mortify* occurs twice in the King James Version (Rom. 8:13; Col. 3:5), and in both instances Paul urges the believers to exterminate evil from their thoughts and actions by his use of this graphic expression. From the sense of chastising or self-discipline the word has acquired connotations of shame, humiliation, and chagrin.

Despite the obsolete nature of the term, the intention is as wholesome now as it was in the time of Paul. The Christian needs to discipline his or her thoughts and deeds continually in order to ensure that they correspond to the high moral and spiritual aspirations represented by the gospel. Since evil deeds proceed from depraved thoughts (Matt. 15:18; Mark 7:20), Christ taught that self-denial must be a daily occurrence (Luke 9:23) and exercised as an act of divine grace through the Holy Spirit.

**MOTIVES AND MOTIVATION.** Motives may be defined as the purposive emotional forces that prompt persons to undertake various kinds of activity. While some motives are superficial in nature, as for example the need to satisfy the immediate pangs of hunger leading to an impulse-purchase of food, others are located deeply in the human mind. These are based upon such emotions as anxiety, greed, ambition, hatred, fear, or love, and may often be of a complex rather than a simple nature. Because of the egocentric orientation of the human personality, the motives that dictate activity are much more likely to be selfish than altruistic. For this reason it is important to distinguish between worthy and unworthy motives, which then brings the matter into the area of ethics.

Having identified the concept of motivation from a psychological standpoint, it merely remains to observe that motivation is the power that arises within the individual to ensure that the desired objectives are attempted, if not actually achieved. If the motive for action is strong, it generates a corresponding degree of energy and enthusiasm for the accomplishing of the goal. But if the motives are uncertain, or come to exhibit internal conflict, the motivation may be attenuated or fluctuate in intensity and could conceivably languish before the motives have been exercised fully. This contingency carries with it various degrees of frustration.

Motives and motivation should always be regarded as complex psychological phenomena, and the professional theorists have advanced various interpretations in order to account for this contingency. These range from a straightforward stimulus-response sequence to an involved psychoanalytical explanation based upon the supposed productive power of unfulfilled desires in the subconscious mind. What does seem clear, however, is that motives and motivation are far less dependent upon external stimuli than earlier, and rather simplistic, explanations suggested.

Because of the omnipresent activity of evil in the personalities of fallen human beings, the Christian who is rejoicing in the new birth must keep his or her motives pure and lofty. To have the "mind of Christ" is fundamentally important in this area. Jesus spoke of the blessings accruing to the "pure in heart" (Matt. 5:8) and taught the fundamental importance of motivation in the assessment of human behavior (Matt. 15:19). Obedience to the truth of Christ through the Holy Spirit exerts a purifying effect upon the human mind and makes love from a pure heart a dominant emotional force (1 Pet. 1:22).

**Bibliography:** Cofer, C. N. and Appley, M. H., *Motivation: Theory and Research* (1964).

See RIGHT AND WRONG.

**MOVIES.** Two ways in which movies are often evaluated are in terms of sex and violence. These are both important concerns. Studies have shown children to be negatively influenced by violence in television and movies. Sex becomes an issue because of scenes that are too explicit and because of attitudes taken. A movie might not be explicit, but portray adultery in a romantic and positive way, for instance. Both sex and violence seem to escalate to new levels as the public becomes jaded at the old levels.

Other movies may be inoffensive in terms of sex and violence, but may create a vision of a world where God doesn't exist or may have values that are totally materialistic. So questions of world view also need to be raised.

Many movies are only commercial entertainments, copying other movies that were financially successful and appealing to the lowest common denominator. Other movies communicate timeless truth through the director's vision and the actors' skill.

Going to a movie involves entering an environment where the size of the screen, the darkness, and the lack of commercial interruptions can produce an impact on all the senses that cannot be matched by other media. But, in contrast with watching television, for instance, going to a movie usually involves a more conscious choice. A person can read reviews and talk to friends before deciding to see a movie.

We are told to "try all things and hold fast to that which is good" (1 Thess. 5:21). Some Christians have thrown out movies categorically as something "not good." Other Christians prefer evaluating films on an individual basis.

The Christians who do not go to any movies ensure that they do not see any bad ones. However, they will miss those movies that give unique and clear expression to questions about world view and values which, as with any good art, can heighten our perception and understanding of the world.

S.M.G.

**MURDER.** Murder is the ultimate act of personal violence and results in an individual losing his or her life. From a legal standpoint murder must be distinguished from manslaughter, in which individual existence is also terminated. Whereas manslaughter constitutes an act of criminal homicide not marked by premeditation, murder is an unlawful killing characterized by "malice aforethought," however long or short the motivating period may have been. Manslaughter is unintentional or accidental; murder is deliberate.

The first recorded crime in human history was murder (Gen. 4:8), and ever since it has been regarded as the most serious of all offenses and deserving of capital punishment. In the ancient Near East murderers were commonly executed when apprehended, and the laws of the ancient Hebrews were no exception to this procedure. The sixth commandment (Exod. 20:13) emphatically prohibited murder, and any rendering of the verb *ratsach* which merely suggests killing in general is a misunderstanding of the original Hebrew. The reason for the highly serious manner in which murder is viewed lies in the fact that it violates the *imago dei* or image of God in mankind (Gen. 1:27) in an irrevocable manner. This image must be protected (Gen. 4:15), and accordingly God decreed a value for human dignity in prescribing capital punishment for murder (Gen. 9:16).

This enactment demonstrated that one person's life is neither more nor less valuable in principle than that of another. The taking of a murderer's life thus constituted an equitable punishment for the crime. In order to protect the dignity of the criminal and avoid the possibility of lengthy and bitter recriminations against his family, the statute on capital punishment was reinforced by the principle of *lex talionis,* or punishment of the same kind as the injury (Exod. 21:24). Under this legislation only the murderer was to be executed and nobody else in his family as an added compensation, so that there would be no blood feuds stretching over several generations.

Murder is a reprehensible crime, however committed; and the ultimate punishment has the sanction of God himself. The killing of enemy soldiers in wartime in defense of one's homeland, or in the support of one's allies, has never been regarded traditionally as murder, although the execution of uninvolved and defenseless civilians has.

See ABORTION; CAPITAL PUNISHMENT; EUTHANASIA; LIFE, SACREDNESS OF.

**MYSTICISM, ETHICS OF.** Some of the greatest moral authorities in the Bible, including Moses, Isaiah, and Paul, apparently had mystical experiences (Exod. 3:1-6; Isa. 6:1-8; Acts 9:3-9). So did later Christian leaders such as Bernard of Clairvaux and Francis of Assisi. Although these moralists stress traditional themes of love and union with God, mystics are frequently distrusted by theologians and church leaders because of their heretical tendencies and because some of them are more interested in their absorbing experiences than in moral and social concerns.

Paul Tillich says that mysticism, with its relentless pursuit of union with God, "neglects the human predicament and the separation of man from the ultimate." Reinhold Niebuhr says that mystics are tempted "to stand, as it were, above the structures and coherences of the world." These omissions occur more radically in some mystics who, attempting to purge themselves of imperfections, reject ideas of God that they perceive as limited, inaccurate, or idolatrous. Striving for perfection, they may also reject all conceptions of morality as relatively wrong. Thus, their quest for worthiness in the sight of God may by degrees change to a quest for a purified, emptied consciousness in which, in Martin Buber's words, "the being stands alone in itself and jubilates, as Paracelsus puts it, in its exaltation." Thus, the mystics' perfected state of illumination is theologically suspect and could hardly be universally recommended as the goal of the Christian life. Its dangers are discussed by the philosopher Arthur Danto, in *Mysticism and Morality.* He points out that a mystic of the extremely pure sort just described experiences "a devaluation of all values save those revealed to him at the high moment of insight," and this causes him to count personal and social attachments as of only secondary importance.

Morally untrustworthy mystics are therefore recognized by their obsession with the experience of mystical illumination. Their narrowly focused activity has been labeled "pure" mysticism, because it is unmixed with any other interest. Although *pure* is a positive adjective, this mysticism is suspect because it has no concern beyond itself. It has been said, metaphorically, that pure mystics polish the mirror of the self, but do not allow the image of God to appear there. On the other hand, Christian mystics who practice a "mixed" mysticism concern themselves with spiritual and moral problems. Albert Schweitzer notes this, when he says, of Paul's commitment to the Christian moral life and to salvation in Christ, that Paul "is not wholly and solely a mystic."

Yet, if mysticism is not sufficient for morality, one can still argue, as Iris Murdoch does, that morality requires it. Mystics are, as stated, perfectionists. Therefore, if a "mixed" mystic focuses on moral questions, and seeks moral perfection as well as union with God, we will discover that he has a vision of his ultimate hope, (called "the Good" by Murdoch), which he takes very seriously. Murdoch argues that such a vision, whether it includes God or not, is necessary in every moral life. Therefore, she says, "The background to morals is properly some sort of mysticism, if by this is meant a non-dogmatic, essentially unformulated faith in the reality of the Good, occasionally connected with experience."

This suggests that mystical morality is characterized, not by the content of its moral advice (which is not unique among Christian moral prescriptions), but by its uncompromising idealism. In dealing with particular moral problems, the Christian mystic is dissatisfied with conventional moral solutions. He takes Christ's demands for perfection (Matt. 5:48) seriously, but he is also frequently aware that in this mortal life he has only choices between evils. For the moral mystic, this creates a desperate dilemma, which he resolves individually in an intellectual or visionary illumination experience that occurs only after intense concentration and discipline in a purification process. Guided by the Holy Spirit, he finds himself called to a particular solution, relative to his historical and individual circumstances. Because of its individuality, mystical moral leadership may appear in styles as different as those of the aggressive, forceful Ignatius Loyola and the peaceful, retiring St. Francis.

Mystical moralists, in their character as inspired exemplary leaders, embody an answer to the "Euthyphro dilemma." That classical criticism of theistic moralities asks, essentially, what knowledge of God's commands can add to our natural moral intuitions and reasoning power, since we seem capable of providing our own ethical guidance. The mystical moralist demonstrates that it is possible for inspired Christians to experience moments of illumination (after ascetic disciplines), when possibilities that were not anticipated by natural morality are revealed. Inspired moralists are rather like athletic champions demonstrating new ways in which games can be played. When they have displayed their unprecedented responses, others can emulate them. Obviously, however, anyone who claims to have had an inspired insight into possibilities for doing the will of God in ways not previously envisaged by our moral rules must be suspect. We must ask whether his highly original moral prescription is consistent with God's moral commands in Scripture as interpreted by the church. In that sense, mystics who are delivering moral advice to us must be regarded as engaged in, not a distinctive ethics of mysticism, but rather a strenuous effort to achieve a highly developed moral and spiritual solution, in which they perceive and respond to idealistic, even saintly moral demands. Whether a given mystic has provided us with valid moral leadership that we should follow is always a serious question.

**Bibliography:** Danto, A. C., *Mysticism and Morality* (1972); Horne, J. R., *The Moral Mystic* (1983); Murdoch, I., *The Sovereignty of Good* (1970); Schweitzer, A., *The Mysticism of Paul the Apostle* (1931).

J.R.H.

# –N–

**NARCOTICS.** The term *narcotic* is applied to drugs derived from the juice of the opium poppy pod, or to synthetic drugs with similar properties. The natural narcotics—those extracted from the poppy—include morphine, codeine, heroin, and dilaudid. Synthetic narcotics include merperidine ("Demerol"), pentazocine ("Talwin"), and methadone. Drugs of this class have been used for centuries for their sedative, analgesic, and euphoriant properties. Morphia, tincture of opium, and opium smoke were at one time used widely for insomnia, for the relief of anxiety, and for relief of pain. Today their chief legitimate use is relief from pain, from disruptive cough, and (rarely) from diarrhea.

These preparations, so potent for pain relief, are dangerous drugs. In moderate overdose they may be rapidly fatal. In continued use they can induce addiction. It is this last quality that has moved Western governments to impose rigid controls on their use.

Persons suffering from chronic or recurrent pain are at risk for dependency upon any drug that offers relief. Acetylsalicylic acid (aspirin) and acetaminophen (Tylenol) are in themselves potent analgesics. But they are frequently combined with narcotic pain killers, usually codeine. These drugs are readily available on the open market, without prescription. The frequency of their abuse is not known with certainty, but it is very high. Patients in whom pain is combined with anxiety (whether the anxiety is related to the pain or to other circumstances or conflicts in life) are at especially high risk for dependency on over-the-counter opiates. The hazards of codeine dependency relate as much to the complications and side effects of the psychologically innocuous drugs with which they are combined than to the codeine itself. The withdrawal syndrome from codeine and its derivative drugs is rarely severe. But because of their availability, the risk of relapse into addiction is extremely high.

The role of genetic factors remains unclear. Research of the last decade has demonstrated that there are "opiate receptors" in the central nervous system. This discovery led to the discovery of naturally occurring opium-like substances in the brain, the endorphins. It may be that persons with a deficient level of these naturally occurring chemicals are at special risk for addiction to opiates. Such a deficiency might be inborn as a result of genetic factors, or might develop later from sources not yet clear. Certain intensely pleasurable activities are thought to be associated with an increased production of these substances in the brain. This may account for the "addict-ing" quality of certain socially acceptable activities, from jogging to computer-mania!

Social factors are also important in the frequency of opiate use. Easy access to opiates correlates with a higher rate of addiction. Potent opiates are easily available to medical and nursing personnel; it is scarcely surprising that the rate of narcotic addiction in this social group is very high.

The use of narcotics among youth and among marginal social groups is a matter of great concern. In a time of uncertainty these drugs offer welcome oblivion to the anxious or the deprived—an immense temptation. The cost of the temptation is high. Outside medical settings, narcotics are hard to find, and they are expensive. Because they are illegal, because the addiction is compelling, and because the financial stakes are high, the trade has fallen under the control of organized crime rings. In many ways the ethical issues of narcotics are much more those of the exploitation of the poor and weak than of addiction itself.

There is, of course, no necessary connection between addiction and crime—but as drugs are restricted and as prices rise, addicts may do almost anything, often quite out of character, to obtain supplies. Theft (usually petty) and prostitution are frequent accompaniments of addiction. The addiction itself promotes poverty, both because of the cost of the drugs and because of the lost productivity that accompanies the illness.

Addictions are hard to cure. In addiction, the body's need for the drug increases. Without an adequate amount of the drug in the bloodstream, the addict develops an extremely unpleasant withdrawal syndrome, accompanied by an intense craving for the drug. Because of this craving, and because of the emergence of anxiety, depression, or other unpleasant emotions held at bay by the narcotics, the compulsion to return to the drug may be overwhelming.

The ethical issues involved in narcotics are complex. Is there any legitimate use of such dangerous preparations? Is addiction in itself a sin, or is it better considered as an illness? Is addiction primarily a social or a personal problem? If it is a personal problem, what volitional aspects are involved? If addiction has a genetic component, what is the level of personal responsibility? If addiction is a social problem, what agencies carry the responsibility for perpetuating this disorder? What agencies are responsible for bringing about change? If addiction is primarily a moral issue (whether personal or social), how does the gospel address it? Does the gospel offer hope to the sufferer? How can the gospel bring about change in the society to make addiction unneeded as well as unacceptable?

The Scriptures themselves do not address the use of narcotics. Our Lord refused a mildly narcotic drink in his Passion (Mark 15:23). This seems related to his determination to offer himself up to the Father in a fully conscious and moral act. The offering of the narcotic is not rebuked.

Since narcotics are powerful analgesics, their short-term use for the control of acute pain poses little ethical difficulty. Modern medicine—and the modern patient—would be hard pressed for relief of suffering if we did not have these drugs in our therapeutic arsenal. The longer term use of narcotics for the management of chronic pain is much more dangerous and is to be discouraged because of the risks of addiction. The ethical considerations of using narcotics for control of long-term pain are great for the doctor. He must take responsibility to ensure that his prescribing practices entail as few harmful consequences as possible. "First do no harm" is the ancient first law of medical practice. In terminal illness with ongoing pain, the life-damaging consequences of addiction are not significant; and the quality of the patient's life may be considerably enhanced by the careful use of maintenance narcotics.

Self-administration of narcotics raises many ethical issues. Anxious persons, or persons with recurring or chronic pain should be aware of the hazards of using over-the-counter pain killers containing codeine or other narcotic drugs. While Christians do not value pain in itself, they recognize that it is not the worst of evils. To be under the dominion of any other agent than the Spirit is a living denial of the redemption that sets us free from principalities and powers, of whatever sort.

The hazards of experimenting with "hard" narcotics such as heroin can hardly be overemphasized in working with vulnerable groups. But the ethical issues at stake are less those of individual addiction than those of the social factors that lead to addiction. Christians will be less concerned about the fact of a person's addiction than by the exploitation that the addiction represents. The sin of the drug dealer, the drug boss, and the pimp is great because they avariciously exploit a human weakness and wield their power viciously over their victims. Christians will be exercised by the illicit wealth concentrated in the hands of such persons. Furthermore, Christians will address the social conditions that are conducive to narcotic addiction: poverty; unemployment; emotional, educational, and cultural deprivation; and especially spiritual impoverishment. In a wider dimension, Christians will be sensitive to the international scope of the narcotic drug trade. Opium poppy is a major cash crop in some underdeveloped countries of the world. The Christian will recognize that stopping drug use in North America or Western Europe may induce great poverty in some other part of the world. Christians will insist that international aid assist in helping the poor develop crops or industry that will provide alternative sources of income.

Finally for the individual addict, of whatever social station, ethical Christians will have the compassion of Christ for the ill. Addiction is an illness with a relapsing course. Whatever moral factors may have entered into the original addiction, may accompany the behavioral changes of addiction, and may be associated with drug trafficking, addiction is an illness; the suffering has both spiritual and psychophysical dimensions. In the course of the treatment, the Christian who serves such sufferers will both live and proclaim the gospel of redemption from all powers and will insure that the best of scientific and psychotherapeutic efforts will be put forward for the treatment of the illness. Addicts are profoundly lonely people. The Christian will attempt to provide the addict with a loving (which implies both a supportive and a confronting) community, will go into the wilderness to rescue the lost, and will forgive as he has been forgiven.

**Bibliography:** Gilman, A. G., et al., (eds.), *Goodman and Gilman's the Pharmacological Basis of Therapeutics* (6th ed., 1980); Goldstein, A., *Science* (1976) CXCIII, pp. 1081–86; van Ree, J. and Tereneus, L., (eds.), *Characteristics and Functions of Opiates* (1978).

J.E.R.

**NATIONALISM.** Anything that can be described as national has to do with the communal interests, attributes, or policies of a specific people or race, bound together either by a common language or historically related ones, a general identity of descent, and a unifying religious and political tradition. Some of these elements may change as the history of the nation progresses, to be replaced by other more or less welcome factors which then proceed to shape the community's interests and perhaps modify its cohesiveness. What may be described as nationalism is that feeling of zeal or enthusiasm for one's country which issues in strong desires for political policies that will establish the identity and selfhood of the nation and give it character and distinctiveness among the other nations.

The motivating forces of nationalism are complex, and therefore not easily understood. From one point of view they are rooted in the egocentricity of fallen human nature, which possesses a sense of selfhood and personal identity that demands recognition to a greater or lesser degree. Individuals who possess strong personalities tend to live uneasily in community unless they have positions of authority or leadership, and under such conditions their own opinions and ideas clash frequently with the selfhood of other authoritarian figures. The differing parties may well be persuaded as to the essential rightness of their own particular ideas for the welfare of the community, but may experience considerable difficulty in obtaining a consensus. From what begins as a simple conflict of ideologies can come political and social movements that can change the shape of national life for many decades. Or, as a perceptive New Testament writer observed, national and social turmoil originate in the kind of personal upheaval that comes from unsatisfied lust and ambition (James 4:1-2).

Turmoil has its basis in another feature of human nature, namely the fact that while certain individuals may not function particularly well outside the membership of a small group, they can often develop, if they are given leadership opportunities, a particular type of tradition that will attract wide attention and diversify their opportunities for ideology. It is when such leaders come into conflict with others who are endeavoring to foster a diverse tradition that the conflict arises. This process can be seen in the various nationalist groups that arise when colonial nations are endeavoring to obtain independence and statehood, or in older European nations where distinct political and cultural entities such as the Serbians and Croatians lived together in an uneasy relationship.

National groups of this kind understandably cherish their own traditions and policies, regarding them inevitably as superior to those of others. While they may be entirely correct in their assumptions, the nature of community within a given country demands understanding and flexibility on the part of leaders and citizens alike. If this is lacking or denied, the internal cohesion of the people is weakened by political and social dissension, and riots, rebellions, and military coups can ensue unless they are aborted by repressive measures.

If this is true of the nationalistic ethos of a given people, it is even more so of the external manifestations of that nation when it is in political relationships with others. The very fact that in the modern world the nations have to live in community, often with those of very different national ideologies, in order to survive, demands that any type of nationalism should be able to exhibit a recognizable degree of flexibility in international dealings, whether or not that same privilege is extended internally to the citizens of any of the given associating nations.

The manner in which nationalism can develop, and ultimately grow out of control, can be illustrated by the attempts over several centuries to secure a policy of home rule for Ireland. The germs of this movement were evident in the sixteenth century, when for political and religious reasons the Irish resisted an increase of English influence in their land under Henry VIII. After many years of rebellion against Britian, the country of Ireland was made part of Great Britain in 1801 and was duly represented in the British Parliament. Economic and other considerations in that century led to a movement for home rule, which would have given Ireland its own Parliament while still remaining a part of Great Britain. Despite considerable Protestant opposition a Home Rule bill was passed in 1914 but never implemented because of World War I (1914-1918). Republican Irishmen, anxious for complete independence, fomented rebellion which was crushed; and in 1920 the country was partitioned by an act of Parliament. Thirty years later the Irish government declared itself independent, and cut its ties with Britian, leaving Northern Ireland alone related politically to Great Britain. Since that time violence has erupted periodically, and although many people in both Northern and Southern Ireland want their country to be reunited, serious political and religious issues still divide the land. Although the hostility is marked by great bitterness, efforts toward peace and unity are being made in the hope of redeeming the disaster that has resulted from self-determination and nationalism.

Scripture has no words of condemnation for those who take a delight in their country. Such pleasure was especially legitimate for the ancient Hebrews, who received Palestine as their inalienable gift from God. It was primarily God's land, and they were the privileged stewards of it. Thus the people could rejoice in the victories of David and in the splendor of Solomon's reign despite all its serious moral and economic undertones. In the New Testament the Christian is instructed to be loyal to king and government alike (Rom. 13:1-7), but notwithstanding this advice the individual's own sense of stewardship will demand a careful assessment of nationalistic ideals and in the interests of peace, order, and good government will avoid the blustering kind of patriotic fervor that has brought countries to the brink of war in times past.

**NATURALISM, ETHICS OF.** Naturalistic ethical theories have an ancient ancestry, but philosophers' use of the term *naturalism* began with G. E. Moore's *Principia Ethica* in 1903. He observed that certain moralists, such as the Stoics, Spencer and Rousseau, say that the morally good life is a life in accordance with nature. Usually the appeal to the natural is used loosely, and often within systems that found ethical conclusions on other considerations as well. Nevertheless, Moore holds that the appeal is a significant one in ethical theory, and he attempts to abstract it from its various contexts and to depict it precisely. He defines as "natural" any object or attribute that exists, has existed, or will exist in time; and he specifies that naturalism ultimately identifies moral goodness with publicly observable features of human life.

Moore's principal example of a naturalistic ethical system is that of Herbert Spencer, who holds that conduct is moral insofar as it is that of beings who, by engaging in it, are becoming more complex and highly evolved. Since Spencer's theory, with its identification of "good" and "more highly evolved," is no longer studied seriously, the appeal of naturalistic ethical systems is best illustrated by later systems.

For example, Ralph Barton Perry's *General Theory of Value* says that anything in which a person exhibits interest is *prima facie* good. This means that an individual or a group will recognize many levels of value that may compete for realization on a given occasion. In moral decisions, therefore, it is decided which values should be realized, relative to a person's or a society's resources. A correct moral decision produces a "good" state of affairs characterized by "harmonious happiness" and achieved by "reflective agreement" among persons realizing an optimal combination of satisfactions or desires. What people want, whether they get it, and whether conflicts have been resolved in mutually satisfying ways are identifiable and observable states of affairs. Thus, Perry's definition of the good in natural terms occurs within a theory that is understandable, plausible, humane, yet not oversimplified.

The most consistent and influential of all ethical naturalists was John Dewey. In such works as *Problems of Men, Human Nature and Conduct,* and *A Theory of Valuation,* he prescribes scientific method as an extension of common-sense problem solving within a democratic society. One of his central contentions is that "good" means desirable things or states of affairs, chosen from the things we naturally desire. Invoking a biological model, he pictures man as an organism intimately involved with its environment, like a fish in water. This delicate situation is in constant change, with desires developing when the organism becomes, for example, hungry or cold. The satisfaction of such desires can occur only at the cost of effort. The organism (person) may therefore picture a state in which the imbalance is redressed and may calculate the cost (in terms of effort and renunciation of other desires) of realizing that satisfaction. If it acts so as to restore the organism-in-environment to a state of comfortable equilibrium, permitting the satisfaction of as many desires as possible with minimal cost in pain and effort, it does that which is morally good. Dewey emphasizes that there is not one final and unchanging good, end, or aim for the moral life. Goods are relative to the needs of persons and societies and can be identified by their character as intelligently conceived solutions to problems. The only "absolutes" in Dewey's rather attractive picture of persons behaving morally are science (the method of intelligence), respect for the judgment of each man, and democracy as the social organization that permits these values to flourish.

Naturalistic ethical systems can be criticized in important ways that the Christian is especially qualified to explain, although his response has been mirrored in some secular philosophical discussions. For example, the first intuitive response of the Christian could be that there is nothing spiritual in this picture of the moral agent. A similar reaction is expressed in the secular criticism that naturalism's depiction of human decision making does not raise interesting philosophical problems. If morality is merely the problem-solving activity of an organism in its environment, it is not a matter of dealing with profound questions about the meaning of life, death, the threat of nothingness, and the complexities of evil and guilt that are characteristic of the human condition. With regard to such matters, the naturalist suggests only further "adjustments" and "restoration of the equilibrium." Such natural responses are not necessarily moral, and might, in fact, be observed in some higher animals.

This suggests, in fact, that naturalistic ethical systems operate in a tight, logical circle. Having defined *good* as "pleasure," "the greatest happiness," or "the intelligent solution to the problem," the naturalist thereafter refuses to consider moral questions that have not been framed in those terms. Although any system has to have assumptions to which it appeals, vicious circularity is suggested if reasons can be found for casting doubts on those fundamental assumptions, and that is what happened to naturalism. In particular, G. E. Moore, in his famous explication of "the naturalistic fallacy," argued that any moral system that identifies "good" with a natural state such as pleasure or happiness actually misrepresents it. This can be illustrated by entertaining the proposition that "good" should be defined as "a state of happiness." If this is done, one finds that the terms cannot consistently be used interchangeably, because one can always legitimately ask, of any particular state of happiness, whether it is good. This "open question" argument justifies Moore's contention that systems such as Dewey's commit the fallacy of oversimplifying the meaning of key moral terms.

Variations of this fundamental criticism of naturalism also occur in the "puzzle cases" that philosophers invent to embarrass the school of naturalists who say that *good* means "happiness." Puzzle cases are constructed to present hypothetical situations in which happiness for the vast majority of those affected can be increased by doing a great injustice (perhaps by torturing an innocent person). Such problems embarrass naturalists, and it is only fair to note that they produce various subtle arguments in reply. However, their efforts in response to the puzzle cases may plausibly be taken as signs that unqualified ethical naturalism, unsupported metaphysically or religiously, does indeed experience great difficulty in accounting for our experiences of moral demands for benevolence, truth, and justice. Naturalism exhibits great stress when it must stretch its basic beliefs to explain these fundamental moral experiences.

The best Christian critique of naturalism, as exemplified by Reinhold Niebuhr, is one that accepts it insofar as it is true, but also corrects it. Naturalism's depiction of man as part of nature is acceptable, reminding us of our creaturely status in a world that is good (Gen. 1:31). Yet it overstates its case by treating the spiritual side of man's life as illusory, imaginative, or mistaken. In doing this, it is both too optimistic and too pessimistic, neglecting the depths and the heights in man's nature. It optimistically neglects the insight that Adam, allowed a free choice, disobeyed God (Gen. 3:2-6). More remarkable is that Adam was not led into sin merely by bodily appetites or his animal nature. A being with only "natural" appetites would remain happily in the Garden of Eden. It is for higher reasons (being "as gods, knowing good and evil," Gen. 3:5) that he and Eve chose the forbidden fruit. Thus man's higher capabilities make him more liable to choose complex and spiritual forms of wrongdoing, and through Adam's sin we are caught, through complex family and social relationships, in a human solidarity of sin in which we are personally and corporately guilty. Such biblical insights into the human predicament are neglected by the naturalist, in his confidence that men can use reason and scientific method to overcome all social ills and ignorance. In contrast, the biblical revelation tells us that we struggle not only against natural psychological or social problems, but against "principalities, against powers, against the rulers of the darkness of this world, against spiritual wickedness in high places" (Eph. 6:12).

Nevertheless, in this struggle our originally good but fallen nature is redeemed and we are continually transformed by the power of God (2 Cor. 4:16). Thus, the Christian who depicts man's moral situation as a problem insoluble in natural terms also depicts it as solved supernaturally. This analysis is presented repeatedly in Scripture, an outstanding occurrence of it being found in the series of paradoxes that Paul presents in 2 Corinthians 4:7-10, where the pattern of dying and rising in Christ is so vividly stated.

The continuity of Christian morality's highest spiritual insights with our natural moral situation is strikingly depicted in Romans 13, where, in only fourteen verses, Paul raises our thoughts from our most mundane moral obligations to profound spiritual experience. He begins by admonishing his readers to obey those laws that guarantee a decent life in any civilized state. Rapidly he expands upon that theme to interpret such laws as expressions of those that have been promulgated in the law and our conscience. Yet, he says, that law and our moral duties are better summed up in the maxim that we should love our neighbors as ourselves. But our duty does not stop there, and Paul calls us to a radical self-transformation that will be like awakening from sleep. Thus, acknowledging that we are natural creatures who live by laws necessary for our survival and well-being, Paul connects that moral awareness to a world of spiritual obligation that goes far beyond the natural. He demonstrates that while the Christian attends to this world's needs

and desires, he does not live by bread alone (Luke 4:4).

Prudent philosophical naturalism and Christian morality therefore agree in prescribing benevolence, honesty, fairness, and other basic virtues. The great difference between them occurs in the additional analyses and prescriptions that the Christian moralist provides. We are, he says, to take no thought about what we shall eat or drink or wear, in the faith that such things are taken care of within God's greater plan (Matt. 6:25). We are not to resist evil, not to return wrongs with wrongs (Rom. 12:17). We are told that he who would save his life must lose it first (Matt. 10:39). The biblical ethic, delivering injunctions whose moral worth and possibilities for redeeming evil times (Eph. 5:16) are immediately obvious to the Christian, advises courses of action that appear to be foolish and self-contradictory from the point of view of a naturalistic theory, whether it be hedonist, utilitarian, evolutionary, or scientific. Yet the Christian, knowing what Scripture says, knowing in his own experience the passage through suffering and despair that is accomplished by Christ's redemption, sees the moral life as more than can be described in natural terms. He heeds the advice that he is not to conform to this natural world, but to be transformed and renewed (Rom. 12:2).

**Bibliography:** Dewey, J., *Theory of Valuation* (1939); Moore, G. E., *Principia Ethica* (1903); Niebuhr, R., *The Nature and Destiny of Man* (2 vols., 1941 and 1943); Perry, R. B., *General Theory of Value* (1926).

J.R.H.

**NECESSITY.** In ancient Greek thought *ananke*, "necessity," was regarded as a cosmic force which was all-powerful in human society and to which even the gods were subject because of their inability to thwart its unremitting intent. It is hardly surprising that necessity was linked with fate by the Stoics and other fatalists and credited with serving the ends that fate (*moira*) or destiny dictated. Necessity could thus be described as a cosmic determinism of a sinister nature that brought whatever limited degree of freedom the individual might have possessed to an end, and with *moira* reduced human existence to nothingness.

In the New Testament the concept of necessity described the obligations of tradition in the releasing by Pilate of a prisoner at a time of festival in Jerusalem (Luke 23:17). It was also applied to the inner drive motivated by the Holy Spirit, which urged Paul onward in proclaiming the gospel. In this case if the necessity was denied, serious repercussions could be in store for him (1 Cor. 9:16). In yet another sense an augmented form of the term, *epanankes*, was used to describe the basic ceremonial requirements for Christian fellowship, as set out in a letter describing the resolutions of the Council of Jerusalem (Acts 15:28-29).

**NECROMANCY.** This term is a combination of two Greek words, *nekros*, "dead," and *mantis*, "seer, diviner." A necromancer is thus one who attempts to establish communication with the dead as a means of divining the answers to such matters as the nature of coming events, the solutions to problems perplexing an inquirer, the plans or intentions of a given individual or group, or merely some attempt at investigating the conditions of existence of a deceased loved one. Necromancy rests upon the ability of a seer or diviner to establish credible contact with the dead and, as an important corollary, his or her ability to furnish an equally credible answer.

In the ancient world necromancers played upon the superstitious and gullible with the kind of results that are obtained with credulous people today. Old Testament legislation condemned such behavior as a capital offense (Exod. 22:18; Lev. 20:27; Deut. 18:11). Thus the terror of the medium of Endor can be imagined readily when she discovered that the man who had requested an act of necromancy was none other than the very king who previously had killed those practicing this prohibited art (1 Sam. 29:9-12).

The Christian regards knowledge of the future as the prerogative of God alone and following the example of the incarnate Christ, who was content to allow matters involving the end of the age to await God's decision (Matt. 24:36; Mark 13:32), commits his or her life on a daily basis to the Lord's will and keeping without desiring to know what a day may bring forth. Since God is the God of the living (Matt. 22:23), the Christian must live with him in faith, conscious of spiritual fellowship with those who have died after years of submission to the claims of the gospel, This "church triumphant" glorifies God in his nearer presence, and the Christian is urged so to live in obedience and sanctification as to join that blessed group at death. Necromancy is regarded in Christian circles as demonic, and as a form of occultism which preys upon the fears and superstitions of credulous people. It actually does nothing to build up Christian faith, but instead can introduce a false spiritism which is condemned in the New Testament (1 John 4:1-3).

**NEIGHBOR.** In modern usage a neighbor is someone who lives in close proximity to oneself, whether in the immediate vicinity or in an adjacent area or district. The word itself is of rather obscure origin, but *nigh* and *bower* have been suggested plausibly as roots. Being a neighbor was an important function in the community of ancient Israel, where brotherhood in the covenant not merely involved physical proximity but spiritual fellowship. The Israelites were commanded to love their neighbors as themselves (Lev. 19:18, 34). The Decalogue specifically prohibited a person from coveting his or her neighbor's

possessions (Exod. 20:17), but encouraged all members of the covenant community to live in fellowship.

Old Testament ideals were continued into the New Testament period, with the love of one's neighbor being commended by Christ (Matt. 5:43) and being extended even to one's enemies. The story of the good Samaritan (Luke 10:30-37) added a new dimension to neighborly behavior, while in the epistles honest dealing with Christian brethren is commended by Paul (Rom. 15:2; Eph. 4:25). These and other references urge the Christian to be a neighbor to others, whether Christian or not, and thus exemplify the love of Christ who in his death accepted responsibility for the fallen and lost, whether of the house of Israel or not.

See NEW TESTAMENT ETHICS; SERMON ON THE MOUNT.

**NEW MORALITY.** The New Morality is another name for situation ethics. This nontraditional approach to Christian behavior became popular midway through this century mainly through the writings of the late Bishop John Robinson and the Rev. H. A. Williams of Cambridge, both of England, and Professor Joseph Fletcher of the United States. Proponents of this ethical system propagate it with a zeal as insistent as that of any evangelical missionary, frequently in open derision of traditional orthodox moral standards, and in hostility to them.

Briefly, New Morality's exponents hold that the supreme value and the highest good in human life is *agape* (love) and that right behavior in any situation can be determined entirely on the basis of this plus the circumstances, unbound by any prescribed rules of behavior such as the Ten Commandments. The circumstances of a situation alone determine the manner in which that love is to be expressed. Any means therefore is justified by the loving end it serves. The rightness or wrongness of a deed does not reside intrinsically in the deed itself. What is good (loving) in one situation might be wrong (unloving) in another. Fornication, homosexual activity, theft, lying, abortion and other killing, for example, are never intrinsically immoral in themselves. The doer has the right to decide in love when they are and when they are not. The results of this attitude are evident daily in Western society, particularly in television, novels, art, and other media. One could call it a morality of "anything goes" as long as the subject feels he or she is doing it in love. There is no such thing as the regrettable "lesser of two evils," a common concept in traditional morality. Every course of action chosen in love after consideration of its expected consequences is considered completely justified and good, no matter what moral code it transgresses.

Proponents of traditional Christian morality would counter that though *agape*love is indeed the ultimate and absolute standard of Christian behavior, such love has to be defined and directed. Christian ethics must be guided not by the subjective love of humans but by the infinite purposeful love of God Himself (John 13:34; 1 John 3:16; 4). Human attempts, no matter how well-meaning, to govern behavior by consideration of its consequences alone are doomed to confusion and failure because no human can know all possible consequences of any deed; only God can.

The goal and purpose of all human action, no matter how loving, has to be determined in the light of the Creator's purpose, not ours alone (Eph. 1:4-6). Even the great Augustine's famous dictum to "love, then do what you like," does not mean that ethics are to be based entirely on subjective love. Love in Augustine, as in the New Testament, is inextricably tied to obedience (John 14:15; Rom. 1:4; 1 John 1:23-24). Human love by itself is creaturely and fallible, inevitably conditioned by human fallenness. The Creator's love is perfect and unfailing. It encompasses within itself, as an essential and inescapable component, the very order of all that God has created, the transcendent determination of what human finite love ought to be (John 13:34). God's love can be primarily understood only as expressed by Him in revelation and derivatively in the order of things, particularly in the revealed order of our own human nature. Human beings cannot fulfill themselves by flying in the face of their own created nature and dependent existence, defying clearly revealed standards of right and wrong.

Actually, love in itself is not a principle or a rule of behavior, nor alone a reliable guide. Rather it is an attitude toward others, a willing of what is best for them and for all. The human motive of love needs laws to guide its behavior. It supplies the energy and spirit and purposiveness to do what on other grounds is recognized to be right. Without laws, love's actions are entirely subjective. Moral laws provide a measuring rod, a divine standard by which to assess love's deeds.

God has provided this standard in the Ten Commandments, endorsed by Jesus and also by His apostles (Exod. 20; Matt. 5:17-20; Luke 18:20; Rom. 13:8-10). Differing situations do indeed affect the particular manner in which the moral law will be lived out. One aspect of Jesus' teaching and that of the apostles consisted of concrete applications of the moral law to varying situations (for example, Matt. 5:21-48; Luke 10:25-37; 1 Cor. 7—8). Even with a strong external moral law, however, two things are desperately needed: (a) a will and wisdom enlightened by God's Spirit to know how to live the absolute standards in each particular situation, and (b) spiritual strength and power to perform it. Both are promised and given in and through the gospel (John 15:4-5; 16:13-14; Eph. 3:20; Phil. 2:13).

**Bibliography:** Dykstra, C., *Vision and Character* (1981); Fletcher, J. and Montgomery, J. W., *Situation Ethics: True or False* (1972); Lewis, C. S., *Mere Christianity* (1955); Lunn, A. and Lean, G., *The New Morality* (1964); Schaeffer,

F. A., *Escape from Reason* (1968); Waddams, H., *A New Introduction to Moral Theology* (1964).

D.N.P.

**NEW TESTAMENT ETHICS.** In order to understand so large a subject as New Testament ethics, it is necessary to place it in the proper context of discussion with a series of introductory remarks. These remarks will be followed by a look at the theological foundations of ethics in the New Testament. Finally, the content of New Testament ethics will be discussed.

New Testament ethics cannot be looked at in isolation from the much larger whole of which it is a part. Most directly related to it are the teachings of the Old Testament; next, that of the rabbis in Jesus' day; then that of the Greco-Roman world in general; followed more remotely by the Christian ethical tradition considered as a whole. In this regard, little that is said in the New Testament is really new or unique. However, it would be a mistake on that account to level it out into a collection of universal maxims to be found, more or less, everywhere. Although the problems discussed are similar and the answers given familiar, what sets them apart is their relation to Jesus, the incarnate Son of God, according to Christian thought. One must approach New Testament ethics, not only with an eye to all that surrounds it and proceeds from it, but with the realization that it has its own distinctive nature.

There is no systematic presentation of ethics in the New Testament, nor are the principles to be found there comprehensive. The Gospels are occupied primarily with the life, death, and resurrection of Jesus; and Jesus' teachings are often evangelistic or in defense of Himself. The book of Acts is designed to be historical/theological narrative. The letters of the New Testament come closest to containing ethical theory, but here again were not designed as ethical treaties. Matters were dealt with as they arose, in a more or less *ad hoc* fashion. Occasionally one gets short ethical/exhortational bursts and so-called *Haustafeln*, but collecting it all together does not create a textbook. This is not to say that the New Testament writers (and Jesus) did not have a well thought-out ethical position, only that the writings we possess were not designed to parallel Aristotle or Seneca.

The literature of the New Testament is written in diverse terms of form and often requires careful analysis to extract the ethical content undamaged from the situation where it is found. Jesus' teaching method, for example, included the use of hyperbole and paradox in order to stimulate interest or thought. It would be a mistake to push his metaphors too far. Paul was writing either letters to churches where specific problems arose or to individuals who required guidance, often, on narrowly specific topics (such as Timothy's digestive problems). The ethical content of Revelation is couched in elaborate cosmic symbol. That principles for life may be found in all this is self-evident, but it requires care (and humility) not to overabsolutize one's own observations. The numerous Christian ethical systems that eventually arose are ample testimony to the difficulty of the task.

The principles found in the New Testament were addressed to believers, not to the world at large. Thomas Jefferson's attempt to universalize the teachings of Christ by removing what he considered objectionable and all such attempts to create "world Bibles" with the so-called best from all religions fail to do justice to any of the traditions thus handled. This is especially true of the New Testament, where the books were designed to be church books, written to believers, presupposing a certain set of ideas and commitments. This is not to say that the ideas would be unintelligible to an outsider. He might very well see what is being said and scorn it or admire it, as the case might be, but to embrace it would require that he become a Christian, because the ethical teaching of the New Testament is part and parcel of a whole theological complex of ideas that cannot be torn asunder. This should not be misunderstood. New Testament ethics is also part of a larger whole, including ethical concerns that cut across time and societies. Everyone is concerned about honesty, family, and authority, and so is the New Testament. But what is said in the New Testament is based on a specific vision of reality that gives the ethical ideas found there a special flavor of their own.

The ethical statements of the New Testament are directed primarily to the life of a person as lived, rather than to the mind of a person for contemplation. This is a matter of emphasis. Paul did send the Philippians a list of virtues and counsel them to "think on these things" (Phil. 4:8), but a reading of just a few pages of Aristotle's *Nicomachean Ethics* and Jesus' "Sermon on the Mount" (Matt. 5—7) is all that is required to highlight the differences of approach. New Testament ethics is not so much a subject for discussion as a life to be lived; the exhortations are not academic, but practical. As a result, there is no attempt made to pull it all together into a neat synthesis, nor to make pronouncements, even on the same subject, fit exactly. We are counseled to embody the truth in such a way that others will see it and glorify our Father who is in heaven.

A specific set of presuppositions that is often taken for granted underlies the ethics of the New Testament. Treaties on ethics usually begin by carefully outlining where the discussion will begin and the parameters within which it will flow. It is not often that such procedures are followed in the New Testament. It is assumed that the reader will know what lies behind the statements made. If it needed mentioning, the writer was free to bring it up; but often it is the obligation of the reader to know it. The theological foundations and nature of New Testament ethics are such that every clear-minded Christian should know them as implicitly as they know the sun comes up in the morning.

*The Theological Foundation and Nature of New Testament Ethics.* In one sense of the word, Christian theology as a whole permeates the ethics of the New Testament. Consequently one would need a comprehensive understanding of the entire belief system of the early believers to do full justice to their exhortations concerning life. It is, of course, not possible to provide that here; but the most significant matters, those most directly related to ethics, can be pointed out.

Absolutely central to the ethical pronouncements of the New Testament is the proposition that God exists and is in control of His creation. What humankind ought to do is not a matter of empirical observation, followed by a general conclusion or principle based on consensus, and then a question of what metaphysical base the behavioral pattern has, if any. In the New Testament it is instead a matter of revelation, given by God. "He has *showed you,* O man, what is good; and what does the LORD require of you but to do justice, and to love kindness, and to walk humbly with your God?" (Mic. 6:8). That is, of course, the Old Testament, but the New Testament agrees with it. God gave His commands to us (see Mark 7:5-13). It is simply inconceivable that life could be understood, or human behavior explained and evaluated, apart from the fact that God exists and has made His will known. One could of course dispute this point (many have), but that is not the issue. To Jesus and all the writers of the New Testament, God exists as an absolutely nonnegotiable fact, and everything is seen in the light of that transcendent reality. A corollary to this is that God is in total control of the universe. He sees every sparrow that falls; He numbers the very hairs on our heads; He has known us from our birth, guides us through the ambiguities of life, and welcomes us home at death. Nothing is left out, nothing is by accident, nothing takes God by surprise and ultimately, His will will be done. Knowledge of this did not answer very question, but it did mean that no question was unanswerable, giving the early Christian believers courage to face their detractors and persecutors without anxiety. It also meant that in perplexing situations there existed One who was able to read our intentions and evaluate fairly, even if no one else did, and who could guide us into the right decision when there did not seem to be any answer.

The New Testament assumes a doctrine of creation, the sanctity of life and the whole created order, and the ultimate ownership by God of all things. "The earth is the LORD's and the fullness thereof; the world and those who dwell therein" (Ps. 24:1). God is good. All of God's thoughts are good, all of God's acts are good, the results of God's acts are good. The earth as the result of God's will is good; everything in it is good, from the winds that blow to the sea creatures in the deep. Humankind, made in God's image is good. This is not to ignore the problem of sin, but sin in the Bible is not seen as something greater than God, nor able to thwart His purposes. It is true that sin has marred God's good creation; but it began as good, stays in principle good, and will be restored in the end as "new heavens and a new earth wherein dwelleth righteousness," thus finding (re-finding) its true identity. Jesus draws numerous images from life and nature—flowers, rain, trees, houses, rooms, walls, lamps, clothes, fishermen, women, children. In none of it is there any sense of ultimate alienation; rather, all is subject to God, living in His grace and open to Jesus as illustrative of God's purposes.

New Testament ethics assumes a soteriological understanding of life. The simple facts are these: God made the world good; humankind fell into sin, becoming something alien to its own being; and God in His love reconciled the world to Himself, graciously offering Himself to His own creation. When one by faith is in Christ, then a new creation exists where the old has passed away and the new has arrived (2 Cor. 5:17). The commands of the New Testament assume that grace is operative in the person's life so that God's requirements may, in fact, be fulfilled (Rom. 8:1-4). Paul did not expect the believer, somehow by his own energy, to generate the strength to raise himself up to the level of God. Rather, by identification with Christ who died, rose, and ascended, we find ourselves seated in heavenly places in Christ Jesus (Eph. 2:6), for we are dead and our life is hid with Christ in God (Col. 3:3).

Salvation in the New Testament is defined as by and through Christ, hence Christ becomes the center of the Christian's existence and the source of all his actions, which, of course, include ethical actions. In fact, this renders all acts ethical, or at least open to ethical scrutiny. We are not compartmentalized, with part of our being redeemed and part unredeemed. Every aspect of our life is God's, by creation and by redemption, so all our acts are sanctified. (That our sinful acts are not included goes without saying. When we sin we are acting contrary to our redeemed nature.) To be saved, or redeemed, is to be in Christ. This powerful and comprehensive figure of speech is used over 180 times in the New Testament and is all-encompassing. Put simply, Christ is our life (Col. 3:4); He lives in us (Gal. 2:20), we are complete in Him (Col. 2:9); and in Him we have wisdom, righteousness, sanctification, and redemption (1 Cor. 1:30).

New Testament ethics is person-oriented, not rule-oriented. It is true that God gave specific commandments, but these were designed to embody principles and to give us guidelines for the outworking of those principles. They were not designed to be straitjackets that restricted our behavior. The laws were like broad roads on which to walk in the right direction, not a razor's edge off which one might fall by the slightest deviation. In time that narrow view had begun to prevail in the popular mind, or worse yet, the commands were being used to negate the very

thing that they were designed to accomplish (see Mark 2:23-28—The sabbath was made for man, not man for the sabbath), but that was not their original purpose. The commands of God were designed to enhance the living of human life, to expand it, and to bring it to fulfillment. Thus, in the New Testament, the emphasis is not upon the minutiae of observance, nor even the overt act *per se,* but upon the principle of action as it opens up a person to himself and others, in love. To the pure, all things are pure (Titus 1:15), and whatever is done may be done to the glory of God. So if one must choose between justice (law) and mercy, choose mercy every time. The episode of Jesus and the woman taken in adultery illustrates this (John 7:53—8:11). By legal right the woman could be executed; Jesus shamed her accusers into letting her go.

New Testament ethics is shaped by an eschatological perspective. The last judgment looms large (not to say ominously) before the minds of the New Testament writers. We must all give an account of ourselves before the judgment seat of Christ. This does two things. Firstly, it tells us that actions are important, and the ethical dimension of everything we do will be evaluated. Secondly, it frees us from rendering any final judgments now. Paul goes so far as to say that not only can he not judge others, nor others him, but he cannot even judge himself, and it does not really matter (1 Cor. 4:1-5). The thought, well expressed by Judah the patriarch, "Know what is above thee—a seeing eye and a hearing ear and all thy deeds written in a book," produced in most Jewish minds a meticulous scrupulosity (the Mishna); but in Paul it produced a release from such scrupulosity and a freedom to be all things to all people (1 Cor. 9:19-23). Thus freedom became a rallying point for Paul early in his ministry (Gal. 5:1) and permeated his understanding of ethics to the point where some were even accusing him of advocating sin so that grace might abound. Paul vehemently denied this, arguing that we are to walk in newness of life (Rom. 6:1-4).

*Principles of New Testament Ethics.* The above ten points must be kept in mind as the principles of New Testament ethics are discussed, because they operate at every level. They are the focus and theological foundation of all that is said in the New Testament concerning human behavior. In order to facilitate discussion, our ethical duties will be looked at under three heads: responsibility to God, responsibility to others, and responsibility to ourselves.

*The believer's responsibility to God.* When a lawyer asked Jesus what the supreme commandment was, His answer was epoch-making as it was simple. He said "You shall love the Lord your God with all your heart, and with all your soul, and with all your mind, and with all your strength" (Mark 12:30), quoting more or less from Deuteronomy 6:5. The context of Jesus' statement must be understood. In the Pentateuch there are 613 commandments to be found, around which vast argument has swirled. If one chose any of them as supreme it would immediately antagonize those who said another was supreme. The lawyer knew this and posed the question of supremacy "to test him" (Matt. 22:35). Jesus knew that the Ten Commandments were considered the epitome of the law—its highest expression, written by the very finger of God—and, that it contained two unequal sections. The first four commandments dealt with our duty to God and the last six with our duty to man. In replying to the crafty lawyer, Jesus in effect was saying that running through all 613 commandments, as epitomized in the ten, is the principle of love, first to God and then to man. The whole law may be summarized in those two words. So, none of the commandments is supreme as such; but all of them are embodiments of the supreme principles of love, providing us with a new way of viewing them, as well as ourselves.

This became the basis for understanding all life for the early believers. God loves us (John 3:16); nothing can separate us from that love (Rom. 8:31-39); that love fills and energizes us (Rom. 5:5); and is ultimately perfected in us (1 John 4:12). Those who love know God (1 John 4:8), abide in Him (1 John 4:16), are controlled by Him (2 Cor. 5:14), and possess that which surpasses all, even faith and hope (1 Cor. 13:13). It is interesting (and perhaps a bit surprising) that, given the centrality of this in the New Testament's teaching, what it meant was not worked out in some detail. This is probably because early Christians already had in their minds rather clearly what it meant in practice. Essentially it meant giving God His due, honoring Him as God, and letting Him be God in our lives. This meant respecting His name (person) (Matt. 5:33-37); perhaps even violating a law in letter, in order to fulfill it in principle (Mark 2:23-28; Luke 14:5); and consciously directing our hearts toward that love (2 Thess. 3:5). Just as God's love to us was creative in sending His Son, so our love to Him is to be creative in doing His will with a glad and willing heart, without worrying about minute details.

The second part of Jesus' reply to the lawyer was that we are to love our neighbor as ourselves. This is a constant refrain, found throughout the whole New Testament (Matt. 5:43; 22:39; Mark 12:31; Luke 10:27; Rom. 13:9; Gal. 5:14; James 2:8). Paul's great hymn to love in 1 Corinthians 13 epitomizes the attitude required of believers. We are to love one another (John 4:9); do good unto all men (Gal. 6:10); love our enemies (Matt. 5:44); and put up with one another in love (Eph. 5:2). If we do not love one another, we do not love God (1 John 4:20) and are not even Christians (1 John 3:10). This love must be translated into concrete action, providing for those who are in need (1 John 3:17-18; James 2:8-26), and sought above all else, for it binds everything together in perfect harmony (Col. 3:14).

All this is stated as a matter of principle in the New Testament; it is the way in which we ought to live. The reason is that love contains within it all the laws that all the ethical systems in all the world could possibly devise. Jesus concluded by saying, "On these two commandments [love of God and neighbor] depend all the law and prophets" (Matt. 22:40). Paul twice worked out the rationale for understanding love in relation to law this way. In Romans 13:8-10 he states "Owe no one anything, except to love one another; for he who loves his neighbor has fulfilled the law. The commandments 'You shall not commit adultery, You shall not kill, You shall not steal, You shall not covet,' and any other commandment, are summed up in this sentence 'You shall love your neighbor as yourself.' Love does no wrong to a neighbor; therefore love is the fulfilling of the law." In Galatians 5:13-14 he says "For you were called to freedom, brethren; only do not use your freedom as an opportunity for the flesh, but through love be servants of one another. For the whole law is fulfilled in one word, 'You shall love your neighbor as yourself.'" The book of James calls this the royal law (2:8-13) and, somewhat paradoxically, the law of liberty, that is, a law that does away with laws. The point is easily grasped. Genuine concern (love) for our neighbor moves us to seek what is ultimately best for him, and under no circumstances would we do what is harmful; so the laws that were devised to protect one's rights become redundant. The one who loves will do all that the law requires and far beyond, because love seeks actively what is good for the neighbor. This is not to say that laws should therefore be thrown out. Far from it. They may act as guidelines for our behavior, channeling our love in understandable and socially familiar directions. There is nothing wrong with that. But they must be seen as only a first word on the subject, not the last word; and if they stand in the way of human freedom and fulfillment, they may be set aside according to higher principle, as Jesus did (Mark 2:23-28) and Paul did (1 Cor. 9:19-23). Paul's discussion is significant. He says, "To the Jews, I became as a Jew, in order to win Jews; to those under the law I became as under the law—though not being myself under the law—that I might win those under the law. To those outside the law I became as one outside the law—not being without law toward God but under the law [ennomos] of Christ—that I might win those outside the law." Notice how difficult it is for Paul to express this idea. He is both under the law and not under it; he is both outside of it and in it. Our freedom from law includes the option to live under laws or not, but does not free us unto license. We are under a higher obligation that includes all lesser formulations, the very law of love itself, indeed of God Himself, for God is love. If love were truly operative in all human life, legislation would not be needed and evil would cease, because love does no wrong to a neighbor (Rom. 13:10).

That is the ideal of New Testament ethics. Unfortunately, love is not always operative and we do not always seek what is best for our neighbor. It is sometimes the case that guidelines need to be given for the outworking of our faltering and tentative, if sincere, love. Who is our neighbor? According to Jesus, everyone, which meant that every individual or group of individuals, in whatever context, must be treated with dignity and respect. In the New Testament, most of the situations were dealt with on an *ad hoc* basis, thus giving it all an unsystematic texture. There is no set of rules, *per se,* that should govern our lives, but only what love and sanctified good sense would indicate.

It is not possible to deal with everything that the New Testament treats at this point, but a list of topics can be given along with the verses where the subject is handled: husbands and wives (Eph. 5:22-33; Col. 3:18-19; 1 Thess. 4:3-8; Heb. 13:4; 1 Pet. 3:1-7); parents and children (Eph. 6:1-4; Col. 3:20-21); slaves and masters (Eph. 6:5-9; Col. 4:1; 1 Tim. 6:13; 1 Pet. 2:18-21); dependence on others (2 Thess. 3:6-13); general relation to others (Matt. 5:43-48; 7:1-5; Rom. 12:9-21; 14:13-23; 15:1-6; 2 Cor. 6:3-10; Titus 3:1-3, 8-11; James 5:1-6; 1 Pet. 4:7-11; 1 John 6:3-10); civil authorities (Rom. 13:1-7; Titus 3:1; 1 Pet. 2:13-17); religious authorities (Heb. 13:17); immorality (Matt. 5:27-28; Rom. 13:1-4; 1 Cor. 5:1-2; Heb. 13:4; 1 Pet. 4:1-6); marriage and divorce (Matt. 5:31-32; Mark 10:1-16; 1 Cor. 7:1-40); gossip (James 3:1-12); wealth (Mark 10:17-45; 1 Tim. 6:10; James 5:1-3); and the conscience of others (Rom. 14:1-4; 1 Cor. 8:1-13).

*The believer's responsibility to himself.* Jesus recognized that the love of one's neighbor in some significant way reflected one's love of himself. That we are loved by God means that we may not despise ourselves. We are not to judge another man's servant, even if that servant is oneself (Rom. 14:4; 1 Cor. 4:1-5). Jesus recognized the legitimacy of our human needs, encouraging us to pray for "our daily bread" (Matt. 6:11), and said to the one who seeks the kingdom of God before all else, that all the things necessary for life will be provided to him (Matt. 6:33). Paul said very simply, "No man ever hates his own flesh, but nourishes and cherishes it" (Eph. 5:29). This meant in practice that any extreme form of self-denial, self-abuse, or asceticism was ruled out. Such practices might have the appearance of self-sacrifice and discipline, but in reality were of no value at all (Col. 2:16-23). Complicated dietary rules fall in this category: "Everything created by God is good, and nothing is to be rejected if it is received with thanksgiving" (1 Tim. 4:4). To forbid eating foods or drink is rejected by Paul as unnecessary bondage (Col. 2:16; 1 Tim. 4:1-3). Likewise, sexual appetite is to be acknowledged, and provision must be made for it (1 Cor. 7:1-9; 1 Tim. 5:11-15; Heb. 13:4). Our thoughts are to be brought into obedience to Christ (2 Cor. 10:5),

our minds are to be filled with virtuous ideas (Phil. 4:8), and our mouths are to speak things edifying to those around us (Eph. 5:19; Col. 3:16). We are to cleanse our spirits from every defilement (2 Cor. 7:1) and our consciences are to be clear (1 Pet. 3:21). There are times when we might find it necessary to deny ourselves certain allowable things in the interest of some higher good (1 Cor. 7:5; 9:26-27), but this in no way denies the goodness of the things set aside. Summarizing, the New Testament encourages us to treat ourselves with dignity and respect, just as we are to treat others in this way.

*Conclusion.* New Testament ethics is a theocentric system that assumes God's control of all things, thus freeing the believer to live without anxiety in the world and without hostility toward his neighbor. The fundamental principle of love pervades all God's dealings with us, and should pervade all our dealings with others. Complex rules are not given to cover every contingency; rather the exhortation is made to do good unto all men (Gal. 6:10). Creative love will find a way to work that out concretely in practice. When we do this we will show that we are truly children of our Father who is in heaven. It is this vision of human life that became the Christian ethic. E. F. Scott put it this way: "The unchanging element in our religion has been its ethical teaching. Its doctrines have been differently understood in each generation; its institutions and ritual have assumed many forms and have given rise to countless divisions. But the ethical demands have never varied. They were set forth two thousand years ago, and in the interval the whole framework of man's life has been remodeled; but they are still valid, in practically their whole extent, for all sections of the church" (*The Ethical Teaching of Jesus*).

**Bibliography:** Bruce, A. B., *St. Paul's Conception of Christianity* (1894); Enslin, M. S., *The Ethics of Paul* (1957); Henry, C. F. H., (ed.), *Baker's Dictionary of Christian Ethics* (1973); Kaye, B. and Wenham, G., (eds.), *Law, Morality and the Bible* (1978); Manson, T. W., *The Teaching of Jesus* (1931); *Ibid., Ethics and the Gospel* (1960); Marshall, L. T., *Challenge of NT Ethics* (1946); Osborn, E. F., *Ethical Patterns in Early Christian Thought* (1976); White, R. E. O., *Biblical Ethics* (1979); *Ibid., Christian Ethics* (1981).

See BEATITUDES; SERMON ON THE MOUNT.

W.A.E.

**NIHILISM.** This term originated in the Latin word *nihil,* meaning "nothing." Nihilism is therefore any form of reductionist ideology that seeks to bring any or all of the phenomena of existence to the level of nonreality or nonbeing. For the nihilist there can be no rational justification in religious belief for such things as metaphysical standards or norms, and therefore any objective basis for morals and ethics is totally illusory.

While it may be possible for the nihilist to speak of such things as social mores, it can only be done by recognizing that they are in fact the expression of community traditions and can have no ultimate or binding authority. As a system of ideas nihilism was a child of the Russian revolution against the Czarist regime and represented the communist rejection of all established religious and secular authority in its various manifestations.

Nihilism not unnaturally exhibits pessimism and cynicism about the prospects for individual and collective human existence. According to its adherents there can be no objective standards for morality, faith, or truth, and hence they fall victim to the misconception of the ancient Greek Sophists that everything is relative and that the individual is his or her own arbiter. For Nietzsche, the sweeping away of the old ideals left human existence without meaning or moral justification, since the relativism espoused by nihilism accorded every deed equal justification, which itself was meaningless morally.

Nihilists in general are agnostic and narrowly empirical, but even in the latter area they experience frustration, since no one person's experience can begin to point to anything that is epistemologically true, but is merely a statement of individual feeling. With emptiness continually on the horizon it is small wonder that the nihilistic writers such as Camus, Heidegger, and Bertrand Russell felt so helpless when surveying the tide of events as to become resigned to ultimate nothingness. Secular existentialists have frequently stressed what for them is the utter lack of meaning in life and the sense of complete futility that was mentioned by one Old Testament author (Eccles. 1:2, 14).

Nihilists betray all the characteristics of those whom the psalmists reviled for dismissing the existence of God as a fact of life (Ps. 53:1). Their personal misery and sense of hopelessness is evident on all sides, and their literary musings make for very depressing reading. Nihilists are often intelligent people, and thus it must have been very disconcerting for a man such as Bertrand Russell, who was one of the prominent intellectuals of his age, to find himself enmeshed irrevocably in an ideology that reduced him in utter helplessness to a neat and precise zero. Paul had encountered *de facto* nihilists in Ephesus (the "beasts," perhaps, of 1 Cor. 15:32), and in his letter to the church there he reminded the members of their own hopeless, lost condition before they accepted Christ as Savior (Eph. 2:12). Conversion to the Christian faith is the only specific means by which new life and lasting hope for the future can be assured, for both the nihilist and anyone else. This occurs through the renewing of the mind (Rom. 12:2), which transforms the unregenerate, lost nature and gives it an eternal dimension based upon the saving work of Christ. He alone is the hope of mankind, and the very antithesis of nihilism, being in fact the fullness of God Himself (Eph. 1:23; Col. 1:19). The Christian life, therefore, is one of hope and joyous expectation of a future existence with Christ, in stark contrast to that of the nihilist, which, ironically enough, will be reduced to nothingness at the final assessment of human values.

**Bibliography:** Rosen, S., *Nihilism, a Philosophical Essay* (1969).

**NONCONFORMITY.** As the term implies, nonconformity is a failure to adapt to a pattern of life or thought which others have accepted as normative and which they may possibly wish to enforce. The failure to conform may result from a conscientious objection to the commonly espoused ideology, or it may be passive in nature and take the form of simple default.

In religious circles it describes those who do not honor the traditions of the majority, but instead formulate and promote their own beliefs and practices on an independent basis. The term was used by the Church of England of Roman Catholics and Protestant denominations such as Anabaptists, Presbyterians, Methodists, and others who dissented from the authority and doctrines of the established church. Not infrequently these groups were treated with great severity, but in the process they managed to lay a foundation of democracy in British life by challenging the autonomy and autocracy of the Church of England. From nonconformist circles came a revival of biblical preaching, a series of enactments for the betterment of social conditions in the nineteenth century, and even a political party, the earliest members of which were devout Christians.

Paul urges nonconformity upon the Christian, not so much in doctrinal or ritualistic terms, but in repudiating the power of worldly living and becoming renewed in Christ (Rom. 12:2).

**NORMS.** This term is derived directly from the Latin *norma*, which among Roman workmen described a square that carpenters and masons used in order to make a right angle. When applied figuratively it came to mean a rule or standard by which situations or people were judged or organized. In these respects *norma* corresponded closely to the Greek *kanon*, which was used originally of a measuring rod, then of a moral rule, and finally of a list of persons known to be governed by such norms. The canon of Scripture comprised a list of spiritual writings that fulfilled certain criteria of internal consistency, and any works which appeared to be deficient in these respects were excluded from the canon. The Latin word *regula*, which was the Roman counterpart of the Greek *kanon*, was synonymous with *norma*.

The general sense of "standard" familiar from antiquity is also one way in which norms are understood today. In a mechanistic or purely descriptive sense it carries the idea of a mean or average, because it constitutes a pattern which exhibits the least amount of deviation. But if the term is being employed in a regulative sense, it then becomes a standard in comparison with which other factors are judged objectively. This is especially the case where morality and ethics are founded upon specific rules, as in various religions. Under these conditions, any divergence from the established standard is immediately self-evident.

Not all ethicists would grant that norms emerge from the same or a similar source. A list of rules by which appropriate conduct may be recognized need not necessarily proceed from a divine authority. Instead, such regulations for conduct may constitute the guidelines as agreed upon by a properly authorized body, and be thoroughly secular in character except where they may involve such theological concepts as honesty and truth.

Totalitarian states have envisaged the source of their ethics as emerging from the struggles of the working class for self-determination. Under such conditions a low level of consistency becomes the norm, and in Marxist societies where egalitarianism is applied rigorously to all except the governing classes, it is maintained by distributing all losses evenly among the peasants.

Each one of the foregoing norms could be regarded as based upon an extrinsic source of origin which is imposed upon the individual by an external authority. But there are some norms that are generated internally on a purely subjective basis of evaluation and decision. Many of these norms seem to arise in the first instance from a residuum of traditional values and are thus intrinsic in the sense of constituting a base of innate, although inchoate, idealism upon which the individual draws whenever necessary. Some ethicists would argue that this value base has been established as the result of genetic processes which transmit racial and other facets of memory. This is not to say, of course, that the behavior consequent upon the norms is governed genetically, since to date no gene has been isolated that could claim such a facility. But there is certainly warrant for the notion that, as with the fallenness of humanity, so certain positive elements of character can be transmitted genetically for some generations.

The New Testament gives an indication of this tendency in Paul's commendation of Timothy's faith, which he attributed to the fidelity of character of Eunice, Timothy's mother, and similarly to Lois, Timothy's grandmother (2 Tim. 1:5). Here it is not so much the Christian faith that has been transmitted, for the acceptance of Christ must be an individual act throughout the various generations, but rather that particular disposition of character which, when stimulated, makes a positive response in divine grace to Christ's gospel challenge.

In a more secular sense, behavioral norms can often be determined intrinsically in terms of feelings of noblesse oblige, where a certain kind of breeding dictates that under given conditions a particular form of behavioral response is expected. While it might take a rather lengthy interval of time for the individual to articulate these norms in the form of language, the response in a given situation to what is right, wrong, or proper, is often instantaneous. The behavior which results has not been learned from habitual response to stimuli, such as would be the case with norms derived from extrinsic sources, but instead is the product of innate characteristics which produce activity that can be evaluated ethically just as adequately as other forms of normative conduct.

In addition to the moral standards which may have been inherited or acquired otherwise, there are certain special factors of an ethical nature which, through the decision of a recognized authority within the social configuration, belong only to selected elements of that group. These commonly have to do with the taking of human life and therefore would involve military personnel, police, juries, medical practitioners, and the like. The special behavioral norms associated with their duties are well understood by the members of these groups, who are deemed to be behaving morally and lawfully when they observe the various statutes and traditions which govern them.

For the Christian, the standards which relate to moral conduct are extrinsic in origin and are specifically the product of divine revelation. Because God's love for mankind is manifested in a concern for relationships, the believer is required to exhibit in his or her own life the kind of ethical and moral behavior that is uniformly characteristic of God's own personality. Thus the norms that are revealed reflect holiness, righteousness, love, fidelity, obedience, justice, and all the other moral and ethical qualities that the believer must manifest in day-to-day living. These norms are of an absolute character and do not admit of qualification. But they are also presented not so much as ironclad standards which demand immediate, implicit, and uncompromising acceptance, but rather as the fruits of spiritual development through divine grace. Instead of being imposed unequivocally upon the Christian community, the individual believer is encouraged to grow into them through the work of the Holy Spirit (Gal. 5:22-23; Col. 3:12-17) as part of the normal development of the Christian's life and conduct.

**NUCLEAR WARFARE.** Nuclear warfare became a reality in the military action that effectively terminated the Second World War—the dropping of a nuclear bomb on Hiroshima (6 August 1945) and another on Nagasaki (9 August 1945), in Japan.

The horror of nuclear warfare is so great that it tends to be regarded as fantasy—like horror fiction. However, to come closer to appreciating its true significance, it is necessary to attempt to envisage its magnitude and potential. The following represent some relevant facts.

During the Second World War, a large bomb dropped from an aircraft contained about one ton of trinitro toluene (TNT). Such a bomb dropped, for instance, on suburban London demolished about half a block of houses and severely damaged the neighboring blocks. Nuclear bombs are measured in their power by comparison with this one ton of TNT.

The bombs dropped on Hiroshima and Nagasaki were about twelve kilotons (i.e., equivalent to twelve thousand tons of TNT). The damage done by these bombs has been fairly well documented. The effect occurs in several steps. First there is the primary release of energy. This creates enormous heat, melting and vaporizing everything around, and forming a large, empty crater. This energy source radiates in all directions, setting fire to anything flammable. However, this energy comes as a short burst of extremely high intensity, causing chemical disruption equivalent to temperatures not readily attainable by other means. At considerable distance (i.e., several kilometers) an effect like strong sunburn is produced. Nearer to the source it could be likened to a very intense microwave oven.

But both sunburn and a microwave oven involve electromagnetic radiation in small wavebands. A nuclear explosion generates all wavelengths from radio waves, through the visible range (i.e., light energy), to ultraviolet, X-rays, and gamma rays, together with high energy particulate radiation of beta and alpha rays, and neutrons. These radiations, particularly the X-rays, gamma rays, and neutrons, give rise to some of the secondary or longer term effects. They damage the fundamental chemical mechanism of the life process, producing (among other things) cancer and leukemia years later. Such radiation damage is of particular significance in the reproductive process, where it can produce sterility or defective offspring, not only in humans, but in all animal and plant life.

Discussion of nuclear warfare has generally centered on the relationship between the USSR (now CIS) and USA. The former Soviet Union operated under a defense policy referred to as damage/limitations. To win a nuclear war they had to be able to inflict overwhelming damage through an initial offensive first strike and then have sufficient defensive capabilities to limit the effectiveness of guaranteed US response. The United States, on the other hand, has operated under a policy referred to as mutual vulnerability. This policy is often shortened to the acronym MAD (Mutually Assured Destruction) and assumes that a nuclear war is not winnable. Therefore, to avoid or deter a nuclear war, US policy has declared that although we will not be responsible for a first strike we will assure an opponent's destruction if it chooses foolishly to attack us.

Today two unfolding and dramatic developments have drastically changed the nuclear picture. The first development is the break-up of the Soviet Union. Who is in control? Who is responsible for their vast nuclear arsenal which is spread over four republics? Who is the US to negotiate with in the future?

The second development is the growing proliferation of nuclear weapons among Third World countries. How many countries now have the capability to use atomic, bacterial, or chemical (ABC) weapons? How many more countries or terrorist groups will have the same capability in the next two decades? The Persian Gulf War made clear that all leaders cannot be trusted to act rationally or depended upon to respect time-honored Just War rules which, in part, attempt to protect the lives of non-combatants.

The fear of the improbable, an unlimited nuclear strike by a superpower possessing thousands of nuclear weapons, has been replaced by the terrorizing probability that an angry Third World country or irrational terrorist group holding a grudge would use nuclear weapons regardless of their consequences.

The realities of nuclear proliferation, the success of the Patriot anti-ballistic missile against the SCUD missile in the Gulf War, and leaders desperate enough to use these weapons have prompted the East and West to reconsider modest missile defenses which could protect both regions from accidental, limited, or terrorist missile use. President Bush has referred to this defensive system as Global Protection Against Limited Strikes (GPALS).

A limited ballistic missile defense against terrorists or disgruntled Third World countries would not only defend participant nations, but also provide those possessing the most nuclear weapons the opportunity to work together on a project which would benefit the rest of humanity.

Today six basic war/peace positions derive from the Just War and Pacifist traditions. Their advocates are equally sincere Christians who desire peace, not war.

Four of these basic positions fall under the umbrella of the Just War tradition: Nonresistance (Herman Hoyt); Nuclear Pacifist (John Stott, Billy Graham); Preventive War (Jerry Falwell, Harold O. J. Brown); Historic Just War (Carl Henry, Kenneth Kantzer).

Two of these basic positions fall under the Pacifist umbrella: Historic Pacifist (Myron Augsberger, John Drescher); Radical Pacifist (Ron Sider, Jim Wallis).

The *Nonresistance* position teaches that government must be allowed to carry out its God-given commission. Christians should support this process up to but not including the taking of human life. The *Nuclear Pacifist* position teaches that government's mandate to punish, reward, and protect must be supported up to, but not including the use of weapons of mass destruction. The *Historic Just War* position teaches that Christians are responsible to support their government in the just use of force. But this use of force must be defensive in nature. Nuclear weapons could be used in a strictly limited fashion on military targets. The *Preventive War* position is an extension of the Historic Just War position. It argues for the possibility that force, including nuclear weapons, could be used preemptively as well as defensively

The *Historic Pacifist* position teaches that government has a God-given obligation to exercise necessary force in carrying out its responsibilities. Christians, however, must not be involved personally in this process except for paying their legal tax debt. The Historic Pacifist position also teaches that the corporate church as well as individual members of the church must support a pacifist policy and that nuclear weapons should never be used under any circumstances. The *Radical Pacifist* position teaches that individual Christians and the church corporately must live by pacifist convictions. Many supporting this position also extend the pacifist obligation to the secular state. They contend that government ought to adopt a national policy of pacifism. Some Radical Pacifists openly encourage the withholding of that portion of their tax liability which could be used to support the military budget.

Advocates of all six positions would agree that no sane person wants to encourage a nuclear war. Their differences emerge from answers to three basic questions and from the way Scripture is interpreted by each position to support its views. These three questions are:

1) Does Scripture give government a divine mandate to exercise necessary force in carrying out its responsibilities of punishing evil, protecting the innocent, and rewarding good?
2) If government is obligated to carry out these responsibilities to what extent can a Christian directly participate in the process?
3) Which alternatives available to government for carrying out these responsibilities are most consistent with biblical principles and a Christian conscience?

Key Bible verses for serious study involved in this discussion include: Gen. 9:6, Lev. 19:18, Deut. 20:10-20, Est. 8:11, Mic. 4:3, Matt. 5:9, 38-39, 22:21, 26:52, Luke 3:14, John 19:10-11, Acts 25:10-11, Rom. 12:17-21, 13:1-7, 2 Cor. 10:3-6, Titus 3:1, 1 Tim. 2:1-2, 1 Pet. 2:13-15.

Nuclear weapons and the ability to make them are a reality. However, from a biblical perspective many of the questions relating to war and the use of force do not change whether we are discussing conventional or nuclear weapons.

- Does the Bible indicate that all killing is considered murder?
- Is the example of Jesus' death on the cross God's most complete revelation to mankind concerning the issue of killing or being killed?
- Does Jesus' teaching in Matt. 5:38-39 supersede

all other biblical instruction concerning the use of force?
- Is the context of Christian discipleship as described in Matt. 5:38-39 personal, corporate, or national?
- Can a secular state be expected to live by standards practicing Christians fail to consistently live by?
- Does the context or language of Rom. 13:1-7 indicate that its application is limited only to local police work or good governments?
- Is there a difference between an individual exercising personal revenge and the state exacting just retribution against law breakers?
- Christ's command to love includes enemies, neighbors, and self. Just War advocates seem to be willing to sacrifice the lives of enemies for the lives of neighbors. Pacifists appear to be willing to sacrifice the lives of neighbors for the lives of enemies. Is one position morally superior to the other?
- Should Christians, regardless of which position they personally embrace concerning the issue of nuclear warfare, support developing a defense policy which purposely attempts to protect all human life rather than the current MAD policy which will guarantee destruction of life by the millions if it is ever exercised?

**Bibliography:** Clouse, R., *War: Four Christian Views* (1981); Payne, K. I. and K. B., *A Just Defense: The Use of Force, Nuclear Weapons & Our Conscience* (1987); Payne, K. B., *Missile Defense In the 21st Century: Protection Against Limited Threats* (1991); Sider, R., and Taylor, R., *Nuclear Holocaust & Christian Hope* (1982); Stott, J., *Involvement: Being a Responsible Christian in a Non-Christian Society* (1984).

See ATOMIC ENERGY; MILITARISM.

C.E.C. K.I.P.

**NUDISM.** As with so many other technical terms, the word *nudism* has its origin in Latin vocabulary, where *nudus* bore a variety of meanings. While it generally meant "naked" or "unclothed," it also described someone who was lightly clad, as in a tunic or some other scanty attire appropriate for one who was working. In both these senses it is the equivalent of the Greek word *gumnos*, which in the New Testament described Peter's attire as he engaged in the task of fishing (John 21:7). In poetry and rhetoric *nudus* also indicated something stripped of a covering, something that was unadorned, spoiled, or defenseless in the presence of a vandal.

In the ancient world *nudus* would only be applied to prisoners of war, who had been stripped of their clothing deliberately to shame them in front of their enemies, or of servants and slaves who normally wore light attire for their work. The Greeks popularized nudity by requiring their athletes to exercise without clothing when in the gymnasium. Greek soldiers similarly disrobed quite frequently before going into battle against the enemy so that they would not be hampered by clothing or unnecessary equipment. By contrast, nakedness was abhorrent to the ancient Hebrews, who associated bodily exposure with shame and fear (Gen. 3:10). This conflict of ideologies was one of the serious points at issue when Hellenism was threatening to swamp Jewish culture in second-century-B.C. Palestine (2 Macc. 4:7-17).

In imitation of the Greek ideal, nudist groups arose in Europe at the beginning of the twentieth century with the aim of producing strong, healthy bodies as the result of vigorous exercise and carefully controlled dieting. Where nudism became popular in other countries, the emphasis upon vigorous physical exercise was replaced by an indulgence in swimming and sunbathing, since most nudist camps were located near secluded beaches. Such groups as are organized to conduct their affairs decorously, the members following the behavioral norms established by the group. They generally maintain their relationships at the level of social intimacy and are usually very discreet about their activities so as to avoid animosity on the part of nonnudist neighbors.

There are, of course, other ways of acquiring physical health quite apart from total bodily exposure, one of which is establishing wholesome habits of mind. The notion that one can dispose of one's problems or inhibitions simply by disrobing is naive and in the main caters only to the exhibitionist. Physical, mental, and spiritual difficulties surely demand a more professional approach to them than mere disrobing in public.

Christians normally find nudism unappealing, preferring instead to follow New Testament traditions of modesty and seemliness, which include appropriate clothing as well as wholesome attitudes of mind (1 Pet. 3:3-5; 5:5).

# -O-

**OATHS.** In legal usage, an oath constitutes a statement or declaration, the content of which is affirmed to be true. When in process of its being sworn, the name of God or some other acceptable substitute is included as a validating factor. In consequence the content of the oath is accepted as true in the sense that it corresponds with the factual reality of the situation or circumstances from which the need for an oath arose.

The taking of oaths is ancient, forming an important part of the judicial system of the Sumerians, who developed the first high culture of human society from about 4000 B.C. They formulated a legal system that allowed for issues to be contested in court before a panel of three judges. The swearing of an oath by the plaintiff and the defendant was a fundamentally important preliminary to the court proceedings, and perjury was regarded as a very serious offense. This pattern, with some variations, has survived the test of time, and forms part of modern legal procedure.

Another ancient Near Eastern form of oath-swearing seems to have had some metaphysical connection with the human life-principle. This was the so-called "phallic oath" and involved an individual taking an oath by a god or gods while grasping the lower abdominal region of the person who had persuaded him to swear an oath that a particular course of action would be undertaken as a result of this procedure.

This oath is well illustrated in the case of the aged Abraham (Gen. 24:2-9), who as a patriarch responsible for the welfare of his family was concerned about the fact that his dearly loved son Isaac was still unmarried. Being anxious for Isaac to avoid a liaison with a pagan Canaanite woman, Abraham summoned his chief household steward and made him swear that he would protect Isaac from such a destiny. The oath involved the servant in a lengthy journey to Mesopotamia to obtain a wife for Isaac from the city of Nahor, where relatives of Abraham were still living. Accordingly the anonymous steward obeyed Abraham's injunction to "please, put your hand under my thigh, and I will make you swear" (Gen. 24:2-3, NKJV). The servant swore by the Lord, the God of the universe, that he would fulfill his master's commands; and in so doing took an oath by the supreme Power who had begotten the cosmos as well as by the procreative powers of the earthly patriarch Abraham. Understandably this type of oath was both tremendously serious and responsible.

In antiquity an oath normally involved deity, whether explicitly or not, because the superstitious people of the ancient Near East confidently expected an outraged deity to punish anyone who failed to keep an oath sworn by his or her name. But in the Old Testament some oaths take the form of covenant agreements (Gen. 26:28-30), which again in antiquity were always ratified by divine witnesses. Oath-taking was an early feature of Hebrew jurisprudence (Exod. 22:11), and the sacrificial rituals of the Mosaic era provided for someone who had pronounced aloud an impetuous oath without realizing fully the implications of his action (Lev. 5:4). An equally important ritual involving oath-taking enabled a woman to be cleared of suspicion of immorality leveled by a jealous husband if she was innocent (Num. 5:12-31).

In the Old Testament period in general oaths were solemn and responsible affairs, but by the time of Jesus the Jews had developed some casuistic procedures for evading vows (Matt. 23:16-22). It was this practice that Christ was condemning in his teaching and not the solemn swearing of oaths and vows found in the Old Testament. The fact that Jesus responded to the high priest under oath (Matt. 26:63-64), even though it sealed his fate, showed that he was not abrogating the Old Testament concept of oaths. There is thus no reason why the practicing Christian should not swear oaths under properly accredited circumstances. The believer is urged, however, not to indulge in extravagant or trivial oaths (Matt. 5:34-36), but to be a person of such credibility that a simple yes or no, whether under oath or not, should be a good and sufficient answer. James warns his readers that the tongue is a very influential member of the body (James 3:5-6), and all Christians will be aware of the ancient prohibition against false witness (Exod. 20:6) when oaths have to be sworn.

**OBEDIENCE.** The basic meaning of *obedience* is to conform oneself to the will, order, or command of another or a law. The Hebrew word most often translated "obey" in the Old Testament (*sama*) has the basic meaning of "listen" or "hear." The connection between hearing and obeying is illustrated in many texts that are translated "obey the voice" (Gen. 27:8; Exod. 5:2; Deut. 13:4; Jer. 7:23). It is also illustrated by texts where *hear* suggests more than listening (Matt. 17:5, "This is my beloved Son, in whom I am well pleased; hear ye him"). Further, the Greek word, *hupakouo*, meaning "listen to," is often translated "obey" in the New Testament (Matt. 8:27; Eph. 6:1; Heb. 5:9). Obedience is a listening that implies an active, affirmative response to the will of the one who requests or commands. It implies not simply a conformity of external action, but, more importantly, the affirmation of the intent of one's heart (Rom. 6:16-19).

Scripture commands obedience to parents (Eph. 6:1; Col. 3:20), masters (Eph. 6:5; Col. 3:22), political rulers and authorities (Titus 3:1), and church leaders (2 Thess. 1:8; 3:14; Heb. 13:17) as well as to God (Deut. 27:10; Jer. 7:23). Obedience to human authorities is commanded because of their God-given roles, but not necessarily because of the moral quality of what they will.

Obedience to the will of God is a necessary requirement for those who would become God's people, whether in the Old or New Testament. This is true for individuals in the Old Testament, such as Abraham, Moses, Joshua, and Saul, as well as for the nation of Israel (Exod. 19:5; Deut. 11:27-28; 1 Sam. 12:13-14). The nation was condemned for its failure to obey God and hear His voice (Neh. 9:17; Dan. 9:10). The prophetic word to a fallen Israel and Judah was a call to obedience (Isa. 1:19; Amos 3:1; 5:1; Jer. 7:23). For both the individual, Saul, and for the nation, God desired obedience more than sacrifice (1 Sam. 15:19; Amos 5:14-20). Obedience is very important in the New Testament as well. Those who truly follow Jesus must hear His word and act on it (Matt. 7:24). The relation of the Christian to God is described as one of obedience to faith (Acts 6:7; Rom. 1:5) as Christ becomes "the author of salvation" for all those who obey Him (Heb. 5:9). Obedience is the faith-response to God's word in Jesus Christ. A faith that does not result in obedience in life is not a true faith (Eph. 2:8-10; James 1:22-23; 2:20). The Holy Spirit is given to those who are obedient (Acts 5:32), so that the fruits of the Spirit result from obedience (Gal. 5:22-23).

The supreme example of obedience in the Bible is Christ, who was "obedient unto death of the cross" (Phil. 2:8). Christ was obedient not only in His death, but also in His life, where He kept the moral law of God so that He was a man without sin and wholly righteous before God (2 Cor. 5:21; Heb. 4:15; 7:26). This obedience in life and in death, according to Paul, provides the basis for our salvation: "For by one man's disobedience many were made sinners, so by the obedience of one shall many be made righteous" (Rom. 5:19).

In traditional Christian ethics, rightness is defined as conformity or obedience to the will of God. Christ, through His life of complete obedience to the will of God that extended to death on the cross, becomes the example of a perfect moral life. The question confronting the Christian ethicist is not whether moral action implies obedience of God's will (for surely it does), but how to determine what God's will for a given situation is. Many followers of God in the Old Testament heard His voice and obeyed it, such as Abraham (Gen. 12:1-4), Samuel (1 Sam. 3:1-18),

Isaiah (Isa. 6), and Jeremiah (Jer. 2). The commandments in the Old Testament are a codification of God's will, especially as summarized in the Decalogue. Thus, obedience to the Ten Commandments becomes central to many Christian ethical theories. But in what way must we be obedient to the commandments in order to conform to the will of God?

The Pharisees interpreted the 613 commandments of the Torah through an elaborate structure by specifying rules for every conceivable situation, and to these rules they were scrupulously obedient; but Jesus condemned them for their approach to the law (Matt. 23:1-23). Jesus stated that obedience is more a matter of the intent of the heart than that of external conformity of action (Matt. 5:27-48). The one who is obedient to God is the one who conforms to the spirit and intent of the law and not simply to its letter. It is here that the life of Christ and the teachings of the New Testament provide a needed amplification on what that intent is. Not all Christian ethical theorists determine the will of God primarily from the Ten Commandments, however. Some look more to Jesus' teachings, especially in the Sermon on the Mount. Others, such as the Thomists, attempt to discover the will of God through natural law, that is, a rational analysis of God's revelation in the created order, as well as through Scripture. Still other theorists look to a direct address from God in a concrete situation.

**Bibliography:** Murray, J., *Principles of Conduct* (1957); Smedes, L., *Mere Morality: What God Expects From Ordinary People* (1983); Yoder, J. H., *The Politics of Jesus* (1972).

See DIALECTICAL ETHICS; SERMON ON THE MOUNT; TEN COMMANDMENTS.

S.D.A.

**OBLIGATION.** An obligation is some form of constraint which makes one person liable or indebted to another because of a favor granted or a service received. The term is derived from a Latin verb *obligare,* which meant originally "to cover up a wound" or "to tie up with a bandage." From the idea of binding or fastening came the legal and religious usage of making someone liable to another person and thus of obligation in general.

In modern usage the legal meaning of a binding contract or agreement is prominent, and this extends to all that is involved in the compiling of such a document and its subsequent implementation. The existence of a contract that has been duly attested binds the signatories to certain conditions, and the legal obligations thus fostered require a response which is known as duty. If, as in the ancient world, this contract or bond was signed under specifically religious auspices, the parties have an additional moral as well as a legal obligation to ensure that the conditions agreed upon are fulfilled. But even if the agreement is entered upon in an entirely secular context, people of any integrity experience a de facto sense of obligation to ensure that the undertaking is honored to varying degrees. In most Western countries this moral sensitivity has been honed by the prospect of costly litigation for those who repudiate their obligations or become delinquent about them.

The tragedy of ancient Israel's history and religion was that the legal and spiritual obligations of the Sinai covenant were not matched by a consistent sense of duty. The legal demands of the Decalogue (Exod. 20:2-17) and associated enactments were largely ignored by a nation that accepted the privileges of the covenantal relationship but disregarded their own responsibilities. The Christian must be admonished not to commit the same error. He or she is saved in order to serve in the larger mission of the church and kingdom and, having accepted Christ as Savior and Lord, is under immediate obligation to obey his teachings and live a life of purity in the Holy Spirit. The absolute requirement of implicit obedience to God's commands cannot be emphasized too greatly in this antinomian age. Innovations can bring with them spiritual disaster, as Israel's own history illustrated amply, but the believer's commitment to Christ imposes an obligation on him and him alone.

**OBSCENITY.** This word emerges directly from a common Latin adjective, *obscenus,* the origins of which are rather obscure, but seem in general to have signified something filthy or foul. In a metaphorical sense, as found in the Roman poets and orators, it indicated something that offended the canons of decency or modesty, while in other connections it carried the sinister sense of a warning sign or an evil omen. In modern parlance obscenity is defined broadly in terms of what is socially or morally filthy, repulsive, or indecent; and in that respect it is not greatly different from one of the principal ancient Roman usages.

Even though it might be thought comparatively easy to afford statutory definition to a word that can be understood to mean "against filth," obscenity has proved to be very difficult to define with any precision. What is regarded as filth by some persons can be lauded by others as enlightened and innovative or artistically daring, depending upon the perspective of those concerned. If this is true of a comparatively narrow segment of the North American public, even more significant divergences of understanding occur when foreign countries are involved. For example, scenes taken from "Old West" movies of North American origin are frequently highly offensive to some Oriental viewers, while the general behavior of Hollywood's female movie stars both on and off the screen has earned for North American women generally an unwholesome reputation among Arab peoples. The popular American finger-sign of approval, made by conjoining the index finger and the thumb in a rough circle, is an obscene gesture in Greece.

In the general understanding of people living on the North American continent, obscenity describes certain types of offensive speech or activities that have sexual overtones of a kind that generate distaste. Obscene language normally contains a generous but boring admixture of Anglo-Saxon quadriliteral epithets which relate in a vulgar manner to such things as sexual activity or the functioning of the human body. Blasphemy is not infrequently included when the speaker, who is often a person with a very restricted general vocabulary, has exhausted his or her supply of regular expressions. Obscene speech is deemed such because to the hearer it contains words that are offensive to good taste and morals, and for whatever purpose it may have been employed it is degrading and derogatory in its nature and content. It is regarded by many, even among those who use it, as the language of the gutter and is unacceptable because of the moral depravity which it reflects and perpetuates.

But to define obscenity as far as sexual matters are concerned is a much more complex affair. While momentary genital exposure might be considered to be disgusting, it could be argued with some plausibility in court as constituting an example of "realistic art" that depicts the depravity of some situation or period in human history. But a verdict of obscenity would no doubt be rendered were such an act of exposure to be accompanied by lewd, suggestive gestures or actions. In point of fact, the United States Supreme Court distinguished in 1966 between sex per se and obscenity by defining the latter in terms of the encouraging of lustful desires in the mind of the observer, or "prurient interest," as the ruling described it.

In Canada the emphasis is somewhat different, concentrating upon what is regarded as the "undue exploitation" of sex. But once again it is not easy to decide just how far prurient interest has been aroused or what is the actual nature of "undue" exploitation of sex. Accordingly, refuge has been taken behind what is engagingly described as community standards, which presumably constitutes legislation by group consent as to what is obscene. Since community traditions vary considerably from place to place, there can be neither consistency nor uniformity in attempts to define the nature of obscenity on such a basis. What would be described as obscene in Salt Lake City, for example, would quite probably pass without notice in New York. Indeed, some pornographers regularly take advantage of the difficulty of defining community standards to infiltrate the market with depraved movies, obscene literature, and other forms of "artistic representation" with the sole objective of quick financial gain.

In order to offset the deficiencies inherent in most definitions of obscenity, a third consideration has been added in some jurisdictions, namely that what is regarded as obscene must also be without any evident redeeming virtue for society. But even this consideration can be challenged in the name of art or realism, and in a permissive society even frank obscenity can expect to be defended under the guise of being "a realistic commentary on contemporary social values." Many critics of this situation have observed that if the degeneration of social values continues to any extent, the time may well come when it will be virtually impossible for anyone to prosecute successfully for obscenity. But the oscillation of social opinion is such that a reaction can be expected once the situation has reached a certain point of saturation, after which even the habituated will be found calling for some sort of remedy if only to keep up with the new trends.

For those Christians concerned with social justice and the effect of pornography and obscenity upon the population, especially on those members who are of school age, the means by which this blight can be removed or at least halted in its tracks gives much food for thought and prayer. Censorship has been suggested by Christians and others, and while such a procedure could affect free speech, it has the undoubted merit of drawing a line between genuine freedom and avowed license. Indeed, censorship of films that can be expected to arouse deep offense in the minds of the general public is already at work in terms of a system of viewer-rating. More active forms of censorship are also employed, and in some countries it is illegal for obscene literature and films to be imported. Those who defy the law risk heavy fines and imprisonment when caught.

The Christian's mission to society includes not merely the condemning of sin in its various forms, but an active participation in the ongoing life of the community in order to influence its mores in the direction of Christian values. The believer is urged to be pure in heart and is promised rich blessings as a result (Matt. 5:8), while being warned about the power for good or evil of the tongue (James 3:5-10). In particular, he or she should study carefully the biblical injunctions against the proper and improper use of sexuality and be prepared to instruct others on this matter. Only as Christians exemplify the high standards of purity and moral behavior as commanded by Christ will society be influenced to consider their desirability and adopt them as a way of life. For that reason alone believers need to become far more involved in the performing arts, in the publishing of secular literature, and in other areas of life from which obscene material might otherwise proceed. It is doubtful if obscenity will ever be halted, if for no other reason than the fiscal greed of its purveyors; but with resolute Christian witness its progress can certainly be impeded.

**Bibliography:** Cotham, P. C., *Obscenity, Pornography and Censorship* (1973).

See CENSORSHIP; PORNOGRAPHY.

**OCCULTISM.** This term has its roots in the Latin verb *occulo,* "to cover, hide, conceal," in the most general sense of those words. As an adjective *occultus* meant anything concealed or hidden, whether relating to plans, emotions, private knowledge, or personal secrets. In modern usage the emphasis is placed upon the esoteric nature of what is concealed, so that the occult is generally identified with mysticism in some form, or the exercise of hidden supernatural powers.

Occultism as practiced historically has always depended for its success upon an element of superstition and gullibility in its adherents. The exercise of what purported to be supernatural powers by mortals began in the high cultures of ancient Mesopotamia, where special branches of the priesthood engaged in divination of various kinds. The Sumerians were the first to develop astrology in the third millennium B.C., and one of the earliest allusions to it was contained in a poem about Gudea, a renowned king of Lagash about 2100 B.C. The patron deity of the city, Ningirsu, appeared to him in a dream and instructed him to build a temple. To help Gudea understand, a woman came bearing a tablet containing a picture of the starry heavens, and showed him how to build in accordance with the "holy stars."

The Babylonians and Assyrians broadened occultism by making it a function of the priesthood. The widespread belief in evil spirits and their influence over human beings necessitated professional intervention in the form of *mashmashu* and *ashipu* priests. These individuals recited incantations and performed rituals to protect people from harm. Pregnant women were deemed especially vulnerable, and thus they would call upon the *ashipu* priest to devise suitable spells and bind the power of the evil spirits by tying mystic knots. The priests also intervened in cases of illness by uttering incantations and indulging in different forms of sympathetic magic. Cures were no doubt often effected by the psychological suggestion inherent in the incantations, aided pragmatically by draughts of salicylic acid that had been brewed by decoction or infusion of the bark and leaves of the willow (*salix*) tree. This medicament, the crude preparation of aspirin (acetylsalicylic acid), the world's most popular drug, apparently had its origin with the Sumerians.

A very important division of priests in Babylonia and Assyria was that of the *baru* or seer, who interpreted and decided which days were lucky or unlucky for commencing some undertaking. He employed the growing number of astrological techniques that were available in Babylonia, among which were horoscopes, to divine the trend of future events. Since superstitious people were preoccupied with their own destinies, then as now, the priests formulated an astrological system which would assist them in their prognostications. They observed the movements of the planets carefully, and any deviations from the observed norms were accorded special significance, generally of a sinister variety. Eclipses of the sun and moon were particularly ominous, as they still are today in primitive societies. Venus, Jupiter, and Saturn were all important planets for divinatory purposes, and the priestly findings of antiquity have been perpetuated in part to the present as elements of astrological tables. The basic tenet of this form of occultism remains unchanged from Babylonian times, namely that the stars and planets exert an influence upon the future of the individual which will vary according to his or her time of birth.

Because the Mesopotamians believed that the future could be controlled and predicted, given the proper conditions, the *baru* priest was extremely important for his ability to observe correctly the movements of the celestial bodies. His findings enabled him to ascertain the future course of events on earth, which were believed to be reflected in what occurred in the heavens. The *baru* priest was especially valuable to the king, because he would accompany the nation's armies on their campaigns and give decisions as to whether or not it was favorable to begin a battle, having observed the omens.

Yet another method of priestly divination consisted of hepatoscopy, which involved the sacrificing of an animal and a careful inspection of its liver and entrails generally. If the liver exhibited an anomaly of any kind, such as an abnormally distended lobe, this was regarded as inauspicious, and the enterprise that had been contemplated was postponed accordingly. A summary of Babylonian divinatory techniques available to the king and state officials at the time of the exile (sixth century B.C.) has been preserved by the prophet Ezekiel. He noted that the king of Babylon stood at the crossroads, shook arrows, consulted the teraphim (some form of idol), and examined a sacrificial liver (Ezek. 21:21-22), preparatory to a major attack on Jerusalem.

The Mesopotamian priests generally were dedicated to work in their various ways for the benefit of society and were the official dispensers of magical relief and divinatory advice. But as early as the time of Gudea of Lagash a competing group of persons arose who were outside the priesthood, but who by some means had acquired the knowledge of spells, magic, and incantations thought to have been restricted to official priestly circles. These rival persons used their knowledge to bring harm to others and became known as sorcerers and witches. As a result they were often held responsible for initiating disease or misfortune in the community, whether or not they were the agents of such calamity. Under Assyrian law such practitioners of evil, if apprehended in the act, could be found guilty of sorcery (*kishpu*), the penalty for which was death, as was also the case among the Hebrews (Exod. 22:18).

As ancient as the combating of evil spirits by spells and incantations is, the use of divination is even older. A "chief diviner" at Lagash was mentioned in a tablet dated about 3000 B.C., and the Sumerian Flood Epic preserved a tradition that divination had been received by the priesthood from the gods. One means of discovering the divine will was through dreams and visions which the seer would interpret in terms of an already-existing dream tradition. Dreams could be spontaneous or induced, and if particular elements such as numbers or the movement of animals occurred during the dream, they were of importance for the explanation of the dream. In order to produce an interpretation, the *baru* priest relied upon his training and his supposed "hidden knowledge;" but he was not always very successful in such an enterprise, even at a late stage in the divinatory tradition (Dan. 2:1-11).

A form of divination that is not completely without parallel in the Rorschach psychological test was popular in both Mesopotamia and Egypt. Known as lecanomancy, it was performed by dropping oil or finely ground flour on the surface of wine or water that had been placed in a container. The configurations which the floating materials ultimately formed were interpreted along traditional guidelines, which might be modified if the shapes suggested some definite object. Some modern fortune-tellers employ tea leaves in divination and are apparently guided by somewhat similar considerations as far as configurations are concerned. The reference to Joseph's divining cup in Genesis 44:5 is evidently to lecanomancy.

Perhaps the least complicated system of divination in ancient Mesopotamia was the casting of lots after a question had been asked which could be resolved by a simple positive or negative response. The Hebrews employed lots for divination in both cultic (Lev. 16:8) and secular (Josh. 18:10; 1 Chron. 25:8) ceremonies, and sometimes sought a direct response from God by this means (1 Kings 22:6).

One of the black arts of antiquity was necromancy, which is based on the belief that by establishing communication with the spirits of dead people, certain elements of one's future life can be ascertained. Necromancy assumes that the human personality survives the death of the body and that it is in a position to communicate with persons on earth. The most familiar act of necromancy in biblical literature is the request by Saul, Israel's first king, for the so-called witch of Endor to bring up the ghost of the prophet Samuel from the grave. Even though Saul himself had prohibited sorcery and witchcraft in the land, his need for prophetic advice was so desperate that he even broke his own strict law. The woman raised the spirit of Samuel by a technique that is not described, and Saul received stern rebukes from the ghost (1 Sam. 28:8-20). The following day Saul was killed in battle, and his body mutilated (1 Sam. 30:3-10).

In modern terms such an experience would be described as a spiritualist séance. Spiritualists, like the ancient necromancers, believe that the human spirit survives bodily death and that the deceased can somehow become available for communicating with the living. For this purpose a medium is necessary, through whom the personality from the spirit world can give messages to loved ones and others. As far as the mechanics are concerned, the communications result either from the medium being possessed and uttering or writing messages as a result, or else speaking directly in a trancelike condition without appearing to be possessed. In other types of séances there are manifestations in the form of ectoplasmic apparitions, or else furniture is moved about by unseen forces, sometimes quite violently.

Unlike the situation involving the witch of Endor, whose occult powers were of a dramatic character, many séances have been shown by psychic researchers to exhibit various degrees of fraud. Yet despite the proven activities of charlatans, there are some psychic phenomena which cannot either be proved or disproved. If more scientific research in the area of extrasensory perception is undertaken, it may be possible to establish a clearer understanding of the nature of these and other psychic phenomena.

A blatant form of demonic occultism is that of Satan worship, the supporters of which engage in various rituals, often under the influence of mind-disorienting chemicals. The devotees are often said to dance in a circle, sometimes around an altar on which an animal has been or is to be sacrificed. The quasi-religious rituals enthrone the devil as the supreme object of worship; and the rites, often held at dead of night under a full moon, have been alleged to be marked by orgiastic practices. In some countries a human being has reportedly been sacrificed to the devil instead of an animal.

The Christian's position on occultism is founded on such Old Testament injunctions as Exodus 22:18 and Deuteronomy 18:10-12, which regarded the activities condemned as abominations. As part of Canaanite religion their pervasiveness helped to destroy the covenant people in the pre-exilic period and were quite rightly condemned by Isaiah (47:13) and others. The superstitious veneration of stars worships the creature rather than the Creator and as such dethrones God from his exclusive position as Lord of all life.

Necromancy is particularly dangerous because it involves dealing with powers that are beyond human control. The Scriptures warn the believer that there are evil as well as good spirits and even provide a test for determining the true nature of the entities in question (1 John 4:1-3). As far as Satanism is concerned, it would be repudiated by any serious Christian without a moment's consideration, since the believer worships Jesus, not the devil (Matt. 4:10, addressed, interestingly enough, to Satan himself).

However intriguing it might be to know what the future has in store, the Christian is commanded to love God exclusively and to walk continuously in faith without being concerned for the affairs of the morrow. If guidance for the future is needed, the believer has the assured help of the Holy Spirit (John 16:13) for his or her problems. All of this is not to say, however, that evil powers do not exist, for the believer will certainly be tempted as the Lord was. Nevertheless the Christian is admonished not to give place to the devil (Eph. 4:27), but to live according to the commandments of Jesus.

If the Christian's spiritual vitality is diverted into one or other of the forms of occultism, the impact of gospel preaching and ministry to others is diminished seriously; and Christ is no longer enthroned supremely in the individual's life. It is therefore fundamentally important for the believer to reject anything that does not glorify Christ, mindful of the fact that Jesus' own mission was to destroy the works of the devil (1 John 3:8). No practice of any kind can be considered ethically, morally, or spiritually suitable for the Christian life if it conflicts with the behavioral norms revealed in Scripture.

**Bibliography:** Nigosian, S. A., *Occultism in the Old Testament* (1978).

See ASTROLOGY; FORTUNE-TELLING; MAGIC; NECROMANCY; WITCHCRAFT.

**OLD TESTAMENT ETHICS.** A spiritual and theological basis for the behavior of God's chosen people and, by implication, all mankind. Grounded in the Ten Commandments, or Ten Words, Old Testament ethics supply an understanding for the entire spectrum of human emotion and behavior.

*Basic Characteristics.* The most distinctive feature of Old Testament ethics is its unique theology. Biblical ethics in both testaments is firmly based on the character and actions of God. The revelation of God and His will to mankind must be the starting points forming the central organizational principle for doing ethics. Such a basis, of course, points to other important characteristics of Old Testament ethics.

Since God's revelation is personal, his ethical expectations of mankind are both personal and internal. The Old Testament reveals a God who enters into a convenantal relation with persons whom He has created in His image, and consequently, with whom He wishes to continue in fellowship. This covenant relationship is personal, expressed both externally and internally, for though "man looks at the outward appearance, the LORD looks at the heart" (1 Sam 16:7). One observes many expressions in the Old Testament connected with the "heart" in the sense of the total person, rather than just the emotions. "The thoughts," "plans," "intents," and "counsels," in short, all the motives and inner aspirations, are to be included in ethical evaluations.

Another characteristic of Old Testament ethics is the social dimension. Social relationships among families, workers, and communities are firmly addressed with ethical demands. One often thinks of murder, adultery, and stealing as personal sins, without realizing that victims are members of the community as well. The Old Testament takes this into consideration and provides ethical underpinnings for the social relations of related groups, such as brothers and sisters, fathers and children, neighbors and friends, magistrates and citizens, employers and employees, and also those not so readily related such as the rich and the poor, the stranger or refugee, the widow, the orphan, and the other outcasts of society. God cares for all these and considers how His people respond in all these social situations.

There is also an eschatological characteristic to Old Testament ethics, as it is not merely concerned with the present, but also considers the future. "Do this and you shall live" is more than a "this life" orientation. It is an expression that clearly anticipates the New Testament concept of "eternal life," suggesting a quality of life in both the here and now and the future. Although the promises of the covenant to Abraham were not fulfilled until the incarnation of Christ, they set forth an implicit end and reward for ethical living as a faithful response of the people of God.

Finally, Old Testament ethics expands to universal dimensions because God is the universal Creator. Israel was granted a special revelation and redemptive relationship with God; but, even though other nations had no such revelation or relationship, it is clear that they remained accountable to God for their actions (Amos 1:2—2:4). The rise of Assyria was under God's sovereign control; nevertheless judgment awaited them for their cruelty and evil designs (Isa. 10:5-19). God's universal control was understood by Israel as early as the time of Abraham (Gen. 18:25). The implications of this universal dominion go beyond international governments, reaching down to include all people throughout all ages. Paul made clear this universal application of judgment in Roman 1—3.

*Governing Principle.* As noted above, the distinctive feature of Old Testament ethics is its unique theology. The ethical norms of the Old Testament are grounded in the very nature of God Himself. Although He is transcendent, God enters into convenant relationship with His creatures in general and with man in particular (Hos. 2:18-20).

*As Creator.* God made man in His image and gave him tasks to perform (Gen. 1:27-28; 2:15-25). In the creation account, God revealed Himself as sovereign over all, giving unity to all creation. In the "creation ordinances" God calls on man to emulate His creative and ruling activity by "serving" the earth (Gen. 2:15), that is, by tilling the ground and caring for the garden, by naming and subduing the animals and by exercising dominion over God's creation. Even the order to "be fruitful and multiply, and fill the earth" was a conscious reflection of the creative activity of the sovereign Creator. All man's activities were to be motivated by a desire to emulate the God who made him. The motivation was to love and honor God by serving Him and His creation. Even the sabbath (Gen. 2:2-3), resting after the six days of labor, was understood as God's pattern to be imitated (Exod. 20:11).

The fact that sin entered into creation does not affect the sovereign God or the essential unity of the universe He created. It makes no difference that man is in rebellion against God, because the Old Testament considers all mankind to be under His authority just because He is the Creator. Furthermore, unbelievers and heathen nations are held responsible to God whether they acknowledge Him or not. By the same token, the creation ordinances continued to apply after the Fall so that "serving" the ground came to include the environmental and sanitary concerns of the community as well as the production of grain and fruit.

*As Redeemer.* God took the initiative to counter the effects of sin on the human race, revealing Himself as sovereign over the forces of evil. This manifestation of God's graciousness also revealed His plan and purpose for man in sin and grace.

The Fall of man was an act of rebellion against the Creator that resulted in the corruption of man's whole character. So great was the alienation of man against God that true understanding was completely distorted. Man's emotions were twisted away from all that was godly. The will of man was placed under bondage so as to avoid God and resist His authority.

Into this desperate condition of mankind, God reveals Himself as Redeemer by graciously condescending to speak to Adam and Eve and promising a Redeemer from their descendants; by graciously calling people to repentance through the preaching of Noah; and more specifically, by graciously electing Abraham and the nation of Israel through whom God would bring the promised Redeemer.

The initiative of redemption was exhibited by the establishment of a covenantal relationship with the elect, whether individually or corporately (Deut. 4:37; Amos 3:2). The key expressions that run throughout the Old Testament reflecting this covenant relationship are: "I will establish My covenant between Me and you and your descendants...to be God to you and your descendants after you" (Gen. 17:7) and "I will take you as my people" (Exod. 6:7; 19:5-6; Deut. 7:6-8). It is clear that the election of Israel stems from the love of God and that the covenant bond is maintained through the covenant love or faithfulness of God. Stipulations are given to Israel within the framework of covenant. General stipulations appear in divine instruction (the Ten Commandments, Exod. 20:1-17; Deut. 5:6-21), while more specific stipulations can be found, in the case law format (Exod. 20:18—24:11; Deut. 12—26). The basis for the normative ethics of these Old Testament covenants was not a code of law, however, but the covenantal God who identified Himself as the great suzerain of the covenant. The benevolent redemptive acts that God performed on behalf of His people required a covenantal response of wholehearted devotion to Him. Note for example, Genesis 17:1, where, after almost twenty-five years of tender nurture and protection, God reveals himself to Abraham. "I am God Almighty," He says, adding the convental stipulation "Walk before me and be wholly devoted [to me]." God's qualities of redemption are demonstrated in the Exodus, which documented His tender care for the protection of His elect as He covenantally called them to be His treasured possessions and a holy nation. The claims of redemption from the bondage of slavery and sin magnificently reveal God's authority over His people.

*Holiness.* As Creator, God made man in His image to reflect Him in dominion and service. As Redeemer, God sovereignly and graciously seeks to remake fallen man to conform to His image. This implies that God's intention for man is to mirror what He is and does. The moral nature through which such ethical demands can be determined and understood is described by the words *holy* and *holiness.*

In words reminiscent of the great preambles to the covenants in Genesis 17:1 and Exodus 20:2, Moses identifies the standard for normal ethical conduct in Leviticus 11:45: "For I am the LORD who brought you up from the land of Egypt, to be your God; thus you shall be holy for I am holy." Holiness has a special meaning in Hebrew, especially as applied to the Lord God. Above all, it expresses the sum total of the attributes of God as transcendent, as separate and distinct from His creation. The holiness of God includes His unapproachability (Exod. 19:11-16; Isa. 6:1), His jealousy and wrath (Exod. 20:5), His covenant love (Exod. 20:6), His glory (Ezek. 1:28), and His majesty (Isa. 6:13). In view of the sinfulness of man, holiness can also reveal the very opposite in man, namely his own limitations and his utter corruption that can only be overcome through forgiveness and pardon (Isa. 6:4-7). Holiness, then, may be considered the sum total of the divine attributes. A good list of these appears in Exodus 34:6-7 as God spoke to Moses after the heinous incident of Aaron's golden calf: "And the LORD passed before him and proclaimed, 'The LORD, the LORD God, merciful and gracious, longsuffering and abounding in goodness and truth, keeping mercy for thousands [of generations], forgiving iniquity and transgression and sin, by no means clearing the guilty, visiting the iniquity of the fathers upon the children to the third and fourth generation.'" This list must be compared with Deuteronomy 7:9-10, which clarifies the thousands "of generations" who are the beneficiaries of his covenant love, and speaks of God as a "faithful God" and the one who "repays those who hate him," "destroying them."

One cannot escape the essential aspects of the character of God that are part of His holiness:

love, faithfulness, justice, truth, forgiveness, and so on. The bases of God's covenantal requirements on His people are summed up by the succinct statement: "You shall therefore be holy, for I am holy." It becomes apparent that this theocentric ethic is also the basis for the New Testament ethics of Jesus (Matt. 5:48), of Paul (1 Thess. 4:7) and of Peter (1 Pet. 1:15-16). Man's need to imitate God is expressed in the New Testament through the Son of God who is "the brightness of [God's] glory and the express image of his person" (Heb. 1:3). Paul exhorted the Corinthians: "Imitate me, just as I also imitate Christ" (1 Cor. 11:1). The Old Testament believer did not have the incarnate "image of his person" that he could imitate, but, through God's actions and words, he did have a significant understanding of God that he could emulate.

*The Content of Old Testament Ethics.* The ethics of the Old Testament must be gathered from all Old Testament teachings regarding human conduct. The Hebrew word *torah* applies to such teaching when used in its broadest sense of "authoritative instruction." Such instructions include the revelation given by God to Moses that is recorded in the patriarchal narratives and wilderness wanderings in addition to the Decalogue, levitical rules, and deuteronomic sermons. But *torah* is also used for the prophetic history, the prophetic books themselves, and the poetic and wisdom literature of the Old Testament. Nevertheless, within the total context of the Old Testament "instruction," there are several summarizing texts, namely the Book of the Covenant, Exodus 20—24; the Book of Holiness, Leviticus 17—26; and the Deuteronomic Stipulations, Deuteronomy 6—26. The prophets (Jer. 7:9; Hos. 4:2; Amos 2:6-8; Mic. 6:8) and Wisdom teaching (particularly in Proverbs) also provided summaries. All these teachings, however, are succinctly stated in two key verses: "You shall love the LORD your God with all your heart, with all your soul, and with all your might" (Deut. 6:5) and "You shall love your neighbor as yourself" (Lev. 19:18).

Four observations concerning ethics in the Old Testament should be made: First, all actions and ethical requirements given in the Old Testament should be interpreted in light of these two summarizing texts. One need only recall our Lord's expression: "On these two commandments hang all the law and the prophets" (Matt. 22:40). Second, the close affinity between the creation ordinances and the Decalogue suggests that the former have never been abrogated, their sanctity and relevance instead having been established through subsequent revelation. Third, these texts proclaim the standard for thought, life, and conduct in relation to God, fellowman, and even oneself. If one follows the basic pattern given in the Ten Commandments, he discovers the basic sanctity of worship, work, and life. Finally, it is of great significance that the Decalogue is referred to in the Hebrew Old Testament as the Ten Words (from Hebrew *dabar*, "word"). The distinct emphasis of this term is to understate the gravity and underscore the graciousness of the divine stipulation. Once again, God demonstrates the grace of His sovereignty in His covenantal relationship with His people.

*Holiness in Worship.* The First Word, "You shall have no other gods before Me," addresses the question of whom one is to worship and what relation one must sustain with Him. It forms the basis for all following teachings on ethics. A right covenantal relationship with God must begin with an internal attitude that ascribes true worship permamentaly and exclusively to the one true and living God. The great *Shema Israel* ("Hear O Israel") of Deuteronomy 6:4 focuses attention on the covenant Lord as "our God," highlighting His uniqueness, His solitariness, and His supremacy. Based on such uniqueness and sovereignty, Israel is commanded to "love the LORD your God with all your heart and with all your soul and with all your strength." This is a very positive expression of the First Word, "You shall have no other gods before me," which demands the exclusion of all other gods. No god, idol, institution, man, or object may usurp His lordship. There is no place for competing loyalty. Hence, polytheism is excluded.

The Second Word. "You shall not make for yourself any carved image...you shall not bow down to them nor serve them..." addresses the questions of *how* one must worship. The mode of worship is only that which God ordains in His word. Clearly forbidden in worship are all idols, or pictures, representing God, or worse, representing the gods of the surrounding nations. It should be noted that this prohibition has to do with "bowing down and serving" these idols, that is, offering religious worship. This word must not be construed as a statement against the expression of artistic talent, as God Himself encouraged the use of artisans for the tabernacle. He specifically required artistic representations on the curtains and specified the cherubim on the ark of the covenant to be sculpted works of gold (Exod. 37:7-9).

The Third Word. "You shall not take the name of the LORD your God in vain" is more than just a condemnation of all profanity. To be sure, the use of the name or names of God in a light, frivolous way, or in meaningless ejaculations and curses is condemned. However, in the Old Testament culture a "name" has a fullness of meaning that our Western culture cannot begin to fathom. God reveals Himself in Scripture by (1) His proper names and titles, such as God, Yahweh, Adonai, El Shaddai, and others; (2) His essential names or attributes, such as holiness, goodness, justice, truth, faithfulness, and so on; and (3) His personal names, such as Father (Isa. 63:16), Son (Ps. 2:7, 12), and Spirit (Isa. 42:1). Using these and other "names" of God in meaningless expletives or even abbreviated as minced oaths is merely an external measure of transgression. Far

more significant, however, is that man, by virtue of his creation, eternally carries the imprint of the divine "name" upon him as image bearer. Furthermore, by virtue of redemption, God's people are called to be a *holy* nation, bearing the imprint of the divine attribute that demonstrates the totality of God's character. "Be holy, for I am holy" might well be regarded as the positive expression of the Third Word. Thus, the Old Testament holds all mankind, at least by virtue of creation if not redemption, responsible to reflect godliness in conduct as well as speech. No mere externalism will suffice. This provides the theological and spiritual foundation for all the following ethical precepts.

A special note is required in regard to this Word. It may not be taken as a prohibition against oath-taking in civil or ecclesiastical courts. In fact, Deuteronomy 6:13 precisely indicates that one is to "serve him only and take your oaths in his name." Oaths such as these are based upon the truthfulness and veracity of God, hence the seriousness of them. In effect, one is simply saying: "As God is true, I swear to the truthfulness of my testimony. God will ultimately be my judge." This actually anticipates the Ninth Word, which addresses the matter of bearing false witness.

*Holiness in Work.* The Fourth Word, "Remember the sabbath day, to keep it holy," serves as a transition from the first three, which call for a right relationship with God, to the last six, which call for a right relationship with other men. As a transition word, the principle of ceasing from the labor of six days and resting on the sabbath is as fitting a conclusion to the first section as it is an introduction to the second section. Here is exhibited the call to imitate God in His work of creation (Exod. 20:11), that man, who was created in God's image, should work six days and cease such work on the seventh. Significantly, Deuteronomy 5:13-15 repeats the injunction but gives another reason, that of God's redemptive work in freeing the Israelites from the slavery in Egypt. The effect of sin is similar to this slavery in that it defies God and places man in bondage. The emphasis of this Fourth Word of grace, then, is to underscore liberation from overwork and the bondage of sin and to exhibit the kindness of God to humanity.

The sabbath is also a day for worship. In this connection, the Old Testament speaks of it as a time for holy convocation, but gives no particular details. The day belongs to the Lord and promotes a time of corporate and family worship. The explication of Jesus appearing in Matthew 12 suggests that deeds of mercy and works of emergency and necessity were certainly appropriate. It would be unfair to say that the day was to be somber, because the concept of assembling together suggested by the sabbath also included designated times for the celebration of festivals and even whole years as sabbatical and jubilee years (Lev. 23—25; Deut. 16:1-17). Indeed, the

Day of Atonement was a solemn day for reflection on sin and the only way of pardon, but, in addition, there was to be celebration of the mighty acts of God, who so wondrously has provided through the previous week and throughout the growing seasons.

As a fitting introduction to the last six words, the sabbath principle emphasizes the Old Testament work ethic, encouraging till and producing food not only for oneself, but for the benefit of others as well. Here we see God's care for the well-being of man reflected in man's care for the well-being of his family, his neighbors, and even his enemies (Prov. 25:21). In short, this Word anticipates the horizontal relationships of the final six words by recognizing the dignity of men and women, an essential element for right relations in society.

*Holiness in Life.* If the first four words are summarized in Deuteronomy 6:5, "You shall love the LORD your God will all your heart," the next six words may be summarized in Leviticus 19:18, "You shall love your neighbor as yourself" (also see Matt. 22:37-39). The principle of love for God should be reflected in love for man because man's dignity comes from God's image in him.

The Fifth Word. This command speaks to the sanctity of the family and, by extension, to other institutions. "Honor your father and mother" means that children are to show respect and reverence for parents (Lev. 19:3) and "to love" them (Ps. 91:15) as representatives of God's authority in the home. Parents have a responsibility to reflect the likeness of God through caring and providing for their children, defending them from harm (Ps. 103:6-14), and above all training and disciplining them in the nurture and admonition of the Lord (Gen. 19:18; Deut. 6:7-25; Prov. 22:6). Failure to reflect God's image as parents may forfeit the respect due them by their children.

The role of husband and wife exists within the institution of the family. Since God created both man and woman in His image (Gen. 1:27), husband and wife must be considered equals before God committed to one another in love and honor. Such a relationship calls for fidelity and monogamy, qualities that are further developed and protected under the Seventh Word. Suffice it to say that the wife shares in her husband's dignity and must never be reduced to a position of chattel or slave. Proverbs 31:10-31 celebrates that godly wife for her managerial talents and business acumen, for being a gracious mother and wife, and for having authority and a clear sense of personal worth. Any reduction of the status of women is a result of sin.

In a broader sense, the Fifth Word applies to other institutions, such as government where kings, judges, and lesser magistrates are to reflect God in their functions as leaders and citizens are responsible to honor and obey them (Deut. 16:18—17:20). Religious leaders such as priests, Levites, and prophets, likewise, are established by God (Deut. 18), and God's people are responsible to hear His word through their instruction. There are limitations, however, to the people's subjection to these authorities. When those in authority reduce a person to the status of slave, they deny his dignity and dishonor his Creator. When such leadership fails to reflect God's image in carrying out their high calling, they may forfeit the right to be followed and obeyed. For example, the extreme abuses in the days of Solomon and the totalitarian insensitivity of Rehoboam were major factors in the rebellion and secession of the ten tribes of Israel (1 Kings 12:1-16). In a similar vein, false priests and false prophets were not to be followed, but were instead liable to capital punishment.

Also included under this heading is social responsibility for the poor (Deut. 15:7-11; Prov. 14:21, 31), for the fatherless and widows (Exod. 32:22-23; Ps. 146:9), and for the oppressed. The economic aspect of such social concerns is addressed in the Eighth Word, but the Sixth Word takes into account the responsibilities of those in authority to avoid oppression and to perform justice for the needy. Isaiah 58:2-12 is a classic expression of the prophetic call for social justice as a concomitant to true worship. Jeremiah associates the knowledge of God with doing justice and righteousness. He pleads the cause of the afflicted and needy by comparing the example of Josiah to the oppression and extortion under Jehoahaz (22:15-17). Governmental officials, judges, employees, religious leaders, join parents in carrying tremendous responsibility under God.

The Sixth Word. "You shall not murder" expresses the sanctity of life. The Old Testament recognizes degrees of sinfulness, such as between deliberate, premeditated murder and unintentional manslaughter (Exod. 21:13-14; Num. 35:15-34; Deut. 19:4-13). The Hebrew *ratsach* "to murder," is used for assassination, killing for revenge, and a lion killing a man. It is not used, however, for killing animals for food or sacrifice, for defending oneself against intruders or burglars, for the execution of murderers by the state, nor even for killing in war. Application of the Sixth Word would extend to suicide, to accessories to murder (2 Sam. 12:9), to man or beast causing the death of a person (Exod. 21:28-36), and even to someone causing the death of woman's fetus (Exod. 21:22-25). The Old Testament considered the dignity of human life so sacred that all reasonable safety measures were to be taken to protect life and limb, such as parapets or verandas around flat roofs (Deut. 22:8) and coverings over pits to keep people from falling (Exod. 21:33-34). A lack of self control that leads to gluttony and drunkenness is immoral because of the damage to one's own body and health, not to speak of the psychological damage to one's self-worth.

Under this heading one must also consider the

Old Testament teaching in three areas: capital punishment, war, and the unborn. Capital punishment begins with God, who delegates to human government the responsibility to requite wrongs. God alone is the giver of life and hence, God alone has the right to recall it. In Genesis 9:5-6, however, he instituted the following: "From the hand of every man's brother I will require the life of man. Whoever sheds man's blood, by man his blood shall be shed; for in the image of God He made man." The starting point must be God who created man in His image. This point needs to be stressed as it is fundamental to the understanding of capital punishment in its further applications in Old Testament ethics. For example, in addition to murder, fifteen other crimes may be requited through the death penalty: striking or cursing parents (Exod. 21:15); kidnapping (Exod. 21:16); use of divination (Exod. 22:18); bestiality (Exod. 22:19); sacrificing to foreign gods (Exod. 22:20); sabbath breaking (Exod. 35:2); adultery, homosexuality, and incest (Lev. 20:10-21); human sacrifice (Lev. 20:2); blasphemy (Lev. 24:11-14); incorrigible delinquency (Deut. 17:21); false prophecy (Deut. 13:1-10); and the unchastity or rape of a betrothed virgin (Deut. 22:20-27). All these are crimes against God or human beings, none against property, suggesting that crimes against people are crimes against God. Hence the seriousness of capital punishment. According to Old Testament traditions, all these call for very careful investigation and evidence. It was only at the word of at least two or three witnesses that a crime was established. God, however, is also a God of mercy and grace. Provisions were made for the appropriate ransom or sacrifice upon the criminal's true repentance. The only exception may be in regard to premeditated murder (Num. 35:30-32), which may turn on the definition of "by man *shall* his blood be shed." One view is that capital punishment is mandated. It takes Genesis 9:5-6 as an order or command that must be followed no matter what other conditions or facts apply to the case. Another view is that the passage provides permission or merely a suggestion. A third position is that death is to be understood as the maximum penalty. The Old Testament has noted the different degree of heinousness between involuntary manslaughter and premeditated and deliberate murder. A further indication of God's intention may be seen in Deuteronomy 16:18—17:13, where a plurality of judges must decide on all cases after carefully garnering all the evidence. The decisions they then make must be based upon the previously established principles and any mitigating circumstances in each case. A careful analysis of the way God's mercy in such capital offenses is revealed through the Old Testament leads to the conclusion that God never delights in the death of even the most violent sinner. Instead, He is always eager to reveal His holiness through mercy and pardon whenever a sinner repents from his wicked ways (as in Ezek. 18).

Therefore, judges are expected to mirror God's attributes of mercy and justice in all their deliberations and decisions.

The problem of war in the Old Testament is another aspect of ethics that is a further extension of governmental responsibility delegated by God. This is what the New Testament calls the power of the sword given to the state (Rom. 13:3-4). The Yahweh wars against the Canaanites must be considered an expression of God's judgment against their heinous religious practices and degraded society. As such, the judgment must be viewed as an intrusion upon the great eschatological judgment when retribution will be meted out to recalcitrant sinners. One must also take note that Rahab and her household were saved from the calamity and judgment through repentance and faith.

The Old Testament establishes principles for the defense of home and country from invasion by criminals or foreign army. Resistance may be taken when an unprovoked invasion of home or country begins. A neighbor or neighboring nation also has a responsibility to come to the defense of the attacked friend or country. God may use an Assyria or a Babylon as His instrument of war for disciplining His own people and nation (Isa. 10:56; Hab. 1:6) and then destroy them because of their pride and cruelty (Isa. 10:15-16). War may be thought of as God's reluctant method of dealing with a rampant evil that refuses to submit to patient and diplomatic encounters.

Finally, the sanctity of life has implications for the life of the unborn human embryo. Exodus 21:22-25 presents a case of a pregnant woman bystander who is hurt by men in a fight. If she or the unborn child dies or is maimed, the *lex talionis* of "life for life, eye for eye," and so on would apply, clearly suggesting that the fetus is just as much a human being as the mother. Such an understanding is further supported by Job's plea to God, "Your hands have made me and fashioned me, an intricate unity.... and knit me together with bones and sinews" (Job 10:8-12), and by David's song, "For you have formed my inward parts, you have woven me in my mother's womb" (Ps. 139:13). The life of the human fetus is holy because God creates that life in the womb.

The Seventh Word. "You shall not commit adultery" establishes the sanctity of sex and marriage. Indeed, the institution of marriage is a creation ordinance for the benefit of mankind (Gen. 2:23-24). It is monogamous and indissoluble. Marriage is symbolic of the eternal covenant relationship between God and His people, as the figure of husband and wife for Yahweh and Israel shows (Isa. 54:5-6; Hos. 2:19; the New Testament figure of the bride used for the church). Therefore, in Old Testament ethics, to violate or abuse sex or marriage is to deny the covenantal relations they symbolize. This is why idolatry is so often considered spiritual adultery or prostitution (Hos. 2:1-13; 3:1-3). A major concern that Moses shows in Leviticus 18 in dealing with the holiness of sexual conduct is about the utter denigration of sex in the Near Eastern world in general and in Canaanite religious practice in particular. Bestiality, homosexuality, transvestism, fornication, and sacred prostitution were part and parcel of the culture and cultus. Such were these distortions that some of the strongest language is used in the Scriptures to outlaw them.

Three problems in the ethics of the Old Testament need to be addressed at this time: divorce, polygamy, and levirate marriages. In regard to divorce, it is clear from the creation ordinance that institutes marriage that the unity it establishes must not be broken, as it is symbolic of the covenant bond between God and man. With the Fall, however, the theological effect of sin is introduced. Moses recognized potential problems and permitted divorce (Deut. 24:1-4; see Christ's corrective to Pharisaic interpretation in Matt. 19:7-8). Such is the devastating effect of sin that divorce is allowed in the most extreme circumstances. What Moses legislated is that after divorce and remarriage, it is illegal for a man to return to the first wife. The precise reason is not clear, but the implication is that the wife has been defiled, that it is an abomination to the Lord, and that the land has been polluted, an allusion to elements associated with incest and sexual offenses in Leviticus 18—20. But what does God think of divorce? Malachi 2:16 expresses it succinctly, "'I hate divorce,' says the LORD God."

In regard to polygamy, once again the creation ordinance clearly establishes monogamy as the norm. The first occurrence of polygamy is identified with Lamech, a descendent of Cain (Gen. 4:19). Nowhere does the Old Testament condone polygamy, but rather it reveals the difficulties and heartaches that result. Close scrutiny of the Old Testament, however, shows that there are only five or six examples of polygamy through the patriarchal period and only thirteen cases through the divided kingdom. Most of these were people with absolute power and hardly representative. The norm in Old Testament ethics is monogamy in spite of the few instances otherwise (see Deut. 28:54, 56; Prov. 5:15-21).

Levirate is an Old Testament institution (Deut. 25:5-10) of which two examples are given—Tamar (Gen. 38) and Ruth. It provides, through remarriage, for the continuation of the name and property of a deceased brother who leaves no son. The brother or next of kin of the deceased husband is permitted to marry the widow in order to raise a family to carry on the deceased's name. It is to be noted that this was contrary to the laws on incest under normal conditions. The overriding concerns in this tradition, however, are to continue the name of the brother, to prevent the God-given property from leaving the family, and possibly to provide for the welfare of the widow as well.

The Eighth Word. "You shall not steal" speaks of the sanctity of wealth and possessions. It addresses the area of personal, social, political, or business economics. The Old Testament views wealth and possessions as gifts from God, suggesting that man has these only as a stewardship rather than as an absolute ownership. To steal someone's property is to steal from God, the rightful owner. To withhold from the poor and needy, from orphans, widows, or refugees is an affront to God both because of the dignity they maintain as image bearers and because of God's concern that wealth be used to aid the destitute. It would be a mistake to think that the Old Testament puts a premium on poverty as a virtue to be desired. Affluence need not be considered an evil, but must be acknowledged as a blessing that God is pleased to give. There are dangers and responsibilities that go along with wealth. Deuteronomy 8:11-18 warns of pride and forgetting God—in essence, idolatry. Other dangers associated with wealth are a distortion of values and blindness to one's own shortcomings and anxieties. On the other hand, stewardship of wealth requires philanthropy and thanksgiving (Deut. 15:7-8; 26:1-11).

Holiness in economics is also related to the Old Testament work ethic and to truth. Honesty in work should reflect the productivity of the Creator and should always be exhibited in commerce (Prov. 20:13-23).

With respect to usury, the Eighth Word is a word of grace and mercy when applied to interest on loans. An Israelite was not to charge interest when lending to fellow citizens who were needy or poor (Exod. 22:25; Lev. 25:35-37; Deut. 23:19-20). The concern was to discourage greed at the expense of people in distress. Loans to foreigners, however, presumably for a business venture, were allowed to be given at interest.

The sanctity of property is also expressed in the law of the year of Jubilee (Lev. 25). This exhibited the sanctification of the whole land, typifying the eschatological kingdom of peace and liberty. It taught that the land belonged to God and that God's people held it only as a stewardship. All business, therefore, was to be transacted in the fear of God and with concern toward the poor and needy. Once again, theology is seen as the basis for Old Testament ethics.

The Ninth Word. Integrity and truth are the ethical norms of holiness expressed in "You shall not bear false witness against your neighbor." Although couched in a concrete statement reflecting legal process in court, its basic principle reflects the sanctity of truth in every area of life. Here again, the overlapping with other ethical norms can be observed, for truth is the essence of the marriage troth, as well as of the covenantal bond between God and His people. Slander may overlap with the sixth commandment, for by ruining the character of innocent parties one is involved in character assassination (Lev. 19:16; see also Ezek. 22:9; Prov. 11:9). It is also closely associated in Old Testament ethics with theft, stealing, and cheating (Lev. 19:11). Truth and purity in the heart are essential to the motives expressed in the Tenth Word (Ps. 51:6). Truth is an attribute of God's very nature, for God cannot lie (Num. 23:19; Isa. 65:16). Theology is again seen as the mainspring of Old Testament ethics.

The concrete legal terminology of the Ninth Word helps define a lie: to bear false witness is to intentionally deceive a person or court who has a right to know the whole truth and nothing but the truth. One may, however, withhold or conceal facts where circumstances make it clear that no one has claim to such knowledge or when there is no violation of moral obligation (as in 1 Sam. 16:1-3).

The seriousness with which perjury and malicious accusation are taken can be found in Deuteronomy 19:15-21. Special attention is to be given to verse 19 where such false accusation is punishable by the same penalty intended for the accused. The *lex talionis* is appealed to not to satisfy personal vengeance but to maintain judicial equity.

The Tenth Word. This commandment speaks to the sanctity of the heart and motives: "You shall not covet...you shall not set your desire on..." This word clearly points to the centrality of a pure motivation of the heart called for in all the commandments and indeed in all Old Testament ethics. Christ brought this clearly into focus in his comments regarding murder and adultery by including "anger" and "looking on a woman to lust for her" as part and parcel of covenantal stipulations (Matt. 5:21-22, 27-28; also 15:19), but even the prophets had been concerned about the inner motives of the heart decrying mere externalism (as in Isa. 1:11-15; Amos 4:4-5). In the selection of a king for Israel, even Samuel was tempted to look on the outward appearance "but the LORD looks at the heart" (1 Sam. 16:7). Finally, when Proverbs 21:4 lumps together "a haughty look, a proud heart, and the plow of the wicked" as sin, the implication is that Old Testament ethics concerns much more than merely external rectitude.

Motives in Old Testament ethics appear to be clearly related to the theology of the covenant. The preamble and historical prologue to the Ten Words of the covenant are "I am the LORD your God, who brought you out of the house of Egypt, out of the house of bondage" (Exod. 20:2). Here God expresses His authority, by reminding His people of a previously established covenant in which He kept His part. He hopes to awaken the minds and hearts of His people to respond in faithfulness and loyalty to their sovereign redeemer. What else would be the meaning of the oft-repeated phrase, especially in Leviticus 18—22, "For I am the LORD your God"? Related to this theological motive must be the gratitude and remembrance of the heart for the great historical experiences given to people of God. Even the curses and the blessings address the motives by appealing to reason and observation. They instill a fear of judgment for disobedience and provide promises of blessings for faith and obedience.

*Limitations of Old Testament Ethics.* Having discussed the basic characteristics, governing principles, and content of Old Testament ethics, we conclude with a brief consideration of their limitations. First, since so much of the Old Testament deals with the nation of Israel as the people of God, there are certain national considerations that must be understood. These include political laws concerning relations with neighboring nations, particularly the problematic relations with the Canaanites who were to be extirpated. Suffice it to say that there is a theological dimension to these relations that is not always apparent when reading the text, such as for example, the intrusion of the eschatological judgment on the Canaanites for their depraved idolatry and heinous religious practices. There is also a clear missionary responsibility that all too often Israel failed to carry out.

Secondly, a limitation that is perhaps more important arises from the nature of progressive revelation. This is to say that, in the Old Testament historical period, some ethical problems were permitted to exist, but were clearly corrected in later revelation, such as polygamy and slavery, to name only two. One must necessarily recognize a long history of the revelation of God's will and any ethical problems must be seen in such a perspective.

Thirdly, there is another caveat that needs to be considered, namely that of the apparent materialism and legalism of the Old Testament. Sometimes Old Testament ethics is couched in legal terms using material blessings as reward for doing good and curses as dire warnings for disobedience. If these aspects are all one sees in the Old Testament Scriptures, he fails to understand the spiritural implications of the covenantal relationship. That relationship is an eternal fellowship with the God who has acted in love, mercy, and faithfulness and has expressed His will for His redeemed people in the whole of Old Testament Scriptures. The limitations of materialism and legalism arise because of the sinful imperfections of men.

Whatever limitations are admitted, it would be a mistake to think that the social and political structures and their laws are monolithic. Even rewards and punishments transcend the temporal and material, making the goal of moral action a blessed fellowship with the covenant Lord. Far beyond the external demands of the law are the ideals expressed by the psalmist, "Your word have I hidden in my heart, that I might not sin against You" (Ps. 119:11), and by the prophet, "I will put My law in their minds, and write it on their hearts" (Jer. 31:33). They understand that the Lord God is and will be their God, and that they are and will be His people.

Old Testament ethics calls for a radical break with one's sinful nature. It demands a heart relationship with God together with actions consistent with His character and activities.

**Bibliography:** Bruce, W. S., *The Ethics of the Old Testament* (1909); Goldingay, J., *Approaches to Old Testament Interpretation* (1978); Kaiser, W. C., *Toward Old Testament Ethics* (1983); Snaith, N. H., *The Distinctive Ideas of the Old Testament* (1964); Wright, C. J. H., *An Eye for an Eye, The Place of Old Testament Ethics Today* (1983).

P.R.G.

**OMISSION, SINS OF.** In the Scriptures sin is described in a number of ways. If it involves the breaking of one of God's Ten Commandments (Exod. 20:2-17) and other similar legal material, it is a sin of commission if the act of transgression has been entered upon in a deliberate frame of mind. The same is true if all other standards for spiritual living that God has established are violated consciously. But it is possible to sin without actually committing some form of direct rebellion against God simply by failing to do what God expects of the believer. Or, as James expressed it, "to him who knows to do good and does not do it, to him it is sin" (James 4:17, NKJV).

A sin of omission is a failure on the part of the Christian to do what is known to be right. This realization can have uncomfortable consequences for the believers who are disinclined to "become involved" with anything that does not appeal to them or does not serve an immediate personal aim. This would apply, for example, to some aspects of service to humanity that may be unappealing or even distasteful, but are nevertheless a fundamental part of the gospel mandate. The person who neglects Christ's commandment regarding love of one's neighbor (Matt. 22:37-40) is therefore not merely guilty of a sin of omission, but also one of direct commission. Fortunately both types of sin yield to the power of Christ's atoning blood when the proper scriptural conditions have been met (1 John 1:9).

**OPEN HOUSING.** This is a technical American term that has arisen out of legislation aimed at halting racial discrimination where housing accommodation for minority groups is involved. The overall aim is to make it possible under the law for people to live in the accommodation of their choice, whether a rental unit or home ownership is involved.

A series of statutes in the United States has established the principle at the federal level, and funds are now available for housing projects that encourage a racially balanced mixture of homeowners. It should be remarked that the intent of the legislation was not to encourage people to indulge in the kind of housing accommodation that was patently beyond their ability to sustain financially, whether by supplementary assistance or not.

Despite the presence of federal enactments, there are many localities where an unofficial type of segregation is practiced. This obviously defeats the spirit of the legislation, but it is difficult to resolve because even Christians are divided on the matter. The New Testament teaches that for those who are living in fellowship with Jesus there is no differences between races, but that all believers are one in him (Gal. 3:28).

**OPPRESSION.** This term is a modified form of "on pressing," which describes the basic idea involved. Oppression is therefore something that lies or weighs heavily upon a person or a situation. In purely personal terms it could be a decision that has been made or has to be made which is of such severity as to cause an individual great distress of mind. In a broad social context, oppression denotes any kind of harsh circumstance that interferes with justice and personal freedom.

Most commonly these are imposed externally, as in the case of a dictatorial government that subjects its citizens to repressive measures of various kinds. The anguish of oppression emerges from the fact that the restrictions were imposed arbitrarily by government and were not a matter of voluntary participation or acceptance by the citizens. The sense of oppression under such circumstances is augmented by concomitant feelings of injustice, and if when these are given public expression they are met with brutal reprisals that effectively quench all opposition to the governing authority, the burden of oppression can become overwhelming. A tyrannous government, by producing its own elite group of rulers, effectively classifies all others as second- or third-class citizens; and without the protection of law they are ripe for exploitation which, depending upon its severity, can reduce them to a socioeconomic level that is little better than slavery.

The final, devastating ingredient of oppression is the awareness that freedom has been lost, whether by default or not, perhaps forever; and the crushing weight of hopelessness that the overall situation engenders may well be more than many people are able to bear. The future, therefore, can only be one of despair, raising the question for some as to the value of the struggle for survival. As hopeless as these conditions may seem, they can become even worse if harsh dictatorial policies are supplemented by unforeseen natural disasters such as earthquakes, floods, and famine. These take their own toll of life regardless of the government that is in power, and even though material aid may be forthcoming from neighboring peoples, it is always too late for some.

The classic instance of oppression to which most biblically literate persons would look is that of the bondage which the Israelites endured at the hands of the ancient Egyptians after the death of Joseph (Exod. 1:11-14). The narratives present a picture of a once-secure people, who had been living on the finest land in ancient Egypt, now being forced to perform unaccustomed and menial tasks along with other workers under rigorous conditions of employment. As commonly interpreted, the Hebrews above all others were discriminated against by being subjected to the indignities of forced labor and punished by being beaten, whipped, or otherwise maltreated when their energies flagged.

Unfortunately an interpretation of this sort fails to take certain important cultural considerations into account. In ancient Egypt anything of significance that was accomplished was achieved to the accompaniment of blows, whether it was the labors of the student in school or the toil of the builder, the stone carver, the worker in metal, or the general laborer. The blows were administered in order to focus the recipient's attention upon his or her work and the procedure was so traditional as to be accepted without complaint as a regular part of everyday life. When the Hebrews were drawn into this milieu, they were in fact not being discriminated against when blows were inflicted upon them, but were merely being integrated into the regular Egyptian work force and treated just like other workers. The "hardness" of the pharoah's heart (Exod. 7:22) had very much less to do either with Hebrew religion or the threats of Moses than with an understandable reluctance on his part to lose such an excellent body of workers such as the Hebrews, who at that time were reputed to be the best workers of metal in the ancient Near East. In the end, liberation came not principally as a relief from years of oppression, or, as we have seen, of normal manual work, but as the beginning of a far larger destiny that was to be quite independent of Egyptian control.

The liberation of the Israelites was thus a unique, nonrepeatable occurrence marked throughout by the direct attention of God to the situation. It is therefore entirely unsuitable for Third World and other theologians to use as a model of aspiration for future political deliverance from some such economic "oppressor" as the United States. As more than one commentator has observed, the true oppressor in Latin America which has held people in bondage for generations while they have been living among incredibly rich natural resources has been the political and economic value system, supported by the traditional national religion. Internal oppression in such countries could be relieved quickly were they to be organized along the lines of democratic capitalism, independent of religious control, and enabled to take a proper and dignified position in the world marketplace.

No Christian could support conscientiously any of the accompaniments of oppression, since he or she has been given a special freedom by receiving the truth of Christ's gospel (John 8:32). The ministry of the Christian in society is to relieve oppression and liberate the captives wherever and however possible (Luke 4:18). If society is to be prevented from falling into the hands of the unscrupulous and dictatorial, it is mandatory for Christians to become involved actively in all the processes of national life, not merely those related to voluntary social welfare, but in decisions at the highest political and military level, to ensure that freedom will be maintained and oppression removed from human society.

**OPTIMISM.** This is the expectation that in the end all things will turn out well. A variety of evils make optimism a difficult philosophy to hold: natural disasters such as earthquakes, hurricanes, drought, and the like are hard to square with it. Perhaps even worse are the moral failures of the race. This includes not only individual evils like crime and selfishness, but evils on the large scale: wars, pollution of the environment, widespread poverty, man's oppression of man, and the like.

In the face of such evils there are humanists who hold firmly to the view that people will ultimately learn to cooperate with one another for the good of all. Evil is seen as a mark of the childhood of mankind, which will vanish when maturity arrives. Sometimes this is put forward as "positive thinking." If we dwell on evil we multiply it, but if we direct our thoughts otherwise we have the power to rise above it. All such views founder on the fact that people so readily do what is wrong (the Christian doctrine of the Fall). This compulsion is not confined to the ignorant and immature. Indeed, the worst evils come from the sophisticated and the civilized. Human culture puts tools into their hands that enable them to engage in evil on a bigger scale by far than their less advantaged neighbors.

Despite all the evil and the suffering this world offers, it is hard to see how the Christian can be anything other than optimistic. For the believer, the ultimate truth is that "God is love" (1 John 4:8, 16). This whole creation was produced by a God whose nature is love. When people went astray in their sins, that loving God sent His Son to die on a cross, and so put their sins away. This is the heart of the Christian faith and not merely a peripheral teaching. Moreover, it is not to be understood as though God made provision for sins to be forgiven and then left us to our own devices. The Bible contains many promises of God's continuing presence with His people (Heb. 13:5). It assures us of the power there is in the gospel (1 Cor. 1:18) and of the indwelling of the Spirit of God in believers (Rom. 8:9; 1 Thess. 1:5). As for the problems with natural disasters, there will in due course be a new heaven and a new earth (Isa. 65:17; 66:22; Rev. 21:1). The optimism of the Christian is founded not on our power to do good, but on the conviction that God, who has begun a good work, will see it through to the end (Phil. 1:6).

L.M.

**ORDER.** The Latin word *ordo,* from which this term is derived directly, had almost as many meanings as its modern counterpart. A familiar ancient concept of lines or rows in series arose from farming, but was also applied to other areas of life that were conceived of organizationally. The interest that the human mind has in the fact of order seems to be one facet of the *imago dei*, or divine image, reflecting inadequately the perfect organizational ability of the One who created the cosmos and mankind.

In human society, order expresses itself in various forms. If community life is based upon a theory of social contract, regulating principles are immediately built into the situation by the general agreement of those involved to submit to certain restrictions on individual liberty for the benefit of the larger social unit. When leadership is involved in the implementing of such community living, the basis of government has been laid. At this stage it can begin to exercise what political scientists and others generally regard as its function, namely the control of behavior in the community. This can be accomplished by enacting and enforcing statutes that will ensure justice for the citizens and by affording a peaceful environment will protect their lives from the disruption and harm that would occur where there was no sense of law and order. The most ancient city-states of the Sumerian empire seem to have been participatory democracies, although some of them degenerated at times into dictatorships, due to political corruption.

Democratic institutions allow each citizen to participate under recognized conditions in the process of ordering the affairs of the state, and these conditions afford excellent opportunities for the believer to bring Christian influences to bear upon secular life. The New Testament requires the Christian to support the government in power, even though its policies may be unchristian and unethical in some areas, for the sake of order in society. The Christian therefore respects the governing authority, conforms to the rules for social order, pays the appropriate fiscal levies with as good a mind as possible, and also prays for those responsible for the ordering of national life (Mark 12:13-17; Rom. 13:1-7; 1 Tim. 2:1-2). Ethically and spiritually all these contributions to social order are good and acceptable in God's sight and should therefore form a prominent part of the believer's witness to Christ in contemporary society.

**ORDERS OF GOD.** This expression refers to the social structures that have been established by God. Luther recognized three such structures, or "orders": the home (including marriage, family, and business); civil government; and the church. Luther believed that every Christian should sense God's call, or "vocation," to a definite place in one or more of these social orders. Everyone shares in secular authority through his or her "office(s)."

Based upon the doctrine of the Fall (Gen. 3), the legislation of capital punishment of the Old Testament (Gen. 9:5-6; Exod. 21:12, 14, 22), and the affirmation of the secular "sword" in the New Testament (Luke 3:14; Rom. 13:1-7; 1 Pet.

2:13-17), Luther believed that civil government is necessary because of sin. But he taught that marriage, work, and property were part of the original order of creation, based upon the creation accounts in Genesis (Gen. 1:26-28; 2:15, 18-25). It is because of sin that all vocations have become distorted by self-interest. However, for the Christian, the meaning of vocation is redeemed and transformed. Every Christian is called to love as he has been loved; but for each, his or her particular calling provides the concrete means and direction for doing so (1 Cor. 4:7; 1 Pet. 4:8-10). Luther thus viewed the so-called "secular" vocations and skills as the gifts of God for fulfilling the love command (Matt. 22:39; Mark 12:31; Luke 10:27; 1 John 4:20-21). Like Brother Lawrence in the monastery kitchen, and Mother Teresa in the streets of Calcutta, the Christian is called by Christ to surrender self-interest and to make Christ and His kingdom known through love for others. Even unbelievers serve God unwittingly in their secular work, by contributing to the social order in which God provides multifarious temporal blessings and preserves a people and an environment for the proclamation of His Son as the Savior of the world.

**Bibliography:** Althaus, P., *The Ethics of Martin Luther* (1972); Brother Lawrence, *The Practice of the Presence of God* (1692/94); Thielicke, H., *Theological Ethics*, Vol. 1 (1979); Wingren, G., *Luther on Vocation* (1957).

See TWOFOLD REIGN OF GOD.

N.J.L.

**ORIGINAL SIN.** The doctrine of original sin attempts to frame a rationale for the universal tendency of mankind to sin, which comes from the depths of his being. Mankind is predisposed or biased to sin. This has been expressed in many theological, philosophical, and psychological forms, all of which come down to the concept of man's inevitable yet willful radical tendency to evil.

An important distinction is often drawn between actual sin and original sin, between sinning and the sinful nature that produces sinful behavior. Augustine epitomizes this in a famous confession: "those sins which I have committed, both against thee, and myself, yea, many and grievous offenses against others, over and above that bond of original sin, whereby we all die in Adam."

Historically, as Paul states in Romans 5:12-21, original sin is related to the Fall. Adam sinned and consequently mankind became universally sin-prone. Paul does not say how the transmission occurs, nor what is transmitted, only that through the one sin of the one man, Adam, all people have been affected. Their sinning by violating the moral law entails something more than personal imitation of Adam's sinning.

Spiritually this is expressed by Paul in Romans 7. By means of a deeply moving self-analysis,

Paul laments that he knows how he ought to behave but fails to do so. No good dwells within himself, he says (18) and then adds, "for I do not do the good I want, but the evil I do not want is what I do" (19). Why? It is the "sin which dwells in me" (20).

This apparent contradiction is the root of the theological problem of how to state this doctrine so as to reconcile inevitability and responsibility. We perceive that sinful acts to which we succumb are beneath moral behavior. Guilt sets in for the wrong done. Nevertheless, in the process of the sinning, we sense a moral obligation and the freedom at hand to avoid it. Experientially this paradox is regarded as a strong attestation to the reality of original sin and for the continuing need of divine grace to break its habit through the use of freedom for its proper ends.

Few recognize the practical social and political values of this doctrine in the history of Western Christendom. This doctrine is a pillar of democracy, because belief in the universal sinfulness of man has forced a recognition of the need to balance the use of power with means to eject those who abuse it.

Human behavior is pervasively sinful. It is impossible to assign responsibility individually for many of the conditions that prevail in the world. No single person has escaped having a sinful nature, and therefore every single person is in need of God's grace and salvation. As well, racial solidarity signifies that no individual escapes sin and that all men and women share in the trauma of humanity that is due to sin. We have a responsibility to change for good our inheritance, which works for evil both societally and racially.

**Bibliography:** Becker, E., *The Structure of Evil* (1968); Dubarle, A. M., *The Biblical Doctrine of Original Sin* (1967); Newbigin, L., *Sin and Salvation* (1956); Neibuhr, R., *The Nature and Destiny of Man* (1946).

S.J.M.

**ORPHANS.** Throughout history, it would appear, the destitution of orphans, rather than their lack of parents, is their primary qualification for pity and assistance. In Old Testament times such destitution could result just from having no father. Special commandments related specifically to the orphans' plight and that of widows (Exod. 22:22-24; Deut. 14:28-29; Isa. 1:17). Their care is also a mark of true New Testament religion (James 1:27), focusing on just one aspect of the biblical virtue of loving one's neighbor as oneself (Lev. 19:18; Luke 10:25-37). Scripture however, describes no institutional provision for orphans. Presumably extended families, neighbors, or congregations absorbed them as so often happens in rural communities today, for example in India.

Early Christianity followed the biblical pattern of caring for orphans. By the fourth century, however, the established church began, with minimal help from the state, to found refuges for all who could not care for themselves, including orphans. Orphanages became, in effect, feeder communities for monasteries, convents, and seminaries, and provided several popes.

Care of orphans is not limited to Christians and Jews. It is to be found in many primitive societies and other world religions such as Hinduism, Sikhism, and Islam. Aristotle urged the state to establish standards of orphan care and organize means of aid. In England it was not until Elizabeth I and her Poor Law, which contained special provisions for orphans, that the state took a major part in their care. This happened chiefly because monasteries, which had been doing such charitable work, were immobilized by Henry VIII. Brian Rodgers asserts that since 1601 more orphans have been cared for by the state than by all private charities put together.

A certain Captain Coram founded the first large orphan institution in Britain in 1739. Vincent de Paul had established one in Paris about a century earlier. These early foundling hospitals, overwhelmed by numbers, at times had a death rate approaching 80 per cent. Research reported by Reuel Howe suggests that lack of continuous physical human contact may have been part of the explanation.

Dr. Thomas Barnardo, an outstanding British nineteenth-century founder of orphanages, discovered what North American children's aid societies have confirmed, that boarding children with foster parents is not only the most financially efficient way of caring for orphans, but is in many ways best for their future life. He emigrated many orphans to Canada and Australia, suffering severe criticism for this action despite its overall beneficence. Dr. Barnardo's homes still exist in various countries. Their purpose is to give children an education, a trade, and a faith in Christ.

The best apparent solution for orphans is adoption. Some adoptions do break down but this is usually because of scars from early childhood abuse and rejection.

Current approaches to orphan care are many and varied. The biblical pattern of care by kin and neighbors seems still the most personal and humane way.

**Bibliography:** Beaudry, J., "Orphan in the Early Church," *New Catholic Encyclopedia* (1966); "Charity, Almsgiving," in Hastings, J., (ed.), *Encyclopedia of Religion and Ethics* (1911); Greenleaf, B. K., *Childhood Through the Ages* (1978); Howe, R. L., *Man's Need and God's Action* (1965); Rodgers, B., "Orphans," in MacQuarrier, J., (ed.), *A Dictionary of Christian Ethics* (1967); Wagner, G., *Barnardo* (1979).

D.N.P.

**OTHERWORLDLINESS.** This term expresses the tension evident throughout Scripture in the life of the believer, as he or she struggles to survive morally and spiritually in a world that is under a divine curse as the result of human sin. It is seen clearly in the life of the ancient Israelites as they lived under the provisions of the Sinai covenant. By the terms of that agreement they were required to be a kingdom of priests and a holy people (Exod. 19:6), living as a community in obedience to a provident God who had furnished them with a home among the peoples of the Levant.

Idyllic as this scene might appear to the casual reader, temptations to sin arose both from within the community, because selfishness and greed displaced holiness, and from outside it in the form of the seductive idolatry and immorality of the people with whom the Israelites had to deal. The history of the nation after the time of Joshua was blighted by repeated violations of the covenant ideals, and groups such as the Nazirites (Num. 6) and Rechabites (Jer. 35) were raised up by God to set a standard of "otherworldliness," which unfortunately proved to be of little avail.

The ministry of Jesus illustrated clearly the tensions in the mind of the Christian between the things of God and those of the world. In his own temptation Jesus resisted the lure of worldly power (Matt. 4:8-10; Luke 4:6-8) and encouraged his disciples to believe that he had overcome "the world" (John 16:33). This assurance was necessary because he was warning them that, as believers, they would encounter antagonism from the "ruler of this world" (John 12:31) and his followers.

As with the ancient Israelites, the Christian is required to be in this world but not of it, living in society but not being corrupted by it. Not everyone is able to accomplish this difficult feat, and historically people and groups have retreated into isolation to contemplate otherworldliness in an atmosphere of silence and prayer. However exemplary this activity may seem to be, it deprives society of the active presence of those very people who could demonstrate holiness within the context of daily life. More commendable are those Christians who in obedience to Christ live by the power of the Holy Spirit as becomes those preparing to be citizens of a heavenly realm while still in the midst of a fallen world.

# –P–

**PACEM IN TERRIS.** Peace on Earth (1963) is the second encyclical authored by John XXIII, the first being *Mater et Magistra* (1961). Both of these encyclicals address a world quite different from that of the encyclicals of Leo XII and Pius XI. The concern of these first encyclicals was limited largely to the condition of labor within the Western world. The encyclicals of John XXIII were global in outlook and more concerned about other types of relationships. Greater socialization and vastly improved communications had brought men and countries together in a way that was unprecedented. More intimate relations of this kind also brought questions of order among men, between men and their governments, between states, and finally within the world community. It was these issues that the encyclical addressed.

In dealing with order among mankind, the encyclical stressed the rights and duties approach. This was based on the truth that every individual is a person endowed with intelligence and free will, or made in the image and likeness of God. The dignity of the human person also stems from the fact of redemption by the blood of Christ. In this section the encyclical offers a lengthy but incomplete list of rights and duties and the corresponding obligations of others.

In its second section, the encyclical deals with the relation between individuals and the state or public authorities. The social nature of mankind calls for authority. It is the function of authority to promote the common good. Authority should fulfill this role by promoting personal rights and duties without favoritism or any kind of suppression.

The third section of the encyclical deals with the relations that should exist between states. They should be based on truth, justice, freedom, and solidarity. Since it is at the international level that peace is largely threatened, observing these demands will be essential to maintaining peace.

Finally, the encyclical discusses the relation of individuals and political communities to the world community. Since the latter has never been politically organized in any adequate way, we are at a disadvantage. But the encyclical recognizes the United Nations and the efforts it has made toward world community.

The encyclical makes reference to what is a very important principle in hierarchical relationships: the principle of subsidiarity. Pius XII had appealed to it in reference to the operation of the social order. In *Pacem in Terris* it has a role in regulating all relationships between individuals and states, smaller states and larger states, and so on. In its conclusion, the encyclical urges all Christians to promote these principles. Peace depends on their observance.

**Bibliography:** Bennett, J. C. and Niebuhr R., *Christianity and Crisis* (1963), XXIII, pp. 81–83; Murray, J., *Studies* (1963), LII, pp. 294–311; Sheerin, J., *Catholic World* (1963), CXCVII, pp. 148–51.

J.C.

**PACIFISM.** *Pacifism* and *pacifist* are early twentieth-century terms that originate from the traditional terms *to pacify* and *pacification*. Pacifism is the doctrine or belief that all wars and armed hostility are wrong and that all national and international disputes should be settled by peaceful means rather than by force. Some extend this doctrine to reject the use of any force or violence including self-defense and law enforcement.

Pacifism has been defined as enthusiasm for love, though critics hold that this ideal is left uncontextualized and is sometimes done to death by a thousand qualifications. Marxists identify love with economics. Liberation theology similarly identifies love with economics and politics. At times liberation theology writers advocate the use of force to achieve their ends, and thus are alienated from other Christian pacifists who also are absorbed with social issues. Critics of nontheological pacifism maintain that advocates of the doctrine frequently defer to social pressures and modify their views to suit current fancy.

Christian pacifism has many roots, the most prominent being the stance of the defenseless Christians in late medieval and Reformation times in Europe and Britain. Most Christian pacifists identify Christian pacifism with Christian nonresistance and take as their golden texts Matthew 5:9, 39 ("Blessed are the peacemakers....Do not resist one who is evil"), along with 1 Peter 2:21-23. Significant differences exist among pacifists as to the precise interpretation and application of these ideals.

The least rigorous pacifism is a generalized feeling that war is wrong without formulating specific injunctions as to what to do in particular cases. Moderate pacifists maintain that all war is wrong but often ignore or say nothing about violence in society, or about homicide such as abortion, euthanasia, family or paramour killing, or manslaughter of various kinds. Moderate pacifists express conflicting opinions about self-defense. Some vigorously defend the right to self-defense; others deny the right.

Strict pacifists reject any use of force and deny that killing is ever right but face the charge of advocating utopian withdrawal. On the one hand they acknowledge that the state is ordained by God to maintain justice and order in non-Christian society. On the other hand as Christians they decline to participate in the state's coercive activities on the ground that "the sword is outside the perfection of Christ." Critics allege that strict pacifists wrongly apply the person-to-person ethics of the Sermon on the Mount to the non-Christian civil sphere and that, failing to make it work, they then abdicate all secular social and civil relationships and responsibilities. This hiatus in the ethical responsibilities of the individual reflects a theological perspective in which an unbridgeable gulf is created between Old and New Testaments. Critics insist that Jesus did not reject Moses, only the distortion of the Mosaic law into loveless retribution (Matt. 5:38). Otherwise, what God commanded in the Old Testament is made morally contradictory to that which he gives in Christ. The Sermon on the Mount does not negate the validity of just civil government, nor national loyalty, nor the civil responsibility of the Christian (Rom. 13:1-7; 1 Pet. 2:13-17).

Many Christians feel apprehensive about the ambiguities of the solutions that pacifists have advocated and practiced. Is patience and resignation in the face of war or violence justified, especially when it may actually facilitate murder and genocide, further anarchy, and increase violence? Does absorption with nonresistance by pacifists result in failure to glorify the positive ideals and values of justice and a just and democratic state?

A damaging criticism of traditional pacifist groups and communes is their tendency to practice psychological coercion and psychological violence, which is a common characteristic of all closed and optionless societies. The Canadian Mennonite-Brethren novelist Rudy Wiebe has dramatically highlighted this issue in his several novels, especially *Peace Shall Destroy Many.*

If the state is divinely ordered, ought not the Christian to take his rightful place and accept his civil responsibilities to repress evil, to redress wrong and to maintain justice, even by force? Nevertheless, the burden of proof to justify the use of force is always on the one who uses force. In view of this the pacifist is often right. As much as pacifism conflicts with powerfully held moral convictions (for example, self-defense), nonresistance can be redemptive and may be the best solution in more instances than the critics of pacifism allow.

Nonviolent resistance is sometimes an acceptable way of bringing about change where structural injustice is present and some form of civilized protest is called for. However, this is a form of aggression which is not consistent in principle with the passivity of strict pacifism.

Most Christians believe that it is impossible to find an absolute fixed point between strict pacifism and anarchy. They hold that the use of force

or lethal force is rarely right and that if it is used an adequate moral statement must legitimize its use.

**Bibliography:** Buzzard, L. and Campbell, P., *Holy Disobedience* (1984); Cizik, R., *The High Cost of Indifference* (1984); Jesudasan, I., *A Gandhian Theology of Liberation* (1984); Lutz, C. P. and Folk, J. L., *Peace Ways* (1983).

S.J.M.

**PARENTHOOD.** The root of this English term is the Latin verb *pario*, meaning "to breed, beget, bring forth, bear," and was used consistently in Latin literature in both a literal and a metaphorical sense. Parenthood thus implies not merely the physical fact of producing offspring, but also of rearing them to be mature human beings.

The biblical tradition related the functions of parenthood to the institution of marriage, which united a man and a woman in a physical, emotional, and spiritual bond (Gen. 2:22-24), and furnished the appropriate environment for the procreation of children. The family unit thus became the cornerstone of all social configurations in the ancient world and has survived in this manner to the present, although with some modifications. For the Hebrews, the concept of parenthood outside the boundaries of marriage or a familial relationship constituted immorality. Two principal family structures existed in antiquity, namely the matriarchal, in which property and inheritance passed through the mother, and patriarchal, where descent and inheritance factors were traced through the male head of the household.

In Old Testament times the primary purpose of marriage was not companionship so much as the procreation of children, and any wife who could not produce offspring became an object of shame, pity, and ridicule. At an early period in Mesopotamian history a system was devised whereby barren wives gave their handmaids to their husbands as concubines so that offspring might be produced for the household. This tradition is reflected in the decision of Sarah to give her handmaid Hagar to Abraham as a concubine (Gen. 16:1-3).

Children were very highly valued in the ancient world for economic and other reasons, and the Hebrew poets lauded them as God's choice gifts (Ps. 127:3-5; 128:3). Jesus Christ maintained this attitude in his ministry and used their trust and obedience to illustrate the character mandatory for believers to exhibit (Matt. 18:1-4; Mark 9:36-37). Paul employed the concept of family to describe the larger divine household (Gal. 6:10; Eph. 2:19) and thereby maintained the consistency of the biblical family tradition.

The human infant is by far the most helpless of all young mammalian life and consequently requires an inordinate amount of care if it is to be nurtured successfully. The feeding habits of the individual child need to be attended to carefully, having regard to possible allergic reactions; and for the child to develop properly under normal circumstances the child must be spoken to much of the time he or she is awake. It is equally important for the infant to be held tightly and caressed so as to convey to the child a sense of physical and emotional security, played with frequently, and encouraged to crawl as soon as it shows an interest in that kind of mobility. No infant should be discouraged from periodic crying, since this is invaluable for developing the lungs. In this general connection it goes without saying that children should not be sedated merely to accommodate the convenience of the parents. From a child's earliest days he or she is able to appreciate the emotional impact of tender, loving care; and if the child is normal physically and mentally he or she will thrive in such an environment.

But parenthood can be attended by tragedy on occasions also, and if certain complications arise in pregnancy the expectation of a live birth can become increasingly remote. Expectant parents understandably grieve when a spontaneous abortion occurs, or when a fetus is born dead; but it has to be realized that the body's own interruption of what is one of the most basic of natural female processes carries with it a message for the parents and their family doctor alike. Equally distressing is the occasion when a baby is born in a badly deformed condition, or has some such genetic disability as mongolism (Down's syndrome). Babies with imperfectly formed hearts, livers, lungs, and other organs seldom survive for long unless their existence is protracted by artificial means, and their decease should be accepted in a mature manner as one of God's blessings in disguise to fallen, undeserving humanity. While Down's syndrome often presents a terrible burden for parents to bear, it is perhaps of some consolation for Christian parents to realize that such children exhibit an unusual awareness of the Lord's presence in their lives and that given appropriate spiritual instruction they can become devout and useful citizens.

The chief responsibility of Christian parenthood is the rearing of children in the knowledge and reverence of God, which is the beginning of all wisdom (Ps. 111:10). This is achieved most satisfactorily by example and precept, in which both parents share in teaching a child to pray and instructing him or her in Bible stories and other forms of Christian education. Above all, Christian parents should be present with their children as much as possible in the formative years, even if this means sacrificing pleasure or selfish ambition, so that the young family members may develop emotional as well as physical security as they grow into society.

The unity of family life for Christians must be based upon biblical, ethical, and spiritual teaching, with Christ established firmly as the head of the household and all the members subject to his will. By this means the temptations of the world, the flesh, and the devil can be resisted as the child grows toward maturity, and an opportunity can be afforded for the young as well as the old to witness to Christian family values in secular society that so frequently stands in desperate need of the kind of parenthood that the Christian faith upholds.

**PATIENCE.** This term is used to describe the calm toleration of such conditions as discomfort, anguish, or suffering, or the attitude of one who exercises restraint under provocation. It is an emotional quality that is marked by a degree of endurance and determination, with the objective of maintaining personal equanimity for as long as is necessary. This restraint is illustrated clearly in Exodus 34:6, where in a passage of propositionally revealed truth God announces himself as a patient (KJV "longsuffering") being. It was only because of this virtue in the divine character that the apostate and disobedient Israelites were saved from destruction. God's patience with them was demonstrated continuously in the pre-exilic period by his sending prophets who in various ways proclaimed the law and sought to recall an idolatrous and carnal nation to the spiritual traditions of the Sinai covenant. When finally even God could be no longer patient with his corrupted people, the covenant curses that were part of the Sinai agreement (Deut. 23:15-68) for violating the sacred oath at Sinai (Exod. 24:7) came upon the northern and southern kingdoms.

The concept of patience was prominent in the teachings of Jesus, as illustrated in the parable of the unforgiving debtor (Matt. 18:23-30), whose brusque, intolerant attitude failed to exemplify God's patience toward his wayward people. In times of tribulation patience would constitute a saving grace (Luke 21:19), the Greek term *hupomone* being used of someone whose convictions remain steadfast when on trial. Paul appealed continually for this kind of patience to be manifested in Christian living (Rom. 5:4; 1 Tim. 6:11; Titus 2:2).

Yet another Greek word for patience, *makrothumia*, occurs in the letters of Paul and Peter. It is quite properly translated "longsuffering" in the King James Version, being used to describe the richness of God's nature (Rom. 2:4), the spirit of endurance that helped to sustain Paul himself (2 Cor. 6:6), and the nature of one element of the believer's character (Eph. 4:2). It is a manifestly Christian virtue which all believers must cultivate (Col. 1:11; 3:12) as they sow the seed of the gospel and then await its growth, or when they labor under discouragement or active persecution (James 5:7-11).

See RESIGNATION.

**PATRIOTISM.** Coming from a Latin root *pater*, "father," patriotism is zeal or enthusiasm for the fatherland, that is, the country of one's birth or adoption. This type of fervor is based upon the acquired traditions of the native land, but also in some circumstances on the expectations that the individual citizen may cherish for the future when, for example, a former colony gains its political and economic independence. The ardor that is engendered by such a prospect may induce the individual to take up arms in defense of his country, or to indulge in considerable personal sacrifice to ensure the successful completion of some project that would bring profound benefit to his or her fellow citizens.

National pride is at least as old as the ziggurats or staged temple-towers of ancient Mesopotamia, which proclaimed magnificently the architectural skills of the builders for all to see. The successive empires of Near Eastern antiquity seemed bent upon outstripping their predecessors in achievements and splendor, and this is seen particularly in the instance of Nebuchadnezzar II (605-562 B.C.). Having reconstructed and extended the ancient city of Babylon to unprecedented proportions, he reflected with pride upon his achievements shortly before experiencing mental illness (Dan. 4:30). Archeological reconstructions have shown that Babylon was indeed a magnificent capital city and one that could readily have aroused national pride. Any enthusiastic citizen could therefore be expected to rally to its defense should danger threaten.

Since the Christian is also a citizen, obeying lawful authority and paying taxes (Matt. 22:21; Rom. 13:1-7), it is legitimate for him or her to exhibit enthusiasm for the homeland, especially where its influence in world society warrants such an attitude. On this basis Paul could speak with guarded enthusiasm about the reputation of his native city (Acts 21:39). Yet he was also aware that Christ's kingdom was of an otherworldly character and that the primary objective of Christian witness in the world was to evangelize with a view to fulfilling the concept of that kingdom, and not merely promoting national interests.

Devotion to one's country is a noble ideal, and if Christ is firmly enthroned in the individual's life it is thoroughly compatible with discipleship. Accordingly the Christian will be ready to serve his or her country fruitfully in peacetime and when hostilities threaten will be ready to defend the best interests of national life in whatever manner is appropriate. But because of the believer's prime loyalty to Christ, the brash, blustering form of patriotism known vulgarly as "jingoism" will be discarded as being an unseemly attitude for the believer to adopt. The same will be true of a melancholy aphorism attributed to Samuel Johnson: "Patriotism is the last refuge of a scoundrel."

See LOYALTY; NATIONALISM.

**PAULINE PRIVILEGE.** This is the title that has been given to a passage of Scripture in which Paul, writing to the Corinthian church, gives his views on certain aspects of marriage (1 Cor. 7:10-15) in a manner which he states clearly as

his own, and not the Lord's. He is speaking to a situation in which an unbeliever is married to a believer. He maintains that as long as there is no conflict in the relationship, the marriage should remain intact, since the unbeliever would be sanctified by the believing spouse. If, however, the unbeliever chooses to abandon the Christian partner, he or she is free to do so. Then Paul adds, "A brother or a sister is not under bondage (*ou dedoulotai*) in such things (1 Cor. 7:15, NKJV).

The concluding verse has been used by some Roman Catholics and Protestants as a means of avoiding the stigma of adultery which Christ laid upon the remarriage of divorced persons while the spouse was still alive (Mark 10:11-12). Based upon this comment of Paul, they claim that they have the "privilege" of remarriage after divorce without falling under the condemnation of adultery, and accordingly many persons have grasped the opportunity of exercising the "Pauline privilege."

Critics of this position have not been slow in pointing out that Paul's advice is, by his own admission, personal and not inspired by the Lord. Since his recommendation conflicts clearly with what is the earliest, unglossed form of Christ's teaching on the subject (Mark 10:11-12; Matt. 19:9), his remarks raise the question as to whether in fact the apparently emphatic teaching of Christ in Mark's Gospel is absolute or only relative. If the former, then Paul is introducing "another gospel" into the ethics and morals of marriage by permitting remarriage after divorce from a living spouse. If the latter, then relativity could apply to other difficult moral and spiritual issues, and with the introduction of the concept of "special cases" Paul could even find himself proclaiming universalism instead of the exclusive nature of eternal salvation in Christ.

Other critics have questioned the nature of the "unbelief" of the spouse and have wondered how such a concept can possibly apply to Christians, who, while honoring the same Lord, still divorce each other and remarry. Aside from specific religious groups such as Jews, Moslems, Buddhists, and the like, most people would be offended if they were to be dismissed as non-Christian whatever the quality of their lives.

It seems clear that Paul's understanding of unbelief involved a rejection of the Christian faith in favor of the contemporary pagan deities, and this raises the real question as to whether Paul's advice to the Corinthian Christians has any relevance at all to modern Christian life. Paul may well have realized the delicate position in which his ruminations placed him, because at the end of the chapter in which the "privilege" section occurs he returns to the theme of remarriage, this time in terms of a widow. Any plans for marriage are perfectly legitimate in such an instance, he avers, but "only in the Lord" (1 Cor. 7:39). Did he mean by this remark the limitations set by Christ in His teachings, which in any event would have no bearing on a widow wishing to remarry unless the proposed spouse was himself divorced, or was he also including his own, uninspired comments which modified Christ's utterance significantly? In the latter event, how could something different from Christ's teachings still be "in the Lord"?

The question as to what is meant by being "under bondage" is important for an understanding of the position of those Corinthians parted from their spouses through pagan unbelief. According to the circumstances outlined by Paul, the marriage bond has been disrupted, and the phrase *under bondage* would therefore seem to mean that the believing spouse is not under any form of subjection to the unbeliever, such as feeling an obligation to dissuade the dissident one from departing. While Paul is sanctioning separation, he never advocates that the believer should seek a divorce or even desire one. While the Christian should therefore be reconciled to separation or divorce should they occur, Paul nowhere gives such a person the freedom to remarry, since this would then constitute an adulterous union.

For those persons who wish to dispose of their current spouses in the hope of uniting with a more acceptable substitute, the "Pauline privilege" may seem a convenient way of securing that objective and possibly successive ones if the proposed substitute proves to be unacceptable. But Christians who regard their marriage vows as a covenant sworn before God will be hesitant to break them, no matter what the conditions may be, following Paul's injunctions (1 Cor. 7:10-17). In the event that marital conditions are intolerable, the couple may separate without further intent to remarry, so as to remain in accordance with Christ's teachings on monogamy.

**Bibliography:** Heth, W. A. and Wenham, G. J., *Jesus and Divorce* (1985).

See FORNICATION; MARRIAGE.

**PEACE AND WAR.** The word *peace* is derived from the Latin *pax*, which carried the same general meanings as the English word. Peace in a political sense indicates a state of affairs that is characterized by a lack of internal or external violence or conflict. This condition may have been arrived at as the result of vanquishing an enemy or entering into a covenant of nonaggression with neighboring peoples, while internal peace is the normal consequence of order and good government. In a metaphorical sense the Romans used *pax* to describe the right relations that ensued in the absence of civil or international strife and, in a still more derived sense, of good will, permission, and graceful concourse. The term was also used as an interjection, a greeting, or a farewell, as is also the case today in ecclesiastical circles. Finally, in *pax* the Romans found an apt term to describe such calmness and serenity of spirit as their way of life permitted.

The term *war* is apparently of Teutonic origin and bears no linguistic semblance to the Latin word *bellum*, "conflict, war." While the Romans used this word both of local conflicts and larger military campaigns, they were careful to modify the noun in cases where careful planning had preceded the enterprise. Thus they could speak of *iustum bellum* to describe a fully fledged military offensive that had been entered upon with the formality due to such an occasion.

The aggressive nature of *homo sapiens* became evident at an early period of history (Gen. 4:8, 23). The Sumerians of southern Mesopotamia were a small-statured but highly militant people who inhabited about a dozen city-states that seemed to prey regularly upon one another. Sir Leonard Woolley recovered from a large burial pit at Ur one of the most beautiful and meaningful artifacts to have come from Sumerian culture. It comprised a mosaic panel which, when restored, depicted the activities of peacetime on one side, and the accoutrements of war on the other. Quite aside from the antiquarian value of this so-called Standard of Ur for furnishing information about lifestyles at Ur in the third millennium B.C., the mosaic panel has a richer significance. The Sumerians had devised a literary technique by which they employed opposite concepts linked in pairs to describe totality. Thus the Standard was not just depicting peace and war as separate entities, but by putting them together on one panel was describing the totality of life at Ur. The aggressiveness of the Sumerians was matched subsequently by that of the Babylonians and Assyrians, and in Old Testament times military violence was a regular feature of life.

For the Hebrews the word *shalom* carried much the same range of meaning as the Latin *pax*, except that it was also used of soundness, wholeness, and health. It could convey a greeting (Gen. 29:6) or a dismissal (1 Sam. 1:17), a sacrificial peace offering (Exod. 24:5), a state of national or personal equanimity, or, more seriously, a misrepresentation of the true state of affairs (Jer. 6:14; 8:11). Despite the natural desire of all for peace (Mic. 4:4), the tendency in Near Eastern antiquity was for nations to be continually at war with one another. Mountain peoples and nomadic Semitic tribesmen were particularly menacing and aggressive and even presented problems of defense for some large settled locations in northern Mesopotamia by the periodic raids which they launched.

As contrasted with these rather desultory attacks, the *iustum bellum* of the later Romans had its counterpart in the Near Eastern concept of "holy war." This signified that the military conflict was not merely between peoples, but between the gods of those nations. Thus when one group conquered another, it was deemed to be a victory of a god over his opponents; and the human participants merely assisted in the process.

War was organized according to certain well-understood procedures in antiquity. An aggressor would give a besieged city an opportunity to surrender, on the understanding that if this occurred, human life would not be taken. If the besieged citizens refused and their city was taken subsequently, they could expect no mercy. When in the days of Joshua the Hebrews placed a city under the ban (*herem*), it meant that nothing would be spared once the city was overthrown. Ambushes and night attacks were infrequent, and fighting normally only took place during the hours of sunlight. On those occasions when people were taken prisoner, the women were sometimes brutalized or mutilated and commonly were stripped of their clothing in order to shame them. Men and women who were enslaved had little hope of ever regaining their freedom if they were transported to distant territories by their captors.

Human life was unfortunately cheap in the ancient Near East, and victorious armies made this abundantly clear to their unhappy captors. The Hebrews were given explicit instructions about the humane treatment of captive women whom they wished to marry (Deut. 21:10-14), which contrasted forcibly with the callousness and brutality of other nations toward female captives. The prospect of war in antiquity was therefore horrifying, and a land bridge such as Palestine was by definition subject to the depredations of foreign armies that were in transition to other destinations.

In the Old Testament God generally used warfare as a means of establishing his people in their land and punishing their enemies. It was not meant for purposes of aggrandizement, however; and David seems to have come under a rebuke for unnecessary killing (1 Chron. 22:8; 28:3). By tradition the Hebrews were not a militaristic people, and being semi-nomadic until the settlement period under Joshua they were ill-instructed in matters of military life and technology. David was conservative in his approach to weaponry, since he did not appear to have possessed the compound Asiatic bow, with its greatly extended range of fire, nor the iron-fitted, horse-drawn chariots of Hittite design. Even after the settlement in Palestine, the Hebrews were dependent for a considerable time upon the Philistine blacksmiths for supplies of weapons, and it was only during the reign of Solomon that the technological deficit was redressed and that at a time when Philistine power was in decline.

During the New Testament period Palestine was firmly in the grip of the occupying Roman power. One out of every two persons in the empire was a slave, and many fanatical groups in Judea sought to incite rebellion against Rome. Had Christ presented himself as a potential conquering king instead of God's Messiah, he would have had an immediate and enthusiastic following of political dissidents. But as against those who envisaged him in that capacity (John 6:15), he made it clear to them and to others that his kingdom was not of this world (John 18:36). He was indeed the peaceful prince (Isa. 9:6) who rode into Jerusalem just before his arrest and trial on a donkey, a symbol of peace and domesticity.

Jesus commended the peacemakers (Matt. 5:9) and promised to give peace (*eirene*) to his followers of a kind that the world could not offer (John 14:27). Peter acknowledged that Jesus preached God's peaceful word, and Paul boldly described the Savior as "our peace" (Eph. 2:14) because his atonement had reconciled man to God. Several of Paul's letters commence with a salutation of peace from God and Christ (Phil. 1:2; 1 Tim. 1:2) and include the prayer that divine peace would keep the hearts and minds of the believers (Phil. 4:7).

In an age that is oppressed by the thought of impending military catastrophe and finds peoples' hearts failing them for fear of what may transpire in the immediate future (Luke 21:26), the Christian is in a paramount position to witness to the peace that alone has eternal value. When Jesus is King and Lord of our lives, his peace rules in our hearts; and even though we may find ourselves in the midst of oppression and turmoil, war and conflict, he gives us that blessed assurance of eternal life with him when he shall have conquered all principalities and powers and is enthroned victorious as King and Lord of all.

**PEACE, SPIRITUAL.** This is that of which Jesus spoke when He said to His disciples during Holy Week: "Peace I leave with you; my peace I give to you" (John 14:27). This peace that comes through, in, from, by, and because of Jesus may be looked at from three angles, each of which has moral implications:

1. Peace as the absence of hostility between man and God as a result of the sacrificial death of Jesus (Col. 1:20). Instead of wrath from heaven, there is friendship for those who are in Christ. For the sinner who believes, there is a positive relationship with the Father as the one who forgives sin, cancels debt, justifies, and adopts into His redeemed family (Rom. 5:1; 8:1). The moral consequences of this relationship include a clear conscience that can function in the way God intended (2 Cor. 1:12; Heb. 10:22), freedom from the guilt and power of sin, and freedom to be God's child in practice (Gal. 5:1, 13).

2. Peace as a condition of the human heart resulting from the work of regeneration and the abiding presence of the Holy Spirit (John 14—16). Negatively this means the absence of guilt, anxiety, fear, and depression; positively, the presence of a deep conviction of God's love and a sense of internal harmony and quietness of spirit. This peace is a fruit of the Spirit (Gal. 5:22) and can be so deep and profound as to pass understanding (Phil. 4:7). The moral implications of such internal peace include a delight in God and His ways and a desire and determination to serve Him and obey His commandments, loving both Him and one's neighbor (Rom. 8:6; 14:17; Gal. 6:16).

3. Peace as the quality of relationships within a

community of believers, who, because of their relationship to God and because of the presence of the Holy Spirit, enjoy an absence of personal hostility and ill will, and a desire and intention to do the best, one for another (John 20:19, 21, 26). By His atonement, Jesus has not only reconciled men to God, but also has reconciled them one to another, removing old divisions (Eph. 2:14). In fact, He has created a new person (Eph. 2:15) who is to be above all racial, class, income, and age divisions. Thus, the peace of God through Jesus Christ in the power of the Holy Spirit is to create a community in which "there is neither Jew nor Greek, slave nor free, male nor female," but new persons created in the image of Jesus (Gal. 3:28). Because of the moral implications of this peace, the apostles urged the churches to put into practice this reality and really and truly to live at peace (2 Cor. 13:11; Col. 3:15; 1 Thess. 5:13). Thus, true believers are genuine peacemakers (Matt. 5:9).

The nature of this peace from God through Jesus is the peace of the kingdom of God. Thus, it can never be the peace for which nations and secular communities aim. Those in whom this peace is found, however, will desire to see the arrival of civil and international peace, which is good relationships between nations and the absence of war.

P.T.

**PENANCE.** Coming from the Greek term *poine*, "penalty" (Latin *poena*), this spiritual discipline is regarded as a sacrament in Roman Catholic and Eastern Orthodox theology. Originating in the postapostolic period, it was intended to chastise those members of the church who were guilty of grave moral offenses such as apostasy and sexual impurity. Offenders had to submit to a lengthy public regimen and could not be admitted to it a second time. From the fifth century penance became a private affair following confession to a priest and was elevated to a sacramental level by Peter Lombard (ca. 1100-1160).

This doctrine was reaffirmed at the Council of Trent (1545-63) over the objections of reforming Protestants, who attacked the concept of absolution by a priest. Luther in particular protested against the abuses that had arisen in the Roman Church, particularly the sale of indulgences, and opposed the general concept of penance by declaring the doctrine of justification by faith.

In current usage the penitent sinner has to exhibit contrition, confession, and some form of satisfaction for sin before the priest can pronounce absolution. Despite all these safeguards the practice is still open to abuse.

James counseled Christians to pray for healing by approaching God in faith and confessing their sins one to another (James 5:15-16), but makes no suggestion that a mediating priest should pronounce forgiveness, since only God can forgive sins (Mark 2:7; Luke 5:21).

**PENITENCE.** Coming from a Latin verb *paenitio*, "to be sorry, regret," penance describes the emotional reaction of an individual who exhibits contrition or repentance for sin. The Greek verb *metanoeo*, "to repent," has the sense of the Hebrew verb *shub*, "to turn back" (Ezek. 14:6; 18:30), but along with the implied change of mind there is the sense of remorse or regret. These elements are present in the teachings of John the Baptist and Jesus (Mark 1:15; 6:12; Luke 10:13). True penitence involves three components, namely sorrow for sin, a recognition that it is a contravention of God's morality, and a solution to forsake the way of sin and death. When the penitent sinner comes for the first time to Christ in faith and accepts Jesus as Savior and Lord, the experience is known as conversion, or spiritual rebirth, which is mandatory for eternal life in the kingdom of God (Matt. 18:3). Penitence should not be confused with the Roman Catholic sacrament of penance, even though some Roman Catholic translators render the gospel injunction *repent* by the phrase *do penance*.

**PERFECTIONISM.** As a theological doctrine, this is the claim that by the grace of God, Christians can be completely delivered from sin and made perfect in love within the present life. Such a claim, however, is very much a minority position. Characteristically, as the Christian church has reflected on the meaning of Scripture, the standards of perfection, the subtlety of sin, and the lives of Christians, it has concluded that moral and spiritual perfection is not attainable in this life. Along with the apostle Paul, the Christian community typically confesses, "Not that I...am already perfect...but I press on to make it my own, because Christ Jesus has made me his own" (Phil. 3:12).

As a moral doctrine, perfectionism is the absolute rejection of evil means in the pursuit of good ends, coupled with a strict construal of what constitutes evil means. Thus the perfectionist rejects as morally unacceptable the use of less-than-perfect means, even in extreme circumstances, to gain an end. In some cases, most Christians (and others) may have judged the necessity of circumstances to demand their use. For example, the perfectionist rejects the use of all lethal force, judging such to always be incompatible with the divine call to love our neighbor as we love ourselves. Therefore, we are not to kill another human being, even as the only means to save innocent life from the murderous assaults of an unjust aggressor. This stance is taken even at times when it is judged that the use of lethal force may actually serve to reduce the overall amount of lethal force in the world. In defense of an absolute ban on lethal force, the empirical claim is sometimes made that the use of force to stop force only increases the amount of force because of various reactions and counter reactions that its use sets in motion. What is said of lethal force is also said about the use of any force, lethal or not, as well as about a range of other less-than-perfect means. Lying, for example, is rejected even in extreme circumstances where it, too, might save innocent lives. To be a faithful Christian, according to such a view, is to renounce the use of evil means totally in response to the counsels of perfection found in the Gospels, especially, the admonition not to resist evil (Matt. 5:38-41). Perfectionists often feel impelled to reject social and political involvement because such involvement, if it is to be effective, must include the use of imperfect means, especially, the threat of force and the use of force.

Those who dissent from perfectionist views often suggest that: (a) the use of coercion to control those who violate the rights of others is not itself an evil; (b) to tolerate violence and the violation of rights passively, as the perfectionist urges, is to be responsible for the ensuing evil, since we are accountable for what we allow to happen as well as what we ourselves do; and (c) the counsel "not to resist evil" is not intended as advice applicable to the public sphere of law and order, but is a rejection of personal revenge.

The perfectionist raises significant questions for the Christian community. If we reject perfectionism, then what limitations do we place on the means used to achieve good ends, personal or public? Further, are we in fact responsible for all the consequences of our failure to act to prevent evil? Finally, is there a point prior to our doing everything we can do to prevent evil where we are to commit the course of events to the sovereignty of God and not take action ourselves?

**Bibliography:** Ellul, J., *Violence: Reflections from a Christian Perspective* (1969); Yoder, J. H., *The Politics of Jesus* (1972).

See JUSTIFICATION AND ETHICS; PACIFISM.

R.W.

**PERJURY.** This term, based on the Latin word *iuro*, "to swear, take an oath," describes false statements or untrue evidence given under oath in a court of law. Inasmuch as it constitutes deliberate deception, it falls under the condemnation of the ninth commandment (Exod. 20:16), which expressly forbids false testimony against one's neighbor. What makes perjury particularly serious is that the lying is intentional and does not proceed from ignorance of the situation. The obligation of a witness to make true statements under oath has been a cardinal tenet of legal proceedings since Sumerian times; and if perjury is not penalized heavily, the entire system of justice fails.

Lying is regarded as a sin in Scripture (Ps. 59:12; Isa. 59:13) because it is in the nature of falseness and as such is the diametric opposite of truth as revealed in God's nature. Perjury is the instrument of Satan, the father of lies (John 8:44) and strikes at the very heart of law and order in society. By definition it will be abhorrent to all Christians, who are bidden to speak the truth with their neighbors (Eph. 4:25).

**PERSECUTION.** This term usually refers to unmerited suffering inflicted on an individual or a group by a person or persons in a place of power. Racial minorities, for example, have often been the objects of persecution on account of their race. People have sometimes had to suffer for no better reason than the color of their skin. Persecution may result from the official attitude of governing authorities, or it may stem from the unreasoning hostility of maddened crowds. It may take the mild form of insult or minor suffering, or it may mean forfeiture of goods, imprisonment, torture, and even death.

While the term may be employed in a wide variety of situations, its most characteristic use is for religious persecution. An individual or group may manipulate the mechanism of persecution against what it sees as a wrong opinion or a wrong religion and aim to eradicate the error, either by conversion or by execution. This can be done from wholly unworthy motives. The persecutors may not hold firmly to any view of their own, but may persecute because they see the opportunity of confiscating the goods of the persecuted, or of ridding themselves of personal enemies.

But persecution can also be the outworking of deeply and sincerely held views. The authorities may be genuinely pious people, who hold such firm views that they can brook no other opinion. They may also see the view they are opposing as so evil, either in itself or in its consequences, that its adherents must be compelled to abandon it. The infliction of suffering becomes, in their eyes, a legitimate means of securing the desired end. Truth must be forwarded no matter what the cost. They see the immortal souls of the persecuted as imperiled by their pernicious doctrines. For their own good, they must be constrained to abandon them. If in the end they will not budge, then it seems better to the persecutors that they should die. At least their deaths will be a warning to others.

The persecution of the people of God goes back a long way. The Jews, for example, were persecuted by Antiochus Epiphanes when that monarch made a determined effort to make them renounce their religion. The Jews themselves, however, have not been guiltless. They sometimes persecuted the prophets (Matt. 5:12; Acts 7:52), and they persecuted the Christ (Matt. 27:18; John 5:16). Jesus warned His followers that this would be their lot (John 15:20; 16:33), and the case of Stephen speedily showed that this was no idle warning (Acts 7:54-60). Paul also experienced persecution (Acts 13:45; 2 Cor. 11:23-27). In due course, the Roman emperors launched serious persecutions against the early church, such as that under Nero.

It is one of the sad features of the history of the Christian church that the followers of Christ have also not been guiltless. Orthodox, Roman Catholics, and Protestants have all at times been so sure of the rightness of their position, and so out of harmony with the Spirit of Christ, that they have used positions of power as the means of coercing others.

In the light of this unfortunate aspect of history it is important to work for better understanding and wider tolerance. It is one of the melancholy aspects of the modern world that religious persecution continues, sometimes at the hands of godless totalitarian states, sometimes from strongly religious motives, and sometimes because lawless men engage in it. In the light of the teaching of Scripture, Christians can expect no less. But that same Scripture teaches them to counter hostility with love.

L.M.

**PESSIMISM.** This term originated with the Latin word *malus*, "bad," of which it is the superlative form, *pessimus*, "worst." A person who exhibits pessimism, therefore, is someone who adopts a negative, if not the worst possible view of the outcome of events, whether of a personal nature or otherwise. This is accomplished by discounting any possible influences of a positive character and emphasizing instead the prospect of impending disaster.

As a psychological phenomenon pessimism can be relative as much as absolute. Many Christians could be considered ontological pessimists, judging from the reflections that they make in speech and in writing about the depravity of human nature and society in general. Paul even gave this attitude a cosmological perspective when he noted the agony under which all of creation was groaning (Rom. 8:22), and he was by no means the first thinker to arrive at this conclusion, having been anticipated in secular society by the philosophies of the Atomists Democritus and Leucippus, the Stoics, Epicurus, and the Skeptics. But the pessimism that Christians may hold in connection with the world and society is by no means absolute, for it is tempered by the realization that in Christ old things have passed away and all things have become new (2 Cor. 5:17). The Christian is also aware that the world is under God's curse because of human disobedience (Gen. 3:17), yet despite this the final assessment of human values (Matt. 25:31-32) will be followed by a new cosmos (Rev. 21:1).

A degree of pessimism is common in the experience of most persons when they review their lives and contemplate with embarrassment and regret the blatant mistakes and lost opportunities of the past. But mentally healthy individuals are not obsessed by such thoughts, regarding them instead as debit entries in the person's balance sheet. Only in certain mental diseases does pessimism assume dominant proportions and can present serious problems for the therapist. The depressive psychotic, for example, is a pathological pessimist who finds it difficult if not absolutely impossible to entertain optimistic concepts.

An induced form of pessimism is encountered in such thinkers as Schopenhauer, who could see nothing positive at all about life and experience, and felt that our world was the worst possible of its kind. Views of this sort are enshrined to varying degrees in existentialism and nihilism, although the sincerity of some of the utterances from these sources may well be questioned.

The Christian can and must be optimistic when realizing that his or her faith is grounded upon the One who said, "Be of good cheer, I have overcome the world" (John 16:33). The presence of Christ's saving grace in the individual's life constitutes the hope of future glory (Col. 1:27). Probably the best scriptural antidote to pessimism is the assurance that all things work together for good to those who love God (Rom. 8:28).

**PHARISAISM, ETHICS OF.** The name *Pharisee* refers to a scholarly group in Judaism who were influential in the period from approximately 70 B.C. to A.D. 150.

They were characterized by a strong knowledge of the Hebrew Bible, by their methods and techniques of interpreting the Hebrew Bible (sometimes referred to as "oral law"), and by an active theology that included speculation on such topics as afterlife and the resurrection of the dead. Unfortunately, the Pharisees have sometimes been described by outsiders as hypocrites and legalists. This estimation, however, is not appropriate to Pharisaism once one examines the group in detail. The beliefs and practices of the ancient Pharisees ultimately set the tone for rabbinic teachings that directed Judaism from the second century A.D. to the present.

The first principle of Pharisaic ethics was a competent and full knowledge of the Hebrew Bible. The spoken language of the day was either Aramaic or Greek, so the Pharisees were skilled in at least two and sometimes three languages. Josephus, a Jewish historian of the first century, tells us that the Pharisees were considered to be the most accurate interpreters of biblical law, a skill resting on the knowledge of sacred Scriptures (*Jewish War*, II. xiii. 14). The Pharisees believed that Scripture was the source whereby both the individual and the community should define themselves. They also believed that a moral God had revealed His character and His expectations for humanity in the sacred texts. The commandments contained therein not only gave direction for the Jewish religious expression, but they also included the primary source for knowing ultimate truth, morality, and the natural order of things.

As a group or school within ancient Judaism, the Pharisees placed specific emphasis on the "reasonableness" and "accessibility" of Scripture as a source for ethical issues—whether it included the proper response to God or dealings on the human plane. Scripture had to do with both dimensions, and it was human responsibility to respond to the revelation of God by understanding what was meant to be accessible and purposeful.

The particularism of the Pharisees was that, although ancient Scripture was divine revelation, it was only one part of the revelation. At Sinai, there was a twofold revelation: a written part known to all and an oral part preserved by Moses, the prophets, and the heroes of ancient Judaism. The dual form of revelation ultimately became the possession of the Pharisees.

Although Pharisaic ethics are complex, their most lasting impact was the formulation of an open-ended process of exploring, reading into, and giving significance to every element of biblical teaching. They were responsible for the beginning of an ethical process rather than an ethical conclusion. Piety was the endless search for the appropriate understanding of God's revelation in Scripture. The act of studying, memorizing, and commenting on the sacred text was holy, allowing Scripture to assume a central role in the religious orientation of Judaism that had not existed before the era of the Pharisees.

**Bibliography:** Goldin, J., *The Jewish Expression* (1970); Heschel, A. J., *God in Search of Man: A Philosophy of Judaism* (1956); Kadushin, M., *Worship and Ethics* (1964); Neusner, J., *From Politics to Piety: The Emergence of Pharisaic Judaism* (1973); *Ibid.*, *The Rabbinic Traditions about the Pharisees before 70* (3 vols., 1971).

See JEWISH ETHICS; OLD TESTAMENT ETHICS.

W.O.M.

**PHILANTHROPY.** A combination of two Greek words, *philos*, "love," and *anthropos*, "mankind," this term describes the practice of acting in love or affection toward humanity. Philanthropy sometimes assumes large proportions, making it distinctive as an act of charity even though the responsible agent may wish to remain anonymous. Philanthropic foundations of this kind have been of immense benefit to religion and culture alike and often continue their benefits long after the death of the founding philanthropist.

The love of humanity was an important concept in the life of ancient Israel and was made specific by the injunction to love one's neighbor as oneself (Lev. 19:18). Such charity, however, was restricted to the members of the covenant community or those who associated themselves with it.

In the teachings of Jesus, Christians were given a broader concept of the ancient Levitical injunction by being made aware that humanity was not just coextensive with Judaism, but included people of other backgrounds also (Luke 10:36-37). The Christian is required to give to those who ask for assistance (Matt. 5:42) and to lend without any expectation of repayment (Luke 6:30).

Historically, Christians have been at the forefront in philanthropic works, ranging from the founding of the earliest hospitals to the abolition of slavery, the ameliorating of oppressive conditions in society, and the promoting of democratic ideals. The Christian ministers in this way because Christ has taught that His followers have an obligation of philanthropic witness to society (Matt. 25:34-45) which must be performed as unto Him.

See CHARITY, WORKS OF.

**PIETISM.** In popular understanding, Pietism represents a form of religion that is world-denying, dreamy, and other-worldly. However, the history of Pietism does not completely support this notion.

Pietism as a movement arose in the seventeenth and eighteenth centuries as a protest against the narrowness and rigidity of Protestant scholasticism. The leader of the Pietist movement was a German teacher, Philipp Spener (1635-1705). According to his teaching, the Christian should reject the worldliness of society, basing his spirituality upon the Bible. The church should pay greater heed to preaching and to the importance of good works. Spener influenced A. H. Franke, who developed significantly the course of Pietism. Franke had a great burden for the poor of Halle, and a whole series of institutions was founded, including a school, a hospital, an orphanage, a teachers' institute, and a Bible training center.

Franke left his mark on a young noble man, Count von Zinzendorf (1700-1760). This influential and gifted man created the Moravian church from refugee groups who had camped on his land. He made of them a major spiritual force that influenced Western Christianity profoundly, because it was through the preaching of a Moravian missionary that John Wesley was converted. Zinzendorf's theology broadened out over the years through contact with other Christian churches, including Roman Catholicism; but essentially his faith was deeply personal, mystical, and experiential. He spoke of "heart religion."

Theologians are divided over the nature of Pietism. There are those who believe that it was fundamentally a Protestant form of medieval monastic and mystical piety shaped by a Puritan ethic. Others argue that it had arisen from a rigid and rather Pharisaic form of Lutheranism, which in developing a system had lost its heart. Whatever view one might take on this issue, however, there can be little doubt that Pietism has made a major contribution to modern Christianity through its threefold emphasis upon holy living, scholarly devotion to the Scriptures, and a commitment to world mission.

Perhaps it was Zinzendorf's form of Pietism that, more than anything else, was to suggest to later generations that the movement was essentially a world-rejecting faith. In one sense this will always remain true because of their belief in the necessity of new birth. Nevertheless, as we have seen, Pietism believed that true faith was anchored in good works, compassion for the poor, and the alleviation of social ills.

It may well be that the example of this interesting movement in Christian history will help reinforce the need for faith and works to go hand in hand. Modern Christianity has much to learn from Pietism. There is a danger in those Christian groups that emphasize the experiential side of the faith of ignoring the fact that it is "by their fruits you shall know them" (Matt. 7). Heart religion is indeed to be encouraged and is of the essence of Christianity, but it should never be divorced from life in the world. True faith is shown in compassion, in response to human needs, and in the welfare and betterment of social conditions.

**Bibliography:** Lewis, A. J., *Zinzendorf, The Ecumenical Pioneer* (1962); Stoffler, F. E., *The Rise of Evangelical Pietism* (1965).

G.C.

**PILFERING.** This word is derived from a French term *pelf*, which was generally used in a disparaging manner to pour contempt upon wealth. Pilfering still carries that disreputable character as a description of petty rather than grand theft. Pilfering frequently begins in early childhood with the theft of small items from exposed counters in stores and in some cases continues for a number of years before it is either discontinued entirely on ethical grounds or grows as habitual behavior to the point where the offender is apprehended and charged.

According to reports, an enormous amount of pilfering by employees takes place; and despite the fact that the items may be inexpensive, the aggregate loss becomes significant over a period of time. The assumption is that the employer "will never miss" the items involved, or that "the company owes it to me," among other specious excuses. But pilfering is theft, whatever alibis may be adduced to support it, and therefore falls under the consistent scriptural condemnation of stealing. To imagine that because pilfering is described in law as "petty theft" it is not as sinful as theft committed on a larger scale is entirely fallacious. Sin is always sin, whatever proportions human beings might assign to it.

Theft was prohibited in the Decalogue (Exod. 20:15) and equally forbidden in the teachings of Christ (Matt. 19:18; Mark 10:19; Luke 18:20). Paul challenged the Christians at Rome on the matter of theft (Rom. 2:21) and pleaded with the believers in Ephesus to abandon the practice (Eph. 4:28).

**PIRACY.** This noun is based upon a Greek verb *peirao*, "to try, attempt," and was used originally of sea brigands who interfered with maritime trading vessels by pillaging them and disposing of the proceeds. With the colonizing of overseas territories by European imperialist powers came an increase in piracy, and even when ships traveled in groups they were not immune from attacks by pirate vessels. Ships journeying from India or the Caribbean to Europe were especial targets for pirates, and the sea-roving thieves of the Spanish Main became known as buccaneers. Pirates would often sail under false colors and having selected a victim for piracy would approach it and hoist what came to be known as the traditional buccaneer's emblem of death. This flag, known as the "skull and crossbones," depicted a human skull surmounting two crossed thigh bones, executed in black on a white background.

The pirates did not always fare very well, however, especially when they encountered armed merchantmen disguised as ordinary trading vessels. Pirates traditionally terrorized their victims at sea by various acts of brutality and by a form of murder known as "walking the plank," the end of which projected well beyond the deck of the particular ship and precipitated the walker into the ocean. Mutineers also employed this punitive device from time to time. Piracy on the high seas still occurs in Oriental waters, and refugees aboard small ships bound for more friendly shores are frequently halted and searched by pirates and having been robbed are set adrift or thrown overboard to drown.

A more sophisticated form of piracy has become evident in the world of computer science. The progress of the technology has unfortunately far outstripped protective legislation, so that computer pirates cannot always be punished adequately even when caught. Skilled thieves, many of whom are juveniles, can violate such copyright as exists and steal the contents of software programs with virtual impunity; and only the most sophisticated encrypting techniques can foil this activity. When computer piracy extends to such sensitive areas as fiscal confidentiality and military secrecy, society as a whole is at the mercy of the pirates.

All the biblical injunctions prohibiting theft, from the Decalogue (Exod. 20:15) to the teachings of Jesus (Mark 10:19) apply also to computer piracy. The Christian will be the first to set an example of honesty and will be courageous enough to become involved in the prosecution of persons caught in the act of piracy. Theft in whatever form is the curse of modern as of ancient society and must be prevented as far as possible if the social fabric is not to deteriorate further.

See COMPUTER ETHICS; THEFT.

**PITY.** This word is based upon the Latin adjective *pius*, which was used widely in the sense of "holy," "affectionate," "filial," and "conscientious." As a noun, *pietas*, it referred mainly to proper conduct toward the gods, respect for one's native land, and in a metaphorical sense of tenderness and pity. In the latter sense the word describes an emotional reaction of compassion for the misfortunes or suffering of another person or of a group that is bearing oppressive burdens.

Such sympathies reflect the image of God in man, because the Scriptures teach that God shows compassion (Pss. 78:38; 86:15; 111:4), an attribute that was noticeable in Jesus also (Matt. 20:34; Mark 8:2; Luke 7:13). The Bible teaches that while God has pity on those who reverence him, just as a loving father behaves towards his children (Ps. 103:13), he has no compassion for those who deliberately flout his laws (Jer. 13:14; Ezek. 5:11). Yet it was his covenant love that sent Jesus into the world to atone for human sin and to call the elect into the Christian church (Rom. 9:15). Christians are urged to have pity on one another in times of affliction (1 Pet. 3:8) and to be kind and tender by nature (Matt. 18:33).

**PLAGIARISM.** Plagiarism is an act in which a person appropriates the thoughts, writings, artistic works, or inventions of another and uses them as his own. Moral sanctions against such behavior are based on the concept that it is possible to "steal" intangible entities as well as material goods, and that such theft is wrong (Deut. 5:19).

Recognizing the cultural and monetary value of such intangibles, the law has developed the doctrine of "intellectual property." Legislators have attempted to protect the integrity of works and the financial interests of those who create and invent. Various legal mechanisms deal with the problem of plagiarism.

First, it is possible to initiate a lawsuit for the civil wrong of making false claims about a product or work, such as its authorship. In almost every jurisdiction, there are also patent, trademark, and copyright acts that protect the owners of intellectual property. A patent will be granted, upon application, for a product or process or design, if the subject of the patent is original and is sufficiently well developed that it can be properly described and investigated. The patent prevents others from using the item or concept unless they receive a license to do so. A trademark offers the same protection where a registered name or phrase is involved.

Copyright acts guarantee the exclusive right to publish and sell artistic, literary, or musical creations during the lifetime of the artist plus fifty years. Like the patent, copyright was designed to encourage artists to create without the fears of losing the financial benefit of their work or seeing it abused or adulterated through plagiarism. Unlike patents, copyright comes into existence automatically upon the creation of any original work, no matter what its merits. They do not prevent others from using the work, but merely require the permission of (and often royalties to) the copyright holder (often the publisher or agent). Copyright laws prohibit not only outright plagiarism, but also the reproduction of significant portions of a work, unless it is for "fair use"—private study, limited distribution in a classroom, or nonprofit entertainment for charitable purposes. Most countries offer reciprocal copyright arrangements through the operation of two major treaties. Patents can also be obtained in foreign countries. Infringement of patent and copyright statutes will usually result in a legal injunction to cease the prohibited action and may also give rise to financial penalties.

**Bibliography:** Burn, P., *Guide to Patent, Trademark and Copyright Law in Canada* (1977).

S.E.R.

**PLEASURE.** As with so many English terms, *pleasure* has its roots in Latin, in this case the verb *placeo,* "to please, satisfy." When used as an impersonal singular form, *placet,* the Romans assigned a certain ethical value to it by understanding it to mean "it seems good" or "it appears right," and this use was common to both orators and writers.

In English usage the word *pleasure* describes a wide range of sensory enjoyment which may include esthetic and bawdy experiences alike, the rowdy excitement of a major public event, or the quiet satisfaction of knowing that some project or task has been accomplished. These and many other experiences produce in individuals what some psychologists would prefer to describe as experiences of positive affectivity. This definition points to the emotional values of pleasure for the personality as a whole, but in the light of the variables furnished above it will be evident that what is pleasurable for one may not be so for another and might even be distasteful.

Ethical questions regarding pleasure often arise from an assessment of an allegedly pleasurable experience in the light of the individual's tastes and standards. Because pleasure is a relative and essentially transient emotional feeling, many Christians do not place a significant emphasis upon it, preferring instead to develop a mature spiritual relationship with God in Christ. One reason for a diminution of personal interest in what is normally regarded as pleasure is the realization that its values are often shallow and sometimes even discreditable. If positive feelings of developing relationships within the community of the family result from various kinds of activities, this outcome for some would represent the height of pleasurable indulgence. But for people whose values are essentially of the carnal order, only something approaching a prurient performance would produce what they would deem as pleasurable.

The latter situation was certainly the case in the culture which Paul addressed. The hedonism fostered by the Epicureans was by no means qualified by the principle of moderation that some of them espoused. Drunken, violent, orgiastic episodes were often the result, not least at large banquets in wealthy households. Such pleasures were the preoccupation of people who have substituted self for God (2 Tim. 3:4) and consequently serve different forms of fleshly indulgence (Titus 3:3; 2 Pet. 2:13). The Christian's ethical responsibility is to take pleasure in those things which delight God, namely obedience to his commands and holiness of life in human society. By comparison with these aspirations, all other pleasures must be evaluated sternly, and if they prove deficient they should be discarded. Thus the believer will delight in the glories of God's creation and the attempts by people to magnify the Lord in art, literature, science, the ministering of the gospel to society, and in other ways. Worldly pleasures which debase and pollute the mind, however subtly that may be done, do not promote Christian growth and will be avoided accordingly.

**POLLUTION.** From the middle of the twentieth century, this word, which generally means spoiling of purity, or contamination, has come to refer particularly to environmental contamination.

Many Old Testament passages speak of the beauty and bounty of the earth, which is God's creation. The Psalms especially praise the Lord for the loveliness of the physical world (Pss. 24:1-2; 33:1-9; 50:1-2; 65:5-13; 72:19). Man's responsibility is that of steward. God has made him dominant over other living things (Gen. 1:28), but man is to have respect for God's creation. Specific references to man's stewardship (Matt. 25:14-28; Mark 12:1-12; Luke 12:42-46; 1 Cor. 4:1-2) are mostly about spiritual things, but it is clear that a responsible approach to the environment is considered in Scripture to be elementary.

Man has become aware of pollution as a serious environmental problem only since World War II. Before that, the general attitude was that the environment could absorb whatever contaminants were dumped into it. However, population explosion is now producing levels of wastes and by-products of industry so high that man's own survival is seen to be threatened.

The problem of pollution is primarily an ethical one because it is susceptible to control. It occurs because man is reluctant to pay the cost of control. It is usually cheaper in the short run simply to discharge contaminants into the environment than to deal with them in ways that promote environmental cleanliness.

Air pollution is caused largely by the combustion of fossil fuels. Carbon dioxide is one of the most serious pollutants. In the atmosphere it absorbs heat and raises air temperature, producing the "greenhouse effect." Rising world temperatures will melt the polar ice caps, raise sea levels, drown the coastlines, increase evaporation from freshwater lakes, and reduce life in the oceans by affecting the circulation of nutrients. Since vegetation uses carbon dioxide in photosynthesis, encouragement of vegetation, especially trees, throughout the world would do much to control

levels of this gas in the atmosphere. Unfortunately, the agricultural industry traditionally looks upon trees and shrubs as unwanted competition, and in urban areas where carbon dioxide levels are highest, trees are usually considered by administrators to be a nuisance, raising the cost of maintenance services.

Carbon monoxide is an air pollutant produced mostly by motor vehicles. It damages blood hemoglobin and impairs sight and hearing. It is removed from the air by plants and soil bacteria, by oceanic absorption, and by photochemical conversion to carbon dioxide. Levels of carbon monoxide become very high over cities and areas of heavy vehicular traffic. Instead of constructing larger motorways in urban areas, municipalities should require most local traffic to use public transport.

Nitrogen dioxide is liberated into the atmosphere mainly by motor vehicles and power plants. It is converted to ozone by ultraviolet light, and both ozone and nitrogen dioxide damage plant and animal tissue.

Sulphur dioxide is released by the burning of coal. In the atmosphere it combines with water to form sulphuric acid, in the same way nitrogen dioxide forms nitric acid. These acids in rainwater destroy the biota of lakes and inhibit tree growth, as well as erodes mortar and stone of buildings and attacks textiles and plastics. Controversy over control is due to the high cost of installing "scrubbing" equipment in offending industries. It is a question of higher profits now or better stewardship in the long term. Society needs to accept that this ethical question is posed to everyone, not just the industries directly involved, since everyone must eventually share the higher costs of production.

Many additional elements and compounds are released into the air by industrial combustion, many of which are highly toxic. Certain of these are present in very small particles and are deposited in the lungs of humans and other animals. Again, the ethical problem centers around the willingness to pay for control.

Water pollution includes oil in the oceans. About half of this comes from petroleum refinery wastes and from drainings from service stations, running out by rivers and sewers into the sea. Vessels discharging oily ballast wastes account for considerable oil pollution, and a smaller amount comes from offshore drilling and natural seepage from the ocean floor. The noticeable contamination of beaches on remote islands is disturbing evidence of the degree to which the oceans are polluted with oil. Besides killing seabirds, oil in the water must affect other marine life; the specifics are still being studied. The control of oil pollution is a practical problem of policing, reflecting an unwillingness on the part of offenders to act ethically.

Sewage wastes in water include disease organisms such as typhoid, bacterial and amoebic dysentery, cholera, infectious hepatitis, and also phosphates, nitrates, and other chemicals including mercury from factories, farms, and homes. Phosphates cause blooms of algae in lakes, which take oxygen from the water as they die and decompose, killing fish and other organisms. Mercury damages brain tissue. In North America some progress has been made in reducing the amount of phosphates in household detergents, but pollution of water by industries seems in many cases to yield only to the pressure of persistent litigation.

Thermal pollution of water occurs especially near cities and power plants where water is used as a coolant. Elevated water temperatures affect aquatic biota, disturbing the ecosystem. In the future, the amount of water needed for cooling will become impracticable to provide, based on extrapolation of present usage.

Pollution on land includes lead, which is released into the atmosphere by the burning of leaded gasoline. It precipitates out from the air as dust, contaminating the soil. It is then absorbed into plants by roots and from the surface of leaves. Chlorinated hydrocarbons are used as herbicides and insecticides. They degrade slowly and so build up in the world's food chains and in the atmosphere. They interfere with calcium metabolism in living organisms. Polychlorinated biphenyls (PCBs) are used in transformers, plastics, solvents, and printing inks. They enter water and the atmosphere from industrial discharges and sewage, degrade slowly, and are highly toxic. Radionuclides enter the environment from atomic weapons testing, nuclear reactors, and radioactive wastes. Their ionizing radiations produce lesions in living tissue.

As in many environmental problems, pollution is primarily ethical. People who would not throw litter on their own properties may do so readily in public places. Industrial leaders who would not tolerate pollution around their own homes may allow it to be discharged from factories and carried elsewhere. As the human population escalates, pollution becomes more threatening to survival. Pollution represents both an act of aggression against society and an abdication of responsibility in the stewardship of the earth. The Christian principles of love for fellowman and accountability to God require every effort to combat it.

**Bibliography:** Smith, R. L., *Ecology and Field Biology* (1980); Tiller, R. M., *The Human Species* (1977).

N.D.M.

**POLYGAMY.** Literally meaning "many marriages" but effectively meaning more than one marriage alliance. It has usually taken the form of polygyny (marriage with two or more women) rather than polyandry (marriage with two or more men). In Western countries polygamy is not allowed by law for permanent residents, but it is allowed by law and custom in most Islamic countries.

The Christian position on polygamy is that God ordained monogamous marriage, one husband and one wife together (Gen. 2:24; Matt. 19:8; the implications of the picture of God and his bride, Israel, for example, Isa. 62:5). This marriage state seems to have been practiced by most Israelites and Jews in Old Testament and later times. Monogamy, in fact, seems to be presupposed in Proverbs 5:15-20; 18:22; and 31:10-31.

Like divorce, polygamy was allowed by God as the second best moral choice. Laws were provided to control its practice and to protect the women involved. The taking of concubines (who had fewer rights than a wife, being little more than slave-women) was allowed, but was also controlled by laws (Exod. 21:7-11). Examples of men who had two or more wives include Jacob (Gen. 29), David (2 Sam. 5:13-16), Solomon (1 Kings 11), and Rehoboam (2 Chron. 11:21). While the last three men took wives for varied reasons (love, lust, desire for male children, foreign alliances, diplomacy), Jacob was actually tricked into having two wives.

Deuteronomy 21:10-14 protects the rights of a female captive in war who is taken as wife (second wife?), and the inheritance law (vv. 15-17) recognizes that the primary moral criticism of bigamy is that one man cannot love two women equally. Hence this law protects an unloved wife and her son. The story of Elkanah and his wives is a comment on the moral dangers of polygamy (1 Sam. 1).

Western missionaries have not always been wise when they have met polygamy and made converts of men who practiced polygyny. Instead of encouraging the man to maintain his present wives and family, they have sometimes insisted that he get rid of all his wives but one. This has often had bad consequences. While a Christian ought not to become a polygamist, a person converted while a polygamist may commit the lesser evil by maintaining rather than dismissing his extra wives and their children.

P.T.

**POPULATION CONTROL.** "And God blessed them; and God said to them, 'Be fruitful and multiply, and fill the earth . . .'" (Gen. 1:28a). This command is part of the Creation Mandate of Genesis 1—2. Today, the great debate about this passage is whether or not the earth has been "filled." That is to say, has the population of the earth reached the level at which its resources are inadequate to meet the needs of all people on earth?

The answer that gets the most attention today is that the earth's population has indeed reached or exceeded that level. Many Christians believe this answer. However, the overwhelming evidence is that the earth's resources and man's technology is quite capable of supporting many times the present six billion people on earth. Some of that evidence follows.

First, Colin Clark estimates that the world could sustain 35 billion people on the "overconsumptive" American diet and 100 billion on an "adequate" Japanese diet. Historically, famines have six causes: war, the prevention of cultivation, the willful destruction of crops, defective agriculture, governmental interference by regulation and taxation, and currency restrictions.

The continuing famine in Ethiopia is an example. For centuries, Ethiopian farmers had stored food after good harvests to provide for years of bad harvests. However, by government decree such storage was labeled "hoarding" and disallowed. Families were relocated and commercial marketing of food was forbidden. Many other governmental "changes" disrupted a fairly efficient system of food production and supply that severely aggravated (if not caused) this continuing famine.

Second, productivity is not necessarily limited where people are closely populated. Taiwan is only two-thirds of the size of Switzerland, with sixteen million people; yet the crowded island has the second highest standard of living in Asia (behind Japan, another densely populated country).

Third, food production has increased more rapidly than the population on a world-wide basis. Even in the United States where large surpluses of food are produced almost every year, *more* could be produced were it not for government controls. But politics is not the only problem. Worldwide, the average work day varies from 45 minutes to seven hours. Surely there is a great deal more time for greater production!

In Creation God gave mankind abundant natural resources to provide for the needs of a planet "filled" with people. In addition, He has given mankind an ingenious mind that is capable of utilizing those resources, provided man is willing and is free to pursue such development.

Why, then, is overpopulation rhetoric so appealing? The answer has to do with short-term vs. long-term costs, apparent consensus of expert judgment, population as a cause of pollution, judgments about people's rational use of resources, one-sided news media exposure, and hidden agendas that include increasing government control and an elite power structure.

Population statistics indicate that 2.2 children per married couple is necessary *to maintain* population at current levels. Thus, the logical conclusion is that couples who are able to have children should be "fruitful" with 3 or more to continue to multiply within God's Creation Mandate. This number should also be adequate statistically to fill the void of those who are physically unable to bear children.

These children will themselves become the resources to feed themselves and others. As long ago as the 18th century, Adam Smith recognized that the surest sign of a healthy economic order was continued population growth. As children multiply, their children's needs (food, shelter, and clothing) increase, and economic expansion occurs. (This reality is certainly a message to the United States in the 1990's with its abortion rate and stagnant economy.)

In addition, an expanding number of children are necessary to provide for the needs of their parents. In the United States, an inordinate burden is being placed upon productive workers because the abortion of one in three pregnancies for 18 years has greatly limited present and future workers.

Population growth creates new economic opportunities and markets. Such growth expands markets, making investments more attractive by reducing risks and increasing total demand for goods and services. Larger numbers of people lead to proportionally larger economies that make large public investments such as highways, bridges, railroads, irrigation systems, and ports less expensive on a per-person basis.

Finally, we must believe God. Every mention of the bearing of children is described in positive terms (e.g., Ps. 127:3-5). This biblical affirmation of children coupled with the Creation Mandate provides the authority to override any scientific objections to population control. God never limited or abrogated that affirmation or mandate. As pointed out, however, the greater scientific evidence points to more-than-sufficient resources to meet a growing population. And likely, God will either terminate history before actual overpopulation occurs or He will continue to give man the ingenuity to stay ahead of population needs until His Second Advent.

**Bibliography:** Beisner, C., *Prospects for Growth: A Biblical View of Population, Resources, and the Future* (1990); Davis, J. J., *Evangelical Ethics* (1985); Payne, F., *Making Biblical Decisions* (1989); Simon, J., *The Ultimate Resource* (1981).

See ABORTION; CONTRACEPTION; EUTHANASIA.

**PORNOGRAPHY.** It is difficult to define pornography absolutely because it tends to be spoken of in descriptive terms. For example, it has been defined as an "obscene or unchaste depiction of sexual organs or behavior." The concept of what is obscene or unchaste is highly subjective and varies widely. Pornography is more than merely sexually explicit material. It has an offensive quality in that it degrades sex, condones anti-social behavior, and assaults the sensibilities of the viewer by its obsessive and unrealistic treatment of sex. It becomes more than a violation of an aesthetic standard.

Pornography is essentially a moral problem and has to be recognized as such if it is to be dealt with effectively. It has been described as "dirt for money's sake" and has been defined as portraying humiliating or abusive sexual situations and using of sex as a weapon of oppression. It can be especially offensive in its sexist treatment of women, who tend to be portrayed as purely sexual beings. They usually are childlike, rarely older than their mid-twenties, and enjoy being sexually manipulated by men. Rape is conveyed as being pleasurable for women. There is also a disturbing trend toward linking extreme violence with sex and portraying sexual acts with children.

Both the Old and New Testaments encouraged morally upright lives (Lev. 18—19; 1 Cor. 6:9). Family life was the ideal and adultery, prostitution, and unnatural sex threatened that ideal (Deut. 27:20-23).

The moral threat posed by pornography and obscenity is still relevant to our present law. In England, Canada, and the United States, pornography is governed by obscenity laws; but definitions of obscenity are not especially helpful. Basically the test is whether the "bounds of common decency" have been exceeded. In the United States it was decided in 1957 that the protection of free speech under the First Amendment to the Constitution does not apply to obscene publications, and obscenity may thus be regulated. The current American guidelines as found in *Miller* v. *California* are (a) whether "the average person, applying contemporary community standards" would find that the work, taken as a whole, appeals to the prurient interest...; (b) "whether the work depicts or describes, in a patently offensive way, sexual conduct specifically defined by the applicable state law; and (c) whether the work, taken as a whole, lacks serious literary, artistic, political, or scientific value." In Canada Section 159(8) of the criminal code states that any "publication, a dominant characteristic of which is the undue exploitation of sex, or of sex and any one or more of the following subjects, namely, crime, horror, cruelty and violence, shall be deemed to be obscene." In England under The Obscene Publications Act, a publication is defined as obscene if, taken as a whole, its effect is such as to tend to "deprave or corrupt" persons who are likely to see it. However, publication can be justified on the grounds of literary or artistic merit. In England pornography involving children is an offense under the Protection of Children Act (1978). Obscenity also includes publications depicting offensive conduct with no sexual elements, such as drug taking and violence. In Canada there is strong pressure to bring in similar legislation dealing with nonsexual obscene publications and child pornography. At the present time pornography is not regulated adequately by obscenity laws.

Pornography is being viewed increasingly as a women's civil rights issue, in that it condones their exploitation and the use of violence for sexual gratification. American municipalities are empowered to enforce civil rights ordinances. To curb pornography one U.S. municipality has defined it as discrimination against women and has drafted an ordinance prohibiting publication and trafficking in pornographic material. Unfortunately, the legislation failed at the municipal level on the grounds that it would violate freedom of speech and expression. However, this approach to the problem will probably be pursued elsewhere.

Pornography is a growing problem. It is becoming increasingly accessible in video-tape form and by cable and satellite transmissions. It is becoming more and more explicit in its obsessive treatment of aberrant sexual behavior, and it is increasingly linked with extreme violence and sadistic subjection of women. Child pornography, too, is growing ever more prevalent. Nonetheless, vociferous arguments are made against controlling pornography in the belief that to do so would fetter rights of free opinion and expression, however distasteful to the majority those minority views might be. It is further argued that no concrete evidence exists that exposure to pornography contributes to increasing violence or sexual abuse.

To counter such arguments it must first be noted that pornography is more than merely sexually explicit material. It advocates the subordination and exploitation of a particular group in society and applauds sadistic and violent practices in relation to them. This would not be tolerated in a nonsexual context. Just as society will no longer accept racial discrimination, so it should not accept sexual discrimination. Freedom of speech and expression have never been unlimited. They have to be exercised within the constraint of defamation laws. Thus, genuine advocates of pornography should be made to express their views in a sexually neutral fashion if they honestly wish to obtain acceptance by the majority. While pornography cannot be specifically linked to increasing violence and sexual abuse, it is naive to assume that it is therefore without influence. Society's educational process is based on the principle that what people read and are exposed to molds their understanding, beliefs, and behavior. Pornography alienates an individual's sexuality from his personality as a whole. The ill effects of exposure to this may be internalized in the individual, but are real enough. Children are particularly receptive and impressionable. Where pornography is now so readily available they need to be protected from it by society.

**Bibliography:** Chine, V., *Sex in Mass Media. Where do you draw the line?* (1980); Copp, D. and Wendell, S., *Pornography and Censorship* (1983); Stevens, I. N. and Yardley, D. C. M., *The Protection of Liberty* (1982); Williams, B.,

*British Commission on Obscenity and Pornography* (1979).

D.E.T.

**POVERTY.** This word is a slight modification of the Latin *paupertas,* "scanty means, poverty," as opposed to complete destitution. As such it is the noun equivalent of the adjective *pauper,* "poor, of modest means." A poor person is therefore one who does not have abundant fiscal resources at his or her disposal, but is not completely devoid of such necessities of life as food, shelter, and clothing. Poverty must therefore be regarded as depicting a low level on the socioeconomic scale, but not in fact the lowest.

Poverty seems to have been a part of human existence from a very early period. Its origins lie strictly within human nature, and therefore it must not be regarded as a state or condition imposed upon humanity by a stern and vindictive God. Indeed, if the Genesis narratives relating to the Garden of Eden (Gen. 2:8-15) are to be given the slightest credence, Adamic man's first habitat was ideal in every respect, including the fact that all Adam needed to do was to tend a fully developed environment. All of this was lost by human disobedience, and thereafter agricultural work assumed its familiar character as a result of God's curse on the ground (Gen. 3:17-19).

The first real indication of the nature of poverty among the covenant people of Israel occurs in the Mosaic law, which governed national and individual conduct in the light of God's desire to have his chosen people living in community as a priestly kingdom and a holy nation (Exod. 19:6). This group was to care for its members in such a manner that there would be few poor people there, although the community would never be free from them (Deut. 15:4, 10; Matt. 26:11).

Five Hebrew words were used in the Old Testament to describe the poor in a socioeconomic sense. The person known as *ani* or *aneh* was not a derelict or a beggar, but one who originally had money and possessions but had become impoverished as a result of the improper disposition of money or property. The word *rush,* "poor," was used in an entirely economic or social context; and the same was true of the infrequently used designation *misken,* "socially inferior," this being the Hebrew equivalent of the Akkadian *mushkenu,* "beggar." In a related sense the words *dal* or *dallah* described a peasant who was without influence or power because of his impoverished social status.

A term that has an interesting linguistic history is *ebyon,* which seems to have described a beggar in the first instance, but was used subsequently of the homeless and very poor. In the pre-exilic period *ebyon* was employed significantly of righteous persons who petitioned God to deliver them from need (Pss. 37:14; 40:17). In the postexilic period, when the Jews felt overwhelmed by the pressures of Hellenistic Greek culture, those who cherished the ideals of the Sinai covenant used the term in a noneconomic sense to describe their fidelity to the ancient Mosaic spiritual ethos. The members of the Dead Sea community described themselves as "the poor," and this could not possibly have referred to their economic state, judging by the wealth of the community as listed in the Treasure Scroll. The Qumran sect regarded itself as the only true representative of Mosaic spirituality and therefore employed the term *ebyon* in the sense of "faithful" or "spiritually loyal" to describe the character of the group. This appears also to be the usage intended by Christ, who in speaking primarily to his disciples taught about the rewards of the "poor in spirit," that is, the spiritually faithful, who in fact alone deserve to inherit the kingdom (Matt. 5:3).

In New Testament times there were many beggars and impoverished people, and these were mostly described by the Greek word *ptochos,* "poor," although the synonyms *penes* and *penichros* were also employed. The Old Testament usage largely influenced New Testament thought, which was given distinctiveness by Jesus in his first synagogue reading in Nazareth (Luke 4:16-21), in which the lection was taken from Isaiah 61:1-3. The "poor" in verse 4 would indeed rejoice in the jubilee-year fulfillment of the ancient prophecy, for they would have an opportunity to redeem their family holdings (Lev. 25:47-55) in the traditional manner. It is characteristic of Luke to stress the Isaianic theme of social and economic restitution for the deprived, since that was the basic jubilee-year message to the *anawim.* Matthew, by contrast, emphasizes the ethical and spiritual condition of the "poor," not their social status (Matt. 5:3). Some interpreters have understood the New Testament concept of giving one's wealth to the poor to have actually meant participating in the jubilee-year activities so as to reduce poverty.

From the foregoing it would appear that God has an inveterate concern for poverty, but that the basic cause springs from ignorant, stupid, or unrighteous conduct either by the individual who was poor or by the community of Israel. Poverty would therefore appear to be a relative condition that is governed to a large extent by the status of a person within his or her environment. It need have no necessary connection with money, which would certainly be true in a bartering environment, and must be evaluated in terms of the situation in which it actually occurs. Thus while there are beggars in both New York and New Delhi, the subsistence levels of the very poor are proportionately higher in the West than in the Orient, due to the way in which various governments subsidize the poor from taxation revenues.

While many persons are born into poverty, many also manage to surmount their economic difficulties and live in a more affluent manner. Enterprise and initiative are largely responsible for such a change, along with educational standing or special manual skills, and given some or all of these factors a person can improve his or her economic situation significantly. Again the relational factor enters into such considerations, for if wealth is the criterion of prosperity there will be many who will remain consistently poor by some Western standards. Once more it is important to stress that for any such comparisons to be fair, the appropriate social status only is to be considered. Thus the rich person of Hollywood must be compared only with Indian moguls, for example, and the modern derelicts of San Francisco with their counterparts in Calcutta.

The gospel message has always manifested a great concern for the underprivileged and the economically deprived. As a consequence the Christian church has been at the forefront of attempts to alleviate the plight of the poor by educating them, evangelizing them, and establishing programs of self-help and medical care. But sometimes church policies have stood in the way of material prosperity among the poor, as in Latin America. Poverty is not infrequently the result of mismanagement of money, whether by individuals or governments; and it is particularly tragic when impoverishment is imposed upon a people by national policies, as in Ethiopia. Vast amounts of aid have been poured by the Western nations into that Communist country, only to be used by the military and not the starving people. When disease and famine stalk the land, the prospect for impoverished bodies and spirits are far from encouraging.

What is true for Ethiopia in the 1980s also holds good for other African countries. It was estimated in 1960 that the continent of Africa was self-sufficient as far as food supplies were concerned. But subsequent political strife, governmental corruption, and economic mismanagement in countries such as Nigeria, Zimbabwe, Uganda, and elsewhere have had the depressing effect of reducing about 40 per cent of the African population to the poverty level. Sadly, enough, the resultant alienation cannot be healed by the expedient of pouring vast amounts of American money or food into countries that are mismanaged or the victims of political aberration.

Some relief agencies receive enthusiastic support from the media for projects involving the feeding of starving children, but the use of such unfortunate subjects in order to solicit funds is frowned upon by the agencies as "pornography of the suffering." The procedures being criticized oversimplify the problem by conveying the impression that money is all that is needed to solve the problem. In general, the media fail to link the problems of the Third World countries to the economic and political policies of those lands and their relationship to the developed world's governments and businesses.

The Christian, understandably confused by all this, will desire guidance as to how to deal adequately with poverty. Certainly the giving of all of one's money for this purpose only increases the problem by adding one extra person to the already vast number. It is interesting to note that Jesus made no attempt to eradicate the poverty of his day on a national or collective basis, but instead he instructed his followers in ways of ministering to the larger needs of the poor (Luke 14:13, 21; 18:22).

The egalitarian notion of a world in which poverty is entirely absent seems unfortunately to be nothing more than an unattainable ideal. Even if it were possible, it would undoubtedly break down in the face of human cupidity, ignorance, duplicity, and stupidity. While the Christian may wish to relieve poverty on an individual basis, it is wise to use well-established agencies which maximize the financial support given. The Christian can then donate freely to relieve the plight of the poor as a privileged response to the saving work of Jesus in ministering to a lost and spiritually impoverished world.

**POWER.** It is customary to define power in terms of a capability to achieve specific goals or objectives. This facility may involve physical force, political maneuvering, or moral persuasion; but in any case it is characterized by a recognized dynamism which has to be respected even if its nature and effect prove distasteful for any reason. The Greeks conveyed the concept by the use of the word *dunamis*, which has been modified and included in the English language in various ways. The word *power* has a Latin background, however, being derived from *possum*, "to have power," and correlatives such as *potestas*, "power, control."

To be authentic, power must be based upon authority; and its exercise is derived from that authority, whether the power ultimately works for good or evil. This relationship between power and authority is evident in the Scriptures, where the source of Christ's power (*dunamis*) is described as the Holy Spirit (Acts 1:8). Correspondingly, Paul's assertion that there is no power but God's (Rom. 13:1) employs the word *exousia*, "authority," to denote the ultimate validating principle. What Paul is doing in Romans 13 is furnishing the believers with a theological basis for the understanding of secular, that is, imperial power, wherever it may be encountered. His remarks were needed greatly by Christians in the Roman Empire, because the enforcing of imperial policy upon the people, approximately half of whom were slaves, was sometimes accompanied by brutality.

Therefore the believers were assured that temporal power was neither autogenous nor self-sustaining, but that in fact it was delegated to the secular authorities by God himself, the one supreme source of power. The book of Genesis indicates that a delegating of divine authority to human beings was an early feature of history (Gen. 1:26-28), the purpose being to ensure a proper degree of order in society. In all ancient Near Eastern religions the various priesthoods believed that they received their authority from the national deities, and on this basis they enacted laws and regulations directed at the organizing of secular life and cultic worship.

The Hebrews were no exception to this general principle, for in the covenant community the high priest and his cultic associates were responsible for ordering the life of the Israelites as God's people. In addition to supervising the community and ensuring its well-being, they were commissioned to teach the law (Mal. 1:7); and when they discharged these duties conscientiously the nation prospered. But when, as in the days of Eli (1 Sam. 2:22-25), the priesthood became corrupt, the abuse of power brought disaster to the nation in a manner that was to recur (Isa. 28:7; Jer. 6:13-14; Ezek. 22:26).

Regardless of the wrong or right use of power, the fact remains that it is a derived, not an inherent, human property. Governments are to be respected as a microcosm of the supreme power, and their injunctions obeyed accordingly in all those matters that pertain to proper social order. Paul clearly expects that this latter concern will be uppermost in the minds of government officials, and here he seems to reflect the spirit of the *pax Romana* instituted by Augustus. There is no expectation of the state persecuting the Christian church in Paul's letter to the citizens of the imperial capital, so the guidelines of obedience to authority and the exemplification of Christian love to members of society are prescribed as the proper attitude for Christians to adopt.

Peter sounds a more serious note, however, in dealing with the same subject along parallel lines (1 Pet. 2:13-25). In verse 19 he sets out the principles that should govern the believer's response to persecution, whether personal or not. Under conditions where power works adversely to the interests of the Christian, Peter advises patient endurance, reminding the believers of Christ who paid the supreme penalty at the hands of a hostile power structure. It is important for the Christian to realize that neither of these two apostles took the view that power was itself evil in nature. Instead, following the traditions of the Old Testament, they regarded it as God's gift for the proper ordering of society.

Yet there have been many occasions in human history when power has not been recognized as a trust from God, but rather as a means of personal or national aggrandizement. Individuals or groups who seize power may justify their actions by purporting to correct the kind of social abuses that arise in dictatorships, but only if those deficiencies are rectified can their claims have any validity. Unfortunately all too many revolutions substitute a worse master for a bad one and present the ethical irony of the new authorities being made subject to those very powers that state leaders were supposed to control. So it is that in some jurisdictions political corruption, genocide, economic mismanagement, and social conditions in general are often worse after an uprising than before. Certain abuses seem to result from an un-

willingness or an inability to exercise power in a determined and ethical manner, which indicates that power can be tempered or even stultified by indecision or weakness of personality.

It is thus insufficient merely to discuss power as an abstract concept, because the reaction of the individual to power is symptomatic of the larger problems of wielding power. We are all authoritarian figures, even if the only thing we dominate is the family pet. Parents represent authority, order, and power in the eyes of their children; and this pattern is repeated at each of the various levels of employer-employee relationships. Some employers wield power in the same unfeeling way that a bullying, emotionally insecure dictator does; and the more absolute the power appears to be, the more Lord Acton's celebrated dictum seems to hold true. The evil of absolute power is really no different in point of fact from that of complete anarchy, for theological as well as social reasons. Because of the "checks and balances," a participatory democracy probably offers the best opportunity for a mature exercise of power, even though a benevolent dictatorship is generally recognized as the most efficient form of social organization.

The Christian will live as though his or her first duty is to the Lord, and on this basis will behave as a responsible citizen ought to do, as indicated by the scriptural guidelines mentioned above. A disciplined moral and spiritual life as directed by God's Holy Spirit will ensure that when the Christian has the opportunity of utilizing power, that exercise will be conducted in the full realization that the power is in fact a mandate from God, with all the responsibilities that such a situation involves.

**PRAGMATISM.** Pragmatism as a philosophical movement has been the most significant and distinctive contribution of American thinkers to the history of philosophy. It was the most influential philosophy in this country during the early decades of the twentieth century. Although many thinkers can be identified in some way with pragmatism, including jurists like Oliver Wendell Holmes, Jr., three philosophers, namely Charles Sanders Peirce (1839-1914), William James (1842-1910), and John Dewey (1859-1952) are the most significant.

Peirce presented the basic ideas of pragmatism in a series of essays that was published in 1877-1878. In "Fixation of Belief," Peirce describes thinking as the procedure we use to remove doubt and to fix belief to guide action. Its character is public and experimental, enabling others to test and confirm or revise its results. In "How to Make Our Ideas Clear," he takes an experimental approach to meaning, stating that a clear idea of an object is gained through a consideration of its practical effects. To say that a diamond is hard means that it will not be scratched when it is rubbed over another surface.

Pragmatism became popular when James presented Peirce's ideas to the public in lectures and essays. For James, the pragmatic method was a way of ascertaining truth in addition to being a method for discovering meaning. In order for an idea to be true, it has to make a concrete difference in some individual's actual life. James states that "truth happens to an idea. It becomes true, is made true by events. Its verity is in fact an event, a process." He connects truth with value because truth is a "species of good," in that truth is "whatever proves itself to be good in the way of belief." In taking this approach, James rejects the notion of absolute truth, that experience could never change, and the view that truth consists of the correspondence between an idea and a fixed reality. In comparison with Peirce, James gives greater emphasis to concrete, individual experience, a fact that caused Peirce to rename his position "pragmaticism."

John Dewey, the most influential of the pragmatists, was influenced strongly by Charles Darwin's theory of evolution. The higher qualities, such as intelligence, were developed so that humans are able to organize and shape their environment for individual or social ends. The problems initiated by the environment are resolved by scientific thinking. This is distinguished from common sense thinking only in that it is more careful and reflective. "Valuation" occurs when a process of deliberation is needed to resolve conflicts between competing desires and immediate values in order to act. The moral life is never completed, and its ends are never ultimate because new conflicts arise and new ends must be sought. It does not consist of following some absolute standard or set of rules that was laid down in the past. The educational process for Dewey is a moral process where "growing, or the continuous reconstruction of experience, is the only end." Education should promote the reform of democratic society through schools that are model societies. Democracy, in turn, should contribute "to the all-around growth of every member of society."

Pragmatism became popular in the United States because it was compatible with the country's optimistic temper, democratic spirit, and trust in ideas that work. Though few professional philosophers would call themselves "pragmatists" today the movement has left a legacy to American thought and life, particularly in educational philosophy, through the considerable influence of John Dewey and his followers.

**Bibliography:** Dewey, J., *Democracy in Education* (1916); Dewey, J., *Reconstruction in Philosophy* (1920); *Theory of the Moral Life* (1908); James, W., *The Meaning of Truth* (1909); *Ibid.*, *Pragmatism* (1907).

S.D.A.

**PRAYER.** In the Bible, prayer takes on a variety of forms: adoration, confession, petition, intercession, thanksgiving, praise, entreaty, meditation, and even at times expostulation. A discussion of prayer must begin with the point that prayer is to be sharply distinguished from magic. The practitioner of magic is concerned to manipulate nonhuman and superhuman forces to bring about his own will. The praying person is concerned to do the will of God (1 John 5:14). Prayer is not a device for ensuring that God does what we want; it is a means of bringing us into conformity with what God wants. A curious feature of much modern praying is that in the instance in which we get what we have asked for, we speak of "answered prayer." If we do not gain our request, we have the problem of "unanswered prayer." But "No" is just as much an answer as is "Yes." Real prayer is more concerned to bring the worshiper into line with God's purpose than to secure what the worshiper wants.

This can be seen when we reflect on some of the conditions of prayer in the Bible. There must be real sincerity involved; prayer is "from the heart" (Hos. 7:14), and it is not concerned with selfish desires (James 4:3). Prayer must always be in faith (Mark 11:24; James 1:6); the person who does not really trust God has no business praying. Prayer is to be "in the name" of Jesus (John 14:13-14). This does not mean that we must always close our prayers with "through Jesus Christ our Lord" or the like (though that is a good way of ending prayers), but that prayer should be in accordance with all that "the name" stands for. Prayer that does not fit in with what Jesus is and what He came to do is not real prayer in the Christian sense.

The person who prays must pray with forgiveness of those who have wronged him (Mark 11:25); to nourish grudges is to nullify our prayers. Prayer is abiding in Christ and having His words abide in us (John 15:7). This is much like praying in faith; to have the wrong attitude to God is to make prayer meaningless. So is it with obedience (1 John 3:22). It is not that our prayers are heard and answered as a reward for our obedience. That would be more or less going back to magic; it would mean doing the things that please God in order to coax Him into doing what we want. Rather, if we are genuinely longing to see the will of God done, then we will be obeying His commandments. This is not meritorious, but is part of the living out of the faith in which we pray. Prayer is never achieved in our own strength or wisdom, but is "in the Spirit" (Eph. 6:18; Jude 20). Such prayer is to be constant (1 Thess. 5:17).

Does all this make prayer an intolerably complicated exercise? Must we keep looking at a multiplicity of conditions before we can pray? Not at all. True prayer flows from the centrality of the cross. When we see that nothing we can do will ever merit salvation, that it is Christ's death alone that brings us forgiveness, this brings about a humble relationship with God. Sincerity, faith, the desire to do God's will, and all the rest flow from this basic fact. True prayer is the natural outworking of a right relationship to God.

**Bibliography:** Hallesby, O., *Prayer* (1948); Thomson, J. G. S. S., *Interpreter's Dictionary of the Bible*, vol. 3, pp. 1257-60; Smith, C. W. F., *Interpreter's Dictionary of the Bible*, vol. 3, pp. 857-67.

L.M.

**PREACHING.** The role of the preacher is by its very nature a contradictory one. He is inevitably buffeted by competing external and internal forces. The generic biblical sense of "to preach" is evangelistic. Preaching is proclamation of the Christian faith to those who are not Christians.

The expansion of this term by Christians to include ministry within the church has broadened the meaning of preaching to embrace didactic and nurturing functions of public Christian ministry. The preacher is required prophetically to rebuke evil and sin in the world and in the church, to invite non-Christians lovingly to become Christians and at the same time pastorally to shelter and nurture Christians in the church. The requirement to be firm and uncompromising about many matters, while at the same time needing to be humble and tenderhearted creates its own special ethical difficulties.

The divine call to preach places the preacher in a unique position. He is driven by an inner compulsion that provides a sense of urgency. The call is God's. This direct call is one of the mysteries of the Christian faith. It places a terrible responsibility upon preachers and impels them with awesome urgency (Amos 7:15). Jesus took this role to Himself (Isa. 61:1; Mark 1:38; Luke 4:18). The early Christians felt this same urgency (Acts 4:20; 5:20). Paul declared "necessity is laid on me" (1 Cor. 9:16). He expands upon the tensions as well as the joy of his preaching efforts in 2 Corinthians 1—6. Failure to answer the divine call and failure to fulfill the divine mandate because of personal moral bankruptcy have always appeared to Christians to be a particularly odious lapses. It is difficult to see how it could be otherwise, given the greatness of the calling.

The preacher's single most important priority must be to guard his personal integrity (1 Tim. 6:11-16). Otherwise, the reputation of the Christian faith and any effectiveness of preaching are undermined (1 Tim. 3:7). Personal purity is crucial.

The preacher must also give attention to competence in sermon preparation, gathering of data, factual honesty, valid observation, and confidentiality of information divulged to him during personal conversations. It is not only indiscreet but immoral to cite attributable information about others in sermon illustrations.

Salary, money management, and spending require careful scrutiny. The preacher is ill-advised to build up consumer debt. He and his family ought to live within a reasonable median range of the economy where they minister. Preachers who leave town without paying or securing all debts are an offense to the faith.

Personal integrity for the preacher includes a good marriage relationship and family life. Most professionals, including preachers, must work long and irregular hours. Their children ("preacher's kids") are sometimes overwhelmed by the role that others expect them to fill. The care with which the preacher attends to these problems reflects on his character. Parents of devout, sterling character are usually held in high regard by their own children, even when responsibilities keep parents away a great deal. Integrity cements love and creates trust.

Integrity is crucial in multiple staff relationships, in dealing with fellow pastors, and in denominational matters. Few Christian denominations have written or detailed codes of behavior for preachers. There is a received consensus among Christians based on New Testament teaching that betrayal of trust, an overbearing manner, manipulation, character assassination, divisiveness, and schism are morally wrong. Cooperation is the hallmark of spiritual maturity. Where theological issues or the integrity of denominational life are clearly at stake, then here too resistance can be mounted and leadership exercised with integrity, even if firmly.

Clarity and authenticity of message are linked by Paul to integrity in 1 Timothy 6:11-16. In Scripture there is the continual warning against false or misleading prophets (Deut. 13:1-3; Jer. 23:25; Matt. 7:15; 2 John 10). The call of God and moral responsibility to communicate accurately the revelation combine in the Bible. The central Christian message concerns Christ incarnate, crucified, risen, and coming again. Therefore a certain sense of greatness is a moral obligation laid on the preacher. He should not trivialize the faith by concentrating on peripheral and divisive issues.

Authenticity and credibility are important criteria when judging the emotional freight of preaching. Persuasion rather than manipulation, moral transformation by God's Spirit instead of mere behavior modification are goals of preaching. Legitimate passion that is fired by Christ's compassion for broken humanity will reach out to more and more people and may not be called mere multiplying of numbers. On the other hand, to major on developing a cult of personality through mass suasion is morally wrong.

The preacher ought also to be a person of grace. The virtues Paul urges for Christians in contrast to vices (Gal. 5:16-26) apply equally to preachers. The preacher must expose evil, pretension, and injustice, but he must not be a trampler. The gospel and beauty are not disjunctives. Thus the preacher is obligated to prepare sermons that are literate, informing, and educating as much as they are persuading and exhorting.

Finally, the preacher must be the man of God that the Scriptures and the Christian church have aspired for him to be. Preaching competence, ethical integrity, and spiritual sensitivity belong together. Great preachers are men who walk with God. Credibility depends upon perceived spirituality (Isa. 57:15). The preacher who spends time with God quietly internalizes those principles and values that do more than shield the mind and heart from moral turpitude. More importantly, they serve as a positive guide in behavior patterns, which include the sanctified use of trust and intimacy for the glory of God.

**Bibliography:** Blackwood, W., *The Preparation of Sermons* (1948); Morgan, G. C., *Preaching* (1937); Mounce, R. H., *The Essential Nature of New Testament Preaching* (1960); Spurgeon, C. H., *Lectures to Students* (n.d.).

S.J.M.

**PREJUDICE.** Prejudice may be defined as a learned emotional response characterized by a biased or preconceived opinion of persons, events, or situations. While in modern parlance the prejudgment tends to be negative in form, this is by no means always the case. An individual can be prejudiced in favor of something just as readily as against another thing, and this applies to persons and situations also.

The term is derived from the Latin *praeiudico*, "to decide beforehand, prejudge." The adjective *praeiudicatus* as used by some Latin orators meant prejudiced in the sense of "'decided before the event." There can be no doubt that prejudice is an acquired and not an intrinsic tendency, since very young children do not manifest it. It is true, of course, that such infants will both like and dislike their peers by turns, but this is due to the fact that their own personal security or possessions are being threatened in some manner, and not for the usual reasons associated with prejudice.

Young children exhibit all the egocentricity of fallen humanity, and when they are in process of being reared by adults they are confronted with preconceived notions about a surprisingly wide range of situations or things. Under such conditions they tend to absorb the opinions expressed if only because they are presented under the guise of authority. Since the ideas assume the character of truth, it is obviously beyond the ability or even the desire of a child who appears to be growing up in an ethical environment to question what he or she has been taught. Consequently the child can grow to adulthood without having subjected earlier knowledge to a critical examination, and as a result is the victim of a good deal of folklore, racial misconceptions, preconceived ideas about the opposite sex, physical or mental disability, and many other hazards of the unexamined life. Having acquired such an unsatisfactory residuum of what passes for knowledge, many adults see no desire to implement critical changes, preferring instead to live and die among the clichés, half-truths, and downright misrepresentations that go to make up prejudice.

But if an individual is willing to examine his or her stock of knowledge rigorously in the light of up-to-date information about the topics in question, a surprising change of attitude can take place as the person unlearns what was acquired in childhood, and replaces prejudice with informed factual opinion in an atmosphere of mental openness and freedom from particular constraints. This process ought to apply consistently throughout a person's lifetime to all areas of knowledge, and not merely to those that concern current social prejudices. The reason for insisting upon the importance of this periodic review is that prejudice in particular thrives upon a lack of factual input, whether it is for or against some particular situation. Conversely, the very deficiencies which support prejudice prevent a balanced intellectual and emotional examination of the subject of prejudice.

The biggest hurdle to surmount in this laudable endeavor of re-education is the unfortunate fact that, in insecure people generally, prejudice offers a high degree of resistance to correction and elimination, principally because such a result would undermine the sense of superiority upon which prejudice often rests. To feel superior in some small respect is fundamentally important in preserving the stability of insecure personalities, but what is not generally realized is that a broadening and maturing of the individual's mind and nature is one extremely valuable result of removing prejudice. This achievement is followed by a developing degree of tolerance, which brings an even more broadly balanced outlook to individual lives, as Christians have discerned in applying biblical principles of tolerance (Rom. 12:18; Col. 3:11, 13).

In contemporary life prejudice is commonly thought of mainly in racial terms, where some nations regard others as inferior in certain ways. This attitude is not restricted to issues of color, but involves inheritance factors as well as social ideologies to the point where even people from different parts of the same country exhibit specific prejudices for a variety of reasons. Where there are recognizable ethnic groups in a nation, it is usually very difficult to avoid expressions of prejudice, if only because ethnic immigrants bring with them the traditions of their native lands, some of which may seem undesirable to the host country, and which in any event usually contain internal tensions and hostilities. When the latter come into the open, suspicion and prejudice are fostered in the minds of many who have no actual involvement in the situation. Yet another important manifestation of prejudice arises from conflicts between the sexes, producing stereotypes of the "male chauvinist" and the "militant feminist," which rightly or wrongly foster prejudice.

Christians are commanded to live at peace, because the peace of Christ arbitrates in their minds (Col. 3:15), and to honor everybody (1 Pet. 2:17). Since there are to be no racial distinctions or discrimination in the community of Christ (Col. 3:11), the Christian church should and must be in the forefront of the fight against prejudice as part of its ministry to the world.

**PRESUMPTION.** This term is based upon the Latin verb *sumo*, "to take up, assume," and appeared in a compound form *praesumo*, "to take first to oneself, forestall, anticipate." The noun *praesumptio* meant either an anticipation of something, a preconception, or a supposition. In current English usage a presumption is something that is accepted as constituting undeniable fact, whether the accuracy of the presumption has actually been checked or not. Presumption also applies to the attitude of mind that can confidently transgress the bounds of propriety without undue concern about possible recriminations. This type of presumption also involves an imposition upon the charity or courtesy of the recipients of such behavior, and not infrequently provokes adverse reactions as a result.

Many ethicists have seen the root of presumption in human pride, which prompts an individual to arrogate to himself or herself powers or expectations that are unreal, or at the very least inappropriate to the time and situation. Moses and Aaron were accused of this very act by two persons who may well have been jealous of their preferred status in the community and wished to have greater prominence themselves (Num. 16:3). In the Torah (Deut. 18:22) the criterion by which a prophet speaking in the Lord's name could be judged accurately as to whether his proclamation was true or false subsisted in the matter of fulfillment. If the prophecy remained unfulfilled, the prophet was false and had spoken presumptuously, not having had the Lord's authority for his proclamation.

Some theologians have conjectures that presumption was the sin that occasioned the expulsion of Satan from heaven, but the Scriptures, while noting the event (Luke 10:18), are silent about the cause. The disciple who realizes that he or she is not above the master (Matt. 10:24) will not be guilty of the sin of presumption, but will walk in obedience and humility in the will and guidance of the Holy Spirit. It is the responsibility of the disciple to follow, and not to attempt to usurp the leadership of the Lord.

In Roman Catholic canon law, presumption describes a reasonable estimate of some dubious circumstance, arrived at after a careful examination of circumstantial and other evidence. It is only employed when full proof is lacking, but similarities or precedents indicate the direction which the verdict should take. This is known as *presumptio iuris* and differs from *presumptio hominis* in that in the latter there are no legal precedents to instruct a judge in a decision that must be made.

**PRIDE.** This term is derived from a French word *prud*, "good," but in English has acquired some unfortunate negative connotations of haughtiness, arrogance, a flaunting of superiority, and other manifestations of an exaggerated estimate of self-worth. As it happens, however, these do not constitute the total meaning of pride in current usage, for there are positive aspects of the term as well. For a person to take pride in his or her work means that the individual concerned respects the particular form of activity sufficiently well as to ensure that it is discharged to the best degree possible. This type of pride ensures good and efficient workmanship, a commodity that is in scarce supply in contemporary society, as well as a finished product in which others can take delight. All these are positive values, representing the best efforts of a person who labors to attain to the standards of performance which the craft demands so as to bring pleasure and even pride of ownership to others. Paul expressed the concept in a negative fashion in 2 Timothy 2:15 in urging his younger brother in the faith so to labor before God that he would appear as a workman who did not need to be ashamed.

Another common expression which places a positive emphasis upon the concept relates to a person taking pride in his or her appearance. This involves self-discipline as well as self-estimate and for the Christian represents an attempt to present the body, which is the temple of the Holy Spirit (1 Cor. 3:16), in a manner that befits such a lofty concept. The element of self-discipline will be manifested in the injunction of Paul for women to dress in modest attire (1 Tim. 2:9-10) so that they are not clothing themselves at an exorbitant price at the expense of other things, nor are they flaunting their purely physical attributes in a manner that could be reminiscent of the courtesan. The estimate of self-worth that the person possesses, whether male or female, will ensure that a neat, attractive appearance is the servant, not the master, of the one who is witnessing for Christ in human society.

The concept of pride is even described under certain circumstances in English as "proper." While this is a somewhat metaphorical use of the term, it is important because it carries moral and ethical connotations. Among those who use it, the expression *proper pride* has a basis in the person's self-estimate because it demonstrates that the individual should only indulge in those thoughts and actions that are deemed worthy of that person and will maintain and promote his or her self-respect. In other words, proper pride is based upon value judgments relating to the rightness or wrongness of behavior, emphasizing propriety rather than arrogance or haughtiness.

The Old Testament vocabulary for pride is extensive and varied, even for a vice, thereby indicating the importance attached to it. Three related words, *geah*, *gaon*, and *gewah*, describe pride in terms of 'swelling," "excellency," or "elevation" with the emphasis upon arrogant behavior and the punishment that it would merit from God (Prov. 8:13; 16:18; Isa. 25:11). Presumption (*za-*

*don*). haughtiness (*gobah*), and self-elevation (*gaawah*) also claim a place in the vocabulary of pride. By contrast the New Testament uses comparatively few terms to express the concept, and most of those are rare. The proud teacher of unrighteous doctrine is described as *tuphoomai*, or "puffed up with conceit," while another uncommon word, *huperephania* (Mark 7:22) characterizes pride as arrogance. A related form, *hupererphanos* (Luke 1:51; James 4:6), "exceedingly proud," describes an extreme form of what in Scripture is consistently vicious and evil.

Any self-respect that the Christian has can only be based upon the atoning work of Christ, which has exalted the sinner to a place in Christ's glorious kingdom. The believer can then exercise proper pride, in the words of Paul, by walking worthily of his or her vocation to ministry. This is accomplished not in a worldly spirit of arrogance, but in "lowliness and gentleness, with longsuffering" (Eph. 4:2, NKJV). Haughtiness of demeanor (Isa. 3:16) is unbecoming to one who is trying to imitate the humility and obedience of Christ (Phil. 2:8) in this world. Paul makes the definitive pronouncement about pride in the Christian's life when asserting that the believer should not think of himself or herself more highly than is warranted, but instead should make a sober assessment of personal ability according to the measure of individual faith (Rom. 12:3).

See PRESUMPTION.

**PRINCIPLES, BIBLICAL.** If we take "principles" to refer to fundamental, comprehensive laws or doctrines, it may be claimed that the following four points represent the general thrust and concern of the whole Bible. "All Scripture," we are told, "is inspired by God and is profitable for teaching, reproof, correction and training in righteousness" (2 Tim. 3:15).

Ethics are to be grounded in the revelation of God's character, will, actions, and purposes. In the Old Testament Israel was often told, explicitly and implicitly, "This is what God is like, follow his example" (Lev. 19:2, "You shall be holy; for I, the LORD your God am holy"; see 1 Pet. 1:15-16), and "This is what God has done for you; out of gratitude you should do the same for others." The Decalogue does not begin with a command, but with a statement of redemption: "I am the LORD your God, who brought you up out of the land of Egypt..." and on this basis the people are told to keep God's commandments.

In the New Testament disciples of the kingdom and members of the church of God are also reminded of the character of God: "You must be perfect as your heavenly Father is perfect" (Matt. 5:48) and, "Be merciful even as your Father is merciful" (Luke 6:36). It is only possible to love God and people because God first loved and loves still: "We love because he first loved us" (1 John 4:19) and "Be imitators of God as beloved chil-

dren; and walk in love as Christ loved us..." (Eph. 5:1; 4:31-32).

The purpose of ethics is to describe and produce a people who reflect the character of God, Creator, and Redeemer. God called Israel into existence as a separate people and entered into a special relationship with this people in order to speak through Israel to the whole world. "If you obey my voice and keep my covenant, you shall be my own possession among all peoples...and you shall be to me a kingdom of priests and a holy nation" (Exod. 19:5-6; Isa. 42:6; 49:3, 6). The very existence and character of Israel as a people and society were to be a witness to and for God. They were to be a model or paradigm of His holiness expressed in the social and political life of a redeemed community.

In the New Testament there is the same emphasis where disciples are urged by Jesus to be "the salt of the earth" and the "light of the world" (Matt. 5:13-14). Peter declared that the churches "are a chosen race, a royal priesthood, a holy nation, God's own people" who are to declare the wonderful deeds of Him who called them out of darkness into light (1 Pet. 2:9). Thus the movement is from the committed, faithful people of God toward the whole population, for God desires that all men should reflect His character.

Ethics are to be grounded in the love (*agape*) that comes from God. When asked which was the greatest commandment in the law, Jesus replied that on two commandments—to love God wholly and to love the neighbor as oneself—all the law and the prophets hang (Matt. 22:36-40). He also told his disciples to love their enemies and to do unto others as they would wish others to do to them (Matt. 5:44; 7:12). Paul claimed that "love is the fulfilling of the law" (Rom. 13:10; Gal. 5:14-15). Such loving is only possible where the love of God through the indwelling presence of the Spirit is present in the heart.

Since God is love, and since He loves the ungodly, it is from this love (together with the knowledge that each person is made in the image and likeness of God) that the dignity of each person, whoever he or she happens to be, is established. Thus the basis of the moral relationship between one person and another (and between the church of God and society at large) ought to be that of the acknowledgment of the value, dignity, and worth of every person. This may be called a bestowed rather than an appraised dignity, for it is given by God's love and not achieved. Thus where there is genuine love, there is also the determination to provide for the true well-being of the brother, neighbor, and enemy.

Ethics are to be consistent with the justice and righteousness of God. Justice is what God himself practices and executes in human affairs (Jer. 9:24; Ps. 103:6; 2 Cor. 9:9-10), and it is what His people are to imitate (Deut. 10:18-19; Isa. 1:17; Amos 5:21-24; Hos. 10:2; Mic. 6:6-8; Matt. 23:23; James 1:27). This justice is unique in that, informed and empowered by love and acknowledging the true worth of people, it has a special concern for those on the fringes of society and those in particular need (the "deserving poor," Exod. 22:21-22; Deut. 14:9; 15:7; Jer. 22:3-4). Thus this is a creative justice bringing into reality what it requires. It is to be contrasted with that secular idea of justice that preserves the *status quo*. It requires a willingness to put the interests of others before self, class, and ethnic interests.

In New Testament terms, ethics are those of the kingdom of God. "Seek first God's kingdom and his righteousness," said Jesus (Matt. 6:33). With the dawning of this reign of righteousness and salvation within human history, there has arrived a new age of righteousness and justice; but the latter needs to be implemented in the power of the Spirit of the Lord. The full demands and outworking of God's creative justice come into being where the kingdom of God is present.

**Bibliography:** Haughey, J. C., (ed.), *The Faith That Does Justice* (1977); Mott, S. C., *Biblical Ethics and Social Change* (1982); Wright, C. J. H., *Living as the People of God: The Relevance of O.T. Ethics* (1983).

P.T.

**PRISONERS OF CONSCIENCE.** This expression was apparently invented by Peter Benenson, a Christian lawyer in England, who on Trinity Sunday, 1961, launched a human rights movement that has become institutionalized as Amnesty International. In its strict sense, a prisoner of conscience is one who has been imprisoned by state authority solely for the peaceable public expression of religious commitments or conscientious convictions. Those who have used or advocated violence are not considered prisoners of conscience. The term is more widely used by Amnesty International itself also to include any person who has been imprisoned as the result of discrimination on grounds of color, sex, ethnic origin, or language. It is estimated that half the countries of the world hold prisoners of conscience in this wider sense, and that one country in three has subjected prisoners to torture or cruelty since 1980. Some prisoners of conscience have been convicted of crimes (almost always of a political nature); many, however, are incarcerated without trial, or, as in Soviet countries, are consigned to "psychiatric hospitals" for "medical treatment."

The term is used normatively. Those who use it understand a prisoner of conscience to be *ipso facto* a victim of injustice. The nature of the injustice suffered by a prisoner of conscience can be different according to whether a person is a prisoner of conscience in the strict or the wider sense.

In the former case, the argument is that, whatever other powers a government may rightly exercise for public order and the common good, it may not claim a citizen's ultimate allegiance. This understanding can be found in Greek antiq-

uity (Plato's *Apology,* Sophocles' *Antigone*), but its more influential development is to be found in the biblical faith. In the Old Testament, God raises prophets to challenge powerful but unrighteous leaders. Jeremiah, for example, was put in the stocks (Jer. 20:3) for his forthright denunciations of King Jehoiakim of Judah, and of the policies of the nation's religious and political establishment (19:3-15). The mission of the prophets thus reflects what the Jewish theologian Martin Buber calls the "theopolitical assumption" that God remains the sovereign of His people in all matters, human sovereignties notwithstanding. In the intertestamental period, the tradition of conscientious witness was strengthened. When, after 175 B.C., Antiochus IV (Epiphanes) attempted to suppress Judaism for political reasons, the Maccabean resistance ensued. As one martyr expressed it, "I will not comply with the king's ordinance; I obey the ordinance of the Law given to our ancestors through Moses" (2 Macc. 7:30). Christ prophesied that his followers would be persecuted for their convictions, and their sufferings are indeed a major theme in Christian history. Imprisonment was not generally used as a means of punishment before the eighteenth century, but early Christians suffered torture, hard labor, and terrible forms of execution for their faith.

The role of conscience continued to be recognized in the later church. The most influential medieval theologian, Thomas Aquinas (1225-1274), believed that Christians might disobey human legislation that transgressed "the eternal principles of law," and that to follow even an erroneous conscience, if it were "invincibly erroneous," was free of guilt. In the sixteenth century, Martin Luther heroically defied the ecclesiastical and imperial establishment on grounds of conscience: "Here I stand; I can do nothing else." His contemporary Sir Thomas More accepted martyrdom for his faith by declaring that he was "the king's good servant, but God's first." The supremacy of conscience was endorsed in a secular forum when the judges at the Nuremberg trials of Nazi war criminals refused to entertain the plea of those accused of unconscionable crimes that they were merely obeying the legal instructions of their rightful leaders.

Christian theology has also, however, provided justification for the coercion of conscience. When Christians came into control of the state in the fourth century, they began to regard schismatics, heretics, pagans, Jews, and other minorities as political problems. Augustine, especially in his famous *Letter 93,* found scriptural support for coercion in New Testament exhortations to church unity, in Paul's insistence on obedience to the established authorities (Rom. 13), in examples of compelled righteousness (Luke 14:23), and in the view that severe discipline is a spiritual medicine (1 Cor. 5:5). Such arguments would later be used to legitimate the medieval Inquisition and other forms of Christian tyranny.

The injustice suffered by prisoners of conscience in the second and wider sense of the term—prisoners as a result of discriminatory treatment—is held to be a violation of their human rights. The argument here is that all human beings, regardless of their race, gender, or social situation, are (in the words of the American Declaration of Independence of 1776) "endowed by their Creator with certain inalienable rights; that among these are life, liberty, and the pursuit of happiness." It is controversial but, on the whole, doubtful whether either biblical or pagan antiquity had an understanding of natural human rights similar to the modern sense. The impetus to human rights theory was not so much reflection on biblical faith as the development of traditions of constitutionally restricted political power, particularly in England. In the eighteenth century, a full-blown theory of the natural rights of all human beings was argued by philosophers. It was institutionalized in the American and French Revolutions. In recent years, especially in revulsion against the Nazi terror, human rights theory has won a high degree of official acceptance in international declarations, treaties, and customary law. This acceptance is often more a matter of rhetoric than of fact, although the countries belonging to the European Convention of 1950, the American Convention of 1969, and the International Covenant of 1976 have accepted the jurisdiction of international courts.

What focused Christian thought on human rights most significantly was probably the antislavery movement, which began gathering momentum in 1787 and which was spearheaded by committed evangelical Christians. The biblical underpinnings of Christian human rights theory include the creation of humanity in God's image, the sense that proper political power rests on covenant with Him, Christ's high evaluation of the worth of the individual person apart from social status, the spiritual equality of all persons as sinners for whom Christ died, the prophetic and messianic concern for social justice, the law of love, and what has been called "the biblical bias for the poor."

But human rights theory is rejected by various groups. First, Communist states understand human rights to be primarily the economic rights of the collective, which the individual exists to serve. Secondly, Third World apologists for persecution believe that their own societies are undergoing a phase of state-building and economic development such as European nations had to pass through before being able to entrench human rights. (Yet these countries have usually made commitments to international standards of human rights.) Third, classical Western conservatives have regarded civil rights not as God-given gifts but as the creation and heritage of a sound system of government. Fourth, neoconservatives have complained that human rights ideology implies restrictions on what they take to be the higher principle of self-interest. Finally, some sectarian Christians take it that, unlike Paul, they should not appeal to worldly protection for themselves and should not trouble themselves over the protection of nonbelievers.

The most noted organization concerned with prisoners of conscience is Amnesty International, which won the Nobel Peace Prize in 1977. Members in about 150 countries seek relief for individual prisoners by writing letters on their behalf, except where this tactic is likely to prove counterproductive. Prisoners are identified equally in Communist, Western, and nonaligned countries.

It may be concluded that the Bible and sound Christian tradition recognize the claims of a conscience led by God and condemn governmental interference with God's will. But the Bible does not condemn (nor does it endorse) the imprisonment of persons acting illegally from a mistaken conscience, or from nonconscientious motives. Of course, in practice, it is not always immediately possible to tell the difference. It is a matter of social policy whether a state will prefer to err on the side of the individual or on the side of the collective. The Bible does not speak of natural human rights; but respect for the oppressed, love of neighbor, and social justice are without doubt biblical norms, to which human rights theory gives equivocal expression. Since prisoners of conscience are so often victims of injustice, we owe them, on biblical grounds, our prayers and our active concern.

**Bibliography:** Brown, P., "Augustine's Attitude," *Journal of Roman Studies* 54 (1964), pp. 107–16; Buber, M., *The Prophetic Faith* (1949); Frend, W. H. C., *Martyrdom and Persecution in the Early Church* (1965); "Perspective," *United Nations Chronicle* 21 (1984); Power, J., *Amnesty International* (1981).

A.L.H.

**PRISONERS OF WAR.** In almost any battle from the earliest periods of human history, some persons, both soldiers and civilians, have been taken captive by the enemy. In ancient Sumeria prisoners of war were frequently carried away by the visitors to serve as slaves, and if the city in which they were living was subsequently attacked and conquered by another enemy, the slaves were often liberated. The ancient Assyrians established a reputation for brutality to prisoners, especially pregnant females, who were often stripped publicly, mutilated, and disemboweled. Male and female prisoners were normally made to disrobe and then marched off into exile without clothing in order to add personal embarrassment to the shame of capture. Women prisoners of war were thus especially vulnerable to atrocious behavior, with beatings and sexual assault being common occurrences. In Roman times it was not unusual for imperial soldiers serving in foreign lands to pursue native women, whether prisoners of war or not, and having assaulted them sexually to kill them. In ancient Israel it was common for male prisoners to have their thumbs and their big toes amputated (Judg. 1:6-7). This was a more humane procedure than killing them, because it merely disabled the captive so that he could not use a bow or flee readily. Atrocities of this kind still persist, unfortunately, and international legislation has been enacted to try to control the situation and to maintain some sort of dignity and honor for prisoners of war.

The ethical concerns of the Bible for prisoners (Ps. 102:20; Zech. 9:11; Matt. 25:36) underlie the legislation which began with the Hague Convention of 1907 and continued with several Geneva Conventions from 1929 onward. The overall aim is to afford humane treatment for prisoners, to protect them from reprisals of any kind, and to arrange for their repatriation whenever possible. Some authorities have criticized the provisions of the 1949 Geneva Convention as making life for prisoners of war more attractive than for combatants, regardless of how the ideals were stated. Communist nations generally have not ratified the enactments, and in World War II the Japanese committed atrocities against Allied prisoners, as did North Korean and North Vietnamese Communists at a subsequent period.

Christians who cherish the image of God in mankind will support resolutely the various conventions aimed at according war prisoners humane treatment and will seek to maintain Christ's attitude toward persecutors and dictators (Matt. 5:44-45).

**PRISONERS, RIGHTS OF.** Any discussion of prisoners' rights presupposes an understanding of both human rights generally and of the purpose and effect of imprisonment as a penalty for lawbreaking. Both of these preliminary topics, whether approached from a secular or Christian perspective, are problematic.

Theorists seeking to find a basis for human rights have traditionally looked either to an implied contract between the members of a society or alternatively to some form of "natural law." Weaknesses of the former approach include the artificiality of pretending that a society is based on a contract that binds its members, despite the fact that they have had neither control over its terms nor an opportunity to consent or refuse to accept its obligations. Furthermore, where rights are supposedly based solely on a social contract, they can just as easily be altered or terminated by means of a further actual or supposed agreement.

There are also fundamental difficulties with many of the natural law theories. In particular, humanistic theories that, without reference to any outside standard, see rights as inherent in or dictated by human nature have difficulty in accommodating the tremendous conflicts between different people's value systems.

For the Christian, an answer to this dilemma must begin with the recognition that God is the ultimate source of all truth and justice (John 1:1-14). The Bible asserts that people are made in God's image (Ps. 8) but also makes it very clear that "all have sinned and fall short of the glory of God" (Rom. 3:23; Ps. 14:1-3). As a result, in terms of absolute justice at least, no one deserves any rights at all. Rather, claims for human rights should be grounded in an understanding of God's grace, mercy, and His plan to redeem and restore fallen humanity. Thus, specific demands for human rights to be respected are essentially claims for God's creation ethic to be put into practice in a particular context.

For the Christian, then, human rights are derived from God's plan for creation rather than from human agreement. The concept of human rights should be founded on a specifically Christian outlook, the characteristics of which have been completely and perfectly spelt out by Jesus. This has significant implications for the administration of criminal justice generally, and in particular for the way in which prisoners are to be treated. If rights were somehow earned by good behavior, then it would of course be reasonable to conclude that people who behaved badly would forfeit their rights accordingly. However, because basic human rights exist regardless of individual merit, it follows that, just as they are not earned through good behavior, neither are they automatically forfeited through bad behavior or criminal activity.

Nevertheless, "rights" only have substance when matched by corresponding duties or obligations. Jesus confirmed the teaching, implicit in the Old Testament, that love for God and love for one's neighbor are the essential commandments on which all rules to govern human behavior should be based (Matt. 22:34-40). What happens when rules based on these basic principles are disobeyed and, as a result, one person's "freedom" infringes on another person's rights? This is where a theory of either punishment or correction becomes necessary.

Leaving aside crude revenge, the most common justifications for punishment are divine or societal retribution, deterrence, and rehabilitation. Of all the forms of punishment that have been used historically, imprisonment is one of the most difficult to make sense of in terms of any of these theories. The fact that in most Western countries the vast majority of the prison population has been in prison before is ample evidence that in most cases prison neither rehabilitates nor deters those who are incarcerated. Not all prisoner are recidivists, but the "success" rate is very low indeed. The extent to which the imprisonment of offenders deters other people from committing offenses is more difficult to assess, but its effectiveness in this area is very seriously doubted in criminological circles. This leaves retribution as a possible rationale for imprisonment. The concept of "just desserts" is of course very familiar to Christian thought. It must not be forgotten, however, that in the Bible, divinely imposed retributive punishment is always tempered by justice and mercy. These fundamental principles dictate that imprisonment, or any other form of punishment, must not be humanly degrading or imposed arbitrarily. In every case the offender's dignity must be respected (Deut. 25:3).

What then might be a Christian perspective on imprisonment? Very little direct comment on the subject can be found in the Bible. This should come as no surprise, however, as the practice of using imprisonment as a form of punishment for criminal offenses only became popular in the early eighteenth century. A century and a half later, there are now hundreds of thousands of people in prison worldwide. Imprisonment is likely to remain a favored correctional tool for many years to come.

In marked contrast to this state of affairs, under Old Testament law the principal penalties for offenses were fines, compensation orders, and corporal or capital punishment. Indeed, there is no express reference at all to imprisonment as a form of punishment under Jewish law, although there is an account of Joseph being put in an Egyptian prison for being accused of offending Potiphar's wife (Gen. 39:20). Normally an offender would completely discharge his or her debt to society almost immediately after a finding of guilt. The considerable emphasis that was placed on securing compensation and practical restitution (Lev. 6:1-5) has been largely neglected in most contemporary criminal justice systems.

New Testament references to imprisonment indicate that it was used as a form of executive punishment without trial (Matt. 14:3), and as a temporary pretrial measure (Acts 5:18; 12:4). It was apparently also used for nonpayment of debts, and perhaps in other civil disputes (Matt. 5:25-26). Although nothing like modern imprisonment, the apostle Paul apparently spent two years living in Rome under house arrest (Acts 28:16, 30).

However, what references there are in the Bible to the way in which prisoners should be treated tend to be extremely sympathetic to the needs of those in custody. For example, in the parable of the sheep and the goats (Matt. 25:31-46), Jesus groups prisoners together with the hungry, the thirsty, the sick, and other members of society in need of compassion. Help given to such people is considered as given to Christ himself and failure to give assistance results in condemnation to eternal punishment. Similarly, the writer of the letter to the Hebrews exhorts his readers to "remember those in prison as if you were their fellow prisoners" (Heb. 13:3).

The failure of imprisonment to achieve the goals of deterring or rehabilitating individual offenders may in large part be attributable to the fact that in many cases so little regard is given to the dignity of those in custody. Moreover, in terms of the fundamental biblical emphasis on restitution and reconciliation, imprisonment is a singularly inappropriate correctional tool. Where an offender is sent to prison, any victim of the crime generally remains uncompensated, and at the same time society pays a high financial cost to keep the prisoner in custody. Considerable stress is placed on family relationships, and the prisoner's alienation from society at large is likely to be exacerbated by involvement in the prison's subculture. Furthermore, arguments in favor of imprisonment that are based on principles of just retribution cannot be sustained if prisons are in themselves manifestly unjust places. Many prisoners live under the threat of violence from their custodians or other inmates. Internal prison rules governing, for example, prison discipline are frequently obscured by administrative secrecy and unchecked discretion. While never denying individual responsibility for wrongdoing, Christians in a position to do so should strive for the development of penal systems in which justice is tempered with mercy, and punishment is administered in a manner that fosters both redemption and reconciliation. It is salutatory to remember that hell will be populated by people who have found justice, heaven by those who have found mercy.

**Bibliography:** Foucault, M., *Discipline and Punish: The Birth of the Prison* (1978); Marshall, P., *Human Rights in Christian Perspective* (1983); Millard, C., *Canadian Criminology Forum* (1982), 5:1, pp. 11–24; Stott, J. and Miller, N., *Crime and the Responsible Community* (1980).

C.J.M.

**PROCREATION.** God's first recorded command to humans was to procreate (Gen. 1:28).. The resultant scriptural attitude toward children, in contrast to moods often prevalent in Western society today, is that children are a blessing from God (Gen. 15:2; 30:1; Deut. 25:5; 1 Sam. 11:20; Ps. 127:3; Matt. 22:24; Luke 1:7, 28). On the scriptural value-scale, children have clear priority over high standards of living. Procreation by married parents is part of God's revealed plan for humanity, a sacred duty to be celebrated in joyful cooperation with God. Important as it is, however, it remains but one of the purposes of marriage, as most wedding liturgies clearly indicate.

Neither 1 Corinthians 7 nor any other New Testament passage should be interpreted as contradicting this creation mandate. The Corinthian chapter was addressed to a particular congregation in response to specific problems being experienced at the time. While the New Testament as a whole focuses strongly on personal transformation and preparation for the *parousia,* it by no means abrogates perennial creation principles and values, including procreation. Rather, following Jesus, who strongly endorsed Old Testament values rightly understood, New Testament Christianity took those values for granted. Life's daily agenda of tasks and functions was not to stop because of the eagerly expected *parousia* (2 Thess. 3:6-15), even though that agenda might have to be adjusted from time to time to the requirements of specific circumstances. Procreation must go on.

Homosexual and lesbian sexual relationships not only fail to fulfill the mandate to procreate, but they contribute to an ambience of nonscriptural anti-procreativity.

Stewardship of one's procreative powers is part of humanity's general responsibility to "have dominion" over all creation (Gen. 1:26-28). When in a couple's sanctified judgment it becomes appropriate to suspend the procreation of children for any length of time (and the reasons might be many, among them the wife's health and responsible "spacing" of children), then the remaining purposes of sexual union, including sexual love, remain valid according to most Protestant thinkers, and artificial means of conception prevention are quite legitimate.

Another limit to procreation must be the obligation to avoid inflicting hereditary diseases on future generations. Persons having this affliction in their genetic background are strongly advised not to have children; nevertheless, for reasons outlined above, this should not prevent them from expressing their love sexually to their spouses, with adequate safeguards against conception. To be ethical, methods of limiting procreation should be as effective as possible, freely chosen by both spouses, have no serious medical or psychological side effects, and, in most instances, be reversible.

Couples who are unable to procreate through normal sexual intercourse can often succeed with unusual methods, all of which have to be tested in the light of God's revealed will and purpose. Christians' opinions differ on the ethics of such methods. *In vitro* fertilization presents a problem because a number of eggs are thus fertilized, but not all these incipient humans are implanted in the womb, the unwanted ones being discarded once pregnancy is achieved. A similar ethical problem arises with the use of intrauterine devices as conception preventatives, which allow the egg to be fertilized but prevent it from being implanted. Artificial insemination with the husband's sperm is an action within the marriage bond, but not insemination by a donor's sperm, which would be adulterous. Some would consider it wholesome to have a husband and wife's fertilized egg introduced into the womb of another woman who would carry their child instead of the wife who cannot. Others would consider this procedure psychologically and socially, and therefore ethically, too risky. These are only some examples of unusual methods of procreation that are possible today and concerning which serious ethical thinking continues to be done.

**Bibliography:** Christian Medical Society,

*Birth Control and the Christian* (1969); *Ibid.*, "A Protestant Affirmation on the Control of Human Reproduction," a written consensus of twenty-five evangelical scholars who took part in an interdenominational consultation on this theme in August 1968 in Portsmouth, New Hampshire, U.S.A.; Fagley, R., *The Population Explosion and Christian Responsibility* (1960); "Procreation" in MacQuarrie, J., (ed.), *A Dictionary of Christian Ethics* (1971); Greer, G., *Sex and Destiny* (1984); Guzzetti, G., "How the Vatican Came to Oppose Use of the Pill," *The Toronto Star* (Sept. 30, 1969); *Lambeth Conference Report* (1958); Pike, J. A., *Birth Control and the Christian* (n.d.).

See ARTIFICIAL INSEMINATION; CONTRACEPTION; SEX.

D.N.P.

**PROFANITY.** This term describes the treatment of a holy person, place, cause, or institution as if it were common or unholy. In particular, it designates the use of language about God that is irreverent, blasphemous, and base, or which uses the divine name as a curse or in swearing.

For such activity or words to be recognized as sin, there must be a general awareness of the existence of the holy Lord and of His demands upon and commands to mankind. Thus, in Israel, profanity was recognized by the law (Lev. 19:8) and by the prophets (Ezek. 36:20-23) as a serious offense against the Lord, deserving His wrath and punishment. Profanity is the opposite of reverence for God, His name, His character, His revelation, and His purposes. Paul referred to "unholy and profane persons" (1 Tim. 1:9), possibly indicating those who scorned the idea that there is one true and living God and that His name, with that of the Lord Jesus, should be reverenced. The writer of Hebrews singled out Esau as a profane person because he sold his birthright for a meal—a birthright had messianic implications, and with which the honor of God's name and purposes were intimately connected (Heb. 12:6).

Today we find those who deliberately and knowingly commit the sin of profanity by their celebration of secularism, their denial of the existence of God, their rejection of the morality of the Decalogue, and their general lack of respect for religious ideas, worship, and institutions. Their atheism makes them confident that there will be no Judge to punish them. Many others encouraged by the jokes from comedians and loose talk of public figures often profane God's name by using it as a swear word. Often this form of speech has become such a habit that it occurs without the person realizing he or she is using it.

Profanity is also a sin of devout and religious people who do believe that God exists and that He is holy. There is profanity of holy things, for example the careless and hypercritical use of the Bible, which is Holy Scripture, and the unworthy receiving of the sacramental body and blood of Christ in Holy Communion. More serious is the profaning of God's name, character, and revealed will, for example, by careless and irreverent use of God's name in prayer, chorus, and song, or by an immoral life that is not compatible with the profession of God's name.

Although by God's holy standards profanity is a most serious sin, it is not the kind of offense that Christians should seek to punish by law. It is only as the general awareness of the existence of a holy God thoroughly permeates society that people will understand this particular immorality. In Muslim countries where Islamic law is followed, profanity is punishable by the state. The West, however, is too secularized for profanity to be punishable by civil law.

P.T.

**PROFESSIONAL ETHICS.** One of the basic problems facing anyone attempting to study professional ethics is the task of defining the term *profession*. At one time the professions included law, medicine, the church, and possibly teaching. Today common usage is much broader. There is little agreement on which occupations fall within the scope of the professions. It may well be that the original concept of the word has been lost.

Traditionally, members of a profession have professed a body of skill and knowledge common only to a few within society, namely, themselves. Furthermore, that knowledge has extended beyond the bounds of ordinary things and was grasped as a result of learning, usually in a university. Thus, a profession has in the past been associated with learning, and the members of a profession were regarded as learned. The exclusive knowledge of professions in former times guaranteed for their members high earnings and wealth. Such wealth has been a feature of the medical and legal professions.

The position of the professions in the old sense has been eroded by the increase of specialization within society and by the consequent increase in the number of groups that can profess special skill and knowledge. Members of such groups consider that they belong to the professions. Their education, as well as that of the established professions, may not now be so exclusive as the training of the professions was in times past. Technology, which in the shape of word processors, computers, and advanced machinery is replacing the need for personal skill and knowledge, may also be undermining the unique place of the learned professions and contributing to the shift in the meaning of the term *profession*. The diminution in the relative economic status of the older professions in countries such as the United Kingdom may have further weakened the claims of a small group to be considered specifically as the professions.

The spread of groups claiming professional status renders it impossible to contemplate the emergence of a single code of ethics that can be called professional ethics. It is clear, and must be stressed, that most groups calling themselves professions will assert that they abide by ethical standards. Indeed, some groups will advance the argument that they should exercise a monopoly because their ethical standards protect the public from the unscrupulous.

Professional ethics encompasses a variety of principles and issues. One aspect of such ethics is regulation. A discussion of ethics must focus attention on principles of law enforced by a society through its legislators and courts, on principles and standards demanded by professional bodies, on standards expected of a profession by society, and on the moral principles of members of the profession.

Another important part of ethics is debate. At issue today are questions dealing with the relationship of law and personal morality, the right of the individual to differ with his peers, and the freedom of the group to assert its own standards against those desired by society or enforced by the law. Abortion and euthanasia are matters of ethical debate within the medical profession and form an important part of medical ethics. Because it is impossible to cover all the regulatory aspects of ethics and the issues of debate, only a few have been selected.

One of the hallmarks of professional conduct that is often jealously guarded is independence. The professions demand that, in giving advice, members should be free from influence and should not be under the control of the client, patient, or any particular pressure group. It is important that when accountants audit the accounts of companies, they should not have to yield to pressures or influences of directors. The medical profession, likewise, must not be placed in the situation of prescribing a given brand of drug because a drug company has bought their professional judgment. There is in such cases a difficult dividing line between testing a new drug on selected patients in return for payment and prescribing the drugs of any company that pays the desired amount. Lawyers must equally resist pressure from governments when deciding whether to sue the state on behalf of the citizen.

Underlying the need for the independence of the professions are honesty and trust. Those who seek the aid of the professions expect honesty and desire to be able to trust the person consulted. Where there is a lack of honesty and trust, public confidence is weakened.

The professions have been noted for service to others. Behind the idea of service is the principle that others come before self. Perhaps one of the tragedies of modern life is that service and personal sacrifice are sometimes regarded as foolishness. Although the professions must undoubtedly protect themselves and have interests that are proper to advance, there is still a central role for denying one's interests and comfort for the sake of others.

Diligence is yet another requirement of the

professions. It is not enough to produce a result; the result must be sought diligently.

It is difficult for people to enforce independence, honesty, trust, service, and diligence. Indeed, in some cases they cannot be enforced directly. The professional bodies seek to set standards that will, in most situations, require proper professional conduct based on the concepts outlined. Where there is the possibility that a member of a profession may be judged adversely the principles and concepts should be reduced to clear prescriptive rules capable of reasonably certain application.

Of the many areas of debate, four can be mentioned. When the members of a profession are employed rather than self-employed, the question of the use of the weapon of industrial strike may arise. Is it right for a professional person to advance self-interest at the expense of the public who is being served? On the one hand, it is argued that unless labor is withheld, there will be no proper settlement of some disputes, and the long-term interests of the public will be hurt. Others, however, contend that self-sacrifice is the only policy. Some groups who achieve good conditions of service are entering into no-strike agreements. The weapon of the strike, therefore, may not be the best means of seeking to force an agreement. Some professions, in fact, may forbid strike action.

A difficult area for doctors is the matter of disclosure to the patient. Is it always right to inform one who has a terminal illness of the nature of the complaint? Opinion seems to be moving in favor of giving the information, but of ensuring that it is given caringly. In some cases, it might prove unwise to disclose too much.

An issue never far from debate is that of conscience over the law. For the professions, the question may be focused on professional standards and principles over the law. In Hitler's Germany, the professions were faced with these issues. The answer of the nations was that obedience to the law is no defense to crimes against humanity. In one celebrated English lawsuit, a doctor who had carried out experiments on Jews sued a publisher for libel. A book in which the doctor was criticized had been published. His defense was that he had carried out the experiments and operations rather than leave the patients to others who would have been less careful and merciful. The jury found for the doctor, but awarded the lowest damages ever given in England, one halfpenny.

It is often difficult to decide where the line should be drawn, and a full discussion of the issue is impossible. Three thoughts are, however, suggested by the lives of Daniel and his friends. They were able to serve an alien king who had ruined the temple of God in Jerusalem. It is, therefore, wrong to assume that Christians may not work for ungodly men. They drew the line when they were required to deny the worship of God. They accepted the punishments intended by the state, but, in their cases, prevented by God. Other examples of disobedience are found in the Bible, but they are examples of extreme situations.

The final point of debate chosen relates to recent developments of science, particularly in the field of genetics and the experimentation on embryos. At stake in such a debate are opposing views of human life. For the Christian, a description of human life based solely on scientific observation is inadequate. Christians must seek to resolve these matters by developing a biblical understanding. Although the Bible does not deal directly with the actual developments under discussion, it is arguable that there are general principles to be found in Scripture and that these principles are against such developments. Decisions in this area are already being made. A report in the United Kingdom has recommended that such experimentation be permitted subject to controls.

For those who seek to follow Christ, the ethical standards being applied in their professions must reflect not only those of the profession, but also Christ's standards.

M.H.J.

**PROHIBITION.** The common understanding of prohibition is that of recognized authority forbidding certain activities. The term has its origins in the Latin verb *habeo*, "to hold, keep." When prefixed by the preposition *pro-* it appears as *prohibeo*, "to hold someone at a distance," or in a metaphorical sense to prevent a person from engaging in some activity or to interfere with its conclusion. The ancient Romans used the word in a legal sense, and it is in that same context that it often appears in contemporary life.

What is known in the United States as Prohibition was the product of temperance movements in the nineteenth century. Societies arose in protest to the depravity caused by alcoholism and along with their counterparts in Britain and Europe were instrumental in bringing the manufacture and distribution of intoxicating beverages under government control. In 1917 the United States federal government prohibited alcoholic beverages entirely in response to pressure from temperance societies, and this state of affairs lasted until the great depression, when the law was repealed in 1933.

Spectacular as the prohibition of alcoholic beverages may be, there are less dramatic but nonetheless real enactments of the same order relating to certain types of weapons and a wide range of mind-disorienting chemicals. In religious circles the Roman Catholic Church endeavored to control the spread of doctrinal views other than their own approved ones and after 1571 drew up a list of works sanctioned by the censors, known as the Congregation of the Index. Any works that were forbidden by this group were then listed on the *Index Prohibitatus*.

The New Testament promotes the concept of

restrained behavior by Christians as they witness to the world in love, but also provides definite moral guidelines which include prohibited conduct (Gal. 5:17-21; Eph. 5:3-4) relating to matters of an immoral and unspiritual nature.

**PROMISCUITY.** Promiscuity is the practice of engaging in sexual activity with a variety of sexual partners. The term is derived from the Latin *promiscuus* and denotes indiscriminate mingling. Promiscuity covers a wide range of sexual behavior, including extramarital escapades by married persons, the so-called "singles bar scene," a series of sexual relationships in which one has exclusive relationships with one partner, and the continuation of a variety of sexual relationships at the same time. The breadth of the term renders it less than precise for moral analysis, dealing as it does both with marital infidelity and with intercourse between single persons with varying degrees of commitment, but in any case it would seem to cover adultery and fornication, both of which are roundly condemned in Scripture.

Promiscuity is a clear example of an area in which biblical and traditional beliefs and practices have met with significant challenge from many in the secular realm. The traditional view had seen promiscuity as harmful, dangerous to society's moral fabric, pathological, and a fit area for legal prohibition in many jurisdictions. Sexual behavior has often been limited to the marital bond and has not been allowed in relatively committed nonmarital relationships, let alone brief and temporary liaisons. Many secular thinkers believe the traditional view to be hopelessly ill-founded, especially since the advent of artificial birth control and effective therapy for venereal disease.

Sexual intercourse, in the thought of such secularists as philosopher Richard Wasserstrom, can be seen as merely an intensely pleasurable physical satisfaction, outside the realm of morality except as it causes harm, is deceitful, or otherwise violates an accepted category of moral duty. The challenge is raised as to how the biblical case against promiscuity can be made compellingly in contemporary culture? What indications can be found in human experience for the moral condemnation of such behavior?

Promiscuity is an emotionally immature and dangerous pattern of sexual behavior, involving a jarring discontinuity between the intimacy of the act and the impersonality of the relationship. Promiscuity may be a way of seeking "love" not found in genuine relationships, proving one's attractiveness in order to overcome feelings of inadequacy, or exerting sexual power over others. Engaging in promiscuity reduces others to an object of one's pleasure, rather than treating them as persons in a genuine human relationship of mutual caring. To engage in promiscuity seeks satisfactions that can only be found in a genuine facing of one's own emotional situation and in a committed relationship that marriage is ideally suited to provide. Christians need not be puzzled or embarrassed to hold their seemingly outdated morality, since it alone provides the context for genuine human relationship and caring, as well as the basis for the stable nurturing of the young.

**Bibliography:** Bertocci, P. A., *Sex, Love, and the Person* (1967); Smedes, L., *Sex for Christians* (1976); Wasserstrom, R., "Is Adultery Immoral?" in *Today's Moral Problems* (1979 ed.).

D.B.F.

**PROMISE.** When a person makes a promise, he or she indulges in a declaration of intent, positively or negatively, to fulfill a particular commitment or perform some specific duty at a future time. A definite promise normally includes a date on which the promise shall have been fulfilled. Indefinite promises, while assuring the recipient of genuine intent, do not specify a time limit by which they will be implemented fully.

The idea of future projection is implied in the Latin verb *promitto*, "to send forth, promise," which in terms of pledging oneself carries the same emphasis as in English. A promise should be distinguished from an oath, which in law is a formal or statutory declaration made binding by including the name of God as witness. Sometimes promises are made emphatic by a statement such as, "I swear to you by God that I will...," but these utterances lack the binding character of an oath because they are made outside a formal legal context.

There does not appear to be a specific Hebrew word for *promise*, although *omer*, "saying" (Ps. 77:8), and *dabar*, "word" (1 Kings 8:56; Neh. 5:12-13; Ps. 105:42), have been translated in this manner. Instead, the concept of swearing is employed (Gen. 24:3) in place of the less rigorously contractual promise. Yet the element of promise is clearly present in God's assurance to Abraham that he would make him the father of many nations (Gen. 15:4-6), and this is in addition to the formal covenantal undertaking that God made with the patriarch to guarantee the promise (Gen. 15:8-18). Abraham's firstborn, Isaac, was in a real sense the seal of that promise, which convinced the dubious parents as nothing else could.

The covenant at Sinai, by which the Hebrew tribes were banded into a single nation, contained stipulations of a general and detailed nature, as in the Hittite international treaties, but also listed many promises of blessing if the covenantal undertaking was honored (Deut. 28:2-14). In general, God's covenants are accompanied by assurances or promises which assist in explaining both the context of the occasion and its significance for the future. Thus God pledged a messianic line of succession to David (2 Sam. 7:12-16), based upon a mating with a woman whom David had not even encountered at that time, and elaborated on the eternal nature of the succession.

Following the pattern of the Sinai covenant, the

Hebrew prophets extended promises of divine blessing upon the homeland and its people, along with pointed warnings as to what would occur were the promises of the covenant to be broken. By contrast the Greek word *epangelia*, "promise," occurs frequently in the New Testament, along with a variant form *epangelma* (2 Pet. 1:4; 3:13). Jesus alluded to the Holy Spirit as "the Promise of My Father" (Luke 24:49, NKJV; Acts 1:4; 2:33). Peter interpreted the intervention of God to liberate the Hebrews from Egyptian control in terms of the fulfilled promise to Abraham (Acts 7:17), while Paul concurred in designating the seed of Isaac as the children of promise (Rom. 9:8-9). It is God's perceived fidelity (Heb. 11:11) that assures the believer that the promise will be implemented without fail, and the coming of the incarnate Jesus does for the new covenant what the birth of Isaac did for the old.

One enormously valuable benefit for the Christian is that when he or she accepts Jesus as Savior and Lord, that person is incorporated into the covenant of God's grace, becoming an heir and a partaker of divine promise in Christ by the gospel (Eph. 3:6). The believer can therefore look back to Abraham in all confidence as a "forefather" in the faith (Rom. 4:1).

The Christian ought therefore to keep promises according to the pattern of fidelity set by God. Yet it should be remembered that promises are not as binding as oaths and can be modified by agreement where circumstances warrant. Believers should avoid making rash or hasty promises, otherwise their spiritual credibility is at risk if such undertakings have to be abandoned for some reason or other. The believer's word at all times should be his or her bond.

**PROPAGANDA.** The term originates from the Congregation for Propagating the Faith, an organization of cardinals established by Pope Gregory XV in 1622 for the administration of foreign missions. It refers to the ideas, doctrines, and practices propagated by some organization or movement. The word *propaganda* came to have a negative meaning after World War I, when the deceptive methods of propagandists during the war were exposed. The term is now used to connote a deliberate manipulation of beliefs, attitudes, and actions through a deceptive use of words and other symbols such as pictures, insignia, and flags.

According to Jacques Ellul, propaganda is "total"; it uses all available media to encircle each person's emotional and intellectual being, providing him with a complete explanation of the world. Modern means of communication provide effective instruments for delivering propaganda to a mass audience. In much of the world the use of propaganda is accepted as a normal part of the political and social process; it is an integral part of the strategy of totalitarian governments to control their populaces. The United States government, operating in the midst of a free society, refrains from suggesting that it uses propaganda to control its citizenry. Nevertheless, it often uses propaganda both at home and abroad to gain support for its policies, especially during the time of war.

Coercion through propaganda, understood as a deceptive use of symbols for a preconceived goal, is unethical because it negates the possibility of a free and reasoned response. Ellul warns that using propaganda to communicate the Christian message reduces it to the level of other ideologies. This does not rule out a legitimate use of persuasion; but the proclamation of the Christian gospel should follow the pattern set forth by the apostle Paul who said, "We use no hocus-pocus, no clever tricks, no dishonest manipulation of the Word of God. We speak the plain truth and so commend ourselves to every man's conscience in the sight of God" (2 Cor. 4:2, Phillips).

**Bibliography:** Ellul, J., *Propaganda: The Formations of Men's Attitudes* (1969); Fortner, R. S., *Christian Scholar's Review* (1977), 7:153–64.

S.D.A.

**PROPERTY.** Property is that which one owns. It means the right to own, possess, or have exclusive use or control of something, often land. Such right commonly includes right of disposition by means of sale, gift, or bequest. There is no capital-free society. All property within societies is owned or controlled either privately (private capitalism) or publicly (state capitalism) to varying degrees. It is useless to postulate absolute ownership of property. Historically all jurisdictions have hedged ownership with myriads of qualifications. These include state power to expropriate; taxation; limiting rights of sale, gift, and bequest; regulations governing use (chattel, land, buildings); and humanitarian considerations (treatment of animals).

Ownership is relative and transient. Christians believe that all property ultimately belongs to God the Creator (1 Chron. 29:11, 14), that men bring nothing into the world, and that they certainly can take nothing out when they die (1 Tim. 6:7). The purpose behind Israel's tradition of the jubilee year (Lev. 25) may have included an implicit reminder of the common humanity of rich and poor, of mankind's common dependence upon God the Creator and Sustainer of life, and of the importance of ethical stewardship in managing property and resources.

Socialist theory inveighs against the private ownership of property, though all modern socialist states have had to concede property ownership to varying degrees. Many have had to allow private enterprise as well. State capitalism is biblically indefensible. Private ownership of property is not only explicitly approved in both the Old Testament and New Testament, it is the social and economic backdrop to life on earth. God gave man dominion over the earth (Gen. 1:28; 9:1-7; Ps. 8). The proscriptions against theft and covetousness in the Decalogue assume right of ownership (Exod. 20:15, 17). This is confirmed in the New Testament (Matt. 19:18; Rom. 7:7; 13:9). Abraham negotiated and paid for land as a family burial plot, which became his "possession" (Gen. 23). Owed wages are earned property and must be paid (Lev. 19:13). Ahab at first respected Naboth's property rights (1 Kings 21), but Jezebel plotted to have Naboth killed in order to wrest away from him and his heirs that which was rightfully theirs. Samuel challenged Israel as to whether he had ever wrongly taken or absconded with anyone's property (1 Sam. 12:3-5).

The common ownership referred to in Acts 2:44-45 and 4:32 does not constitute a universal prescription. More likely this event signifies accommodation to the exigencies of the moment, namely, social assistance in a time of need during the formation of the church. This practice did not become the pattern of early Christian life, or else it proved to be inadequate to their circumstances, judging from Paul's campaign to secure welfare for them (Acts 24:17; Rom. 15:25). Dispersal from Jerusalem forced Christians to adapt to life in the world at large within varying cultures. The second-century Epistle to Diognetus states that such adaptation enabled them to expedite their missionary mandate and that this was preferable to life in closed communities. Communal life may be a useful expedient, but it cannot be advocated on biblical grounds that purport to deny right of private ownership of property.

A serious danger of modern times is dominant ownership in perpetuity, which in principle excludes or limits others from opportunity to own property and to create wealth. Examples of this are exclusive state capitalism (communism) and religious bodies such as churches, corporations, and communes, where such bodies are closed entities, unlike public stock companies. In modern times these may lock up land for generations, even more completely than the traditional superwealthy. Impersonal entities are immune to death and laws governing bequest, which in the past have facilitated transfer of property through wealth creation and acquisition. A crucial Christian principle is to avoid repression and to encourage opportunity.

Christian stewardship of property and resources entails far more than prudent use of wealth, tithing, and altruistic help to the needy. It also entails wealth creation as a moral obligation. This is inherent in man's gifts and abilities and in the divine mandate given to man to have dominion over creation. Wealth creation ought to result in creation of opportunity for others. The message of Amos should not be seen merely as an appeal to help rather than to oppress the poor. It is an appeal to create opportunity. Jesus taught that uninvested resources are bad stewardship. It is striking that Matthew places the parable on effective wealth creation (25:14-30) in series with the injunction to help the needy (25:31-46). Paul does indeed caution against avarice (1 Tim. 6:6-10;

also note Pss. 73; 82); however, he also urges avoidance of idlers. He alludes to a received tradition regarding diligence (2 Thess. 3:6), which complements wealth creation and proportionate, altruistic giving (1 Cor. 16:2; Eph. 4:28).

The rich farmer in Luke 12:16-21 is not censured for his good and successful farm management, but for his selfishness. Repressive ownership, whether private or public, is wrong. Wealth creation and economic development are parallel concepts. For the Christian steward, the ability to maximize wealth and opportunity is a divine gift and an ethical responsibility.

**Bibliography:** Chilton, D., *Productive Christians in an Age of Guilt Manipulators* (1981); Novak, M., *The Spirit of Democratic Capitalism* (1982); Sider, R., *Rich Christians in an Age of Hunger* (1977); Wogaman, J. P., *The Great Economic Debate: An Ethical Analysis* (1977).

S.J.M.

**PROSTITUTION.** This term describes the activity of a man or woman who trades in sexual services as a temporary or permanent way of life. The word is derived from the Latin root *statuo* as an augmented form of the verb *sto*, "stand, stand firm." *Statuo* means to set up or place something in position and with the addition of the preposition *pro* was used of something exhibited for sale or an article that was sold dishonorably. The noun *prostituta* was employed by Latin authors of a harlot.

There are two commonly cited historical reasons for prostitution. The first is that it supplies a demand for sexual activity by men when they are unwilling or unable to acquire it by any other means. From very early times, men going on long journeys have had recourse to harlots in order to gratify their alleged sexual needs. In some countries their hosts have supplied female members of the household for purposes of coitus, a tradition which still survives in various parts of the world and has been perpetuated in Western society by the availability of "companions" or "escorts" at large business conventions as part of the hospitality.

In cultures such as that of the ancient Hebrews, there could be some argument for the availability of prostitutes inasmuch as a husband did not normally cohabit with his wife for up to three years after childbirth. This abstention, combined with the months of pregnancy, could conceivably constitute legitimate sexual deprivation, for which a harlot would suffice unless there were servant women available in the household. But in Hebrew culture adultery was forbidden (Exod. 20:14), and the Levitical laws regulated sexual behavior very carefully in any event (Lev. 18:6-23; 20:10-21) so as to preserve the community's purity and guard against pagan religious practices in which harlotry was common. This is illustrated by the cultic practices of Israel's neighbors, where ritual prostitution was part of religious worship; and this was naturally condemned frequently in the Hebrew Scriptures (Num. 25:1-5; Ezek. 16:15, 25, 28, 36-41).

The second reason for prostitution, which is often advanced by the harlots themselves, is that it is a fiscally profitable enterprise which in most jurisdictions escapes the rigors of income tax. Many prostitutes concede that, moral factors aside, their occupation is distasteful and incites a hatred of their clients, many of whom make no secret of their desire to degrade the harlots. When a prostitute has to support a parasitic pimp as well as a possible drug habit, her personal share of money is apt to be quite small. Nevertheless, the prostitute regards it as easily, if somewhat dangerously, acquired. Some married women work as part-time "call girls" simply to provide for personal expenses, while others are employees of brothels. Prostitution has become a public health hazard in recent years, with male and female prostitutes spreading syphilis, gonorrhea, and herpes, along with AIDS (Acquired Immunodeficency Syndrome), which is being transmitted increasingly by heterosexual activity. Consequently various jurisdictions are enacting strict legislation in an attempt to control prostitution.

Whether married or single, the Christian is urged to abstain from all irregular sexual conduct because it is one of the abhorrent fleshly works (Gal. 5:19) which result in spiritual death. The prostitute is nevertheless a legitimate object of an evangelistic ministry and can be expected to listen to the gospel message just as harlots did in the days of Christ. Believers will therefore support the various efforts made to rehabilitate such sexual deviants and restore them to a legitimate place in society.

**PROTEST.** As a verb, this word means to make an objection to some situation or to issue a formal statement expressing innocence with regard to certain actions or events. In fiscal circles it describes the issuing of a written declaration that such monetary items as bank drafts are not acceptable, or have not been tendered. As a noun, *protest* signifies a formal statement of renunciation, disapproval, or rejection of a policy or procedure. When things are done "under protest," the implication is that the participant has not been free to act otherwise.

The ability to protest is one of the precious legacies of participatory democracy and can assume many practical forms, from active membership in an opposition party of a parliament to kindergarten complaints about inadequate washroom facilities. Protests normally require an ethical basis, consisting of a sense of right and wrong, and the application of such ethics to the object of protest, which is generally lodged with a politically superior person or body, or with some other form of authority.

The protester draws attention to perceived, or sometimes imagined, faults in or abuses of the particular matter under protest, and if ignored may resort to violent means in order to convey the message that was not accepted previously. Protests frequently result in some modification of earlier patterns of life or behavior, though few are as far-reaching as the uprising of British barons against King John which produced the Magna Charta, or the dramatic nailing by Martin Luther of ninety-five theses to the church door at Wittenberg, resulting in social revolt by the peasantry and a devastating assault upon the doctrines and temporal authority of the Church of Rome.

While Christians are bidden in Scripture to respect authority (Rom. 13:1-6), peaceful protests help to prevent decadence in all organizations. The Christian protester, whether an activist in peace, anti-nuclear, or anti-Communist concerns, must first have his or her moral values established firmly upon fact rather than hearsay. Unless the situation in question is assessed carefully and critically, the protester can simply become a dupe of clever propagandists. No behavior can be countenanced by Christian protesters that does not glorify God or fails to respect the rights and views of those who do not share the views of the protesters. Even the Christian protester is required by Scripture to live peaceably in society, if at all possible (Rom. 12:18).

**PROTESTANT WORK ETHIC.** The term *Protestant Ethic* derives from Max Weber's famous study, *The Protestant Ethic and the Spirit of Capitalism*, (first ed. 1904/5). Weber's argument, from the view of the social and economic historian, is that certain aspects of Protestant teaching and religion contributed (alongside a "tremendous confusion" of other influences) to the development of capitalism. The writings of Martin Luther, John Calvin, and the Puritans are among the teachings and religious movements examined by Weber. R. H. Tawney, in *Religion and the Rise of Capitalism* (1922), also seeks to explore the social and economic effects of Protestant thought, although he too recognizes that, at certain points, such effects may be out of harmony with Protestant values and ideas themselves. ("Little do those who shoot the arrows of the spirit know where they will light.")

Both Weber and Tawney examine the Protestant doctrine of calling. In medieval times, it is argued, vocation was largely identified with the monastery, with the call to a life of monastic asceticism. (This is a view now challenged by some historians). In contrast, Luther affirmed that "secular" responsibilities are laid upon us by God, in addition to the "religious" ones. Indeed, for Luther, certain forms of religiosity could actually become excuses for idleness. God calls man to serve his fellow creatures and to glorify his Creator by being conscientious and morally diligent in his work—as merchant, clerk, doctor, tradesman, farmer, scholar, prince. A "wide" doctrine of vocation was also a characteristic of

Calvin's thought and of Puritanism. Thus Calvin, for example, talks of the individual's daily tasks as a "station assigned him by the Lord": one to be fulfilled under the "superintendency" of God.

In natural extension of this view of calling, Protestant ethics also emphasized the evils of sloth and of misused wealth. But alongside these emphases there was a simultaneous development: a growing openness to "commercial necessities." Take the evolution in attitudes toward usury as an example of this. The earlier medieval theologians had proscribed it altogether—as had Luther. Calvin, however, accepts it within careful conditions, because it can advance economic life in a way that is for the good of both lender and borrower. Many of the English Puritans held positions that were similar to this.

Protestant teachings about salvation and assurance are also studied by Weber and Tawney. The Catholic received assurance of his salvation through the sacraments and priestly absolution. Within Protestant spiritualities, however, there is a different religious dynamic. The repeated doctrinal emphasis of the first generation of Protestants was that salvation was through grace and faith. But how does one know that one is of the elect—that grace has done its work? The answer was: "By their fruits shall you know them." One is assured of one's salvation not through the rites of the church but through the fruits of one's life. A daily existence characterized by moral order and by ardent devotion to one's spiritual and temporal affairs could bring to the believer certainty that God's grace was effective in him. One cannot be saved through one's works, but one does need them to bring the assurance of that salvation. Weber and Tawney both see this as part of the essential "inner-psyche" of Protestant piety, brought about through the original Protestant theological revolution.

The distinctiveness of Weber's original thesis was his understanding of the relationship between the Protestant ethic and wider social and economic developments. Summarizing briefly, we may say that Weber's study of Protestant movements led him to believe that;

a. their emphasis on the Christian calling to work diligently at all one's affairs and responsibilities,

b. their general frugality (including a greater commitment to earning than to consuming: a trend that itself encourages capital investment and business growth),

c. their belief that success in one's work was one indication that the Christian was living a well-ordered, disciplined life, and

d. their evolving commercial attitudes.

All these factors combined to create a dynamic approach to commercial life, and one that ultimately served to strengthen the development of a certain form of capitalism. Tawney's thesis is similar in many respects. He writes of Puritanism being most "congenial to the world of business" and of its giving the "capitalist spirit" a bracing and fortifying "tonic."

The writings of Weber and Tawney continue to draw attention to significant questions for the theologian and the student of Christian ethics. Certainly the Reformation and Puritan views of vocation continue to point us toward important truths. The idea can still lurk in the subconscious that one is only truly involved in God's work when one is involved in the religious ministries of the church: in mission, pastoral care, teaching, and so on. This position is to be repudiated strongly. In creation, God has called mankind to exercise dominion over nature—to till and to keep, to order and to organize—and to serve his fellowman in the context of human community. In this respect it must be affirmed that our covenant responsibilities as the people of Christ do not abrogate our continuing responsibilities as God's creatures.

The debate about the Protestant work ethic raises warnings. To the extent that Weber, Tawney, and others are correct in their analysis of the early Protestant religious experience, we are warned about just how easy it is for a profound (and fully understandable) psychological desire for Christian assurance to translate into forms of motivation that may actually contradict the very heart of Reformation concerns: It may be forgotten that salvation is through grace and faith alone. Striving to produce works "for assurance" can be but a hairbreadth from striving to produce works "for salvation."

There is also a danger that, without due care, we could take a narrow, rather one-dimensional view of work from the Protestant work ethic. The proper fears that the Reformers and Puritans had about the dangers of idleness called forth a distinctive view of day-to-day life. The individual has not necessarily to cease from his labor once his basic financial and physical needs have been met. One may have labored enough to pay the bills and keep one's business on a secure footing, one may have grown enough food to feed the family; but this does not necessarily mean that one has fulfilled one's obligations to God. Clearly such a mental approach could do wonders for one's business life, at least in terms of the quantity of hours invested. Clearly, too, there are very often immensely strong moral and social reasons for working beyond one's own material necessities. But nevertheless such an approach, if taken too far, must run the danger of creating unbalanced attitudes to both life in general and to work in particular. There are many important forms of human activity other than work. And there are many important forms of work, many callings, which will not come within the sphere of one's labor. These might include, for example, looking after one's neighbors, unpaid work in the local community or church, or participation in educational or artistic activities. Labor must never be considered to be the only alternative to sloth.

**Bibliography:** Baxter, R., "The Christian Directory" in, *The Practical Works of Richard Baxter* ed. Orme (1830); Green, R. W., (ed), *Protestantism and Capitalism* (1959); Hill, C., *The Century of Revolution 1603-1714* (1961); Tawney, R. H., *Religion and the Rise of Capitalism* (1938); Weber, M., *The Protestant Ethic and the Spirit of Capitalism* (1930, 1st. English ed.).

See EMPLOYMENT; SABBATH; WORK.

M.D.G.

**PROVOCATION.** In one sense of the term, provocation is a state of mental or emotional anger, irritation, or resentment that has resulted from the application of some disturbing stimulus, which may have been accidental or deliberate. In a less malign sense it can become the means of initiating thought or stimulating discussion by the way in which concepts have been presented. On such a basis it evokes activity of the kind demonstrated by the Achaian church in their charitable contributions to the fledgling Christian churches of Paul's day (2 Cor. 9:2).

For the most part, however, provocation in Scripture is of a sinister character. The Hebrew *kaas* means "to make angry," as when the Israelites provoked God by their wickedness (Deut. 4:25; 1 Kings 14:15), or made him bitter (*marah*) because of their apostasy (Pss. 78:40, 56; 106:43). Provocation in the sense of blasphemy is indicated in the Torah by *maatz* (Num. 14:11; 23:16; Deut. 31:20). In the New Testament *parazeloo*, "to be very zealous," is used principally of provoking to jealousy, while *parorgizo* means "provoking to the point of anger."

The Christian may well be encouraged to evoke and stimulate enthusiasm for the cause of the gospel (Rom. 11:14; Heb. 10:24), but is admonished not to cause needless antagonism and is especially warned not to provoke family members, especially children, to anger (Eph. 6:4). In the same way Christians must be extremely careful not to provoke God's wrath through idolatry or antinomianism. Instead they must manifest Christian love, one consistent feature of which is that it is not easily provoked (1 Cor. 13:5).

**PRUDENCE.** As with many other ethical terms, this word has its roots in Latin and specifically in the word *prudens*, which originally meant "far seeing, conscious, with eyes open." Subsequently Latin authors employed in to mean "knowing" or skilled." The noun *prudentia* described foresight, but more commonly circumspection, discretion, and sound judgment.

In the Old Testament, prudence was interpreted in terms of perception (Prov. 8:12) and understanding (2 Chron. 2:12; Prov. 18:15), while in Isaiah 3:2 it was associated with the insights of prophecy and divination. To be prudent (Hebrew *bin*) meant to possess understanding or intelligence (1 Sam. 16:18; Hos. 14:9), a sense which was also found in the New Testament Greek term *sunetos* (Matt. 11:25; 1 Cor. 1:19). *Phronesis*,

"understanding, perception," occurs in Ephesians 1:8 to describe a characteristic manifestation of God's grace.

Prudence was one of the natural virtues in Greek ethics and was included in the seven cardinal virtues formulated by the medieval church. In the Scriptures it is commended as a concomitant of wisdom, but Jesus taught that even wisdom and prudence are no substitute for the simple faith of babes in Christ (Matt. 11:25; Luke 10:21; 1 Cor. 1:19).

**PSYCHIATRIC PRACTICE, ETHICS OF.** Psychiatry is a medical discipline and profession. For centuries the Hippocratic Oath guided the professional behavior of physicians. More recently the Geneva Convention oath has been widely used to guide professional behavior in the medical professions. Psychiatry has also developed its own criteria for professional conduct.

One of the prevalent liberal myths of psychiatry has been that psychiatry can be "value free." On the contrary, psychiatry is deeply concerned with ethical questions—as any discipline involving human relationships and behavior must be. The behavioral problems that come to psychiatric attention, the dominance of liberal values in modern psychiatry, and the heavy responsibility psychiatrists bear for those in their care, all make ethical reflection important for the practicing psychiatrist.

Knowing and doing truth is a major ethical concern for psychiatry. No medical discipline remains so uncertain of its facts. Despite advances in both psychological and neurological sciences, many of the theories held to account for psychiatric disorder are largely conjectural. Insofar as these conjectures raise questions for investigation they are useful. To the extent that they are regarded as doctrine to be believed, they betray truth. Psychiatric illnesses are profoundly debilitating; psychiatric patients suffer enormously. For their sake psychiatry must concern itself more ardently with knowing and doing the truth than it has in the past.

The ethics of psychiatric practice also include considerations and problems of love. The problems have become notorious because of the nonsensical claims of a few psychiatrists for the therapeutic value of having sexual intercourse with their patients. The profession has firmly refuted this, recognizing that sexual encounter between therapist and patient represents at the very least an abuse of a privilege, exploiting the patient's weakness and needs.

More positively, the psychiatrist must demonstrate love for the patient by being at the disposal of the patient's need. This implies that the psychiatrist will continue an education in order to maintain knowledge and skills and will not take advantage of the weakness of the patient in order to enhance personal self-esteem, financial status, or to satisfy personal pathological drives. The psychiatrist who loves his neighbor, the patient, will make his skills available to the patient regardless of the patient's ability to pay the standard professional fee. Some psychiatrists will choose to work in community mental health teams and mental hospitals where the most disadvantaged and least attractive psychiatric patients are concentrated.

Psychiatric practice is rooted in a trusting relationship of commitment to the patient and to the patient's welfare. This has implications ranging from the frequency and punctuality of appointments, to availability at crisis times, to a rigid maintenance of confidence, to providing alternative care when the relationship breaks down.

One of the most vexed ethical questions for the psychiatrist is the matter of medical committal for enforced treatment. Most psychiatrists are loathe to exercise this power. In those jurisdictions where committal is primarily a medical procedure, psychiatrists are willing to do so only when it is clear that the patient is incapable of caring for himself, or that he is at risk to himself (for self-injury or suicidal attempt), or that he is a risk to others.

Psychiatrists cannot ethically ignore social conditions. The work of social psychiatric investigators has demonstrated amply the correlation between social decay and an increase in psychiatric disorder. Poverty, alcoholism, family breakdown, and other signs of social breakdown are proper subjects for psychiatric concern, investigation, and comment.

Psychiatrists are transmitters of cultural values through the diagnoses they make, the treatments they undertake, and the process of the treatment. As ethical physicians, they must be conscious of the values they hold in each of those activities and of the way in which those values are transmitted to the patient. The Christian psychiatrist will value his patient as created in the image of God, and will desire continually to minister in Christ, through Christ, and with Christ, to the troubled people in his care.

**Bibliography:** *American Journal of Psychiatry* (1973) *130*, p. 9; Fine, S. H., [et al.], (eds.), *Today's Priorities in Mental Health* (1980), pp. 145–54; Levine, M., *Psychiatry and Ethics* (1972); Moore, R., *American Journal of Psychiatry* (1978) *133*, p. 158; Runions, J. E., *Canadian Journal of Psychiatry* (1984) *29*: 4, p. 223–7.

J.E.R.

**PUBLISHING, THE ETHICS OF.** By its very nature publishing functions best when it is characterized by mutual trust among all involved parties. Author and publisher have mutual obligations. Many of these are spelled out in their contract, but others remain implicit. Trust and trustworthiness are keys to a satisfactory author/publisher relationship. Author and publisher also have a responsibility to the public that buys their product or that is dependent on them for information. This responsibility involves the trust of the public in the ethics of the author and the publisher. In sum, all responsible publishing involves ethics at almost every turn, and Christians involved in any aspect of publishing should be especially aware of these ethical obligations. The following discussion focuses on book publishing, but the application to other forms of publishing is obvious.

1. Publishers' ethical obligations to authors include the following:

a. To represent honestly and fairly to the author the extent of their interest in a book proposal or manuscript and to explain how the manuscript will be edited, published, and promoted. This explanation should be realistic, including explanation of the uncertainties of publishing such as editing time, advertising budgets, publishing success or lack thereof, and criteria for keeping books in print.

b. To spell out clearly how they want to see a proposal developed into a book or how they want to see a manuscript revised.

c. To review the proposal or manuscript and to make a final publishing decision within a reasonable period of time. Authors need to realize that the review and decision-making process is by its nature time-consuming. But publishers have an implicit ethical obligation to make the process move efficiently and to keep authors informed of its progress, especially if there are any undue delays.

d. To edit the manuscript so as to help the author communicate effectively and cogently by improving style, logic, and organization, and calling attention to errors in fact. But it is unethical to edit an author's expressed viewpoint to make it conform to the house viewpoint. Authors should be kept informed of progress on their manuscripts, and the publisher is ethically bound to allow an author to approve the edited manuscript. In turn, though, the authors must realize that they may forfeit this opportunity by failing to meet publisher's deadlines.

e. To abide by all provisions of both contractual and informal agreements. These can (but do not necessarily) include deciding on the manuscript's acceptability within the stated time limit, publication within a certain time limit, payment of advances and royalties as specified in the contract, and book promotion.

f. To pay authors a fair return on their investment of time, effort, expertise, and money. In "Christian" publishing there has been a tendency to take undue advantage of an author's sense of ministry and underpay him or her. This results in books that are underpriced or subject to unreasonably high discounts. The author is usually the one who is hurt by this. The beneficiaries are the publishers, the distributors and bookstores, and the buying public. Books should be sold at realistic prices (neither underpriced nor overpriced), allowing the author a fair return.

2. The author has ethical obligations to the publisher that are equally important. The provisions of the contract and what may have been agreed to informally should be conscientiously fulfilled. Primary among these responsibilities are:

a. To inform all parties if a book proposal or manuscript is being submitted to more than one publisher at a time. Multiple submissions are not unethical, but publishers should be told when this is being done.

b. To negotiate in good faith with a publisher. In other words, one publisher should not be used merely as leverage against another publisher to improve the contractual terms.

c. To submit the manuscript at the agreed-upon time. Publishers must plan their budgets and release schedules months in advance, and the arrival of manuscripts plays a key role in this planning. This is especially important if the publisher has advanced money to the author. If unforeseen circumstances prevent an author from meeting the deadline, this should be discussed with the publisher. Authors have an ethical obligation to make no new commitments that might take precedence over prior publishing commitments and deadlines. Other publishers act unethically when they try to persuade authors to take on new commitments that will cause the author to default on prior commitments.

d. To submit a completed manuscript of the highest possible quality, conforming to the publisher's style manual, and living up to what was promised in the proposal in terms of subject, approach, reading level, and so on. If the author's perception of the book changes significantly as the book is being written, the publisher should be so informed.

e. To submit an original work, that is, a work that is not plagiaristic. This is not to suggest that one has no dependence on the work of others. But such dependence should not be slavish and should be appropriately acknowledged. In this connection, the author should be acquainted with the principles of "fair use," especially as interpreted by the publisher, and when appropriate, obtain permissions to quote.

f. To represent fairly viewpoints with which one disagrees. The quest for a better understanding of the truth is not helped by slanted misrepresentations of what one considers error.

g. To use fairly and accurately the authorities one quotes as support. It is unethical to quote someone else in a way that suggests that that person is supportive of the author's viewpoint when in fact he or she is not.

h. To abide by the usual contractual commitment not to publish a work derivative from that work with another publisher without permission of the first publisher.

i. To honor the "option clause." This clause, routinely placed by most publishers in their standard contracts, is subject to much misunderstanding. The usual wording of the option clause simply obliges the author to grant the publisher the first option of (or first offer of) his or her next book. In other words, the publisher in question will be given the first chance to see the next book and negotiate with the author. However, the option clause obliges neither the publisher to accept the book nor the author to accept the publisher's offered contract. For whatever personal reasons he or she may have, the author, having given the manuscript to the publisher and considered their contract offer, is free to offer the book to another publisher. Although the author should fulfill an option clause, in the final analysis it is practically meaningless. In this writer's opinion, under normal circumstances authors should not hesitate to strike the option clause from the contract before signing; they are a meaningless nuisance to the author. The loyalty of author to publisher is best earned by the publisher.

3. The author and publisher have ethical obligations to the general public. When author and publisher join together to produce a book, they assume certain ethical obligations toward the clientele they serve. When Christians publish, it is especially important that they be aware of these obligations.

a. Author and publisher have a responsibility to produce those books that make genuine contributions to our understanding of and appreciation of truth—whether that be of the Christian faith or of God's creation. Unfortunately, Christian publishing all too frequently fails to meet high standards of excellence and significance.

b. Author and publisher have an ethical obligation to produce some books that may have only marginal financial success, if such books have an especially significant contribution to make. Author and publisher should assume the risk of publishing controversial books when such books courageously address significant issues from a truly Christian perspective.

c. They share an obligation to represent the book accurately and fairly in marketing and promotion. They should refrain from extravagant or misleading claims.

d. They should not camouflage the true nature and message of a book. They should not reprint and promote previously published books under new titles without also clearly indicating the original title on the cover and copyright page.

e. Misleading titles should be avoided. This is not to suggest that titles should not be enigmatic or tantalizing. But they should not be misleading.

In summary, the relationship of author and publisher to one another should be governed by the highest ethical standards. These standards should not be applied legalistically without reference to unique and unforeseen circumstances that may arise. But taking these standards seriously will enhance the mutual trust and understanding that are so essential to a happy and successful author/publisher relationship. With a relationship based on these principles, they will also have a basis upon which to assume their ethical obligations to the public they serve.

S.N.G.

**PUNISHMENT.** This term is based upon a Greek word, *poine*, "penalty," the Latin equivalent of which was *punio*. Punishment is thus the treatment administered to a transgressor as a response of discipline or retribution. Punishment presupposes the existence of certain authoritative pronouncements that have been violated by an apprehended offender. Since law is not concerned so much with concepts of "right" or "wrong" as with what is or is not permissible at a given time and place, moral or ethical issues as such are not the basis upon which a legal decision for punishment is rendered, contrary to much popular opinion.

Since, however, human beings are moral entities, their actions have a consequent moral value and according to Scripture (Gal. 6:7-8) are part of a cause-effect sequence. Thus God can be expected to punish evildoers and reward those who live according to his commandments by "visiting" (Hebrew *paqad*) his people in ways appropriate to their deeds.

Punishment consists of a penalty inflicted upon the offender as an appropriate recompense for transgression, and in Scripture this is the primary aim. Rehabilitation of the criminal was not prescribed except in terms of fellowship with the community once the punishment had been endured. Capital punishment in Israel was strictly retributive, but was restricted in scope by the *lex talionis*, which controlled retaliation by prescribing a limit to the amount of the punishment to be imposed. While God punishes the sinner for wicked deeds, he is quick to forgive and restore the penitent to fellowship with himself (Jer. 18:21; 1 John 1:9).

See CAPITAL PUNISHMENT; CHILDREN, REARING OF; CRIME.

**PURITY.** This word is derived from the Latin verb *puto*, "to cleanse, purify." As an adjectival form, *purus* meant "clean, free from dirt, uncontaminated"; and this is the sense of its English counterpart. Purity is thus a condition which is marked by freedom from contaminants or pollutants of any kind. In a developed ethical and religious sense it describes a state of wholesomeness unimpaired by sin or transgression.

The ancient Near Eastern religions seem to have had certain standards of holiness or purity for their priests and priestesses, but these were not of a moral order. They involved dedication to the service of a particular deity and the keeping of certain behavioral rules that formed part of the tradition of the particular cults. Thus while Babylonian high priestesses copulated ceremonially with the king at the annual enthronement ceremonies, the vestal virgins of ancient Rome were required to be chaste.

Among the Hebrews the moral aspect of purity went hand in hand with certain ritual regulations for participating in worship. The ceremonial rules for approaching God on Mount Sinai, for example, required fasting, ritual ablutions, and abstinence from coitus (Exod. 19:10-15). Ceremonial washings were part of the priestly preparations for offering sacrifices in the sanctuary (Exod. 30:17-21), and these were emblematic of the moral cleanliness which God demanded of his worshipers. The emphasis upon the moral over against the ceremonial appeared forcibly in the prophetic teachings (Amos 5:21-24; Micah 6:7-8), where emphasis was laid upon that holiness of life which results from obedience to God's commands.

Jesus was constantly in conflict with the Pharisees over such matters as washing the outside of a vessel but ignoring its interior (Matt. 23:25). He commended the pure in heart (Matt. 5:8) because their motivation was in harmony with God's will. Similarly Paul urged Timothy to hold to love out of a pure heart (1 Tim. 1:5) and to maintain the mystery of the faith in a pure conscience (1 Tim. 3:9). For James, pure religion involved practical ministrations to the desperately needy elements of society and the exercise of personal moral and spiritual cleanness. In the current world, as in that of Christ and the apostles, purity in thought, word, and deed is a challenge that will try even the most dedicated persons. But if we are to serve the God who is the embodiment of purity, no options are available.

See FORGIVENESS.

# -Q-

**QUARRELING.** This word describes a process of altercation or contention between individuals or groups that involves acrimonious exchanges and sometimes even erupts into violence. The term originated from the Latin verb *queror,* "to complain, lament," and points to the basis of quarreling in terms of a complaint about some person or thing. Quarrels become particularly intense when there is a real ethical or moral factor at stake, and so intense do the resultant feuds often become that they may be perpetuated for generations. This is not just a characteristic of Arab peoples, for example, but is widespread among humanity.

John the Baptist ultimately lost his life because Herodias disliked him intensely for condemning her immoral union with Herod (Mark 6:17). Ironically enough, the trial of Jesus resulted in an earlier quarrel between Herod and Pontius Pilate being resolved (Luke 23:12). Paul instructed the Colossian Christians to forgive one another instead of quarreling (Col. 3:13) and also the believers in Rome to live at peace with everybody if at all possible (Rom. 12:18). While Christians will desire to express a wide range of opinions about the concerns of everyday life, they are required at the same time to be imitators of Christ, who preached peace instead of strife. Dignified, legitimate protests must never be allowed by believers to degenerate into ill feeling, bitter contention, or evil conflict.

# -R-

**RACE RELATIONS.** The principle of racial equality is espoused by most nations. It is usually upheld in a negative fashion by laws that penalize the majority for discriminating against the minority, rather than by laws that confer special rights on the minority. Race relations came under scrutiny only when previously homogeneous nations changed as a result of widespread immigration. Where such immigration was voluntary, the influx of new customs, religions, and languages caused extreme anxiety and distrust among the indigenous population. The fact that the majority of immigrants came, in the case of Britain, from what had been colonial dominions fostered an attitude that such immigrants were inferior. In the United States after the Second World War, immigration from Puerto Rico and Mexico heightened the existing racial tension that was the legacy of slavery. Frustrated by the economic and social deprivation that they suffered, some members of racial minorities began to express their anger by riots and destruction of property.

In Britain the concept of equality at law is considered to be central to the system of justice. Nonetheless, there was no equivalent of the American Bill of Rights to uphold racial equality. No significant racial problems were perceived until after the Second World War. Color discrimination against immigrants, however, was recognized as a serious problem by 1965 when the first Race Relations Act was passed. That Act has been amended and extended by subsequent legislation. Racial discrimination was defined to include both direct and indirect discrimination; a complaints procedure for individuals was set up; and the Commission for Racial Equality was established with powers to enforce the Act and to promote good race relations. Inciting racial hatred was made an offense, and segregation was deemed to be discrimination. To what extent the Act protects cultural and religious practices is not clear. The areas that are covered by the Act are discrimination in employment, education, housing, the supply of goods, facilities and services, property transactions, and membership of associations and clubs, including trade unions. There is widespread concern, however, that the immigration laws discriminate on a basis of color; and this in turn does not enhance racial harmony in the country.

Enforcement of the Act varies with the area of discrimination. The machinery of enforcement is cumbersome and has been used by relatively few individuals, provoking criticism that the Act is comparatively ineffective. Britain's immigration laws have become increasingly restrictive to limit immigration from her former Empire. Immigration policy and its enforcement have been inconsistent.

In the United States slavery was abolished in 1863. The Bill of Rights gives all persons the equal protection of the law and forbids the denial of voting rights "on account of race, color, or previous condition of servitude." Over the next several decades, however, the Supreme Court interpreted the Bill of Rights so as to permit discrimination against blacks. In 1896 the Court held that segregation could be practiced without creating inequality, and in 1906 the Court defined the Thirteenth Amendment as "the denunciation of a condition, and not a declaration in favor of a particular people." Following this, many of the southern states enacted segregationist "Jim Crow" laws that effectively subordinated the blacks. The Supreme Court struck a blow for racial equality with the *Brown vs. the Board of Education* decision in 1954, when it overturned segregation in the public school system by stating that "separate but equal has no place in public education." This principle was soon applied to all public facilities, guaranteeing equality of opportunity and accommodation. Thus, individual states were required to do more than merely refrain from passing discriminatory legislation. A succession of Civil Rights Acts provided for equal voting rights and employment opportunities. Blacks still lag behind whites, however, both economically and socially. To compensate for this, official programs of preferential hiring and preferential educational admissions have been instituted. These affirmative action programs focus on group needs, sometimes permitting an unworthy individual to benefit from them. They are criticized as practicing reverse discrimination. The Supreme Court has never pronounced on their constitutionality, and thus their status remains unclear. However, it is hard to believe that the social status of the majority whites is endangered by such programs. The current trend, however, is to cut back affirmative action programs. This is unlikely to ease the tensions of racial minorities.

In Canada human rights legislation is framed as a conciliation procedure, that is, it aims to correct people's practices and behavior rather than punish offenders. There are rarely any prosecutions for violations. The threat of unwanted publicity appears to spur people to behave appropriately. However, racial tension is growing in Canada; and it remains to be seen if the present law is sufficient to cope with it.

Biblical law sees all men as creatures of God. Individuals should thus behave considerately to one another and live in harmony. The Jews were God's chosen people but were forbidden to oppress non-Jews (Exod. 22:21 and 23:9). They had been subjected to oppression themselves and understood that it was not appropriate treatment for any person. Jesus expanded this principle to one of loving people different from oneself. The Gospels make it clear that redemption is not for a single race but is offered to all people and that all peoples should endeavor to live in harmony with one another.

**Bibliography:** Caporti, F., *Study of the Rights of Persons Belonging to Ethnic, Religious and Linguistic Minorities* (1977); Newman, J., *Race Migration and Integration* (1968); Santa Cruz, H., *Racial Discrimination* (1971); Sigler, J. A.,

*Minority Rights: A Comparative Analysis* (1983); Stevens, I. N. and Yardley, D. C. M., *The Protection of Liberty* (1982).

D.E.T.

**RACISM.** Racism embraces the beliefs that hereditary biology determines the differences between groups, that cultural differences are predetermined and immutable, and that the distinguishing social and cultural features of the subordinate group are inferior. These false beliefs foster prejudice and discrimination.

Pure races do not exist as such. While many physical differences can be seen among various groups of peoples, one cannot make clear and precise distinctions on the basis of race. The Jews form an ethnic rather than a racial group. In northern Europe many Jews have blonde hair and light eyes, and non-European Jews also have many variations. A combination of social, biological, environmental, political, and cultural factors makes any group distinctive. These factors are all essentially mutable.

Population movements have been a major cause of racism. In the seventeenth century when the Spanish conquistadores came to America, they speculated that the Indians they found were of another race because they were unlike any people they had encountered before. They enslaved the Indian population, apparently because they deemed them inferior. Subsequent English immigrants brought in African slaves to replace the less hardy Indians. Thus, blacks and Indians were held to be inferior because of their menial circumstances from an early period. Western colonialism, culminating in the Victorian Empire and its attendant population displacement, contributed greatly to the growth of racism, such as in South Africa, in the Middle East between Jews and Arabs, on the Indian subcontinent with the establishment of Pakistan and Bangladesh, and finally in Britain itself.

Specific groups have long perceived themselves as the norm and all outsiders as inferior. Thus, the Greeks viewed all non-Greek-speaking peoples as barbarians fit only for slavery. The Jews saw their own exclusivity in racial terms, although God's covenant with Noah (Gen. 9:1-17) indicates clearly that all peoples are to be equal in the sight of God. Old Testament Scripture emphatically denounces oppressive nations. God's judgment on them is set out in Isaiah 13. Again, in Isaiah 34:1-10, God vows vengeance on them for their oppression of the Jews. Specific instances of their punishment are to be found in the deliverance of the Jews from Egypt (Exod. 12:29-36) and from the Moabites (Judg. 3:7-31). Christian philosophy is firmly anti-racist, preaching a universality of salvation (Rom. 9:22-32). Salvation is essentially an individual rather than a group concept. All people will be joined together as one in Christ.

Prejudice and discrimination are learned attitudes. They may occur as outlets for more general frustration or they may be used to exploit for gain. Their cost to the victims, oppressors, and society as a whole is great. Their victims are humiliated and disadvantaged socially, politically, and economically. They breed unhealthy social conditions that affect the whole community including the discriminators and that break down communication between different groups in society. Prejudice and discrimination hinder social mobility and are expensive, both where the state tries to enforce institutionalized prejudice and where it works to combat discrimination.

Prejudice and discrimination lessen the freedoms of all persons. Prejudice, which is so often motivated by fear and frustration, is clearly linked to other kinds of rigid thinking, causing an inability to accept new ideas and adapt to new situations. This merely serves to intensify the frustration on the part of the prejudiced. In their denial of universal human dignity, prejudice and discrimination break down the idea of equality at law. A general disrespect for the law results in violence, tearing the fabric of society apart. Racism is a moral and social abomination. Although prejudice is hard to eradicate, a strong stand should be taken to wipe out discrimination and to aid the disadvantaged.

See KU KLUX KLAN; RACE RELATIONS.

D.E.T.

**RAPE.** Rape is legally defined as sexual assault in which vaginal penetration by the penis is accomplished without the woman's consent, although in everyday usage the term refers to any nonconsenting sexual activity. Other uses of the term include sexual assaults by men against other men, and by women against men, although the latter is rare. In addition to such "forcible rape," the category "statutory rape" is used to refer to intercourse with a girl below the legal age of consent.

The word *rape* comes from the Latin *rapere*, meaning "to seize." Rape is prohibited in the Old Testament law, which prescribes the death penalty for the offense when the woman is betrothed (Deut. 22:23-28). Although popularly considered a sexual act, psychologists recognize rape to be an act of aggression. Significantly, the Deuteronomy passage recognizes this, saying of rape in places that "this case is like that of a man attacking and murdering his neighbor" (Deut. 22:26, RSV). In the Old Testament, as well as in the Babylonian Code of Hammurabi and other ancient and medieval codes, distinctions were made between rape of a betrothed virgin, of a virgin who is not spoken for, and of a married woman. In the eleventh century, rape was judged more serious if it was perpetrated against a woman who was a virgin or who was of the upper classes. Such distinctions did not disappear from English common law until the thirteenth century, although it may well still be the case that rapes of promiscuous women, racial minorities, and wives tend to receive milder recompense in courts of law today, despite our policy of equality.

The immorality of rape is based primarily on the fact that it is a violation against the victim, a deeply traumatic experience in which the aftermath may include guilt, shame, anger, fear, and sexual dysfunction. Physical repercussions may include injury, venereal disease, and pregnancy.

Forcible rape has been categorized into power rape, in which a sort of dominance is sought, accounting for an estimated 55 per cent of rapes; anger rape, in which the woman is made to suffer for the rapist's generalized hostility toward women, which accounts for 40 per cent of rapes; and sadistic rape, in which the rapist wishes to cause suffering to the victim, approximately 5 per cent.

Research has debunked the common misconceptions that rapists are oversexed men and that rape victims behave in sexually provocative ways and thus "ask for it." It is estimated that one out of every six women will be the target of an attempted rape, and one in twenty-four will be actual rape victims. Rape victims include elderly women and children.

One of the most tragic possible consequences of rape is pregnancy. Christian ethicists, as well as the public at large, are divided over whether abortion is justified in such cases. On the one hand it is argued that a fetus conceived in rape has no less right to life than any other fetus, while on the other, it is argued that since the fetus was conceived in a way that totally bypassed the woman's consent, she is under no obligation to carry it to term.

Society's misguided attitudes toward rape seem to be connected with warped, unbiblical views about sexuality and about women's worth and dignity. Philosopher Ann Garry has pointed out that in our culture sexuality has long been seen as the male inflicting harm on the female, a theme she sees carried through in typical male-oriented pornography. Susan Brownmiller, among others, considers rape as an extension of society's acceptance of male victimization of women through sexual behavior.

The biblical insistence upon justice for victims of oppression implies that the present difficulty experienced by rape victims in prosecuting their attackers is contrary to the will of God. Christians are called upon to oppose the heinous crime of rape by insisting on justice for rapists, by providing counseling for the victims of rape and for would-be perpetrators, and by calling society to a healthier view of sexuality and of women's status.

**Bibliography:** Brownmiller, S., *Against Our Will: Men, Women, and Rape* (1975); Garry, A., "Pornography and Respect for Women," in Bishop, S. and Weinzweig, M., *Philosophy and Women* (1979); Geisler, N., *Ethics: Alternatives and Issues* (1971).

See CRIME; VIOLENCE.

D.B.F.

**RASHNESS.** The word *rash*, when used in a nonclinical sense, describes some reckless, ill-considered, or precipitate thought, decision, or action. Rashness is thus a characteristic response of a person who engages in such activities. The difference between being rash and being bold seems to be the same as that between ill-considered action resulting in failure and a decision that is translated into success, however tenuously grounded that decision may have been in the individual's mind. The speed with which a decision is actualized need have nothing to do with rashness, however. In medicine, for example, decisions that are a matter of life or death often have to be made within minutes or even seconds; but for all their quickness they are formulated on the basis of knowledge and experience. Where rashness is concerned, however, the decision characteristically lacks a comprehensive basis of knowledge which the situation would demand and instead seems often to be based upon impulse.

Most Christians would concede that they are rational beings, and therefore any irrational thought, or actions based upon such thought, can hardly glorify their Creator. The believer is commanded to honor the Lord in heart (that is, with will and purpose) and mind (that is, intellectually); and by exhibiting rashness he or she would not therefore be manifesting the loving forethought and careful planning characteristic of God's nature. The admonition of Paul that the believer should live soberly (Greek, *sophronos,* "prudently") in this world and think in a sound-minded manner (Rom. 12:3, Greek, *eisto sophronein*) should counsel all Christians against the practice of overly bold, impetuous conduct.

**RATIONING.** A ration is a predetermined allotment of some article or commodity that is distributed according to an established pattern. Rationing is the authoritative process by which the distribution procedures can take place, whether this is done by informal agreement among a group of people or by legal enactment such as might occur during a state of emergency.

In peacetime, rationing of commodities is normally unnecessary unless a sudden demand is crated which far outruns the supply. Even then, rationing is only a temporary measure and is usually administered on an informal basis. Under emergency conditions such as occur in wartime, rationing is enforced by law in order to prevent profiteering and black-market activity. The aim is not to distribute available commodities evenly to all, but to ensure that noncivilian needs are met in full first before the remaining supplies are released to the general population. In totalitarian states this concept of rationing is particularly in evidence as a feature of everyday life and is likely to remain so since Communist theory requires all deficiencies to be distributed equally among the proletariat.

Christians who are involved in rationing schemes in various parts of the world will want to ensure that the items being handled are being distributed as fairly as possible on the basis of genuine need and without respect of persons (James 2:2-4). By this means the believer will exemplify the scriptural "royal law" of loving one's neighbor as oneself (James 2:8).

**REBELLION.** Derived from the Latin noun *bellum,* "war," this term denotes any expressed resistance to a promulgation or enactment issued by a recognized authority. The act of rebellion can vary from a domestic dispute between parents and children to a well-organized civil revolt against government, but the intent is exactly the same where defiance of legal authority is involved.

Revolts in effect proclaim openly that the previously acknowledged authority is no longer lawful or worthy of obedience, and that a state of war therefore exists. This does not necessarily mean that the conflicting parties will resort to violence, but challenges the promulgating authority to suspend further action until the tensions have been resolved reasonably.

It is sometimes affirmed by ethicists and others that the aim of rebellion is independence, but this is not necessarily so where peaceful revolt is concerned. Quite often all·that is intended is a display of disapproval which will bring to the notice of authority the fact that there is a lack of satisfaction with a given situation. Picketing is a peaceful form of rebellion, that has the function of making a public protest against certain conditions imposed by the particular authoritative body. When the dispute has been resolved there is no further need for peaceful rebellion of that type.

Militant rebellion against a government, however, assumes other and more sinister aspects. On some occasions there are excellent reasons why the government should be overthrown, as for example when there is blatant corruption, injustice, and gross exploitation of the people. But there are situations in which rebellion is the conscious act of a political opportunist and his supporters and merely has personal aggrandizement as its objective. Rebellions of this character are usually terminated with considerable brutality if they prove unsuccessful.

Christians are exhorted to submit to secular rule as to power delegated by God for the legitimate ordering of human society (Rom. 13:1-7). If the nature of government is distasteful, the modern believer in North America or Europe has peaceful means at his or her disposal by which protests can be registered. Christians who have to choose whether or not to participate in rebellion should be mindful of Paul's admonitions and in any event must assess carefully the cost of participation. If the cause is deemed worthy of the supreme sacrifice, the moral responsibility for that choice must still remain with the individual.

See OPPRESSION; PERSECUTION; REVOLUTION.

**RECIDIVIST.** This term is derived from the Latin *cado*, "to fall," and with the prefix *re-* describes a backward motion or a restoration to an earlier or normal condition. In current English a recidivist is a person who has relapsed into a former way of life, and the term is used predominantly of criminals who return to illegal activities after they have been released from prison.

One of the greatest disappointments that would-be reformers of the modern penal system experience is the rate of recidivism among prisoners. Experts in penology have expended considerable effort in attempting to discover causes for the phenomenon, but without much unanimity of opinion. If imprisonment is intended to be a deterrent, it has clearly failed for the recidivist.

This then leads to questions as to the nature of the deterrent and whether in fact it should be replaced by something that would leave with the criminal a lasting sense of society's disapproval of his or her doings. If a prison sentence is meant to have some rehabilitative elements, that has failed also because the criminal goes back again to his or her old way of life. Some geneticists have endeavored to assess the problem clinically and have claimed the discovery of a genetic factor common to habitual criminals. These findings, however, have had doubt cast on them by other geneticists; and therefore such a line of inquiry is no more profitable than its precursors. A study of recidivism itself reveals little about its true nature. Not all prisoners return to crime on release, nor does recidivism have any connection with a given social level, since recidivists come from all classes of society.

The Christian believes that the only certain cure of recidivism is a solid experience of spiritual conversion and salvation through the work of Christ, who makes new creatures of those who commit their lives to him (2 Cor. 5:17). Such a new believer will need to be nurtured carefully in the fellowship of the Christian church, receiving support and reinforcement that may be necessary for a lifetime. Those Christians acquainted with prison ministries will recount sadly the persons who have made a Christian profession, only to fall into recidivist ways at a subsequent time. This unhappy fact merely underlines the need for the solid experience mentioned above.

See CRIME; CRIMINAL PERSONALITY.

**RECONCILIATION.** This term describes the procedure, or the effect of the procedure, whereby persons who were previously at enmity have been restored to friendship and made compatible once more. The idea is ancient, being an important element in the Hebrew sacrificial system when an atonement was being offered for sin (Lev. 6:30; 16:20). In such cases the Hebrew verb *kaphar* meant "to cover," in the sense of making an atonement for sin. In the New Testament the Greek word *diallattomai*, "to be

changed entirely," was used in Christ's prescription concerning reconciliation (Matt. 5:24); and the same change of attitude characterized Paul's use of *katallasso* and *katallage* (Rom. 11:15; 2 Cor. 5:18-19).

The Christian basis for reconciliation is the atonement for sin made by Christ's death upon the cross. In this act, Jesus is the new Adam making good the damage done by the old Adam in his act of disobedience (1 Cor. 15:22, 45-49). Sinful mankind has been redeemed by this act of divine love and grace and can now enter upon the way of eternal life by confession of sin and the accepting of Jesus by faith as personal Savior and Lord. As a result of forgiveness through Christ's atoning work, the barrier which the fact of sin had created between God and the individual is broken, and the sinner is reconciled to God (2 Cor. 5:20). It is important to notice the direction which this spiritual movement takes. It is not God who is reconciled to man, as is sometimes thought, but the exact opposite (Col. 1:21-22), the intention being to present the converted sinner as a holy and blameless member of Christ's body, which is the church. Once this has been accomplished, any sense of reconciliation on God's part toward the sinner has also been achieved.

On such a basis of theology the believer ought to have little or no difficulty in pursuing and achieving reconciliation with another person, whether a believer or not. If we are indeed exemplifying the person of Jesus the redeemer, we have a moral obligation to forgive as we are forgiven by the work of Christ (Matt. 6:12). Jesus taught that the believer cannot expect divine blessing if unresolved resentments, quarrels, disagreements, and the like are allowed to continue (Matt. 5:23-24), even if the other party is the offender.

For true reconciliation to take place, the person who instigated the offense must be fully persuaded as to the nature of his or her action and be sufficiently penitent as to ask for forgiveness. The one who had been offended by whatever occurred must be able to accept the contrition of the other party as a genuine response and extend his or her forgiveness accordingly. The offender must not be cajoled or persuaded into asking for pardon, if only because the approach must be of a voluntary nature. Similarly the forgiveness must be equally free on the part of the person offended. All enmity and animosity must be dispensed with on that basis and the relationship pursued as in earlier days. The reconciliation of a husband and his estranged wife (1 Cor. 7:10-11) should proceed on the same basis of mutuality and spiritual integrity. It is imperative for Christians not to hinder the Lord's work by perpetuating petty quarrels, but instead to live together in the unity of the Spirit and the enfolding peace of Christ (Eph. 4:3).

See FORGIVENESS.

**RECREATION.** This term means literally a "refreshing" or "renewing" of the individual by engaging in such procedures as will stimulate the person concerned and bring new creative energies and insights to bear upon his or her life. Recreational pursuits should thus be considered as a means to an end and not an end in themselves.

What passes for recreation is as varied as those who participate in it. For some it involves membership in a team that engages in sports activities of different kinds, while for others recreation consists of being a spectator to such sports and deriving enjoyment from them. The recreation of some individuals involves work on the part of others, who are occasionally exploited in the process, and this may present ethical problems. While many persons prefer outdoor activities as their form of recreation, there are others for whom such a prospect, though desirable, is impossible. These individuals are left to find other forms of diversion with which to refresh their minds, and fortunately the range is again extensive. The world of television has opened up vast new vistas for housebound invalids, and although television needs to be viewed selectively and critically, there is a good deal of wholesome instruction and diversion to be had in the process.

Recreational pursuits which damage an individual's character or deface the image of God in that person must be avoided strictly. These include any kind of amusement that would involve drunkenness, immorality, gambling, or involvement with mind-disorienting substances. The Christian needs to remember that it is times when the spiritual guard is relaxed somewhat that the devil sweeps in and will lead the believer into sin if not checked. Recreation, therefore, should be chosen in such a manner that it achieves the objective inherent in the term and so refreshes the body and mind of the participant that he or she is invigorated and renewed to continue witnessing in human society to Christ's atoning work.

See AMUSEMENTS; ENJOYMENT; ENTERTAINMENT; LEISURE.

**REFORMED ETHICS.** The Reformed approach to ethics began with the practical approach of Ulrich Zwingli (1481-1531), was organized and taught by John Calvin (1509-1564), and codified, at least for British and American Calvinists, by the Westminster divines (1643-1649). The key doctrines that shaped the ethical system developed by Reformed theologians were (1) revelation, (2) unity of the covenants, (3) God's sovereign grace, and (4) a Reformed world-and-life view.

*Revelation.* Reformed ethics is Bible-based. It insists that ethical standards be derived from Scripture through accurate exegesis rather than natural law. Basing ethical norms on natural law came into the Roman Catholic Church through the influence of Aristotle and Thomas Aquinas. Although Reformed ethics seeks to encompass all

human existence, and thus may include insights drawn from philosophical reflection and the empirical study of natural phenomena, all ethical standards, both personal and social, with authority over the life of the Christian must be demonstrably of divine revelation.

Because of commitment to this doctrine of "Scripture only," some, especially in the twentieth century, have stressed "Christian liberty," rejecting what they consider extra-biblical legalisms imposed by many Christians. Others hold that this is an inconsistency. If room is made for considering natural law and philosophic reasoning as legitimate sources of ethical insight, it is asked, how much more room should there be for the application of biblical principles beyond that which is directly and explicitly taught in Scripture?

*The Unity of the Covenants.* An alternate name for "Reformed Ethics" might be "Covenant Ethics." Reformed theologians believe in the unity of the old and new covenants, forming one covenant of grace. Thus they accept the Old Testament as a revelation of the will of God for Christians. Although the New Testament is viewed as modifying the application of Old Testament law in some instances (for example, the *lex talionis*, "eye-for-eye" doctrine; the law of divorce), the Old Testament moral law, especially as it is summarized in the Ten Commandments, is normative. Only those elements of the law that are no longer normative are fulfilled in Christ or explicitly set aside by Jesus Christ Himself or the apostolic authors.

Reformed theologians laid great emphasis on expounding the implications of the Ten Commandments for contemporary obedience. This was almost an innovation on the part of Calvin, but was followed in the Westminster Larger and Shorter Catechisms and in the work of Charles Hodge, premier Reformed theologian of the nineteenth-century Princetonian school.

In recent years a viewpoint called theonomy has been advocated in what many mainstream Reformed theologians consider an extreme form. These concepts, enunciated by Rousas John Rushdoony, have been developed by Greg L. Bahnsen into a form that most in the Reformed school view as being contrary to historic Reformed principles. Theonomy holds that the entire Old Testament legal system is applicable today in society as principle and as "case law." The specific cases to which Old Testament law is applied in Israel reveal God's moral law and are binding as such on society today. In contrast, Reformed theologians historically have held that the New Testament church, though having a basic continuity with the church of the Old Testament (Israel), is nevertheless released by the teaching of Christ and the Apostles from obligations to the Mosaic system such as ceremonial, civil (judicial), and dietary regulations. Old Testament "case laws" were specific applications of the moral law to Israel as a theocracy; but with the change of the church from the form of a state (Old Testament) to the form of a spiritual body (New Testament), the civil laws no longer directly apply. Only the basic moral principles, particularly epitomized in the Ten Commandments, are viewed as being normative for the Christian under the new covenant.

In the other direction, away from theonomy, Reformed theology stands against dispensational views of law. It holds that typical dispensational teaching is antinomian, since it disallows Old Testament teaching as normative for the Christian.

The law was given as part of God's common grace, designed for all humankind. Its requirements are part of the human conscience, inscribed in the heart of all people. Furthermore, revelation of God's will for humankind is equally beneficial to believer and unbeliever and equally the basis of judgment. To the extent that any society subjects itself to the law of God, that society will benefit. Reformed theologians have identified three uses of the law. The civil or political use of the law is to restrain evil in human society. The second use of the law is pedagogic or evangelistic. This purpose is to bring the sinner to conviction so that he may seek salvation. The third purpose of the law is didactic, setting a standard of behavior for the Christian.

The law is viewed as a reflection of the character of God, which is the standard for human attitudes and behavior. It is not optional, but obligatory, and thus is rightly called "law."

*God's Sovereign Grace.* As distinct from all other religions, with the possible exception of Shin Buddhism, and as distinct from some branches of the Christian church, such as the Roman Catholic, one does not obey the law to become acceptable to God or gain merit with Him. Rather, one is justified by God's sovereign grace and responds to it in obedience through the enabling gifts of faith and the Holy Spirit and with the motivation of love. In this way, Reformed ethics stands over against any form of legalism. Legalism is not defined as it is among some contemporaries as honoring the law and meticulous observance of the law, but rather in its historic sense as gaining merit or even salvation through obedience to the law. Only because of sovereign grace is the believer assured of final salvation. The perseverance of the saints means that the true believer will continue to pursue holiness by the grace of God. This is not to imply, however, that the Christian will achieve perfect holiness in this life. Reformed theology is strongly opposed to all forms of Christian perfectionism. The classic work by Reformed theologian B. B. Warfield articulates the Reformed position on perfectionism.

Since ethics deals primarily with that function of human personality called "the will," the key ethical question is: what kind of will does a person have? Is it free? Because of God's sovereignty, Reformed theologians have emphasized what to those outside Reformed circles must appear its most distinctive and prominent tenet, namely the denial of free will. Humankind in its fallen state is viewed as unable to consistently choose to do right. Reformed theologians insist that the idea of a free will is nowhere taught in Scripture (though responsibility for one's choices is), is far too high a view of man's capacity for moral good, and inevitably leads to some form of attempted self-salvation. But man does not have an autonomous will, a self-sufficient moral consciousness. He is totally depraved—fallen in all aspects of his being and totally incapable of satisfying the demands of the law. His only hope, therefore, is in the sovereign intervention of the God of grace who chooses to impart saving faith and regeneration to the elect. This impartation enables the redeemed sinner to live a life increasingly conformed to God's moral likeness.

God's sovereign grace in the life of the believer is not a quietism, as though growth in holiness devolved wholly on God's activity. There is the need for faithful use of the means of grace (such as prayer, Bible study, the church) and diligence in the pursuit of holiness in dependence upon the indwelling Holy Spirit.

*Reformed World-and-Life View.* Finally, Reformed ethics, particularly in the twentieth century with the impetus of the teaching of Abraham Kuyper (1837–1920), has emphasized the unity of all life so that a Reformed world-and-life view affirms the cultural mandate along with the evangelistic mandate. All culture is seen to be under the authority of God, requiring participation from the consistent believer in accomplishing the will of God in all aspects of culture, not merely in religion and personal ethics. This has provided a rationale for involvement in various ways of promoting good in society as a whole.

While this emphasis has been stronger and more clearly articulated in the twentieth century, it certainly has its roots in the earlier Reformed doctrine of Christian vocation. Every vocation in the will of God is viewed as "holy." Such teaching contrasts with the teaching of the medieval church that held that "holy orders" were distinct from secular vocations. From this and other doctrines, such as the priesthood of all believers, according to some historians, came the Protestant work ethic, capitalism, and even representative democracy.

In conclusion, we must consider the Reformed view of each of the three basic questions with which all ethical systems must deal: (1) What is the purpose or end toward which an action is directed? What is the *summum bonum,* the highest good? (2) What is the standard (law or duty)? What should a person do? (3) What is the motive; why does he do what he does?

The end toward which all attitudes and actions must point is not the happiness of the individual who makes a moral choice, nor the welfare of the others in his life, though these purposes may be included. The chief end is the glory of God. This not only brings great emphasis to the God-ward virtues, but it controls the answers to the other two questions as well.

The standard is the character of God Himself. Good is good because God says so, not merely because it proves rational or beneficial. God says it is good because that is the way God Himself is. We know what God is like and what He desires of humankind by divine revelation in the incarnate Son and in Scripture. Ethical standards may be informed legitimately by innate moral judgment (conscience) and by rational observance of things as they are, but no ethical question can be answered authoritatively except on the basis of written revelation and by the illumination of the Holy Spirit.

The highest motive for ethical behavior is love for God. Love for others and love for self are not thereby excluded in Reformed ethics, but the order is clear and must be determinative in ethical choices. Personal rights and desires must give way before the demands of the highest welfare of one's neighbor, and all choices must yield to that which most glorifies God.

Thus the ultimate consideration regulative of human disposition and conduct is the perfection of God. God Himself is the reason for right conduct, the criterion for right conduct, and His honor the ultimate goal of right conduct.

**Bibliography:** Bahnsen, G. L., *Theonomy in Christian Ethics* (1979); Henry, C. F. H., *Christian Personal Ethics* (1957); Murray, J., *Principles of Conduct* (1957); Van Til, C., *In Defense of the Faith Vol. III: Christian Theistic Ethics* (1980); Warfield, B. B., *Perfectionism* (2 vols., 1931).

J.R.McQ.

**RELATIVISM.** Relativism is the theory that all knowledge, particularly judgments in ethics, science, and religion are not absolute but depend upon culture or varying social perspectives.

Philosophically, relativism began when Heraclitus (d. 486 B.C.) taught that everything is in flux; we cannot step into the same river twice and therefore man cannot discover any fixed, immutable knowledge. The great Sophist Protagoras (c. 490-421 B.C.) observed that a cool breeze is stimulating to a man in good health but disagreeable to a man with a fever. Hence, the breeze is both pleasant and unpleasant, and each man is telling the truth. In fact, no one can be mistaken. If there were no men and one tried to consider the wind itself, it would be neither cold nor hot nor gentle or breezy; in fact, it would be nothing. Other similar observations led Protagoras to conclude, "Man is the measure of all things." Plato interpreted this to mean that there can be no absolute knowledge since each man's views are equally valid. Pyrrho (c. 360-270 B.C.) was an influential skeptic whose teachings were preserved by his students. He taught that we must always suspend judgment, since our sensations may deceive us. If we cease striving to know things in themselves, we shall be content to live a peaceful life. As a consequence of his theory, Pyrrho taught that nothing made any difference.

Relativism holds that all knowledge is individual and personal, and hence no universal judgments can be made. Furthermore, since ideas exist only in the mind, we have no way of knowing whether these ideas actually correspond to reality. Individual persons perceive the same objects in various ways. There is no way of knowing under what conditions we can grasp the true nature of things.

*Relativism in Knowledge.* Since relativism is based on the assumption that we cannot make any knowledge claims that go beyond immediate experience, its roots lie in empiricism. This belief, that all knowledge comes through the senses, received its most consistent expression in David Hume. Beginning with the supposition that man's knowledge was limited to his impressions, Hume even denied the so-called inviolable law of cause and effect. All that we can do, says Hume, is observe that B follows A; but since we never have an impression of causality, we cannot be sure of the principle.

If all knowledge is based on impressions, it follows that the knowledge of God, immortality, or the soul is impossible. Hume argued that it is illicit to construct any theory that would go beyond the evidence. He went so far as to concede that we have no proof of the existence of the external world since all that we can have is an impression of it inside our minds, with no way of knowing how these impressions correspond to the real world. Furthermore, even if the external world was the cause of these impressions, we have no proof that it is still there after we no longer perceive it. Such relativism actually led to the skeptical conclusion that knowledge of anything was impossible. At best, we have a series of impressions about which nothing intelligent can be said.

*Relativism in Religion.* Immanuel Kant, who said that he was awakened from his dogmatic slumbers by reading Hume, tried to construct a theory of knowledge that would avoid Hume's skepticism. Kant saw clearly that if Hume were correct, science itself would be in jeopardy. Kant agreed with Hume that experience gives us a rather chaotic manifestation of sensation, but that the mind arranges it according to innate categories. Regardless of how unconnected the raw data may be, the mind gives it unity and necessity. But, according to Kant, the mind organizes only the data of experience. The knowledge of God, immortality, and the soul, therefore, is always beyond reach.

Kant had a profound effect on the philosophy of religion, particularly with his arguments that God in unknowable. The result is that religion, as traditionally understood, is an impossible science.

Since Kant, religion has been at best interpreted as an individual and private experience without any verifiable basis. Such relativism affirms that there is no objective standpoint from which religions may be judged, and thus we have only personal religious feelings and nothing more, hence Schleiermacher's definition of religion as "a feeling of dependence." The argument follows that there is good in all religions and none can claim superiority. It does not matter what one believes, just as long as he is sincere and his own beliefs are of help to him.

*Ethical Relativism.* Ethical relativism has had a variety of contemporary expressions. John Dewey, for example, believed that morality could be based on a scientific foundation, but that there are no fixed standards by which actions can be judged. He said that whatever standard people use, it remains "subject to modification and revision...on the basis of the consequences of its operational application.... The superiority of one conception of justice to another is of the same order as the superiority of the metric system...although not of the same quality."

Though Dewey's illustration of the metric system actually proves the opposite of what he intended (when measuring lines the result is the same whether we use inches or centimeters), he taught that an act can be moral according to one standard and immoral by another. He believed that an action was not inherently moral, but depended upon whether it was a means to something else. Dewey's theory provided the basis for other relativistic ethical theories. For example, both situationism and cultural relativism hold that there is no fixed absolute by which actions can be judged. Either the social context or the consequences of the action in a given situation is the sole arbiter in moral choices.

The fact that all autonomous theories collapse into relativism is ample proof that human reason left to itself cannot judge moral matters. As Hume himself showed so clearly, human reason cannot move from what *is* to what *ought* to be. Through empirical observation we learn that murders occur. But we cannot on that basis conclude that they ought not to occur. We can *describe* but we cannot *prescribe*. Human reason cannot jump from a fact to a moral judgment. Thus the best that man can do is adopt an undefined relativism that cannot even give direction in the simple choices of life.

*The Weaknesses of Relativism.* Several arguments may be advanced against relativism. First, those who argue in its favor do not live consistently with their conclusions. For example, Pyrrho, who taught that nothing made any difference, stepped back quickly one day as a chariot swung around a corner. One of his students chided him for his lack of consistency: He should not have stepped out of the way for it made no difference. Pyrrho, however, cleverly replied. "That is why I stepped back, for it makes no difference."

Hume admitted that although he could not prove the existence of the external world, he did act as if it were there. Though human reasoning left to itself ends in relativism, human beings created in the image of God will act inconsistently with such conclusions. Ultimately relativism fails because it is unable to satisfy the demands of human experience and behavior.

Second, all relative theories are logically inconsistent. If truth is in flux then relativism itself is caught in that flux. If what was right yesterday is wrong today, then perhaps relativism itself is already obsolete. In fact, one cannot even suggest that this theory is relatively true, unless the person assumes the existence of an absolute standard by which views may be judged. Without such a moral yardstick we cannot distinguish between an opinion that is relatively true and one that is relatively false. Augustine argued correctly that relativism that ends in skepticism can only be overcome by revelation and a theistic view of the world. Truth is not changing, nor did it begin when we were born. It had always existed. Truth is hence *discovered* by the human mind. Logical forms, for example, are known to be true the moment they are pointed out because they are independent of experience.

Factual information about the world is also based on an absolute theory of truth. Columbus either discovered America or he did not; George Washington was either the first president of the United States or he was not. To speak of truth as changing as the relativists do is to misuse both language and logic.

Man's inability to find absolutes is a tacit admission of his need for revelation in moral and religious matters. Only one who has special knowledge that goes beyond human experience can say, as Christ did, "I am the Way and the Truth, and the Life; no one comes to the Father, but through Me" (John 14:6).

**Bibliography:** Clark, G., *A Christian View of Men and Things* (1952); Dewey, J., *Logic, the Theory of Enquiry* (1938); Erickson, M., *Relativism in Contemporary Christian Ethics* (1974); Lutzer, E., *The Necessity of Ethical Absolutes* (1981).

E.W.L.

**RELIGIOUS FREEDOM.** (see **FREEDOM, RELIGIOUS**).

**REMARRIAGE.** References to the dissolution of marriage in Scripture carry the implication of the right to remarry (Deut. 24:1-4; Matt. 5:31-32; 19:9; Mark 10:11; Luke 16:18). Christ's words on the subject, variously reported in the Gospels, must be understood in light of the dilemma the Pharisees posed and of the unacceptable practices implied in the words "from the beginning it was not so."

The Pharisees hoped to criticize Christ, whether He advocated either position too loose or too tight. Jesus' reply is, first, that easy divorce by easy procurement and flaunting of legal papers is, in fact, adultery. There must be no trifling with marriage. Second, while divorce may occur due to adultery, God's purpose in creation is a real, lifelong union of one man and one woman. Remarriage must thus constitute commitment to that goal. While this allows for the concessionary nature of divorce in Deuteronomy 24:1-4, it proscribes the ancient and modern practice of the easy shuttling of men and women back and forth and reinforces the ideal of creation, which is enduring, monogamous marriage. Jesus' words ought not to be seen as legislative enactment, but as moral indignation at gross abuse and as strong reinforcement of the creation ideal.

Paul's limited discussion of marriage and divorce in 1 Corinthians 7 includes the so-called "Pauline privilege" (vv. 10-11, 17, 25, 40). Some scholars believe that what Paul says is offered not as blank apostolic authority, but as informed apostolic opinion on what makes sense and is emotionally possible while maintaining moral standards in a sinful world and in difficult situations. Marriage is normal (vv. 8-9). Marriages ought not to be broken up (vv. 10-11). Mixed marriages should be conserved (vv. 12-16). If the unconverted partner wishes divorce, the spouse should accept it. Presumably severing such a tie allows ("not bound" v. 15) for remarriage of the forsaken partner, although this is not stated in the text. Widows (and presumably widowers) are free to marry, only in the Lord (v. 39).

Marriage is clearly the preferred state. The proscriptions in Scripture are aimed to prevent wife-swapping or easy passage of women from one man to another, or of men from one woman to another. The creation ideal is affirmed, concessions to human frailty are noted, and balanced judgment is encouraged. Some remarriage is equivalent to adultery, Scripture says, but apparently not all remarriage.

The union of one man and one woman in marriage is central to God's purposes for mankind. Through marriage God ordained the continuance of the human race and human emotional well-being. As such marriage and remarriage ought to be viewed as more than issues of civil and ecclesiastical law. Those who reject remarriage in the church give to the state the right to frame its own laws respecting divorce and remarriage. Christians should regard marriage as a creation gift for the good of all men and women and seek to enhance its permanence and values.

Marriage as the normal state of mankind is accepted more realistically in Eastern Christian traditions than in some in the West where there persists a strong ascetic tendency. In the Eastern rite of remarriage, reconsecration includes the words "being unable to bear the heat and burden of the day and the hot desires of the flesh, are now entering into the bond of second marriage." This poignantly highlights Paul's words in 1 Corinthians 7:1-8. However, full recognition of the legitimacy and importance of conjugal union

to human beings means more than that marriage is an emotional escape-valve. Thus the Eastern rite, along with most other Christian traditions, emphasizes that true love is the necessary condition in which full personhood can blossom.

In certain circumstances divorce and remarriage may disqualify one from ministry. Paul insists that marital stability is crucial to effective ministry (1 Tim. 3:2-5). Those who divorce and remarry must allow to others, especially in cases of previous flagrant behavior, the right to discount potential effectiveness in ministry. Thus, a distinction needs to be preserved between forgiveness, which God freely gives to the penitent, and qualifications to minister in view of the reputation of the gospel (1 Tim. 3:7).

**Bibliography:** Besson, C. C., *Picking Up The Pieces* (1983); Hosier, H. K., *The Other Side of Divorce* (1975); Krebs, R., *Alone Again* (1978); McRoberts, D., *Second Marriage* (1978).

See ANNULMENT; DIVORCE; MARRIAGE.

S.J.M.

**REMORSE.** This word is usually defined in terms of deep repentance or sorrow for something that has happened. While remorse is normally the emotional response of an individual to wrongdoing that he or she has committed, it is possible to feel bitterly sorry about something that another person has done, as when relationships have been destroyed unilaterally, or when circumstances entirely beyond one's control have supervened to bring about serious personal loss.

As a response of penitence or contrition, remorse can be a powerful healing mechanism for the believer if, as Paul puts it, the sorrow is genuine, is directed toward God for forgiveness, and issues in repentance that leads to salvation (2 Cor. 7:10). Deep sorrow over the deaths of loved ones whom he might have been able to save had he been present was displayed by King David in the case of Saul and Jonathan (2 Sam. 1:17-27) and also of Absalom (2 Sam. 18:33; 19:4), but in both instances the outpouring of bitter grief began the process of restoration in David's personality. By contrast, the worldly grief resulting in death (2 Cor. 7:10) can be illustrated by the remorse of Judas Iscariot, who betrayed Christ. Overcome with regret and sorrow at the result of his deed, he went away and committed suicide (Matt. 27:3-5). The remorseful Christian always has the consolation of being able to approach a powerful and loving Savior who heals as he forgives the sinner.

See REPENTANCE.

**RENUNCIATION.** To renounce something is to relinquish or abandon formally all claims, rights, and titles to it. Not merely is it an act of absolute surrender, but it involves complete repudiation of ownership, association, or relationship. Renunciation, therefore, is the act or process of renouncing. It has its origins in a Latin verb *renuntio,* which originally meant "to bring back a report" to someone such as an official. But in the Latin orators it was also used of retracting a promise or revoking or canceling something, and this is close to the current English usage.

As with other aspects of spirituality, Abraham is an excellent example of one who renounced the delights of life in ancient Ur to follow God's leading (Gen. 12:1-5). Christ demanded of his followers a similar renunciation of the ideals and objectives of the world (Matt. 19:16-30; James 4:4), including family ties if necessary. Jesus must be the supreme Lord of the believer's life, and anything that intervenes displaces his true lordship. But God not only demands and receives, he also gives generously as promised (Luke 6:38) and encourages the believer to renounce this world's values in order to receive everlasting life.

**REPARATION.** This noun denotes the compensation, amends, or recompense due, payable, or discharged where any kind of damage has been caused. The nature or amount involved may be decided either by mutual agreement between the parties concerned or as the result of legal action. Reparation can be effected privately among individuals or on a much larger scale between governments for damage inflicted for various reasons. The noun comes from a Latin verb *reparo,* meaning "to make good, restore, repair," which is the current English sense.

For the Christian, reparation is an important part of ethical behavior. Respect for the property of a neighbor, for example, should be of such a quality in Christian love as to urge the believer to make proper, indeed ample, settlement if and when such restitution is required. While insurance normally covers this and other kinds of liability, the Christian ethic demands scrupulously fair dealing in any kind of debt situation (Rom. 13:8), whereas the unbeliever might try to lie or cheat his or her way out of the liability.

See RESTITUTION.

**REPENTANCE.** Repentance is an emotional response of contrition, regret, penitence, or sorrow for something that one has done that is clearly wrong. It is often accompanied by deep sadness that the occurrence ever happened, as well as by the complete inability of the offender to reverse the trend of events. Repentance for certain misdemeanors can last a lifetime, because while atonement and reconciliation may have been achieved, the memory of the event or situation still remains and can recur intermittently without either warning or control.

The idea of repentance has its roots in the Old Testament, where the Hebrew *naham* implies a change in God's previously stated or implied intentions (Gen. 6:6-7; Exod. 32:14). A similar change is also inherent in the verb *shub,* "to turn back, repent," where God's people are asked to

renounce their idolatry and espouse the moral and spiritual ideals of the Sinai covenant (1 Kings 8:47; Ezek. 14:16; 18:30). In the New Testament the Greek words *metanoeo* and *metamelomai* express respectively the concepts of "being of another mind" concerning things previously said or done or "having remorse, regretting."

John the Baptist preached repentance as the theme of his ministry (Matt. 3:2; Mark 1:4), and while Jesus supported this message he taught that he himself embodied the kingdom about which John had preached (Luke 17:21). Yet he also was calling sinners to repentance (Mark 2:17) and commanded his apostles to proclaim repentance and forgiveness of sins through the cross to all peoples (Luke 24:47).

Repentance leads first to spiritual conversion and thereafter to forgiveness of sin incurred in the believer's daily life. Repentance affects the total personality (Luke 19:8) and represents the outward turning away from sin. By being forgiven, the Christian then turns in renewed faith to God and seeks his will for future witness and ministry. As some ethicists have pointed out, the life of the believer has a positive ethical motivation in consequence of repentance and forgiveness; and this is characteristic of the grace of Christ.

See REMORSE.

**RERUM NOVARUM.** This is the first of the social encyclicals. It was published in 1890 under Leo XIII and dealt with the problems which the working class of the time was facing. The English title is *The Condition of the Working Class.* The encyclical was inspired by the miserable conditions of the working class that resulted from the industrial revolution and its underlying philosophy of liberalism. The situation called for some remedy.

The first part of the encyclical condemns the solution proposed by the socialists, which traced the cause of the whole problem to private property and saw the solution as the elimination of private property. The encyclical defended private property as a basic right and argued that it was necessary to maintain human dignity. Without it the human being would be entirely dependent. The encyclical also condemned socialism for attempting to reduce all human beings to the same level, pretending that suffering can be eliminated, denying any value to it, and promoting class conflict instead of Christian love.

According to the encyclical the purpose of the state is to help its people, especially those who are least able to help themselves, but it should not absorb the individual and his family or make them subservient. It should promote free associations of workers for their protection. Such associations, of course, should respect the rights and duties of employers. Laborers violating the rights of employers would be as bad as employers violating the rights of laborers.

**Bibliography:** Baerwald, F., *Catholic Mind*

(1951) XLIX, pp. 632–34; De la Bedoyere, M., *Catholic Digest* (1941) V, pp. 35–38; Delaney, J., *Catholic Mind* (1941) XXXIX, pp. 13–22; Keane, J., *American Catholic Quarterly Review* (1891) XVI, pp. 595–611.

J.R.C.

**RESIGNATION.** In Christian theology resignation means uncomplaining endurance in the face of persecution, sorrow, or some other form of evil. It does not comprise apathy, indifference, or a rejection of previously held spiritual values, nor is it some form of technique such as nonviolent resistance for dealing with particular situations. It consists of the full surrender to God of whatever problems overwhelm the believer, in the knowledge that Jesus is all-powerful (Matt. 28:18) and in his good time he will overrule the evil and work all things in consonance with his will for the benefit of the believer.

Resignation of this kind was counseled in the Old Testament (Amos 4:13) when circumstances were inappropriate for direct human action. Although believers complained periodically in times of hardship (Pss. 42:8; 44:24), the experience of Job makes it clear that divine blessing only occurs when the believer is fully surrendered to God's will, especially in circumstances for which he cannot be held accountable, finds difficult to understand in consequence, and is powerless to change (Job 42:1-10). The passive attitude toward authority which Christ manifested at his trial demonstrated resignation in the face of a larger issue, namely that the Scriptures must be fulfilled by his death and resurrection (Matt. 26:54). Peter also laid down the principles of Christian resignation, describing such an attitude as "thankworthy" (1 Pet. 2:19, KJV). Patient endurance in faith is the key to Christian resignation, and this is quite different from a total abandonment of concern or the relinquishing of all responsibility inherent in the secular use of the term.

See PATIENCE.

**RESPONSIBILITY.** This term denotes a condition of moral, and sometimes legal, accountability because of the position or status which a person occupies. Since they are moral creatures by nature, human beings can be held morally responsible for their actions on the basis of "natural" law (Rom. 2:14-15), to say nothing of the gospel of Christ. Whether a person is a believer or not, nobody can be excused from responsibility for failing to meet the challenge of God to an obedient, dedicated, and holy life since the law has already been written in Gentile hearts.

Responsibility is thus based upon knowledge and is therefore a cognitive response rather than an intuitive moral reaction. While responsibility and duty are closely related concepts, they should not be identified or confused. Duty consists of the legal or moral obligation to discharge properly the functions of one's mandate in life, whereas responsibility stresses the accountability of the individual in the performance of his or her duties. Many Christians need to become increasingly conscious of the fact that their own responsibilities for witness in the world will come ultimately under divine scrutiny (2 Cor. 5:10) and should govern their activities accordingly.

See DUTY.

**RESTITUTION.** This term properly describes a form of compensation (Latin *restituo*) in which stolen or misappropriated belongings are restored or returned to their rightful owners. In instances where liability is admitted but the property cannot be returned in its original form, restitution can be made by agreement in other terms such as monetary compensation. Restitution is different from reparation in that the latter normally involves the repairing or replacement of damaged goods or property, whereas restitution has a much wider legal and ethical scope. Retribution is different from both because it involves the repayment of an individual or a group for violations of laws or ethics.

Specific acts of restitution were prescribed under the Mosaic law, based broadly on equivalence of value (Exod. 21:26-36). But some transgressions demanded double restitution (Exod. 22:4, 7) or more (Prov. 6:30-31), according to the seriousness of the offense. The restitution of property to the original owners was a feature of the Hebrew jubilee year (Lev. 25:13). It should be remembered, however, that this was not done because of any damage that had been sustained, or from any form of criminal activity, but instead to preserve the inalienable nature of the land that God had given to his people.

Where required, restitution is mandatory for the believer before there can be any expectation of a continuing relationship with God (Matt. 5:24). Evil must not be rewarded with evil (Rom. 12:17), but the Christian must be scrupulously honest in all such dealings, thereby proclaiming love for his or her neighbor.

See REPARATION; RETRIBUTION.

**RETRIBUTION.** This term is normally used in a negative sense to describe the penalty imposed upon someone convicted of wicked behavior. It is derived directly from the Latin verb *retribuo,* "to give back," that is to say, to give a person what was due to him or her. The implication in both Latin and English is that the recompense is for evil deeds, otherwise the repayment would have been phrased in terms of a reward.

The ethical character of retribution is made clear in Scripture in terms of the punishments prescribed for physical and moral evil. There is an ominous degree of consistency attached to retribution in the aphorism that assures a person of reaping what he or she has sown (Gal. 6:7). Since the tendency of the human heart is for evil rather than good (Gen. 6:5), retribution of a specifically punitive nature would appear to be the inevitable lot of the unbeliever (Matt. 25:46) as a consequence of sin (Rom. 2:5). The Christian, by contrast, will receive in the final evaluation of human conduct a recompense that will be appropriate to works of love performed in the faith, grace, and strength of Christ.

See RESTITUTION; REVENGE.

**REVENGE.** Revenge is the process or act of securing appropriate retaliation for some offense that has been committed, whether against oneself or another person. Depending upon the circumstances, legal proceedings might be necessary in order to achieve the desired effect, in which case a civil suit would probably be the most appropriate means of dealing with the situation. Self-motivated acts of revenge involving violence are forbidden to the ordinary citizen, since violence has now become the monopoly of the state. Nevertheless, feuds of varying kinds do occur periodically and can be perpetuated through a number of generations.

The ancient Hebrews sought to prevent blood feuds by means of the *lex talionis,* or law of revenge (Exod. 21:23-25). This principle provided punishment similar in nature to the offense, but to a specified maximum limit. This had considerable moral value in replacing individual acts of hostile recrimination by retributive measures performed with the sanction of the community.

The Christian is urged never to seek revenge for real or fancied injuries. The believer is to commit his or her situation to God, who alone claims the privilege of revenge (Deut. 32:35; Rom. 12:19). While the offended Christian may well be angry, he or she can count upon appropriate retribution from the One who judges righteously, following the example of Jesus (1 Pet. 2:23).

**REVOLUTION.** In a general sense this word describes an ordered rotational movement such as a cyclic repetition of time. This is one of the meanings of the Latin verb *revolvo,* from which the term is derived. A more common understanding of the Latin, however, was "to roll back," which has elements in common with modern political usage, in which revolutions seek to impede the progress of existing government and return to a different, perhaps more traditional way of life. The sudden upheaval characteristic of most modern revolutions is the normal expression of powerful ideological motivation, and the intent of change may be either toward a totalitarian or a democratic state. The cyclical nature of human experience is such that these patterns tend to succeed each other, especially in unstable countries.

Not all sociopolitical revolutions are violent in nature, however. In the participatory democracies it is possible for a capitalist economy to become largely socialist in character when a government with a large parliamentary majority passes legislation which involves radical changes of a socialistic nature. These result from massive government intervention in the lives of private citizens, such as the nationalizing of various services and the introduction of compulsory contributive schemes of various kinds. These are invariably extremely expensive to maintain if only because they result in an expanding bureaucracy and are only tolerated by many individuals because the measures have been imposed by a democratically elected group of citizens. But the fact is that a decade of such legislation can produce a social revolution of a kind that is virtually impossible to reverse and, for more conservatively minded politicians, one that is extremely difficult to control fiscally. All socialist health-care services in the world are bankrupt by definition, for example, and are only maintained by heavy, and sometimes hidden, subsidies from taxpayers' monies.

Revolution claims a long history and is not without its benefits, as the experience of the United States demonstrates. Christianity itself has sometimes been described as revolutionary in the peaceful sense, and there is no doubt that when a person confesses his or her need of salvation and accepts Jesus as Lord and Master of life, changes of the most fundamental order take place as a result of the "new creation" (2 Cor. 5:17, KJV). This kind of revolution, which contributes new strength to the church of God, should be the prime aim of witness and evangelism. Practitioners of the "theology of revolution" might well consider liberation in terms of people being reborn in Christ and liberated within their circumstances, instead of initiating the overthrowal of regimes, usually in favor of a Marxist-type state, without reflection upon whether the change is in fact either morally justified or a truly beneficial move for the society involved. Christian revolutionary idealists need to remember that both the oppressing rulers and the revolutionaries themselves are sinners and that therefore the pathway of social revolution is not guaranteed to lead to either a physical, moral, or spiritual utopia.

See REBELLION.

**REWARDS.** A reward is a form of recompense for, or a recognition of, specific or general services that have been rendered over a shorter or longer period of time. In contrast to retribution, a reward normally has a pleasurable, positive connotation such as might be associated with something that has been fully merited. In Scripture the idea of a reward can be both positive and negative, but in each case refers to the end product or effect of a sequence of causation (Gal. 6:7) upon which a judgment of value has been pronounced by God.

The pragmatic nature of Hebrew society emphasized the great rewards that came from diligence, honesty, and perseverance (Prov. 11:1; 16:7; 31:15, 18). Yet at the same time the Israelites were reminded that the reward for finding wisdom far surpassed the profit made from trading in gold and silver (Prov. 3:13-14). In the same way the Israelites who waited upon God in faith and obedience, keeping his commandments, also received a great reward (Ps. 19:11). The final recompense for human activity, both good and bad, will be dispensed by God at the final judgment and will be based upon his evaluation of human response to Christ's atoning work on Calvary.

See RETRIBUTION.

**RIGHT AND WRONG.** In general terms, what is right is what is morally required; what is wrong is what is morally prohibited. In the context of the Christian faith, talk of right and wrong is intimately linked to the will of God and, more specifically, to the will of the God and Father of Jesus Christ. For the Christian, then, to specify that an action is wrong is to declare that it is contrary to the will of a holy, loving, and just God. To specify that an action is right is to declare that it conforms to the will of a holy, loving, and just God, either as permitted or commanded. This provides a standard of human conduct that is *objective* (determined by facts independent of social consensus or individual human will), *universal* (applicable to all human beings), *eternal* (not rendered obsolete by the passage of time), and *exalted* (possessing a sanctity worthy of an ultimate respect). Thus the common conviction that there is an important difference between actions that are right and actions that are wrong has a basis in that conviction. The Christian, then, views the moral life as obedience to the divine will. This transforms the search for moral truth into a search for the will of God and the act of honoring a moral conclusion into an opportunity for obedience to God.

*Subjective Right vs. Objective Right.* Objectively, right actions are those actions that *are* right (as judged by correct moral standards and correct factual information). Subjectively, right actions are those actions that are sincerely and conscientiously believed to be right (whether or not they actually are right). Many times, of course, what a person sincerely and conscientiously believes to be right actually is right (subjective and objective right correspond), but at other times this is not the case (the two diverge). A moral belief is sincerely and conscientiously held when it is not only one's actual belief (no pretense or hypocrisy is involved), but it is also a belief that one has come to as a result of both an openness to truth and an adequate effort to secure truth. But are individuals to be judged by reference to what actually is right (or wrong), or are they to be judged by what they sincerely and conscientiously believe to be right? A number of considerations favor the latter view. How, we may wonder, can we expect people to turn their backs on their sincerely and conscientiously held moral beliefs? To be unfaithful to moral truth, as one understands it, would be personally corrupting. Consistent with this, the apostle Paul affirms that

it is sinful to eat meat offered to idols if one believes such an act to be wrong, even though in fact, as Paul himself tells us, it is not actually wrong (1 Cor. 8). Thus the one who eats meat offered to idols is judged by reference to subjective right. One can act sinfully, in this case not because what is done is objectively wrong, for objectively it is morally permissible, but because it is sincerely and conscientiously believed to be wrong. Thus divine judgment falls, appropriately, not only upon those who fail to live up to their correct moral beliefs, but also upon those who fail to live up to their mistaken moral beliefs when those beliefs are sincerely held and conscientiously acquired.

*Egoism vs. Altruism.* A classic answer to the question of how one decides issues of right and wrong is found in the appeal to self-interest. Finding expression in the ancient world of Epicurus with his egoistic hedonism, its most famous contemporary exponent has been the late novelist, Ayn Rand. According to ethical egoism, an agent is obliged only to do what ultimately benefits the agent. Right actions are those that serve the agent's own long-term interest; wrong actions are those at odds with those interests. It does not follow from this that the ethical egoist is never to do that which helps others, for helpful deeds may be the price one pays for being a member of a community (or other social group) from which one receives desired benefits. Nevertheless, one is to help others only in order to gain some advantage or benefit for oneself.

Such a moral outlook excludes as unacceptable all sacrifice for others that does not involve an adequately compensating benefit. In contrast to such views, an ethical altruist contends that people are at least sometimes obliged to do what benefits others at the expense of their own interest. One does, in other words, have a genuine obligation to help others, an obligation that is not reducible to a more fundamental obligation to benefit self. In this debate between egoist and altruist, the Christian will side with the altruist, for there is too much in biblical teaching that contradicts the egoist's position. There is the command to love our neighbor as we love ourselves (Matt. 19:19). Establishing a dedication to the welfare and well-being of other human beings (who also are in the image of God and equally the object of God's love) is as morally basic as a dedication to one's own welfare and well-being. In accord with this perspective, the apostle Paul admonishes, "Let each of you look not only to his own interests, but also to the interests of others" (Phil. 2:4). In doing so we share in the example of Christ, whose servanthood and ultimate sacrifice for others is the Christian's supreme moral and spiritual paradigm (Phil. 2:5-8).

Nevertheless, there are emphases in Scripture that indicate that when eschatological considerations are taken into account, there are no ultimate sacrifices for those making temporal sacrifices in the name of Christ. Indeed, "great is their reward in heaven" (Matt. 5:12). But it does not follow that the existence of heavenly rewards is to turn Christians into egoists. For it is what is done for Christ's sake, not for the reward's sake, that is finally rewarded (Matt. 19:29). Genuine concern for others is granted a heavenly reward, not a prudential self-serving that seeks only advantage for self (Luke 6:32-36).

*Utilitarianism vs. Rights Theory.* Utilitarianism is a moral theory with both able advocates and capable critics on the contemporary scene. Its attraction for many modern thinkers is that it provides a single unifying principle for the whole of morality. It is, from the Greatest Happiness Principle that utilitarians purport to deduce all obligations, all moral rules, and all virtues. Because there is only a single supreme principle of morality, there cannot be irresolvable moral conflicts, as conceivably can occur when one recognizes several fundamental principles that are all equally basic. Further, utilitarianism provides a rational means for evaluating actions and selecting moral rules. This involves calculating their impact on human happiness. Thus, according to the utilitarian, one's fundamental commitment is to maximize the happiness of the greatest number. This is the ultimate right-making property.

Today utilitarianism has various sophisticated versions, not all of which are open to the same criticisms. It is widely felt by critics, however, that utilitarianism does not adequately protect the individual against the interests of the larger group. It is the greatest amount of happiness that is of primary concern; and as a consequence, a few individuals can (in principle) be used, sacrificed, and made to suffer in order to benefit the larger number. The danger, in other words, is that the Greatest Happiness Principle allows individual rights to be infringed in order to secure certain social gains. This is a possibility because in some circumstances violating rights may maximize overall human happiness and because, for the utilitarian, it is the Greatest Happiness Principle that has moral priority rather than rights possessed by individuals. Because of this perceived danger, "rights theorists" affirm that rights are morally basic and are not to be sacrificed for the sake of increasing total happiness. In this debate, Christians will identify with rights theorists. The respect owed to human beings is grounded not in the temporal interests of society, as utilitarians contend, but in the absolute claim of God, as Christian theology requires. For it is God who has called the individual into existence for His purposes and ends, and these cannot be set aside for utilitarian ends. Thus the right to life and the right to religious liberty, to mention but two examples, are not grounded in the Greatest Happiness Principle, but in the Creator's purpose for His creation. In charting a Christian ethic of right and wrong, individual rights will be given a place of priority.

*Consequentialism vs. Formalism.* Moral theories are typically divided into these two categories. Consequentialist moral theories place exclusive stress on the consequences of actions or adoption of rules in determining their moral acceptability. It is not the intrinsic character of stealing, lying, or adultery that counts against these activities and renders them wrong—that would be formalism—but rather what results from our doing them. It is argued by advocates of certain forms of utilitarianism and by advocates of situation ethics (both of which are consequentialist theories) that an action is right when it impacts human welfare and well-being more favorably than any alternative. According to the consequentialist perspective, acts such as stealing, lying, and adultery are in-and-of-themselves morally neutral and take on a moral character only as they bring about certain positive or negative results. Should the results be favorable, these acts become right. Such a view, however, has implications in sharp conflict with common moral sense and the Christian conscience. It would follow, since consequences alone make an action right, wrong, or indifferent, that in a situation where the consequences of lying or telling the truth are identical, it would not matter whether one lied or told the truth. But surely that is to underestimate the respect we should have for truthtelling.

Because of the morally unsatisfactory implications of consequentialism, at least in the versions alluded to, one may be attracted to the formalist alternative. In its unqualified form it recognizes only the intrinsic character of an act in establishing its rightness or wrongness, the consequences for human welfare being a moral irrelevancy. It is solely the "form" of one's action that has moral significance. This, however, may seem extreme just as consequentialism is extreme or one-sided. The possibility of human pain, suffering, unhappiness, and so on being caused or prevented surely cannot be relegated to a moral irrelevancy. Nor can the fact that happiness is secured or frustrated be of no concern. Quite sensibly the Christian community will be attracted to a view that acknowledges the moral importance of both intrinsic features and consequences.

How do these two factors fit together in making moral decisions? Here there will be debate. One could give primacy at all times to intrinsic features, concluding that good consequences are to be diligently sought but never by doing what is intrinsically objectionable. Such would provide that when there is a conflict, the inherent features always override consideration of consequences. Thus, if one recognized lying as inherently objectionable, then one is not to lie, no matter the good that can be achieved by doing so. Perhaps a war can be prevented or innocent life saved from unjustified lethal assault; but no matter, one is not to lie. One can modify this position, however, by arguing that consequences do override intrinsic features on occasions, when, that is, the consequences are weighty and certain. But the less weighty and the less certain the good consequences are, the greater the moral risk and the greater the likelihood of moral error in choosing to pursue desirable ends by means of inherently flawed means.

*Rules and the Rights.* The existence of intrinsic properties that make actions right or wrong leads to a morality that is rule-based. This is so because rules ascribe intrinsic value or disvalue to certain kinds of actions. When one fails to bring one's behavior into conformity with the appropriate body of moral rules, one is performing actions that are intrinsically objectionable, having, as they do, morally negative features attached to them. Rules serve, then, to point out intrinsic features of actions that must be taken into account when making moral decisions, hence their importance. Moral rules are not, however, mere summaries of what usually helps or hurts people, though the helpful or hurtful nature of these actions may also contribute to their moral status. Because moral rules are more than utilitarian summaries, one cannot set aside rules whenever the utilitarian gain of doing so is only slightly better than keeping them. If actual consequences of individual acts were the only relevant consideration, then it would be morally appropriate to do so. But because, on the contrary, intrinsic moral features have "weight," they cannot simply be ignored for small utilitarian gain.

Despite the importance of moral rules as ascribers of intrinsic value or disvalue, the determination of what is right or wrong is still not easily and quickly accomplished by straightforward appeal to moral rules. In part this is because moral reasoning involves appeal to facts as well as to moral principles, and there may be genuine uncertainty over the facts. If we are uncertain about what the facts are, we will be uncertain about what moral conclusions we should draw, even though we are quite clear about our moral principles. This underscores the need for Christians to be factually informed and knowledgeable about the world in which God has placed them. For ignorance of facts can be as morally disastrous as ignorance of moral principles.

It is not merely factual uncertainty, however, that complicates moral decision-making and makes arriving at the correct moral conclusions difficult. Often we have the added complication of not possessing precise moral rules but only general advice to be, for instance, generous, brave, or helpful. For example, Christians will struggle typically with the question: "What proportion of my financial resources should I give to humanitarian and missionary efforts, and what proportion should remain for family needs and luxuries?" There are no formulas for answering this kind of question (for some persons, 10 per cent will be too much, and for other 10 per cent will not be enough). One must simply struggle with this question, never completely certain of the correctness of the decision made. To use another example, it is correctly believed that burdens borne to fulfill obligations can become

sufficiently onerous that a person can be relieved of obligations that otherwise hold—such as the obligation to keep a promise. But at what point does the burden become sufficiently great so as to release one from that obligation? Once again formulas do not exist to answer this question nor a host of other such questions that arise in the course of living our moral lives. Christians will therefore seek the Holy Spirit's guidance, gain inspiration from biblical models, learn from experience, and operate with a wary attitude toward the distorting influence of self-interest. But still they will not automatically be saved from the agony, uncertainty, and possibility of error that is involved in moral decision-making.

**Bibliography:** Frankena, W. K., *Ethics* (1973); Geisler, N. L., *Ethics: Alternatives and Issues* (1970); Hospers, J., *Human Conduct* (1972); Long, Jr., E. L., *A Survey of Recent Christian Ethics* (1982); White, R. E. O., *Biblical Ethics* (1979); Wogaman, J. P., *A Christian Method of Moral Judgment* (1976).

See MOTIVES AND MOTIVATION; VALUES.

R.W.

**RIGHT TO DIE.** Because of what are alleged to be the intransigent attitudes on the part of the law, medicine, and the church regarding the termination of life by the incurably ill, a number of people in several countries have begun crusading for the so-called right to die. This right is meant to be implemented when the patient is suffering from a terminal and painful illness for which there is no cure. Promoters of the movement have formulated what they call a "living will," which contains the following statement: "If there is no reasonable expectation of my recovering from an illness or injury, I request that I be allowed to die in dignity and not kept alive by heroic measures. I ask that drugs be administered to me only for the relief of pain and not to prolong my earthly life, even if these pain-killing drugs may hasten my death."

In its present form the living will assumes the nature of an option more than a right and is very little removed from much standard medical practice under circumstances where irreversible diseases are allowed to take their natural courses. It is the concept of "dying with dignity" that provokes ethical concern, however, because of the possible implications of suicide and active or passive euthanasia which the living will appears to condone. Suicide would occur if the patient was assisted in some way to terminate his or her own life, and in many jurisdictions such conduct is illegal, although suicide as such may not be adjudged a crime. Active euthanasia would take place with the assistance of the doctor and the consent of the relatives, while passive euthanasia would allow the sufferer to die without the intervention of life-promoting techniques.

Just how "dignified" any of these approaches is has been a matter of heated debate. When definitions of *dignity* are attempted, the concerns that dominate the discussion have to do with patients dying with a clear mind against a background of minimal pain, thereby passing from this life in congenial surroundings and being spared the agonies of enduring short-lived periods of the extension of biological existence at the expense of human life of familiar quality.

The compassion that family members feel for a loved one dying in agony from an incurable disease is understandable, but hardly to the extent that would permit them to put an end to that life, as is sometimes done. The expression *right to die* is apt to mean different things to different people, and to expect legislation on euthanasia to cover all the contingencies adequately is unrealistic. Many Christians and others feel that the matter of euthanasia simply does not lend itself to legislation, if only because of the interpersonal relationships involved. A large segment of opinion is in favor of leaving matters of life or death to the wisdom and experience of the medical profession, whose members alone can inform the public about the medical issues characterizing the process of dying. As some doctors have pointed out, even if legislation were enacted to permit medical practitioners to indulge in active or passive euthanasia in cases of painful, terminal illness, it is the doctors alone who could certify these clinical conditions.

While some practitioners employ elaborate life-support systems for their own protection as well as to satisfy relatives of the sufferer that all possible help was being extended to the patient, many others concentrate upon making the patient comfortable in the absence of life-prolonging measures.

For terminally ill patients the hospice movement has provided an alternative to suicide or euthanasia. A hospice was originally a place of shelter for travelers on long journeys, and in the medieval period was a highly prized institution. The best-known of the modern hospices was founded in London, England, in 1967, and the movement has spread to Canada, the United States, Australia, and elsewhere.

The dying person finds little of the normal hospital routine in a hospice, but instead is encouraged to enjoy the company of visiting relatives and friends. The patient is given an honest and forthright prognosis and is supplied with a narcotic medicine called a "Brompton cocktail" which can be sipped periodically whenever the pain becomes intense. Self-administration of the medicine gives the patient the sense of participating in his or her own therapy and has an important beneficial effect upon the personality. When all of this is supplemented by spiritual ministrations, the dying person is able to leave behind the best of all possible worlds.

Laudable as the intentions of those who promote the right to die concept may be, the guilt that could result from such activities may more than offset the humanitarian values originally envisaged. For the Christian, the emphasis should be on promoting the activities of the hospice movement and adding a dimension of spiritual quality to it as a means of demonstrating their loving concern for the terminally ill.

**Bibliography:** Humphry, D., *Let Me Die Before I Wake* (1985 ed.); Rollin, E., *Last Wish* (1985).

See AGED, CARE OF THE; EUTHANASIA.

**RIGHT TO WORK.** It is a common contemporary dictum that every adult human being has an inherent, inalienable right to work. Within present social assumptions this is usually taken as meaning a right to paid work—to employment or labor.

While Christian thought stresses the importance of work and labor for human existence, the concept of "right to work" needs to be handled critically. Most contemporary thinking about rights has its roots in the enlightenment view of the individual rather than in a biblical/theological view of man. Christian thinking about work starts from the biblical view that God summons man to exercise dominion over his environment, to order and organize it, and to serve his fellowman in the context of society. Thus from a theological point of view, work is to be regarded primarily as an obedience to be rendered by the creature to his Creator, rather than as an autonomous and inherent right. An individual can, if he so desires, choose to renounce a right unilaterally. (Indeed, following their Master, Christians are sometimes called upon to set aside what, in legal or secular moral terms, are their rights.) But an individual cannot renounce unilaterally the moral obligation to work placed upon him by God. This is not mere semantics. These basically express two fundamentally different ways of understanding moral value. One stems from a philosophical perspective that sees man, and the intrinsic qualities residing in him, as the ultimate source of moral judgement. The other places all ethics—all obligations to self and to neighbor—under the transcendent authority of God. In recognizing the "rights" of others, we must, in strict theological terms, recognize the fact that God requires us to treat others in a certain way. And in recognizing the importance of work for others, we must, above every other consideration and factor, recognize the importance of their fulfilling their obligations to God. Such obligations, if fulfilled, serve in God's creative providence to enhance the life of both the individual worker and the wider community.

In terms of responsible citizenship, then, Christians should be concerned with the promotion of the cultural conditions in which "working life" can flourish. Christian concern about the present unemployment crises and "the future of work" should be as marked as that of any other group. It is important, however, that such concerns are rooted in a recognizable theological rationale.

**Bibliography:** Cranston, M., *What are Human Rights?* (1973); Wright, C. J., *Human Rights; A Study in Biblical Themes* (1979).

See EMPLOYMENT; HOMELESSNESS; WORK.

M.D.G.

**RIGHTEOUSNESS.** In Scripture, righteousness means fairness, conformity to a standard, and conduct that is fitting and good. For the Hebrews the norm of righteousness was God Himself. They saw His character as that of utter purity, total goodness, and holiness.

The standard, then, of holiness is set by God himself. He requires from His people that which He is.

The twin Hebrew words *tzedeq* and *tzedeqah* are used to show two strands of development. First, these words, representing justice and righteousness that God expects from all people, convey a strong ethical meaning. The eighth-century prophets, Amos, Hosea, Isaiah, and Micah put particular stress upon the ethical demands of religion. They insist with great firmness upon fair dealing between man and man, as well as between man and God. A marked bias toward the needs of the poor and destitute is revealed in these turbulent prophets, whose writings show that they, apparently unlike many of the hierarchy of the Temple, believed that social justice is indissolubly linked with righteousness.

However, while retaining a strong ethical basis, righteousness also conveys the notion of salvation. God's righteousness is never cold and judgmental. Mercy and love are integral parts of His character in the Old Testament. This is brought out in the later chapters of Isaiah, where redemption of God's people is an aspect of his mercy and righteousness. He is a "righteous God and a Savior" (Isa. 45:21).

In the New Testament the word usually translated "righteousness" is the Greek word *dikaiosune*. Its corresponding verb form is invariably translated "to justify." Paul is the New Testament writer who uses these words predominantly, and he does so in a way that brings together the ethical and the salvational elements. We can go as far as to say that he uses the word in three main ways. First, he traces man as under the condemnation of sin. We are guilty and utterly helpless of ourselves (Rom. 7). Second, he uses it for salvation, which is a free gift in Christ. We have no righteousness of our own (Rom. 3:10-20), and therefore salvation is not a thing we can buy. Third, once a man is reconciled to God, a new life is required of him, in which he embraces the ethics of Christ.

It is important to observe that, because righteousness is primarily set within the context of salvation, grace plays a major role in its interpretation. Remove grace from the heart of Christianity and righteousness will be misinterpreted as a law-centered way of living. So it was in the early centuries of Christianity. Legalism swept aside a gospel of grace, and church discipline was erected upon a basis of obedience to the commandments and laws of the Christian faith.

During the Reformation, interpretation of *righteousness* was at the center of the controversy separating Christians. Martin Luther (1483-1546) made his wonderful discovery that the righteousness of God is revealed in Jesus Christ apart from the law (Rom. 3:21). Instead of seeing God's standard of justice as a retributive aspect of His character, Luther realized that the gospel of Jesus Christ revealed God's righteousness, which may be reduced to this simple statement: "that the just man lives by faith." This was, of course, a return to biblical teaching. God's righteousness is not an impossible standard of perfection that we must all somehow attain if we are to be saved; it is rather an element of His salvation that is the apex of our calling. Righteousness, according to Luther, is something God confers upon us through His grace.

Where the Reformers parted company from their contemporaries was in their rejection of good works as the means of salvation: man was simultaneously a saint and a sinner. In himself man is utterly sinful, but in Christ he is accounted righteous. Medieval Catholicism disagreed emphatically with this notion. It seemed to them that Luther was in serious danger of ignoring good works entirely, suggesting instead that the heart of man was untouched by the grace of God. While it is true that major misunderstandings made it impossible for either side to fully appreciate the points of the other, Luther had actually discovered something very important about righteousness—that it is a gift of grace.

Nevertheless, we cannot avoid the ethical implications of righteousness. It is indeed firmly anchored in the context of salvation, but God's laws still remain God's laws and are binding upon all people. By ourselves we cannot keep God's standards. We fail constantly and we need His grace to persevere. For those of us who claim to follow Christ, the ethical claims are not less but more demanding. Yet we follow and obey, not because we must, but because we want to. Not because by them salvation is earned, but because it has already been given to us as a gift. We live righteous lives because we know that it delights our heavenly Father. It is our love gift to Him.

**Bibliography:** Kung, H. *Justification by Faith* (1957); Reid, G. *The Great Acquittal* (1981).

G.C.

**ROMAN CATHOLIC ETHICS.** Roman Catholic ethics (or "moral theology") has had many forms and sources.

*Historical Outline.* Early Christian texts often mix brief moral instructions or exhortations with other teachings. The first six chapters of *The Teaching of the Twelve Apostles*, (i.e., the *Di-*

*dache,* probably a second-century work) give a rather full collection of ethical instructions. The *Stromata* of Clement of Alexandria (c. 150-c. 220) give extensive discussions of the duties of Christians. Many of the great patristic writers such as Tertullian (c. 155 to after 220) and Augustine (354-430) composed treatises on particular ethical topics: marriage, virginity, lying, patience, faith, hope, and charity.

The earliest Christian ethical writings were primarily practical. Toward the end of the second century, however, some Christians began to respond to intellectual attacks on Christianity. Tertullian and Clement provided a more fully reasoned justification for their ethical conclusions, although they did not elaborate complete ethical theories.

The earliest converts to Christianity learned that they were not bound by every Mosaic law, but maintained many of the Old Testament laws as guides to life. Their principal ethical guidelines, however, were Christian in character, involving the imitation of Jesus Christ in His love and obedience to the Father, His love and forgiveness toward mankind, His humility, and the fuller life made possible by the Holy Spirit.

Accordingly, early patristic ethics was primarily scriptural and included common sense applications to particular situations and warnings against dangers. Paul had stated, however (Rom. 2:15), that God's law is written in the hearts of pagans. Different patristic writers might interpret this in slightly variant ways, but they generally agreed that human reason can reach some ethical truth even without sacred Scripture.

Tertullian rejected Greek philosophy (in theory at least) but maintained that the "naturally Christian soul" (preferably uncontaminated by philosophy) retained some knowledge of the moral law implanted in it by God. Other patristic ethicists, however, made considerable use of philosophy. Clement used middle Platonism mixed with Stoic and Aristotelian elements. Basil (c. 329-379) and Ambrose (339-397) borrowed from the Stoics. Augustine freely acknowledged his debt to Platonism. These writers, however, took from philosophy only what they judged to agree with the truth they discovered in the sacred Scriptures.

With the coming to power of Constantine (312), Christians ceased to view the empire as a persecuting enemy and began to dream of a regime embodying Christian values. Catholic ethics, accordingly, commenced grappling with great affairs of state. Ambrose and other bishops were in frequent conflict with Christian rulers, and the church-state problem has occupied social ethicists ever since.

The continuing task of raising the level of religious and moral awareness of the baptized masses proved as difficult as the earlier challenge of resisting persecution. Writers such as John Chrysostom (354-407) and Basil advocated a somewhat radical economic equality. Chrysostom believed that the amassing of great private fortunes was normally the result of injustice.

Moral guidance was a question not only for individual teachers but of corporate concern. Accordingly, local church councils such as that of Elvira (309) spelled out guidelines for several areas of Christian life.

After the patristic age, theology, including moral theology, declined in the Western church. From the sixth to the eleventh centuries the relative few who theologized usually repeated teachings of patristic authors, particularly Augustine. By the sixth century, private confession to a priest began to replace public penance for grave sins. Penitentials began to appear, the first ones being little more than lists of sins with suggested penances, often involving years of fasting. These books were composed of decrees of local councils, opinions of learned men, and the author's own opinions. Bishops frequently objected to the use of private penitentials and tried, with limited success, to replace them with others based more exclusively on church decrees.

Penitentials remained an important source of moral guidance for clergy and the faithful for many centuries. Although later penitentials included some theological background or pastoral advice, too often these books left people with rules lacking any sufficient vision of the meaning of Christian life. They did, however, provide useful guidance for uneducated and sometimes barbaric people.

Twelfth-century scholars collected and systematically organized scattered and often confusing church laws. Robert of Flamborough introduced some of the products of this legal scholarship into his penitential, composed between 1205 and 1213. A close relationship between law and ethics persisted into modern times, adding clarity and precision to ethical thought, but often explaining Christian life in overly legal categories.

The twelfth-century revival of philosophy and theology influenced ethics. Peter Abelard (1079-1142), for example, emphasized that guilt and sin depend on intention and consent and called attention to the subjective elements in moral life.

The great ethical treatise of the thirteenth century, Part Two of the *Summa Theologica* of Thomas Aquinas (1225-1274), was the most comprehensive Catholic ethic up to this time. It was developed systematically from fundamental principles and integrated within a total theological synthesis. Aquinas borrowed heavily from both Augustine and Aristotle, but contributed an original theological vision of his own. For Thomas, natural law meant that ethics must take account of the nature of things and persons and of their natural orientations toward certain ends. These orientations or "appetites," however, play a role in moral life only insofar as they are recognized by reason and integrated by reason and free choice into a total human life oriented toward God.

John Duns Scotus (1265-1308) proposed a notion of divine freedom and omnipotence that had ethical consequences. Scotus reasoned that if God can do whatever He wills, then He could change many of the moral laws. William of Ockham (1280-1348) adopted a nominalist philosophy that rejected any notion of intrinsic natures that govern ethics. This allowed him to draw from the notion of divine freedom and omnipotence certain conclusions more radical than those of Scotus. According to Ockham, God could decree that falsehood, killing of the innocent, or even hatred of God Himself, is morally good. Where Aquinas maintained that God is "bound" by His own nature to act in certain ways in establishing ethical norms, Ockham saw no reason for such limits. His view has greatly influenced later ethics.

By the fifteenth century the influence of Ockham probably outweighed that of Aquinas or Augustine at a number of universities. During the sixteenth century Thomism revived, especially in Spain, where Francisco de Vitoria (c. 1483-1546) introduced Thomas's *Summa Theologica* as the basic theological text at the University of Salamanca and applied the principles of Aquinas to legal and social issues of the time. In Northern Europe, Erasmus (1466-1536) and other Catholic humanists abandoned the scholastic tradition and tried to renew moral theology by relating it more closely to sacred Scripture, to personal piety, to patristic thought, and to everyday experience.

The faithful and many of the clergy found moral guidance less from the great thinkers than from the *Summae Confessorum*, practical guidebooks for confessors that had replaced the penitentials. The Council of Trent (1545-1563) insisted that priests be better trained to hear confessions. Seminaries established courses on "cases of conscience," and manuals of moral theology were composed for use in these courses. The manual-type of text remained the standard reference for education of the clergy until quite recently. Perhaps the most influential manual author was Alphonsus Liguori (1697-1787), who strove to counter the legalism of some texts by stressing the love and mercy of God and other central truths of faith.

The manuals included discussion of moral cases (casuistry) but added systematic theological background. Often the elements were not well integrated. Texts from Aquinas might be mixed with ideas of nominalist inspiration, and the practical casuistry often had little relation to the preceding theology. The isolation of moral theology from dogmatics and Scripture sometimes gave the impression that Christian life is mainly an observance of a detailed code of law. On the other hand, many manuals contained a wealth of practical wisdom about how to find equitable solutions to difficult problems.

In the nineteenth and twentieth centuries some Thomists composed manuals that tried to apply the theological vision of Aquinas in a consistent way to solving cases. Others, like Johann Baptist Hirscher (1788-1865) in Germany, rejected Thomism and tried to relate moral theology more closely to contemporary philosophy, to concrete experience, and to an awareness of historical change.

Roman Catholic social ethics has developed considerably in the last hundred years, encouraged by the social encyclicals of Leo XIII and subsequent popes. Recently, national hierarchies have become more vocal on social issues, exemplified by the 1983 statement on nuclear arms by the American bishops.

In recent decades several moralists, such as Bernhard Haring, have attempted to renew Roman Catholic ethics by bringing it closer to its scriptural roots, by using material from psychology and the social sciences, and by addressing new issues raised by social, economic, and technological change. A lively controversy exists between those who insist that acts can be judged as morally good or evil only in their particular context and those who argue that certain types of action are morally evil regardless of the situation in which they occur. Controversy exists also concerning whether the modernization of Catholic ethics has involved uncritical acceptance of too many modern attitudes.

*Characteristics of Roman Catholic Ethics.* Roman Catholic ethics presupposes a particular understanding of justification by faith. Catholics, like other Christians, believe that sinners are justified not because of merit on their part, but by God's gratuitous gift in view of the merits of Jesus Christ. Catholics also believe that the Christian, justified by faith, is inwardly transformed by God's grace and can perform actions that are truly meritorious, not because they are human actions, but because they are the product of God's grace. Accordingly, Christian moral life has two aspects. First, it is a grateful response to God's love and forgiveness, an aspect stressed by Luther. Second, it involves actions, particularly loving actions, which move the person effectively toward the object of that love, God. This second aspect allows the moral life to be viewed teleologically, a view many Protestants find unacceptable. Some Catholic moralists also stress the second aspect as to obscure the first. In this they depart not only from Protestant ethicists, but also from the authentic Catholic notion of justification by faith.

Roman Catholic ethics generally presupposes a particular attitude toward nature. Catholics believe that people are "wounded" by original sin and made prone to evil, but not fundamentally corrupted. Human nature, they believe, retains good tendencies. In the Catholic view, grace builds on nature and heals the wounds inflicted by sin. The healing and perfecting of nature is seen as an integral part of sanctification, begun in baptism, but not finished in this life.

Natural law plays a larger part in Roman Catholic than in Protestant ethics. Different Catholic moralists have different theories of natural law, but nearly all grant that people can know important moral truths without Scripture, and that this knowledge is to be incorporated into Catholic ethics.

The Protestant-Catholic difference concerning natural law is to some extent a matter of emphasis. Many Protestants (e.g., Luther, Grotuis) made room for natural law. While some Catholics have so stressed natural law as to obscure the scriptural basis for ethics, others give much more scriptural emphasis. All agree, however, that on certain basic questions human reason by itself is quite adequate.

Roman Catholic moralists speak frequently of the development of virtues. Virtues are acquired qualities that enable one to act well. Honesty, courage, temperance, and others are considered to be natural virtues because they develop naturally from repeated action. One becomes more temperate by behaving temperately. Faith, hope, and charity are called "supernatural virtues" because they require the special help of God beyond His normal sustaining of our natures in being and action. Progress in Christian life involves development of these virtues.

Church authority (of general and local councils, of popes and bishops) plays a significant role in Roman Catholic ethics, both in positive teaching and in warning against objectionable positions. Official statements vary in authority. There have been few, if any, pronouncements on ethics that have been considered infallible, but major statements by general councils or popes carry great authority. (The recent dissent by many Catholics against official church teaching on artificial contraception is unusual.) However, Roman Catholic ethics is hardly a monolithic system imposed by the hierarchy. Usually (except when repeating a point already established as official church teaching) official statements are made only after a question has been thoroughly discussed among moralists.

Catholics and Protestants can agree that, insofar as Christians are inspired by the gospel and moved by the Holy Spirit, they tend to unify on major ethical issues. Differences arise on how best to respond to existing disunity. The Catholic church insists on the need for authority as an instrument of unity, to challenge individuals to move beyond a private and overly subjective view. Many Protestants find it hard to reconcile this use of authority with the need to respect individual freedom and responsibility.

Roman Catholic ethics often involves casuistry, going beyond general principles to provide more precise guidance by discussing and "solving" typical cases. Some writers have given the impression that the textbooks can provide, in advance, a solution to almost any situation that might arise, leaving little scope for individual prudence. Others, notably Thomas Aquinas, give greater scope to individual prudence. While casuistry runs the risk of leaving too little scope to individual prudence, it does foster objectivity in solving moral cases by bring it into the domain of public and critical discussion.

Protestant ethicists have often rejected casuistry, being content to discuss ethical issues in general terms and have left to the individual, aided by the Holy Spirit, the task of applying general norms to particular situations. The Protestant-Catholic difference on this point is in some respects narrowing. In the expanding field of medical ethics, for example, some Protestant ethicists discuss cases and draw detailed guidelines in a way not unlike Catholic casuistry. Most Catholic ethicists, meanwhile, stress more than formerly the responsibility of persons to make their own ethical judgments. This leaves the problem of helping people achieve the level of knowledge and information required to assure that their making their own judgment is in fact to make a decision based on objective truth.

**Bibliography:** Fuchs, J., *Human Values and Christian Morality* (1970); Gustafson, J., *Protestant and Roman Catholic Ethics* (1978); Haring, B., *Free and Faithful in Christ*, Volumes I–III (1978-1981); Vann, G., *Morals and Man* (1960).

See CONFESSION; MORTAL SIN; PENANCE; VENIAL SIN.

J.R.C.

# –S–

**SABBATH OBSERVANCE.** In the ancient Near East, rhythms of work and rest were not peculiar to Israel. The creation narrative, however, makes it clear that the theological justification for the Jewish sabbath (literally, "ceasing") is rooted in the actions and values of God Himself. This is reaffirmed in the fourth commandment (Exod. 20:8-11). God placed a special significance of His own "ceasing" from the work of creation, thereby assigning special significance on human rest as well. Even here the imitation of God emerges as a central concept in Old Testament ethics. The moral and social codes of the Pentateuch lay a repeated emphasis on sabbath observance; not least through the scale of punishment that they prescribe for its violation (Exod. 31:12-17; 34:21; 35:2-3; Lev. 19:3, 30; 23:1-3). The codes extend sabbath principles beyond the use of time to the ordering of the land (Exod. 23:10-11) and of property (Lev. 25).

Some conceptions of sabbath tend to re-subjugate its meaning and importance to work. Here the function of rest is seen in terms of recuperation and personal replenishment, which will enable people to work more efficiently. Certainly better work is a demonstrable product of proper systematic rest. Various studies have shown the importance of regular time off for productivity. Scripture, however, does not give particular stress to this dimension of rest (see Exod. 31:17). Rest does not exist for work. Rather, in the Pentateuch we see that ceasing is given a positive value of its own. Above all the sabbath is to be holy, sacred, a day set apart for the Lord—a day for public worship and for making special offerings to God (Lev. 23:1-3; 24:8; Num. 28:9; Ps. 92). Primarily then, sabbath rest exists to uphold the necessity of regularly turning away from one's daily labor in order to focus on other precious dimensions of human existence and fulfill other aspects of one's obligations to God. It stands as a protection against the individual's own preoccupation with work, as well as against the exploitation of the worker by others (Exod. 20:10; Deut. 5:12-15).

The prophets both uphold this conception of the sabbath (Isa. 56:2; 58:13-14; Amos 8:5) and offer stern warnings against its corruption and empty observance (Isa. 1:13; Hos. 2:11). After exile, the nation is called to once more honor the sabbath (Neh. 13:15-22).

By the time of Jesus, however, certain Pharisaic schools had clothed the concept of sabbath rest with a precise code of legalistic obligations. Jesus' liberation of the sabbath is to be understood against this background (Matt. 12:1-14;

Mark 2:23—3:6; Luke 6:1-11). The Pharisees had developed a concept of the sabbath divorced from human well-being. In contrast, Jesus reaffirms the original ordinance by proclaiming that the sabbath is made for man, not man for the sabbath. It is there to protect, serve, and enrich human life.

On the first day of the week, Jesus rose from the grave. From very early in its history, the primitive church met together on the first day (the Lord's Day: Rev. 1:10) to celebrate His great resurrection triumph (Acts 20:7; 1 Cor. 16:2). However, Christianity has also absorbed much of the concept of sabbath rest in its approach to Sunday. Church historians differ as to how quickly and in what forms this absorption evolved. Certainly after the conversion of Constantine, the state took a hand in freeing Sunday from certain forms of labor.

The theological principle underlying this coming together of sabbath rest and resurrection celebration is to be affirmed. God's intentions for mankind in creation have not been abrogated. If God still calls man to work, He still calls him to rest. But it is natural and proper that Christians should clothe the doctrine of sabbath with the gospel of Jesus Christ.

In terms of contemporary discussion, two key issues may be identified. First, it is to be noted that there is a diversity of opinion among Christians as to how Sunday should be approached. The concept of "ceasing" originated to protect those precious dimensions of human existence that might otherwise be squeezed out by the often intimidating demands of labor. Some Christians now apply this widely. Sunday is for worship, but it is also a day for the family and perhaps for other forms of experience that might be threatened or submerged. Others maintain a more rigorous, religious interpretation. Whatever we make of these different approaches, most will agree that the central focus of Sunday is to be the individual and corporate worship of God.

A second key issue concerns the place of Sunday in a non-Christian culture. There is a Christian obligation to point toward the need for systematic rest and for a systematic turning away from daily labor to contemplate the ultimate questions and concerns of human existence. The church should be concerned to protect the freedom of its own members to rest and worship on Sundays. But whether or not there should be a legal obligation upon all members of society to "rest on the first day of the week" raises difficult questions about the nature of Christian ethics and of legal and political obligation.

**Bibliography**: Blanch, S., *The Ten Commandments* (1981); Davidman, J., *Smoke on the Mountain* (1963).

See EMPLOYMENT; WORK.

M.D.G.

**SAINTLINESS.** The concept of saintliness is that of the behavior which saints exhibit. The saints of the Old Testament period were the "godly ones" (*hasidim*), the "holy person" (*qadosh*), the "man of God" (*ish elohim*), or, as in Psalm 85:8, the "people of God." In the New Testament the common term for a saint was *agios,* a holy person committed to Christian service.

Because this entry has to do principally with the characteristics of saintliness, it is important to recognize certain behavioral differences which the general terminology reflects. The individual known as *hasid* was pious or godly because he had experienced divine mercy in a living relationship, and this placed him in a special category as a consequence. The "holy person" was someone separated from secular life and dedicated to divine service, with no apparent prerequisites of advanced spirituality (Lev. 10:1-2; 1 Sam. 2:12). The "man of God," by contrast, was both separated to God and spiritual, acting as a prophet and divine counselor. The Lord's people could be described as saints when they were living holy lives, separated from paganism, in accordance with the prescriptions of the Sinai covenant.

The New Testament saints were simply those persons who had responded to the challenge of the gospel and had become converted through faith in Christ. In this sense they had been "called to be saints" (Col. 1:2) and brought into a relationship of developing spirituality with Christ. From Paul's exhortations and admonitions to his readers it is possible to see some of the elements of saintliness that Christians ought to be exhibiting. Uncompromising loyalty to God in Christ through faith and obedience is mandatory, as is the conscious effort to manifest in society those qualities of altruism, purity, justice, and separation from all forms of evil and worldliness that are typical of the divine nature.

The Christian is commanded, as a saint, to grow into God's holiness (1 Pet. 1:16), and this involves a relationship with the Holy Spirit as the guide to godly living. The Christian must pursue a distinctively different life from the person of the world in order to be recognized as saintly, not of an artificial or bizarre order, but of a kind in which Christ increases and self decreases. It goes without saying that such a life will be of the highest moral and ethical character, emphasizing honesty and integrity, purity, and love of one's neighbor, pursued in the power of the Holy Spirit and in fellowship with other Christians.

See SANCTIFICATION.

**SANCTIFICATION.** This word describes a condition of holiness such as would be characteristic of a saint. Those who in Bible times were described as "saints" or "holy persons" had been set apart in some manner or called by God for a specific purpose. In Leviticus 11:44 the covenant nation of Israel was bidden to be holy as God is holy. This meant that all the high moral and ethical elements evident in the divine nature through revelation were to be fostered by the covenant community as a whole. No impurity of the kind forbidden by the Sinaitic legislation was to exist among the Israelites, and altruism was to be practiced consciously in community life. Honest dealings one with another were mandatory, as was the consistent observance of God's laws and statutes, which themselves reflected his altruism, justice, and loving care for his obedient people. The Sinai covenant revealed God as a merciful, provident father of the nation, whose most pressing demand was that he should be supreme in the affections and worship of his people (Exod. 20:3-6). On such a basis the faithful Israelite could expect material and spiritual blessing, one important aspect of the latter being the growth in divine grace as the relationship of obedience and holiness progressed.

The conditions which formed a prerequisite for holiness in the old covenant were imposed upon Christians also (1 Pet. 1:16). The believer sanctifies God by being obedient and especially by pursuing all those elements of morals, ethics, and spirituality that are known to be "good" (1 Pet. 3:13-15). While the Christian belongs to a special body that has been called out of the world and is being sanctified through the work of the Holy Spirit (Eph. 5:25-26) as a consequence of God's gift of Christ to the world (1 Cor. 1:30), the individual Christian's life must be one of spiritual growth in which the moral values of holiness demand constant attention (Heb. 12:14). Paul states specifically that God's will for the believer is his or her sanctification (1 Thess. 4:3), and the New Testament makes it clear that divine grace is available to help in the achievement of that objective. The Holy Spirit plays a fundamentally important part in individual sanctification. Described by Christ as the "spirit of truth" (John 16:13), he will guide the believer into what is true, and through this kind of revelation will enable him or her to glorify Christ. The Holy Spirit reminds the believer of the ethics of Christian living by urging the necessity of walking worthily of the vocation of faith (Eph. 4:1) and manifesting humility, tolerance, and loving forbearance (Eph. 4:2), as becomes those who are being sanctified.

But the process of sanctification, imperfect as it will always be in mortal experience, demands not merely gifts from God, but determined human effort to grow into the knowledge of Christ. Sanctification does not come about because someone has been exposed to a holy person or some consecrated object. Rather, it is a process of spiritual development in which, by God's grace, the works of carnal living are rejected in favor of the high ethical and moral qualities of God's nature. Paul speaks of "walking in the Spirit" (Gal. 5:16) and promises that the attributes of a life that is sanctified by the Holy Spirit will include love, joy, peace, gentleness, self-control, and humility, which are described as the "fruit of the Spirit" (Gal. 5:22-23). On the basis of these divinely bestowed attributes, the Christian can claim quite legitimately an experience of sanctification through the Spirit, not however as a matter for personal pride or selfish satisfaction, but for the task of proclaiming Christ's gospel in society and as a practical example of holy living.

See SAINTLINESS; PERFECTIONISM.

**SCANDAL.** This word owes its origin to the Greek word *skandalon,* which in classical times occurred in the rather more complex form of *skandalethron.* This word referred to the lever by which a baited trap was sprung and in a metaphorical sense to some word or expression used to trap an opponent in a debate. By New Testament times *skandalon* had come to be used of a "stumbling block," that is, some sort of impediment that causes a person to miss his or her footing in life or an obstacle that hinders proper progress.

Among the ancient Hebrews it was strictly prohibited under the Mosaic legislation for anyone to place a stumbling block (*mikshol*) in the path of a blind person because such inconsiderate behavior took shameful advantage of a serious human disability. The New Testament used three words for "stumbling block," one of which, *proskomma,* was similar to the Hebrew *mikshol* in constituting a significant obstacle to progress. Paul used the rare expression *lithos tou proskommatos* in Romans 9:32-33 regarding Israel's failure to attain to the law of righteousness. Elsewhere (Rom. 11:9; 1 Cor. 1:23) Paul employed *skandalon* in the older sense to signify a snare or a trap in connection with Israel's spiritual blindness or as illustrating the way in which the preaching of the Crucifixion was an obstacle to belief among the Jews.

In modern times, *scandal* is generally understood to be consequent upon scurrilous behavior and normally constitutes a verbal report of such activity, whether exaggerated or not, which results in disrepute or injury to a person's reputation. When scandalous reports are untrue they constitute a form of false witness, which is prohibited in the Decalogue (Exod. 20:16).

Jesus has stern warnings for those who cause innocent young believers to stumble or those who find themselves stumbling into sin because some part of the body had tempted them successfully. For the Christian, the cross of Christ is an object of glory, not an impediment, but the individual believer must be very careful not to present Christ's saving work in such a manner that it does in fact become an obstacle to true belief. Similarly the believer will do everything possible to follow a way of life that will avoid any taint of scandal through unethical or immoral behavior. By this means the body of Christ will be honored and not brought into disrepute.

**SCIENCE AND ETHICS.** The process by which we derive our knowledge is of great importance in that research may be a humane, honest, enjoyable, creative process, or a politicized, partisan, self-serving, even vicious process attended by unnecessary waste and human and animal suffering. Thus, the process by which scientific knowledge is derived, its validity, and its application, are all in human hands and subject to the ethical principles held and practiced by those involved.

In considering ethics, it is necessary to distinguish nature from science. Nature has been defined as the "the external material world and its phenomena, considered primarily as these manifest themselves to the senses, without reference to the underlying forces, causes, and processes" (Webster). On the other hand, science represents the current, incomplete state of human understanding of nature. The term encompasses the method (empirical) by which such knowledge is derived, as well as the systematic accumulation of knowledge that can be studied, integrated, and reflected upon by students and mature scholars in a rich variety of disciplines.

The scientist's world view might be regarded by some as necessarily influencing the shape and outcome of the scientific process, but this is only selectively true. Relatively few experimental "wet bench" scientists are consciously guided by a rigorously formulated philosophy. They simply "do science," which when done properly, results in findings that seem to be minimally influenced by the scientist's philosophy and can be readily shared by scientists of different philosophical persuasions.

It should be recognized, however, that even vague and unsystematized philosophical positions define the scientist's state of being, affecting the person doing the work even if they do not perceptibly influence the work itself. The person is guided by an ethical system rooted in a philosophy, and the extent to which both influence the work may well vary with its nature. For instance, investigating the chemical structure of a hormone is less ethically sensitive than investigating the use of that same hormone as a contraceptive.

Fundamentally, the scientist's view of "the underlying forces, causes, and processes" built into the very definition of the word *nature* are crucial. To the atheist, these may be blind, mechanistic forces operating at random, toward no discernable goal. At best, in the case of living things, the goal may be defined as "survival of the species," the value and purpose of which are not necessarily considered. To the Christian, "underlying forces, causes, and processes" may still be acceptable as inherent in nature. At a purely scientific level of consideration the Christian may validly use such terms to describe natural phenomena. Behind all, however, is the Creator, who through all such agencies fulfills His divine purposes. With this perspective, the Christian scientist experiences the sense of "walking in God's footsteps after Him" when making discoveries. This is bound to influence attitudes and the mode of daily operation in the laboratory.

In simple, idealistic terms, the Christian scientist exercises an inborn curiosity and drive to discover the secrets of nature. Personal ambition and the need for material reward are undoubtedly present, but so is the understanding of entering God's world, responsible and responsive to Him, and uncovering His handiwork in a manner that honors Him and subserves the material and spiritual welfare of his own and other societies. On the other hand, the unbelieving scientist is alone, lacking the spiritual, God-honoring dimension of the believer's experience. The unbelieving scientist has much in common with the believer; may cooperate happily with others in the laboratory; may make discoveries of lesser, equal, or greater significance; but nevertheless, be operating within quite a different framework.

An operating framework that ignores or denies the creatorship and sovereignty of God has given rise to the following presuppositions regarding ethics in science. For the most part, these beliefs are so subtle and implicit as to be virtually unrecognizable, but, in essence, undoubtedly exist.

1. The scientific enterprise "embodies" the ethical principles that properly guide its progress. Starting with their undergraduate and graduate traineeship, it is all too commonly assumed that our future scientists will "automatically" pick up the required ethical principles along with all the other skills required. Unfortunately, the channels for transmitting scientific skills are clearer and more likely to be valid and coherent among faculty supervisors than those for ethical principles. One is reminded of a cartoon depicting a bewildered looking worker in a huge mechanized bakery asking a fellow worker, "Have you ever discovered exactly where the bread gets enriched?"

Frankly, it is hard to place where our future scientists get enriched with ethical principles. At best, it happens through rather relativistic courses or appropriate role models. The most influential role model is probably the student's graduate supervisor, with whom most of the traineeship is spent. However, in a pluralistic scientific community, the perspectives of such role models could cover a very broad spectrum indeed. An East Indian Hindu supervisor could provide a very different ethical perspective from that of an Orthodox Jew or a Scottish Presbyterian. What the student absorbs may be attributed to science but, in reality, has its origins in the personal perspective of the supervisor himself. In this case the perspective may represent a coherent view firmly rooted in the particular religion, or

some kind of hybrid position representing more than one set of religious and/or cultural roots.

Thus, in the formative apprenticeship years, scientists are heavily influenced by a rather haphazard assortment of ethical positions, primarily reflecting those of their mentors that they may mistakenly believe to arise out of science itself. These principles may or may not receive adequate scrutiny, depending on the personality and previous environmental influences, particularly home and church, of the scientist concerned.

2. The best interests of the scientific enterprise encourage sound ethical behavior by scientists. It is commonly supposed that scientists will behave altruistically "for the good of science." Unfortunately, there exists too much evidence to the contrary, including well-publicized accounts of blatant fraud. In the highly competitive struggle for research grants, jobs, and prestige, scientists may readily succumb to the intense pressures placed upon them by "smoothing out" their data, exaggerating its importance or relevance to the cure of dreadful diseases, publishing questionable results prematurely, and so forth. An impressive bibliography and its promise of career advancement becomes much more compelling than the dutiful observance of a borrowed set of weak ethical concepts absorbed by "osmosis" from mentors to whom one is no longer accountable. Financial considerations may prematurely launch a dangerous drug onto the market, or withhold life-saving information, each time with tragic consequences upon the lives of numerous unsuspecting consumers.

3. Concerns for the "common good of society" will compel ethical behavior. The inadequacy of this ethical basis can be elaborated along the same lines. Moreover, individual perceptions of "the common good" will vary widely, depending on one's perspective. For instance, developing a better, more readily available drug for inducing abortion may be a worthy ideal for some, but objectionable to others. Or, research on germ warfare organisms may be considered essential to national defense by some and morally wrong by others. All this indicates that "for the good of society" is not a primary ethical yardstick but rather a reflection of prior values rooted in a particular belief system.

Even well liked and respected scientific colleagues can be singularly unhelpful when it comes to issues of right and wrong involving their immediate sphere of work. A "Don't rock the boat!" attitude, political expedience, other career considerations, or even lack of courage due to lack of conviction can often loom larger in their advice than anything else. Regrettably, idealistic and courageous behavior is more frequently exhibited in relation to moral issues situated at a safe distance from the workplace. War and peace in distant countries, the fate of dissidents in the Soviet Union, abortion on demand, and other valid but removed concerns tend to generate a more impressive display of conviction and courage than issues of right and wrong on one's own doorstep with one's future promotion at stake. Christian scientists continually have to rely on a biblical perspective for guidance. Of course, not every issue of current relevance is explicitly dealt with in Scripture, but the framework of essential principles properly understood and balanced can be brought to bear on any situation.

In a nutshell, ethics in science do not arise out of the science itself but reflect the prior perspectives of a diverse group of scientists. The best ethics observed in the scientific enterprise are largely borrowed from other sources in the Judeo-Christian sphere, unmistakably from the Bible itself. With such diversity there is also a lack of consistency and coherence, such that conflicting advice may be obtained on many, or most, ethical questions making it necessary to make an individual choice. In particular, the authority on which a particular ethic is based must be intrinsically valid, convincing, and gripping if it is to work in the crunch, when personal interest or security is clearly at stake. It is relatively easy to articulate ethical/moral sentiments about wars, justice, and freedom in faraway places, but difficult to take a firm stand on day-to-day issues in the workplace. God must be the ultimate source of the wisdom, strength, and courage required by the scientist to "do what's right" in daily life (Eph. 3:20; 6:10-20). "What's right" should be no less than the application of God's revealed principles, which are relevant to the entire spectrum of human experience, in and out of the science laboratory.

**Bibliography:** Osmond, D. H., "Malice's Wonderland: Research Funding and Peer Review", *Journal of Neurobiology*, XIV.2, 95–112, 1983.

D.H.O.

**SCRUPLES.** This term describes the hesitant feelings experienced when an individual has doubts, mental reservations, or misgivings about the morality or propriety attaching to a particular course of action. The scruples may arise because the question of honesty has been raised by the projected activity or because what has been suggested is open to hesitation on grounds of conscience or religious faith. If the individual so involved declines to participate in the proposed course of action, he or she is said to have been deterred from it by scruples. An unscrupulous person is one who would have no compunction whatever about acting in an unprincipled or unethical manner.

The term originated with the Latin noun *scrupus,* which meant "a rough or sharp stone," but in a metaphorical sense referred to uneasiness of mind, doubt, or hesitation. It is mandatory for the Christian to avoid every appearance of evil (1 Thess. 5:22), to say nothing of participating actively in it. Moral and ethical conduct by the believer is one means of demonstrating practical love for one's neighbor, as well as honoring God in purity, honesty, and truth.

See MENTAL RESERVATIONS.

**SECRECY.** Secrecy is the act or habit of guarding from public scrutiny or knowledge certain information that has been deemed to be, or has been classified as, confidential. Secrecy need not be restricted to an individual, but can be the function of a group that has agreed, or been sworn, to secrecy. The best results are obtained from a policy of secrecy when as few individuals as possible are in possession of the secret information. Even so, secrets can be extracted from people by skilled, nondirective interrogation, or by blackmail consequent upon the person possessing the secret being compromised as the result of sexual or fiscal misdemeanors.

Many areas of professional life have long cherished the traditions of secrecy for certain members. The lawyer-client relationship, the journalist and his source of leaked confidential information, and the doctor-patient right of privacy are all examples of this tendency. The "seal" of the Roman Catholic confessional is another area where secrecy is cherished and honored. In government circles "official" secrecy surrounds many policies and plans that affect diplomacy, military operations, and related matters; but such secrecy is by no means impregnable, as has been demonstrated periodically. Secrecy in other areas has been contested in various jurisdictions by public-information acts which seek varying degrees of disclosure.

Christians who are sworn to secrecy are under direct obligation to keep their oath, and if matters of conscience or scruples are involved they should withdraw their participation in order to preserve their integrity and credibility, whatever the personal cost. To be party to secret information, and then to release it surreptitiously or to gossip about it, as some Christians are wont to do, is base, reprehensible, and unethical conduct which represents a grave breach of trust and is entirely unworthy of a follower of Jesus.

**SECRET SOCIETIES.** This is a popular term applied to a number of groups or associations that restrict their membership and bind participants to secrecy in certain areas of activity by means of oaths. The impression commonly gained is that all the proceedings and activities are highly secret in nature, but this, of course, is untrue. Indeed, instead of speaking about "secret societies" it is more accurate to talk about "societies that have secrets." These secrets normally consists of passwords, ritual procedures of initiation, symbols, secret handshakes, and so on. The oaths of nondisclosure that most initiates are required to take enhance the elitist nature of the organization and help maintain the authority of the hierarchy established by the society in question.

Probably the most familiar organization of this kind is Freemasonry, which claims to go back to sixteenth-century European life, and was firmly established in Britain in the eighteenth century. Its emphasis was thoroughly Protestant and upper-class, and for many generations it made Roman Catholicism the target of its attention. It had elaborate rituals formulated in part upon traditions concerning the building of the Solomonic temple, and its adherents were sworn to secrecy about most of the proceedings in the various lodges and councils. In later years Freemasons became involved increasingly in educational and charitable causes, which enhanced their public image and allayed fears about the real nature of the society.

Groups of this kind have not infrequently attracted church members, particularly those with racist or bigoted tendencies. This is true especially of the Ku Klux Klan. Other individuals of milder disposition have favored societies with secrets because the quasi-exclusive or elitist atmosphere appeals to some immature romanticism in them. Although this tends to be disguised by demonstrations of philanthropic activity, the organizations are distinctly reminiscent of childhood gangs with their passwords, secret signs, and other tokens of exclusivity. The most sinister secret society of modern times is the Mafia, which binds it members by stern oaths and rituals preparatory to engaging in a life of crime.

In its very early days Christianity was something of a secret society (John 20:19), but this situation altered radically as a result of Christ's command to preach the gospel throughout the world (Mark 16:15). The Christian church will not be expanded by secret disciples such as Nicodemus (John 3:2), nor is it honored by puerile esoteric rituals, even though they might claim a quasi-religious character. While many persons regard these organizations as relatively harmless forms of amusement, some Christians who dislike the idea of swearing oaths refuse to participate in them, whatever charitable objectives they may avow.

See KU KLUX KLAN; OATHS.

## SECULARISM, SECULARIZATION.

Secular comes from the Latin saeculm, meaning "time" or "age," and thus secularism is a view of life that causes the secularist to be totally of this age, without any vision of eternity. It maintains that, as history moves on, so values and rules, laws and norms, change. Thus morality is merely that accepted or tolerated by the society in which one lives. For secularism, morality cannot consist of norms, values, and laws dictated by religious faith; it must be worked out freely and chosen by people for themselves. While secularism is a philosophy of life, secularization is a social process that both prepares the way for, and actually aids, the former. Secularism may be viewed either as a body of teaching or as a set of assumptions that insist that the real meaning of this world is found within itself, that we need not concern ourselves with any future life, and that morality can be based on this-wordly principles rather than on claims of revealed truth. It comes in varied forms, sometimes explicity (as in the *Humanist Manifesto II* of 1973), but often implicity (as the underlying assumptions of advertising, entertainment, and affluence). The term *secular humanism* is often used to describe the content of secularism. The *Humanist Manifesto II*, signed by some very influential people, states:

> We affirm that moral values derive their source from human experience. Ethics is autonomous and situational, needing no theological or ideological sanction. In the area of sexuality, we believe that intolerant attitudes, often cultivated by orthodox religions and puritanical cultures, unduly repress sexual conduct. The right to birth control, abortion, and divorce should be recognized.

Secularization is a term used in a variety of ways. It has been used to refer to a loss of religious faith, a weakening of confidence in Christianity, and the demise of Christian values in the West. These usages point to the growing emphasis on this *saeculum* (age) and less interest in, or reference to, the transcendent reality of the kingdom of God. A better way of understanding secularization is to view it as a social process involving both the way society is structured and organized and how people in the society believe and act. Here the emphasis is upon the removal of religion and religious ideas and values from important areas of society, so that the practice and presuppositions of religion are seen as belonging properly only to the private sphere. In Western society there has been a major retraction of what has been called "the sacred canopy." This once covered government, politics, education, medicine, and welfare, but now it has shrunk and covers only parts of these; and where it does cover it cannot prevent some amount of secularism getting through. This process is well illustrated by the skyline of cities like Paris and London. Once they were dominated by the towers and spires of churches (symbolizing the dependence of human beings upon God), but now they are dominated by office-blocks (symbolizing the search for dominance in this *saeculum* by modern people).

While the assumptions on which society was formerly organized in the West were primarily religious (belief in God and in His providence, blessing, judgment, moral law, and rule via human agents), they are now dependent upon what has been called "functional rationality" or "technique orientation." This works on the basis of, "Simply figure it out and it can be don," and thus has no meaningful place for prayer or reference to God. The arrival of the computer represents a significant advance in the possibilities for a greater commitment to such technique orientation.

The process of secularization is not identical in all countries or societies, since various factors affect the way in which it proceeds. These factors include the type of culture, the extent of the processes of modernization and urbanization, the use of the dependence upon technology, the presence of heavy industry, the use of migrant labor, the strength of the nation-state, and so on. Thus, while most of Western society is deeply secularized, the effect of this on church attendance is much greater in Europe than in America. However, within America, the strength of evangelicalism (and church attendance) is to be found not in and near the centers of secular power (major universities, higher socioeconomic classes, urban culture, and professions), but rather among the less well educated and in rural areas, the Midwest and South.

Is secularization a truly modern phenomenon, or has it occurred before? As far as the West is concerned, it is certainly a novelty. While there was pluralism (belief in different deities and ethical systems) in the Roman Empire, there was also a common belief that the source of all things was not within this world but was, rather, a transcendent reality. The modern West is the first society that knowingly and deliberately organizes itself without any meaningful or major reference to a dependence upon the living God. Earlier societies may have neglected their religion or acted contrary to its teaching, but they were organized on the assumption that God did exist and that this world is dependent upon another transcendent reality, namely God's kingdom. What communist countries do dogmatically in their official denial of the existence of God and the value of religion, the 'free" countries of the West appear to do functionally by effectively excluding God and religion from the centers of government, education, politics, medicine, trade, industry, advertising, entertainment, and so on.

Is secularization inevitable and irreversible? On both counts the answer is no, as the recent history of Iran has shown. However, to change the direction of Western society will require a tremendous effort by a lot of people who are fired with the vision of the holy and righteous Lord.

How does secularization affect the place of Christian faith and practice in Western society? First, it leads to what has been termed "privatization": Christianity is seen as one amongst many leisure activities and as suitable for the home. This is well illustrated by the statement of the founder of the McDonald hamburger empire who said: "I believe in God, the family, and McDonald's—and in the office that order is reversed." In other words, God is pushed from the centers of power into the private areas of life. Secondly, it leads to the church being moved to the perimeters of society, the result being "marginalization." Instead of occupying the center of the stage or plan of society, the church is envisaged as belonging to the margins. This is because it is not seen as having anything functionally useful to contribute to the running of the major organs of modern society.

Since the process of secularization is so broad and deep, it is inevitable (or seemingly so) that it has affected the life of the churches and the life of professing Christians. In terms of morality, it is seen entering the churches through such systems as those called "situation ethics," by the adoption of a double-standard morality (what applies at home does not apply at work), and by the erosion of teaching concerning the human conscience as the judge and guide to behavior. There is need among Christians for a greater awareness of the process and content of secularization, as well as for a combined determination to halt its progress by a great commitment to the Lord and His ways.

**Bibliography:** Berger, P. L., *The Social Reality of Religion*, (1973); Chadwick, O., *The Secularization of the European Mind* (1975); Guinness, O., *The Gravedigger File: Secret Papers on the Subversion of the Modern Church* (1983); Martin, D., *A General Theory of Secularization* (1978); Toon, P., *Your Conscience as Your Guide* (1984).

P.T.

**SEDUCTION.** This term originated with the Latin verb *seduco*, "to lead aside, lead apart." A person who seduces is therefore one who seeks to divert others from a behavioral or ideological pattern that has been established previously. Seduction is the process by which persons are led astray or perverted in various ways. It can assume a purely intellectual form, in which a person is made to succumb to doctrinal blandishments that divert him or her from the truth. Jesus warned that in the course of history false Christs would arise and attempt to seduce Christians by their signs and wonders (Mark 13:22), and therefore believers need to be on their guard against the influence of false doctrines. Seduction can also form the kind of persuasion that results in persons committing crimes or indulging in various acts of folly or stupidity. But the commonest use has to do with sexuality, in which seduction involves a man persuading a woman to indulge in sexual relations with him, or less frequently of a woman who deprives a man of his chastity by tempting him to lust after her. This form of moral and spiritual defilement was found in the Christian church at Thyatira (Rev. 2:18), where not merely false teaching but fornication and idolatry were being promoted.

Any criminal behavior is abhorrent to sincere believers, who are commanded to be honest in their dealings (Rom. 13:13). In the same way the Christian is commanded to flee from sexual sins (Rom. 6:18), which by nature debase and deprave the divine image in mankind. Seduction is especially reprehensible because it involves someone deliberately and unscrupulously manipulating another by a demonstration of superior persuasive power, thereby callously exploiting a weaker neighbor and bringing moral shame upon that person. Behavior of this kind is diametrically opposed to the teachings and examples of Jesus Christ.

**SEGREGATION.** This noun is derived from the Latin noun *segrego,* which was used originally in a pastoral setting to mean "separate from the flock." When employed in a metaphorical sense by the Roman authors and orators it signified a separation from others or the process of setting apart. Segregation therefore occurs when someone or something is removed from the rest and isolated for a particular reason. This type of separation is calculated and deliberate, as opposed to the involuntary form that animals and human beings practice when they separate from a larger group and associate with their own kind.

Involuntary segregation among children and adults is evidently an instinctive reaction of the personality to that of others. It is a complex of factors which may or may not have to do significantly with facial appearance, racial origins, or religious persuasion. The segregating factors do rest heavily upon a perception of compatibility, however, which in adults is expressed periodically by a group of such people separating themselves from the larger social unit and pursuing an independent existence as a community.

By contrast, the deliberate form of segregation is an institutionalized procedure associated predominantly with attempts to maintain law and order, or to control the economy in some manner. In the Middle Ages Jews were segregated in Europe, deprived of access to professions that were regarded as Gentile-Christian perquisites, and forced to live apart from others in ghettos. Segregation with official approval has been in operation among Hindus for centuries through their caste system. This procedure divided up the Hindu population into social classes of a rigid nature, and it was not until after World War II that the Indian government began to legislate against that type of segregation.

Law and order are also maintained in society by detaining convicted criminals and accommodating them in prisons which effectively segregate them from the general public. Further segregation also takes place within the prisons themselves in the case of inmates whose lives are at risk from other prisoners because of the particular nature of the crimes that they have committed.

On a larger scale segregation involves the separation of whole groups from the community, predominantly on the basis of race, as is done under the apartheid conditions of South Africa. According to this system, segregated persons are accommodated on reserves of land, as with the Indians of Canada and the United States; and unless local conditions are controlled carefully by the authorities these locations become hotbeds of crime, drunkenness, and squalor. While the political and social ideal may be for the complete integration of the various races that go to make up a community or a nation, there are occasions when other considerations make that ideal difficult if not impossible, as, for example, where national and racial differences conflict. In such an event, all the criticisms that relate to racism would be applicable and would be noted by Christians accordingly.

The separateness of the Christian church from worldly concerns has sometimes been interpreted along the lines of voluntary segregation, and in fact certain religious sects have done much to confirm this impression by the isolationist social patterns that they have adopted. The Christian church, however, is called to service and ministry in the world, not segregation, just as ancient Israel was once extended a vocation to become a holy, priestly nation (Exod. 19:6). Where segregation exists, it is the responsibility of the Christian to minister to that situation, making every effort to relieve distress and injustice while witnessing to spiritual freedom among those in bondage.

See APARTHEID; CIVIL RIGHTS.

**SELF-CONTROL.** Among the Greeks of the Socratic period, *sophrosune* or "self-control" was one of the ethical ideals that was commended in the expectation that a proper balance of action and restraint would result in a more integrated individual life. In the New Testament *sophrosune* was replaced by *enkrateia* (Acts 24:25; Gal. 5:23; 2 Pet. 1:6), where the term seems to describe continence or self-restraint. The closest approach to *sophrosune* in Hellenistic Greek is in Titus 2:2, where the more senior believers are urged to be *sophron* (temperate KJV), that is, to behave as mature, prudent people.

The exercising of self-control in sexual matters was urged upon Corinthian Christians by Paul (1 Cor. 7:9), while the general Greek sense of self-discipline appears in 1 Corinthians 9:25, where an athletic metaphor is involved. The believer is bidden to manifest self-control as one of a number of qualities that should distinguish Christian living. Even though Jesus may have been recognized as lord of individual existence, self-discipline is still needed in order to combat those temptations that would dethrone Christ from his preeminent position. Just as the athlete must train rigorously if he or she is to attain success, so the life of the individual Christian must be disciplined by applying consistently the ethical and spiritual demands of the gospel of Jesus if the great prize of eternal life in Christ is to be gained.

**SELF-DECEPTION.** The classical early modern statement about self-deception and falsity is given by Roger Bacon (1561–1626) in a series of parables at the dawning of the modern scientific method. He calls them idols or false notions and identifies them thus: Idols of the Tribe (given in human nature itself as men make themselves to be the measure of all things), Idols of the Cave (prejudices of individual men due chiefly to the predispositions generated and sustained by their egocentric predicament), Idols of the Marketplace (errors due to the associations of men which reinforce the ambiguous and erroneous use of words), and Idols of the Theater (error deriving from received dogma, categories, and method which, because wrong at bottom, can yield only wrong conclusions).

Modern psychological research has endeavored to discover the mechanisms of the brain which facilitate self-deception and the relation between the disposition of the person toward his own well-being and the function of those mechanisms. A sociological correlation is then made. For some, such as the Jewish writer Elie Wiesel who has in his writings probed the meaning of the holocaust, memory serves the vital function of retaining painful awareness of past evils in order to warn against repeating them in the future. The new research claims that human beings commonly practice the "vital lie" as individuals, groups, and societies. This entails denial, buried secrets, and fantasy in situations such as perpetuating the myth of a happy family which is anything but happy, masking the problem of drug addiction or alcoholism, "group-think" situations in which no dissenting voice dare be raised, unquestioned assumed consensus, white lies as the lubricant of social well-being, frames of reference which become a Procustean bed for the truth, and the tendency of societies to rewrite painful history. While some suggest that self-deception may serve a useful function, such as the claim that some patients who purposely avoid seeking out information about impending surgery tend to recover more quickly than those who do, most authorities see self-deception as a destructive force.

On the basis of biblical teaching, Christianity has always advocated commitment to truth. This is so closely woven into Christian faith that it is as much a subtle, pervasive pattern as an explicit statement. Anything less than commitment to truth is a betrayal of what is fundamental to Christian faith. Truth, appreciation for and authentic knowledge of the created order, and revelation by God of himself to man are seen to be a coherent whole. Christian faith does not undercut respect for nature or the scientific enterprise. Rather, it reinforces the importance of fact, verification, and truth.

Paul in 1 Corinthians 1—2 does not depreciate reason, only the abuse and errors of reason. His play of words on "things that are not" (1 Cor. 1:28) is a reference to a Greek philosophical phrase which means nonbeing. Paul, like Bacon, is saying that things men imagine to be ultimate reality may well be nonbeing, while the truth about God which some men by their categories exclude is reality.

Similarly, in 2 Timothy 2:23—26 Paul refers to those of untrained mind who, while purporting to teach others, are themselves a contradiction and lead others into error. Paul urges Timothy to be patient with contradiction and to try to lead such persons back to their sober senses (note also 2

Tim. 3:7). Important in this context is Paul's relating of ethics to intellectual pursuits: character and the pursuit of truth are inextricably linked, hence his call to repentance. P. T. Forsyth comments that the truth we see depends upon the men we are. Athenagoras, the second-century Christian apologist, wrote to the Emperor Marcus Aurelius that Christians center their attention not upon specious logic nor upon the skill of making speeches, but on the proof and lessons of actions.

For Christians, truth is accurate statement of that which is actually the case. This entails rigorous logic, careful attention to data, screening of historical record, and recurring scrutiny of hypotheses. This is laid upon Christians because of the Christian claim to historical revelation, to objective truth which is more than merely existential ("truth to me"), and to events which are reportable, not merely events to faith. The claim to truth and the demand for truth are powerful and demanding emphases in Scripture.

**Bibliography:** Goleman, D., *Vital Lies, Simple Truths: The Psychology of Self-Deception* (1985); Holmes, A. F., *All Truth Is God's Truth* (1977); Laing, R. D., *The Divided Self: An Existential Study in Sanity and Madness* (1965).

S.J.M.

**SELF-DEFENSE.** This term describes the act or process of resisting attacks upon one's person, reputation, or possessions. Self-defense may involve an individual in resisting physical violence and in some jurisdictions comprises a valid defense where a charge of murder has been laid as a consequence of the resistance. Some ethicists have adduced the Old Testament law of proportional retaliation (Exod. 21:23-25; Lev. 24:19-21; Deut. 19:21) as justification for self-defense, but this is improper because the legislation in question refers to the restrictive penalties for various acts of violence or aggression in which self-defense need not necessarily have been a part.

Jesus apparently did not favor self-defense and emphasized his teachings by his way of life (John 18:11; 1 Pet. 2:23). His insistence that his followers should not resist evil (Matt. 5:39) seems to have been consonant with the advice of prophets such as Amos (5:13), where resistance would have been futile because the time was inopportune (Luke 22:53). The New Testament teaches that the believer is required to counter violence with love (Rom. 12:17-21) instead of retaliation (1 Thess. 5:15), but the true ethical nature of such an approach is only valid where the aggressor is already aware of its significance. Where this is not the case, an arrogant, bullying opponent merely assumes that nonretaliation is a sign of weakness, which is frequently the case.

Christ desires his followers to be strong and well-armed against potential or actual opposition (Eph. 6:10-18). If such strength and preparedness is clearly in evidence, it can act as a deterrent to hostile action. The taking up of arms in warfare for the defense of one's country against an aggressor has long been recognized by the Christian church as a legitimate duty to society. Some individuals, Christian and otherwise, have endeavored to avoid such responsibilities on conscientious grounds, and accordingly have questioned the morality of armed resistance to an aggressor in the light of Christ's teachings.

Some biblical scholars have maintained that Jesus was not imposing a universal law of nonresistance to aggressors in his teachings, since such a promulgation would have disrupted totally the stability of society. Instead, they argue that Jesus was speaking primarily to his newly assembled group of disciples (Matt. 4:18; 5:1) and advising them on how they were to meet opposition from the religious authorities of the day. Those persons were not authorized by the occupying Romans to use physical violence, especially of a militaristic nature, in order to gain their objectives. Nevertheless, because Christ and his followers threatened the established religious hierarchy in Judaism, they could expect to be the targets of attacks by the scribes, Sadducees, and Pharisees. When this eventuality occurred, Christ followed the instructions that he himself had given to his followers. If this interpretation is correct, the local Judean situation in the time of Jesus was totally different from one involving armed aggression on purely imperialistic grounds. This latter ought always to be resisted as a moral duty to one's country and fellow citizens by every freedom-loving individual, Christian or not.

**SELF-DENIAL.** Any attempt to renounce personal interests, appetites, possessions, pleasure, and so on, or to make them subject to discipline in order to achieve some high moral purpose, can be regarded as self-denial. If such activity is indulged in so that others may benefit, it is regarded as an ethical act, but where self-denial has no altruistic goals in view it is normally regarded as unacceptable by ethicists and liable to a charge of salvation by works from theologians.

Christ advocated self-denial in his teachings (Matt. 16:24), and several New Testament writers stressed that discipleship involved the complete renunciation of sin and self and total surrender to the will of Christ. Where self-denial led to self-sacrifice, it was regarded as the most meaningful expression possible of Christian love (John 10:15; 15:13). Christian groups throughout the centuries have endeavored to emulate the example of Christ by indulging in certain practices of self-denial. Some of these reached extreme proportions of physical abuse and seem to have been motivated more by psychological than spiritual considerations. All Christians are expected to keep Jesus enthroned as King and Lord of their lives and to deny any credence or authority to anything that would interfere with the Christian's obligation to live in obedience, purity, and holiness toward God (1 Pet. 1:14–16).

**SELF-EXAMINATION.** In Christian circles this term describes the kind of stocktaking or critical examination of one's moral and spiritual life that is invaluable in estimating growth or progress. This type of examination involving a study of motives was prescribed for the undisciplined Corinthians by Paul (1 Cor. 11:28) so that the spiritual integrity of the primitive *agapé* service might not be violated. At a subsequent time the same group of believers was urged to examine themselves as to their doctrinal orthodoxy (2 Cor. 13:5).

Some writers of a psychological bent have associated self-examination with self-awareness or self-knowledge, as though the main objective in Christian life was to grow in an understanding of self rather than Christ. Even the Socratic maxim "know yourself" is interpreted wrongly in this connection, since his real intent was to warn his hearers that they were only human, and therefore subject to the frailties of body and mind. Christian self-examination is a test of the extent to which the believer is abiding by the divine requisites of obedience, purity, and love.

Certain Christian denominations take advantage of Lent, a period which precedes Easter by forty days, for purposes of self-examination in the light of Scripture. Others believers prefer more frequent tests of the relationship with God and use the Ten Commandments frequently to ascertain the degree of their fidelity to God's basic commands. All self-examination should be indulged in as a means of promoting further growth in grace and not as neurotic self-flagellation.

**SELFISHNESS.** This word describes a motivating condition of the personality in which individual egocentricity normally prevails above all other considerations. Correlatively it is marked by an absence of concern for other persons, whether it be on an emotional, material, or social level.

Selfishness is the most obvious attribute of fallen human nature, and constitutes the dominating force of unregenerate individuals. Its fundamental denial of the rights, interests, and welfare of others renders it reprehensible morally and by contrast makes the altruism of the practicing Christian conspicuous. Selfishness is at the root of much of the social and moral evil in life, and from a theological perspective is a denial of divine supremacy and a flaunting of human nature in all its corruption. Some of those who are aware of the ethics involved excuse their selfish preoccupations by talking about the "survival of the fittest" or the "struggle for existence" in apparent unawareness of the divine assertion that the race is not necessarily given to the swift, nor the battle to the strong (Eccles. 9:11).

The New Testament teaches that when a person accepts Jesus as Savior and Lord, the old, selfish nature is surrendered and the love of Christ replaces love of self, guiding and impelling the believer to acts of grace and altruism in the service of Christ (2 Cor. 5:14; Gal. 2:20; Phil. 3:14). In all things Jesus must have the preeminence (Col. 1:18) and self must be negated.

**SENSUALITY.** Anything that can be described as sensual is connected specifically with one or another of the body's functions by which sensation is quickened. Sensual experience therefore does not occur as the result of spiritual or intellectual activity and can thus be defined exclusively in terms of carnal indulgence of various kinds, principally greed, pleasure, addiction, and the different forms of appetite.

In common parlance sensuality is identified with the pursuit of sexual relations to the virtual exclusion of almost all other sensual pleasures. It has thus become associated with sexual orgies of the kind that were typical of degenerate Roman society in New Testament times.

Sensuality has nothing whatever in common with the Christian ethic, which speaks of the products of physical sensation as the "works of the flesh" (Gal. 5:19-21). These are set in direct antithesis to the "fruit of the Spirit," which includes the graces and qualities that typify Christian character (Gal. 5:22-23). Jesus warned of the dangers of unregulated carnal passion (Matt. 5:28), while Paul emphasized that the believer has "crucified" the flesh, that is, human nature, with all its longings and lusts (Gal. 5:24). The Christian is not required to live an ascetic life, but must submit his or her desires obediently to Christ's will and "put to death" all that partakes of sensuality (Col. 3:5).

**SERMON ON THE MOUNT.** The Sermon on the Mount is the most significant passage in the New Testament for Christian ethics. It is widely regarded as giving the fullest, clearest, and most characteristic description of the kind of people Jesus wanted his followers to be. Probably no passage of Scripture has been more frequently quoted or more often discussed: the ante-Nicene church fathers, for instance, cite Matthew 5—7 more often than any other three chapters in the Bible. Indeed, the popularity of the Sermon has extended far beyond the confines of the church. Even non-Christians, such as Gandhi, have considered the Sermon to be one of the most important ethical statements ever made. So influential has been the Sermon in Western culture that much of its language has become proverbial: "turn the other cheek"; "the salt of the earth"; "don't cast your pearls before swine"; "wolves in sheep's clothing"; "the narrow path"; and so on. How often do we hear people say that, although they do not believe in Jesus Christ as the Son of God, they "try to live by the Sermon on the Mount"?

This sentiment illustrates the fact that the popularity of the Sermon has not always been matched by an adequate understanding of its intent and message and still less often by a serious submission to its demands. Indeed, obedience to the Sermon is sometimes short-circuited by frustration at being unable to understand its overall intent or the meaning of specific commands. Does the Sermon show us how to become Christians? Or does it show people who are already Christians how to live? How can we be expected to live up to the radical demands of Jesus? Must we, and can we, always refuse to "resist an evil person" (Matt. 5:39)? These questions, and others like them, can be answered only if we understand the original intent of Jesus in the Sermon. Before investigating this issue, a fuller description of the Sermon is necessary.

*Description.* It was apparently Augustine who first designated Jesus' teaching in Matthew 5—7 as "the Sermon on the Mount." Characterizing this teaching as a "Sermon" seems justified since Matthew frames the teaching with a solemn introduction: "And he opened his mouth and taught them, saying" (Matt. 5:2), and conclusion: "And when Jesus finished these sayings, the crowds were astonished at his teaching, for he taught them as one who had authority, and not as their scribes" (Matt. 7:28-29). Moreover, the Beatitudes serve as an effective sermon "introduction," while an equally appropriate conclusion is provided by the parable of the two builders, with its call to obedience.

The accuracy of the title *sermon,* however, has been widely questioned. For one thing, all of Matthew 5—7 could have been spoken aloud in fifteen minutes—hardly a "sermon" by ancient standards. More important is the problem posed by a comparison of Matthew 5—7 with parallel material in Luke's Gospel. Luke 6:20-49 contains material that, though much shorter, is closely parallel to Matthew 5—7. Beatitudes introduce this teaching, the parable of the two builders concludes it, and most of the material in between is similar to the teaching in Matthew 5—7. But, in addition to this, some of the material in Matthew's *sermon* is found scattered in other parts of Luke's Gospel. One popular explanation of these phenomena is that Matthew 5—7 and Luke 6:20-49 are collections of sayings that Jesus taught on many different occasions. While possible, this explanation has difficulty accounting for the rather clear opening and closing statements in Matthew.

It is better, therefore, to consider Matthew 5—7 and Luke 6:20-49 as two versions, or summaries, of a single sermon taught by Jesus on a specific occasion. Differences between the two versions are due to the fact that each evangelist has selected material that is most relevant to his respective audience. Luke, for instance, writing to Gentiles, omits all the teaching about the Jewish law. Material from Matthew's Sermon that has parallels elsewhere in Luke may be explained as similar teaching, given on more than one occasion. The Lord's Prayer, recorded in Matthew 6:9-13 and Luke 11:2-4, is an obvious example.

The occasion for this sermon, which is important for our understanding of it, is given most fully by Luke. According to Luke 6:12, Jesus "went out to a mountain to pray"; after spending all night in prayer, he chose twelve men as his apostles (6:13-16). He next "came down with them and stood on a level place," where he healed many people and proceeded to preach the Sermon (6:17-20). Matthew sets the stage for the Sermon much more briefly. After narrating Jesus' call of Peter and Andrew (4:18-22) and summarizing Jesus' activity in Galilee (4:23-25), Matthew depicts Jesus going "up on the mountain" and giving the Sermon from there. (Luke's "level place," 6:17 is best seen as a plateau area in the mountains.)

One fact of significance that emerges from this discussion is the context of discipleship in which both evangelists set the Sermon. Their introductions suggest that the Sermon is basically intended for those who were already followers of Jesus. To be sure, Matthew specifically states that "the crowds" also heard the Sermon (7:28), but it seems clear both from the context and content of the Sermon that Jesus had in mind mainly those who had already chosen (or been chosen) to follow Him. As Charles Gore put it, the Sermon "was spoken into the ear of the church and overheard by the world."

*Intention.* What was Jesus' purpose in preaching the Sermon on the Mount? What kind of "ethic" emerges from it? Perhaps surprisingly, Christians have been far from unanimous in giving an answer to this question. Yet the answer is decisive if we are truly to understand and obey Jesus' teaching. It will be help to approach this issue by delineating eight of the more important viewpoints on the ethic that Jesus presents in the Sermon.

1. *An outmoded ethic.* Although most people, Christian and non-Christian alike, have been effusive in their praise of the Sermon, there have been some who considered its message wrongheaded or out-of-date. They think that Jesus misunderstood the course of history or was "naively utopian" in His ideals. At any rate, these people argue, Jesus' teaching in the Sermon can be disregarded in making ethical decisions.

2. *An absolute ethic.* At the opposite extreme are those who take the commands of the Sermon simply and literally as an exact, timeless description of the behavior expected of all Christians in all their relations. This viewpoint is associated above all with the Anabaptist movement at the time of the Reformation. It accounts for the teaching of their modern-day descendants, such as the Mennonites and the Amish, that taking oaths is always wrong (Matt. 5:34), that violence is always to be avoided (Matt. 5:39), and that Christians cannot serve as judges (Matt. 7:1). Most Christians have felt that such a literal application of the Sermon was neither necessary nor practicable. On the other hand they have not wanted to jettison the relevance of the Sermon either. Therefore, most approaches to the Sermon have sought to qualify its language in some way.

3. *An interim ethic.* It is generally agreed that Jesus' teaching in the Sermon has to be related to His central message, the kingdom of God. According to Albert Schweitzer, famous missionary doctor and theologian, Jesus taught that the kingdom of God was going to dawn within His generation and that it would replace the present world order. The Sermon could then be regarded as providing Jesus' disciples with a sort of emergency "martial law" ethic to be followed in the brief "interim" before the Kingdom came. Since Jesus was wrong about the Kingdom coming so quickly, Schweitzer maintained, we cannot take the ethic literally. We can, however, apply some of its principles.

4. *An ethic for the future Kingdom.* Classic dispensationalism also teaches that Jesus proclaimed the imminent appearance of the Kingdom, but that it was "postponed" when the Jews refused to receive Jesus. The Kingdom will come after Christ's second return, and it is then that the commands of the Sermon, literally interpreted and applied, will be fully applicable. In the meantime, however, the "ethical principles" of the Sermon are binding on the believer.

5. *An ethic for "super-saints."* Traditional Roman Catholic teaching has distinguished between "precepts" that are binding on all Christians and "evangelical counsels" that only *some* Christians need to choose to follow. The Sermon on the Mount falls into the latter category: only those who are called to this radical form of discipleship are bound by its strong demands.

6. *An ethic of repentance.* It has been popular to view the Sermon, especially in the Lutheran tradition, as designed to stimulate repentance. Jesus sets forth, in uncompromising form, the demand of God so that people may recognize their inability to meet it and will consequently embrace the gracious offer of free pardon in the gospel.

7. *An ethic for personal relations.* Luther himself, and many in the Protestant tradition, have confined the Sermon to the realm of personal relations. There are two "realms," the secular and the spiritual: God rules the secular through human government, the spiritual through His Word. The Sermon, then, is intended to regulate the conduct of the Christian in his personal relationships with others, not his conduct as a citizen or "officer" of the state.

8. *An ethic of principles.* One of the most popular alternatives, held in a variety of forms, is that Jesus, in the Sermon, is setting forth basic ethical principles and that He does not intend all His commands as literal, universal precepts. The Christian should read at least parts of the Sermon as forthright illustrations of the root attitudes that they are to adopt. Depending on the circumstances, these attitudes may or may not manifest themselves in the ways Jesus suggests.

In deciding which of these options has best claim to represent Jesus' actual intention, two issues are decisive: the relationship between the

Sermon and the kingdom of God; and the proper interpretation, or hermeneutics, of the Sermon.

*The Sermon and the Kingdom.* That the kingdom of God was the central topic in Jesus' preaching is generally agreed. Some people have sought to divorce the Sermon from Jesus' teaching about the Kingdom, so that they could give credence to the "simple ethic" of the Sermon without having to accept the theological implications of the Kingdom. T. W. Manson, in a memorable image, dismisses any such attempt: "The notion that we can wander at will through the teaching of Jesus as through a garden, plucking here and there an ethical flower to weave a chaplet for the adornment of our own philosophy of life, is an idea that is doomed to disappointment, for the nature of plucked flowers is to wither." The teaching of Jesus in the Sermon must be tied closely to His proclamation of the kingdom of God.

But what did Jesus proclaim about the Kingdom? Both Albert Schweitzer and dispensationalists, though disagreeing radically on other points, are agreed that Jesus initially preached that the Kingdom was near, but not yet present. This is questionable, however. Passages such as Matt. 12:28 ("But if it is by the Spirit of God that I cast out demons, then the kingdom of God has come upon you") strongly suggest that the Kingdom was already present, in some sense, during Jesus' ministry. But that He also expected a future manifestation of the Kingdom is clear from the petition in the Lord's Prayer: "thy Kingdom come." It is best, then, to consider the Kingdom as both present and future. If we understand by *Kingdom* the reign of God, rather than a realm, then we can understand how this could be. With Jesus' first coming, people could experience the reign of God in their lives ("the kingdom of God") as never before; but at His second coming, Christians and the world will be subject to that reign in a final, climactic, all-encompassing manner.

The Sermon provides guidelines for life in the Kingdom; it "portrays the ideal of the man in whose life the reign of God is absolutely realized." The Sermon is, therefore, fully applicable to the believer in the present age. At the same time, the fact that God's reign has not been consummated, and that believers have not been glorified, means that the demands of the Sermon may not be ultimately attainable in this life. But this leads us to the second consideration.

*The Sermon and Interpretation.* How did Jesus intend His commands in the Sermon to be understood? First, there is no evidence that He intended them only for some disciples. The Sermon presents "the greater righteousness" that is necessary for entrance in the Kingdom of God (5:20); all of Jesus' followers are bound by it. Second, it is evident that Jesus expected His disciples to obey it, not just to be convicted by it. The concluding parable calls clearly for an absolute submission to what Jesus has taught in the

Sermon; and it is "he who does the will of my Father in Heaven," spelled out in the Sermon, who will enter the Kingdom (7:21). Third, it is difficult to confine the relevance of the Sermon only to personal relationships. The disciple is one who owes allegiance first of all to God in all his affairs, and it is impossible to think that a Christian could be guided by one principle in his personal relations and another in his "official" relations.

We are left, then, with two of the views outlined above: the "absolute ethic" and "the ethic of principles." Both have an element of truth and an element of falsehood. Those who maintain that the Sermon is to be taken with full, unmitigated force are to be commented for recognizing that Jesus' teaching is not to be avoided, even when it places the Christian in a difficult position. Too often Christians have applied literally only those parts of the Sermon that they considered relatively easy to obey. The Anabaptist tradition reminds the whole body of Christ that Jesus' ethic is not an "easy" one, and that we must strenuously avoid forcing Christian discipleship into the mold of our own culture.

On the other hand, the "absolutist" position has failed to integrate the Sermon adequately with other Scriptures, often ignoring the original context, and has not taken seriously the possibility of hyperbole and illustration in the Sermon. For example, Jesus' command never to swear must not be treated in isolation from the apparent oaths that God (Heb. 7:21) and Paul (Phil. 1:8) swore, and the context of Matthew 5:33-37 strongly suggests that Jesus is prohibiting oaths that His contemporary Jews were using to avoid telling the truth. Similarly, Jesus' teaching about not resisting evil must be interpreted in the light of God's commands to Israel to wage war in the Old Testament. That hyperbole, or exaggeration, is present in the Sermon can hardly be doubted: only fanatic extremists, such as Origen, have literally obeyed Jesus' teaching to "cut off" any member of our body that causes us to sin (Matt. 5:29-30).

The "ethic of principles" approach correctly recognizes the necessity to look at these factors in interpreting the Sermon, but often goes too far in eliminating specific, concrete forms of behavior from Jesus' demands. Clearly He is not only setting forth basic "attitudes," although these are undoubtedly of central importance. He is also showing how certain attitudes must be expressed in action.

We conclude that Jesus intends in the Sermon to describe the attitudes, lifestyle, and approach to life that is incumbent on all who acknowledge Jesus as Savior and Lord. Because the Kingdom has not yet come in its fullness and our sinful tendency is not yet eradicated, our obedience to that ideal is necessarily incomplete. But this in no way lessens our obligation to meet that demand; and when we fail, we must ask forgiveness.

*The Sermon: Gospel or Law?* In the Sermon itself, Jesus says nothing about conversion or the work of the Holy Spirit. But in addressing people who had already chosen (or been chosen) to follow Him, it is safe to assume that He presumes conversion as the necessary condition for obedience to the Sermon. The Sermon is not "gospel," telling us how we can be saved; it is "law," setting forth the radical, uncompromising will of God for those who have been saved. Indeed, if conformity to the demands of the Sermon were necessary for salvation, who would be saved? Who is never angry, never lustful, consistently loving his enemies, or perfect as the heavenly Father is perfect? No, these are the fruits of conversion, not its basis. Jesus' failure to mention the work of the Spirit here is no doubt due to the fact that His death and resurrection, the necessary basis for the indwelling work of the Spirit, had not yet happened. Yet it is fair, in the light of the whole of Scripture, to recognize that it is only by the work of the Spirit that such character traits as those described in the Beatitudes can be achieved.

*Exposition.* So many important issues are treated in the Sermon that even a survey of all of them is impossible. But a brief outline of the central ethical thrusts of the Sermon is in order.

The Other-Worldly Character of the Disciple (5:3-16). The Beatitudes promise an eschatological blessing for certain character traits and attitudes that are often the antithesis of what the world would consider attractive. It is the "poor in Spirit," "the mourners," and "the meek" who will receive God's gracious response. Even persecution is to be gladly embraced, for it signifies the pursuit of godliness (vv. 11-12). Jesus begins the Sermon, then, by zeroing in on basic attitudes and qualities that exemplify the disciples' pursuit of the other-wordly, spiritual kingdom of God, rather than a kingdom of this world.

The Greater Righteousness of the Disciple (5:17-48). These verses delineate the attitudes and actions that make up the righteousness required for the Kingdom against the background of the Old Testament and Judaism. Jesus claims that His teachings "fulfill" the law and the prophets (5:17), by which He means that His teaching brings to its final, definitive form the will of God already enunciated in the Old Testament law. In six "antitheses" Jesus compares His teaching with the Old Testament and contemporary Judaism. Jesus "radicalizes" the law by showing that God prohibits the attitudes of anger and lust as well as the actions of murder and adultery (5:21-30). He reasserts the Old Testament teaching on divorce (5:31-32) and corrects perversions of the Old Testament teaching concerning oaths, retaliation, and attitudes toward enemies (5:33-47). The ultimate righteousness is nothing less than a character that imitates the very character of God Himself (5:48).

The Religious Practices of the Disciple (6:1-18). Jesus uses the three most prevalent religious practices of his day (almsgiving, prayer, and fasting) to illustrate the absolute necessity of sincerity in devotional duties. Our motivation must not be the praise of men, but the praise of God.

The Priorities of the Disciple (6:19-34). Materialism is attacked boldly by Jesus in this section. The disciple is to focus on the treasures of heaven (6:20), on the Kingdom of God and His righteousness (6:33), instead of on the treasures of this world. Anxiety, a concern about material things that short-circuits our devotion, is prohibited because it manifests too great a concern about these things. To be anxious is to be questioning implicitly God's providential care (6:26-32).

The Relationships of the Disciple (7:1-12). This section has less coherence than the others in the Sermon. Jesus prohibits a judgmental attitude (*not* decision-making and "rebuking in love" where needed, 7:1-5), and warns against letting the gospel be tarnished by its violent, unrepentant opposers (7:6). Verses 7-11 focus on prayer, emphasizing that the very character of God should encourage us to make our requests known to Him. The "Golden Rule" is a helpful principle in guiding our relations with others, although it should not be singled out as the most important ethical principle of the Sermon or of Christianity, since the principle is found also in both Judaism and paganism.

The Decision of the Disciple (7:13-27). As is appropriate in a sermon, Jesus concludes with a call to obedience, for the "narrow gate," the "hard way" of obedience of Jesus' teaching is the only path that leads to eternal life. As beautiful as are Jesus' figures of speech, as penetrating as are His insights into human conduct, His words are useless, indeed dangerous, if they are not obeyed.

At the conclusion of the Sermon, Matthew tells us that "the crowds were astonished at his teaching." To be sure, much of what Jesus said in the Sermon can be paralleled in pagan and Jewish writings. But nowhere will one find so succinct, so clear, and so compelling a statement of ethical principles. More important, nowhere will one find so authoritative a proclamation of the will of God for His people, coming from the One uniquely qualified to reveal that will to us.

**Bibliography:** Bonham, T., *The Demands of Discipleship: The Relevance of the Sermon on the Mount* (1967); Davies, W. D., *The Setting of the Sermon on the Mount* (1964); Henry, C. F. H.; *Christian Personal Ethics* (1957); Hunter, A. M., *Design for Life* (1953); Kissinger, W. S., *The Sermon on the Mount: A History of Interpretation and Bibliography* (1975); Mason, T. W., *The Teaching of Jesus* (1935); McArthur, H. K., *Understanding the Sermon on the Mount* (1960); Ryrie, C. C., *Dispensationalism Today* (1973); Windisch, H., *The Meaning of the Sermon on the Mount* (1951; original German Edition, 1937).

See BEATITUDES; JESUS, ETHICAL TEACHINGS AND EXAMPLE OF; THE LORD'S PRAYER; NEW TESTAMENT ETHICS.

D.J.M.

**SERVICE.** This word describes the activity that forms the normal routine of one who is employed as a male or female servant. In a household thus equipped it is the norm for the servant to attend punctiliously to the needs of the master and mistress, and to safeguard their interests in all possible ways. Being a household servant of one sort or another in antiquity was usually the result of having been captured in battle, and in unenlightened households such servants were often brutally exploited. This was less so in ancient Hebrew society, since servants received protection under the Decalogue (Exod. 20:17). Occasionally a servant would become so attached to his master that at the time of manumission, when slaves were normally set free, the servant would enter into a permanent compact with his master in a special ritual (Exod. 21:4-6).

As contrasted with the very limited degree of service in private households, there are many public servants in modern times who are either government or civic employees. They are engaged in a wide variety of administrative duties in the interests of good government, and so numerous have they become that in some areas of the world the central governmental authority is the largest single employer in the country.

From the idea of secular household service it was but a small step to designate those who serve Jesus as Savior and Lord as the "household of faith" (Gal. 6:10). Christ taught his disciples about the servant-master relationship (John 13:16) but promoted them and all subsequent disciples to the position of "friend" (John 15:15). This gave the concept of service a much deeper significance because now the servant would be fully apprised by Christ of the heavenly Father's plans.

To be in the service of God was a high privilege in Bible times, and this is no less the case for the modern Christian. Service to God and mankind is the most advanced form of avocation possible and finds its fullest expression in the Christian faith and its ethic.

**SEX.** The development of sexual identity begins at conception. The embryo will develop male or female genitalia depending upon whether the fertilizing sperm carried respectively the Y or the X sex chromosome. The child's external genitalia will define its sexual identity from the moment the delivery room staff say, "It's a girl!" or, "It's a boy!"

Gender identity (the psychological awareness of masculinity or femininity) arises from both sexual identity and the parents' expectations and training. Gender identity is usually well-consolidated by about age four. The gender role assigned by the parents will be almost impossible to change after that age. If, for psychological reasons of their own, the parents raise a child as though he or she were a member of the opposite sex, they lay the groundwork for much later difficulty, as, for example, transsexualism (in which

persons insist that they are members of the opposite sex and demand reconstructive surgery).

Gender identity is further enhanced by prevailing social attitudes toward masculine or feminine roles. Public media, peer pressure, education systems, and early sexual experiences will all contribute to sexual self-awareness.

Gender role arises from a fusion of sexual identity, gender identity, and the object of sexual desire. Gender role refers to the sexual behavior by which a person expresses his or her gender identity. In most people, gender identity and gender role lead to exclusive heterosexual behavior. In a minority of the population (between 5 and 10 percent of males and about 1 percent of females) sexual interest, arousal, and satisfaction occur within the same sex.

*Physiology.* At puberty the brain gives the testes and ovaries the signal to start producing male or female hormones (testosterone or estrogen/progesterone, respectively). With the rapid rise of these hormones, there is a correspondingly rapid development of both the internal and external genital organs. The centers of the brain concerned with sexual appetite are also stirred by these hormones, leading to the psychological awareness of sexual appetite. Gender identity converges with these physiological changes to direct sexual appetite. Girls become aware of boys as more than a nuisance; boys become aware of girls as more than pests. By midadolescence both sexes agree, "Vive la différence!"

Sexual arousal can occur as the result of fantasy (whether during waking or sleeping states) or as the result of physical or psychological contact with a member of the opposite sex. Sexual intercourse is the normal adult means of achieving satisfaction of sexual appetite.

In males, sexual arousal is associated with a rapid increase in awareness of the sexual organs, accompanied by changes in blood flow that cause penile erection. In females, sexual arousal often occurs more slowly, but is similarly associated with a heightened sensitivity of breasts and sexual organs, with the accompanying change in the blood flow in the pelvic structures leading to erection of clitoris and engorgement of the vulva.

During sexual intercourse the friction produced upon the man's penis and the woman's clitoris by the rapid thrusting movements leads to a rhythmic contraction of the muscles surrounding the base of the penis and the vagina. In the male, these contractions ejaculate semen (the fluid carrying the sperm cells) from the penis into the upper vagina. This physical release, in itself often nearer pain than pleasure, is accompanied by an intense emotional feeling of pleasure, warmth, and closeness. The term *orgasm* applies to the combined physical and emotional experience, applicable to both male and female. Following orgasm, the genitalia rapidly diminish in size and sensitivity. The post-discharge emotional states are often intense and may range from elation to sadness.

*Psychological satisfactions.* The psychological aspects of sexual desire, release, and fulfillment are complex. Men typically have a compelling sexual drive from late adolescence to midadulthood. Women's sexual appetite becomes more piquant in midthirties until menopause. Most men will achieve temporary satisfaction through masturbation if sexual intercourse is not available. For many men, the psychological satisfactions are relatively simple. Few men, however, will be able to perform sexually in a relationship marked by derision or hostility. Some men fuse intense aggression with sexual activity that may lead them into practices that are (usually unconsciously) humiliating to their partner. This is seen at its rawest in rape, but is present in many other sexual behaviors. Sometimes the partner, because of complementary psychological drives (for example, the need to be punished) will be a willing participant.

Men who have developed or inherited a Christian understanding of sex or marriage will have a different psychological set. They will find their psychological satisfaction in the context of love and will see the sexual act not only as a way of discharging sexual energy, but also as an expression of the most tender aspects of love. No piece of literature so beautifully describes the physical and psychological satisfactions of either male or female as The Song of Songs. This set of erotic poems celebrates sexual appetite, sexual anatomy, and sexual satisfaction in the context of a loving relationship.

Sexual satisfaction is physiologically no more difficult for women than for men. But the psychological aspects are more vulnerable. Women typically are willing to engage in sexual activity only to the extent that it is understood to be a pledge of assured love, fidelity, and security. They are more likely to require the emotional stimuli of expressions of love and endearment along with physical stimulation in order to achieve either arousal or satisfaction. Unpleasant emotions are more likely to interfere with satisfactory sexual experience in women that in men. Unrealistic guilt about having sexual feelings, uncertainty about the man's intentions or attitude, marital conflict, fear of pregnancy or injury—all may interfere with a woman's sexual satisfaction.

*Ethical principles.* In the Christian view, sexual relations are acceptable only within the bonds of marriage (Heb. 13:4; 1 Cor. 6:12-20; 1 Thess. 4:3-7). Nonmarital sexual intercourse (for example, with a prostitute) is regarded as fornication; extramarital sexual intercourse, whether by man or woman, is adultery. The stringencies imposed by the early church, based upon the teaching of Christ (Mark 10:2-9), were in studied contrast to the prevailing mores of the Gentile world (where casual sexual relations were widely accepted and even applauded) and the Jewish world (where sexual morality was superior to the pagan world, but where divorce and remarriage were readily available).

Christian strictness is not based upon suspicion of the body, but upon the integrity of persons and the inner meaning of marriage. More radically even than the Old Testament, our Lord taught that pre—, non—, or extramarital sexual relations violate the basic nature of humanity. No longer is the woman a chattel: she is a wife to whom the husband owes devotion, love, fidelity, and sexual satisfaction (1 Cor. 7:4-5; Eph. 5:21-33). No longer is the man a master: he is a husband to whom the wife responds with love, reverence, and sexual responsiveness.

In contemplating the mystery of sexual union in a committed, publicly acknowledged union; in reflecting upon the claim implicit in sexual intercourse; in meditating upon the creation story; in recalling the marital imagery of the prophets and the lush romance of the Song—the ancient church, under the guidance of the Spirit, discovered that Christian marriage is a symbol of the relationship between Christ and the church. Saint Paul's teaching in Ephesians so entwines the themes of Christ and the church with husband and wife that it is hard to say which theme is more illuminating of the other. Marriage is an effective sign of the relationship between Christ and the church. In faithful and loving marriage, sealed by sexual union, the couple participates in the mystery of Christ's love for the church and the church's devotion to its Lord. In Christ's effectual and self-giving love for the church, and in the church's loving acceptance of His love, with its claims, husband and wife find the pattern for their responses to each other.

Because the sexual relationship stands at the heart of the marital union, sealing it, constituting it, making it fruitful, any violation of fidelity destroys the living parable of marriage. It is for this reason that the Apostle thundered over illicit sexual relations (1 Cor. 5:1-5; Gal. 5:19-21). Fornication and adultery betray the mystery of Christ in the church as well as violating the integrity of the offender and the trust of the offended spouse.

With the rise of feminism and the demands women have rightly made for equal treatment, traditional sexual roles in marriage have been challenged. While the New Testament confers identical and equal sexual rights upon both husband and wife, the notion that sex-on-demand is the husband's right is deeply engrained culturally in most civilized societies. The women's movement has battled this notion to the ground in our century. Women, too, have sexual rights—including the right to be treated tenderly, to have their wishes consulted, and to make sexual claims upon their partners. Confusing as the situation may be in a culture long dominated by male strutting, the new situation offers the Christian churches an opportunity to reassert the sublime values which invest marital sexual relations in New Testament thought.

The relationship between sexual intercourse and human reproduction is not explicated in the New Testament. That new life will result is assumed as a matter of course. In the New Testament the emphasis falls more upon the relationship between the spouses which sexual intercourse effects, seals, and nourishes than upon procreation. The idea that sexual intercourse is moral only if it is potentially procreative does not appear in the New Testament. However, the view that every act of martial intercourse must be open to the transmission of life was universal throughout the Christian world until the present century. While the use of contraception has become widespread within Western Christian marriage, there has been little serious discussion among Protestants of the significant theological and philosophical points which the traditional teaching raises.

As contraceptive measures have become legalized (usually because of militantly secular pressures), most Christian couples have availed themselves of the freedom and flexibility which contraceptive measures allow the sexual intimacy. Whether this has led to more marital bliss or more sexual conflict is far from clear; certainly it has eroded the notion of sexual discipline. (1 Cor. 7:5).

A further complicating factor as the result of the freedom imposed by contraceptive measures is the so-called sexual revolution. Since pregnancy need not be a consequence of sexual activity, the utilitarian and gallant motives for chastity no longer are cogent. Promiscuity is no longer a pleasure reserved for the court or the slum: it is available to (and widely accepted) by both men and women. The dangers of promiscuity are no longer those of unwanted pregnancy, nor of incurable disease. But new hazards have become evident: the unrealistic quest for ultimate sexual satisfaction is one of them. Unbridled lechery is never satisfied; and despite the sensory intensity, emotional satisfactions wane. In the end, the person who has been promiscuous is in danger of being jaded, sexually bored, cynical in using others, and alienated from genuinely intimate relationships. In trivializing the most intimate and intense human act we debase ourselves and violate the confidence of others.

**Bibliography:** Small, D.H., *Christian: Celebrate Your Sexuality* (1974); Thielicke, H., *The Ethics of Sex* (1964); Vincent, M.O., *God, Sex and You* (1972).

J.E.R.

## SEXUAL MORALITY AND PERVERSIONS.

Human sexuality is first mentioned in Scripture in the context of creation in the image of God (Gen. 1:27-28). Sexuality, created in the divine image, enables mankind to manifest divine qualities in human society. The relationship between man and woman is marked by complementarity (Gen. 2:23), mutuality (Gen. 2:25), unity (Gen. 2:24), and love (Gen. 2:25). Any sexual

behavior which fails to exhibit these qualities is either inadequate or perverse.

Human sexuality is also a means to share in God's work. God's first word to humanity is directed toward sexuality (Gen. 1:28), which becomes an instrument of doing the will of God. Any sexual behavior outside God's lordship falls short of the divine standard.

These implications are not worked out all at once in the Old Testament. Although the ideal of a committed, monogamous relationship inheres in the creation story it is not, in fact, required for valid Old Testament marriage. And, although sexual activity is fully acceptable only within marriage, a variety of sexual behaviors is tolerated. Polygamy persists throughout the Old Testament period. Prostitution is acknowledged, and regulated—with studied disapproval (Lev. 19:29; 21:7,14). Many passages in Proverbs deplore prostitution, and in the prophets, the theme is a favorite image for denouncing the fickleness of Israel's religious commitments. Pre-marital intercourse is practiced, but entails either a forced marriage or a fine (Ex. 22:16-17).

On the other hand there were capital sexual crimes in the Law. Adultery, narrowly interpreted, is severely proscribed (Lev. 20:10). A pair commit adultery, however, only if the woman is married, and the woman's husband is the offended party. The offending man's marital state is irrelevant. Any form of incest is also condemned rigorously (Lev. 20:10-14, 17-21). Male homosexual intercourse is forbidden (Lev. 20:13). Curiously, lesbianism is not noted, although some sexual contact must have been known in harems.

The New Testament sets human sexual morality in the context of the New Creation in which Christ is the New Man, the Last Adam. In all things, including sex, we now take our cue from Him. Henceforth, any sexual behavior must not only manifest the image of God but also the mystery of Christ. Marriage remains the only acceptable setting for sexual activity.

The New Testament calls God's people to a high ethical plane in the matter of sexual behavior. Premarital intercourse is forbidden. The Christian who consorts with a prostitute is debasing the body of Christ (1 Cor. 6:15). Christians are liberated from the snares of sexual revelry (1 Pet. 4:1-4). Homosexual activity is acknowledged briefly, as a pagan debasement, and condemned (Rom. 1:26-27; 1 Cor. 6:9, 19; 1 Tim. 1:10). Incest is tackled with apostolic vigor (1 Cor. 5:1-5). Persons who violate dominical morality are to be excommunicated (1 Cor. 5:3-5).

This rigorous containment of sexual activity does not rise from a morbid puritanism bent upon sexual repression, but from a revelation that sexual activity must serve more than physical, psychological, or procreative values if it is to be authentically human. It must also serve the spiritual values of self-giving love, mutual meeting of need, unimpaired unity (as a living parable of reconciliation in Christ), and sacramental participation in the relationship between the bridegroom (Christ) and the bride (the church). Any sexual activity that does not subserve these values and that does not portray christological and ecclesial realities is unacceptable.

Such ideals are manifestly impossible to achieve by human resolve. Experience demonstrates that they are fragile, rarely realized in their fullness, and frequently betrayed. The sexual morality of the New Testament requires the filling, gifts, and power of the Spirit (1 Cor. 7:7; Gal. 5:22).

The witness of the New Testament has been tragically ignored in the easy sexual relations of our century—relations made easier by the availability of effective contraceptive measures. Our own society has fused abundant leisure with self-gratifying hedonism—"If it feels good, do it." Scripture takes full account of the voluptuous pleasures of sex, confining them to marriage (Prov. 5:15-20). When an act so totally absorbing as sexual intercourse has no significance beyond its immediate pleasure, all values are in danger of being made relative to pleasure. Any morality of the person or of the relationship becomes impossible. The good is defined by fleeting feeling.

A prevailing romantic naturalism treats sex as a natural appetite of the same order as hunger and thirst, a natural urge of the same order as the need to empty bladder or bowels. Scripture fully recognizes the biological pressure and goal of the sexual urge. But the reduction of sexual behavior to biological function bleaches sexual activity of meaning. If an act that involves the totality of two persons' attention and experience is merely biological, there is little room for any significance beyond the biological in other human experiences.

Another common rationalization for freer sexual activity arises from popular misunderstandings of psychoanalytic theory. According to this popular notion, neurosis is the result of sexual restraint. At its worst, this rationalization of sexual behavior outside of marriage is a prevaricating version of the pleasure rationale for casual sex. At best it treats sexual activity as a means to individual well-being, which is selfishness.

The most seductive contemporary view holds that romantic love legitimates sexual behavior. "It's all right if you're in love." The Bible, of course, could not be any clearer in teaching that moral sexual activity requires self-giving love (Eph. 5:28). It does not shrink from the delights of romantic love (Song of Songs). Paradoxically, however, romantic love is more nourished by sexual restraint than by sexual activity. Romantic love is notoriously unstable, especially after sexual intercourse (2 Sam. 13:14-15).

The sexual urge is easily contaminated by the experiences and emotions of early life. When sexual drive is fused with negative experience with members of the opposite sex, or with negative feelings such as aggression or rejection, sexually deviant behavior may result.

Homosexuality (same sex attraction), fetishism (in which a specific object or nonerotic part of a person is sexually exciting), sadism (in which sexual excitement is enhanced by cruelty to the sexual partner), masochism (in which sexual excitement is sustained by injury to oneself), exhibitionism (in which sexual excitement is achieved by displaying one's sexual organs, without sexual contact), voyeurism (in which sexual pleasure is vicarious through watching the sexual activity of others), bestiality (in which an animal is a sexual partner)—all fall short of the divine standard and meaning for sexual behavior.

Sexual behavior (however motivated, consciously or unconsciously) that directs an individual to a nonperson (bestiality or fetishism) is clearly the most deviant form of sexual aberration. Such behavior violates the interpersonal intention, which is the goal and significance of sex. Sexual behavior that insults, degrades, or injures another person (sadism, masochism, rape, exhibitionism) is perverse because it debases and destroys the sexual partner and makes the sexual act an instance of aggression rather than a parable of love. Sexual behavior that avoids sexual encounter (compulsive masturbation, exhibitionism, and voyeurism) is evidence of a pathetic failure to establish intimate contact with another person.

Homosexuality in men and lesbianism in women are the most complex forms of deviant sexuality. The causes of homosexuality are obscure. Such behavior is common is settings in which men (less commonly, women) are thrown into close contact without the possibility of heterosexual outlet. Prisons, boarding schools, barracks, and ships on the high seas are notorious. Individuals engaging in homosexual acts under these circumstances are rarely homosexual in their self-identity, usually prefer heterosexual activity, and revert to heterosexuality when circumstances are propitious. This voluntary homosexuality is a form of fornication.

Involuntary homosexual identity remains a poorly understood and perplexing condition in which the person (whether male or female) usually has had a keen sense of himself as being different from childhood. There is no evidence that early sexual seduction by an older member of the same sex produces the condition. Contemporary research suggests that a variety of factors may be implicated. There is accumulating evidence for an inborn factor, either hereditary or consequent upon hormonal abnormalities during fetal development. Some writers stress the impact of adverse early experiences with the child's mother (or father). Much work remains to be undertaken before we shall have an adequate understanding of the condition.

About 5 percent of the male population have an exclusively homosexual inclination; up to 10 percent have predominant homosexual preference although they may also be capable of sustaining heterosexual activity. Some homosexual couples form stable relationships that are analogous to heterosexual marriage. In most cases, however, the fragility of homosexual relationships is notorious, and many male homosexuals avoid enduring relationships by pursing casual contacts frenetically.

In any form, and whatever its origins, homosexuality must be regarded as a deviation from the divine intention. Homosexual promiscuity falls within the range of behavior that the Bible calls "fornication" or "uncleanness." It is a parody of the marriage relationship, since the element of unifying disparate sexes is not present. The notions of complementarity and mutality are truncated by the identical sexual identity of the partners.

The pastoral care of any persons with aberrant sexual behavior requires great skill, much patience, and deep compassion. For while the behavior is ethically reprehensible, it is rooted in drives that move outside the normal range of volition. The person with aberrant sexual drive is often deeply troubled by it, struggles futilely against it, and in the very struggle tends to have the behavior reinforced. Such people are often unwilling to consider change because of repeated prior failures. For many people the behavior is so appropriate to their self-awareness that they can see no reason to make a change. Applying the evangelical counsels of sexual morality to these conditions will require the greatest pastoral care, acceptance of the person, and skill in assisting in control and change of powerfully reinforced behavior patterns.

**Bibliography:** Bailey, D. S., *Sexual Ethics* (1962); Bell, A. P. and Weinberg, M. S., *Homosexualities: A Study of Diversity Among Men and Women* (1978); Twiss, H. L. (ed.), *Homosexuality and the Christian Faith* (1978); White, J., *Eros Defiled* (1980).

See ADULTERY; FORNICATION; HOMOSEXUALITY; INCEST; LESBIANISM; MARRIAGE; MASTURBATION.

J.E.R.

**SHOPLIFTING.** Shoplifting is a form of petty theft in which articles of various kinds are removed surreptitiously from stores without payment being made. It is a very common form of behavior in the Western world and is punishable by law, although such a drastic step is not always taken. This inaction is sometimes governed by the age or mental condition of the offender, who may simply be released with a warning. Even when professional shoplifters are apprehended, they are not infrequently released without charges being laid because of the bad publicity that the prosecuting store might receive as a result.

Many courts tend to treat shoplifting as a matter of minor importance, and consequently they seldom impose deterrent sentences. So costly an enterprise is shoplifting to the general public, however, that a minimum of 5 percent is added to the cost of articles to cover losses by petty theft. While shoplifting is generally perceived as a crime committed by potential or actual customers in stores, studies have shown that much of the shoplifting is the work of employees who are able to conceal their thefts because of a familiarity with store procedures.

Since shoplifting is stealing, all the biblical prohibitions against theft apply to it also, beginning with the proscription in the Decalogue (Exod. 20:15) and continuing to Paul's exhortation in Ephesians 4:28 and beyond. The Christian will shrink in abhorrence from this criminal denial of property rights, and will endeavor to live an honest and upright life in obedience to God's commands.

See CRIME; THEFT.

**SICK, CARE OF.** In the ancient world the various nations had branches of the priesthood that cared for the needs of the ill by means of spells, incantations, mystic rites, and foul-tasting medicines, some of which had a genuinely therapeutic effect. Among the Hebrews God had revealed himself as the great Healer (Exod. 15:26), but in cases of suspected leprosy the priest acted as diagnostician and as one who could pronounce a leper cured, should such a situation ever occur (Lev. 13–14).

Physicians who were really herbalists gradually arose in Israel (2 Chron. 16:12) but were of little repute (Job 13:4). By the time of Christ they were using incantations as well as empirical herbal treatments, but with little improvement in their general effectiveness (Mark 5:26). Jesus revealed himself as an effective healer to the point where he was sometimes overwhelmed by the sick, whom he healed nevertheless (Matt. 4:24; Mark 1:34), often by the imposition of hands. This gift of healing was promised as an accompaniment to evangelistic activity in the primitive church (Mark 16:18) and was in evidence during the New Testament period (Acts 3:7; 20:10). The epistle of James spoke of fervent prayer being made on behalf of the sick, as well as their anointing, which when characterized by the "prayer of faith" resulted in the sick person recovering (James 5:14-16). Confession and prayer were also prescribed for the sick (James 5:16) independently of anointing. The hospital movement is believed to be a specifically Christian innovation which has brought much blessing and comfort to the sick over many centuries. Vast numbers of Christians have dedicated their lives to ministering to the sick, following the example set by the Great Physician.

**SIMONY.** Simony is an offense under canon law, constituting the unworthy or unethical acquisition of an office in the church by means of monetary payments for that purpose, or by other devious methods. The name has its origins in the account of Simon Magus, who in the days of the primitive church sought to purchase the gift of imparting the Holy Spirit through the imposition of the apostles' hands (Acts 8:17-24). Peter castigated him for thinking that divine gifts could be acquired for money, and when he understood the situation Simon appeared to be penitent.

Simony was an important consideration in European countries at a time when church livings ("parishes") were comparatively few in quantity. Such as were in existence were generally well-endowed from various sources, and to be inducted into the "temporal possessions" of such a benefice as rector assured the holder of a degree of affluence such as was enjoyed only by the wealthy. To maintain the appearance of fiscal integrity in the successful candidate, he was required to swear at the time of institution and induction to the living that he disclaimed any motives of simony.

After churches grew in number, and particularly in Britain after the Evangelical Revival of the eighteenth and nineteenth centuries, the Ecclesiastical Commissioners who disbursed money invested for clergy salaries gradually introduced more equitable means for dealing with clergy stipends, so that at the present time simony is not by any means the temptation to clergy that it once was. Simony as a general description of any trafficking in ecclesiastical preferment is reprehensible to Christian morals wherever in the world it may be practiced. Christ demands of his followers complete commitment to service without thought of financial gain or purely personal considerations (Matt. 5:24-25; 6:19-21). Spiritual gifts by definition are given and can only be acquired as the individual grows in divine grace.

**SIN.** Evil and wrongdoing are only described as "sin" or "sinful" when they are understood as directed against God. They are, therefore, primarily religious words denoting the position of mankind before God.

As Emil Brunner points out, however, "sin is never the beginning; it always comes second. Sin has a history behind it." The idea of man as a sinner rests upon the presupposition that we are creatures made for communion with God, but now are separated from Him by our sin. This unique relationship is expressed in the word *image*. Human beings are made in the "image and likeness of God" (Gen. 1:26). Although the Bible nowhere gives us a definition of *image*, it suggests a moral and spiritual bond between God and mankind that is at the heart of what it is to be human. Thus, sin gives us a clue about our relationship with God. His love is primary, but sin has soured and broken the intimate link between creature and Creator.

There is no special Hebrew word for sin, although three words stand out to describe man's propensity for evil. *Hattat* means "to miss the mark"; *awon* represents "going aside from the right way"; while *pesha* is translated "transgres-

sion" or "rebellion." The first and third come together in Job 34:37: "he adds rebellion (*pesha*) to his sin (*hattat*)."

Jesus in the Gospels never speculated about the origin of sin, but we find in His teaching the same acceptance of its reality and power. He addressed people as lost and in need of God's forgiveness and grace (Mark 1:15; Luke 15) and spoke with a clear understanding of the inner nature of man, preaching that sin and evil have their origin in the "heart" of the individual (Matt. 15:19). Paul was in hearty agreement with this stress. His is the fullest theology of sin in the New Testament. The word *sin* occurs more than sixty times in his Epistles. He treats sin as mankind's tragic predicament from which only God in Christ can deliver us. Human beings are "under sin"; sin "lords it" over us leading to hardness of heart and despair (Rom. 3:11-18; 5:6; Eph. 2). Paul sees man's bondage consisting not only in the acts we do, but also in the fact that we cannot help doing sinful things. Thus, sin proceeds from a sinful nature (Rom. 7:24).

But where in the Bible do we find the statement of the holiness God requires from us? It is a mistake to single out isolated proof texts as if these alone present us with the answer. There are, of course, passages like the Ten Commandments (Exod: 20) and Jesus' restatement of the Commandments (Luke 10:27) that set forth the ideal that God requires. But the Bible urges us to look at the character of God as our standard of holiness. "Be holy as I am holy," Yahweh appeals in Leviticus 19:2. Isaiah (in Isa: 6), on seeing the glory of God in the temple, is made aware of his own guilt as well as that of his society (see also Amos 5:21-24).

*Original Sin.* What does it mean to say that sin proceeds from a sinful nature? If we cannot help doing evil things, how can we be held accountable? As we have noted, the Bible concentrates upon the fact of sin and makes little attempt to explain it. There are, however, two passages in the Bible that theologians view as crucial for our interpretation. The first is Genesis 1-3, which is the story of Adam's sin and expulsion from the Garden. It sets forth man's situation as a sinner and a being separated from Almighty God. The second passage, Romans 5:12-18, is the sequel of the Genesis story. It is Paul's explanation of the origin of sin. In this passage he compares Christ's obedience with the disobedience of Adam and shows that mankind "fell" when Adam trespassed against God. But Paul avoids a bare attribution of sin to Adam. He writes: "therefore as sin came into the world through one man and death through sin; and so death spread to all men because all men sinned." Here Paul combines two ideas: that humanity's problem is inextricably linked with Adam and that sin occurs in varying ways throughout the whole of human life, providing our share in the blame.

*The Interpretation of the Fall in Christian Thought.* There have been two major interpretations of the Fall in the early church, both of which have influenced later theology. The first, associated with the name of Irenaeus of Lyon (d. A.D. 200), viewed it as a tragic event that contained the seed of a greater hope and blessing. Irenaeus visualized Adam not as a developed and mature individual, but as a young creature with unfulfilled possibilities of growth in his relationship with God. This progress was cut short tragically through sin. At the heart of this Irenaean view of the Fall are two elements, the reality of Satan's power and the potential good in the Fall. On the latter point, Christ as Second Adam not only heals the breach opened up by sin, but takes man on to a greater level of spiritual attainment and blessing with God than He would have had if he had not sinned.

By contrast, the Augustinian view of the Fall saw nothing good in it. Saint Augustine (354–430), on the basis of his own personal experience of sin together with his interpretation of Paul's teaching, saw Adam's fall as a great poison that has affected human life, culture, and social relationships, as well as mankind's walk with God. Humanity is a "mass of perdition," corrupt and unable to find God unless He comes to his aid. The complete weakness and helplessness of mankind is contrasted with the gift of grace offered freely in Christ. Thus, Augustinianism has a bleak and pessimistic view of human nature, but a big concept of God in Christ.

Although Augustine's view was the most popular in the medieval and Reformation periods and was followed by both Catholic and Protestant scholars, Catholic and Protestant interpretation differed greatly on the question: "What did Adam actually lose when he fell?" The Catholic position, typified by Thomas Aquinas (twelfth century) was that Adam lost his original righteousness, affecting the soul of man, but that his mind was still free to discover the works of God. Luther, however, disagreed with this. Following the traditional teaching, he argued that sin has affected every level of human nature—mind, soul, and body. The image of God is lost in man and without God's grace man is totally unable to find God.

*The Fall in Contemporary Thought.* In secular thought the problem of the individual and his inclination toward evil has been the central issue in the nature-nurture controversy. The "naturists," who include such thinkers as Hobbes, the Social Darwinists, and recent writers such as Robert Ardrey, argue that we are children of a natural world and must not be held responsible for biological drives. This is true in part. We are products of nature and aware of the appetites of the flesh. Nevertheless, we transcend our lowly origins. Unlike all other creatures, we know the difference between what is and what ought to be. It will not do to make heredity the sole ground for explaining man's dilemma. There are also the "nurturists" like Locke, Rousseau, T. H. Huxley, and Marxists who blame man's evil upon his environment. According to this viewpoint, if one changes man's environment, man himself will be improved. Of course there is truth in this, but not the whole truth. We know only too well that universal education, better conditions, full employment, improved housing, and modern social amenities do not necessarily lead to a reformed humanity and a more moral outlook.

While, then, it is easy to scoff at the Bible's picture of mankind dead in trespasses and sins, it sums up accurately our situation. G. K. Chesterton once remarked that the doctrine of original sin is the one directly ascertainable doctrine in Christianity. He meant, of course, that it summed up our experience as well as our reality. Man's nature is in a real sense "fallen." We are all aware of the bias toward evil and are conscious of our inability to do anything about it. We echo Paul's frustration, "the evil I do not want, I do" (Rom. 7:19).

But what about this link with Adam? Is it fair to blame it all on him? What is being rediscovered today is the nature of human solidarity. Western individualism is a false understanding of human nature. We are members, one of another, and an individual's sin affects others as their sin affects the individual. An intricate network exists in human life that makes it impossible to allot blame based upon individual acts. Modern theology has begun to understand this, and we currently talk about "structural sin," that is, wrongdoing which hurts, influences, and shapes others. It is a mistake to lay all the blame, therefore, on Adam and his sin. We share in his act of rebellion against God, but we ourselves perpetuate and extend the network of sin by our own acts of rebellion and disregard of God's laws.

*The Consequences of Sin.* The consequences of turning our back upon God and His laws and rejecting His claims upon our lives are threefold. First, we are divided within. Sin affects our nature so that God is dethroned and we substitute ourselves as sovereign: "You will be like God," says the temptor, "knowing good and evil" (Gen. 3:5). Second, it affects our social lives and leads to alienation between the sexes, classes, and races. Our experience shows us daily how evil infects society, spreading from one person to another, alienating brother from brother and community from community. It is not surprising that every ambition for the reform of society, and every visionary dream for a utopian community invariably end up as a disappointed expectation.

But, third and possibly more importantly, the effect of sin is the destruction of the relationship between God and mankind. Formerly he shared warmth, love, and fellowship with God; but sin has become a tyrant separating man from a holy God and sentencing him to a bondage from which he cannot free himself. Only in Christ can he find deliverance.

**Bibliography:** Anderson, R. S., *On Being Human* (1983); Brunner, E., *Man in Revolt* (1939);

Carey, G. L., *I Believe in Man* (1977); Fagan, S., *Has Sin Changed?* (1979).

G.C.

**SINS OF OMISSION.** When Christians fail to practice the positive actions and virtues which Christ commanded us to do, we are guilty of committing sins of omission. In the parable of the final judgment, Jesus condemned those who failed to provide food and water, clothing, and hospitality to those who were hungry, poor, and homeless (Matt. 25:41-45). He made it clear that actions of this type rank high on His list of service priorities: "As you did it not to one of the least of these, you did it not to me" (Matt. 25:46, RSV).

**SINGLE-MINDEDNESS.** Single-mindedness is a state of attention in which one's dedication or devotion to a person or an objective is unimpaired by any form of counterattraction or competition. Single-mindedness exemplifies constancy, determination, and unflagging energy in the realization of the goal that inspires it and is thus a peculiarly exclusivist activity.

Service to God and mankind is the highest form of commitment that it is possible for human beings to perform, and it was to this type of dedication that God called the Israelites in the Sinai covenant. They were to worship him exclusively; and despite the varied temptations to sin that their pagan neighbors offered, they were to remain constant and loyal to him, living lives of ceremonial and moral purity and holiness.

Jesus demanded the same dedication from his own followers, with the addition that now their motives were to be under scrutiny as well as the outward manifestations thereof (Matt. 5:27-28). The believer's life must be Christ-centered (Matt. 22:37) and lived in total commitment to the Savior and in Christian witness and service to others, as a slave would serve a master (Col. 3:22). In this way the believer grows in spiritual grace and in fellowship with other committed members of the Christian church.

See DOUBLE-MINDEDNESS.

**SITUATIONAL ETHICS.** The ethical position known as situational ethics arose in the 1960s as a radical response to a view that saw Christian ethics chiefly in terms of rule-keeping. Situational ethics emphasized three things: the overwhelming value in Christian ethics of self-giving love (*agape*); the need for Christians to be autonomous in their moral reasoning and to come to moral judgments as the result of free-decision; and the solidity of the moral life. In the last of these emphases, situational ethics is undoubtedly influenced by existentialism, which stresses the importance of individual choice and the idea that no person can know beforehand what ethical demands a particular situation may make upon him. Such freedom and spontaneity of moral action is, it is claimed, stifled by an unthinking obedience to impersonal laws. The slogan "people before principles'" is an apt summary of the position of the individual and of the moral judgment he is to make of situations.

Situational ethics can be held in varying degrees of strength. At its mildest and most conventional or traditional, it is to be understood as an urging for the need to think about how the general and abstract moral principles of Christianity apply concretely, as suggesting the importance of not taking up inherited moral attitudes uncritically, and as a possible response to situations in which there is a clash or conflict of principles. In such a context, situational ethics is hardly distinguishable from Christian casuistry, which studies how particular cases might be handled from the standpoint of Christian moral principle.

A stronger form of situational ethics would regard moral principles merely as advice to be overridden when there is good cause. A still stronger form would regard such principles merely as summaries of past ethical judgments. The strongest form of all would be one in which moral rules were totally disregarded, each act being judged individually on whether or not it furthered some particular value. In this system, the decisions about what to do in the absence of rules must be made either in terms of some version of consequentialism, or in a series of disconnected "authentic" choices in which God speaks His moral word directly. It is doubtful whether this extreme form of ethical intuitionism (for this is what the position comes to) is intelligible, because any rational assessment of a situation must involve employing some general principles.

The extent to which this ethical position might justly be called "antinomian" is debatable. It is antinomian in the strict sense, for it holds that the Christian is freed from any reliance on God's moral law as a rule of life. Whether situational ethics is antinomian in the further sense that its advocates support behavior that is immoral is not something that can be determined *a priori*, but can be determined only by an examination of what individual thinkers say. Presumably, however, there would be little point in situational ethics if the possibility of moral justification of what, by conventional Christian standards, is unjustifiable were not a real one. So situationalists must think that there are situations in which various courses of action would be justified. To this extent situational ethics is antinomian.

The basic assumption of situational ethics, that law and love are opposites, is not one that can be supported from the Bible, where love is the content of the divine law (Matt. 22:36-40) and is said to be the fulfilling of that law (Rom. 13:10), and where unlawful behavior is unequivocally condemned. The Bible also stresses that the observation of the law of God is not to be legalistic, that is, concerned with minor matters at the expense of major, nor blind to the possible conflicts of laws in the daily living of life, such as situations in which the lesser of two evils ought to be followed. But situational ethics appears to pay scant regard either to the real nature of ethical conflict or to the depths and subtleties of the development of moral character.

**Bibliography:** Fletcher, J., *Moral Responsibility* (1967); Outka, G. H., and Ramsey, P. (eds.), *Norm and Context in Christian Ethics* (1969); Ramsey, P., *Deeds and Rules in Christian Ethics* (1965).

See ABSOLUTES, MORAL; ANTINOMIANISM; RELATIVISM; UTILITARIANISM.

P.H.

**SKEPTICISM.** This noun comes from a Greek word *skeptomai,* "to examine, look carefully at," and in philosophy and ethics properly denotes a questioning attitude with regard to such matters as epistemology or religious tenets. In its developed form, however, skepticism becomes a subjective, rather dogmatic rejection of traditional ethical or moral principles which often does not even admit the possibility of doubt about the validity of its own position. This latter is understandable, of course, since to doubt one's doubtings is not the way to inspire confidence in one's already uncertain epistemology.

Philosophical skepticism developed in Greece about the sixth century B.C. and continued in various forms into the Christian period, when it encountered defeat at the hands of Christian writers, notably Augustine (354–430). The modern phase began with David Hume and was continued in various ways by Nietzsche, Dewey, and Russell. Skepticism in ethical and religious matters received an impetus from nineteenth-century scientism, which purportedly only accepted data that could be verified empirically. Since ethical and religious traditions were essentially subjective and in some cases conditioned culturally, they were objects of skepticism by many adherents to "scientific method."

More recent studies in all areas of science have shown that there are many postulates that have to be accepted at face value because they cannot be validated empirically. These would include what philosophers designate as first and final causes. Skepticism is misplaced in these and other cases, since if a scientist is being true to science, he or she will only be concerned with what can be observed experimentally and quantified or measured in other ways. With regard to these concerns only can scientific skepticism be justified and not in connection with areas of life which stand outside a narrow scientific empiricism.

The New Testament encourages the believer to honor God with the mind as well as the heart (Matt. 22:37), implying that a critical evaluation of people and phases of thought is a legitimate and important activity of the Christ-centered life (1 Tim. 6:3-5). The believer must not be tossed to and fro by false doctrine (Eph. 4:14), but must proclaim the truth in love, confident that the gospel message is true (1 Thess. 2:13) and worthy of human acceptance in faith (1 Tim. 1:15).

**SKYJACKING.** This term represents the aviational equivalent of hijacking and is a form of piracy which involves the seizure in some manner of airplanes. Skyjacking is normally attempted either by psychologically disturbed individuals or by one or more politically motivated terrorists when the airplane is in flight and takes the form of threatened or actual killing of some passengers or crew as part of a predetermined demand. This latter sometimes involves the payment of a large ransom, the delivery of the skyjacker to some particular destination, or the release of political prisoners or captured members of fanatical groups.

Because terrorists who indulge in skyjacking are frequently individuals who will sacrifice their own lives for their particular ideology, attempts at resistance while airborne are fraught with grave danger. The usual procedure is to secure approval for landing the airplane at a particular location and thereafter either to negotiate with the skyjackers or to enlist the aid of specially trained military units to board the airplane and kill or capture the terrorists. According to United States Federal Aviation Administration records, there have been more than 775 illegal seizures of airplanes between 1931 and 1985. Until 1958 almost all skyjackings occurred in Communist-dominated countries, but thereafter involved other nations as well. While the outcome of many instances of skyjacking is unknown, authorities believe that the success rate is disturbingly high as air pirates manage to reach their destination or achieve such goals as acquiring ransom money or the liberating of political prisoners. Consequently skyjacking is unlikely to be eradicated entirely, despite the increasingly stern nature of reprisals by the United States and other nations.

All Christians will deplore the violent means which skyjackers employ in their attempts at extortion, as well as the low estimate that they place on human life, especially their own. It seems clear that vigorous punitive measures will have to be pursued consistently if the menace of skyjacking is to be controlled.

**SLANDER.** Slander constitutes the act or effect of false rumors that have been circulated in such a manner as to produce an adverse view of a person's reputation or integrity. Such information is defamatory because it is false and in general legal usage describes something that has been spoken. In a nonverbal sense it can also include gestures and other signs. Slander thus differs from libel, which normally describes published statements injurious to a person's reputation.

By definition, slander comes under all the strictures associated in Scripture with false witness, beginning with the Decalogue (Exod. 20:16; 23:1-2). The New Testament condemns those who speak evil of their fellows (Acts 19:9; Rom. 1:30) and relates such activity to the father of sin (1 John 3:8). While the Christian can expect to be slandered and defamed (2 Cor. 6:8), as

Christ was, he or she must requite such reports with blessing (Rom. 12:14; 1 Cor. 4:12). It is mandatory for the believer to live a life of unquestioned integrity so that shame and rebuke will not fall upon the body of Christ (2 Cor. 6:3).

**SLAVERY.** Slavery is an institution in which persons become the chattels or property of another. The Mesopotamians of old obtained their slaves principally by conquering rival city-states and taking their inhabitants captive. At various periods slave markets were established in the hill country east of Mesopotamia, and the early nature of these enterprises is indicated by the Sumerian ideogram for (female) slave, which was a combination of the signs for "mountains" and "woman." For various reasons people would sometimes offer themselves voluntarily for service in households, and if they had special talents such as financial management they could rise to an important position in the household and have their own slaves. If another city-state conquered its rival, all those enslaved previously became free once more, sometimes to their disadvantage.

In the Old Testament, slaves, referred to euphemistically in the King James Version as "servants" or "bondservants," were given special consideration under the law (Exod. 20:17; 21:2, 11, 26, 27, 32); and the exploitation of widows and orphans, whether slaves or not, was expressly forbidden. The sexual violation of a betrothed female slave (Lev. 19:20) carried with it a penalty similar to that found in second-millennium-B.C. Nuzi legislation. The humane nature of the Mosaic laws concerning the poor of the land forbade them being exploited as slaves and in any event ensured their liberation in the jubilee year (Lev. 25:35-42).

By New Testament times slavery had become a thoroughgoing political as well as a social instrument, and one half of the imperial population was categorized as slave. The humane provisions of the Old Testament had long been replaced by harsh, repressive conditions, and women in particular were exploited callously. Jesus made no pronouncements on the morality of slavery, while Paul, probably with economic considerations in view, exhorted slaves to remain with their masters and serve them loyally. Householders in turn were instructed to treat their slaves with consideration (1 Cor. 7:21-22; Col. 3:22-23). Following Paul's tradition, the early Fathers asserted that the slave and his or her master were equal before God.

In the Middle Ages, slaves in Europe were recruited from captives taken in war, or from the ranks of free persons who wished to secure economic shelter in a large household. Population increases and the decline in economic prosperity made the lot of the slave and the free laborer very similar, and this led to serfdom. Domestic slavery declined in Europe in the thirteenth century, but the wars between Christians and the African Moors ensured a certain number of slaves. Two

centuries later several European nations were trading openly in African slaves by royal warrant, although the British did not engage in this kind of commerce until 1631. In the next century British churchmen of various denominations rose in protest against the slave trade. A bill for its abolition was finally passed in 1807, and by 1833 slavery in Britain's overseas territories was terminated also.

In the United States there were comparatively few slaves in the north, and due to economic conditions the abolition of slavery was accomplished quite readily. But in the South the slaves had become integral to the social system and actually formed a majority in the states of South Carolina and Mississippi. Lincoln's Emancipation Proclamation (1863) began the process whereby slavery was abolished, and this was finally implemented by the Fourteenth and Fifteenth Amendments to the Constitution (1868-70). One extremely unfortunate result of this movement was that many of those liberated found themselves in extremely difficult economic circumstances and came to regard their freedom as a mixed blessing.

No Christian would countenance the deliberate imposition of servitude upon another human being, if only because Scripture requires the believer to treat all others with decency and consideration as persons for whom Christ died. Modern labor laws, which have their roots in the British Evangelical Revival, endeavor to ensure that workers are treated with some dignity, but in jurisdictions where such legislation does not apply it is not uncommon to discover working conditions that are very close to traditional slavery.

**Bibliography:** Longenecker, R. N., *New Testament Social Ethics for Today* (1984).

**SLOTH.** This word, derived from the adjective *slow*, describes laziness, inactivity, or general indolence, whether symptomatic of some pathological condition or a hereditary tendency. In the way in which the term is employed in current speech there is an implied deliberateness about sloth, as though the individual concerned had the ability to indulge in a more active way of life but was simply unattracted by such a prospect. The Greeks were familiar with this tendency, which they called *notheia* and understood it to mean "sluggishness" or "torpor".

Sloth has presented ethical problems for Christians for many centuries and was included in the list of the "seven deadly sins" by Pope Gregory the Great. In a spiritual environment where the King's business demands haste (1 Sam. 21:8), sloth, while not as spectacular a vice as its companions in Gregory's list, is nevertheless just as debilitating because it involves an inhibiting of effort and energy that could be used constructively for Christ's ministry to the world. Commitment to Christ compels discipline instead of inertia, for the proclamation of the gospel demands that the sleeper must awake because of the lateness of the eschatological hour (Rom. 13:11) and the need for urgent work in consequence. When others are toiling rigorously, it is sheer self-indulgence for a believer to be slothful. Instead, inertia must be banished, the sleeper aroused, and the slothful quickened (Eph. 5:14).

**SMOKING.** This common term describes the process by which tobacco products and other addictive substances are ingested into the body. Normally this is achieved by inhaling the combustible products of the tobacco plant, a weed known botanically as *Nicotiana tabacum*, to which is sometimes added another species, *Nicotiana rustica*. Variations of the inhalation procedure include the chewing of tobacco, a habit that was socially acceptable a century ago, and its introduction into the nostrils or on the gums in a finely powered form known as snuff.

The first mention of tobacco is generally attributed to Christopher Columbus, who in 1492, noted its use among the North American Indians, particularly in the peace-pipe rituals. Some historians think that Columbus introduced the smoking of tobacco to the inhabitants of the Caribbean countries; but, regardless, what was described as the "fashionable Indian weed" was brought to Europe in 1556, and to England in 1565, where wealthy people smoked it for its alleged medicinal properties.

King James I, however remained unpersuaded by such arguments, objecting both to the pungent aroma of the weed and also to to the effect that it appeared to be having upon his courtiers. In his celebrated *Counterblast to Tobacco* (1604), he complained that by the "immoderate taking of tobacco the health of a great number of people is impaired and their bodies weakened and made unfit for labour," which also resulted in "a great part of the treasure of our land spent and exhausted by this only drug." To ensure that "a less quantity of tobacco will hereafter be brought into this our realm England," the outraged monarch raised taxes on imports of tobacco by an unprecedented 400 percent. But the addictive nature of the weed was more than adequate to meet such a challenge, and almost four centuries were to pass before the monarch's opinions became common currency.

Sir Francis Bacon summarized the situation quite aptly in 1623 when he said that tobacco "conquers men with a certain secret pleasure, so that those who have once become accustomed thereto can hardly be restrained therefrom." Modern experiments, unfortunately, have not been able to dispute the force of this observation. Confirmed smokers experience an inner compulsion that, surprisingly enough, is similar to that of a heroin addict. Medical researchers assign smoking to the category of "dependence disorders" and attribute to it a particularly obstinate character. Many regard nicotinic acid as the most addictive substance known to mankind, since it takes only seven seconds to make an impact upon the brain as compared with eleven seconds for heroin. In view of these findings it is surprising that so many smokers are ultimately able to break the habit.

While men predominated as smokers from the time of King James I, the suffragette movement saw women gradually joining their ranks; and smoking ultimately became socially acceptable. The dilettantes brought a new dimension to the practices of serious smokers by constructing a form of glamour associated with the various gestures and postures of smoking. With the public advertising of tobacco there was promoted a supposed connection between cigarettes and pipes and manly virility, or more subtle sexual activity. A cigar in particular came to be symbolic of riches, or at the very least of an aspiration thereto. Smoking was also taken to involve a reflective activity, and this was particularly the case when men smoked pipes. Woman allegedly had their own sexual symbols as they sat in a state of languor, waving a cigarette protruding from a long holder. As an extension of their advertising, cigarette companies ultimately began sponsoring various types of athletic events. At the present they seem bent on associating the "good life" with smoking against a background of luxurious settings or expensive recreational facilities.

Smoking was at a peak during World War II, but after that time a number of studies began to show that nicotine-based gratification carried with it some serious side effects. Nicotinic acid and other alkaloids that make the plant addictive also have an adverse effect upon bodily nutrition. Thus, nicotinic acid and acetaldehyde deprive the blood of vitamins in the B group and also reduce the utilization and storage of vitamin C. According to Surgeon General C. Everett Koop of the United States, smoking is the chief cause of chronic obstructive lung disease, the most important of which are chronic bronchitis and emphysema. He has also estimated that smoking costs the United States about $40 billion annually in health-related expenses and lost productivity. Some researchers at the United States National Institute on Drug Abuse have concluded that smoking is far more deadly than excessive drinking and more resistant to treatment than heroin addiction because of its intensely strong habit-forming properties. In the area of genetics, research at the Sergievsky Center at Columbia University has revealed a connection between cigarette smoking and the frequency of trisomy (the presence in human beings of an additional chromosome) as observed from spontaneous abortions. The association of an environmental agent with the frequency of trisomy is new and seems to be correlative in some way to the age of the woman. If a young woman smokes before or during the time of conception, the risk of tobacco affecting her chromosomes is decreased. Because in the case of an older female smoker, the risk of trisomy is increased This phenomenon, needless to say is very difficult to explain medically.

The dramatic increase of lung cancer among

men has been attributed to the fifty or more carcinogenic factors that affect the body in so-called "mainstream" cigarette smoking. Although some deaths from lung cancer occur among non-smokers, the relationship between smoking and pulmonary cancer has been attested so well statistically that in some countries packages of cigarettes carry a health-hazard warning. These statistics are so awesome that they need neither repetition nor emphasis here.

When women smoke, as about 30 percent apparently do in Western nations, they discover that lung cancer can affect princesses as well as professional women, housewives, and others. Since lung cancer often shows itself only after about thirty-five years of addiction, the social changes of the post-World War II period, during which increasing numbers of woman adopted the practice of smoking, are only now becoming evident from a pathological standpoint. When women are pregnant, smoking may result in miscarriages, premature births, or infants whose birth weights are lighter than normal. The children of smokers appear to suffer from more pulmonary diseases and are more subject to poisons of various kinds than nonsmokers. At least some of these ailments will probably not be related to cigarette smoking, since such women tend to be less affluent, less well educated, heavier drinkers of coffee and alcohol, and less likely to have received good prenatal care. The cancer situation for women smokers has changed significantly of late, with the result that lung cancer is more common than breast cancer. A lung cancer "epidemic" has been predicted by the United States Center for Disease Control in Atlanta, credited to the "historic increase in the exposure of women to tobacco." Cervical cancers have also been blamed on cigarette smoking by some authorities, who claim that female smokers have four times as many cervical cancers as female nonsmokers.

A good deal of heart disease is caused by smoking, according to statistical reports, and it has been estimated by the United States Surgeon General that one in ten American cigarette smokers may die prematurely from cardiac disease. The apparent effect of the carcinogens in cigarette smoke is to accelerate the processes of arteriosclerosis; and the risk of death is said to increase with the numbers of cigarettes smoked, the degree of inhalation, and the length of time involved. In addition to the absorption of "mainstream" smoke into the lungs, smoke issuing from the burning tips of cigarettes or released from the mouths of smokers ("sidestream" smoke) has also been found to cause cancer of the lung in nonsmokers who have inhaled it over many years. According to the United State Environmental Protection Agency, such "passive smoke" is a greater risk to public health than hazardous air pollutants of the nature of benzene, vinyl chloride, and arsenic. It should be noted in passing that statistics endeavoring to link cigarette smoking with various diseases are contested vigorously by cigarette manufacturers, who claim that the evidence is inconclusive.

Campaigns against smoking are very much in evidence in Western society and are directed increasingly at children in the eleven to thirteen year age group that, according to statistics, is the one most subject to peer pressure to commence smoking. While a "soft sell" approach is usually adopted, certain hard facts are often introduced. These could range from such slogans as "lung cancer cures smoking" to the information that young women who smoke a minimum of one package of cigarettes a day for twelve years or more increase the risk of cervical cancer by at least twelve times. Most campaigns directed at young people stress the fact that teenagers who smoke are on average considerably less healthy than their nonsmoking counterparts.

Cancer societies also sponsor a number of ingenious programs such as Smokebusters, Great American Smokeout, and Cold Turkey Week to help smokers "break the habit." In response to the need for assistance, some commercial concerns have arisen to provide lectures, aversion therapy, hypnotism, acupuncture, and behavior modification programs. At a different level, various groups from Christian denominations have instituted publicity campaigns in the press and elsewhere in an attempt to secure a ban on the advertising of cigarettes. Public disapproval of smoking has been further recognized by the enactment of legislation in various jurisdictions to provide for nonsmoking areas in restaurants, hotels and motels, on public vehicles, and in certain work areas. As society becomes more health-conscious and better informed about the damaging effects of smoking, the habit will become less and less acceptable. It seems unlikely that it will dwindle to extinction, however, if only because the psychologically frail will continue to use it as an emotional crutch and succumb to its addictive properties.

The sale of tobacco products provides vast revenues for governments, which are understandably reluctant to lose them. While some governments make modest attempts to warn smokers of the dangers inherent in the habit, they also provide subsidies for those farmers who grow tobacco as a cash crop, an action that has been condemned as hypocrisy. Advocates of "rights" for nonsmokers feel that the best chances of success in the war against tobacco lie in full-scale attacks on the cigarette manufacturing industry itself. The objective would be to restrict tobacco advertising in newspapers, on billboards and other outdoor signs, and especially the sponsorship by cigarette manufacturers of various kinds of athletic events.

At the time of writing, most North American cigarette companies submit voluntarily to an ethical code in which they affirm their intention of advertising only to adults of eighteen years or older and without stating or implying that cigarette smoking promotes physical health or is an essential element of personal success, romance, and the like. Critics of this code maintain that the tobacco manufacturing industry breaks its own rules by associating such healthy activities as sports and athletics with smoking.

In view of the enormous health hazards connected with tobacco consumption, the Christian church could well demonstrate its real concerns for society as a whole by vigorous attacks upon smoking. This has already begun in some Christian denominations and is expected to gain considerable support both inside and outside the church. So addictive is the habit that its victims need massive support of the kind that Alcoholics Anonymous provides for its members. This help is needed badly, if only because many smokers who are considering breaking the habit once and for all find themselves in the position of Samuel Clemens, who is reported to have said that giving up smoking was easy, he had done it many times. Faced with all the available evidence, it is difficult to believe that anyone who continues to smoke is anything other than irresponsible and foolhardy. Certainly no Christian who treasures his or her body as the temple of the Holy Spirit and is aware of the penalties attached to its defilement (1 Cor. 3:16-17; 6:19-20) would wish for one moment to become involved with such as enslaving and health destroying activity as smoking.

## SOCIAL CONCERN, EVANGELICAL.

Evangelicalism is both a theological position and a historical phenomenon that has emerged at various times in the history of the church, particularly since 1700 in Great Britain and the United States. Evangelical doctrines coincide with the historic orthodox teachings of the Christian church on the nature of the Trinity, the sovereignty of God, the virgin birth, man's fallen condition and need for salvation, the person and work of Jesus, and the personal return of Christ. The distinguishing features of evangelical theology are its view of Scripture and its emphasis on missions and evangelism. Scripture is the inspired, infallible, and inerrant revelation of God to humanity that is the ultimate guide for faith and practice. The major task of Christians in this age is to evangelize, that is, to proclaim the gospel found in the inspired Scripture in order to bring individuals to personal faith in Jesus Christ. Social service is both logically a result of saving faith and a means of preparation for the proclamation of the gospel. Evangelicals, however, would not tend to equate social service with the gospel.

Christians who have manifested the spirit of evangelical belief can be found throughout church history, including the apostolic age. During the German Reformation, the term *evangelical* was applied to those Lutherans who sought to reform Christianity by an emphasis on the study of the Bible and on salvation by faith alone. Later, the term was applied to both Reformed and

Lutheran Christians, and today, in Germany, *evangelical* means Protestant. Evangelical elements are evident especially in German pietism with its emphasis on biblical authority and a life of piety and devotion.

In Great Britain, evangelicalism arose out of the Methodist revival in the eighteenth century led by the Wesleys and George Whitefield and an evangelical revival within the Anglican church a few years later. A similar revival occurred in Scotland that led to the founding of the Free Church in 1843 under the leadership of Thomas Chalmers. John Wesley had a holistic view of salvation, connecting the material with the spiritual and the personal with the social. He opposed slavery, supported prison reform and the development of educational institutions, and established organizations to meet various social needs. Other evangelicals, including members of the Clapham Sect, a group of wealthy individuals living in Clapham, were active in social reform. Will Wilberforce, a member of the Sect and also of Parliament, Granville Sharp, and other evangelicals provided leadership to the movement that led to the abolition of slavery. The leader of the movement for prison reform was another evangelical, John Howard. Working conditions, especially for women and children, were improved in the nineteenth century through the efforts of Lord Shaftesbury, a member of Parliament and an evangelical.

Evangelicalism in the United States is associated with revivalism beginning with the Great Awakening in the early eighteenth century under George Whitefield, Jonathan Edwards, and others, and the Second Awakening in the late eighteenth and early nineteenth centuries. Revivalism continued throughout the nineteenth century, with many antebellum evangelists such as Charles Finney being in the forefront of social reform, particularly the abolitionist movement.

During the first half of the twentieth century, a reversal occurred when Christians with evangelical beliefs withdrew from efforts aimed at social reform. Most of the mainline white denominations in the north were overtaken by modernism with its emphasis on social action rather than evangelism and its rejection of many of the orthodox Christian doctrines, such as the virgin birth, the inerrancy of Scripture, and the substitutionary atonement. In reaction, Christians who came to be called "Fundamentalists" emphasized the traditional doctrines and a gospel of personal, not social, salvation.

Although many Christians in many denominations hold evangelical beliefs, contemporary evangelicalism in the United States is most clearly identified with the National Association of Evangelicals, founded in 1943 by Harold J. Ockenga, pastor of Park Street Church in Boston, and others, *Christianity Today*, the work of Billy Graham and his Evangelistic Association, and a group of colleges and seminaries, such as Wheaton College, Fuller Theological Seminary,

Gordon College, Gordon-Conwell Theological Seminary, Westmont College, and Bethel College and Theological Seminary. Men associated with this movement during its formative period in the 1940s had fundamentalist backgrounds and include Ockenga, Carl F. H. Henry, who was the founding editor of *Christianity Today* in 1956, and Edward J. Carnell. In 1946, Henry wrote *The Uneasy Conscience of Fundamentalism*, in which he derided fundamentalists for their narrowness, otherworldiness, anti-intellectualism, and unwillingness to apply their faith to culture and social concern.

Until recent years, evangelical Christians in the United States have been more active in responding to private moral sins and in ministering to the overly concerned about evils that result from the ways society is structured, such as racism, sexism, poverty, unemployment, and inadequate housing. On many social issues, most evangelicals have supported conservative social and political positions. The reasons for this are both theological and sociological. The fact that evangelicalism arose historically out of fundamentalism has caused many evangelicals to react negatively to anything that is suggestive of the social gospel. Further, the theological position widely held by evangelicals does not directly support involvement in changing social structures. Evangelicals operate under the thesis that the problem of mankind is a broken relationship between the individual and God, a relationship that is mended through personal conversion when an individual responds in faith to the atoning work of Jesus on the cross and in the Resurrection. Man is not saved through a change in his environment. Therefore, evangelicals emphasize the evangelism of individuals and tend to view social service wholly as a means of preparing people for evangelism. In addition, the fact that fundamentalism, and thus evangelicalism, has been strongly influenced by dispensational theology, which emphasizes the imminent personal return of Christ and the social catastrophe that will precede it diverted attention from social reform. Sociologically, most evangelicals belong to middle-class families whose ancestors immigrated to the United States in the late nineteenth or early twentieth century, and thus share the ideals and values of conservative middle-class America. As a result, they will tend to support the institutions that have brought them material benefits and social standing, rather than to oppose them for the sake of those who are maltreated by them.

In recent years, evangelicals have become much more active in their social and political involvement. This is best illustrated by the Moral Majority, founded and led by Jerry Falwell. Even though Falwell calls himself a fundamentalist rather than an evangelical, his followers include a large number who are evangelicals. He and those in his movement are involved in political and social action, especially in attempts to influence party platforms, elections, and legislation. His agenda includes opposition to abortion, pornography, the Equal Rights Amendment, and support of the free enterprise system, democracy, and a strong national defense including the development of nuclear weapons. He believes America is a nation chosen by God to exemplify Christian morality and the free enterprise system, to protect the freedom of the Western world from communist domination, and to defend the chosen nation of Israel.

A rather different approach was taken by a group of about fifty evangelicals who met in Chicago in 1973 and set forth the "Chicago Declaration." They acknowledge that God requires both love and justice, and admit that the evangelical community has perpetuated attitudes and structures in support of racism, sexism, and a maldistribution of wealth in the world. They call on evangelicals "to demonstrate repentance in a Christian discipleship that confronts the social and political injustice of our nation" and to "challenge the misplaced trust...in economic and military might."

Ronald Sider and Jim Wallis represent a radical approach to social concern among evangelicals, taking the position that Christians should develop a counter-culture in opposition to the present secularist, materialistic, and militaristic culture in the United States. Sider is a professor, now at Eastern Baptist Seminary, and most well-known for his book *Rich Christians in an Age of Hunger*, while Wallis leads the Sojourner Community in Washington, D.C., and edits *Sojourners*, a monthly periodical. Their theological positions center on the kingdom of God, which is characterized by separation from the values of worldly culture and a simple lifestyle of nonviolence, love, and concern for the hungry, the poor, and other individuals maltreated by various social institutions. They tend to oppose existing social institutions, such as the government of the United States, rather than to work within them for social betterment. They are both pacifists, strongly opposing military expenditures and the development, possession, and use of nuclear weapons.

Another evangelical position on social concern is represented by people such as Richard Mouw, Lewis Smedes, and Arthur Holmes. Borrowing heavily from the Calvinist tradition, they emphasize the reforming of culture through involvement in traditional social institutions. The starting point of their theories is the order of creation, by which men and women were brought into being as social creatures along with social institutions such as family, business and trade, and government. The institutions, as well as, individuals, were perverted from their rightful purposes and order in the Fall. Jesus Christ came and wrought a work of redemption not simply for individuals, but for all of creation, including social institutions. The kingdom of God represents a vision of a new order when men and women will be right with God and live in peace and justice. That

Kingdom, which will be fully realized in the future age, is to be partially realized in the present as Christians work to reform the current social institutions in accordance with their vision of the future. Mouw calls for a Christian emphasis on evangelism that is not only individual, but social and political as well. In particular, the church is to be the model of the new order. Representatives of this position are opposed to abortion and evils brought about by social institutions such as racism and sexism. Though they generally fall within the just war tradition, they tend to be nuclear pacifists.

Evangelical Christians are not only active in articulating positions advocating social concern, but they have formed many organizations to meet social need and to change unjust social institutions. These include agencies such as World Relief, a relief agency associated with the National Association of Evangelicals, and World Vision, both involved in combating world hunger; Prison Ministries, an organization founded by Charles Colson to minister to prisoners and to work toward prison reform; and Voice of Calvary, founded by John Perkins in Mississippi, to provide models for economic and social development, particularly among blacks.

**Bibliography:** Falwell, J. (ed.), *The Fundamentalist Phenomenon: The Resurgence of Conservative Christianity* (1981); Marsden, G. M., *Fundamentalism and the American Culture: The Shaping of Twentieth-Century Evangelicalism: 1870–1925* (1980); Mouw, R., *Political Evangelism* (1973); Wallis, J., *Revive Us Again: A Sojourner's Story* (1983); Webber, R., *The Secular Saint: A Case for Evangelical Social Responsibility* (1979).

S.D.A.

**SOCIAL ETHICS, CHRISTIAN.** The term *social ethics* refers to the area of moral questions, problems, and issues that arise from man's relation to social structures, as well as the principles and applications that are developed in response to them. Social structures are those systems and organizations that humans form in order to respond to the natural world, the spiritual world, and other social structures. These include family, tribe, business and trade, school, and government. Examples of social problems are divorce, child abuse, poverty, disease, abortion, alcoholism, pornography, malnutrition, war, and racial injustice.

The questions of how Christians should respond to ethical problems within society and should relate to social structures, especially when these structures are dominated by those who oppose Christian values, has faced the church since its inception. Most Christians in the first three centuries did not participate in the Roman social structures because of the deification of the emperor, idolatry, and pagan rites. After the conversion of Constantine in the fourth century,

however, Christians came to dominate the social structures, making necessary the development of a Christian social philosophy. This was provided, in part, by Augustine, who advocated Christian participation in government and military service because they were ordained by God to curb violence and evil. In the thirteenth century Thomas Aquinas developed a model where church and society were complementary, with Christians being responsible for participating in both. He emphasized the positive role of social structures in promoting the common good, basing it on his understanding of natural law. The Reformers, Calvin and Luther, built on Augustine's position and developed theories supporting the participation of Christians as part of their duty to God. Calvin emphasized the role of Christians in reforming social structures perverted in the Fall. Luther's view was more dualistic, with Christians being required to operate simultaneously within the spheres of secular society and of the kingdom of God, even though some conflict might exist between them. In the same period, Anabaptists and other radical reformers rejected military participation and withdrew from the established structures to develop their own societies, patterned on their understanding of the kingdom of God as set forth in the New Testament. In the nineteenth and early twentieth centuries, liberal Christians or modernists argued that social reform is central to the mission of the church and that the church must modernize its view and be active in the change of social structures. Conservative Christians, those who came to be called "fundamentalists," responded by emphasizing the "fundamentals" of historic orthodox Christianity and the need for an individual response to a gospel of personal salvation. The question of the primary mission of the church still divides American Christians, though in recent years many fundamentalist and evangelical Christians have been active in seeking social change.

The question of how the Bible is to be used in response to issues of social ethics depends on how one applies the teachings of the Old Testament to contemporary Christians and on how one interprets the teachings of Jesus, Paul, and the rest of the New Testament. If the principles behind the moral and social law in the Old Testament are normative for Christians currently operating within society, then not only are Christians obliged to minister to the needs of individuals, but they are also responsible for ordering social structures and for changing unjust structures. God in creation mandated social structures; He created man and woman because it was not good for man to dwell alone (Gen. 1:27; 2:18-25). The Decalogue commands respect for the authority of parents, and thereby of government in the patriarchal society. It also forbids the desecration of the societal structures of marriage through adultery (Exod. 20:14; Deut. 5:18), of property through stealing (Exod. 20:15; Deut.

5:19; 25:13-16), and of communication through lying (Exod. 20:16; Deut. 5:20).

The Torah in its civil regulations emphasizes the structuring of a just society (see Deut. 16:18-20). Debtors are to be released from their debts every seven years (Deut. 15:1-3), protected from usury (Deut. 23:19-20), and provided with the basic means for life (Deut. 24:6, 12-13, 17). Property is to be returned to original owners in the year of jubilee (Lev. 25:8-17). Wars are to be fought humanely (Deut. 20:10-20). The calls for revival by the prophets are in large part calls for social justice. The prophets give priority to justice for the poor and disenfranchised (the widow, the orphan, and the alien) over acts of worship (Isa. 1:10-17; 10:1-4; Amos 5:5-12, 21-27). They condemn the leaders of Judah and Israel for materialism (Amos 3:12-15; 6:4-7), oppressing the poor (Jer. 22:13-17; Amos 5:11), bribery (Isa. 5:23; Amos 5:12), and injustice in the courts (Amos 5:10-12).

The New Testament presents a message of social as well as individual salvation. The song of Mary portrays the Messiah as one who feeds the hungry and humbles the rich and the proud (Luke 1:46-56). Jesus, at the beginning of His ministry, entered the temple in Nazareth to claim that the text from Isaiah that describes the Spirit of the Lord coming up one who is anointed "to preach the gospel to the poor,...to heal the broken-hearted, to preach deliverance to the captives, and recovering of sight to the blind, to set at liberty them that are bruised" (Luke 4:17-21) was being fulfilled through Him. This text has spiritual implications, but it also shows that Jesus came to deal with evil structures as well as to minister spiritually to individuals. Jesus, in His earthly ministry, met the social as well as the spiritual needs of people; He gave sight to the blind, healed the sick, cured the lame, and ministered to the condemned. Much of his teaching, including the Sermon on the Mount, has implications for social ethics. The great division between the sheep and the goats, for example, is based on how people responded to the social and physical needs of others (Matt. 25:31-46). Jesus also condemned the Pharisees for their lack of concern for justice and mercy (Matt. 23:23).

Paul appears to be a conservative in his response to social structures. He indicates that Christians are to be subject to the higher powers because government is ordained by God (Rom. 13:1-7; 1 Pet. 2:13-18). They are to pray for kings and others who are in authority (1 Tim. 2:1-4). Slaves are to be obedient to their masters, and wives are to be submissive to their husbands. Underlying Paul's teaching, however, is the view that social structures are perverted (Rom. 1:18-32; 8:19-23). In response to this problem, he offers a vision of the church where barriers between human beings are broken down and social injustices are overcome (Gal. 3:26-28; Eph. 2:11-22; Col. 3:8-11; Philemon). James criticizes those who have become rich through the misuse

of social structures (James 2:1-9; 5:1-6) and equates true religion with a ministry to orphans and widows (James 1:27). Revelation, along with Isaiah and Micah in the Old Testament, presents a vision of a new age when God will reign over social structures that are truly just and when all humanity will be at peace (Isa. 9:2-7; 11:1-10; 65:17-25; Mic. 4:1-5; Rev. 21—22).

In summary, the Bible teaches that social structures are essential to God's order for humanity and that Christians have a responsibility not only to minister to the social needs of individuals, but also to make social structures, perverted by the Fall, more just.

**Bibliography:** Moberg, D., *Inasmuch: Christian Social Responsibility in the Twentieth Century* (1965); Mott, S. C., *Biblical Ethics and Social Change (1982);* Mouw, R., *Political Evangelism* (1973); *Politics and the Biblical Drama* (1976); Smedes, L., *Mere Morality: What God Expects From Ordinary People* (1983).

S.D.A.

**SOCIAL GOSPEL.** As a term, *social gospel* may be understood in two ways—as a movement that attempted to combine political and social insights with Christian theology and as a way of understanding the implications of the gospel for society.

As a movement, we must trace early attempts to achieve a biblical vision for a just society. In the nineteenth century, through the impact of the Evangelical Revival, schools, hospitals, and orphanages were built and many social projects such as prison reform were initiated. William Wilberforce and Lord Shaftesbury attacked the causes of social evil and attempted to introduce legislation which would prevent exploitation. In America, prominent evangelical leaders fought against social problems such as prostitution, alcoholism, and racism.

In 1848 F. D. Maurice, J. M. Ludlow, and Charles Kingsley started a new movement that they called Christian Socialism. Based upon F. D. Maurice's "Kingdom Theology," Christian Socialism embraced three statements concerning the individual, the community, and the nation. First, concerning the individual before God, they emphasized that God's love embraced all men. Instead of starting from the wrath and holiness of God, they approached theology from the character of God as a being of love, who has revealed His concern for mankind in the incarnation of His dear Son. Second, concerning the community, they argued that no man has the right to call anything his own. Third, they suggested that if any nation sanctions one law for the rich and another for the poor, it goes against the maxims and ideals of the kingdom of God. From this soil the Social Gospel Movement rose in the late nineteenth century to oppose the evils of laissez-faire capitalism. In 1912 this movement produced the Social Creed of the Christian Churches, which was accepted by the Federal Council of Churches later in the year. It argued for the abolition of child labor, a minimum living wage, reduced hours of work, and the equitable distribution of resources.

Although the Social Gospel Movement waned after World War I, its benefits percolated into mainstream Christianity, influencing, for example, the Life and Work aspect of the ecumenical movement, and William Temple's thinking. In general the movement challenged the accepted Christian thought of the period. Today the values for which the Social Gospel Movement fought are largely agreed upon by most Christians, and its theoretical principles are at the heart of many peace and protest movements.

As a way of understanding the gospel, the term *social gospel* often stands for the following concern: that the mission of Jesus Christ compels the church to work out the "ethic of the Kingdom." That is to say, the issues of poverty, injustice, and inequality must not be avoided by people who confess that God loved humanity so much that He gave His Son for its salvation. Theologians of Third World countries, particularly, are reminding Christians in richer churches that the vision of the Kingdom means that we must analyze society from the perspective of the oppressed. A gospel that is "social," they argue, will inevitably have implications for economic, social, and political structures.

See THIRD WORLD.

G.C.

**SOCIOBIOLOGY.** Sociobiology is a recent doctrine and discipline in which aspects of genetics converge with evolutionary biology, population biology, sociology, and philosophy. Sociobiological theory was first articulated in a 1975 book by Harvard University entomologist Edward Osborne Wilson. At first glance, "morally good" behavior, such as altruism or self-sacrifice, would be incompatible with evolutionary theory. Such behavior would be disadvantageous to the individual as a competitor in the race for survival and reproduction and would thus not survive the competition for individual survival. In short, altruistic behavior would doom an organism to extinction. Sociobiology attempts to explain how such traits have emerged in human evolutionary history, thus purporting to give a naturalistic account of the emergence of morality.

Sociobiology holds the challenging thesis that basic moral concepts of the philosopher and theologian, such as duty, self-sacrifice, rights, and obligations, are manifestations of altruistic behavior, which itself can be explained biologically. It would be profitable, sociobiologists contend, for the study of such concepts to be taken from the humanities and given to the natural scientists. The sociobiological explanation for morality is totally dependent on evolutionary process. Wilson argues that an organism, such as the hu-

man being, is really but a carrier for genetic material that seeks to replicate itself. To do so, the genes direct behavior in the organism that is advantageous to the future welfare of the genes. The welfare of the genes is not the same as that of the individual, since, as W. D. Hamilton has argued, the genes are also distributed among the individual's kin. Thus, the genes of individuals are advantaged by behaviors that promote the group as well as the individual, since, according to Hamilton's kin selection theory, organisms seek to increase the survivability and fitness of the relatives who share their genes. A bird will give an alarm of an approaching predator to the flock to which the bird belongs, thereby "altruistically" decreasing its own survival prospects while increasing that of the group. Robert Trivers's theory of reciprocal altruism holds that populations programmed to aid one another will be more successful at survival and reproduction than will other populations. Thus, altruism can be seen to be an evolutionarily advantageous trait.

Sociobiology as applied to human morality implies several theses that strain heavily against traditional and Christian perspectives of ethics and human life. It is reductionistic, explaining away noble ideals and actions as merely genetically advantageous phenomena and the individual as a mere carrier of DNA. It is deterministic, as it explains all behavior in terms of genetics. It thus joins other determinisms based on psychological, economic, or physiological factors. Implications more acceptable to traditional views are the falsities of psychological egoism, the doctrine that self-interest alone can motivate our actions, and of ethical relativism, which holds that no moral values are universal.

**Bibliography:** Caplan, A. L., (ed.), *The Sociobiology Debate* (1978); Wilson, E. O., *Sociobiology: The New Synthesis* (1975).

D.B.F.

**SODOMY.** This term is derived directly from Sodom, one of the ancient cities of the plain area located on the southeast corner of the Dead Sea (Gen. 14:2; 19:1). Sodom has gone down in history because of the infamy of its inhabitants, as illustrated in the account of the two divine messengers visiting Lot, who had made his home in Sodom. He extended to his visitors the usual Oriental courtesies (Gen. 19:2), but the evening was disturbed by all the male inhabitants of the place who demanded that the visitors be sent out to them so that they might "know them," that is, have homosexual relations (otherwise known as *sodomy*) with them.

Lot even offered his virgin daughters to satisfy their lust in order to avoid violating the canons of hospitality, but the visitors averted calamity by bringing amaurotic blindness upon the Sodomites. The following day the city and its neighbors were destroyed (Gen. 19:24-25). Lot's wife, who had evidently been reluctant to leave her home and possessions, was also killed when God's judgment descended upon the city.

Some modern homosexuals, in an attempt to deny the equating of sodomy with homosexual perversions, have suggested that the desire of the Sodomites to "know" the visitors was merely a gesture of hospitality. The Hebrew verb *yada,* translated "know," is frequently used as a euphemism for sexual relations, and this is evidently the case in Genesis 19:5. Had hospitality been the real reason for the mob scene outside Lot's house, he would not have offered his daughters to the men for purposes of sexual gratification and certainly would not have described the citizens' actions as "wicked" (Gen. 19:7), which would have been a correct designation of homosexual perversions. The tradition of sodomy as homosexuality persisted throughout the biblical period, being mentioned in the New Testament as late as the epistle of Jude (verse 7).

All forms of sexual perversion (Rom. 1:24-27; Gal. 5:19) are forbidden to Christians, who are commanded to live moral and holy lives as a witness to their evil and adulterous generation. Homosexuality in particular is expressly prohibited under pain of death in the Old Testament (Lev. 20:13) because it was a pagan form of sexual defilement that, if permitted, would corrupt the moral and ceremonial life of the covenant community, as it did successively with ancient Canaan, Greece, and Rome. Christians are only permitted to indulge in sexual activity involving members of the opposite sex and, at that on the basis of a legal, monogamous marriage relationship.

**SORCERY.** In modern usage this term is thought of as synonymous with witchcraft, and this perpetuates the Old Testament meaning of the verb *kashaph,* "to employ witch craft or sorceries" (Deut. 18:10; 2 Chron. 33:6), despite the fact that the Hebrew word conveys nothing about what was involved in the procedures. By New Testament times sorcery had come to be associated with magical spells, potions, and charms (*pharmakeia,* Gal. 5:20), and this was significantly different from the ancient Roman understanding of sorcery. The Romans conceived of *sors,* the root from which *sorcery* is derived, as a lot or small ticket which was placed in a bag or some other container preparatory to being drawn for some purpose. The term then applied to the castings of lots in order to arrive at a decision and in religious circles to an oracular response which was determined by lot. The main emphasis of the term for the Romans was thus of a divinatory nature, which in metaphorical language caused the *sors* to symbolize a person's "lot in life."

Magic as a whole has been regarded as a degenerate form of religion in which the practitioners seek to emulate the mysterious powers commonly attributed to the pagan gods. This is certainly true of sorcery, which sought by various means to persuade its adherents that the wizard,

sorcerer, or sorceress could employ mystic, quasi-divine powers of personality to know the will of the gods, bring about communications between the gods and mankind by means of ritual performances, and reveal the future through such procedures as divination and necromancy.

In the Old Testament the world commonly rendered *sorcerer* or *witch* by most English versions was *mekashshephah* and apparently could apply to persons of either sex. It is not altogether easy to discover precisely what was involved in the functions of such a practitioner. Certainly sorcery was a commonplace procedure among the Canaanites and was strictly prohibited in the Hebrew community in consequence (Exod. 22:18; Deut. 18:10-12). The term *mekashshephah* has been related to an Arabic root meaning "to cut off," and may have referred to the kind of ecstatic stimulation that the Baal priests of Jezebel attempted to induce by cutting their flesh with knives (1 Kings 18:28). Alternatively, the cutting implied by the Arabic word could have referred to the shredding of various herbs in order to produce an intoxicating drink. In Jeremiah 27:9 some oracular or divinatory response seems to be involved, and the same is true of Daniel 2:2, whereas with other references (Exod. 22:18; Deut. 18:10; Isa. 47:9, 12) it is impossible to determine the function of the *mekashshephah.* It may have been that drug-induced divination was the function of the sorcerer principally, but that cannot be determined with any assurance. The deities that were being invoked were certainly "strange gods," as far as the Hebrews were concerned, hence the prohibitions against witchcraft and sorcery.

In modern times witchcraft has gradually gained a following that is more in evidence in a pluralistic society than in earlier days. Though still illegal in many Western countries, witches and sorcerers operate in covens or groups and indulge in various kinds of rites, often in a secluded country location under a full moon. Early in World War II, British covens reportedly danced surreptitiously in a circle, unclothed (in itself an extremely unhealthy procedure in the English climate), and then stood facing continental Europe as they pushed with their hands in a symbolic gesture of repelling an expected Nazi invasion. Meanwhile, more orthodox-minded citizens were either busily praying or manning coastal artillery.

In various parts of the Western world the worship of Satan is practiced, and the accompanying rites allegedly involve some sort of animal sacrifice on occasions. Sorcerers still appear to be using charms, incantations, rituals, magic potions, spells, and the like in their attempts to manipulate powers of a demonic nature.

The New Testament urges Christians to avoid all spurious spirits (1 John 4:1-3) because they originate with the devil. Only those spirits which confess the incarnate Christ are trustworthy, and all others, along with sorcerers and witches, are ultimately to be destroyed (Rev. 21:8). Christians do not need any guidance from such sources as stars, cards, devils, or mediums, but have only to look to God's Holy Spirit for true leading in life (John 16:13).

**Bibliography:** Nigosian, S. A., *Occultism in the Old Testament* (1978).

**STERILIZATION.** In industrial usage this term designates a process by which substances are rendered free from germs, bacteria, and similar agents which could promote infection. In medical circles it also refers to processes ensuring that equipment used in treating patients is not merely clean, but does not harbor any germs.

The need to prevent infectious bodies from reproducing has led to the term being used of surgical attempts to inhibit human reproduction. This is accomplished by vasectomy for men and tubal ligation for women. The effect is to prevent the union of sperm and ovum by impeding the normal progress of these substances through the vas deferens and the Fallopian tubes respectively. The procedures are alleged to have no effect of an adverse nature upon sexual functioning other than preventing conception.

Voluntary sterilization is indicated for socioeconomic, genetic, therapeutic, and personal reasons. It is generally thought unnecessary for husband and wife to undergo joint sterilization, since the failure rate is reputedly very small. As a form of contraception voluntary sterilization has been condemned by Roman Catholic moral theologians, and this attitude was maintained in the encyclical *Humanae Vitae*.

Roman Catholic males who undergo vasectomy could therefore experience guilt at having contravened their church's enactments, but Protestants would certainly not be affected in that manner. Those who adhere to sterilization procedures claim it is an efficient means of contraception and relieves married couples of nagging worries about economics should the wife become pregnant. Ethically the procedure has been criticized as providing pleasure without responsibility, but this is a specious argument since pleasure and responsibility are not normally associated in the minds of those involved in hedonism.

Quite clearly both parties must be in agreement with the concept of voluntary sterilization if only to avoid suspicion of infidelity on the part of the sterilized person later on. With the full cooperation of husband and wife, the surgeon is assured of legal protection for the sterilization procedures. Undoubtedly such steps constitute a sophisticated form of contraception which will commend itself to those who are otherwise inhibited by ecclesiastical pronouncements. It is a serious and dramatic decision, however, since the operation is generally regarded as permanent; and this fact should be considered by anyone contemplating voluntary sterilization.

Compulsory sterilization has been advocated periodically, and indeed enforced in some jurisdictions, for purposes of selective breeding such as the prevention of conception in feeble-minded women or as one form of treatment for sexual deviates. But many persons regard such a procedure as an unwarranted invasion of a person's privacy, a violation of rights, or some similar argument; and these arguments, allied with fears of genetic engineering or eugenics has made the concept generally unattractive.

See CONTRACEPTION; EUGENICS; GENETIC ENGINEERING.

**STEWARDSHIP.** A steward is someone who is responsible for the property of another. He has no legal claims on it; but, rather, he is in a position of trust, accountable to his superior. Stewardship, therefore, is the task of such an undertaking. In Scripture mankind is viewed as a steward of God's riches, ordered in the creation narrative to "subdue the earth, to till and keep it." This provides us with a unique and privileged responsibility to share in God's work of creation. At the heart of stewardship is an understanding of the "symbiosis" of all things, in which the whole of creation works harmoniously together.

Two aspects of stewardship stand out in Christian theology. First, we are, as individuals, answerable to God for the lives we lead. This is the area that is called personal ethics. Three examples of stewardship in this area may be given. First of all, we are accountable to God for the use of our time. The Israelites were commanded to give to God one day a week to spend in His company and worship Him. This was a day of re-creation (Exod. 20:10). Also, according to the Old Testament, we are accountable to God for the way we use our money. Again, the Israelites were given a guide. One-tenth of their goods was to be set aside for God as their tithe. It was, we must note, the "bottom line"; it was their duty. Actual self-giving began after they had given the tithe. Finally, the Old Testament clearly expected the people of God of offer their gifts and talents to Him (Exod. 28:3; 31:1-10).

The New Testament develops and intensifies personal stewardship quite significantly. Worship on the Lord's Day was clearly very important for the early Christians (Acts 2:42) but now because of the warm and personal relationship that existed between the Christian and his God life itself was worship, and true worship flowed from the believers' hearts and lives (Col. 3:16). The New Testament says very little about the tithe, but goes beyond it in terms of commitment (1 Cor. 8-9). The pattern for giving is now the radical self-offering of Christ. Sacrificial giving for the benefit of others must, Paul urges, be the way that Christians approach the distribution of their wealth. Perhaps it is in the area of talents, however, that the New Testament shows its greatest advance upon the Old Testament. All members of Christ's family have talents and abilities to offer, and we must use them generously in His service (1 Cor. 12).

The second level of stewardship in theology delves into social ethics. It is common to distinguish two aspects of social ethics. First of all, man's relationship to the rest of creation must be considered. In recent years there has been an urgent need to work out the ethics of our relationship with our environment. The sin of man is evident in the way in which nature is exploited for wrong reasons. Indeed, there is a striking relevance about the words uttered by Isaiah long ago: "The earth lies polluted under its inhabitants. For they have transgressed the laws and violated the statutes, broken the everlasting covenant. Therefore a curse devours the earth and the inhabitants suffer for their guilt" (24:5-6).

There has been for many years a growing realization that resources are running down, that pollution is growing, and that we are recklessly allowing technology to dictate the pathway of progress. The Christian shares in the dilemma facing mankind, namely, how may we maintain a proper, respectful attitude to creation while at the same time enjoying its fruits?

A second level of social ethics concerns our relationship to society and one another. It was common at one time in the Christian church to separate social and personal ethics. The personal was the concern of Christianity, but the social was the province of secular society. It is currently agreed by most thinking people, however, that we cannot separate life into such compartments. The demands of the gospel influence the way in which we live in society as well as our relationships with others. Thus, today we are more inclined to recognize the effect of sin in society that affects the structures of political and social life. We recognize that the equality of races, sexes, creeds, and colors (Gal. 3:28) must be allowed to make its profound and powerful impact upon society.

Stewardship, therefore, has important repercussions for both the individual and society. The Christian, basing his discipleship upon his Lord who went to the cross for the sake of others, will recognize, as Paul said long ago: "You have been bought with a price, so glorify God in your body" (1 Cor. 6:20).

G.C.

**STRIKES.** A strike occurs when a group of workers in industry or business refuses to continue with normal work in order to protest real or fancied injustices, actual or potential danger associated with working conditions, or more commonly to impress upon management the need for higher wages, more "fringe benefits," or improvements in other areas of work.

Strikes originated with the industrial revolution in nineteenth-century Britain, when employees formed trade unions in an attempt to force unconcerned owners of mines and factories to provide better working conditions for their employees. In Britain the trade unions also founded a political party, and this example was followed elsewhere in Europe. Early British socialists were often devoutly Christian individuals with a genuine altruistic concern for their fellows. But as the labor movement developed, the Christian social emphasis was largely replaced by purely political considerations, influenced by Marxist-Leninist ideology.

In the current free-enterprise system, relations between labor and management are dominated by the concept of collective bargaining. These procedures are initiated at the request of one or the other of the two parties, and the issues that are of concern are then discussed. Typically an offer is met by a counteroffer, and thereafter negotiations center upon the prospect of an agreement, which in the usual course of events involves concessions on both sides. If it proves impossible to reach a consensus, the labor representatives use the threat of a strike as their ultimate bargaining weapon. If it is still impossible for an agreement to be reached, the union involved authorizes the employees to withhold their services in the form of a strike.

This kind of action is controlled by law in Western countries, usually in the form of a Labor-Management Relations Act. Such legislation normally prescribes the procedures by which a strike may be called legally. If they are ignored or defied the consequent work stoppage is illegal, and the union responsible can be prosecuted under the law. Different employment situations result in various kinds of strikes. Where there is union-management disagreement about such matters as wages or working conditions, the strike is regarded technically as economic in nature. Where violations of legal enactments are alleged by unions, the proposed strike is based on allegations of unfair labor practices by management. Sometimes workers in a different area of industry are persuaded by their unions to demonstrate solidarity with another union that is on strike, and the resultant walkout is known as a sympathy strike.

In order to draw attention to their real or supposed grievances, striking unions are permitted by law to establish picket lines consisting of striking workers who carry placards and walk outside the factory or business involved. Picketing is normally controlled by law to ensure peaceful protests, but sometimes tempers flare and violence erupts. The number of pickets on duty at any one time can be limited by a court injunction in most jurisdictions. Some strikes are long and bitter, producing bad relations among the workers themselves as well as with management. On occasions strikers ultimately force a company to close its operations, an achievement which by any standards is a hollow victory.

Employers can also stage their own version of a strike, in which they simply close the factory or business; and this prevents employees from working until the matters at issue have been settled. This procedure is known as a *lockout*, which along with strikes is normally prohibited by law during the period of a previously established contract. In some countries strikes by public employees are illegal, while in totalitarian countries any kind of strike by members of the work force is prohibited on pain of severe reprisals.

During a strike, workers are usually supported financially from a strike fund established by the union, but such payments represent only a fraction of what the worker would normally earn. If a strike cannot be settled by labor and management, a mediator is frequently employed, or the matter is submitted to arbitration, either voluntary or through legislation. The decision of an arbitrator is then binding upon both parties.

Taking a cue from the labor movements, strike tactics have been employed by others besides industrial workers. Thus prisoners have gone on *hunger strikes* in prison, and some have even died in the process. University students and others have adopted a strike procedure known as the *sit-in*, whereby premises are invaded and occupied until whatever matter at issue was solved.

Since striking is the worker's ultimate weapon in the Western democracies, it is unlikely to be abandoned unless it is legislated out of existence. It is perhaps noteworthy that in Russia, whose political policies tend to be admired so much by socialists worldwide, all strikes are forbidden by law, and anyone found defying such enactments is dealt with summarily.

In the light of the democratic process, the individual Christian will need to evaluate the moral issues involved in striking. If the protest is to ensure safety and reasonable working conditions, the Christian might be justified in supporting such an endeavor. If, however, the strike mostly serves the interests of individual aggrandizement and does little or nothing for the benefit of the workers, its morality must be called into serious question. Workers need to remember that they are under a moral obligation to labor honestly and conscientiously for the wages that they receive and that any form of corruption, whether in the factory or the marketplace, is basically theft from an employer.

**SUBJECTIVISM.** In subjectivism, an action is ultimately rendered right or wrong by the approval of human beings, either individually (personal subjectivism) or collectively (societal subjectivism or cultural relativism). Accordingly, if individual response or societal consensus should change, then right and wrong change correspondingly.

Ethical subjectivism can take the form of asserting that moral propositions are true or false; but it can also add that, when there is variation in fundamental moral attitudes, truth varies from person to person or from culture to culture. Alternatively, it can take the form of an outright denial of any moral truth, only acknowledging personal or cultural tastes. In neither case, would it seem, is there an adequate basis for taking moral questions seriously. Indeed, moral seriousness presupposes that there is a significant and

important difference between actions that are right and actions that are wrong. But individual human will or social consensus is not adequate to account for that difference in a way that will retain the significance and importance that people see attaching to moral matters.

In contrast to ethical subjectivism, ethical objectivism asserts that moral propositions are rendered true or false by some fact independent of what human beings believe or approve. The Christian tradition is objectivist, affirming that the character of a loving and just God provides the standard for right and wrong, and good and evil, and stands in judgment of human response. Ethical subjectivism is, then, at odds with Christian belief.

Two considerations have prompted some Christians to become ethical subjectivists: first, the existence of widespread moral disagreement among persons and cultures, and, second, our inability to construct successful proofs for the first principles of morals. An argument based on the first consideration, however, is unsatisfactory. For, from the fact that different people or different cultures disagree over the correct answer to a moral question, it does not follow that there can be no ultimately correct answer to that question. The second argument is also inconclusive. The first principles of any discipline are beyond proof, including, for example, the first principles of logic or science. Being first principles, they are the ultimate court of appeal and thus not establishable in the same way that other beliefs are. This leads to the suggestion that, if we are to avoid total skepticism, there are some propositions that we know to be true independently of formal argument and proof-giving. The first principles of morals may be in this category.

R.W.

**SUFFERING.** This term originated from the Latin word *suffero,* meaning "to bear up" under something such as work or illness. In a nonphysical sense the Romans used the verb to describe an expense or a penalty that had been incurred. Such usage has laid the foundation for the common English understanding of suffering as the unpleasant things that an individual has to endure in life. Suffering is the common lot of humanity, although a large proportion of it is either unnecessary or largely imaginary.

The Scriptures base all of human suffering upon the pristine rebellion of our first parents against God's commands. Because of this simple act the whole face of nature was changed by being placed under a divine curse (Gen. 3:17), and human suffering began. It is well to reflect at this point upon the intense seriousness with which God regards his command for human obedience, and the dread consequences contingent upon disobedience. So much suffering has been caused unnecessarily over the centuries because human beings flatly refused to obey God's laws for behavior in human society. Those individuals who bleat the incessant question about how can God possibly be a God of love if he allows this or that calamity to happen either do not know or fail to remember that God punishes iniquity to the third and fourth generation of those who hate him (Exod. 20:5). But if we obey him and keep his commandments, he brings blessing, not calamity, upon us.

Some Christians are profoundly disturbed when suffering comes into their lives, imagining that they are somehow exempt from the consequences of human fallenness. By virtue of being human we are subjected, as is all of nature, to the law of entropy. This law can only be held in abeyance for individuals by an influx of power that will halt the process of inevitable deterioration, an eventuality for which a loving God has provided in the regenerating atonement of Jesus on the cross. But because we have altered the conditions of life as originally given and insist upon leading unnatural and unhealthy lives, we suffer the consequences of serious pollution of the human genetic reservoir, to say nothing of our own particular stupidities and ignorances. If only Christians were alert to these matters, much suffering would be avoided. This would include the tragedies of famine and death in Third World countries that are largely the result of fallacious political ideologies, corruption, and bad management.

Christians who encounter suffering in their lives despite their best attempts to avoid it should assess its nature and origins carefully, using professional help if necessary. The situation should then be committed to a loving heavenly Father in complete submission, with a prayer for his mercy and sustaining grace. Out of such a relationship will grow a greater awareness of the range and power of divine love that makes God's strength perfect in human weakness (2 Cor. 12:9) and shows, as with Job, the all-sufficiency of divine grace.

See EVIL; HOMELESSNESS; THIRD WORLD.

**SUICIDE.** Suicide is the deliberate taking of one's own life. It has long been considered immoral in the Christian moral tradition, at least since the Synod of Arles in A.D. 553. While not confirmed in Scripture, suicide seems to be prohibited by the Sixth Commandment, which prohibits murder, as suicide may plausibly be seen as murder of oneself (Deut. 5:17). Scripture may be ambiguous in its treatment of suicide, as in the story of Samson. While in captivity, Samson, praying for divine assistance, ended his life by pulling down the pillars of the Philistine temple, destroying himself along with the Philistines (Judg. 16). Similarly, Scripture seems to tolerate Saul's deliberate falling on his sword to keep from being captured and humiliated by the Philistines (1 Sam. 31:4).

From the standpoint of Christian ethics, however, Thomas Aquinas (1224-1274) argued that suicide was a sin against the natural law, which taught individuals to love themselves and further their own welfare. It was, as well, a sin against the community of which we are all in integral part, and a sin against God who has sole prerogative to determine when we are to die.

This Christian perspective shaped the historical position of the West. Christians rejected the Stoic notion that the option of suicide was an important element of freedom. It was not until David Hume's (1711–1776) famous counterargument that the traditional Christian view on suicide met with serious challenge. Hume's argument responds to each point of this tradition. He claimed that suicide is not an offense to God, since God's concern is only in maintaining the regular order of nature. The community's legitimate expectations toward an individual are reciprocal, and an individual is no more sinning against them by suicide than by emigration. The natural inclination to self-preservation, which formed the basis of Aquinas's claim that natural law prohibited suicide, established for Hume a belief that anyone seriously considering suicide must have very good reasons to overcome such a deep-seated urge. While Immanuel Kant (1720–1804) reaffirmed the strict prohibition on suicide, current secular thought seems more drawn to Hume's view that suicide can, at times, be morally acceptable.

Closely related to the question of suicide is that of the ethics of suicide prevention. Is it justifiable, and possibly even mandatory, for persons serving on behalf of society to act to prevent people from committing suicide? Some have argued that the individual's liberty is always to be respected in such decisions, at least when reasonably assumed that the decision is not based on delusions or emotional imbalance. Others have argued for paternalism of a limited sort, preventing such suicides either for the subjects own good, because the subject is irrational, or because of a desire to prevent a bad example for society.

This debate is relevant to the considerable philosophical, theological, and popular interests in the application of such questions of morality to certain bioethical dilemmas. These include the patient's possible right to refuse or demand cessation of life-prolonging treatment or to receive pain-reducing medications that have as a side effect the shortening of life. Much discussion surrounds the issue of voluntary euthanasia, the cessation of a patient's life at his or her own request, either by passively withholding treatment or actively instituting a death-dealing procedure. One of the most widely discussed suicide-related issues today is the so-called "Living Will," by which people express their desire not to receive extraordinary medical care to extend their lives should they come to suffer from any disease with a prognosis of death. In such areas, strongly held values in the contemporary moral arena, such as the individual's right to self-determination, come into conflict with concerns that might well lead to a general devaluing of human life.

**Bibliography**: Brandt, R. B., in Perlin, S., et al., (eds.), *A Handbook for the Study of Suicide* (1975); Donagan, A., *The Theory of Morality* (1977); Kant, I., *Lectures on Ethics*; Smedes, L., *Mere Morality* (1983).

D.B.F.

**SURROGATE MOTHERHOOD.** This expression has been used in the situation in which a couple is unable to have children, due to the wife's infertility of incapacity to carry a child to term. A second woman is impregnated with the husband's sperm through artificial insemination, bears the child, and relinquishes it at birth to the original couple, often in return for payment for her services. A variation of this involves the surrogate acting as "host womb" for a child of the couple, conceived through *in vitro* fertilization.

The chief legal issues involved are those of the legality and enforceability of the arrangements between the parties. Should a woman be permitted to contract to give up a baby she has borne and to receive money in return? Though numerous bills and reports have been presented in the U.S., Canada, and the U.K., there is, as yet, no specific legislation on the subject.

Those in favor of surrogate motherhood argue that the surrogate, as a free adult, should be able to enter into such a contract. Likewise, the father has a right to arrange the conception of his own child, to support the woman who bears it, and to receive, with his wife, custody of that child. Opponents argue that the practice is equivalent to baby-selling; offering money in conjunction with adoption is illegal in most jurisdictions. Present laws respond by turning a blind eye toward most problem-free transactions, which is facilitated if the participants falsify hospital and birth records in order to cover up the nature of the arrangement. If a dispute erupts between the parties, the case is handled by judges not as a contractual matter, but through a consideration of the best interests of the child involved, as in ordinary custody cases.

The clinical procedures of surrogate motherhood involve cooperation between a physician and a woman who has undertaken to accept AID (artificial insemination, donor) from the husband of a couple who have been prevented from conceiving their own child because of the wife's infertility. The introduction of the donor semen into the surrogate, or substitute, womb is a simple matter which may need to be repeated if ovulation has been mistimed. Otherwise pregnancy follows in the usual manner. Once the child has been born it is handed over to the adopting parents, who proceed to rear it as their own.

The ethical aspects of this matter came into prominence in England when Britain's first-known commercial surrogate mother gave birth to a baby girl for an American couple. This much-publicized case brought a demand from the Royal College of Obstetricians and Gynecologists that the use of surrogate mothers be barred in Britain. At a meeting in 1985 of the British Medical Association, doctors voted narrowly in favor of supporting surrogate births, but only "in select cases with careful controls." Meanwhile, legislation outlawing surrogate motherhood agencies and imposing jail sentences upon offenders was passed by the British parliament.

Part of the outcry resulted from the surrogate mother's admission that she was paid $8,300.00 by the American family for her services, which were offered for "love and money." In addition, the twenty-eight-year-old housewife received $22,000.00 from a sensationalist British tabloid to tell of her experiences through much of the pregnancy. The moral revulsion expressed in the ensuing outcry turned as much on the crass, mercenary instincts of the surrogate mother as upon the surrogate adultery involved. The Honorable. Norman Fowler, Britain's Social Services Minister, stated the feelings of most persons when, in presenting the legislation barring surrogate mother agencies in the United Kingdom, he said, "Surrogate motherhood for commercial gain is wrong."

Prior to the legislation being enacted, an American "womb leasing" agency based in Maryland was planning to expand its activities to Britain. The organization, known as the National Center for Surrogate Parenting, had apparently leased the wombs of two British women previously for American wives who were unable to carry a fetus to full term. British doctors have been divided in their approach to the medical ethics involved in surrogate motherhood, depending partly upon whether they believe that embryos constitute genuine human life from the moment of fertilization, or alternatively that they do not actually take on accredited human form until several weeks have elapsed after conception.

Another point at issue is the nature of the real mother, with many Christians and others insisting that the biological mother must always be deemed to be the true mother when the child is born, whether acting as surrogate or not. Many doctors regard AID as condoning adultery and are opposed to it on moral grounds. In addition, they feel that by supporting such a procedure they would be trafficking in the sale of babies, which in unlawful and offensive to medical ethics. Doctors in other parts of the world are having to grapple with the same social and ethical problems.

Viewed from a Christian standpoint, surrogate motherhood remains controversial. The earliest documented instances of the practice occurred in the Old Testament stories of Abraham, Sarah, and Hagar, and Jacob, Rachel, and Bilhah (Gen. 16:1; 21:9; 30:1). Surrogate motherhood could be considered an answer to the commandment "Be fruitful and multiply" (Gen. 1:28). The surrogate might equally be regarded as an example of Christian charity, providing the gift of life to a childless friend.

On the other hand, the practical details of surrogacy have been fraught with problems since the unhappy days of Hagar. In Old Testament times, surrogates were slaves. There is a danger that the agencies that organize most modern surrogate transactions may be similarly exploitative of disadvantaged women, just as they may prey upon desperate, childless couples. There is also a significant possibility in such an emotionally charged situation that someone will refuse to comply with the terms of the agreement. In the worst case scenario, this can leave the couple penniless, the surrogate emotionally scarred, and the child unwanted by either party.

The underlying theological argument against surrogate motherhood is grounded in the Christian view of marriage and the parent-child relationship. Surrogate motherhood seems to promote the view that a child is an object to be ordered from a catalogue of potential mothers. If the child does not meet the desired specifications, he may be deemed "inferior merchandise." Likewise, surrogate motherhood relies upon the notion that a third party may step in to fulfill the procreative function of marriage, doing so by giving up for money the child that through biology and birth is her own. Although assisting a couple in reproduction is certainly not contrary to Christian teaching, the commercialization of children, the trivialization of motherhood, and the significant imposition of an outsider into the marriage bond all suggest that surrogate motherhood may not be compatible with Christian beliefs.

**Bibliography:** Keane, N., *The Surrogate Mother* (1981); Mady, T., *American Journal of Law and Medicine* (1983), 7:524; O'Donovan, O., *Begotten or Made* (1984); Wadlington, W., *Virginia Law Review* (1983), 69:465.

See ARTIFICIAL INSEMINATION; GENETIC ENGINEERING; PARENTHOOD.

S.E.R.

**SYMPATHY.** This term is derived from the Greek verb *sumpatheo,* meaning "to suffer with" another person. Interestingly enough the verb appears once only in the New Testament, in Hebrews 10:34, relating to the sympathy which the recipients had extended to the author when he was "in bonds." Elsewhere the Greek follows the tradition of the Hebrew in expressing the emotional rapport of sympathy in terms of the "bowels" (Hebrew *rachamim*; Greek *splangchnoi*). The Hebrews associated certain physical organs with emotional states and not incorrectly assigned to the bowels the capacity for intense feeling, especially of compassion for others.

Following the example of Jesus (Matt. 9:36), Christians cherish sympathy as an essential ingredient of the moral and spiritual life. It arises out of a consciousness of altruistic love, because the believer realizes that he or she was once unworthy of Christ's gift of salvation (1 Pet. 2:10). Suffering with those who suffer (Rom. 12:15) is a manifestation of Christ's love to the world and a means of helping some in difficulty to bear a burden which might otherwise be crushing. By demonstrating genuine sympathy in this manner, the believer is fulfilling the law of Christ (Gal. 6:2).

# -T-

**TAXATION, ETHICS OF.** There is no agreed definition of the term *taxation.* It covers payments exacted by governments from persons within their power to pay governmental expenditure. In this sense, taxation is imposed on a person irrespective of the benefit he may or believes he may obtain from the authorities. A government may choose to use its revenues for defense, health, education, law and order, public works, or for the personal benefit of its rulers. Taxes are often levied on citizens or residents according to the value of their incomes, capital, or spending. These are direct taxes, paid by the person on whom the tax has been levied.

In another sense, taxation can be regarded as covering not only payments exacted by governments for general purposes, but also payments required by governments for particular rights, licenses, or benefits conferred. In the English courts, for instance, the cost of television licenses has been treated as a tax. Similarly, customs duties are considered a form of taxation. These types of taxes are often considered indirect taxes, passed on to the consumer rather than absorbed by the licensee or importer.

The ethical problems of taxation arise in four main areas; the limits of taxation; equality and taxation; freedom and avoidance; and the payment of taxes to immoral governments or to governments that use the money for evil ends.

*Limits of Taxation.* Taxation can be viewed both as a means of achieving social goals, such as the redistribution of wealth or the funding of worthwhile projects, and as a tool with which governments can attempt to control or direct economic activity. In either of these contexts, it is arguable that taxes may and should be levied until the general purpose for which they are imposed is achieved. Some questions arising in this area are whether governments can achieve such purposes through taxation and whether taxation is the most efficient method of achieving the desired result. Such questions, however, require pragmatic answers and belong to the study of economics. On these premises, taxation is regarded as a means to an end, the fundamental problem being the value of the end itself.

Against the view that taxation is merely a means to an end, it may be argued that excessive taxation is an attack on freedom and a disincentive to the hardworking. The argument on freedom will be considered under that heading. As regards any disincentive effects of high tax liabilities, it must be pointed out that there has been no clear proof that such effects occur.

*Equality and Taxation.* There are numerous classifications of taxes that can be levied by governments. Taxation may cover direct or indirect taxes, capital or revenue taxes, poll taxes, customs and excise duties, duties on particular goods and services manufactured in or entering into a territory, stamp duties, estate duties, capital transfer taxes, or property taxes. One purpose served by employing so many diverse taxes is that of spreading the burden throughout the community. Another purpose is that of ensuring that taxes are levied under circumstances suitable to the government.

There are so many methods of levying taxes, however, that, cumulatively, they can result in vast disparities between the amounts paid by some citizens and those paid by others. The question arises, therefore, as to whether there should be an equal imposition on everyone. Few governments could survive by levying the same duty on everyone, which could only be achieved by taxing all on the amount that the poorest could afford. It has to be accepted that equality in taxation does not mean that every person pays the same amount.

Another approach to a more equal taxation might be to charge a flat-rate tax on the income or capital assets of a person within that tax system. That procedure would not result in equality of payment, but would enable everyone to pay an equal percentage of their income or net worth. Each would pay according to his or her means. Once more, however, the problem would be either a low rate of tax or a heavy rate on the poor.

In most of the states of America a sales tax is levied on goods and services at a flat rate. Each state, however, sets its own rate. In European, countries this is called "value added tax" or "VAT." The total sales tax that a person pays in one year depends upon how much he or she spends. Such a tax is often criticized because, although it is levied at one rate for all and, in that sense, seeks equality, it nonetheless affects rich and poor in different ways. The rich pay according to the amount they choose to spend on luxury items and the poor pay according to the amount they must spend on necessities. Exemptions for certain classes of necessities do not wholly ameliorate the harsh effects of the tax on the poor, and in part create benefits for the wealthier members of society.

Generally, the modern state uses a variety of taxes, many of which are imposed by reference to scales that increase as wealth increases. It should not, however, be assumed that all the wealthy pay the largest tax bills. Through the use of tax havens and avoidance schemes, rich members of society are often able to reduce their tax burdens substantially. A gap may exist between the aims of a tax system and its realities.

There is another aspect of the problem of equality that cannot be ignored. The effect of tax policies is not only felt in the amount taken from citizens, but also in the benefits conferred on citizens. Taxation cannot usefully be analyzed on its own. It must be regarded as a part of the total operation of the state.

A knowledge of what a system achieves is a matter for economists and social scientists. Whether these achievements are good or just is a matter of moral and political debate.

*Freedom, Taxation, and Avoidance of Payment.* Taxation has been an instrument of governments throughout recorded history. Attitudes concerning taxation and the willingness or unwillingness to pay have been wide ranging. They have generally depended upon all other contemporary attitudes toward government.

One of the cornerstones of the American Revolution was a defiance of "taxation without representation." The colonists objected to the British Empire's levy of taxes upon them with neither their knowledge nor consent. Until the mid-eighteenth century, the colonies had been responsible for their own taxes and revenues. The colonists' reaction to newly imposed taxes was more than tax avoidance—it was tax rebellion.

Attitudes within the post-Colonial United States have also been wide ranging. Supreme Court Chief Justice John Marshall once said, "The power to tax is the power to destroy." A later member of the Supreme Court, Oliver Wendell Holmes, however, said, "Taxes are the price we pay for civilization."

Income tax is one of the easiest taxes to avoid. Britain has had the longest history of income taxes. Introduced in 1799, the tax existed on and off until it became permanent in 1842. During the 1930s, the Duke of Westminster won an important legal case in which the courts asserted the freedom of anyone to avoid paying taxes. On the basis of this case, there arose in Britain a massive tax avoidance industry in the 1960s and 1970s, employing schemes known as artificial avoidance schemes. Faced with such a massive growth in avoidance, which appeared to undermine the integrity of the tax system, the courts overruled their decision in the Duke of Westminster case. As a result, tax avoidance schemes began to prove ineffective.

The United States has had a shorter, if no less troublesome, history of income tax. Some income taxes were used as a measure to raise revenue during the Civil War, but it was not until 1913, with the sixteenth amendment to the United States Constitution, that income tax became permanently legal. Its top rate was a mere 6 per cent on income above $500,000. The American tax system evolved, initiating tax withholding as a war-time measure during World War II. The tax laws have been often amended since that time,

bowing to the pressures of special interest groups. Cries for tax reform and fairness become more and more frequent as wealthy individuals and corporations can, by using legal loopholes and tax shelters, pay very little tax or avoid payment altogether.

In moral terms, it may be possible to object to British artificial avoidance schemes and American loopholes and tax shelters on the grounds that the manipulation of law by artificial means involves some degree of pretense. Another objection is that excessive avoidance of payment can destroy the system, and, with it, the concept of government itself. It is, probably, not sufficient to reply that such avoidance of payment is part of a person's freedom.

*Payment of Taxes to Immoral Governments.* Recent protests about the activities of governments in areas such as nuclear arms, chemical warfare, nuclear power, and abortion have caused members of various pressure groups to attract publicity by withholding tax. In some instances, it has been argued that a person is not obliged to pay taxes to governments that perpetrate evil acts. The arguments that play a large part in this debate concern the relationship of the individual to law and to the state. In particular, the moral argument rests on whether it is ever right to break the law.

In religious terms, some would assert with Peter and John, "Judge for yourselves whether it is right in God's sight to obey you rather than God" (Acts 4:19). The problem with the use of this quotation is that we cannot always tell which action is "right in God's sight." The quotation was also a declaration to a religious authority rather than a secular one.

Others would argue that Jesus paid taxes to the authority which committed the ultimate evil of crucifying Him. One should rely on Jesus' words in Matthew 22:21: "Give to Caesar what is Caesar's, and to God what is God's." Yet again, Paul's contention in Romans 13:1-7 appears to support payment:

> "This is also why you pay taxes, for the authorities are God's servants, who give their full time governing. Give everyone what you owe him. If you owe taxes, pay taxes; if revenue, then revenue."

M.H.J.

**TECHNOLOGY, ETHICS OF.** Technology is the systematic modification of the environment for human ends. Often it is a process or activity that extends or enhances a human function. A microscope, for example, extends man's perception. A tractor extends man's physical ability. A computer extends his ability to calculate. Technology also includes devices that make physical processes more efficient. The many chemical processes we use to make products fit this description of technology.

The biblical mandate for developing and using

technology can be found in Genesis 1:28. God gave us dominion over the land, and we are obliged to wisely use and manage these resources in building His kingdom. God's ideal was not to have a world composed exclusively of primitive areas. Before the Fall (Gen. 2:15), Adam was to cultivate and keep the garden. Today we are still called to apply technology to this fallen world that groans in travail (Rom. 8:22). Technology can benefit man in exercising proper dominion, and thus remove some of the effects of the Fall (such as by curing disease or breeding better crops).

The Bible provides a number of important principles for using the earth's resources in an ecologically sound and responsible manner. For example, the Israelites were instructed to bury their waste (Deut. 23:13), to practice soil conservation (Lev. 25:1-23), to conserve trees (Deut. 20:19-20), and periodically to rest the animals (Exod. 23:12).

Technology in and of itself is neither good nor evil. The world view behind the particular technology determines its value. In the Old Testament, technology was used both for good (the building of the ark in Gen. 6) and for evil (the building of the Tower of Babel in Gen. 11). Therefore, the focus should not be so much on the technology itself as upon the philosophical motivation behind its use. Here are three important principles that should be considered.

First, technology should be seen as a tool, not as an end in itself. There is nothing sacred about technology. Unfortunately, our culture tends to rely on it more than is appropriate. If a computer, for example, proves a particular point, we have a greater tendency to believe it than if the answer was a well-reasoned conclusion from a person. If a machine can do the job we are prone to mechanize, even if human labor does a better or more creative job. We have come to the place where we have unconsciously placed machines over man. We are their servants rather than they ours.

We often look today only to science and engineering to solve problems that may be due to human sinfulness (wars, prejudice, greed), the fallenness of the world (death, disease), or God's curse on Adam (finite resources). In Western culture especially, we tend to believe that technology will save us from our problems and thus use technology as a substitute for God. Christians must not fall into this trap, but instead we must exhibit our ultimate dependence upon God. Moreover, we must differentiate between problems that demand a technological solution and ones that can be remedied by a social or spiritual one.

Second, technology should be applied in different ways according to specific situations. For example, there are distinctions between man and animal that, because we are created in God's image (Gen. 1:27), call for different applications of medical science. Just because artificial insemination is used to improve the genetic fitness of livestock does not justify using it on human beings. Just because we can do something does not mean we should do it.

Another important aspect of this principle is to recognize the diversity of cultural and social contexts. American farmers may use a high-energy, green revolution-type of agriculture, but that does not mean it is the best form of agriculture to export worldwide.

Many commentators, most notably E. F. Schumacher, have focused upon the notion of appropriate technology. In Third World countries, for example, sophisticated energy and capital-intensive, sophisticated forms of agriculture may be inappropriate for the culture as it presently exists. Industrial advance often brings social disruption and increasing havoc to a society. These countries must use caution in choosing the appropriate steps to industrialize, lest they be greatly harmed in the process.

Third, ethics, rather than technology, must determine the direction of our society. Jacques Ellul has expressed the concern that technology moves society instead of vice versa. Today we seem all too motivated by a technological imperative in our culture. A technological ability to do something is not the same as a moral imperative to do it. Technology should not determine ethics.

We possess the technological ability to be gods, but we lack the capacity to act like such. Too often, man has tried to use technology to become God. He uses it to work out his own physical salvation, to enhance his own evolution, or even to attempt to create life. Christians who take seriously human fallenness (Gen. 3), will humbly admit that we often do not know enough about God's creation always to use technology wisely. Because we take human sinfulness seriously, we will be careful to prevent the use of technology for greed and exploitation.

Technology's fruits can be both sweet and bitter. Christians must bring strong biblical critique to each technological advance and analyze its impact. In so doing, we will help ensure the positive effects of technology, restraining negative ones by setting up appropriate constraints against abuse.

**Bibliography:** Ellul, J., *The Technological Society* (1964); Elsdon, R., *Bent World* (1981); Schaeffer, F., *Pollution and the Death of Man* (1970); Schumacher, E. F., *Small Is Beautiful* (1973); Wilkinson, L., (ed.), *Earthkeeping: Christian Stewardship of Natural Resources* (1980).

See COMPUTER ETHICS; ECOLOGY.

J.K.A.

**TELEOLOGICAL ETHICS.** Teleological theorists argue that all moral decisions should aim at consequences such as pleasure, happiness, or self-realization (ends hereafter designated as "happiness"). They claim that people naturally seek such things, and they challenge nonteleological moralists to justify the moral life without appealing to such consequences. Kant nearly succeeds in doing so, but even he argues that dutiful persons ultimately are rewarded with happiness. Apparently, consequences must be considered in moral judgments. The best reply to teleologists may be Bishop Butler's, in *A Dissertation upon the Nature of Virtue.* Presenting counterexamples of cases in which an act of fraud or violence could produce greater general happiness than could an act of honesty or kindness, he argues that our conscience and duty would still compel obedience.

Since happiness and duty both provide moral constraints, how can we choose between them? The accepted philosophical wisdom has been that happiness emerges as a quality of the moral life. Virtuous living provides happiness. Aristotle states this clearly in the *Nichomachean Ethics,* Book X. Despite this, however, virtuous people often suffer. The belief that happiness ultimately supervenes upon morality, therefore, must be either assumed as a metaphysical principle or accepted on faith. Kant holds it as a metaphysical principle. Paul, however, embraces it through faith, declaring that, "...all things work together for good to them that love God" (Rom. 8:28). This emphasizes duty rather than consequences, not telling us to love God in order to achieve happiness, but to trust that happiness will accompany commitment in the love of God.

Christian morality is therefore not teleological, aiming at neither happy results here, nor "pie in the sky" hereafter. Instead, Christians follow the priorities set by our Lord: "But seek ye first the Kingdom of God and his righteousness; and all these things shall be added unto you" (Matt. 6:33).

**Bibliography:** MacIntyre, A., *A Short History of Ethics* (1966); Melden, A. I., *Ethical Theories* (1967).

J.R.H.

**TELEVISION.** Television is an audiovisual medium of communication, programmed by a variety of corporations (at present commercial, public, governmental, religious, local cable, and pay television). It has grown over the last thirty years to dominate other means of communication in North America and to replace newspapers as the medium first in the public favor.

*Purpose.* The primary programming purpose of commercial and pay television, which is controlled by profit-seeking corporations, appears to be popular entertainment employing fiction, fantasy, and athletic competition. Other purposes include instruction, the influencing of public opinion, and the creation of markets for products.

American public television, which is supported by charitable contributions and government subsidies, tends to have different emphases: children's programming, news and public affairs, and a variety of forms of artistic and cultural entertainment. Where commercial television attempts to appeal to the widest possible audience, public television targets quite specific groups ("narrowcasting").

Governmentally sponsored television, for example, corporations like the British Broadcasting Corporation and the Canadian Broadcasting Corporation, combine educational and entertainment purposes. They may also have purposes of political policy; for example, the CBC is mandated to promote national unity and Canadian cultural expression.

Cable television, which is controlled by publicly licensed private companies, is usually required to provide opportunities for programming by community organizations.

Whether the purpose of religious television is to be seen primarily as public service or private aggrandizement depends on a number of theological presuppositions. There is little evidence to suggest that the "electronic church" has led people toward a deeper commitment to a community of faith. On the contrary, it has possibly privatized religious involvement and siphoned religious donations to itself, away from broader, mission-oriented giving.

*Effects.* Television has helped democratize entertainment by giving wide access to high-priced performances. It can be a companion (though sometimes a crutch) for the lonely and the infirm. It has at times sensitized the public conscience to important world events; for example, its coverage of the American war in Vietnam during the 1960s may well have hastened an end to that conflict. Cable television can give minorities access to a wider public, and noncommercial television has become a primary instrument of education both for children and adults.

According to research into viewing habits, television has a diversionary effect on viewers. They tend to decide first whether to watch, and only then what to watch. Partly because of this tendency, television programming has entered into people's lives in ways they do not always recognize and has reshaped their perceptions and values.

For a first example, television has in the past generation reshaped political reality. Fifteen-second film clips on the evening news and selective broadcast reporting are major contributors to our perception of our social context and the public "images" of politicians. Television journalism fights for freedom but does not always report the news responsibly, being often influenced by theological, national, racial, gender, political, cultural, and economic biases. Commercial television tends either to sensationalize or avoid controversial topics, neglecting complex or nonvisual ones. Curiously, although television is the main source of political information, it apparently fails to increase interest in politics.

Second, television has not only reinforced social values connected with the interests of those who control it, but it has created new values through a slow and subtle process of conditioning. The depiction of illegal or socially unacceptable means to achieve socially approved ends is common. The portrayal of a limited number of occupations—such as law enforcement and crime, medicine and other professions, and idleness based on independent wealth—encourages viewers to depart from reality into the fantasy of violence, of upper status, and of freedom from economic restraint. There is evidence that television increases aggression by depicting hostile acts, frequently in a favorable light, and by devaluing gentleness. (Public pressure may perhaps have helped reduce depictions of killings, but portrayals of other forms of brutality have probably increased.) Television may also contribute to the early sexual focus of children.

Third, it has formed attitudes toward groups of people. Minorities, the elderly, and children, for example tend to be stereotyped. Women are portrayed in programming and commercials to a large extent as sexual objects, as victims or as supporters of the male characters, and only rarely in professional roles.

Fourth, television guides daily decision making, for example, by weather reports, by commercials and programming related to diet, exercise, and nutrition, and by its timetabling of popular programs. Family conflict over viewing habits often leads to the purchase of separate sets or to power struggles, breaking down family harmony.

Fifth, television usurps time available for other activities, such as church involvement, charitable activities, educational or cultural events, homework, music, conversation, social gatherings, travel, movies, household tasks, or sleeping.

*Response.* When used discriminatingly by a family and as a basis for family discussion, television can be a helpful educational tool. Noncommercial television, as well as public service programming on commercial television, can provide helpful programming for a variety of age, interest, ethnic, and ability and disability groups. It can further the general welfare and model the values of human diversity, imagination, initiative, and excellence.

Studies show that advertising and depictions of sex and violence are widely criticized by the viewing public, who are especially concerned with possible effects on children. Many would like to see television meet a wider variety of educational goals, especially adult vocational and personal development.

For the Christian in particular, there is much in television programming that raises questions. The depiction of humanity is frequently brutalizing; faith is neglected or trivialized; and social values are subordinated to profitability or a self-serving sense of artistic license.

In pastoral counseling of families with problems, pastors should watch for the influence of television upon the children in the area of rela-tionships, particularly among their peers and with members of the opposite sex. Removing television for a short or prolonged period may be a help in "normalizing" childhood development and stabilizing family life.

In the public forum, Christians should oppose repugnant programming and promote education about values that are essential to the Christian faith.

**Bibliography:** Comstock, G., *et al., Television and Human Behaviour* (1978); Macy, J. W., Jr., *To Irrigate a Wasteland* (1974).

M.M.M-H.

**TEMPER.** In an ethical and psychological sense this word is used of the personality to describe either a positive or negative condition of composure. In the former, temper is described as *good* when it is characterized by kindness, love, peace, generosity, consideration, and the like, and *bad* when the personality exhibits such negative reactions as anger, hatred, malice, bitterness, and cognate emotions. The Christian is urged to develop and express the graces of the Holy Spirit (Gal. 5:22-23) as contrasted with the evidences of bad temper (Eph. 4:31-32). The King James Version used the term *temper* on four occasions (Exod. 29:2; 30:35; Ezek. 46:14; 1 Cor. 12:24) in a nonpsychological sense to describe mixing or mingling.

**TEMPERANCE.** This noun is derived from the Latin verb *tempero*, which means variously "to keep in due proportion, to regulate, to exercise forbearance," and "to abstain," all of which express the sense of control or moderation. The idea of temperance as a rigorously supervised way of life is seen in such Old Testament movements as the Nazirites (Num. 6) and the Rechabites of Jeremiah's day (Jer. 35). The latter were stern advocates of desert mores, including abstention from wine, in contrast to the luxury of upper-class life in pre-exilic Judah, thereby reinforcing the strictures of prophets such as Amos (4:1; 6:4-7). The concept of the Christian exercising self-control in sexual matters was stressed by Paul (1 Cor. 7:9) and was included among the graces evident in Christian character (Gal. 5:23, "temperance," KJV, "self-control," NKJV).

Temperance has long been used to describe movements to combat alcohol, and in the minds of some has come to be synonymous with total abstinence. This can hardly be supported by Scripture, however, even though the Nazirites and Rechabites were abstainers. Rather, the idea of the moderate use of alcohol of those who are able to tolerate it is seen in Paul's medicinal remedy for Timothy's dyspepsia (1 Tim. 5:23). Even Jesus drank wine without renunciation or complaint at different times in his ministry. Temperance is best understood in the Latin sense of keeping things in due proportion, which brings an ethical dimension to all habitual processes.

**TEMPTATION.** It is important to distinguish two primary meanings of this term in biblical and Christian usage: testing or proving someone or something without inducement to sin, and enticing someone or being enticed to sin.

In the Old Testament God tested individuals, such as Abraham (Gen. 22:1), and nations, such as Israel (Deut. 8:2; 13:3). These tests were not intended to undermine faith, but to rebuke unbelief and confirm faith. In the New Testament Christians may be allowed by God to undergo testing, most notably persecution. James 1:12-15 and 1 Corinthians 10:1-13, often wrongly thought to center upon sinful appetite or sinful enticement, refer primarily to the allurement of apostasy as a result of persecution or extreme hardship. Christians should be ready for the test of persecution (Matt. 6:13; James 1:2-4). The prayer "lead us not into temptation, but deliver us from evil" (Matt. 6:23) may refer to such testing. It is always wrong, however, for man to test God (Matt. 4:7; Exod. 17:7).

Enticement to sin is the more common understanding of temptation. Being tempted without succumbing to the temptation is not sin. God does not tempt to evil (James 1:13). However, succumbing to temptation in the heart is sin (Matt. 5:28). Thus, mind-set, inclination, and intention are important. Fondling temptation entails consent to sinning.

The incarnate Lord is presented strikingly in the Bible as the second Adam, which metaphor includes His triumph over the tempter and temptation. He has set a new path for a new humanity (Col. 2:12) and is the file leader of the new race (Heb. 4:14-15). He has fully experienced our condition and can now help us sympathetically in times of testing (Heb. 2:18).

Since early Christian times expositors have recognized in Scripture a link between Adam's temptation, Christ's temptation in the wilderness, and temptations the Christian undergoes. Indeed, among the early church fathers, Christ was seen to be the second Adam, defeating Satan on the same ground on which man's first parents fell morally. A parallel may thus be drawn between "good for food," "pleasant to the eye," and "to make one wise" (Gen. 3:6); the three temptations of Jesus (Matt. 4:1-11); and the evil trilogy of the lust of the flesh, the lust of the eye, and the pride of life (1 John 2:16-17).

Christ's victory over the kingdom of evil has taken place through the perfection of His humanity, His incorruptible death on the cross, and His resurrection. The Christian, therefore, should enter the fray of life confident that victory over the powers of evil is already behind his back. Hence the strong urging to "resist the devil and he will flee from you" (James 4:7).

Modern understanding of human nature rarely includes advice to resist temptation, especially with regard to appetite. With human nature being viewed purely behaviorly, gratification of appetites is said to be no more and no less moral than any body function. Christians, however, refuse to reduce all human acts to such a nonmoral footing. Lust is a morally qualified feeling that is sinful (Matt. 26:41; James 1:14).

Others discourage resistance to temptation on psychological grounds, claiming that resistance causes repression and that repression causes neurosis, unhealthy fantasy, and isolation, which may lead to violence. Here the Christian replies that guilt and neurosis are not caused by restraint, but are the consequence of dalliance with and succumbing to temptation. The best antidote to immoral allurement of any kind is to fasten the mind upon that which is good (Gal. 5:16-26).

**Bibliography:** Fairlie, H., *The Seven Deadly Sins Today* (1978); Neill, S., *The Christian Character* (1955); Olsson, K. A., *Seven Sins and Seven Virtues* (1959); Pieper, J., *The Four Cardinal Virtues* (1966).

S.J.M.

**TEN COMMANDMENTS.** These injunctions, sometimes known as the Decalogue (a Greek expression meaning "ten words"), are vital to Christian ethics. They are recorded twice in the Old Testament (Exod. 20:1-17; Deut. 5:6-21), quoted as authoritative by Jesus Christ (Mark 10:18-19), and cited by theologians and church leaders throughout subsequent history as a concise summary of God's demands for human behavior.

The Old Testament stresses the importance of the Decalogue in several striking ways. Unlike any other part of the revealed law, these commandments were spoken directly by God to the people of Israel (Exod. 19:16) and written by His hand on stone (Exod. 32:15; Deut. 4:13). The accompanying audiovisual phenomena (thunder, lightning, earthquake, and trumpet blast) ensured that everyone realized an event of momentous significance was taking place. After the first two tables were broken by Moses in anger at the people's apostasy during his absence (Exod. 32:19), God provided a second set (Exod. 34:1), which were later deposited, on His instructions, in the ark of the covenant as its sole original contents (Exod. 25:16; 40:20).

Scholarly debate continues about the origin and literary history of the Decalogue, but its centrality is not in dispute. As a foundational statement of God's will it was accepted in Old Testament times as definitive (Deut. 5:22). Though not strictly a law code in the modern, technical sense (in that it lacks detail and penalty clauses), it formed the basis of the main blocks of civil and criminal law set out in Exodus, Leviticus, and Deuteronomy. It also sharpened the divinely revealed messages of the prophets (Jer. 7:9; Hos. 4:2; 13:4) and aided the psalmists as they sang of God's majesty and royal demands (Pss. 50; 81).

As far as the numbering of the commandments is concerned, the Bible leaves some room for flexibility, providing three main traditions. Orthodox Judaism regards the historical prologue (Exod. 20:2) as the first commandment and combines the prohibition of false gods and image-worship as the second. Roman Catholics and Lutherans also treat the vetos on other gods and images as a single commandment (the first), but divide the closing ban on coveting into two (the ninth and tenth). The Greek Orthodox and Protestant Reformed traditions treat the prohibition of coveting as one (the tenth) and divide the opening commandments on false gods and images (the first and the second).

These differences are not crucial, but they can lead to misunderstanding. The seventh commandment, for example, will convey "stealing" to a Roman Catholic and "adultery" to a Reformed Protestant. This article will use the third of the numbering schemes listed above.

The two versions of the Decalogue (in Exod. 20 and Deut. 5) do not differ in the content of the commandments themselves, but do have important variations in the wording of the supportive material. One significant difference is in the order of people and property listed in the tenth commandment. In the Exodus version *wife* comes after *house*, while in Deuteronomy the order is reversed—probably to counter any impression that a wife was of no more value than part of her husband's property.

The other most interesting variation is in the reason given for obeying the sabbath commandment. In Exodus the focus is on creation, with a reminder of the Lord's work and rest recorded in Genesis. In Deuteronomy the spotlight falls on redemption, as readers are reminded of the Lord's mighty rescue of Israel from Egypt.

*The doctrinal base.* This double support for the fourth commandment, highlighting the doctrines of creation and redemption, vividly exposes the theological foundations on which the whole Decalogue is built. It also helps account for the Christian conviction that these commandments can never become obsolete. The doctrine of creation is fundamental to Christian ethics. Because man and woman are created in God's image (Gen. 1:27), the "good" in them is always what reflects His character. And because the Creator set out a fundamental pattern for human behavior and lifestyle from the beginning, the "right" thing for men and women to do is always that which best accords with their Maker's instructions.

Both motifs appear strongly in the Decalogue. Indeed, it is possible to trace the roots of each of the commandments to the biblical account of creation. In addition to the explicit appeal to the Lord's sabbath rest in the fourth commandment, there is an echo of the creation of human sexuality in the seventh (Gen. 2:18-24) and an implicit reference to the divine image in the sixth (Gen. 9:6). The tenth commandment even has a verbal link with the account in Genesis of mankind's first failure. The word for *covet* (Hebrew *cha-mad*) in Exodus 20 is the same as the word for "desire" in Genesis 3:6.

The Decalogue, then, is a republication and reinforcement of the morality of creation. The fact that most of its commandments are reflected in nonbiblical texts from the ancient Near East should not surprise us. Nor should Amos's assumption that pagan nations ought to observe them (Amos 1:1—2:3). The Ten Commandments "ring bells" in the minds of non-Jews and non-Christians of all cultures and generations, simply because they express rules for living that their Creator provided for them.

Tertullian, the third-century catechist from North Africa, saw this link between creation and the Decalogue especially clearly. The Ten Commandments, he declared, were written on the hearts of men long before they were engraved on blocks of stone. Centuries later, Thomas Aquinas, in his exposition of natural law suggested that the commandments were given only to remind men and women of the duties that their sin had obscured.

If the doctrine of creation undergirds the Decalogue, the doctrine of redemption does so even more explicitly. Significantly, the commandments are prefaced by a reminder of the way in which God rescued His people from slavery in Egypt—a single verse in Exodus (20:2) and four whole chapters in Deuteronomy (1—4). This, as Alec Vidler puts it, is "the proclamation of the divine indicative on which all human imperatives depend." God's act of redeeming love came first. His demands followed.

This order is important. God did not impose the Ten Commandments on Israel arbitrarily or capriciously, demanding the nation's obedience in the face of terrible sanctions. He acted first in saving grace, and only then spelled out the ways in which His redeemed people could respond freely and gratefully to His love. Those who kept His commandments were those who loved Him (Exod. 20:6; John 14:15).

Such is the language of covenant relationship. The Decalogue is, in fact, often described by the Old Testament with covenant terminology; sometimes as "the words of the covenant" (Exod. 34:28; Deut. 4:13), and at other times as "the tables of the covenant" (Deut. 9:9, 11, 15). Seen in this light, Jesus' choice of two love commandments to sum up the Decalogue's demands becomes strikingly logical (Mark 12:29; see Deut. 6:4; Lev. 19:18). The Ten Commandments set out the parameters for maintaining a healthy relationship with God and with other people. Some scholars think that they were used liturgically in Old Testament times to remind worshipers of their covenant God's "entry requirements," always to be met if they were to enjoy genuine fellowship with their Redeemer.

*Interpretation and Application.* As demonstrated, the roots of the Ten Commandments lie deep in the doctrines of creation and redemption. That is enough to persuade Christians of their contemporary relevance, both to the church and to secular society. It does not, however, always explain how they should be interpreted and applied.

The culture gap that separates Old Testament times from our own is nowhere more apparent than in the detailed wording of the second, fourth, and tenth commandments. People in Western society do not, as a rule, make idols out of wood or stone. Nor do very many of them work a six-day week, have a manservant, or own an ass. The fact that the Ten Commandments allude to the particulars of everyday life is a salutary reminder that every thought, word, and action matters to God. But it also highlights the uncomfortable truth that some of the Decalogue's details do not apply strictly to life in an industrial society today.

An important point in understanding the Decalogue is that the covenant love that motivates Christians is not quite the same as the gratitude that originally inspired obedience to the Ten Commandments. Christians look to the cross of Christ for their redemption, not to the Exodus from Egypt. There is discontinuity, as well as continuity, between the old covenant and the new, and the Christian has to approach the Decalogue with the mind of Christ.

The interpreter's main task is first to discover how a particular commandment was understood in its original context, and then to discern the basic moral principle it expresses. That principle (or "middle axiom") can be related to the conditions of a different culture, allowing specific application to be made. The underlying principle is like an unchanging chapter heading. The chapter itself has to be rewritten for every age.

We find this hermeneutical process at work in the Bible itself. In First Timothy, for example, Paul parallels the Decalogue closely (without quoting it) in explaining the right use of the Old Testament law (1:8). He takes the seventh commandment as a ban on homosexual practice, as well as on adultery, and he uses the eighth to cover kidnapping—a refined form of stealing prevalent in Ephesus, the city in which Timothy was working.

The interpreter must bear four things especially in mind as he applies the Ten Commandments to his contemporary culture: (a) *Their Theocentric Emphasis.* As in the Sermon on the Mount, duty to God and duty to neighbor interlock in the Decalogue. It is simply not possible to split the religious from the ethical without severely mutilating the whole. (b) *Their Positive Implications.* The majority of the commandments are cast in a negative form. That was necessary in order to curb human lawlessness and to preserve the freedom God had gained for His people. But, latent in each negative there is a positive. As the Westminster Larger Confession puts it, "where a sin is forbidden, the contrary duty is commanded." (c) *Their Social Dimension.* Although each commandment is set in the singular,

the "You" is addressed to Israel as a corporate personality. The Decalogue's precepts are for social as well as for personal morality. (d) *The Priority of Attitudes.* As they are phrased, all but one of the commandments (the tenth) deal with deeds and words. Jesus, however, exposed inward motives and attitudes that lead to the actions that the Decalogue condemns (Matt. 5:21-28). In so doing, he laid bare the Decalogue's deeper meaning and sharpened its challenge.

With these guidelines, we can attempt an outline analysis of the commandments themselves and set up some signposts for their contemporary application.

*Analysis.* The first commandment sets the theocentric tone for all that follows. The distinctive mark of Jewish and Christian ethics is that God's character and will determine what is good and right. The Israelites were surrounded by people who worshiped different deities of nature, which set conflicting ethical standards (Hos. 4:11-14). They themselves, in contrast, were called to serve the one supreme God who allowed no competitors and laid down His own high, coherent set of obligations. Jesus stressed the positive side to this commandment by highlighting the love-demand of Deuteronomy 6:4 (Mark 12:30). Refraining from polytheism is an inadequate response unless it is matched by devoted commitment to the Lord.

The second commandment shifts the focus from the object of people's worship to the way in which they conduct it. In Old Testament times, the purpose of making an image was to enlist the deity's help to bless and protect. In other words, the aim was not to serve but to control. The Lord makes it clear in this commandment that His power can never be manipulated to serve human ends. Today, it is common to create mental images of the Almighty. Many can cope with the idea of a God who is indulgent and tolerant, but find it hard to accept the picture drawn here of a God whose love burns so powerfully that those who commit spiritual adultery suffer his lasting judgment (which is one possible meaning behind the Hebrew word for *jealous*).

The third commandment and the entire Bible take names seriously. The name of a person expressed his or her character. The Lord's name, therefore, stands for His Person (Pss. 20:1; 22:22; Mic. 4:5; John 1:12). To use His name superficially or contemptuously (*vain* means "empty") is to insult Him. One of the more obvious ways of disobeying this commandment was to use the divine name to fortify a promise that was then broken (Lev. 19:12; Eccl. 5:1-6). Jesus exposed the hypocrisy that marked this practice (Matt. 5:33-37).

The fourth commandment sets out the value and the danger of work. Both in its unfashionable description of God as a worker (Ps. 8:3, 6) and in its outspoken attacks on laziness (Prov. 6:6-11; 2 Thess. 3:6-12), the Bible underlines heavily the value of work for human fulfillment. But each version of this commandment makes it clear that work must be balanced by rest and relaxation. God set the example Himself in creation (Exod. 20:11), and at the time of the Exodus He rescued his people from a life of forced labor (Deut. 5:15). There is an implied challenge here to some aspects of the traditional "Protestant work ethic" and the beginnings of a much-needed Christian doctrine of leisure.

Is Sunday the Christian sabbath? Opinions within the churches differ. The New Testament never makes an explicit link between the sabbath and the Lord's Day (compare Gal. 4:8-11; Col. 2:16 with Acts 20:6-12; 1 Cor. 16:1-4; Rev. 1:10). Yet Sunday, the day of Jesus' resurrection, is the supremely appropriate day of the week for Christians to celebrate their redemption.

In the fifth commandment, the word *honor* means "treat as of weighty importance," and the theme of respect for parents figures strongly in both Old Testament and New (Lev. 19:3; Eph. 6:1). Those who despise their parents (or worse) were subject to severe penalties under Old Testament law (Exod. 21:15; Lev. 20:9). Such callous conduct in family life amounts, the New Testament adds, to a denial of the faith (1 Tim. 5:8). The promise attached to this commandment is addressed to the nation rather than to the individual. Israel would survive and thrive in Canaan if the structures of family life remained strong. This underlying principle is clearly applicable in every age. A threat to the family is always a threat to the community.

The sixth commandment condemns all unjust killing, particularly the violent murder of a personal enemy. The word used for killing deliberately excludes capital punishment and killing in war, both of which were accepted in the Old Testament era (Exod. 21:12; Lev. 24:17; Deut. 20:10-13). This commandment is based on the special status any human being enjoys as a person created in God's image (Gen. 9:6). Here is a principle that should inform Christians in their attitudes to modern issues like abortion, suicide, and euthanasia. Jesus extended it also to cover hatred in the mind (Matt. 5:21).

The seventh commandment also looks back to the Bible's account of creation for its basis (Gen. 2:18-25). No matter what claims modern experts make for the therapeutic benefits of variety in sexual experience, the Bible bans adultery absolutely as a major threat to the unique "one flesh" relationship that intercourse was always intended to seal (Matt. 19:9). As with the ban on murder, Jesus made this commandment even more radical by applying it to the thought-life (Matt. 5:27). Positively, we have here a full-blooded advocacy for the value of chastity, seen both as abstinence from intercourse of any kind outside marriage (1 Cor. 6:12-20) and as lovingly committed fidelity within it (Eph. 5:21-33).

The eighth commandment raises social and political questions about the ownership and distribution of wealth. The Bible does not teach that the right to private property is sacrosanct, but the principle of stewardship implies that robbing a person of his or her belongings is equivalent to stealing from God. At the political level, the Old Testament's provision for sabbatical and jubilee years ensured that the accumulation of property was kept in regular check (Exod. 21:1-6; Lev. 25). These laws also stress the virtue of generosity. In the New Testament, Paul echoes the same positive theme when he brackets his own ban on stealing with an appeal for charitable giving (Eph. 4:28).

Because it is not in God's nature to deceive (Num. 23:19; Titus 1:2), the ninth commandment calls His people to imitate him. A person who lies is displaying Satan's image, not the Lord's (John 8:44). The main aim of this commandment was to insure truthful witness in the law-courts (Exod. 23:1; Deut. 19:16-19), but elsewhere in the Old Testament the value of integrity in any kind of relationship is heavily stressed (Ps. 15; Prov. 12:19). In today's world it is a principle that might be carefully but boldly applied to accepted standards in advertising and electioneering, among other things.

The tenth commandment, with its stress on attitudes, paves the way perfectly for the Sermon on the Mount, where Jesus exposed the inward demands of other items in the Decalogue's list. As Paul discovered (Rom. 7:7), even a first-class Pharisee (Phil. 3:5) could founder on this rock. The obverse of covetousness is contentment (1 Tim. 6:6-10). By this the Bible understands not indifference to material things, but happy acceptance of either little or much with trusting dependence on God the Giver (Phil. 4:11).

Throughout the history of the church, Christian people have believed that the Ten Commandments, correctly interpreted and applied, convey God's will for man's personal and social living. Early church fathers, like Irenaeus and Origen, related them to the Sermon on the Mount as two ends of the same ethical spectrum. Medieval schoolmen identified them with natural law and incorporated them into manuals for the instruction of penitents. In Reformation times, Luther elaborated them as a social code, while Calvin described sanctification as "ever more complete obedience to the Ten Commandments."

Today, sovereigns of the United Kingdom promise to "maintain the laws of God" at their coronations and presidents of the United States place their hands on a copy of the Decalogue when taking their inauguration oaths. The simple but comprehensive principles of the Ten Commandments are as necessary as ever in the perplexed and uncertain moral climate of the twentieth century.

**Bibliography:** Kaiser, W. C., *Towards Old Testament Ethics (1983); Stamm, J. J. and Andrew, M. E., The Ten Commandments in Recent Perspective* (1962); Vidler, A., *Christ's Strange Work* (1963); Wallace, R. S., *The Ten Command-*

*ments* (1965); Wright, C. J. H., *Living as the People of God* (1983).

D.H.F.

**TERRORISM.** A terrorist is one who brings extreme fear and violence into a person's life, and terrorism is the process by which such intimidation is introduced and results. Historically, terrorism has expressed itself consistently as a political activity, either as an anarchistic protest against established civil authority or as a form of piracy that was mounted without warning.

Terrorism claims a lengthy history, being a feature of the predatory raids of the Habiru in second-millennium-B.C. Mesopotamia. This group, which does not seem to bear any relationship to the ancient Hebrews, was blamed in several ancient Near Eastern records for wanton acts of killing and pillaging. The ancient Assyrians used terrorist tactics as a psychological weapon, and in their annals boasted of the various ways in which they had struck deep fear into the hearts of their enemies. These included making examples of city elders by entombing them alive and mutilating and disemboweling pregnant women. In consequence of these tactics only the most resolute were prepared to withstand the attack of an Assyrian army (2 Kings 18—19).

Rebellion against government rule was a common occurrence in Palestine during the Roman occupation. Terrorist groups made periodic attempts to cause riots in the hope that a general uprising against the Roman authorities would result in their overthrow and the establishing of a Jewish state such as had occurred during the Maccabean period. The condemned Barabbas, who was liberated when Jesus was sentenced to death, had been arrested for murder during an insurrection in Jerusalem (Mark 15:7). What appears to have been another terrorist group made a compact to fast until they had killed Paul (Acts 23:12-13), which resulted in his being taken to Caesarea under heavy military escort preparatory to leaving for Rome.

Modern terrorism dates from the nineteenth century in Russia, where Mikhail Bakunin (ob. 1876) advocated the overthrow of the government by terror and violence. Alexander II of Russia was only one head of state to be murdered by terrorists, whose activities also led to the commencement of World War I (1914-1918).

With the resurgence of nationalism and a consequent desire for independence from colonial powers, terrorism began to increase after World War II (1939-1945). One such group, the Mau Mau tribesmen, perpetrated many acts of terrorism in Uganda in an attempt to obtain political independence from Britain. Between 1945 and 1948 terrorist groups in Palestine made similar attacks upon British forces in an effort to hasten the end of the political mandate and bring about independence.

Renewed efforts to reunify Ireland and break the affiliation of Northern Ireland with Britain led to innumerable acts of terrorism in the 1970s and a great loss of life in Ulster. The matters at issue have long passed the stage of religious acrimony, and the violence that erupts periodically is obviously motivated by purely political considerations, in which communist agents appear to be playing a part. It is possible, however, that some sort of peace may yet be restored to Ireland by cooperative political policies.

A resurgence of political activity in Near Eastern Moslem countries, inspired by a stricter emphasis upon religious beliefs and practices, was accompanied by the growth of terrorist groups which had Israel and the allies of the United States as their general targets. The single-minded character of Moslem terrorism is reinforced by the fanatical religious dedication of the perpetrators who indulge in various acts of piracy and destruction by land, sea, and air in order to achieve their political objectives, which in essence comprise the defeat of Israel and her allies.

The Western world generally has been slow to appreciate the deadly nature of terrorism and even slower to adopt stern retaliatory measures. Unfortunately unpreparedness and weakness play directly into the hands of these fanatical killers, who place an extremely low value on peoples' lives, including their own. Until quick and effective deterrents to terrorism are developed, nobody in the Western world is safe. The Christian is under obligation to honor and obey the government in power (Rom. 13:1-5), regardless of his or her private feelings. This recognition of lawful authority must be the base for the establishing of effective countermeasures to terrorism, so that all offenders will see at firsthand that anarchy and assassination have no place whatever in civilized human society.

**THANKFULNESS.** This term describes the expression of gratitude for favors received, whether from God or human beings. Such a response is quite frequently complex in nature, containing elements of relief, happiness, emotional elation, genuine appreciation, a sense of personal satisfaction, and the like.

While thankfulness is a response that believer and unbeliever alike can express, it is peculiarly a characteristic of the practicing Christian. Gratitude for the saving work of Christ, which has brought the believer from spiritual darkness into the light of the gospel (1 Pet. 2:9), should constitute a prime element in any act of thanksgiving. Thereafter God ought to be thanked in every circumstance (1 Thess. 5:18) for his divine mercy, which sustains the believer in good and evil times alike. Prayer and supplication to God must also be accompanied by thanksgiving (Phil. 4:6), which must continue unabated as the believer grows into the knowledge and love of Christ (Col. 2:7). While it may appear to the unbeliever difficult if not ridiculous for a Christian to be thanking God in the midst of adversity, such an action is in fact the full expression of the prayer of faith that God will restore and bless.

**THEATER.** This term is derived from the Greek *thea*, "spectacle," and thus refers to some sort of dramatic presentation, usually on a stage or raised platform. Where such performances are held consistently in a building, that structure is described as a theater. The ancient Greeks perfected the design of outdoor theaters to the point where a speaker standing anywhere on the stage could be heard by all members of the audience seated in the amphitheater.

The Hebrews had no such spectacles as theatrical performances in their culture, although their religion contained a great deal of solemn ritual, especially ceremonies such as the Day of Atonement (Lev. 16) and the Passover (Exod. 12:1-28). Indeed, theatrical displays were resisted by orthodox Jews during the second century B.C., when Hellenistic Greek culture threatened to engulf the ancestral Sinaitic faith.

In the medieval period the Christian message was dramatized for illiterate people and others by such devices as passion plays, but contemporary secular theater was already acquiring an unsavory reputation. The bawdiness and immorality of much theater in the eighteenth century was repudiated by the ethos of the Evangelical Revival, and this has influenced many Christians since that time.

The libertinism of the twentieth-century world of theater does not commend itself to the majority of believers, yet at the same time it can produce religious epics of timeless value, as well as affording artistic expression to individuals who themselves are Christians. Participation in theater will naturally be a matter of personal taste and guidance, as with other diversionary matters, but in any event the dedicated Christian will do all to the glory of God (1 Cor. 10:31) and will not engage in any activity that will lead a brother or sister astray in faith or morals (1 Cor. 8:13; 2 Cor. 6:3).

**THEFT.** This term describes the act or process by which the money or property of someone is abstracted surreptitiously in part or whole. This form of behavior was expressly prohibited to humanity in the Ten Commandments (Exod. 20:15), although the frequency with which it is mentioned in Scripture indicates that theft was a regular feature of ancient life, the Decalogue notwithstanding. Christians were reminded in the New Testament of the fact of stealing and the necessity of avoiding such misbehavior (Matt. 19:18; Eph. 4:28). A related activity expressed by the Greek verb *nosphizomai*, "purloin," described the action of secreting someone else's goods and taking them away, as a servant might in lieu of payment.

Theft of various kinds is probably the most common form of crime in the modern world, and estimated losses from theft are usually retrieved by increasing the purchase prime of commodities by up to 5 per cent. No sincere Christian will countenance any kind of theft, however petty, for one moment, since to do so would violate one of God's major commands relating to human behavior.

See CRIME; SHOPLIFTING.

**THEOLOGICAL VIRTUES.** The word *virtue* is derived from the Latin noun *virtus*, which had a variety of meanings including "manliness, vigor, ability, worth," and "virtue." Its Greek counterpart, *arete*, was equally comprehensive, embracing meanings such as "goodness, excellence, rank distinction," and "skill." Plato used the plural form (*aretai*) to described noble deeds, and he and other philosophers employed the singular when virtue was being discussed.

In this connection Plato taught that there were four natural or inherent moral qualities in individuals, namely wisdom, justice, prudence, and temperance. These corresponded to the alleged fourfold division of the soul's nature, reflecting social justice, intellect, will, and feeling.

Christian theology repudiated the pagan concepts of virtue, teaching that virtue was a divine endowment and not a matter of human effort. Paul enunciated a famous triad of ethical and spiritual qualities which for him constituted virtues, that is, faith, hope, and love (1 Cor. 13:13). These abiding spiritual values were stressed in various letters to the Christian communities in Asia Minor (Gal. 5:5-6; Col. 1:4-5; 1 Thess. 1:3) and are known as the theological virtues, in contrast to the intrinsic or natural virtues of Plato. During the medieval Christian period these two groups were combined to produce the seven cardinal virtues.

The theological virtues are based upon the redemptive and saving work of Christ on the cross and can only be seen fully in the life of a person who has committed himself or herself to Jesus as Savior and supreme Lord. This itself is an act of faith on which subsequent belief builds and grows. This leads Paul to enunciate his doctrine of salvation by faith rather than by human works (Eph. 2:8). The virtue of faith is defined in Hebrews 11:1 as "the substance of things hoped for, the evidence of things not seen" (NKJV). Hope is stimulated by faith to expect God to fulfill his great and precious promises in Christ, who is described as the hope of the Christian (1 Tim. 1:17). The believer's hope of eternal life is guaranteed by the resurrection of Jesus, and this points directly to the future; whereas faith is rather more involved with the past and present. Love, regarded by Paul as the greatest of the theological virtues, is that spiritual attribute which characterized Christ's atoning death for sinners (John 3:16) and which saves to the uttermost those who are lost spiritually. Love is defined from a Godward perspective in 1 John 4:10 and assures the believer of salvation and blessing (Eph. 6:23; 2 Thess. 2:16; 1 John 3:1).

See CARDINAL VIRTUES; VIRTUE; VIRTUES.

**THIRD WORLD.** The "Third World" is a popular though not wholly accurate designation of those nations who are not strictly aligned politically with the United States and its partners, representing the "free world," or with Russia and its satellites, comprising the "communist bloc." These unaligned nations appear quite willing to accept financial and other assistance from any quarter and are represented by India, Pakistan, Indonesia, most of the African nations except South Africa, and Latin American peoples.

Third World problems began to emerge in clear focus when the colonial powers granted independence to their former overseas holdings. Some of the emerging nations were poorly prepared for their newfound freedom; and in their anxiety to take their place as developing peoples, borrowed large sums of money from a number of lending agencies. Unfortunately most of this financial assistance was linked to the American dollar, and as this currency grew stronger the balance of payments deficit increased.

Those who borrowed American dollars in 1970, before interest rates increased dramatically, are now faced with the prospect of repaying the original loan at very much higher levels of interest. Estimates in 1984 by the World Bank and the United States Federal Reserve Board placed the Third World's indebtedness at a staggering $800 billion. Because the majority of loans to developing countries are linked to the prime rate, any increases in that rate could add an estimated additional $1.25 billion to Third World debt. To talk of the full repayment of such indebtedness seems increasingly unrealistic in the eyes of many, since most debtor nations have experienced great difficulty in their attempts to meet interest charges, to say nothing of repaying the principal amount.

To try to deal with this problem, certain nations in close proximity to one another have banded together in an attempt to reschedule debt payments to foreign banks. The nations of the Caribbean and South America have formed the Latin American Parliament in an attempt to restructure their debts and work toward a solution of the larger problem. Members of this group have charged that the terms of repayment hitherto demanded have denied resources to developing countries by reducing the availability of imports, while, at the same time, enriching the creditor nations, who should actually be opening their markets more widely to Latin America imports and, presumably, be loaning money at significantly moderated rates. While it is true that, for various reasons, Third World nations are living well above their incomes, it is difficult not to be sympathetic to those who are increasingly uneasy about extracting huge sums of money from their seriously ailing economies and demonstrably restive populations merely to service already existing debt.

Crushing debt is not the only problem facing some Third World nations. The African Development Bank has complained that apart from debt, African countries are harassed by disease, drought, famine, and the rapid growth of desert areas. Of these factors, "desertification" is probably the most serious because it seems to result from climatic shifts involving changing temperatures at the North Pole, fluctuations that are beyond human control. It is tragic that the growth of desert land in Africa, which has some of the finest topsoil in the entire world, should be so pronounced, despite attempts at reclamation and irrigation. The resultant hunger and malnutrition make a mockery of the 1974 World Food Conference resolution that chronic hunger would be a thing of the past within a decade. While agronomists and others know how to make the deserts "blossom as the rose," as the ancient Hebrew prophet foresaw (Isa. 35:1), the costs are unfortunately prohibitive.

It is merely a matter of record that, unfortunately, too many Third World countries are working against their own interests. This is due in no small measure to political corruption, which effectively retards social development and caters to the unscrupulous elite rulers at the expense of the poor. Africa is a prime example of this kind of corruption. When Nkrumah became leader of independent Ghana in 1957, he was penniless, but when deposed less than a decade later he had an estimated 2.3 million pounds in British and numbered Swiss bank accounts, as well as property in Egypt and Morocco, all purchased with government funds. When the civilian government of Nigeria was overthrown at the beginning of 1984, evidence was adduced to show that government ministries had illegally appropriated billions of dollars from the coffers of that oil-rich country.

According to diplomatic reports, President Mobutu of Zaire has at least $20 million in European bank accounts and property investments. Zambia, which contains extremely rich deposits of copper, is in a state of virtual bankruptcy through political corruption and poor management. Nigeria has the unenviable reputation of being the most corrupt country on the continent of Africa, while life in Uganda under Milton Obote is reportedly even worse than it was when Idi Amin ruled because of the corruption and violence that are condoned. In socialist Zimbabwe, whose prime minister Robert Mugabe vowed to avoid the social cancer of corruption, a series of scandals has disclosed that millions of dollars cannot be accounted for by various government ministries and departments. The corruption in Mozambique had reached such a state that its Marxist president Samora Machel executed a number of corrupt politicians in an attempt to dissuade others from following the same dishonest path.

In Ethiopia, which has been a Marxist state from the time of the overthrow of Haile Selassie, the sorry tale of human cupidity, mismanagement, and political corruption precipitated a famine, which by 1985 had attracted world attention and attained the status of a "good cause" for people to support. The conditions had been forecast well in advance by United Nations experts, but their report was suppressed by the communist government of Ethiopia because its tone and recommendations were politically unacceptable to Ethiopia's president, Mengistu Haile Mariam. What is not generally known about Ethiopia is that this man, aside from vowing to wipe out the five thousand Christian churches in the land, proclaimed Ethiopia fully communist after he became president and spent $200 million to celebrate the event. While communist Russia has been pouring over $3 billion worth of armaments into the country, an amount that, if it had been in cash would have fed the nation for at least a decade, UNICEF was also giving Ethiopia about $45 million in assistance for development purposes.

As with some other countries in the Third World, the Mariam government has worked against its own long-term interests by spending almost half its budget on defense, resulting in the largest standing army in black Africa, and using much of the remainder to develop its industrial capabilities. Support for agriculture has been diverted from the needy peasants to inefficient state farms, which attempt to provide food for the army and the comparatively small number of people living in cities. The peasants, who comprise 85 per cent of the population, are the hardest hit by this sorry picture of political mismanagement, greed, dishonesty, and ambition. These factors have combined with harsh climatic conditions to produce the worst famine ever known in Ethiopia, the effects of which will most probably leave a permanently damaging mark upon the country's economy, no matter what assistance is offered by other nations.

It is commonly assumed by uninformed persons that Third World nations are the innocent victims of brutal capitalist oppression by the Western powers. The facts are that the governing classes of the nations named above have displayed a zeal for corruption, viciousness, and callous exploitation of their own peoples that is unmatched by any Western capitalist nation, but instead is in accord with the treatment by the Russians of their satellite peoples. In an age of professed concern for human dignity, it is distasteful to report that the human rights records of the African nations are despicable and have drawn vigorous protest from persons both inside and outside Africa. Although many atrocities and acts of brutality have been committed by military personnel, some are also the result of intertribal warfare. While for the purposes of this article Africa has been the center of attention, the same lamentable tale of political corruption, human greed, and appallingly bad administration can undoubtedly be duplicated in other Third World nations.

The concerned Christian will naturally be anxious to implement some measures aimed at helping remedy this extremely serious state of corruption. First and foremost the fiscal situation must be dealt with, since it also affects the rest of the world. The debt crisis for Third World countries is of ominous proportions, and if insolvency is to be prevented, some means of rescheduling interest payments must be devised. Additional financing from creditor nations would enable debtor countries to achieve better economic growth, provided that the funds are applied properly. Since bankers are understandably reluctant to contribute to the private fortunes of officials in debtor countries, it is important for proper safeguards against corruption to be established.

Concurrently with these measures, firm steps should be taken to control population growth until local food supplies have been developed to the point where the countries can be self-sustaining. Communist-related nations will experience considerable difficulty in achieving the latter goal, since the members of the Soviet bloc seem to be in perennial trouble in the matter of food production and need generous help from the Western nations. The emphasis must be upon significant practical action, since the situation demands much more than an agreement to the effect that agricultural development is the key to national economic viability, as occurred at a meeting of African nations in Lagos during 1982. However distasteful it may be for cultural or economic reasons, the controlling of population growth must rank high on the list of priorities. It seems that for the foreseeable future large amounts of seed grain will be needed in order to increase food supplies. Aid of this kind will need to be monitored carefully, lest it be used for food, stolen, or sent to Russia in exchange for armaments, as has happened in the past. In addition to this, engineers, agricultural experts, and others will be needed to devise possible means of combating the ravages of drought, as well as instructing native peoples how to produce food by utilizing modern techniques, a task that is far from easy given the highly conservative nature of peasants.

The Western world can continue the good work already undertaken by maintaining short-term emergency food supplies and by fostering realistic means of meeting acute need. This latter consideration involves such things as refraining from adding to Third World misery by offering them anabolic steroids to treat malnutrition and promote growth rather than providing normal foodstuffs. Third World countries are desperately in need of expanded markets in capitalist countries where they can sell legitimate national products instead of introducing illegal commodities such as heroin to the lucrative Western market. Many Christians prefer to patronize those charitable organizations that already have experience of work in specific areas of the Third World, rather than some large, amorphous group where so much of the donated money is absorbed by administrative costs.

Whatever form of assistance Christians choose to offer to the Third World must be governed by the most stringent measures in order to forestall any possibility of dilution through corruption. This is mandatory in order to protect the donors of the particular form of aid, whether they be individuals or groups, from callous exploitation by the recipients, and also from the inference that the donors are supporting, or appearing to support, a corrupt form of Third World government. Christians have long brought benefit to underdeveloped parts of the world in terms of a wide variety of social programs associated with the more specifically spiritual aspect of missionary work, and this is especially true of the contribution made by Christian medical personnel. All these activities have been outstanding and have manifested the sense of Christian dedication that has inspired and undergirded them. They also represent the most economical method of disbursing assistance to the needy, and are an example for the secular world to follow.

**TOLERANCE.** This word is derived from the Latin verb *tolero*, which meant "to endure," but also in a metaphorical sense "to hold out against someone." As an adjective, *toleratus* meant "able to be endured," and hence "tolerable." On this linguistic basis tolerance is the enduring of views, beliefs, and behavior without active interference, whether by intellectual censure or physical repression. At its best tolerance demands in its adherents an equable disposition and a willingness to consider opinions and approaches that are different from one's own without necessarily becoming committed to them. Self-control and an absence of prejudice are other necessary ingredients of tolerance, and when all these factors are combined with a general attitude of studied indifference toward life as a whole, an individual can be tolerant about almost any issue.

It is significant that the greatest threats to tolerance have existed historically in the areas of politics and religion. Both of these are ideologies, and both have deep roots in human culture. When adherents to these ideologies have felt threatened they have lashed out vigorously against their opponents, and human history is littered with examples of this tendency. The more dedicated the supporters proclaim themselves to be, the more utterly convinced they are of the rightness of their position and the totally erroneous nature of all opposing concepts. As a result they naturally feel a moral obligation to defend "the truth" by every means at their disposal, regardless of whether or not "the truth" claims divine or human inspiration. There is a real sense, therefore, in which intolerance will always be part of human existence; and advocates of tolerance in various areas of life should be aware of these facts.

Perhaps as a reaction to millennia of intolerance from the time of the Sumerians to that of modern Communist oppression, the late twentieth century witnessed a definite assertion of tolerance based principally upon legal enactments providing for equality under the law. Some moves toward tolerance were also made by certain religious denominations and interfaith groups, with varying degrees of success. But the best intentions and interests of this movement encountered resistance due to the migrations of people after World War II, who brought their historic prejudices with them in addition to those acquired during hostilities and demanded a variety of concessions from their democratic hosts while being unwilling to reciprocate in favor of majority rights. This attitude, in both religious and political areas, did not exactly commend itself to hosting nations, who discovered that in many cases they were also supporting the immigrants financially through unemployment, health, and welfare programs. When North Americans and Europeans visited totalitarian states such as Russian and Islamic regimes, they were shocked to find that tolerance was strictly a democratic notion.

Although religious tolerance has been included in the Universal Declaration of Human Rights (1948), it cannot be regarded as binding upon humanity in more than an idealistic sense, and whenever the convenience of nations or groups so requires, it can be expected to be ignored. Tolerance necessarily meets with considerable resistance from a religious point of view if only because certain aspects of it are inimical to the faith of all groups. In a pluralistic society the most that can be expected is a cool respect for the beliefs of others.

Tolerance is not a biblical term, and while the concept of love and service to all peoples is prominent in the New Testament, it is only expressed on the basis of the superiority of the Christian faith over all other religions (Acts 4:12). The Christian is well aware that God is supremely intolerant of sin, apostasy, unbelief, and infidelity, while at the same time loving the sinner and making eternal salvation in Christ available to all who respond in faith and obedience. Christian tolerance will therefore be best expressed in the loving, dedicated ministry of the gospel to all in need, regardless of race or creed.

**TRANQUILLITY.** This abstract noun is derived directly from the Latin *tranquillitas*, "quietness, calmness, stillness," and with its cognates bears consistently the notion of peace and serenity. In modern English tranquillity has come to be used largely in a poetic or rhetorical setting, and though comparatively infrequent in occurrence it is by no means obsolete.

From the beginning of history the world has been a place of strife and insecurity, and usually the only way that an individual or group could ensure a tranquil existence was to separate from society and live on a self-sustaining basis. One important product of spiritual experience is that it supplies the means whereby one can enjoy an inner peace and serenity because of the sustaining, comforting, reassuring power of a provident God. Jesus illustrated this inner calm at the greatest moments of stress in his life, and promised his disciples that he would give them his peace also (John 14:27). Subsequent New Testament writings confidently affirm the fact of inner tranquillity as one of the believer's precious spiritual possessions (Eph. 2:14; Phil. 4:9; 1 Thess. 5:23).

**TRANSPLANTING OF ORGANS.** This term describes the transferring of certain parts of the body from a donor to a recipient, in whom they are implanted as a substitute for, or perhaps in addition to, an organ that is so impaired by disease as to be useless. Whatever organs are involved in the transplanting process, there are always risks to be considered, not least in the recuperative period following the operation, which needs to be monitored as carefully as the surgery itself. Purely mechanical problems such as the rejection of the donor organ, despite careful matching, can jeopardize the success of the procedure and the life of the patient, to say nothing of side effects such as blood clots, major or minor strokes, or different forms of paralysis or pneumonia.

When a pragmatic value is being put upon the procedure by doctor and patient, all these factors have to be taken into account before a decision can be made. But a judgment of value, which would estimate the possible worth of the operation to the patient, is an extremely sensitive philosophical, ethical, and spiritual matter which must be settled positively and confidently if the procedure is to result in healing. This is an especially important consideration for the doctor, because any emotional turmoil in the patient can and does inhibit healing, as surgeons know well.

The morality or organ transplantation has been a matter for considerable debate at all levels of society. While many people would support it in theory, others regard it as too experimental in nature and consequently reject the idea. A good deal depends upon the individual's concept of the essential worth of life and the resultant lengths to which he or she would go to maintain that life. In cases where major organs are involved, the recipient may well wonder if the donor's final hours of existence were prejudiced in any way so that the recipient might enjoy a viable transplant.

Most thoughtful Christians would agree that the prolonging of individual existence by organ transplantation is only a rather more spectacular, and possibly dangerous, means of extending a person's life than other, more orthodox procedures employed in medicine, some of which also place the patient at considerable risk. Scripture, of course, offers no guidance on this modern problem, but the Christian who is considering submitting to organ tranplantation will need to have direct guidance from the Holy Spirit to proceed so that divine peace and healing may attend all who participate in the surgery and in postoperative treatment.

See HEART TRANSPLANTATION; MEDICAL ETHICS.

**TREATIES.** A treaty is a solemn agreement, usually in writing, between two or more sovereign states creating rights and duties binding on those states in international law. Generally speaking, only sovereign states can become bound by treaties. Rights and obligations that arise from treaties are normally only applicable to the states party to them through signature and later ratification. In modern practice the term *convention* is sometimes used of treaties. Occasionally, *covenant* is also used, as, for example, the International Covenants on Civil and Political and Social and Economic Rights (1976). International law regarding treaties is to be found mainly in the Vienna Convention on the Law of Treaties (1980).

Treaties are essential to a well-regulated world order and allow for civilized relations among nations, such as treaties relating to postal and telephonic communications. The present complex web of treaties reflects international interdependence. Treaties are used to enhance cooperation among states, to settle disagreements, and to reduce the potential for conflict. Even in time of war, treaty obligations exist that seek to maintain a minimum standard of humanity, as, for example, the Geneva Conventions (1949) dealing with rights of sick and wounded, prisoners of war, and civilian populations.

The leading ethical issue involved in treaties is *pacta sunt servanda*, namely, that obligations entered into freely are binding and should be observed in good faith. This principle is recognized by International Law (Vienna Convention, Article 26) and the exceptions to it, such as fraud, duress, and change of circumstances, are narrowly defined. It is also recognized biblically. The prophets castigated not only Israel, but pagan nations for breach of covenant undertakings, as well. The upholding of these covenants is still incumbent on nations as well as individuals in the eyes of God (Josh. 9:3-27; Ezek. 17:15-21, especially v. 15 and vv. 18-19; Amos 1:9; Ps. 15:4).

Another ethical question in the international community has been the insistence that treaties should be public documents. There are requirements for treaties to be publicized (Article 102 of the United Nations Charter), the purpose of which is to preserve a measure of stability in international relations, especially as secret treaties have been a cause of war.

Treaties are the primary source of International Law, another other main source being international custom (that is, practices accepted by states as legally binding; see Article 38 of the Statue of the International Court of Justice). The lawmaking effect of treaties can be most clearly seen in multilateral treaties, which are akin to domestic legislation. Examples of such treaties are with regard to Antarctica and outer space. Another main type of treaty is the bilateral treaty, which is more akin to a contract. In the present fragmented world order, enforcement of international legal obligations is less than complete, and such duties are easily avoided by recalcitrant states. A measure of observance of them, either on principle or for self-interest, does take place, however.

Treaties have been seen to be as ancient as political communities, and many examples of texts have been discovered in the ancient Near East. Indeed, it is suggested by some Old Testament scholars that the then current style of treaties between a client state and a superior empire was used as a teaching model in the Mosaic legislation, displaying the relationship between God and Israel, including God's ethical demands. Israel was, moreover, prevented from entering into treaties with the inhabitants of Canaan (Exod. 32:33; 34:12). During the monarchy period, treaties were joined by Solomon and the kings of Israel and Judah with neighboring nations (1 Kings 5:12; 2 Chron. 16:2). In more modern times, treaties have been historic milestones of the reorganization of European politics in post-war periods, for example, Westphalia (1648), Vienna (1815), and Versailles (1919).

**Bibliography:** Kitchen, K. A., *Ancient Orient and Old Testament* (1966); McNair, A., *The Law of Treaties* (1961).

A.J.G.

**TRUST.** The ability of an individual to trust implies the prior existence of an object or person that has already demonstrated credibility and therefore furnishes the assurance that trust will not be misplaced or abused. On such a basis, trust as a conscious act of will implies a relationship between the individual and the source of trust that is characterized by complete reliance. This relationship may be temporary or of a more permanent nature, but it is only valid as long as the credibility of the object of trust is sustained.

Since trust involves strong belief and shares the character of faith, it may appear rather surprising that the biblical terminology creates a difference between them. The Hebrew word commonly used for *trust* is *batah*, which as a verb means "to lean on" a person, or "to have confidence in" someone, whether God (2 Kings 18:5; Ps. 37:3), human beings (Prov. 28:26; 31:11), or inanimate objects (Prov. 11:28; Jer. 7:4). Another term, *hasah*, means "to take refuge in" and is used predominantly of trust in God. In the New Testament the Greek verb *elpizo*, "to hope," and its cognates are often translated by *trust* in the King James Version because it carries a different emphasis from that of *faith* (*pistis*).

As part of the act of faith by which a sinner becomes converted spiritually, trust is place in the efficacy of Christ's substitutionary atonement to cleanse the penitent offender from sin and initiate

spiritual reconciliation with God. Having received Christ as Savior and Lord by faith, the believer then has confidence in God to fulfill all the promises that Scripture makes to the Christian concerning day-to-day provision, spiritual guidance in this life, and blessings in eternity. Thus confidence furnishes an added dimension to the faith which justifies a person (Eph. 2:8). As faith grows, trustful expectation of the Lord's mercies increases, enabling the Christian to stand firm in the faith and witness to society with boldness and confidence in the atoning work of Jesus.

**TRUTHFULNESS.** This word characterizes the customary attitude of an individual who exhibits the quality of "fullness of truth" in whatever he or she says or does. It designates an extremely high state of morality that has been checked and verified by observation in various ways and found to be consistently true in belief and practice. The word *truth* is used in several different senses, not all of them connected explicitly with morality. In modern society we speak of *truth* in terms of such disciplines as the descriptive sciences, mathematics, history, and philosophy. Yet since these are functions of human beings who are moral, they are still amenable to moral interpretation, and the *truth* that they manifest may only differ from spiritual *truth* in degree rather than in kind. In assessing truthfulness, the majority of people employ what is known to philosophers and ethicists as the "correspondence theory" of truth. Statements are thus regarded as true if they match in detail the manner in which the events described actually occurred. Corroboration by another witness is generally required for this kind of authentification, a situation which it is not always possible to accommodate.

Spiritual truth, however, transcends mere factual correspondence, and as an attribute of life, touches all areas of ethics and morals. Truthfulness is one of God's supreme qualities, and it is this habitual manifestation of his nature that inspires the trust and confidence of those who come to believe in him. The Hebrew *emunah*, "truth, truthfulness," denotes stability or steadfastness, which is also true of the more common word *emeth*, "truth." In the New Testament the Greek word *aletheia* describes truthfulness in terms of a genuine attitude (John 4:23), an honest revelation from God (John 8:40), and the nature of Christ's own witness (John 18:37).

Following the example of Christ, all believers are urged to speak truthfully to their neighbors (Eph. 4:25) instead of bearing false witness in society, an activity that was prohibited in the Torah (Exod. 20:16). Paul proclaimed the truthfulness in Christ of his preaching (Rom. 9:1) and by contrast stated that divine anger would fall upon those opponents of Christ who disobeyed the truth (Rom. 2:8). Paul described God as the quintessence of truthfulness (Titus 1:2) because it was impossible for God to do other than maintain his integrity (2 Tim. 2:13). When the character of the individual Christian comes to be recognized as typified by truthfulness, the gospel message that is proclaimed gains enhanced credibility.

**TWOFOLD REIGN OF GOD.** This expression, originated by Luther, refers to the difference between God's internal way of governing the individual Christian and His external way of governing society. Based upon the apostolic affirmations of secular authority in Romans 13:1-7 and 1 Peter 2:13-14, Luther taught that God works through human reason, natural law, and the "offices" of earthly government with His "left hand." Here God's temporal purpose is to restrain sin and maintain peace, for which the use of force and punishment is often necessary. But, based upon New Testament passages like the Sermon on the Mount (Matt. 5:1—7:27), Luther taught that God works through Christ, Scripture, and the Holy Spirit with His "right hand." Here God's eternal purpose is to reveal sin, bring about repentance, preach the gospel, and win eternal life and the voluntary obedience of faith. Here Christ rules without force.

The perennial difficulty for the Christian is to determine how he or she is related to these two, sometimes opposing, forms of divine government. On the one hand, Christians are subject to a secular authority that resists evil and uses force—to the extent that such authority does not obstruct God's revealed will (Acts 4:17-20; 5:29). On the other hand, they are subject to Christ alone, who calls for nonresistance to evil and repudiates the use of force (Matt. 5:38-48). The solution, Luther suggested, is to ask in each particular case whether the issue concerns "self" or "others." Insofar as it concerns oneself, the Christian stands under Christ's radical command to forgive and to suffer injustice. However, insofar as it concerns others, the Christian is called to seek justice on his neighbor's behalf. This may lead to the death of an enemy, as in capital punishment or a defensive war. Even then the Christian is to pity and pray for the salvation of his enemies.

**Bibliography:** Althaus, P., *The Ethics of Martin Luther* (1972); Bornkamm, H., *Luther's Doctrine of the Two Kingdoms* (1966); Luther, M., "The Sermon on the Mount," *Luther's Works,* Vol. 21 (1956); *Ibid.,* "Temporal Authority: To What Extent It Should Be Obeyed," *Luther's Works,* Vol. 45 (1962).

See ORDERS OF GOD.

N.J.G.

# –U–

**UNBELIEF.** The prefix of this term indicates a sense that is contrary to the word to which it is attached. Thus unbelief basically implies a lack or nonexistence of confidence or trust in whatever factors are involved in a given situation. Whereas disbelief may refer to a particular incident, statement, or the like, unbelief is a more comprehensive frame of mind that applies to whole areas of life and existence and not just to a special circumstance. It is an overall attitude of distrust that influences opinions and excludes from credible consideration all phenomena that do not conform to the narrow criteria in the mind of the unbeliever. Such an attitude is especially inimical to religious faith and can even inhibit creativity by its negative response, as Christ indicated when he was unable to work many miracles in Galilee (Matt. 13:58).

In terms of religious faith, unbelief is not a matter of pursuing a way of life without any serious consideration being given to spiritual issues, especially the matter of divine existence. In Scripture, and especially in the New Testament, it has much the much more sinister attribute of a deliberate and conscious repudiation of God's person and work as revealed particularly in the incarnate Christ (John 5:38; 10:24-25; Acts 19:9). Unbelief is therefore connected to the individual's intelligence and will, resulting in an attitude described biblically as "hardening the heart" (Exod. 8:15, 32; Prov. 28:14). It cannot be excused on the grounds of ignorance, by constitutes an obdurate, conscious rejection of God's revelation in Christ.

Unbelief is particularly demonic because, in setting himself or herself up as a judge who pronounces on history and divine revelation alike, the unbeliever's rejection of God's witness to his son Jesus makes God himself a liar (1 John 5:10). Having engaged with apparent success in this rejection of divine activity in history, the unbeliever is subject to no moral or ethical code save that of his or her own devising. Not infrequently the unbeliever is in the position of having once been among the many called by Christ, but has not succeeded to divine election.

Needless to say, the unbeliever is condemned roundly in Scripture for the presumption involved in the conscious rejection of God's claims upon his or her life (Deut. 1:32, 34-35; John 3:18, 36; 2 Thess. 2:12), and the penalty prescribed for such sinful action is death (John 8:24). Paul attributed the rejection of Israel by God and its replacement by the Christian church to unbelief (Rom. 11:20).

Improbable as it ought to appear, unbelief was apparent in the primitive Christian church (Gal. 1:7; 2 Tim. 3:8), and Paul waged a continuous battle against those who repudiated God's revelation in Christ (Rom. 1:28; Titus 1:15). These unbelievers were the forerunners of the various heretics with whom the Church Fathers had to deal, culminating in the repudiation of Arianism at the Council of Nicea in 325. During the period of the Holy Roman Empire an orthodox approach to the principal doctrines of the faith was the norm, and the Reformation's emphasis upon faith, justification, and other biblical doctrines was in accord with this position.

Only in the Enlightenment period did atheism, skepticism, and other forms of unbelief come into increasing prominence; and with the rise of scientism in the nineteenth century many scientists took advantage of the popularity of their subject to denigrate or reject religious beliefs as inferior and belonging to a past age of myth, legend, and religious credulity. At this time an antinomian movement took shape among freethinking clergy, supported by a European literary-critical view of Scripture which largely denied its inspiration and authority. Philosophers of various schools adopted naturalistic, positivist, existentialist, and Marxist positions, all of which demonstrated hostility to traditional biblical belief.

For the Christian, the works of the devil must be under constant attack as the church moves forward to break down the gates of hell (Matt. 16:18). Believers are now working in unprecedented numbers with modern, sophisticated equipment to proclaim Christ's saving gospel to mankind. Meanwhile the spiritual bankruptcy of liberal theology has brought a new generation of evangelical thinkers and writers to the forefront in the assault on unbelief.

**UNCLEANNESS.** This term is used in a physical and also a religious and moral sense in the Scriptures. The Old Testament employs the word *tame* and its cognates to describe what was unclean or defiled, while in the New Testament the most common word is *akathartos*, "unclean, impure," supplemented by the rare use of *koinos*, "profaned, polluted" (Rom. 14:14; Heb. 9:13) and *miasmos*, "pollution, defilement."

In purely physical terms uncleanness was used in connection with the classification of animals (Lev. 11:10-48; Deut. 14:3-21) and also for the group of diseases known as leprosy (*tsaraath*). The rationale of the laws which prohibited certain things as unclean is not explained, although hygienic as well as idolatrous considerations have been suggested. In the case of leprosy diagnosed as malignant, the sentence of uncleanness and banishment that was imposed (Lev. 13:45-46) had an important preventative significance for the whole community. Appropriate cleansing rituals were also provided for in the Torah (Lev. 12:1-8; 15:1-33).

Religious or ceremonial defilement resulted from transgression of the divinely prescribed laws for worshiping God. Levitical sacrificial rituals had to be followed to the letter, and deviations were punished dramatically (Lev. 10:1-2) so as to prevent the introduction of defiling, pagan innovations. Sins of ritual omission, accident, or inadvertence were forgiven the Israelites on the Day of Atonement (Lev. 6:1-34), but sins committed in deliberate violation of the covenant provisions could not be forgiven under any of the sacrificial rituals (Num. 15:30).

Because the Israelites were required to live as a priestly kingdom and a holy nation (Exod. 19:6), moral purity was of the highest importance; and various sections of the Torah specifically prohibited sexual practices current among pagan nations (Lev. 18:6-23), as well as other forms of spiritual defilement (Lev. 19:29-31; Deut. 17:2-5). These regulations underlay Jewish life in New Testament times, but were given a wider dimension by Christ's teaching that defilement really issues from the heart, that is, from human will, purposiveness, and intelligence (Matt. 15:1-20). The Christian who has allowed his or her life to become unclean in some manner can be reconciled to God through repentance and cleansing in the blood of Christ (1 John 1:7). The believer is warned to avoid uncleanness (2 Cor. 6:17) and reminded that no defiled person has any inheritance in Christ's kingdom (Eph. 5:5).

**Bibliography:** Douglas, M., *Purity and Danger* (1966).

**UNEMPLOYMENT.** Unemployment may be defined as the denial of opportunities for paid work, usually understood as a result of economic reasons outside the individual's control. As such, unemployment (and especially the significant rise in long-term unemployment) stands as one of the great ethical, social, and politico-economic issues of our time. The principle foci of Christian ethical concern are, (1) that employment is, in our society, a primary means of organizing the work to which God summons the human race (though work should not be identified wholly with employment); (2) that there is an important moral connection between work and the maintenance of one's livelihood; and (3) the pain that frequently characterizes the experience of unemployment in our society.

The latter fact itself reflects the very wide range of benefits that employment confers on the individual. The felt experience of unemployment is not only one of financial deprivation and "letting one's family down," but often also of loneliness (deprivation of community), an erosion of self-confidence, an unstructured lifestyle, and atrophy. It is not uncommon to find the feeling of redundancy compared to that of bereavement in terms of certain distress symptoms that are frequently exhibited. In turn, unemployment is linked to a range of other social problems: deep bitterness and resentment, vandalism, addiction, and marital and family breakdown. Above all else, the experience of unemployment is usually one of a sense of failure and loss of self-esteem.

The Christian doctrine of man is not one that affirms that a person's value resides in what he or she produces or achieves. Instead, it locates the worth of each and every individual in the fact that they are made in God's image and are those for whom the Son of God gave up His life on a Roman cross. In Christian understanding, human worth is not achieved, but is graciously bestowed. In weighing human value, we start not with the works of men but with the works of God. Such theological truths are at once important and liberating. In a culture, however, that embraces such a strong ideological connection between human work and human worth they need to be applied with the utmost pastoral sensitivity.

While unemployment does not only affect certain groups, it is a reality that emphasizes and reinforces particular social divisions. Unemployment is highest among the young, the unskilled, and ethnic groups.

Unemployment has become a major political issue in Western democratic societies, not least because many people still look to politicians to solve it. In reality we should recognize the vast range of interlocking factors at work in the creation and destruction of employment possibilities: technological innovation, fluctuations in international trade, environmental and climatic conditions, population distribution, and so on. Some political approaches are no more than attempts to bring down unemployment at the expense of one's rivals in the international marketplace: included here are modifications of trade tariffs and exchange rates as well as drives to increase business competitiveness through the "short-term medicine" of inflation control and increased efficiencies. Justice may require some such modification, and inefficiency is not a virtue. But Christian ethics cannot ultimately accept the nationalistic response of "solving" one's own problems through making them somebody else's. We have to seek some degree of equilibrium here.

Other political approaches emphasize the need to go on expanding the overall economic cake. Certain forms of economic expansion, however, need to be subjected to careful scrutiny on environmental grounds. In human terms as well, we must ask whether it is desirable for us to seek yet further extensions of the consumer society.

See EMPLOYMENT; HOMELESSNESS; RIGHT TO WORK; WAGES; WORK.

M.D.G.

**USURY.** This term designates the unjust exaction of interest on loans. Our English word *usury* is derived from the Latin noun *usura*, which originally meant "enjoyment" but later also came to mean "interest."

Although the Mosaic law allowed interest on loans to foreigners, it prohibited the practice among fellow Israelites because of opportunities to exploit desperate people in unfortunate circumstances, thus disrupting the social unity of the people of God (Exod. 22:25-27; Lev. 25:35-37; Deut. 23:19-20). Given that bartering basic necessities was the chief means of exchange in an agarian society such as ancient Israel, the law sought to protect the borrower from being stripped of his sustenance as the only means of repayment. There is little evidence this legislation was practiced or enforced during the monarchy, although after the Exile a major effort was made to apply the law and eliminate the social oppression of usury (Neh. 5:1-13).

Jesus never explicitly addressed the issue of interest taking, except to use it to illustrate his parables (Matt. 25:14-30; Luke 19:11-27). Although usurous practices illustrate faithful stewardship in these parables, it does not necessarily follow that Jesus condoned charging interest on loans. The Lord frequently employed otherwise negative images to reach a positive conclusion in his teaching (for example, the parable of the unjust steward who is commended for his sagacity but not for whatever made him unjust, Luke 16:1-9). A more accurate opinion could be that usury was a familiar enough practice to his listeners that Jesus could use it to great effect. Judea under Roman rule was less dependent on the barter system than in earlier times, which meant the extreme oppression associated with usury was somewhat eased and therefore not a prominent social issue. However, the disciples could not enter too facily into lending and taking interest: "Give to everyone who asks of you. And from him who takes away your goods do not ask them back" (Luke 6:30). For whatever reasons disciples lent their goods (or asked for reparations), the Lord reminded them to consider the merciful treatment God had offered them as a model for dealing charitably with others (Luke 6:36; Matt. 18:23-25).

The early church had no clear or consistent policy concerning usury. The medieval church, however, condemned it universally (except for Jews) and formally at the Third Lateran Council (1179), having accepted Aristotle's idea that money is "barren" and cannot reproduce itself. Usury was not only uncharitable but unnatural as well. The lender, therefore, could not expect more in return than he lent without imposing an unjust burden upon the borrower.

By the time of the Protestant Reformation (the sixteenth century), the enormous increase in trade and wealth caused money to be understood as a commodity that could be bought and sold at a profit as could any good. This conception of money was strongly held in northern and central Europe, despite the opposition of Reformers such as Martin Luther. Soon the demand for money created "money markets" which in turn caused the founding of great banking houses to serve these new markets. These developments laid the groundwork for the modern understanding and acceptance of interest taking.

Today the major Christian churches, including the Roman Catholic Church, distinguish between charging interest as a valid commercial enterprise and usury as unethical exploitation. Modern usury is commonly found in transactions between a desperate borrower and a "loan shark" who is only concerned with keeping the borrower in debt indefinitely with huge interest payments beyond the market value of money. Such practices are strictly regulated and punished by civil authorities in most places. As the usurer under the Mosaic law, the loan shark has no interest in the welfare of the borrower and often leaves him in a worse situation than before he borrowed. Unfortunately, the victims of this maliciousness are often the poor who cannot afford loans at reputable banks or savings and loans.

Although Christians may find few objections to the principle of charging interest, they should be more circumspect than is naturally expected in accepting the usual business applications of this principle. Christians cannot, if Jesus is truly Lord of all, make an uncritical distinction between their business and personal lives. They must balance their obligations to be faithful stewards of property (especially in regard to the property of others) and their obligations to be merciful servants to financially demoralized individuals. They must weigh what is in their power to correct and what harm or benefit will result from their decisions. Above all, Christians must guard against the "business as usual" attitude that insulates them from the financial distress of others.

G.S.L.

**UTILITARIANISM.** Utilitarianism is an early nineteenth-century formulation by Jeremy Bentham and James Mill of ancient Cyrenaic and Epicurean hedonism into a modern ethical theory which is opposed to intuitionism. The son of the latter, John Stuart Mill, gave the theory its traditional definition in his 1851 essay *Utilitarianism*: "The creed which accepts as the foundation of morals utility, or the greatest happiness principle, holds that actions are right in proportion as they tend to promote happiness, wrong as they tend to produce the reverse of happiness. By 'happiness' is intended pleasure, and the absence of pain; by 'unhappiness,' pain, and the privation of pleasure." Ever since, the popular short definition of Utilitarianism has been the doctrine that the greatest happiness of the greatest number should be the guiding principle of action.

In England, the traditional rigorous doctrine that pleasure is the only good (at least that the actual or probable maximizing of pleasure is the preferred action to be taken by an agent) was later balanced by ideal forms of Utilitarianism, which granted that other things besides pleasure are good and might command priority. In America, following the work of William James, R. B. Perry, and John Dewey, Utilitarian ethics took a more pragmatic and instrumentalist bent and were used to reinforce the interest theory of value.

The root of Utilitarian doctrine is the idea that intrinsic value lies in pleasure or pleasant consequences and that actions are therefore to be judged in relation to the net value of these. The early form of Utilitarianism was philosophical and ethical in character: the pursuit of happiness ought to be the chief end of action. Later, American versions of Utilitarianism especially became much more psychological and descriptive, claiming that pleasure is in fact the chief end of the actions of all organisms, including man. Recent formulations make this a biological-behavioral response, in the sense that actions are understood to be behavioral not intentional, that is, organisms are programmed or conditioned to seek fulfillment of needs and to maximize pleasure for themselves.

Nineteenth-century criticism of Utilitarianism was severe, especially by Christians, some of whom used the charge of defection to Utilitarianism as a slur. It was seen to be selfish, with no provision for overriding ideals which direct behavior. Mill was forced to defend the doctrine by conceding that as a system of ethics it could achieve its end only by the general cultivation of nobleness of character. With the development of evolutionary theory late in the century, questions were put as to whether, in the absence of sentiment, ideals, and altruism, Utilitarianism becomes the justification of savage evolutionism (nature red in tooth and claw). In modern times, Utilitarianism is, paradoxically, strongly criticized as a theory of behavior while continuing to be powerfully influential in practical day-to-day ethics and politics.

The theoretical question as to how to measure pleasure and happiness quantitatively remains, as does the traditional hedonistic paradox that the direct pursuit of pleasure or happiness entails missing them. True happiness invariably accompanies, or is a function or correlative of, some other constructive activity.

The idea that everything is to be judged by its utility is offensive to many. It is one thing to say this about concepts and abstractions, but it is another to say it about persons. Utilitarian theories with an economic bias are charged, as are aspects of Marxism, with valuing humans merely as production units: if they contribute to the general economy, they are of value; if they do not, they are of little or no value or are even of negative worth. Christians strongly deny that human beings, or any individual human being, are simply a means to a universe of happiness or a means to maximize happiness per capita. Rather, human beings are ends in themselves and are of infinite worth in themselves. For Christians this is a critical foundation stone of ethics.

Parallel to the foregoing is the charge that Utilitarianism is only superficially altruistic; that its genius is fundamentally egoistic and selfish. If the fundamental principle of action is egoistic satisfaction of need, as modern hedonists claim, why should anyone care for anyone else? It remains a question whether altruism does not logically mark the death of any consistent hedonism.

Nevertheless, Utilitarianism is widely regarded in modern societies as a useful, practical social and political tool, especially in the age of polls and poll-taking. The principle of the greatest happiness for the greatest number furnishes a rough-and-ready method of balancing the demands of interest groups. Theoretically, it leaves unanswered the question of what to do with the dissident, the outcast, and the minority. Utilitarianism is the ethical palliative of an affluent society. Only as other values and ideals are superimposed upon it can utilitarian principles be made to function in a civilized manner.

**Bibliography:** Blackham, H. J., *Objections to Humanism* (1963); Downie, R. S. and Telfer, E., *Respect for Persons* (1970); Graham, B., *The Secret of Happiness* (1955); Mill, J. S., *Utilitarianism* (1851).

S.J.M.

**UTOPIANISM.** Utopianism is a political and social outlook that derives its name from, but antedates, the title of Thomas More's book *Utopia* (1516). Utopianism advocates, or dreams of, the establishment of a perfect or ideal society lacking violence and oppression and having whatever ideals the promoter of the vision favors. Sometimes the word *utopian* is used as a term of approval, sometimes as a criticism. Occasionally the word is used in a narrower and more theoretical fashion to indicate the construction of a political model or an ideal for intellectual purposes. Utopians are criticized for escapism and for naivete in their understanding of human nature and human affairs; there is a tradition of anti-utopian, or dystopian, writing, well-known examples of which are Aldous Huxley's *Brave New World* (1931) and George Orwell's *1984* (1948), in which the nightmarish possibilities of so-called utopias are explored. Utopianism would also be objected to by conservatives, holding either a more organic or a more laissez-faire views of society and its institutions.

Advocates of a return to a supposed Golden Age are also said to be affected by utopianism. Karl Marx (1818-1883) contrasted his supposedly scientific theory of socialism (scientific because it was claimed to be in accordance with the objective laws of historical development) with the utopian socialism of Robert Owen (1771-1858) and Francois Fourier (1772-1837). Their socialism allegedly disregarded such scientific laws and proceeded in abstraction from actual historical circumstances.

Sir Karl Popper (1902- ), in *The Open Society and Its Enemies* (1945), claims that there are two sorts of social change: utopian, which attempts to implement some definite political blueprint for the whole of society, and that which involves what he calls "piecemeal social engineering," that is, social change through the meeting of individual social problems on an entirely *ad hoc,* trial and error basis, with no ideal end-result in view.

Certain millenarian and perfectionist movements within the Christian church may also be said to be infected with utopianism. They see certain aspects of the teaching of the Bible, particularly, parts of Daniel and other Old Testament prophecies, the Sermon on the Mount, and Revelation, as outlining an achievable political goal. These movements have then attempted to bring about such goals by a political platform involving the reform of land-tenure or bloody revolution or by the establishing of the Fifth Monarchy.

Christian attitudes to ward utopianism as a political movement will clearly depend upon views both of the nature of Christian eschatology and of what the Christian's or church's attitude toward politics ought to be. In general, however, utopian attitudes have been viewed by Christians with extreme suspicion, because the Bible portrays the ideal end-state as being brought about redemptively, by the intervention of the risen and glorified Christ in grace and judgment, and not through mere human political activity. This intervention is the consummation of the kingdom of Christ and the inauguration of that kingdom in its final, glorious expression. This is a divine gift, no more the product of utopian activists than it is the result of piecemeal social engineers. Utopian attitudes are also suspect on biblical grounds because of the view of human nature and of the limited possibilities open to the human race, unaided, that they imply. According to the Christian church, the consummation involves not merely divine intervention, but the final stage of the transformation of human nature as it now is.

**Bibliography:** Bury, J. B., *The Idea of Progress* (1920); Cohn, N., *The Pursuit of the Millennium* (1957); Mannheim, K., *Ideology and Utopia* (1936); Popper, Sir K., *The Open Society and Its Enemies*, 2 vols. (1945).

See MARXISM, PERFECTIONISM.

P.H.

# -V-

**VALUES.** A theory of value seeks to determine what states of affairs are good and desirable, and therefore worthy of promotion and preservation. If attempts at promoting and preserving various states of affairs are to make sense, there must be ends that are worthwhile in-and-of-themselves. There must be, in other words, what is called "intrinsic value." For not all values can be instrumental, desirable solely as a means to something else. If A is valued because it brings about B, and B is valued because it brings about C, *ad infinitum*, but nothing along the way is valued for its own sake, then the whole process of valuation makes no sense. Means have worth only if there are ends that have worth, and there are ends that have worth only if there are intrinsic values. Theoretical discussions, among moralists and others, focus on intrinsic value and seek to identify those ends that are desirable for their own sake. In discussing intrinsic value, there is a crucial distinction made between nonmoral value and moral value. Candidates for nonmoral value include: pleasure, happiness, beauty or aesthetic experience, knowledge, and freedom. Candidates for moral value include: love of God, love of neighbor, justice, conscientiousness, and various character traits. Moral values are properties of persons (singly or in groups) and do not include rightness and wrongness, which are ascribed to actions, not to the person doing the action.

A human life is complete, it might be judged, when both the full range of desirable nonmoral and moral values (or goods) are a part of that life. There are, however, two mistakes that can be made in relating moral and nonmoral value. First, the importance of nonmoral values and goods can be underestimated, especially by various forms of religious otherworldliness. It may be believed either that pleasure, happiness, and so on, are relatively unimportant as long as one is good and spiritual, or, which is more likely, that moral and spiritual goodness is sufficient to guarantee happiness. In such a case, however, are nonmoral factors of no importance in securing happiness? To answer this question one need not long ponder the force of Aristotle's comment, "No man is happy on the rack." For is it not true that we contribute significantly to a human life, even the life of a good and spiritual person, by securing release from the rack? It seems clear that we do. Great pain can detract from the happiness of even the best of persons, and we surely make life better by relieving the pain and suffering produced by the rack or by illness, poverty, psychological disturbance, and the like. Indeed, to downgrade the importance of nonmoral goods for a life undercuts the basis for a Christian social ethic and is incompatible with the biblical concern for the poor, the sick, the homeless, and those suffering in various ways. Surely the appropriate response to such need is the provision of various nonmoral goods (for example, food, clothes, and medical care). Such a response, of course, is a recognition that nonmoral goods contribute significantly to the happiness of people who, as created by God, are beings with bodies and minds as well as souls, and therefore beings with physical as well as spiritual needs.

The second mistake in relating moral and nonmoral value is to interpret the significance of moral value solely in terms of its production of nonmoral value. Whereas the first mistake downgrades the legitimate importance of nonmoral goods, this second mistake downgrades the independent importance of moral value. In such a utilitarian interpretation, moral value has only instrumental significance, being judged important solely as a means to various nonmoral goods, especially happiness or pleasure. Thus, a loving or caring person will contribute significantly to the happiness of others, engaging in happiness-producing activities such as feeding the hungry, helping the sick and so on. Hateful persons will not do so but, on the contrary, will seek to harm by word and deed. Therefore, love is good and hate is bad. But if this is all that can be said on behalf of love (although this certainly is significant), then love is solely of instrumental value and of no intrinsic worth.

There is, perhaps, reason to draw back from such a utilitarian conclusion, especially as an analysis of all moral value. Consider, for example, the love of God. There can be no doubt that the person who truly loves and worships God is on the only path that can secure genuine and ultimate happiness. Therefore, this particular moral and spiritual value will lead to a most significant nonmoral value, and therefore, certainly has crucial instrumental worth. But the full value of a person's love for God is not to be accounted for solely in terms of the happiness it brings to the one possessing it. Rather, God is, by virtue of who He is and what He has done as sovereign Creator and Redeemer, a proper and fitting object of love and worship, and ought, therefore, to be worshiped. Love of God is intrinsically desirable, and its absence in any given life is a moral tragedy, independent of the negative consequences that it will inevitably have for that life.

This is true also of love of neighbor and of conscientiousness (faithfulness to one's moral principles), to take but two additional examples. Though clearly of instrumental value, these moral goods are not valuable solely in terms of the happiness they usually secure for others and for oneself. A loving friend and a conscientious policeman, the one motivated by love and the other by duty, who attempt to save a life at great personal risk but fail in their attempt, have nevertheless done something of great value. This is true even if their efforts are known to no one but God. True, no life was saved, the unhappiness caused by death was not prevented, and a good example was not provided for others, but nevertheless something good was done, something that may be deemed to be of significant value. What we must suppose from this is that the exercise of love and conscientiousness have intrinsic worth, over and above the happiness that they may secure.

Value theories can be monistic (a single intrinsic value is recognized) or pluralistic (multiple intrinsic values are recognized). Christians may be attracted to a monistic value theory that acknowledges glorification of God as its sole intrinsic value. Such a theory would argue that a state of affairs takes on value only to the extent that it glorifies God. There is, then, a single intrinsic good, spiritual or theological in character, from which all other values derive their worth. But, on the other hand, Christians may wish to opt for a pluralistic theory, contending that God can be glorified only by states of affairs that themselves have intrinsic value. Thus, being a loving person, being a person faithful to one's duty, or being a just society are possible ways to glorify God only because these are states of affairs valuable in themselves. On such a view all the intrinsic goods (moral and nonmoral) discussed above could be recognized as such, but it would be claimed that glorification of God is the supreme good (the so-called *summum bonum*). This means that should there be a possible conflict between glorifying God and lesser goods, then the lesser goods are to be forfeited. This forfeiture (and other forfeitures as well) is morally possible because given the fact that a state of affairs is valuable for its own sake, it does always not follow that its promotion and preservation is always obligatory. Among other reasons, promotion or preservation of this state of affairs might require a sacrifice of other values of even greater worth.

Values are frequently contrasted with facts. The comment "That's a value judgment" is often made with this very contrast in mind. The implication of such a statement is that value "judgments" are only expressions of personal preference and not, like factual matters, something in the objective realm. Christians, on the contrary, will affirm the existence of an objective order of value and obligation, independent of social consensus or personal preference, and grounded ultimately in the character of God. Actually, in both Christian and non-Christian realms, there is often wide agreement over what basic values are to be acknowledged. Little discussion is required to convince people that love is better than hate, pleasure is better than pain, and happiness is better than unhappiness; that justice is a good, along with freedom, knowledge, aesthetic experience, and so on. Disagreement more frequently enters when: (a) determining the best means to these acknowledged ends, (b) adjudicating conflicts between competing values (freedom versus welfare considerations, for example), and (c) providing a theoretical account of our value structures. Christians will not always be in agreement, but they will seriously confront value questions, because a search for an answer to these questions is a search for the will of God, and because they can be taken seriously as God does have a will in these matters.

**Bibliography:** Lamont, W. D., *The Value Judgment* (1955); Pepper, S. C., *The Source of Value* (1958); Perry, R. B., *General Theory of Value* (1926).

R.W.

**VANDALISM.** This term is derived from the name of an aggressive group of Germanic tribes that inhabited Scandinavia before the Christian era but moved eastward about 100 B.C. and resettled in central Europe. There they lived undisturbed for almost four centuries until they were menaced by the westward advance of a Mongolian tribe known as the Huns. In 406 the Vandals invaded the northwestern area of the Roman Empire, raided Gaul, and then after three years of consolidation they advanced into Spain, conquered North Africa and pillaged Rome in 455, causing a great deal of damage. The following century Justinian conquered the Vandals, and by 534 their power had disappeared.

Although they behaved no differently from any other invading barbarian group, the Vandals became notorious for the damage and destruction that resulted from their pillaging. Consequently anyone who engages in the wanton damage or destruction of valuable property is known as a vandal. The modern offender stands in the same tradition by damaging, defacing, or destroying public and private property alike.

The psychodynamics of vandalism are not easy to assess, but since the classic Vandals destroyed anything that they did not understand, ignorance and stupidity must be included with selfishness, undiscipline, and willful aggression as causative factors. The Christian is commanded to demonstrate neighborly love, and this includes respect for the property of others. In consequence the believer will do everything possible to discourage vandalism and promote order and good behavior in society. Vandalism is a costly crime, particularly if irreplaceable items of personal or national value have been damaged beyond repair. The vandal, like the sneak thief, represents one of the lowest levels of criminal life and merits strong punitive treatment when apprehended.

**VENEREAL DISEASE.** Venereal diseases are infectious diseases that are transmitted primarily by sexual contact. These diseases are personally devastating: they destroy relationships; they are costly to society; and they are hard to control, especially in a permissive society.

Scripture says little about venereal disease. Leviticus has strict laws of sexual hygiene (Lev. 15:1-33), possibly directed at reducing the spread of disease. Certainly the requirement that any person having a sexual discharge abstain from sexual intercourse would have limited the spread of the most common and most highly contagious disorders. The requirements of bathing after sexual intercourse and of abstaining from sexual relations during the menstrual period would also help to reduce the spread of infection.

This spread is primarily from mucosal surface to mucosal surface, since the organisms of infection will ordinarily not penetrate normal skin. Any contact between healthy and infective mucosa of genitalia, mouth, urinary tract, or rectum is likely to result in transmission. These organisms may occasionally be transmitted nonvenereally as a result of contact with contaminated objects. They may also be transmitted from mother to child, either by passage through the placenta or by contamination from the vagina during delivery.

Most of the venereal diseases can be treated with antibiotics. At the present time there is an epidemic of venereal disease in North America, the result of widespread sexual permissiveness. Some of the organisms are becoming resistant to the usual antibiotics, making them more serious because they are less easily treated.

At the personal level, venereal disease damages, or destroys, not only sexual organs, but may also spread through the bloodstream to affect many other organs. For example, gonorrhea may cause not only infertility in both sexes, but may spread to joints, causing an arthritis, and to eyes, causing an iritis. Syphilis is notorious for its spread to blood vessels in all parts of the body, with devastating consequences in the circulatory system and the central nervous system. In the early years of this century, syphilitics filled the mental hospitals. Effective treatment for syphilis was one of the first great steps forward in the treatment of psychiatric patients.

A discussion of ethical issues in relationship to venereal disease must move at several levels. At the level of the individual, prevention is important. Sexual continence is clearly a primary preventive measure. Few males contract a venereal disease unless they have engaged in illicit sexual relations. Wives are at greater risk, since men may carry the more common diseases without symptoms. Premarital sexual activity (especially promiscuous behavior) or extramarital sexual activity (especially with prostitutes) puts both sexes at high risk. A second preventive measure is the consistent use of condoms in doubtful sexual situations. If a person is unable or unwilling to restrain himself sexually, he has at least an ethical obligation to minimize the risk of spreading disease. If a person has contracted a venereal disease, there is an ethical responsibility to inform sexual contacts of their risks. Because of the hazard these diseases pose to the person, to others (including the unborn), and to society, any person who has contracted a venereal disease has an ethical obligation to secure effective treatment.

At the social level, several ethical principles exist. Since venereal diseases spreads more rapidly in promiscuous populations, the need for a social ethic that advocates sexual continence and that effectively disapproves of promiscuity and prostitution is important. Because of the social cost of these diseases, society has an ethical responsibility to try to limit their spread. For this reason, many Western jurisdictions require mandatory blood tests prior to marriage, mandatory reporting to state authorities of any cases diagnosed in a physician's practice, and mandatory treatment. Rigorous preventive measures and treatment can help reduce the waste caused by venereal disease.

The treating physician is often placed in a difficult ethical position. Since he is bound by statute, oath, and habit to confidentiality, he is not at liberty (except within the requirements of the law) to advise the patient's sexual contacts of their risk. At the same time, his knowledge of the risk, especially to spouses and families, places him in an awkward moral position. Probably the best means of resolving such a conflict is through counseling the patient to inform any contacts of their risk, and to support the patient through the intense family difficulties that such a disclosure might precipitate.

**Bibliography:** Ma, P. and Armstrong, D., *The Acquired Immune Deficiency Syndrome and Infections of Homosexual Men* (1984); McCormack, W. M., *Diagnosis and Treatment of Sexually Transmitted Disease* (1983); Petersdorf, R. G., *et al.*, (eds.), *Harrison's Principles of Internal Medicine* (10th ed., 1983), pp.891–902.

J.E.R.

**VENIAL SIN.** The term *venial* originated in the Latin *venia*, which carried a range of meanings having to do with goodwill. It was held to be a characteristic of the gods, and thus meant "indulgence, favor, grace," and the like. These senses were also applicable to humans under proper circumstances, with the interesting addition of "forgiveness." In a moral, ethical, or legal sense, anything venial was pardonable.

In the medieval Roman Catholic Church, venial sins were regarded as offenses that were insufficiently severe in nature to cause the spiritual death of the soul or deprive it wholly of sanctifying grace. The Scriptures state that all sin tends toward death (John 8:34; Rom. 6:23), but Roman Catholic moral theologians have claimed that in 1 John 5:16-17 the author distinguishes between venial and mortal sins. For them the "sin unto death" is deliberate apostasy, the unforgivable sin against the Holy Spirit (Mark 3:28-29), by comparison with which every other moral offense paled into insignificance.

Protestant Christians, while agreeing on the seriousness of apostasy, do not normally make an official distinction between degrees of sin, regarding all spiritual transgressions as defiling and causing separation of the individual from fellowship with God. While all sin is therefore very serious, it can be forgiven when the penitent offender comes in faith to Christ and begs for remission, claiming the atoning blood of Christ for pardon (1 John 1:7, 9).

See MORTAL SIN; SIN; SINS OF OMISSION.

**VICE.** This term is derived from the Latin word *vitium*, meaning "fault, blemish, defect," and used by the Romans of defects or imperfections in structures and commodities, as well as of environmental inadequacies. In a metaphorical sense it was applied to morals to describe behavior that was unacceptable even by the depraved standards of Roman culture. Along with gluttony and greed, the most serious offenses committed in the New Testament period were of a sexual nature. Lacking the moral restraints of Hebrew culture, the Greeks and Romans indulged in the grossest forms of sensuality, including homosexual practices, incest, and bestiality.

For them, prostitution could hardly be considered a vice, since it formed a normal part of the cultic rites of heathen temples. Rape, adultery, and premarital coitus were also unexceptionable, and these practices were common to rich and poor alike. It is small wonder, then, that the Christian ethic contrasted so powerfully with contemporary social behavior and hardly surprising that groups such as the Corinthians, who had a traditionally bad reputation for indulging in all forms of immorality, should have found it difficult to relinquish their former dissolute ways once they became Christians. While it is untrue to say that chastity was unknown in the Roman Empire, since it was a requirement for vestal virgins, the proclamation by Paul and others of chastity as a Christian virtue that was mandatory in life must have shaken profoundly those pagans who heard this aspect of Christ's teachings being proclaimed.

For ethicists, vice is the antithesis of virtue and comprises sin against individual selfhood. It is habitual by nature, often has powerful sexual overtones, and depraves the individual and others who come into contact with it. Medieval church theologians combined biblical and secular ethics to produce a list of vices known as the "seven deadly sins," which included both carnal and spiritual evils. The Christian will be instructed by Paul's catalog of fleshly sins in Galatians 5:19-21 as to the true nature of vice and will be cautioned to avoid sedulously the modern counterparts of these sins against God and mankind.

**VIOLENCE.** Ethically, violence must not be defined in terms of natural disasters such as tornadoes, floods, landslides, lightning strikes, or animal savagery, but in personal terms. Violent acts are functions of persons and are to be judged morally in relation to the motives of persons as moral agents (whether God, man, or other rational creatures) and the nature and quality of their acts.

Violence is the use of physical or psychological force so as to injure or coerce someone either physically or psychologically or both or to damage something. The physical and psychological consequences may well interlock, for example, physical maladies due to psychological abuse, as in the case of the abuse of a spouse or a child.

Modern forms of violence differ little from traditional forms, except that the inventions of modern technology and psychological techniques make violence easier to mask. Common modern forms are:

1. Terrorism (including assassination, kidnapping and hostage-taking), random or indiscriminate violence, and sadism.

2. Torture, maiming, and judicial amputation.

3. Homicide, including murder and other forms of killing such as abortion, infanticide, assistance to commit suicide, and euthanasia (whether voluntary, nonvoluntary as in the case of an unconscious person, or involuntary).

4. Fighting, and striking or threatening to do so, which at times may include some sports such as boxing, ice hockey, and football.

5. Robbery and mugging.

6. Vengeance, vigilante activity, and mercenaries who are not ethically motivated.

7. Abuse of a spouse, child abuse, abuse of the elderly, and abuse of employees.

8. Anarchy, unjust war, and some civil disobedience including aggressive pacifism.

9. Certain controversial medical, clinical or quasi-medical procedures including lobotomy, leucotomy, and electroconvulsive therapy, forced treatment of various kinds, claims for beneficent confinement, surgical alteration of the sex of an individual, and clinical or surgical alteration of personality. Many regard some or all of these as violent acts.

10. Psychological roughness or aggression including lie detector or other similar tests, malicious psychological injury, the use of truth serums, some forms of conditioning including brainwashing, the use of mood or mind-altering substances, threats, summoning a prisoner for execution only to halt it at the last instant, and various forms of aggression theory and practice in business administration.

In the past, apart from one's actually witnessing a violent act, violence could be depicted only in still-life drawings or paintings, simulated (acted out in a staged drama), or imagined through literature. Modern communications techniques such as television and video graphically portray violence in action. Television has the capacity to sensitize the public against the horrors of violence. As well, many claim that television violence blunts moral sensitivity and increases the potential for violence. Modern communications techniques are powerful tools for good or ill. Some believe that television readily brutalizes people, for example the showing of an actual killing such as the shooting of a felon in a police action.

In the hands of the unscrupulous, television or video may readily be used for evil purposes such as exploiting prurient interests. Repressive regimes use nationally controlled television to suppress truth and to foster violent attitudes for political purposes. Thus television depiction of violence can as much contribute to violence as it can deter violence, depending upon the moral intention of the presenter and the capacity of the viewer to deal with it morally.

Despite the fact that violence can be progagated via television it can be a powerful tool against violence. As in the case of shortwave radio, satellite television makes repressive control of the media more difficult in closed societies so long as some free countries exist. Balanced programming from countries which are democratic and free tends to foster longings for liberation, especially among women and minorities in cultures where they are abused and repressed.

Jesus rebuked naked violence and urged peace. His gospel brings peace among men. Christians abhor violence and the anger which accompanies it. In the seven New Testament lists of vices, four mention anger: 2 Corinthians 12:20; Galatians 5:20; Ephesians 4:31; Colossians 3:8. Violence is uniformly condemned: Psalms 7:16; 18:48; Ecclesiastes 5:8; Matthew 5:39; 26:52; Luke 3:14; 2 Corinthians 11:20; 1 Timothy 3:3; Titus 1:7; 1 Peter 2:23. As much as is humanly possible, Christians should be peaceable: Matthew 5:9; Romans 12:18; 2 Corinthians 13:11; 1 Thessalonians 5:13; 1 Timothy 2:2.

A distinction must be drawn between the customary meaning of violence and the lawful use of force, coercion, and infliction of pain. Scripture is replete with references to the just anger and wrath of God and to his smiting evil people. The state is God's instrument to withstand and judge evil (John 19:11; Rom. 13:1-7; 1 Pet. 2:13-17). While to some the forcible restraint of evil (Rom. 4:15; 13:4-5) in relation to the law of love (Rom. 13:8-10; Gal. 5:6) is a puzzle, both are consistent with the nature and rule of God. They attest to the realities of the present evil-infected world as well as to the presence of God's kingdom in the evil-infected world.

Legal use of force is legitimate, but it must be exercised within the terms of a legal code based on principles of justice, equity, and compassion. Thus, just war, policing and imprisoning, capital punishment, and legitimate self-defense against criminal activity (which is distinct from persecution) are not specifically prohibited to Christians. Jesus did not denounce participation in war, even though he urged his followers to peace. However, a purely vengeful view of justice (an eye for an eye) is alien to the righteousness of God as taught in the Bible.

Physical force has little place in family relations. This includes the discipline of children. Spanking should be rare; it must be carefully controlled and must flow from and be practiced in love.

The root causes of human violence are a puzzle to modern, sophisticated man. Violence occurs in all social, economic, and educational levels of society. Nineteenth-century German society was one of the most educated and culturally advanced of the era, yet a Hitler could subsequently arise and with him the indescribably cruel and violent Nazi regime. Violence characterizes sinful man. Christians may well have to suffer violence in this life for the sake of their faith. Scripture has long pointed to the close relation between anger and violence on one hand and the importance of forgiveness and faith on the other in the ultimate justice of God.

The imprecatory psalms are an important paradigm (Pss. 35; 55; 58; 59; 69; 109). How can a Christian heap abuse upon and pray for violence to come upon his enemies? It should be noted that the psalmists recall the goodness and severity of God upon both the just and the unjust. Evil is not excused. It is seen to be real, reprehensible, and worthy of judgment. The sentiments of the imprecatory psalms are offered in prayer and are a dialogue between the troubled soul and God who is just. The psalmists' anger is vented. Destructive anger is not stored up to cultivate guilt and depression, eventually to break out in uncontrolled violence. These are prayers to purge the soul, not formulas for action. The final judgment is left to God, and the faith is expressed that God judges men severely in this life as well as in the future in many ways, through disaster, armed might, and the judicial process.

**Bibliography:** Devine, P. E., *The Ethics of Homicide* (1978); Fromm, E., *The Anatomy of Human Destructiveness* (1973); Sider, R. J., *Christ and Violence* (1979); Ungerleider, C. S., *Television and Society* (1984).

S.J.M.

**VIRGINITY.** This term has its roots in the Latin word *virgo*, meaning "maiden, virgin, young woman." The classical understanding of the word was that of a girl or woman who had not experienced carnal relations. Formerly this condition was attestable at marriage, when the hymen was ruptured with a consequent slight loss of blood. But nowadays a perforated hymen need only mean that the woman concerned has used tampons to deal with her menstrual periods, and hence its value as an indication of virginity has depreciated. The notion that a woman who has not indulged in carnal relations is therefore pure is a quaint poetic fantasy, if only because all women (as are all men) are by nature defiled by sin, whether they are virgins or not.

The Hebrews laid great moral stress upon virginity as a token of ceremonial and social purity, and all women were expected to be virgins at the time of marriage unless they were widows or harlots. For a Hebrew male to marry a whore, as Hosea did at God's command (Hos. 1:2), was therefore unthinkable under normal circumstances. The great gift to the Hebrews of a messianic Prince was to be the offspring of a virgin (*almah*, Isa. 7:14). This word is always used in Hebrew of an unmarried female, whereas another term, *bethulah*, frequently rendered "virgin" in the King James and other versions, did not refer exclusively to a sexually unsullied female. For example, in Joel 1:8, the prophet instructs the people to "lament like a virgin girded with sackcloth for the husband of her youth" (KJV).

For the Hebrews, virginity had an abiding and significant moral value because it enhanced the distinctiveness of covenantal traditions as compared with the gross immorality of contemporary pagan cultures. The New Testament authors maintained this tradition, enhanced by the fact that Jesus was conceived miraculously and born of a virgin (*parthenos*, Matt. 1:23; Luke 1:27). While virginity was respected, it was never regarded in the New Testament as a morally superior state of life; and Paul himself did not receive any special revelation concerning virgins. If they so desired, and opportunity availed, they were free to marry (1 Cor. 7:28); but Paul's personal preference in view of the shortness of the time before Christ's expected return was for people to remain as unencumbered as possible. In 2 Corinthians 11:2 Paul uses the imagery of virginity when describing his desire to present the local Christian community to Christ as "a chaste virgin," that is, in the height of moral and ethical purity.

In the current evil and adulterous generation, women who manage to preserve their virginity until marriage are to be respected greatly for their stout resistance to the unprecedented seductive pressures to which young women have been subjected as one result of the feminist movement. Christians are required to set examples of moral living and to adopt a chaste and morally pure manner that will view both virginity and marital chastity as equally precious gifts from God for those called to pursue such ways of living.

**VIRTUE, VIRTUES.** This term is derived directly from the Latin *virtus*, a word which referred originally to masculine properties such as those characteristics associated with manhood. *Virtus* was thus a collective noun which summed up or reflected elements such as strength, bravery, resourcefulness, excellence, and reliability.

Since these qualities were sought after in a good soldier, it is hardly surprising that this usage occurred in literature and speeches dealing with war.

In a metaphorical sense the Romans employed *virtus* of the qualities exhibited by superior breeds of animals, while orators, poets, and philosophers found in it a ready designation of such abstract concepts as power, goodness, value, and general worth. In religious circles the Romans used the expression *deum virtute*, which in a literal sense meant "by the merit of the gods" (where *deum* is a contracted form of the genitive plural *deorum*), but became common currency as an expression of gratitude for divine mercy, roughly equivalent to the modern "Thank God!" *Virtus* ultimately found widespread usage as a description of moral perfection in the abstract or of a person or group that exemplified such a concept. In poetic and rhetorical passages virtue was sometimes personified and regarded as a deity.

The classical Greek counterpart of *virtus* was the common word *arete*, which in broad terms described excellence or goodness of any variety. As with *virtus*, *arete* was used at an early period to portray manly characteristics of strength, endurance, loyalty, ingenuity, and so on; and this was especially noticeable in Homer. He even reflected the anthropomorphism of Greek religion by describing these qualities as exhibited by the gods of the Greek pantheon. Outside Homer, *arete* was used occasionally as a designation of nobility or rank, comparable to the Hebrew expression *gibbor hayil* (Judg. 11:1), literally "man of valor," but more accurately describing a person of title by virtue of land tenure.

The Greeks employed *arete* widely in prose to describe excellence or high qualities of various kinds as encountered in animals and people alike. As their epic poetry and other writings show, this ancient race admired noble and courageous deeds greatly and described outstanding feats of valor readily in terms of *arete*. Yet it is interesting to note that, while they assigned a high value to such exploits, their prose writings do not seem to indicate that they associated a concomitant moral or ethical quality with them. What they did admire were the unusual, superior features that had been brought to their notice, but their evaluations. Even when the concept of uniqueness or distinction led to public recognition or fame as the result of excellence, the concept of *arete* which underlay the situation still did not seem to carry anything more than a nonethical judgment of value, being regarded as the equivalent of *doxa*, "glory, praise, renown."

But it was in the Greek philosophical writings that *arete*, the normal term for virtue, came into its own as a moral and ethical quality. This was not a spontaneous development, however, because in the days of Socrates and Plato a group of teachers known as Sophists professed to teach *arete* to all who would listen. Their "virtue," however, was of a pragmatic variety which comprised the art of managing both states and families so as to attain public success in a democratic community. Plato built upon the central concern of Socrates, namely the care of the human *psyche*, which for the average Greek simply meant the "life principle," to emphasize the unity of all existence under the control of reason.

For Plato this was virtue, and even though it might be categorized under such moral forms as prudence, courage, justice, and temperance, these were not to be regarded as separate ideals to be assigned their own independent status as virtues. In his teaching Plato in fact made no particular distinction between these four moral qualities, which subsequently came to be designated four moral qualities, which subsequently came to be designated as the "four cardinal virtues," but instead regarded them as different aspects of a life lived under the control of reason. Because of the concept of the fundamentality of virtue which Plato espoused, there could be no rigid line of demarcation between public and private morality, any more than there could be between politics and ethics.

Aristotle's ethical concern was teleological in nature, involving a scrutiny of the end or purpose of human activity. For him there was only one final end, since his concept of unified wholes or systems precluded any form of diversification. This end was *eudaimonia* or "well-being," an activity of humanity's highest faculties ("soul") in accordance with the dictates of reason. Such activity must accord with whatever virtues were recognized and be perpetrated in a complete life, not just in sporadic efforts. For Aristotle, virtue was not an emotion so much as an established disposition of character acquired through the practice of virtuous deeds, which he regarded as ends in themselves.

Aristotle maintained that human behavior, to be truly ethical, must be controlled by the "doctrine of the Mean," since the conduct of a virtuous individual must always be correct and appropriate. He also distinguished between moral and intellectual virtues, regarding the former as justice, courage, prudence, temperance, and the like, while the latter comprised science, art, wisdom of a practical nature, intuitive reason, and theoretical wisdom. Whereas Plato unified the concept of virtue, Aristotle separated each virtue and defined it carefully and independently, although his treatment is far from being systematic. Aristotle maintained that virtue, like vice, is the consequence of an individual's free choice, but otherwise seemed to understand motivation very inadequatley.

Platonic and Aristotelian thought passed in various ways into Christian theology, As far as the concept of virtue is concerned, the four moral qualities described as "cardinal virtues" were expanded to seven in the medieval period by the addition of Paul's three "theological virtues" (1 Cor. 13:13). By contrast with Greek thought, the New Testament does not speculate upon the "virtuous life" as understood by the Greeks and Romans. Indeed, *arete* occurs in the Greek New Testament only in Philippians 4:8; 2 Peter 1:3, 5; and in the plural form, *aretai*, in 1 Peter 2:9. These references indicate that the virtues mentioned are imparted by God as the believer grows in fellowship with Christ and are not the consequence of rigorous human self-discipline.

See CARDINAL VIRTUES; THEOLOGICAL VIRTUES.

**VIVISECTION.** Vivisection is the use of animals for experimental and teaching purposes. It is a mainstay of modern research in biology, toxicology, veterinary medicine techniques, biomedical research, and so on. Peter Singer and Tom Regan have said that "the use of animals as subjects in research is as commonplace in the scientific community as is the use of animal flesh for food in the world at large." This claim is substantiated by their citation of 1971 statistics that show that in that year American researchers used 45 million rodents, 700,000 rabbits, 200,000 cats, 85,282 primates, 46,264 swine, 22,961 sheep, 1,724,279 birds, more than 15 million frogs, 190,415 turtles, 500,000 dogs, and numerous other animals.

Descriptions of the gruesome and agonizing nature of many of the studies prick the conscience of humane individuals. Is it morally justified to treat animals the way we do in research? If so, under what conditions is it justified, and how are we to limit unjustifiable research? Animals have been shown to suffer great agony at the hands of researchers. Experiments have been conducted in which electrical shock, physical trauma, surgical distress, psychological upset, and many other effects have been produced in various animals.

In view of the manifest suffering caused animals by such procedures, several attempts have been made to reduce the moral blame that might attend such activities. Two main lines of argument have been advanced: either animals are not truly conscious of pain, but merely manifest behavior that is similar to our pain response; or that their pain, however real it may be, is morally justified by the humanitarian benefits to be produced. The first line of argument was used by Rene Descartes, who argued that animals are merely automata that only appear to be conscious and aware of pain. Descartes's view came at a time when science, in which the extensive use of animals would serve, was in rapid ascendancy. Other major figures in the philosophical-ethical tradition, such as Immanuel Kant, believed that only rational beings merit moral consideration.

Many have argued that, while it is highly likely that animals are made to suffer by such research, the benefits of science are sufficient to justify their use. This falls prey to two different sorts of criticism. On the one hand, it is a sheer consequentialism, a case of the "end" (in this case, scientific advance) "justifying the means," namely, the sufferings and deaths of huge numbers of animals. On the other, it is said to betray an objectionable perspective called *speciesism.* This view suggests that the human species is so far above all others that the slightest whim of humanity outweighs the most basic claims of animals. Some have argued to the contrary that animals indeed have rights, because they are either sentient beings capable of conscious suffering (Peter Singer), or "interest bearers," beings for which some things are important (Joel Feinberg).

The move to respect the welfare of animals seems to come from two different sources. Some argue that the differences between human beings and other species are differences of degree rather than qualitative distinctions. These people would elevate animals, in effect, by degrading the human. Others accept the traditional Judeo-Christian distinction between person and less-than-person, but argue that this tradition does not mandate treating animals as mere objects in the world. Scripture speaks often of animals, stating that they are of concern to God and are His subjects (Gen. 9:10; Exod. 20:10; Ps. 50:10-11; Jonah 4:11; Matt. 10:17; 23:34; Mark 1:13). As respected a thinker as C. S. Lewis represents a strong Christian anti-vivisectionist approach.

Most Christians, regardless of their views on animal rights, would agree that a more responsible approach to stewardship is in order, which recognizes that animals, as part of God's creation, merit consideration above that of mere objects. Most Christians would argue for a responsible use of animals in research, an approach that would attempt to reduce both the numbers of animals used and the suffering produced to an absolute minimum, while doing what is scientifically necessary to advance human welfare.

Bibliography: Hume, C. W., *The Status of Animals in the Christian Religion (1957); Lewis, C. S., God in the Dock* (1970); Regan, T., *Environmental Ethics* 2(2):99–120; Regan T. and Singer, P., (eds.), *Animal Rights and Human Obligations* (1976); Schaeffer, F. A., *Pollution and the Death of Man* (1970).

D.B.F.

**VOCATION.** The concept of vocation is a peculiarly continental Reformation derivative from the theology first of Luther, then Calvin. It was not used commonly by Christians of the Reformed traditions in Britain. The concept continues to appear in the literature of the Lutheran and Reformed traditions in the United States, though common use is declining.

The term *calling* is almost wholly a Pauline concept, with a parallel use in First Peter. Paul's primary meaning is as a calling to salvation (Rom. 8:30) through the gospel (2 Thess. 2:14), and, as a necessary corollary of this, to "lead a life worthy of the calling to which you have been called" (Eph. 4:1; 1 Peter 2:9). This is the primary sense in which the Christian life is a vocation, namely a calling to follow Christ and to fulfill the pattern of His life in our lives (Phil. 3:14; 1 Peter 2:21; 3:9). Such vocation embraces love, forgiveness, reconciliation, peace, and goodness as its frame of reference.

A derived sense of calling to special ministry sometimes occurs (Acts 16:10; Rom. 12:6-8; 1 Cor. 1:1; Eph. 4:11). However, it is doubtful that the biblical term *calling* can be understood to mean vocation. Luther was wrong to translate 1 Corinthians 7:20 as "vocation" *(Beruf).* This passage probably refers to the environment or circumstances in which one finds oneself (1 Cor. 1:26).

More important than vocation is the crucial Reformation doctrine of the universal priesthood of believers. Those who are called, justified, and sanctified by grace and by faith alone are called to serve as well. Christian vocation is not the prerogative of a priestly class only, nor is ministry legitimated only by ordination. Every believer is called to minister, from which comes the concept of Christian vocation.

In Neo-orthodox theology of modern times, Karl Barth has given a powerful impetus to the concept of vocation through his teaching regarding the election of Jesus Christ to servanthood. The vocation of the eternal word was to go into the far country, becoming obedient by offering and humbling Himself to be the brother of man; to take His place with the transgressor; and to judge him by judging Himself and dying in his place *(Church Dogmatics* 4.1.157). It follows that Christ's commitment to His vocation ought to elicit humble obedience from us, His followers.

The Christian's vocation, therefore, is to be the Lord's servant in the world, whatever one's occupation. In practical, day-to-day terms, the ethics of such a life implied in general biblical principles, specific biblical prohibitions, and the pattern of Christ's life.

Christian vocation ties in closely with the theology and ethics of work. Not work, however, merely as drudgery nor to maintain subsistence existence, but the more positive sense of contributing to the well-being of others through careful utilization of the earth's resources. Scripture abounds with references to the values of useful work. Jesus learned carpentry. Several of His disciples were fishermen. Paul was a tentmaker. Lydia traded in fine cloth. Philemon was probably a businessman.

Three important principles follow from biblical teaching. First, as much as lies within their power, each Christian and each Christian family should strive to be self-reliant. This is not merely to avoid becoming a drain on others, but to produce more than their own needs so that others can share in the abundance. Second, Christians should strive for excellence. When men and women do good work and produce dependable products, they bless and enrich the lives of others. Third, Christians ought to strive to improve the world, making it a better place than it was when they came into it.

To accomplish these things, biblical writers urge Christians to give daily attention not only to their general deportment and interpersonal relations, but also to specific actions in the marketplace. While the Christian is free, not all things are helpful, nor do they build up. Some things actually enslave (1 Cor. 6:12; 10:23). These should, therefore, be avoided. Seek the good of one's neighbor (1 Cor. 10:24). Don't pilfer from the job. Guard the reputation of the Christian faith by doing good work (Titus 2:8-10). As a general rule, therefore, the Christian ought to work hard in a useful vocation, striving to contribute to the good of humanity.

**Bibliography:** Hatfield, C., *The Scientist and Ethical Decision* (1973); Reich, R., *The Next American Frontier* (1983); Richardson, A., *The Biblical Doctrine of Work* (1952); Trueblood, E., *The New Man For Our Time* (1970).

See WORK.

S.J.M.

**VOLUNTARISM.** This philosophical term originated from the Latin *voluntas*, meaning "will, choice, inclination." Voluntarism thus describes the philosophical theory which exalts the exercise of the human will over the deliberations of reason. Many ethicists trace voluntarism back to the Sophists and their disputes with Plato as he endeavored to base human action upon rational thought and decisions.

Since that period the conflict between will and reason as behavioral determinants has found expression in the writings of numerous prominent philosophers. David Hume (1711-1776) gave an important dimension to the concept by arguing that reason alone could do no more than choose means toward ends and was incapable of selecting the goals themselves. This latter task was for him the function of will, which not merely identified ends as such but achieved them with the people of reason. Because of his repudiation of the principle of causality as generally understood, the realizing of goals would constitute a separate identifiable activity, unconnected with previous behavior.

Schopenhauer (1778-1860) concurred with Hume in giving the will priority over the intellect, although for him will was a cruder and less sophisticated force than Hume envisaged. Like some other voluntarists, Schopenhauer interpreted will in terms of self-preservation. Nietzsche (1844-1900) also gave a central place to will, regarding it as the supreme motivating factor in all human endeavor. Ethical voluntarism was also espoused by William James (1842-1910), as well as by modern existentialist writers, who in general agree that reason alone is an inadequate basis upon which to establish moral theory.

James supported an earlier form of Christian fideism, holding that a person could make a commitment to religious faith on the basis of will alone in the absence of any purely rational grounds for belief. Since for most voluntarists God's existence cannot be proved, rational considerations would provide no impediment to the existence of faith.

In social ethics, voluntarism expresses itself in terms of voluntary rather than compulsory support for state-controlled education, health, and welfare programs. Voluntarists are also at the forefront of movements opposing compulsory military service. Since self-preservation has generally constituted the goal of life for most voluntarists, they would come under all the biblical condemnations of selfish rather than altruistic behavior. In the view of the writer they commit a very common methodological error in setting two postulates in diametrical opposition and imposing a choice between them rather than regarding them as components for concerted action. One's world may well consist of will and idea, but the latter always needs the former to implement it, since wishing alone does not suffice.

**VOTE.** As a verb this word denotes the action by which a person makes a choice, either by ballot, a vocal response, or a show of hands, in favor of or in opposition to a particular proposal. As a noun it describes an individual's verdict on a motion presented for consideration, under whatever form it has been cast. While some ballots are secret and others are not, the importance of the individual vote is constant except in those cases where there has been fraudulent interference with the voting process. Voting is only meaningful where there is a genuine choice and individual freedom to exercise that choice. In Communist Russia a facade of democracy is maintained by mounting an election process, but since the list of candidates has already been predetermined and the ordinary citizen is under compulsion to vote for that list and none other, freedom of choice is nonexistent.

Truly democratic voting allows for a negative vote by abstention, as well as positive, declared support for a proposal or a candidate for office. The freedom to vote or abstain has long been a cherished privilege of the Western participatory democracies, which by law provide their citizens with regular opportunities to exercise their franchise. By maintaining this tradition the electorate is guaranteed the continuance of democratic government. So seriously is the principle of the individual vote regarded in Australia that those who refuse to vote, or abstain for any reason other than of a serious medical nature, are subject to a heavy fine.

The New Testament teaches that the Christian must always regard civil authority as a delegated function of a larger divine power, designed to inculcate law and order in human society (Rom. 13:1-7). Since the believer is thus by definition a citizen also, an important form of Christian witness to society can be undertaken by active participation in the political process. In this way Christian values will be at the forefront of discussion, and evil persons and motives will be restrained. To allow the cherished privilege of voting to go unused is absolutely unpardonable for the practicing Christian, if only because of the sense of social irresponsibility which it indicates.

See RESPONSIBILITY.

**VOWS.** This term is derived from a Latin verb *voveo*, meaning "to promise solemnly." Among the Romans it was used in a secular sense of a solemn undertaking, sometimes given under oath, and also in a religious sense of something promised by a worshiper to a god in a solemn act of dedication. The highest form of a vow was the self-offering of an individual for service in a shrine or temple, and in the ancient world such persons were known as votaries. The vow was thus a solemn promise or undertaking that was often attested by an oath or some form of sacred ceremony and had the same general character whatever its implications. All ancient Near Eastern nations were superstitious, and therefore the gods were always significantly present in daily life. In the last analysis, therefore, a vow was invariably a religious affair.

In the Old Testament the common Hebrew words *nadar* and *neder* were used to describe a vow, whether made by a man or woman (Num. 30:2-3). Sometimes the vows assumed the form of bargaining with God (Gen. 28:20-21; Num. 21:2), while on other occasions they involved a ritual of a distinctive character. Such was the undertaking described as the vow of the Nazirite (Num. 6:2-21). The object of this vow was to enable a man or woman to be separated unto the Lord. It involved abstinence from the fruit of the vine and its products, as well as including acts of discipline which embodied the ideals of personal holiness. The vow was undertaken for a specific period, and when that period had ended the person could resume a normal life if such was desired.

Vows were normally discharged by peace offerings (Prov. 7:14), which in effect reinforced the fellowship engendered by the vows. They seem frequently to have been a test of sincerity on both sides, but were normally of such a solemn nature that they were discharged in the proper spirit of the undertaking. One tragic vow was that made by Jephthah, who pledged to God that, were he to be victorious over the Ammonites, he would sacrifice as a burnt offering whatever emerged first from his house on his return (Judg. 11:31). His dismay when his only daughter rushed out to greet him was tempered by the inviolable nature of his oath as a patriarchal figure. Occurrences of this kind from Greek culture were also by no means unknown.

Vows in New Testament times seem to have been infrequent, judged by the paucity of references to them in Scripture. In Acts 18:18 Paul was spoken of as having taken a vow of an unspecified nature, which he discharged in the temple at Jerusalem (Acts 21:26) in conjunction with four other persons (Acts 21:23), but these are the only occasions on which vows were mentioned. Blessing normally accompanied the discharging of a vow (Job 22:27), while the one who defaulted was cursed (Mal. 1:14), indicating that fulfillment was God's expectation of the one who entered into a vow. While a vow may imply a sense of deep dedication, it was not made mandatory for anyone in Israel. Since it was a voluntary act, no sin was committed by those who abstained from vows (Deut. 23:21-22). The Christian is warned against rash oath-taking (Matt. 5:34-37), and should therefore avoid becoming entangled in a solemn undertaking from which escape is possible only at great cost.

See OATHS.

# -W-

**WAGES.** All societies, other than the most economically primitive, need to maintain some system of wage-rewarding work. Christian ethics affirms both the importance of labor and that labor transactions should be governed by justice.

The Covenant Codes of the Old Testament (Lev. 19:13; Deut. 24:14-15) insist that wages be paid promptly and that the wage earner not be cheated. Similarly, the wide-ranging concern for social righteousness that characterizes so much Old Testament prophecy is relevant here. Jeremiah declares God's judgment upon the man who extends his business by injustice and dishonesty and by defaulting on his wage payments (22:13).

The New Testament also points toward the moral responsibilities of those who hire laborers (Matt. 20:1; James 5:4). But Luke (3:14) warns wage earners—particularly those in places of special power, and so special temptation—not to escalate their wages through immoral means, in this particular context, intimidation. The practice of paying wages in return for Christian ministry also emerges in the New Testament (Luke 10:7; 2 Cor. 11:8; 1 Tim. 5:18).

Medieval Catholicism developed a detailed teaching to establish what was just in various forms of economic exchange, including wages. Its central moral principle was that there should be a demonstrable link between economic reward and economic contribution. This was seen as a clear implication of the natural moral law, which lay behind the medieval condemnation of usury. By the fourteenth century, however, some theologians were willing to admit usury within certain conditions. The principle of reward equal to contribution also lay behind the development of medieval just wage theory, which demanded equal pay for equal work. This was understood in a highly conservative fashion, that wages should maintain persons in their relative status. Alongside this, it was affirmed that one must take account of the actual work done, not exploiting extraneous factors (such as a large supply of local labor or an individual in dire financial circumstances) in setting wage rates. Both Luther and Calvin affirmed this principle of "equivalent value."

There has been little sustained examination of the just wage in more recent eras. Indeed, it is virtually impossible to assess equivalent value in modern industrial society, with its massive variety of labor tasks. In reality, the modern marketplace has evolved its own complex system of forces to establish wage rates and differentials, which reflects a whole array of human values. In the future, the development of automation may render the notion of equivalence even more unworkable. Indeed, according to one school of thought, we should respond to the automative revolution by bringing an end to the social connection between labor and the distribution of wealth. Others call for the termination of the current Western situation in which wages-growth continues alongside increasing unemployment. They suggest reductions in the labor week and the development of schemes for the sharing of employment.

**Bibliography:** Catherwood, F., *The Christian in Industrial Society* (1964); Fogarty, M. P., *The Just Wage* (1961); Ivens, M., (ed.), *Industry and Values* (1970).

See EMPLOYMENT; WORK.

M.D.G.

**WAR.** War may be defined as the use of armed force by a state to secure its will against the will of another state or states. It is possible to broaden this definition to include the use of force by or against recognized international authorities that are not states (such as the United Nations) and bodies that have been given the *de facto* status of governments-in-exile.

Warfare between states has always been a feature of human society. Wherever men have bonded together into communities, one of their chief intentions has been to find the security to pursue their social and economic activities. While this has not always involved their going to war, a preparedness to do so has often been seen as a prerequisite of peaceful coexistence with potential adversaries.

The principal war recorded in the Bible is the conquest of Palestine by the Israelites after the Exodus from Egypt. This is a holy war, commanded by God, with the twin purposes of punishing the Canaanite tribes and establishing a homeland for His people. In its pursuit, all conventional wiles of warfare are engaged, placing spying and ambushes alongside a dependence on God. Other wars reported in Scripture are sometimes presented as the will of God, sometimes condemned, but do not share the peculiar character of the conquest.

The contrast between the prominence of war in the Old Testament associated with the will and character of God (the "Lord of Hosts," the "man of war"), and in the New, with the teaching of Jesus on meekness and nonresistance, has led to a diversity of Christian responses to the problem of war itself. Several ethical dilemmas are posed for the believer today. It was widely assumed in the early church that war was evil and could never be justified. The conversion to Christianity of the Roman Empire brought about a rethinking of this wholesale rejection of war, taking its lead from the classical concept of the *bellum justum,* which was originally more concerned for propriety than for morality in warfare. Augustine's doctrine of the "Just War" has since been the paradigm of the church's thinking. The pacifist tradition became, and has remained, a minority report.

The general rejection of pacifism by the church has focused upon the pacifist misapplication of Jesus' teaching concerning personal relations and the affairs of nations. It was no more intended to preclude armed communal defense than to dismantle systems of criminal justice. To suggest that nations are not to be regarded ethically as individual persons is not to imply that they should therefore, be free from all moral constraints. For example, a fundamental biblical theme is that the nation is morally obliged to defend its weak and unprotected people.

Augustine's criteria of Just War suggest a framework for Christian assessment of particular wars. These criteria are generally taken to include the waging of the war by a competent authority, its righteous ends, and its proper and proportionate means. But the advent of modern weapons technology, with its chemical, biological, and nuclear options, has raised new problems concerning, for example, the inviolability of noncombatants and the scale of conflict. Contemporary approaches to the ethics of war require their own biblical and theological foundations and cannot limit themselves merely to restatements of the Just War theory developed in the Middle Ages. That theory was a biblical adaptation of natural moral thinking to particular circumstances. The church has yet to come to a biblical mind on contemporary questions. It must do so through a biblical critique of the several moral options, all of which, from pacifism through varieties of Just War theory to an unqualified acceptance of current war-fighting possibilities, have their origins in natural moral thinking.

**Bibliography:** Bainton, R., *Christian Attitudes Toward War and Peace* (1960); Craigie, P. C., *The Problem of War in the Old Testament* (1978); Curry, D. C., (ed.), *Evangelicals and the Bishops' Pastoral Letter* (1984); Hare, J. E. and Joynt, C. B., *Ethics and International Affairs* (1982); Ramsey, P., *War and the Christian Conscience* (1961).

See ARMAMENT; DISARMAMENT; JUST WAR CRITERIA; MILITARY SERVICE.

N.M. de S.C.

**WEALTH.** The term *wealth* is used broadly to describe an accumulation of something that is particularly abundant and valuable, as with the phrases "wealth of information" or "wealth of experience." Most commonly, however, the word is used of material riches, in whatever form they have been amassed.

From early times people have struggled to attain to wealth, impelled very frequently by ambition and greed. In antiquity wealth was represented by such diverse elements as flocks and herds, rings, crowns, ornaments, statues made from precious metals, furnishings of various kinds plated with gold, and a domestic treasury replete with costly items from foreign lands. Before money was invented, about the sixth century B.C., traditionally by the fabulously rich king Croesus of Lydia (561-546 B.C.), goods and services were frequently paid for in weighed amounts of gold and silver (Gen. 23:16). Since silver was much more plentiful than gold, it was always the prominent metal used as a medium of exchange. The Hebrew word for silver (*kesep*) is often rendered *money* in modern versions (Gen. 17:13, RSV), but it must be remembered that until the postexilic period (after 538 B.C.) *money* denoted a particular weighed amount of a precious metal rather than a coin.

Both the Hebrew Scriptures and the Greek New Testament reflect the Semitic view of human existence, refusing to make any artificial distinction between material prosperity and divine blessing. A person was blessed with wealth because he or she revered and obeyed the God of Sinai. Abraham is not merely an exemplar of faith in God for Jew and Christian alike, but also of the way in which divine blessing was indicated by great wealth. The Hebrew poets celebrated the crowning of a person's fidelity to the covenant ethos by the divine bestowal of abundant riches (Pss. 1:3; 112:1, 3). In the New Testament, wealth is again emphasized as one of God's rich gifts, bestowed on the true believer for his or her enjoyment (1 Tim. 6:17). While Jesus Christ occasionally made demands upon certain individuals by challenging them to sell their possessions and give to the economically deprived (Matt. 19:21; Luke 12:33), He was not indulging in a condemnation of wealth in itself. Instead, He was endeavoring to inform His followers as to priorities (Matt. 6:33), urging them to be preoccupied with the Kingdom rather than with material things. While Christ warned His followers about the deceitfulness of riches, He also commended the unjust steward for His business acumen (Luke 16:9).

The New Testament in particular draws attention to the responsibilities of the wealthy believer, of which there must have been a significant number. Of prime importance are fidelity and scrupulous honesty in the way in which riches are used. If the believer has been a unfaithful or dishonest in his stewardship of "the unrighteous mammon," he can scarcely be expected to receive the true riches of God (Luke 16:10-12), namely his spiritual blessings. In exercising stewardship of material wealth, the believer is exhorted to be generous to those in need (1 Tim. 6:18). Here Paul appeals to the example set by Christ, who, though He was rich, became poor for humanity's sake, that by His poverty many might become rich (2 Cor. 8:9).

It need hardly be said that wealth is by no means the only divine gift over which stewardship has to be exercised. All gifts possessed by believers are from God (1 Pet. 4:10) and are to be held in trusteeship, a concept to which the Christian must be entirely faithful. Consequently, if we take the Christian ethic seriously, we must give as God has given to us, without reserving any part of our gifts for purely personal satisfaction or gain. By being rich in good deeds, the believer establishes a firm basis of fidelity toward God, in anticipation of the time when he will enter into eternal life (1 Tim. 6:19).

While the privileges and opportunities of wealth are enunciated clearly in Scripture, there are equally plain warnings about the pitfalls that sometimes accompany them. Discontent with the degree of one's prosperity could be interpreted as an implicit condemnation of God for an apparently inadequate provision of material resources. Contentment with what God has provided is encouraged in Scripture (Ps. 62:10; 1 Tim. 6:8; Heb. 13:5). Probably the gravest offense is that of refusing or failing to recognize that God alone is the true source of the bounty (Deut. 8:17-18). Unless the individual's spiritual priorities are kept clearly in view, wealth can become the prime object of one's attainments, and, in some instances, can lead to a trust in riches rather than in God (Ps. 52:7).

For those in this perilous condition it is very difficult, Jesus said, to enter the heavenly kingdom (Mark 10:23), simply because their preoccupation with material wealth has resulted in their becoming "poor toward God" (Luke 12:21). Instead of a covetous attitude, therefore, Christians must strive consistently to enlarge Christ's church and kingdom and to be content with whatever material benefits accrue, in the knowledge that they have first given themselves unto God (2 Cor. 8:5). In general, therefore, while Scripture does not condemn wealth as such, it issues stern warnings against preoccupation with riches, condemning those rich people who have succumbed to the dangers inherent in it.

In the apostolic period the circumstances of the Jerusalem church made the pooling of private property desirable and necessary for a period of time (Acts 4:32-35). This procedure was not unlike the one followed by the Dead Sea Scrolls community at Qumran. Evidently a measure designed to meet a specific emergency, it should not be seen as a blueprint for a socialistic or communistic way of life. Both these political concepts are in effect protests against private possession of property, professing that property should be owned and managed by the state or community. Classical communism in particular has sought, in addition, to emphasize state control of finances, of the production and distribution of goods and services, and of the entire educational system as means of eliminating existing capitalists and of bringing about a classless society.

Modern socialism disavows private enterprise in favor of government ownership of the means of production, and, like communism, upholds the concept of centralized management of the economy. The fact that there are many wealthy individuals living in socialist and communist countries is, understandably enough, seldom a matter for public discussion. From the foregoing, it should be evident that the symbiotic activities of the primitive church in Jerusalem have nothing whatsoever to do with either modern socialism or communism. What occurred, in fact, was a desperate response to the absence of wealth, not an attempt to eradicate it. Apparently some years elapsed before the financial problems of the Jerusalem Christian community were alleviated, partly as the result of donations from other churches (2 Cor. 8:2-5).

Just as there will always be poor people in the world, so there will always be wealthy ones. The biblical ethic imposes upon the latter a responsibility to minister to the needs of the former and to exhibit compassion toward those who will not or cannot provide for their own needs. In addition to the problems and temptations that the wealthy already have in virtue of possessing riches, they are open to abuse and different kinds of violence from those who, through greed, envy, or malice, would like to deprive them of at least a part of their monetary resources. Kidnapping and other forms of banditry are commonly used to exploit the affluent, and these attempts sometimes lead to murder. Consequently, the wealthy often take elaborate precautions to protect themselves and their interests. This places a certain restriction upon individuals who might otherwise be much more free to indulge in charity and philanthropic activity.

It is not always realized that the rich pay a high price for their wealth in the form of taxation, since even the most ingeniously devised tax shelters have distinct limits to their effective functions. The most wealthy person known to the writer once complained that, when he had taken advantage of all possible methods of legal tax avoidance, he still paid in excess of $1 million annually in income taxes. As is the case with all taxpayers, a portion of that money would be allocated by the government for the relief of poverty through such social schemes as unemployment and other benefits. Modern taxation systems thus make involuntary philanthropists of us all, which raises the question of whether governments have the moral right to disburse taxpayers' monies on schemes or projects with which the individual citizen may be in disagreement.

One final point should perhaps be raised in connection with wealthy Christians, or those who can convey the appearance of affluence. This concerns the periodic abuse that they endure at the hands of zealous reformers who imagine, quite mistakenly it would appear, that the Christian ethic requires the believer to sell all of his or her property and distribute the proceeds to the poor. In the first instance, as was pointed out above, Christ's instructions were to specific persons for special purposes and were not meant to be normative in any sense for the Christian church.

Second, the fact is that God has a definite need for our money in order to promote His work in the world. The money, which is God's gift to us in the first place, is, when donated to His work, a symbol or token of our commitment to Him and His creatures. If it represents a tithe, or more, of personal income, the donor will be the recipient of divine blessing, and the one to whom the money is given will profit similarly. Quite clearly there can be little realistic charitable relief for the impoverished unless there is a significant degree of fiscal input at some stage in the process.

If the wealthy were to liquidate their assets and give the proceeds to the poor, as they are urged to do periodically by those who imagine riches to be somehow tainted with evil, they themselves would then join the ranks of the poor, thereby increasing the magnitude of the very problem that they are trying to diminish. But if the wealthy remain wealthy, they guarantee the presence of a solid fiscal base from which future philanthropic work may proceed, as they submit their resources to the guidance of the Holy Spirit.

At the lowest level, wealth can be used in a manner that corrupts, depraves, exploits, and enslaves people, bringing some of the worst motivating factors of human behavior to the forefront of activity. But, if the scriptural ethic is acknowledged and obeyed, wealth is seen to be a matter of stewardship rather than absolute ownership or possession. The rich person will, therefore, express continual gratitude to God, who is the source of material and spiritual blessings alike, and will direct his or her thanksgiving into works of a charitable or philanthropic nature. The quality of commitment will ideally be such as to demonstrate true spiritual compassion for the disadvantaged and underprivileged and will help in some small way restore the rather tarnished image of God in them by reflecting altruistic, Christian love.

**Bibliography:** Sider, R., *Rich Christians in an Age of Hunger* (1978).

See AFFLUENCE; PROSPERITY.

**WIDOWS.** A widow is a married woman of any age whose husband has died and who has not contracted a subsequent marriage. Widows, especially childless ones, have always been vulnerable socially, not least so in the ancient world, where a childless widow had no option but to return to her father's home if he was still alive. Since everyone belonged to some family in Old Testament times, independent survival was impossible, and in many cases parentless widows

were forced into slavery and concubinage unless they were able to remarry. The widow of Zarephath whom God appointed to sustain the life of Elijah (1 Kings 17:9) was in a desperate plight due to famine, and doubtless many of her contemporaries died (Luke 4:25-26).

The Torah forbade anyone to afflict a widow (Exod. 22:22), lest God should take speedy revenge upon the offender. Widows were classed with the stranger and the fatherless as those whom the Israelites were required to protect (Deut. 24:17-21) and include in their festivals (Deut. 16:11). In the primitive church one of the earliest acts of social ministry was to the widows, although the performance of the duty was apparently somewhat uneven (Acts 6:1). At a later period believers were encouraged to assist widows privately (1 Tim. 5:16). For James, true religion involved altruistic service to widows "in their affliction" (1:27), indicating that their situation was frequently extremely stringent. James's criterion is still true for the modern believer, and many Christians have devoted themselves tirelessly to the needs of the elderly and widowed in the best biblical tradition.

**WIFE ABUSE.** In North American society, this particular type of assault has either been generally disregarded or dismissed as largely coincidental to the marriage relationship. The offense tends to go unreported, one possible reason being that the majority of people in Western society live very private lives, preferring to "mind their own business" rather than become involved with the affairs of others, particularly where possible danger might result.

The question arises, however, as to whether supposedly Christian countries, such as those in North America and the European continent, continue to ignore the civil liberties of one group of their citizens. According to such sources as the Canadian Charter of Human Rights and comparable legislation in the United States, wife abuse is an offense under the law. In countries such as Great Britain, which does not have a Charter of Rights as such, it is generally treated as a form of assault when and where it is reported.

There can be no doubt that, judging by the publicity engendered, wife abuse has become increasingly prevalent in recent times. Statistics are notoriously difficult to obtain for this offense, but it has been estimated that between one and three women out of every ten in Canada and the United States have been subjected to this form of assault at some time during their marriage. For those who are concerned with the welfare of society, particularly from a Christian point of view, it is a problem that has not merely legal dimensions, but moral ones as well.

All of this was brought home to the present writer with startling suddenness some fifty years ago, when she, a naive daughter of the manse, was horrified to witness the man next door coldbloodedly pounding his wife's head into the wall of their house and proceeding to beat her in the abdomen with his fists. He was quite clearly intent on assaulting his wife in parts of the body that could not be seen easily by the public. This scene of marital abuse took place in a quiet country location on the Bay of Quinte. It was never reported to the authorities.

Since this type of assault takes place in many countries, it is difficult to believe that it is either a new ethical problem, or one confined to the North American continent. Indeed, it seems highly probable that women, as well as children, have been the victims of assault from time immemorial. Various reasons for this type of behavior have been advanced, and, of possible causes, alcoholic intoxication ranks high on the list. Some men who have personality disturbances of an anti-social or psychopathic variety are prone to express their aggressive drives on marriage partners, typically smaller in size and far less physically powerful.

There are, however, reasons other than those of a characterological nature that provoke wifebeating. Sometimes it is simply an expression of the intolerable degree of stress that the wage earner experiences in the highly competitive society of modern times. Resentment and frustration thus find an outlet in the act of aggression against the spouse, for which the offender is frequently sorry when his temper has cooled. At other times, it is a protest against conditions of poverty. This type of assault is often associated with child abuse and even incest in extreme cases. There are even some cases where the woman herself provokes the assault by a mindless and entirely unsympathetic attack upon her spouse's deficiencies, bringing quick retaliation. While the reasons may be manifold, the end result is still an offense against a person.

One turns in vain to Scripture for instances of wifebeating, for while there are indications that slaves were beaten, there is nothing about such treatment being meted out to a wife. Sarah abused her handmaiden Hagar, whom she had given to Abraham as a concubine because she herself was childless (Gen. 16:6), but such is not recorded in connection with a legal wife. Either this was so common that it was considered unworthy of record, or it was simply unheard-of behavior. The closest that Scripture comes to recording an assault on a married woman is in Exodus 21:22, which deals with compensation for a pregnant woman who has been accidentally harmed as two men began a fight.

The Old Testament makes it abundantly clear that the marriage contract was a very serious matter, which became even more important in New Testament times. Ten days of feasting marked the marriage celebration, a time at which all the relatives of the bride and groom were present. This was followed by a full year of "honeymoon," when the bride and her husband lived alternate months with each other's families. After this, the bridegroom left his wife for a time to prepare a home for her, and, according to Jewish tradition, he repeated to his new wife words very similar to those spoken by Jesus to His disciples, as recorded in John 14:1-3. In Matthew 19:5, Christ also emphasized that the man must become one flesh with his wife, quoting Genesis 2:24. This commitment of marriage involved love, honor, and respect between the two contracting parties.

Paul stated clearly the kind of relationship that ought to exist between husband and wife (Eph. 5:25-29), being particularly careful to emphasize the love that a husband should demonstrate toward his spouse. From this teaching it can be concluded that any man who beats his wife is certainly not treating her as though she were his "own flesh," but instead is dealing with her as one might with a chattel, a thing, or a slave. The children of such a union who witness the beating of the mother will no doubt grow up in fear and learn to hate and despise both parents. Such brutality, therefore, can only breed terror and dishonor.

One curious trait commonly exhibited by "battered wives," as they are sometimes known, is a tendency to "forgive all" once the actual abuse has ended. Whether such "forgiveness" is the result of love for the abuser, once tempers have subsided, or, more importantly, of outright fear for the future is often very difficult to establish. In theory, wives who have been beaten can summon police aid. All too frequently, however, investigation into family disputes is hampered by the reluctance of the battered wife to have charges of assault or bodily harm brought against the husband. Cases have been known where a woman complainant finally refused to testify against her husband, or common-law mate, in court, and was promptly given a jail sentence for contempt. For those who maintain that the courts are far too lenient in cases of wifebeating, this turn of events must come as a surprise. In actual fact this is the normal procedure in those jurisdictions where judges are required to proceed on all domestic assault cases, even when the victim wishes the charges to be withdrawn or declines to testify. Such a stand has been generally applauded by sociologists and feminist movements, but some other segments of the public have been less enthusiastic in their appraisal of such court action.

For those persons for whom battered wives are an entirely new social phenomenon, the question might well arise as to why women continue to endure such barbaric treatment within a marriage or a common-law relationship. One answer is that the masochistic female derives what would seem to others to be a perverted emotional satisfaction from the experience. It apparently meets some deeply concealed need. Other battered women are very much afraid of even worse treatment or reprisals if they resist or report the beatings. If a woman has children and is living in a common-law situation, she may be in dread of losing her children and the modest kind of shelter that they have. In cases where wifebeating arises from a background of poverty, the victim is often almost completely lacking in any kind of training and expertise that would enable her to obtain work and support herself and her children. Even if such a mother qualifies for support under a welfare program and can be accommodated in some kind of a shelter or similar institution, survival is still often a delicate matter, both for economic and emotional reasons.

Fortunately, there are organizations that can assist battered wives and try to direct them to a better future, away from physical violence. Those trying to help victims of wifebeating recommend that the woman should be examined by a doctor immediately after the assault to determine the nature of any injury. The next step is to secure legal advice, in which the victim will be advised of her basic rights and ascertain the procedures to be followed in such matters as the custody of children, the possession or repossession of the family property, if any, and access to any monies that might be available from bank accounts. The vast majority of battered wives have very little funding available for legal counsel, and therefore have to rely upon a small percentage of lawyers who accept legal aid cases.

Another important step for the victim to take is consultation with a nurse who works in the area of public health and is experienced with the problems of battered women. In fact, a nurse is often preferred to a doctor for a consultation, because battered wives fear that doctors will compel them to notify the police about the assault. Public health nurses not merely provide professional medical assistance, but, because they are usually well informed on wife abuse, are also a source of great emotional support. They know about the locations of shelters where the victim and her children can go until other arrangements can be made. Once in the shelter, the woman can apply for public welfare assistance and perhaps even be admitted to one of numerous retraining and upgrading programs that can enable her to make a fresh start in life for herself and her children.

While these steps toward the alleviation of the problems caused by wife abuse are of great importance, they cannot substitute for the removal of the offense itself. Here the Christian church must speak out clearly and decisively against a background of biblical teaching about the family and the responsibilities of individual members. Wife abuse must be stigmatized as completely incompatible with the code of family ethics contained in Scripture. In the Christian church all persons are equal before God (Gal. 3:28), and if the husband is not prepared to keep his promise to love and cherish his wife as his own body, the wife must insists on her right to leave the family situation until the husband is rehabilitated. The same is true to a lesser extent for non-Christian couples, since, if they are legally married, they are required by law and by their own public commitment to respect each other. It is unfortunate that women who are living in the so-called "common-law" relationship have no such protection, but that has been a matter of personal choice.

Wife abuse is a reprehensible example of the exploitation of the weak by the stronger. It robs the victim of individuality and personal dignity, and, as far as the purely physical violence involved is concerned, it is an offense under the law. No responsible modern society ought to tolerate or condone wife abuse for one moment.

**Bibliography:** Dobson, J. C., *Love Must Be Tough* (1983).

See CRIME; FAMILY; VIOLENCE.

A.P.

**WITCHCRAFT.** In common usage a witch is a female who indulges in magical practices of various kinds such as divination, necromancy, the casting of charms or spells, soothsaying, and so on. These elements of witchcraft were also practiced in antiquity by males, who were known as wizards; but whenever they are referred to collectively it is under the term *witchcraft*, regardless of the sex of the practitioner. Among the ancient Hebrews a witch was known as *mekashshephah* (Exod. 22:18), a term that is sometimes rendered *sorcerer*. Unfortunately this term does not convey a very clear idea as to what was specifically involved in ancient Near Eastern witchcraft.

Arguing from the supposed relationship of the Hebrew to an Arabic root meaning "to cut," some scholars have thought that witchcraft involved self-mutilation with knives, combined with a whirling dance similar to that of the Arab dervishes, as a means of inducing an ecstatic experience of deity which would be accompanied by some form of revelation (1 Kings 18:28). Others have rejected this notion in favor of a different form of cutting, namely that of slicing herbs so as to make some kind of heady brew by decoction or infusion. When imbibed, this liquid could conceivably produce such diverse reactions as hallucinations, torpor, or sexual excitement, depending upon the herbs or toxins employed; and these in various ways would serve as vehicles of divine communication.

By the period of the Exile (sixth century B.C.), the term *mekashshephah* seems to have involved some form of mental divination, as in Jeremiah 27:9 and Daniel 2:2, instead of an altered degree of consciousness induced by means of potions. Ancient Hebrew law specifically prohibited witches, wizards, and whatever arts they practiced (Exod. 22:18; 1 Sam. 15:23) because of their involvement with the idolatrous practices that were in fundamental violation of the covenant ethic. The God of Sinai had demanded of his people the absolute repudiation of any other kind of deity than himself and had stigmatized the gods of other nations as vain and false idols. Any Israelite who sought to worship them or to communicate with them in any way was therefore repudiating one of the express prohibitions of covenant legislation (Exod. 20:3-6). There were, of course, appointed means by which the Hebrews could know God's will for them, such as the mechanical casting of lots (Num. 27:21); but anything approaching the magical practices of pagan nations constituted a denial of Sinaitic monotheism. But even those who normally adhered to such laws sometimes broke them in times of great anxiety, as with King Saul, who immediately before his death had recourse to a spiritualistic medium (1 Sam. 28:7-19).

Witches and wizards continued into New Testament times (Acts 8:9; 13:8) and were promised a fiery destruction because of their doings (Rev. 21:8). In the medieval period the Roman Catholic Church condemned witchcraft, and legislation forbidding it was passed in many countries. Despite this, however, black magic and witchcraft have survived; and those who have rejected Christianity have not unpredictably replaced it with magic and superstition.

In addition to the casting of a wide range of spells, modern witchcraft has included the resurgence of Satanism or devil worship, which involves esoteric, often immoral rites, and reportedly human sacrifice under certain circumstances.

See ASTROLOGY; OCCULTISM; SORCERY.

**WOMEN, STATUS OF.** In the twentieth century the status of a person in society has acquired the meaning not only of legal rights and privileges but also of the attitudes afforded to position in society. Throughout history, revolutions have resulted in dramatic changes in social and legal positions. While such changes have improved the quality of life for some, for others such revolutions have had disastrous results—the mixed benefits and abuses of the industrial revolution being an obvious example. Fortunately, in current Western culture, most changes in status have been gradual, effected over long periods, as the requirements of the culture altered.

In the earliest subsistence societies, the differences between the roles of men and women were effectively slight, as the greatest motivation of all members of society was survival itself. As various societies developed and maintenance of life became less difficult, the role of the sexes changed. Biological differences resulted in women's work becoming principally that of bearing and nursing children. While men were providers of food and shelter for the family, women prepared the food, made the clothing, and protected the young. As affluence developed, it became a mark of wealth and "status" for men to have women who were little more than ornaments. By the time of Christ, the demarcation of the roles of the sexes seems to have been well-defined (1 Pet. 3:7).

Certain Christian views and morality were reflected in the English Common Law. Paul's views, especially as found in his letter to the Ephesians (5:23) were particularly influential. Thus, Blackstone, in his *Commentaries on the Common Law,* summarized a wife's theoretical position:

> By marriage a husband and wife are one person in law; that is, the very being or legal existence of a woman is suspended during the marriage, or at least as incorporated or consolidated into the husband, under whose wing, protection and cover she performs everything, and is, therefore, called in our law a *femme covert.*

The English Common Law provided the basis for codes of law in America and other English colonies. The treatment of and attitude toward women was uniform in these areas and throughout most of the Western world. From time to time some pockets of resistance or progress developed, but were primarily ignored or, at best, short-lived. Margaret Brent, in 1647, was denied the "place and voyce" in the Maryland Assembly she called for. Women with property, however, were allowed to vote in the Massachusetts Colony between 1691 and 1780. New Jersey, between 1790 and 1807, allowed women to vote through an election law which read "he or she."

Despite these isolated incidents, nothing of merit was written on the subject of women's equal status until 1790. The atmosphere of freedom, democracy, and egalitarianism surrounding the American and French Revolutions spilled over into the area of women's rights, resulting in the first major work on the subject, *The Admission of Women to Full Citizenship* by the French *philosophe* Condorcet. It was followed very quickly in 1792 by the first English writing in the area, Mary Wollstonecraft's *A Vindication of the Rights of Woman.* Both works, however, were largely ignored.

The status and rights of women remained unchanged. The dominance of a husband over his wife in marriage continued to be upheld by the courts of many countries. In marriage, a woman lost her ability to own property, to contract, to sue or be sued. If she earned any money from employment, it belonged to the husband. Her status was that of a chattel of her husband, and she could not acquire a domicile independent of her husband.

In exchange for this loss of identity and independent status, a wife acquired the right, often illusory, to be maintained by her husband. The husband was not allowed to remove a wife from the matrimonial home against her will, unless the wife was found to be an adulteress. Conversely, a wife was never obliged in law to maintain a husband; nor had the wife any recourse if the husband was found to be an adulterer. A husband had the legal right to sue a man with whom his wife committed adultery for alienation of his wife's affections, and, if she were injured, for loss of her services and sexual availability. A corresponding legal right was not given to the wife because it was considered that she, as a chattel herself, held no proprietary rights.

Ironically, unmarried women never suffered from the legal disabilities of married women. An unmarried woman could own property, contract, sue, and be sued. Such women, however, suffered from a severe handicap if they were required to earn their own living. Women, married or single, were regarded as intellectually inferior to men, an attitude reflected in the law. Thus, women, outside of such incidents as already noted were denied the right to vote or participate in public life. They were not allowed into the professions of law or medicine, nor were they allowed to teach in universities. An unmarried woman, without family, wealth, or support, was relegated to certain kinds of menial work in factories, or as a servant. At the most, a woman could find a post as that elevated servant, the governess.

It was inevitable that women should rebel against the laws and attitudes that stereotyped them as being inferior to men. The most effective area to disprove such inferiority was in the realm of education. During the 1830s, many women's colleges were founded in the United States. Some established American universities accepted women students during the 1860s, and, by 1900, 70 per cent of American colleges and universities were coeducational.

Advances in women's rights were being made outside the realm of education, as well. The Seneca Falls Convention, meeting to discuss the issue at Seneca Falls, New York, in 1848, issued its *Declaration of Sentiments and Resolutions,* signed by sixty-eight women and thirty-two men. Based upon the American Declaration of Independence ("We hold these truths to be self-evident: that all men and women are created equal"), the *Declaration* addressed injustices forced upon women in all areas of life, including theology and religion:

> The history of mankind is a history of repeated injuries and usurpations on the part of man toward woman, having in direct object the establishment of an absolute tyranny over her. To prove this, let facts be submitted to a candid world....
>
> He allows her in Church, as well as State, but a subordinate position, claiming Apostolic authority for her exclusion from the ministry, and, with some exceptions, from any public participation in the affairs of the Church....
>
> He has usurped the prerogative of Jehovah himself, claiming it as his right to assign for her a sphere of action, when that belongs to her conscience and to her God.

The Seneca Falls Convention provided the basis for the American women's suffrage movement. As a result of a seventy year struggle, women were given the right to vote in 1920 with the ratification of the nineteenth amendment to the United States Constitution.

The women's suffrage movement in England started a bit later, in 1866. These women tried by persuasion and discussion to have the government in Westminster extend the franchise to women. A militancy was later acquired by the movement, and many women were imprisoned for their cause. Happily, the suffrage movement succeeded and British women were ultimately allowed to vote in 1928.

Individual women of intelligence also fought for the right to be admitted to the professions, and legislatures have continued to open the law for women, both married and single.

By the last half of this twentieth century, women have mostly been accepted as having equal legal and social status to men. All professions and careers are potentially open to women, whether single or married.

The adverse social sanction that formerly applied to married women who chose to work outside the home has changed. Further, women in the home have been freed from much of the former drudgery of housework by advances in technology and medicine. Available and inexpensive sources of energy in Western society have resulted in the discovery and development of labor-saving household appliances. Advances in medical knowledge and discovery of drugs have lessened the dangers of childhood diseases so that mothers are relieved of the nursing role that formerly could occupy so much of their time.

Since the Second World War, the number of working women has increased dramatically, and more and more married women continue to work after marriage and childbirth. Families with two incomes can afford more luxuries and a higher standard of living, although in some economies, two incomes are becoming more of a necessity. Women have enlarged their traditional limited sphere of vocations from secretarial, nursing, and teaching, to professions of law, medicine, accounting, the church, and politics.

As Christians, we must examine the impact on our society and on the family unit of this changed status of women. Also as Christians, we must be thankful that women are finally accepted as persons with opportunities to use their abilities to the best effect. Clearly we must be concerned with the maintenance of family life, which is affected by the changing role of women; now men must play a greater role in the establishment and functioning of the home.

It is in the confines of the family that children traditionally acquire emotional stability and learn Christian values. It is now the responsibility of both parents to ensure that the family is kept intact and that Christian examples are followed. Throughout the Bible we are reminded of the importance of women in the propagation of faith (e.g., Prov. 3:1). The important role of mothers in teaching Christian values to their children must not, and need not, be neglected in view of the changed status of women, although responsible fathers should now play an equal role as teachers.

Ironically, the great significance of early childhood education is only now being elevated to its proper status.

Perhaps the Christian church should be concerned that married women with children not be forced to work outside the home. All women do not have the same interests or skills, and those who choose to manage a house and care for children as a full occupation should have legal protection to allow them to do so. There is an unfortunate trend in many jurisdictions, as women have been granted equal status with men, to remove certain protections in law that a married woman formerly had. In such jurisdictions, for example, a woman who marries, has children, and remains at home may be in great difficulty at the break-up of the marriage. The married woman who is deserted can no longer rely on support from her husband for any extended period. Husbands are now being relieved of responsibility for the former wife who has borne the immense workload of the home and raising children. Feminists have recently begun to argue that the value of a woman who keeps house should indeed be recognized in terms of the labor involved and especially in terms of the economic worth of that labor. Keeping a home and family should be recognized as a career, they argue, which uses a number of valuable skills worthy of dignity and even economic recompense.

In many cases a deserted wife forced to return to the workplace must now do so to the detriment of her children's well-being. A mother's freedom to remain with her children is being lost as married women realize that they are responsible for their own livelihood. It has become more important than ever, in light of changing attitudes, for Christians to regard their marriage vows as a sacrament of the church, not to be put aside lightly. Women must be allowed to retain the freedom of choice to remain at home with their children without fear of economic hardship.

The role and status of women in society has changed, resulting in women having a more stimulating and satisfactory life. But Christian men and women must be certain that this changed status enhances, rather than threatens, the stable home. Both husband and wife must, now more than ever, ensure cooperation in maintaining the stability of marriage, as well as in sharing careers and work inside and outside the home. Even the influential and radical American feminist, Betty Friedan, has recently emphasized that family and career for women are not irreconcilable polarities. Instead, she stresses that the family has a critical role to play for society in nurturing the individual, and that the family remains of the utmost concern to women, whatever the kind or extent of career they may choose.

As Christians, we must accept our role and status in society with a certain good grace—so long as we are each able to put forth our best effort to employ all our talents in our chosen life's work.

**Bibliography:** Clark, W. H., *Women and Equality: Changing Patterns in American Culture* (1979); Friedan, B., *The Second Stage* (1982); Giele, J. Z. and Shrock, A. C., (eds.), *Women: Roles and Status in Eight Countries* (1977); Hollis, P., *Women in Public, 1850-1900* (1979); Iglitzer, L. B. and Ross, R., (eds.), *Women in the World: A Comparative Study* (1976); Scarzoni, J., *Sex Roles, Women's Work, and Marital Conflict* (1978).

L.L.

**WORK.** The concept of work occupies a prominent place in the creation narratives in the book of Genesis. Chapter one (vv.26-28) twice affirms a relationship between the fact that man is made in God's image and that he has been called to exercise dominion over the earth. Because man is made in the image of God, after His likeness, he is capable of ruling over the rest of the created order. Similarly in chapter two, man is given the charge of "tilling" and "keeping" (15). Work—in the sense of taking charge of the environment, of maintaining, ordering, and organizing it—is thus fundamental to God's purposes for human life. Human work, as worship, is an activity in which the divine image is set forth. Given the ancient Near Eastern context, rule (dominion) here is to be understood in terms of monarchy. Man is a king, set over nature by God. He is, therefore, the vice-regent, responsible to his Creator for how he uses and organizes the creation.

So the creation narratives affirm that God calls man to work. In turn, mankind's responsibility for harnessing the potentialities of nature involves various characteristics. Work is linked to the meeting of basic physical needs (Gen. 1:29) and is to be a creative exercise. The magnificent diversity that characterizes nature's resources means that man's working tasks abounds with different possibilities and options. Work demands decision, commitment, a great investment of human imagination, ideas, and energy. God has graciously allowed humankind enormous scope to exercise their own creativity, ingenuity, and choices on the "canvas of creation."

There seems in this sense, to be a scientific mandate actually implicit in the call to creative dominion. In order that he might be able to manage his environment, man must gain an understanding of its inner nature, its varied possibilities. In this respect, some commentators have argued that the fundamental conception of nature implicit in the creation narratives is one that is highly congenial to the needs of scientific endeavor. In other ancient understandings, the natural world is still often perceived in "sacral" terms: The stars, the plants, and the animals are seen as enshrining deities, and so are only to be approached with much religious trepidation. But the Genesis cosmogonies make a clear distinction between God the Creator and His creation. The natural order, while being God's, is not itself divine. It is "desacralized." Thus the way is opened up for rational investigation. In early Israel, to name a person or an object was not only to exercise parental or political authority over it; it was also to express insight into its essential nature (Gen. 35). Thus, when God invites man to "name the animals" (Gen. 2:19-20), he is being summoned to bring the natural realm within his own systems of perception, understanding, and classification. God calls man to a dominion of knowledge respectful of His creation. Calvin affirms that those who neglect the study of nature are as guilty as those who, when investigating God's works, forget the Creator.

It also seems right to uphold the importance of the "aesthetic" element in the responsibilities of human dominion. A glance at the character of the created order demonstrates that God's creative work goes far beyond the necessities of function and utility to an overwhelming affection for diversity, vastness, color, and wonder. Of course, evolutionary explanations for diversity and color can be given. But unless God is wholly excluded, such intermediate explanations cannot detract from the basic point being affirmed here. God cherished an order in which function was vast, diverse, and awesome (see Job 38:25-27). And, if beauty is of such importance for the Creator King, then surely it is to be important for the vice-regents too. The gifts of the worker and the materials that he or she handles both come from the one creator God. And in this sense all good work, whether aesthetic or functional, gives glory to Him.

The final point to be made here about the concepts of dominion and "keeping" in the Genesis narratives concerns the relationship between the sexes. It ought to be noted that in chapter one (v. 28), the charge to dominion, just as the charge to procreation, is specifically given to both male and female. Similarly, in chapter two (v. 18), we note that woman is first introduced to man not as his lover, or even as the mother of his children, but as his co-worker. The artificial restriction of men and women to separate spheres of life finds no justification here.

In understanding the nature and meaning of human work, we have to consider more than the relationship between man and nature. Work also calls men into a network of social relationships. It is a corporate human responsibility, to be done in the context of human fellowship and interdependence (Gen. 2:18; 1 Cor. 12). It is also a fundamental means through which we serve one another and create community. The ethical codes of the Pentateuch make it very clear that our work is not done only for ourselves and our families, but for the good of society as a whole (Lev. 23:22; Deut. 24:19-22). Paul instructs Christian people to work hard because it will enable them to help those in need (Eph. 4:28). Clearly, there is a great variety of ways in which our endeavors can serve, protect, encourage, enlighten, or inspire those around us.

In theological terms, work is to be defined as the investment of one's energy in dominion over nature and the service of others. While employment, and other forms of work for direct economic benefit, are of crucial importance, we should not think of work wholly in terms of them. Activities of dominion and human service should be considered as work—irrespective of whether they involve selling one's wares in the marketplace. In this sense we need to maintain a very broad conception of human work. We are to see ourselves as fulfilling God's call when we are working on the construction site, in the laboratory, in the flower garden, in the shop, or in the hospital, and not just when involved in "religious" ministries.

The theological and scriptural ideals for man's working life contrast vividly with a great deal of actual human experience. This is in part due to social constraints and necessities. There will always be many working tasks to do that are less rewarding and stimulating. It is also due to the fact that work, as with the whole range of human relationships and experiences, has been distorted and corrupted through human fallenness (Gen. 3:14-19).

Human endeavor may show great achievements in art, science, and the development of civilization. But work is also often made an idol, a means of worshiping the creation rather than its Creator. The history of work is frequently a history of frustration, corruption, exploitation, bitter competitiveness (rather than cooperation), and hurt. However, we should not identify the toil of the Genesis story with the monotonous and soul-destroying labor that characterizes so much of modern industry. Repairing an engine, developing a garden, running a business, creating music, writing an article—all these tasks can involve toil. But none of them are inherently boring or stunting. Soul-destroying work is a social invention, though one fostered by human greed and selfishness. In the face of this we should seek to uphold God's rich ideals for human existence.

**Bibliography:** Agrell, G., *Work, Toil and Sustenance* (1976); Richardson, A., *The Biblical Doctrine of Work* (1952); Schumacher, E. F., *Good Work* (1979).

See EMPLOYMENT; SABBATH; UNEMPLOYMENT; WAGES.

M.D.G.

**WORLDLINESS.** The term *world*, in English translations of the Bible, refers to several things: the earth, the created universe, the people who inhabit the earth, the sinful behavior of fallen humankind, this age as opposed to that which is to come, and possibly, secular as opposed to religious.

Because of these various meanings, it is possible for Scripture to say both that God loved the world (John 3:16) and that we must not love the world (1 John 2:15). The people of the world, as the object of God's love and saving purpose (John 1:29; 3:16-17; 1 John 2:2), constitute humanity as a whole. On the other hand, these same people, until redeemed, are ruled by the devil (John 12:31; 1 John 5:19), in fact are opposed to God and His people (John 17:14), and are "in darkness" (1 John 2:15) or spiritually unenlightened. It is this world of fallen human behavior that is in opposition to God and that all those who love God must oppose. This sinfulness is the world that Jesus overcame (John 16:33) and that we must overcome (1 John 5:4). Again, the term *world* can refer to a period of time as opposed to a world in eternity that will endure forever. In this usage the world is temporary (1 Cor. 7:31; 1 John 2:15).

Though Jesus and Paul use the term *world* in the same sense as John, John explains the evil of worldliness in much greater detail. It is interesting to note that in a single passage he uses the term in four of its basic meanings: creation (John 17:5), earth (v. 11), mankind (v. 6), and the sinful way of thinking of fallen human beings (v. 14).

There are several levels of thinking, then, that can rightly be called *worldly*. At the lowest level, worldliness can refer to the way of thinking and behaving that is characteristic of fallen human beings. To think like this is to adopt the values of sinful humanity. But this is not the only way in which one can be worldly.

A person whose way of thinking is limited to the visible affairs of this planet and his own lifetime would be worldly in the sense of being thoroughly secular. He might be materialistic or altruistic, covetous or generous, but his life is worldly in either case because it rules out the realm of the Spirit and life beyond death.

There is a way in current usage in which the term *worldly* refers to a person who is aware of what happens in the world and has an understanding of its implications. A "worldly-wise" person in this sense would be somewhat like the people who are commended for "understanding the times" (1 Chron. 12:32; Esther 1:13). This idea of worldliness is not condemned in Scripture.

Perhaps the clearest passage in Scripture that analyzes worldliness is 1 John 2:15-17. Here a love for the world is contrasted with a love for God in such a way that there can be no reconciliation. Basically the contrast is between doing the will of God, resulting in eternal life, and identifying with the sinful behavior of fallen humankind and suffering the consequences. Here "the world" is defined as the lust of the flesh, the lust of the eyes, and the pride of life. Note that each of these drives is a distortion of God-given desire. We are built on the image of God with the desire to enjoy, to possess, and to achieve. Sin distorts these into fleshly lusts such as gluttony, illicit sex, covetousness, and pride. When these behaviors become a pattern of life, the lust becomes sensualism, the covetousness becomes materialism, and the pride becomes egoism. These root sins define worldliness and from them proceed most, if not all, sinful behavior.

In the first half of the twentieth century, *worldliness* came to refer to participation in certain recreational activities, particularly drinking alcohol, smoking, social dancing, attending motion pictures, and playing cards. This understanding of *worldliness* had several unfortunate results. Some felt that abstinence from these activities was proof that a person was not "worldly" but "spiritual." Some, in fact, seemed to feel that by adopting this lifestyle of abstinence, a person became a genuine Christian. Good behavior as a way of salvation has always been with us as a basic heresy, but this particular list of bad behavioral items became for some a heresy of the heresy, because of its shallow and narrow understanding of the good behavior necessary to earn salvation. Even for the majority of believers, who would reject the idea of salvation by any kind of mere human effort, there was nevertheless a great deception in that a truly biblical concept of worldliness—all the subtle nuances of lust, covetousness, and pride—could be fully indulged while a person felt quite "spiritual," having rejected "worldliness." Some of these activities may well be worldly in the biblical sense, but, as a representative list, they lead one far astray from a biblical understanding and condemnation of worldliness.

What is the biblical antidote to worldliness? Historically, some form of monasticism or withdrawal from the world has been offered as the most spiritual solution to the problem. Others, without taking monastic vows, have adopted, or at least admired, lesser levels of *otherworldliness*. This is an error that may come from Greek dualism that affirms the realm of the Spirit, setting it against the material. This idea has been reinforced by a confusion of the distinct ways in which Scripture uses the term *world*. When we are enjoined not to love the world, but to oppose it, Scripture is never referring to leaving the earth or the people of earth. Rather, it speaks of abstaining from the sinful behavior of this world and opposing evil behavior in all its manifestations. The biblical way is to remain *in* the world while refraining from being *of* the world. John 17:13-18 (see also 7:7; 8:23; 15:19) clearly demonstrates that God intends His people to remain in the world, not only on earth, but among fallen people, partaking of their life, while remaining pure from its defilement and way of thinking. If anyone loves the world, the love of the Father is not in him (1 John 2:15).

**Bibliography:** Kittel, G. (ed.), *Theological Dictionary of the New Testament:* I, pp. 197–208; III, pp. 867–98.

See MATERIALISM.

J.R.McQ.

**WRATH.** This term is a rhetorical and poetic word for anger and is used widely in the King James Version in that connection. In the Old Testament the Hebrew *aph* denotes "face" or "person" as well as "anger" and is commonly used of God's intense displeasure with sin and sinners alike. This wrath was not a petulant display of bad temper such as is common among human beings, but rather the reaction of a righteous and holy God whose laws and statutes had been disobeyed.

But despite dramatic displays of divine anger (Num. 11:33; Ps. 78:31), God reveals himself as one who loves and forgives the penitent sinner and would even reverse the appointed punishment were repentance to be in evidence (Jer. 26:3). Words such as *hemah* and *haron* expressed the heat of divine anger (Deut. 29:23; Neh. 13:18), while the general concept of God's displeasure with sin was described by *ebrah* and *qetseph* (Ps. 85:3; Josh. 22:20). In the New Testament the common Greek words *thumos* and *orge* are normally used to express human (Luke 4:28; Col. 3:8) and divine (Rom. 1:18; Eph. 5:6) anger respectively. Paul's doctrine of last events includes a demonstration of God's anger against those who have rejected the saving gospel of Christ (Rom. 2:5; 1 Thess. 1:10), but this is not the only expression of divine wrath that unbelievers will experience (Rom. 1:18; 1 Thess. 2:16).

Jesus laid great emphasis upon God's wrath toward all who manifest the sin of unbelief. He had received from the Father a mandate which entailed dying for human sin (Mark 10:45), and so great a price was this to pay that anyone who spurned such a saving act would not see eternal life, but instead would experience the full weight of God's anger (John 3:36). Because human wrath carries the potential for serious damage both to the individual concerned and others, Christians are required to forsake anger (Gal. 5:20; Eph. 4:31; Col. 3:8) in favor of emotional reactions that are less likely to issue in recriminations or a demand for vengeance. Similarly anything that might provoke a believer to anger should be resolved as expeditiously as possible (Eph. 4:26), lest the devil gain an advantage and harm the believer.

# -Y-

**YOUTH ETHICS.** The term *youth ethics* can be understood in three ways: (1) the ethical practices of young people; (2) the views and concerns young people have about ethical issues; and (3) the ethical principles that apply especially to their lives.

1. The ethical practices of the younger generation have been decried by their elders since ancient times. Nevertheless, many who work closely with teenagers find strong reasons for reassurance:

—While racial prejudice continues, millions of young people today cooperate in integrated schools their grandparents would have resisted.

—"The Sexual Revolution Is Over," a popular magazine announced in 1984. The headline was premature, but there are signs of improvement.

—Each year a higher percentage of youth goes on to college.

—The Gallup Poll reports that 87 per cent of teenagers pray.

—Any reader will know dozens of young people who have volunteered to spend many hours raising money for worthy causes, worked with unfortunates, participated responsibly in valuable school organizations, or served sacrificially in church activities.

Nevertheless, one may still note that:

—Over 1 million American teenagers become pregnant each year, 30,000 being girls under fifteen.

—Annually there are 1.5 million legal abortions in the United States.

—An estimated 90 per cent of teenage fathers eventually abandon their children.

—Most youth have at least tried marijuana by high school graduation; and alcohol has become such a menace, particularly on the highways, that in 1984 state after state in the U.S. was raising the legal drinking age to twenty-one.

2. The views on ethics that young people profess are surprisingly conservative. In 1984 Gallup survey summarizes its findings, "The nation's teen-agers strongly endorse such fundamental values as respect for authority, emphasis on traditional family ties, and plain hard work. They approve emphasis on self-expression and technological improvement, endorsed decreased emphasis on money, and reject more acceptance of marijuana use, all by a wide margin." Gallup found young people evenly split concerning whether or not there should be more sexual freedom.

For good or bad, the views of most adolescents reflect those of their parents. According to a 1984 survey by the National Association of Public School Principals, three-fourths agree with their parents about drug use, education, and the work ethic, and most agree with their parents' views on sex. Most do disagree about clothes and curfews, and older teens complain that their parents treat them "like children."

A 1976 Gallup poll of adolescents in Dayton, Ohio, found that only 12 per cent said religious beliefs had no effect on their conduct. The Princeton Religion Research Center's 1984 report found that those who regard religious beliefs as important are much more concerned about family ties and much less concerned with greater freedom in regard to sex or drug use.

3. Some ethical principles apply especially to young people. Youth are the recipients of a great deal of biblical wisdom. Much of Proverbs is addressed to the young. (See Prov. 1:8, 10; 2:1; 3:1; 4:1). The Passover ritual included instructions for them (Exod. 12:26). The law was to guide young as well as old (Ps. 119:9). The New Testament frequently includes passages especially related to young people (Matt. 19:16-22; Eph. 6:1; all of First and Second Timothy). Although ethical principles apply to all ages, certain concerns are especially relevant to the particular opportunities and tensions of adolescence and young adulthood. Such "developmental tasks" as completion of school, vocational choice, and sexual adjustment obviously call for religious guidance. A glance at church school materials will show concern to deal directly with temptations to promiscuity, drug abuse, and the like. Most Christian educators, however, seek to avoid a legalistic approach, and attempt instead to deal with the underlying tensions of adolescence.

Strommen, in his influential *Five Cries of Youth*, found one young person in five suffering from self-hatred. One-third of church youth were bothered by inability to communicate with their parents, many feeling themselves "psychological orphans" (a "cry" closely related to suicidal tendencies). Many cry out for social justice. A fourth cry, however, is the prejudice of many who have been taught a narrow-minded legalism. The fifth and final cry is that of joy, found in about one-third of the church young people surveyed, springing from a sense of identity and secure love. Many Christian educators have emphasized the provision of a Christian environment and fellowship in which young people can deal with these *cries*, feel loved, and thus practice the ethical principles they are taught.

Wycoff and Richter have listed the responses of parents and educators in six varied denominations: Roman Catholic, Episcopal, Methodist,

Presbyterian, Church of God, and Baptist. Asked to rank in order of importance sixty-two goals of youth work, the respondents listed these as the top ten: (1) "Has a healthy self-concept about his or her value and worthiness as a person" (all but the Baptist and Church of God respondents putting this first); (2) "Sets an example of Christian behavior among his or her friends and associates;" (3) "His or her religion is meaningful in everyday life;" (4) "Takes a responsible view toward moral questions such as drug use and sexual behavior;" (5) "Has a personal relationship with Jesus Christ" (rated highest by Baptist and Church of God respondents); (6) "Understands sexual feelings and has responsible ways of handling them;" (7) "Discovers the meaning of love through personal relationships;" (8) "Is acquiring knowledge about human sexuality and has formed a responsible Christian approach in sexual matters;" (9) "Is not embarrassed to identify himself or herself as a Christian and to speak of Christian beliefs;" and (10) "Considers helping others as central to Christian commitment."

It may be noted that goals one, five, and nine have to do with the sense of personal identity, the Christian answer to the adolescent's perennial question, "Who am I?" Clearly these educators believe that foundations for dealing with the ethical problems of sex, drugs, and interpersonal relationships are being loved, developing Christian self-understanding, and growth toward Christian maturity.

**Bibliography:** *Religion in America: The Gallup Report* (1984); Strommens, M., *Five Cries of Youth* (1974); Wycoff, D. C. and Richter, D., *Religious Education Ministry with Youth* (1982).

See CHILDREN, REARING OF; JUVENILE DELINQUENCY.

W.M.R.

# –Z–

**ZEAL, ZEALOT.** These terms are derived from a Greek root *zelos*, which has the basic meaning of "eager rivalry" or "zealous imitation." Zeal is therefore an emotional state characterized by passionate dedication to some ideal or to a cause. Because of the fervor involved in zeal, direct action is invariably a concomitant of such an experience. Hence the zealot is a person consumed with enthusiasm for the cause espoused, and such is the state of dedication engendered that the objective or cause is pursued with single-minded devotion, no sacrifice being considered too great to make in order for the goal to be attained.

As with any other emotion, zeal needs to be controlled carefully, and history is littered with examples of misguided enthusiasm. In the Old Testament, passionate devotion (Hebrew *qinah*) for God's house was regarded as wholesome, even though it was accompanied by rebukes from those who misunderstood its nature (Ps. 69:9). An outburst of religious zeal for the laws of the covenant resulted in the slaughter of many apostate Israelites (Num. 25:1-13). But religious zeal also produced an adverse result in the case of the penitent apostle Paul, who confessed to having persecuted the church through misguided enthusiasm (Phil. 3:6). Christians are encouraged to manifest ardent and wholehearted devotion to the cause of the gospel (Gal. 4:18; Rev. 3:19), following Christ's own example (John 2:17).

In Christ's time a fanatical group of religious revolutionaries known as Zealots provoked periodic uprisings in Palestine. Simon, one of Christ's disciples, was a Zealot (Luke 6:15; Acts 1:13), though he gave no evidence of political activity during Christ's lifetime. Jesus himself has been thought by some scholars to have been a Zealot also and to have paid for this political affiliation with his life. But his teachings indicate clearly that such was not the case. His kingdom was declared to be "not of this world" (John 18:36) in the presence of the political leader who allowed Jesus to be crucified. Zealot behavior was terrorist and revolutionary in nature and thus entirely out of harmony with Christ's teaching about loving one's enemies (Matt. 5:44). In fact, the Gospels contain no evidence whatever to indicate that Christ even had contact with the Zealots or that he gave any support to their cause. While political enthusiasm is quite proper for the Christian, it must be subjected, like all other forms of behavior, to the overlordship of Christ and its objectives pursued by peaceful rather than violent means.

# SCRIPTURE INDEX

## to the

## Encyclopedia of Biblical and Christian Ethics

## PROVERBS

## ECCLESIASTES

## SONG OF SOLOMON

## ISAIAH

# PERSONALITIES INDEX

## to the

## Encyclopedia of Biblical and Christian Ethics